W9-CCX-939

Encyclopedia of
SOUTHERN
BAPTISTS

IV

BROADMAN PRESS
Nashville, Tennessee

Dewey Decimal Classification: 286.03
Subject Heading: BAPTISTS—ENCYCLOPEDIAS
Library of Congress Catalog Card Number: 58-5417

Printed in the United States of America

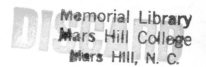

EDITORIAL COMMITTEE

ROBERT JAMES DEAN, A.B., B.D., Th.D. (Chairman), Editorial and Curriculum Specialist, Church Programs and Services Office Staff, Sunday School Board of the Southern Baptist Convention

HAROLD CLARK BENNETT, B.A., M.Div., L.L.D., Executive Secretary-Treasurer, Southern Baptist Convention Executive Committee

CHAUNCEY RAKESTRAW DALEY, B.A., B.D., Th.M., Ph.D., L.L.D., Editor, *Western Recorder*

F. WILBUR HELMBOLD, A.B., M.A., Librarian, Samford University

ERNEST EARL KELLY, JR., B.A., B.D., Th.M., Th.D., D.D., Executive Secretary-Treasurer, Mississippi Baptist Convention Board

HARRY LEON McBETH, B.A., M.Div., Th.D., Professor of Church History, Southwestern Baptist Theological Seminary

LOULIE LATIMER OWENS (MRS. OLLIN J.), A.B., D. Letts., South Carolina Baptist historian

WILLIAM MORGAN PATTERSON, B.A., M.Div., Th.D., D.D., Dean of Academic Affairs and Professor of Church History, Golden Gate Baptist Theological Seminary

RICHARD DONALD PATTON, B.S., M.Div., Pastor, First Baptist Church, Portland, Tennessee

WALTER BYRON SHURDEN, B.A., M.Div., Th.D., Dean, School of Theology, and Professor of Church History, Southern Baptist Theological Seminary

JAMES LENOX SULLIVAN, B.A., Th.M., D.D., former President, Sunday School Board of the Southern Baptist Convention

MANAGING EDITOR
LYNN EDWARD MAY, JR., B.A., M.A., B.D., Th.D.

ASSOCIATE EDITORS
CHARLES STEPHEN BOND, JR., A.B., M.A., Ph.D.
CHARLES WILLIAM DEWEESE, B.A., M.Div., Ph.D.

THE GENERAL COMMITTEE

I. SOUTHERN BAPTIST CONVENTION AGENCIES

AMERICAN BAPTIST THEOLOGICAL SEMINARY
Walker, Arthur Lonzo, Jr., B.A., M.Div., Th.D.
Executive Director-Treasurer, Southern Baptist
Convention Education Commission; Secretary-
Treasurer of the Southern Baptist Commission
on the American Baptist Theological Seminary

ANNUITY BOARD
Bloskas, John D., B.A.
Former Vice-President and Director of Public
Relations

BAPTIST JOINT COMMITTEE ON PUBLIC AFFAIRS
Wood, James Edward, Jr., B.A., M.A., B.D.,
Th.M., Ph.D.
Director of J. M. Dawson Studies in Church
and State, Baylor University, Waco, TX

BROTHERHOOD COMMISSION
Jennings, Harold Royce, B.A.
Former Director, Communications Division

CHRISTIAN LIFE COMMISSION
Tillman, William Morris, Jr., B.S., M.Ed.,
M.Div., Ph.D.
Assistant Professor of Christian Ethics,
Southwestern Baptist Theological Seminary

EDUCATION COMMISSION
Walker, Arthur Lonzo, Jr., B.A., M.Div., Th.D.
Executive Director-Treasurer

EXECUTIVE COMMITTEE
McClellan, Albert Alfred, B.A., Th.M., D.D.
Retired, former Associate Secretary and
Director of Program Planning

FOREIGN MISSION BOARD
Hill, Thomas Willard, B.A., B.D., Th.D.
Administrative Assistant to Vice-President for
Office of Overseas Operations

GOLDEN GATE BAPTIST THEOLOGICAL SEMINARY
Patterson, William Morgan, B.A., M.Div.,
Th.D., D.D.
Dean of Academic Affairs and Professor of
Church History

HISTORICAL COMMISSION
Tonks, Alfred Ronald, B.A., B.D., Th.M., Ph.D.
Assistant Executive Director

HOME MISSION BOARD
Morris, Orrin Delbert, B.A., B.D.
Director, Research Division

MIDWESTERN BAPTIST THEOLOGICAL SEMINARY
Wamble, G. Hugh, A.B., B.D., A.M., Ph.D.
Professor of Church History

NEW ORLEANS BAPTIST THEOLOGICAL SEMINARY
Howe, Claude Leodis, Jr., B.A., M.S., B.D.,
Th.D.
Chairman, Division of Theological and
Historical Studies; Professor of Church History

RADIO AND TELEVISION COMMISSION
Duncan, Clarence Edgar, B.J.
Director, Personnel/Purchasing

SEMINARY EXTERNAL EDUCATION DIVISION
Rigdon, Raymond May, Jr., A.B., M.Div., Ph.D.
Executive Director, Seminary External
Education Division of the Southern Baptist
Seminaries

SOUTHERN BAPTIST FOUNDATION
Johnson, Hollis Eugene, III, B.A.
Executive Secretary-Treasurer

SOUTHEASTERN BAPTIST THEOLOGICAL SEMINARY
Meiburg, Albert Lunney, B.S., B.D., Th.D.
Dean of the Faculty

SOUTHERN BAPTIST THEOLOGICAL SEMINARY
Hinson, Edward Glenn, B.A., B.D., Th.D.,
D. Phil.
David T. Porter Professor of Church History

SOUTHWESTERN BAPTIST THEOLOGICAL SEMINARY
Elder, Prentice Lloyd, B.A., M.Div., Th.D.
Executive Vice-President

STEWARDSHIP COMMISSION
Fagan, A. Rudolph, A.B., B.D.
Executive Director-Treasurer

SUNDAY SCHOOL BOARD
Lesch, Gomer Rupert, B.S.
Special Assistant to the Executive Office

II. ASSOCIATED ORGANIZATIONS

BAPTIST WORLD ALLIANCE
Bryant, Cyril Eric, Jr., A.B., Litt.D.
Associate Secretary

WOMAN'S MISSIONARY UNION
DeVault, Doris, B.A., M.R.E.
Coordinator of Special Services

III. STATE CONVENTIONS

ALABAMA
Allen, Lee Norcross, B.S., M.S., Ph.D.
Dean, Howard College of Arts and Sciences, Samford University

ALASKA
Meeks, Allen Henry
Executive Director-Treasurer, Alaska Baptist Convention

ARIZONA
Canafax, Jesse Lee, B.S., D.D.
State Missions Director, Arizona Southern Baptist Convention

ARKANSAS
Selph, Bernes K., A.B., Th.M., Th.D.
Retired pastor, First Baptist Church, Benton, AR

CALIFORNIA
Hepburn, Donald Stewart, B.A., M.R.E.
Director of Communications and Public Relations, Southern Baptist General Convention of California

COLORADO
Young, James Lee, B.A., M.R.E.
Editor, *Rocky Mountain Baptist*

DISTRICT OF COLUMBIA
Langley, James Arthur, B.A., B.D., Th.M., Th.D.
Executive Director, District of Columbia Baptist Convention

FLORIDA
Joiner, E. Earl, A.B., B.D., Th.M., Th.D.
Professor and Chairman, Department of Religion, Stetson University

GEORGIA
Lester, James Adams, B.A., B.D., Th.M.
Director of Public Relations, Baptist Convention of the State of Georgia

HAWAII
Walker, Edmond Richmond, A.B., Th.M., Th.D.
Executive Secretary-Treasurer, Hawaii Baptist Convention

ILLINOIS
Chaney, Charles Leonard, B.A., B.D., Th.M., M.A., Ph.D.
Dean of Redford School of Theology and Church Vocation, Southwest Baptist College

INDIANA
Springs, Frances Stovall (Mrs. Edward W.)
Historical Secretary, State Convention of Baptists in Indiana

KANSAS-NEBRASKA
Shope, James Henry, B.A., M.Div.
Director of Missions, Tri-County Valley Baptist Association

KENTUCKY
Crismon, Leo Taylor, M.S.L.S., Ph.D.
Retired Librarian, Southern Baptist Theological Seminary

LOUISIANA
Poe, William Allen, B.A., B.D., M.A., Ph.D.
Professor of History, Northwestern State University, Natchitoches, LA

MARYLAND
High, Larry Eugene, B.A., M.R.E.
Editor, *Maryland Baptist*

MICHIGAN
Wilson, Robert B., B.A., B.D., D.D.
Executive Director-Treasurer, Baptist State Convention of Michigan

MISSISSIPPI
Kelly, Ernest Earl, Jr., B.A., B.D., Th.M., Th.D., D.D.
Executive Secretary-Treasurer, Mississippi Baptist Convention Board

MISSOURI
Moore, David O., A.B., B.D., Th.M., Ph.D.
Chairman and Professor, Department of Religion, William Jewell College

NEVADA
Myers, Ernest Boyd, B.A., Th.M., L.L.D.
Executive Director-Treasurer, Nevada Baptist Convention

NEW MEXICO
O'Brien, Bonnie Ball (Mrs. Chester C., Jr.), B.A., M.R.E.
New Mexico member of Historical Commission, SBC

NEW YORK
Lowndes, Jack P., B.A., M.Div., D.D., L.L.D.
Executive Director, Baptist Convention of New York

NORTH CAROLINA
Ray, Cecil Armstrong, A.B., Th.M.
General Secretary-Treasurer, Baptist State Convention of North Carolina

NORTHERN PLAINS
Owen, Roy W., B.A., B.D.
Executive Director, Northern Plains Baptist Convention

NORTHWEST
Harvey, Samuel Allen, B.A., B.D., Th.M., S.T.D.
Pastor, Calvary Baptist Church, Renton, WA

OHIO
Sommerkamp, Theo Enoch, B.S., M.S.
Editor, *Ohio Baptist Messenger*

OKLAHOMA
Gaskin, Jesse Marvin, A.B., D.D.
Director, Oklahoma Baptist Historical Commission

PENNSYLVANIA-SOUTH JERSEY
Bush, Ellis Marion, B.A., B.D., Th.M., D.D.
Executive Director-Treasurer, Baptist
Convention of Pennsylvania-South Jersey

SOUTH CAROLINA
Clayton, John Glenwood, A.B., B.D., Ph.D.
Special Collections Librarian, Furman
University Library

TENNESSEE
Madden, Thomas J., B.A., Th.M., D.D.
Executive Secretary-Treasurer, Tennessee
Baptist Convention

TEXAS
Charlton, Thomas Lee, B.A., M.A., Ph.D.
Associate Professor and Director of Program for
Oral History, Baylor University

UTAH-IDAHO
Lemke, Anita Tetzloff
Executive Assistant, Utah-Idaho Southern
Baptist Convention

VIRGINIA
Moore, John Sterling, B.A., Th.M.
Pastor, Manly Memorial Baptist Church,
Lexington, VA

WEST VIRGINIA
Walls, Jackson Cecil
Editor, *West Virginia Southern Baptist*

IV. SPECIAL AREAS

BIBLE
Jones, Peter Rhea, B.A., M.A., M.Div., Th.M.,
Ph.D.
Pastor, First Baptist Church, Decatur, GA

CHURCH ADMINISTRATION AND RELIGIOUS
EDUCATION
Terry, Jack Doutree, Jr., B.A., M.R.E., Ed.D.
Dean, School of Religious Education,
Southwestern Baptist Theological Seminary

CHURCH MUSIC
Reynolds, William Jensen, B.A., M.S.M., M.M.,
Ed.D.
Associate Professor of Church Music,
Southwestern Baptist Theological Seminary

ETHICS AND SOCIAL CONCERN
Valentine, Foy Dan, B.A., Th.M., Th.D., D.D.,
L.L.D.
Executive Director, Christian Life Commission
of the Southern Baptist Convention

EVANGELISM
Hogue, Charles B., B.A., B.D., D.D.
Vice-President, Evangelism, Home Mission
Board of the Southern Baptist Convention

HISTORY
Shurden, Walter Byron, B.A., M.Div., Th.D.
Dean, School of Theology, and Professor of
Church History, Southern Baptist Theological
Seminary

MISSIONS
Falls, Helen Emery, A.B., M.R.E., M.A.,
Ed.D., D.D.
Professor of Missions, New Orleans Baptist
Theological Seminary

OTHER BAPTIST BODIES
McBeth, Harry Leon, B.A., M.Div., Th.D.
Professor of Church History, Southwestern
Baptist Theological Seminary

PASTORAL CARE
Lester, Andrew Douglas, B.A., B.D., Ph.D.
Associate Professor of Psychology of Religion,
Southern Baptist Theological Seminary

PREACHING
Carlton, John William, B.A., B.D., Ph.D.
Professor of Preaching, Southeastern Baptist
Theological Seminary

PUBLIC AFFAIRS AND RELIGIOUS LIBERTY
Wood, James Edward, Jr., B.A., M.A., B.D.,
Th.M., Ph.D.
Director of J. M. Dawson Studies in Church
and State, Baylor University

SPECIAL ARTICLES
Patterson, W. Morgan, B.A., M.Div., Th.D.,
D.D.
Dean of Academic Affairs and Professor of
Church History, Golden Gate Baptist
Theological Seminary

STEWARDSHIP
Fagan, A. Rudolph, A.B., B.D.
Executive Director-Treasurer, Stewardship
Commission of the Southern Baptist
Convention

STUDY AND RESEARCH
Bradley, Martin Bird, B.S.
Manager, Research Services Department,
Sunday School Board of the Southern Baptist
Convention

THEOLOGY
Ashcraft, Jesse Morris, B.A., B.D., Ph.D.
Dean of the Faculty and Professor of Theology,
Southeastern Baptist Theological Seminary

CONTRIBUTORS

Acree, A. Troy
Adams, Bert N.
Adams, Bob E.
Adams, Laddie Ray
Adams, Leonoar Craig (Mrs. George William)
Adams, Roy G.
Aderholt, Elmer Dessel
Adkins, Paul R.
Adkins, Samuel Thurman
Adkinson, Loretta Jean
Aldridge, Dennis Merrill
Aldridge, Marion Douglas
Allen, Catherine Bryant (Mrs. Lee Norcross)
Allen, John H.
Allen, Lee Norcross
Allen, William Fletcher
Alley, John Gallemore
Amos, William E.
Anders, Sarah Frances
Anderson, Frederick J.
Anderson, Gerald Harry
Anderson, Justice Conrad
Andrus, Carla D.
Anthony, H. Everett
Asher, Louis F.
Atkinson, Ernest Edwin

Babb, Marguerite Skinner (Mrs. Roy W.)
Bagby, Edward Booker, Jr.
Baggett, Hudson Doyle
Bagley, George Edwin
Baker, John Wesley
Baker, Larry Nathan
Baker, Randall
Baldwin, Vanita M.
Ball, William Lockhart, Jr.
Ballenger, Isam E.
Barnes, Charles R.
Barnes, Paul Gordon
Barry, James Clinton
Baumgartner, Leslie Raymond
Beacham, James Leon
Beall, Jewell (Mrs. Noble Y.)
Bearden, Carter E.
Beasley, James R.
Beck, Frances (Mrs. Samuel H.)

Beck, Rosalie
Belew, Marion Wendell
Bellue, Eloise Virginia (Mrs. Vernon M.)
Belvin, B. Frank
Bennett, Harold Clark
Bentley, Fred B.
Bergstrom, Herbert Eugene
Bess, Christine McFarlin (Mrs. Ewing W.)
Biggs, Johnny Gilbert
Binkley, Olin Trivette
Bird, Craig Aubrey
Blackaby, Henry Thomas
Blackmore, James Herrall
Blair, Richard Charles
Bland, Thomas Albert
Blattner, Robert Eugene
Bloskas, John D.
Blount, Evelyn
Bolin, William E.
Boling, Fencher Daniel, Jr.
Bolton, John David
Bonner, Harry G.
Borders, George
Bowen, Evans Buford
Bowles, Bruce W.
Boyce, William Arthur
Boyd, Kay
Boyd, Lester Charles
Boyd, Robert Melville
Boyle, Clifford Ervin
Bradley, James Curtis
Bradley, Martin Bird
Brady, Otis Walter
Bragg, Eugene
Brannon, Thomas J.
Brantley, Elizabeth Jones (Mrs. Russell H., Jr.)
Brantley, Russell H.
Brasington, J. Bryan
Braswell, Glen Edward
Brewer, Ben R.
Bridges, Elise Nance (Mrs. Fred Thomas)
Bridges, Tommy Lee
Brissie, Samuel Carlton
Brister, Commodore Webster
Broach, Claude W.
Brock, Clarence R.
Brooks, Lamar Judson

Brooks, Nathan Cohn, Jr.
Brown, Aquilla Ann
Brown, Archie Earl
Brown, Ellen Kuniyuki
Browning, James V.
Bryant, Cyril Eric, Jr.
Bryant, James Cecil
Bryant, Orvell, Jr.
Bryson, Newman Larry
Bullard, George Woodrow
Burcham, Arthur Denson
Bush, Ellis Marion
Byrd, David Q., Jr.

Cadle, Betty Lynn
Cain, Clyde Ray
Cain, M. Don
Caldwell, Carroll Dana
Caldwell, William Gerald
Callaway, Joseph Atlee
Cameron, Harold Edward
Camp, Berniece
Campbell, Robert Clinton, Jr.
Canzoneri, Antonina Mabel
Canzoneri, Joe G.
Capps, George E., Jr.
Carlton, John W.
Carleton, Stephen Paul
Carpenter, Kathryn Ellen
Carswell, William Jones
Carter, Benjamin Carroll
Carter, Thomas Edwin
Cashwell, Thomas Leary
Causey, Joseph Newman
Chamberlain, Horace Eugene
Chandler, John R.
Chaney, Charles Leonard
Chapman, Fred M.
Charlton, Thomas Lee
Cheatham, James Douglas, Sr.
Claiborne, Frank
Clark, Howard Wilson, Jr.
Clark, James Wilbar
Claybrook, Prince Edward
Clayburn, Mary Elizabeth
Clayton, Clyde C.
Clayton, John Glenwood
Clayton, Lynn Parks

Clinton, William Lee
Coates, Edwin Smith
Coldiron, James Owen
Cole, Archie Harold
Collier, Thomas William
Colvin, Achel Buford
Comish, Allen Beza
Compton, Bobby Dale
Conner, Barbara Rhea (Mrs. Ray)
Conner, Raymond Joseph
Conrad, Carl E.
Constanz, Nell Marie
Conyers, Mark R.
Cook, Donald Eugene
Cook, L. Katherine
Cook, M. Judson
Cook, Shelly Smith (Mrs. Michael L.)
Cooper, Edgar R.
Cooper, Lawrence Owen
Cooper, Margaret Neal (Mrs. W. David)
Cooper, Nancy Blanche
Copeland, E. Luther
Corder, Benjamin Loyd
Corts, Thomas E.
Cothen, Grady C.
Cox, Elmo
Cox, Michael
Cox, William Russ
Craft, Mel C., Jr.
Craig, Robert E.
Crawley, James Winston
Crisman, Larry Smith
Crismon, Leo Taylor
Croslin, Harrison C.
Crotts, Glen Edmond
Crowder, Rowland Edmund
Cruse, Irma Russell (Mrs. J. Clyde)
Cullen, Joy Souther
Currin, James Harvey
Curtis, Edward N.
Cuthbertson, William Welsh

Dacy, Jennifer Alice (Mrs. Joe, II)
Daley, Chauncey Rakestraw
Daniel, J. Nixon, III
Daniels, Velma Seawell (Mrs. Dexter, Jr.)
Danielson, Betty Hortense (Mrs. Alan Dale, Sr.)
Darby, Wade Edwards
Davenport, William Randolph
Davidson, Minor
Davis, C. Anne
Davis, Frederick Michael
Davis, Jo McDonald (Mrs. Donald Ray)
Davis, Lynn Marcellus, Jr.
Day, Clayton E.
Day, Frederick Emerson
Dean, Robert James

Deane, Charles Bennett, Jr.
Delamarter, Walter R.
Delozier, Ferrall (Mrs. Homer)
DeVault, Doris
Deweese, Charles William
Dexheimer, Frances Willyne (Mrs. David Andrew)
Diaz, Doris
Dilday, Russell Hooper
Dillow, Don Eugene
Dillow, Myron Delene
Dixon, Robert Ernest
Dobbins, Austin Charles
Dodson, Dennis Michael
Dominy, Bert Buckner
Doom, James Burdette
Dorris, Rivos Hycel
Downs, Cleamon Rubin
Downs, David William
DuBose, Joseph Palmer, Jr.
Dudley, John
Duett, A. Rudy
Duke, Richard Leighton
Duncan, Charles C.
Duncan, Lillie Roberts (Mrs. George C.)
Dyer, Gerald Eugene

East, Wade B.
Edens, John Davis
Edgemon, Roy T.
Edwards, Charles Richard
Elder, Prentice Lloyd
Elder, William Henry, III
Elkins, Clifford
Eller, Frances Greer (Mrs. Eugene R.)
Elliott, John Hackett, Jr.
Eskew, Harry Lee
Estep, William Roscoe, Jr.
Estrada, Leobardo Cuesta
Ethington, W. Howard
Ezell, Mancil Charles

Fagan, A. Rudolph
Falls, Helen Emery
Farmer, Arthur E.
Fasol, Albert Delio
Faulkner, Brooks Russell
Ferguson, Milton U.
Ferguson, Robert Uriel
Fielder, L. Gerald
Fields, Wilmer Clemont
Finlator, William Wallace
Fisher, Benjamin Coleman
Fite, James David
Flowers, Glen Dale
Flynn, Jean Martin
Flynt, James Wayne
Foster, Luther Adolphus
Foust, Wayne
Fox, Bill
Fricke, Hans Walker
Fulbright, Robert G.

Gabhart, Herbert Conway
Gallimore, Howard Hamilton
Gallman, Lee
Gardner, Robert Granville
Garlow, John Lyle
Garrett, James Thomas
Garrett, Wilkins Barry
Garrison, Searcy S.
Gary, Howard Edwin
Gaskin, Helen Isom (Mrs. Jesse M.)
Gaskin, Jesse Marvin
Gatwood, Charles Stewart
George, Timothy Francis
Gera, George M.
Giddens, Howard Peterson
Gilmore, Margaret Taylor
Glasser, Arthur F.
Godfrey, C. Norman
Godsoe, James Edward
Godwin, Johnnie Charles
Goerner, Henry Cornell
Goodner, James M.
Goodson, James Lenard
Goodwin, Edward C.
Goodwin, Mary Helen Johnson (Mrs. Jack Milton)
Goss, Beverly Ann
Graham, William Smith
Grant, Daniel R.
Grant, J. Marse
Graves, Harold K.
Graves, William Walthall
Gray, Elmer Leslie
Green, Atton Jackson, Jr.
Greene, Glen Lee
Gresham, Felix Morris
Gresham, Roy
Grey, James David
Griffin, Marvin C.
Grizzard, Richard Stuart
Groner, Frank S.
Gruver, Kate Ellen
Guajardo, Alcides

Hacker, Jamesy Leland
Haggard, William Charles
Halbert, William Hibbard
Halbrooks, G. Thomas
Hall, Johnnie
Hamlet, Charles Buck, III
Hammer, Donald Eugene
Hammock, H. Rex
Hammonds, Richard Donald
Hancox, Jack Donald
Handy, Robert Theodore
Haney, David Preston
Hannah, Gene Austin
Harmon, Richard W.
Harms, Donald Harvey
Harrell, Flynn Thomas
Harris, O. Ray
Harris, Philip B.
Harris, Robert Lawson
Harrop, Clayton K.

Hart, Alfred Carl
Harthcock, Edward Gary
Harvey, Samuel Allen
Harwell, Jack Upchurch
Haskins, Robert Eugene
Hastey, Stan L.
Hastings, Carroll Brownlow
Hastings, Robert Jean
Hatfield, Lawson Gerald
Hatley, James Wayman
Havlik, John Franklin
Hays, George Howard
Hays, Marguerite Johnston
   (Mrs. Thomas F.)
Heacock, Joe Davis
Hedquist, Timothy Alan
Heironimus, Rick Edward
Helmbold, F. Wilbur
Henderson, Eula Mae
Hendricks, William L.
Henley, Odus Taylor
Henry, Auguie
Henry, Margaret Hill (Mrs.
   Dolan Edward)
Hepburn, Donald Stewart,
   III
Herring, Reuben
Herrington, Annette Horton
   (Mrs. Russell)
Hester, Hubert Inman
Hester, Richard L.
Hickey, Dewey
Hiett, Dollie E.
Higgins, George L.
High, Larry Eugene
Highlan, June
Hill, Leonard Edmund
Hill, Ronald C.
Hill, Thomas Willard
Hillis, William Daniel
Hinkle, Joseph W.
Hinson, Edward Glenn
Hobbs, Herschel H.
Hobbs, Joseph Dewey, Jr.
Hoffman, Harvey W.
Hogue, Charles B.
Holcomb, Daniel Harrell
Holcombe, Edna Olean
Holland, Curtis
Hollaway, Ernest Lee, III
Hollinger, Herbert Vern
Hollis, Harry N., Jr.
Hood, Roland Parks
Horton, James T.
Hough, Raymond
   Franklin, Jr.
House, Aubrey L.
Householder, Lloyd Thomas
Howard, Marjorie G.
Howe, Claude Leodis, Jr.
Howell, Doris Dooley (Mrs.
   John C.)
Howell, Elmin K.
Howell, Walter Gerald
Howerton, Robert F.
Huddleston, J. R.

Hudgens, Wana Jean
Hudgins, Ira Durwood
Hudson, Carl A.
Huffman, Jacquelyn
   Upchurch (Mrs. Keith)
Huggins, Kay Martin
Hughey, John David
Humphreys, Fisher Henry
Hunke, Edmund William,
   Jr.
Hunt, Thomas W.
Hurt, John Jeter, Jr.
Huss, John Ervin
Hustad, Donald Paul
Hyatt, Leon Miles, Jr.

Igleheart, Glenn A.
Ingram, Joe Lynn
Inman, Gary L.
Irby, Galen Francis
Irwin, Leonard Gayle
Ivins, John C.

Jackson, Don
Jackson, George Huddleston
Jackson, Robert Scott
Jackson, Walter Coleman,
   III
Jacobs, Wynona Holley
   (Mrs. John I.)
Jasper, Mary Kathryn
Jenkins, James Lineberry,
   Jr.
Jennings, Harold Royce
Jepson, Marsha Kay
Johnson, Bob I.
Johnson, Daniel Bramlet, Jr.
Johnson, Gustave Edward
Johnson, Hollis Eugene, III
Johnson, Mary Lynch
Johnson, Roy Lee
Joiner, Edward Earl
Jones, George Alexander
Jones, J. Olan
Jones, Peter Rhea
Jones, William H.
Jump, Chester Jackson, Jr.
Junker, C. William

Keefer, Yvonne Kelsoe (Mrs.
   James A.)
Keller, Ella Mae
Kelley, Elwood G.
Kelly, Ernest Earl
Kelly, Marjorie Cole (Mrs.
   Earl)
Kendall, William Frederick
Kennedy, Harvey H.
Kennedy, James Hardee
Kennedy, Philip Edward
Kerr, Truman Carroll
Kidd, Gene
Kilgore, Robert H.
Kimbler, George Harvey
Kindrick, Stephen B.
King, Bernard Dodson

Kirkland, Donald Milton
Kitchings, Harold Tribble
Knight, Calvin Stinson
Knight, Malcolm Buckner
Knight, Walker L.
Knott, Linda Brumley (Mrs.
   Emerson Perry)
Koehler, Arthur Harold
Konig, Cherry Linda

Laird, David Elmo
Lambert, Erin Ewing (Mrs.
   Franklin T.)
Lamborn, Lois Moeller
   (Mrs. Richard S.)
Lamborn, Richard S.
Lamm, Wilbur Clayton
Land, Richard Dale
Landers, William Houston
Landes, James H.
Landgrave, John Phillip
Langley, James A.
Langston, Paul T.
Lankford, Vernon Thomas
Lantrip, Gordon Len
Ledbetter, Donald H.
Lee, Christin Morrow (Mrs.
   William Eugene)
Lee, G. Avery
Lee, H. Page
Lee, Howard William
Lee, Robert E.
Lee, Robert L.
Lemke, Anita Tetzloff
Leonard, Bill J.
Lesch, Gomer Rupert
Lester, Andrew Douglas
Lester, James Adams
Lewis, Allan E.
Lewis, Kirk
Link, William Calhoun, Jr.
Lockwood, Quentin
Looney, Floyd
Lord, William Harvey, Sr.
Loring, Ben Edwin, Jr.
Love, Charles Peyton
Lowndes, Jack P.
Lowry, James A.
Lumpkin, William Latane
Lycan, Gilbert Lester

Madden, Thomas J.
Maddox, Jesse Cordell
Magar, Paul Dean
Magruder, Charles Emerson
Maguire, John Henry
Mallory, Hazel (Mrs. C. C.,
   Jr.)
Marcum, Richard Tandy
Marler, Martha Ellen
Martin, Reginald Wayne
Martin, Rondel T.
May, Jean Barrett (Mrs.
   Spurgeon)
May, Lynn Edward, Jr.
McAdams, Howard Douglas

McBeth, Harry Leon
McCall, Emmanuel Lemuel
McCann, Norman Ewell
McClain, Howard Gordon
McClanahan, Herman Lee
McClellan, Albert Alfred
McCrummen, Norman H.
McCullough, Paul
McDonald, James M.
McDonough, Reginald M.
McElrath, William Nold
McGlaughlin, Leonard
Douglas
McGlon, Jessie Lowe (Mrs.
Charles A.)
McGregor, Donald T.
McIntyre, Jesse Ralph
McKibbens, Ben M.
McKinley, James Frank, Jr.
McKinney, Ruth Elizabeth
McLeod, H. Eugene
McManus, Uriah Alonzoe,
Jr.
McMillan, Edward L.
McNabb, Polly Anna
McSwain, Larry Lee
McWilliams, Anne
Washburn (Mrs. William
D.)
Means, Frank Kester
Medlin, Tandy Shad
Meiburg, Albert Lunney
Mercer, Earl D.
Merchant, Thomas L.
Miebs, Shirley F.
Milburn, Lowell Duane
Miles, Linda
Miller, Richard Alvey
Miller, William Starr
Mills, John Edwin
Mills, Watson Early
Mitchell, Joyce Arlene
Moore, David Otto
Moore, E. Harmon
Moore, John Allen
Moore, John Sterling
Moore, Lamire Holden
Moore, Margaret Ross (Mrs.
E. Harmon)
Moore, Martha Paulette
(Mrs. John S.)
Moore, Sterling Hale
Morgan, Bruce M.
Morris, G. Gwin
Morris, Orrin Delbert
Morris, Russell Allen
Morrow, Hazel B.
Moseley, Fred Baker
Mosley, Ernest Edward
Murrie, B. J.
Myers, Ernest B.
Myers, Lewis I., Jr.
Myers, Vern Caperton

Nagy, Ora Sue
Nash, Stanton H.

Naylor, Rebekah A.
Neal, Charles Edward
Neal, Henry Kirkland
Neal, Lillie Joy
Neely, H. K., Jr.
Neely, Herbert Willingham,
Sr.
Neely, Jacqulyn Marie Sloan
(Mrs. Herbert)
Nelson, James Winfred
Nelson, Ronald Lynn
Nelson, Thomas Wheeler
Nethery, Mary Jane
Nettles, Thomas Julian
Nicholas, D. Jack
Nicholas, Timothy Alan
Norman, James Eugene
Norman, William Edward
Northcutt, Jesse J.

O'Brien, Janice
O'Brien, Robert J.
O'Dell, Daniel R.
Oglesby, David C.
Oldham, Robin Clay
Omanson, Roger Lee
Orr, Robert Alvin
Owen, Dorothy Duke
Owen, Franklin Pearce
Owen, Roy W.
Owens, John Joseph
Owens, Loulie Latimer
(Mrs. Ollin J.)
Owens, Ollin J.
Owens, Paul Edwin

Page, Evelyn Jackson (Mrs.
John W., Jr.)
Painter, Elizabeth A.
Pair, Charles L.
Palmer, Gerald Burton
Parker, Bobby Eugene
Parker, Sara Frances (Mrs.
Leroy)
Parks, Alva G.
Patterson, William Morgan
*Pedigo, Oliver Leonard, Jr.
Pentecost, Julian H.
Peterson, Monte Raymond
Pettus, Herschel Crockett
Pharr, L. Keener
Phillips, James Wilbur, Jr.
Philpot, James Morgan
Pillow, Jerome Baird
Pitts, William Lee
Plemmons, Erskine V.
Poe, William Allen
Poole, William Augustus
Porch, Luther Quentin
Porter, Lee
Potter, James S.
Potts, Alton Earl
Price, Linda Dianne
Prince, Myra Sherman (Mrs.
John R.)
Provence, Ruth

Pryor, Dorothy Marion
Psalmonds, Walter Gordon
Puckett, Richard Gene
Pyles, Wilford Allan

Queen, Alonzo Calvin
Quinn, Emily Esteen

Raley, Helen Thames (Mrs.
John Wesley)
Randolph, Grady L.
Ransdell, John William
Ratliff, F. William
Ray, Cecil Armstrong
Redford, Francis Jackson
Reynolds, William Jensen
Rhea, Claude H., Jr.
Richardson, Charles Ray
Richardson, Frank C.
Richardson, Harold D.
Richardson, Russell G.
Ricker, George E.
Rigdon, Raymond May, Jr.
Riggs, William Russell
Ritchey, George A.
Rives, Elsie
Roberson, William Thomas
Roberts, John Elgin
Roberts, John Ewing
Roberts, Johnson Thomas
Roberts, Theodore K.
Robertson, Michael D.
Robinson, Carolyn
Covington (Mrs. Orville
A.)
Robson, John H.
Rockett, Arthur D.
Roden, Charles Pentecost
Rodgers, Luther London
Rodgerson, Phillip E.
Rogers, William H.
Romo, Oscar I.
Rose, Morton Frank
Roselle, Charles Marion
Ross, Jerry Edward
Ross, John Wilson
Routh, Porter W.
Rowe, Susan
Rudick, June
Rushing, Stanley Ballard
Russell, Maude Marie (Mrs.
Clyde)
Rutledge, Harold Lee

Sagert, Stanley Adolph
Salley, Charles Landrum
Sanders, Perry Ray
Sapp, W. David
Sawyers, Conway H.
Scanlon, Alton Clark
Schroder, Gladys
Scott, Jimmie Wayne
Scott, John Daniel
Selph, Bernes K.
Severance, W. Murray
Sewell, William Lamar

Shacklee, Larry
Shackleford, Alvin Cicero
Sharp, Charles E.
Shelley, Bruce Leon
Sheppard, Carl Wayne
Sheridan, Richard C.
Sherouse, Craig Alan
Shope, James H.
Shurden, Walter Byron
Simmons, Paul D.
Simms, Stewart Broadus, Sr.
Sims, Cecil
Sims, Richard B.
Sinclair, Helen Stuart
Sisk, Ronald D.
Skaggs, Jay Lynn
Skogman, Earl G.
Smith, Doyle
Smith, Elliott Marek
Smith, James Hillman
Smith, James Neron
Smith, Robert E.
Smith, Sam Mayer
Smith, Sidney, Jr.
Smothers, Hubert Bon
Sneed, John Everett
Snider, Robert Larkan
Snider, Ruby Herrick (Mrs.
  Roy E.)
Sommerkamp, Theo Enoch
Sorrill, Bobbie
South, Gilbert Eugene
Spain, Rufus B.
Sparrow, Bonita Marie (Mrs.
  Eldon K.)
Speer, Michael L.
Spencer, Richard A.
Springs, Frances Stovall
  (Mrs. Edward W.)
Spruell, Malcolm Eugene
Stagg, Evelyn Owen (Mrs.
  Frank)
Stagg, Frank
Stamps, Stanley Duthiel
Standerfer, Ernest Dale
Stanford, Keith W.
Stapp, Robert Norville
Starkes, M. Thomas
Stassen, Glen H.
Steely, John Edward
Stephens, Mary Essie
Stephenson, Richard Murrell
Stevens, Paul W.
Stewart, Jonas Lee
Stocksdale, Alan H.
Storm, Edward E., Jr.
Stowe, Darty Fay
Strickland, Phil Dowell

Stringer, Lynn Terry
Stripling, Paul Wayne
Stroupe, Henry S.
Stubblefield, Jerry M.
Stuckey, Robert Homer
Summerlin, Travis L.
Sutton, Beverly Faye
Swinford, Maurice L.

Talmadge, Paul Anderson
Tampling, Andrew W.
Tate, Marvin E.
Taulman, James Edwin
Taylor, Bob R.
Taylor, Raymond Hargus
Terry, Bobby Sweede
Terry, J. Murphy
Thomas, Frank H., Jr.
Thomas, J. V.
Thomason, John W.
Thommarson, Robert Lane
Thompson, Archie Paul
*Thornton, Everett Whitfield
Tidsworth, Floyd, Jr.
Tidwell, Charles A.
Tidwell, Donavon Duncan
Tillman, William Morris, Jr.
Tonks, Alfred Ronald
Treadway, Charles Franklin
Trotter, Donald Francis
Trulove, Harry David
Tull, James E.
Tupitza, Victor
Turner, Maynard P., Jr.
Turner, Robert M.

Valentine, Foy Dan
Van Sciver, Mark R.
Vaughan, Carrie S.
Venosdel, Donald F.
Verdery, Eugene Augustus
Voda, Melba B.

Wagoner, Elizabeth Carlton
  (Mrs. Walter R.)
Wagoner, Walter Raleigh
Waldrop, C. Sybil
Walker, Arthur L.
Walker, Arthur Lonzo, Jr.
Walker, Betty R.
Walker, Charles Orville
Walker, Edmond Richmond
Walker, Freddie
Walker, Oval
Walls, Jackson Cecil
Walser, Richard Gaither
Walters, Terrill Duke (Mrs.
  Ernest J.)

Waltz, David C.
Wamble, Gaston Hugh
Wardin, Albert William, Jr.
Warren, Sibyl Brame (Mrs.
  Casper Carl)
Waters, Michael C.
Watkins, Loretta Rees
Watson, Stanley Jack
Watson, W. Joe
Weaver, William K., Jr.
Welch, Grady Ellis, Sr.
Wellmon, Wayne Kenneth
West, G. Allen, Jr.
Westmoreland, Newton
  Jackson
Whitaker, Bruce E.
White, Walter Bel
Whitlow, C. Eugene
Whitlow, June
Whitt, William Martin
Wilkinson, Louie L.
Willard, Conrad Raymond
Williams, Clovis Fred
Williams, Craven Edward
Williams, George Yeargan
Williams, Jack L.
Williams, Judy Elaine
Williams, Wayne
Willing, Elizabeth Leighton
Willis, Charles Gentry
Wilson, Mrs. Anita
Wimpee, W J
Winningham, Otha, Jr.
Wilson, Betty J.
Winter, Jimmye Simmons
  (Mrs. Charles)
Womack, William Lloyd, Sr.
Wood, James Edward, Jr.
Wood, John Atkins
Wood, Presnall H.
Woodard, John Raynor, Jr.
Woolf, Elbert Warren
Wrenn, Paul E., Jr.
Wright, Charles I.
Wright, Harvey J.
Wright, Morris Jesse

Yarbrough, Slayden Alex
Yates, Kyle Monroe, Jr.
Yeager, Barbara Sue
Yoder, James Grant
Young, Chester Raymond
Young, James Lee
Young, John Terry

Zeman, Jarold Knox

*Deceased

INTRODUCTION
TO
VOLUME IV

This volume was planned, supported, and produced by Southern Baptists themselves, working together through their organized agencies and state Baptist bodies. Volumes I and II (1958) and Volume III (1971) have proven the validity and utility of the ENCYCLO-PEDIA OF SOUTHERN BAPTISTS as a comprehensive, authentic source of information on Baptists in general and Southern Baptists in particular. The ENCYCLOPEDIA has provided Southern Baptists, as well as those interested in them, with historical insight, objective evaluation, and adequate information for a consistent understanding of Southern Baptists—their past and present life and their work. By the end of 1981, 14,500 sets of the initial volumes were in circulation. Volume III was reprinted in 1981 to meet the continuing demand for this first supplemental volume. The ENCYCLOPEDIA has been widely utilized as a basic resource on this second largest religious body in the United States.

Volume IV of the ENCYCLOPEDIA is supplemental to the first three volumes. Incomplete in itself, this volume should always be used as a companion to Volumes I-III. The present volume expands and updates the content of the first three volumes by presenting significant developments in the life and work of Southern Baptists, 1970-80, and articles on some subjects inadvertently omitted in the earlier volumes. Following the same format as its predecessors, Volume IV was produced as a cooperative venture. Eight hundred twenty-two writers contributed 1,272 articles, and a qualified editorial staff prepared the manuscript for publication. In the four volumes of the ENCYCLOPEDIA, readers should find the facts that are essential for a genuine understanding of Southern Baptists in the context of their history, their theology, their methodology, and their present organization.

History.—The significant developments in Southern Baptist life and work in the seventies prompted officials of Broadman Press and the Historical Commission, SBC, to confer regarding the need for updating the ENCYCLOPEDIA. After considering this and other factors, such as the broad circulation of Volumes I-III, these officials in 1979 agreed to publish a fourth volume which would supplement and update the content of the first three and thus record for future generations the significant developments of the 1970s. By nature and content many of the articles in earlier volumes of the ENCYCLOPEDIA were complete and needed no revision. It was determined that Volume IV would therefore contain: (1) supplemental material to update the content of original articles needing revision, (2) articles on important subjects not included in Volumes I, II, or III, and (3) monographs on new developments in the life and work of Southern Baptists since 1970.

Broadman Press requested that the Historical Commission develop and coordinate the project for producing a manuscript for Volume IV as it had done earlier in producing the earlier volumes. Lynn E. May, Jr., executive director of the Historical Commission, devised a plan for publishing Volume IV of the ENCYCLOPEDIA, following the basic format of the plan utilized by the Commission in the production of the first three volumes. In April, 1979, the Historical Commission approved the plan and authorized its executive director to implement the project in cooperation with Broadman Press. Jointly appointed by the Commission and Broadman as managing editor, May procured the commitment of each state Baptist convention, Southern Baptist Convention agency, and related organization to cooperate in the preparation of Volume IV, making it a Convention-wide cooperative venture similar to the production of the first three volumes.

The plan called for an editorial committee composed of representatives from the following agencies or groups: Sunday School Board, SBC; state executive secretaries; state editors; Historical Commission, SBC; Executive Committee, SBC; Southern Baptist Historical Society; seminary historians; college and seminary librarians; state historians; former Convention presidents; and pastors. The editorial committee that was appointed consisted of Robert J. Dean, chairman; Earl Kelly, Chauncey R. Daley, Walter B. Shurden, Harold C. Bennett, W. Morgan Patterson, H. Leon McBeth, F. Wilbur Helmbold, Loulie Latimer Owens, James L. Sullivan, and Richard D. Patton. Johnnie C. Godwin, C. Stephen Bond, and Thomas L. Clark of Broadman Press and Lynn E. May, Jr., Charles W. Deweese, and A. Ronald Tonks of the Historical Commission staff also participated in committee meetings. Beginning its work in September, 1979, the committee formulated all editorial policies, took an active part in planning the project, and in numerous other ways made a creative and indispensable contribution.

To provide additional leadership for the project, the managing editor enlisted a general committee, composed of a representative of each of the twenty-three Convention agencies and related organizations, each of the thirty-four state Baptist conventions, and the fifteen background areas to be included in Volume IV. Designated as agency chairmen, state chairmen, and special area chairmen, these individuals were made responsible for proposing subjects to be included, selecting writers, and assigning monographs to be written for their agency, state, or area on topics approved by the editorial staff. They also were responsible for content editing and verification. The editorial committee and staff developed guidelines and procedures and provided training for ENCYCLOPEDIA chairmen at an orientation meeting held in Nashville, Tennessee, December 10, 1979. The seventy-two persons who served as chairmen played a vital role in planning and preparing the copy for Volume IV.

The content of this volume was planned around the same basic categories of information formulated for the earlier volumes, except for the addition of public affairs and religious liberty as a background area. Material covering the history and work of each Baptist state convention and each Southern Baptist Convention agency since 1969 is also included. With guidance and correlation from the managing editor and his staff in Nashville, each chairman planned, procured, edited, and submitted monographs for Volume IV. Through this systematic approach, the material procured for this volume presents a comprehensive picture of Southern Baptists, 1970-80.

Staff and writers.—More than nine hundred people served on the committees, the editorial staff, and the writing staff which planned and produced this work. These people are recognized leaders of the denomination who have freely contributed their time and talents because they realized the importance of the project. The articles for the ENCYCLOPEDIA were written and edited by persons qualified for the assignment by training and experience.

Editorial procedure.—The procedure employed in editing copy for Volume IV was similar to that used in the production of the first three volumes. The ENCYCLOPEDIA chairman of each agency, state, and area was responsible for basic verifying, editing, and revising, as required, on all monographs which he assigned. He then forwarded the manuscripts to the managing editor. The editorial staff in the office of the Historical Commission accessioned, evaluated, provided further verification as needed, edited, styled, retyped when required, and arranged the monographs for submission to Broadman Press. The editorial staff revised material as needed to eliminate needless detail and subjective evaluation, to correct omissions and duplications, and to make terminology consistent. The goal of the staff has been to make the content as complete, consistent, accurate, and objective as possible. A Broadman copy editor gave each monograph a final check before the manuscript was submitted to the printer.

Pictures.—Photographs which illustrate many facets of Baptist life and work are included in this volume. Each Convention agency and state Baptist convention was given an opportunity to submit photographs illustrative of its work. The editorial staff made the final selection of pictures from those submitted. Most of them portray structures erected since 1970.

Acknowledgments.—Like its predecessors, Volume IV of this ENCYCLOPEDIA is the product of a cooperative venture. It is not possible to mention here the hundreds of people, institutions, and agencies involved in this project; but we must acknowledge some who have made highly significant contributions. Gratitude is expressed to the sponsoring agencies: the thirty-four state conventions and the Executive Committee, boards, commissions, institutions, and auxiliaries of the Southern Baptist Convention which cooperated in the work. They contributed time, material, and financial support to help underwrite the costs of planning and preparing the manuscript for publication. Their subsidy has helped to make it possible for this volume to be sold at a far more reasonable price than would otherwise be possible.

Gratitude is due to members of the editorial committee and the general committee who contributed freely of their time and skill in planning, preparing, and processing the materials for this volume. Special appreciation is due Robert J. Dean, chairman of the editorial committee, for his counsel and assistance to the managing editor in planning Volume IV, implementing the project, and revising the style guide. To all writers whose names appear as contributors, appreciation is expressed for their dedicated research and for the writing of the monographs.

Acknowledgments should also be made of the contributions made by the employed staff of the Historical Commission. As associate editor of Volume IV, Charles W. Deweese shared major responsibility in the editorial processes. He and A. Ronald Tonks assisted the managing editor in developing plans and procedures, approving monograph titles, evaluating manuscripts, and in verifying, revising, and rewriting of monographs. Mrs. Caroline M. Patton and Mrs. Frances P. Goeller deftly handled the complex stenographic work and manuscript control so that each item was properly acknowledged, accessioned, processed, styled, retyped as needed, and filed. They also assisted in the editorial processes. The competence and the careful attention to the details of publishing Volume IV given by these four colleagues are greatly appreciated. Gratitude must also be expressed to Mrs. Sue Jones and Mrs. Shirley Rose for assisting with ENCYCLOPEDIA correspondence and the duplication of manuscripts and for assuming some of the routine duties normally performed by the staff members working on the ENCYCLOPEDIA. These workers constituted a capable team, without which this work could not have been accomplished.

The ENCYCLOPEDIA staff worked closely with the staff of Broadman Press in the production of this volume. Chief editor of Broadman Press, C. Stephen Bond, served as an associate editor for Volume IV. Bond and his associates Myra Carver and Rhoda

Russell Royce, and an outside editorial consultant, George W. Knight, shared in the editorial and publishing processes.

Content and usefulness.—The Encyclopedia includes many kinds of material, all of which is especially relevant to Southern Baptists. However, in addition to materials dealing specifically with Southern Baptist work, history, personalities, and methods, other information has been included which Southern Baptists need in order to understand themselves in their setting and relationships. The facts contained in this volume will prove that Southern Baptists have much they can learn from one another. A common awareness and understanding of this rich heritage can help strengthen their cooperative unity.

Pastors, teachers, students, denominational leaders, and others will find in this volume a compendium of information that will serve them well. Those who prepare programs, teach, or have to answer questions can find help in all four volumes of this basic reference source. All who use the Encyclopedia will find it to be the gateway to a genuine understanding of Southern Baptists. Volume IV supplements the content and extends the usefulness of Volumes I-III by portraying the major developments in the life and work of Southern Baptists from 1970 to 1980.

Lynn E. May, Jr.
Managing Editor

ACKNOWLEDGMENT

In making available Volume IV of the Encyclopedia, the Historical Commission and Broadman Press have performed a service to all of us. The broad participation in this project is a demonstration of the cooperative spirit of Southern Baptists. The Introduction appropriately acknowledges the support and participation of Southern Baptist agencies and groups; the editorial committee; the agency, state, and special area chairmen; the writers; and others who worked on the project. Special thanks is due Lynn E. May, Jr., for initiating this project and for serving as managing editor. He and his staff worked long and hard to provide this reference volume on Southern Baptists' life and work in the 1970's. Leading in the development of Volume IV, the managing editor has carried on in a worthy way the work of his predecessors, Norman W. Cox and Davis C. Woolley.

Robert J. Dean
Chairman, Editorial Committee

HOW TO USE THIS VOLUME

Arrangement of Material.—The monographs are in alphabetical order. Those on associations are arranged alphabetically under the name of the state. Alphabetizing of articles was done according to the main word in titles. For example:

Arkansas Associations
Dawson, Joseph Martin
Hunger, World
Liberia, Mission in
Refugee Resettlement
Texas, Baptist General Convention of
Wake Forest University

References.—A Roman numeral I, II, and/or III following a title in this volume denotes that an article by that identical title appears in Volume I, II, and/or III. A "cf." reference following a title refers the reader to an article in the earlier volumes on a similar subject but with a different title. Cross references are included to make all the material in this volume more accessible. "See also" references at the end of monographs refer to supplementary information in related monographs. "See" references arranged alphabetically with monographs direct the user from subject areas to the monographs in which those subjects are treated. Bibliographies appearing with monographs refer to sources of additional information. A "(*q.v.*)," following an incidental reference to a person, refers the reader to a biographical sketch in Volume IV. Biographical monographs in the previous volumes are referred to by "(*q.v.* I)" or "(*q.v.* II)" or "(*q.v.* III)." A "(*q.v.*)" in a cutline to a photograph indicates that a monograph relating to the subject preceding the "(*q.v.*)" appears in Volume IV.

Abbreviations.—The names of organizations are often abbreviated after their initial appearance in a monograph. Abbreviations most commonly used include FMB for Foreign Mission Board, HMB for Home Mission Board, SBC for Southern Baptist Convention, and WMU for Woman's Missionary Union.

Biographies.—This volume contains biographical sketches of 385 deceased Baptist leaders. Most of these are persons whose deaths occurred 1970-80. Also included are sketches of earlier Baptist leaders inadvertently omitted in Volumes I-III. Biographies were selected by special state and agency committees from among deceased leaders who rendered significant service as pioneers, scholars, authors, leaders, preachers, missionaries, editors, statesmen, educators, or philanthropists.

Scope.—The breadth of subject matter in this volume will soon become evident to those who use it. Numerous definitive articles are included in the following areas: Bible, Church Administration and Religious Education, Church Music, Ethics and Social Concern, Evangelism, History, Missions, Other Baptist Bodies, Pastoral Care, Preaching, Public Affairs and Religious Liberty, Stewardship, Study and Research, Theology, and miscellaneous general articles. Monographs on the Southern Baptist Convention, SBC agencies, agency programs, publications, etc., are included. An article may be found on each state convention, institution, publication, etc. Associational monographs are limited to new associations and changes in associations. Biographical articles provide basic information on the life and ministry of deceased leaders. Special monographs reflect the numerous changes in organization, programs, and publications of Southern Baptists, 1970-80.

Users should note that this volume contains numerous brief monographs related to the longer monographs on major organizations. For instance, the main article on the Foreign Mission Board is supplemented by separate articles on each mission of the board plus special articles on related subjects such as Baptist Spanish Publishing House, English-Language Churches Overseas, Foreign Missions, Directions in, etc.

For reference and Reading.—Like other encyclopedias, this volume is primarily a reference work. Users will find its pages inviting them to explore its content further and are encouraged to read it like any other book. Pastors will find the volume useful in sermon preparation. Church program leaders will find helpful material for conducting mission studies (or studies of any facet of SBC life in the 1970s). Denominational leaders can use the volume in writing and planning.

HOW TO USE VOLUMES I-III

Volumes I and II, published in 1958, contain monographs covering the period from Southern Baptist beginnings up to 1956. Volume III, published in 1971, contains monographs covering the years from 1956 to 1970. The arrangement and scope of these monographs are the same as in Volume IV. The use of abbreviations is also similar to that in Volume IV.

References in Volumes I-III differ at two points from those in Volume IV. First, an asterisk (*) by a title in Volume III denotes that an article by that identical title appears in Volume I or II. Second, in Volume III a "(q.v., Vol. I)" or "(q.v., Vol. II)," following an incidental reference to a person, refers the reader to a biographical sketch in Volume I or II.

A "cf." reference following a title in Volume III refers the reader to an article in the earlier volumes on a similar subject but with a different title. "See," "See also," and "(q.v.)" references in Volumes I-III mean the same as in Volume IV.

HOW TO USE THE INDEX TO VOLUMES I-IV

Published separately, the *Index to Volumes I-IV* can help the user of the ENCYCLOPEDIA OF SOUTHERN BAPTISTS by pinpointing the volume(s) and page number(s) containing monographs on desired subjects or biographies. Each entry in the index has three parts: (1) monograph title, (2) volume number, and (3) the initial page number of the monograph.

The *Index* contains an entry for every monograph in the four volumes. It also groups related monographs under selected subject areas (such as Bible, Evangelism, Preaching, etc.), under state convention related entities (such as Hospitals and Children's Homes), and under the Southern Baptist Convention and its agencies.

"See" references between entries direct the user from subject areas to the monographs in which those subjects are treated.

ILLUSTRATIONS

A

ABERNATHY, JOHN ARCH (b. Iredell County, NC, Jan. 3, 1896; d. Hot Springs, AR, Mar. 19, 1973). Foreign missionary. The son of Sarah Lackey and John Abernathy, a carpenter-farmer, he attended the University of North Carolina, University of Chicago, Southwestern Baptist Theological Seminary (B.Ed.), and New Orleans Baptist Theological Seminary (B.C.T., 1928). He married Jewell Leonard, June 20, 1925. First serving in China under the Baptist China Direct Mission, 1920-24, he was appointed by the Foreign Mission Board, Dec. 5, 1924. He served in north China, 1925-48, was interned, 1941, and repatriated, 1942. He was Southern Baptists' first missionary to Korea, 1950, 1951-61, and founder and president of Korea Baptist Seminary, 1952-57, but was briefly assigned to the Philippines during the Korean War, 1950-51. He is buried in Memorial Gardens, Hot Springs, AR.

FRANK K. MEANS

ABERNATHY, ZENOBIA JEWELL LEONARD (b. Huntington, AR, Apr. 2, 1894; d. Hot Springs, AR, Feb. 16, 1977). Missionary. Daughter of Frank and Amanda Leonard, farmers, she attended East Central Normal School, Ada, OK, and New Orleans Baptist Theological Seminary. She went to China with a Baptist faith mission, Aug., 1920, serving as principal of a girls school in Taian, and teaching the Bible to women. After her marriage to John Arch Abernathy (q.v.), June 20, 1925, she transferred to the Foreign Mission Board, 1927. When her husband was imprisoned by the Japanese in World War II, she returned to the United States. She joined him again in China in 1945 and continued working there until the country fell to the Communists. She is buried in Memorial Gardens, Hot Springs, AR.

DOLLIE E. HIETT

ABORTION (III). The serious issue of abortion has received much attention among Southern Baptists in recent years. In 1971 the SBC passed a resolution expressing the view that "society has a responsibility to affirm through the laws of the state a high view of the sanctity of human life." This resolution also called for legislation to "allow the possibility of abortion under such conditions as rape, incest, clear evidence of severe fetal deformity, and carefully ascertained evidence of the likelihood of damage to the emotional, mental, and physical health of the mother." In 1974 the SBC voted to reaffirm this resolution.

In 1976 the SBC passed a resolution which rejected any indiscriminate attitude toward abortion as being contrary to the biblical view of the sacredness and dignity of human life. The messengers said that government should have a limited role in matters related to abortion, and that expectant mothers should have the right "to the full range of medical services and personal counseling for the preservation of life and health."

In 1977 the Convention reaffirmed the 1976 resolution on abortion, as did the messengers to the 1978 and 1979 SBC meetings. In 1980 the SBC passed a resolution favoring "appropriate legislation and/or a constitutional amendment prohibiting abortion except to save the life of the mother."

The Christian Life Commission, SBC, has provided resource materials about this moral problem. Such resources as "Issues and Answers: Abortion" explore the issues related to the problem and make suggestions for ways to eliminate the conditions which lead to abortions. Other denominational publications also provide help on the abortion problem. The CLC has also dealt with abortion in conferences and workshops.

HARRY N. HOLLIS, JR.

ABSTINENCE (I). See ALCOHOL AND OTHER DRUGS.

ACADIA BAPTIST ACADEMY (I, III). This coeducational boarding high school experienced declining enrollment and escalating operational costs in the early 1970s. The Louisiana Baptist Convention executive board authorized borrowing of funds to complete the 1972-73 session. In July, 1973, the trustees suspended the academy's operation for the 1973-74 session. In Nov., 1973, the convention approved the trustees' recommendation that it be closed.

GEORGE L. HIGGINS, JR.

ACCENT (III). See WOMAN'S MISSIONARY UNION, AUXILIARY TO SBC.

ACHIEVEMENT GUIDES (III; cf. Standards of Excellence, Vol. II). The correlated church program Achievement Guides were updated and promoted for use as planning and evaluation tools with the new programs and materials made available in Oct., 1970. As program designs were updated later in the 1970s, each church program revised its guides as required by program needs.

In late 1978 the Church Training Department of the Sunday School Board introduced new

General, Adult, Youth, Children's, Preschool, and Associational Standards of Excellence. The elements of program design used as headings in the guides were replaced by Organization, Training, Planning, Resources, and Growth. Three levels of recognition in the guides were replaced by two, standard and advanced.

The Sunday School Department replaced Achievement Guides in Feb., 1979, with a set of Sunday School Standards having these sections: Outreach and Growth, Bible Study, Evangelism, Member Involvement, Organization, Learning Environment, Planning, and Leadership Development. No levels of recognition were provided; all requirements must be met for standard recognition.

The Brotherhood Commission officially abandoned Achievement Guides in 1979 and did not replace them, except by setting standards through suggested goals in planning guides. Woman's Missionary Union approved revised WMU and age-level guides somewhat similar to the previous guides in Jan., 1980, for the 1981-82 year. Church Music guides were scheduled for revision by the end of 1980.

ROBERT ORR

ACKISS, ERNEST LEE (b. Oceana, VA, Sep. 16, 1887; d. Atlanta, GA, Sep. 17, 1961). Military chaplain. The son of William H. Ackiss and Mary Ann Senca Ackiss, schoolteachers, he attended Richmond College (B.A., 1910), Southern Baptist Theological Seminary (Th.M., 1913), and Chicago University (Ph.D., 1916). In Feb., 1917, he married Susan Rich Davison. Their children were Ernest L., Jr., Mary, and Sue. Ackiss served several pastorates and was assistant professor at the University of Richmond before serving in the United States Navy as a chaplain, 1918-51. He was appointed to the Chaplains Division, Home Mission Board, on Apr. 1, 1953, as a field secretary for military personnel. He is buried in Arlington National Cemetery, Arlington, VA.

CARL HART

ACTEENS (III). Beginning in Oct., 1970, Acteens succeeded Girls' Auxiliary and Young Woman's Auxiliary as the missions organization for girls 12-17 years old (or school grades 7-12). As one of the five missions education organizations of Woman's Missionary Union, SBC, Acteens provides opportunity for girls to experience mission study, mission action and direct evangelism, and mission support. In 1979 Acteens organizations totaled 13,115 with a membership of 115,944. *Accent* and *Accent, Leader Edition*, the monthly magazines for Acteens and leaders, provide the basic resources for all Acteens activities.

Through Studiact, the Acteens individual achievement plan, Acteens may engage in individual missions experiences. The five Studiact achievement levels are Queen, Queen with a Scepter, Queen Regent, Queen Regent in Service, and Service Aide.

Three National Acteens Conferences mark the progress of the organization. The first conference, held at Glorieta Baptist Conference Center, July, 1972, attracted a capacity crowd of 900 Acteens. In June, 1975, the second conference was held in Memphis, TN, with 10,716 participants. Approximately 11,500 persons attended the third conference in Kansas City, MO, in July, 1979.

In 1977 six Acteens members were chosen to serve as the first Acteens National Advisory Panel. In 1980 the fourth selection of panelists served in this capacity.

BEVERLY SUTTON

ADAMS, THEODORE FLOYD (b. Palmyra, NY, Sep. 26, 1898; d. Richmond, VA, Feb. 27, 1980). Pastor, civic leader, president of Baptist World Alliance, and author. Son of Floyd Holden, a Baptist minister, and Evelyn (Parkes) Adams, he attended public schools in Oregon and Indiana and was a graduate of Denison University (B.A., 1921) and Colgate Rochester Divinity School (B.D., 1924). He received 10 honorary doctorates from universities in the United States and Canada and was a member of Phi Beta Kappa, Beta Theta Pi, Phi Mu Alpha, and Omicron Delta Kappa. On Feb. 26, 1925, Adams married Esther Josephine Jillson. They had three children: Theodore F., Jr., John Jillson, and Betsy Ann. Ordained in 1924, his Baptist pastorates included: Cleveland, OH, 1924-27; Toledo, OH, 1927-36; and First Church, Richmond, VA, 1936-68 (pastor emeritus, 1968-80).

Adams served on the executive committee, Baptist World Alliance, 1934-80. He was vice-president of the Alliance, 1947-50, and president, 1955-60. In 1925-26 he was vice-president of the Baptist Young People's Union of America. Assisting in the organization of the World Council of Churches, he was a vice-president in 1946. A member of the Foreign Mission Board, SBC, 1940-50, 1961-67, he also served as a trustee of Virginia Union University, Denison University, the University of Richmond, Southern Baptist Hospital, Virginia Baptist Children's Home, and Virginia Institute of Pastoral Care. A member of the boards of the Rockefeller Fund for Theological Education and the Council on Religion and International Affairs, Adams was also an organizer of CARE, serving as a vice-president and board member.

Instrumental in founding Richmond Memorial Hospital in 1957, he became chairman of its board. For 22 years he conducted a daily radio broadcast in Richmond and did extensive work in television. Upon his retirement he was visiting professor of preaching at Southeastern Seminary, 1968-78. He received the Freedom Foundation Award in 1960, the E. Y. Mullins Denominational Award in 1967, the National Brotherhood Citation, and the Upper Room Citation for outstanding leadership in the World Christian Fellowship.

Adams' books included: *Making Your Marriage*

Succeed (1953), *Making the Most of What Life Brings* (1957), *Tell Me How* (1964), and *Baptists Around the World* (1967). He is buried in Westhampton Memorial Park, Richmond, VA.

JOHN S. MOORE

ADAMS, WILLIAM WALTER (b. Shelby County, AL, Sep. 16, 1892; d. Kansas City, MO, Dec. 24, 1977). Seminary professor. Son of William Ferguson and Nancy Rebecca (Martin) Adams, he graduated from Howard College (B.A., 1919) and The Southern Baptist Theological Seminary (Th.M., 1922; Th.D., 1925). He married Beulah Elemna Reeves, June 6, 1924. They had two sons, William and Bert. After teaching at Eastern Baptist Theological Seminary from 1925 to 1946, he became president and New Testament professor at Central Baptist Theological Seminary. From 1954 to 1963, he was James Buchanan Harrison professor of New Testament interpretation at Southern Seminary.

BERT N. ADAMS

ADULT WORK. See AGE GROUP WORK IN THE CHURCHES.

AGE GROUP WORK IN THE CHURCHES (cf. Children's Work, Vol. III; Youth Work, Baptist, Vol. III). *Adult Work.* — Age spans are designated in three groups: young adults, 18 years of age (or high school graduation or marriage) through 29 years; median adults, 30 through 59 years; and senior adults, 60 years and on. Age-group work is evident primarily through church program organizations. Each organization has areas of work and study materials for adults, and each seeks to keep adults informed about the work of the church and denomination.

Sunday School for adults begins with the basic unit of a class focusing on Bible study, outreach, witnessing, and ministry. An adult department is organized to include two or more classes. Church Training provides studies and training in the area of discipleship. Using a variety of topics, adults participate in ongoing and short-term study groups.

Woman's Missionary Union includes Baptist Young Women (18 through 29 years) and Baptist Women (30 years and older). The work is carried out through mission action, direct evangelsm, mission study, and mission support. Brotherhood includes Baptist Men, a fellowship organized to involve men in mission learning experiences, witnessing, ministering, and missions support. Adults in Church Music participate in adult choirs and in vocal, instrumental, and handbell groups.

As society in general experiences changes, churches are feeling the influence of the changes. For example, the increases in the number of single adults, median adults, senior adults, single-parent homes, and women in the work force are challenging churches to adapt schedules and approaches for these adults.

A trend in the 1969-80 period focused on ministry with single adults and senior adults. As the 1980s began, churches were becoming increasingly aware of the need to reach and train median adults, now comprising the largest segment among adult population age groups.

Children's Work. — The period from 1969 to 1980 saw churches being oriented and adapted to the new grouping-grading plan and literature designed in the late 1960s. This period produced marked changes in attitudes of churches toward teaching children. As in preschool work, in keeping with recommended design and sound educational methods for teaching children, many churches moved from teacher-centered to child-centered teaching.

The 1970s saw a significant increase in the churches' efforts to train children's teachers to understand the child and use properly the new literature within the context of the church setting. Also, children's enrollment declined, which brought about a new emphasis on reaching children for Bible study.

Approved and added to the Foundation Series (for children) was a second curriculum built on Convention Uniform Series outlines. This curriculum includes *Bible Study: Younger Children* and *Bible Study: Older Children* (weekly leaflets) and *Children's Bible Study: Teacher.*

Preschool Work. — During 1969-80, leaders in Southern Baptist churches grew in awareness of the crucial nature of the first five years of life and began taking more seriously the need to reach and teach preschoolers. As a result, Cradle Roll came to the forefront. In 1979 enrollment approached 63,000. HomeReach, a new ministry to preschoolers who cannot attend Sunday School regularly, was initiated.

New quarterly literature was designed especially for use during extended sessions of Sunday School and Church Training while parents attend worship services.

A new emphasis on parenting has emerged. *Living with Preschoolers,* a quarterly magazine for parents, was published in the early 1970s. *Beginning,* a quarterly periodical for parents of babies and toddlers, began early in the 1980s.

The trend has been toward a more child-centered approach to teaching; that is, teaching the child at his or her level of understanding and need. There has been a coordinated effort among preschool leaders in all areas of preschool work to apply new insights into child development to church literature, leadership training, and products. The trend is toward more men becoming involved in preschool work.

While the objective of preschool work continues to be enriching the child's present spiritual development and laying foundations for conversion, the percentage of preschool baptisms is increasing.

The number of churches reporting kindergartens has declined with the increase in public school kindergartens. Other weekday education programs continue to increase.

The decrease in Sunday School enrollment of preschoolers corresponds to the decrease in population of this age group from 1960-70 and projected for 1980.

Youth Work.—"Youth ministry," the over-arching term for everything a church does with youth, began to come into its own in the 1970s. More and more churches of all sizes in the SBC began to call full-time ministers of youth or part-time youth directors. In 1973 the Church Administration Department of the Sunday School Board began offering materials for and guidance to youth ministers through a consultant in youth ministry coordination.

The emphasis of this work was twofold: (1) to help youth ministers become more aware of and to appreciate more fully the values of the basic youth education programs (Sunday School, Church Training, youth choir, Acteens, and Pioneers) in building youth ministry; and (2) to help youth ministers clarify their calling, sharpen their ministry and leadership skills, and improve their roles in administration, coordination, and outreach.

LOUIE L. WILKINSON, ELSIE RIVES,
C. SYBIL WALDROP, BOB R. TAYLOR

AGENCY STUDIES BY COMMITTEE OF FIFTEEN. In 1970 the Executive Committee, SBC, authorized a Committee of Ten (later changed to Fifteen) to review the assignments made in the 1959 report of the Committee to Study the Total Southern Baptist Program and report any possible changes. The major differences between the Committee of Fifteen and the Committee to Study the Total Southern Baptist Program were that the 1959 committee was a Convention committee and that it employed a professional consultant.

The Committee of Fifteen met 21 times and accumulated nearly 5,000 pages of reports. Most of the recommendations, in keeping with Convention polity, had to do with areas of concern which were transmitted to the agencies for their own study and recommendation.

Recommendations dealing with agency observation of the Brotherhood Commission and the Radio and Television Commission were adopted, but a recommendation that would transfer the work of the Stewardship Commission back to the Executive Committee was defeated.

Perhaps the two most significant recommendations to the Convention that came out of the Committee of Fifteen were:

Recommendation No. 14:
That the two mission boards review thoroughly their present mission plans, and consider the implementation of bold new plans where needed, presenting their plans to the Executive Committee in February, 1976, and to the Convention with such recommendations as they deem advisable in June, 1976.

Recommendation No. 11:
That the Convention authorize the Convention officers elected in 1974 to appoint a committee of seven persons widely experienced in denominational life to study and evaluate the Executive Committee in the light of Bylaw 9, and that it report to the Convention in 1975. . . . None of the seven should be an active member of the Executive Committee.

The first recommendation led to the Mission Challenge Committee and the Bold Mission Thrust movement. The second led to the report on the Executive Committee by the Committee of Seven.

See also BOLD MISSION THRUST; MISSION CHALLENGE COMMITTEE.

PORTER W. ROUTH

AGING. Even as late as the 1960s and early 1970s, few SBC agency programs related to older persons. However, the 1973 SBC passed a resolution asking the Executive Committee to conduct a feasibility study for a major survey of present and future ministries to and with senior adults and to take appropriate action. In Sep., 1973, the Coordinating Committee of the Inter-Agency Council requested Albert McClellan and Leonard Hill of the Executive Committee staff to design such a study.

The project culminated when a Southern Baptist Conference on Aging was held in Nashville, TN, Oct. 23-25, 1974. Approximately 200 persons attended, all professionally related to work with the aging. As a result of that meeting, several important things happened. The Coordinating Committee established a Group on Aging. In Apr., 1977, the Sunday School Board began publishing *Mature Living,* a monthly periodical for Christian senior adults. Other SBC agencies and institutions, along with state conventions and general associations, also initiated or further developed work with the aging. Also in 1976 and 1977, the Southern Baptist Association of Ministries with the Aging was created. This association meets annually and provides a channel of involvement for more persons throughout the field of aging in the SBC.

In 1977 plans were initiated with appropriate SBC agencies to plan and conduct a 1980 Conference on Aging at Ridgecrest Conference Center. This meeting was cancelled in early 1980 due to low preregistration resulting from bad economic conditions and the energy crisis.

By action of the Convention, the program assignment of aging was moved from the Christian Life Commission to the Christian Social Ministries Department, Home Mission Board, in Jan., 1972.

PAUL R. ADKINS

AIKEN, JEFFERSON BOONE (b. Pickens County, SC, May 24, 1889; d. Florence, SC, May 6, 1978). Businessman and philanthropist. The son of Jefferson Davis and Mollie D. Aiken, he was an alumnus of Furman University (B.A., 1914). He married Pearl Ellis, of Florence, SC, Dec. 28, 1909. They had six children. An active supporter of Furman, Aiken served as a trustee and alumni association president. He served as vice-president of the South Carolina Baptist Convention in 1943. This convention honored him in 1970 with the E. A. McDowell Award for Distinguished Christian Service. He is buried in Mount Hope Cemetery, Florence, SC.

W. FLETCHER ALLEN

ALABAMA ASSEMBLIES (SHOCCO) (cf. Shocco Springs Assembly, Vol. III). George

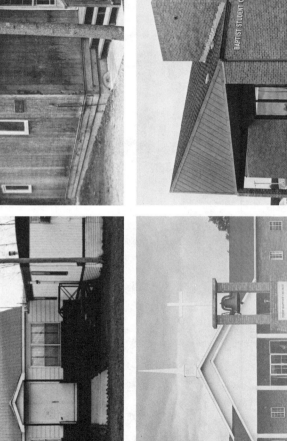

HIGHLAND LAKES BAPTIST CENTER LODGE, near Monrovia, IN. A lodge which houses cafeteria facilities and a conference area for approximately 100 people.

MISSOURI BAPTIST STUDENT CENTER, Crowder Junior College, Neosho. Serves also as office for Shoal Creek Association.

INTERNATIONAL SEAMAN'S CENTER, Port of Indiana, near Portage, IN. A ministry of the Northwest Baptist Association in cooperation with the Home Mission Board and the State Convention of Baptists in Indiana. Ministers in various languages through Bible distribution and other ways to crewmen on about 120 ships per year.

FIRST BAPTIST CHURCH, Mountain Grove, MO. Architecture is typical of Missouri Baptist churches built since 1970.

GEORGE E. BAGLEY CONFERENCE CENTER at Shocco Springs Baptist Assembly, Talladega, AL. Built in 1976.

Ricker became director of Shocco Springs Baptist Assembly in 1970, upon the retirement of Waymon C. Reese. Shocco Springs then began hosting year-round conferences. Since that time all buildings in the main camp have been renovated and air conditioned. Improvements included completion in 1972 of Springview Inn, a four-story motel. The George E. Bagley Conference Center, built in 1976, includes 13 conference rooms, a media center, gift shop, recreation room, fireside lobby, and auditorium. The Mary Essie Stephens Activities Center, built in 1980, at the Woman's Missionary Union Camp of Shocco, includes a multipurpose meeting room, lodging for the camp director, a dining hall, and an infirmary. Attendance for the decade increased to a record 22,275 (with 2,273 public decisions) in 1980.

See also ALABAMA BAPTIST ENCAMPMENTS, Vol. I.

GEORGE RICKER

ALABAMA ASSOCIATIONS (I).

I. New Associations. HALE. Constituted Oct. 18, 1956, at Stewart Baptist Church by 10 churches formerly in Cahaba Association, after earlier organizational meeting. In 1979, 13 churches reported 73 baptisms, 2,545 members, $382,891 total gifts, and $36,771 mission gifts.

TUSKEGEE-LEE. Formed in 1969 by merger of Lee and Tuskegee Associations. In 1979, 35 churches reported 325 baptisms, 13,523 members, $2,146,919 total gifts, and $248,061 mission gifts.

II. Changes in Associations. CLEAR CREEK. Organized in 1874, this association changed its name to Winston County on Oct. 7, 1959.

LEE. First organized in 1929, it disbanded in 1931. The association reorganized, Oct. 29, 1958, at First Baptist Church, Opelika, with 16 churches from East Liberty and Tuskegee Associations. It dissolved, Oct. 20, 1969, to join with churches of Tuskegee Association to form the Tuskegee-Lee Association.

MADISON-LIBERTY. Organized in 1838 as Liberty, Madison County, and renamed Madison-Liberty in 1920, the association changed its name to Madison in 1964.

MINERAL SPRINGS. Organized in 1893, the association changed its name to North Jefferson in 1971.

NORTH JEFFERSON. Organized as Mineral Springs in 1893, the association changed its name in 1971.

TUSKEGEE. Organized in 1846, it merged with Lee to form Tuskegee-Lee Association in 1969.

WINSTON COUNTY. Organized in 1874 as Clear Creek, the association changed its name in 1959.

III. Associations not Affiliated with Alabama Convention. Most of the following are Primitive Baptist associations which were extant in 1979. Statistics are cited from latest available records.

ANTIOCH (# 2). A Primitive association, constituted by some churches from the main associa-

tion of the same name in 1945 or 1946. In 1963 two churches in Escambia County reported 41 members.

CANE CREEK. A Primitive association constituted around 1850 by churches from Cleburne, Randolph, and Calhoun Counties, with one other each from Clay and Cherokee Counties. In 1962 it reported two churches from Calhoun and one from Cleburne Counties.

CHATTAHOOCHEE VALLEY. A Primitive association constituted Aug. 23, 1940, by three churches in Chambers, Lee, and Russell Counties. In 1946 four churches reported 168 members.

CHOCTAWHATCHEE. A Primitive association constituted in 1839 by churches in southeastern Alabama. In 1952, 11 churches reported 429 members.

CLAY BANK. A Primitive association constituted in 1845 by churches in southeastern Alabama. In 1962 six churches reported 93 members.

FELLOWSHIP. A Primitive association constituted in 1891 by churches in Jefferson, Blount, Cullman, Winston, and Marshall Counties disclaiming any connection whatsoever with Mount Zion Association, embracing the same general areas, which it deemed to be in disorder. In 1961 seven churches in Cullman, Blount, Jefferson, Winston, and Marion Counties reported 112 members.

FIVE MILE CREEK. Constituted as a Primitive association about 1868 by churches from Mount Zion and Lost Creek Associations. In 1961 seven churches in Cullman, Blount, and Jefferson Counties reported 89 members.

HILLABEE. A Primitive association constituted Oct. 15, 1870, at Bethlehem Church, Tallapoosa County, with 12 churches and 368 members. The churches apparently were in Tallapoosa, Clay, and Coosa Counties. In 1962, 13 churches reported 327 members.

HOPEWELL. A Primitive association constituted about 1884, by churches in Lamar, Fayette, Pickens, and Tuscaloosa Counties (not to be confused with a Primitive association of the same name, constituted about 1867 by Mississippi churches). In 1961, 10 churches reported 93 members.

LITTLE HOPE (Footwashers) (#1). A Primitive association apparently constituted 1876. In 1948 it corresponded with Wetumpka, Mt. Zion, and Lower Wetumpka Associations. The two affiliated churches, both in Bibb County, were Hopewell and Mt. Olive. By 1960 two other churches had previously affiliated: Pleasant Home, Lipscomb, Jefferson County, and Selma Church, Dallas County. In 1975 two churches reported 73 members.

LITTLE HOPE (STREETMAN/DEASON PARTY) (#2). A Primitive association apparently constituted in 1881. In 1929 this association received "correspondence" from Mt. Zion and Wetumpka Associations. Two churches were affiliated: Little Hope and Hopewell, both from Bibb County. In 1939 the association admitted two churches, Cluster Springs, near Birmingham, and Mt. Olive, near Columbiana. In 1941 it voted to correspond with "Trumpet Baptists" in Texas and other western states, plus Echeconee Association of Georgia. In 1951 the association exchanged "correspondence" with Cane Creek and Hillabee Associations.

LITTLE VINE. A Primitive association constituted about 1855. At the 1894 session, seven churches reported 84 members. Association minutes of 1931 and 1934 record the sessions as though it was constituted in 1857, two years later than the previously cited body. In 1934 that association reported four churches (one in Mississippi and one each in Franklin, Winston, and Marion Counties, Alabama) with total membership of 70. Association minutes of 1949 record the session as though it began in 1859, four years later than the first cited body. In 1949 the association reported four churches, one in Mississippi, and three in northwest Alabama. In 1963 three churches reported 26 members.

LOST CREEK. A Primitive association constituted Nov. 15, 1844, by eight churches, all in Walker County, except New River Church in Fayette County. In 1958 two churches reported 38 members.

LOWER WETUMPKA. A Primitive association constituted Oct. 9, 1914, by four churches from Elmore County, two from Coosa County, one from Tallapoosa County, and one from Macon County, all from the Wetumpka Association. In 1958, 12 churches reported 437 members.

MOUNT PLEASANT (#1). A Primitive association constituted in 1861 by churches in Jackson and DeKalb Counties. In 1961, 19 churches in De-Kalb and Jackson Counties in Alabama and one each in Georgia and Tennessee reported 2,301 members.

MOUNT PLEASANT (#2). A Primitive association constituted about 1910 by dissident churches from Mount Pleasant (#1). In 1961, 12 churches in DeKalb and Marshall Counties reported 1,226 members.

MOUNT PLEASANT (#3). A Primitive association organized about 1956. That year it reported one church in DeKalb County, AL, two churches in Georgia, and 206 members.

MOUNT ZION. Constituted in 1823 by churches in Blount, St. Clair, Shelby, Walker, and Jefferson Counties. It was originally a body allowing both Primitive and Missionary attitudes and practices, having in its early leadership Sion Blythe and Hosea Holcombe (q.v. I). With the departure of Blythe to Texas and of Holcombe to the Canaan Association, the association took on a decidedly primitive cast. It suffered a serious division in 1878, with the Allredge-Stewart-Copeland faction (#1) continuing as the main body numerically to the present.

MOUNT ZION (#5). A Primitive association constituted in 1911 by churches in southwest Alabama which had been in the Antioch Association (Primitive). In 1938 five churches reported 100 members.

MUD CREEK. A Primitive association constituted at Mud Creek Meeting House in 1821 by nine churches in Jackson County. In 1962 six churches in Jackson, DeKalb, and Marshall Counties reported 293 members. This body is to be distinguished from another Mud Creek Association which is comprised of churches in Jefferson County and which is affiliated with the Alabama Baptist State Convention.

MUSCLE SHOALS STATE LINE. A Free Will association constituted about 1921. In 1957, 28 churches in the border counties of North Alabama and Middle Tennessee reported 1,928 members.

PATSALIGA. A Primitive association apparently constituted Nov. 13, 1891, at Ivey Creek Church, Crenshaw County, by 14 churches from Conecuh River and Clay Bank Associations. Total membership in churches then affiliated was 465. Around 1911 widespread division among Primitive Baptists occurred and another Patsaliga Association (#2) resulted. In 1950, 12 churches, 10 of which had clerks in Alabama, reported 278 members. Churches function in Covington, Crenshaw, and Geneva Counties.

SAND MOUNTAIN. A Primitive association, differing from the cooperating missionary association by same name, was constituted about 1917. In 1959 four churches, one each in Blount, De-Kalb, Jackson, and Marshall Counties, reported 126 members.

SEQUATCHIE VALLEY ASSOCIATION. A Primitive association apparently constituted in 1833 from churches chiefly from Mud Creek Association (Alabama). Churches were primarily in Southeastern Tennessee, Northeastern Alabama (Jackson and DeKalb Counties), and Northwestern Georgia. In 1960 the association reported three churches from Tennessee and two from DeKalb County, AL.

WEOGUFKA. An association, perhaps extinct, constituted in 1882 when "some three or four churches in the northwestern part of Coosa, not being in sympathy with mission work, withdrew." At various times the association included churches from Shelby, Chilton, Autauga, and Talladega Counties. An anti-mission attitude is reflected in the minutes of the association. In 1922 Weogufka Missionary Baptist Association reported six churches. The word *Missionary* in the name implies some connection with the Landmark movement.

WETUMPKA. A Primitive association constituted at Wetumpka in Oct., 1843, by churches in Coosa and Macon Counties. By 1857 Wetumpka reported 21 churches affiliated, including some from Autauga, Tallapoosa, Talladega, and Shelby Counties. In 1961, 10 churches in Chilton, Elmore, and Shelby Counties reported 507 members.

WILLS CREEK. An association constituted Nov. 4, 1836, at Harmony Baptist Church, St. Clair County, by churches principally dismissed from Mount Zion Association. It had a "divided" attitude toward missions, which characterized its subsequent history. Originally constituted as Wills Creek United Baptist Association, the word *United* was deleted in 1842. In 1882 the word *United* was restored to the name, and in 1962 the word *Primitive,* which had been printed in the title for years but had not been adopted as a constitutional change, was officially dropped to conform to the constitution and the original name. Although not affiliated with the state convention or the SBC, the association has followed progressive principles for several decades and is a growing body. In 1968, 28 churches in Marshall, DeKalb, Etowah, Blount, Calhoun, and St. Clair Counties reported 4,332 members.

WILLS CREEK (#4). A Primitive association constituted about 1924 by some churches which held dual affiliation with both the original Wills Creek Association and this body. In 1962 five churches in Marshall, DeKalb, and Jackson Counties reported 169 members.

See also ALABAMA ASSEMBLIES (ASSOCIATIONAL), VOL. III.

F. WILBUR HELMBOLD

ALABAMA BAPTIST (I, III). Hudson Baggett, continuing as editor, strengthened the financial position of the paper. A new building, located in Homewood, to house the editorial and business offices was constructed and dedicated debt free in 1976 at a cost of $500,000. Jack Brymer is managing editor. The circulation increased from 140,000 in 1969 to 154,000 in 1979.

HUDSON BAGGETT

ALABAMA BAPTIST CHILDREN'S HOME, THE (I, III). Residential care for dependent children now exists at Troy, Decatur, Gardendale, and Mobile. A program for mentally handicapped children began in Mobile in 1978. Other services include foster homes, family aid, and assistance to students in college and vocational schools. A total of 271 children receive care. T. W. Collier succeeded R. Hobson Shirey as general superintendent in 1975.

T. W. COLLIER

ALABAMA BAPTIST FOUNDATION, THE (I, III). The foundation structure was changed in 1978 to provide for the chief executive officer to be designated as president. U. A. McManus, Jr., was elected president, Sep. 1, 1978. Vernon Yearby, who had served as chief executive since 1966, retired in Jan., 1979. N. J. Bell, III, who had served as president of the board since 1964, was elected chairman of the board. The assets of the foundation increased from $2,292,538 in 1969 to $10,022,458 in 1980. In 1980 foundation personnel were giving enthusiastic support to the recently inaugurated $45,000,000 Alabama Baptist State Convention Endowment Program for Christian Higher Education.

U. A. MCMANUS, JR.

ALABAMA BAPTIST HISTORIAN (III). Semiannual publication of the Alabama Baptist Historical Society. F. Wilbur Helmbold, librarian at Samford University and curator of the society, continues as editor. Irma R. Cruse became assistant editor, Jan., 1979. Publication

was suspended for a five-year period (1971-75) in order to publish a special issue of *A History of the Rise and Progress of the Baptists in Alabama* by Hosea Holcombe. Publication resumed with the Jan., 1976, issue.

IRMA R. CRUSE

ALABAMA BAPTIST HISTORICAL COMMISSION (III). This agency of the Alabama Baptist State Convention is composed of 16 members elected for four-year terms. The convention approves its organizational, financial, and program structures. The commission promotes the historical interests of the convention through collection, organization, and dissemination of historical information. Its collection at Samford University Library facilitates historical research and writings. The commission promotes oral history and microfilming of church, association, and denominational records. It sponsors the Alabama Baptist Historical Society and cooperates in the publication of the *Alabama Baptist Historian*. Major achievements in the 1970s included participation in the Baptist Information Retrieval System and the production of indexes to *The Alabama Baptist,* 1974-79, and the Alabama Baptist State Convention *Annuals,* 1823-1875.

QUENTIN PORCH

ALABAMA BAPTIST HISTORICAL SOCIETY (I, III). The Alabama Baptist Historical Society, an agency of the Alabama Baptist Historical Commission, publishes *The Alabama Baptist Historian*. Annual meetings held in the spring focus on the presentation of papers dealing with Alabama Baptist history. The society occasionally holds workshops dealing with historical research and writing. Presidents usually serve two-year terms. The presidents since 1969 have been J. Albert Hill, Hoyt Harwell, William D. Jones, Herbert M. Newell, and Lee N. Allen.

LEE N. ALLEN

ALABAMA BAPTIST RETIREMENT CENTERS. The Alabama Baptist Retirement Centers came into existence with the election of a 20-member board of directors by the Alabama Baptist State Convention, Nov., 1975. Andrew W. Tampling, pastor of First Baptist Church, Birmingham, became first executive director in Sep., 1976, with offices in the Baptist Building in Montgomery. Assisting senior adult Baptist family members in retaining their dignity, independence, health, and sense of belonging has been the thrust of this ministry from the beginning. In 1980 Clara Verner Towers in Tuscaloosa, with 201 apartments, and Baptist Village of Dothan, with 50 spacious townhouses, were the developing centers ministering to some 300 senior adults.

ANDREW W. TAMPLING

ALABAMA BAPTIST STATE CONVENTION (I, III). The Alabama Baptist State Convention in 1973 celebrated its 150th anniversary. Alabama Baptists in 1979 reported 3,046 cooperating churches with a membership of 961,401. Record Cooperative Program gifts totaled $12,006,277; designated gifts $7,054,195. Total receipts in the churches amounted to $153,620,240.

I. Executive Board Program of Work. A constitutional change altered the number of members on the executive board. A maximum of 125 regular members plus the president of the convention, if he is not already a board member, compose the membership of the board. One member is chosen from within the territory of each of the 75 associations. Remaining members are selected on the basis of each territory's percentage of the total state membership of the ABSC. A minimum of five women and a proportionate percentage of laymen must be elected to serve on the board.

Administration. — The executive secretary-treasurer is responsible for all the programs of work of the executive board. George E. Bagley continues to hold this position. An assistant was added to the Office of General Administration in 1977. The Department of Stewardship and Cooperative Program Promotion and the Office of Public Relations are based in administration. Two new programs added to administration are the Office of Church-Minister Relations and the $45,000,000 Endowment Program. The executive board is involved in the Program of Disaster Relief. A new disaster relief van is in operation in disaster areas. Voluntary crews move the van to provide the following services: Food preparation and distribution, communications, first aid, counseling, and disaster recovery.

Church Development Division. — The division office, the Sunday School Department, the Church Training Department, the Church Music Department, and the Brotherhood Department are located in the Church Development Division.

Church Ministries Division. — The division office, Associational Missions Department, Special Missions Department, Campus Ministries Department, Evangelism Department, and Retirement and Insurance Department are located in the Church Ministries Division.

Business Management Division. — This division directs Accounting and Services, Computer and Office Services, Shocco Springs, and is responsible for insurance and maintenance on all convention properties.

Convention Budget. — The ABSC increased the percentage of gifts through the Cooperative Program to the SBC in the 1970s from 35 percent to 35.5 percent of the budgeted amount and 55 percent of the Challenge Goal. For the 1980s, the convention approved the dollar-base budget procedure removing all percentages except for SBC causes. Beginning in 1980, 45 percent of the budget will go for SBC causes after deducting expenses generally designated for the promotion and collection of Cooperative Program funds. Such expenses are designated and set aside in the budget as general denominational causes. Alabama Baptists adopted a goal increasing SBC causes .5 percent per year during the 1980s provided Cooperative Program receipts increase a minimum of 10 percent over the previous year.

Shocco Springs Baptist Assembly. — Springview Inn, a modern motel-type building, was constructed in 1975 and furnished at a cost of $330,000. A fourth floor was added in 1976. It provided 80 new rooms with a capacity of 314 persons.

A major building renovation project, the new George E. Bagley Conference Center, was completed and dedicated in Dec., 1976. The center provides a media center, a spacious lobby, several conference rooms and classrooms, a refreshment center, an auditorium seating 220 persons, and an auxiliary dining room.

The new Mary Essie Stephens Chapel-Dining Hall, located at the Shocco Springs Girls in Action Camp, was completed in July, 1980.

Baptist Building. — When the convention office building was completed in 1963, the third floor was left unfinished for future expansion. A major portion was finished for occupancy in July, 1980, providing space for conferences and seminars, an enlarged executive board room, the computer section, the Baptist Foundation of Alabama, the office for the Alabama Baptist Retirement Centers, Inc., and the $45,000,000 Endowment Program.

II. Convention Agencies and Institutions. *The Alabama Baptist.* — The convention weekly paper had a circulation of 154,000 in 1980. The new office building, completed in 1976, provides an attractive and spacious facility for staff members. The convention supplements the income from gifts from the churches through the Cooperative Program.

Alabama Baptist Children's Homes. — The main campus for the convention child care ministry is located in Troy. A new campus is being developed in Mobile, along with a satellite home for ministry with mentally handicapped children. The Decatur campus began receiving children in 1969. Four cottages are located on a spacious campus.

Higher Education. — The ABSC owns and operates three schools of higher education: Samford University, Birmingham; Judson College, Marion; and Mobile College, Mobile. The convention authorized the development of an endowment program with a goal of $45,000,000 for the convention's program of Christian higher education as carried out by the three schools. Lamar Jackson provides leadership for the program. The Education Commission (formerly the Educational Advisory Committee) coordinates the endowment program.

Retirement Centers, Inc. — The retirement centers, one of the newest ministries of Alabama Baptists, provide for senior citizens on two locations: Clara Verner Towers, Tuscaloosa, and Baptist Village, Dothan.

Baptist Student Union Centers. — Seven new BSU centers were constructed or acquired dur-

ALABAMA STATISTICAL SUMMARY

Year	Associations	Churches	Church Membership	Baptisms	SS Enrollment	VBS Enrollment	CT Enrollment	WMU Enrollment	Brotherhood Enrollment	Ch. Music Enrollment	Mission Gifts	Total Gifts	Value Church Property
1969	76	2,927	830,110	28,327	532,186	284,503	245,187	95,837	37,951	85,657	$ 8,641,753	$ 58,107,915	$271,481,758
1970	75	2,932	843,840	28,615	524,986	240,058	239,913	88,728	39,454	87,457	9,069,572	61,135,913	280,182,156
1971	75	2,942	858,630	31,580	516,824	238,622	221,799	84,834	41,890	86,311	10,311,941	68,061,804	301,902,228
1972	75	2,950	876,237	32,265	516,821	232,873	221,991	85,073	42,451	94,471	11,516,723	74,537,554	332,358,743
1973	75	2,954	892,206	30,375	519,264	237,004	216,569	83,877	42,325	99,719	12,519,438	80,787,744	347,765,529
1974	75	2,970	907,579	29,889	522,308	246,887	216,378	86,150	44,332	106,289	14,371,322	89,676,075	385,365,867
1975	75	2,990	926,007	29,961	529,064	259,453	217,174	88,173	47,452	111,532	16,226,540	98,705,443	430,711,414
1976	75	2,993	937,204	27,063	534,506	236,352	215,402	89,861	47,694	112,559	18,883,457	109,699,441	478,829,977
1977	75	3,009	945,181	22,116	529,055	236,352	208,774	87,231	48,229	111,102	19,827,243	119,550,598	533,395,442
1978	75	3,004	952,318	21,944	526,049	232,204	204,711	85,364	47,354	115,499	20,478,212	134,476,447	586,870,161
1979	75	3,003	966,296	25,024	525,593	236,882	203,494	84,406	47,879	118,894	22,825,462	146,935,654	667,121,713
1980	75	3,002	976,793	28,356	529,894	250,147	204,227	86,036	49,507	122,952	24,896,660	159,843,781	736,857,338

GEORGE E. BAGLEY

ing the 1970s. The locations are University of South Alabama, Mobile; Livingston University, Livingston; University of Montevallo, Montevallo; Jacksonville State University, Jacksonville; University of Alabama in Tuscaloosa, Huntsville and Birmingham; and Auburn University, Auburn. The BSU Center at the University of Alabama in Tuscaloosa has undergone major renovation.

The Christian Life and Public Affairs Commission.—The commission assists Alabama Baptist churches and associations in the development of Christian morality, strengthening family life, working for prevention of crime, ministering to the imprisoned, and applying Christianity to all areas of life.

Special Emphases.—Good News Alabama was a cooperative effort by the Baptists in Alabama to share the gospel of Christ with every person in the state and to provide every person with an opportunity to participate in the ministry and witness of a New Testament fellowship of believers. Good News Alabama, the greatest cooperative effort ever undertaken in the state by black and white Baptists, precipitated the organization of Inter-Baptist Committees in all the associations. The director of the Special Missions Department coordinated the leadership in this assignment.

Alabama Baptists joined with other Southern Baptists in accepting the challenge of Bold Mission Thrust. Upon recommendation of the Bold Mission Committee, Alabama Baptists adopted in the 1978 convention these two emphases for the 1980s: The Bold Mission Program: Bold Believers on Mission, and The Bold Mission Program Part II: Action Plans.

GEORGE E. BAGLEY

ALABAMA NEGRO BAPTISTS (III). Four Negro Baptist conventions are active in Alabama. Reporting 2,522 churches and a total membership of 610,000, they are the Alabama State Missionary Baptist Convention, Inc., New Era Progressive Missionary Baptist State Convention, Progressive Baptist Mission and Education Convention of Alabama, and the New Era Missionary Baptist State Convention of Alabama. The predominantly black conventions work cooperatively with the predominantly white Alabama Baptist State Convention.

Cooperative ministries between National, Progressive, and Southern Baptists include inter-Baptist ministries, summer missions, pastoral training in extension centers, human relations conferences, funding the Birmingham Baptist Bible College and Selma University, inter-Baptist fellowship committees, scholarships for students in church-related vocations in college and seminary, church programming, revivals, and leadership conferences and retreats.

The single most successful cooperative venture among Baptists in Alabama occurred in the 1970s. As part of the Bold Mission emphasis, the leadership from the five Baptist conventions jointly conceived and planned "Good News Alabama," an evangelistic effort designed to involve Baptist churches in witnessing to every person in the state. A concentrated advertising campaign involved bumper stickers, billboards, spot commercials on radio and television, and newspaper ads. A toll-free telephone service provided personal answers to inquirers. County "Good News Alabama" task forces, including both blacks and whites, were used to implement these projects.

A major commitment by leadership in the five Baptist conventions is the establishment of inter-Baptist fellowship committees within the counties of Alabama. These committees are planned to foster better communication, fellowship, and joint ministry between black and white Baptists.

A. EARL POTTS

ALASKA ASSOCIATIONS. See ALASKA BAPTIST CONVENTION.

ALASKA BAPTIST CONVENTION (III; cf. Alaska, Baptists in, Vol. I).

I. History. The years 1969-80 brought rapid social and economic changes to Alaska. The discovery in 1968 of the largest oil field in North America on Alaska's North Slope and the subsequent construction of the 800-mile Trans-Alaska Pipeline from Prudhoe Bay on the Arctic Ocean to Valdez brought thousands of people and an economic boom to the state. In 1971 Congress settled the aboriginal land claims of Alaska's Eskimos, Indians, and Aleuts by granting them title to 40,000,000 acres of land and a financial settlement of almost $1,000,000,000 to be paid over a 20-year period. A revitalized fishing industry followed the extension of the protective fishing zone 200 miles along Alaska's extended coastline.

As the 1980s arrived, construction of a natural gas pipeline along the route of the Alaska Highway was anticipated, and the state was pitted against the federal government over the withdrawal of over 100,000,000 acres of public lands for national parks and monuments, wildlife refuges, national forests, and wild and scenic rivers to preserve Alaska's pristine wilderness for future generations. Members of the churches and missions of the Alaska Baptist Convention were involved in all of these activities.

In 1969 the convention had 37 churches and 17 missions. In 1980 it had 41 churches and 28 missions. There were three black churches, one church and six missions predominantly Eskimo in the Northwest Arctic, two Indian villages in the Central Arctic, and one native church in both Anchorage and Fairbanks.

In 1969 there were 5,805 resident members, compared to 6,624 in 1980. The convention staff in 1969 included: E. W. Hunke, Jr., executive secretary; E. C. Chron, state missions director; Allen Meeks, director of religious education; and Judy Rice, Woman's Missionary Union secre-

tary. In Dec., 1970, E. W. Hunke, Jr., resigned to become western regional coordinator for the Home Mission Board. His successor, elected in May, 1971, was J. Troy Prince of Baton Rouge, LA. Upon the resignation of E. C. Chron, in 1972, responsibilities of the state missions director were assigned to the executive secretary. In 1973 Hollis V. Bryant of Juneau became church extension director and Chugach associational missionary. He served in this dual capacity until Jan., 1976, when he became full-time associational missionary. In 1975 W. R. Canary of Arkansas became associate in the area of religious education with responsibilities for music, student work, and church administration. In 1976 John H. Allen, associate director of the Church Extension Department of the Home Mission Board, was elected director of state missions. In 1978 W. R. Canary resigned as religious education associate, and J. Troy Prince resigned as executive director, a title change approved by the convention in 1978. Allen H. Meeks served as interim executive director from Jan., 1979, to Aug., 1980, when he was elected executive director of the convention.

In May, 1969, a special session of the convention revised the Articles of Incorporation to make them comfortable to state law. Another document called the Restated Articles was adopted in 1971. Conflicting statements in these two documents were corrected by convention action in 1977.

Planning for a new Baptist Building was begun in the fall of 1970. The old convention office building, a converted dwelling in downtown Anchorage secured with the help of the HMB, was sold and the proceeds used to construct the new Baptist Building on O'Malley Road, seven miles from the city's center. The structure, completed in 1978, was constructed near the Turnagain Children's Home on approximately 120 acres of property deeded to the convention by the First Baptist Church, Anchorage, in 1971. The building cost approximately $160,000.

In 1971 as part of its 25th anniversary celebration, the convention published *In This Land,* by Naomi Ruth Hunke. The 334-page book tells the story of the growth of Southern Baptists in Alaska.

The convention, which had been given Orton Ranch near Ketchikan for a Southeast Alaska camp, did not develop the property and in Nov., 1972, deeded the property to the First Baptist Church, Ketchikan.

An era of Baptist life in Alaska came to an end in Jan., 1974, when Felton H. Griffin, pastor of the First Baptist Church, Anchorage, since 1945, resigned. Griffin was not only the senior pastor in the state but the person most responsible for the formation of the convention and its recognition by the SBC.

Alaska experienced a population growth from 302,361 in 1970 to approximately 414,197 in 1980. The number of resident church members, the enrollment in Sunday School, and the number of baptisms in the churches of the convention remained relatively constant and lagged behind previous growth patterns of the convention. For example, in the metropolitan Anchorage area where almost half of Alaska's population lives, only one church and one mission were begun during the period, while one church left the convention to join another Baptist body, and two churches disbanded or united with other congregations.

The period was not without denominational conflicts. The question of receiving members by alien immersion was a problem in Anchorage in 1970-71. Individual churches in almost every area of the state experienced problems with charismatic pastors and laymen. In 1978 the convention learned that designated monies had been used to cover operation expenses. Budget cuts and increased giving by the churches enabled the convention to begin repayment of those designated funds. In 1979 the convention decided the office of executive director was not to be filled until all designated money had been repaid. The repayment of these funds was expected to be completed late in 1980.

After over one half of the deficit was repaid by the annual meeting of the convention in Aug., 1980, and after financial responsibility was restored, the convention elected Allen Meeks as executive director. Meeks had served as interim director on three occasions.

The convention continues to publish the monthly paper, *Alaska Baptist Messenger*. The executive director continued to assume responsibility as editor.

II. Program of Work. *Alaska Baptist Family Service Center.*—The Turnagain Children's Home, begun in 1949, had been supported through the years by the First Baptist Church, Anchorage, the Chugach Association, and the convention. The board of trustees elected by the convention was dissolved in 1971 and supervision of the home placed under the executive board. In 1972 the convention voted to phase out the cottage-type orphanage operation and start a new type of ministry. In Jan., 1973, C. J. Lawrence of Texas became the first director of Christian Social Ministries for the convention. Through the sale of 100 acres of convention property on O'Malley Road, the construction of the new Alaska Baptist Family Service Center was begun in May, 1974. The center, which cost $290,000 to construct, opened in May, 1975. The facility provides space for a staff and 12 children in need of temporary care. The center also provides space for personal and family counseling. Following the death of C. J. Lawrence in Sep., 1975, Harold Hime of Texas was elected director of Christian Social Ministries. His successor in Dec., 1979, was Will Miles. In 1978 the convention again elected a separate board of trustees for the Alaska Baptist Family Service Center.

Associational Developments.—The Chugach Baptist Association in 1980 reported 19 churches and 11 missions, nearly half of the churches and missions in the convention. Edward Wolfe became director of missions for the association in 1977. The association reactivated its camp near Wasilla and built a road to it. The churches con-

structed five new cabins. The camp was named the Laverne Griffin Baptist Camp in honor of the wife of Felton Griffin. New churches or missions were established in the 1970s in the following communities of the association: Willow, Kenney Lake, Sutton, Wasilla, Mountain View, Anchorage, and a Korean congregation in Fairview. Trinity Church, Mountain View, disbanded in 1979, and turned the property over to Chugach Association. The site was used to house Faith East, a satellite of Faith Baptist, the associational office, the Native Training School, and the new Native Mission. New sites were purchased on Rabbit Creek Road in south Anchorage and in Sutton, north of Palmer.

The Tanana Valley Association serves interior Alaska. Bill Duncan became the association's first director of missions in 1978. The association purchased land near Delta Junction for an associational camp and began construction on facilities in 1979. The association had 10 churches and four missions in 1969. In 1977 a new church was organized in Fairbanks. Missions were established in Badger Road, Fairbanks, and in Northway, near the Canadian border. A new site was purchased at Healy.

The Tongass Association has seven churches and one mission which are located in Southeast Alaska.

Lewis and Alma McClendon were appointed as missionaries to the logging camps on Prince of Wales Island, the second largest island in USA possessions. They moved to Coffman Cove, traveling to their other camps during the week by airplane, boat, hiking trails, and by an all-terrain vehicle. In 1980 Lewis McClendon was appointed as the association's first director of missions.

The Trinity Baptist Church of Ketchikan, organized in 1972, developed fellowship problems in 1978 and ceased to meet. First Church, Petersburg, built their first church unit in 1978 after meeting in rented facilities for many years. Trinity Baptist of Juneau was established in 1979 and was looking for a site and facilities as 1980 began. The First Baptist Church of Ketchikan owns and operates Orton Ranch Camp which was once given to the convention for a state encampment. Several new constructions have been added.

Tustumena Association was organized in May, 1968, on the Kenai Peninsula. Maurice Murdock, first moderator in 1968, was killed in a logging accident in 1980. There are four churches and three missions in the association. The HMB and the convention have funded a new director of missions for the association, effective Jan. 1, 1981. New construction included Kodiak Baptist Church after years of renting, and a new parsonage and music director's home for First Baptist Church, Soldotna. New church sites have been purchased at Funny River Road and Kalifonsky Beach Road. A new mission was established at Homer in 1978.

Alaska Baptist Native Work.—Alaska Baptist native work was given a major emphasis with the beginning of a statewide Native Baptist Bible Conference in 1977 at the Friendship Mission in

ALASKA STATISTICAL SUMMARY

Year	Associations	Churches	Church Membership	Baptisms	SS Enrollment	VBS Enrollment	CT Enrollment	WMU Enrollment	Brotherhood Enrollment	Ch. Music Enrollment	Mission Gifts	Total Gifts	Value Church Property
1969	4	36	10,539	791	7,420	6,896	3,547	1,306	334	906	$131,059	$1,037,026	$ 5,807,415
1970	4	36	10,740	674	7,305	5,112	3,401	1,139	278	832	129,389	1,095,946	6,013,415
1971	4	37	12,404	832	7,468	3,888	3,103	1,065	354	959	231,577	1,283,113	7,152,315
1972	4	37	12,961	773	7,355	4,629	2,835	1,016	371	840	260,279	1,397,110	7,609,322
1973	4	37	12,699	656	6,955	4,429	2,166	829	352	911	236,149	1,413,394	7,880,015
1974	4	37	12,842	684	6,639	4,882	2,133	785	406	960	225,593	1,478,018	9,472,120
1975	4	38	13,562	679	6,553	5,439	1,921	876	431	1,010	294,186	1,914,350	14,042,800
1976	4	37	14,597	645	6,648	4,374	1,711	800	430	1,158	345,782	2,556,671	15,739,000
1977	4	39	14,076	718	7,257	4,343	1,908	841	384	1,355	486,161	2,696,808	16,160,238
1978	4	40	14,837	837	7,122	5,144	1,912	1,038	570	1,758	588,481	3,037,188	21,160,633
1979	4	40	13,696	597	7,417	4,841	2,170	984	516	1,502	561,279	3,129,627	17,765,734
1980	4	40	15,282	894	6,883	5,613	1,629	836	544	1,397	555,597	2,934,171	20,587,653

SHIRLEY F. MIEBS

Fairbanks. It was so successful that it became an annual affair. The Native Training School was reopened in 1978 with five students. Don Rollins came to Anchorage to direct the school in 1980. Work was opened in Nome and Ekwok, and reopened at Ft. Yukon. Valeria Sherard was transferred to Friendship, Fairbanks, after 17 years in Kiana. In 1978 the convention named its state mission offering "The Valeria Sherard Offering for State Missions." Alaska mission funds increased greatly through the State Mission Offering, 2000 Club, and Cooperative Program.

Mission Support and Social Ministries.—The 2000 Club was raising about $18,000 a year by the end of the 1970s, having averaged only less than $10,000 for most of its 20-year life. The State Mission Offering averaged $5,000 for the first half of the 1970s but reached $15,000-$16,000 for the last four years of the 1970s.

Harold H. Hime, director of the Christian Social Mission program, 1976-79, was succeeded by Will Miles in 1979. The basic work centers in family services, with active child-care programs at Anchorage and Nome. Fairview Center at Anchorage and Friendship Mission at Fairbanks conduct programs of Christian Social Ministries. Friendship of Fairbanks and Grandview Church of Anchorage conduct programs of literacy and citizenship.

JOHN H. ALLEN and RICHARD MILLER

ALASKA BAPTIST MESSENGER. See ALASKA BAPTIST CONVENTION.

ALCOHOL AND OTHER DRUGS (cf. Abstinence, Vol. I). American drinking patterns are a result of the mixture of imported practices and their interaction with the American frontier life-style. In colonial days alcoholic beverages were consumed by a large portion of the American people. As the rowdy drinking patterns of frontier life developed, moderation and abstinence received more attention from the churches. The American Society for the Promotion of Temperance, founded in 1826, initially emphasized moderation, but by 1850 abstinence from all alcoholic beverages was declared as the goal, although there was considerable opposition to total abstinence within the society. This disagreement initiated the big controversy between "wets" and "drys," which has characterized much of the discussion on alcohol in America.

The Prohibition movement, which culminated in the passage of a constitutional amendment in 1919, had its beginning as early as 1851. Some view Prohibition, which was repealed in 1933, as a total failure, while others point to the marked decrease in alcohol consumption and in alcohol-related problems.

Since its founding, the SBC has been actively involved in opposing alcohol consumption. As early as 1887 a Committee on Temperance was appointed. In 1908 the SBC voted to appoint a standing committee on temperance, which later was expanded to the Committee on Temperance and Social Service. Chaired by A. J. Barton (*q.v.* II), the committee was active in efforts to achieve Prohibition. Although the committee dealt with other moral issues, alcohol received by far the most attention during the 28 years of Barton's leadership.

Nearly every SBC meeting has passed a resolution condemning alcohol use and abuse. During the 1960s and 1970s, the SBC often included other drugs in resolutions on alcohol.

Illicit drug use, other than alcohol, was a limited occurrence in the United States before the early 1960s. In a short time illicit drugs, such as marijuana, heroin, cocaine, and "angel dust," were available in most places. In addition, much concern existed over the nonmedical use of drugs legally available by prescription. These included barbiturates, tranquilizers, and amphetamines. Studies on smoking revealed the serious health hazards posed by the drug nicotine.

JOHN A. WOOD

ALDERSON, JOHN, JR. (b. New Jersey, Mar. 5, 1738; d. Greenbrier County, VA, Mar. 5, 1821). Pioneer preacher in western Virginia. Son of John Alderson, Sr., a Baptist pastor, and Jane (Curtis) Alderson, he moved at age 17 with his parents from New Jersey to Rockingham County, VA. He married Mary Carroll. Succeeding his father as pastor of Lynville Creek Baptist Church in Rockingham in 1775, he moved in 1777 to Monroe on the Greenbrier River and helped organize the Greenbrier Church, Nov. 24, 1781. Alderson helped begin other Virginia churches, including Indian Creek and Big Levels, and was pastor at Indian Creek for many years.

In his latter years Alderson devoted most of his time to preaching and to the work of Greenbrier Association, which he served often as moderator. He helped evangelize and establish the reputation of Baptists in a large area of the Virginia frontier. Alderson, WV, was named for him and his family. He is buried beside the Greenbrier church.

WILLIAM L. LUMPKIN

ALLEN, THOMAS ROBERT, JR. (b. Atlanta, GA, Nov. 25, 1906; d. Miami, FL, June 9, 1975). Seminary staff member. The son of Thomas Robert, an auto parts department manager, and Ouida Ragsdale Allen, he attended Georgia Tech, Stetson University (B.A., 1931), and Southern Baptist Theological Seminary (Th.M., 1934). He married Eunice C. Fuller of Trigg County, KY, Oct. 29, 1929. They had one daughter, Christine. As a student at Southern Seminary, he began working with the maintenance department, Sep., 1931. In Nov., 1939, he became superintendent of buildings and grounds for the seminary, retiring July 31, 1972. He is buried at Scottsdale, AZ.

LEO T. CRISMON

ALLEN, WILLIAM COX (b. Dillon County, SC, June 22, 1879; d. Columbia, SC,

Feb. 19, 1971). Pastor and editor. The son of William Benjamin and Theodosia Cox Allen, he attended Furman University (B.S., 1900), the University of South Carolina (M.A.; Ph.D., 1931), and The Southern Baptist Theological Seminary. Pastor of several churches in South Carolina, he served as assistant recording secretary of the South Carolina Baptist Convention for 20 years; member of the general board of the state convention; trustee of various South Carolina Baptist institutions; editor of the *Baptist Courier*, 1935-40; and vice-president of the SBC, 1940. He married Eva Eula Padgett, Dec. 25, 1907. She died the following year. He married Annie Laura Sherwood, June 11, 1911. Their children were Wilton, Gwendolyne, and Anne. He is buried in Riverside Cemetery, Dillon, SC.

W. FLETCHER ALLEN

ALLISON, FRANCIS PAUL (b. Lockwood, MO, Feb. 19, 1921; d. Nashville, TN, Aug. 9, 1971). Pastor and denominational worker. The son of Wilfred Harold Allison and Geneva Cordelia Allison, he attended Southwest Baptist College, South Missouri State College, William Jewell College (B.A.), and Central Baptist Theological Seminary. He married Wilma Rapier, Nov. 4, 1945. They had two children, Pamela and David. His Missouri pastorates included Swope Park Chapel, Kansas City; Beverly Hills Church, Independence; and Calvary Church, Columbia.

Allison served as associate executive secretary-treasurer of the Kansas-Nebraska Convention of Southern Baptists, 1958-69, filling the roles of director of the programs of stewardship and finance, public relations, and promotion and missions. As director of promotion, he edited the *Baptist Digest*, 1959-67. From 1969 until the time of his death, he was director of stewardship development for the Stewardship Commission, SBC. He is buried in Woodlawn Cemetery, Nashville, TN.

N. J. WESTMORELAND

ALMAND, CLAUDE MARION (b. Winnsboro, LA, May 31, 1916; d. Jacksonville, FL, Sep. 12, 1957). Composer and music educator. The son of Pearl Almand and Claude Almand, a Baptist minister, he was the first director of graduate studies in church music at Southern Baptist Theological Seminary. Almand held the position while also serving as associate dean of the School of Music at the University of Louisville, 1944-53. Prior to those positions, he was professor at Peabody College, 1940-44. From 1953 until his death, he was dean of the School of Music at Stetson University.

Almand was educated at Louisiana College (B.A., B.M., 1934), Louisiana State University (M.M., 1938), and Eastman School of Music of the University of Rochester (Ph.D., 1940). Highly regarded among Southern Baptists for upholding high musical standards for churches, Almand was one of several outstanding composers awarded commissions by the Louisville Orchestra, 1948, 1949. His best known sacred composition is *The Resurrection Story* (1959), an Easter cantata. He married Lenoir Patton, July 27, 1950. He is buried in Oakdale Cemetery, Deland, FL.

PAUL T. LANGSTON

AMERICAN BAPTIST ASSOCIATION

(I, III). A national body of missionary Baptist churches which are fundamentalist in biblical interpretation, premillennial in eschatology, and separatist in interchurch relations. The national meeting of the association, to which each cooperating church may send three messengers, elects each year the following committees or agencies—a missionary committee to solicit support and channel funds to home and foreign missionaries; a missionary service trust to serve as a liaison between the foreign missionaries and governmental agencies; a literature committee for publications; a history and archives committee; and youth encampment trustees to manage the youth encampment facilities.

The association's constituency supports nine schools in the United States, primarily colleges or institutes, and four institutes in foreign countries; publishes 15 periodicals; and sponsors 66 missionaries on 15 foreign fields. While an independent survey, based on associational records and correspondence, discovered for 1971 a membership of only 207,000 in 1,540 churches, the association in 1981 claimed about 1,500,000 members in about 5,000 churches. About 40 percent of the membership is in Arkansas with some associational strength in the neighboring states of Texas, Oklahoma, and Louisiana, as well as in Florida and California.

BIBLIOGRAPHY: Conrad N. Glover and Austin T. Powers, *The American Baptist Association, 1924-1974* (1979).

ALBERT W. WARDIN, JR.

AMERICAN BAPTIST CHURCHES IN THE U.S.A.

(cf. American Baptist Convention, Vols. I, III). About 6,000 local congregations affiliate with the American Baptist Churches (ABC), which have an estimated total membership of over 1,300,000. Denominational headquarters are at Valley Forge, PA. Formerly the Northern Baptist Convention (1907-50), then the American Baptist Convention (1950-72), the new name was adopted in 1972. In 1968 the Convention appointed a Study Commission on Denominational Structure and accepted the commission's report on reorganization at the Convention's last annual meeting in Denver, CO, in 1972. The work of a Study Commission on Relationships, created in 1974, further clarified the relationship of the new national structures to regional, state, and city societies. The commission's report (1976) led to the adoption and ratification of a new set of bylaws which went into effect, Jan. 1, 1979. Hence the decade of the 1970s was marked by a thorough reorganization of the ABC.

The adoption of the new name symbolized a shift from a "society" to a "churchly" concept of organization. In the interests of economy, stewardship, and inclusiveness, the ABC changed its former annual gathering of representatives of churches to a biennial meeting. Both the local churches and the various regional organizations which enter into covenant relations with the denomination elect delegates to the biennial meeting, which elects the ABC officers, and which alone can amend the bylaws. The other functions of the biennial meeting are celebration, inspiration, fellowship, sharing information, training in leadership and mission, and expressing the will of the delegates on issues of concern.

A General Board of about 200 members, which serves as the "board of directors" of the ABC, now conducts most of the major legislative functions once carried out by the annual convention. The board must meet annually and usually meets twice a year. Members normally serve a four-year term, so arranged that about 25 percent of the board is replaced each year. Approximately 75 percent of its members are elected by about 150 election districts, which rotate their representatives among the categories of clergy, laymen, and laywomen. The other 25 percent are at-large members elected by the biennial meeting. This provides a balance with respect to age, sex, ethnic and language groupings, and needed skills.

The board has a long list of functions, including the giving of general oversight and direction to the life of the denomination; serving as its legislative body; setting policy in the areas of program functioning, planning, coordinating, and evaluating; adopting policy statements and resolutions; and electing the general secretary. Robert C. Campbell served in that capacity throughout the decade.

What were once independent and autonomous national societies for home and foreign missions and for education and publication are now under the control of the General Board. The legal existence of the societies continues, but the board determines their functions and selects out of its membership the national program boards—the Boards of Education Ministries, of International Ministries, and of National Ministries. The Board of Educational Ministries (BEM) and its staff direct the preparation and distribution of curricular materials for Sunday Schools and other educational settings, supervise the work of Judson Press, and provide the administrative support for American Baptist Men, American Baptist Women, the American Baptist Assembly at Green Lake, WI, the American Baptist Historical Society, and the Commission on the Ministry. The BEM also maintains relationships with schools, colleges, and seminaries related to the denomination.

The Board of International Ministries (BIM) guides all mission and relief work outside the United States and Puerto Rico. In the 1970s, churches in Asia, Africa, and Latin America related to the BIM enjoyed remarkable growth with more than 400,000 baptisms recorded.

This board continued historic emphases on meeting basic human needs through educational, medical, agricultural, and community development programs.

The Board of National Ministries (BNM) provides support and resources for local congregations and for regional, state, and city agencies in the areas of evangelism, public mission, social action, and relief. Much attention in the 1970s focused on developing an evangelistic lifestyle for individuals, churches, and boards, and on emphasizing work towards justice for all people. The BNM has been active in refugee work and in providing nonprofit housing.

In sum, these arrangements of program boards of about 40 members each, functioning under the General Board of which they are all members, have implemented the shift from a society to a churchly concept of organization for the ABC. The board also has representation on the fourth national board, the Ministers and Missionaries Benefit Board.

The regional, state, and city agencies which enter into the "Covenant of Relations" with the General Board elect representatives to the biennial meeting and participate in the raising, collecting, and distributing of contributions for carrying out the American Baptist mission beyond the local church. The covenant, one of the significant achievements of the 1970s, begins with affirmations about the nature of covenant relationship and declares that "It is appropriate, therefore, that American Baptists join together in local congregations and in denominational organizations by way of covenant in order to accomplish common purposes related to the Gospel of our Lord Jesus Christ."

The covenant essays to bridge the gap between congregational autonomy and denominational order by stating a dozen biblical and theological assumptions about the nature of the church, beginning with "The Church is all the people of God who have committed themselves to live under the Lordship of Jesus Christ," and "While the primary expression of the Church is the local congregation, the Church is also expressed in groupings of interdependent congregations in associations, regional units, or national bodies."

The American Baptist Churches are members of the North American Baptist Fellowship, the Baptist World Alliance, and the National and World Councils of Churches. They have an "associated" relationship with the Progressive National Baptist Convention, Inc., and the Church of the Brethren.

BIBLIOGRAPHY: Robert T. Handy, "American Baptist Polity," *Baptist History and Heritage (July, 1979).*

ROBERT T. HANDY

AMERICAN BAPTIST CHURCHES IN THE U.S.A. INTERNATIONAL MINISTRIES (cf. American Baptist Foreign Mission Society, Vol. I; American Baptist Foreign Mission Boards, Vol. III). An important element in the reorganization of the American Baptist Churches in the U.S.A. in the 1970s was the

transfer of outreach responsibility in Latin America from the Board of National Ministries to the new Board of International Ministries.

The successful completion of a denominational capital funds campaign produced more than $16,000,000 in new resources for capital projects and short-term programs sponsored by both the National and International Ministries. The churches in Asia, Africa, and Latin America related to International Ministries experienced spectacular growth with more than 400,000 baptisms being recorded in the 10-year period and the total membership reaching over 1,260,000. A strong emphasis continued upon educational, medical, agricultural, and community development programs that speak to basic human need.

The increasing maturity of churches in a number of areas made possible the redeployment of personnel and finances. American Baptist missionaries were sent for the first time to such places as Bangladesh, Israel, Nepal, and Nigeria. International Ministries also forged closer, supporting relationships with Baptist communities and leaders in Eastern Europe.

Periodic meetings of the Baptist Council on World Missions, formed in 1968 in Bangkok, brought together the leaders of the Baptist conventions and unions related to American Baptists for interchange of programs and ideas and gave these overseas leaders a stronger voice in the determination of mission policy and strategy.

National Ministries continued its emphasis on both parish and public ministries and also continued to be one of the leading agencies in refugee resettlement. Through representation at the Church Center at the United Nations and its Washington office, meaningful contacts occurred at these two nerve centers of international and national decision making.

CHESTER J. JUMP, JR.

AMERICAN BAPTIST CONVENTION (I, III). See AMERICAN BAPTIST CHURCHES IN THE U.S.A.

AMERICAN BAPTIST THEOLOGICAL SEMINARY (I, III). Enrollment at American Baptist Theological Seminary grew in 1969-80 to 190 students. A scholarship program begun in 1977 by the Southern Baptist Commission on the American Baptist Theological Seminary provides support for 100 church vocation students from National Baptist churches.

Title to the main campus property was transferred from the Holding Board to the trustees in 1977. A major renovation of campus buildings was completed in 1979. The SBC approved in 1978 an agreement with the National Baptist Convention of the U.S.A., Inc., specifying a governing board of 32 trustees equally divided between the Conventions and a Holding Board of eight Southern Baptist and four National Baptist members.

Financial support for the seminary in 1978-79 included $53,510 from National Baptist sources and $176,945 from Southern Baptist sources. Tuition and other income provided additional funds for a total budget of $332,941 for the academic year.

On June 1, 1980, Odell McGlothian, Sr., formerly director of publications for the Sunday School Publishing Board of the National Baptist Convention of the U.S.A., Inc., became the 11th president of the seminary. Charles E. Boddie was named chancellor to serve as a goodwill ambassador for the institution.

GEORGE E. CAPPS, JR.

AMERICAN BAPTIST THEOLOGICAL SEMINARY, HOLDING BOARD OF. The 1922 agreement related to the American Baptist Theological Seminary called for the creation of a board of eight Southern Baptists and four National Baptists to "hold and control property" of the seminary. Under the 1964-65 agreement, the campus was conveyed by deed to the seminary trustees in 1977. Two parcels acquired for the seminary's discontinued farming operation were sold. The funds were invested by the board. The Holding Board continues to hold title to the remaining property.

GEORGE E. CAPPS, JR.

AMERICAN BAPTIST THEOLOGICAL SEMINARY, SOUTHERN BAPTIST COMMISSION ON THE. In 1913 the SBC appointed a committee (commission) of nine to "advise and confer with the colored brethren" regarding establishing a Negro Theological Seminary. E. Y. Mullins (q.v. II) was chairman of this committee (commission) until 1925. In 1919 O. L. Hailey (q.v. I) became the first paid secretary of the commission. The Southern Baptist Commission on "the Negro Baptist Seminary" which had acted jointly with a commission of the National Baptist Convention was dissolved in 1925 and replaced with the Commission on the American Baptist Theological Seminary.

The new commission had eight members who were also members of the Holding Board for the seminary. In subsequent actions the SBC has elected 16 members to the commission who also serve as trustees of the seminary.

As approved by the SBC, the objective of the SBC Commission on the American Baptist Theological Seminary is to "act as liaison between the National Baptist Convention of the U.S.A., Inc. and the Southern Baptist Convention in matters relating to the American Baptist Theological Seminary and through the Seminary to assist generally in developing a strong program of ministerial education for National Baptists."

The executive director-treasurer of the Education Commission was asked to serve as secretary-treasurer of the Southern Baptist Commission on the American Baptist Theological Seminary in 1962. Secretaries of the commission have been: O. L. Hailey (q.v. I), 1919-34; Eugene Perry Aldredge (q.v. I), 1934-49; Leland Stanford Sedberry (q.v. III), 1949-61; Rabun

Brantley, 1961-70; Ben Coleman Fisher, 1970-78; and Arthur L. Walker, Jr., 1978- .

ARTHUR L. WALKER, JR.

AMERICAN SOCIETY OF MISSIOLOGY. This society was organized in June, 1973, at Concordia Seminary in St. Louis, MO, as an outgrowth of the Association of Professors of Missions. The purpose of the society is to promote the scholarly study of theological, historical, social, and practical questions relating to Christian missions; foster fellowship among missiologists; facilitate mutual assistance and exchange of information; and encourage research and publication in the field of Christian missiology. The organization is made up of evangelicals, conciliar Protestants, and Roman Catholics. Membership includes professors of missions and staff members of various social services and mission boards, society executives, missionaries, and writers. The society publishes the journal, *Missiology: An International Review*. The membership of more than 600 includes many Southern Baptist missions professors, administrators, and missionaries.

M. WENDELL BELEW

ANABAPTIST HISTORIOGRAPHY (cf. Anabaptists, Vols. I, III). The study of sixteenth-century Anabaptism during the years 1970-80 was marked by increasing specialization and refined methodology among scholars of varying perspectives. George H. Williams' masterful synthesis, *The Radical Reformation* (1962), remains the standard survey, although recent scholars have questioned placing Anabaptism within the Radical Reformation. The appearance of new editions and translations of primary source materials has contributed to Anabaptist research.

Four general trends exist in current Anabaptist research: (1) Interest in the origins and typology of Anabaptism. James M. Stayer, *Anabaptists and the Sword* (1972), has challenged the theory of homogenous origins, and other scholars have argued for a "polygenetic" understanding of Anabaptist beginnings. Kenneth R. Davis, *Anabaptism and Asceticism* (1974), has restated the case for the influence of medieval lay piety on early Anabaptism. (2) Studies of the impact of Anabaptism within a localized area. Notable are Cornelius Krahn, *Dutch Anabaptism* (1968); Irvin B. Horst, *The Radical Brethren: Anabaptism and the English Reformation to 1558* (1972); and Claus-Peter Clasen, *The Anabaptists in South and Central Germany, Switzerland, and Austria* (1978). (3) Focus on individual Anabaptist leaders. This includes reinvestigations of major figures: Christolf Bornhäuser, *Leben und Lehre Menno Simons* (1973), and Christolf Windhorst, *Täuferisches Taufverständnis* (1976), on Balthasar Hubmaier, as well as new research on lesser-known characters; and Gottfried Seebas on Hans Hut in Hans-Jürgen Goertz (ed.), *Radikale Reformatoren* (1978), and Klaus Deppermann, *Melchior Hoffman* (1979). (4) Studies on the relationship of Anabaptism to the mainline reformers. Examination of the complex interaction of Anabaptists with Reformation leaders has shed new light on both the radicals and their ''magisterial'' opponents. Scholars who have written on this subject include W. Balke, *Calvijn en de doperse Radikalen* (1973), and M. Lienhard (ed.), *The Origins and Characteristics of Anabaptism* (1977).

TIMOTHY GEORGE

ANDERSON, JANE AGNES WALKER CREE BOSE (b. Ware, Hertsfordshire, England, Apr. 12, 1880; d. Knoxville, TN, Apr. 25, 1971). Woman's Missionary Union leader. Daughter of Scottish preacher Archibald Cree and Agnes Walker Cree, she attended Limestone College. On July 28, 1908, she married Charles Alfred Bose. They had one child, Frederick. She served the Kentucky WMU as office secretary, 1913-16, and corresponding secretary, 1916-25. In 1925 she became principal of the WMU Training School. She resigned to marry James Hughes Anderson, June 10, 1930. She is buried in Highland Memorial Cemetery, Knoxville, TN.

DORIS DEVAULT

ANDERSON COLLEGE (I, III). In 1971 J. Cordell Maddox became vice-president and in 1973 the eighth president, succeeding John E. Rouse, who had served since 1957. The enrollment increased to over 1,000 students. The curriculum of the college expanded as several new courses and programs were added. The faculty increased to 49 full-time members.

In the 1970s the college achieved national recognition in athletics through achievements in men's basketball, tennis, and golf. The women's basketball teams won four consecutive national junior college championships.

The library building constructed in 1956 was more than doubled in size in 1975 through the gift of Gladys Atkins Johnston (*q.v.*) and named for her late husband, the former South Carolina governor and senator, Olin D. Johnston.

Two successful financial campaigns secured funds for endowment and building needs, and the Abney Athletic Center was begun before Maddox left in 1977 to become president of Carson-Newman College.

Ray P. Rust became the ninth president of the college in Mar., 1978. During his presidency the college achieved a record enrollment of over 1,200 students. The annual giving program of the college increased substantially, and endowment reached its present level of $1,616,350. The Abney Athletic Center was completed without increasing the capital indebtedness of the college, and plans have been drawn for a fine arts center. Over $1,000,000 are designated for the initial phase of this project from funds on hand and pledged. Other plans for the immediate future include the building of a new dormitory for 100 students and a faculty office building.

The college annually graduates approximately 200 students with associate degrees in arts, fine arts, business education, and fashion merchandising.

PAUL TALMADGE

ANGELL, CHARLES ROY (b. Boone Mill, VA, Oct. 8, 1889; d. Miami, FL, Sep. 11, 1971). Pastor. He was a graduate of Richmond University (B.A.), Penn University (M.A.), Crozier Theological Seminary (B.D.), and Johns Hopkins University (Ph.D.). Stetson University awarded him an honorary D.D. degree, June 1, 1942. Angell married Ilma Meade of Elizabeth City, NC, Oct. 8, 1915. Their children were Charles Roy, Jr., Pattye Kathryn, and Ilma Louise. His pastorates included Elizabeth City, NC; First, Charlottesville, VA; Fulton Avenue, Baltimore, MD; First, Baton Rouge, LA; First, San Antonio, TX; and Central, Miami, FL, where he served from 1936 until his retirement in 1962.

He was a frequent speaker at campfire services at Ridgecrest, especially during Student Week and Training Union Week from 1937 to 1960. He was the author of several sermon books noted for their apt illustrations. Included are: *Iron Shoes* (1953), *The Price Tags of Life* (1959), *God's Gold Mines* (1962), *Shields of Brass* (1965), and *Rejoicing on Great Days* (1968). All were published by Broadman Press. Angell served as vice-president of the SBC, 1945-46; president of the Florida Baptist Convention, 1949; and as trustee of Baptist Hospital of Miami and of Stetson University. In 1951 he delivered the annual sermon at the SBC in San Francisco. He is buried in Woodlawn Cemetery, Miami, FL.

CONRAD WILLARD

ANGOLA, MISSION IN (III). Continuing work was established in 1968. During the 1970s Baptist mission work expanded from Luanda into several major population centers. By 1975 four missionary couples were projecting plans for agricultural, radio, Bible correspondence, theological training, and evangelistic ministries. On Aug. 10, 1975, political instability necessitated their evacuation. Conditions after independence from Portugal on Nov. 11, 1975, prevented permanent return, and by 1977 all missionaries except Curtis and Betty (McCown) Dixon transferred to other countries. The Dixons, living in Portugal since 1977, continued to provide Sunday School literature, Bibles, radio programs, Bible correspondence courses, and Theological Education by Extension materials to Angola. The Dixons transferred to the mission in Portugal in 1981. In 1979 the Angola Baptist Convention reported 72 churches and 160 students in five theological education centers. The Baptist Book Store continued to operate in Luanda.

JOY NEAL

ANNIE ARMSTRONG EASTER OFFERING. See WEEK OF PRAYER FOR HOME MISSIONS AND ANNIE ARMSTRONG EASTER OFFERING.

ANNUITY BOARD, SBC (III; cf. Relief and Annuity Board, Vol. II).

I. History. The year 1970 represented a period of innovative change for the Annuity Board. In that year elected trustees authorized the reorganization of the board, the installation of new business systems, and a change in staff titles. The installation of the new accounting system, which allowed the board to credit benefits more swiftly than ever before, provided the method for upgrading benefits. Through the new system, members both received benefits based on current values of funds held in trust and received extra credits similar to dividends for members in Plans A10, A11, and A25. Titles of all officers were changed to comply with those used in the financial world. Darold H. Morgan, who later would become president, was elected to serve as senior vice-president and understudy to R. Alton Reed, the president. Frank Durham, a retired business executive, was also elected senior vice-president of investments. In 1970 assets held in trust stood at $230,049,237, a total that would increase dramatically in the next 10 years.

Reed retired as chief executive officer in 1971. During the two decades of his leadership, assets grew from $35,091,515 to $292,705,482. Accomplishments in 1971 included additional payments to retired persons which involved a guarantee of not less than 4 percent in their monthly checks, as well as an 8.33 percent bonus paid in one month and a 16.67 percent bonus in another for a total of 29 percent. A record 6 percent interest compounded monthly was credited to all benefit reserves in 1971.

The year 1972 saw the dawning of a new era when Morgan became president. Noteworthy achievements under Morgan that year included the payment of a 13th check amounting to 16.67 percent of an annual benefit to certain annuitants and the allocation of a record 10 percent good experience credit to the accounts of most Plan A members. Underwritten by a new insurance carrier, a health benefit plan for church employees was developed and scheduled for implementation in 1973. Aetna Life & Casualty Company was named the new insurance carrier to underwrite programs.

In 1973 the widow benefit under Plan A increased from 40 to 50 percent, and a temporary income benefit was incorporated in Plans A10, A11, A12, A13, and A14. The benefit provided assistance to widows during critical financial periods which normally follow a husband's death. Economic and political upheavals both at home and abroad made 1973 "among the most difficult times in memory," observed Morgan. Still, the board paid out a record $15,506,663 in retirement benefits and an estimated $9,000,000 in insurance claims. The largest number of annuitants receiving benefits for the first time included 767 in Plan A, 531 in Plan B, and 74 in Plan C. Annuitants received an eighth consecutive 13th check, despite the adverse investment climate. The extra benefits amounted to 16.67 percent of an annual retirement benefit. In 1973

the board inaugurated the Designed Insurance Program for churches.

Despite a depressed stock market, the board recorded a good year for new enrollments in retirement plans in 1974, as 1,969 members joined plans. Almost $16,500,000 in contributions to retirement plans held by Baptist agencies were received, a record at that time.

The years 1975 and 1976 were times of far-reaching decisions. The board spent much effort establishing new policies and creating innovative programs geared to meet future needs of plan members. In 1976 the basic interest assumption for calculating retirement annuities increased from 4 to 6 percent, and work began on a new retirement program for ministers and church employees.

Contrasts characterized the board's ministry in 1977. Strong growth in new retirement accounts occurred, along with a poor stock market performance on the national scene. But the board paid out $19,100,000 in retirement and protection benefits as assets approached the $500,000,000 mark. To undergird the new Southern Baptist Retirement Program which would replace the Southern Baptist Protection Program a year later, the board created two new investment funds. Joining the Variable Fund were the Fixed and Balanced Funds—a move which gave Southern Baptists participating in board programs an even greater voice in how their retirement programs were to be invested.

The Southern Baptist Retirement Program began on Jan. 1, 1978. Offering members a choice of investment funds, high earnings, and flexible benefits, the program was termed a worthy successor to Plan A, the obsolete program which had served the denomination for many years.

In 1979 the board's assets in trust swelled to $667,521,000, exceeding 1970 assets by $437,471,763. In 1979 government involvement in private pension programming, a reality the board had been facing for several years, intensified. Meeting in early 1980, the board's executive committee formally approved the staff's planning administrative steps to comply with the federal pension law, in case the board should come under the jurisdiction of the Employee Retirement Income Security Act of 1974 in 1983.

II. Insurance Services Department. The Life and Health Benefits Department, established in 1964, became the Insurance Services Department in the reorganization of the Annuity Board in 1970, with insurance programs designed separately for churches, agencies, and seminary students.

Church Insurance.—In Oct., 1969, the board offered to church employees a new life insurance program underwritten by Aetna Life Insurance Company. All Life Benefit Plan participants covered through the old Group Life & Health were allowed to transfer. The Life Benefit Plan was then closed to future participants. Many participants transferred to new Plans 122 and 123, with life schedules based on annual compensation. Long Term Disability Plan 124 was begun.

In Aug., 1972, the board closed Long Term Disability Plan 124 and transferred participants to the new Long Term Disability Plan 224, as underwritten on a standard or nonstandard basis. New applicants for disability coverage were then required to provide evidence of insurability with coverage being extended only to standard insurance risks. The board added Life Plans 127 (for Texas residents only) and 205 to the insurance program in Jan., 1973.

A new medical program underwritten by Aetna became available to church employees. Life insurance became a prerequisite for medical coverage. Evidence of insurability was required on all employees and dependents to be covered. All persons in the old Blue Cross plan were included in Aetna's medical program without evidence of insurability, and without requiring participation in the life program. Four plans of insurance were available. Rates for these were broken down by five geographical regions. The rates were also divided into under-age-50 and over-age-50 categories. In Mar., 1973, the board removed the premium waiver provision originally included in the church life coverage. Plan 299, which supplemented Medicare on a limited basis for persons over 65, was added Apr., 1974, to the medical program and underwritten by Aetna. The five geographical regions for the purpose of medical rates were consolidated into four regions in Oct., 1974. In May, 1975, the board initiated case underwriting for church medical plans and closed two medical plans, 252 and 253, with participants transferring to one of the two remaining plans of their choice in July, 1976.

In Feb., 1977, modified coverage became available for medical and long term disability. Denominational employees and dependents not insurable on a standard risk basis became able to obtain coverage on a modified basis as nonstandard risks through the waiver program.

Step rating was established in Mar., 1977, for church medical plans in five-year increments. A comprehensive medical plan supplementing Medicare went into effect in Jan., 1978, for church senior medical participants (age 65 and over).

The board discontinued case underwriting in Apr., 1979, and removed the maternity exclusion benefit at the same time. In Sep., 1980, premium waiver became a part of the church life program for persons disabled.

Agency Insurance.—The board phased out the Blue Cross/Blue Shield plan for agencies and transferred them to the Aetna group plan for life and medical coverage as of Apr., 1969. In Feb., 1970, the board employee medical account changed from Blue Cross/Blue Shield to Aetna Life & Casualty. In Nov., 1970, a comprehensive medical plan was added to the agency program. In Sep., 1971, the board implemented special risk accident insurance for trustees (directors) of SBC agencies. The agency program was opened to churches with 25 or more employees in 1973. In 1975 the board permitted churches with 10 to 24 employees to enroll in the group program. Long term disability was opened to the latter group in 1979. The board added associational groups to the agency program in 1976.

In Jan., 1976, dental coverage became a part of the insurance program for agencies and institutions to offer to their employees. The board cancelled separate basic medical coverage in 1976 and separate major medical coverage in 1978. The continuing comprehensive medical plan thereafter provided these types of coverage for agency employees and dependents. In Jan., 1980, pooled life maximum increased to $100,000, and in July, 1980, the special rate for pooled life was eliminated.

Seminary Student Insurance.—The seminarian program began offering life and medical insurance through Aetna in Sep., 1971. The original group included five of the six Southern Baptist

	RELIEF AND ANNUITY BENEFITS			TOTAL ASSETS AND INVESTMENT EARNINGS	
Year	Relief Benefits	Retirement & Protection Benefits	Totals	Total Assets	Investment Earnings
1919-68	$ 8,710,020	$ 57,743,398	$ 66,453,419	$208,218,706	$ 77,831,548
1969	176,165	7,087,686	7,263,851	221,303,261	10,375,296
1970	162,507	8,241,799	8,404,306	239,066,046	10,617,731
1971	164,186	9,887,604	10,051,790	277,631,190	16,636,795
1972	171,581	11,192,951	11,364,532	316,814,692	22,295,543
1973	189,742	15,837,988	16,027,730	333,273,607	10,001,735
1974	216,513	15,692,198	15,908,711	337,656,912	(8,577,381)
1975	254,204	15,734,003	15,988,207	377,321,187	23,149,064
1976	285,505	17,138,343	17,423,848	440,745,783	41,393,317
1977	324,096	19,085,316	19,409,412	464,897,826	6,508,022
1978	345,978	25,558,637	25,904,615	531,422,040	47,932,401
1979	392,484	31,806,393	32,198,877	667,474,987	55,582,067
1980	413,980	37,015,444	37,429,424	806,518,757	101,812,175
	$11,806,961	$272,021,760	$283,828,722		$415,558,313

HAROLD D. RICHARDSON

seminaries. Medical insurance was available without evidence of insurability at matriculation, and long term disability was added one year later. In Oct., 1974, Southwestern Baptist Theological Seminary joined the seminarian insurance program with Bible schools eligible a year later. Student long term disability was closed in Mar., 1977, to new applicants due to lack of interest. Life insurance without underwriting at matriculation was implemented in Sep., 1980.

JOHN BLOSKAS and JOHN DUDLEY

ANTIGUA, BRITISH WEST INDIES, MISSION IN. Antigua is an island of 73,000 people and 108 square miles in the eastern Caribbean. Members of the General Association of Regular Baptists began the earliest Baptist work in Antigua. Because of various difficulties and calls for help from the Baptists on the island, Southern Baptists became involved in 1968 by sending missionaries and financial help. Three Baptist churches with a combined membership of about 526 and three missions with a combined average weekly attendance of about 125 organized the Antigua Baptist Association in Jan., 1980. Southern Baptist missionaries engage in an agricultural ministry.

GARY E. HARTHCOCK

ARCADIA BAPTIST HOME (III). This retirement facility admitted its first residents in 1960. The original purpose of providing Christian fellowship for the elderly in a family-like atmosphere has not changed. Licensed by the state of Louisiana as an intermediate care facility, a full-time staff provides 24-hour care. It is supported by the Cooperative Program, gifts from individuals and churches, and by receipts from residents. L. T. Stringer succeeded Raymond W. Gaudet as administrator in 1975. In 1978 the home was enlarged to accommodate 80 persons.

L. T. STRINGER

ARCHAEOLOGY, BIBLICAL (I). Techniques for reaching the objectives of biblical archaeology are changing. Excavation projects are more regionally than site oriented, requiring more staff with multidisciplinary skills and fewer laborers for digging. Systematic study of climate, soils, flora, fauna, settlement patterns, subsistence strategy, trade, microbiology, ethnoarchaeology, and related matters has added new dimensions to the discipline and enabled an integrative approach to the ancient world out of which the Bible came. Interactions with history and environment are now sought to provide benchmarks of political, religious, and social information essential to a knowledge of the people of God in their own world. This knowledge cultivates perspective and understanding which comprise the basic legacy of archaeology to the Bible and its interpreters.

JOSEPH A. CALLAWAY

ARCHITECTURE, CHURCH (I, III). For three-quarters of a century, the Sunday School Board has offered architectural consultation services to Southern Baptist churches. The philosophy has been that building design must begin on the inside with the many program aspects of the church. Every line on paper must bear its proper relationship to the intended use of the building before an attempt is made to set it in frame, mortar, steel, and stone. In 1980 the board's Church Architecture Department was servicing approximately 700 requests per month. In the period 1970 to 1980 Southern Baptist churches increased from 34,360 to 35,605; total membership from 11,629,880 to 13,379,073; and church property evaluation from $4,127,738,253 to $9,609,575,477.

Programming and building planning have become somewhat routine; however, three factors will likely affect the future of Southern Baptist church architecture: (1) Exorbitant, inflated building costs, (2) excessively high interest rates on borrowed building funds, and (3) increasing utility (energy) prices. As a result, many congregations are planning their programs on the basis of multiple uses of space. The trend is toward two and three Sunday Schools and two or three morning worship services. Flexibility of space is being demanded in planning. Areas can thus be shifted and rearranged for several different purposes two or three times a day.

ROWLAND E. CROWDER

ARGENTINA, MISSION IN (I, III). The mission mourned with Argentine Baptists the loss during the 1970s of two honored leaders: Carlos de la Torre, pastor, physician, and educator; and Santiago Canclini, pastor, teacher, and champion of religious liberty. The Argentine Convention restructured itself organizationally, sent a missionary to Peru, set up a Baptist Men's organization, and constructed a new communications building on the International Seminary campus in Buenos Aires. The cities, especially Buenos Aires, were of particular concern. An extension plan was designed to reach the unchurched and mobilize the churches in fostering missions. A major city evangelization project was launched in Rosario. The International Seminary expanded its library space, established an extension department, chose its first national director, and moved toward greater national participation and identification with Argentine Baptists. Seventy-two missionaries were serving in 1979.

FRANK K. MEANS

ARIZONA, BAPTIST FOUNDATION OF (I, III). From 1962 to 1979-80, the foundation grew from a budget of $15,000 and a staff of one to a budget of $345,000 and a staff of eight. Glen E. Crotts continued to serve as president and executive director. Trust assets grew to approximately $4,300,000 as of Jan. 31, 1979, most of which was earmarked by donors for the ultimate benefit of Baptist causes. In addition, as of 1979-80, the foundation managed $5,300,000 in assets. The income from those assets was used to provide the foundation operating budget.

The board of directors increased in 1978 from 15 to 21 to provide additional leadership and exposure of foundation emphases to Arizona Southern Baptists. In Aug., 1978, the foundation established the Foundation Plan of Church Finance which gave assistance to the churches in selling revenue bonds to raise money for church construction. In 1978-79 churches were assisted in raising more than $690,000 for financing.

GLEN CROTTS

ARIZONA ASSOCIATIONS (I, III).

I. New Associations. Arizona has added no new associations since 1970.

II. Changes in Associations. LAKE MEAD. Organized in 1956 by churches in Clark County, NV, formerly affiliated with Mohave Association. Its name was changed in 1977 to Southern Nevada Association.

SOUTHERN NEVADA. Organized in 1956 as Lake Mead. Name was changed in 1977. In 1979 it became a part of the Nevada Baptist Convention.

TROY BROOKS. Organized Nov. 3, 1957, as Hassayampa Association. Its name was changed to Troy Brooks in 1958 and to Yavapai Association in 1974.

YAVAPAI. Organized in 1957 as Hassayampa Association, the name was changed to Troy Brooks in 1958 and to Yavapai in 1974.

BEVERLY A. GOSS

ARIZONA BAPTIST CHILDREN'S SERVICE (cf. Arizona, Baptist Children's Home of, Vol. III). In 1970 George Wilson, hired as the first director of the home in 1960, retired and was succeeded by Don Cain. Also in 1970, the board of directors surveyed the childcare needs throughout Arizona in order to continue current services of the home and to expand to meet new needs. In 1971 the legal name of the agency was changed to Arizona Baptist Children's Services to reflect more accurately the new nature of the organization.

The 1970 study indicated that two major areas of need in Arizona were abused and neglected children and teenagers with serious problems. To meet these needs ABCS opened a temporary sheltered-care home for children in 1971 and began several new programs for teenage children. These programs have expanded and developed into well-established, accredited programs. ABCS now cares for more than 1,000 children each year.

DON CAIN

ARIZONA SOUTHERN BAPTIST CONVENTION (III; cf. Arizona, Baptist General Convention of, Vol. I).

I. History. *Numerical and Financial Growth.* —

The Arizona Southern Baptist Convention experienced growth during the 1970s, but in 1979 the organization of the Nevada Baptist Convention subtracted one from the number of associations and decreased the number of churches and members. Church Training and Woman's Missionary Union enrollments showed a definite decline in this same period. Cooperative Program gifts increased from $444,840 in 1970 to $1,113,757 in 1979, and the value of church properties from $26,384,000 in 1970 to $78,653,000 in 1979. Gifts to the ASBC totaled $16,779,409 for 1979.

North Phoenix Baptist Church experienced outstanding growth during the decade, mostly adult converts. Membership increased from 2,447 members to 8,730 (5,606 by baptism). The congregation moved to a 40-acre site in the heart of Phoenix with an auditorium seating 5,000 and a $20,000,000 property. Total receipts for 1969 were $332,483; these increased in 1979 to $3,478,877.

Convention Properties. —Significant changes occurred in property ownership and development in hospitals, Baptist Student Union centers, and camp facilities. In Nov., 1969, the convention voted to sell Parkview, Scottsdale, and Phoenix Baptist Hospitals. In the ensuing controversy between the ASBC executive board and the Arizona Baptist Hospital Association regarding legal title to ownership and authority to operate the hospitals, a settlement agreement was executed on Jan. 15, 1971, whereby the convention, for a monetary consideration, relinquished all claim to the hospitals, it being stipulated that the action was not regarded as a sale of properties but a transfer of authority.

Contributing to the growth of Baptist Student Union ministry in Arizona colleges during the decade was the acquisition of student centers on the three university campuses. The University of Arizona center, Tucson, which had been acquired in Oct., 1965, gave way to a new structure which was started in 1974. On Dec. 17, 1975, a building was purchased to serve Northern Arizona University students in Flagstaff. At Arizona State University, Tempe, construction of a center was completed in 1977 at a cost of $175,000.

During 1976 and 1977 Paradise Valley Baptist Ranch near Prescott, ASBC's encampment, underwent extensive renovation and refurbishing, particularly the kitchen and dining hall and Yavapai Lodge. With construction of Smithey Lodge, a large motel-type dormitory with living room adequate for group meetings, the encampment became operable year-round. In Dec., 1976, the convention acquired Mt. Lemmon Encampment in the Catalina Mountains of Southern Arizona near Tucson from Catalina Association.

Organization of the Nevada Area Baptist Convention. —The Nevada Area Baptist Convention (later called Nevada Baptist Convention), with the cooperation of both ASBC and the Southern Baptist General Convention of California, was organized, Oct. 16-17, 1978, at Las Vegas' Red-rock Baptist Church. A number of gifts, including pledges of state mission monies by the sponsoring conventions, helped to smooth the path for the new convention. The NBC became operational on Jan. 1, 1979.

Changes in Leadership Personnel.—Upon the resignation of Charles Lloyd McKay as executive secretary-treasurer, Sep. 1, 1970, Roy Forreston Sutton became the acting secretary-treasurer. The following Dec. 1, the board chose Sutton as executive secretary-treasurer. On Nov. 11, 1975, the board requested Sutton to postpone his retirement until the jubilee year, 1978, and he consented. Upon Sutton's retirement, Jess L. Canafax became interim executive director-treasurer (new title) and served until the coming of Jack Bernhardt Johnson, who was elected by a called convention, May 8, 1979, as the new executive director-treasurer.

Grand Canyon College likewise experienced a change of leaders in this period. Arthur K. Tyson resigned as president in 1972, and was succeeded by William R. Hintze (*q.v.*), 1973-77, who in turn was succeeded by Bill R. Williams in 1978.

Jubilee, 50th Anniversary.—At the state convention of 1977 Richard Jackson, president, appointed a steering committee for the 50th anniversary celebration. The committee, chaired by Fayly Cothern, held its first meeting, Feb. 10, 1978, naming subcommittees. Advance publicity included newspaper and *Baptist Beacon* coverage, and personal visits by Fayly and Gaylon Cothern to 58 churches of the convention.

Plans and participation culminated in a service which featured a parade of flags by individual churches; recognition of the winners of awards to churches and individuals in song writing, history writing, and sermon competition; a 400-voice jubilee choir; presentation of gifts to retiring convention leader Sutton, and a closing message by W. A. Criswell.

II. Program of Work. *Executive Board.*—The board is responsible for all the work of the convention in the interim between sessions. The board consists of 30 members plus the president and vice-president of the convention. The president is chairman of the board. The board presents to the convention annually for its adoption a comprehensive budget. The board studies the affairs of the boards and institutions of the convention, makes recommendations concerning needed adjustments, and makes whatever other recommendations it deems advisable.

Evangelism.—Irving Childress served as director during the entire decade of the 1970s. In 1975 Nathan Pillow assumed the position of associate director. During this period the division developed saturation witness techniques and summer youth witness teams. Since 1970 baptisms have totaled 46,936.

Sunday School.—Harvey Kimbler was director during the entire decade. Enrollment in 1970 was 46,831 and reached a peak of over 61,000. In 1979 the Nevada Convention was organized and

ARIZONA STATISTICAL SUMMARY

Year	Associations	Churches	Church Membership	Baptisms	SS Enrollment	VBS Enrollment	CT Enrollment	WMU Enrollment	Brotherhood Enrollment	Ch. Music Enrollment	Mission Gifts	Total Gifts	Value Church Property
1969	15	227	68,282	3,391	46,827	23,784	20,524	7,474	2,526	5,751	$ 672,388	$ 4,948,019	$25,948,011
1970	15	225	70,190	3,621	48,392	26,573	19,533	7,192	2,678	5,943	823,819	6,468,765	26,253,216
1971	15	230	73,695	4,291	49,357	25,542	15,593	6,448	2,797	6,220	1,030,348	6,128,437	28,563,824
1972	15	232	78,187	4,792	49,911	27,168	14,936	6,178	2,767	6,148	1,080,420	6,749,552	31,500,014
1973	15	232	81,638	4,782	49,840	29,280	13,889	6,070	2,764	7,294	1,222,266	7,693,053	36,713,802
1974	15	233	85,375	5,530	51,593	29,431	13,894	6,142	2,908	8,339	1,510,281	8,827,106	42,341,133
1975	15	236	88,817	5,360	53,438	31,394	14,167	5,811	2,784	8,046	1,648,821	10,321,622	47,516,175
1976	15	234	92,267	4,759	56,884	26,115	13,439	5,690	2,559	8,199	1,847,849	11,263,367	52,908,428
1977	15	237	94,882	4,537	57,413	26,335	13,061	5,445	3,060	8,980	2,023,627	13,241,000	61,278,331
1978	15	244	97,742	4,495	56,584	24,953	12,758	5,786	2,842	9,077	2,141,898	14,522,353	67,921,262
1979	14*	230	90,983	4,748	54,143	25,215	13,427	5,885	3,605	9,063	2,353,871	16,061,192	78,689,234
1980	14	232	96,167	5,554	56,051	25,739	14,440	6,309	4,401	9,376	3,029,049	17,624,838	86,838,823

*One association of Nevada churches previously affiliated with the Arizona Convention united with the new Nevada Convention.

GLADYS SCHRODER

took more than 8,000 of this enrollment. Enrollment in 1979 was 54,338. Vacation Bible School enrollment was 22,339 in 1970 and has reached a peak enrollment of over 31,000. Kimbler also serves as church building consultant, director of family ministries, and church library consultant.

Church Training.—Robert Lynn Warren served as Church Training director in 1970. In 1971 Cecil Edward Archer returned and served through 1975. Amos Coffee succeeded Archer and served during 1976-77. In 1978 Bill May became the director. Enrollment in 1980 was 13,406. May also serves as director of Church Administration and Church Recreation.

Missions.—The Missions Division involved itself in 15 associations in 1970-78. Jesse L. Canafax succeeded Dan Stringer as director in 1971. In 1974 Delbert Fann became director of Language Missions, and in 1975 Tom Sykes became director of Church Extension. In 1977 Earl Stallings became director of Christian Social Ministries and senior adult work. During the 1970s the division consisted of 60 language congregations. In 1980 there were two mission centers in Phoenix and two in Tucson.

Woman's Missionary Union.—In Oct., 1970, WMU was reorganized. Enrollment dropped at this time, but it was on an upward trend in 1980, when enrollment totaled 7,597. In 1972 director Mary Jo Stewart was appointed to Ecuador as a missionary under the Foreign Mission Board. In Aug., 1973, Beverly Goss became director. State presidents included Louise Fuller, Sierra Vista, 1970-74; Bertha Secrest, Phoenix, 1974-78; and Beth McGhee, Tucson, 1978-present.

Stewardship.—Cooperative Program gifts increased from $444,840 in 1970 to $1,113,000 in 1979. The long-range goal is for church receipts to increase 14 percent per year for the next four years and for an increase in Cooperative Program giving of at least one percent per year. While many churches give upwards of 20 percent through the Cooperative Program, the goal is one percent annually until the desired goal of 10 percent average from the churches is reached. L. D. Parker is director.

Brotherhood.—Cecil Archer served as director until 1975 when he was succeeded by Thomas Edwin Sykes. Sykes served until Dec., 1979, when he was succeeded by Nathan Pillow. Enrollment in 1970 was 2,457 and is presently 3,605.

Church Building.—Lowell Billy Parker served as consultant until 1976 when Ernest B. Myers assumed the responsibility. Myers served through 1978 and was succeeded by Harvey Kimbler. The church building consultant serves as a liaison with the Church Architecture Department of the Sunday School Board, SBC.

Baptist Student Union.—In 1970 Harvey Kimbler succeeded Irving Childress as director. Bob Warren succeeded Kimbler in 1972 and served until Bill May became director in 1978. In 1980 there were 175,000 students on the campuses served by the BSU.

Music.—C. E. Archer, Bob Warren, and Macon Delavan, the present director, served during the 1970s. In 1970 the enrollment in the music ministry was 5,875 and was 9,052 in 1980.

See also NEVADA BAPTIST CONVENTION.

HARVEY KIMBLER

ARKANSAS ASSOCIATIONS (I, III).

I. New Associations. CURRENT-GAINES. Organized in 1975 by the merger of Current River and Gainesville Associations, it is comprised of churches in Randolph and Clay Counties in Northeastern Arkansas. In 1980, 30 churches reported 188 baptisms, 6,555 total members, $854,964 total gifts, and $181,083 mission gifts.

II. Changes in Associations. BOONE-NEWTON. Formed in 1961, the association changed its name to North Arkansas Association, Oct. 17, 1974.

CARROLL COUNTY. Organized in 1950, the association disbanded and became part of North Arkansas Association, Nov. 25, 1974.

HOPE. Organized in 1907, the association changed its name to Southwest Arkansas Association, Oct. 14, 1976.

NORTH ARKANSAS. Name changed from Boone-Newton in 1974. When Carroll County Association merged with North Arkansas in 1974, the association covered the three counties of Boone, Carroll, and Newton in Northwest Arkansas.

SEARCY COUNTY. Organized Aug. 1, 1971, after Stone-Van Buren-Searcy Association disbanded. Searcy County Association disbanded in Oct., 1978.

SOUTHWEST. Name changed from Hope to Southwest Association in 1976.

STONE-VAN BUREN-SEARCY. Organized in 1932, the association disbanded May 4, 1971.

CONWAY H. SAWYERS

ARKANSAS BAPTIST ASSEMBLY AND CAMPS (cf. Arkansas Baptist Assembly, Vols. I, III; Camp Paron, Vol. III).

The Arkansas Baptist State Convention operates its assembly near Siloam Springs, AR, and a missionary education facility, Camp Paron, 42 miles west of Little Rock.

Lawson Hatfield, director of the convention's Sunday School department, has also been business manager and program director of the assembly since 1968; Don Cooper has been assistant director, and Gene Devor resident manager. Youth oriented, the program provides educational activities for all age divisions in the mornings, afternoon recreation, and evening worship. In 1969 in three weekly sessions, enrollment was 2,170 with 70 professions of faith and 159 commitments to church-related vocations. In 1979 there were six weekly sessions, and enrollment was 5,585 with 309 professions and 85 vocational decisions. The highest one-week attendance in the 1970s was 1,415, recorded July 16-21, 1979.

During the decade, church-owned dormitories were replaced by convention-owned structures and family units, providing 1,660 beds. Other improvements included: connection to city water, improved food services, air-conditioned family rooms, dining hall, and tabernacle; construction of a choir room, a residence, camper space, and teaching pavilions; and the acquisition of adjacent property. Recreational facilities include 13 fields and courts, plus jogging, swimming, and adult crafts. Weatherized facilities provide for group retreats up to 100 people. Property value of the 175-acre site, including 33 buildings and 29 teaching pavilions, was $610,525 in 1980.

Camp Paron, developed in 1964 on a site of 271 acres, now includes 12 dormitories, an activities building, cafeteria, snack shack, and infirmary, with property value of $483,668. An annual average of 650 campers attended summertime week-long camps for mission education in the 1970s. Church retreats were scheduled the rest of each year. The capacity is 200.

Business managers have been John Cutsinger, 1969-70; C. H. Seaton, 1971-78; and Robert U. Ferguson, 1979-   Royal Ambassador camp directors have been C. H. Seaton, 1971-78, and Neal Guthrie, 1979- . Woman's Missionary Union camp directors in the 1970s were Sara Wisdom, Marsha Shappach, Julia Ketner, Betty Jo Lacy, Karen Russey, and Debbie Moore.

BIBLIOGRAPHY: E. Glenn Hinson, *A History of Baptists in Arkansas* (1979).

LAWSON HATFIELD

ARKANSAS BAPTIST COOPERATING MINISTRY WITH NATIONAL BAPTISTS. The history of the Cooperative Ministries Department of the Arkansas Baptist Convention began in 1954 with the election of Clyde Hart as secretary of Race Relations. Prior to this, Arkansas Southern Baptist efforts in race relations were spasmodic and local depending upon the relationship of the churches and people. Occasionally, black representatives would visit state conventions to bring greetings or address the body, and the state convention would contribute money to black work. The Home Mission Board, SBC, offered financial aid in 1954, which has continued until the present. In 1957 a full department was established. Clyde Hart served until retirement in 1968. The program he directed included Vacation Bible Schools, leadership clinics, student work, youth camps, extension centers for the adult Christian education, and general encouragement to churches, associations, and state conventions.

In 1970 Robert Ferguson became department director, and the work was renamed Cooperative Ministries with National Baptists. The emphasis changed from doing something for blacks to working with blacks in Christian ministries. Since 1970 the traditional aspects of the program have continued. In addition, black regional associates teach and promote the program; state and associational joint committees bring black and white Baptists together for consultation and program planning; scholarship programs assist ministerial students; the assistant chaplaincy program at the Tucker Reformatory ministers to first offenders; area fellowships bring Baptists together for fellowship and inspiration; and joint state convention sessions and joint evangelism conferences lead to joint Christian efforts.

See also ARKANSAS BAPTIST STATE CONVENTION, Vols. I, III.

ROBERT V. FERGUSON

ARKANSAS BAPTIST FAMILY AND CHILD CARE SERVICES (cf. Bottoms Baptist Orphanage, Vol. I; Arkansas Baptist Home for Children, Vol. III). Arkansas Baptist Family and Child Care Services, the name adopted in 1970, is an arm of the church reaching out to help heal the hurts of troubled children and families resulting from abuse, neglect, abandonment, and a multitude of other circumstances. Troubled children are given a chance to develop their full potential. The agency also ministers to the broken families of these children in some situations.

This ministry has changed over the years to meet changing needs. A statewide ministry is designed to meet the needs of the total family. The children's home in Monticello serves children ages 6-18. Family-style living is provided in cottages. Area offices in Little Rock, Jonesboro, and Fayetteville provide counseling, intake evaluations for children needing care, work with families, foster home recruitment, and supervision of group home for boys and emergency receiving homes for children.

JOHNNY G. BIGGS

ARKANSAS BAPTIST FOUNDATION (I, III). The 1970s were years of change for the foundation. Ed McDonald, Jr., resigned as director, Jan., 1972. Harry D. Trulove was elected, Mar., 1974. By the end of the decade, 40 tax and estate seminars were being staffed each year. Roger Harrod was employed as vice-president and legal counsel in May, 1979. In 1979 more than 200 persons celebrated the agency's 30th anniversary with a banquet. Assets grew from $258,445 on Jan. 1, 1970, to $4,008,000 on Dec. 31, 1979.

HARRY D. TRULOVE

ARKANSAS BAPTIST NEWSMAGAZINE (III; cf. Arkansas Baptist, Vol. I). Editor Erwin Lawrence McDonald retired, Dec. 31, 1971, completing 15 years as editor, and was named editor emeritus in Aug., 1974. Charles H. Ashcraft served as interim editor, Jan. 1, 1972-May 11, 1972.

J. Everett Sneed, a native of Batesville, AR, and a graduate of Arkansas College, Southwestern Baptist Theological Seminary, Baylor University, and the University of Heidelberg, was elected editor, effective May 18, 1972.

Changes in content of the magazine included adding a weekly column by a layman, beginning in 1972, and a departmentalization approach, increasing the number of churches mentioned in news brief items, beginning in 1972. The staff was increased by one in 1976 and again in 1979.

In spite of inflation, the paper's circulation increased from 59,989 in 1972 to 72,619 in Dec., 1979. A readership survey in 1977 revealed that the majority of the readers are longtime subscribers who are regular readers of a select portion of the magazine.

In Nov., 1979, the state convention in annual session set up a three-year trial for the *Arkansas Baptist Newsmagazine* to function under a separate board, 1980-83.

Besides Sneed, the staff in 1980 included Betty Kennedy, managing editor; Millie Gill, reporter and photo lab technician; Danna Sample, reporter; Mary Giberson, secretary to the editor; and Ann Taylor, bookkeeper and mailing clerk.

J. EVERETT SNEED

ARKANSAS BAPTIST STATE CONVENTION (I, III).

I. History and Program of Work. Charles H. Ashcraft assumed the role of executive secretary, July 1, 1969, coming from the executive secretaryship of the Utah-Idaho Southern Baptist Convention. On the threshold of the 1970s, he led the Arkansas Convention to adopt the themes, "Living the Spirit" and "Sharing Christ." One or more of the departments of work were assigned the full responsibility for each year's planning, development, and application of the themes in the life of the convention.

Roy F. Lewis, employed as assistant executive secretary in 1971 specifically to promote the Cooperative Program and stewardship, remained in the position until 1979. He initiated a missionary-in-residence program in 1973 in cooperation with the Foreign Mission Board. Gilbert Nichols, missionary to Paraguay, was named the first missionary to spend his furlough promoting the Cooperative Program in Arkansas churches. He and his successors gave much-welcomed credibility to all aspects of stewardship and missions.

Church extension was the first major emphasis of the Missions Department in 1971 when R. H. Dorris became director. The convention showed a net gain of 59 churches during the 1970s, compared to 25 in the 1960s. Total membership in the churches in the 1970s grew by 18.38 percent to a record 428,402 by 1980. The decade ended with approximately 35 missions in strategically developing communities.

Cooperative Program giving in the 1970s reflected this growth in church extension, as well as the status of the economy. Giving increased by 38.14 percent with a record $6,773,588 in 1979. The percentage of undesignated receipts forwarded to SBC causes remained approximately the same. However, the 1978 meeting of the state convention authorized the executive board to formulate plans to move to a 50 percent figure by 1985.

A phenomenal program of giving to Christian higher education also characterized the 1970s. The convention authorized an Ouachita-Southern Advancement Campaign for 1971-73, with a goal of $4,000,000. More than 56 percent of the churches participated. With gifts and pledges outside the church phase, a total of $5,682,937 was committed. With Ouachita Baptist University looking ahead to its centennial year, the 1976 convention session approved specific goals for the university during its centennial decade, 1976-86. For Southern Baptist College the 1978 convention approved a 10-year campaign for $5,100,000. A portion of this amount will be sought through the churches.

The general affluence of the 1970s also resulted in an increase of 14.7 times the 1970 assets handled by the Arkansas Baptist Foundation. Harry Trulove became executive director of the foundation in 1975.

The Woman's Missionary Union and all Arkansas Baptists honored Nancy B. Cooper upon her retirement in 1974 after 26 years of service as executive secretary-treasurer. In 1975 Julia Ketner was elected her successor. Emphasis on mission education and support continued. The decade showed a 33 percent increase in the annual giving to the Dixie Jackson Offering for State Missions and Annie Armstrong Easter Offering for Home Missions, and a 37 percent increase in giving to the Lottie Moon Christmas Offering for Foreign Missions.

The 1970s witnessed great strides in Cooperative Ministries with National Baptists led by Robert U. Ferguson. This work became a full department in 1974. Joint meetings of Arkansas Baptists and National Baptists became frequent events on all levels of church and denominational life. Major assistance was given to Arkansas Baptist College in its attempt to solicit gifts of $106,000 in order to obtain a matching gift of like amount.

The Mission Department's Small Church Revolving Loan Fund for building aid to small churches grew from $13,500 in 1970 to $278,239 by the end of the decade.

The 1976 convention approved a Third Century Endowment Campaign by the Baptist Student Union. The goal of $1,000,000 was to be handled by the Baptist Foundation with the earnings designated annually to support student work. By the end of 1979, more than $875,000 had been obtained in gifts and pledges.

In 1975 Arkansas Baptists gave $100,000 to fight world hunger. The convention subsequently took other positive steps to help meet this need.

A Stewardship Department was established in 1976 with James A. Walker as director. The Bold Mission Thrust goal of doubling Cooperative Program giving by 1982 became the first order of emphasis.

As early as 1972 the convention was looking ahead to the nation's bicentennial year. That year a Spirit of '76 Committee was named to plan a major thrust in evangelism and missions. Simultaneous revivals were planned for the spring of 1976 to be known as Life and Liberty Crusades.

On July 3, 1976, a Life and Liberty Rally was held in War Memorial Stadium in Little Rock.

Guests were Paul Harvey, popular news analyst, Anita Bryant, singer, and Malcom Scott, National Baptist preacher. The estimated attendance was 20,000 persons, making the rally by far the largest gathering of Baptists in the state's history. The emphasis was both evangelistic and patriotic. The rally was telecast live by a local television station.

The ministry of evangelism was separated from the Missions Department in 1972, becoming a full department under Jesse Reed. Later, a state evangelist and a director of youth evangelism were added to the staff.

During the 1970s the number of baptisms reported by the churches fluctuated. Though no firm explanation has been given, during those years when the major thrust of the churches was evangelism and missions, the number of baptisms was up; during those years when the fellowship of the convention was threatened and attention was diverted to internal problems, the number of baptisms dropped. During the 1970s, 129,955 baptisms were reported in Arkansas.

The Division of Deaf Ministries became Language Missions in order to provide a ministry for ethnic groups beginning to settle in Arkansas. The convention's first Hispanic congregation was organized in Little Rock in 1975. Many opportunities opened for helping churches minister to Vietnamese and Laotians who became Arkansas residents.

The Special Ministries Division assisted churches in serving the underprivileged, minorities, drug abusers, the elderly, vacationers, and recreational enthusiasts. As many as 36 student summer missionaries served each year in resort and recreational areas.

In 1971 the Missions Department opened a Migrant Mission Center at Hope, AR, near a government labor camp. Annually, between 40,000 and 50,000 migrant persons stop at this camp. Most of them are Mexican-Americans. Bob Gross, director of the center from the beginning, reports a ministry to thousands of visitors each year.

Chaplaincy ministries caught the imagination of Arkansas Baptists in the 1970s, particularly in correctional institutions. At the end of the decade, the convention had five chaplains employed full time in state institutions.

In 1974 the Missions Department assumed responsibility for developing a program of continuing education. The principal development for this ministry was the establishment in 1975 of a branch of Boyce Bible School with Withrow T. Holland as director. By the end of 1979 a total of nine students had earned fully accredited diplomas from Southern Baptist Theological Seminary through this program.

In 1978 the convention joined in Bold Mission Thrust by linking with Indiana Baptists to help double the number of congregations in that state by 1982. Approximately 200 Arkansas pastors and laypersons were enlisted for simultaneous revivals in Indiana in Apr., 1979. More than 1,000 professions of faith were reported.

J. Everett Sneed became editor of the *Arkansas Baptist Newsmagazine* in 1972, upon the retirement of Erwin L. McDonald. Circulation grew during the decade by 8.25 percent. The 1979 convention authorized a study to be made of the feasibility of a separate board of control for the publication.

With continuing sociological changes involving family structure and behavior, the sociological changes of the 1960s precipitated new articles of incorporation and a new name for the Arkansas Baptist Home for Children in 1970. With new goals and concepts of ministry, the institution became the Arkansas Baptist Family and Child Care Services.

II. Major Convention Issues. During the 1970s, several proposals brought heated discussions, differences of opinions, and some polarization among the constituency of the convention. The Committee of Twenty-Five, appointed in 1969 to seek a resolution for the fellowship problem that erupted late in that decade, reported in 1971. It recommended that the convention define "regular Baptist churches" as those which in doctrine and practice adhere to the principles and spirit of the Baptist Faith and Message as adopted by the SBC in 1963. After considerable discussion the state convention adopted the recommendation in amended form to read "The Baptist Faith and Message shall not be interpreted as to permit open communion and/or alien immersion."

The fellowship problem remained with the convention throughout the 1970s. Messengers from several churches to the annual meeting of the convention as late as 1979 were being challenged on grounds that they were violating this interpretation of the Baptist Faith and Message.

A study committee was authorized in 1975 to examine the need for a crisis support ministry for pastors and other church staff personnel. In 1977 the convention voted to establish such a ministry. In late 1979 Glenn McGriff was employed to begin his work, Jan. 1, 1980, in an office away from the Baptist Building.

The convention in its 1976 session rejected the executive board's recommendation for expansion of the Baptist Building with a new structure on a nearby parking lot. However, the 1978 convention authorized a study committee to determine space needs for future expansion of departments of work housed in the Baptist Building. The committee's report in 1979 confirmed need for growth space and recommended four possible alternatives. It also recommended that a new committee make an in-depth study to determine the most feasible alternative, provide cost estimates for the project, and with other pertinent information report to the 1980 convention.

The 1977 convention adopted ordination as the proper credential for Arkansas Baptist ministers to perform weddings.

In 1977 convention messengers authorized an updated history of the convention. The result was *A History of Baptists in Arkansas* (1979) by E. Glenn Hinson.

The 1978 convention established a Christian

ARKANSAS STATISTICAL SUMMARY

Year	Associations	Churches	Church Membership	Baptisms	SS Enrollment	VBS Enrollment	CT Enrollment	WMU Enrollment	Brotherhood Enrollment	Ch. Music Enrollment	Mission Gifts	Total Gifts	Value Church Property
1969	44	1,187	346,422	10,731	209,219	91,260	95,172	31,672	8,584	28,906	$ 4,036,304	$24,201,880	$109,713,397
1970	44	1,190	349,724	11,195	207,165	81,937	91,911	28,835	7,811	28,697	4,180,078	25,165,094	113,761,898
1971	44	1,186	356,674	12,331	205,856	86,574	84,326	27,606	9,001	29,429	4,915,221	27,585,219	119,949,146
1972	44	1,192	367,020	14,551	212,555	92,414	84,772	27,184	9,324	31,183	6,048,726	31,672,637	126,828,907
1973	44	1,197	378,117	13,899	215,927	91,797	84,009	26,103	8,645	35,381	6,451,592	33,316,149	137,574,301
1974	44	1,198	390,333	14,606	222,551	95,866	83,364	26,296	8,491	37,850	7,709,938	38,613,987	154,653,737
1975	43	1,201	398,166	14,086	226,387	103,956	83,514	26,276	8,940	38,378	8,327,892	42,974,406	170,103,869
1976	42	1,213	406,878	13,237	233,211	98,205	83,173	26,298	9,016	38,740	9,180,311	49,053,439	189,890,847
1977	42	1,229	416,338	11,492	232,694	95,783	80,321	26,958	9,664	40,935	10,862,849	53,933,303	214,659,968
1978	41	1,233	422,146	11,822	232,935	99,234	80,105	25,499	9,214	41,991	13,114,272	61,215,545	248,416,508
1979	41	1,241	428,348	12,705	233,680	100,774	76,865	25,265	9,133	44,588	12,636,514	68,615,288	281,535,919
1980	41	1,245	435,619	15,507	242,792	107,632	80,654	26,505	10,225	46,916	14,131,317	75,290,470	320,669,809

ORA SUE NAGY

Life Council, and Robert A. Parker of Florida came as director in mid-1979.

The 1979 convention authorized a study for an expansion of the Paron Camp facility to include a lodge-type building for year-round use.

The Arkansas Baptist History Commission, Bernes K. Selph, director, is actively engaged in collecting, processing, and preserving matters of historical interest to Arkansas Baptists. The Riley Library on the Ouachita Baptist University campus is the repository of the commission's materials. Former director of the commission, George Truett Blackmon (q.v.), died in 1979.

The 1979 convention adopted the Bold Mission Thrust goals of the SBC for 1979-82.

Charles H. Ashcraft retired as executive secretary in 1980. He was succeeded by Huber L. Drumwright, formerly dean of the School of Theology at Southwestern Baptist Theological Seminary.

RIVOS H. DORRIS

ARMS CONTROL, DISARMAMENT, AND WORLD PEACE (cf. Peace and Southern Baptists, Vols. II, III). The recognition of the global-destructive threat of the atomic bomb following 1945 led to serious thought concerning international agreements that would control, stop, or reverse the steadily growing danger of nuclear arms. In 1945 Secretary of War Henry L. Stimson wrote a memo to President Harry S. Truman indicating that the bomb is "the climax of the race between man's growing technical power for destructiveness and his psychological power of self-control and group control—his moral power."

"Disarmament" refers to efforts to decrease or eliminate some or all weapons. "Arms control," more limited in scope, is the effort to stop particular kinds of weapons from being built. Weapons covered by arms control agreements are those that would tend to destabilize the international balance, make war more likely, or make foreseeable war more murderous for both sides. Thus far, actual disarmament has appeared too difficult to achieve, except for a treaty that caused biological weapons to be destroyed, and SALT I (Strategic Arms Limitation Treaty number I). The SALT I agreement required the Soviet Union to destroy 258 land-based intercontinental ballistic missiles in compensation for additional submarine-based missiles that they had built.

Some important arms control achievements have occurred, however. A test-ban treaty has stopped the testing of atomic bombs in the atmosphere, thus eliminating a major source of radiation fallout and international hostility across the globe. Several treaties have banned nuclear weapons from outer space, the seabeds, Antarctica, and most of Latin America. The Non-Proliferation Treaty has hindered the spread of nuclear weapons to other nations. The Hot-Line Treaty has provided an emergency communication link between the superpowers in times of crisis, and it has been used. SALT I and II attempted to limit the building of major weapons of mass destruction. These agreements allowed both sides to forego the cost of constructing expensive systems such as the antiballistic missile.

Resolutions passed and reports adopted at SBC meetings in 1891, 1895, 1911, 1940, 1943, 1944, 1945, 1946, 1955, 1967, 1978, and 1979, as well as the statement of Baptist Faith and Message in 1925 and 1963, called upon Southern Baptists and government leaders to pray, work, and take initiatives for peace and peacemaking. The resolutions of 1959, 1978, and 1979 specifically called on Baptists to support and urge efforts to reach multilateral agreements leading to arms control and disarmament. The 1979 resolution urged United States Senate ratification of SALT II. Resolutions of the Baptist World Alliance also have been explicit and frequent in calling on Baptists to pray and work for peace, to support arms control and disarmament measures, to urge their political leaders to work for arms control and disarmament, and for the United States and the Soviet Union to ratify SALT II.

See also WAR AND PEACE, VOL. II; PEACE, WAR AND, VOL. IV.

GLEN H. STASSEN

ARMSTRONG, ALICE (b. Baltimore, MD, Nov. 13, 1846; d. Baltimore, MD, Dec. 15, 1928). Writer and editor. Daughter of Mary Walker Armstrong and James Dunn Armstrong, a wealthy tobacconist, she attended Southern Home School for Girls, Baltimore. Four years older than her sister, Annie (*q.v.* I), she promoted the formation of the Woman's Missionary Union through several articles under the pen name, "Ruth Alleyn," in 1887 and a paper read at the WMU organizational meeting in 1888. Later she was editor for the woman's department in *Kind Words* and *Foreign Mission Journal*. She is buried in Greenmount Cemetery, Baltimore, MD.

DORIS DEVAULT

ART, RELIGIOUS (I, III). The variety of media using art continues to expand. Large video screens make possible the projection of charts and pictures at the annual SBC meetings. Displays, both complex and simple, in exhibit halls educate messengers and promote and advertise programs, services, and materials. An identification symbol for use by Southern Baptist churches was approved by the 1979 Convention. Television and videocassettes used as teaching and training tools make use of illustrations, photos, maps, and charts. State papers communicate information quickly through photos. Art from around the world on display in mission organizations shows the mixture of cultures where the gospel is proclaimed. Portraits of Baptist leaders are part of the record of the history of the denomination.

Questions and some controversy have been raised by the increased effect of visuals. The depiction of biblical people, places, and events; different ethnic, racial, and language groups together; the various roles for women; and the composition of the family have been objects of study and concern. But the use of art by Southern Baptists remains true to the universal pattern of using art as well as words for religious instruction.

JERRY ROSS

ASSOCIATION OF BAPTIST CHAPLAINS. See CHAPLAINS, ASSOCIATION OF BAPTIST.

ASSOCIATION OF BAPTIST FOUNDATION EXECUTIVES, THE. An association organized on May 7, 1947, in St. Louis, MO, to consider mutual problems, share ideas, and promote fellowship among the members. The association adopted its constitution and by-laws on Feb. 21, 1955. From a charter membership of 10 persons representing nine states, the association has grown to a membership of 50 persons representing 26 state Baptist foundations and the Southern Baptist Foundation. Six associate members whose responsibilities relate to the procurement of endowment or other trust funds for Baptist causes represent other SBC agencies.

THOMAS E. CARTER

ASSOCIATION OF BAPTIST PROFESSORS OF RELIGION. See BAPTIST PROFESSORS OF RELIGION, ASSOCIATION OF.

ASSOCIATION OF BAPTISTS FOR SCOUTING. See SCOUTING, ASSOCIATION OF BAPTISTS FOR.

ASSOCIATION OF BAPTISTS FOR WORLD EVANGELISM. See WORLD EVANGELISM, ASSOCIATION OF BAPTISTS FOR.

ASSOCIATION OF CHRISTIAN SCHOOLS, SOUTHERN BAPTIST. See SOUTHERN BAPTIST ASSOCIATION OF CHRISTIAN SCHOOLS.

ASSOCIATION OF PROFESSORS OF MISSIONS. See MISSIONS, ASSOCIATION OF PROFESSORS OF.

ASSOCIATION OF SOUTHERN BAPTIST COLLEGES AND SCHOOLS, THE. See SOUTHERN BAPTIST COLLEGES AND SCHOOLS, THE ASSOCIATION OF.

ASSOCIATION OF STATE EXECUTIVE SECRETARIES, SOUTHERN BAPTIST. See SOUTHERN BAPTIST ASSOCIATION OF STATE EXECUTIVE SECRETARIES.

ASSOCIATIONAL ADMINISTRATION SERVICE, HOME MISSION BOARD PROGRAM OF (cf. Associational Administration Service, Program of, Vol. III). The program of Associational Administration Service (AAS) encourages and equips associations in making decisions based on an adequate understanding of their own purposes, needs and resources, and of state convention and SBC resources.

Two principles—full partnership of associations on the denominational team and "positive neutrality" of AAS among SBC programs—are fundamental to the program.

AAS engages in research and development and provides materials and events as it works with associations, state conventions, and other SBC programs to achieve four major purposes: (1) To increase Southern Baptists' understanding of and commitment to associations as "churches in fellowship on mission in their setting"; (2) to develop stronger, more effective associations; (3) to develop stronger, more effective associational leaders; and (4) to represent the associational perspective in SBC interprogram relationships.

Achievements of the 1970s included approval of the Associational Base Design, 1972, SBC approval of a revised program statement, 1973, National Consultation on the Baptist Association at Ridgecrest, 1974, SBC approval to include Associational Emphasis Week in the denominational calendar, 1976, increased publications on the association, revision and coordination of associational planning concepts, and increased attention to research.

Leaders of the program have been Loyd Corder, 1966-74, F. Russell Bennett, 1974-75, and J. C. Bradley, 1975-

J. C. BRADLEY

AUDIOVISUALS/ELECTRONIC MEDIA (cf. Audio-Visual Aids, Vol. I). In 1963 Broadman introduced the CAVE (Church Audiovisual Education) Plan in which all Broadman film items, except films, are sold to churches in the plan at a discount. Certain manufacturers permitted Broadman to sell their audiovisual equipment through the plan at a discount also. The plan continued into the 1980s.

In 1976 Broadman Films released its first videotapes. In the same year seven videotapes concerning the various age groups in the Sunday School were produced and released dually with motion pictures to take advantage of the large number of 16mm projectors available in churches. The standard release medium at the time was 3/4 inch U-matic. In 1979 Broadman also released in 1/2 inch VHS and 1/2 inch Beta.

Beginning in 1977 Broadman also released its first product in four formats: motion picture, videotape, recorded filmstrip, and audiocassette. This was the January Bible Study material on Exodus. Based on a program need of the Church Training Department of the Sunday School Board, Broadman Films coproduced with Family Films in 1976 a motion picture entitled "Bold Discipleship." Broadman retained SBC rights for distribution. Special promotion planned with directors of associational missions led to the distribution of prints of the film to the associations as well as the Baptist Film Centers,

resulting in broad circulation. In 1978 Broadman initiated and then coproduced with Family Films a film entitled *Being Born Again,* which was also circulated in the so-called "Associational Plan."

Another unique product, released in 1975, was "Pronunciation of Bible Names," consisting of two audiocassettes, a manual, and a plastic case. Through a distinctive system of respelling, all 3,600 proper names in the Bible were presented in such a way as to be difficult to mispronounce with the system used.

Broadman continues to produce, sell, or lease audiovisual materials and equipment. Motion pictures, videotapes, filmstrips, slides, overhead transparencies, and audiocassettes are produced and released under the Broadman Films label.

In 1979 representatives of several state conventions and SBC agencies met to propose a coordinated program of video for churches. This action represented the first venture by the states to inaugurate a Conventionwide program of audiovisuals. According to the developing plan, videotape equipment will be sold by the SSB to churches and associations on a minimum cost basis. Videotapes will be produced by the various agencies on some formulated release cycle and distributed to churches.

W. MURRAY SEVERANCE

AUDITORIUMS (CHURCH) MULTIPURPOSE. See CHURCH AUDITORIUMS, MULTIPURPOSE.

AUSTRIA, MISSION IN (III). Twelve missionaries were engaged primarily in youth work in 1979. The Salzburg church (dedicated in 1977) and the historic Mollardgasse church in Vienna sponsor English-language work and promote various youth ministries. These provide the hope for future evangelistic efforts in this traditionally oriented society of less than 1,000 Baptists. Churches and missions in the Baptist Union total 13.

ELISE NANCE BRIDGES

AUTHORITY IN SOUTHERN BAPTIST THOUGHT, SOURCES OF. In locating ultimate authority in the will of God, Southern Baptists do not differ from their fellow Christians. To identify the divine will as the source of all authority, however, does not resolve other questions that arise once that affirmation is made. These questions focus upon the more immediate authorities, the instruments through which God's purpose is communicated, and the resources Christians may use in seeking to understand that purpose. In the context of these further questions, Baptists seek to offer a distinctive witness to the world.

While theological discussion at a technical level will distinguish the manifestations of authority of the three persons of the Trinity, in ordinary usage no such distinction is made. When Baptists speak of the lordship of Jesus Christ or of the Holy Spirit as the final arbiter in issues confronting them, they are speaking of the authority of God as it is manifested in Jesus Christ or of the Holy Spirit's interpretation of that authority by guiding the Christian's choices. In a famous address delivered on the steps of the United States Capitol in 1920, George W. Truett (*q.v.* II) said, "The doctrine of the absolute Lordship of Jesus Christ . . . is for Baptists the dominant fact of all their Christian experience." By this he did not mean to exclude God the Father or the Holy Spirit from the exercise of authority, but he intended to focus attention upon the divine authority manifested in Jesus Christ. Similarly, a speaker may vary expressions of divine authority without intending to change the emphasis or draw a contrast. Thus in everyday usage the following expressions may be taken to mean the same thing: "God is leading us," "It is the Savior's bidding," and "Under the Holy Spirit's guidance."

This divine authority is manifested in different ways and through various channels; the ones most frequently cited are the Bible, personal experience, and the influence of other Christians. Baptists would be reluctant to enlarge this list indefinitely, but in practice there are other channels of authority, even though they may not be acknowledged as such. These include tradition, confessions of faith, and offices (or officers) in the church and in the denomination.

Prominent persons in any society, whether they hold a formal office, possess an authority that, although unspecified, is often quite weighty. Churches and denominations share in this characteristic. Although in some instances the authority may appear first, to be followed with recognition by being named to an office, in other instances the office may be bestowed for other reasons, and only subsequently is the person then acknowledged to possess an authority by virtue of the office. While some denominations specify such authority and its limits, among Baptists it is highly variable, depending upon personalities, issues, and prevailing moods of the people.

Tradition is the most difficult to define among all the sources of authority. By its very nature it can never be totally summarized in written form. Tradition also defies any attempt to specify its use. An observation in a church business meeting that "we've always done it this way" may be translated to mean, "We must continue to do it this way." In this way tradition—even if incorrectly remembered and partially handed down—assumes an authoritative role.

Creeds and confessions of faith (Baptists have preferred the latter term) also possess varying authority. William L. Lumpkin stated in *Baptist Confessions of Faith* (1969):

The Baptist Movement has traditionally been noncreedal in the sense that it has not erected authoritative confessions of faith as official bases of organization and tests of orthodoxy. An authority which could impose a confession upon individuals, churches, or larger bodies, has been lacking, and the desire to achieve uniformity has never been strong enough to secure adoption of a fixed creed even if the authority for imposing it had existed.

Although those who formulate a confession of faith and those who adopt it originally may not intend to claim for it an authoritative voice, there is nothing to prevent its being used as though it possessed such a voice. This kind of use is occasionally advocated among Baptists.

Central to almost all Baptist statements on authority is the affirmation that the Bible communicates the divine will and is the only definitive and sufficient rule for faith and practice. Baptists acknowledge that the Bible is not an independent authority but is an instrument of God's authority. It declares God's truth and provides divine guidance for the life of the individual believer and for the company of believers, the church. The first article of the Second London Confession of 1677 states: "The Holy Scripture is the only sufficient, certain, and infallible rule of all saving Knowledge, Faith, and Obedience." Similar language appears in subsequent confessions down to the present time.

Two specific points of disagreement among Baptists arise in this context. One of these appears in response to the question, "In what areas is the Bible authoritative?" In other words, is it to be taken as definitive in matters of science and history, or is its authority specifically in the realm of "saving Knowledge, Faith, and Obedience"? There is no significant divergence of opinion among Baptists on the latter point; the Bible is the reference book for matters of church polity as well as for questions on the human condition, the plan of salvation, the deity of Christ, and the vocation of the believer. When a question is not addressed in the Bible—as for example the Christian response to ethical issues that are peculiar to the modern situation, or the organization for a church's ministry in the modern world—Baptists strive to respond in harmony with the biblical revelation. On the former part of the question, about the Bible's scientific and historical authority, the most that can be said is that differences exist among Baptists, and these differences do not appear to be approaching resolution.

The second area of disagreement among Baptists on this point arises in response to the question, "How much authority is to be ascribed to the interpretation of the authority?" Where there is disagreement on interpretation, and where no agreed-upon principles exist for the delineation of permissible variations, the biblical authority itself and the authority of one interpretation or another can be kept distinct only with the most careful thought and enunciation. Hence, while Baptists agree in declaring the Bible to be the unique and inspired written word of God, they hold divergent views on the authority that can rightfully be claimed for a specific interpretation of the Bible as a whole or in its various parts.

One reason for the diversity of opinion on

biblical authority is the Baptist conviction that personal experience, under the guidance of the Holy Spirit, is one of the instruments by which God makes his will known to his people. This conviction is expressed in various terms, depending on the specific focus of interest. The "autonomy of the individual" is sometimes stressed to insist that no other human authority may be interposed between the individual believer and God. Another more affirmative declaration speaks of the "priesthood of the believer," insisting that each person is responsible to God and is not dependent upon the priestly ministry of another to gain access to God or to receive the disclosure of the divine will. These and other similar expressions give voice to the central conviction that God's authority, which is definitive and all-encompassing for the believer, may be made known to the Christian not only in confessions of faith and in the Scripture, but in the promised presence of the Holy Spirit who, in the words of Jesus, would "guide you into all truth."

See also AUTHORITY, VOL. I; AUTHORITY OF THE SOUTHERN BAPTIST CONVENTION, VOL. I.

BIBLIOGRAPHY: W. L. Lumpkin, *Baptist Confessions of Faith* (1969). "The Nature and A. of Baptist Confessions of Faith," *Review and Expositor* (Winter, 1979). J. L. Garrett, "The Concept of Biblical A. in Historic Baptist Confessions of Faith," *Review and Expositor,* (Winter, 1979). P. M. Harrison, *A. and Power in the Free Church Tradition* (1959). Bernard Ramm, *The Pattern of A.* (1957). E. Y. Mullins, *Freedom and A. in Religion* (1913).

JOHN E. STEELY

AVERETT COLLEGE (I, III). The 1970s began with Averett moving to a coeducational four-year program, graduating the first class with bachelor's degrees in 1971. In the same year the Mary B. Blount Library was completed with room for 100,000 volumes. Enrollment increased to 1,200, requiring the college to consider more property and a master plan for additional space and buildings. A major was offered in Christian studies with opportunities for emphasis in religious education and pastoral ministries. Departments of business administration and social work were established. As the decade ended, the department of education qualified to offer a master's degree in that field. Conwell A. Anderson resigned as president in June, 1979, and was succeeded by Howard W. Lee, who was inaugurated on Apr. 26, 1980. Total assets on June 30, 1979, were $6,959,130.

HOWARD W. LEE

AVERYT, EDWIN FRANKLIN (b. Shelby, AL, Jan. 6, 1902; d. Columbia, SC, July 3, 1978). South Carolina layman and philanthropist. The son of John Francis Averyt, a merchandiser, and Ella Mosely Averyt, he graduated from the University of Alabama (B.A., 1926). He married Asenath Pratt Murfee, Nov. 8, 1930. They had three children: Ella, Dorothy, and Gayle. He was president of Colonial Life and Accident Insurance Company, Columbia, SC, from its founding in 1937 until he retired in 1970.

Averyt served as director of Carolina Children's Home and as a trustee of Newberry College and Furman University. He was also on the board of advisers for North Greenville College, which named its library for him. A wing at South Carolina Baptist Hospital is also named for him. The Averyts endowed a scholarship fund at the University of Alabama. A member of Shandon Baptist Church in Columbia, he donated a building that bears his name. He is buried in Elmwood Cemetery, Columbia, SC.

TERRILL D. WALTERS

AWARE (III). See WOMAN'S MISSIONARY UNION, AUXILIARY TO SBC.

B

BACONE COLLEGE (I, III). The 1980 capital worth of this Oklahoma school was $5,673,541, including $1,776,645 endowment. There were 506 students and 46 faculty. The budget was $2,000,000. On Mar. 11, 1974, Charles D. Holleyman succeeded Garold D. Holstine as president. Pasqual Dean Chavers became president, Mar. 11, 1979.

J. M. GASKIN

BAHAMAS, MISSION IN (I, III). In 1971 the mission began working with the reorganized Bahamas National Baptist Missionary and Educational Convention. Missionaries served as consultants on the various convention committees in the areas of Sunday School, Church Training, and Vacation Bible School; Men and Boy's Work; Women and Girl's Work; Youth and Student Work; Music; Evangelism; Stewardship; Home and Foreign Missions; and Theological Education. The Bahamas Baptist Bible Institute has extension classes on three other islands. The Baptist Young People's Fellowship was formed in 1973. Vacation Bible Schools are totally in the hands of Bahamians.

In 1980, 13 missionaries were working in the

Bahamas, including a journeyman couple and a couple working with the Caribbean Baptist Fellowship Media Center.

ANTONINA CANZONERI

BAILIE MEMORIAL BOYS' RANCH (III). After 15 years of struggle to provide properly for this work, the Northwest Baptist Convention voted in May, 1978, to give the assets of the ranch to a board of directors not related to Baptist work. Increasing pressures from the state of Washington and inadequate support from the churches strongly influenced the convention's decision. Leon Bailie, William Fleming, Herman Klindworth, Joe Hall, and Marie Carr were major contributors to the work of the ranch.

CECIL SIMS

BAKER, AZRA CURTIS (b. Clay County, AL, Jan. 9, 1894; d. Louisville, KY, May 13, 1976). Pastor and religious broadcaster. Son of John Baker, a farmer, he attended Mercer University and Southern Baptist Theological Seminary. He married Gertrude Woods, June 26, 1919. They had one daughter, Cora Lee. He owned Seymour, IN, radio station WJCD, broadcasting the gospel. His pastorates included Baptist churches in Kentucky and Tabernacle Church, Macon, GA. He is buried in Cave Hill Cemetery, Louisville, KY.

E. HARMON MOORE

BALL, WILLIAM LOCKHART, SR. (b. Honaker, VA, May 5, 1875; d. Rock Hill, SC, June 12, 1953). Pastor. Son of Isaiah Drake and Rebecca Lockhart Ball, farmers, he attended Tazewell College, Richmond College, and Southern Baptist Theological Seminary. He married Marion Swann Terrell, Dec. 20, 1911. Their children were Marion and William. He served as pastor of Tabernacle Baptist Church, Richmond, VA, 1905-19; First Church, Spartanburg, SC, 1919-32; and Earle Street Church, Greenville, SC, 1932-46. He served on the Foreign Mission Board, SBC, 1906-19; the Executive Committee, SBC, 1927-41; preached the annual sermon at the SBC meeting, 1929; and was president of the South Carolina Baptist Convention, 1930-32. He is buried in Woodlawn Memorial Gardens, Greenville, SC.

W. L. BALL, JR.

BANGLADESH, MISSION IN (cf. Pakistan, Mission in, Vol. III). This country was part of India up to 1947. Then it existed as part of Pakistan until 1971, when Bangladesh won its independence after war against Pakistan. Southern Baptist missionaries have been deeply involved in various development projects since Bangladesh won its independence. Eighteen missionaries, including two journeymen and a Mission Service Corps couple, are under appointment for Bangladesh. Progress in church growth had been slow until recently. In 1979, 11 churches were related to the Bangladesh Baptist Union, and five were added during the year in areas where Southern Baptist missionaries serve.

JAMES F. MCKINLEY, JR.

BAPTIST AND REFLECTOR (I, III). James A. Lester resigned as editor, Apr. 30, 1974, following a six-month leave of absence. Ralph L. Norton, executive secretary of the Tennessee Baptist Convention, assumed responsibility for the publication. Eura Rich Lannom, an employee of the publication since 1943, became acting editor in Aug., 1974, holding that position until Alvin C. Shackleford became editor, Nov. 1, 1976. Bobbie Durham became editorial assistant, Aug., 1971.

In a reorganization in Feb., 1979, the position of circulation manager (which had been vacant since the resignation of David Keel in Oct., 1975) was changed to associate editor, and Lannom's position was changed from assistant to the editor to advertising and subscription manager. Charles Warren became associate editor, July 15, 1979. The format of the publication changed from a 16-page magazine to a 12-page tabloid newspaper in Jan., 1979. The circulation in 1980 was 82,462.

In May, 1977, the executive board of the convention created the position of public affairs and Christian life consultant, which was assigned to the *Baptist and Reflector* office. Jerry M. Self was elected to that position and began his service on Mar. 23, 1978.

ALVIN C. SHACKLEFORD

BAPTIST BACKGROUNDS (cf. Baptists, Vol. I). The historical roots of modern Baptists go back to the radical Puritans during the reign of Elizabeth I (1558-1603) who withdrew from the Church of England and formed themselves into voluntary consociations of "visible saints." One of their leaders, Henry Barrow, cited four reasons for their separation from the established church: false membership, false ministry, false worship, and false church government. The Separatist churches gathered by a "covenanting" ceremony and maintained church order through the strict enforcement of congregational discipline.

The first Separatist to make believer's baptism the basis for church membership was John Smyth. In 1608/09 he baptized himself and his entire congregation which had fled to Holland under threat of persecution. Smyth also abandoned the Calvinist tenets of original sin and absolute predestination. The General Baptists who moved to England in 1611 under Smyth's disciple Thomas Helwys embraced an Arminian doctrine of grace. The Particular Baptists, who believed in particular or limited atonement, also developed out of the Separatist milieu, although by a different route. The Particular Baptist churches, whose theology was first codified in the London Confession of 1644, were offshoots in the 1630s from an independent congregation founded at Southwark by Henry Jacob in 1616. Its members included both strict Separatists and semi-Separatists, those who advocated withdrawal from the Church of England but permitted a measure of fellowship with godly members of the established church.

The Separatist tradition has had a profound effect on Baptist ecclesiology. Separatists articulated and practiced the concepts of a covenanted community, regenerate membership, church discipline, separation of church and state, and local congregational autonomy.

BIBLIOGRAPHY: C. Burrage, *The Early English Dissenters in the Light of Recent Research* (1912). B. R. White, *The English Separatist Tradition* (1971).

TIMOTHY GEORGE

BAPTIST BASKET, THE. A paper published monthly in Louisville, KY, by the Central Committee of Kentucky Women's Missionary Societies from Jan., 1888, through Sep., 1895. The paper stressed tithing. Mrs. Thomas Osborne, sister-in-law of Agnes Osborne, who edited *The Heathen Helper,* was the editor. She was assisted by a staff of editors, one from each state that had a central committee. In addition to articles and quotes on giving, the paper published a complete Women's Missionary Society program each month.

BOBBIE SORRILL

BAPTIST BEACON (I). Irving Childress became editor in Oct., 1970. C. L. Pair succeeded him, Jan. 15, 1973. The circulation was 12,500, Jan. 1, 1980. About 250 of the 295 churches and missions which cooperate with the Arizona Southern Baptist Convention subscribe to the state paper through the church budget plan. The *Beacon* receives its income from subscriptions, advertising, and the Cooperative Program.

See also ARIZONA SOUTHERN BAPTIST CONVENTION, Vol. III.

C. L. PAIR

BAPTIST BIBLE FELLOWSHIP INTERNATIONAL (cf. Baptist Bible Fellowship, Vol. I). A nondenominational sending agency of independent Baptist and fundamentalist traditions with emphasis on evangelism and church planting. John Rawlings is the current president. In addition to their three-year Bible college and graduate school in Springfield, MO, they also maintain a seminary in Arlington, TX. This group supports 458 missionaries in 45 countries with Brazil, the Philippines, and Mexico having the largest number of missionaries. The total income for missions is approximately $7,000,000.

M. THOMAS STARKES

BAPTIST BIBLE INSTITUTE, GRACE-VILLE, FLORIDA (III). In Jan., 1969, ground was broken for the Frank Faris Student Center. The institute had an enrollment of 320 for the academic year 1969-70. Maximum enrollment allowed was increased from 300 to 400 by the Florida Baptist Convention in Jan., 1972. Enrollment for the 1979-80 school year was 426. The year 1979-80 produced 98 graduates as compared to 42 for 1969-70. Library holdings advanced from 17,000 volumes in 1970 to 30,986 in 1980. The institute's budget increased from $386,103 in 1969-70 to $959,590 in 1979-80.

In 1972 the institute was licensed as a school of higher learning in Florida by the State Board of Independent Colleges and Universities. In June, 1979, the Southern Association of Colleges and Schools granted the institute candidacy for accreditation status. During the 1975 meeting of the Florida Baptist Convention the Bachelor of Ministry degree was approved. This is a four-year, 130-semester-hour program in biblical studies, music, and religious education.

President James E. Southerland retired, Dec., 1977, completing 20 years of service. He was succeeded by Joseph P. DuBose, Jr., who previously served as pastor of East Hill Baptist Church, Pensacola, FL. J. D. Allen and Cecil L. Davis retired from the faculty in June, 1978. Jerry W. Batson and R. C. Hammack succeeded these two teachers.

The 1979 fall semester began with 16 faculty members. James T. Owens was employed as assistant professor of music, while Michael Burns succeeded Joe Wood as assistant professor of religious education. In Sep., 1979, the institute's trustees conferred the rank of emeritus professor upon Josiah D. Allen, Cecil Loring Davis, and Martin Valca McKinster; the rank of emeritus president upon Arthur House Stainback and James E. Southerland; and the rank of emeritus public relations director upon Hal D. Bennett.

Permission was received in Nov., 1979, to begin construction of a preschool center. Groundbreaking activities took place in Mar., 1980, for the McRae-Morrow Preschool Teaching-Training Center.

JOSEPH P. DUBOSE, JR.

BAPTIST BOOK STORES. See BOOK STORES, BAPTIST.

BAPTIST BULLETIN SERVICE (III). The service provides local churches a bulletin for each Sunday of the year with a full-color front cover and appropriate text on the back cover, often related to the programs and work of the SBC. Approximately 1,400,000 are used weekly by the churches. W. C. Fields was editor, 1959-72. Albert McClellan, who had served as editor, 1949-59, served a second time as editor, 1972-80.

LEONARD E. HILL

BAPTIST CENTER, SWITZERLAND (III). See SWITZERLAND, BAPTIST CENTER.

BAPTIST CHILDREN'S AID SOCIETY (III). See MARYLAND, INC., BAPTIST CHILDREN'S AID SOCIETY OF.

BAPTIST CHILDREN'S HOME AT SAN ANTONIO (cf. Mexican Baptist Orphans

Home, Vol. II; Mexican Baptist Children's Home of Texas, Vol. III). The home serves 100 children of all races. The Baptist General Convention of Texas provides 50 percent of operating funds, and the other 50 percent comes from gifts, wills, and memorials. A member of the National Association of Homes for Children, the home was licensed in Mar., 1980, to begin a foster care and adoption program. Total assets in 1980 were $3,303,270. The home has $750,000 in endowment administered by the Baptist Foundation of Texas. Leland Hacker is administrator. The home was called Mexican Baptist Children's Home until 1980 when it was given its present name by the Texas Baptist Convention.

LELAND HACKER

BAPTIST CHILDREN'S HOMES OF NORTH CAROLINA, INC. (III).

Group care is provided for children at the Mills Home, Thomasville; Kennedy Memorial Home, Kinston; Odum Home, Pembroke; and Broyhill Home, Clyde. Other services include family social work, foster care, emergency care, therapeutic camping, care for unwed mothers, advanced education, counseling, referrals, programs of family life education, and a demonstration day-care and weekday early education center. The program is directed toward cooperation with pastors, directors of missions, and denominational leadership in efforts to strengthen Christian family life.

Charity and Children has been the official publication of the homes since 1887. The statewide ministry of the homes is directed by 36 trustees, elected by the state convention. Administrative offices are located in Thomasville, with regional administrators in strategic areas throughout North Carolina.

ELIZABETH T. WAGONER

BAPTIST CHILDREN'S VILLAGE, THE (III;

cf. Mississippi Baptist Orphanage, Vol. II). Paul N. Nunnery's title as head of the institution was changed in 1975 to executive director. From 1972 to 1979, the village acquired three residential care facilities outside the central campus in Jackson. The New Albany group home opened, Feb., 1972; the Tate County branch campus opened, Sep., 1975; and Dickerson Place in Lincoln County opened, Dec., 1979. Two new cottages were built on the Jackson campus in 1970 and 1974, raising to 13 the total number of cottages on that campus.

The voluntary system of foster care across the state continued into the 1980s, averaging 30 children in the program. Approximately 65 percent of the children placed in village facilities, rural and urban, are court referred; the rest are voluntary placements. An average of 425-430 different children per year between 1975 and 1980 were in village care. The average daily enrollment was 225. This reflected the emphasis on family reunification. Weekend visitation with families was stepped up, and in May,

1980, the village held its first Family Day on the Jackson campus. One weekend a month approved families invite village children into their homes.

The institution served in 1974-75 as an organizer of the National Association of Homes for Children, a group of nonprofit child-care agencies. In Mar., 1980, Patricia Nash Dean, widow of Jay Hanna (Dizzy) Dean, contributed the residence which was their home at Bond for a group home for village children, effective at her death.

TIM NICHOLAS

BAPTIST COLLEGE AT CHARLESTON (III).

The college achieved accreditation from the Southern Association of Colleges and Schools in Dec., 1970, just five years after opening. John A. Hamrick continues as president. The holdings of the L. Mendal Rivers Library, dedicated in 1970, total over 100,000 volumes. Now referred to as the Library and Learning Center, facilities include a well-equipped and professionally staffed audiovisual center.

A second dormitory complex allows for a combined total of 900 resident students. A maintenance building accommodates the college's printing facilities. With assistance from supporters particularly interested in athletics, new tennis courts, a baseball field, and a field house have enlarged the physical education facilities.

Academic and career counseling offices are in operation. Special options, such as College Level Examination, veterans credit, advanced college credit, course challenge, and credit through subject examinations and fast-track opportunities for high academic achievers in the President's Scholars group, provide ways to shorten time spent in classrooms and speed the student with special abilities and experiences toward the desired degree. An English Language Institute for International Students has opened college doors to many students from around the world. Twenty countries were represented among students in the 1980 fall session. Cultural and social exchanges are arranged through cooperation with Woman's Missionary Union groups from the surrounding associations.

Under the NASDTEC program, several areas are offered for teacher certification: art, biology, business, chemistry, education, English, foreign languages, history and social studies, physical education, mathematics, music, physics, psychology, sociology, and speech-drama. Special concentrations have been added in areas of accounting, management systems, computer science, biology, and chemistry, plus a degree in general studies.

In 1971 the college was one of the first colleges in the state to offer a four-year degree in criminal justice and the first to offer a major in music therapy. Ann Whitworth Howe, South Carolina's first registered music therapist, initiated the program in 1971. In 1972 a unit of the Air Force ROTC was begun on campus.

Continuing education began in 1974 with a

CAMPBELL UNIVERSITY (*q.v.*), Buies Creek, NC. D. Rich Building houses social sciences, English, speech and drama, business, art, and the J. Clyde Turner Auditorium, which seats over 1,000 people.

BAPTIST CHILDREN'S HOMES OF NORTH CAROLINA, INC. (q.v.) *Top, left:* Broyhill Home, Waynesville-Clyde, established in 1971. *Top, right:* Kennedy Home, Kinston, Cedar Dell mansion renovated to house Family Services Center. *Lower, left:* Mills Home Campus, Thomasville, Mills Home Baptist Church and Cottage. *Lower, right:* Odum Home, Pembroke, residence and general office building.

few workshops, seminars, and lectures in the area of business administration. By fall, 1980, the program had greatly expanded. In addition to a new, accelerated evening degree program, the continuing education catalog, *Horizons,* listed 119 classes, workshops, and seminars offered for personal and professional enrichment. The college's enrollment totals of 2,500 do not include the more than 600 students in noncredit continuing education programs.

A chapel-religion building is in the planning for the 1981-82 school year, with a new science building, an additional classroom building, an administration building, and a music building needed to complete the master plan.

MARGARET T. GILMORE

BAPTIST CONVALESCENT CENTER.
A convalescent center founded in Newport, KY, by Northern Kentucky Association in 1951, owned and operated by the association, and incorporated under the laws of Kentucky. The bed capacity is 167, with 108 for intermediate care and 59 for skilled nursing care. The center is licensed to accept Medicare, Medicaid, and Veteran's Administration patients. Total assets are $6,000,000 with an operational budget for 1980 of $1,700,000.

GEORGE ALEXANDER JONES

BAPTIST COURIER, THE (I, III).
Weekly news journal of the South Carolina Baptist Convention. The office building for the *Courier* was enlarged in 1978 to 7,200 square feet. The additional space accommodates new typesetting and composition equipment and the computer operations, which maintain the subscription list. Circulation grew from 102,000 in 1970 to 127,000 in 1980. In 1980 the building, equipment, and furnishings were valued at $500,000. The staff has eight news and office personnel. The annual operating budget is $650,000. John E. Roberts has served as editor since 1966.

JOHN E. ROBERTS

BAPTIST FAITH AND MESSAGE FELLOWSHIP, THE.
An organization independent of the SBC, composed of Southern Baptists who are dedicated to the principles of biblical inerrancy, evangelism, and missions. Its headquarters are in Buchanan, GA.

On Mar. 5, 1973, 52 persons meeting in the First Baptist Church, Atlanta, GA, voted to form the Baptist Faith and Message Fellowship (BFMF) and thereby signaled their concern for upholding the Baptist Faith and Message, a statement of faith adopted by the SBC in 1963.

On Sep. 5, 1973, the BFMF was chartered in Georgia with M. O. Owens of North Carolina as president of a 24-member board. This board meets semiannually. An eight-member executive committee functions throughout the year. Other presidents during the 1970s were Laverne Butler from Louisville, KY, and Harold Lindsell, former editor of *Christianity Today.*

William A. Powell, the motivating force behind the organizational efforts, left the Home Mission Board, SBC, and became editor of the *Southern Baptist Journal,* publication of the BFMF, on Nov. 1, 1973. In 1979 he became the vice-president in charge of fund raising and publication. Russell Kaemmerling of South Carolina then became editor of the *Journal* in 1980. He served only a few months before resigning, and Powell again became editor. In-house publications have been an occasional "Membership Bulletin," which was discontinued because of the perennial financial problems of the BFMF, and "1200 Comments," which is copyrighted and sent to those who contribute substantially to the fellowship.

Through its publications and activities, the BFMF has sought to convince all Southern Baptists to embrace its views of biblical orthodoxy and has endeavored to expose Southern Baptist leaders who have advocated views unacceptable to the BFMF.

See also BIBLE, CONTROVERSIES ABOUT THE; CONSERVATIVE THEOLOGY, RESURGENCE OF; INERRANCY; SOUTHERN BAPTIST ADVOCATE; SOUTHERN BAPTIST JOURNAL.

BOB D. COMPTON

BAPTIST FEDERATION OF CANADA.
See CANADIAN BAPTISTS.

BAPTIST FOUNDATION OF OKLAHOMA, THE
(cf. Oklahoma Baptist Foundation, Vols. II, III). In 1969 the operating budget was $126,178, with endowment, capital needs, and personal trusts held by the foundation totaling $7,748,037. Income distribution to agencies, institutions, churches, and individuals was $434,628. In 1980 the operating budget had increased to $399,149, with endowment, capital needs, and personal trust funds totaling $24,274,231. Income distribution in 1979 was $1,677,194.

Thomas Edwin Carter, executive secretary-treasurer, retired, June 1, 1973. The board of directors elected Clovis Fred Williams as his successor. The foundation's articles of incorporation and bylaws were amended and restated, Dec. 20, 1974. Board officer titles were changed from president and vice-presidents to chairman and vice-chairmen. The executive secretary-treasurer's title was changed to president-treasurer. The office of corporate secretary was filled by a staff member who also served as secretary to the president. Vice-presidents serving on the staff were assigned responsibilities of Church Loan and Property Management Services, Estate Planning Services, Communication and Estate Stewardship Services, and Computer and Special Investment Services.

Investment pools of the foundation administered by committees of the board are:

Church Building Loan Trust.—On Oct. 31, 1969, 156 churches had loans totaling $4,200,091. By Oct. 31, 1979, this figure had increased to 193 churches, with loans totaling

$10,341,611. Income from the Church Building Loan Trust Fund for 1969 was $761,349. By 1979 this had increased to $2,183,913.

Equity Investment Pool.—On Jan. 1, 1969, $1,357,380 was invested in the pool. By Apr. 30, 1980, this figure had climbed to $4,211,901. Income from the pool in 1969 was $55,487; in 1979 it was $289,684.

Fixed Income Pool.—This pool was formed in Jan., 1972, when bonds valued at $872,913 were placed in the pool for administrative purposes. On Jan. 1, 1980, $3,175,504 was invested in the pool. Income received during 1979 was $262,725.

In 1978 the foundation began special attorney orientation dinner meetings. By June 1, 1980, 354 attorneys had attended these meetings. Area foundation offices were opened in Lawton in 1978 and in Shawnee in 1979.

C. FRED WILLIAMS

BAPTIST GENERAL ASSOCIATION OF NEW ENGLAND. See NEW ENGLAND, BAPTIST GENERAL ASSOCIATION OF.

BAPTIST GENERAL CONFERENCE. Swedish Baptists in America trace their origin to Aug. 8, 1852, when Gustaf Palmquist, a teacher from Sweden, baptized three converts in the Mississippi River near Rock Island, IL, and organized a Baptist church. The Swedish Baptist General Conference was organized at Village Creek, IA, June 12-14, 1879. The conference dropped the word *Swedish* from its name in 1945.

A theological seminary, organized in 1871 at Milwaukee, WI, became a department of the Divinity School of the University of Chicago in 1888. The seminary moved to St. Paul, MN, in 1914 and merged with Bethel Academy. It is now known as Bethel College. The conference initially worked extensively among Scandinavian immigrants and received some support from the American Baptist Home Mission Society and the American Baptist Publication Society. From 1888 until 1944, foreign mission efforts were channeled through the American Baptist Foreign Mission Society. The conference established its own foreign mission work in 1944, in part as a desire to be independent, and as a reaction to the policies of the American Baptist Foreign Mission Society.

Offices of the conference are located in Arlington Heights, IL. Warren R. Magnuson has served as general secretary of the conference since 1969. Beginning with *Zions Wäktare (The Watchmen of Zion),* May, 1871, a chain of denominational papers has continued unbroken from that time until the present. The official organ of the conference is the *Standard,* a monthly periodical. The conference incorporates churches in Canada, the United States, and the Caribbean. In 1979 there were 772 churches, 4,671 baptisms, and a total membership of 131,999. Contributions for all causes in 1979 totaled $53,363,138. In Apr., 1981, the churches in Canada voted to incorporate as the Baptist General Conference of Canada.

BIBLIOGRAPHY: David Guston and Martin Erikson (eds.), *A Centenary History: As Related to the Baptist General Conference of America, 1852-1952* (1952); *Fifteen Eventful Years, A Survey of the Baptist General Conference, 1945-1960* (1961).

A. RONALD TONKS

BAPTIST HISTORIOGRAPHY. See HISTORIOGRAPHY, BAPTIST.

BAPTIST HISTORY AND HERITAGE (III). This quarterly journal of the Historical Commission, SBC, advanced in several ways during the 1970s. More issues focused on single themes, enhancing the publication's resource value. More seminary classes used various issues as texts. The Norman W. Cox Award, presented annually since 1975 by the commission and Southern Baptist Historical Society, goes to the writer of the best article published by the commission and society in this journal or *The Quarterly Review.* Recipients during 1975-80 were, respectively, Ira V. (Jack) Birdwhistell, James E. Tull, Thomas R. McKibbens, Jr., H. Leon McBeth, Claude L. Howe, Jr., and David W. Music.

CHARLES W. DEWEESE

BAPTIST HOME, THE (cf. Missouri Home for Aged Baptists, Vol. III). Edward C. Goodwin became administrator in 1974 upon the retirement of John H. Burney. Occupation of a new 64-bed medical facility in 1977 increased the resident capacity to 210. The name of the home was changed in 1979, and the home was licensed as an intermediate care facility in 1980. The operating budget of $1,700,000 in 1980 included the wages for a staff of 113 and provided funds for ministries in other nursing homes through the outreach program.

EDWARD C. GOODWIN

BAPTIST HOME FOR CHILDREN, JACKSONVILLE (III; cf. Florida, Baptist Home for Children, Vol. I). Financial support for the home comes from churches, individuals, aid from relatives, child support payments, Florida Baptist state mission offering, income from a trust fund, and other sources. Operating expenses rose from $113,500 in 1969 to $231,680 in 1979.

The regular program cares for 50 boys and girls coming primarily from northeast Florida. An emergency shelter program, begun in 1979, cares for up to 12 neglected and dependent boys, ages 12-17, waiting adjudication by the state of Florida. The period of care is not to exceed 60 days. A full school program is conducted on campus for boys in the emergency shelter program. Other children attend the public schools.

The John and Aliese Price Building, including the chapel, administrative offices, dining room, and kitchen, was erected in 1974. George E. Norton serves as director, assisted by 19 staff members. In 1977 Norton was elected president of the Child Care Executives of the Southern Baptist Convention.

MALCOLM B. KNIGHT

BAPTIST HOMES FOR THE ELDERLY, INC. (Louisville, KY). Interest in care for the elderly in central Kentucky was expressed as early as 1915 with the founding of the Kentucky Baptist Children's Home. This interest, developed further in a Home for the Aged Committee appointed by the Long Run Association in 1953 and appearing again in the General Association of Baptists in Kentucky (Kentucky Baptist Convention) in 1958, was stimulated by a gift designated by Sarah H. Wigginton at her death in 1957. A board of directors was established in 1963 from Baptist churches in Long Run Association (limited to those in Jefferson County). The directors authorized a board of trustees who opened and operated the N. B. and Sarah H. Wigginton Home for Men in Louisville, Oct., 1968, to Apr., 1979. Changes in laws and conditions made it possible to care for others than "men who were residents of Jefferson County."

A 210-bed nursing home, called Baptist Home East, was developed and opened in northeastern Jefferson County on June 27, 1979. The cost was $950,000. In early 1980 the residents, men and women, in personal care and intermediate care, averaged 90 persons. The annual operating budget of the home is $1,000,000.

LEO T. CRISMON

BAPTIST HOSPITAL, INC. (cf. Baptist Hospital, Inc. (Mid-State), Vols. I, III). This 724-bed, full-service, general hospital owned by the Tennessee Baptist Convention, consists of 12 buildings in a two-block complex. Statistics for 1979 were as follows: patients admitted, 29,737; emergency room visits, 41,688; births, 4,614; surgical procedures, 16,175; number of employees, 1,848; and medical staff members, 547. Students receive training in medical technology, X-ray, nursing, and inhalation therapy.

The full-service concept of health care has been enlarged since 1970, with more emphasis placed on emergency room services, pediatrics, obstetrics, hemodialysis, and charity care. Programs such as short-stay surgery, outpatient endoscopy, and the Progressive Care Center for nonacute patients are offered to cut the cost of hospitalization. Three full-time, trained chaplains work on an around-the-clock basis in the Department of Pastoral Services.

GENE KIDD

BAPTIST HOSPITALS, INC. (III; cf. Hospital Commission of Kentucky Baptists, Vol. I). In 1973 Homer D. Coggins succeeded Hubert Lee Dobbs as president. In 1980 the three executive vice-presidents were Ben R. Brewer, in charge of the Louisville Baptist Hospitals (Highlands, 276 beds, and Baptist East,

253 beds); H. Earl Freezor at Western Baptist Hospital in Paducah (319 beds); and Tom J. Smith at Lexington (297 beds). Total property value in 1979 was $45,303,470, and total assets were $65,913,518. Indebtedness stood at $14,092,104. The total number of beds is 1,136, with 98 bassinets. The medical staff of 925 is assisted by 3,000 employees. Admissions in 1979 were 49,667.

In 1974 Baptist Hospitals, Inc., acquired Mallary Taylor Hospital through a trust agreement with Oldham County. This hospital, located in La Grange, KY, was a 31-bed unit in financial difficulty and desired a linkage with a large hospital for financial reasons. This sharing arrangement benefited the hospital and kept it in business until 1979 when the trust agreement and working arrangements were concluded.

BEN R. BREWER

BAPTIST HOUR, THE (I). See RADIO AND TELEVISION COMMISSION, SBC.

BAPTIST INFORMATION RETRIEVAL SYSTEM (BIRS). A computer-based information service on Baptist life and history operated by the Historical Commission, SBC, since 1974. The commission established an Indexing Study Committee in June, 1972, to survey the feasibility of developing an indexing system proposed by F. W. Helmbold, former president of the Southern Baptist Historical Society, at the Apr., 1971, society meeting. The committee, meeting at Samford University, Sep. 15-16, 1972, included Lynn E. May, Jr., A. Ronald Tonks, Belden Menkus (consultant), Walter B. Shurden, J. Wayne Flynt, Loulie L. Owens, John H. Woodard, J. M. Crowe, Martin B. Bradley, and F. W. Helmbold, chairman. Observers from Samford were: Fanna K. Bee, William D. Jones, and John Burrows. Intensive discussions persuaded the committee that it was possible to create a computer-based information system without bankrupting Baptist agencies and without confining its usability to particular interest groups.

The Historical Commission staff and consultants Helmbold and Menkus began to develop a *Thesaurus for Baptist Indexing and Baptist Information Retrieval System* containing subject headings which could be indexed and searched. The commission employed Smith, Murray, and Associates, computer firm of Birmingham, AL, to provide computer services in the development of the *Thesaurus* and other elements of the information system. Eventually, a Thesaurus Control Committee was established representing agencies from a broad spectrum, e.g., missions, publishing, education, states, and the commission. The *Thesaurus* has gone through three separate and expanded editions (1973, 1976, 1978).

The ad hoc committee called for the commission to enlist representatives from several Baptist agencies to meet at the Home Mission Board in Atlanta, GA, Aug. 29, 1973. With broad representation of leadership from SBC and state agencies, the commission projected beginning a pilot project in 1974, on authorization of the cooperating agencies. The proposed pilot project envisaged a period of 18 months (later extended to 24 months), six or seven input locations geographically, and a varied assortment of types of input material.

Orientation for BIRS indexers and their supervisors took place in Nashville, TN, Nov. 26, 1973, at which time the *Thesaurus* was available. The ad hoc committee met again following that orientation meeting to consider policies and procedures for operation of BIRS during the pilot project which began in 1974.

By Jan., 1975, the input was of sufficient variety and extent of data that the commission staff initiated retrieval tests. Index printouts for the *Southern Baptist Periodical Index, The Alabama Baptist,* the *Biblical Recorder* (including retroactive indexing beginning with 1834 issues), and the *Baptist Standard* were tested and proved suitable. Lynn E. May, Jr., developed a thorough *Report on the Baptist Information Retrieval System (BIRS) Pilot Project,* Oct. 1, 1973-Dec. 15, 1975, which detailed progress of the system and reflected a development cost of only $22,123 to that date.

With a proven capability, BIRS expanded to include indexing of the *Western Recorder,* begun in 1977, and of Alabama Baptist State Convention *Annuals,* 1823-1875. Both have been issued in printout form.

BIRS also includes indexed materials for 48 Southern Baptist periodicals (1973-   ), Baptist Press releases (1974-   ), Executive Committee, SBC, minutes (1974-   ), and miscellaneous other sources. By early 1981 the total data file included more than 325,000 bibliographical data entries.

BIRS annually produces indexes arranged by subject and author, including the *Southern Baptist Periodical Index;* indexes to the state Baptist papers of Alabama, Kentucky, North Carolina, and Texas; and a few periodicals, such as *Missions, USA.* BIRS also produces each year dozens of bibliographical reference printouts on selected subjects and authors for individual inquirers through a regularly scheduled retrieval format. Occasional special printouts are produced, such as the 390-page "Bibliography on Mission-Related Subjects" (1980).

A BIRS Advisory Committee meets annually to evaluate the ongoing operation, plan strategies for the future, and consider proposed new subject headings which need to be entered into the constantly expanding *Thesaurus.*

"An Information Service for You" brochure, describing BIRS, available from the Historical Commission, has attracted retrieval inquiries of writers, students, and agency staffs.

See also HISTORICAL COMMISSION, SBC.

F. WILBUR HELMBOLD

BAPTIST INTERNATIONAL MISSIONS, INC. A nondenominational sending agency of fundamentalist and Baptist traditions engaging in evangelism, church planting, education, broadcasting, aviation, and a ministry to servicemen. Organized in 1960, by 1981 the body had about 600 missionaries under appointment to 55 countries. The first fields of work were the Caribbean and Nicaragua. At present the largest work is in the Bahamas with Brazil and Japan next in size. Tom Wallace became president in 1980, succeeding J. R. Faulkner who had served since 1972. Headquarters are located in Chattanooga, TN.

HELEN E. FALLS

BAPTIST JOINT COMMITTEE ON PUBLIC AFFAIRS. See PUBLIC AFFAIRS, BAPTIST JOINT COMMITTEE ON.

BAPTIST MEDICAL CENTER, GADSDEN, AL (cf. Memorial Hospital, Baptist, Gadsden, Vols. II, III). In Oct., 1978, Baptist Memorial Hospital became Baptist Medical Center, Gadsden. Cecil Hamiter continues as chief executive officer. Bed capacity is 327. The board of directors authorized the Baptist Memorial Foundation, Aug., 1976, with Pink V. Love as executive director. Family Practice Residency Program, begun July, 1978, moved into its permanent building, Oct., 1979, housing 12 doctors specializing in family practice. Professional management services were arranged, Aug., 1978, with Mountain View Hospital, with 102 beds for progressive care patients and alcoholic detoxification and rehabilitation services.

GEORGE Y. WILLIAMS

BAPTIST MEDICAL CENTER, MONTGOMERY, AL (cf. Montgomery Baptist Hospital, Vol. III). Baptist Medical Center, Montgomery, W. Taylor Morrow, president, has expanded to 454 beds and employs 1,100 people. Surrounded in a one-mile radius by offices of more than 100 physicians, it is a major referral center of central Alabama. It offers medical residency programs, internships and clerkships, and clinical programs for registered and practical nurses.

GENE A. HANNAH

BAPTIST MEDICAL CENTERS, BIRMINGHAM (cf. Birmingham Baptist Hospitals, Vol. I; Baptist Medical Center, Birmingham, Vol. III). Known as the Baptist Medical Center until 1975, the Baptist Medical Centers of Birmingham (BMC), owned by the Birmingham Baptist Association, are operated by a board of 25 trustees. Hospitals in Birmingham are the 439-bed BMC-Princeton and the 485-bed BMC-Montclair. BMC operates hospitals in Fort Payne, Cullman, Homewood, and Jasper. BMC supports physician residency training in internal medicine, general surgery, pathology, and diagnostic radiology. It operates a nursing school, a school of anesthesia for nurses, and a residency program for clinical pastoral education. BMC provides health care administration residencies and education programs for LPN (Licensed Practical Nursing), radiologic technology, dietetics, medical/social work, and pharmacology.

ROBERT F. HOWERTON

BAPTIST MEDICAL-DENTAL FELLOWSHIP.

A national organization of Southern Baptist physicians and dentists. Organized in 1976, the purpose of the group is to provide Christian fellowship and spiritual strength for the members and to provide opportunities to witness through vocation. Membership is open to all Southern Baptist physicians and dentists and medical and dental students.

DAVID HANEY

BAPTIST MEMORIAL HOSPITAL.

Affiliated with the Missouri Baptist State Convention, this general acute-care, 359-bed hospital opened its doors for patients, Jan. 20, 1960. The first unit consisted of 183 beds, 20 bassinets, and four upper floors unfinished. Goldman S. Drury served as first hospital director, closing the first year's operation with total assets of $3,170,520. Hamilton V. Reid succeeded Drury as hospital administrator in 1960, serving until 1977. Russell D. Harrington was administrator, 1977-78. Since July 31, 1978, Michael C. Waters has been the executive director.

Features of the hospital include: The Eye Institute of Mid-America, Curry Center for Health Education, Arthur Land Cardiac Intensive Care Unit, Goppert Family Care Center, and a complete Department of Pastoral Care. Assets totaled $28,424,158 in the 1978 audit. The Missouri Baptist State Convention elects the 39 members of the board of trustees.

See also MISSOURI BAPTIST CONVENTION, Vol. III.

MICHAEL C. WATERS

BAPTIST MEMORIAL HOSPITAL SYSTEM, SAN ANTONIO

(cf. Memorial Hospital, Baptist, San Antonio, Vols. II, III). The hospital system consists of three full-service hospitals: 688-bed Baptist Memorial, built in 1902; 190-bed Northeast Baptist, opened in 1970; and 189-bed Southeast Baptist, opened in 1971. A major $11,000,000 modernization project was completed in 1977, adding new emergency room facilities at each hospital and additional space at Baptist Memorial for nuclear medicine. The old hospital was renovated in 1978 into an educational center for the Institute of Health Education, which operates schools in nursing, medical technology, medical transcription, radiologic technology, surgical technology, cytotechnology, dietetic interns, and clinical pastoral education.

The hospital system has two cardiac catheterization labs, an eye treatment center, total body scanners, and computerized laboratory equipment. Its property was valued at $30,300,000 in 1979. The hospital system admitted 43,962 patients during the fiscal year 1978-79 and employed 3,500 persons. David Garrett was executive director.

JANICE O'BRIEN

BAPTIST MESSAGE

(I, III). The official newspaper of the Louisiana Baptist Convention. The printing plant owned and operated by the newspaper since 1963 was sold in 1970 because of insufficient capital for further development. The *Message* began offering a news-page service to churches in 1970. A growing number of churches now print their local news on the back page.

James F. Cole resigned as editor in 1977. He was succeeded by Lynn P. Clayton on July 15, 1978. Clayton had been editor of the *Baptist Digest*. Skyrocketing postage and printing costs produced a near crisis during the 1970s. Between 1970 and 1980, annual postage costs went from $3,000 to $180,000. Budget subscription rates increased from $1.00 to $2.35. In 1980 the circulation was approximately 70,000.

LYNN P. CLAYTON

BAPTIST MESSENGER

(I, III). Weekly newspaper of the Baptist General Convention of Oklahoma. The circulation was 97,448 in May, 1979. Installation of new offset printing equipment in 1979 expedited production and made possible a larger number of special church editions. Jack L. Gritz concluded a 30-year editorship in Sep., 1979. Richard T. McCartney, director of public relations for the Baptist General Convention of Texas, became editor, Dec. 1, 1979.

JOE L. INGRAM

BAPTIST MISSIONARY ASSOCIATION OF AMERICA

(III; cf. North American Baptist Association, Vol. II). The Baptist Missionary Association of America (BMAA), consists of 1,487 churches in 29 states. Craig Branham continues as the general secretary of missions. In 1978 the number of BMAA churches reporting statistics was 1,418, with a membership of 219,697. Total church contributions to outside causes such as missions, education, and benevolence in 1978 was $4,472,474. The grand total to all causes was $31,075,115. BMAA churches support 141 missionaries: 66 in 19 foreign countries, 75 in the United States, 17 on interstate fields, and 58 on state and local mission fields.

The BMAA owns and operates one seminary (in Jacksonville, TX); one radio and television ministry (Harvest Gleaner Hour, Conway, AR); one national encampment (Daniel Springs Memorial, Gary, TX); a Baptist publications committee (with business offices in Little Rock, AR, and editorial offices in Texarkana, AR-TX); a research and public relations department (Baptist News Service, Jacksonville, TX); two Baptist book stores (one in Little Rock and one in Texarkana, AR); an armed forces chaplaincy department; and a national youth department.

A national Woman's Missionary Auxiliary and a national Brotherhood are additional organizations supporting the mission projects of the parent organization. Various departments of the BMAA publish six periodicals and support at least 17 other mission and miscellaneous ministries. Supporting associations own and operate three book stores, three colleges, several Bible schools, and four Baptist children's homes, and publish 42 supporting periodicals (state Baptist papers).

LOUIS F. ASHER

BAPTIST MISSIONARY CONVENTION OF ILLINOIS. See ILLINOIS, BAPTIST MISSIONARY CONVENTION OF.

BAPTIST MISSIONARY SOCIETY (of Great Britain) (I, III). In India, original field of the Baptist Missionary Society, government restrictions made the entry of new missionaries difficult; in 1980 only 16 BMS missionaries served there. Many churches with which the society was associated joined the Church of North India in 1970. In the state of Orissa the two bishops of this united church were former Baptist pastors. Two groups of Baptist churches remained outside the united church, each claiming to be the continuing Baptist Union. BMS tried to maintain relations with all.

Following a period of natural disasters and civil war, East Pakistan broke with West Pakistan in 1971 and formed the state of Bangladesh. Missionaries and churches related to BMS were much involved in relief work and agricultural improvement. Church growth was most evident among Hindu villagers in western border regions.

BMS, a member of the United Mission to Nepal, had 16 missionaries assigned to that country engaged in medical work, education, and community development.

In Zaire, until 1971 the Democratic Republic of the Congo, churches associated with BMS became a community within the Church of Christ of Zaire. The churches experienced problems of communications and oversight in a large country of sparse population and deteriorating economy.

Angola, which became independent in 1975, was ravished by civil war, the north being to a considerable extent depopulated. Of about 200 Baptist churches in that area, only two survived. Under a Marxist government, churches were allowed to continue most of their activities. Those in the north enjoyed remarkable growth.

In Brazil, BMS missionaries worked in Mato Grosso state, which the society entered in 1976, in agreement with Baptist conventions of the area.

In 1980, 210 BMS missionaries were in overseas service, and a record number of candidates were in training. The society's budget for that year was £1,531,631.

JOHN ALLEN MOORE

BAPTIST MUSIC. See MUSIC, BAPTIST.

BAPTIST NEW MEXICAN. Official publication of the Baptist Convention of New Mexico. C. Eugene Whitlow, who came as editor from the pastorate of First Baptist Church,

Alamogordo, NM, in 1967, retired in 1981. The style of the publication was changed in 1973 from a 16-page format to an 8-page tabloid. The 1980 circulation was slightly over 16,000.

C. EUGENE WHITLOW

BAPTIST PEACEMAKER, THE. A quarterly paper intended to encourage Southern Baptists in the mission of peacemaking. It originated within the World Peacemaker group of Deer Park Baptist Church, Louisville, KY, and publication was begun, Dec., 1980. E. Glenn Hinson (Southern Baptist Theological Seminary professor) and C. Carman Sharp (Deer Park pastor) serve as coordinating editors, assisted by 21 additional consulting editors from throughout the SBC. Its contents include worship and teaching aids, news, issues analyses, and editorials.

CRAIG A. SHERAUSE

BAPTIST PRESS (I, III). In 1979 Baptist Press, the Southern Baptist news service, distributed 1,040 news stories and 165 features. They went to approximately 450 religious and secular news media in the USA and abroad. Stories used were selected and edited by the central office in Nashville, TN, from copy submitted by the six bureaus, the 34 Baptist state papers, approximately 300 special correspondents among Southern Baptist organizations, and about 100 stringers who work for daily newspapers.

The central office is operated by the SBC Executive Committee. Wilmer C. Fields is the director. Robert J. O'Brien, news editor, 1973-80, was succeeded by Dan Martin, Aug. 1, 1980. James Lee Young, the first feature editor, 1973-77, was succeeded by Norman Jameson in 1977.

A sixth bureau was opened at Memphis, TN, in 1973 with Roy Jennings as bureau chief. Stan R. Hastey became chief of the Washington, DC, bureau in 1978. Richard M. Styles was chief of the Richmond, VA, bureau, 1975-77, followed by Robert M. Stanley. This bureau handles news submitted by press representatives in approximately 95 countries.

Walker Knight has been chief of the Atlanta, GA, bureau since its establishment in 1959. In the Dallas, TX, bureau Orville Scott, chief, 1972-76, was succeeded by Richard T. McCartney, 1976-79. Scott then became chief again. At the Sunday School Board bureau, the chiefs were Gomer R. Lesch, 1966-77; L. Bracey Campbell, 1977-79; and Lloyd T. Householder, beginning in 1979.

WILMER C. FIELDS

BAPTIST PRIVATE SCHOOLS MOVEMENT. Numbering only 12 in 1940, Baptist elementary and secondary schools increased to 341 with approximately 50,000 pupils by 1978. Much of that growth came in the 1970s. In 1966 in 14 southern states from Virginia to Texas, Baptists sponsored 54 elementary and secondary schools. The 1980 Sunday School Board mailing list showed 328 schools in those same states and a total of 416 schools, 391 elementary and 25 secondary, in 33 states.

Several reasons accounted for this growth. One was the desire for schools with a Christian perspective, including instruction in Bible and Christian values. Many schools attempting to meet this need, however, were less than satisfied with the materials available. Consequently, the SSB began producing in 1978 a graded Bible curriculum specifically for private schools designed not only to teach what the Bible says, but also to enable students "to apply its truths to their lives." Materials for two grade levels were added each year with plans for material for all 12 levels to be available by 1983.

The desire for quality education was a second reason. Students in some private schools tested above local and national averages. Some schools selected their textbooks primarily from state-approved lists. Some used books from various evangelical publishers, citing higher academic quality as well as a more Christian perspective. But a 1976 SSB study indicated that only 20 percent of the responding schools were state-accredited, and some did not desire it, fearing any external control, including accreditation. Further, whereas 38 percent had some personnel with master's degrees, 21 percent had some teachers or administrators with only a high school diploma. The level of academic quality appeared to be uneven.

A final reason for growth cited by opponents and admitted by some supporters was the desire to escape racial integration. The greatest growth occurred after the implementation of court-ordered integration and busing to achieve racial balance. Opponents charged that by creating havens for racism and negative public school images, the private schools were detrimental to the mission of the churches, for even if their motives were right, they were not so interpreted by the people of the community who perceived racism, classism, and hypocrisy.

That perception of racism also led to a difficult church-state issue. The Internal Revenue Service in 1978 issued a ruling denying tax-exempt status to any private school they determined to be racially imbalanced. The ruling divided Baptists. The Christian Life Commission praised the ruling; the Baptist Joint Committee on Public Affairs denounced the ruling as containing "serious church-state constitutional problems." The 1979 SBC reflected the dilemma, passing resolutions supporting public schools, opposing racism, and denouncing the IRS ruling.

The private school movement may make a significant contribution to future Baptist life. But some feel that it must overcome the charges of racism and classism, attain a more uniform level of high academic quality, and maintain a basic Christian perspective in order to do so.

See also SOUTHERN BAPTIST ASSOCIATION OF CHRISTIAN SCHOOLS.

BIBLIOGRAPHY: Research Services Department, SSB, *Southern Baptist Day Schools* (1976).

G. THOMAS HALBROOKS

BAPTIST PROFESSORS OF RELIGION, ASSOCIATION OF. Founded in New Orleans, LA, in 1928, the association is an independent, professional organization for teachers of religion in accredited colleges, universities, seminaries, and divinity schools. In 1980 it had about 275 members. The organization meets annually in conjunction with the Society of Biblical Literature, Southeastern Region; publishes a journal and a monograph series; and promotes discussion of literature, movements, curricula concepts, and methodologies in the field of religion. Its journal, *Perspectives in Religious Studies,* is published three times annually.

WATSON E. MILLS

BAPTIST PROGRAM, THE (I, III). General program journal for the staff leadership of the churches and related organizations of the Southern Baptist Convention. The circulation in 1979 averaged 58,630. Wilmer C. Fields served as editor, 1959-1972. Albert McClellan, who had been editor, 1949-59, became editor a second time and served from 1972 until his retirement in 1980.

LEONARD E. HILL

BAPTIST PUBLIC RELATIONS ASSOCIATION (III). The association had about 200 members in 1970. At its 25th anniversary in 1979 membership stood at 315. Another 175 were eligible for membership. In 1980 membership was running two-thirds men, one-third women. The annual BPRA awards competition attracted 300 to 400 entries. The organization continued to be the largest and most active denominational public relations organization in the world. The 1979 membership carried 32 different titles, reflecting the diversity of structure and emphasis in Southern Baptist utilization of the profession. Members' common responsibilities were communication, interpretation, and persuasion.

BPRA holds two meetings annually—a workshop and business session each winter or spring and a breakfast meeting during the SBC. Seven officers are elected annually at the workshop. Through the years BPRA has performed several communications projects for Southern Baptists.

See also PUBLIC RELATIONS.

WILMER C. FIELDS and C. WILLIAM JUNKER

BAPTIST RECORD, THE (I, III). Joe T. Odle (*q.v.*), who became editor in 1959, retired, Aug., 1976, and was succeeded by Donald T. McGregor, associate editor since Jan 1, 1975.

In 1980 the paper, the official newspaper of the Mississippi Baptist Convention, continued to function in public relations activities for the state convention and its board.

In 1969 the circulation was 109,000; by 1980 it was 128,600. In 1969 the paper had 10 employees; in 1980 there were seven. The position of business, circulation, and advertising manager had been abolished; and the editor had taken on those functions with the help of the office staff.

Expenses increased substantially in the 1970s because of increased costs in postage, labor, and newsprint. The paper received no Cooperative Program subsidy prior to 1975, but $30,000 was necessary that year. The subsidy continued to climb until it reached $163,878 in 1980.

In 1980 almost 1,600 of the state's more than 1,900 churches subscribed to the paper's Every Family Plan, which was introduced in 1936 by Josie McEachern of Sunflower, MS, and adopted by Baptist state papers nationwide.

DONALD T. MCGREGOR

BAPTIST SPANISH PUBLISHING HOUSE (III; cf. Spanish Baptist Publishing HOUSE, Vol. II). Thomas W. Hill succeeded Frank W. Patterson as general director in 1970. The publishing house's work expanded in 1973 to include English and French materials for overseas use. An international board of trustees was formed in 1975. In 1977 N. Aldo Broda, an Argentine citizen, became the first Latin American general director. In 1980 the publishing house celebrated its 75th anniversary. Its net worth, excluding buildings and land, reached $2,700,000. Annual sales were $2,250,000, personnel included 35 missionaries and 80 employees, and production included 1,325,000 books, 2,900,000 copies of periodicals, 7,250,000 tracts and miscellaneous pieces, and 375,000 pieces on contract. Wholesale book deposits were maintained in 16 countries.

J. WILSON ROSS

BAPTIST STANDARD (I, III). John J. Hurt retired as editor on July 14, 1977, after an 11-year tenure in which the circulation of the *Standard* grew to 375,000. A $1,200,000 building, located five miles west of the Dallas business district and designed for the operations of the paper and the printing company, was dedicated debt-free in May, 1975. The *Standard's* former building, on the edge of the Dallas business district, was sold. Hurt was succeeded, July 15, 1977, by Presnall H. Wood, a Texas pastor and co-author of *Prophets with Pens (1969)*, a history of the *Standard*.

More than 300 churches use the front or back pages of the paper for their local news. Circulation at the close of 1979 was at an all-time record of 393,000.

PRESNALL H. WOOD

BAPTIST STUDENT UNION (I, III). The 1970s brought a marked growth to BSU work. The ministry expanded to 1,138 campuses by 1980. This came about by a rapid expansion of leadership. In 1980 there were 464 full-time professional, 118 part-time professional, and 375 volunteer directors of Baptist student ministries. Thirty-four state conventions and three state fellowships have departments of student ministries which provide administrative leadership. Nationally, National Student Ministries, a department of the Sunday School Board, leads BSU work. The department head since 1969 has been Charles M. Roselle. National Student Ministries is responsible for the publication of materials, field services, and the national student conferences held at Ridgecrest and Glorieta.

The philosophy and objectives which were approved in 1962 have remained the same. Actions to fulfill these have focused around ten emphases. Five represent Christian growth: Worship, Bible study, churchmanship, stewardship, and fellowship. Five represent Christian outreach: Evangelism, missions, social action, ministry, and international student ministry.

The Student, the official periodical for students and leaders, is now supplemented by a Student Ministry Curriculum for study and leadership development. *The Baptist Student Union Guidebook* is the organizational manual. The *SHARE Seminar Workbook* is the evangelism training instrument which is supplemented by the *Master Plan* witnessing materials. The *Spiritual Journey Notebook* is the training instrument for personal growth and discipleship.

Baptist Student Centers were located adjacent to 260 campuses in 1980. Valued at $43,532,000, they serve as places of operation for the BSU. Where there are no centers, meetings are held on campuses or in nearby churches. State conventions supplemented by local associations provide ongoing financial program support for the BSU. Endowments for BSU held by Baptist foundations total $2,591,000.

BSU missions have received major attention. A large number of students have responded, particularly to short-term volunteer missionary service. The students normally give their time for a summer or a semester in mission service. In addition special teams from the campuses work for one or two weeks during school breaks. A total of 6,471 students served in these activities in 1979. To supplement the funds provided by missionary agencies to support these activities, the students in 1979 raised $641,595 through special efforts called student missions. Special projects to alleviate hunger have been popular in BSU outreach activities.

The SSB through National Student Ministries operates in keeping with the actions of the SBC on June 2, 1970. Several SBC agencies have actions involving college students. A Student Ministries Advisory Group representing SBC agencies, state student directors, local campus directors, and students meets annually to coordinate these actions.

CHARLES M. ROSELLE

BAPTIST TRAINING UNION (I, III). See CHURCH TRAINING.

BAPTIST UNIVERSITY OF FLORENCE, ALABAMA. A women's college founded by the Florence Land, Mining, and

Manufacturing Company in 1889 to promote development of the town. James Boardman Hawthorne (*q.v.* I) became president of the proposed institution which was chartered on Feb. 26, 1889. A large three-story brick building of Renaissance architecture was completed in 1890. Hawthorne was unable to obtain the necessary endowments, and plans for a Baptist school were soon abandoned.

L. D. Bass, a Baptist minister and educator, established a nonsectarian college at the site in 1891, known as the Southern Female University, with an enrollment of 100 girls, mostly from Baptist families. It moved to Birmingham in 1892, and the building remained vacant until purchased by M. W. Hatton of La Grange, GA, in 1908. He operated it as Florence University for Women until the building burned, Mar. 2, 1911. It was never rebuilt.

RICHARD C. SHERIDAN

BAPTIST VILLAGE, INC. (cf. Georgia Baptist Village for the Aged, Vol. I; Baptist Village, Vol. III). A home for the elderly supported by Georgia Baptists which experienced consistent growth during the 1970s. In May, 1974, a 55-room intermediate care unit was occupied. This raised the resident capacity to 338, thus making operational for the first time three distinct levels of care: (1) 84 apartments for the care of residents who need some regimentation but little or no assistance in their routine activities of daily living, (2) 106 beds available in the intermediate care category for individuals who are largely ambulatory or very active wheelchair patients, and (3) the skilled care section, containing 148 beds, for individuals requiring a greater degree of skilled and professional nursing services.

Harvey R. Mitchell retired as administrator on Dec. 31, 1979. He was succeeded by J. Olan Jones, administrative assistant for 11 years.

J. OLAN JONES

BAPTIST WOMEN (III). Since 1970 the Woman's Missionary Union, SBC, organization for women, ages 30 and up, in Southern Baptist churches. *Royal Service* is the publication for Baptist Women. In Jan., 1973, two important decisions were made pertaining to Baptist Women organizations. The first was to make provisions in the organization structure to add "other officers as needed," and the second was to add a series of books on spiritual growth. The books were identified as "The Woman I Am" series. One book was provided each year for group or individual study.

To make books for Baptist Women Round Table Group more accessible, a quarterly plan known as Round Table Book Club began, Sep., 1976. Mission books could be purchased at discount using a Baptist Book Store charge account. In 1977 TransCom materials, known as the "Big A" Club, for unchurched children ages 6 through 11, were provided for women to use in mission action.

In 1978-79 one of the major emphases of WMU, Baptist Women Year in the Church, resulted in an increase of 686 Baptist Women organizations and 1,817 members over the previous year. Baptist Women organizations totaled 26,183 with a membership of 494,273.

EVELYN BLOUNT

BAPTIST WOMEN'S WORLD DAY OF PRAYER. Sponsored annually by the Women's Department of the Baptist World Alliance as a time of prayer and fellowship, this day has been observed on every continent. The European Baptist Women's Union suggested a day of prayer as a means of furthering reconciliation in war-torn Europe in 1948. The suggestion of European women resulted in the establishment of a Baptist Women's Day of Prayer to be held on the first Friday in December, beginning in 1951.

In 1963 the date was changed to the first Monday in November. BWA Women's Department changed the official title to Baptist Women's World Day of Prayer in 1980. The offering taken on this day supports the work of the Women's Department.

BARBARA YEAGER

BAPTIST WORLD, THE. Founded in Jan., 1954, as the official publication of the Baptist World Alliance. The Jarman Foundation gave the "seed money" to begin the publication. Arnold T. Ohrn (*q.v.*), general secretary of the BWA, was the founding editor, with Marjorie Moore Armstrong serving as managing editor, 1954-56. Cyril E. Bryant became managing editor in 1957 and editor in 1960. The publication reports on Baptist life in all areas of the world. In 1980 the monthly circulation of 7,000 went on a gratis basis to Baptist leadership in 104 countries and on a paid basis to other interested subscribers. Baptists in several countries translate the publication into their own languages.

C. E. BRYANT

BAPTIST WORLD ALLIANCE. (I, III). *1980 World Congress.*—A total of 19,812 delegates from Baptist conventions and unions in 92 countries attended the 14th Baptist World Congress in Toronto, Canada, July 8-13, 1980. The congress celebrated the 75th anniversary of the Baptist World Alliance with a program around the theme, "Celebrating Christ's Presence Through the Spirit," and also adopted a new statement of objectives looking toward greater "internationalization" of the fellowship in the future.

An almost completely new BWA staff was elected. Gerhard Claas of West Germany, who had served as associate secretary for Europe since 1976, was named general secretary to succeed Robert S. Denny who retired. Denny had joined the BWA staff as associate secretary in 1956 and became general secretary in 1969. Eight others also were named to the multinational, multilingual professional staff. They came from five countries and speak eight languages in addition to English.

The BWA elected as president Duke K. McCall, president of Southern Baptist Theological Seminary. Twelve vice-presidents from 10 nations support him.

Highlighting congress business action and setting more positive directions for the future was the adoption of a report from a Long-Range Planning Committee, chaired by Theodore F. Adams (*q.v.*). Adams was BWA president, 1955-60, and had long been active in its outreach. The recommendations amended the Preamble to the Constitution to read:

PREAMBLE

The Baptist World Alliance, extending over every part of the world, exists as an expression of the essential oneness of Baptist people in the Lord Jesus Christ, to impart inspiration to the fellowship, and to provide channels for sharing concerns and skills in witness and ministry. This Alliance recognizes the traditional autonomy and independence of churches and general bodies.

The revised Statement of Objectives was aimed at bringing the focus of BWA activities to all its member bodies rather than simply the older and more affluent members in Europe and North America.

OBJECTIVES

Under the guidance of the Holy Spirit, the objectives of the Baptist World Alliance shall be to:

1. Promote Christian fellowship and cooperation among Baptists throughout the world.

2. Bear witness to the Gospel of Jesus Christ and assist unions and conventions in their divine task of bringing all people to God through Jesus Christ as Savior and Lord.

3. Promote understanding and cooperation among Baptist bodies and with other Christian groups, in keeping with our unity in Christ.

4. Act as an agency for the expression of biblical faith and historically distinctive Baptist principles and practices.

5. Act as an agency of reconciliation seeking peace for all persons, and uphold the claims of fundamental human rights, including full religious liberty.

6. Serve as a channel for expressing Christian social concern and alleviating human need.

7. Serve in cooperation with member bodies as a resource for the development of plans for evangelism, education, church growth, and other forms of mission.

8. Provide channels of communication dealing with work related to these objectives through all possible media.

Other constitutional changes placed the election of the entire secretariat in the hands of the General Council (formerly executive committee), rather than the congress, and designated the General Council as the nominating committee for officers of the Alliance, i.e., the president, 12 vice-presidents, and treasurer.

BWA Staff.—Robert Denny, who succeeded Josef Nordenhaug (*q.v.* III) as general secretary when Nordenhaug died in Sep., 1969, presided over the executive staff throughout the period. Frank H. Woyke, associate secretary with responsibility for relief and the work of study commissions, retired in 1971. Cyril E. Bryant, director of communications since 1957, was made associate secretary for communications in 1971, and Theo Patnaik, a native of India, was made associate secretary for youth the same year. Carl W. Tiller, a United States government executive who had served as western treasurer since 1956, became associate secretary for relief and development and study and research in 1972. Fred B. Rhodes succeeded Tiller as treasurer.

C. Ronald Goulding, associate secretary for Europe, with offices in London since 1965, moved to Washington, DC, in 1976 to become associate secretary with responsibility for evangelism and education and relief and development. Gerhard Claas, formerly general secretary of the Baptist Union of West Germany, was elected associate secretary for Europe, moving the European office from London, England, to Hamburg, Germany. Meanwhile, Alan C. Prior became associate secretary for Asia in 1975, with offices in Sydney, Australia. Following the resignation of Carl W. Tiller in 1978, Charles F. Wills of the American Baptist Churches staff was named associate secretary with responsibility for study and research and the North American Baptist Fellowship. Betty Lee Smith, a member of the staff since 1966, was elected assistant secretary in Nov., 1976, with responsibility for conferences and youth work.

Other major staff changes followed the 1980 congress in Toronto. Denny, Goulding, and Wills retired. Reinhold Kerstan, director of communications for the North American Baptist Conference, was made associate secretary with responsibility for communications and the division of study and research. Denton Lotz, a member of the faculty of the Baptist Seminary at Ruschlikon, Switzerland, became associate secretary with responsibility for the divisions of evangelism and education and of relief and development. Erna Redlich, a member of the Washington staff since 1968, was made assistant secretary with responsibilities in relief and development. Betty Smith continued as assistant secretary for conferences. C. E. Bryant became administrative assistant to the general secretary, to serve until his retirement in Sep., 1982.

Kund Wumpelmann, formerly general secretary of the Baptist Union of Denmark, was selected secretary-treasurer of the European Baptist Federation and regional secretary of BWA to head the European office, now removed to Copenhagen, Denmark. He succeeded Claas in this position. Edwin I. Lopez, formerly general secretary of the Convention of Baptist Churches in the Philippines, was named to succeed Alan C. Prior as regional secretary for Asia, and the regional office moved from Sydney to Manila.

1970 World Congress.—The 12th Baptist World Congress at Tokyo, Japan, July 12-18, 1970, the first congress to meet in Asia, drew 8,500 participants from 78 countries despite its distance from the traditional Baptist population centers of Europe and North America. The theme, "Reconciliation Through Christ," was taken from 2 Corinthians 5:19. The program dealt largely with evangelism (reconciliation with God) and brotherhood (reconciliation with man). A program innovation included symposiums each morning with representatives from various parts of the world discussing informally and unrehearsed the topics of human existence, family life, peace with justice, freedom of faith, and race relations.

The congress chose V. Carney Hargroves as president for the 1970-75 quinquennium. The congress also voted enthusiastically to continue the congress's theme as a five-year program, "The World Mission of Reconciliation—Through Christ." The SBC Foreign Mission Board responded to a BWA invitation by placing its own evangelism consultant, Joseph B. Underwood, as director of the worldwide reconciliation program. Underwood conducted inspirational rallies and led training institutes in 45 countries, setting up ministries to serve people with diverse and particular needs. Evangelistic fires were lighted in many areas, with more than 26,000 decisions reported in Nigeria and 13,000 baptisms in less than five weeks in the Telegu area of India. Underwood was assisted in the program by 12 regional leaders, BWA staff and departmental personnel, and an international advisory committee of 36.

Success of the World Mission of Reconciliation was so evident when the BWA executive committee met in Louisville, KY, in 1974 that the committee voted to recommend to the 1975 congress in Stockholm, Sweden, that a Division of Evangelism and Education be established as a permanent BWA action agency.

1975 World Congress.—The 13th Baptist World Congress met in Stockholm, July 8-13, 1975, with a registration of 9,936 persons from 92 nations. The theme continued the reconciliation emphasis from 2 Corinthians 5, "New People for a New World—Through Christ." Bible study sessions by language groups opened each day's program. The work of the study commission was featured in a daily interview, continuing the panel discussion innovation of the Tokyo congress, using representatives from many nations.

The BWA elected as president for 1975-80, David Y. K. Wong, the first Asian and the first layman to hold that office. The congress also adopted a series of amendments to the BWA constitution, as proposed by a Committee on Constitutional Revision and Structural Changes, chaired by David S. Russell of Great Britain.

The revised constitution provided for four primary divisions of Alliance activity, each directed by an international committee and under supervision of an associate secretary. These divisions are: Communications, Evangelism and Education, Relief and Development, and Study and Research. Strengthened emphasis was placed on the work of the Departments for Men, Women, and Youth which give attention to training for lay evangelism and witness.

The name of the Alliance's governing body was changed from executive committee to General Council, and the smaller advisory group known as the administrative committee was renamed executive committee.

C. Ronald Goulding, associate secretary for Europe, was invited to move to Washington to direct the new work in Evangelism and Education.

Evangelism and Education.—The program for evangelism and education began by preparing an inventory of available source materials on soul winning and discipleship training, as originated by BWA member bodies. A series of three guidebooks, published in Washington, aimed at helping denominational leaders and pastors in every country to select ideas and programs most adaptable to their areas of the world. These were followed by a series of regional, often continent-wide, conferences, in which an international faculty discussed with local leaders possible answers to problems related to evangelism and training particular to each area. These conferences, held during the 1976-80 period, met in India, Malaysia, the Philippines, Australia, Switzerland, Kenya, Mexico, Guatemala, and Canada.

Goulding evaluated the conferences: "This joining together of individual Baptist groups to learn from each other lent great motivation to both witnessing and Christian teaching. Each union, each convention remained uniquely as they were—but each learned the most effective methods for their individual country or culture."

The Alliance became a basic center for evangelistic outreach in still another way: The organization of a Conference of International Mission Secretaries. Sixty-seven of the Alliance's 120-member bodies have mission work outside their own countries. Their leaders met first in conjunction with the BWA executive committee at Einseideln, Switzerland, in 1973, electing Sven Ohm, mission secretary of the Baptist Union of Sweden, as the conference leader. There have been annual meetings since then, plus a continuing exchange of correspondence on matters of current and common concern. Surveys have been made of areas not yet reached by Baptist or other Christian missions, and also of theological schools offering scholarships to students for the ministry in Third World countries. Strategies are being developed to reach out to provide cooperative and maximum mission outreach without duplication.

Cooperative mission effectiveness also has been sought in two forums conducted in 1977 and 1979 dealing with relationships between mission-sending and mission-receiving BWA bodies.

Issues of conflict, especially charges of paternalism, were discussed candidly. Plans for partnership, or interdependence (avoiding both dependence and independence), were projected, dealing with finances, leadership training, and cooperative effort. The Alliance was asked to serve as a channel for mutual consultation and cooperation.

Sven Ohm of Sweden observed in his report

to the General Council at Toronto: "All churches, old and new, are called to obey the Great Commission, regardless of age or resources. Today's partnership missions can learn from mistakes in the past and become increasingly fruitful." He added that both the mission-sending and the mission-receiving bodies should work "in a climate of trust and in genuine partnership, including the planning of the missionary program and the mutual responsibility for it."

The First World Conference of Baptist Men met in Hong Kong, Nov. 26-30, 1974, and the Ninth Baptist Youth World Conference met in Manila, Philippines, July 19-23, 1978.

C. E. BRYANT

BAPTIST WORLD ALLIANCE, FRIENDS OF THE. A voluntary association of individuals pledged to give annual financial support to the operating budget of the BWA. Their gifts supplement regular allocations made by the BWA's member bodies. The gifts also help because many of the BWA's member bodies exist in currency controlled areas, from which contributions cannot be made.

Formal fund-raising activities for the BWA began in 1963 when the BWA executive committee, meeting in Waco, TX, authorized a Sustaining Gifts Committee, with Walter Pope Binns as chairman. V. Carney Hargroves, Esther J. Jillson Adams, and Owen Cooper served as chairmen in succeeding years. Friends arose in 1975 with the guidance of fund-raising officials at the University of Richmond. Linda T. Brown became the first office coordinator, under the direction of BWA General Secretary Robert S. Denny. W. A. Criswell has been chairman of Friends since 1975.

C. E. BRYANT

BAPTIST WORLD ALLIANCE, MEN'S DEPARTMENT OF THE. The Baptist World Alliance organized the Men's Department at Rio de Janeiro, Brazil, during the Baptist World Congress there in 1960. A committee had been named at the 1955 Congress in London, England, to study the feasibility of such an international fellowship of Baptist men.

John A. Dawson, Chicago, IL, was first chairman of the department, 1960-65. His successors have been Robert L. Mills, Georgetown, KY, 1965-67; George W. Schroeder (q.v.), Memphis, TN, 1967-70; David Y. K. Wong, Hong Kong, 1970-75; and Stephen S. Steeves, Moncton, New Brunswick, Canada, 1975-80.

The department has sponsored two World Conferences of Baptist Men, the first in Hong Kong in Dec., 1974, and the second in Indianapolis, IN, in Apr., 1978. Additional worldwide meetings are planned in connection with the Baptist World Congress sessions.

The Men's Department program has five objectives:

1. Encourage men to realize the importance of getting involved in their local church.

2. Encourage men in every association, union, convention, or country to be involved in aggressive evangelistic lay witness penetration.

3. Encourage men in all areas around the world to set aside one day each year for a Baptist Men's Worldwide Day of Witness and Prayer, to develop a real concern for each other.

4. Encourage closer involvement of laymen with their pastors, to work together as a team— that all may feel a part of the work of the Men's Department.

5. Encourage Baptist men to have local, regional, and continental rallies and to organize and promote the World Conference of Baptist Men every five years.

C. E. BRYANT

BAPTIST WORLD ALLIANCE, WOMEN'S DEPARTMENT OF THE (III). The department continued its activities at BWA Congresses in Tokyo, Japan, 1970; Stockholm, Sweden, 1975; Toronto, Ontario, Canada, 1980; with pre-Congress conferences for national leaders, as well as two open women's sessions. Meetings of the six continental organizations took place in intervening years.

At the 1970 session a procession of women in national costumes accompanied a discussion of continental work. Marie Mathis, USA, was elected president (reelected 1975); Ayako Hino, Japan, was elected recording secretary (reelected 1975); and Letha Casazza, Canada, was elected to the new position of promotion secretary (includes the treasurer's office, reelected 1975).

The 1975 meeting on the theme, "One World, One Lord," included a summary of Baptist women's activities worldwide.

In Toronto bylaw changes combined the offices of secretary and treasurer, created the salaried position of executive director, and officially changed day of prayer title to Baptist Women's World Day of Prayer. Kerstin Ruden, Sweden, was elected president; Judith Clanton, USA, was elected secretary-treasurer.

See also BAPTIST WOMEN'S WORLD DAY OF PRAYER.

DORIS DEVAULT

BAPTIST WORLD ALLIANCE, YOUTH DEPARTMENT OF THE. The Youth Department of the Baptist World Alliance directs its attention to the promotion of international fellowship and the encouragement of youth in Christian witness activities in their own communities and around the world.

A Youth Committee, composed of representatives of Baptist conventions and unions holding membership in the Alliance, directs the department. A member of the Alliance secretariat is designated as the BWA youth secretary.

Baptist Youth World Conferences are held every five years unless war or other international problems interfere. Such conferences have met in Prague, Czechoslovakia, 1931; Zurich, Switzerland, 1937; Stockholm, Sweden,

1949; Rio de Janeiro, Brazil, 1953; Toronto, Ontario, Canada, 1958; Beirut, Lebanon, 1963; Berne, Switzerland, 1968; Portland, OR, 1974; and Manila, Philippines, 1978

The Youth Department had its beginnings when a World Baptist Young People's Union was organized at the Baptist World Congress in Stockholm in 1923. This was changed to the Young Peoples Committee of the BWA when the Congress met in Toronto in 1928. T. G. Dunning, London, England, was its first chairman; and Frank H. Leavell (q.v. II), Nashville, TN, its first secretary.

Joel Sorenson of Stockholm, Sweden, became the first full-time youth secretary in 1950, with Robert S. Denny of the USA serving as committee chairman. Denny succeeded Sorenson in Jan., 1956, and moved to the Alliance's Washington office as BWA associate secretary. Theo Patnaik of India became youth secretary in 1971, after Denny became BWA's general secretary. Patnaik was succeeded in 1976 by Betty L. Smith.

Committee chairmen, succeeding Dunning and Denny, have been Sorenson, 1955-60; W. G. Wickramasinghe of Ceylon, 1960-65; Gunnar Hoaglund of the USA, 1965-70; Karl-Heinz Walter of West Germany, 1970-75; and Daltro Keidann of Brazil, 1975-80.

C. E. BRYANT

BAPTIST WORLD ALLIANCE MEMBER BODIES. Autonomous national Baptist groups affiliated with the Baptist World Alliance at the close of the 1980 Baptist World Congress in Toronto, Canada, totaled 120. They have headquarters in 85 nations and a total of 117,357 churches in 121 nations.

In the table that follows, the date beside the member body indicates the year of organization of that body. All figures are the latest submitted to the BWA office in Washington, DC, as of Sep. 1, 1980.

	Churches	Other Preaching Places	Church Members
AFRICA			
Angola—Baptist Convention of Angola (1966)	50	100	21,125
Baptist Evangelical Church in Angola (1977)	300	——	18,658
Burundi—Union of Baptist Churches of Burundi (1928)	8	43	4,465
Cameroon—Cameroon Baptist Convention (1954)	497	5	31,931
Union of Baptist Churches of Cameroon (1957)	120	13	38,528
Ethiopia—Baptist Evangelical Association of Ethiopia (1958)	57	55	1,652
Ghana—Ghana Baptist Convention (1957)	87	44	5,548
Kenya—Baptist Convention of Kenya (1971)	600	60	30,000
Liberia—Liberia Baptist Missionary and Educational Convention, Inc. (1880)	70	67	33,850
Malawi—The African Baptist Assembly Malawi, Inc. (1945)	518	19	42,876
Baptist Convention in Malawi (1971)	171	72	13,184
Mozambique—Baptist Convention of Mozambique (1957)	7	9	500
Nigeria—Nigerian Baptist Convention (1914)	1,275	1,355	261,200
Rwanda—Union of Baptist Churches in Rwanda (1962)	20	158	20,352
Sierra Leone—Baptist Convention (Sierra Leone) (1974)	10	8	743
South Africa—Baptist Union of South Africa (1877)	325	825	56,369
Tanzania—Baptist Convention of Tanzania (1971)	269	115	17,364
Togo—Togo Baptist Association (1964)	7	6	1,090
Zaire—Baptist Community of Bandundu (1970)	26	170	22,543
Baptist Community of Western Zaire (1958)	310	100	115,000
Baptist Community of the Zaire River (1972)	186	1,400	106,282
Zimbabwe—Baptist Convention of Zimbabwe (1963)	78	106	18,000
Baptist Union of Central Africa (1959)	17	3	1,632
TOTALS FOR AFRICA	5,008	4,733	862,892
ASIA			
Bangladesh—Bangladesh Baptist Sangha (1935)	201	20	9,426
Bangladesh Baptist Union (1920)	23	14	1,500
Garo Baptist Union, Bangladesh (1890)	116	81	8,941
Burma—Burma Baptist Convention (1865)	2,840	1,950	357,891
Hong Kong—The Baptist Convention of Hong Kong (1938)	46	13	28,587
India—Baptist Church of Mizoram (1903)	228	——	30,229
The Baptist Union of India (1939)*			
Bengal Orissa Bihar Baptist Convention (1850)	73	57	5,893
Convention of Baptist Churches of the Northern Circars (1874)	195	200	100,000
Council of Baptist Churches in Northeast India (1950)	3,305	2,997	330,468

Council of Baptist Churches in Northern India (1957)	470	371	60,000
Karnataka Baptist Convention (1976)	27	——	1,997
Samavesam of Telugu Baptist Churches (1962)	673	531	288,430
Indonesia—Kerapatan Baptist Churches of Indonesia (1951)	107	——	2,500
Union of Indonesian Baptist Churches (1971)	67	135	15,084
Japan—Japan Baptist Convention (1906)	183	67	25,394
Japan Baptist Union (1901)	53	13	4,114
Korea, Republic of—Korea Baptist Convention (1950)	730	60	100,000
Malaysia—Malaysia Baptist Convention (1953)	41	48	4,375
Philippines—Baptist Conference of the Philippines, Inc. (1954)	48	——	3,800
Convention of Philippine Baptist Churches, Inc. (1935)	434	400	51,000
General Baptist Church of the Philippines, Inc. (1958)	38	10	1,661
Luzon Convention of Baptist Churches, Inc.	80	——	——
Mindanao Convention of Southern Baptist Churches (1968)	378	1,020	25,000
Ryukyu Islands—Okinawa Baptist Convention (1955)	18	12	1,504
Singapore—Singapore Baptist Convention (1975)	16	6	2,500
Sri Lanka—Sri Lanka Baptist Union (1932)	21	17	2,023
Taiwan—Chinese Baptist Convention (1954)	74	45	12,325
Thailand—Thailand Baptist Convention (1976)	125	——	8,508
TOTALS FOR ASIA	10,610	8,067	1,483,150

CENTRAL AMERICA AND CARIBBEAN ISLANDS

Bahamas—Bahamas National Baptist Missionary and Educational Convention (1936)	194	——	45,000
Costa Rica—Baptist Convention of Costa Rica (1946)	24	25	2,058
Cuba—Baptist Convention Association of Western Cuba (1905)	102	30	6,786
Baptist Convention of Eastern Cuba (1904)	125	25	6,211
El Salvador—Baptist Association of El Salvador (1939)	41	77	3,839
Guatemala—Convention of Baptist Churches of Guatemala (1946)	63	152	6,215
Haiti—Baptist Convention of Haiti (1955)	86	584	40,776
Honduras—National Convention of Baptist Churches (1958)	27	37	2,287
Jamaica—Jamaica Baptist Union (1849)	275	329	36,445
Nicaragua—Baptist Convention of Nicaragua (1937)	47	108	4,522
Panama—The Baptist Convention of Panama (1959)	57	66	6,316
Trinidad and Tobago—Baptist Union of Trinidad and Tobago (1816)	24	34	2,330
TOTALS FOR CENTRAL AMERICA AND CARIBBEAN ISLANDS	1,065	1,467	162,785

EUROPE

Austria—Baptist Union of Austria (1953)	9	2	691
Belgium—Union of Evangelical Baptist Churches (1903)	8	4	512
Bulgaria—Union of Baptist Churches in Bulgaria (1908)	10	4	650
Czechoslovakia—Baptist Union in Czechoslovakia (1919)	28	84	3,978
Denmark—The Baptist Union of Denmark (1839)	41	70	6,362
Europe—European Baptist Convention (English language) (1964)	40	3	3,847
Finland—Finnish Baptist Union (Finnish speaking) (1925)	10	5	771
Swedish Speaking Baptist Union of Finland (1883)	24	38	1,712
France—Federation of Baptist Evangelical Churches (1896)	28	39	2,997
Germany, Democratic Republic—Union of Evangelical Free Churches in the GDR (1849)	215	298	21,193
Germany, Federal Republic—Union of Evangelical Free Churches in Germany (FRD) (1849)	356	267	68,012
Hungary—Baptist Union of Hungary (1846)	200	250	12,000
Italy—Baptist Evangelical Christian Union of Italy (1957)	80	20	4,200
Netherlands—Union of Baptist Churches in the Netherlands (1881)	81	8	11,951
Norway—The Norwegian Baptist Union (1879)	64	86	6,299
Poland—Polish Baptist Christian Union (1858)	55	88	2,539
Portugal—Portuguese Baptist Convention (1923)	52	10	2,800
Romania—Baptist Union of R. S. Romania (1923)	662	442	160,000
Spain—Baptist Evangelical Union of Spain (1929)	61	73	4,800
Sweden—Baptist Union of Sweden (1889)	422	——	21,651
Switzerland—Union of Baptist Churches in Switzerland (1924)	15	5	1,425
Union of Soviet Socialist Republics—All Union Council of Evangelical Christians-Baptists (1909)	5,000	——	545,000
United Kingdom—Baptist Union of Great Britain and Ireland (1813)	2,091	——	174,578
Baptist Union of Scotland (1869)	157	3	14,429

Yugoslavia—Baptist Union of Yugoslavia (1926)	61	70	3,484
TOTALS FOR EUROPE	9,770	1,869	1,075,881

MIDDLE EAST

Israel—Association of Baptist Churches in Israel (1963)	6	16	402
Jordan—Baptist Community of Jordan (1957)	7	7	256
Lebanon—Lebanese Baptist Convention (1955)	12	6	650
TOTALS FOR MIDDLE EAST	25	29	1,308

NORTH AMERICA

Canada—Baptist Federation of Canada (1944)	1,106	80	124,772
Mexico—National Baptist Convention of Mexico (1903)	427	600	37,000
UNITED STATES OF AMERICA			
American Baptist Churches in the USA (1907)	5,897	——	1,231,646
Baptist General Conference (1852)	772	23	132,000
General Association of General Baptists (1870)	894	——	73,046
Lott Carey Baptist Foreign Mission Convention, USA (1897)*			
National Baptist Convention of America (1880)	12,400	1,173	3,500,000
National Baptist Convention, USA, Inc. (1880)	27,000	2,575	6,300,000
North American Baptist Conference (1851)	355	10	57,241
Progressive National Baptist Convention, Inc. (1961)	1,534	145	700,000
Seventh Day Baptist General Conference (1801)	65	5	5,181
Southern Baptist Convention (1845)	35,605	2,312	13,379,073
Union of Latvian Baptists in America (1950)	8	2	563
TOTALS FOR NORTH AMERICA	86,063	6,925	25,540,522

OCEANIA

Australia—The Baptist Union of Australia, Inc. (1926)	701	42	52,148
New Zealand—Baptist Union of New Zealand (1882)	162	15	18,937
Papua New Guinea—Baptist Union of Papua New Guinea (1976)	208	17	18,000
TOTALS FOR OCEANIA	1,071	74	89,085

SOUTH AMERICA

Argentina—Baptist Evangelical Convention (1908)	327	154	25,000
Bolivia—Baptist Convention of Bolivia (1947)	14	9	700
Baptist Union of Bolivia (1936)	90	250	10,500
Brazil—Baptist Convention of Brazil (1907)	2,811	3,481	464,000
Chile—Baptist Evangelical Convention of Chile (1908)	178	146	15,760
Colombia—Baptist Convention of Colombia (1952)	82	53	10,000
Ecuador—The Baptist Convention of Ecuador (1972)	56	87	3,000
Guyana—Baptist Cooperative Convention of Guyana (1973)	15	15	1,600
Paraguay—Baptist Evangelical Convention of Paraguay (1908)	32	34	4,000
Peru—Baptist Evangelical Convention of Peru (1966)	47	73	4,193
Uruguay—Baptist Evangelical Convention of Uruguay (1908)	38	14	2,568
Venezuela—National Baptist Convention of Venezuela (1951)	55	115	3,500
TOTALS FOR SOUTH AMERICA	3,745	4,431	544,821

GRAND TOTALS (120 bodies, 85 nations and dependencies)	117,357	27,595	29,760,444

*While it is believed that all the churches of this body are also members of other BWA affiliates, they are counted there.

C. E. BRYANT

BAPTIST YOUNG WOMEN (III). Since 1970 the Woman's Missionary Union, SBC, organization for women 18 through 29 years in Southern Baptist churches. *Contempo* is the publication for BYW. In Jan., 1976, approval was given to have BYW organizations on college campuses without these organizations being directly related to churches. Working with the National Student Ministries Department of the Sunday School Board, a design for Campus BYW groups was developed. The organization was piloted in 1977 and 1978. In 1978-79 it became an official organization of WMU.

Two important changes were approved in Jan., 1972. The first was to provide for "other officers as needed" in BYW organizational structure and the second was to add a series of books on spiritual growth called "The Woman I Am" series. The first in the series was produced in 1976.

Additional features in the organization came with the beginning of the Round Table Book

Club and the introduction of TransCom materials (the "Big A" Club) for use in mission action with unchurched children, ages 6 through 11. In 1975-76 *a tempo* was a BYW emphasis in WMU. The emphasis included Kaleidoscope '76, first National BYW Conference, June 11-13, 1976, Virginia Beach, VA. In Jan., 1979, a new BYW insignia was introduced. In 1979 BYW organizations totaled 6,463 with a total membership of 71,155.

EVELYN BLOUNT

BAPTISTS FOR FREEDOM. A small movement designed to curb alleged authoritarian forces in the SBC following the 1962 dismissal of Professor Ralph Elliott from Midwestern Baptist Theological Seminary. Though primarily designed as a pro-Elliott group, the group also opposed creedalism while supporting freedom and integrity in all phases of denominational activity.

During the 1963 meeting of the SBC in Kansas City, MO, the group distributed newsletters, sponsored a hospitality room, and hosted a fellowship dinner for over 300 guests. G. Avery Lee, pastor of St. Charles Avenue Baptist Church in New Orleans, LA, spoke at the dinner on "Areas of Tension Between Freedom and Responsibility." Headquartered in Kansas City, MO, the organization soon dissolved for lack of financial support. Chairman of the movement was Robert T. Latham.

WALTER B. SHURDEN and LINDA PRICE

BAPTISTS TODAY, ANALYSIS OF (III). Baptists in the United States in the 1970s were probably more in the public eye than at any time in their history, partly because of two prominent political persons, President Jimmy Carter and former White House aide Charles Colson. Both openly admitted to "born again" experiences, and both identified themselves as Baptists. Especially for Southern Baptists this new prominence increased contact with the media and gave them opportunity to explain their doctrines and views more fully.

Biblical conservatism increased among most American evangelicals, with Southern Baptists receiving much publicity. More conservative than some other Baptist bodies, Southern Baptists in 1970 banned the distribution of a commentary on Genesis, thought by many to contradict the meaning of the Scriptures. Rather than merely signal an end to the theological controversy of the 1960s, it signaled the beginning of the restive 1970s which climaxed with a dispute over the "inerrancy" of the original manuscripts of the Bible. After about 1970, an emphasis on Bible study, church renewal, and personal spirituality began to grow.

The "charismatic" movement touched most Baptist groups during the 1970s. In some instances Southern Baptist associations withdrew fellowship from affected churches. In others uneasy compromises were reached. American Baptist churches welcomed charismatics with "a cautious openness," and they planned conferences between charismatics and noncharismatics. Most Baptist churches in the 1970s maintained a fairly constant attitude toward charismatics. Baptist views were generally conciliatory, while resisting the extremes of charismatic behavior.

Ecumenical activity lessened among Baptists in the 1970s. American Baptist participation in the Consultation on Church Union was minimal and left the denomination intact and separate. The SBC continued a policy of isolation from both national and world ecumenical movements, though some individual churches and pastors seemed inclined to cooperate locally with other denominations.

Church growth was generally less marked, and in some cases it actually diminished. For example, American Baptist membership declined from 1,396,900 in 1970 to 1,231,646 in 1978. In the same period Southern Baptists gained from 11,629,880 to 13,196,979, but Southern Baptist Sunday School growth showed a loss from 7,418,067 in 1969 to 7,317,960 in 1979. Some smaller Baptist groups showed marked increases. The Baptist General Conference, for example, gained in membership from 104,000 to 132,000.

The supply of ministers generally gained in number. The Baptist General Conference reported an increased number of ministers. Southern Baptists enrolled 5,848 ministers in their six seminaries in 1969. Ten years later they enrolled 10,954. American Baptists are said to have a sufficient number of ministers, about half coming each year from other denominations. Conservative Baptists produced in two seminaries more ministers than they could place in their churches. At the end of the decade, more black Baptists were enrolled in accredited seminaries than ever; 121 in six SBC seminaries and over 600 in all accredited seminaries.

Cooperation among Baptist groups continued about as it had been for many years. With the formation of the North American Baptist Fellowship in 1965, participating Baptists were brought closer together. The NABF attempts no programs and does not involve the churches. It is mostly an organization for communication among Baptist leaders, most of whom meet in connection with the executive committee of the Baptist World Alliance. One of the larger Baptist groups, the Conservative Baptist Association of America, is not affiliated with either the NABF or the BWA. Many of the smaller groups are also not affiliated.

Baptists were not in complete agreement on social issues. Three times in the 1970s Southern Baptists approved a moderate resolution against abortion, rejected "any indiscriminate attitude toward abortion, as contrary to the biblical view," affirmed "the limited role of government in dealing with matters relating to abortion," and supported "the right of expectant mothers to the full range of medical services and personal counseling for the preservation of life and health." In 1980 this moderate view was rejected for a resolution with strong pro-life implications. Southern Baptists did not take a stand for the Equal Rights Amendment until 1980 when a resolution on women was amended not to endorse the Equal Rights Amendment. On these two issues Southern Baptists were more conservative than some other Baptist groups. On most other social issues, they showed the same strong, sympathetic interest displayed by major Baptist groups. Some of these issues are world hunger, civil rights for minorities, the energy crisis, concern for the aging, and protection of children from pornographic use.

Missions continues to be a predominant concern of most Baptist groups, though the form of missions has changed for some of them. In 1971 in a major mission address, an American Baptist mission leader declared, "the foreign missionary era is ended." Nine years later the same leader said, "I am not sure that the 1970's have seen a radical change in mission philosophy in American Baptist churches." American Baptists reported four recent major developments: (1) the internationalization of their missionary force, (2) involvement of mission churches in the decision-making process, (3) increased mission communication, and (4) dialogues with other faiths. The Southern Baptist approach continued to be more traditional. In 1974 Southern Baptists appointed a Missions Challenge Committee from which finally emerged Bold Mission Thrust, an effort to witness to the whole world by the year 2000. Bold Mission Thrust involves traditional methods such as career missionaries, schools and hospitals, evangelism, and church development. It also involves the wide use of laypersons in mission work, and radio and television as a major evangelistic means. Many of the smaller Baptist groups conduct vigorous missions programs fully as effective as the larger ones except on a more limited scale.

The larger Baptist groups showed both unity in life and work and diversity in policy and practice. In the 1970s some of the major shifts in Southern Baptist life were: (1) reintensification of missions as a major denominational purpose for the last quarter of the century, (2) full support of the seminaries as a strategy for Bold Mission Thrust, (3) renewal of the spiritual life of the churches, (4) revival of local church Bible study groups, (5) development of more intensive modern evangelism methods, and (6) a recommitment to the Sunday School as a major means of church growth.

American Baptists shifted in quite different ways: (1) protection of the Christian conscience with reference to military service, (2) growing acknowledgment of women's concerns, (3) strong emphasis on church growth through evangelism and social action, (4) a cautious openness to charismatics, and (5) consolidation of newly instituted denominational structures.

Black Baptists also made interesting shifts: (1) limited openness to women preachers, (2) from strong emphasis on social action to evangelism, (3) movement away from strong associa-

tional and state conventions, (4) less interest in integration of churches, (5) less interest in denominational cooperation, and (6) more reliance on public sectors for educational support.

ALBERT MCCLELLAN

BARBADOS, MISSION IN. Responding to a request from a Christian group, the Foreign Mission Board sent missionaries to Barbados in 1972. Work began with three existing churches in the areas of lay leadership and evangelistic outreach. In 1974 the Barbados Baptist Convention formed with four churches. Each church has its own pastor and facilities for anticipated growth. Major emphasis is on leadership development. The Barbados Baptist College, opened in 1978, is a theological center for training leaders for the Caribbean. A dental ministry was being carried on in a permanent clinic as well as a mobile dental clinic which was donated by a dentist in the USA. Eight missionaries were serving in 1979.

WILLIAM L. WOMACK

BARKER, LILLIE EASTERBY (b. Columbia, SC, Jan. 4, 1865; d. Richmond, VA, July 10, 1925). Woman's Missionary Union leader. The daughter of Samuel R. and Lizzie Easterby, she was a graduate of Chester Female Institute of Virginia (1887). She married John Alexander Barker, June 6, 1888. They had no children. The same year they went to Bahia, Brazil, as Southern Baptist missionaries but resigned in 1890 because of her health. Barker served as president of the Virginia WMU, 1899-1901, 1902-05, then as president of WMU, SBC, 1903-06. During her presidency, the Margaret Home (later Margaret Fund) was established and missionary education of youth gained in momentum. She is buried in River View Cemetery, Richmond, VA.

DORIS DEVAULT

BAYLOR UNIVERSITY (I, III). During the 1970s Baylor enjoyed steady growth. The 300-acre Waco, TX, campus contains the College of Arts and Sciences, the Graduate School, and the Schools of Business, Education, Music, and Law. The School of Nursing is located in Dallas. Baylor also offers advanced degrees through the United States Academy of Health Sciences in San Antonio and the College of Dentistry in Dallas—a total of 35 degrees in more than 100 areas of study.

In addition to traditional academic and professional courses, Baylor offers special programs in American studies, church-state relations, environmental research, international journalism and business, and other fields. Students may also receive credit for study abroad in Europe, Latin America, the Middle East, and the Far East.

Enrollment increased in the 1970s from 6,900 to 10,000. Seventy-nine percent of the students reside in Texas; the remainder come from all the other states and territories and 30 foreign countries. Female students outnumber males 51 to 49 percent. Over 18,000 students received degrees during the past decade—almost as many as graduated during Baylor's first 100 years.

The operating budget for the Waco campus increased in the 1970s from $13,907,000 to $35,237,000; property values grew from $32,169,000 to $72,676,000; and endowment rose from $23,431,000 to $55,136,000. New construction changed the appearance of the campus, and older buildings underwent extensive renovation, most notably Old Main and Burleson Hall.

The university also improved its academic status. The average ACT score for incoming freshmen is 24, compared to the national average of 18. Ninety percent of the arts and sciences faculty hold doctorates.

Baylor continues to maintain strong ties with its historic Christian tradition and with the Baptist General Convention of Texas. Sixty-one percent of the students are Baptist. A full-time chaplain and staffs from the Baptist Student Union and other similar denominational organizations provide religious activities for students on and off campus. Over 2,000 Baylor students are preparing for the ministry or other church-related vocations. Abner V. McCall retired as president in May, 1981, and was succeeded by Herbert H. Reynolds, former executive vice-president.

RUFUS B. SPAIN

BAYLOR UNIVERSITY MEDICAL CENTER (cf. Baylor University Hospital, Vols. I, III). With 1,275 beds, Baylor in 1980 was the second largest church-related hospital in the country with a net value of $150,000,000. The decade opened with Boone Powell, Sr., executive director, receiving the highest award bestowed by his profession, the Gold Medal Award for Excellence in Hospital Administration.

Major philanthropic gifts and broad community and denominational support made possible the following new facilities in the 1970s: Erik and Margaret Jonsson Hospital; Carr P. Collins Hospital; A. Webb Roberts Center for Continuing Education; Beulah Porter Beasley Memorial Auditorium; the $20,000,000 Baylor Medical Plaza containing physicians' offices, diagnostic and treatment centers, a 75-room hotel, and related facilities; Charles A. Sammons Cancer Center; and the H. L. and Ruth Ray Hunt Heart Center. Another milestone was the establishment of the Baylor University Medical Center Foundation. Since 1909, Baylor has provided health care for 1,640,000 hospitalized patients.

JUDY WILLIAMS

BEARD, ROSS ROE (b. Pangburn, AR, May 22, 1900; d. Muskogee, OK, Nov. 10, 1978). Missionary to the Indians. The son of William and Hettie Beard, he married Grace Mae Honea, Nov. 1, 1922. He attended Arkansas State Teachers College, 1928-31. Under ap-

pointment by the Home Mission Board, he worked with Ponca and Pawnee Indians, 1931-39, and the Cherokees, 1939-66. With the Cherokees he averaged conducting nine Vacation Bible Schools per year. He is buried in Beryl Baptist Cemetery, Conway, AR.

B. FRANK BELVIN

BEASLEY, TITUS WALKER (b. Appomattox County, VA, June 2, 1890; d. Bolivar, MO, Oct. 21, 1965). College professor. The son of Benjamin Walker and Isabella Day Beasley, farmers, he attended Fort Union Military Academy and Richmond Academy before entering the University of Richmond (A.B., 1918) and Southern Baptist Theological Seminary (Th. M., 1922). He never married.

Beasley went to Missouri in 1923 to teach at LaGrange College. From LaGrange he moved to Mayfield Baptist College at Marble Hill, MO, in 1928. After this college closed in a financial crisis, Beasley moved to Bolivar, MO, to teach history and government at Southwest Baptist College. He taught at this school from 1930 until his retirement in 1961. He is buried in Greenwood Cemetery, Bolivar, MO.

H. K. NEELEY

BELGIUM, MISSION IN (III). Although Belgium has state-supported churches, the Belgian Baptist Union, the smallest in Europe, has legal standing. In 1971 the European Baptist Federation established the Interior Mission to aid churches in evangelization and development. For several years a missionary served as pastor of a French-speaking church (in Nivelles) which in 1972 sponsored its first International Gospel Music Festival. Six missionaries assist primarily with English-language work. In the Jurbise church a day-care center was opened in 1973 and a new educational unit in 1980. The Brussels church was constituted in 1973. Baptists number 520 in 11 churches and 2 missions.

ELISE NANCE BRIDGES

BELIZE, MISSION IN. Formerly British Honduras, Belize lies on the east coast of Central America. Baptist work was begun here in 1822 by British Baptists, and it continued with some assistance from the Jamaica Baptist Union. Southern Baptist missionaries Otis W. and Martha (Yates) Brady arrived in Belize in 1977 and officially started work in May, 1978. Two churches have been established with a total membership of 81. Three young men have been called to preach and are now pastors-in-training. The missionaries and churches started by Southern Baptists are cooperating with the already existing Belize Association of Baptist Churches. F. Wayne and Janie (White) Blanton were appointed to Belize in 1979.

OTIS W. BRADY

BELL, PAUL CARLYLE (b. Leakey, TX, Oct. 9, 1886; d. Dallas, TX, July 24, 1952). Home Missionary. Graduated from the University of Texas, he attended seminary and the *Universidad International* (Panama). On June 3, 1913, he married Ida Pearl Elliot. They had seven children: Paul C., Jr., Ida Ruth, Irma Pauline, Beatrice, Dorothy, Esther, and Caroline, three of whom became foreign missionaries. Bell married Gladys Harmon, Nov. 14, 1941. Appointed by the Home Mission Board in 1919, Bell served in New Mexico, Texas, and from Dec., 1941, until his retirement, Jan., 1952, as superintendent of missions in Panama. He also began the work in Honduras, Guatemala, and Costa Rica, fields later transferred to the Foreign Mission Board.

KATE ELLEN GRUVER

BELMONT COLLEGE (I, III). With 33 states and 23 foreign countries represented in the student body, the fall enrollment, 1979-80, totaled 1,483 with 77 faculty members. Three new buildings added during the last decade are the Center for Business Administration, Hitch Science Building, and Humanities Building. A new student center was completed in 1981. The 1979 audit showed assets in excess of $12,000,000 with an annual operating budget of $4,500,000 and endowment of approximately $1,500,000.

During the past 10 years, 2,336 students have graduated, bringing the total number during the college's short life to 3,630. The college has just finished its second 10-year self-study under the auspices of the Southern Association of Colleges and schools, its accrediting agency.

Belmont grants six degrees: Bachelor of Arts, Bachelor of Business Administration, Bachelor of Music, Bachelor of Science, Associate of Arts, and Associate of Science in Nursing. These comprise 40 major areas and 50 minor fields from which students may select courses. New programs recently begun include music business, commercial music, criminal justice, health-care management, and information systems management. Herbert C. Gabhart continues as president.

HERBERT C. GABHART

BELOTE, JAMES DALBY (b. Washington, DC, Oct. 15, 1913; d. Richmond, VA, Mar. 4, 1975). Missions administrator. The son of Theodore T. Belote, he attended George Washington University, Columbia Bible College (B.A., 1935; Th.M., 1938), Wheaton College (B.A., 1936), The Southern Baptist Theological Seminary, and New Orleans Baptist Theological Seminary (Th.D., 1946). He married Martha Bigham, Sep. 9, 1937. They had five children: James, Jr., Theodore, Virginia, Martha, and Linda. Appointed a missionary by the Foreign Mission Board, Apr. 10, 1940, he served in Hawaii, 1941-45; China, 1947-50; and Hong Kong, 1951-68, where he was president; Hong Kong Baptist Theological Seminary, Kowloon, beginning in 1952; and Asia Baptist Graduate Theological Seminary, Hong Kong, beginning in 1960. Elected secretary for East

Asia, he gave oversight, 1968-75, to the board's work in Hong Kong, Macao, Taiwan, Okinawa, Japan, and Korea. He is buried in Westhampton Memorial Park, Richmond, VA.

FRANK K. MEANS

BENIN, MISSION IN (cf. Dahomey, Mission in, Vol. III). Southern Baptist missionaries have been able to establish stations in Cotonou, 1970, Abomey, 1974, and Porto Novo, 1976, in the Peoples' Republic of Benin (formerly called Dahomey). Activities are primarily evangelism and church development. They include three centers with reading rooms, a Bible correspondence school, youth and student activities, and a limited medical program carried on by a missionary nurse. A missionary dentist arrived from language study in 1980 and opened a clinic in Abomey. The staff in 1980, including language students, numbered 14 working in 25 churches and preaching stations. Baptist constituents at the end of 1979 totaled 517.

JOHN E. MILLS

BENNETT, JOSEPH JOHNSON (b. Jackson County, GA, Oct. 18, 1872; d. Atlanta, GA, Dec. 30, 1945). Pastor and denominational worker. He attended Martin Institute, Jefferson, GA, Mercer University, and the University of Georgia (A.B., 1895). Recognized as a scholar and orator, he was ordained to the ministry at age 19. He served as president of Hearn Institute, Floyd County, GA. He married Mary Elizabeth Conyers, of Stilesboro, Oct. 14, 1896. Their children were Joel Conyers, Joseph, Jr., William, and Mary.

Bennett's Georgia pastorates included Second Church, Athens, while a student; Jackson Hill, Atlanta, 1899-1902; and Griffin First, 1902-06. After the Griffin pastorate, he became corresponding secretary, Georgia Baptist State Mission Board, and served until 1914 when his health failed. During his term of office 50,000 members were added to Georgia Baptist churches. Upon regaining his health, Bennett returned to Jackson Hill and in 1923 was called to Prince Avenue Church in Athens. He is buried in Crestlawn Cemetery, Atlanta, GA.

BRUCE M. MORGAN

BERMUDA, MISSION IN (III). A mission opened in St. George's in 1975. It was constituted as Wellington Park Baptist Church in Dec., 1979. In May, 1979, the Bermuda Baptist Fellowship formed, including First Baptist, Wellington Park, and Emmanuel Baptist Churches. Robert and Ruth (Sims) Harris and Reginal and Mary Ellen (Kemp) Hill were serving in pastoral ministries and a weekly television ministry.

ROBERT L. HARRIS

BERRY, JAMES EARL (b. Magazine, AR, Dec. 18, 1885; d. El Dorado, AR, July 26, 1961). Businessman and philanthropist. Son of William Thomas Berry, planter, and Nancy

Catherine Berry, he attended Ouachita Baptist College (B.A., 1914; LL.D., 1958). He married Ruby Middlebrook, Nov. 3, 1921. They had two daughters, Margaret and Robin. After moving to Smackover, AR, in 1921, he opened Berry Drug Store, serving later as president of Arkansas Pharmaceutical Association. He was also president of Smackover State Bank, a member of the Arkansas Baptist Hospital Board, and a deacon at First Baptist Church.

Berry moved in 1952 to El Dorado, AR, where he organized the Berry Company. A deacon at the First Baptist Church of El Dorado, he served many years as a member and trustee chairman of Ouachita Baptist College. The J. E. Berry Building at this school is named to honor his gift which made it possible. He is buried in Arlington Cemetery, El Dorado, AR.

SAMUEL ADKINS

BESS, VERA MINGA PAYNE (b. Nettleton, MS, Dec. 26, 1901; d. Pickens, SC, Aug. 17, 1979). Home missionary. Daughter of Walter and Josie Minga, she attended Mississippi Normal Institute. She married Ewell Payne, June 10, 1923. Their children were Tommy and William. The Paynes were missionaries to the Cherokee Indians, Cherokee, NC, 1948-57. She worked jointly with her husband as director of missions for Pickens and Twelve Mile River Associations in South Carolina, 1957-67. After the death of her first husband, she married Evert Bess, June 14, 1975. She is buried in Hillcrest Cemetery, Pickens, SC.

FRANCES G. ELLER

BETHEA BAPTIST HOME (I, III). See SOUTH CAROLINA BAPTIST MINISTRIES FOR THE AGING.

BIBLE, CONTROVERSIES ABOUT THE. Southern Baptists engaged in continuous controversy about the Bible from 1960 to 1980. Controversy smoldered in the early 1960s as a reaction to the book, *The Message of Genesis* (1961), by Ralph Elliott, professor at Midwestern Baptist Theological Seminary, and exploded at the SBC in 1962 where messengers reaffirmed faith in "the *entire* Bible as the authoritative, authentic, infallible Word of God," urged SBC agency and institutional heads to preserve Baptists' "historic position" concerning "the historical accuracy and doctrinal integrity of the Bible," and started the process which led to adoption of the Baptist Faith and Message in 1963.

Waning after 1963, controversy flared anew in late 1969 when volume I of *The Broadman Bible Commentary* was published. Criticism, directed at the exposition of Genesis by G. Henton Davies, an English Baptist, quickly erupted in state Baptist papers, local pastors' conferences, and an ad-hoc "Affirming the Bible Conference" held prior to the 1970 SBC meeting.

The 1970 Convention instructed the Sunday School Board to withdraw and rewrite volume I

of the *Commentary* "with due consideration of the conservative viewpoint." Subsequently, Davies was asked to rewrite his material, but in June, 1971, the SBC instructed the board "to obtain another writer."

The controversy was one of heated charges, numerous resolutions in conventions, and little discussion of issues. The discussion suggested that the real issue was not validity or integrity of the Bible, but a theory of inspiration, a type of biblical interpretation, and Convention control. Ultraconservatives tended to call anyone a "liberal" who did not assert that the Bible, in its original manuscripts, was inerrant and infallible. Moderate conservatives responded that the assertion was meaningless since original manuscripts no longer exist, that the Bible nowhere claims inerrancy or infallibility, and that apparently only one major Baptist confession of faith (Second London Confession, 1677) uses the term *infallible*.

The controversy spawned organized groups among ultraconservatives. The Baptist Faith and Message Fellowship was organized in Mar., 1973, publishing the *Southern Baptist Journal*. In the late 1970s leadership moved beyond the fellowship. In 1979 Paige Patterson, president of the Criswell Center for Biblical Studies, Dallas, TX, and Paul Pressler, layman from Houston, TX, conducted caucuses in numerous states, campaigning for an acceptable SBC president. Their candidate, Adrian Rogers of Memphis, TN, was elected, although Rogers disavowed connection with the group. In Apr., 1980, Patterson and Pressler announced formation of state groups to seek to control the election of the SBC president, boards, and committees for a period of 4 to 10 years in order to rid the Convention of "liberals."

See also BAPTIST FAITH AND MESSAGE FELLOWSHIP, THE; BROADMAN BIBLE COMMENTARY, THE; CONSERVATIVE THEOLOGY, RESURGENCE OF; INERRANCY; MIDWESTERN BAPTIST THEOLOGICAL SEMINARY, Vol. III.

J. TERRY YOUNG

BIBLE CORRESPONDENCE COURSE, RADIO-TELEVISION. See RADIO-TELEVISION BIBLE CORRESPONDENCE COURSE.

BIBLE INSTITUTE, THE (I, III). An educational institution offering courses in biblical and theological studies, religious education, church music, and other pastoral training for more mature students who are not college graduates. Since 1969 two Southern Baptist seminaries have developed institute programs, Boyce Bible School at Southern Baptist Theological Seminary and the School of Christian Training at New Orleans Baptist Theological Seminary, to supplement the institutes supported by or affiliated with state conventions. Both seminary programs sponsor centers in urban areas away from the seminary campus as well as classes offered on the campus.

In several states other programs have been

inaugurated which imitate the program of the Bible Institute. Two models are dominant. One relates to a post secondary institution and offers a program very similar to the seminary plan, offering work at a variety of locations. The other model is basically an extension program and is offered through the state convention office or a division of the state office.

Baptist Bible Institute, Graceville, FL, has changed its curriculum to offer a greater number of courses at the collegiate level in a four-year program. The institute offers the Bachelor of Ministry degree with emphasis in biblical studies, religious education, and church music.

ARTHUR L. WALKER, JR.

BIBLE READING, DAILY (cf. Bible Readers' Course, The, Vol. I; Bible Readers' Courses, Vol. III). In 1967 the Sunday School Board moved the responsibility for producing daily Bible reading references and the magazine *Open Windows* from the Training Union (now Church Training) Department to the Sunday School Department. Because of the multiple curriculum offerings in various programs, no effort existed to relate the devotional readings to curriculum content. The readings selected for inclusion in *Open Windows* were for use in all appropriate Sunday School, Training Union (Church Training), Woman's Missionary Union, and Brotherhood publications, as well as in *Home Life*.

In 1974-75 the board expanded the basic devotional passage to be highlighted each day into a larger passage to provide a plan which would result in reading the Bible through during the year. Similar plans were offered in 1976 and 1980.

DONALD F. TROTTER

BIBLE STUDY, HOME. See HOME BIBLE STUDY.

BIBLICAL CRITICISM, NEW TESTAMENT. In order to understand the meaning of New Testament writings for today, one needs first to discover their meaning for both the authors and the original readers. To this end, New Testament scholars have developed several methods of study.

Textual criticism attempts to establish the Greek text as closely as possible to the original writings by examining the extant ancient manuscripts, the style of the authors, and the writing habits of scribes. *Source criticism* attempts to determine the oral and written sources which the writers used in composing their own writings. *Form criticism* seeks to isolate and categorize by their form earlier oral traditions which have been incorporated into the written text. This allows one to catch a glimpse into the life of the early Christian communities prior to the writing of the Gospels and Epistles. *Redaction criticism* examines the way in which the author selected and arranged his material and altered the traditions which he used. This enables one to discover the writer's own theological concerns and the milieu in which he wrote. *Literary criti-*cism inquires into the form and structure of a writing with the assumption that this is related to the meaning of the text.

See also FORM CRITICISM; REDACTION CRITICISM; SOURCE CRITICISM; TEXTUAL CRITICISM, VOL. III; LITERARY CRITICISM, THE BIBLE, VOL. II.

BIBLIOGRAPHY: W. A. Beardslee, *Literary Criticism of the New Testament* (1970). W. R. Farmer, *The Synoptic Problem* (1964). G. E. Ladd, *The New Testament and Criticism* (1967). E. V. McKnight, *What is Form Criticism?* (1969). B. M. Metzger, *The Text of the New Testament* (1968). N. Perrin, *What is Redaction Criticism?* (1969).

ROGER L. OMANSON

BIBLICAL CRITICISM, OLD TESTAMENT. The methodologically consistent use of the procedures of modern historical and literary criticism in the study of the texts that compose the canon of the Old Testament. Critical study of the Old Testament involves textual criticism, source criticism, form criticism, tradition history or transmission history, redaction criticism, and rhetorical criticism. The critical reconstruction of Israel's history is usually considered a separate area of study.

The conclusions reached in critical study of the Old Testament sometimes differ from traditional assumptions. For example, the Pentateuch can no longer be explained merely on the basis of Mosaic authorship, especially with authorship understood in modern terms. Critical analysis reveals a long history involving traditions, sources, and texts. The Pentateuch is more of an expression of Mosaic authority than of Mosaic authorship. The critical interpreter knows that authority was more important than literary authorship in ancient literature.

Critical study of the Old Testament has been controversial among Southern Baptists. Seminary professors Crawford H. Toy (*q.v.* II) and Ralph H. Elliott were both forced from their teaching positions largely because of their interpretations of the Old Testament. In Southern Baptist seminaries, critical study of the Old Testament became common only after World War II. *The Broadman Bible Commentary*, which reflects the use of moderate and constructive critical exegesis, was vehemently opposed by some and Broadman Press was forced to have the commentary on Genesis rewritten. The debate over critical study continues.

See also FORM CRITICISM; REDACTION CRITICISM; SOURCE CRITICISM; TEXTUAL CRITICISM, VOL. III; LITERARY CRITICISM, THE BIBLE, VOL. II.

BIBLIOGRAPHY: Ronald E. Clements, *One Hundred Years of Old Testament Interpretation* (1976). John I. Durham, "Contemporary Approaches in Old Testament Study," *The Broadman Bible Commentary*, I, revised (1973). John H. Hayes, *An Introduction to Old Testament Study* (1979).

MARVIN E. TATE

BIBLICAL RECORDER (I, III). Weekly news journal of the Baptist State Convention of North Carolina. J. Marse Grant, editor since

1960, has the longest tenure of any editor in the paper's history. Woodrow W. Hill joined the staff in 1972 as assistant editor and field representative. Toby Druin, associate editor, resigned in 1973 to join the Home Mission Board news staff. Charles Richardson, assistant editor of the *Baptist Standard* in Texas, succeeded Druin in 1976. Under Grant the paper took strong stands on such issues as world hunger, Christian citizenship involvement, disaster relief, and state liquor laws. The 1980 circulation was 119,000.

CHARLES RAY RICHARDSON

BIBLICAL SCHOLARSHIP IN SOUTHERN BAPTIST COLLEGES AND UNIVERSITIES. Several hundred persons engage in the teaching of religion in Southern Baptist colleges and universities; a majority teach in the biblical field. Many belong to the Association of Baptist Professors of Religion and other professional organizations. Several hundred journal articles, curriculum materials, and books have grown out of their research.

See also BIBLICAL STUDIES, SOUTHERN BAPTIST, VOL. I.

WATSON MILLS

BIBLICAL STUDIES, DERWARD W. DEERE LECTURESHIP ON. See DEERE, DERWARD W., LECTURESHIP ON BIBLICAL STUDIES.

BICENTENNIAL BELL, MISSISSIPPI. See MISSISSIPPI BICENTENNIAL BELL.

BICENTENNIAL (1976), BAPTISTS AND THE UNITED STATES. Baptists of the United States observed the Bicentennial in a variety of ways through their respective denominational programs and agencies. The SBC assigned the Baptist Joint Committee on Public Affairs (BJCPA), Christian Life Commission, and Historical Commission the responsibility for a Convention-wide project for 1975-76, "Let Christ's Freedom Ring." Plans, programs, and resource materials were prepared in cooperation with the SBC Sunday School Board and other agencies on this Bicentennial theme.

In response to a recommendation of the North American Baptist Fellowship in 1972, the BJCPA accepted responsibility for coordinating and implementing a national Baptist observance of the Bicentennial. A Baptist Bicentennial committee, chaired by James E. Wood, Jr., executive director of the BJCPA, was formed to plan "a national Bicentennial convocation." Members of the committee included: C. C. Goen and Winthrop S. Hudson of American Baptist Churches in the USA; Lynn E. May, Jr., and W. Morgan Patterson of the SBC; E. C. Smith of the Progressive National Baptist Convention; and Frank Woyke of the North American Baptist Conference.

Planned on behalf of eight national Baptist bodies, the convocation was held in Washington, DC, Jan. 12-15, 1976, with participants from across the nation, representing all the sponsoring Baptist bodies along with a representation from the Baptist Federation of Canada. The theme chosen for the convocation was "Baptists and the American Experience." The event was termed "convocation" because it was a calling together of Baptists to a deeper awareness of the commitments and realities of the American experience in the light of Baptist faith and practice.

Far more than a celebration of 200 years of America's nationhood, the observance of the Bicentennial had profound implications for the community of faith as well as the nation as a whole. The convocation provided a practical means whereby national Baptist bodies, independently of official civil observances, could join hands to review and reevaluate, both appreciatively and critically, Baptists and the American experience. Admittedly, the American Revolution remains unfinished in many ways so long as the promise for the American dream, "liberty and justice for all," remains unfulfilled. In both its breadth and its focus the event was unprecedented for the Baptists of America.

While the convocation was consciously planned so as to come at the beginning of the Bicentennial, the dates of the convocation were chosen as symbolically appropriate. The convocation was held between the birthdays of Isaac Backus, Jan. 9, the champion of religious liberty at the time of the founding of the Republic, and Martin Luther King, Jr., Jan. 15, the nation's foremost leader of human rights in the twentieth century.

The 20 essays prepared for the convocation were published as *Baptists and the American Experience* (1976), edited by J. E. Wood, Jr.

See also MISSISSIPPI BICENTENNIAL BELL.

JAMES E. WOOD, JR.

BINNS, CARLTON WILBUR (b. Washington, GA, Nov. 24, 1897; d. Atlanta, GA, Dec. 6, 1977). Denominational worker. Son of Laura Binns and James Walter Binns, a minister, he attended Mercer University (A.B., 1919; L.L.B., 1920). He was assistant solicitor and solicitor of Fulton County Criminal Court, 1926-29. He served as attorney for the Home Mission Board, 1949-65, and as Georgia Baptist Convention vice-president. He married Marie McLean, June 24, 1931. Their children were Mary Arnold and John Carlton. Binns is buried in Westview Cemetery, Atlanta, GA.

LEONOAR C. ADAMS

BIOETHICS. The treatment of both the moral problems that arise from the interface between biology and medicine and the interaction between ethics and the sciences, particularly the life sciences. V. R. Potter used the term "bioethics" in 1971 to denote the latter, broader meaning, while others use it in the former, more restricted sense. In both senses, technological advances in the life sciences, coupled with humanity's uncertain future, heighten the tension between the possible and the desirable and undesirable.

In the narrower sense, bioethics covers such areas as behavior control, control of reproduction, experimentation on human subjects, euthanasia and allowing to die, mass screening programs, and genetic engineering. More broadly conceived, bioethics treats also quality-of-life decisions, medical economics, definitions of health and disease, health care delivery systems, ecological imbalances, and concepts of a just society which include health care delivery systems.

Bioethics received limited attention in the SBC during the 1970s. No resolutions on this subject were passed. Resolutions dealing with abortion, family planning, and the handicapped and the 1978 Declaration of Human Rights alluded to health care delivery. The Christian Life Commission, SBC, sponsored a Biomedical Ethics Conference, Aug. 26-27, 1976, in Nashville. The proceedings were published in a book entitled *A Matter of Life and Death* (1977).

                                   BOB E. ADAMS

BIRMINGHAM BAPTIST HOSPITALS
(I). See BAPTIST MEDICAL CENTERS, BIRMINGHAM.

BIVOCATIONAL MINISTRY.
In 1980 bivocational pastors were serving 9,845 Southern Baptist churches. Many more staff persons served in such a role. Bivocational ministers are "persons who serve more than one vocation or institution and/or whose income is partly derived from some source other than the institution of their primary religious employment." The title "part-time" is considered offensive and nondescriptive of a calling to ministry with a complete commitment, even though there are financial limits in some settings.

The historical pattern of SBC ministry in smaller churches prior to the 1920s was an ordained person whose financial support was secular employment. From the 1920s to the 1970s churches of all sizes increasingly stressed the single role minister fully employed by the local church. With the church extension emphases of Bold Mission Thrust and the large number of small churches, renewed attention was given in the 1970s to bivocational ministry. This attention included specially designed Seminary Extension curricula, a Home Mission Board consultant, and conferences and resources for linking persons with ministry opportunities through the HMB Department of Associational Services.

Studies indicate that 60 percent of bivocational pastors have more than high school education, 25 percent are students, and 46 percent prefer single-role ministry. Nearly 84 percent serve nonmetropolitan churches, and 80 percent are in churches smaller than 300 members. Rates of baptism and new missions are comparable with other SBC churches, but per capita giving is lower. Bivocational pastors report a sense of freedom in focus upon essential tasks of ministry and prophetic action which financial independence gives.

BIBLIOGRAPHY: Doran McCarty, "The Bi-Vocational Minister and His Ministry," *Associational Administration Bulletin* (Mar., 1979). Lewis Wingo, "The Needs of Bi-Vocational Pastors," *The Quarterly Review* (Apr., 1979).

                                   LARRY MCSWAIN

BLACK, HUGO LAFAYETTE (b. Clay County, AL, Feb. 27, 1886; d. Bethesda, MD, Sep. 25, 1971). Baptist Supreme Court justice. The son of Martha Ardella Toland and William Black, a merchant, he attended the University of Alabama (L.L.B., 1906). He married Josephine Foster, Feb. 23, 1921. Their children were Hugo, Jr., Sterling, and Mary. He married Elizabeth Seay DeMeritte, Sep. 11, 1921. On the Supreme Court, 1937-71, he was a member of the "liberal bloc" and the foremost defender of civil liberties. He is buried in Arlington National Cemetery, Arlington, VA.

BIBLIOGRAPHY: John P. Frank, *Mr. Justice Black* (1949). Virginia Hamilton, *Hugo Black: The Alabama Years* (1972). James J. Magee, *Mr. Justice Black: Absolutist on the Court* (1980).

                                   LEE N. ALLEN

BLACK BAPTISTS IN ALABAMA. See ALABAMA NEGRO BAPTISTS.

BLACK BAPTISTS IN ARKANSAS. See ARKANSAS BAPTIST COOPERATING MINISTRY WITH NATIONAL BAPTISTS.

BLACK BAPTISTS IN ILLINOIS. See ILLINOIS, BLACK AND ETHNIC CHURCH GROWTH IN.

BLACK BAPTISTS IN LOUISIANA. See NEGRO BAPTISTS IN LOUISIANA.

BLACK BAPTISTS IN THE UNITED STATES. See BLACK SOUTHERN BAPTISTS; NATIONAL BAPTIST CONVENTION OF AMERICA; NATIONAL BAPTIST CONVENTION, U.S.A., INC.; PROGRESSIVE NATIONAL BAPTIST CONVENTION, U.S.A., INC.

BLACK BAPTISTS IN VIRGINIA. See NEGRO BAPTISTS IN VIRGINIA.

BLACK CHURCH RELATIONS, HOME MISSION BOARD PROGRAM OF (cf. National Baptists, Home Mission Board Program of Work With, Vol. III). Black Church Relations is the new title for what was formerly called the Department of Cooperative Ministries with National Baptists. The SBC approved the revised program statement in 1980. The substance of the program's activity has not changed. The revision more accurately recognizes the three aspects of the program's continuous ministry: (1) Leading the Convention in cooperative activities with the three National Baptist Conventions; (2) assisting black Southern Baptist churches; and (3) assisting Southern Baptists desiring help in interracial ministries.

In 1980 the program had 3 staff persons, 2 national consultants, and 92 missionaries, interns, and contract consultants. Illustrations of the kinds of ministries of this program include:

1. Annual, regional, and associational confer-

ences for churches in racially changing communities.

2. Seminary extension units reaching more than 4,000 persons.

3. Scholarships to more than 275 black youth preparing for full-time Christian vocations.

4. Cosponsorship of the National Baptist Student Retreat, a weekend missions conference reaching over 1,800 collegians.

5. Orientation activities for black Southern Baptist pastors, churches, and seminarians.

6. Development of resources to assist churches in racially changing communities, black church development, and interracial ministries.

7. Conferences to assist black churches in their development.

8. Nine internships both for service and the development of black seminarians.

9. Cosponsorship of the C. D. Hubert Religious Institute, a national theological forum for black churches.

10. Consultative services to SBC agencies needing help in their ministries with black persons.

Emmanuel McCall has directed the department since Jan., 1975, upon the retirement of Victor Glass. Edward Wheeler and Chan Garrett are associates to McCall.

EMMANUEL MCCALL

BLACK SOUTHERN BAPTISTS. Black Southern Baptists are the largest minority constituency in the SBC. Approximately 3,500 churches, located in every state convention, report about 150,000 black members.

Black Southern Baptists in the 19th Century. — When the SBC was founded in 1845, approximately one-third of its members were black. Although slave membership was the most common practice, sometimes blacks had their own separate churches. While integration was the dominant church style, there was no racial equality in Southern Baptist churches.

During the pre-abolition period (1845-65), black Southern Baptist existence was dominated by the institution of slavery in church as well as society. Having been a major factor in the controversy which led to the founding of the SBC, blacks were the object of evangelism and were often included in the membership of the church of their owner. Thus, the first black Southern Baptists were members not by conviction but by condition.

In pre-abolition churches black Southern Baptists suffered from the imposition of second-class membership. They were usually systematically excluded from pastoral leadership of the whole integrated church. They were often segregated in a slave gallery. They suffered ministry by proxy. They were exploited in their religious education. They were disfranchised except in slave affairs. They usually could not assemble without white supervision. Even in the black churches pastors were often white, due to distrust of indigenous black gatherings exacerbated by Nat Turner's revolt in 1831.

In 1845 the SBC instructed the new Board of Domestic Missions "to take all prudent measures for the religious instruction of our colored population," and programs were initiated to work with blacks.

The abolition of slavery brought a black exodus from white-dominated churches and the formation of black Southern Baptist churches. These black churches organized Southern Baptist associations in some locales and were a major part of the Southern Baptist population. In some places, like the Florida Baptist Convention in the 1880s, they were even a majority. These post-abolition black Southern Baptists were mission-minded and sent some of their members as Southern Baptist foreign missionaries to Africa.

By 1900 most black Southern Baptists had found alternative membership in the National Baptist Convention of America. Most Southern Baptist work with blacks shifted from church involvement to relationships through the Home Mission Board, SBC.

Black Southern Baptists in the 20th Century. — After a half-century absence, black churches began affiliation with the SBC again. In 1951 Community Baptist Church of Santa Rosa, CA, and Greater Friendship Baptist Church of Anchorage, AK, affiliated, and by 1980 there were approximately 600 predominantly black Southern Baptist congregations with an estimated 100,000 members. Predominantly white Southern Baptist churches had attracted about 50,000 black members. Most of the black Southern Baptist churches are dually aligned with a National Baptist convention.

Black Southern Baptists have served the denomination in various capacities at many levels and have been elected to the following offices: (1) Associational moderator, vice-moderator, Sunday School director, Brotherhood director, finance committee chairman, student work chairman, missions committee member, pastors' conference president, and others; (2) state convention president, vice-president, board members, commission members, and president of the pastors' conference; and (3) SBC vice-president, Home Mission Board member, Foreign Mission Board member, Christian Life Commission member, and American Baptist Seminary Commission member.

Black Southern Baptists have been employed in various denominational staff positions: (1) Associational associate director of church extension and consultant on black church ministries; (2) state convention area directors of Christian social ministries, center directors, teacher-missionaries, directors of cooperative ministries, pastoral interns, and state director of a department of black church relations; and (3) SBC home missionaries, foreign missionaries, consultants, book store manager, seminary professor, accountant, associate department director, and department director.

A recent development among some black Southern Baptists was the forming of a Black Southern Baptist Fellowship in 1979 to deal with issues of Southern Baptist life from black perspectives.

BIBLIOGRAPHY: Research Services Department, SSB, SBC, "Study of Black Southern Baptists" (Dec., 1980).

SIDNEY SMITH

BLACKMON, GEORGE TRUETT (b. Titus County, TX, Sep. 19, 1903; d. Arkadelphia, AR, Aug. 16, 1979). Minister, educator, and historian. Son of Jesse Lee Blackmon, a farmer-carpenter, and Queen Ann (Whitley) Blackmon, he married Bessie Grace Hicks, June 8, 1930. Their children were James, Lillian, and Kenneth. He attended Ouachita Baptist College (B.A.) and Southwestern Baptist Theological Seminary (M.R.E., Th.D.). He served as chaplain with rank of captain in the United States Army, 1942-45. He was professor of biblical and Christian history, Ouachita Baptist University, 1946-69.

A state director of the Southern Baptist Historical Society, 1960-70, he was chairman of the Arkansas Baptist History Commission, 1958-65; executive secretary, History Commission, Arkansas Baptist State Convention, 1965-75; and member, board of trustees, Ouachita Baptist University, 1969-75. He was named distinguished alumnus of Ouachita in 1976. He is buried in Salem Cemetery, Saline County, AR.

BERNES K. SELPH

BLANCHARD, JOHN (b. Cooke County, TN, Mar. 30, 1821; d. Pope County, IL, May 21, 1901). Baptist pastor and medical doctor. Son of John and Sarah Blanchard, farmers, he married Charlotte Justice, Mar. 24, 1842. They had seven children: Eliza, Mary, John, James, William, Maranda, and Isaac. On Sep. 23, 1849, he was ordained into the ministry at Little Grand Pier Baptist Church in Illinois. He served as pastor of 14 churches in southern Illinois, sometimes five at a time, traveling much of the time on foot. Most of his work was done in Big Saline Baptist Association. In 1869 he graduated from the Eclectic Medical College, becoming a doctor. He is buried in the Old Concord Church cemetery, Pope County, IL.

RONALD L. NELSON

BLANDVILLE COLLEGE (Blandville, KY). A private school incorporated in 1866 at Blandville, then the county seat of Ballard County, KY, which failed by 1885 and was purchased by West Union Baptist Association in 1886. Among the presidents and instructors during the school's Baptist years (1885-1910) were J. N. Robinson, W. H. Witty, Z. J. Amerson, T. A. Scott, A. Slaughter, J. C. Neville, W. D. Powell, J. H. Greenwell, and Arthur M. Wilson. The school, which served several educational levels, reached enrollments of 120 (1894) and 130 (1903). Its first building was destroyed by fire in 1905, and the rebuilt structure was sold to the county for a high school in 1910.

R. CHARLES BLAIR

BLEDSOE, THOMAS W. (b. Greene County, GA, Apr. 11, 1811; d. Bossier Parish, LA, Jan. 10, 1871). Deacon and denominational leader. Reared by an uncle, Thomas Stocks, following the death of his parents, Bledsoe served as a judge in Talbot County, GA, before settling in 1848 near Fillmore, LA. There he helped to found a church and labored long as a deacon. Four times elected moderator of Red River Association, he was the first layman elected president of the Louisiana Baptist Convention. His tenure (1854-57; 1864-71), totaling 10 years, was the second longest in the history of the convention.

GLEN LEE GREENE

BLUEFIELD COLLEGE (I, III). During the 1970s Bluefield became a four-year college. The new program led to the graduation of the first baccalaureate class on May 21, 1977. Fully accredited by the Southern Association of Colleges and Schools, in 1979 the college had a faculty of 24, including 11 Ph.D.'s. Enrollment was 428. A new dormitory housing five married couples and 40 single students was completed in 1979. The men's dormitory was named Cruise Hall in honor of George Cruise, former chairman of the board of trustees.

In Sep., 1978, the enlargement of shelf space in the library was completed, and the collection increased to 47,988 volumes by 1979. Charles L. Tyer succeeded Charles L. Harmon as president on July 1, 1972. Total assets on Aug. 31, 1979, were $3,244,895 with a projected budget of $1,195,000 for 1979-80.

STEPHEN B. KINDRICK

BOLD MISSION THRUST. The term "bold missions" as applied to Southern Baptist programs probably originated with Marie Mathis during the early stages of '70 Onward planning, possibly in a meeting of the '70 Onward Steering Committee, Feb. 21, 1966. A point made in the meeting was that whatever else Southern Baptists emphasized in the 1970s, the decade should close with a bold emphasis on missions. Kept alive in the committee's thinking, the idea emerged as one of the major purposes of the 1977-79 emphasis period, "LET THE CHURCH REACH OUT—by boldly confronting the secular world through bold missions." Both the Home Mission Board and the Foreign Mission Board made extensive plans for promotion of bold mission in 1977-79, and the HMB subsequently adopted "Bold Mission Thrust" to describe its promotional program.

In 1974 the SBC authorized a special committee to "measure Southern Baptists' human and financial resources and potential for mission advance." Two years later this committee brought 15 recommendations to the Convention, all of which were approved. The first recommendation asked the Convention to set as "its primary missions challenge that every person in the world shall have the opportunity to hear the gospel of Christ in the next 25 years, and that in the presentation of this message, the biblical faith be magnified so that all men, women, and children can understand the claim that Jesus Christ has on their lives.''

One year later three reports from three different groups provided the basic thrust for Bold Mission Thrust. The Executive Committee, on instruction of the Convention in 1976, brought a coordinated report on behalf of the agencies involved in missions challenge. It called for affirmation of the years 1977-79 as years of ''Bold Missions: Through Bold Witnessing, Bold Committing, and Bold Teaching.'' The Executive Committee also joined with a group of lay leaders in an effort to secure 5,000 short-term lay missionaries who would be supported by private resources by 1982. The Stewardship Commission, reporting for its Bold Mission Task Force, brought a proposal that as a part of Bold Mission Southern Baptists double the 1977 Cooperative Program at least three times by the year 2000. All three proposals were approved, and the Executive Committee was assigned the responsibility for coordination.

In the fall of 1977 the Executive Committee adopted a general plan for coordination that called for a Bold Mission Thrust Leadership Group and a Bold Mission Thrust Steering Committee, with members from the involved agencies, the state conventions, the associations, and the Executive Committee. Leadership for the emphasis was provided by the agencies involved. Albert McClellan, associate executive-secretary of the Executive Committee, was appointed the first coordinator. In 1978 the Steering Committee developed a plan for 1979-82 under the title Bold Mission Thrust with emphases in three general areas: Growing, Going, and Giving. It was approved by the Executive Committee and the Convention. In 1980 the SBC adopted a plan for 1982-85 under the title of ''Bold Mission Thrust'' and emphasizing ''Reaching People, Developing Believers and Strengthening Families.'' This plan included Convention approval of an interprogram leadership group to work with the Bold Mission Thrust Steering Committee in the promotion of Bold Mission Thrust, 1982-85.

Bold Mission Thrust as approved in 1977 incorporated the mission interests of all the agencies. Six specific components were named: The Cooperative Program, the Mission Service Corps, other programs of Volunteer Involvement in Missions, the Missions Education Council, Missions Challenge, and Coordinated Promotion Planning. Other interests included career missionaries and program support for missions.

The annual Bold Mission Thrust report of the Executive Committee to the Convention in 1980 contained a significant paragraph developed by the Bold Mission Thrust Steering Committee which described Bold Mission Thrust as follows:

The program is as much a local church emphasis as it is a denominational emphasis. Bold Mission Thrust is:
   Churches responding to God's mission in world missions.

Churches carrying out God's mission purposes.
   Churches strengthened to provide a base for missions.
   Churches involving their people in missions.
   Churches cooperating with other churches in meeting world needs.
   Churches supported by denominational resources.

The report also outlined the way the denomination does the work of Bold Mission Thrust as follows:

1. Bold Mission Thrust is the cooperative expression of the mandate for missions given to the churches by Jesus Christ.
   2. It utilizes existing church organizations and programs.
   3. It focuses on the church council or similar group as the planning and expediting agent.
   4. It recognizes the pastor as the primary leader for Bold Mission Thrust.
   5. It promotes church growth as the way for building a base for Christ's conquest of the whole world.
   6. It employs missions education as the basic motivational tool, especially education in the biblical mandate for missions.
   7. It utilizes existing denominational structures and programs.
   8. It depends on the career missionary both at home and in foreign lands as the major part of the mission thrust.
   9. It enlists lay persons for special short term missionary service, and it enlists other lay persons to directly support them.
   10. It recognizes the Southern Baptist Convention agencies with direct programs to the churches as primarily responsible for Bold Mission Thrust leadership, and the other agencies as supportive.

ALBERT MCCLELLAN

BOLIVIA, MISSION IN. The Baptist Convention of Eastern Bolivia organized in 1947 through Brazilian missionary efforts. In 1976 the convention invited the Foreign Mission Board to work with the Bolivians and Brazilian missionaries in the evangelization of eastern Bolivia. This invitation was accepted in 1977, and the first Southern Baptist missionary couple arrived in Bolivia in June, 1979. Six months later a second couple joined them. The delegates of the 16 churches of the convention voted at the 1979 annual meeting to enter a three-year program of evangelism with the theme, ''Bolivia for Christ.''

J. BRYAN BRASINGTON

BOLTON, CHARLES HOUSTON (b. Belgreen, AL, Sep. 13, 1886; d. Thomasville, GA, Nov. 11, 1973). Pastor and denominational executive. Son of Franklin Marion and Josephine (Hall) Bolton, farmers, he attended Atlanta Theological Seminary (1912-14) and Southern Baptist Theological Seminary (1915-17). He married Lena Mae Painter, Sep. 20, 1904. Their children were Charles, Elinor, and Edith. He served as a pastor in Kentucky, Alabama, and Florida, 1916-39. Pastorates included Southside Church, Montgomery, AL, 1917-24; Norwood Church, Birmingham, AL, 1924-27; and First Baptist, West Palm Beach, FL, 1927-39.

He served as associate secretary, Relief and

Annuity Board, SBC, 1939-41, and as executive secretary-treasurer, Florida Baptist Convention, 1941-49. During his term of service, the Rogers Building (convention headquarters) was freed of debt, a plan of rural and city mission work was initiated in cooperation with the Home Mission Board, a reserve fund was established, the convention moved toward greater unity, and the foundations were laid for better relations between Stetson University and the convention. In 1944 he assumed the pastorate of Riverside Baptist Church, Miami, FL, where he served until 1949. Then he served as the first executive secretary of the Southern Baptist Foundation, 1949-53. In his work for the foundation, Bolton established its professional services, secured an image of security and integrity, and negotiated the transfer of major funds from the agencies to the care of the foundation.

Bolton returned to the pastorate in 1953, serving First Baptist Church, Avon Park, FL, 1953-56, his last pastorate. After retiring in 1956, he served 40 interim pastorates before his death. He also served as trustee and chairman of Stetson University's board of trustees between 1937 and 1963. He is buried in Oaklawn Cemetery, Jacksonville, FL.

JOHN HENRY MAQUIRE

BOOK STORES, BAPTIST (I, III).

A group of more than 60 retail, religious book stores owned and operated by the Sunday School Board, including six seminary stores, two conference center stores, and three Lifeway book stores. Five of the stores operate film centers which rent religious films to churches. Since 1975, five regional mail-order centers have been opened to provide mail-order services for several states and to serve as regional warehouses for other Baptist Book Stores. Lifeway stores, started in 1972, are in shopping centers to serve persons who might not consider shopping in a store bearing a denominational label. In 1979 a new direct sales department began to offer customers another channel through which to buy. Baptist Book Stores sell program materials from Broadman Press, Convention Press, Woman's Missionary Union, Brotherhood Commission, and the Home and Foreign Mission Boards. They also sell a variety of Bibles, religious books, music, church supplies, and gift items from Broadman, Holman, and more than 300 other vendors.

WILLIAM S. GRAHAM

BOPHUTHATSWANA, MISSION IN.

The Bophuthatswana nation was created on Dec. 6, 1977. Dale and Ann (Puckett) Beighle, Southern Baptists' first missionaries there, had arrived six days earlier. Initial Southern Baptist involvement was in response to an appeal from top-level government officials for Christian personnel to fill vacancies. "On loan" to the Bophuthatswana government, Beighle taught veterinary assistants at Taung College of Agriculture in the southwest area.

Early in 1978 Edmond and Mary Ann (Pugh) Moses arrived to begin pharmacy work in the northeast area. Within a year Southern Baptist missionaries lived in five of the country's six districts. They were serving in medical, educational, social, and direct evangelism ministries. At their 1980 planning meeting the 18 missionaries approved strategy emphasizing church development and youth evangelism.

JOY NEAL

BOTSFORD, EDMUND (b. Woburn, Bedfordshire, England, Nov. 1, 1745; d. Georgetown, SC, Dec. 25, 1819). Pastor. Son of Mary Botsford and Edmund Botsford, grocer and hardware dealer, he migrated to Charleston, SC, in 1766. Converted under the preaching of Oliver Hart (q.v. I), he was ordained, Mar. 14, 1773, by Hart and Francis Pelot. An itinerant along the South Carolina-Georgia border for several years, he served briefly as a chaplain in the Revolutionary War. He was pastor of Welch Neck Baptist Church, 1779-97, and Georgetown Baptist Church, 1797-1819. He is buried at Georgetown, SC.

J. GLENWOOD CLAYTON

BOTSWANA, MISSION IN (III). Having begun work in Botswana in 1968, Southern Baptist missionaries participated in the organization of the country's first Baptist church in 1970 in Francistown. In 1973 Marvin and Elizabeth (Haley) Reynolds moved to Selebi-Pikwe, and in 1975 Roy and Patsy (Dodds) Davidson moved to Gaborone, the capital city, to begin radio work. Kasane became the fourth center of missionary residence in 1976 when Albert and Virginia (Cox) Sutton established an agricultural ministry there.

Bible Way Correspondence School began in 1976 and reported almost 2,000 students in 1979. Dental clinics begun in 1970 were discontinued in 1977 but resumed in 1980. Preparations were under way for beginning a teaching ministry in government secondary schools. Theological Education by Extension was undergirding the mission's goals of establishing strong indigenous churches.

JOY NEAL

BOTTOMS BAPTIST ORPHANAGE (I). See ARKANSAS BAPTIST FAMILY AND CHILD CARE SERVICES.

BOWMAN GRAY SCHOOL OF MEDICINE.

A continuation and expansion of the two-year Wake Forest Medical School established in 1902 at Wake Forest, NC, Bowman Gray moved to Winston Salem, NC, in 1941. This school and North Carolina Baptist Hospital form one of 126 academic medical centers in the nation with major responsibilities for medical education, research, and patient care. About 100 students make up each class. In addition, 1,000 train annually through teaching programs, including biograduate students, house officers, and allied health students.

See also NORTH CAROLINA BAPTIST HOSPITALS, INC., VOLS. II, III, IV.

RUSSELL BRANTLEY

BOYCE BIBLE SCHOOL. A division of Southern Baptist Theological Seminary's Ministry Training Center, which provides the supplemental and special education programs of the seminary. Approved by the SBC on June 13, 1974, the primary purpose of the school is to provide training for practicing ministers who have not completed college.

James Pettigru Boyce (q.v.I.), whose name the school bears, stated in an address on theological education on July 30, 1856: "A Baptist theological school ought not merely to receive college graduates, but men with less of general education . . . offering to every man such opportunities of theological study as he is prepared for and desires."

The recommendation to establish the Boyce School was made by the Southern Seminary trustees with the approval of the SBC Executive Committee. As authorized by the Convention, a board of overseers was elected by the seminary trustees, and Boyce was begun in the fall of 1974 with Allen W. Graves, dean of the seminary's School of Religious Education, serving as executive director. Graves developed the format and curriculum for the school and enlisted the faculty.

The goal from the beginning was that the school should have a faculty of experienced teachers and pastors. Veteran educators Gaines S. Dobbins (q.v.) and George W. Redding of Georgetown College were enlisted to teach. Among others who served on the first faculty were H. C. Chiles, Carroll Hubbard, Verlin Kruschwitz, James H. Smith, Harold Purdy, and James W. Middleton.

James L. Ryan succeeded Graves as executive director in 1976. Following Ryan's resignation in July, 1977, Arthur Walker, the seminary's vice-president of student affairs, became interim director. On Jan. 1, 1978, David Q. Byrd, Jr., pastor of First Baptist Church, Jackson, TN, became the director.

In the fall of 1975, an off-campus center of Boyce Bible School was begun in Little Rock, AR, under the direction of Withrow T. Holland. Sponsored jointly by the Arkansas Baptist State Convention and Southern Seminary, classes met in the Central Baptist Hospital in Little Rock.

The second off-campus center was begun in Columbus, OH, in the fall of 1976 under joint sponsorship with the State Convention of Baptists in Ohio. Orville Griffin, director of evangelism and stewardship for the convention, was named local director, with classes meeting in the Boyce Building adjacent to the state convention building.

In the fall of 1979, Boyce began the operation of its third center. At the request of the Peninsula Baptist Association of Virginia and with the approval of the Baptist General Association of Virginia, Boyce assumed the operation of the Peninsula Bible Institute in Hampton, VA. This center convened in Liberty Baptist Church in Hampton under the direction of J. B. Flowers.

In the spring of 1980 Boyce began its fourth off-campus center in Springfield, IL. Sponsored jointly by Boyce and the Illinois Baptist State Association, classes began in the association's building in Springfield under the direction of Rick Heironimus, director of leadership training for the association.

See also SOUTHERN BAPTIST THEOLOGICAL SEMINARY.

DAVID Q. BYRD

BOYS RANCH TOWN, OKLAHOMA (I, III). New programs begun since 1969 include individualized training through a vocational shop project, individual work for pay as incentive for boys to develop talents, and recreational-counseling services. The latter service is called LUV (for Learning, Understanding, and Venture). In 1980 property value was $2,750,000. A staff of 24 cared for 42 boys in residence, plus a few in foster care. The annual operating budget exceeded $380,000. As of Mar., 1980, 828 boys had entered the ranch since its founding in 1953. Charles T. Boldin has been superintendent since 1956.

J. M. GASKIN

BRANTLEY, CLOVIS AUGUSTUS (b. Lily, FL, Oct. 18, 1912; d. Decatur, GA, Mar. 31, 1979). Missionary and denominational leader. The son of John and Martha Brantley, citrus growers, he was baptized in 1927 at First Baptist Church, Mt. Dora, FL. He married Gladys Beall, Dec. 30, 1935. They had three daughters: Lolita, Martha, and Tessa. He attended Stetson University and Baptist Bible Institute, New Orleans, LA.

Appointed a home missionary in 1937, Brantley served in the Baptist Rescue Mission, New Orleans, and founded the Baptist Baby Home in 1948 as part of the work in the Woman's Emergency Home, New Orleans (Sellers Home and Adoption Center). During his years of service in New Orleans, 1937-51, he also led in establishing mission centers and developing community weekday ministries. He served as founding director of Baptist Center, Memphis, TN, 1955-57. He served on the staff of the Home Mission Board, SBC, 1957-77.

Brantley served as pastor of Blake Memorial Baptist Church, Lake Helen, FL, and First Baptist Church, Plateau, AL. He authored *God Can* (1946). His body was cremated.

PAUL R. ADKINS

BRAZIL, MISSIONS IN (I, III). New work and better financial support contributed to the rapid growth of Brazilian Baptists during the 1970s. Various Home Mission Board projects, like "Trans-Amazonica," extended gospel witness to remote, neglected parts of the country.

Brazil led the media advance in Latin America as the Radio and Television Board of Religious Education and Publications acquired new headquarters facilities. Increases in seminary enrollments also occurred. As the new decade dawned, Brazilian Baptists looked toward 1982, the centennial of Baptist work among Brazilians. The Brazilian Baptist Convention set challenging goals for the years leading up to the centennial. In 1980, 49 missionaries served in Equatorial Brazil, 90 in North Brazil, and 166 in South Brazil.

FRANK K. MEANS

BRENTWOOD BAPTIST CENTER (Denver). In Apr., 1975, the Colorado Baptist General Convention secured the former facilities of Brentwood Baptist Church, and renamed them Brentwood Baptist Center. The facilities included an auditorium and educational space totaling 16,000 square feet.

Four ministries initiated at the Baptist Center included: A preaching ministry, with services begun by Dwight Braswell; a ministry to children under the direction of the Roy Cyrs; a Christian training institute; and a Christian social ministry in a joint endeavor with the Home Mission Board, under the direction of Autry Brown.

The preaching ministry developed from a Sunday morning service to a church-type mission, which constituted into a church in 1979, and meets in the center for worship.

The ministry to children is approved and licensed by the Social Services Department of Colorado. The program averages 60 children in daily attendance. The weekday director at the Baptist Center is Jo Ann Fisher who is jointly employed by the state convention and HMB. The Child Care Ministry is under her supervision. Bill and Betty Cartee, Mission Service Corps volunteers from Georgia, supervise an active ministry to Asian refugees.

The Christian training institute evidently did not meet a need in the Denver area and was discontinued. However, a Korean mission ministry was begun under language missionary-pastor Sung Seuh Lee. The Korean mission, sponsored by Ward Road Baptist Church, Arvada, CO, meets weekly at the Baptist Center.

GLEN E. BRASWELL

BREWTON-PARKER COLLEGE (cf. Brewton-Parker Junior College, Vols. I, III). Although the institution is still a junior college, it dropped the word *Junior* from its name in 1977. W. Starr Miller succeeded J. Theodore Phillips as president in July, 1979. The student body in 1980 totaled 900. The endowment was $1,350,000. The college offers programs in liberal arts, the fine arts, business, and in vocational fields. Through a cooperative program with Tift College at Forsyth, GA, Brewton-Parker offers four-year programs on campus.

W. STARR MILLER

BRISBANE, WILLIAM HENRY (b. near Robertville, SC, 1806; d. Arena, WI, 1878). Minister, editor, and abolitionist. Son of Adam F. Brisbane and Mary Anna Mosse, he married Anna Lawton. They had several children who died young, in addition to B. Lawton Brisbane, a Baptist minister. Educated by Bishop England of the Roman Catholic Church at Charleston, SC, William T. Brantley at Beaufort College, and at a military school in Middletown, CT, he became "skilled in theology, a masterful writer and speaker." The terms of his Uncle William Brisbane's will in 1821 made him wealthy. By the time he was 20, he was active as a messenger to the Savannah River Baptist Association and the South Carolina Baptist Convention. He supplied churches, served on committees, and in 1833 became pastor of Beech Branch Baptist Church.

In 1834 Brisbane became editor of *The Southern Baptist and General Intelligencer,* published in Charleston. At that time he held proslavery sentiments and wrote editorials supporting them. But within several months he read a chapter on "Personal Liberty" from *Elements of Moral Science* (1835) by Francis Wayland which stirred him deeply and he completely reversed his position. His editorials condemning slavery led to much abuse and dismissal as editor.

Following several efforts to satisfy his conscience regarding his own slaves, he eventually took them with him and fled to Ohio where he settled them in new homes and trades. "He became a radical and uncompromising leader in the cause of human emancipation." He was once nominated for President of the United States on the Abolition Party ticket. Brisbane moved to Wisconsin where he lived for 25 years before his death.

LOULIE LATIMER OWENS

BRITISH VIRGIN ISLANDS, MISSION IN. See TORTOLA, MISSION IN.

BROADMAN BIBLE COMMENTARY, THE (III). Broadman Press completed this 12-volume work in Apr., 1972. However, the original Volume 1 was withdrawn from publication in 1970 and replaced with a revised Volume 1 in Oct., 1973. This action resulted from a 1970 SBC vote to ask the trustees of the Sunday School Board that Volume 1 be withdrawn "from further distribution and that it be rewritten with due consideration of the conservative viewpoint." When the SSB trustees met two months after the Convention, they voted to comply with the Convention request.

In Jan., 1971, a special committee of the SSB trustees recommended that the original authors be asked to rewrite their works from a conservative stance. The 1971 Convention, however, voted to ask the SSB to "obtain another writer and proceed with the commentary according to the vote of the 1970 Convention." Clyde T. Francisco replaced G. Henton Davies as the writer of the Genesis part of the volume. Although an article on "The Scriptures in Translation" was not an object of controversy, the author, Robert G. Bratcher, asked that it not be used in the revised volume, so Barclay H. Newman, Jr., rewrote that article. All other material is identical with that published in the 1969 volume.

This set of Southern Baptist commentaries was directed toward ministers and serious lay students of the Bible as an advanced resource to help in Bible interpretation. Over 333,000 volumes have been sold, and the commentary has become a standard resource for Bible students. Although the commentary's interpretations reflect the diversity of Southern Baptists, they also reflect the unity of their commitment to Christ.

See also BIBLE, CONTROVERSIES ABOUT THE.

JOHNNIE C. GODWIN

BROADMAN PRESS, (I, III). Reorganization, expanded production, and growth in sales characterized the 1970s. In Oct., 1971, the new Broadman Division came into being as a streamlined organization that compactly and efficiently brought together editing, production, and distribution for all lines of Broadman products except music, which is edited by the Church Music Department under contract. This new freedom and responsibility allowed Broadman to publish more quickly to match the times and to venture with new authors and broader markets within the publishing assignment guidelines. Between Oct., 1971, and Oct., 1980, sales more than doubled from $4,500,000 to over $10,000,000 per year, and the net contribution moved from a negative figure to about $750,000.

Broadman Audiovisuals.—During the 1970s Broadman averaged adding 82 items per year to this line. Almost 900 films, filmstrips, videotapes, and audiocassettes are in release. Major additions to the line in the 1970s included: Films, *Bold Discipleship* and *Being Born Again*; filmstrips, *What Baptists Believe* (Series III) and 16 age-group teaching resource filmstrips; videotapes, seven age-group teaching tapes (first Broadman-produced videotapes, 1977); and audiocassettes, children's tapes that appear quarterly on the Church Literature Order Form.

Broadman Books.—During the first half of the 1970s, Broadman released an average of 65 titles per year; the last half, an average of over 100 titles per year. Some major publishing ventures of the 1970s were: (1) Completion of the 12-volume *Broadman Bible Commentary* in 1972 (Vol. 1 revised in 1973); (2) beginning of the 24-volume *Layman's Bible Book Commentary* (one volume per quarter from July, 1978, through July, 1984; over 250,000 books sold in the first two years); (3) reentry into the children's book market with the 24-volume BibLearn Series (with sales of almost 400,000 books in the first four years); (4) design and production of a complete line of Broadman Vacation Bible School curricula for the general trade; (5) development of a plan for systematic production of textbooks

for seminaries; and (6) publication of a layman's witness, *Why Not the Best?* by Jimmy Carter. Between 1969 and 1980, the total number of books in print more than doubled from 464 to 1,026.

Broadman Music.—Significant products released during the 1970s included: *The New Broadman Hymnal*; handbell music; and *Celebrate Life* (released in 1972 with sales of over 250,000 copies). Approximately 1,700 different music items are in print. Efforts are under way to expand the music sales force to meet denominational needs more effectively and to strengthen Broadman's position in the music industry.

Broadman Supplies.—The Broadman supply line is of major importance because of the variety of materials offered to meet church needs. Broadman's selection of supplies with more than 1,600 items is among the largest of any religious publisher in the world.

Major additions to the line during the 1970s were choir robes, pulpit robes, playground equipment, church furniture, Weekday Early Education materials, Vacation Bible School supplies, baptistries, puppets, handbells, audiovisual equipment, and supplies that bear the recently adopted SBC logo.

Broadman intensified its efforts to serve Southern Baptists by the newly created position of publication services coordinator (begun in 1976) and by a strong acquisitions program that includes visiting or contacting all SBC agencies each year. Broadman publications have not elicited unanimous agreement from all Southern Baptists. However, the publications reflect the diversity of the denomination itself within the guidelines assigned Broadman by the Sunday School Board. The dual focus on Southern Baptists and the broader Christian community continues to place Broadman in a strategic position to serve boldly in publication ministry.

See also AUDIOVISUALS/ELECTRONIC MEDIA; CONVENTION PRESS; SUNDAY SCHOOL BOARD, THE.

DESSEL ADERHOLT

BROADUS, ELIZA SOMMERVILLE (b. Charlottesville, VA, Oct. 1, 1851; d. Louisville, KY, Oct. 8, 1931). Pioneer Woman's Missionary Union leader. The daughter of John A. Broadus (*q.v.* I) and Maria Harrison Broadus, she was educated by her father in history, literature, mathematics, philosophy, and languages. She was chairman of the Kentucky Central Committee (*q.v.* I), 1903-19, and charter member of WMU, SBC, being elected vice-president from Kentucky at Richmond, VA, in 1888. She declined reelection in 1920.

Encouraged by William O. Carver (*q.v.* I), she called a mass meeting of Baptist women, Oct. 12, 1904, to consider ways of helping the four single women attending classes at Southern Baptist Theological Seminary. From this beginning, the WMU Training School came into being in 1907. She is buried in Cave Hill Cemetery, Louisville, KY.

DORIS DEVAULT

BROTHERHOOD BUILDER. See Brotherhood Commission, SBC.

BROTHERHOOD COMMISSION, SBC
(cf. Brotherhood, Baptist, Vols. I, III). The
number of men and boys in church Brotherhood
units fluctuated from year to year during the
1970s while showing some growth over the
10-year period. The enrollment in 1970 was
422,527, compared with 469,315 in 1979. Part of
the growth was attributed to the shift of boys six
through eight from the Woman's Missionary
Union Sunbeam organization to the Crusader
Royal Ambassador organization in Brotherhood.

Brotherhood enrollment in 1971 showed
219,702 Royal Ambassadors, 216,662 Baptist
Men, and 25,174 general officers, compared
with 204,721 Royal Ambassadors, 220,966 Baptist Men, and 43,598 general officers and com-
mitteemen in 1979.

In terms of funding, the commission's budget
grew from $623,175 in 1970 to $2,468,964 in
1980-81. Gifts from the Cooperative Program
were $264,609 in 1970 and $650,000 in 1980-81.

Leadership Changes.—Richard L. Sherrick retired on Dec. 31, 1970, as director of the agency's
Supporting Services Division after 10 years of
service and was replaced by Norman Godfrey,
also assistant to executive secretary George W.
Schroeder (*q.v.*).

Schroeder retired May 1, 1971, and died May
29, 1971. His successor, W. Glendon McCullough (*q.v.*), director of the Division of Personnel
at the Home Mission Board, took office on Nov.
1, 1971, and served until his death on Aug. 23,
1978, in a traffic accident. After 13 months of
agency leadership by a cabinet composed of four
section directors, including Bob Banks, program; Norman Godfrey, ministries; Roy Jennings, communications; and Lynette Oliver,
business, trustees elected James Hillman Smith,
executive secretary of the Illinois Baptist State
Association, as the new executive director of the
commission. He began his duties on Sep. 16,
1979. Influenced by budget and scope of programs, the size of the staff fluctuated during the
decade from a high of 53 to a low of 40.

Leading the agency's trustees as chairmen
were Solon G. Freeman of Memphis, TN, 1971;
John Smarge of Silver Spring, MD, 1972-73;
Hovie D. Revis of Greenville, SC, 1974; P. A.
Stevens of Louisville, KY, 1975-76; William E.
Hardy of Columbus, MS, 1977-78; and Jack
Deligans of Livermore, CA, 1979-80.

Expansion and Development in New Areas.—With
the arrival of McCullough in 1971, the commission turned its atention from introducing an enlarged Brotherhood program to Southern Baptist
churches through Shaping the Seventies conferences to a redefinition of priorities and implementation.

The eight priorities were better cooperation
with other SBC agencies and state Brotherhood
leaders, accelerated promotion of Royal Ambassadors as a missions organization, harnessing the
potential of senior men and young men, greater
involvement of men and boys in mission action in
creative and imaginative ways, preparation of
men to witness, undergirding the stewardship
program of Southern Baptists, developing a
sound theological base for Brotherhood work,
and improving the Brotherhood image.

In an effort to make the priorities realities,
McCullough led the agency in 1974 to form a
special study group known as the Direction '84
Committee to make specific proposals for involving men and boys in missions in the 1980s.

A report from the committee, approved by
agency trustees, Aug. 22, 1975, recommended a
statement of purpose for Brotherhood work,
reaffirmed such church Brotherhood tasks as
engaging in missions activities, teaching missions, praying for and giving to missions, undergirding the church and denomination, and proposed a fifth, developing personal ministry. In
the new task Brotherhood units were encouraged
to help persons understand what it means to be
called to ministry and to call forth the gifts that
are in all people so they may do their ministry on
behalf of the whole body of Christ.

The committee also urged the agency to continue publication of quality Brotherhood materials for the churches, continue the Royal Ambassador program at a high level of efficiency,
keep priority needs compatible with available
funds, seek to reach young people and young
adults, and give more attention to family and
coeducational activities.

Finally, the committee recommended expanding the functions of the agency to: (1) provide for
a communications and promotion plan aimed at
pastors, church staff, church leaders, associational leaders, state leaders, denominational
agencies, SBC committees, and laity; (2) include
a development program; (3) develop a marketing
plan for periodicals and merchandise; (4) develop and promote a program of World Missions
Conferences; (5) develop a leadership training
program for church and associational leadership
and professional-type training for state Brotherhood personnel; and (6) initiate and provide
leadership for special mission projects.

Trustees agreed to implement the recommendations through long-range objectives and goals.
The objectives were: (1) to communicate a distinctive identity of the Brotherhood Commission
and its work; (2) to improve continually and communicate a comprehensive mission education
program; (3) to help churches lead men and boys
to grow in quality and quantity of involvement in
missions; (4) to practice good stewardship in
managing resources; (5) to employ, equip, and
develop a staff professionally and spiritually
qualified to implement the agency's goals; and
(6) to obtain the funds needed to reach agency
goals.

To implement the church tasks, the agency in
1979 published three basic books, *The Purpose and
Plan of Baptist Brotherhood, Baptist Men's Guide,*
and *Royal Ambassador Guide.*

When McCullough took the reins of the commission in 1971, a Committee of 15, subcommittee of the SBC Executive Committee, was in the process of studying the program assignments of agencies. The following year SBC messengers approved the following changes:

1. That the charter of the Brotherhood Commission be changed to provide for a Commission composed of one man from each eligible state convention, plus ten local members, and consisting of two-thirds laymen and one-third ordained persons.

2. That the Brotherhood Commission establish an advisory committee, without vote, composed of each state Brotherhood department director, a representative of the seminaries, a representative of the state executive secretaries, and one staff member each from the Sunday School Board, Foreign Mission Board, Home Mission Board, Radio and Television Commission, Christian Life Commission, Woman's Missionary Union, and Stewardship Commission. Each respective group will appoint its representative.

3. That the Commission develop, project, and implement plans and programs involving men and boys in the total mission scope of Southern Baptist Convention activities (such emphases as mission learning experiences, mission involvement, personal involvement, personal witnessing, evangelism, and financial support); and make plans and programs available to the local churches. The program statement should be rewritten accordingly in keeping with established procedure.

4. That consistent with the Commission's program assignment, all activities of Baptist men and boys be continually studied, analyzed, developed, and implemented by the Commission in cooperation with the agencies of the Convention that could most effectively promote and successfully expedite the work.

During this same period there was a growing interest among Southern Baptist men in the denomination in lay ministries, particularly lay renewal. To respond to that interest, the commission employed James Johnson, an Arlington, TX, computer specialist, to direct the lay ministries program on a part-time basis.

Interest in lay renewal continued to expand and the agency chose David Haney, a Southern Baptist pastor and author, in 1974 to direct lay ministries on a full-time basis. Haney launched an extensive program design and field program in cooperation with the HMB to provide guidance for churches in church renewal. During the next five years, Haney led in developing a variety of renewal approaches for churches, including a life-style of ministry and witness, a bold new laity program, and couples involved in ministry and witness.

In 1973 the commission began assuming the coordination and promotion responsibility for World Missions Conferences (Schools of Missions). Each year thereafter, more than 1,000,000 Southern Baptists from 3,000 churches participated in these conferences to hear firsthand accounts of Southern Baptist progress in the mission fields.

James W. Hatley, a former Southern Baptist home missionary and rural-urban consultant for the Texas Baptist Convention, accepted a call, June 15, 1976, to direct the World Mission Conference Department for the commission.

Other innovations McCullough introduced for involving men in missions included regional and national prayer breakfasts, national World Missions Conferences at Glorieta Baptist Conference Center, and Baptist responses to disasters in the nation and world.

In 1973 the commission sponsored a national prayer breakfast for home missions in Atlanta, GA, attended by 1,000 men from the southeastern United States. The principal speaker was Georgia Governor Jimmy Carter, also a member of the Brotherhood Commission trustees as a representative of Georgia Southern Baptists. Governor Carter shared the podium at a national prayer breakfast in Dallas, TX, the following year with Vice-President Gerald Ford, one of three major prayer activities for missions sponsored by the commission. The commission sponsored 16 vocational breakfasts and a Bold Missions rally in Atlanta on June 16, 1978, which attracted 8,000. Jimmy Carter, then President of the United States, was the principal speaker at the rally.

In 1977 the commission began a national leader training program by renewing sponsorship with WMU of a Bold Mission Leadership Conference for a week each summer at Glorieta, attracting about 2,000 members of Southern Baptist families. During the same year the agency also expanded Brotherhood services to Southern Baptist ethnic churches and arranged with the HMB for consultant Daniel Moon to direct the assistance. Moon led in publishing Brotherhood materials in Spanish, Korean, and Chinese and in training church leaders.

In an effort to improve cooperative planning and promotion with state Baptist conventions, the agency employed Bob Banks, director of Brotherhood work for Oklahoma Baptists, in 1974 to implement a cooperative process for planning and promoting Brotherhood work.

In succeeding years Banks led in designing and conducting two-year growth projects known as mission education dialogues, and in launching a national leader training program. Banks also was instrumental in carrying out major materials revisions to reflect 1979 program changes, and in expanding a campcraft program to include adults.

Under Godfrey's leadership as director of the ministries section, the agency coordinated a series of disaster relief projects. The denomination's two mission boards identified the areas needing disaster relief, and the commission worked with state Brotherhood departments to enlist skilled laymen for the short-term volunteer service.

The commission also sponsored a series of national meetings for Royal Ambassadors. A national missions congress attracted 3,000 Pioneer Royal Ambassadors to St. Louis, MO, in 1973, and another in 1979 at the Opryland Hotel in Nashville, TN, brought almost 2,500 registrations.

Beyond the normal emphasis on the Cooperative Program, the commission sponsored a Royal Ambassador Torch Run from Memphis to Miami Beach, FL, in 1975 as part of the fiftieth anniversary of the Cooperative Program. A total of 2,153 Royal Ambassadors carried the torch 1,438 miles during the 29-day project, climaxing the celebration with a presentation on the opening night of the SBC.

Shortly after Smith became executive director in 1979, he led the agency to adopt a succinct purpose: "Helping Churches Involve Men and Boys in Missions." One of the strategies for reaching this objective was to realign the organization into five divisions. Division directors were James H. Smith, Administration; Lynette Oliver, Business; Roy Jennings, Communications; Bob Banks, Royal Ambassadors; and David Haney, Baptist Men. Norman Godfrey was elected to a new position as associate executive director.

Smith specifically strengthened the Baptist Men's Division, adding two associate directors, Larry Yoder, Richmond, VA (curriculum and training), and Frank Black, Memphis (men's ministry projects). One of Smith's expressed hopes was 1,000,000 men involved in missions through Baptist Men by 1990.

The agency asked Hatley to include associational Brotherhood promotion in his duties and brought Moon, language missions consultant, into the administrative unit under Godfrey. The commission also responded to a request by the SBC Executive Committee to conduct 10 regional conferences to gather information from concerned laymen on how the laity could contribute uniquely to Bold Mission Thrust, using their skills and spiritual gifts. The findings seriously influenced other agency strategies for helping churches involve men and boys in missions.

Publications.—The commission published six periodicals for men and boys and their leaders during the 1970s. It also produced an institutional newsletter for the agency staff and trustees and state Brotherhood leaders and families of the three groups.

Crusader, a monthly magazine for Crusader Royal Ambassadors, 6-11, was edited by Ernest Lee Hollaway, III, until his resignation in 1977. Jack Childs succeeded him and was followed by Phil Burgess. Connie Davis was named managing editor of the publication in 1979 upon Burgess' resignation. Circulation of the magazine ranged between 67,000 and 108,000. Content of the magazine focused on Southern Baptist missions and mission-related activities.

Probe, a monthly magazine for Pioneer Royal Ambassadors, 12-17, was edited by Everett Hullum until 1970. Replacing Hullum was Mike Davis, associate editor. James Johnson of Pine Bluff, AR, became editor, Aug. 1, 1980. Circulation of *Probe* fluctuated between 32,000 and 68,000.

World Mission Journal replaced *Baptist Men's Journal* in 1973 and Jim Newton, assistant editor of Baptist Press, news service of the SBC, was employed to edit the monthly tabloid for Baptist

men. Dana Driver had been editor of *Baptist Men's Journal.* Circulation of the tabloid opened in 1973 at 50,000, climbed to 65,000, but leveled off at 43,000 during the latter part of the decade.

Crusader Counselor, a quarterly publication begun in 1969 for leaders of Crusader Royal Ambassadors, was edited by the *Crusader* magazine staff. Circulation was about 20,000.

Pioneer Plans, initially an insert in *Probe* but since 1977 a separate quarterly magazine for leaders of Pioneer Royal Ambassadors, was edited by the *Probe* staff. Its circulation average was about 12,000.

Brotherhood Builder, quarterly magazine for general church and associational Brotherhood officers, was edited by Roy Jennings when editor Darrell Richardson resigned in 1972. Jennings was succeeded as editor in 1977 by Tim Fields, former editor of *Pioneer Plans* and *Crusader Counselor.* When Fields resigned on June 1, 1980, Mike Davis succeeded him. Circulation averaged 10,500.

In an effort to build a family relationship between agency trustees and staff and state Brotherhood leaders and families of the three groups, the commission began publishing a four-page monthly institutional periodical in Jan., 1972. Named *The Family,* the periodical, edited by Jennings, focused on new developments in Brotherhood, rationale for changes, employee benefits and their comparison with those of other agencies, features on new trustees, staff members, and state Brotherhood leaders, and general achievements of these groups.

Coordination.—Throughout the decade the agency maintained inter-agency relationships through personnel assigned to subcommittees of the Coordinating Committee of the Inter-Agency Council. The agency also accepted assignments from the SBC to work with other agencies through a Missions Education Council to reach the goals of Bold Mission Thrust.

See also DIRECTION '84 COMMITTEE; ROYAL AMBASSADOR CONGRESSES, NATIONAL; WORLD MISSIONS CONFERENCES.

ROY JENNINGS

BROTHERHOOD LEADERSHIP WEEK. Begun in 1978, this special week appears on the SBC denominational calendar the first full week of September each year. Its purpose is to lead churches to prepare their Brotherhood officers to lead Brotherhood units effectively the next 12 months. Activities include training, planning, coordination, and evaluation.

ROY JENNINGS

BROUSSARD, EUGENE (b. Grand Chenier, LA, July 5, 1899; d. Sulphur, LA, July 30, 1956). Pioneer missionary to the French in Louisiana. Son of Tholand and Rhoda Broussard, farmers, he married Mae Lee, Mar. 8, 1921. They had five children: Rosalee, Joyce, Wanda, Wilda Mae, and Gene. Ordained Aug. 20, 1931, by Memorial Church, Port Arthur, TX, he was educated at Acadia Baptist Academy, Eunice, LA. He worked as a Baptist missionary in Cameron Parish for six years before the first conversion was recorded. He established churches in Oak Grove, Grand Chenier, Cameron, Johnson Bayou, and Hackberry. He is buried in Mimosa Pines Cemetery, Sulphur, LA.

ARTHUR D. ROCKETT

BROWN, FRANCES ELIZABETH (b. Cobden, IL, Dec. 5, 1913; d. Cobden, IL, Jan. 15, 1979). Woman's Missionary Union leader. The oldest of 13 children born to Herman and Ruth Brown, farmers, she attended Southern Illinois University (B.S.) and Carver School of Missions at Southern Baptist Theological Seminary (M.R.E.). Following her graduation, she was involved in good will center work in East St. Louis, IL, West Frankfort, KY, and Birmingham, AL.

She was serving as director of education and church secretary at First Baptist Church, Barbourville, KY, when she was asked to become the first WMU director for Michigan Baptists, Nov. 1, 1958. She served in Michigan 20 years. Under her leadership, as the Baptist State Convention of Michigan grew, so did the number of mission organizations. Her career was punctuated with "firsts" as she led the first group of women to Ridgecrest in 1959 and held the first week of girls' camp and the first women's retreat. Over 450 Michigan Southern Baptists celebrated her years of service during the annual meeting in Apr., 1978. The state missions offering received by Michigan Baptists is named in her honor. She is buried in the Cobden, IL, cemetery.

JOYCE MITCHELL

BROWN, HENRY CLIFTON, JR. (b. Bossier City, LA, Sep. 16, 1921; d. Fort Worth, TX, June 10, 1973). Seminary professor of preaching. Son of H. C. Brown, a railroad employee, and Ruby (Yarborough) Brown, he graduated from Louisiana College (B.A., 1946), The Southern Baptist Theological Seminary (Th.M., 1949), and Southwestern Baptist Theological Seminary (Th.D., 1954). On May 25, 1945, he married Dorothy Ruth Ware. They had two children, Mary Kathryn and Clifton Scott. Brown married Velma Lynn Darbo, Nov. 17, 1967, following his first wife's death, Nov. 6, 1966.

During Brown's college days, he was pastor of Mora, LA, Baptist Church, 1943-44; president of the Baptist Student Union council, 1944-46; state BSU president, 1946; and associate pastor of the Pollock, LA, Baptist Church, 1945-46. The Pollock Church ordained him, Aug. 4, 1946. He was pastor of Pigeon Fork Church, Waddy, KY, 1947-49.

In Aug., 1949, he became an instructor of preaching at Southwestern Seminary. He was named professor of preaching in 1954. He wrote, edited, or contributed to 27 books. Prominent among these was his coauthorship of *Steps*

to the Sermon (1963) and his book, *A Quest for Reformation in Preaching* (1968). These books reflected Brown's desire to move preaching away from being labeled as expository, topical, or textual to an organized procedure of following specific steps in developing biblical sermons. Two of his books, *A Search for Strength* (1967) and *Walking Toward Your Fear* (1972), were biographical. The former described his grief experiences at the loss of his first wife. The latter examined how he adjusted to life as a heart patient. He is buried in Forest Park Cemetery, Shreveport, LA.

AL FASOL

BROWN, RAYMOND BRYAN (b. Winnfield, LA, Nov. 16, 1923; d. Raleigh, NC, Dec. 16, 1977). Pastor, educator, and author. Son of George Franklin and Lovie Phenald Brown, he attended Louisiana State University (A.B., 1944), Yale Divinity School (B.D., 1947; S.T.M., 1948), and The Southern Baptist Theological Seminary (Th.D., 1950). He also did postdoctoral study at the University of Tuebingen. Brown married Caralie Nelson, Sep. 2, 1946. They had three children: Bonnie, Raymond, and Helen.

He served as pastor of Beth Car Baptist Church, Halifax, VA, 1950-52, Tabernacle Church, Richmond, VA, 1955-60, and was interim pastor of numerous churches. He taught at the University of Richmond (assistant professor of Bible and religion, 1952-55); Southern Seminary (associate professor of New Testament interpretation, 1960-64); and Southeastern Baptist Theological Seminary (professor of New Testament interpretation, 1964-73; distinguished professor of New Testament interpretation, 1973-77), where he was also academic dean, 1966-74.

Brown served as editor of articles in the biblical area for the *Encyclopedia of Southern Baptists,* Volume III, and was a member of the Historical Commission, SBC, 1956-60, the Association of Baptist Professors of Religion (president, 1971), and the Society of Biblical Literature. His writings include *Professor in the Pulpit* (1963) with W. Morgan Patterson; *A Study of the New Testament* (1965), with Velma Darbo; "1 Corinthians," *Broadman Bible Commentary,* Volume 10 (1970); and *Mark: Savior for Sinners* (1978). He is buried at Richmond, VA.

RICHARD A. SPENCER

BRUCE, HENRY BYRON (b. Kell, IL, Sep. 16, 1925; d. Tempe, AZ, July 7, 1971). Pastor, Navy chaplain, and denominational officer. The son of Alice and H. G. Bruce, farmers, he was ordained by Pleasant Hill Baptist Church, Mt. Vernon, IL, Oct. 17, 1943. He married Doris O. Guffey, of Vandalia, IL, Dec. 20, 1947. They had three sons: Ronald, David, and Mark. Bruce attended Southern Illinois University (B.A., 1947) and Central Baptist Theological Seminary (M.Div., M.R.E., 1954). He served as pastor of churches in Missouri,

Texas, Illinois, and Arizona. He is buried in East Resthaven Cemetery, Phoenix, AZ.

JOE CAUSEY

BRYAN, ANDREW (b. Goose Creek, SC, c. 1722; d. Savannah, GA, Oct., 1812). Early black minister in Georgia. Born to unknown slave parents, he was converted and baptized at Savannah, GA, about 1782 by George Liele, black Baptist minister later active in Jamaica. Beginning to preach within a year after his baptism, Bryan was ordained, Jan. 20, 1788, by Abraham Marshall (*q.v.* II) as he assumed the pastorate of the first black Baptist church in Georgia, located at Savannah. His wife was Hannah, whom he married about 1774.

Bryan bought his freedom at Savannah, May 4, 1789, from a son and heir of his former owner and master, Jonathan Bryan, prominent Georgia Revolutionary War patriot. However, his wife continued a slave to the heirs of his former master.

Bryan and his followers were encouraged by Christian friends, but others abused them. Once in 1800, while baptizing converts, he and the other worshipers were attacked by an armed band. During the 24 years following his ordination, black Baptists in and about Savannah grew from 63 in one church to 2,416 reported by three churches.

W. J. CARSWELL

BRYAN, GAINER E., SR. (b. Riddleville, GA, Apr. 5, 1894; d. Waycross, GA, Oct. 24, 1974). Denominational worker and educator. The son of John Young and Mary Fulghum Bryan, merchants, he graduated from Draughon's Business College, Atlanta (1914), and Mercer University (1928). On Dec. 28, 1915, he married Lila Smith. They had two children, Grace and Gainer E., Jr.

At age 21 Bryan joined the Baptist Young People's Union at Riddleville, attended his first state convention in 1916, and returned home to organize unions in 22 of the 23 churches in Mount Vernon Association by 1918. On Apr. 1, 1922, he began service as Sunday School-B.Y.P.U. worker for Hephzibah Association. Upon his resignation in 1923 to enter Mercer, he was employed to do the same work by the Rehoboth Association from 1923 to 1928. For one year, 1926-27, he was assistant professor in Mercer's School of Religious Education. The Sunday School Department of the Georgia Baptist Convention employed him in 1928, and on Mar. 11, 1938, he became state Training Union secretary.

Under Bryan's direction the Training Union work centered around organizations in every association, one-day regional meetings, a six-day state convention, a one-night simultaneous meeting called "M" Night, major emphasis on rural churches, and development of department staff and volunteer workers.

Bryan received an honorary doctor's degree from Atlanta Law School in 1954 and Mercer

University in 1959. The Georgia Baptist Convention elected him as vice-president in 1964. He served on the Historical Commission, SBC, 1960-66. He retired Dec. 31, 1962, after 24 years as state Training Union secretary.

CHARLES O. WALKER

BRYANT, THERMAN VIRGIL (b. Pontotoc County, MS, Feb. 5, 1913; d. Jackson, MS, July 4, 1977). State convention leader. Son of Bailey and Mattie Bryant, farmers, he was educated at the University of Mississippi (B.A., 1951; M.Ed., 1953). He married Annie Grace McCord, Sep. 21, 1934. They had two sons, Therman Harold and William Bruce. His educational career included teacher, principal, superintendent, and elementary school supervisor in Pontotoc County, teacher at Batesville, MS, and academic dean and assistant to the president of Clarke College, 1956-65. He was listed in *Who's Who in American Education.* Bryant was one of the authors of "An Introduction to Baptist Work," a required course in Mississippi Baptist colleges. From 1960 to 1965, he served as a member of the Mississippi Convention's Board of Ministerial Education.

In 1965 the Mississippi Baptist Convention Board elected Bryant as an associate in the Department of Cooperative Missions, where he served until his death. During his years of employment by the board, he served as director of in-service guidance and world missions conferences, rural church consultant, and interfaith witness consultant. He also directed the Seminary Extension program in Mississippi. He is buried in Bethel Cemetery, Pontotoc County, MS.

EARL KELLY

BRYANT, WADE HAMPTON (b. Easley, SC, Feb. 11, 1898; d. Richmond, VA, Oct. 3, 1970). Pastor and denominational leader. The son of Wade Hampton and Mamie (Robinson) Bryant, he was educated at Clemson College (B.S., 1918) and The Southern Baptist Theological Seminary (Th.M., 1927). Bryant married Lillian Ethel Martins, Sep. 21, 1927. They had no children. He served as pastor of six Baptist churches: Second Highland Park Church, Louisville, KY, 1924-27; Clemson University Church, Clemson, SC, 1927-29; Barton Heights Church, Richmond, VA, 1929-43; University Church, Baltimore, MD, 1943-45; First Church, Roanoke, VA, 1945-61; and Derbyshire Church, Richmond, VA, 1961-67. In retirement he was minister of visitation, Northminster Church, Richmond, VA.

In 1932 at Barton Heights Church, Richmond, he instituted an annual school of missions, a forerunner of the world missions conferences. He then proposed the "Wade Bryant Club Plan" to help remove the staggering debt of the Foreign Mission Board, SBC. The plan called for individuals to pay 25 cents weekly on the debt. Virginia's Woman's Missionary Union promoted the plan, and thousands gave until Virginia donated more than $75,000.

Bryant served as president, Baptist General Association of Virginia, 1951, and as a trustee of the University of Richmond, the FMB, and Southern Seminary. He is buried at Greenville, SC.

FREDERICK J. ANDERSON

BUCKNER BAPTIST BENEVOLENCES (I, III). Buckner Benevolences celebrated its 100th anniversary in 1979. The oldest Southern Baptist agency of its kind, Buckner offers a multiservice program of social care, including resident child care, foster care, in-home mother's aid, maternity care for unwed mothers, adoption, retirement and nursing care for older persons, and family counseling.

Major child-care operations are in Dallas, Lubbock, Beaumont, Burnet, and San Antonio. Group foster homes or emergency shelters for children, cosponsored by local Baptist churches, are located in Tyler, Vernon, San Antonio, Lubbock, Brownsville, Kerrville, Odessa, and Conroe. More than 1,200 children receive care each year in these 24-hour residential programs. Another 620 children receive help through mother's aid and foster care.

A home for unwed mothers operates in San Antonio. Outpatient maternity care is offered in metropolitan areas of the state, and the related services of adoption are centered in Dallas and San Antonio.

Buckner's retirement home in Dallas has been expanded to include retirement cottages and apartments and intermediate and skilled nursing care. Custodial and intermediate nursing care is now provided in Houston and Austin. Buckner serves more than 930 older persons annually.

Buckner's total property value as of Aug. 31, 1979, was $12,592,839. Its operating budget for all units in 1979-80 was $10,200,000. Buckner receives approximately five percent of its budget from the Texas Baptist Cooperative Program. The remainder comes from individuals, churches, private foundations, business and corporate gifts, trusts, bequests, endowment, and resident support.

R. C. CAMPBELL

BUDGET OF THE CONVENTION (I, III). See COOPERATIVE PROGRAM ALLOCATION BUDGET PLANNING.

BUILDERS FOR CHRIST, INC. An organization which serves as an information clearinghouse for organizing volunteer teams of Southern Baptists to help churches in their construction projects. An outgrowth of mission trips sponsored by members of First Baptist Church, Greenwood, LA, it was started in 1963 when 25 members assisted a Colorado church in its building project. In following years, participation quickly expanded to include team workers from other churches and states. By 1979 teams had worked on 126 projects, and the organization's newsletter had a mailing list of 2,650 interested people. The organization became a nonprofit corporation in 1980, with an office in Wascom, TX.

HOWARD MCADAMS

BULDAIN, FELIX (b. Navarra Province, Spain, Dec. 20, 1872; d. Waco, TX, June 5, 1956). Bible scholar and teacher. The son of Javier Ernaut and Silveria Buldain, he was baptized in 1910 by J. E. Davis (*q.v.* I) and worked as redactor of *El Atalaya Bautista.* He married Irene Westrup, Apr. 5, 1912. They had one son, Francisco. After her death, he married Luisa Rodriguez, Apr. 14, 1914. They had four children: Luis, George, Mary, and Martha. A Catholic priest before he became a Baptist, his ministry in Texas was as pastor, director of Spanish Department of Baylor University, Mexican Bible Institute, Bastrop, and editorial work for Baptist Spanish Publishing House, El Paso. He is buried in Memorial Park, Waco, TX.

ERNEST E. ATKINSON

BULLETIN SERVICE, BAPTIST. See BAPTIST BULLETIN SERVICE.

BUNN, BONNIE DAVID (b. Franklin County, NC, June 25, 1892; d. Wilmington, NC, Sep. 15, 1977). College president. Son of David Thomas and Annie (Johnson) Bunn, farmers, he graduated from Wake Forest College (B.A.) and the University of North Carolina (M.A.). Bunn served as principal at Tabor, Lillington, and Apex, NC. He served also as superintendent of schools in Buncombe County and Granville County, NC. Appointed president of Chowan College in 1949, Bunn led in the reopening of the college following World War II. From 1951 until his retirement in 1965, he served as supervisor of Columbus County Schools, NC.

Bunn married Iola Val Finch on Aug. 20, 1920. They had two daughters, Blonnie and Anna Frances. A Mason and Shriner, Bunn served as president of North Carolina Rotary and the state Baptist Brotherhood. He is buried in Maple Springs Cemetery near Louisburg, NC.

BRUCE E. WHITAKER

BURKE, WILLIAM EDMUND (b. Olyphant, PA, Jan. 5, 1904; d. Olyphant, PA, Oct. 6, 1977). Denominational worker. The son of Nellie Burke and John Burke, a contractor, he attended St. Bonaventure College and Seminary (B.A., 1927; M.A., 1929). A former Roman Catholic priest, 1931-41, in 1942 he became a field representative of Christ's Mission, New York City, 1943-50. He and wife, Margaret, were married in 1945. Baptized in 1948 by Calvary Baptist Church, New York City, he was the Catholic information field worker for the Home Mission Board, 1954-61, and assistant secretary, Department of Work Related to Nonevangelicals, 1961-69. He is buried in Sherwood Gardens Cemetery, Jonesboro, GA.

C. B. HASTINGS

BURNETT, JESSE MCGARITY (b. Del Rio, TN, Aug. 29, 1870; d. Greenville, SC, Oct. 30, 1947). Editor, educator, and pastor. The son of Henrietta Cody and J. M. L. Burnett, a Baptist minister, he attended Richmond College (B.A.) and The Southern Baptist Theological Seminary (Th.M.). He married Lucile Phillips, Oct. 6, 1897. They had seven children: Hamilton, Katherine, Dorothy, Margaret, Laura, Jesse M. and Henrietta. Burnett was professor of Greek and philosophy at Carson-Newman College, 1895-1912; president of Carson-Newman College, 1912-17; pastor, First Baptist Church, Belton, SC, 1917-39; and editor of the *Baptist Courier*, 1939-47. He is buried at Belton, SC.

JOHN E. ROBERTS

BURNETT, SIBLEY CURTIS (b. Trimble County, KY, Aug. 25, 1899; d. Nashville, TN, Aug. 21, 1972). Denominational worker. Son of Charles Burnett and Mary (Sibley) Burnett, farmers, he married Anita Vaught on June 26, 1936. They had two children, Sibley and Mary. After graduating from Peabody College (B.S., M.A.) and The Southern Baptist Theological Seminary (Th.G., Th.B.), he served as pastor and college professor at Tennessean College, Murfreesboro, and Union University, Jackson, TN. From 1938 until his retirement in 1967, he was a consultant in Vacation Bible School work at the Sunday School Board, SBC. Author of *Better Vacation Bible Schools* (1957), he is buried in Woodlawn Cemetery, Nashville, TN.

JAMES C. BARRY

BURNEY GIFTS (III). A supplementary $100 gift formerly provided to each Margaret Fund student from interest on the Burney Gift Fund together with contributions from state Woman's Missionary Unions. Larger numbers of students made the funding of this program increasingly difficult, and in 1971-72 the gifts were terminated.

DORIS DEVAULT

BURTON, JOE WRIGHT (b. Miles, TX, Sep. 7, 1907; d. Nashville, TN, May 6, 1976). Denominational leader. Son of William Thomas Burton, farmer, and Martha (Davison) Burton, he married Lula Grace Williams, Sep. 9, 1931. They had three children: Mary Lu, John, and Robert. A graduate of Hardin-Simmons University (B.A., 1929) and Southwestern Baptist

Theological Seminary (Th.M., 1932), he was secretary of education for the Home Mission Board, SBC, 1936-45, and secretary of the Family Life Department of the Sunday School Board, SBC, 1946-66. Before his retirement in 1972, he served as the first editor of *Home Life* magazine for more than 25 years.

The author of books on marriage and family life, Baptist history, and missions, Burton received a citation from Lambda Lambda Lambda for distinguished service to religious journalism in 1947. He was registration and recording secretary of the SBC, 1947-65. He is buried in Woodlawn Cemetery, Nashville, TN.

REUBEN HERRING

BURUNDI, MISSION IN. Baptist work in Burundi was begun in 1928 by Danish Baptists. Half a century later they joined Burundi Baptists in asking Southern Baptists to assist in their ministry. In 1978, following a visit to Burundi, Dale and Nelda (Plank) Gann agreed to transfer from Tanzania to become Southern Baptists' first representatives there. After language study in France, they arrived in Bujumbura early in 1980 to begin studying a second language and to prepare for work in church development and leadership training. Two additional missionary couples, one to work in church development and one in agriculture, were appointed in 1980.

JOY NEAL

BUS EVANGELISM. See EVANGELISM, BUS.

BUZBEE, VIRTUS LOWELL (b. near Vienna, IL, Oct. 12, 1902; d. Jackson, MI, Oct. 21, 1979). Pastor and pioneer in Michigan. Son of Shepherd A. Buzbee, a schoolteacher, and Laura Ellice Buzbee, he attended Union University, Jackson, TN (B.A., 1929) and The Southern Baptist Theological Seminary (Th.M., 1936). He married Sylvia Ella Cochran, Apr. 17, 1929. They had one daughter, Geraldine. After pastorates in Illinois, Kentucky, and Tennessee, Gorham Street Baptist Church, Jackson, MI, called him as pastor, 1936-72. Organized in 1923, the Gorham Street Church affiliated with the Southern Baptist Convention through Franklin Association in Illinois in 1927. The church eventually affiliated with five associations, illustrating the growth of Southern Baptist churches in the western Great Lakes area. Buzbee is buried at Jackson, MI.

CHARLES L. CHANEY

C

CABLE TELEVISION. See TELEVISION, CABLE.

CAGLE, RICHARD H. (b. Courtney Flat, Indian Territory, OK, June 3, 1905; d. Colorado Springs, CO, Oct. 25, 1972). Pastor, area missionary. The son of farming parents, he married Nancy King of New Mexico in 1925. They had two children, Nancy and Richard. He attended Baylor University (B.A.) and Southwestern Baptist Theological Seminary (Th.D.). He served churches in Texas until called to Bellevue Baptist Church, Colorado Springs, CO, in 1955. From June 1, 1956, until July 1, 1970, he served as an area missionary for the newly formed Colorado Baptist General Convention. He is buried in Evergreen Cemetery, Colorado Springs, CO.

WAYNE WILLIAMS

CALDWELL, CLAUDE W. (b. Liberty Hill, LA, Jan. 29, 1902; d. Little Rock, AR, May 24, 1977). State missions and evangelism executive. The sixth of nine children of Andrew Marshall and Mary Frances (Smelley) Caldwell, he graduated from Louisiana College (B.A., 1925) and Southwestern Baptist Theological Seminary (Th.M., 1928). On May 25, 1928, he married Lela Jane Armstrong, who predeceased him, Nov. 14, 1972. They had two children, Carroll Dana and Peggy Jane. On Feb. 5, 1974, he married Ratliff Ludwick Bullard.

Caldwell served as pastor of First Baptist Church, Arcadia, LA, 1928-42, and First Baptist Church, Fordyce, AR, 1942-47. He became superintendent of missions for the Arkansas Baptist State Convention on Feb. 15, 1947, serving in this position until his retirement in 1966. He is buried in Pinecrest Mausoleum, Little Rock, AR.

CARROLL D. CALDWELL

CALIFORNIA, SOUTHERN BAPTIST GENERAL CONVENTION OF (I, III).
I. History. Expansion and growth characterized the 1970s as the convention entered its fourth decade. Twenty years after the 1960 convention had adopted a long-range planning report, the document continued to provide direction for the convention's Executive Board and administrative staff. Following the request by the 1978 convention for an updated version of the document, the 1980 convention received and approved the revised report. For the most part the revised document reflected changes in organizational structure and administrative

procedure adopted by the convention and Executive Board during the prior two decades.

Administrative structure did not change appreciably during the 1970s, with only the title of the executive secretary being changed as executive director Robert D. Hughes completed his 14th year on Dec. 1, 1980. Ralph E. Longshore, as assistant executive director, continued to lead the Missions Division, a post he had held since Sep. 9, 1963. Richard Kay served as assistant executive director in the area of Church Services from Nov. 27, 1961, to May, 1980. He resigned to accept an administrative position at the Sunday School Board, SBC. Glen E. Paden, pastor, First Southern Baptist Church, Sacramento, CA, succeeded Kay in Aug., 1980. David C. Oglesby continued to serve as business manager and as the third member of the management team, a post he had held since Sep. 9, 1963.

In 1977 the convention approved the creation of an Office of Communications and Public Relations to relate directly to the executive director's office. In Apr., 1978, this office was filled with the election of Donald S. Hepburn, an accredited public relations practitioner who came from a similar position at Southwestern Baptist Theological Seminary.

The question of church qualification for affiliation with the convention continued to be debated during the 1970s without a final resolution of the issue. Article III, Section 3, of the convention's constitution had prevented affiliation by churches which practiced open communion or alien immersion. The bylaw was the subject of discussion at nearly every convention in the 1970s, with seven amendments being offered in one year to modify the statement.

In 1978, after 27 years of effort to change the statement, it was amended to read: "The messengers shall be elected and certified by the churches cooperating with this convention." Since the new statement also presented problems, the 1979 convention approved the appointment of a study committee to develop guidelines as to what constituted a cooperating church.

Cooperative Program support continued to grow as the ministry and outreach of the convention grew. In 1973 an attempt to cut the state convention's allocation from 26 to 21 percent to SBC causes in order to increase financial assistance to California Baptist College was defeated. In 1974 California's total Cooperative Program contribution to the SBC exceeded $1,000,000.

In 1969 a convention-approved committee

studied the work of the Cooperative Missions Division and reported 13 recommendations to the 1971 convention. Included were recommendations that the division lead in a renewed emphasis on new work; that the suggestion be made to associations to make annual surveys for places to start new work; that an assistant director of the division be employed; that job descriptions be provided for associational missionaries; and that the Language Missions Department develop a program to assist churches in establishing language work. In response to the committee's recommendations, the convention established the Department of Associational Work and Church Extension in 1974.

In 1974 the convention approved a two-year program, known as "1006 by '76," which sought to increase the number of new churches started. Growth in the number of non-Anglo congregations characterized the decade. By 1980 nearly one third of the convention's 1,169 churches and missions, which had 329,781 members, were ethnic. Among the 30 major ethnic and language groups represented are black, Spanish, Korean, Chinese, Middle Eastern, and Slavic congregations.

The growth in churches and membership resulted in the call for greater representation on the convention's Executive Board. In 1978 the convention increased the board's size from 32 to 40 members.

The total number of churches affiliated with the convention decreased in Jan., 1979, when 34 churches, geographically located in the state of Nevada, chose to affiliate with the newly organized Nevada Baptist Convention.

As the SBC developed its Bold Mission Thrust, the state convention began a program in 1976 called "The California Challenge." At the heart of the endeavor were four objectives: (1) present the claims of Christ to every person in California by the year 2000; (2) establish a Southern Baptist witness in every city; (3) increase the number of churches to 2,000; and (4) increase the total membership to 750,000. To facilitate the objectives, a series of goals were developed and tied into the program services by the convention's departments of work.

On Nov. 11-12, 1980, the state convention met in Bakersfield to observe its 40th anniversary. A record 1,362 messengers attended.

II. Program of Work. The Sunday School Department, since Jan. 1, 1981, has been directed by Jerry L. Harris, a former Sunday School promotion specialist with the Foreign Mission Board. He succeeded R. L. (Pat) Patillo, Jr., who had served as department director 1959-80. Jacob Gurley, a graduate of Carson-Newman College and Golden Gate Baptist Theological Seminary, was elected as Sunday School associate in 1975, succeeding Walt G. Crabtree, who served as associate, 1969-74. In 1975 the convention's Executive Board authorized a second full-time associate position and elected Concepcion Padilla. A Spanish-speaking minister, Padilla became the first ethnic to be

employed in a department of the Church Services Division. He served until Sep. 1, 1980, when he accepted a position with the Sunday School Board, SBC.

The Church Training Department is led by Valton Prince, who has served since 1964. Darrell Adcock was elected associate in 1974, succeeding Jerry Brumbelow, who resigned to join the staff of Magnolia Avenue Baptist Church, Riverside, CA.

The Brotherhood and Church Music Departments were combined on Jan. 1, 1969, under the direction of Duane Barrett. At its Sep., 1975, meeting, the Executive Board separated the responsibilities of the two departments and changed the name of the Brotherhood Department to Men's Ministries. Edd L. Brown, a graduate of Hardin Simmons University and Southwestern Baptist Theological Seminary and area missionary for nine years, was elected director of the Men's Ministries Department.

The Stewardship Education and Promotion Department is under the direction of Ronald E. Chandler, who assumed his duties, July 1, 1974, succeeding William H. Bell who had resigned in Oct., 1973, to take a Home Mission Board appointment as pastoral missionary to the First Baptist Church of Cucamonga, CA. Bell, elected in 1971, had followed James Graves, who had served as director of the department from its beginning until his resignation, May 31, 1971.

The Department of Evangelism is led by Harry D. Williams, who was elected to that post in 1969. Monty McWhorter, pastor of the First Southern Baptist Church, Santa Paula, CA, was elected to serve as evangelism associate in 1979. McWhorter succeeded Robert D. Lewis, who was employed as evangelism intern, 1975-77, under a pilot program with the HMB. Lewis was elected evangelism associate, Jan. 1, 1978, and served until October of that year, when he resigned to become pastor of the First Southern Baptist Church, Lodi, CA.

In Sep., 1969, Wendell J. Foss, an associate in the Sunday School Department, was elected director of the Student Work Department. By the end of 1979, under the direction of Foss, the Student Work Department employed four full-time Baptist Student Union directors and six part-time directors.

The Language Missions Department is directed by Lonnie S. Chavez, who was elected effective May 1, 1980. He replaced E. Jack Combs, who served as director, 1955-79. When elected, Chavez was a catalytic missionary for the San Diego and Trinity (CA) Baptist Associations. Chavez directs the work of five general language missionaries who provide special assistance to local churches and associations in ministering to over 40 different language groups.

The Church Music Department is directed by John McGuckin, who assumed the post, Nov., 1979. McGuckin succeeded Duane Barrett, who had held the dual directorship of Church Music and Brotherhood from 1969 to 1974 when the

Church Music Department was made a full-time department. Barrett directed the Church Music Department until he resigned in 1979.

The Department of Black Church Ministries, under the direction of Jack O'Neal, 1960-80, underwent two name changes. First known as the Department of Work with National Baptists, its name was then changed to Department of Cooperative Ministries with National Baptists in 1975. In Jan., 1979, the name was changed to Department of Black Church Ministries.

Currently, 120 black Baptist churches are affiliated with the state convention. Willie T. McPherson, a Southern Baptist black church consultant in Long Beach, CA, was elected director effective May 1, 1980, thus becoming the first black to direct a Southern Baptist state convention's work with National Baptists.

Filling a vacancy which had existed for 19 months, Dixie L. Hunke became director of the Woman's Missionary Union Department, Jan. 1, 1981. She had previously served as a California-based single adult ministry consultant for the HMB. Hunke succeeded Louise Scott, who served between 1975 and May, 1979, when she resigned to take an editorial position at the SSB. Scott succeeded Bernice Popham, a graduate of Georgetown College and Carver School of Missions, Louisville, KY, who served, 1972-74, following the retirement of Eula Stotts in Dec., 1971.

During the 1960s and early 1970s the HMB provided funds to develop several Christian social ministries programs under the convention's Cooperative Missions Division. The funding provided specialized ministries in the inner-city areas of San Francisco, Oakland, and Watts-Compton (Los Angeles); to military personnel on Coronado Island (San Diego); and to migrant farm laborers.

With the merging of the Child Care Board under the auspices of the Executive Board, a Department of Christian Social Ministries was established in Jan., 1972. Robert A. Williams, who had been executive director of the Child Care Board, was elected director of the new CSM department. L. G. Chaddick was made an associate in the department and worked out of a Los Angeles office. The existing inner city mission and service centers were incorporated into the CSM departments.

Expansion of CSM services continued in 1977 with the establishment of a ministry center in San Jose. In 1979 a ministry at the Olympic Training Center at Squaw Valley and a state-wide single adult ministry were added.

The Associational Work and Church Extension Department was implemented, Nov., 1974, and is directed by Donald F. Venosdel, a former director of missions and California pastor. Venosdel succeeded William Bell, who resigned May, 1977, to become pastor of the First Southern Baptist Church, Fountain Valley, CA.

DONALD S. HEPBURN and CARLA D. ANDRUS

CALIFORNIA STATISTICAL SUMMARY

Year	Associations	Churches	Church Membership	Baptisms	SS Enrollment	VBS Enrollment	CT Enrollment	WMU Enrollment	Brotherhood Enrollment	Ch. Music Enrollment	Mission Gifts	Total Gifts	Value Church Property
1969	36	857	243,488	11,256	168,172	110,591	80,471	22,585	8,212	18,891	$2,168,903	$18,788,000	$104,093,884
1970	35	861	253,016	11,891	163,504	82,473	66,357	19,455	7,021	19,592	2,319,618	20,104,035	106,080,252
1971	34	873	258,530	13,820	156,870	82,949	51,716	17,514	7,049	20,743	2,721,727	21,523,507	109,336,749
1972	34	890	267,745	14,747	156,545	82,221	46,808	17,204	7,034	22,604	2,757,815	23,133,920	115,148,623
1973	35	903	279,734	14,155	155,263	83,513	44,156	17,373	7,178	23,575	3,318,636	23,797,746	126,121,795
1974	35	904	289,492	14,526	157,529	77,551	41,486	17,340	6,932	25,575	3,600,015	26,519,326	142,525,153
1975	35	919	299,844	14,976	160,957	78,478	40,458	18,479	7,559	26,930	4,097,784	29,993,460	155,754,797
1976	34	931	306,439	14,382	168,419	72,341	39,145	17,502	7,959	27,113	4,361,251	32,633,377	178,598,422
1977	34	941	315,625	13,679	169,226	69,441	37,432	17,572	8,360	27,092	5,608,558	36,647,204	205,424,127
1978	35	951	319,210	13,523	167,553	72,167	39,102	17,366	7,776	29,836	5,792,417	41,105,763	234,345,628
1979**	34	931	323,964	14,824	163,434	71,171	36,700	18,499	7,666	30,040	6,620,983	46,170,405	269,485,857
1980	32	956	338,818	16,134	169,954	67,005	37,699	18,861	9,154	32,627	7,148,332	50,118,484	314,202,599

**The 1979 decrease reflects the 34 churches which joined with the Nevada Area Baptist Convention.

DONALD S. HEPBURN

CALIFORNIA ASSOCIATIONS (I, III).

I. New Associations. ASOCIACION BAUTISTA. Organized Feb. 27, 1979, consisting of nine Spanish-speaking Southern Baptist churches and missions in the Los Angeles area. Statistical data from the churches was not available.

CENTRAL COAST. Organized Apr. 22, 1980, in Watsonville, CA, by the merger of the Monterey and Santa Cruz Associations. In 1980, 24 churches reported 351 baptisms, 7,490 members, $843,161 total gifts, $132,534 mission gifts, and $598,200 property value.

TAHOE. Organized Jan. 1, 1978, at Tahoe City, CA, by two California churches and a mission, which had been a part of the former Nevada Association, when they elected not to go into the new Nevada Baptist Convention. In 1980 two churches and two missions reported 9 baptisms, 196 members, $116,766 total gifts, $2,437 mission gifts, and $585,000 property value.

II. Changes in Associations. LIVERMORE-AMADOR VALLEY. Organized in 1968, the association disbanded in 1971. Some of its churches affiliated with the East Contra Costa Association while others affiliated with the East Bay Association.

MONTEREY. Merged with Santa Cruz, Apr. 22, 1980, forming Central Coast.

MT. DIABLO. Organized in 1953 as East Contra Costa Association, the name was changed in 1979.

NEVADA. With the formation of the Nevada Baptist Convention, the churches in this association discontinued their ties with the California Convention, Jan. 1, 1979, to become affiliated with the new Nevada Convention.

ORANGE COAST. Organized in 1973 with five churches and two missions coming out of Orange County Association. It existed for about three years and disbanded.

SANTA CRUZ. Merged with Monterey, Apr. 22, 1980, forming Central Coast.

YOKAYO. Changed its name to the Mendo-Lake Association at the annual meeting held Oct. 14-15, 1977. At the time of the name change, the association had 14 churches and missions.

DONALD F. VENOSDEL

CALIFORNIA BAPTIST COLLEGE (I, III). In the summer of 1970, James R. Staples, editor of the *Baptist Beacon*, the state paper of Arizona Southern Baptists, was elected president of California Baptist College, succeeding Loyed R. Simmons. Staples had served 20 years in Arizona as pastor, college administrator, and editor. Under his leadership the campus physical plant has been extensively developed: the construction of the Wallace Book of Life Building, containing an auditorium (Little Theatre) and classrooms; the renovation of the W. E. James classroom and office building; completion of a new maintenance facility and two 24-unit apartment complexes; remodeling of three wings of the Annie Gabriel Library; and the improvement of campus landscaping. Plans for a new student activities center have been approved.

The college offered 17 majors leading to bachelor's degrees in 1980. The library, with holdings of 97,000 volumes, includes a media center, replete with color videotaping equipment.

Enrollment climbed to a high of 822 in 1976 and leveled off at 750 in 1977-80. Eighty percent of the students come from California with representatives from most of the 50 states and about 20 foreign countries. A high percentage of students have an interest in Christian ministry.

The administrative team serving with President Staples in 1980 were Stephen P. Carleton, executive vice-president and academic dean, who has served on the faculty since 1967; Patrick McGrew, vice-president for business affairs since 1970; and H. Keith King, dean of student affairs since 1977. J. L. Harden, who served as vice-president for development until his retirement in 1979, previously served as business manager, 1957-70.

The campus in 1980 was valued at $15,000,000 with an indebtedness of $2,117,464. The proposed 1980-81 budget was $3,952,670.

Two programs are unique to California Baptist College. In 1976 the college founded a Chair of Discipleship, the first in the nation and perhaps in the world. An academic minor was developed with courses covering the disciplines of Christian growth: Bible study, prayer, witnessing, and disciple-making. Jimmy L. Frost served as the first professor in the program and built the curriculum as well as an annual conference featuring speakers from across the nation.

A second unique program is the Book of Life Collection assembled by the late L. E. Nelson. This collection of books and artifacts illustrates the impact of the Bible on Western civilization. Displays appear on a rotating basis in the Wallace Book of Life Building, the most-used facility on the campus.

STEPHEN P. CARLETON

CALIFORNIA BAPTIST FOUNDATION (cf. California, Southern Baptist Foundation of, Vol. I; California, Baptist Foundation of, Vol. III). Cecil J. Pearson, executive secretary of the foundation, reported $1,386,002 in endowment and trust funds in 1970.

R. Bates Ivey, assistant executive secretary, designed and instituted a new debenture program in 1975. This program accelerated the issue of debentures with all issues together reaching $18,000,000 by 1979. The debenture business was made an auxiliary enterprise of the foundation under the name, California Plan of Church Finance. B. LaVern Lewis helped Ivey administer the California Plan of Church Finance, 1975-78.

In 1975 the California Foundation reported $2,500,000 in its endowment and trust funds. By the end of Pearson's 10th year as director in 1976, the foundation had operated 10 years without a deficit. In 1979 the combined total in the foundation's three funds (trust, endowment, and current) was more than $6,500,000.

As Pearson and Ivey looked toward retirement, two people were elected assistant directors in 1979. The idea was to train these new staff members under Ivey and Pearson's leadership. In Apr., 1979, Dennis M. Schmierer was elected assistant director to be associated with Ivey. He had worked for 12 years in financial management and accounting. He attended California Baptist College and graduated from the University of San Francisco. In Aug., 1979, Dan H. Coker was elected assistant director to be associated with Pearson. A graduate of Golden Gate Baptist Theological Seminary, he had served in California 11 years as a pastor and director of missions.

In its management of funds, the foundation assists churches and missions through loans and gifts. Loans to churches amount to about $500,000 a year, with many on an emergency basis. From some of its funds the foundation receives income directed by the original donors to mission ventures. Gifts from this income go to churches, missions, evangelistic campaigns, and student work.

ELMER L. GRAY

CALIFORNIA SOUTHERN BAPTIST, THE (I, III). J. Terry Young, editor since 1963, resigned in 1971 to join the faculty of New Orleans Baptist Theological Seminary. Donald T. McGregor, who had been on the Texas *Baptist Standard* staff for 15 years, was elected editor in Sep., 1971. McGregor resigned in Sep., 1973, and soon became associate editor of the Mississippi *Baptist Record*. Elmer L. Gray, who had been pastor of three California churches, manager of the Sunday School Department of the Sunday School Board, and academic dean of Golden Gate Baptist Theological Seminary, became editor in Mar., 1974. Polly A. McNabb, associate editor, completed 30 years of service with the paper in 1979. The 1980 circulation was about 28,000.

ELMER L. GRAY

CALIFORNIA SOUTHERN BAPTIST CHILD CARE AND FAMILY SERVICES (III). By 1968, the Child Care Board's role had begun to change from primarily child care services to an agency providing referrals to public assistance agencies and direct personal, family, and crisis/stress counseling. The restraints of financial resources made it increasingly difficult for the Child Care Board to expand its ministry and services. Action by the state convention in 1968 limited the board from conducting fundraising activities apart from the Convention's unified giving effort, the Cooperative Program. In addition, Robert A. Williams, executive director of the Child Care Board, and other convention leaders, began to express concern over the increasing duplication of services being offered by the board and the convention's programs of Christian social ministries.

In June, 1971, upon the recommendation of Williams, the Child Care Board took official action to recommend to the convention that the responsibility of the Child Care Board be transferred to the Executive Board. It also requested that family services and child care programs be merged with the Christian social ministries work of the Cooperative Missions Division. The convention approved the recommendation, and on Dec. 10, 1971, the Child Care Board voted the dissolution and liquidation of the board at the close of business, Dec. 31, 1971, with all assets transferred to the Executive Board. The Executive Board in Jan., 1972, officially designated Christian Social Ministries as a full department of the Cooperative Missions Division, and Robert A. Williams was elected director.

DONALD S. HEPBURN

CALIFORNIA SOUTHERN BAPTIST STATE ASSEMBLY (I, III). In the 1970s, lack of funds continued to hamper the development of Jenness Park, located in the High Sierras of central California. However, the summer youth assemblies gained in popularity with increased programming help from the state convention's Church Training Department. The park was widely used by churches and associations during winter months for weekend snow retreats with over 33,000 persons using the park between 1968 and 1978. In 1979 over 4,200 persons registered in retreats and camps.

In 1977 the state convention's executive board authorized the administrative staff to undertake a study of the long-range development of Jenness Park. The staff developed a use plan projecting through the rest of this century. The master plan was adopted in 1979. John R. Lindsey became resident camp manager on Oct. 15, 1979, following the retirement of Joe January, who had served since 1970.

DAVID C. OGLESBY

CAMP CARSON AND CAMP LINDEN (III; cf. Camp Carson, Vol. I; cf. Camp Linden, Vol. I). Departments of the Tennessee Baptist Convention use the camps during the summer to promote their work. Both camps, each of which can accommodate 330 in summer and 250 in winter, are winterized and available for church use on weekends throughout the year. The camp program receives $30,000 from the state mission budget in addition to $200,000 income for operation. Capital funds for equipment and improvements total approximately $250,000 each year. Attendance for 1978-79 totaled 9,370.

JAMES M. MCDONALD

CAMP HUDGENS (III). New facilities erected for this Royal Ambassador camp for Oklahoma have included a director's residence, 1970; water storage, boat house, shop, Pennington Lodge, 1973; and Unit Lodge III, 1980. A total of 15,841 persons have registered since the camp opened in 1960, including 734 in 1979.

The estimated value of grounds and facilities exceeds $500,000. The 1980 budget was $92,000. Paul McCullough has been director since Mar. 1, 1974.

PAUL MCCULLOUGH

CAMP LINDEN (I). See CAMP CARSON AND CAMP LINDEN.

CAMP NUNNY-CHA-HA, OKLA-HOMA. Founded in 1956 on the Falls Creek Assembly grounds, this camp for girls was named for the Choctaw Indian church near McAlester, OK, where organized Baptist women's work in Oklahoma began in 1876. The name means "high hill." Margaret Hutchison (*q.v.* III) led in founding the camp. Under the auspices of Oklahoma's Woman's Missionary Union, six camps for Girls in Action and Acteens were held in 1979, with 667 persons registered. Campers for the years 1956-79 totaled 24,196. The capital value of 16 cabins, a tabernacle, dining hall, and administration building in 1979 was $241,452.

J. M. GASKIN

CAMP PARON (III). See ARKANSAS BAPTIST ASSEMBLY AND CAMPS.

CAMPBELL, ARTHUR CARLYLE (b. Buies Creek, NC, Nov. 28, 1894; d. Raleigh, NC, July 27, 1977). Educator and college president. He was the son of James Archibald Campbell (*q.v.* I) and Cornelia Pearson Campbell. He married Marian Lee Newman, July 21, 1925. Their children were Carlyle, Jr., and Virginia.

Educated at Wake Forest College (A.B., 1911; A.M., 1916) and Columbia University, Campbell taught at Buies Creek Academy early in his career. He chaired the English department of Coker College, Hartsville, SC, 1923-25, where he served as president, 1925-27. He served North Carolina State College in Raleigh as president, 1927-39. Although postdepression and war years clouded his administration as president of Meredith College, where he became president in 1939, the campus had grown by seven buildings and the enrollment by 73 percent when Campbell retired in 1966. He is buried in Buies Creek Cemetery, Buies Creek, NC.

CAROLYN C. ROBINSON

CAMPBELL, LESLIE HARTWELL (b. Buies Creek, NC, Apr. 3, 1892; d. Raleigh, NC, Nov. 25, 1970). Educator and college president. Son of James A. (*q.v.*) and Cornelia Pearson Campbell, he was a graduate of Wake Forest College (A.B., 1911; M.A., 1916). He married Viola Haire in 1914. They had one son, A. Hartwell. In 1925, after his first wife's death, he married Ora Green. Their four children were Catherine, Elizabeth, Ora, and James A. Campbell, II. He served 17 years as associational moderator, also serving one term

as vice-president of the Baptist State Convention of North Carolina in 1940.

Preferring English and Latin, Campbell taught several subjects at Buies Creek Academy, beginning in 1911. He became dean when the academy moved to college status in 1926. He was president of Campbell College from 1934 to 1967, succeeding his father, J. A. Campbell, who founded the school. Under his presidency, the school achieved senior college accreditation in 1966. He is buried in Buies Creek Cemetery, Buies Creek, NC.

PHILIP KENNEDY

CAMPBELL UNIVERSITY (cf. Campbell College, Vols. I, III). The institution became a university in 1979, offering study in 30 major areas for six undergraduate degrees, and graduate degrees in law, education, and business administration. One of America's few undergraduate programs in trust management was established in 1968. Campbell participates in men's NCAA Division I and women's NAIW athletics. The law school, founded in 1976, is accredited by the North Carolina Bar and was provisionally accredited in 1979 by the American Bar Association. For 1979-80, student enrollment exceeded 2,700. Alumni number 15,000. The main campus is located in Buies Creek, with auxiliary campuses in Sanford, NC, and Fort Bragg, NC. Norman Adrian Wiggins has been president since 1967.

BIBLIOGRAPHY: J. Winston Pearce, *Campbell College; Big Miracle at Little Buies Creek* (1976).

MARK R. VAN SCIVER

CAMPBELLSVILLE COLLEGE (I, III). Enrolling about 800 students, this senior, coeducational, liberal arts college offers 35 liberal arts, professional, and preprofessional areas of study, maintains a teacher-student ratio of 1 to 15, and a library with 99,000 volumes. Students represent 20 denominations, but 75 percent are Baptist. They come from 25 states and several countries, but 75 percent are from Kentucky. Approximately one-third are preparing for church-related vocations. A 75th anniversary celebration planned for 1981 included a $2,000,000 financial campaign. In 1981 property was worth $6,000,000, endowment was $750,000, and the annual budget was $3,000,000.

William Randolph Davenport, president since Aug., 1969, has led the college to emphasize strong Christian values, closer church relations, upgrading of faculty and academic programs, stabilizing the enrollment, and improved financial management.

WILLIAM RANDOLPH DAVENPORT

CAMPERS ON MISSION. A fellowship of Christian campers who desire to share their faith. The movement, whose direction is determined by the commitment of its members, began in 1970. There are no membership fees, and Christian campers from many denominations participate. The Special Mission Ministries Department of the Home Mission Board, SBC, promotes this work. In 1979 about 11,500 persons were members, most of whom were Southern Baptists.

R. DONALD HAMMONDS

CANADIAN BAPTIST OVERSEAS MISSION BOARD (cf. Canadian Baptist Foreign Mission Board, Vol. I). The Canadian Baptist Foreign Mission Board was renamed the Canadian Baptist Overseas Mission Board in 1970. It is the mission arm of four Canadian conventions within the Baptist Federation of Canada—the Baptist Union of Western Canada; the Baptist Convention of Ontario and Quebec; l'Union d'Eglises Baptistes Francaises au Canada (French Baptist Union); and the United Baptist Convention of the Atlantic Provinces.

Canadian Baptists entered the 1980s with 107 missionaries serving in India, Bolivia, Zaire, Kenya, Indonesia, Brazil, and Liberia. Personnel are prepared for Angola when permission to reenter is given. Types of ministry include agricultural assistance, church planting, theological education, and medicine. *The Enterprise,* a quarterly publication, gives current information about mission activities and missionaries. Headquarters are in Toronto, Ontario, Canada.

WILLIAM H. JONES

CANADIAN BAPTIST THEOLOGICAL COLLEGE. This school was founded in 1972 at Saskatoon, Saskatchewan, Canada, as the Christian Training Centre. A ministry of Faith Baptist Church, Saskatoon, "for the training of Christian leadership to minister across Canada and the world," it has attracted students from Canada and the United States, offering diplomas in Bible, religious education, and theology. Henry T. Blackaby, pastor of Faith Church, served as president until Glen Allen assumed the role in Jan., 1980. Allen served until Jan., 1981. In 1979-80 the college had 40 students and eight faculty members.

HENRY BLACKABY

CANADIAN BAPTISTS. Baptists in Canada have lived under strong American influences from the beginnings in the 1760s to the present. however, the large influx of immigrants from the British Isles and Europe modified the southward orientation and led to striking diversity in beliefs and practices among Canadian Baptists.

I. Historical Development. The two oldest congregations were planted by Baptist pastors from Massachusetts in the Atlantic region: in Sackville, New Brunswick, 1763, and in Horton (now Wolfville), Nova Scotia, 1765-66. Following the departure of their leaders, both churches ceased to exist but were reconstituted before the end of the century. The Wolfville Church, reorganized in 1778, is the oldest continuing Baptist church in Canada.

The Great Awakening during the 1770s and 1780s and recurrent revivals in the 1800s produced rapid growth. In several counties of New Brunswick and Nova Scotia, Baptists became the largest Protestant denomination, with nearly half of the population reporting nominal Baptist affiliation for census purposes as recently as 1971.

The majority of Baptist churches adhered to the Regular (Calvinist) position while a minority followed the Free Will (Arminian) orientation. The two streams merged to form the United Baptist Convention of the Maritime Provinces (i.e., New Brunswick, Nova Scotia, and Prince Edward Island) in 1906. In 1963 the word *Maritime* was replaced by *Atlantic* so as to include Newfoundland, the youngest Canadian province (since 1949). Baptist work began there only in 1954 in cooperation with Southern and American Baptists stationed at bases of United States armed forces. The Atlantic area is the only region of Canada where, up to now, Baptists have avoided organizational schism.

In the two central provinces of Ontario and Quebec, known as Upper and Lower Canada prior to 1867, Baptist witness was initiated by ministers and missionaries from Vermont and New York in the 1790s. Before long, the Regular Baptists, with their roots in the USA and their emphasis on closed communion, encountered open communion views espoused by Baptist immigrants from England. The protracted communion controversy hindered effective cooperation in education and missions for most of the 1800s.

In addition to the conflicting American and English influences, immigrants from Scotland who established Baptist churches between Ottawa and Montreal from 1815 onward brought to Ontario a strong revivalistic tradition, which was later modified by concern for higher education. French-speaking immigrants from Switzerland arrived in Quebec in the 1830s and under the leadership of Henriette Feller (1800-68) launched work among French Canadians, to be known as the Grande Ligne Mission. Later, the French churches formed an association within the Baptist Convention of Ontario and Quebec. In 1969 the French Association was replaced by the Union of French Baptist Churches in Canada, affiliated with the Baptist Federation of Canada.

From the 1820s onward, several thousand blacks from the southern USA reached Ontario by escape routes known as "the underground railway." In several towns and cities, including Toronto (1826), they established the first Baptist churches. They formed their own Amherstburg Association (1841), which later joined the convention. A similar development occurred among the black Baptists of the African Association in the Atlantic region.

Since the 1850s, the Baptist mosaic in Ontario has been fragmented further by the influx of immigrants from many European countries. The oldest German Baptist churches were organized in the 1850s, followed by Swedish churches in the 1880s. In the 1900s, Baptists in Ontario and Quebec have proclaimed the gospel in at least 30 languages. In the 1970s, the Chinese Baptist churches grew faster than any other Baptist congregations in Canada.

Cooperation in associations led eventually to the formation of The Regular Baptist Missionary Convention of Canada, West (i.e., Southwestern Ontario) in 1851 and The Canada Baptist Missionary Convention, East (i.e., Eastern Ontario and Quebec) in 1858. In 1889 the two were replaced by the Baptist Convention of Ontario and Quebec (BCOQ).

The fundamentalist-modernist controversy in the mid-1920s resulted in a major division within the convention. About one-seventh of the churches (70 out of 490, with 8,500 out of 60,000 members) left the convention. Several rival organizations were formed by the dissident churches.

The Baptist witness spread to Western Canada from Ontario and from Oregon and Washington. Commissioned by the Baptists of Ontario, Alexander McDonald (1837-1911) went to Winnipeg in 1873 and established the First Baptist Church there in 1875. With new churches planted in the other two prairie provinces, Saskatchewan and Alberta (known as the Northwest Territories prior to 1905), the Baptist Convention of Manitoba and the Northwest Territories was organized in 1884.

On the Pacific coast, the First Baptist Church in Victoria was established in 1876 through the combined efforts of lay-people, a pastor from Ontario, and the Baptist Convention of Oregon and Washington, which provided a salary grant. The First Baptist Church in Vancouver was founded in 1887, and the Convention of Baptist Churches in British Columbia was formed in 1897.

In 1907 the churches in the four western provinces joined in The Baptist Convention of Western Canada. Two years later, it was renamed The Baptist Union of Western Canada to indicate a degree of autonomy enjoyed by each provincial organization within the Union, and in particular by the convention of British Columbia.

The pioneering spirit which permeates the Western Canadian culture and the influence of many nondenominational Bible schools strengthened the trend to independent Baptist churches and contributed to divisions within existing bodies. Baptist life in Western Canada has greater organizational diversity than anywhere else in the country.

II. Baptist Bodies in Canada. 1. *The Baptist Federation of Canada (BFC).*—The BFC, the largest national body representing about two-thirds of all Baptists in Canada, was formed in 1944 as a federation of the three historic regional conventions and unions: The United Baptist Convention of the Atlantic Provinces, The Baptist Convention of Ontario and Quebec, and The Baptist Union of Western Canada. The Union of the French Baptist Churches in Canada joined the BFC in 1970. The consti-

tution provides for affiliation by other national or regional bodies.

The regional conventions administer most of the regular denominational work, such as evangelism, Christian education, church extension, stewardship, and missions. The limited responsibilities of the BFC include the following:

1. So far as may be possible to express the common judgement of the constituent churches and organizations on matters of national, international, and interdenominational importance.
2. To afford opportunities for consultation, study, and united policy-making and action . . . including home missions, overseas missions, education, ministerial training and credentials, superannuation, social service, evangelism, Sunday School and Young People's work, the publication of religious literature, and any other matters of common interest and urgency. . . .
3. To speak for Canadian Baptists in the Baptist World Alliance and in other contacts with Baptists abroad.

Between triennial assemblies, a council, made up of elected and ex officio representatives of the four constituent bodies, carries on the work. The major recent BFC projects include the production of a hymnal (1973) and a massive program of global relief and development.

While the population of Canada grew from 14,000,000 in 1951 to 24,000,000 in 1980, the total membership of churches affiliated with the BFC declined during the same period. The 1980 statistics (including nonresident members) were as follows: The Atlantic Convention, 570 churches with 61,130 members; The Convention of Ontario and Quebec, 380 churches with 46,340 members; The Union of Western Canada, 150 churches with 19,200 members; and The French Union, 15 churches with 600 members. Totals for the BFC include 1,115 churches with 127,270 members.

Since 1912, the churches now affiliated with the BFC have cooperated in their overseas missionary work through the Canadian Baptist Foreign Mission Board, renamed the Canadian Baptist Overseas Mission Board (CBOMB) in 1970. In 1980 the board was assisting indigenous churches in seven countries (Angola, Bolivia, Brazil, India, Indonesia, Kenya, and Zaire) and supporting 115 Canadian missionaries. The projected target was 135 missionaries by 1983.

Substantial support for missionary work at home and abroad has been provided through the years by members of the Baptist Women's Missionary Societies, with "mission circles" organized in most local churches. A national coordinating committee, the Dominion Committee of the Affiliated Women's Missionary Societies, was formed in 1935.

2. *The Fellowship of Evangelical Baptist Churches in Canada (FEBC).*—The second largest Baptist body in Canada, FEBC, dates back to a merger in 1953 between the Union of Regular Baptists (organized in Ontario in 1927 by churches which had left the BCOQ during the fundamentalist-modernist controversy) and the Fel-

lowship of Independent Baptist Churches in Ontario (a rival group formed in 1933).

In 1965 the corresponding bodies in Western Canada, the Convention of Regular Baptists of British Columbia (formed in 1927), and the Prairie Regular Baptist Missionary Fellowship (formed in 1930) joined the FEBC after lengthy and often frustrating negotiations. The FEBC as a national body lacks constitutional and geographical balance comparable to that within the BFC.

Of the 405 churches reported as affiliated with the FEBC in 1979, 295 (including 48 French-speaking congregations) were located in Ontario and Quebec. Of the remaining 110 congregations, 66 were in British Columbia, 30 in the three prairie provinces, and 14 in the four Atlantic provinces. Among the 405 churches, 50 were classified as "not officially received into the Fellowship." The level of affiliation varied from one part of the country to the other. The churches in the Atlantic and Central provinces, as well as those in Manitoba and Saskatchewan, were "under direct supervision" of the national office in Toronto. The affiliated Convention of Regular Baptists of British Columbia retained its own administration while the churches in Alberta worked "under a partially functioning (constitutionally undefined) regional set-up."

Estimate of total membership released by the FEBC office in 1979 stood at 46,950. The total submitted by 239 reporting churches was 27,200.

3. *North American Baptist Conference (NABC).*—The first German-speaking Baptist church in Canada was organized in Bridgeport, Ontario, in 1851 as a result of missionary work by August Rauschenbusch, father of the well-known theologian Walter Rauschenbusch (*q.v.* II). With increasing immigration, German congregations were planted in Ontario and later in the prairies. In the early years the German churches received support from and were affiliated with Canadian Baptists. However, tension over several issues in the 1920s led to a unilateral alignment with the North American Baptists in the USA.

Caught in the problems of transition from the German language to English, the NABC churches appear to have made fruitful outreach among Canadians, regardless of their ethnic origin. Ninety churches affiliated with the NABC in the western provinces reported a total membership of about 13,000 in 1980 while 15 congregations in Ontario had a combined membership of nearly 2,000.

4. *Baptist General Conference (BGC).*—The earliest Baptist witness in the Swedish language was recorded in the town of Waterville, Quebec, in 1885. A small Swedish church was organized there in 1892. However, the main thrust developed in Western Canada, beginning with Winnipeg where the First Scandinavian Church was established in 1894. By 1930 there were 23 churches with a total membership of 929. After half a century of cooperation with the Baptist Union of Western Canada, the Swedish

churches decided in 1948 to affiliate exclusively with the BGC in the USA. In 1980 the churches affiliated with the BGC were all English-speaking and belonged to one of the three regional conferences, with the following estimated memberships: The Central Canada Baptist Conference (Ontario, Manitoba, and Saskatchewan), 45 churches with 2,500 members; The Baptist General Conference of Alberta, 20 churches with 1,000 members; The Columbia Baptist Conference (British Columbia and the Northwest in the USA), 20 churches with 3,000 members (in Canada). The estimated total is 85 churches with 6,500 members.

5. *Canadian Southern Baptists.*—Since 1953, a number of Baptist churches in Western Canada have sought affiliation with the Baptist General Convention of Oregon-Washington (SBC), now the Northwest Baptist Convention. Although precedents for such links with Baptist bodies in the USA had been set by churches affiliated with the NABC and the BGC, the Southern Baptist "invasion" into Canadian territory was viewed with concern by the BFC. A special Committee on Canadian Baptist Cooperation appointed by the Executive Committee of the SBC and by the BFC met regularly between 1957 and 1968 to discuss areas of possible tension. Since 1969 its functions have been assigned to SBC and BFC representatives in the North American Baptist Fellowship.

While the BFC churches, on the whole, have welcomed the assistance and leadership provided by SBC agencies and their staff to Canadian Baptists in such fields as evangelism, leadership training, and Sunday School literature, uneasiness about the spread of SBC affiliated churches in Canada has not diminished.

In 1978 the Canadian Baptist Conference, associated with the Northwest Baptist Convention, SBC, reported 32 churches with 2,600 members. In 1979 Southern Baptists in Ohio sponsored a church in Burlington near Toronto, Ontario.

6. *Other Baptist Bodies.*—The Primitive Baptist Conference of New Brunswick was founded in 1875 by George W. Orser. The group reports about 1,000 members, all in northern New Brunswick.

The Alliance of Reformed Baptist Churches was formed in New Brunswick in 1888 as part of the non-Pentecostal holiness movement. In 1966 it merged with the Wesleyan Methodist Church which subsequently joined with the Pilgrim Holiness Church to become The Wesleyan Church (1968).

The Association of Regular Baptist Churches (Canada), organized in 1957, comprises a small cluster of churches in Ontario, led by the Jarvis Street Baptist Church in Toronto.

Cooperation Among Baptists.—Churches affiliated with the BFC and the NABC are committed to cooperation with other Baptists through the North American Baptist Fellowship and the Baptist World Alliance. They hosted the Baptist World Congress in Toronto in 1928 and again in 1980. They were also partners in the Baptist Jubilee Advance program and celebration, 1959-64. Other Baptist groups in Canada have stayed aloof from the wider Baptist fellowship.

III. Cooperation With Other Denominations. Canadian Baptists are divided in their attitudes toward cooperation with other denominations and involvement in the ecumenical movement. The majority of churches affiliated with the BFC are involved in cooperative efforts at local, regional, and national levels. Joint summer services with the Presbyterian and United churches has been a widespread practice in the large cities and some smaller towns. Up to the 1960s, many Baptist churches used a hymnal and Sunday School literature produced jointly by Baptists and the United Church of Canada (a merger of Methodists, Congregationalists, and some Presbyterians in 1925).

However, changes in theological outlook within the United Church and their merger talks with the Anglican Church led to a gradual loosening of ties between Baptists and the United Church. Concern over clearer understanding of Baptist identity and distinctive beliefs led to termination of cooperation in the production of Sunday School materials. When the United and Anglican churches issued a common hymnal, Baptists published their own hymnal in 1973.

In ecumenical relations the three regional conventions within the BFC joined the Canadian Council of Churches (CCC) when it was founded in 1944. After the BFC was formed as a national body, it became the Baptist member body of the CCC. In 1971 the Atlantic Convention withdrew its support and membership in the CCC, as did the French Union in 1973. The convention and union represent one half of the BFC membership.

Since the BFC no longer had the necessary mandate to represent Baptists in the CCC, the BFC council voted, Feb., 1980, to terminate its CCC membership at the end of 1980. By precedent and interpretation of its constitution, the BFC council made the decision on the premise that BFC membership in interdenominational bodies must be based on the consensus among the four constituent conventions and unions. The same principle was applied when the BFC could not join the World Council of Churches. The BCOQ voted in favor (1949), the Atlantic Convention opposed it (1951), and the Western Union never took action.

At the 1980 annual assembly, the BCOQ delegates did not challenge the ruling of its Convention Council that the BCOQ retain its membership in the CCC as one of its founding members.

When Canadian Baptists were invited to participate in church union talks with the Methodist, Presbyterian, and Congregational churches in 1907, and again with the Anglican and United churches in the 1960s, they declined and stated their convictions about the concept of the church, believer's baptism, and other issues in published statements.

Through the 1970s, the BFC Baptists took the initiative in seeking closer relations with denominations in the believer's church tradition, such as Mennonites and Pentecostals. A large Study Conference on the Believer's Church in Canada was sponsored by the BFC and the Mennonite Central Committee (Canada) in Winnipeg, May, 1978.

Other Baptist bodies in Canada have either ignored or opposed ecumenical cooperation at local, national, and international levels. On a personal basis, some, including members of BFC churches, support the Evangelical Fellowship of Canada, formed in 1964. The only cooperative event of national significance to which nearly all Baptists in Canada gave support was the Canadian Congress on Evangelism held in Ottawa in Aug., 1970.

See also CANADIAN BAPTIST OVERSEAS MISSION BOARD; CANADIAN SOUTHERN BAPTISTS; CANADIAN—SOUTHERN BAPTIST CONVENTION RELATIONS; NORTHWEST BAPTIST CONVENTION.

BIBLIOGRAPHY: Barry M. Moody (ed.), *Repent and Believe: The Baptist Experience in Maritime Canada* (1980). J. K. Zeman (ed.), *Baptists in Canada: Search for Identity Amidst Diversity* (1980).

JAROLD K. ZEMAN

CANADIAN SOUTHERN BAPTISTS (III). Southern Baptist churches in Western Canada affiliated with the Northwest Baptist Convention doubled in number and total membership between 1968 and 1979, when 53 congregations reported a total membership of 3,154.

The Canadian work has been supported by mission funds and loan funds from the Fleming Church Loan Trust of Texas from 1955 to the present. During the 1970s a growing number of churches in Texas, Oklahoma, Arkansas, Alabama, Georgia, and other states directly aided new mission work in Canada.

At the 1976 SBC meeting in Norfolk, VA, a motion that the SBC give encouragement and financial support "to Southern Baptists dwelling and working in Canada" was referred to the Foreign Mission Board for study. In 1977 the SBC in Kansas City, MO, adopted a FMB recommendation that SBC agencies provide help to Baptist churches in Canada upon request. As a result, the Home Mission Board began in 1978 to channel support into western Canada through the Northwest Baptist Convention. The Northwest Convention elected Cecil Sims as associate director of missions for Canada in 1978.

Cooperative Program support from Canadian Southern Baptist churches grew from a total of $8,121 in 1968 to $61,246 in 1979. The rural Worsley Baptist Church in northern Alberta gave $9,400 to the 1979 Lottie Moon Offering.

Language missions began in 1968 with the formation of a Chinese Baptist congregation in Vancouver, British Columbia, which reported 400 members in 1979. Chinese Baptist work in Alberta opened in Edmonton in 1974 and in Calgary in 1978. The Korean Baptist Church in

Vancouver was constituted in 1976. A Spanish Sunday School class arose in the Royal Heights Baptist Church, Delta, British Columbia, in 1978.

Beginnings in the province of Manitoba came in 1972 with the arrival of Eugene Laird from McKinney, TX. He helped form in the capital city of Winnipeg a mission which was organized as Friendship Baptist Church in 1973. In 1979 the church reported 168 members and the sponsorship of missions in Winnipeg, Ile de Chene, and Brandon; and it fostered a Baptist Student Union at the University of Manitoba by 1976.

An era of growth in Saskatchewan dawned in 1970 when Canadian-born Henry Blackaby came from Downey, CA, as a pastoral missionary to lead the small Faith Baptist Church in Saskatoon and its mission in Prince Albert. Carroll Memorial Baptist Church at North Battleford and its Indian Mission at Cochin were the only other congregations. Faith Church started a BSU at the University of Saskatchewan in 1971 and established Canadian Baptist Theological College in 1972. Churches have been organized at Cochin, Prince Albert, and Regina, with new missions at Love, Deschambault Lake, Little Red Indian Reserve, Kyle, Allan, Young, Elstow, Colonsay, Broadview Indian Reserve, and Moose Jaw. A BSU has begun at the University of Regina.

In the province of Alberta, new Baptist churches constituted since 1968 included First Church, Airdrie, 1970; Willow Park Church, Calgary, 1971; Edmonton Chinese Church, Edmonton, 1977, along with missions at Cochrane, St. Albert, Grovedale, Fairview, and Fort McMurray. BSU work began in 1975 at the University of Alberta in Edmonton, and in 1977 at the University of Calgary.

In British Columbia new Baptist churches organized included Vancouver Chinese Church, 1969; Gertsmar Road Church, Kelowna, 1978; Victoria Church, Victoria, 1978; and Valley View Church, Creston, 1979, with new missions in Prince George, Surrey, Delta, and Vancouver. A BSU at the University of Victoria began in 1977. Capilano Association has sponsored a prison ministry since 1978 in several institutions.

During the 1970s a marked increase in young adults training for Christian ministry stimulated Canadian-Southern Baptist church planting.

See also CANADIAN BAPTISTS; CANADIAN—SOUTHERN BAPTIST CONVENTION RELATIONS; NORTHWEST BAPTIST CONVENTION.

BIBLIOGRAPHY: Roland P. Hood, *Southern Baptist Work in Canada* (rev., 1977).

JAMES G. YODER

CANADIAN—SOUTHERN BAPTIST CONVENTION RELATIONS (cf. Canadian Baptist Cooperation, Committee on, Vol. III). In 1954 R. E. Milam of Oregon urged the SBC to aid workers of the Baptist General Convention of Oregon-Washington in their ministry to Canadian churches. His request was approved.

In 1957 the SBC approved the appointment of a Joint Committee to guide SBC—Canadian Baptist relations. In 1958 the SBC president ruled that the SBC constitution did not allow for messengers from Canadian Baptist churches, and the Convention sustained the ruling. In 1959 a motion to amend the SBC constitution to include Canadian churches was withdrawn. For 12 years, 1957-69, W. Bertram King, an employee of the Home Mission Board, served as the SBC liaison representative with Canadian Baptist churches. With the approval of the North American Baptist Fellowship, the SBC voted to discontinue the Joint Committee in 1969.

Guidelines for cooperation were adopted jointly by the SBC Committee on Canadian Baptist Cooperation and a corresponding committee of the Baptist Federation of Canada in 1968. These recognized the freedom of individuals to extend their witness, the autonomy of each church, the primacy of fellowship, and the validity of "indigenous affiliation."

In 1977, on recommendation of the Foreign Mission Board, the SBC reaffirmed the 1968 guidelines and authorized its agencies to help Baptist churches of all groups in Canada in keeping with agency program statements. It stipulated also that no workers salaried in whole or in part would encourage Canadian churches to affiliate with the SBC and that requests for assistance be met with an effort to "cultivate fraternal and cordial relations."

See also CANADIAN BAPTISTS; CANADIAN SOUTHERN BAPTISTS; NORTHWEST BAPTIST CONVENTION.

PORTER W. ROUTH

CANNON, CLARENCE ANDREW (b. Elsberry, MO, Apr. 11, 1879; d. Washington, DC, Mar. 4, 1964). Baptist statesman. Son of John Randolph and Ida Glovina (Whitesides) Cannon, merchants, he married Ida Dawson Wigginton of Elsberry, MO, Aug. 30, 1906. Their children were Ida Elizabeth and Ruby Melinda.

Cannon graduated from LaGrange Junior College (1901), William Jewell College (1903), and the University of Missouri (1908). He was admitted to the bar in 1908, beginning practice in Troy, MO. He taught history at Stephens College in 1908 and began his political career as clerk in the office of Champ Clark, speaker of the United States House of Representatives. Cannon was elected to Clark's seat, Mar. 27, 1923, and held that seat for 42 years. He was chairman of the House Appropriations Committee, 1941-64, excepting the 80th and 83rd congresses. He is buried at Elsberry, MO.

L. DOUGLAS MCGLAUGHLIN

CANZONERI, JOE (b. Palazzo Adriano, Sicily, Sep. 24, 1886; d. Jackson, MS, July 11, 1975). Evangelist and pastor. Son of Guseppe and Antonina Canzoneri, grain millers, of Sicily, he came to the USA as a Roman Catholic in 1903 at age 17. At 22 he first saw a Bible in a Baptist Sunday School in Purvis, MS. He soon bought a Bible and after a year of study was converted and called to preach. Having little education, he started school in the third or fourth grade and went on to graduate from Mississippi College (B.S., 1918). He married Mabel Barnett, July 11, 1918. They had four children: Mabel, Joe, Robert, and George.

Canzoneri did YMCA work in Camp Jackson, SC, and after a 1919 interim pastorate in Eatonton, GA, attended Southwestern Baptist Theological Seminary (diploma in gospel music, 1922). He did evangelistic work with Perry F. Evans until he went to San Marcos, TX, Baptist Academy and San Marcos Baptist Church in 1924 to teach and direct music. During 1926-27 he worked with William W. Kyzar, Sr., in tent evangelism under the Mississippi Baptist Convention Board, starting new churches. After 13 months as associate pastor at Calvary Baptist Church, Jackson, he went back into evangelistic work. He is buried in Lakewood Memorial Cemetery, Jackson, MS.

JOE G. CANZONERI

CAPITAL BAPTIST. See DISTRICT OF COLUMBIA BAPTIST CONVENTION.

CARAWAY CONFERENCE CENTER. An outgrowth of the development of Camp Caraway. The North Carolina Baptist Brotherhood led in the purchase of 1,047 acres in the Uwharrie Mountains in Jan., 1962, as a camp for approximately 150 boys. Use of the property for retreats and leadership conferences led in 1973 to the erection of a motel-type building, separate from the camp, containing 51 bedrooms with private baths, conference rooms, and food service. Without interfering with the camping activities, meetings of the state convention's general board, staff retreats, and a variety of programs are conducted here. The director is B. W. Jackson.

NATHAN C. BROOKS, JR.

CARLETON, WILLIAM AUGUSTUS (b. McGee, OK, June 19, 1905; d. San Rafael, CA, Mar. 28, 1980). Educator, denominational leader, and pastor. Son of Edward and Ethel Carleton, he attended East Central State College, Ada, OK, and Southwestern Baptist Theological Seminary (Th.M., 1937; Th.D., 1945). He married Opal Brown, Mar. 17, 1928. They had two sons, William Jr., and John.

Carleton served pastorates at Comanche, OK; Walnut Street Church, Carbondale, IL; and First churches of Duncan and Ponca City, OK. Elected professor of church history at Golden Gate Baptist Theological Seminary in 1953, dean in 1956, and vice-president in 1959, he retired in 1970 and was named dean emeritus in 1972. In 1979 he received an award for outstanding service to the seminary.

Active in denominational affairs, he served as associational moderator and as president of three state Baptist conventions: Illinois, 1940; Oklahoma, 1950; and California, 1966. He

served on the SBC Social Service (Christian Life) Commission, Education Commission, and Historical Commission, as well as on the board of trustees, Southwestern Seminary. After retirement, he taught part time at Golden Gate, the Southern California Center, and in Arusha, Tanzania. He wrote three books: *Not Yours But You* (1954), *The Dreamer Cometh* (1960), and *The Growth of the Early Church* (1970).

HAROLD K. GRAVES

CARLSON, CARL EMANUEL (b. Gwynne, Alberta, Canada, Mar. 2, 1906; d. Dundee, FL, Feb. 23, 1976). Educator and public affairs executive. Executive director of the Baptist Joint Committee on Public Affairs from 1954 to 1971, Carlson was associated with Bethel College, St. Paul, MN, as teacher, 1927-53, and as dean, 1945-53.

Carlson was the son of Evelina and Swan Carlson, immigrants from Sweden who homesteaded in Alberta, Canada, in the late 1800s. Educated at the University of Alberta, Edmonton, Alberta (B.A., 1927), and the University of Minnesota (M.S., 1932; Ph.D., 1950), he became a naturalized citizen of the USA on Sep. 25, 1940. He married Lucille Byllemos. They had two children, Keith and Jocelyn.

Carlson was one of the leading Baptist interpreters in his day of the complex problems of freedom of conscience, religious liberty, and church-state relations. He served as chairman of the Commission on Religious Liberty and Human Rights of the Baptist World Alliance and as a leader of similar church-related organizations.

During Carlson's tenure with the Baptist Joint Committee, the agency developed strong programs of information services, research services, correlation services, and legislative analysis. Many church-state problems of the nation came into focus while he was in office, such as federal aid to religious schools, the place of religion in public education, tax policies as related to the churches, and the intertwining of church or denominational programs of social services with governmental programs.

Four achievements of Carlson's career stand out: (1) A renewed emphasis on the concepts of the biblical basis of religious liberty, (2) the promotion of dialogue and conference as methods of arriving at Baptist positions on complex church-state issues, (3) sending a Baptist press correspondent to Vatican Council II, thus opening the way to ensuing Baptist-Catholic dialogue, and (4) participation in the development of the Elementary and Secondary Education Act of 1968.

Carlson is buried at Winter Haven, FL.

See also PUBLIC AFFAIRS, BAPTIST JOINT COMMITTEE ON.

W. BARRY GARRETT

CARNETT, ALBERT LEWIS (b. Chafee, MO, June 22, 1911; d. Winter Haven, FL, Sep. 29, 1970). Pastor. The son of Dora Carnett and Frank Carnett, a minister, he attended Stetson

University (B.A., 1936) and Southern Baptist Theological Seminary (Th.B., 1937; Th.M., 1940). He and Lois Johnson of Altoona, FL, were married, June 5, 1931. They had two daughters, Marion and Carol.

Carnett served as president, Florida Baptist Convention, 1951-52; president, Jacksonville Baptist Ministerial Alliance; president, Winter Haven Ministerial Association; and also served several terms on the state board of missions. In 1960 he received the Distinguished Service Award at Stetson University, where he served as trustee. Preaching missions included Jamaica and Alaska. He also served as director of Southern Baptist Memorial Hospital, Jacksonville, FL, and was pastor of First Baptist Church, Winter Haven, from 1954 until his death. He is buried in Lakeside Cemetery, Winter Haven, FL.

VELMA SEAWELL DANIELS

CARSON-NEWMAN COLLEGE (I, III). J. Cordell Maddox succeeded John A. Fincher as president in 1977. The 1979 fall enrollment was 1,649. Valued at $15,000,000, the physical plant of the college now includes Dougherty Science Center, Henderson Humanities Building, and a new music building occupied in 1980. Library holdings have increased to 137,031 items. Endowment funds reached $3,630,559 by mid-1979.

The college offers majors in 35 fields of study, including an expanded music curriculum with a concentration in church music. Among the major innovations in the academic program have been a popular three-week miniterm at the conclusion of the spring semester and a church recreation major. Carson-Newman College Bible School, established to provide educational opportunities in biblical interpretation and techniques of church leadership, offers a diploma in Christian ministry to persons with a high school education.

The Southern Baptist Theological Seminary, Louisville, KY, offers two courses each semester at Carson-Newman. Credit from these courses may be applied toward a Master of Divinity degree at Southern or toward a Carson-Newman degree.

J. CORDELL MADDOX

CARTER, BRUCE GILBERT (b. Elgin, TX, July 29, 1904; d. Miami, OK, Oct. 5, 1976). Oklahoma lay leader and educator. The son of Jefferson Lee and Emma Condon Carter, he graduated from Oklahoma Baptist University (A.B., 1928) and the University of Oklahoma (M.A., 1932; Ed.D., 1950). He married Nola Funderburk, July 4, 1929. They had three children: Robert, Marilyn, and John. He was president of Northeastern Oklahoma A&M College, 1943-69; Brotherhood president for Oklahoma Baptists in 1955; and he also served as first president of the National Conference of Southern Baptist Men in 1957, a position to which he was elected again in 1961. For 14 years

he served as a trustee of Oklahoma Baptist University. He is buried in the GAR cemetery at Miami, OK.

J. M. GASKIN

CARTER, ROBERT (b. Nomini Hall, VA, 1729; d. Baltimore, MD, 1804). Baptist lay leader of the Revolutionary era. Son of Robert and Priscilla (Churchill) Carter, wealthy planters, he was educated at the College of William and Mary and in England. Carter married Frances Tasker in 1754; they had 17 children. Inheriting about 70,000 acres and 500 slaves, he became the wealthiest man in Virginia. He broke with inherited Anglican connections and became a Deist in 1776. Severely ill in 1777, he was converted to experiential religion. After studying the various denominations, he was baptized in Aug., 1778, into the Morattico Baptist Church. He was chosen clerk of the church and led in founding other Baptist churches at Nomini and Yeocomico, assisted in the education of ministers, and took leadership roles among Virginia Baptists.

A diligent theologian, Carter reacted against highly Calvinistic views, espoused Arminianism, then adopted the views of Emmanuel Swedenborg. Moving to Baltimore in 1793, he sought new religious insight. His supposed instability has caused historians to overlook his large contributions to Baptists and to reckon him an eccentric. He is buried at Baltimore, MD.

WILLIAM L. LUMPKIN

CASH, AMOS BOYD (b. Gainesville, GA, June 6, 1901; d. Rome, GA, Feb. 2, 1981). Pastor and home missions administrator. The son of Milton Lafayette and Ida Wood Cash, farmers, he was ordained by East Side Baptist (Tabernacle) Church, Cartersville, GA, June 13, 1926. He attended classes at the University of Georgia, other colleges, and several seminaries. He married Cappie Cope, Dec. 19, 1926. They had two children, Jacquelyn and Amos Boyd, Jr.

Cash served pastorates in Georgia and North Carolina for 20 years. In 1944 he became superintendent of missions in Columbus, GA, and in 1949 he became field secretary responsible for mountain missions with the Home Mission Board. In 1952 the HMB assigned him to work with rural churches throughout the nation, with special assignments in the Great Lakes area. Becoming director of Pioneer and Mountain Missions for the HMB in 1955, two years later his duties were narrowed to the expanding work of pioneer missions. In 1959 Cash was named secretary of the Department of Pioneer Missions. During his period of leadership, 1952-67, Southern Baptists achieved their greatest geographic expansion, and churches were started in every state. More than 3,000 churches and missions were established with membership in excess of 700,000. He is buried in East View Cemetery, Adairsville, GA.

M. WENDELL BELEW

CARSON-NEWMAN COLLEGE (q.v.), Jefferson City, TN. Henderson Humanities Building was occupied in the spring, 1977, and houses the Religion, Foreign Language, Philosophy, and Communication Arts Departments.

BELMONT COLLEGE (*q.v.*), Nashville, TN. *Top:* Erected in 1972, the Center for Business Administration Building houses the Departments of Religion, Business, Music Business, and the Computer Center. *Bottom:* Gabhart Student Center. Dedicated in Apr., 1981. Total cost $2,750,000.

Channeling Denominational Information

CASTLEBERRY, VAN BOONE (b. Marshall County, KY, Jan. 10, 1898; d. Hamilton, OH, Dec. 21, 1976). Missionary, pastor, and pioneer Baptist leader. The son of William and Fronia Castleberry, he married Pocahontas Trevathan, Oct. 31, 1918. They had four children: Daniel, Margaret, John, and William. He attended Bethel College, Russellville, KY, and Hall-Moody, Martin, TN. Supported by First Baptist Church, Murray, KY, he served as a missionary in Brazil, 1923-26, and as associational missionary for the Kentucky Baptist Convention, 1927-43.

As pastor of West Side Baptist Church, Hamilton, OH, 1943-46, he encouraged Whitewater Association to begin churches. He also served the association as missionary, 1947-51. Moving to Indiana in 1951, he assisted in establishing Grand Avenue Church, New Castle; First Church, Portland; and Kingston Avenue Church, Anderson. In Nov., 1951, Indiana Association of Missionary Baptists elected him missionary. With R. E. Sasser and C. E. Wiley, he sought affiliation with the Illinois Baptist State Association, laying the groundwork for an Indiana convention. Castleberry served also as the first historian of the State Convention of Baptists in Indiana. He is buried in Rose Hill Cemetery, Hamilton, OH.

CLARENCE R. BROCK

CATTS, SIDNEY JOHNSTON (b. Pleasant Hills, AL, July 31, 1863; d. DeFuniak Springs, FL, Mar. 9, 1936). Pastor and politician. The son of Adeline Catts and Samuel Walker Catts, a merchant and planter, he attended Auburn University and Howard College but received his only degree (L.L.B.) from Cumberland University in Tennessee. He married Alice May Campbell in 1886. Their children were Ruth, Elizabeth, Alice, Sidney, Rozier, Walter, and Edward.

Catts practiced law and managed the family store briefly. Following his conversion at a revival, he entered the Baptist ministry with no formal theological training, experiencing stormy pastorates in Dallas, Lowndes, and Macon Counties in Alabama. In DeFuniak Springs, FL, 1911-14, he resigned over a salary dispute and became an insurance salesman. He ran for governor and in a stunning upset won on the Prohibitionist ticket in 1916. His administration enacted many reforms, although others were blocked. He ran for the United States Senate, 1920, and for governor, 1924 and 1928, narrowly losing each time. He is buried at DeFuniak Springs, FL.

J. WAYNE FLYNT

CAUTHEN, BAKER JAMES, CHAIR OF WORLD MISSIONS. A chair approved by the trustees of Golden Gate Baptist Theological Seminary, Oct. 11, 1977, honoring Cauthen, executive director of the Foreign Mission Board, 1954-79. Cauthen became the first professor to occupy the chair, beginning with the fall semes-

ter of 1980. The major emphases of the chair are to prepare seminary students for mission service and to train church leaders to develop mission-oriented churches.

STANTON H. NASH

CAYMAN ISLANDS, MISSION IN. The Cayman Islands are a British Crown Colony, comprising Grand Cayman, Cayman Brac, and Little Cayman with a population of approximately 17,000 and an area of 100 square miles. Baptists of the Jamaican Baptist Missionary Society began work on Cayman Brac in 1886. Baptist Student Union summer missionaries were the first Southern Baptists in Cayman Brac. Carl Schooling went to Cayman Brac as a journeyman missionary in 1975, and Herbert and Jackie (Sloan) Neely went to Grand Cayman as career missionaries in 1977. Randall Von Kanel was the first journeyman missionary to Grand Cayman, arriving Aug., 1978. Five churches related to the work in 1980 included a church on Grand Cayman organized in 1978.

HERB AND JACKIE NEELY

CENTER FOR URBAN CHURCH STUDIES. See URBAN CHURCH STUDIES, CENTER FOR.

CENTRAL HILLS BAPTIST RETREAT. A camp at Kosciusko, MS, owned and operated by the Mississippi Baptist Convention Board. In 1968 Hurricane Camille destroyed Camp Kittiwake which had operated since 1955 at Pass Christian, MS. Baptist leaders began a search for a future inland campsite which would provide adequate terrain and acreage for a boys' camp. Several available sites were considered but were found inadequate for program needs.

In 1974 Harold Kitchings, pastor of First Baptist Church, Kosciusko, brought to the attention of the board a 220-acre tract of timberland seven miles west of Kosciusko. The board met on July 23, 1974, at his church to consider the property. Later that same day, the board voted to purchase the property for $300 an acre. On May 27, 1975, the camp was increased to 300 acres with the purchase of an adjoining tract. A construction committee of boys and men was appointed to develop a long-range development plan for a camp.

A 25-year master plan has been developed for the site. As of 1980, approximately $1,500,000 had been expended in its development. The Brotherhood Department of the convention began the operation of Royal Ambassador camps at Central Hills Baptist Retreat in 1979. Tents are being used until permanent cabins can be built. As finances permit, cabins will be built to provide a year-round retreat center.

EARL KELLY

CHANNELING DENOMINATIONAL INFORMATION (cf. Programing for the Churches, 1959-69, Vol. III). The process by which certain SBC programs carry information and concerns of other SBC programs directly to the churches. Though the concept includes channeling through field services, the two most common types are (1) curriculum channeling, whereby the concerns of an emphasis program are incorporated into curriculum units or teaching procedures, and (2) noncurriculum channeling, whereby information about a program's work is carried in any publication that will provide space for articles, features, awareness boxes, art, and other items, usually on a much shorter range schedule than through curriculum channeling.

Channeling was developed in response to recommendations from various SBC committees from 1923 to 1959. The process began at the Sunday School Board in 1962 as Project 600, which provided for using Sunday School, Training Union, and Church Music organizations and materials in a more formal way than before to enrich Southern Baptists' understanding of the work of other Convention agencies. Later in the 1960s, the process was broadened to include WMU, Brotherhood, and other service and emphasis programs.

In Jan., 1979, the Church Program Services Coordination Subcommittee of the Coordinating Committee of the Inter-Agency Council approved an update of the noncurriculum channeling process which has significantly increased participation in channeling by SBC agencies. In Jan., 1980, it approved for pilot testing a new approach to curriculum channeling for emphasis programs.

ROBERT ORR

CHAPLAINCY MINISTRIES, HOME MISSION BOARD PROGRAM OF (III; cf. Chaplain, Vol. I). The number of military chaplains declined after 1970 while civilian chaplaincy experienced a slow but continuing growth. The Chaplains Commission now endorses approximately 1,400 chaplains with over 800 about equally divided between active military duty and full-time civilian duty. The other 600 are part-time serving in the Reserves, National Guard, Civil Air Patrol, law enforcement, hospitals, industries, jails, motels, fire departments, and rest homes.

George W. Cummins, who retired as director of the Division of Chaplaincy in 1971, was succeeded by James W. Kelly, former chief of chaplains for the United States Navy. With Richard W. McKay's resignation in 1973, Lowell F. Sodeman served as associate director for hospital chaplaincy and business-industry until his retirement in 1979. Willis Brown retired in 1974 as an associate to the director. Upon Kelly's retirement in 1974, William L. Clark became division director. In 1975 Pat H. Davis was appointed as associate director for military chaplaincy. Clark retired in 1976 and Alfred Carl Hart, who had served in the division since 1970, was named division director.

Huey D. Perry became associate director in

1977 for correctional and other institutional chaplaincy. In 1979 Royce C. Williams was appointed administrative assistant to the division director.

ALFRED CARL HART

CHAPLAINS, ASSOCIATION OF BAPTIST. Prior to 1968 the Association of Baptist Chaplains was known as the Southern Baptist Association of Hospital Chaplains. The organization's membership was limited to Southern Baptist ministers who were working as chaplains in a hospital setting. In recent years, this organization has opened its membership to any Southern Baptist minister serving any institution (hospital, correctional, industrial, or other) as a chaplain. The group meets annually in conjunction with the College of Chaplains, American Protestant Hospital Association.

See also CHAPLAIN, VOL. I; CHAPLAINCY MINISTRIES, HOME MISSION BOARD PROGRAM OF, VOLS. III, IV.

CARL HART

CHARISMATIC MOVEMENT AND SOUTHERN BAPTISTS. Charismatics regard the baptism of the Spirit as a second blessing beyond conversion and consider speaking in tongues (*glossolalia*) as evidence of this blessing. They often emphasize other gifts such as healing, exorcism, and prophecy. Individual charismatics belong to Southern Baptist churches, and perhaps 100 churches are charismatic, but no association or state convention is dominated by charismatics and no prominent denominational leader propagates this outlook. Tendencies toward elitism, reductionism, and divisiveness reduce the appeal of the movement for Southern Baptists, who are committed to evangelism, missions, and denominationalism.

The charismatic movement appears to have peaked among Southern Baptists in 1975-76 following a series of strong actions by several associations. At least five associations in four states (Dallas in TX, Cincinnati in OH, Trenton and Plaquemines in LA, Harmony in CA) excluded charismatic churches, and three others adopted statements of disapproval or warning (Rogers in OK, Union and Guadalupe in TX). Most state conventions, however, as well as the SBC, have been content to allow local churches and associations to deal with problems as they arise. Most of the charismatic churches disfellowshipped by associations consider themselves as still belonging to the respective state conventions and the SBC.

Faced by increasing opposition, charismatic churches and pastors encouraged one another by convening a series of regional and national conferences. Regional meetings in Louisville, KY, in 1974 and 1975 attracted several hundred participants as did a third at Monroe, LA, in 1975. A National Southern Baptist Charismatic Conference met in Dallas, TX, in July, 1976, and again in 1977. The vitality of the charismatic movement in American religion continues, but the impact upon Southern Baptists has been limited and continues to decline. National polls and articles that identify large segments of Baptists as charismatic define the term so ambiguously that results are deceptive.

A general consensus based on what Southern Baptists have said and done regarding the movement appears to include the following elements. First, they react positively toward a renewed emphasis upon the Holy Spirit and agree that in the past they have given too little attention to the work of the Spirit in the life of believers and churches. Second, they affirm anew that a believer is baptized of the Spirit in conversion and requires no second blessing subsequent to that experience. Third, many of them agree that repeated fillings of the Spirit are possible, but such experiences are largely equated with deeper consecration, commitment, or commissioning for special tasks.

Fourth, most Southern Baptists would not deny that speaking in tongues is a biblical gift. But they note that it is a minor gift that should be restricted in use, not actively sought, and not claimed as an evidence of the baptism of the Spirit. It is not a uniquely Christian gift since it is often practiced in other religions. Fifth, most affirm that tongues in Acts and 1 Corinthians are different, the former being understandable language and the latter ecstatic utterance. Modern tongues are regarded as Corinthian—not actual language.

Sixth, none deny the power of God to heal, but most are skeptical about claims of healing gifts and special services where individuals are declared healed. Seventh, most regard the charismatic movement as divisive, since it encourages spiritual pride and emphasizes a minor gift out of proportion to the biblical evidence. Eighth, charismatics are to be tolerated and loved as Christians, but they should not be allowed to disrupt fellowship and engage in militant proselytizing activities.

Finally, local Baptist pastors and churches have the primary responsibility for dealing with problems that arise because of charismatics. Sound biblical exegesis and Christian nurture, allied with meaningful worship and witness, will enable believers to identify and utilize gifts of God's grace in a manner that will honor Christ and edify the church.

BIBLIOGRAPHY: C. L. Howe, Jr., "The Charismatic Movement in Southern Baptist Life," *Baptist History and Heritage*, XIII (July, 1978).

                                                    CLAUDE L. HOWE, JR.

CHEROKEE ASSEMBLY (cf. Cherokee Indian Baptist Assembly, Vol. I). Registration for the 29th session in 1979 was 543. More than 9,000 have enrolled since the assembly's beginning. The 21 acres of land, tabernacle, dorms, dining hall, and Woman's Missionary Union building are valued in excess of $250,000. The annual budget is $5,000. The Cherokee Indian Baptist Association of Oklahoma owns the assembly. Three weeks of camp are held each summer for all ages.

                                                    J. M. GASKIN

CHILD CARE EXECUTIVES OF SOUTHERN BAPTISTS. At the suggestion of H. Truman Maxey, superintendent of Oklahoma Baptist Children's Home, executives of Southern Baptist homes for children met during the 1948 SBC in Memphis, TN, to make plans for forming an organization of chief administrators. The first official meeting of Child Care Executives of Southern Baptists was held in Jan., 1949, at Baptist Children's Village, Jackson, MS, with W. G. Mize as host. Twenty-four from 13 states attended. Officers named included H. Truman Maxey, president, and Wade B. East, secretary. The organization, which has met annually since 1949, has as its purpose and function the exchange of ideas, methods, and procedures of caring for children and developing fellowship among administrators.

See also CHILDREN'S HOME, THE DENOMINATIONAL, VOL. I.

                                                    WADE B. EAST

CHILDREN'S AID SOCIETY, MARYLAND BAPTIST (I). See MARYLAND, INC., BAPTIST CHILDREN'S AID SOCIETY OF.

CHILDREN'S WORK (III). See AGE GROUP WORK IN THE CHURCHES.

CHILE, MISSION IN (I, III). The Baptist Clinic in Antofagasta ministers to about 300 babies weekly. Nearly 1,000 students are enrolled in the school in Temuco. The Woman's Missionary Union is strong, and Vacation Bible Schools continue to be effective. The Chilean Baptist Convention has given greater emphasis to stewardship during this decade. The nationwide Sunday School high attendance goal was reached on Mar. 28, 1976, with 21,315 in attendance. Georgia Mae Ogburn retired in 1976 after 36 years of missionary service and was honored by the Chilean government with the Bernardo O'Higgins Award, the highest award given to a foreigner. At the end of 1979 there were 172 Baptist churches and 250 missions. Seventy Southern Baptist missionaries were under appointment for Chile.

                                                    J. BRYAN BRASINGTON

CHINA, MISSION IN (I, III). The end of the 1970s brought some hope to the Christians in China. The Peking government reactivated the Religious Affairs Bureau and gave authority to the Three Self Movement to open Protestant churches in key cities in 1979. Pastors were receiving pay from the government and preaching on a rotating basis. Large crowds responded, though many older Christians were cautious about identifying themselves. In Canton the former Tung Shan Baptist Church building was refurbished, and weekly worship services were being conducted. Matthew Tang, former pastor of the church, was one of four pastors selected by the government to lead the worship services. Words of hymns and Scripture texts were being printed in bulletins since there are no Bibles or hymnbooks. House churches continued to meet in various parts of China.

GEORGE H. HAYS

CHOWAN COLLEGE (I, III). The only two-year college sponsored by the Baptist State Convention of North Carolina, Chowan offers a strong emphasis on the liberal arts, with 85 percent of its graduates transferring to senior colleges or universities. The college also provides career education programs in secretarial science, merchandising management, commercial art, printing technology, photography, and newswriting-advertising. As a reinforcement of its commitment to meeting the needs of its students, Chowan has increased its personnel and services in the areas of guidance and counseling, residence hall living, financial aid, and extracurricular activities.

Under Bruce Whitaker, president since 1957, 14 buildings have been constructed, including a new $2,500,000 gymnasium-physical education center in 1980. Total assets have increased from $750,000 in 1957 to over $15,000,000 in 1979. With an enrollment of 1,118 in 1979-80, the college operated on a budget of $5,150,000.

BRUCE WHITAKER

CHRISTIAN ACTION COUNCIL, INC. South Carolina inter-church agency of which the South Carolina Baptist Convention is one of 17 member denominational bodies. It works with and for the denominations in the state in behalf of "Christian Cooperation" and "Christian Witness in Public Affairs." The organization began in 1933 when leaders of Baptist, Methodist, and other denominations banded together to oppose the repeal of the Eighteenth (Prohibition) Amendment to the United States Constitution. It was named the South Carolina Federated Forces for Temperance and Law Enforcement. Charles E. Burts (*q.v.* I), then pastor of First Baptist Church, Macon, GA, became its first executive secretary. Other executive leaders have been A. D. Betts, 1939-47; Maxie C. Collins, Jr. (*q.v.*), 1938-49; and Howard G. McClain, 1950- . All except Betts were Southern Baptists. In 1951 the name was changed to Christian Action Council, Incorporated, and its purposes became more inclusive.

The South Carolina Baptist Convention's Christian Life and Public Affairs Committee works closely with the council. The convention, as well as many Baptist congregations, are financial supporters, and its leadership includes Baptist pastors and lay members.

Through the 1950s and 1960s, the council gave special attention to public issues related both to desegregation and alcoholic beverages. A series of ecumenical conferences on racial change, Communism, television, Vietnam, poverty, and civil rights brought together representatives from many denominations to consider those issues and also increased participation in the council by denominations that had not previously

been members. In the 1970s the council focused attention on such issues as race relations, public education, capital punishment, and the role of women in the church.

HOWARD G. MCCLAIN

CHRISTIAN CITIZENSHIP CORPS, THE. A grass-roots network of Southern Baptists sponsored by the Christian Life Commission, SBC. Begun in 1979, the corps consists of Southern Baptist citizens who are interested in what government is doing locally, statewide, and nationally, and who are willing to make their voices heard appropriately in those arenas. The functions of the corps are based on an understanding of Christian citizenship as application of the principles of the gospel to society through appropriate involvement in the political process.

Members of the corps receive a newsletter entitled *Moral Alert* which presents pressing public policy issues along with suggestions as to the Christian ethical principles which ought to be used in evaluating those issues. *Moral Alert* also provides practical information to help corps members understand how the political process works and how to amplify their opinions with government decision makers.

WILLIAM H. ELDER, III

CHRISTIAN INDEX, THE (I, III). Weekly newsmagazine of the Georgia Baptist Convention. Jack U. Harwell has been editor since 1966. In 1980 circulation was 124,000 weekly. In 1972 the *Index* celebrated its 150th anniversary by publishing a 108-page sesquicentennial issue giving highlights of Georgia and Southern Baptist history. It also published a history, *The Index, An Old Friend with New Credentials*, by Jack U. Harwell. In 1976 a bicentennial issue celebrated America's 200th birthday. In 1979 the *Index* published *Louie D., A Photographic Essay on the Life of "Mr. Baptist," Louie D. Newton*, also written by Harwell. Also in 1979, it published *Bedrock Beliefs of Baptists*, by Dick H. Hall, Jr.

JACK U. HARWELL

CHRISTIAN LIFE COMMISSION, SBC (I, III). As the Christian social concerns and Christian social action agency of the SBC, the Christian Life Commission experienced significant development in its life and work during the 1970s. The 1960s were characterized by more active attention to social concerns than Southern Baptists had ever before shown in the history of the Convention. The next decade saw that social awareness and commitment to active involvement on behalf of public righteousness substantially solidified and enlarged in Southern Baptist life. In working during the 1970s to conserve the Christian social concerns gains of the 1960s, the CLC continued its long-standing emphasis on Christian social ethics and led Southern Baptists in the development of some important new initiatives in applied Christianity.

The commission's professional staff members serving at the end of Mar., 1980, were: Foy Valentine, executive director; Harry N. Hollis, Jr., associate executive director and director of family and special moral concerns; William H. Elder, III, director of Christian citizenship development; Tim Fields, director of communications; W. David Sapp, director of organization; William M. Tillman, Jr., director of research and editorial services; Mary Elizabeth Tyler, administrative assistant; and John A. Wood, director of program development. Raymond E. Higgins, II, served as a special coordinator of Christian social concerns and Christian social ministries in a position jointly sponsored by the CLC and the Christian Social Ministries Department of the Home Mission Board; and John H. Buchanan served as special consultant to represent Southern Baptists in Washington, DC, in areas of Christian social concern and Christian social action assigned to the CLC by the SBC. Other professional staff members who served with the CLC at some time during the decade were Pauline P. Barnard, Floyd A. Craig, David Currie, C. Welton Gaddy, David Gooch, W. L. Howse, III, Lee Porter, Elmer S. West, Jr., and David Wilkinson. In 1970 the budget of the CLC was $227,400; and in 1980 it was $600,000.

In 1970 the Baptist state conventions with Christian Life Commissions or the equivalent were Texas, Mississippi, North Carolina, and Virginia. By 1980, five more conventions had moved to establish departments to deal with Christian social concerns: Tennessee, Kentucky, Arkansas, Georgia, and Missouri. Most of the other state Baptist conventions reported having standing committees to study and work in the area of applied Christianity. Approximately 1,000 churches registered in the annual associational letters as having Christian life committees in 1980, and many associations throughout the nation maintained active Christian life committees.

The CLC worked in close cooperation with these state counterparts, with the Christian ethics professors in the Convention's six theological seminaries, and with the other Southern Baptist agencies to help Southern Baptists move forward together in Christian social concern and Christian social action.

Reactivating its publication, *Light,* the commission used this Christian ethics journal to communicate regularly with more than 7,000 Southern Baptists who expressed a special interest in Christian ethics. Under the editorship of William M. Tillman, Jr., *Light* became again an important part of the agency's outreach to Southern Baptists on behalf of applied Christianity.

In the 1970s the commission continued its practice of presenting, almost every year, its "Distinguished Service Award for Leadership in Christian Social Ethics" to some outstanding Southern Baptist ethicist. Recipients were Henlee H. Barnette in 1971, Jimmy R. Allen in 1972, Walker L. Knight and Arthur B. Rutledge in 1973, W. Randall Lolley in 1974, J. Clark Hensley in 1975, William M. Pinson, Jr., in 1977, Sarah Frances Anders in 1978, and James M. Dunn in 1979. G. Willis Bennett was chosen to receive the award in 1980.

Christian citizenship development took on special importance for the commission when C. Welton Gaddy was employed in 1973 as the first director of this program. When he resigned to become pastor of Broadway Baptist Church in Fort Worth, TX, he was succeeded in that position in 1978 by William H. Elder, III. The director of Christian citizenship development is responsible for maintaining the nongovernmental observer relationships of Southern Baptists at the United Nations and for developing and relating to the Christian Citizenship Corps, a loosely knit organization of Southern Baptists committed to working with government representatives at all levels in support of public righteousness.

In support of the cause of applied Christianity among Southern Baptists, the CLC enlarged its development and distribution of pamphlet literature; was responsible for the writing and publishing of many books in the field of Christian ethics; prepared hundreds of articles, stories, guest editorials, and columns, such as the regular weekly release called "On the Moral Scene"; distributed audiocassette tapes primarily from its seminar programs; and inaugurated the distribution of television cassette tapes dealing with such subjects as strengthening families. Educational materials were released each year in support of Race Relations Sunday, Christian Citizenship Sunday, and World Hunger Sunday.

By appointment of President Jimmy Carter, commission staff member Harry N. Hollis, Jr., served as a director of the White House Conference on Families in 1979-80; and the commission's executive director served in 1980 as a commissioner of the President's Commission for a National Agenda for the Eighties. In the 1975-80 period, the executive director also served as chairman of the Christian Ethics Commission of the Baptist World Alliance.

By the mid-1970s there was in Southern Baptist life a growing awareness of the grave moral issue of world hunger. In 1976 and again in 1980 the commission mailed to every Southern Baptist pastor an especially prepared packet of materials to heighten awareness of world hunger. As the Convention agency with primary responsibility for providing information and support related to this pressing moral issue, the commission worked to encourage an expanding sensitivity to hunger and to elicit a united and worthy Southern Baptist response to it.

In 1977, with a strong recommendation which the SBC adopted that year, the commission launched an ambitious program of providing help for television viewers.

A "Statement of Principles for Christian Social Concern and Christian Social Action" was prepared and widely circulated, including special distribution at the SBC in 1979 and at the BWA Congress in 1980.

The commission's conference program grew significantly in the 1970s with the national seminar attracting an average of about 500 registrants each year, with annual Ridgecrest and Glorieta conferences, and with specialized national and regional conferences on such subjects as energy, economics, peace, preaching on ethical issues, and applying the gospel in the local church.

The CLC's continuing responsibility has been reflected in its widely used motto, "Helping Changed People to Change the World."

                                    FOY VALENTINE

CHRISTIAN LIFE COMMISSION
(Texas) (III). The Christian Life Commission of the Baptist General Convention of Texas continues its assignment of applying the gospel to race relations, family life, citizenship, daily work, religious liberty, and moral issues. Its work parallels that of the SBC Christian Life Commission and the Baptist Joint Committee on Public Affairs. The commission also relates to the Family Ministry Department of the Sunday School Board.

During the 1970s the commission expanded its staff and work. Ben E. Loring, Jr., joined the staff in 1973 as an associate, later becoming director of program planning. Bill Blackburn became the family life consultant in 1977, and H. Joe Haag was named research associate in 1978. James M. Dunn, director since 1968, and Phil D. Strickland, director of citizenship education since 1968, complete the professional staff.

The commission's approach to its family life assignment was strengthened during the decade. In addition to providing materials and conferences on family concerns, the commission began training lay personnel for leadership of family programs in local churches. These programs include marriage enrichment and interpersonal communication. Work with single adults was also developed as a part of the family assignment.

Legislative issues occupied much of the commission's concern in the 1970s. In 1974 and 1978, the commission led statewide coalitions to defeat the legalization of pari-mutuel gambling. The commission was involved in other legislative matters such as the revision of the Texas family law code, the establishment of a Texas commission on jail standards, the licensing of child care facilities, bilingual education, welfare reform, criminal justice, and church-state concerns. Two groups of lay persons were organized to enhance the commission's citizenship work.

For the commission the major moral issue of the 1970s was world hunger. Through conferences, articles, and literature, the commission sought to sensitize the consciences of Texas Baptists to hunger concerns.

                                    BEN E. LORING, JR.

CHRISTIAN SOCIAL MINISTRIES, HOME MISSION BOARD PROGRAM OF
(III). Paul R. Adkins, who had served as the first secretary of the department, 1966-68, returned to that position in Jan., 1971. The department was reorganized in 1971. The original five programs were expanded into 13 subprograms: Baptist centers, domestic hunger and disaster relief, literacy missions, ministry with older persons, youth and family services, ministry with single persons, alcohol and drug abusers, migrants and seasonal farm workers, Sellers Baptist Home and Adoption Center, church community ministries, criminal justice system, blind ministry, and handicapped persons.

The department is comprised of the director, one associate director, four assistant directors, and two national consultants. The staff has geographical assignments and expertise in one or more of the subprograms.

                                    PAUL R. ADKINS

CHURCH ADMINISTRATION (I; cf.
Leadership, Vol. III). Administration provides the means through which a group can fulfill its purpose. Church administration discovers and clarifies a church's mission and objectives and then moves in a coherent, comprehensive manner to accomplish those ends. Purposeful church administration involves the congregation in discovering its mission and provides experiences that use all resources and personnel in fulfilling that mission.

Nature of Church Administration.—Among Baptists, each local congregation governs itself. Baptist polity places on church members responsibility for governing the church. However, the burden of administrative activity prevents the church assembled from attending to every detail. A church works effectively if it limits congregational work to decision making and delegates certain decisions to subgroups within its fellowship. Church leaders, the church council, program organizations, deacons, and committees study, plan, and recommend actions to the congregation for decisions. In business meetings, the church receives and acts on reports and recommendations from those subgroups. Each church member has an equal voice and vote in decision making. Administrative responsibilities of the church are:

> Govern the life and work of the church under the lordship of Christ; determine the church's programs, services, and emphases; establish organization to conduct and coordinate the church's program, services, and emphases; determine the church's cooperative work with other churches; establish and maintain appropriate external relationships; select pastor, staff, and volunteer leaders and assign responsibility; provide and allocate resources for the total work of the church.

Trends.—Literature on church administration from 1900 to 1930 emphasized tasks, efficiency, the value of organization, and the minister as the center of the local ecclesiastical circle.

From 1930 to 1960, literature tended to parallel the first 30 years with five additional concepts emerging: (1) the local church organized around functions of worship and education, (2) the local church as an organization (contrasted with earlier views of the local church as a cluster of unrelated and semi-independent organizations), (3) the adaptation of secular advertising approaches to present the Christian gospel, (4) the publication of books by laymen with administrative expertise suggesting how skills and methods of business could be used by churches, and (5) a shift in emphasis from organization- to people-centered approaches.

Since 1960 content of church administration literature and professional development conferences and studies for ministers have moved to include broader understandings of leadership roles of pastors, staff members, volunteer leaders, and deacons; elevated effectiveness of leaders as persons as foundational for developing administrative efficiency on the premise that a church will seldom, if ever, exceed the quality of its leaders; and focused on needs of ministers in areas of personal and spiritual growth, role understanding, personal support systems, and leadership skill development. During the 1960s and 1970s, SBC agency leaders reexamined church program purposes, conducted intensive program design work leading to formal program task statements, and restated church functions as worship, proclamation and witness, nurture and education, and ministry, thereby impacting all levels of administration within a church.

Administrators.—The pastor provides administrative leadership for the total church, leads the pastoral ministries team of staff members and deacons, and leads the church in accomplishing its mission. Many churches employ staff members to lead specialized areas and administer assigned programs. Staff positions include associate pastor, minister of education, minister of music, minister of recreation, age-group directors, and church administrator. A staff member may be salaried or a volunteer elected to work with an employed leader, such as a volunteer music director. Church officers and committees perform general administration functions for the church. Program directors (church-elected lay leaders) provide administrative leadership for Sunday School, Church Training, Woman's Missionary Union, and Brotherhood. Leaders fill three leadership roles in performing their responsibilities: generalist, specialist, and exemplar.

Coordination.—A church council guides planning, coordination, operation, and evaluation of the total church work.

See also CHURCH ADMINISTRATION, LEADERSHIP AND MANAGEMENT FOR; CHURCH COUNCIL.

BIBLIOGRAPHY: James D. Anderson, *To Come Alive* (1973). Jerry W. Brown, *Church Staff Teams That Win* (1979). Robert D. Dale, *Growing a Loving Church* (1974). Roy T. Edgemon, *Equipping Disciples Through Church Training* (1981). Brooks R. Faulkner, *Getting on Top of Your Work* (1973). Allen W. Graves, *A Church at Work* (1972). Robert K. Greenleaf, *Servant Leadership* (1977). Bruce Grubbs, *Helping a Small Church Grow* (1980). Paul Hersey and Kenneth Blanchard, *Management of Organizational Behavior* (1977). Alvin J. Lindgren, *Foundations for Purposeful Church Administration* (1965). Alvin J. Lindgren and Norman Shawchuck, *Management for Your Church* (1977). Reginald M. McDonough, *A Church on Mission* (1980), *Growing Ministers Growing Churches* (1980), *Keys to Effective Motivation* (1979), *Working with the Volunteer Leaders in the Church* (1976). Ernest E. Mosley, *Called to Joy* (1973). Harry M. Piland, *Basic Sunday School Work* (1981). William J. Reynolds, *Building an Effective Music Ministry* (1979). Lyle E. Schaller and Charles Tidwell, *Creative Church Administration* (1975). James A. Sheffield, *Church Officer and Committee Guidebook* (1976). Robert C. Worley, *A Gathering of Strangers* (1976).

REGINALD M. MCDONOUGH and JOHN R. CHANDLER

CHURCH ADMINISTRATION, LEADERSHIP AND MANAGEMENT FOR. In 1965 the SBC launched comprehensive plans for determining its emphasis for the 1970s. As these plans began to actualize in local church life, it became increasingly obvious that new administrative competencies must be developed. Those involved in church administration began to emphasize leadership and management in the local church.

This new emphasis gave rise to creative problem-solving situations. Although the concepts of leader and manager are by no means synonymous, the effective manager is also a leader. As Harold Koontz and Cyril O'Donnell have said:

> Managers should be leaders, but leaders need not be managers. In numerous studies during the past decade, it was assumed that leadership was merely a synonym for managership. While this is not true, it is apparent that the part of the manager's job which involves getting things done through people is undoubtedly made easier when a manager is a skillful leader.

A major problem with the traditional description of leadership and its characteristics is not that they were all invalid, but that they were expressed in rather vague terms and were considered absolutes. They implicitly assumed that there is one best way to lead, or there is one best type of leader personality. Most training materials and seminars tried to mold the individual into a pattern that approximated this ideal leader. Yet, the evidence from research clearly indicates that there is no single all-purpose leadership style.

Fred E. Fiedler, for example, has emphasized recently that effective group performance depends upon the proper match between the leader's style of interacting with the subordinates and the degree to which a situation yields control and influence to the leader. This leadership theory has been successfully researched and tested by others and stands as one of the most important breakthroughs in the study of leadership.

Management, like leadership, is as old as civilization. The study of how managers achieve results is predominantly a twentieth-century endeavor. Each of the managerial functions (planning, organizing, directing, and controlling) has been analyzed and described in a systematic way.

If management is becoming a science, as many authors believe it is, basic management fundamentals should have applicability to all managerial situations, including church administration. Basically, management is a set of skills that an ordinary person can acquire and develop. But management may also be thought of as a kind of work in which an individual performs.

How a person performs the work is referred to as style. Leadership style has to do with influence that goes beyond routine uses of organizational power. When considering leadership styles, distinctions are related to the degree of authoritarianism, participativeness, or permissiveness. This differs from managerial style—the activities of a manager which reflect a combination of concerns for people and production.

The reluctance of some to apply management skills to the local church is real. Some have questioned the practice of spiritual men using worldly management tools. Olan Hendrix pointedly answered this reluctance when he said, "The point is not whether these tools are spiritual or not—the whole point is whether WE are spiritual or not."

See also CHURCH ADMINISTRATION.

BIBLIOGRAPHY: Harold Koontz and Cyril O'Donnell, *Principles of Management,* 4th ed. (1968). Fred E. Fiedler, *Improving Leadership Effectiveness: Leader Match Concept* (1977). Olan Hendrix, *Management for the Christian Worker* (1976).

TOMMY L. BRIDGES

CHURCH AUDITORIUMS, MULTIPURPOSE. A growing architectural trend among Southern Baptists has been the construction of multipurpose buildings for worship, fellowship, recreation, and education. For many years churches have designed one of their first units as a future or present recreation center which they have used for worship. A new concept being introduced is the worship center used for recreation and fellowship.

This type of building has several advantages. It is a worship center with multiple uses which can be a permanent or an interim auditorium. It enables the smaller or beginning church to have a worship center and to provide a broad-based program of ministry. Less money is invested for buildings and land in order to have a well-rounded program ministering to the total person. More use of the building is achieved. If another worship center is constructed, there is little or no conversion expense or disruption of program. Quick changeover by the membership from worship to recreation can be a fellowship builder. Prospective members are introduced to the worship area by recreational involvement.

Careful planning in the design stage must be devoted to selecting durable, low-maintenance, beautiful surface materials and flooring; to acquiring flush-mounted, multipurpose lighting fixtures; and to providing large, accessible storage areas adjacent to the worship-recreation area. Special equipment needs and safety must be remembered.

Policies, procedures, and guidelines which recognize limitations because of multi-use must be explained to the church and approved. Adequate personnel for maintenance, changeovers, and programs must be secured, and time for changeovers allocated.

See also ARCHITECTURE, CHURCH.

NERON SMITH

CHURCH COUNCIL (I). The church council is a forum where church organization leaders plan, coordinate, and evaluate the total work of a church. Church organizations then implement the church's program according to their assigned tasks. The council's principal function is to help the church determine its course, coordinate its effort and activity, and evaluate its work. Duties include: (1) help the church understand its mission and define its priorities; (2) coordinate studies of church and community needs; (3) recommend to the church coordinated plans for evangelism, missions, Christian development, worship, stewardship, and ministry; (4) coordinate the church's schedule of activities, special events, and use of facilities; and (5) evaluate progress and the priority use of church resources.

Membership of the council varies among SBC churches but usually includes persons responsible for directing church organizations. Members usually include the pastor; church staff members; directors of Sunday School, Church Training, Woman's Missionary Union, Brotherhood, Media Services, Recreation Services, and Church Music; and chairpersons of the deacon body, stewardship committee, evangelism committee, missions committee, and other committees as needed. The pastor serves as chairman. Leaders serve on the church council as a result of election to designated church leadership positions. Their term corresponds to the term of office of their church-elected position.

The church council concept grew out of an expressed need among churches for help in selecting program plans suited to their specific needs. In 1923 SBC messengers asked for a correlation of activities suggested for the churches, and a definition of responsibilities of organizations. In 1937 and 1946 resolutions passed by SBC messengers called for a study of problems resulting from multiple church organizations, overlapping activities, and lost effort; and recommendations defining the functions and spheres of each organization. The 1937 Committee on Coordination and Correlation recommended the formation in churches of a church council

representing the several agencies of the church . . . to formulate an integrated and comprehensive church program; to devise a calendar of activities; to co-ordinate the work of all the church agencies; and to discover and develop the needed workers and leaders.

Churches reporting a church council on the Uniform Church Letter to the association increased from 36.1 percent in 1972 to 40.8 percent in 1979.

See also CHURCH ADMINISTRATION.

BIBLIOGRAPHY: Truman Brown, Jr., *Church Council Handbook* (1981).

REGINALD M. MCDONOUGH and JOHN R. CHANDLER

CHURCH EXTENSION, HOME MISSION BOARD PROGRAM OF (cf. Churches and Church-type Missions, Program of Establishing New, Vol. III). In 1971 the Home Mission Board set up the Department of Church Extension, bringing together the church planting assignments from the Departments of Metropolitan, Rural-Urban, and Pioneer Missions. Church planting among ethnic populations remained under the Language Missions program. Three major efforts dominated activities during the 1970s: the increase in the number of new churches started, the development of a corps of church planting specialists, and the development of church extension literature.

In 1979, 1,097 missionaries, mission pastors, and other personnel served through the Church Extension Division (the department was structurally elevated to a division, Sep. 1, 1979). Church Extension emphases this past decade included Extend Now, 1971-73, and the Bold Mission Thrust "congregationalizing" objective, 1976-80. Church planting is not new to Southern Baptists as noted by the fact that approximately one-third of the more than 35,000 Southern Baptist churches in 1980 were less than 30 years old. In 1979 a record number of 1,040 church-type missions were started, with 395 churches constituted.

See also CHURCH GROWTH, PRINCIPLES OF; CHURCH GROWTH PHILOSOPHY.

F. J. REDFORD

CHURCH GROWTH, PRINCIPLES OF (I). "Church growth is the divine-human process of adding to a church those who are saved through Jesus Christ equipping them for responsible discipleship resulting in witnessing, ministering, and establishing new fellowships of believers."

The following biblical principles of church growth presuppose that the church is built upon Jesus Christ (1 Pet. 2:4-8; 1 Cor. 3:10-16). Growth in Scripture is seen as (1) increase in number of believers (Acts 2:41,47; 6:1; 9:42; 11:21-24; 16:5); (2) deepening of discipleship of believers (Acts 2:42; Col. 2:6-7); (3) development of the body, the corporate church, under the direction of its Head, Jesus Christ, according to his gifts (Eph. 4:15-16); and (4) multiplication of the number of churches (Acts 9:31).

God intends that churches should grow (1) to bring all things together in Christ (Eph. 1:10); (2) to reconcile the world to himself (2 Cor. 5:19); (3) to gather a people of his own (1 Pet. 2:9-10); and (4) to bring abundant life to mankind (John 4:13-14). Growth results from God and man working together. Through the work of the Holy Spirit, (1) persons are convicted of sin and brought to faith (John 16:7-11); (2) believers are empowered for witness (Acts 1:8); and (3) the body is gifted for ministry (Rom. 12:1-8; 1 Cor. 12:1-11). Through the witness and ministry of believers, Southern Baptists communicate the gospel through proclaiming the death, resurrection, ascension, and second coming of Jesus (John 12:32; Acts 2:14-47; 1

Cor. 1:18-21; Eph. 3:8-11). Churches communicate the gospel through witnessing (Acts 1:8), caring for the flock of God (John 21:15-17), and applying the gospel in the world with an attitude of prayer, service, and love (Mark 10:35-45; 1 Pet. 5:1-5).

A church is responsible as God's agent to fulfill his purpose in the world (2 Cor. 5:18-20; 1 Pet. 2:9). While God builds up the body (Eph. 2:19-22; 4:7-16), a church must take the initiative as God's agent (Matt. 28:19-20; Acts 1:8). A church witnesses and ministers. It recognizes social, racial, and cultural distinctions and acknowledges the power of the gospel to transcend them and unite persons in Christ (Gal. 2:14-15; 3:28; Eph. 1:10; 2:14-15).

The characteristics of growing Southern Baptist churches reflect the practical application of biblical principles. These characteristics can be observed in various ways in different churches: (1) Pastor, staff leaders, and lay persons committed to and involved in growth; (2) priority commitment to winning lost persons to faith in Jesus Christ; (3) equipping new believers and other members for personal growth, witness, and ministry; (4) worship including music and preaching that is dynamic, challenging, joyful, and expectant; (5) fellowship that expresses acceptance, concern, and love; (6) centrality of the Bible in preaching and study; (7) use of the Sunday School as the major growth outreach arm of the church; (8) a caring concern for meeting the needs of all persons; (9) making specific plans to grow in the context of the church's setting; (10) expressing a world concern through scriptural giving and individual participation; and (11) a prayerful sensitivity to the leadership of the Holy Spirit.

Southern Baptist churches which experience growth have used many of the following actions, under the direction and power of the Holy Spirit: (1) Pastors are personally committed to church growth and share that commitment with the church, (2) the church's leadership team is challenged and equipped to accept growth as a priority concern, (3) the unreached and the lost in the community are located, (4) specific growth goals are established and accepted by the church leadership, (5) a strategy for growth is developed and personally directed by the pastor, and (6) constant reevaluation of the church's growth plans takes place. The church celebrates the work of the Holy Spirit in its life.

See also CHURCH EXTENSION, HOME MISSION BOARD PROGRAM OF; CHURCH GROWTH PHILOSOPHY.

BIBLIOGRAPHY: Grady Cothen and William Tanner, *Growing Southern Baptist Churches* (1979).

J. RALPH MCINTYRE

CHURCH GROWTH FUND, COORDINATED. See COORDINATED CHURCH GROWTH FUND.

CHURCH GROWTH PHILOSOPHY (cf. Church Growth, Principles of, Vol. I). While the term "church growth" has been popularized since 1955 by a clearly defined movement headed by such persons as Donald McGavran and Peter Wagner, Baptists have always expressed concern with the growth of churches. Baptists have sought to use various methods to bring people into the kingdom of God and into a local congregation. They have kept statistics on how well they accomplish that part of the Great Commission.

Church growth for Baptists has occurred through missions and evangelism, church extension, and education. A number of confessions of faith adopted by Baptists through the years included articles on missions and evangelism. The church has been variously defined to indicate that those who share a common life with one another as Christian disciples should seek to bring all persons into that same relationship. Southern Baptists' approach to church growth differs from the formalized church growth movement in that it does not hold to the homogeneous unit strategy; rather, it emphasizes the theological concept that Jesus Christ removed the barriers between persons.

Church extension, illustrated by the Thirty Thousand Movement, 1956-64, and the Home Mission Board's emphasis on evangelizing and congregationalizing, figures also as a major approach to church growth by Southern Baptists. Emphases and programs are developed and promoted to aid churches and associations in establishing new preaching and teaching stations that are designed to grow into functioning churches.

Southern Baptists have become increasingly committed to growing churches through individual evangelism and religious education, especially since the earlier part of the twentieth century. They place significant emphasis on lay evangelism and the Sunday School as the growth arm of the church. Arthur Flake's (*q.v.* I) formula for Sunday School growth has served as a standard still followed by churches.

With the popularity of the church growth movement at a significant level and because Southern Baptists traditionally prioritize growth, Grady Cothen of the Sunday School Board and William Tanner of the Home Mission Board joined efforts in 1980 to define church growth: "Church growth is the divine-human process of adding to a church those who are saved through Jesus Christ, equipping them for responsible discipleship resulting in witnessing, ministering, and establishing new fellowships of believers." This definition, while emphasizing numerical growth, points out a longstanding belief of Baptists about the equally important areas of growth in influence and spiritual maturity. Baptists also believe that all growth itself must mesh together with all other aspects of Christian teaching and practice.

See also CHURCH EXTENSION, HOME MISSION BOARD PROGRAM OF; CHURCH GROWTH, PRINCIPLES OF.

BIBLIOGRAPHY: James E. Carter, "Outreach Theology: A Comparison of Southern Baptist Thought and the Church Growth Movement," *Baptist History*

and Heritage (July, 1980). Grady Cothen and William Tanner, "Growing Southern Baptist Churches" (1979).

BOB I. JOHNSON

CHURCH LIBRARY. See LIBRARY, CHURCH.

CHURCH LOANS, HOME MISSION BOARD PROGRAM OF (III). The Division of Church Loans is responsible for "assisting churches, associations, and state conventions to provide financing for the purchase of church sites and for construction of church buildings." The division staff includes Robert Kilgore, director; associate directors Olin Cox, Bennett Cook, W. C. Dudley, Joe Carl Johnson, Bob Stidham, and William Updike; and assistant directors T. V. Haynes and Thomas Thrailkill.

At the close of 1979 the assets of the Division of Church Loans were divided into four separate funds as follows:

The Church Building Loan Fund.—This fund totals $7,500,000. These funds have been received from special gifts from individuals and churches and through wills, trusts, annuities, and other such gifts designated to be used as loans for churches.

The Church Extension Loan Fund.—This fund contains assets of $40,000,000. These funds have been received over the years from the denomination and from capitalized earnings. Of this amount, $17,000,000 has been borrowed from "banks, insurance companies, and other financial institutions" in keeping with authorization granted by the SBC in 1967.

The Site Fund.—This fund totals $6,500,000 and is designed for the purchase of unimproved real estate for future church usage. The Site Fund is interest free until the church begins to use the property but not to exceed two and one-half years.

The Negro-Ethnic Loan Fund.—This fund has assets of $1,150,000. This fund was created as a result of the "statement on the national crisis" adopted by the SBC in 1968. This fund provides financing to those ethnic Baptist churches not members of the SBC. Loans from this fund are not to exceed $40,000 per church.

The total of all assets of the Division of Church Loans is $55,150,000. In addition the division is servicing $4,000,000 in loan participations which it has sold to other investors. Assets of the division plus loans serviced total almost $60,000,000. During the 1970s an average of about 16,500 churches each year reported debt aggregating $1,250,000,000. Also during the decade, about 11,000 churches put in place nearly $300,000,000 in new construction, remodeling, and land acquisition each year.

Because the assets of the Program of Church Loans are relatively small when compared to these figures, the HMB has had to set priorities in using the assets of the Program of Church Loans. These assets are directed toward the newer areas of the SBC and the new church needing its first unit building. The HMB has defined these newer areas as those state conven-

2161   **Church Music, Vocational Training for**

tions organized since 1940. Loans in the older states are processed only under the most exceptional circumstances.

Interest rates charged by the Program of Church Loans vary from time to time according to the commercial market, with terms that also vary up to 20 years.

ROBERT KILGORE

CHURCH MEMBER ORIENTATION

(III). The basic purpose and design of new member orientation is to lead individuals to reflect upon their salvation experience, to understand the nature of the Christian life and the demands of church membership, and to become increasingly committed to living out the commands of Christ.

Churches vary widely in their handling of new members. Some simply receive them and do nothing more; others present them with membership packets; some receive them and enroll them in new member classes; and some receive members after a prescribed course of study has been completed.

Responsibility for the local program of new church member orientation rests with the individual church. The program design and the creation of materials, however, are the responsibility of the Church Training Department of the Sunday School Board. In keeping with the demands of the churches, both a 13-week and a four-week course of study have been provided, with graded curriculum for children, youth, and adults. The study emphasizes the salvation experience, Baptist doctrines, the denomination's work (or Baptist history), and the work of the local church.

In general, these courses are taught on Sunday night during the Church Training hour. While the greater percentage of churches with such programs provide orientation principally for new converts, some include persons who join the church by transfer of letter.

In 1978-79, 4,172 churches reported new member training for adults, 2,867 for youth, and 2,604 for children. In June, 1979, a new resource, *Survival Kit for New Christians,* by Ralph Neighbour, Jr., was introduced along with other materials which have been favorably received.

ROY T. EDGEMON

CHURCH MUSIC, VOCATIONAL TRAINING FOR.

The ministry of church music among Southern Baptists has experienced phenomenal growth and development. The continuing demand by local churches for adequately trained church musicians shows no let-up. Increasing interest, commitment, and support by Southern Baptists for competently prepared music ministers are at a record high. Enrollments in church music curricula on both the undergraduate and seminary levels are at their highest point.

Historically, Southern Baptist colleges have provided some music training since the late nineteenth century when Furman, Stetson, Howard Payne, Mary Hardin-Baylor, and Meredith cataloged professional music course offerings. During the first three decades of the twentieth century, music became a recognized discipline in many Baptist colleges both as a cultural addition to traditional liberal arts curricula and as a practical tool in the training of ministerial students.

Church music as a specific vocational major began to flourish after World War II. Baptist educational institutions, in response to developing and escalating needs of Baptist congregations in the South and Southwest, took definite steps to minister educationally to the burgeoning numbers of church music volunteers. Traditional college music curricula were expanded during the 1950s and 1960s to encompass functional church music courses.

During the past 30 years, one of the most rapidly growing segments of many Baptist colleges has been the church music department. A 1979 survey of Baptist institutions of higher learning revealed that 46 senior colleges and universities and seven junior colleges offered a major in church music. Each, almost without exception, had a vocational core of hymnology, music in worship, service playing, and sacred choral and vocal literature. In 1979, 1,952 students of the 121,464 enrolled as undergraduates in Southern Baptist colleges and universities were identified as vocational church music students.

The earliest sacred music department in a Southern Baptist theological seminary was organized and headed by Isham E. Reynolds (*q.v.* II) at Southwestern Seminary in 1915. The music department of New Orleans Seminary (then Baptist Bible Institute), was established in 1918 by E. O. Sellers (*q.v.* II). Church music at Southern Seminary was instituted in 1921, and the School of Church Music there began its first session in the fall of 1943. Golden Gate Seminary began music classes in 1945. Southeastern Seminary began church music training in 1956. In 1980 trustees approved a church music major at Midwestern Seminary to begin in the fall of 1981.

The musical training offered in each of the six Southern Baptist seminaries is designed to prepare students for specialized ministries within the expanding field of church music. Seminary music divisions seek to provide within their proscribed program statements competent musical leadership for local churches, colleges, denominational agencies, and worldwide mission fields. A balanced approach which synthesizes biblical knowledge, evangelism, theoretical and practical musicianship, and scholarship is sought.

The music curriculum in the seminaries is structured to offer students a broad spectrum of musical experiences. Areas of concentrated study are available in such fields as church music education, music history, music theory, composition, conducting, music ministry, organ, piano, voice, and ensembles.

Degrees offered by one or more of the seminaries include Master of Church Music, Master of Music, Doctor of Education, and Doctor of Musical Arts. A Diploma in Church Music for noncollege graduates is also available. In 1979 approximately 875 graduate music students were enrolled in Southern Baptist seminaries.

CLAUDE H. RHEA

CHURCH MUSIC CONFERENCE, SOUTHERN BAPTIST. See SOUTHERN BAPTIST CHURCH MUSIC CONFERENCE.

CHURCH RECREATION. See RECREATION, CHURCH.

CHURCH-STATE DECISIONS, THE COURTS AND. The 1970s provided the courts a wide range of experience in interpreting religious liberty guaranteed by the First Amendment.

Establishment Clause Cases.—The Supreme Court drew together, in *Lemon* v. *Kurtzman* (1971), the tests it had developed in several other cases to determine whether government action violates the Establishment Clause: (1) Does the action have a secular purpose? (2) Does the action have a primary effect which neither advances nor inhibits religion? (3) Does the action foster excessive government entanglement with religion or foster political divisiveness on religious grounds? These tests have been applied to a variety of fact patterns.

The Supreme Court voided a New York law which provided for reimbursement of tuition paid to church-related schools and appropriated public funds to maintain and repair those schools. Both of these actions were held to have the primary effect of advancing religion *(Pearl* v. *Nyquist* [1973]).

Even though the Court reaffirmed the constitutionality of lending textbooks to children in parochial schools, it held that state financial programs of remedial instruction, counseling, and testing, as well as speech and hearing services, unconstitutionally aided religion *(Meek* v. *Pittenger* [1975]). The Court further held that public expenditures for instructional equipment and field trips for parochial schools not only aided religion but also led to "excessive entanglement" *(Wolman* v. *Walter* [1977]).

In 1971 the Court held unconstitutional two state laws which provided state funds to pay a part of the salaries of teachers who taught secular subjects in church-related schools *(Lemon* v. *Kurtzman),* and then held that the states could not reimburse those schools for expenditures contracted for before the decision in *Lemon* was handed down *(Lemon* v. *Kurtzman II* [1973]).

Similarly, the Court found a plan to reimburse church-related schools for expenses incurred in state-required testing of children to be in violation of the Establishment Clause *(Levitt* v. *Pearl* [1973]).

While not deciding directly on the constitutionality of the practice, the Court intimated that federal funds, appropriated under Title I of the Elementary and Secondary Education Act of 1965, could be used to help educationally deprived children even if they were enrolled in church-related schools *(Wheeler* v. *Berrera* [1974]).

The Court refused to review a decision by a court of appeals that the requirement of forced attendance at Sunday church or chapel services by students in the federal military academies violated the Establishment Clause *(Anderson* v. *Laird* [1972]).

The Supreme Court made a distinction between higher education and elementary and secondary education. It sustained a federal law which provided for grants to church-related colleges and universities for construction of buildings which would be exclusively used for secular education purposes *(Tilton* v. *Richardson* [1971]). It approved a state-funded scheme to finance campus construction *(Hunt* v. *McNair* [1973]). Finally, the Court sustained state per-student subsidies to church-related colleges which were not so permeated with religion that the Establishment Clause would be offended *(Roemer* v. *Board of Public Works* [1976]).

The Court also held that the National Labor Relations Board does not have jurisdiction over parochial schools *(N.L.R.B.* v. *Catholic Bishop of Chicago* [1979]), and, in what may appear a change from the Bible and prayer decision, two lower federal courts have upheld the rules adopted by a public school board permitting the observance of certain religious holy seasons because, the Court stated, they were not promulgated to serve a religious purpose *(Florey* v. *Sioux Falls School District* [1979]).

Free Exercise Cases.—As with the Establishment Clause, the Supreme Court established tests to determine whether government action infringes the free exercise of religion: (1) Is the activity affected by the action pervasively religious? (2) Does the action place a burden or inhibition on free exercise rights? (3) Assuming an affirmative answer to these two tests, is the burden justified by a compelling state interest which cannot be served by less restrictive means *(Wisconsin* v. *Yoder* [1972])?

The *Yoder* decision declared that the Free Exercise Clause was violated by a law which required Amish children to continue in public schools beyond the level which Amish, for religious reasons, believed their children should go. The Court recognized the state's interest in universal education but held that interest was not compelling enough to override the First Amendment rights of the Amish.

In *McDaniel* v. *Paty* (1978), the Supreme Court held that a state law banning ministers from serving as delegates to a limited constitutional convention interfered with the free exercise of religion.

Two federal courts have held that the leasing of classrooms in parochial schools and assigning public school teachers to conduct secular courses in those rooms—a form of dual enrollment—is unconstitutional *(Americans United* v. *Pair* [1974], and *Americans United* v. *Board of Education* [1974]), though a number of state courts have held that the Free Exercise Clause permits released time programs in which students are dismissed from secular classes in order to undertake off-campus religious instruction.

There have been many other church-state cases during the 1970s, but these demonstrate that although the wall of separation may at times seem as Chief Justice Warren E. Burger said, "a blurred, indistinct, and variable barrier," it is still standing firm.

See also PUBLIC FUNDS AND CHURCH INSTITUTIONS.

BIBLIOGRAPHY: Robert T. Miller and Ronald B. Flowers, *Toward Benevolent Neutrality: Church, State, and the Supreme Court* (1977). *Journal of Church and State.*

JOHN W. BAKER

CHURCH STUDY COURSE (III; cf. Study Courses, Vol. II). The Church Study Course is the basic training system for lay leaders in Southern Baptist churches. Courses for members are available also. From the small beginning in 1902, more than 300,000 study course awards were issued in 1979.

The 1970 CSC system was revised and simplified effective Oct. 1, 1975. Three types of diplomas are now available: Leadership, Subject Area, and Christian Development.

Leadership diplomas are designed for church leaders and potential leaders. Each diploma requires six courses specified by the sponsoring program. An advanced leadership diploma requires eight courses. Leadership diplomas in 1980 included: Sunday School, Sunday School Advanced, Church Training, Church Music, Woman's Missionary Union, Brotherhood, Deacon Ministry, Media Services, Media Skills, Church Recreation, Senior Adult Ministry, and Associational. Seals are added to many of these diplomas to indicate an age-group or area specialization.

The first Subject Area diplomas were added to the system in 1978. Designed for all Christians who desire an in-depth understanding of major areas of Christian knowledge, each diploma requires six courses. Diplomas now offered are: Bible Survey, Baptist Doctrine, Missions, Christian Family Life, Life Enrichment for Senior Adults, Bible Survey for Youth, and Baptist Doctrine for Youth.

Christian Development diplomas for adults and youth, approved in 1975, required that eight courses be earned each two years. These were replaced in 1979 by a new series of five Christian Development diplomas, which measure the total number of courses a person has completed in the CSC since Jan. 1, 1970. Each diploma has three seals. The first diploma is awarded when any five courses are completed. For each additional five courses the next seal or diploma is awarded in sequence. These five diplomas, each with three seals, will measure up to 100 courses. The diplomas in this series are: Christian Development, Advanced Christian Development, Master Christian Development, Distinguished Christian Development, and Special Citation Christian Development. The first

diploma is also available in Spanish. Many courses in Spanish are included in the CSC.

The more than 400 courses in the CSC system are divided into 23 subject areas. Requirements for class study are simply to read the course material and attend classes. Sessions missed must be made up by completing written assignments. Requirements for individual study are simply to read the course material and complete the personal learning activities. Other types of study such as "Educational Institution Study" and "Lesson Course Study" continue to be offered.

Complete information about the CSC system is published annually in a catalog. The Church Program Services Coordination Subcommittee of the Inter-Agency Council supervises the CSC through a coordinator at the Sunday School Board.

WILLIAM R. COX

CHURCH TRAINING (cf. Baptist Training Union, Vols. I, III). The 1970s demanded the total energy of the Church Training Department of the Sunday School Board in amplifying and developing the program as redesigned in 1968 and 1969. Thus, 1970 was the most crucial year in the history of Church Training (Baptist Training Union) since 1935.

The department implemented the new Grouping Grading Plan to provide four age divisions: Adult (ages 18 and up), Youth (ages 12 to 17), Children (ages 6 to 11), and Preschool (birth through 5). The department also introduced new dated curriculum periodicals and a variety of undated resource materials, and offered five new administrative manuals, one general and one for each age division, to facilitate the program changes, define new terms, and explain the usages of materials. The program magazine acquired a new title, *Church Training*.

During the 1970s, flexibility and balance served as organizing principles for the preparation of materials. Designers sought to provide a wide variety of study materials while striking a balance with the Church Training task subjects: Theology, ethics, history, church polity, and organization. New member orientation, church member training, and church leader training continued as the distinctive responsibilities of Church Training.

The launching of CHURCH: The Sunday Night Place at Fort Worth, TX, on Mar. 18, 1973, set in motion plans to give the Church Training program high visibility in the churches and in the Convention. The first edition of *CHURCH: The Sunday Night Place Guide* was published in 1974. The publication was issued annually through Oct., 1978.

In 1976-77 the department developed a pilot project testing the Equipping Center concept of training. After being field tested in approximately 200 churches, the Equipping Center concept was approved. As the Equipping Center materials were being tested, written, and produced, the department strengthened ongoing curriculum materials.

Developing Your Church Training Program and new administration books for each age division were released in 1977.

In Jan., 1978, Roy T. Edgemon, a native of Wichita Falls, TX, assumed his role as director of the department, replacing Philip B. Harris, who retired in 1977 after 17 years of service in the position.

In the late 1970s, the department reassessed its program, analyzed its priorities, and redefined the tasks of Church Training in relationship to other programs of the SSB and other SBC agencies. In 1979 the department stated its task in three parts: (1) Equip church members in discipleship and personal ministry, (2) teach Christian theology and Baptist doctrine, Christian ethics, Christian history, and church polity and organization, and (3) equip church leaders for service.

In 1979 seven priorities emerged as the means for implementing Church Training tasks: Ongoing curriculum materials, Equipping Centers, new church member materials, Build Up: A Church Training Enrollment Plan, Baptist Doctrine Study, *MasterLife: Discipleship Training for Leaders,* and the National Youth Discipleship Program. Equipping Centers were launched in Oct., 1979, with eight modules in six Equipping Centers ready for use by the churches.

The department and other programs of the SSB approached the 1980s with a firm commitment to join other SBC agencies in support of Bold Mission Thrust. A close working relationship developed particularly between the department and the Evangelism Section of the Home Mission Board as evidenced by materials produced to support the National Youth Evangelism Discipleship Strategy and other mission efforts.

Periodical plans were developed to emphasize personal growth and church growth in support of Bold Mission Thrust goals. Special effort was made to make the materials biblical, sequential in content, practical, and personal. The department prepared to launch new youth periodicals and a new approach to Sunday night youth activities in an effort to involve every youth in discipleship training.

Also on the horizon was *MasterLife,* a sequential, developmental, group-discipling process that enables one to make Christ master and to master life.

See also EQUIPPING CENTERS.

RICHARD B. SIMS

CHURCHES AND CHURCH-TYPE MISSIONS, PROGRAM OF ESTABLISHING NEW (III). See CHURCH EXTENSION, HOME MISSION BOARD PROGRAM OF.

CHURCHILL, RALPH DEES (b. Murray, KY, Mar. 10, 1905; d. Fort Worth, TX, Oct. 21, 1978). Seminary professor. The son of Maude Churchill and James Churchill, a mortician, he served as professor of religious journalism, Southwestern Baptist Theological Seminary, 1944-70; director of publicity and extension at Southwestern, 1944-56; and minister of music in numerous churches in the Dallas-Fort Worth area. He attended Murray, KY, State College (B.S., 1934), serving as Baptist student secretary there, 1934-40. He earned three degrees from Southwestern (B.S.M., 1946; M.R.E., 1946; and D.R.E., 1956). He married Ruth George Stone, Nov., 1934. They had three children: Esther, Sheryl, and Kenneth.

From 1951 until retiring in 1970, he served as a commissioner of the Seminary Extension Department, SBC. From 1947 to 1956, he was secretary-treasurer, Southwestern Seminary Alumni Association, and editor of *Southwestern News* and other seminary publications. He is buried in Laurel Land Cemetery, Fort Worth, TX.

CHARLES A. TIDWELL

CITIZENSHIP. See CHRISTIAN CITIZENSHIP CORPS, THE.

CITY MISSIONS (I). See METROPOLITAN MISSIONS, HOME MISSION BOARD PROGRAM OF.

CIVIL RIGHTS. The modern civil rights movement may be said to have started, Dec. 5, 1955, when Rosa Parks, a black woman, refused to give her bus seat to a white man in Montgomery, AL. The resulting Montgomery bus boycott catapulted Baptist minister Martin Luther King, Jr. (q.v.), into the national limelight. Another major event occurred in Greensboro, NC, Feb. 1, 1960, when four freshmen from North Carolina A & T University were refused service at a lunch counter at a Woolworth store. The resulting "sit-in" led to a wave of demonstrations across the South that captured the attention of the nation.

The civil rights movement entered a new phase in 1966 when Stokely Carmichael, during a march in Mississippi, spoke of "Black Power." The rhetoric and the tactics became more militant. The Black Panthers became the symbol of the new black militancy.

Congress passed important civil rights legislation under the Lyndon Johnson administration. Federally funded programs were initiated to deal with problems which particularly affected minorities.

In the 1970s considerable attention was focused on court-ordered busing to achieve integration and on affirmative action programs. These concerns highlighted the complexity of civil rights issues by illustrating that racial issues were inextricably interwoven with fundamental political and economic issues.

During the 1970s some Southern Baptist agencies and churches were active in civil rights issues. Most Southern Baptists who were concerned about racial issues, however, preferred ministries to minorities rather than involvement in the more politically oriented civil rights movement. SBC meetings during this period passed several resolutions pertaining to race but did not address specifically the matter of civil rights.

See also RACE RELATIONS.

JOHN A. WOOD

CLEAR CREEK BAPTIST SCHOOL (I, III). Dennis Merrill Aldridge has served as president since 1954. There are 325 former and present students who now serve as ministers in Kentucky. The 1,000 graduates of Clear Creek are pastors or missionaries in 43 states and six foreign countries.

Improvements in the 1970s included: renovation of Industries Building to an administration building with six classrooms, chapel, 20 offices, bookstore, post office, and student lounge; building a two-story library-music building with classrooms, library, offices, piano, voice and organ practice rooms, and medical clinic; addition of 56 student apartments and houses and two faculty homes plus five faculty-owned homes on campus, a four-room children's center, and a print shop; and renovations and additions to student housing.

Currently there are 196 students enrolled and a faculty-staff of 32. Endowment increased to $1,000,000. Three programs are taped in the campus studio for 64 radio stations.

DENNIS MERRILL ALDRIDGE

CLEM, ORBIE RUSSELL (b. Prairie Dell, TX, Apr. 2, 1902; d. Houston, TX, Apr. 12, 1978). Pastor. Son of William M. and Elizabeth Clem, he attended Arkansas' Mountain Home Baptist College Academy, Decatur College, and Oklahoma Baptist University. In 1934-36, he served as pastor of a pioneering Southern Baptist church at Sunland, CA, predating the California Southern Baptist Convention by six years. He married Lois Maurine Bondurant, Nov. 3, 1935. They had one son, Russell. Clem helped organize the Kansas Convention of Southern Baptists, Mar. 19, 1946. He was elected vice-president and named editor of the *Kansas Southern Baptist Beams,* serving eight years while leading the First Southern Baptist Church, Wichita. He is buried in Forest Park Cemetery, Houston, TX.

N. J. WESTMORELAND

CLINARD, HAROLD GORDON (b. Springfield, TN, Apr. 14, 1922; d. Abilene, TX, Dec. 4, 1973). Minister, educator, author. Son of Louis Clinard, a businessman, and Lydia (Tucker) Clinard, he graduated from Union University, Jackson, TN (A.B., 1944). Ordained by Springfield Baptist Church on Dec. 1, 1940, he married Christine Browder, May 28, 1941. They had three children: Patricia Christine, Glen Truitt, and Tracye.

While in college, Clinard served as pastor of Mt. Olive Baptist Church, Union City, TN, 1940-42; Bethel Baptist Church, Yorkville, TN, 1941-43; Spring Hill Baptist Church, Trenton, TN, 1942-45; and First Baptist Church, Rutherford, TN, 1942-45. While attending Southwestern Baptist Theological Seminary (B.D., 1949; Th.D., 1958), he served Joshua Baptist Church, Joshua, TX, 1945-46; First Baptist Church, Burleson, TX, 1948-52; and First Baptist Church, Huntsville, TX, 1952-55.

Clinard was professor of preaching at Southwestern Seminary, 1955-66. He was pastor of the First Baptist Church, San Angelo, TX, 1966-70. While at San Angelo, he served two years as president of the Baptist General Convention of Texas, 1968-69. He served as the Billy Graham Professor of Evangelism at Southern Baptist Theological Seminary, Louisville, KY, 1970-72. In 1972 he became distinguished professor of Bible at Hardin-Simmons University. During his seminary career he was in popular demand as interim pastor, supply preacher, and conference and assembly preacher. He conducted numerous revival campaigns and was in great demand for special occasion sermons.

Clinard was author of *The Message We Proclaim* (1966), *Evangelism: The Cutting Edge* (1974), and coauthor of a basic text in preaching, with Henry C. Brown, Jr. and Jesse J. Northcutt, *Steps to the Sermon* (1963). He is buried in Laurel Land Cemetery, Fort Worth, TX.

JESSE J. NORTHCUTT

CLINICAL PASTORAL EDUCATION. See PASTORAL CARE.

COLEMAN, LUCIEN EDWIN, SR. (b. near Lonoke, AR, Aug. 28, 1904; d. Louisville, KY, Sep. 2, 1975). Attorney and denominational leader. The son of Hettie Dickerson and Elmer Minor Coleman, a merchant and planter, he received a law degree from Cumberland University, Lebanon, TN, in 1925 and practiced law in Arkansas for 21 years. He was Brotherhood secretary, Kentucky Baptist Convention, 1954-57, and associate secretary and projects coordinator, Brotherhood Commission, SBC, 1958-69. He is buried in Forest Hill Cemetery, Memphis, TN.

ROY JENNINGS

COLLEGE, THE DENOMINATIONAL. See HIGHER EDUCATION, TRENDS AMONG BAPTISTS IN.

COLLEY, WILLIAM W. (b. Prince Edward County, VA, Feb. 12, 1847; d. c. 1919-20). Foreign missionary. Graduating from Richmond Institute (1873), he was appointed a missionary to Nigeria, 1874, serving under the Foreign Mission Board, SBC, until 1879. Returning to the United States, he led black Baptists to organize for foreign missions in 1880, serving as first secretary of the Baptist Foreign Mission Convention, USA, until 1883, when he went to Liberia as a missionary of that board. Colley served under various black Baptist mission boards in West Africa until his death.

H. CORNELL GOERNER

COLLINS, MAXIE C., JR. (b. Lake City, SC, Apr. 15, 1904; d. Columbia, SC, Dec. 31, 1972). Pastor, public leader, and counselor of alcoholics. The son of Maxie C. and Ophelia (Matthews) Collins, he studied at Furman University (B.A.) and Southern Baptist Theological Seminary (Th.M.). He married Mildred Kincaid, Oct. 15, 1928. They had two sons. Collins created an alcoholic rehabilitation program, known as Fairview Center, in Ridgeway, SC, in 1950, and served as its director for nearly two decades. In 1966 he published *Defeating Alcoholism the Fairview Way.* He is buried in Greenlawn Cemetery, Columbia, SC.

HOWARD G. MCCLAIN

COLOMBIA, MISSION IN (I, III). As the 1980s began, the Baptist hospital in Barranquilla was ministering to about 900 persons weekly. Medical caravans traveled to remote areas with medical aid and the gospel. The seminary in Cali had moved from an international board of trustees to an administrative board elected by the Colombian Baptist Convention. "Telephone Friend" provided a telephone devotional to thousands who dialed in weekly. The radio programs were reaching an estimated 500,000 persons daily. Thirteen branch book stores facilitated book and literature distribution. More than $25,000 in Foreign Mission Board hunger and disaster relief funds went in 1979 to aid fire, flood, and earthquake victims. At the end of 1979, 82 missionaries served in 11 cities.

J. BRYAN BRASINGTON

COLORADO, BAPTIST FOUNDATION OF (III). Bill Landers has served as president since 1965. Current assets total more than $400,000. Primary functions are in wills and trusts. Short-term interim loans are made as monies are available. William Harold (Tony) Anthony became associate to the president in 1978.

BILL LANDERS

COLORADO ASSOCIATIONS (III). The 10 associations which were active in 1970 continued throughout the decade without name changes. One new association was formed.

New Associations. HIGH COUNTRY. Organized Oct. 10, 1977, by messengers from eight churches and six missions. All the churches withdrew from Grand Valley Association, and one mission was received from Continental Divide Association. In 1979 seven churches and one mission reported 101 baptisms, 849 members, $219,580 total gifts, $40,909 mission gifts, and $1,753,500 property value. Five missions' totals were included with the respective sponsoring churches, with four of the missions sponsored by churches in the High Country Association.

JAMES LEE YOUNG

COLORADO BAPTIST GENERAL CONVENTION (cf. Colorado Baptist General Convention, History of, Vol. I; Colorado, Baptist General Convention of, Vol. III).

I. History. With the withdrawal of Southern Baptist churches in North and South Dakota, Montana, and Wyoming at the end of 1967 to form the Northern Plains Baptist Convention, the Colorado Baptist General Convention became a one-state convention with 114 churches, 10 associations, and 32,390 members. Thus, 1968 was a year of adjustment from the loss of 35 percent of the churches, 32 percent of the church membership, two staff members (John Baker and Nicy Murphy who went to the new convention), and reduced Cooperative Program receipts. Glen E. Braswell has served as executive secretary since 1967.

At the annual session of the convention in 1970, the executive director recommended to the messengers that the starting of new churches be the major priority in the 1970s, with a goal of 180 churches by 1980. The recommendation was approved. Although the goal was not achieved, there were 167 churches and 33 church-type missions at fiscal year-end 1980.

Roy Owen resigned as associate executive director and director of missions to become executive director-treasurer of the Northern Plains Baptist Convention, Oct. 15, 1976. On May 1, 1978, the Colorado Convention employed W. H. Anthony to serve as its business manager. Anthony has also served part-time with the Baptist Foundation of Colorado.

The CBGC's Silver Anniversary was 1980. A highlight of the year was the completion of a new Baptist building at 7393 S. Alton Way and Yosemite in Englewood. The new building contains more than 19,000 square feet of space at a cost of just over $1,000,000. The new building was occupied, July 1, 1980, and dedicated in August during the meeting of the Executive Board.

A second highlight of the year was the approval by the Executive Board of the first million dollar Cooperative Program budget. The proposed budget of $1,113,334 was considered by messengers at the convention's annual session. Total anticipated receipts were $1,965,982 for fiscal 1980-81.

The Executive Board continues to employ all convention employees, except the executive director-treasurer, who is hired by messengers to the annual convention session, and is the authorized legal agent in transacting business of the convention and responsible for directing the convention's business in the interim session.

Colorado Southern Baptists' state newspaper, the *Rocky Mountain Baptist,* continues to be the official news publication of the convention and is published 48 times per year. With a circulation of 9,400 at the end of 1979, the paper is financed by advertisements, subscriptions, and the Cooperative Program. James Lee Young became editor following the retirement of O. L. Bayless in Dec., 1977.

II. Church Development Division. The Church Development Division was brought into

COLORADO BAPTIST MANOR BUILDING, Denver. Purchased in 1978; valued at $2,000,000. Retirement complex owned and operated by Colorado Baptist Manor, Inc., subsidiary corporation of the Baptist Foundation of Colorado.

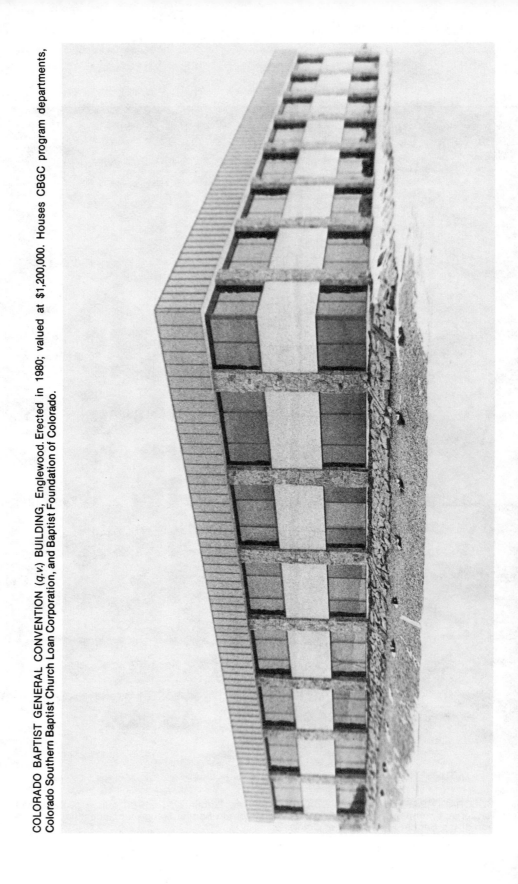

COLORADO BAPTIST GENERAL CONVENTION (*q.v.*) BUILDING, Englewood. Erected in 1980; valued at $1,200,000. Houses CBGC program departments, Colorado Southern Baptist Church Loan Corporation, and Baptist Foundation of Colorado.

being in 1978 through a major change in organizational structure of the Executive Board staff. The division is made up of the departments of Missions, Evangelism, Stewardship-Brotherhood, and Woman's Missionary Union. The division director is Don Murray, who serves also as state missions director.

Evangelism Department. —In Dec., 1978, Harold P. McGlamery retired as state director of evangelism, having served since Jan. 1, 1965. Glen E. Braswell, executive director-treasurer of the CBGC, served as interim evangelism director until W. Michael Wilson was named to head the evangelism department, Nov., 1979. Baptisms continued to climb from 1978-80, reversing a downward trend of previous years. From 1969 through 1979, baptisms reported statewide totaled 29,544.

Evangelism directors since the convention's organization in 1956 have been: Jack Stanton, 1956-59; O. L. Bayless, 1960-65; Harold McGlamery, 1965-78; and W. Michael Wilson, 1979.

Missions. —Don Murray has served as state missions director since 1977. The missions department works through 11 associations. In 1956 the CBGC entered a cooperative agreement with the Home Mission Board to coordinate missions in the state. A missions task force consists of 58 missionaries on permanent assignment, including wives. This force is strengthened by approximately 50 summer missionaries (for 10 weeks) and between 3,500 to 4,000 special project missionaries during the summer.

In the next two decades Colorado Baptists will be attempting to encourage every person in Colorado to respond in a positive manner to the gospel of Christ. They will attempt to establish churches in every community. Already at least 150 places are recognized as needing a church.

As the result of an ethnic study made in 1978, the number of language congregations has increased from 8 to 14. Two new deaf church-type missions and two new Korean congregations have been established. A ministry to refugees has been established at the Brentwood Baptist Center which is owned and operated by Colorado Baptists. Colorado is approximately 26 percent ethnic with the projection of being 33 percent by 1982.

Work continues with the Ute Indians in the Ignacio area, and Hispanic work in the state is growing, enhanced by the efforts of a language missions coordinator for the state. A new emphasis on bivocational ministry also was begun in 1979.

A Christian Social Ministries program was begun through Riverside Baptist Center, Grand Junction, in 1978. Resort ministries continued to be emphasized through cooperative ministry with the HMB. Each year, mission work in the state has been aided and augmented by groups from other states who came to Colorado to do surveys, evangelistic outreach, Vacation Bible Schools, Backyard Bible Clubs, and construction of church buildings, among other projects.

In 1978 more than 6,000 persons came to the state as short-term mission volunteers, most of them with church groups.

Metro Denver has been designated a "Key City" in Bold Mission Thrust. The counties of Moffatt, Rio Grande, Garfield, Eagle, and Routt have been designated as "Key Counties." Much attention will be given to evangelizing and congregationalizing in these areas in order to reach the state and nation for Christ by the year 2000.

Missions directors since the convention's formation have been: Leroy Smith, 1956-57; Cecil Pearson, 1957-59; C. A. Dabney, 1959-62; John Baker, 1962-67; Robert Lambert, 1968-75; Roy Owen, 1975-76; and Don Murray, 1977- .

Stewardship-Brotherhood. —Jimmy R. Rich became director of the Stewardship and Brotherhood Departments in Dec., 1975. Harold P. McGlamery had the Brotherhood responsibility, along with evangelism, from the time of his joining the convention staff in 1965 until Rich's employment. Stewardship was assigned to the state director of missions, 1957-75, when Rich assumed the stewardship duties. Other Brotherhood directors for the convention have been: Philip T. Card, 1956, and Bill Landers, 1958-65. Brotherhood enrollment was 1,519 in 1969 and 1,801 in 1979.

Woman's Missionary Union. —Nicy Murphy was the CBGC's first WMU director, beginning in Dec., 1956, and serving until Feb., 1968, when she became WMU director for the newly-formed Northern Plains Baptist Convention. Betty Lynn Cadle succeeded Murphy and served until she resigned in 1970 to enter foreign missions service of Southern Baptists. Sydney Portis became the state WMU director, May 1, 1971, and has continued to serve in that capacity. WMU enrollment was 3,084 in 1979.

III. Church Services Division. The Church Services Division was brought into being in 1978 in the same organizational restructure that brought about the Church Development Division. The services division is made up of campus student ministries, church administration, family ministries, church training, church media, church recreation, Bible teaching, church music, and church architecture. The division director is D. G. McCoury, who also directs campus student ministries, church administration, and family ministries. McCoury formerly served as Sunday School director, 1975-78.

Bible Teaching (Sunday School), Church Music, Church Architecture. —As a part of the staff reorganization in 1978, Bob Lawrence, statewide Church Music director, became the director also for Bible Teaching (then referred to as Sunday School director). He retained responsibility also for the CBGC's Church Architecture Department.

Sunday School, church music, and church architecture responsibilities were shifted from Philip T. Card, who initially had charge of several departments when the convention was orga-

COLORADO STATISTICAL SUMMARY

Year	Associations	Churches	Church Membership	Baptisms	SS Enrollment	VBS Enrollment	CT Enrollment	WMU Enrollment	Brotherhood Enrollment	Ch. Music Enrollment	Mission Gifts	Total Gifts	Value Church Property
1969	10	122	36,873	1,991	25,314	14,232	13,718	3,942	1,545	3,828	$ 367,790	$ 2,918,408	$13,392,662
1970	10	122	38,344	2,377	25,454	14,054	11,491	3,664	1,548	4,274	425,591	3,259,344	14,496,107
1971	10	122	40,821	2,643	26,122	17,865	9,242	3,357	1,732	4,161	489,645	3,636,610	15,417,565
1972	10	129	43,102	2,980	27,049	19,516	8,516	3,002	1,642	4,711	578,855	4,323,470	16,993,508
1973	10	134	45,996	2,592	27,854	18,409	8,880	2,961	1,633	5,344	721,862	4,887,179	20,648,229
1974	10	137	48,424	2,915	28,348	20,035	7,704	3,270	1,649	5,523	1,032,448	5,584,369	26,350,497
1975	10	142	50,629	2,915	29,716	19,738	7,962	3,276	1,627	5,555	1,224,898	6,918,797	29,849,519
1976	10	146	52,703	2,804	30,523	18,373	7,861	3,299	1,811	5,057	1,802,167	7,633,085	32,734,292
1977	10	150	52,267	2,575	29,363	16,946	7,547	3,022	1,851	5,452	1,682,250	8,496,456	37,757,280
1978	11	152	53,465	2,473	28,847	17,656	7,412	2,860	1,743	5,861	1,906,544	9,504,839	44,400,410
1979	11	156	54,828	2,830	29,497	16,844	7,665	3,093	1,827	6,098	1,856,706	10,590,761	51,286,799
1980	11	164	56,126	3,397	30,395	16,658	7,636	3,074	1,867	6,737	2,505,077	11,906,911	55,696,641

JAMES LEE YOUNG

nized, and given to a new staff member, R. Bates Ivey, 1958-59. He was succeeded in 1961 by John D. Matthews, who had the same three departments as Ivey, retiring in Dec., 1974. Lawrence joined the staff in Jan., 1975, as director of church music and church architecture and is still serving the convention. Sunday School enrollment went from 25,305 in 1969 to 29,650 in 1979.

Campus Student Ministries, Church Administration, Family Ministries.—The reorganization in staff assignments in 1978 saw Campus Student Ministries shift from Philip T. Card to D. G. McCoury, who continues in that position. During Card's 22-year term as campus ministries director, Baptist Student Union grew to have six full-time directors by 1979. The department presently has work on 16 campuses. The most recent annual retreat for international students drew 275 persons.

Church Training, Recreation, Media.—Philip T. Card serves as Church Training director, having held that position since the CBGC was organized in 1956. Training Union enrollment in 1978 in the state reversed a downward trend of several years and climbed back to 7,580, the reported figure for 1979. Card worked with Baptist Student Union, church recreation, and church library until organizational changes were made. He presently is responsible for Church Training, recreation, and media.

JAMES LEE YOUNG

COLORADO SOUTHERN BAPTIST CHURCH LOAN CORPORATION (III). The corporation has issued and sold approximately $10,000,000 in debenture bonds since its beginning in 1957. It had more than $400,000 in reserves in 1980 and has suffered no losses on any of the more than 200 loans made. William H. Landers has served as the only president and director since 1958.

BILL LANDERS

COMMITTEE OF FIFTEEN, AGENCY STUDIES BY. See AGENCY STUDIES BY COMMITTEE OF FIFTEEN.

COMMITTEE OF SEVEN. See EXECUTIVE COMMITTEE STUDY BY THE COMMITTEE OF SEVEN.

COMMUNICATIONS SATELLITES. As of June, 1980, 55 active communications satellites were orbiting the earth, and others were in various stages of construction. The Southern Baptist Radio and Television Commission's actual experience in the use of such satellites includes the following events:

Project Look Up, 1976-77: Participation with other religious groups in the use of NASA's ATS-6 satellite to transmit commission programming from North Carolina to Puerto Rico.

SBC, Kansas City, MO, 1977: Production of the Foreign Mission Board report, including a satellite transmission segment from Hong Kong to Kansas City.

CTS Demonstration, Apr. 26, 1978: Transmission of the afternoon session of the annual Southern Baptist Radio-TV and Cable Consultation from the commission's facilities in Fort Worth, TX, to the First Baptist Church in Nashville, TN.

Radio and Television Commission/Baptist Sunday School Board video distribution for cable television systems, 1977-78: One hour per week contracted through the Public Service Satellite Consortium with Hughes TV Network on the RCA SATCOM system. "At Home with the Bible" and "The Human Dimension" were the program series involved.

SBC, Houston, TX, 1979: Transmission of the Bold Mission Rally from the Astrodome via the WESTAR satellite to public TV stations and via the RCA SATCOM satellite for cable TV access.

"Circulo Tres"/"Puntito" distribution, Sep., 1980, via the Spanish International Network: "Circulo Tres," produced by the commission for the Foreign Mission Board, and "Puntito," the commission's Spanish version of the popular "JOT" series, are scheduled for the full SIN interconnection of 48 stations plus six non-interconnected affiliates.

In 1980, the international implications of satellite use by the SBC Foreign Mission Board were under study. This study could result in opportunities for new telecommunications initiatives of vital importance.

See also RADIO AND TELEVISION COMMISSION, SBC.

                                    CHARLES RODEN

COMPUTERS, SOUTHERN BAPTIST USE OF. Between 1969 and 1980, the computer began to occupy a prominent place among SBC agencies as an instrument to process accurately the volume of information necessary for proper administration and communication. Also, some individual churches began to utilize the computer for similar reasons.

In 1969 the Administrative Committee of the Inter-Agency Council approved a project entitled "Computer Equipment, Systems, and Financing." Its purpose was to assist executives, managers, and boards of trustees as they considered computer equipment, systems, and economics. The appointed work-group consisted of John H. Williams, Frank Traver, William K. Dawson, R. C. McLemore, and Dan McQueen. They submitted their report in Oct., 1969, along with other reports on: "The Use of Computers by Southern Baptist Convention Agency Management and Administration," "The Use of Computers by Southern Baptist Convention Agencies for Program Planning," and "The Use of Computers by Southern Baptist Churches."

The staff directors of four work-groups, John Marvin Crowe, Lloyd Thomas Householder, Howard Bryce Foshee, and John Hayden Williams, formed a committee to coordinate and correlate the reports and bring recommendations to the Coordinating Committee. The Coordinating Committee made three recommendations to the IAC which were accepted: (1) That the Administrative Committee determine interest in a seminar for top executives in the use of the computer, with the seminar conducted by a consulting firm; (2) that Williams convene a meeting of computer executives within the SBC to discuss elimination of duplications and correlation of computer work among agencies; and (3) that such computer executives explore the feasibility of centralizing two computer uses as follows: (a) Church Profile Master Record System, which would contain the name and address of each church and other essential information; and (b) a mailing list of pastors, ministers of education, ministers of music, church officers, associational superintendents of missions, and state and SBC agency personnel.

From a meeting of agency representatives in Nashville, TN, in Oct., 1969, came a recommendation that an association of data processing executives of SBC agencies and institutions be formed. The association's main goal would be to assist in the data processing needs of all the boards, agencies, institutions, and state conventions. The IAC officially sanctioned the Southern Baptist Computer Users Association in 1972, and the association was organized in Mar., 1972. William K. Dawson of the Foreign Mission Board was elected president, and a constitution and bylaws were adopted.

Simultaneously, other agencies began to utilize the computer. The Historical Commission, SBC, developed the Baptist Information Retrieval System to accumulate, categorize, and make available data from published and unpublished Baptist materials. Growing numbers of state conventions, colleges, hospitals, seminaries, and other Baptist agencies initiated the use of computers for accounting and other types of record keeping.

Individual churches began to utilize the computer to communicate with their members, process membership rolls, and provide skills inventories and demographic information. Many churches buy these services while larger churches have their own computer equipment.

Through annual meetings of the association, members shared their experience and explored more effective methods of computer usage. In 1973 the association conducted a survey of computer equipment in use by Southern Baptist organizations. The results indicated use of all sizes of computers with applications as varied as the organizations themselves. The association recommended to the IAC a project to develop a Church Profile Master Record System using the information accumulated by the Sunday School Board from the Uniform Church Letter. This system was implemented in 1978 as a significant effort to share with Southern Baptists the benefits of the computer. The use of the system is growing, and it foreshadows the more efficient sharing of information and ideas within the SBC through computer services.

As the 1970s ended, Southern Baptists had

apparently become sophisticated in the use of computers including large on-line, real-time, data-base methods of data processing in a multiple-job-processing environment. These applications utilized the most up-to-date computer equipment which ranged from small personal computers to the very largest and complex systems. Applications have grown beyond business and accounting practices into areas of communication, management, information, and real-time processing which encompasses all aspects of the individual agencies, institutions, and churches.

See also BAPTIST INFORMATION RETRIEVAL SYSTEM.

HARVEY H. KENNEDY

CONFERENCES, STUDENT MISSIONS.

The first Student Missions Conference for college students was held on the campus of Southwestern Baptist Theological Seminary in 1949. Originally conceived by a group of seminarians as a means of conserving missionary vocation among students, it later came to be viewed as a means of career missionary recruitment.

Since that beginning every Southern Baptist seminary has promoted such conferences. They are usually held sometime in the early spring, but the time varies from campus to campus. The seminary furnishes the leadership, hospitality, and coordination but depends on the Baptist Student Union leadership in each state to promote the conferences. Each group of students provides its own transportation.

The Foreign and Home Mission Boards provide personnel, and the National Student Ministries Department of the Sunday School Board helps coordinate the six seminary conferences and provide aid for the programs.

The format varies from year to year and from campus to campus. Generally, there are worship services with the opening night having a theme interpretation. Furloughing missionaries, seminary professors, mission board personnel, Baptist Student Union workers, and many students participate in the planning and execution of the program. Small group conferences are always a popular part of the weekend activities. A commitment service brings the weekend to a climax. Thousands of students have made life commitments to missions through these conferences.

JUSTICE C. ANDERSON

CONLEY, JOSEPH MORGAN (b. College Park, GA, Nov. 5, 1920; d. Nashville, TN, Apr. 5, 1973). Home missionary and educator. Son of Judge Brayton and Othello Carmichael Conley, he graduated from Emory University (A.B.) and The Southern Baptist Theological Seminary (B.D., Th. M., 1950). He married Mary Evelyn Strong, June 28, 1947. They had three sons: Joseph, Robert, and William. Employed by the Home Mission Board, 1954, as teacher-missionary and director of extension for Selma University in Alabama, he was professor of New Testa-

ment and ethics and director of extension, American Baptist Theological Seminary, Nashville, TN, 1957-73. He is buried in College Park Cemetery, College Park, GA.

MARJORIE HOWARD

CONNECTICUT, SOUTHERN BAPTISTS IN. See MARYLAND, BAPTIST CONVENTION OF; NEW ENGLAND, BAPTIST GENERAL ASSOCIATION OF.

CONNIE MAXWELL CHILDREN'S HOME (I, III). Child care ministry of South Carolina Baptist Convention, located at Greenwood, SC. The services, involving children and families from South Carolina, are foster home care, community-based group home care, care for children in their own homes, family assistance, adoption (limited), campus care, student aid, and crisis care. During a 12-month period, beginning Sep. 1, 1978, 299 children received direct in-care services. An additional 132 children received various degrees of counseling, support, and referral services. On Jan. 22, 1976, the Connie Maxwell trustees signed a statement of compliance with the Civil Rights Act of 1964.

Sam M. Smith retired as executive director, June 30, 1976, after serving in that capacity for 30 years. John C. Murdoch (q.v.), who then served as executive director for nine months until his death, was succeeded by J. Heyward Prince in Sep., 1977.

The campus facilities consist of more than 900 acres of land and 40 permanent buildings. All of the campus buildings in which the children live, the administration building, the church, the activities building, the food and clothing center, the maintenance building, and the print shop have been constructed since 1948. The Connie Maxwell Alumni Association, organized in 1932, has contributed more than $100,000 for improving physical facilities of the home. The latest project of the alumni involved the provision of more than half the funds needed for the swimming pool which replaced the old one in 1979.

In 1979, total assets were $12,330,000, including land, buildings, equipment, invested contingent fund, and a permanent endowment of $5,000,000. The budget for the fiscal year 1979-80 was $1,600,000, with 72.8 percent of the current income derived from direct offerings of churches and the Cooperative Program. The remaining 28 percent came from personal gifts, receipts from relatives of children under care, endowment, and income from productive enterprises. The home had a staff of 98.

Since 1977, Connie Maxwell has developed a crisis care program on campus, opened a group home in Greenville, SC, in response to a request of the South Carolina Baptist Convention in 1975, and begun in Oct., 1979, the operation on campus of a Family Building, which was developed around the concept of the importance of a child's family to the child.

More than 6,000 children have been served since the arrival of the first child at Connie Maxwell, May 22, 1892.

E. BOOKER BAGBY, JR.

CONSERVATIVE BAPTIST ASSOCIATION OF AMERICA (I).

During the 1970s this conservative "movement" of 1,200 churches faced second-generation problems. The foreign mission society (CBFMS) observed its 30th anniversary in 1973 and the association of churches observed its 30th anniversary in 1977.

The decade brought new executive officers to several agencies which lost "founding fathers": Warren Webster to CBFMS in 1971; Haddon Robinson to Denver Seminary in 1979; and Jack Estep to the home mission society (CBHMS) in 1979.

The movement continued to search for greater expressions of unity. In 1977 a Study Commission, led by William Thomas of West Los Angeles, CA, replaced the Inter-Society Commission. With greater funding and wider representation from the movement, the Study Commission secured approval in 1979 for three resolutions: an objective of "one constituency" for the movement; adoption of a single-stated purpose for the movement embracing evangelism, discipleship, edification, and service; and a statement of the functions through which the purpose might be achieved. These signs pointed to a more traditional denominational character for Conservative Baptists rather than their past voluntary society organization.

Another concern was church growth. In 1971 the CBHMS launched a church planting program for small towns and suburbs, called New Churches Now. By 1979 the program counted 44 new churches.

Most Conservative Baptist agencies showed healthy increases during the decade. CBFMS passed $9,000,000 in income for 600 missionaries. CBHMS received $2,500,000 for 250 missionaries. All four schools showed increased enrollments. More than 900 seminarians were enrolled in the two seminaries, Denver and Western, at Portland, OR.

See also CONSERVATIVE BAPTIST FOREIGN MISSION SOCIETY, Vols. I, III, IV; CONSERVATIVE BAPTISTS, Vol. III.

BRUCE L. SHELLEY

CONSERVATIVE BAPTIST FOREIGN MISSION SOCIETY (I, III).

The Conservative Baptist Foreign Mission Society entered the 1980s with 604 career and short-term missionaries appointed to 24 geographical locations in Africa, Europe, South America, and Asia. They serve in evangelism, church planting, Christian education, theological institutes, colleges and seminaries, medicine, literature, and limited development.

The society is governed by a board of 24 directors and three officers, elected by Baptist churches of like faith who contribute to the society's overseas ministries. The administration in the United States is staffed by the general director, Warren Webster, three overseas secretaries (Africa, Asia, and Europe/South America), a personnel secretary, treasurer, and public relations secretary. Area offices are located in New York, Minnesota, Michigan, Colorado, Oregon, and California with the headquarters in Wheaton, IL. The 1979 income of the society was $9,057,000 for all causes.

The *Impact* gives current information on mission activities and missionaries.

H. WALTER FRICKE

CONSERVATIVE THEOLOGY, RESURGENCE OF.

Southern Baptists are, and traditionally have been, conservative in theology. Conservative means that which preserves or conserves insights and values from a received norm or source. In the decade between 1970 and 1980, a resurgence of extremely conservative theology occurred in Southern Baptist life. Three explanations may account for this resurgence, which is by no means limited to Southern Baptists.

First, theology and culture are interrelated. The American political and economic setting of the 1970s was expressly conservative. Numerous political threats, an inflated economy, and a disaffection with the programs of more liberal, socially oriented political administrations gave rise to this political conservatism. These political and social attitudes concomitantly expressed themselves in the religious structures of the day.

Second, in this decade the leadership of Southern Baptist institutions underwent an almost complete turnover. Five of the six seminaries had new presidents. The Sunday School Board, Foreign Mission Board, and Home Mission Board all received new executive leadership. In most instances the retiring personnel were of long-term service in the denomination, and their conservative theology and administrative policies were known and trusted. Although the replacements for these positions are, without exception, conservative and from the mainstream of Southern Baptist life, a transitional time of leadership always provides opportunity for those who feel outside of central power-making decisions to express their opinions and make their bid for a share of power that comes with executive positions.

Finally, accompanying these two phenomena was the rise of schools and seminaries not officially authorized by the denomination.

Two powerful influences outside of Southern Baptist life helped to bring about the resurgence of an exceptionally conservative theology. These influences were the success of large independent Baptist and other evangelical churches and the vitality of dispensational and other forms of evangelical theology. Many large Southern Baptist churches adopted as model in method and theology stellar independent Baptist congregations. Many independent churches, Baptist and others, had withdrawn from denominations because of what they considered liberal theology and policies. Among these groups denominational institutional programs and formal education were often considered suspect. Southern Baptist pastors and churches who moved within this sphere began to share these attitudes about their own programs and educational institutions. At the same time, Neo-Protestant scholasticism, with a rationalist theology indebted almost exclusively to the Calvinist tradition and greatly suspicious of religious experience and any subjective elements in theology, underwent rapid growth and popularity. The dispensational theology of Dallas Theological Seminary is a prime example. Increasing numbers of young seminarians were influenced by and went to such schools. Both the hermeneutic and the concept of Baptist heritage held by these young men, who became pastors in the denomination, differed from that which Southern Baptist ministers had most frequently held.

The principal theological issue involved is biblical hermeneutics—how to interpret the Bible. But proponents of the resurgent neo-conservatism have asserted that the primary theological issue is the authority of the Bible. A particular standard of orthodoxy as to biblical authority surfaced in the terms *infallible* and *inerrant*. The former had been used in at least one major Baptist confession of faith (Second London Confession, 1677) to signify integrity in matters of faith and doctrine, so the majority of the scholarship of the denomination understood it. The latter (inerrant) has apparently not been used in other major Baptist confessions until recently. Inerrant can bear two interpretations: without error in all matters, scientific and others; or without error in matters of faith and doctrine. The inclusive view of inerrancy has been espoused by Harold Lindsell, former editor of *Christianity Today*, whose views of inerrancy have been widely accepted by neo-conservatives. Lindsell attacked Southern Baptists in general in his *Battle for the Bible* (1976) and in particular in his *Bible in the Balance* (1979).

The exclusivist view of inerrancy (that which excludes nonfaith matters) was espoused by Jack Rogers of Fuller Theological Seminary in *Biblical Authority* (1977) and *The Authority and Interpretation of the Bible: An Historical Approach* (1979). The majority of Southern Baptist scholars have refused to enter the debate on the basis of a term that is not a part of most of their heritage and is based on the mathematical model of seventeenth century scholastic debates. Two Southern Baptist seminary professors, L. Russ Bush and Tom J. Nettles, published a work, *Baptists and the Bible* (1979), sympathetic to the inclusivist view of inerrancy. In their view infallibility and inerrancy are equivalents.

For the majority of the denomination's scholarship, the issue has been clouded further by the qualification that the Bible is the infallible, inerrant Word of God in the original manuscripts. Since no original manuscripts are known, and since it seems more expeditious to use the biblical expression "inspired" or the SBC Baptist Faith and Message statement of 1963, which uses the phrase, "truth without any mixture of error," most Southern Baptist scholars have taken these as their basic expression about Scripture.

The strongest evidence of the neo-conservative resurgence was the election of Adrian Rogers as SBC president in 1979. The two most visible arms of neo-conservative resurgence are the Baptist Faith and Message Fellowship and the political coalition organized by Paige Patterson, president of the Criswell Center for Biblical Studies, Dallas, TX, and Paul Pressler, layman from Houston. The Baptist Faith and Message Fellowship was organized by William A. Powell, a former employee of the Home Mission Board. The fellowship publishes the *Southern Baptist Journal* of which Powell is the principal editor. The group had sessions at several SBC meetings. Patterson and Pressler organized a political coalition whose acknowledged purpose is to gain control of the boards of Southern Baptist agencies and institutions.

See also BAPTIST FAITH AND MESSAGE FELLOWSHIP, THE; BIBLE, CONTROVERSIES ABOUT THE; INERRANCY.

WILLIAM L. HENDRICKS

CONSULTATION ON WOMEN IN CHURCH-RELATED VOCATIONS. See WOMEN IN CHURCH-RELATED VOCATIONS, CONSULTATION ON.

CONTEMPO (III). See WOMAN'S MISSIONARY UNION, AUXILIARY TO SBC.

CONTINUING EDUCATION FOR MINISTRY. In the early 1970s, Southern Baptists began to question seriously the assumption that education for ministry is completed with the earning of a theological degree. Competent ministry, many affirmed, requires continuing education as long as a minister is in active service.

Several prominent developments influenced this change in viewpoint: (1) Rapidly changing conditions in contemporary society created needs, demands, attitudes, and situations virtually unknown when many ministers were seminary students; (2) technological developments and the knowledge explosion provided resources also unknown during the periods of formal training of many ministers; and (3) the increasing prominence of continuing education in other professions created a challenge to ministers to keep abreast with the professional development of their lay colleagues.

Among persons interested in continuing education for ministry, consensus on the precise meaning of the term did not exist. A definition approved in 1972 by the Inter-Agency Council of the SBC expressed one key viewpoint: "Continuing education is the area of adult education which is concerned with involving adults, regardless of the extent or the limitations of their formal schooling, in guided learning experiences designed to improve vocational proficiency." Another major viewpoint was that continuing education is possible only for persons who have completed a theological degree program.

All six SBC seminaries responded to the emerging movement by making special provisions for the continuing education of their alumni and other qualified ministers. Southwestern Baptist Theological Seminary was the first to appoint a director of continuing education. Other seminaries followed with the assigning of responsibilities for continuing education to certain staff personnel. All of the seminaries increased their offering of continuing education projects for seminary alumni.

See also SEMINARY EXTENSION DEPARTMENT.

RAYMOND M. RIGDON

CONTROVERSIES ABOUT THE BIBLE.
See BIBLE, CONTROVERSIES ABOUT THE.

CONVENTION EMPHASIS PRIORITY PLANNING.
Convention emphasis priority planning provides coordinated promotion planning for the SBC and state conventions. SBC program representatives, with two state convention program leaders and two associational leaders, lead in developing the concept, planning the content, and designing the emphasis priority promotion plans based on the needs of the churches. The process has existed since early 1967 and is known as Coordinated Promotion Planning.

The 1973-74 emphasis priority, "Sharing Christ Through His Word," centered promotion efforts in Bible study, church extension, and personal witnessing. The next year, 1974-75, placed major emphasis upon revitalizing the Sunday evening activities, involving more people in witness and ministry, and related areas. The theme was "Share His Love Now."

"Let Christ's Freedom Ring" was the theme for the nation's 200th anniversary year. Christian citizenship, religious freedom, personal liberty and Baptist heritage received attention in an effort to lead church members to understand freedom in Christ. Young families were encouraged in Christian growth through involvement in church life. Greater human and financial resources for proclaiming the gospel also received major emphasis during 1975-76.

The theme for 1976-77 was "Let the Church Stand Up." Biblical stewardship and an emphasis on strengthening the major church program organizations were highlighted. Emphasis went to crucial issues in the modern secular society and preparing church members to deal with this society. Church members were encouraged to study basic Baptist beliefs and to deepen their spiritual lives. Enlistment of unchurched persons was also included.

"Let the Church Reach Out—Bold Mission" provided the only two-year priority emphasis during the 1970s. This was an emphasis on missions and evangelism for 1977-79.

In 1977 the SBC adopted a theme for 1979-80 entitled "Equipping for Church Advance."

The content included three emphases: Equipping leaders for service, planning together for growth, and understanding vocational ministry. This emphasis was not implemented due to action of the SBC in 1978 when it approved a major denominational emphasis on Bold Mission Thrust for the period 1979-82. In 1979 the SBC approved another three-year emphasis for 1982-85, continuing Bold Mission Thrust. Areas of emphasis were reaching people, developing believers, and strengthening families.

LYNN M. DAVIS, JR.

CONVENTION PRESS (I, III). Retail sales for Convention Press products increased from $2,991,191 in 1969 to $9,012,627 in 1980 (more than 200 percent). Dramatic fluctuations occurred throughout the period due to the release of new materials. The most notable change was in 1975 when the *Baptist Hymnal*, 1975 edition, was released. Sales increased from $4,192,676 in 1974 to $8,374,343 in 1975. The materials that produce the majority of sales are Vacation Bible School materials, the *Baptist Hymnal* (1975 edition), and Church Study Course materials.

Convention Press materials are usually sold through Baptist Book Stores. However, they also may be sold through Southern Baptist college and school book stores, the extension department of Baptist colleges and seminaries for resale to faculty members and students, any Baptist denominational publishing house for resale to and for use by its own constituency, to Baptist state conventions for promotional purposes, and to foreign trade accounts.

AUBREY L. HOUSE

COOKE, LAWSON H. (b. Richmond, VA, Jan. 1, 1885; d. Memphis, TN, Nov. 20, 1972). Banker and Chamber of Commerce and Brotherhood executive. The son of Benjamin Franklin Cooke, he married Mary Ethel Goodin, who died in 1947. They had two children. A banker in Richmond and later the first general secretary for the Virginia State Chamber of Commerce, Cooke won attention of Southern Baptist leaders for his organization and promotion skills. He became the second general secretary of the Brotherhood of the South (predecessor of the Brotherhood Commission) in 1938 after two years in the Memphis office as an associate to J. T. Henderson (*q.v.* I).

During the next 13 years under Cooke's leadership, the enrollment of men in Brotherhood grew from 10,000 to almost 200,000, and the number of churches with Brotherhood units climbed from 250 to almost 6,000. He considered one of his finest developments a mailing list which, within only a few days, could deliver to 25,000 key laymen any Baptist message. He magnified Layman's Day (now Baptist Men's Day) in Southern Baptist churches while emphasizing stewardship and evangelism. Cooke retired from the Brotherhood Commission, Jan. 1, 1952. He is buried in Memorial Park, Memphis, TN.

ROY JENNINGS

COOKE, VINYARD VIVIAN (b. Butler County, KY, Jan. 7, 1897; d. Delray Beach, FL, Jan. 9, 1973). Businessman and philanthropist. The son of John Martin and Iona Elizabeth (McCoy) Cooke, farming parents, he attended Western Kentucky University. He married Elva Fields Bivens of Greenville, KY, Jan. 26, 1921. They had three children: June, Jane, and V. V., Jr.

Cooke entered the automobile business in Greenville, KY, in 1921. In 1930 he opened Cooke Chevrolet in Louisville, KY. He contributed about $5,000,000 to charitable organizations during his life. After his death the V. V. Cooke Foundation carried on the philanthropic work. Cooke was a deacon at Walnut Street Baptist Church, Louisville, for 40 years. He served Kentucky Baptists as a trustee of Georgetown College, Kentucky Baptist Children's Home, Kentucky Baptist Hospital, and Kentucky Southern College.

In 1944 Cooke gave a building to Southern Baptist Theological Seminary which became the first location of the School of Church Music and later the president's home. He served the seminary as a trustee for 29 years. He is memorialized in Cooke Hall, the music building erected in 1971, and in the V. V. Cooke Chair of Organ, established in 1975. He is buried in Cave Hill Cemetery, Louisville, KY.

DONALD P. HUSTAD

COOPER, DANIEL DAVID (b. Stigler, OK, Jan. 24, 1884; d. Shawnee, OK, Dec. 10, 1968). Pastor and missionary. A Choctaw Indian, he attended public schools, Armstrong Academy, and Oklahoma Baptist University. He married Martha Jane Perry, Aug., 1910. Ordained by the First Baptist Church, Shawnee, OK, about 1920, he was appointed by the Home Mission Board, 1929. He served among several Indian tribes, including Kickapoo, Shawnee, Sauk, and Fox. Cooper Memorial Church near McLoud is named for him. He is buried in Resthaven Cemetery, Shawnee, OK.

B. FRANK BELVIN

COOPER, DAVIS CLAY, JR. (b. Anniston, AL, July 26, 1889; d. Montgomery, AL, Sep. 12, 1973). Businessman, educator, and denominational leader. The son of Annie (Constantine) Cooper and Davis C. Cooper (*q.v.* I), a businessman and bank president, he attended Howard College (B.S., 1908), Vanderbilt University, Louisiana State University, Southwestern Baptist Theological Seminary, and Columbia University. He married Claire Hill, Dec. 12, 1911. They had one son, Davis Clay, III. Cooper was involved in the business community in Oxford, AL, 1912-22, then became an educational director in Kentucky and Georgia.

Cooper returned to Alabama in 1928 as secretary of the Alabama Baptist Sunday School Department. In 1929 he was elected secretary of the newly formed Department of Education and Training with responsibilities for promotion of

Sunday School, Baptist Young People's Union, student work, and Brotherhood work. He served also as secretary of the Sunday School and Vacation Bible School Department, 1938-45, and financial secretary of the Alabama Baptist Executive Board, 1945-60, as well as statistical secretary and recording secretary of the Alabama Baptist State Convention. He is buried in the Oxford, AL, cemetery.

WILLIAM K. WEAVER, JR.

COOPERATIVE PROGRAM (I, III). The Cooperative Program continues to be the main channel of financial support for SBC agencies and the 34 state conventions. A study of the Cooperative Program receipts and disbursements during the past decade reveals that approximately 90 percent of the Cooperative Program funds received by the SBC are allocated for the Foreign Mission Board, the Home Mission Board, and the six theological seminaries.

The 10-year record of Cooperative Program giving is as follows:

Year	Total Cooperative Program: State and SBC	Cooperative Program: SBC	Cooperative Program: SBC Percent of Total	Cooperative Program: Percent of Total Church Gifts
1970	$ 80,609,946	$27,925,302	34.64	9.40
1971	85,435,745	29,970,527	35.08	9.14
1972	91,538,458	31,561,729	34.48	8.95
1973	100,583,695	33,832,932	33.64	8.85
1974	111,637,003	38,036,809	34.07	8.87
1975	122,948,760	41,114,253	33.44	8.86
1976	136,471,299	46,725,721	34.24	8.83
1977	149,105,673	51,940,459	34.83	8.82
1978	164,886,284	57,418,384	34.82	8.82
1979	184,169,263	64,165,480	34.84	8.83

In 1971 the SBC adopted a recommendation from the Executive Committee reaffirming a statement of Cooperative Program principles. A summary of these principles is as follows:

1. The statement recognized the essential unity of all denominational work both in the state conventions and the SBC.

2. The state convention boards were recognized as the principal promotional and collection agencies for all Cooperative Program funds. Yet, the Convention retained as inalienable and inherent the right to direct appeal to the churches.

3. The statement recognized that neither the SBC nor state conventions had the authority to allocate funds for or divert funds from any object included in the respective budgets. However, this principle did not preempt the right of the churches to make designated contributions to any program or agency of the denomination.

4. The principle of a single percentage distribution of Cooperative Program funds between state and SBC causes was encouraged. This principle did not imply that states do not have the choice of deducting agreed-on items before the division is made.

5. The statement encouraged state conventions not to decrease the percentage of Cooperative Program funds allocated for the SBC until representatives from the SBC shall have had an opportunity to present SBC needs.

6. The statement encouraged periodic conferences between leaders of the SBC and the state

conventions to reexamine the cooperative relationships.

In 1976 the Research Services Department of the Sunday School Board conducted a study of the Cooperative Program to identify knowledge about, attitudes toward, and concerns about the Cooperative Program which exist among Southern Baptists. The study included pastors, church staff members, and laypersons. Conclusions of the study were summarized as follows:

1. Respondents had a positive overall image of the Cooperative Program, feeling that it was important, valuable, practical, and desirable.

2. Respondents tended to have positive attitudes concerning the Cooperative Program but expressed a need for more information about the administrative costs of the Cooperative Program and the division of Cooperative Program funds between state and SBC causes.

3. Respondents seemed to be aware of the general purpose of the Cooperative Program.

4. Respondents' knowledge of the budget development and adoption process decreased as the distance from the process increased. Pastors knew more about the process than the lay groups.

5. Respondents did not know the cost of administering the Cooperative Program at the SBC level.

6. A significant number of respondents were incorrectly informed concerning who receives Cooperative Program funds at the SBC level.

7. Respondents indicated some knowledge of the history of the Cooperative Program.

As Southern Baptists entered the 1980s, a growing number of Convention leaders felt that the Cooperative Program should be restudied and its purposes reaffirmed.

See also COOPERATIVE PROGRAM ALLOCATION BUDGET PLANNING; GIVING TRENDS IN THE 1970s.

                                    HAROLD C. BENNETT

COOPERATIVE PROGRAM ALLOCATION BUDGET PLANNING (cf. Budget of the Convention, Vols. I, III). Since 1928 the SBC Executive Committee has been responsible for recommending agency Cooperative Program allocations to the SBC. In the early years, operating allocations were listed as percentages; but as the Convention assumed responsibility for more agencies, this method became complex and inflexible. The Convention found it difficult to respond to developing new priorities. The shift to dollars, which began with the 1951 budget, grew out of a 1946 plan to provide SBC capital needs. This required a fixed fund operating budget. The idea had been first proposed to the Executive Committee in 1927 as a "plan germinal and far-reaching: that the financial objectives of the Southern Baptist Convention be stated in terms of money rather than in percentages." In some years dollars only were used but generally percentages were continued, and it was not until 1958 that percentages were finally dropped from the recommendation to the Convention.

In 1973 the Executive Committee developed a 10-step Cooperative Program allocation budget procedure to begin in July and end the following June. The five most important steps included (1) agency presentations of budget needs to the Executive Committee in September, (2) compilation and distribution of comprehensive budget data in the fall, (3) detailed agency presentations to the Program and Budget Subcommittee and formulation of the proposed budget by the subcommittee in January, (4) approval by the Executive Committee in February, and (5) approval by the Convention in June. Discussions were under way for the improvement of the process in 1979-80.

See also SOUTHERN BAPTIST CONVENTION, CAPITAL NEEDS.

                                    ALBERT MCCLELLAN

COORDINATED CHURCH GROWTH FUND. Funds designated each year by the Sunday School Board to assist state conventions in the promotion of SSB programs. The SSB appropriates the funds to be used for honoraria and expenses of special workers who are enlisted to engage in projects with state conventions, associations, churches, and campus programs. These funds may also be used for expenses of special workers to participate in training meetings for such projects.

The maximum appropriation for use in each state convention or state fellowship is $4,000 plus $90 per association for the year. The Coordinated Church Growth Funds are administered in each state by the state executive secretary or someone he designates. The plans for the use of these funds are made in accordance with priority concerns expressed by the SSB. The amount of funds given to the state conventions by the SSB through this Coordinated Church Growth Fund from 1973 to 1979 was as follows: 1973-74, $218,353; 1974-75, $218,486; 1975-76, $253,898; 1976-77, $244,796; 1977-78, $243,441; and 1978-79, $285,766.

                                    ROBERT G. FULBRIGHT

CORPUS CHRISTI, UNIVERSITY OF (cf. University of Corpus Christi, Vols. II, III). Chartered on Apr. 1, 1947, the university operated for 26 years under the Baptist General Convention of Texas. It suffered many setbacks, including hurricanes Carla, 1961, and Celia, 1970. During the administration of Kenneth A. Maroney, the sixth president, the Texas legislature authorized an upper-level university for Corpus Christi, and the property and assets of the Baptist university were transferred to the state. Corpus Christi State University opened on the site in the fall of 1973.

                                    RICHARD MARCUM

COSTA RICA, MISSION IN (I, III). The Costa Rica mission made strides in long-range planning as it formulated a program base design in the early 1970s. Baptist work entered a new level of partnership as the mission and the Costa

Rica Convention meshed programs of work in 1977. Twenty-eight self-supporting churches and 13 missions were a part of the convention in 1980. They enrolled over 3,000 persons in Bible study and listed some 2,250 members. Eight missionary units served in the fields of evangelism, literature, music, theological education, and women's work.

ANNETTE (HORTON) HERRINGTON

COUNSELING. See PASTORAL CARE.

COUNSELING OF MINISTERS. See MINISTERS, COUNSELING OF.

COUSINS, SOLON BOLIVAR, JR. (b. Luthersville, GA, Nov. 13, 1885; d. Richmond, VA, Jan. 28, 1971). Pastor, teacher, and denominational leader. The son of Solon Bolivar, a Baptist minister, and Lou Ella (Fuller) Cousins, he was a graduate of Mercer University (B.A., 1905) and did further studies at Harvard University, Union Seminary in New York, and Edinburgh University. He received degrees from Mercer University (D.D., 1920) and William Jewell College (L.L.D., 1948). He married Hattie Llewellyn Glousier, Aug. 17, 1912. They had one child, Solon Bolivar, III.

Cousins' pastorates included: Montezuma, GA, 1910-12; First Church, Waynesboro, GA, 1912-15; First Church, Liberty, MO, 1915-18; First Church, Columbus, GA, 1918-21; and Second Church, Richmond, VA, 1921-37. From 1932 to 1937, he taught Bible and religion part-time at the University of Richmond. In 1937 he assumed full-time responsibilities as professor of Bible and department chairman, retiring in 1959.

He served as president, Baptist General Association of Virginia, 1935-37; member, Foreign Mission Board, SBC, 1923-41, 1944-60; member, Virginia Baptist Board of Missions and Education, 1926-29; and trustee, *The Religious Herald*, and the Virginia Baptist Home for the Aged, 1953-59. He served as interim pastor of 26 churches in the Richmond area. He preached the annual SBC sermon in New Orleans in 1937 and was a popular speaker at seminaries, colleges, and denominational gatherings. In 1979 the University of Richmond established in his honor The Solon B. Cousins Grants to Students Preparing for Church-Related Vocations. He is buried in Hollywood Cemetery, Richmond, VA.

JULIAN H. PENTECOST

COX, OLA SHIPP (b. Little Rock, AR, Dec. 19, 1912; d. Charleston, WV, Nov. 27, 1974). State Woman's Missionary Union director. The daughter of Dow and Fanny Shipp, farmers, she was a graduate of Central High School, Memphis, TN. She married Elmo Cox, July 3, 1934. Their two children were Michael and Paul. In Memphis she was teacher of a large (227 members) Sunday School class at Bellevue Baptist Church. After her husband

became vice-president of Charleston (WV) National Bank, she led in the official organization of West Virginia's WMU in 1971. Because of her knowledge of WMU work and speaking ability, she was invited to speak frequently in the convention's churches. She prepared the first state missions program and state missions offering emphasis. The Ola Cox State Missions Offering bears her name.

She became paralyzed by cancer in July, 1972, and was hospitalized until her death 28 months later. Even while confined to the hospital, she carried on WMU work throughout the state from her bedside and by telephone. She is buried in Sunset Memorial Cemetery, South Charleston, WV.

BIBLIOGRAPHY: Mary Ida Tidsworth, *Give Me This Hill Country* (1979).

JACKSON C. WALLS

CRAIG, WILLIAM MARSHALL (b. Anderson, SC, May 28, 1889; d. Dallas, TX, Sep. 15, 1970). Pastor and evangelist. Son of Sam M. Craig, a pharmacist, and Mamie Partlow Craig, he attended Furman University (B.A., 1913) and Baylor University (1936). He married Loulie Ann Cullum of Batesburg, SC, Oct. 31, 1915. They had no children. He served as pastor of First Baptist Church, Kinston, NC, 1916-20; First Church, Petersburg, VA, 1921-27; and Gaston Avenue Church, Dallas, TX, 1927-53. Under his leadership, the Gaston Church became one of the largest in the SBC. He retired in 1953 to enter evangelistic work. He is buried in Old Silver Brook Cemetery, Anderson, SC.

PAUL STRIPLING

CRANE, CLARIS ISABEL (b. Baltimore, MD, Sep. 14, 1880; d. Towson, MD, Jan. 9, 1968). Woman's Missionary Union editor. The daughter of Clara Merryman Crane and Henry Ryland Crane, an insurance executive and merchant, she attended Bryn Mawr College, Philadelphia, PA (A.B., 1902), majoring in English and Greek. She was editor of *Our Mission Fields*, July, 1912, until Sep., 1914, when it became *Royal Service*. She was also author of *Daughter of the Covenant, Edith Campbell Crane, 1876-1933* (1966). She is buried in Greenmount Cemetery, Baltimore, MD.

DORIS DEVAULT

CREASMAN, MYRTLE ROBINSON (b. Chattanooga, TN, Oct. 11, 1887; d. Nashville, TN, May 30, 1980). Author and conference leader. The daughter of William F. Robinson, a railroad employee, and Elizabeth Kirkpatrick Robinson, she graduated from Virginia Intermont College (B.A., 1907) and attended the Chicago Conservatory of Music in 1910. On May 15, 1915, she married Clarence Dixon Creasman. She contributed writings for Sunday School Board publications; edited materials for the Woman's Missionary Union's *Royal Service*,

1931-48; and produced several anniversary pageants for WMU.

Creasman served as president, Tennessee WMU, and as a vice-president of WMU, SBC, 1922-23, 1939-47. She was employed by WMU, SBC, as stewardship director, 1949-53. She was author of four books: *Working with Juniors* (1925), *Plays and Pageants* (1930), *Pageants of the Kingdom* (1943), and *Stewardship Scrapbook* (n.d.). She is buried in Forest Hills Cemetery, Chattanooga, TN.

LINDA KNOTT

CREECH, OSCAR (b. Johnston County, NC, Feb. 3, 1886; d. Ahoskie, NC, Mar. 27, 1974). Pastor and educator. Son of Ransom and Henrietta (Sullivan) Creech, farmers, he attended Wake Forest College (B.A., 1912) and Southern Baptist Theological Seminary (1919-20). He served as pastor of several churches in eastern North Carolina, including Nashville, 1915-19; Crocker's Chapel, 1915-19; Castalia, 1915-19; Oak Level, 1915-18; Red Oak, 1920-24; and Ahoskie First, 1925-51.

A leader in the effort to reopen Chowan College in 1949—following six years during which the institution had suspended operations—Creech became vice-president for development in 1951. For 10 years he rallied support for both capital needs expansion and operating funds. He also served as acting president, Oct., 1956-May, 1957, following the death of President F. O. Mixon.

Creech married Martha Louise Gulley on Aug. 6, 1907. Their children were Orville Ransom, Leah Jessica, Oscar, Jr., Judson Yates, and Elva Louise. He is buried at Ahoskie, NC.

RAYMOND HARGUS TAYLOR

CRISLER, EVA (b. Kentucky, Dec. 25, 1887; d. Colorado Springs, CO, Jan. 4, 1961). Philanthropist and church planter. A registered nurse, she practiced in New York and Chicago before moving in 1937 to Colorado Springs, where she became a charter member of First Southern Baptist Church. Through gifts and loans secured by her personally, the present buildings of First Southern Baptist Church were constructed. In 1959 she moved to Garden Grove, CA, where she assisted many California churches. A trust fund was established in her name by the William Flemings of Fort Worth, TX, to assist churches in Colorado. She is buried in Evergreen Cemetery, Colorado Springs, CO.

WAYNE WILLIAMS

CRISWELL CENTER FOR BIBLICAL STUDIES. Proposed in Oct., 1969, by W. A. Criswell (first president and chancellor), Criswell Bible Institute was established by First Baptist Church, Dallas, TX, in Oct., 1970. H. Leo Eddleman assumed the presidency in July, 1972, and was succeeded by Paige Patterson in Feb., 1975. Eddleman's inauguration of a fully-accredited baccalaureate degree commenced a period of rapid growth. The school became Criswell Center for Biblical Studies in Feb., 1976. Seventeen faculty members, supported by an 87,000-volume library, instructed a cumulative enrollment of 501 (95 percent of whom were Southern Baptists and 80 percent ministerial students) in the 1980-81 academic year.

RICHARD D. LAND

CRITTENDON, ATHA FLOYD (b. Martin, TN, Mar. 10, 1891; d. Colorado Springs, CO, Aug. 28, 1962). Pastor, denominational leader, and state executive. The son of William Lee, a farmer, and Lelia (Boyd) Crittendon, he was educated at Union University (B.S., 1914), and Southwestern Baptist Theological Seminary (Th.M., 1920). He married Birdie Louise Canady, Mar. 8, 1895. They had three children: Robert, William, and Anne. He was pastor of Baptist churches in Tennessee, Arkansas, Missouri, Mississippi, Oklahoma, and New Mexico. He also served on the staff of the Mississippi Baptist Convention before moving to Ponca City, OK.

He left the pastorate of First Baptist Church, Ponca City, in June, 1945, to become executive secretary of the Southern Baptist General Convention of California. In its fifth year, the convention at that time had 76 churches and 5,085 members. His emphasis on expanded rural and city missions programs brought rapid growth. At the close of his administration in Nov., 1950, California had 266 Southern Baptist churches and 33,771 members.

Crittendon faced opposition as the state executive secretary from the very beginning. By 1949 differences between him and some of the convention's organization heads had become public, as had differences with the editor of the *California Southern Baptist*. That same year he was criticized because he favored accepting members from Northern Baptist churches. Friction with the staff continued. Several organization heads resigned prior to the 1950 convention. Crittendon was dismissed that year, C. E. Wilbanks, who had resigned as state secretary of evangelism, was nominated to oppose him and was elected, but he declined the call.

Crittendon suffered a fatal heart attack in Colorado Springs, CO, while en route from Glorieta, where he had attended Foreign Missions Week, to the World's Fair in Seattle. He is buried at Dyersburg, TN.

ELLIOTT SMITH

CROSLIN, HARRISON C., SR. (b. Franklin County, IL, Feb. 16, 1889; d. Ziegler, IL, Apr. 16, 1942). Pastor and pioneer in religious education. Son of Alonzo and Ella Nora Croslin, farmers, he was crippled by polio at age seven. He attended Ewing College, Ewing, IL, and The Southern Baptist Theological Seminary. He married Zella Johnston, Grayville, IL, Oct. 3, 1915. Their children were Harrison C., Jr., Clyde, Carol, and Kenneth.

Croslin supervised the establishment of Baptist foundations (Christian educational institutions with college accreditation) at Southern Illinois University, Carbondale, 1938, and at State Teacher's College, Cape Girardeau, MO, 1939. He served on the Executive Board of the Illinois Baptist State Association for 20 years. He is buried in East Fork Baptist Church cemetery near West Frankfort, IL.

H. C. CROSLIN, JR.

CRUMPLER, WILSON LEWIS (b. Sylacauga, AL, May 26, 1907; d. Falmouth, KY, Oct. 25, 1978). Pastor and associational missionary. Son of Lewis Henry, a druggist, and Flossie Crumpler, he was converted in 1920. First Baptist Church, Bessemer, AL, ordained him, Sep. 23, 1928. He was educated at Howard College (A.B., 1929), and The Southern Baptist Theological Seminary (Th.M., 1939). Crumpler served as pastor in Alabama, Texas, and Kentucky for 30 years and as Kentucky Baptist Convention field worker-missionary for 20 years. He married Imogene Bates, Sep. 19, 1930. They had one son, Joseph Andrew. Crumpler is buried at Birmingham, AL.

A. B. COLVIN

CRUSADER. See BROTHERHOOD COMMISSION, SBC.

CRUSADER COUNSELOR. See BROTHERHOOD COMMISSION, SBC.

CUBA, MISSIONS IN (III; cf. Cuba, Baptists in, Vol. I). Baptist work has continued to flourish amidst government regulations. The clinic (Clinica Bautista) was the only facility appropriated. Churches continue their activities within their facilities. The seminary (Seminario Bautista) has had an average of eight students yearly. The Baptist Convention of Western Cuba includes 114 churches with more than 6,700 members. The Yumuri Camp provides training opportunities.

Oscar Romo and Gerald Palmer, both of the Home Mission Board, SBC, were permitted to visit among Baptists of Western Cuba in 1978. This provided opportunities to speak in several churches to large crowds, to meet with pastors and leaders, to fellowship, and to view how people continue to witness in their contemporary setting.

OSCAR ROMO

CUMBERLAND COLLEGE (I, III). For the fall semester of 1979, 1,705 students were full-time and 376 were part-time. A two-year degree in nursing and a unit of the Army Reserve Officers Training Corps were begun in 1973. Twelve other academic programs were introduced during 1970-78. Of special significance was the progress of the program for training ministers directed by Leon D. Simpson. This activity involved 192 ministerial students in the fall of 1978. During that semester 135 others were also preparing for church vocations.

During the 1970s the college erected three structures: a student center, a dormitory for nurses, and a music building. At the end of the decade the value of the physical plant was $7,352,898. Endowment funds more than tripled during the decade, reaching the total of $4,280,000; and the operating budget of 1979-80, amounting to $5,890,000, almost doubled. Contributions from the Kentucky Baptist Convention increased from $227,053 in 1969-70 to $745,000 in 1979-80.

After almost 35 years as chief administrator, president James Malcolm Boswell retired on July 31, 1980. During his tenure he presided over the school's advancement from a junior college of 152 students to the largest Baptist college in Kentucky. He was succeeded by James H. Taylor, Cumberland's vice-president for development since 1976.

CHESTER RAYMOND YOUNG

CURL, WILLIAM HAYDEN (b. Ammons, KY, Oct. 1, 1891; d. Orlando, FL, Oct. 11, 1973). Pastor and state convention leader. The son of William Kellem and Lela Mae Ammons Curl, farmers, he was converted in 1907 and ordained in 1908. Educated at Bethel College, Russellville, KY, he attended Southern Baptist Theological Seminary, 1921-24. He married Gladys Smith, Jan. 1, 1926. Their children were William and Elsie. He served as missions worker in Kentucky, 1935-45; as director of missions and stewardship training, Kentucky Baptist Convention, 1945-59; and as pastor and interim missionary, 1959-73. He is buried in Macedonia Cemetery, Burning Springs, KY.

A. B. COLVIN

CURRICULUM, SOUTHERN BAPTIST CHURCH (III). During the 1970s Southern Baptists defined a church's curriculum as "the sum of all learning experiences resulting from a curriculum plan used under church guidance and directed toward achieving a church's objective." The design and development of Southern Baptist church curriculum plans and materials was assigned to the Sunday School Board, the Brotherhood Commission, and Woman's Missionary Union. The SSB produced curriculum plans and materials for Sunday School, Church Training, and Church Music. The curriculum plans provided by denominational agencies were contained in a variety of curriculum materials. Each church selected the curriculum plans and materials that most closely matched its own needs and sense of mission.

Numerous changes in curriculum plans and in curriculum materials were introduced in Oct., 1970. This was the fruition of intensive and extensive work by personnel of the SSB, WMU, and the Brotherhood Commission.

A new grouping-grading plan was implemented in Oct., 1970. The Preschool Division was for persons through age 5 or prior to entrance to grade 1. Children were defined as grades 1-6 or ages 6-11, and youth were grades 7-12 or ages 12-17. Adults were divided into three focus ages: Young adults (age 18 or high school graduation through age 29), median adults (ages 30-59 or retirement), and senior adults (age 60 or retirement and up).

The curriculum series at the beginning of the 1970s were the Life and Work Series (for adults and youth in Sunday School, Church Training, Church Music, WMU, and Brotherhood), the Convention Uniform Series (for adults and youth in Sunday School and Church Training), the Forefront Series (for adults in Sunday School), and the Foundation Series (for preschoolers and children in all five church program organizations).

As the decade unfolded, some adjustments and additions were made in curriculum series. During the early 1970s, the Forefront Series was dropped, and its materials were transferred to the Life and Work Series. Church Training dropped the Convention Uniform Series and introduced the Baptist Training Series. In Oct., 1978, the Bible Book Series, which provides a nine-year study plan of books of the Bible, was introduced as a third option for youth and adults in Sunday School.

The concept of curriculum areas, begun in the 1960s, continued throughout the 1970s, but the lines between the curriculum areas were not always rigidly maintained. A case in point was the area of missions education. Responding to the Missions Challenge Committee report to the SBC in 1976, the Missions Education Council was organized in 1977 to promote missions involvement of every person in every Southern Baptist church. Participating in the council were not only the Foreign Mission Board, Home Mission Board, WMU, and Brotherhood but also the SSB. One result was more missions education in materials produced by the board. As the 1970s ended, missions education was still defined as primarily the responsibility of WMU and Brotherhood, but some missions education also was appearing in Sunday School, Church Training, and Church Music materials.

See also SUNDAY SCHOOL BOARD, WOMAN'S MISSIONARY UNION, and BROTHERHOOD COMMISSION.

ROBERT J. DEAN

CURRY, CHARLES FORREST (b. Kansas City, MO, Nov. 20, 1889; d. Kansas City, MO, July 4, 1975). Businessman and philanthropist. Son of Charles S. and Loula Gordon Curry, realtors, he married Janet Boone, Dec. 5, 1917. Their children were Charles Ewing and Carolyn Jane. Educated in engineering at the University of Missouri, he was assistant city engineer, Kansas City, MO, 1919-20. He organized Curry Real Estate Company, 1924; Home Savings Association, 1934; and Mid-America Securities, 1955. Curry served as director for Missouri Baptist Foundation, and as trustee, 1943, and president of the board, William Jewell College, 1956-68. The college library was named in his honor, 1970. He served also as vice-president of Baptist Memorial Hospital, Kansas City, MO. He is buried in Forest Hills Cemetery, Kansas City, MO.

DAVID O. MOORE

CUTTS, LOOMIS CLINTON (b. Oglethorpe, GA, Nov. 9, 1895; d. Vienna, GA, Feb. 21, 1972). Educator. Son of William Loomis, a minister, and Susan Clark Cutts, he attended Reinhardt College, Waleska, GA (1916), Mercer University (1914, 1917, 1921), and Southern Baptist Theological Seminary (Th.G., 1933). He married Vera Evelyn Harrison, May 30, 1922. They had three children: Susie, Sarah, and L. C., Jr.

Ordained in 1933, he taught public school while serving as pastor of First Church, Blue Ridge, GA, 1933-34. From 1934 to 1947 he was pastor of First Church, McCaysville, GA. On June 25, 1946, he was elected as the first president of Truett McConnell Junior College at Cleveland, GA. He led in fund raising, securing faculty, and purchasing of the first buildings. On Jan. 1, 1950, he resigned as college president to become pastor of First Church, Vienna, GA, where his father had served previously. After 15 years as pastor in Vienna, he retired and served as interim pastor for many Georgia churches.

Cutts is buried in the city cemetery of Vienna, GA.

CHARLES O. WALKER

D

DAHOMEY, MISSION IN (III). See BENIN, MISSION IN.

DALLAS BAPTIST COLLEGE (III). During the 1970s, under the administrations of

Charles P. Pitts and William E. Thorn, the college grew in value to more than $10,000,000 through capital improvements and increased budgets from $889,987 to a current $4,025,000. Enrollment in 1979 reached 1,008. W. Marvin

Watson, former postmaster general of the United States, became president in 1979.

CLAYTON E. DAY

DANIEL, JAMES NIXON, JR. (b. Chipley, FL, Mar. 22, 1927; d. Pensacola, FL, May 7, 1975). Attorney. Son of James Nixon and Villeta (McGeachy) Daniel, he married Christine Ziegler, June 4, 1949. They had four children: James Nixon, III, John, Robert, and Christine. Following studies at Washington and Lee and the University of Florida (L.L.B., 1951), Nixon practiced law in Pensacola, 1951-75. He was active in civic affairs and held office in numerous professional legal societies.

Nixon was an active member of First Baptist Church, Pensacola, serving as Sunday School teacher and chairman of deacons. He was vice-president of the board of directors of Baptist Hospital, Pensacola, and vice-president of the Florida Baptist Convention. At the time of his death he was vice-president of the board of trustees of Southeastern Baptist Theological Seminary. He is buried at Pensacola, FL.

J. NIXON DANIEL, III

DANNELLEY, JAY CHARLES (b. Caldwell County, TX, Dec. 12, 1914; d. Midland, MI, Apr. 18, 1975). Home missionary. Son of Emmet and Sally Dannelley, farmer-ranchers, he married Fern Heath on Nov. 20, 1945. They had four children: Joy, Deborah, Rebekah, and Sarah. Dannelley attended Howard Payne College (B.A., 1944) and Hardin-Simmons University (M.A.), and did further study at Southwestern Baptist Theological Seminary, North Texas State University, and Eastern Michigan University.

After serving as a pastor in Texas, Dannelley entered pioneer missions by going to Michigan. His first Michigan pastorate was Glen Eden Baptist Church, Taylor, MI, which began in Feb., 1956. He was named a member of the executive board of the Baptist State Convention of Michigan in 1960. The SBC Home Mission Board appointed Dannelley in December of that same year to serve as superintendent of missions for the western area of Michigan, including Woodland, Western, and Central associations. He was vice-president of the Michigan Convention in 1966. The HMB reassigned Dannelley in 1967 to serve as superintendent of missions for the northeastern part of Michigan (Bay Area). He is buried at Austin, TX.

BETTY WALKER

DARGAN-CARVER LIBRARY (I, III). The Dargan-Carver Library continues to provide resources and services to support research, publishing, and other ministries. On Mar. 1, 1971, the library joined the Management Services Division of the Sunday School Board, SBC.

The library contains 53,000 hardback volumes, 6,000 volumes of bound periodicals, 6,000 collections and/or items of historical documentation, and 10,860,000 pages of microfilm; it receives 1,054 serial publications. The library offers microfilming, photocopying, media programming, and other audiovisual services.

The executive director-treasurer of the Historical Commission, SBC, and the director of the Management Services Division of the SSB direct the total operation. The staff includes one supervisor, four professionals, and six clerical-support employees.

HOWARD GALLIMORE

DAVIS, FANNIE BREEDLOVE (b. Pittsylvania County, VA, Nov. 24, 1833; d. San Antonio, TX, Jan. 1, 1915). Educator, writer, and Woman's Missionary Union leader. Daughter of Hannah Moxley Crump Breedlove and Pleasant Ellis Breedlove, a tobacco plantation owner, she studied in the Female Department of Baylor University after her family moved to Texas in 1847. In 1854 she taught at Baylor College. She married George Bowen Davis, Jan. 4, 1855. The couple had two daughters.

She served as president of the Texas Central Committee of the Home Mission Board, 1878-80; president of the WMU of Texas, 1880-95; and representative to the organizational meeting of the WMU, SBC, 1888. As editor of the *Texas Baptist Worker* and contributor to *The Heathen Helper,* she promoted the cause of missions. She also was active in work with college students, in Young Women's Christian Association activities, and in the temperance and woman's suffrage movements. She is buried at San Antonio, TX.

DORIS DEVAULT

DAVIS, HARWELL GOODWIN (b. Marengo County, AL, Nov. 23, 1882; d. Birmingham, AL, Aug. 5, 1977). Attorney, educator, and denominational leader. Son of Judge Thomas Wyley Davis and Mary Kate (Goodwin) Davis, he graduated from South Alabama Institute (A.B., 1901) and the University of Alabama (LL.B., 1903; LL.D., 1939). Davis practiced law, 1903-15; served as assistant attorney general of Alabama, 1915-17; was commissioned captain in U.S. Infantry, 1917, and later was cited for gallantry in action and promoted to major. He married Lena Vail of Jackson, MS, Dec. 15, 1917. They had three children: Harwell, Jr., Betty, and Dorothy. He was attorney general of Alabama, 1921-27; collector of internal revenue for Alabama, 1933-39; president of Howard College, 1939-58; and chancellor of the college, 1958-77.

Davis served as trustee of The Southern Baptist Theological Seminary, 1938-53; president, Association of Southern Baptist Colleges and Schools, 1949-53; first vice-president, Alabama Baptist Convention, 1961-62; and member, Historical Commission, SBC, 1965-73. At 94 he published a biographical novel, *The Legend of Landsee.* He is buried in Elmwood Cemetery, Birmingham, AL.

ARTHUR L. WALKER, JR.

DAWSON, JOSEPH MARTIN (b. Ellis County, TX, June 21, 1879; d. Corsicana, TX, July 6, 1973). Pastor, denominational leader, author, civil libertarian, and public affairs executive. Son of Martin Judy Dawson, Jr., and Laura Underwood Dawson, he received degrees from Baylor Universtiy (B.A., 1904; D.D., 1916) and from Howard Payne College (LL.D., 1936). He married Willie Turner Dawson of Dallas, TX, June 3, 1908. She predeceased him, Apr. 18, 1963. Five children survive the parents: Alice (Cheavens), Leighton, Joseph, Matthew, and Donna (Van Hoove).

Widely regarded as an eloquent spokesman for the social application of Christian faith to contemporary society, he was also recognized as one of the most ardent and articulate defenders of religious liberty and the separation of church and state in America. He came to exert a wide influence far beyond his own denomination and the Southwest out of which he came and where he lived most of his life.

Ordained by the First Baptist Church of Waco, TX, in 1900, he served as pastor of First Church, Hillsboro, TX, 1908-12; First Church, Temple, TX, 1912-15; and First Church, Waco, TX, 1915-46. Elected as the first executive director of the Baptist Joint Committee on Public Affairs in Washington, DC, he served from 1946 to 1953.

His denominational involvements included: Assistant secretary of the Texas Baptist Education Commission, 1904-05; editor of *The Baptist Standard*, 1907-08; founder of Hillcrest Baptist Hospital, Waco; chairman of the committee which authorized creation of SBC Relief and Annuity Board; state publicity director of Texas for SBC Seventy-Five Million Campaign; chairman of the SBC Executive Committee, 1945; and chairman of the SBC Committee on World Peace, 1944-46. He served for 30 years on the boards of trustees of Baylor University and Bishop College.

In recognition of his concern for religious liberty, Dawson was chosen to represent Baptists of the United States at the founding of the United Nations in San Francisco to which he carried petitions with more than 100,000 signatures calling for a declaration of religious liberty to be incorporated in the charter of the United Nations.

A passionate civil libertarian, he saw religious liberty as integral to the American Bill of Rights and genuine religious faith. A member of the Baptist World Alliance Commission on Religious Liberty, the Department of Religious Liberty of the National Council of Churches, and the American Civil Liberties Union, he helped found Protestants and Other Americans United for the Separation of Church and State, and, upon its organization, served as temporary executive director, 1947-48.

A prolific author, Dawson was a person of remarkably rare gifts. A former president of the Texas Institute of Letters, which he helped found, he was elected a permanent Fellow of that organization. He was the author of 12 books and contributed to many others. His major works include: *The Light That Grows* (1924), *The Spiritual Conquest of the Southwest* (1926), *Christ and Social Change* (1937), *Separate Church and State Now* (1948), *The Liberation of Life* (1950), *America's Way in Church, State, and Society* (1953), *Baptists and the American Republic* (1956), *A Thousand Months to Remember: An Autobiography* (1964), and *José Antonio Navarro: Co-Creator of Texas* (1969). In addition he served as Southwestern correspondent for *The Christian Century*, 1926-46; book review editor, *Homiletic Review*, 1936-45; editor, *The Baylor Century* (forerunner of *The Baylor Line*), 1943-46; founder and editor, *Report from the Capital*, 1946-53; and a member of the editorial council of *Journal of Church and State*, 1959-73.

In 1957 Baylor University established the J. M. Dawson Studies in Church and State, named in honor of its distinguished alumnus. In addition to a graduate degree program in church-state studies, the program administers the J. M. Dawson Church-State Research Center and sponsors annually the J. M. Dawson Lectures in Church and State.

Unafraid of controversy, which he often encountered because of his deep convictions for the rights of persons and his commitment to religious liberty, he saw his Christian faith always in terms of the total arena of life. Profoundly influenced by Roger Williams, Walter Rauschenbusch, and B. H. Carroll, throughout his life he showed a passion for social justice, the free society, civil rights, world peace, religious liberty, and public morality. Dawson is buried in Oakwood Cemetery, Waco, TX.

See also PUBLIC AFFAIRS, BAPTIST JOINT COMMITTEE ON.

BIBLIOGRAPHY: James E. Wood, Jr., "The Legacy of Joseph Martin Dawson: 1879-1973," *Journal of Church and State* (1973).

JAMES E. WOOD, JR.

DEACON, MINISTRY OF THE (cf. Deacon, Vol. I). Since the first century, deacon ministry has been an important part of the work of churches. Many Bible scholars consider the seven mentioned in Acts 6:1-7 to be the forerunners of deacons. Set apart by the Jerusalem church, they were to minister to members who felt neglected and to heal the church fellowship, which was being threatened.

Two concepts of deacon ministry have strongly influenced Southern Baptist churches since the beginning of the SBC in 1845. One concept gives deacons primary responsibility for the material or business affairs of a church. In 1846 R. B. C. Howell (*q.v.* I) wrote *The Deaconship*, strongly advocating that deacons be assigned responsibility for the physical needs of the church so the pastor could be free to care for the spiritual needs. In 1929 Prince E. Burroughs' (*q.v.* I) book, *Honoring the Deaconship*, promoted the same concept. For more than 100 years, these and other books influenced deacons to become administrators of the physical and financial needs of churches.

Another concept emphasizes that deacons should serve as spiritual leaders alongside the pastor to meet the needs of church members. This concept received support from such leaders as Edwin Charles Dargan (*q.v.* I); Gaines S. Dobbins (*q.v.*); Robert E. Naylor, president, Southwestern Baptist Theological Seminary, 1958-78; Howard B. Foshee, director, Christian Development Division, Sunday School Board; Ernest E. Mosley, supervisor, Pastoral Section, SSB (now executive director of the Illinois Baptist State Association); and Charles F. Treadway, deacon ministry consultant, SSB (now retired).

The 1970s saw unusual growth in deacon ministry. Key resources supporting this growth were *The Deacon* magazine, first published by the SSB in Oct., 1970, and *The Deacon Family Ministry Plan,* published by the SSB in 1972. In 1979 Charles W. Deweese, staff member of the Historical Commission, SBC, presented research on the history of deacon ministry in a book, *The Emerging Role of Deacons.*

See also WOMEN DEACONS.

ERNEST E. MOSLEY

DEACONS, WOMEN. See WOMEN DEACONS.

DEANE, CHARLES BENNETT (b. Anson County, NC, Nov. 1, 1898; d. Richmond County, NC, Nov. 24, 1969). Attorney and public official. The son of John and Florence Deane, tenant farmers, he attended Pee Dee Academy, Rockingham, NC; Trinity Park School, Durham, NC (1918-20); and Wake Forest College, graduating from the law school in 1923. On Oct. 15, 1927, he married Agnes Cree. They had three children: Betty Cree, Carol, and Charles.

Deane served eight years as register of deeds of Richmond County; compiled the United States Congressional Directory, 1935-39; and served as administrative attorney, Hearings Branch of the Wage and Hour Divsion, U. S. Department of Labor, 1938-39. He was elected Representative of the Eighth Congressional District in 1946, serving for 10 years. From 1956 until his death he practiced law, including serving as city attorney, in his hometown of Rockingham, NC.

Deane served as a trustee of both Wake Forest University and Meredith College. In 1959 he was elected president of the Baptist State Convention of North Carolina. In 1969 Wake Forest University presented him with the Distinguished Citation. In 1961 the Baptist school conferred upon him an honorary degree, Doctor of Humanities. Deane served also as chairman of the Committee on Boards of the SBC. He is buried in Eastside Cemetery, Rockingham, NC.

CHARLES BENNETT DEANE, JR.

DECLARATION OF HUMAN RIGHTS. Drafted by the Christian Life Commission, SBC, presented to the 1978 Convention by the CLC, and adopted without amendment by the SBC messengers, the declaration urged Southern Baptist laypeople, pastors, churches, and agencies to be aware of denials of human rights and to deal in a "forthright and corrective way with social structures which abuse and violate human rights." The full text of the declaration appears in the 1978 SBC *Annual.*

WILLIAM M. TILLMAN, JR.

DEERE, DERWARD W., LECTURESHIP ON BIBLICAL STUDIES. A lectureship begun in 1971 at Golden Gate Baptist Theological Seminary honoring Derward W. Deere (*q.v.* III), longtime professor of Old Testament. For several years Deere had sought to raise funds to endow a chair in Old Testament interpretation. Simultaneously, various faculty members were contributing toward the establishment of a lectureship. The two funds were combined to establish and perpetuate this annual lecture series.

CLAYTON K. HARROP

DELAWARE, SOUTHERN BAPTISTS IN. See MARYLAND, BAPTIST CONVENTION OF.

DEMEREE, MURIAL RAYMOND (b. Canon City, CO, Mar. 14, 1904; d. Niceville, FL, Jan. 31, 1977). Missionary to the deaf. The son of Lewis Demeree, gold miner, and Edith Talmadge, he attended Colorado School for the Deaf, Colorado Springs, CO. He married Helen Madeline Wood, May 6, 1927. Their children were Helen and Robert. He worked with the deaf in Louisville, KY, and Tampa, FL, before his ordination in 1956. Appointed by the Home Mission Board, Mar. 1, 1958, to serve the deaf in Florida, South Carolina, and Georgia, he transferred to Colorado in 1962. He is buried in Beal Memorial Cemetery, Fort Walton Beach, FL.

CARTER E. BEARDEN

DENMARK, ANNIE DOVE (b. Goldsboro, NC, Sep. 29, 1887; d. Goldsboro, NC, Jan. 16, 1974). Educator and college president. Daughter of a tax collector, Willis Arthur, and Sarah Emma (Boyette) Denmark, she attended Meredith College (Artists Diploma in Piano, 1908) and Anderson College (B.A., 1925). She taught at Buies Creek Academy (now Campbell University), Tennessee College, Murfreesboro, TN, Shorter College, Rome, GA, and in 1917 became instructor in piano and harmony at Anderson College.

After serving as a faculty member at Anderson College for eight years and dean of women for three years, she was named president in 1928. She was the first woman to head a college in South Carolina. Under her leadership, Anderson College became a junior college, and male students were admitted in 1931. She labored tirelessly to keep the college open during the difficult years of the Depression. In 1950 Denmark was elected vice-president of the South Carolina Baptist Convention, the first woman to hold that position. She served as a trustee of Woman's Missionary Training School, Louisville, KY, for 15 years and from 1934-35 served as president of the Southern Association of Colleges for Women.

In 1953 she presided over her last graduation of Anderson College students and became president-emeritus, ending 25 years of service. She is buried in Willow Dale Cemetery, Goldsboro, NC.

PAUL TALMADGE

DENNY, EMERY BYRD (b. Surry County, NC, Nov. 23, 1892; d. Raleigh, NC, Apr. 24, 1973). Lawyer and judge. Son of Sarah Denny and Gabriel Denny, a minister, he married Bessie Brandt Brown, Dec. 27, 1922. They had four children: Emery, Betty, Sarah, and Jean. He studied law at the University of North Carolina and was admitted to the bar in Aug., 1919. He received honorary degrees from the University of North Carolina (L.L.D., 1946) and Wake Forest College (L.L.D., 1947).

Denny practiced law in Gastonia, NC, 1919-42, and was active in civic affairs. He was elected mayor of Gastonia for four successive terms. His capacity for legal insight and sound judgment was recognized, and he served with distinction as an associate justice, 1942-62, and as chief justice, 1962-66, of the Supreme Court of North Carolina.

Throughout his career, Denny's counsel was eagerly sought in church and state. He was a member, deacon, and teacher in the First Baptist Church of Gastonia and Hayes Barton Baptist Church of Raleigh. He was a member of the board of trustees of the University of North Carolina, 1941-43. In 1950 he was elected a trustee of Southeastern Baptist Theological Seminary and, except for the year 1963-64, served continuously until his death. In appreciation of his counsel and service, the seminary library building was named for him in 1969.

OLIN T. BINKLEY

DENOMINATIONAL INFORMATION, CHANNELING. See CHANNELING DENOMINATIONAL INFORMATION.

DIMENSIONS (III). See WOMAN'S MISSIONARY UNION, AUXILIARY TO SBC.

DIRECTION '84 COMMITTEE. A committee organized by the Brotherhood Commission, SBC, Apr., 1974. Its purpose was to examine the total Brotherhood program as it related to men and boys in churches, associations, state conventions, and the SBC, and to propose ways to meet the needs of men and boys more effectively during the next 10 years. The committee was composed of 29 persons from churches, associations, state conventions, and SBC agencies. The proposal for the committee was made

by Glendon McCullough (q.v.) following his election as executive director of the Brotherhood Commission in 1971.

ROY JENNINGS

DIRECTORS OF MISSIONS, SOUTHERN BAPTIST CONFERENCE OF. A conference organized in 1960 in Miami Beach, FL, through the initiative of Harold Gregory, director of missions for the Nashville Baptist Association in Tennessee. Its purposes were to provide fellowship, share information, and help effect changes for the mutual good of members and the denomination. Slow in getting started, the conference took on new life in the 1970s. It had about 300 members in 1980.

G. ALLEN WEST, JR.

DISARMAMENT. See ARMS CONTROL, DISARMAMENT, AND WORLD PEACE.

DISASTER RELIEF. During the late 1960s Southern Baptists began to be concerned about providing volunteers and services, in addition to money, to assist people affected by disasters. With the experience of sending volunteers to Alaska in 1968, the Brotherhood Commission, SBC, began encouraging the use of volunteers, both in the United States and other countries, such as Honduras, Guatemala, and the Dominican Republic. Disaster relief units were built in Texas, Oklahoma, Louisiana, Mississippi, Florida, and Tennessee by Brotherhood departments. The Brotherhood Commission has worked with the Christian Social Ministries Department of the Home Mission Board to produce a *Mission Action Group Guide: Disaster Relief* (1976), written by Laddie Adams, and develop and coordinate other disaster relief training approaches. The Brotherhood Commission belongs to National Volunteer Organizations Active in Disasters.

NORMAN GODFREY

DISASTER RELIEF PROGRAM, TEXAS BAPTIST. The official response team for natural disasters began in Texas following Hurricane Beulah in Oct., 1967. Under Charles McLaughlin, who is responsible for the total response of Texas Baptists, Robert E. Dixon became director of the emergency task force. A tractor-trailer unit was organized after Hurricane Celia and was financed from the state missions offering in 1971. Texas Baptist Men enlists and trains the ministering crew. One of the main contributions of the disaster unit is emergency food. About 260,000 were fed in Honduras in 1975. The disaster relief unit is self-contained, carrying large amounts of water, food, bedding, and facilities for the crew.

R. E. DIXON

DISCOVERY (III). See WOMAN'S MISSIONARY UNION, AUXILIARY TO SBC.

DISTRICT OF COLUMBIA BAPTIST CONVENTION (I, III).

I. History.—Since 1970, 12 churches have joined the convention: Johenning (formerly Southeast Chapel), Nineteenth Street, Rehoboth, and Zion, 1970; Ritchie, 1971; Holy Comforter and Shiloh (of Maryland), 1972; Ravensworth (which also maintained its ties with Virginia Baptists), 1973; New Jerusalem and Second, 1976; Mt. Gilead and First Spanish of Silver Spring, 1979.

Two churches, Broadview and Village, applied for membership in the convention in the fall of 1980 and received approval for membership at the annual convention meeting. These two churches had maintained their Maryland Baptist affiliation while seeking dual alignment with the District of Columbia Convention.

In 1973 Brookland merged into the Hyattsville Church. Withdrawing from fellowship in the convention were: Forestville, Morningside, Capitol Heights, Whitehall, Wheaton Woods, Grace, and Centennial. The Fairland Chapel (sponsored by Takoma Park Church) and Northside Church disbanded in 1969 and 1976, respectively.

The convention was composed of 62 churches in 1979, with 46 churches reporting a membership of 30,088 (the membership of 16 nonreporting churches was estimated at 4,500 for a total of 34,588). Church membership apparently declined in the decade, but the reasons are not clear. Data reported for 1970, with one church failing to report, showed 40,049 members.

Other key statistics at the close of the decade were: total contributions, $6,060,393; mission contributions, $730,116; and total property value, $46,704,710, with outstanding indebtedness of $4,279,340. In 1979, 569 baptisms and 773 other additions were reported.

Following the retirement of M. Chandler Stith, who served as the convention's executive secretary, 1943-1970, James A. Langley, pastor of the Pennsylvania Avenue Church in Washington, was elected executive secretary (now executive director). He began serving on Nov. 1, 1970, and has remained in the post to the present.

After 19 years as editor of *Capital Baptist*, the convention's paper, and director of evangelism and stewardship, James O. Duncan resigned in 1973 to engage in private business interests. James Langley served as editor of *Capital Baptist* from 1973 to the present, and also took the post of director of stewardship.

Carrol Bruce became director of missions and evangelism in Sep., 1976. Roy E. Godwin succeeded him in 1980. Paul Kesterson, director of the Department of Christian Education until 1971, was succeeded by J. Finney Williams, who served for five years. Williams' successor was Carl R. Sapp. Kathryn S. Grant became director of the Department of Baptist Women in 1971, replacing Retha Tillman, and continued in this ministry until Aug., 1980. Howard Rees, who led student work (now Department of Ministries in Higher Education) for 39 years, retired in

1973, and was followed by Joseph M. Smith. For a brief time Edna Woofter ministered as consultant for Christian Social Ministries. In 1974 Harry Hearne assumed this convention post.

II. Program of Work. *Witness and Ministry.*—Convention churches increasingly overcame racial lines. By the close of the decade, 15 convention churches were predominantly or all-black. Many formerly all-white churches now have members of other races and have a large percentage of black members. Johenning Baptist Center, which ministers to a black community, has received wide interest and participation by convention churches.

International and intercultural horizons have expanded. For several years the convention had a staff position for International and Language Culture Ministries, held by Minor Davidson. More recently the Home Mission Board, SBC, assigned Mario Acacia as minister to embassy personnel with the convention. Specific work with the growing Spanish-speaking community began in 1973, and by 1979 one Spanish-language and two Spanish-speaking missions were part of the convention. This work was first under the direction of Ivan Ramirez, and later Ivan Lapinell, with Esther Gonzalez as outreach director.

The Korean congregation affiliated with the convention claims to be the first Korean Baptist church formed in the United States. This congregation dedicated their new building in 1980. Congregations of Haitians, Portuguese, and Vietnamese were also formed.

Beginning in 1976 the convention gave special attention to refugees from Indochina, as it had done in earlier years to refugees from Cuba. Some 700 Indochinese were resettled, and follow-up "case work" was done. The Indochinese use part of the Baptist Building in downtown Washington as a community center, directed by Pat Swain.

Notable changes occurred in convention institutions. The Baptist Home of the District of Columbia instituted a day-care program which it operated in the facilities of University Church. The home waived its former requirement that limited its residents to persons physically able at time of entrance, began management and community services for other nonprofit institutions, and in 1976 purchased the 205-apartment Thomas House in downtown Washington to provide an additional living center for older citizens. William P. Harris, administrator, resigned in 1979 and was followed by David Lyon. Gilbert Smith became executive director of the home and of Thomas House in Dec., 1980.

As the decade ended, District of Columbia Baptists prepared to celebrate 100 years of ministry to the elderly. The Baptist Home for Children dedicated two attractive and spacious new cottages to house youth on its Bethesda, MD. campus. The children's home successfully weathered a storm which attracted public attention over some phases of its management. Wayne Crosby succeeded Marion W. Freeman as administrator in 1977. In recent years the staff of the home has increased with the development of several innovative programs for youth. Crosby resigned in mid-1980 and was succeeded by Jarrett Fishpaw.

The Johenning Baptist Center had three directors during the 1970s: Ted Overman, William H. (Bill) Smith, and William Rountree. In the early 1970s, a small group of Black Panthers arranged with the director to set up a medical clinic at the center. Though this group was strictly nonviolent (they declared that they had broken with the California organization), and were in the main unsuccessful in establishing a clinic, some criticism came to the convention. The group soon left the center. Funds raised in a National Capital Area Mission Offering helped establish a medical clinic at the center as the decade closed. Under Smith's leadership a school opened at the center for preschool children and the early elementary grades. The school has rendered a much-needed service and has prospered. Other programs have also been successful.

As part of its growing concern for deeply troubled persons, the convention became affiliated with and has given financial support to the interdenominational Washington Pastoral Counseling Service, beginning in Feb., 1969. The Department of Baptist Women led women in the churches in a regular ministry with federal prisoners attending seminars sponsored by Prison Fellowship in the nation's capital. The women expanded this service with weekly ministry in three Washington-area prisons.

Campus ministries expanded significantly. In addition to Joseph Miles Smith, the director and a minister to the deaf at Gallaudet College, Clifford Bruffey, the convention has two chaplains, Jerry Buckner and Margaret Rust Smith, and two US-2 workers, Clarence Harris and Mary High. Ministry continues at the University of Maryland, George Washington University, and American University. More recently, ministry was begun at Howard University and the University of the District of Columbia. A volunteer Baptist "chaplaincy" is also maintained at Georgetown University, Catholic University of America, and Columbia Union College.

Social concerns received greater emphasis. A consultant for Christian Social Ministries was added to the staff. The convention approved the Christian Life Witness Committee as a standing committee and gave it a new name, "Committee on Public Affairs and Social Concerns." Although the convention's resolutions varied greatly in subject matter and boldness from year to year, the convention spoke firmly to the effect that restrictions on abortion constitute class legislation against the poor; that the courts should recognize the right of a person to covenant that extraordinary medical means not be used to prolong life where no reasonable hope of recovery exists; and that women should have an equal opportunity to serve as deacons of the churches. The convention contributed financially, and the

staff and others shared in a successful effort to defeat legalized gambling in the District of Columbia in a May, 1980, referendum.

Harry Hearne led volunteers from convention churches in lending direct aid to victims of flood disasters in Kentucky and Pennsylvania. Convention staff aid went, at HMB request, to several United States camps for Indochinese refugees, and later to a camp for Cuban refugees.

The circulation of *Capital Baptist* grew as the convention adopted a program to send the paper to all members of convention churches without charge. An effort was made to set dates of the annual meeting more convenient for lay persons. Due to financial considerations, the executive board in Mar., 1975, voted to begin publishing *Capital Baptist* on alternate weeks, rather than weekly, which for many years had been the publishing schedule.

III. Other Developments. *Relations Beyond the Convention.*—Relations with Baptists of various denominational affiliations, black and white, in nearby Virginia and Maryland showed improvement in some respects and decline in others. In 1973 the Ravensworth Church joined the convention, the first member church from the Virginia side of the Potomac River. However, four of the churches leaving the convention during this decade joined the Baptist Convention of Maryland. In 1980 two Maryland Convention churches applied for membership in the District of Columbia Convention while maintaining their Maryland Convention and association ties.

District Baptists and Maryland Baptists worked out a joint arrangement for conducting a student ministry at the College Park campus of the University of Maryland. Maryland Baptists, however, withdrew from the Joint Committee on Maryland-District of Columbia Cooperation, expressing the general feeling that the committee had not achieved its objectives. After that action, Maryland and District Baptists began conducting separate evangelism conferences after holding joint conferences for many years. The HMB announced that no more financial assistance would be forthcoming to establish District of Columbia Convention churches outside the District boundaries.

The Baptist Committee on Wider Cooperation, formed in the late 1960s with representatives of the six major Baptist bodies in greater Washington, discontinued after only modest success in several interracial projects. A similar effort occurred under the HMB's key cities program. A fruitful cooperative effort among Baptists in the national capital area has been the ad hoc missions group representing the three conventions, Maryland, District of Columbia, and Virginia, and the SBC associations adjacent to the District. Three annual music camps have been one of the most effective joint District of Columbia-Maryland projects.

Relations within the larger Baptist work became stronger. The convention in 1972 approved a formal "Cooperative Agreement" with the HMB in keeping with the board's procedure.

The convention accepted a facilitating role with regard to a special financial campaign of American Baptists and Progressive National Baptists known as the Fund of Renewal. The fund was designed to aid blacks, Hispanics, Indians, and other minorities. The convention in turn was the recipient of some of these funds for its ministry with minorities.

The Department of Christian Education demonstrated a growing readiness to assist in whichever denominational programs—American or Southern Baptist—they chose. In both planning and implementation of programs, the Department of Ministries in Higher Education was involved with both national conventions. Disaster relief programs of the ABC, SBC, and the Baptist World Alliance are commended to the churches, and relief funds are channeled to all three Baptist bodies.

The executive director became one of the administrative group of the Interfaith Conference of Washington, and Baptist lay and staff persons serve on the IFC task forces. The convention contributes financially to the work of the IFC, which is composed of Protestant, Roman Catholic, Jewish, and Moslem representatives. The IFC's purpose is to provide a forum for interfaith dialogue, but equally to address needs of greater Washington from the broadest religious strength.

Convention Finances.—The convention felt pressures on its operation finances during most of the decade. The first years of the Langley administration witnessed strong and successful efforts to "catch up" on the previously-delayed transmittal of funds intended for the American Baptist Churches in the USA and the SBC. Convention programs and operations required austerity to enable the convention's moral commitment to be fulfilled. That commitment was met through a number of sources, but primarily by a grant of $46,000 from the District of Columbia Baptist Foundation. John A. Holt chaired the committee which secured the funds to meet this obligation. Out of this experience, an ongoing convention finance committee was established.

Stewardship in the 1970s did not follow a steady pattern. In some years mission giving declined, with many churches making a disproportionately large cut in mission gifts. In those years the convention received grants from its foundation. The generous sharing of certain costs by the national denominational bodies, especially the HMB and the Sunday School Board, made possible the staffing and implementation of many convention programs.

National Capital Area Mission Offering.—For many years the convention's state mission offering had been designated solely for the support of the Johenning Baptist Center. In 1973 the convention approved a new name for this offering, "National Capital Area Mission Offering," with corresponding enlargement of the goal and distribution of its funds. Over the years this offering has funded many projects, such as Bicentennial Mission on the Mall, summer student

missionaries, "Project Support" to provide start-up funds for churches engaging in community missions, prison ministries, property leased as an International House, and a medical clinic at the Johenning Center in cooperation with the Hadley Memorial Hospital.

Role of Women.—The convention in 1971 elected Letha Casazza as its president, thus becoming the first state convention affiliated with the SBC to elect a woman for its highest honorary office. In 1976 Alliene Tilley was elected president, the third woman in the SBC to serve as state convention president.

Official mandate places women in key convention leadership roles. Bylaw provisions (approved in 1964) require that one third of the executive committee and each standing committee of the convention be laywomen.

During the decade, five women were ordained to the ministry: Sharon Scott (by Takoma Park Church), Vicki Cowell (Hyattsville), Dianne Wisemiller (Briggs Memorial), Sharon Harris-Ewing (Twinbrook), and June Totten (Calvary).

First Family Joins First Church.—The first Sunday following his inauguration, President Jimmy Carter and other members of his family joined First Baptist Church of Washington. Within a relatively short time, Amy Carter, his daughter, professed faith in Christ and was baptized in the church. Except for the Sundays when away from Washington, the President and his family attended Bible class and worship services at First Baptist Church. On many occasions the President taught the Bible class of which he was a part.

United States Bicentennial and Convention Centennial.—The convention shared in the national Bicentennial in a variety of ways. Among these was the sponsoring of Bicentennial essay, songwriting, and art contests with monetary prizes awarded. The convention sponsored a HMB musical drama presentation, "The Fabric of Freedom," on the Ellipse. Through many weeks of the Bicentennial summer, the convention conducted a Ministry on the Mall—a witnessing ministry to the many thousands of visitors on the mall near the Washington Monument, centering around performances of a college student puppet group.

In 1976 the convention adopted eleven "Centennial goals" for the convention's centennial year—1977. John W. Laney chaired the committee, appointed by President Alliene Tilley. The goals were: (1) to develop historical resources, including monthly articles in the *Capital Baptist* in 1977, a history of the convention, and oral history resources; (2) to establish five new fellowships; (3) to baptize at least 1,200 persons in 1977, increase membership in the churches by 10 percent and increase financial support of the convention by 10 percent; (4) to encourage each church to take at least one identifiable step toward increased involvement in the life of the convention and in increased support of its programs and ministry; (5) to encourage each church to enter into a creative and supportive fellowship

DISTRICT OF COLUMBIA STATISTICAL SUMMARY

Year	Associations	Churches	Church Membership	Baptisms	SS Enrollment	VBS Enrollment	CT Enrollment	WMU Enrollment	Brotherhood Enrollment	Ch. Music Enrollment	Mission Gifts	Total Gifts	Value Church Property
1969	1	61	38,159	1,282	23,411	7,363	4,136	3,922	580	3,780	$608,743	$4,472,057	$29,270,863
1970	1	60	37,437	965	21,223	7,972	4,303	3,699	417	3,275	601,618	5,237,677	31,637,688
1971	1	64	37,005	1,174	21,383	6,754	3,500	3,535	431	2,765	612,412	5,034,954	32,947,097
1972	1	64	38,256	1,428	19,722	8,808	2,638	3,444	368	3,127	645,826	5,641,624	33,481,593
1973	1	66	38,947	1,100	18,523	6,513	2,642	4,333	435	3,375	586,302	5,161,976	33,037,472
1974	1	65	35,440	830	15,686	5,313	2,002	3,058	248	2,936	666,696	5,194,253	32,811,930
1975	1	65	34,805	782	14,586	5,189	1,775	2,898	234	3,000	724,131	5,695,264	29,294,648
1976	1	62	30,605	594	13,958	5,238	1,461	3,095	280	2,482	633,969	4,772,869	31,221,432
1977	1	62	33,127	725	12,995	6,227	1,477	2,336	200	2,241	519,520	4,389,664	30,827,868
1978	1	61	33,606	780	13,039	4,940	1,103	2,850	249	2,623	723,316	6,128,070	39,212,287
1979	1	60	34,588	569	11,684	3,175	990	2,273	160	2,375	730,116	6,060,393	46,704,710
1980	1	56	32,552	499	10,810	3,689	924	2,377	392	2,083	719,230	5,463,452	42,054,080

JAMES A. LANGLEY

with another church of complementary or contrasting strengths; (6) to establish in 1977 two new student ministries, and provide two continuing education experiences for clergy and laity; (7) to unite churches in prayer that there be a calling out of volunteers for church-related and missionary vocations; (8) to place renewed emphasis on the National Capital Area Mission Offerings with a focus on some new ministries in this centennial year; (9) to prepare a brochure welcoming newcomers to the area, introducing them to ministries of the convention, inviting them to any of the member churches, and providing a list of the churches; (10) to create a task force to develop recommendations for changes in the convention's name, structure, and staffing which would contribute to a more dynamic, effective witness in the entire metropolitan area; and (11) to use a task force to explore the most effective use of present property and the feasibility of developing new or alternative facilities for a variety of ministries.

Wider Leadership for Baptists.—In 1970 Earl L. Harrison (Shiloh) became president of the Progressive National Baptist Convention. In that same year Fred B. Rhodes, Jr., of Briggs Memorial Church was elected first vice-president of the SBC. The following year American Baptists elected Warner Ragsdale (Wheaton) as second vice-president. The women of the North American Baptist Woman's Union chose Letha Casazza (Takoma Park) as president for a five-year term beginning in 1972.

JAMES A. LANGLEY

DOBBINS, GAINES STANLEY (b. Langsdale, MS, July 29, 1886; d. Birmingham, AL, Sep. 22, 1978). Educator and denominational leader. The son of Charles Wesley and Letitia (Gaines) Dobbins, farmers, Dobbins became printer's devil for the Hattiesburg, MS, *Progress* (now *American*) at the age of 12. He was foreman, city editor, and Associated Press correspondent for South Mississippi at age 17. He served also as editor of *The Saturday Evening Eye,* 1904-05, one of the largest weekly newspapers in Mississippi. He was a graduate of Mississippi College (B.A., 1908), Southern Baptist Theological Seminary (Th.D., 1914), and Columbia University (M.A., 1925). He married May Virginia Riley, Dec., 1909. They had three children: Gaines, Riley, and Austin.

From 1914 to 1916, he was pastor of Galilee Baptist Church, Gloster, MS, and First Baptist Church, New Albany, MS. He was editor of *Home and Foreign Fields,* 1916-32. Professor of church efficiency and Sunday School pedagogy at Southern Seminary for 36 years, 1920-56, Dobbins served as first dean of the School of Religious Education from 1953 to 1956. He served at various times at Southern Seminary as professor, dean, publicity director, development officer, treasurer, and interim president.

Following his retirement from Southern Seminary, Dobbins taught as distinguished professor of church administration at Golden Gate

Baptist Theological Seminary from 1956 to 1966. During this time, as cochairman and chairman of the Baptist World Alliance Commission on Bible Teaching and Training, he engaged in mission tours of Europe, South America, Canada, Africa, and the Orient. In 1958 he taught at Baptist Theological Seminary, Ruschlikon, Switzerland; in 1962 at Instituto Filadelfia, Rivoli (Torino), Italy, and Nigerian Baptist Seminary, Ogbomosho, Nigeria.

In 1966 Dobbins moved to Birmingham, AL, where he served as chaplain of South Haven Nursing Home, 1967-73, and was director of leadership training for his local church, 1969-78. He returned to Louisville, KY, to teach at Southern Seminary and Boyce Bible School in 1975-76. A prolific author, he wrote 32 books and more than 4,900 articles during his career. He is buried in Elmwood Cemetery, Birmingham, AL.

BIBLIOGRAPHY: *Who's Who in America* (1922-77). "Religious Education: Festschrift for Gaines S. Dobbins," *Review and Expositor* (Summer, 1978). "Dobbins' Collections" at Southern Seminary Library, Louisville, KY, Dargan-Carver Library, Nashville, TN, and the home of Austin Dobbins, Birmingham, AL.

AUSTIN C. DOBBINS

DOMINICA, MISSION IN. Southern Baptist missionaries began formal work in Dominica in 1975. Work continues with the Deliverance Baptist Church in the capital city of Roseau, the Boetica Baptist Church, and the Tete Morne Baptist Church. Missionaries have utilized dozens of volunteers for medical, dental, and construction projects. Perhaps the most far-reaching effort to date was reconstruction projects carried out in the aftermath of Hurricane David as missionaries distributed food, led in building more than 80 houses, and repaired numerous others. Reaching youth through a youth center has also been a significant ministry. Missionaries serving Dominica are Fred and Betty (Akery) Walker, Jonathan and La-Homa (Martin) Singleton, and journeyman Colleen Thompson. John Ross, special project dentist, and his wife, Lisa, completed one year in July, 1980.

FREDDIE WALKER

DOMINICAN REPUBLIC, MISSION IN (III). The Dominican Republic occupies approximately two-thirds of the island of Hispaniola just east and south of Cuba. Approximately 5,100,000 people live in this Spanish-speaking community. In 1980, Baptists with nine churches and about 800 members were part of an evangelical community of 45,000. Special ministries in medical clinics, literature, pastor training, music, Christian day schools, and religious education were strengthening the ministry of the churches.

BILL GRAVES

DONNAN, MURPHREE CLAUDE (b. near Pelham, SC, Jan. 11, 1892; d. Greer, SC, Aug. 1, 1976). College president. Son of Hugh and Lula (Burnett) Donnan, he entered Furman University (B.A., 1924) following service in World War I. Ordained in 1918, he married Ernestine Hawkins, Aug. 4, 1924. They had three children: Murphree Yates, Lois Elizabeth, and Hugh Hawkins. Graduating from Southern Baptist Theological Seminary (Th.M., 1928), Donnan soon became principal of North Greenville Baptist Academy in South Carolina, guiding it from an academy to a high school to a junior college in 1934. He continued as president until 1962. He was elected president of the South Carolina Baptist Convention in 1959. He is buried at Tigerville, SC.

JEAN MARTIN FLYNN

DOUGLASS, RICHARD BARY (b. Sayre, OK, Jan. 19, 1936; d. Okarche, OK, Oct. 15, 1979). Pastor and missionary. Educated at Oklahoma Baptist University (A.B., 1958), the University of Oklahoma, and Southwestern Baptist Theological Seminary (B.D., 1962), he married Marilyn Sue Lacy, July 8, 1961. They had two children, Richard Brooks and Leslie Don. Appointed missionaries by the Foreign Mission Board, July 11, 1968, they served in Brazil until they resigned, May 31, 1972.

Prominent in radio and television ministries, Douglass was selected by the Central Oklahoma Multimedia Association for the 1977-78 award as outstanding leader in religious media. President of the state convention in Oklahoma in 1976-77, he was pastor of Oklahoma City's Putnam City Church from Apr., 1972, until he and his wife were brutally murdered in their rural Okarche, OK, home.

J. M. GASKIN

DOWIS, SOLOMON FRANKLIN (b. Fulton County, GA, May 19, 1891; d. Atlanta, GA, Nov. 5, 1967). Pastor and denominational worker. The son of William and Hannah Dowis, farmers, he attended Norman Institute (1912), Mercer University (1917), and The Southern Baptist Theological Seminary (Th.M., 1927). He married Frances Mae Freeman, Nov. 5, 1915. Their children were Frances, Sarah, Solomon, Jr., and William. Following her death, he married Frances Flury, Dec., 1955.

Dowis served pastorates in Georgia and Kentucky. While pastor of Carlisle Avenue Baptist Church, Louisville, he developed a church-centered mission emphasis which prepared him for work with SBC agencies. After serving as pastor of Virginia Avenue Baptist Church, Atlanta, he became superintendent of missions, Atlanta Baptist Association, and developed a city mission program. In 1943, he became superintendent of city missions for the Home Mission Board.

In 1946 Dowis became secretary of the HMB's newly-created department of Cooperative Missions which included city missions, rural missions, mountain missions, and pioneer program. The establishment of new churches in pioneer areas of the SBC was the primary aim of this new department. Dowis gave counsel and established guidelines for the organization of associations and state conventions and led associations and churches to select missions committees. In 1947 he began writing a correspondence Bible course for people who did not have opportunity for Bible study. After retirement in 1958, he was interim pastor of eight different churches. He is buried in Westview Cemetery, Atlanta, GA.

                                                                M. WENDELL BELEW

DRIGGERS, SAMUEL WYATT (b. Mount Pleasant, TX, Jan. 24, 1890; d. Juneau, AK, Oct. 29, 1962). Pastor and evangelist. Son of W. T. and Ollie (Mitchell) Driggers, he was educated at Baylor University (B.A., M.A.) and Southwestern Baptist Theological Seminary (Th.D., 1935). Driggers married Leola Harris of Wartrace, TN, in 1912. Their children were Samuel, Doris, Horace, Carl, and Spencer. A pastor in Texas and Missouri, he served as Stewardship and Brotherhood secretary for the Missouri Baptist Convention. He moved to Colorado where he was the first editor of the *Rocky Mountain Baptist,* 1952-55, turning it over to the Colorado Baptist General Convention, which began publication of the journal in Mar., 1956. He is buried in Mt. Airy Cemetery, Mount Pleasant, TX.

                                                                JAMES LEE YOUNG

DRUGS. See ALCOHOL AND OTHER DRUGS.

DUNCAN, ROBERT SAMUEL (b. Lincoln County, MO, Apr. 27, 1832; d. Montgom-

ery County, MO, Apr. 21, 1909). Pastor and author. Son of Lewis and Harriet (Kinnard) Duncan, he married Sarah Jane Irvin on Oct. 18, 1953. Their children were Thomas Thornton, Henry Kinnard, Annie Belle, Nellie Grey, Malcom Henry, Corey Perkins, Sue Carr, and Mollie Yeaman.

Although not formally educated, Duncan followed in the steps of his father when he was ordained to the ministry by Bethlehem Baptist Church, Lincoln County, MO, on Aug. 27, 1855. From 1869 to 1889, he was Missouri's secretary (or agent) for the Foreign Mission Board, SBC. From 1891 until 1894, he was connected with the American Baptist Publication Society of St. Louis. He wrote many books, including *The History of Sunday School* (1876) and the first history of Missouri Baptists, entitled *A History of Baptists in Missouri* (1882). He is buried at Montgomery City, MO.

                                                                L. DOUGLAS MCGLAUGHLIN

DURHAM, JAMES CHESTER (b. Kingston, KY, Oct. 13, 1914; d. Louisville, KY, Sep. 8, 1975). State convention student director. Son of Green Durham, farmer and salesman, and Bertha Powell Durham, he was educated at Eastern Kentucky University (A.B., B.S.) and the University of Kentucky (M.A.). He married Vera Wilborn, Jan. 20, 1939. They had one son, Thomas Leo Durham. He served as student director for the Kentucky Baptist Convention, 1942-72, and as assistant to the convention's executive secretary-treasurer, 1972-75. He is buried in Memorial Garden East, Louisville, KY.

                                                                A. B. COLVIN

E

EAGLE EYRIE ASSEMBLY (I, III). During the 1970s Eagle Eyrie purchased additional land, bringing the total to 425 acres. The White House, a landmark on the grounds, was replaced by a new small conference center and administration building at a cost in excess of $1,250,000. It was dedicated on June 30, 1980. This building includes administrative offices, a dining hall, a kitchen, conference rooms, and bedrooms for 64 persons. Another new structure housing a gift shop, bookstore, and ice cream parlor was dedicated on June 25, 1979.

A 15-minute color movie featuring a family at Eagle Eyrie was produced to acquaint Virginia Baptists with the assembly. More conferences than ever before were held during the 1970s in

spite of inflationary rises in costs. Total assets on Dec. 31, 1979, were $8,000,000. Malcolm Burgess has served as manager since 1960. John M. Tubbs became assistant to the manager in 1979.

                                                                MARTHA P. MOORE

EAST AFRICA, MISSION IN (III). See KENYA, MISSION IN; TANZANIA, MISSION IN; UGANDA, MISSION IN.

EAST TENNESSEE BAPTIST HOSPITAL (I, III). Since opening in 1948, the hospital has grown to a 312,000-square feet complex, with an additional 122,000 square feet added in July, 1980. Two medical office buildings containing 140,000 square feet, a School of Nursing representing 36,000 square feet, and approximately 1,200 parking spaces brought the medical center's total asset value to $45,000,000.

Containing 425 beds, the hospital offers a full range of general and specialty services, including open heart surgery. In recent years, the hospital has strengthened its coronary care services; improved diagnostic services; updated original facilities; expanded various medical teaching programs; and, in an effort to fight inflation, expanded outpatient services.

EARL G. SKOGMAN

EAST TEXAS BAPTIST COLLEGE (I, III). The 1970s witnessed several major changes in the college. Jerry F. Dawson succeeded Howard C. Bennett as president in 1976. New buildings included the Bennett Student Center, Charles Fry Hall for men, a new home for the president, and the $1,500,000 Mayme Jarrett Learning Center, which opened in 1979. Major renovations were made to all other buildings. By the fall of 1979, the enrollment reached 851 students.

At the end of the 1979-80 academic year, the endowment reached $4,800,000, while the total value of all property reached $13,600,000. The operating budget for 1980-81 was $3,700,000. During the decade the college expanded its degree programs to three associate and five baccalaureate degrees. In 1979, 41 full-time faculty members taught in 13 academic departments offering 16 majors and 20 minors, teacher certification in 12 areas of specialization, and pre-professional studies in five areas.

C. GWIN MORRIS

EASTERN EUROPE, MISSION IN. In 1966 John Allen Moore, a faculty member of the Baptist seminary in Ruschlikon, Switzerland, and a former missionary to Yugoslavia, became Southern Baptists' fraternal representative to the Baptists in Eastern Europe. Ten years later John David Hopper received this assignment, with Austria as his residence. Another couple was appointed for Eastern Europe in 1977. The missionaries maintain regular contacts with the Baptists of Eastern Europe, lecture to pastors and future pastors, preach in churches, and evaluate financial requests to the Foreign Mission Board from a few of the Baptist unions. In 1980 the Baptists of Eastern Europe constituted two-thirds of the Baptists of Europe.

J. D. HUGHEY

ECONOMICS. In any society the church has at least a two-way relationship with the economic system—it is financially affected by fluctuations in the economy, and it serves as a moral guide in helping to shape economic values.

Southern Baptists have fared well financially under the prevailing economic system. Particu-

larly in the twentieth century, the SBC has experienced a dramatic increase in funds available for the various causes which it supports. Between 1923 and 1980, for instance, total gifts to Southern Baptist churches increased from $34,000,000 to more than $2,315,000,000.

The SBC has also addressed the moral dimensions of the economy in a number of ways. First, in the annual reports of the Christian Life Commission, which has Convention responsibility to work actively in this area, and its forerunner, the Social Service Commission, numerous references have been made to the economic ills of the world. In addition, the editors of Baptist state papers have often editorialized on economic issues; and the SBC has passed occasional resolutions related to economics.

At times these reports, editorials, and resolutions have been critical of the prevailing economic system on such matters as labor-management relations, child labor, and greed. In general, however, Southern Baptists have been supportive of the economic system and have seen economic morality as an individual rather than a corporate matter. Strong emphasis has been placed on such personal virtues as honesty, diligence, generosity, and stewardship. The ideas of corporate economic responsibility and economic justice as appropriate concerns for religion have only recently begun to emerge among Southern Baptists.

W. DAVID SAPP

ECUADOR, MISSION IN (I, III). The Ecuadorian Baptist Convention was organized in Oct., 1972. Trained national leaders have emerged. The churches have assumed responsibility for their home mission program. In 1980 the Quechua-speaking mountain Indian churches continued to suffer persecution, but statistical reports showed they were the fastest growing churches. The Second International Baptist Youth Congress met in Guayaquil in 1978. Theological Education by Extension has grown with centers of instruction located throughout the country. In 1980 there were 56 churches and 87 missions.

J. BRYAN BRASINGTON

ECUMENISM AND SOUTHERN BAPTISTS (cf. Ecumenical Movement, The, Vols. I, III). The ecumenical or Christian unity movement underwent a vast revolution between 1960 and 1980. Until 1960 almost exclusively a Protestant concern, it broadened dramatically to include Orthodox and Roman Catholic churches and to focus on unity with humankind. Entrance of Roman Catholics boosted concern for dialogue and cooperation at various levels of church life. As it did, the movement ignited ecumenical participation among groups typically cautious and aloof, such as Southern Baptists. Though the latter did not join ecumenical organizations such as the National or World Councils of Churches or consider merger with other Protestants, they did get involved more extensively in dialogue and cooperation.

From Vatican II on, ecumenical efforts gravitated toward the major participant in it, the Roman Catholic Church, partly because of its size and also partly by design. With full backing in Rome under Pope Paul VI (1963-78) and Pope John Paul II (1978-   ), Roman Catholics took an active part in existing ecumenical organizations, whether local or national or international, stopping short of formal membership in the National or World Councils. They set up liaison with as many denominations as were open to it and organized both bilateral and multilateral dialogues from the grass roots up. They cooperated in numerous inter-church projects at several levels and shared in a variety of interdenominational worship services.

With a radically altered ecumenical climate, Southern Baptists, heretofore almost entirely outside the ecumenical mainstream, found themselves pulled into it. Though the SBC issued no formal statements delineating a different stance, Southern Baptists became significantly involved in ecumenism.

At the grass-roots level many Southern Baptist churches, associations, or agencies cooperated with other religious bodies in dealing with common concerns. Local or regional ecumenical groups sustained numerous services scarcely within the means of individual churches, such as housing for the elderly, day care for children of working mothers, mothers' day out programs, personal and family counseling, health care, after-school recreation, and neighborhood rehabilitation.

As soon as Pope John XXIII gave the signal, informal dialogues with Roman Catholics began. Southern Baptists also took part in dialogue with members of other communions. In 1969 the Ecumenical Institute at Wake Forest University, headed by Brooks Hays (q.v.), former congressman from Arkansas and twice president of the SBC, sponsored the first more or less formal Southern Baptist-Roman Catholic dialogue. Subsequently, the Department of Interfaith Witness of the Home Mission Board worked both with the institute and separately in organizing other dialogues. The latter included local, regional, and national conferences and extended to a wide range of participants. They also involved religious groups besides Christians, such as Muslims and Jews.

Southern Baptists also conducted worship services jointly with other groups, especially on special occasions such as Thanksgiving, Christmas, and Easter. Though not new to Protestants, the number and range of participants grew substantially in this period.

The observance of baptism and the Lord's Supper continued to pose serious obstacles to the relations of Christians with one another. For Southern Baptists, strongly influenced by Landmarkism, the validity of baptisms performed in non-Baptist churches and the prerequisites for communion remained in dispute. Almost all Southern Baptist churches refused to recognize infant baptism and thus to insist on baptism following profession of faith. As a result of changes in cultural outlook, however, more and more churches practiced open communion.

See also ECUMENICALISM, Vol. I.

E. GLENN HINSON

EDNA MCMILLAN OFFERING. Named for Edna McMillan (q.v. III) in 1939, Oklahoma's state missions offering is promoted by the state Woman's Missionary Union annually in September. Receipts grew from $79,534 in 1969 to $269,582 in 1979. Allocations for 1980 were $244,175 for 21 causes including language missions, National Baptist work, scholarships, Baptist Student Unions, camps, retirement centers, disaster relief, chaplaincy, ministries to the blind, and work with internationals.

J. M. GASKIN

EDUCATION, CONTINUING. See CONTINUING EDUCATION FOR MINISTRY.

EDUCATION, SOUTHERN BAPTIST HIGHER. See HIGHER EDUCATION, TRENDS AMONG BAPTISTS IN.

EDUCATION COMMISSION, SBC (I, III). The program of Christian higher education leadership approved by the SBC in 1972 stated five functions as necessary to the purpose of the commission: (1) Christian education leadership and coordination, (2) college studies and services, (3) teacher-personnel services, (4) student recruitment, and (5) Convention relations. At the request of the Program Committee of the Executive Committee, SBC, in Aug., 1970, the commission's publication, *College and Career,* and all vocational guidance materials were transferred to the Vocational Guidance emphasis of the Sunday School Board.

The third full-time executive secretary, Ben C. Fisher, served from Oct. 1, 1970, until Sep. 30, 1978, when he retired for health reasons. He was succeeded as executive director-treasurer on Nov. 1, 1978, by Arthur L. Walker, Jr.

In 1971 the commission staff began a program of annual workshops for admissions personnel. The first workshop for state education committee chairmen was held in 1972. This became an annual event. The H. I. Hester Endowed Lecture Series for the Association of Southern Baptist Colleges and Schools was established in 1972. All Southern Baptist colleges were accredited by the regional accrediting association by 1972.

Throughout the 1970s, the commission placed a major emphasis on the purposes of denominational education. Through the Association of Southern Baptist Colleges and Schools, the commission conducted a National Colloquium on Christian Higher Education at Williamsburg, VA, in 1976. As part of the follow-up to the colloquium, a study was made by Earl J. McGrath, executive director of the Program in Liberal Studies at the University of

Arizona and senior advisor to the Lilly Foundation, to determine the purposes of Southern Baptist colleges and universities and to assess their programs and activities in terms of their goals. The analysis of financial data was made by John Minter Associates. The study, highly complimentary of the commitment of Southern Baptist colleges to their purposes, was published under the title, *Study of Southern Baptist Colleges and Universities, 1976-77.*

The commission and the association also sponsored a National Conference on Bold Christian Education and Bold Missions at Galveston, TX, in 1979, and cooperated with 24 other denominations in sponsoring the two sessions of the National Congress on Church-Related Colleges and Universities in 1979 and 1980.

The papers delivered at Galveston were edited by Arthur Walker for publication in the book, *Educating for Missions* (1981). The commission also published a book for trustees written by Fisher in 1968. The original title of the book was *An Orientation Manual for College Trustees.* The fourth edition was enlarged and published with the title, *An Orientation Manual for Trustees of Church-Related Colleges* (1980). The updated history of the Education Commission, *Partners in Progress,* by H. I. Hester was published in 1977.

Under Fisher's leadership the commission placed a major emphasis on national and international educational relationships. Fisher made several trips to overseas institutions to advise and establish connecting programs. He also led in establishing national organizations through which denominational education could be strengthened.

ARTHUR L. WALKER, JR.

EDUCATION CRISIS. Beginning in the 1970s, anxiety about public schools became intense enough to suggest that the problems were qualitatively different from those of the past. Five basic issues surround the crisis in education.

(1) *The Back-to-Basics Movement.*—The Scholastic Aptitude Test scores have declined since 1941, indicating that students are less proficient in the basic skills. But some educators have pointed out that in earlier years only the best students took the SAT, whereas now all students take it.

(2) *Integration.*—Integration, often accomplished through busing, has been a divisive issue in American life. Some feel that segregation is an illness of society and the public schools should not be asked to remedy it. Others feel that the school is the best place to achieve harmonious race relations.

(3) *Financing.*—The cost of public education increased 150 percent during the 1970s. Escalation of educational costs came when taxpayers were frustrated about high taxes and the spending of tax monies. In the division of tax dollars, education does not appear to enjoy the priority it once had.

(4) *Private Schools.*—Baptists have been among the strongest supporters of public education, but desegregation prompted many churches to start private schools. Race, however, was not the only factor. Supreme Court decisions, which ruled out compulsory prayers and Bible reading in the public schools, boosted the private school movement.

(5) *Discipline.*—Several factors are cited for increased disciplinary problems: young people raised in the "me generation," nurtured by television's glamorization of the tough, cool image; low self-esteem among young people; and the revolution which occurred in race relations often making it harder for white teachers to discipline minority children.

The SBC passed resolutions on education in 1970, 1971, 1972, 1974, 1975, 1976, and 1978. Consistently, these resolutions gave support to the public school system, supported the right of every child to have an equal opportunity in education, and opposed the use of tax monies for church-related and other nonpublic schools.

JOHN A. WOOD

EL SALVADOR, MISSION IN. American Baptists began work in El Salvador over 70 years ago. On Feb. 20, 1974, the Baptist Association of El Salvador (nationwide) requested the Foreign Mission Board, SBC, to establish a Baptist book store and deposit to provide Christian literature. In Aug., 1975, the board transferred Chester and Dorothy (Bell) Cadwallader, Jr., from Guatemala. In Jan., 1977, William and Elizabeth (Graeff) Stennett transferred from Guatemala. In Sep., 1978, Hoyt and Marie (Sadler) Eudaly moved from literature assignment in Nicaragua to direct the wholesale operation. Stennett completed a modern bookstore and deposit building in downtown San Salvador in Feb., 1979. Ernie and Lee Ann (Brittain) McAninch were appointed in 1979 and scheduled to begin their term of service in Dec., 1980.

A. CLARK SCANLON

ELIZABETH LOWNDES SCHOLARSHIP. In 1934 the Woman's Missionary Union, SBC, established within the Margaret Fund a special endowment honoring its retiring treasurer, Elizabeth C. Lowndes (*q.v.* II). The income was to provide an annual award to the outstanding senior Margaret Fund student. Beginning in 1973-74 two separate awards of $200 each have been made to students related to the Home and Foreign Mission Boards.

DORIS DEVAULT

ELLER, EUGENE ROBERT (b. Moravian Falls, NC, Sep. 21, 1900; d. Easley, SC, Feb. 13, 1976). Pastor. The son of William and Sarah Holloway Eller, he attended Mercer University (B.A.) and Southwestern Baptist Theological Seminary. He married Frances Greer, Dec. 23, 1930. They had two children, Bonnie and Thomas. He was pastor in Cuthbert, Fort

Gaines, Coleman, Pelham, and Augusta, GA; Franklin, NC; and Pickens, SC. Director of missions for South Carolina's Piedmont Baptist Association for 13 years, 1956-69, he was president of the Southern Baptist Conference of Directors of Associational Missions, 1962. He is buried in Hillcrest Cemetery, Pickens, SC.

FLYNN T. HARRELL

ELLIOTT CONTROVERSY. See BIBLE, CONTROVERSIES ABOUT THE.

ENGLISH-LANGUAGE CHURCHES OVERSEAS (III). The term, "English-language churches overseas," usually refers to churches ministering largely to an international constituency. Such churches grew in number significantly in the 1970s. The Foreign Mission Board gave continuing encouragement and provided assistance through personnel and funds for buildings. By the end of the 1970s, the FMB listed 168 English-language congregations in 55 countries and territories. Not all were organized churches. Some were mission chapels. Others were English-language congregations of churches worshiping primarily in another language. Over one-third had missionary pastoral leadership. The largest concentration was in Europe, where 46 congregations were members of the European Baptist Convention (English language).

WINSTON CRAWLEY

ENGLISH SEPARATISTS. See BAPTIST BACKGROUNDS.

EQUIPPING CENTERS. The Church Training Department of the Sunday School Board conducted during 1976 and 1977 a pilot project related to Equipping Centers as an additional approach to training for adults. This project was designed and implemented in response to a priority to "Equip the Saints" established by the SSB trustees in Feb., 1976. Approximately 200 churches in five states participated in the project. The Equipping Center concept was validated and materials were introduced and made available to churches in Oct., 1979.

The Equipping Center modules, or courses, are developed around six content areas. By the end of 1985, about 48 modules will be available, eight in each content area. The content areas are Evangelism and Missions, Christian Doctrine, Family Life, Leadership, Church and Community, and Christian Growth.

Equipping Center modules are undated materials, designed to be used in short-term training and on flexible schedules. Materials are provided for both the leader and group members. Modules are reusable and require minimal organization. Equipping Center modules are Bible-based, person-oriented, need-centered, skill-developing, and ministry-motivating.

Each module suggests two or more learning approaches. A learning approach is the basic methodology suggested. Modules may be studied individually, in a seminar, in small groups, one-to-one, or by using a combination of all these learning approaches.

See also CHURCH TRAINING.

ROY T. EDGEMON

ETHIOPIA, MISSION IN (III). In 1970 the first veterinarian appointed by the Foreign Mission Board joined the Ethiopian mission team, which projected a community development program, including medical, handcraft, agricultural, veterinary, engineering, and Bible teaching ministries in rural districts. Radio, cassette tapes, Bible correspondence courses, and business management were based in Addis Ababa. In Apr., 1977, four missionaries were arrested and detained from 2 to 16 days. By June 15 all missionaries had left Ethiopia, most of them later accepting other assignments. In Apr., 1978, Lynn and Suzanne (Knapp) Groce returned to Addis Ababa. Jerry and Rosetta (McIntire) Bedsole followed in June. With their residence confined to the capital, the missionaries were ministering through veterinary medicine, Bible distribution, and discipleship classes.

JOY NEAL

ETHNIC BAPTISTS IN ILLINOIS. See ILLINOIS, BLACK AND ETHNIC CHURCH GROWTH IN.

EUROPEAN BAPTIST MISSION. The European Baptist Mission was first called the European Baptist Foreign Missionary Society when formed in 1954 by the Baptist Unions of France, Germany, and Switzerland. Unions of Austria, Belgium, Italy, and Yugoslavia were added in 1955, Finland and Spain in 1956, the Netherlands in 1965, and Portugal in 1978. The EBM offices are presently in Bad Hamburg, West Germany. Helmut Grundmann is the general secretary.

Baptist work by Europeans had begun in Cameroon, Africa, as early as 1884 but was interrupted by two world wars. The EBM's first endeavors took place in 1956 in Northern Cameroon where no earlier work had taken place.

In 1965 the EBM began work in Sierra Leone, Africa, following the concept adopted in Cameroon involving direct evangelism to build churches and indirect evangelism to meet needs for medical and educational assistance.

In 1979, when MASA (Missionary Action in South America) was integrated into the EBM, orphanages and pioneer evangelistic work in Brazil and Argentina became activities of the EBM.

See also EUROPEAN BAPTISTS, Vol. I.

ISAM E. BALLENGER

EVANGELICAL BAPTIST MISSIONS, INC. An independent, fundamental Baptist mission agency founded in 1928 to sponsor the work of Joseph McCaba to the Niger Colony in

West Africa. An approved agency of the General Association of Regular Baptist Churches, its purpose is to evangelize and to establish local, indigenous Baptist churches. Supported mainly by independent Baptist churches in North America, receipts in 1979 were $1,357,847. In 1980, 130 missionaries were serving in Argentina, Australia, Benin, Canada, France, Germany, Great Britain, Ivory Coast, Mali, Martinique, Niger, Sweden, USA, and Zambia. David L. Marshall is the general director. The Board of Trustees is self-perpetuating. Offices are in Kokomo, IN.

J. TERRY YOUNG

EVANGELISM, ASSOCIATION OF BAPTISTS FOR WORLD. See WORLD EVANGELISM, ASSOCIATION OF BAPTISTS FOR.

EVANGELISM, BUS. The ferment of church renewal in the late 1960s and early 1970s led to the rise of bus evangelism. Churches enlisted drivers, bus pastors, and counselors. Through personal visitation, usually on Saturday, persons were enlisted to ride the bus to Sunday School on Sunday morning.

The Home Mission Board in 1971 employed a coordinator of church bus evangelism who initiated a denominational program to assist churches in bus evangelism. The HMB supported church bus evangelism through materials, resources, and conferences. The first conferences on church bus evangelism in 1971 were conducted in Tallahassee, FL, Fort Worth, TX, Baltimore, MD, Los Angeles, CA, and Louisville, KY. In 1973 this program shifted to the Sunday School Board. Beginning in 1973, Lewis White served as a consultant in church bus evangelism at the SSB.

An estimate made in 1971 projected more than 5,000 Southern Baptist churches involved in church bus evangelism.

JOHN F. HAVLIK

EVANGELISM, E. HERMOND WESTMORELAND CHAIR OF. See WESTMORELAND, E. HERMOND, CHAIR OF EVANGELISM.

EVANGELISM, HOME MISSION BOARD PROGRAMS OF (I; cf. Evangelism Development, Home Mission Board Program of, Vol. III). The 1974 SBC tabled a motion "that a commission on evangelism be established" and asked the Home Mission Board to study the matter and report to the Convention in 1975. In Mar., 1975, the HMB directors, "in response to the action of the Convention," elevated evangelism from division status to section status in the HMB internal structure and requested the SBC to add two evangelism programs to the board's 12 programs.

The directors said these two actions would: (1) Make the evangelism director accountable directly to the executive director-treasurer and make him a member of the executive council of the board; (2) clarify board responsibilities in two basic categories—evangelism and missions; and (3) recognize the large base for evangelism input in board planning and Southern Baptist program planning. The 1975 SBC approved the action of the HMB directors. The new programs of Mass Evangelism and Personal Evangelism were created.

The Evangelism Section staff includes director C. B. Hogue and two specialists attached to his office, John F. Havlik, director of evangelism education and writing, and Glenn Sheppard, director of spiritual awakening. The Evangelism Development Division staff includes director Joe Ford and department directors Ken Carter, Frank Crumpler, and Reid Hardin. Dale Cross is director of metropolitan evangelism strategy. The Direct Evangelism Division staff includes director Fred White and department directors Bobby Sunderland and Howard Ramsey.

The Program of Evangelism Development.—The Program of Evangelism Development is in the Evangelism Development Division, which includes the Associational Evangelism Department, the Specialized Evangelism Department, and the Evangelism Support Department. This program is the major channel "to work with and assist Southern Baptist churches, associations, state conventions, and agencies in interpreting, promoting, and properly relating the message, methods, motivation, and spirit of New Testament evangelism."

Evangelism Development designs strategies, services, and materials for short- and long-range planning in establishing and conducting evangelism; trains and equips associational evangelism chairmen; provides evangelism consultative services; develops annual evangelism themes, emphases, and projects; and, upon request, provides financial assistance to state conventions.

The Associational Evangelism Department develops associational strategies of evangelism, working closely with associational mission directors and evangelism chairmen in enlisting churches to cooperate in evangelistic endeavors. Metropolitan evangelism strategy is part of the Associational Evangelism Department. The Specialized Evangelism Department promotes seminars on growing an evangelistic church and distributes correspondence Bible course material. The Evangelism Support Department relates to volunteers to assist in evangelistic endeavors.

The Program of Mass Evangelism.—The Program of Mass Evangelism is in the Direct Evangelism Division. The purpose of the program is "to work with and assist churches, associations, and state conventions with all types of mass evangelism ministries and projects, including local church revivals, ethnic crusades, area crusades, simultaneous revivals, and other specialized types of mass evangelism." This purpose is accomplished through the development of strategies, services, and materials for planning, conducting, and following up all types of mass evangelism; through the use of mass media for evangelism; and through leadership training conferences.

The Program of Personal Evangelism.—The Program of Personal Evangelism is in the Direct Evangelism Division. The purpose of the program is "to work with and assist churches, associations, and state conventions in motivating, equipping, and involving lay persons, groups of lay persons, pastors, and lay evangelism leaders for a life-style of personal witnessing and the ability to train others for such a life-style." Personal Evangelism develops strategies, materials, and services in establishing and conducting activities and projects; provides Convention-wide leadership training in evangelism; and enlists and trains lay persons for special evangelistic assignments.

C. B. HOGUE

EVANGELISM CONFERENCES, STATE. The statewide evangelistic conference is perhaps the most important meeting for promoting the Southern Baptist program of evangelism. An evangelism program adopted by the SBC in 1947 and ratified in 1948 included the provision that "each state plan and promote a statewide conference on evangelism." The threefold purpose of the statewide evangelistic conference is to inspire, to provide methods for evangelism, and to plan and promote specific objectives for action. Each state conference is planned and organized by the state director of evangelism.

Every state convention continues to have such a meeting each year, with 35,000 total attendance, including more than 15,000 pastors. In the early 1970s, state youth evangelism conferences, growing out of the state evangelism conferences, began to emerge.

JOHN F. HAVLIK

EVANGELISTIC SINGERS. A term generally used to denote musicians associated with evangelists in revival meetings as soloists, song leaders, and choir directors. One of the earliest musicians to accompany a major evangelist was Thomas Hastings (1784-1872), who in 1832 was a musical assistant to Charles G. Finney in New York City. The first singer to accompany an evangelist on an extended basis was Ira D. Sankey (1840-1908), who achieved international fame as Dwight L. Moody's singer in America and Britain from the mid-1870s. Sankey sang solos and led the singing, accompanying himself on a small reed organ on the pulpit platform. Other singers associated with Moody were Philip P. Bliss (1838-76), James McGranahan (1840-1907), George C. Stebbins (1846-1945), and Daniel B. Towner (1850-1919). An important model for Sankey was Philip Phillips (1834-95), renowned in America and England for his services of sacred songs conducted from the reed organ.

While these singers were active in the Northeast, a contemporary in the Southwest was the Texas Baptist evangelist William E. Penn (*q.v.* II). Penn used several singers during his career: George R. Cairns, Vallie C. Hart, J. M. Hunt, Horace N. Lincoln, J. F. Parker, and L. B. Shook.

The two most important successors to Sankey's generation of evangelistic singers in the early twentieth century were Charles M. Alexander (1867-1920) and Homer A. Rodeheaver (1880-1955). Alexander, who was associated with evangelists Reuben A. Torrey and J. Wilbur Chapman, established a new style of evangelistic singers who led singing with exaggerated hand motions and in general assumed a more light-hearted approach to music in revivalism. Rodeheaver, who from 1910 to 1930 was associated with evangelist William A. (Billy) Sunday, continued this trend.

From 1910 to 1928 the Southern Baptist Home Mission Board had a staff of evangelists and singers who held simultaneous meetings in churches of the larger Southern cities. Haas lists 43 evangelistic singers employed by the HMB in this period, including such pioneer church music leaders as Isham E. Reynolds (*q.v.* II) and W. Plunkett Martin (*q.v.*). Reynolds, Martin, and several others in this group had studied at Moody Bible Institute under D. B. Towner. Baylus B. McKinney (*q.v.* II), although not a full-time evangelistic singer, led the music for numerous revival meetings during his career, and wrote many gospel hymns in connection with this work. This era's chorus choir and children's "booster band" of singers were forerunners of the graded choir program that developed among Southern Baptists from the 1940s.

The best known evangelistic singers in recent decades have been Cliff Barrows and George Beverly Shea, song leader and soloist, respectively, for Billy Graham. A number of Southern Baptists are active vocationally as evangelistic singers, engaged exclusively or primarily in evangelistic meetings in Southern Baptist churches. The 1980 directory of Southern Baptist evangelists listed more than 100 music evangelists, including many women.

HARRY ESKEW

EWING, SAMUEL EDGAR (b. Sandoval, IL, May 12, 1865; d. Maryville, MO, Sep. 11, 1941). State convention leader. The son of Robert Ewing and Minerva Jane Martin, he attended William Jewell College (A.B., 1893) and The Southern Baptist Theological Seminary (Th.M., 1896). He served as recording and statistical secretary of the Missouri Baptist General Association, 1917-41; as secretary of the board of Missouri Baptist Hospital, 1914-41; as a member of the Home Mission Board; and as trustee of Southern Seminary and Baptist Hospital, New Orleans, LA. He married Martha James McCount, Sep. 23, 1896. After her death in 1923, he married Eunice E. Ringer, 1926. He is buried in Valhalla Cemetery, St. Louis County, MO.

L. DOUGLAS MCGLAUGHLIN

**EXCEPTIONAL PERSONS, MATE-
RIALS FOR USE WITH** (III). In 1971 the
Sunday School Board transferred work with the
mentally retarded from the Church Training
Department to the Sunday School Department.
A Church Ministry to Retarded Persons was published as a basic guide in 1972. In 1977 a resource kit for use in group study of the book was
released. *Sunday School Resource Kit for Teaching
Deaf Children* was introduced in 1976 as a quarterly release. In 1977 the Special Ministries Section was created. Initially it provided materials
and promoted work with these groups: the mentally retarded, the deaf, the blind, persons with
other handicaps, and language and ethnic
groups.

El Interprete, a member's resource for Spanish-speaking adults, was initiated in 1978. It
was translated from *Sunday School Adults. El Interprete: Maestros,* translated from *The Adult Teacher,*
was released in 1979. In 1979 *Sunday School Resource Kit for Teaching the Mentally Retarded* replaced earlier materials designed for this purpose. In 1980 responsibility for language and
ethnic work was transferred to the Church Program and Services Language Unit. *The Braille
Baptist, The Youth Braille Baptist, Sunday School
Lessons Simplified,* and *Simplified Bible Study* were
continued through the decade.

EUGENE CHAMBERLAIN

EXECUTIVE COMMITTEE, SBC (I,
III). The Executive Committee, SBC, continues
to function as an enabling body to assist the
churches and the agencies of the SBC in carrying
out the Great Commission of Christ. It serves as
the fiduciary, fiscal, and executive agency of the
Convention in all of its matters not specifically
committed to some other board or agency. The
Executive Committee is "specifically authorized, instructed, and commissioned . . . to act
for the Convention ad interim in all matters not
otherwise provided for" [SBC Bylaw 20(5a)].

The following persons served as chairmen of
the Executive Committee during the 1970s:
1969-71, James L. Monroe, pastor; 1971-72,
Owen Cooper, layman; 1972-74, Stewart B.
Simms, pastor; 1974-76, Charles E. Harvey,
pastor; 1976-78, W. Ches Smith, III, pastor;
1978-80, Brooks H. Wester, pastor; and
1980-81, J. Howard Cobble, pastor.

Staff Changes.—Harold C. Bennett succeeded
Porter W. Routh as the executive secretary-
treasurer of the Executive Committee, Aug. 1,
1979. Bennett moved to this position from Jacksonville, FL, where he had served as the executive secretary-treasurer of the Florida Baptist
Convention since 1967.

Porter W. Routh was the executive secretary-
treasurer of the Executive Committee, 1951-79.
During these years the number of Southern Baptist churches increased from 28,289 to 35,605;
membership increased from 7,373,498 to
13,379,073; total mission gifts through the
churches increased from $37,200,000 to
$318,300,000; Cooperative Program receipts in-

creased from $21,500,000 to $150,000,000; and
the SBC portion of the Cooperative Program increased from $8,100,000 to $57,400,000.

Billy D. Malesovas was elected in 1975 to succeed John H. Williams as assistant to the treasurer and director of financial planning. The
Executive Committee elected Tim A. Hedquist
to succeed Malesovas in 1977. Albert McClellan,
associate executive secretary and director of program planning, retired on Dec. 31, 1980, after 31
years on the staff of the Executive Committee,
and was succeeded by Reginald M. McDonough, who had served since 1977 as secretary,
Church Administration Department, Sunday
School Board. W. C. Fields continues to serve as
assistant executive secretary and director of public relations, having served in this position since
1959.

Convention Building.—Since 1963 the SBC
Building has provided offices for the Executive
Committee, Christian Life Commission, Education Commission, Stewardship Commission,
SBC Foundation, and the Seminary Extension
Department. In 1980 the Executive Committee
authorized a special committee to study the
building and determine the necessary course of
action in light of limited space and SBC agency
expansion.

Reorganization.—During the 1970s, the Executive Committee reorganized its subcommittee
structure, reducing the number of subcommittees from four to three: Administrative and Convention Arrangements, Business and Finance,
and Program and Budget. These subcommittees
are divided into appropriate work groups. In
1979 a special committee was appointed to study
the Cooperative Program budgeting process.

Budget Recommendations.—The Executive Committee recommends annually the SBC Cooperative Program Allocation Budget and the SBC
Operating Budget for consideration by the Convention. The following budgets were recommended and subsequently adopted by the Convention:

Year	SBC Cooperative Program Allocation Budget	SBC Operating Budget
1970	$28,858,229	$ 535,000
1971	30,250,000	567,000
1972 (9 months)	24,630,589	429,000
1972-73	33,042,506	598,000
1973-74	35,000,000	666,000
1974-75	40,000,000	715,000
1975-76	51,000,000	817,000
1976-77	55,000,000	909,000
1977-78	63,400,000	989,500
1978-79	75,000,000	1,062,000
1979-80	83,000,000	1,164,000
1980-81	90,000,000	1,335,000

During the same years the Executive Committee operating budget was as follows:

Executive Committee Operating Budget	
1970	$317,200
1971	343,000
1972 (9 months)	259,200
1972-73	420,000
1973-74	479,000

1974-75	531,000
1975-76	569,000
1976-77	616,200
1977-78	667,200
1978-79	736,100
1979-80	744,020
1980-81	860,275

Seminary Allocation and Distribution Formula.— In 1976 the Executive Committee approved an allocation and distribution formula for the six SBC seminaries. Since the early 1950s Cooperative Program funds available to theological education had been distributed to the seminaries on the basis of formulas agreed upon by the seminary presidents. R. Orin Cornett, college administrator and consultant, was employed by the Executive Committee to develop the allocation and distribution formula. The formula has two purposes: (1) To express quantitatively the principles of the equitable distribution of Cooperative Program funds, and (2) to make possible the application of those principles through variations in enrollment and other perimeters. In this case, full-time equivalent enrollment is the basic perimeter. The Convention allocates approximately 24 percent of the Cooperative Program funds to the six seminaries.

Capital Needs.—The Executive Committee developed a capital needs program for the SBC agencies which provided the agencies an orderly method to plan for future capital needs. Upon recommendation of the Executive Committee, the SBC adopted the following capital needs program for 1978-84.

Agency	Capital Needs Allocation
Golden Gate Seminary	$ 4,297,046
Midwestern Seminary	2,000,000
New Orleans Seminary	2,701,295
Southeastern Seminary	2,547,444
Southern Seminary	2,000,000
Southwestern Seminary	2,000,000
Brotherhood Commission	160,200
Radio and Television Commission	1,000,000
	$16,705,985

SBC Symbol.—Upon recommendation of the Executive Committee, the 1978 SBC adopted an easily recognizable symbol for voluntary use by Southern Baptists. The symbol depicts the cross, the Bible, and the world.

Plan for Denominational Planning.—The Home Mission Board requested the Executive Committee to conduct a study related to a plan for denominational planning. The Inter-Agency Council developed a long-range planning model which is summarized in the following steps:

1. Analyze the present situation
2. Project the present situation into the future
3. Identify future problem areas
4. Develop alternative models
5. Select the most feasible alternative model and identify objectives
6. Set strategies for reaching objectives
7. Set goals to quantify strategies
8. Make action plans to reach goals

Special Studies.—As a result of its assignment from the SBC, the Executive Committee must conduct special studies from time to time. Some of these studies conducted during the past 10 years were: Study of SBC Hospitals; Study by the Committee of 15; Study of the Cooperative Program; BSU Study; Study by the Committee of Seven; Study by the Missions Challenge Committee; Study of Possible Merger of Sunday School Board and Brotherhood Commission; and Study of Use of Laypersons.

Bold Mission Thrust.—In 1978, upon recommendation of the Executive Committee, the SBC adopted the major denominational emphasis of Bold Mission Thrust for 1979-82. Bold Mission Thrust is an effort to enable every person in the world to have an opportunity to hear and to respond to the gospel of Christ by the year 2000. The objectives for 1979-82 are as follows (*Annual, SBC,* 1978, p. 47):

1. Bold Growing . . . by providing New Testament based churches and missions for all people

2. Bold Going . . . by seeking out and equipping the called and cooperating in support of persons participating in the activities of Bold Mission Thrust

3. Bold Giving . . . by providing adequate financial resources to accomplish Bold Mission Thrust.

In 1980 the SBC adopted the recommendation of the Executive Committee related to the 1982-85 Bold Mission Thrust Program Emphasis as follows (*Annual, SBC,* 1980, pp. 37-39): Scripture: Matthew 28:18-20

Reaching People

1. 8.5 million in Bible study through Sunday School

2. 1.5 million baptisms: 445,000 in 1982-83; 495,000 in 1983-84; 560,000 in 1984-85

3. 1,500 new churches organized

4. 30,000 churches increase percentage of budget giving through Cooperative Program

5. 2,554 newly appointed missionary personnel and 300,000 short-term mission volunteers, including Mission Service Corps volunteers

Develop Believers

1. Every church involved in regular prayer support of Bold Mission Thrust

2. 1 million church members trained to witness

3. 3.5 million in discipleship and doctrine training through Church Training

4. 1.9 million involved in missions through WMU (1,300,000) and Brotherhood (600,000)

5. 20,000 churches engaged in an emphasis to develop Christian stewards

Strengthen Families

1. 500,000 family units committed to family worship and Bible study in the home

2. Every church providing Christian family enrichment activities to strengthen family relationships and moral values

SBC agencies have developed the following projects to assist each church in accomplishing these goals:

Reach People

1. *Church Growth Thrust:* A three-year project to effect church growth through pastor-led ongoing churchwide climate building, priority

planning, and allocation of resources toward reaching the lost and unchurched.

2. *Bold New Work:* A three-year project to lead churches to reach new people through starting new Sunday Schools and church-type missions. The project includes actions to reach pockets of people such as ethnics, deaf, blacks, socioeconomic, urbanite, etc. that have not responded to other approaches.

3. *8.5 By '85—Sunday School Enrollment Goal Plan:* A three-year promotion plan to reach a Sunday School enrollment of 8.5 million by Sep., 1985.

Develop Believers

1. *Bold Growth in Discipleship:* A three-year project to follow up new Christians and involve church members in discipleship and doctrine training.

2. *Growth in Bold Prayer and Mission Involvement:* A three-year project to lead the entire church to pray for missions, to call out the called for missionary service, to train church members to share their Christian faith through mission action, and to enlarge the enrollment of WMU and Brotherhood.

3. *Bold Witness Training:* A three-year project to equip church members to share their Christian faith with unbelievers.

4. *Bold Giving for Bold Missions:* A three-year project to increase church income and giving for world missions through the Cooperative Program.

Strengthen Families

1. *Opening the Word Together:* A three-year project to enlist church families in daily Bible study and family worship at home.

2. *Marriage—Growing in Oneness:* A two-year project to strengthen husband-wife relationships and bring Christian enrichment to family life.

See also AGENCY STUDIES BY COMMITTEE OF FIFTEEN; BOLD MISSION THRUST; COOPERATIVE PROGRAM ALLOCATION BUDGET PLANNING; EXECUTIVE COMMITTEE STUDY BY THE COMMITTEE OF SEVEN; LAY UTILIZATION STUDY; MISSIONS CHALLENGE COMMITTEE; SEMINARY ALLOCATION AND DISTRIBUTION FORMULA; SOUTHERN BAPTIST CONVENTION CAPITAL NEEDS; SOUTHERN BAPTIST CONVENTION LOGO.

                                        HAROLD C. BENNETT

EXECUTIVE COMMITTEE STUDY BY THE COMMITTEE OF SEVEN. During the 1974 SBC meeting, the officers of the Convention were authorized to appoint a committee of seven persons to study and evaluate the Executive Committee in light of Bylaw 9 (now Bylaw 20) of the SBC Bylaws.

The following persons constituted the Committee of Seven: Harold C. Bennett (Florida), Olin T. Binkley (North Carolina), W. A. Criswell (Texas), C. R. Daley (Kentucky), Daniel R. Grant (Arkansas), Herschel H. Hobbs (Oklahoma), and Alma Hunt (Alabama). Daley was elected chairman and Bennett the recording secretary. The committee worked for two years and made its report and recommendations during the 1976 SBC meeting.

The study centered on the structure and functions of the Executive Committee as set forth in Bylaw 9. The study included a review of the history of the Executive Committee, an examination of recent studies, a survey of the reports and minutes of the Executive Committee, a careful study of Bylaw 9 and the Executive Committee bylaws, interviews with the Executive Committee staff and other Convention leaders, and general hearings related to the Executive Committee.

A summary of the findings and suggestions of the Committee of Seven follows:

1. The Committee on Boards, Commissions, and Standing Committees should nominate members for the Executive Committee only after careful consideration of adequate biographical information and knowledge of the experience and background of the nominees.

2. Prospective nominees should be highly qualified and fully informed of the responsibilities and demands upon Executive Committee members.

3. A more adequate orientation program should be provided for Executive Committee members.

4. Executive Committee members should be more involved in the decision-making process of the committee.

5. More adequate communication and cooperation between the Executive Committee and other SBC agencies should be implemented.

6. The budgetary function of the Executive Committee should involve more members rather than just the members of the Program Subcommittee (now the Program and Budget Subcommittee).

7. The Executive Committee should be cautious in its use of authority and power.

8. The Executive Committee can rightly act for the Convention *ad interim,* but it is inappropriate to assume that the Executive Committee is the Convention *ad interim.*

9. The advisory role of the Executive Committee should never become supervisory.

10. The Executive Committee should recognize the principle of trusteeship as related to the trustees of the other Convention agencies.

11. The role of the Executive Committee in relationship to other Convention agencies is to "advise with them" and not exert power and authority inappropriately.

12. Uniform report forms should be maintained in order to help the agencies present to the Executive Committee adequate information on program plans, accomplishments, and costs.

13. Bylaw 9 should be revised to reflect uniformity of style.

The recommendations of the Committee of Seven included suggested revisions in Bylaw 9. The committee referred its findings and suggestions to the Executive Committee for consideration and a report back to the 1977 SBC meeting. The response of the Executive Committee to the report of the Committee of Seven was positive. The Executive Committee appointed a special subcommittee to study the findings and suggestions and to compile a report and recommendation for consideration during the annual meeting of the SBC in 1977.

HAROLD C. BENNETT

E. Y. MULLINS FELLOWSHIP, THE. An organization designed to promote a progressive spirit of free inquiry in all affairs of the Southern Baptist Convention. In its charter meeting prior to the 1969 SBC annual meeting in New Orleans, LA, the 279-member group drew up statements affirming the importance of the historical-critical approach to biblical studies, criticizing the addition of special offerings above the Cooperative Program, and calling for an increased response of the denomination to social issues. Other concerns were the SBC's basis of representation, the relationship of the Sunday School Board to Broadman Press publishing policy, and ecumenism. The fellowship dissolved by 1971.

WALTER B. SHURDEN AND LINDA PRICE

F

FALLS CREEK ASSEMBLY (I, III). In 1976 Falls Creek went to five identical encampments each summer with registration reported at 37,506. The total for all camps on the grounds that year was 42,807. Both of these figures stand as record highs. In 1979 regular camp registration was 34,838, with a total for the year of 40,539. The total registration from 1917 to 1979 was 913,758, with 101,988 personal commitments recorded. New buildings added in the 1970s included the Northrip Medical Clinic, Leadership Lodge, Scantlan Building, and Book Store. In 1979 the total number of assembly-owned buildings was 117. The annual budget exceeds $500,000, with one-half of that sum provided by the Cooperative Program. The estimated value of assembly-owned property in 1978 was $1,000,000, plus an equal amount for 165 units owned by churches and associations.

BIBLIOGRAPHY: J. M. Gaskin, *Sights and Sounds of Falls Creek* (1980).

J. M. GASKIN

FAMILY LIFE (cf. Family Ministry, Vol. III). Family life is a major concern of Southern Baptists. Meeting in Miami Beach, FL, in 1975, SBC messengers expressed the view that "the family has been ordained by God as a means of bringing order to human society, continuing the race, and providing enriched fellowship and emotional nurture for all people." The messengers further stated that "the restoration of happy and biblical family relationships is one of the most critical moral imperatives of our time," and the messengers urged "the appropriate agencies of the Southern Baptist Convention to give top priority to providing resources for Christian family living," and urged "churches not only to proclaim that monogamy is Christ's teaching for marriage but also to provide compassionate help for couples who face marital problems."

The work of every Southern Baptist agency has some impact on family life. Special responsibilities related to family have been assigned to the Family Ministry Department of the Sunday School Board and to the Christian Life Commission.

The CLC focuses on family through a program of literature distribution, conferences and workshops, and consultation with churches and agencies. A basic pamphlet on family entitled "The Bible Speaks on Family" receives wide distribution throughout the SBC. This pamphlet sets forth the biblical guidelines for family living. In a series of 15 pamphlets on family needs, the CLC provides help for families on a variety of issues including communication, moral values in the home, discipline, planned parenthood, divorce, aging, conflict, one-parent families, roles in marriage, and parents and teenagers.

Conferences, seminars, and workshops sponsored by the CLC frequently deal with family issues. The proceedings of some of these meetings are reproduced and made available for distribution. The CLC also works to help shape public policy which affects family life by participating in national family programs and by testifying before congressional committees.

The importance of family life to Southern Baptists is reflected in one of the major themes selected for emphasis throughout the SBC for 1982-85, "Strengthening Families."

See also FAMILY MINISTRY.

HARRY N. HOLLIS, JR.

FAMILY MINISTRY (III). A Southern Baptist Convention program assigned to the Sunday School Board. The purpose is to "develop the services and materials acceptable for use by Southern Baptist churches, associations, and state conventions in establishing, conducting, and improving family ministry services of marriage and family enrichment, parent enrichment skills, ministries to single persons, premarriage and remarriage education, and personal and spiritual enrichment for senior adults and leaders of senior adults."

Family ministry functions were transferred from Sunday School and Church Training to the Church Administration Department in 1972. Joseph W. Hinkle was named supervisor. In 1975 the trustees of the SSB authorized the establishment of the Family Ministry Department. Hinkle was named secretary.

A church may plan, coordinate, and implement its family ministry program through a family ministry committee, a lay leader, or a minister of family life. Much of a church's family ministry program is channeled through basic organizations, but projects such as Christian Home Week, retreats, workshops, and conferences may be planned and conducted by family ministry leaders. The base design also provides for weekday senior adult clubs and for weekday single adult activities coordinated by a single adult council. *How to Minister to Families in Your Church* (1978), by Joseph W. Hinkle and Melva Cook, and *How to Minister to Senior Adults in Your Church* (1980), by Horace L. Kerr, interpret the designs.

Two new monthly magazines, *Mature Living* and *Christian Single,* were started during the 1970s. *Living with Preschoolers,* a quarterly, and *Home Life,* a monthly, were transferred to Family Ministry from Sunday School, and two additional quarterlies, *Living with Children* and *Living with Teenagers,* were also started during the decade.

The Southern Baptist Marriage Enrichment Retreat system has been developed and implemented. The system is based on the concept of making good marriages better through improvement of communication skills and basic attitudes in the context of biblical teachings and Christian values.

Family Ministry has provided since 1972 an annual series of age-graded books called the Family Enrichment Series for use in Christian Home Week, Family Enrichment Conferences, or other projects.

The National Association of Baptist Senior Adults was begun in 1977. Approximately 30,000 members were enrolled by 1980.

The Family Ministry Department has made extensive use of Ridgecrest and Glorieta Conference Centers. Conferences for families, senior adults, and single adults are held during the fall, winter, and spring. In addition, family ministry consultants assist in association and state projects.

The department is organized in two sections, with Douglas L. Anderson as supervisor of the Family Enrichment Section and Horace L. Kerr as supervisor of the Senior/Single Adult Section.

JOSEPH W. HINKLE

FARMER, FOY ELIZABETH JOHNSON
(b. Scotland County, NC, Oct. 6, 1887; d.

Raleigh, NC, May 29, 1971). Teacher and missionary. The daughter of Frances Johnson and Livingston Johnson (*q.v.* I), a minister, she attended Baptist Female University, now Meredith College (B.A., 1907). After four years of teaching, she and missionary Calder T. Willingham were married, June 6, 1911. They went to Kokura, Japan, where she did evangelistic work and taught cookery, English, and Bible. Her husband died in 1918, and she went back to Japan alone in 1920. The following year illness forced her to return to the United States. In 1922 she married James S. Farmer. Their children were Fannie and James.

Three years as mission study chairman, three years as prayer chairman, and five years as vice-president of the Woman's Missionary Union of North Carolina preceded her seven years as president of that organization, 1942-50, and as vice-president of the national WMU. She served on the Foreign Mission Board, 1954-60; as a director of the University of Shanghai, 1943-63; as a trustee of Shaw University, Raleigh, NC, 1946-53; and as a trustee of Meredith College, 1933-63. She also was the author of seven books. She is buried in Oakwood Cemetery, Raleigh, NC.

MARY LYNCH JOHNSON

FELLOWSHIP OF EVANGELICAL BAPTIST CHURCHES IN CANADA. See CANADIAN BAPTISTS.

FIELDER, JOHN WILSON (b. Comanche County, TX, Jan. 27, 1880; d. Houston, TX, Nov. 30, 1961). Missionary to China. Son of William Anderson and Martha Elizabeth (Carter) Fielder, ranchers, he was a graduate of Baylor University (A.B., 1910). He married Maudie Ethel Albritton, Oct. 9, 1914, in Shanghai, China. Their children were Golda Jean, Richard Byron, Lennox Gerald, and Florence Ann.

In 1911-12, he served as pastor of the Miles, TX, and Comanche, TX, Baptist churches while teaching Latin and mathematics in community schools. He was appointed to China in 1912. His initial assignment was as an educational missionary at the Baptist College, Kaifeng, Honan Province. In 1916-48, his work centered in the railroad industrial center of Chenghsien, and in surrounding areas. He worked at a school for boys and a religious life center providing worship services and instruction. His nurture of outlying chapels in surrounding villages included both Bible teaching, preaching, and training of Chinese people for the ministry.

Fielder's service in China spanned years of turbulence and turmoil following the Republican Revolution after 1911. These multiple crises moved toward Dec. 7, 1941, and his subsequent internment in Shanghai for two years as a prisoner of war. He was exchanged for Japanese POWs at Goa. His repatriation to the United States came in 1943. He resumed his assignment in China in 1946, under the threat of mounting civil war. Clouds of conflict and approaching retirement led to his termination of service in China in 1948. He is buried at Houston, TX.

LENNOX GERALD FIELDER

FINDLEY, HERBERT (b. Jonesboro, AR, Aug. 21, 1898; d. Chula Vista, CA, May 13, 1979). Minister of music and education and director of missions. Son of Jefferson Milford and Ulemma Townsend Findley, he graduated from Southwestern Baptist Theological Seminary (diploma in Church Music, 1922). Findley then began his career as a fund-raiser for Jonesboro Baptist College, Jonesboro, AR. On May 19, 1923, he married Stella Ferguson. They had one child, Mary. His Oklahoma service included First Churches, Talinia, Cushing, and Guthrie; Nogales Church, Tulsa; Kelham Church, Oklahoma City; and Central Church, Muskogee. He was director of missions for Northwestern Association in Oklahoma from 1955 to 1964, when he retired.

CLYDE CLAYTON

FLETCHER, ALFRED JOHNSTON (b. Ashe County, NC, Oct. 10, 1887; d. Raleigh, NC, Apr. 1, 1979). Attorney and philanthropist. Son of James and Louisa Fletcher, pioneer Baptist missionaries in North Carolina and Virginia, he attended Wake Forest College and was licensed to practice law in 1911. Fletcher founded Southern Life Insurance Company, Capitol Broadcasting Company, Inc., National Opera Company, National Grass Roots Opera Foundation, Inc., Montlawn Memorial Park, and the A. J. Fletcher Education Foundation, Inc. His gifts benefited various Baptist bodies and schools, plus other schools. Named in his honor is the North Carolina Baptist State Convention's media center, 1975. Among other honors, he was presented the D.Hum. degree by Duke University, 1975, and the Abe Lincoln Railsplitter Award by the SBC Radio and Television Commission, 1977.

In Jan., 1910, Fletcher married Elizabeth Hardy Utley. They had four children: Fred, Frank, Floyd, and Betty. His second marriage was to Margaret Harrington of Raleigh in Sep., 1967. He is buried in Montlawn Cemetery, Raleigh, NC.

T. L. CASHWELL

FLETCHER, JAMES FLOYD (b. Ashe County, NC, Nov. 11, 1858; d. North Wilkesboro, NC, July 27, 1946). Pioneer mountain missionary. The son of John B. Fletcher and Barbara Alzera Johnston, he served a two-year apprenticeship as a printer. After a few months training at Jefferson Academy, Jefferson, NC, he began teaching at Pugh School House on New River near Meadows of Dan, VA, in 1876. While leading in spontaneous prayer meeting revivals, he felt called to the ministry and was ordained, Dec. 10, 1876. Sixteen days later he

married Louisa Barker. Thirteen children were born to them: Byrd, Arthur, James, Louisa, Dolly, Alfred, Charles, Barbara, Birdie, Mattie, Herbert, Annie, and Gladys.

Fletcher's first church was White Top in Grayson County, VA, where he walked 32 miles round trip monthly for an annual salary of $6.92. Taylor's Valley Church (State Line) in Johnson County, TN, a 50-mile monthly round trip on foot, enjoyed his services for three years without salary. Fletcher organized or helped to organize 13 churches and served more than 30 churches, as many as seven at one time. For 40 years he served under commission from the Baptists of North Carolina and Virginia as a missionary. His churches were among the first in the mountain area to take mission offerings. While Fletcher was serving at Young's Chapel in 1893, the first Woman's Missionary Union in the area was organized. He was a leader in enlisting the Home Mission Board, in 1911, to include Oak Hill Academy in its mountain school program. A member of its first board of trustees, he was the school's pastor and chaplain for 20 years.

Fletcher wrote *A History of the Ashe County, North Carolina and New River, Virginia Baptist Associations* (1935). He is buried at Raleigh, NC.

PHILLIP E. RODGERSON

FLOOD, NOAH (b. Shelby County, KY, June 14, 1809; d. Columbia, MO, Aug. 11, 1873). The Son of Joshua and Mary Flood, he attended Marion College, Marion County, MO, and Shurtleff College, Alton, IL. He moved to Woodford County, KY, and was ordained in 1838 by the Baptist church at the Forks of Elkhorn. He married Livisa Jane Ayres, June 19, 1838.

Flood moved to Callaway County, MO, and found himself in the middle of the antimissionary movement among Baptists. Most of the churches were closed to him, so he preached in schools, homes, and outdoor settings. He signed the constitution organizing the Baptist Central Society of Missouri, 1837, and then served as second general agent, 1839-41, and as moderator, 1869-70. He is buried in Richland Cemetery, Callaway County, MO.

L. DOUGLAS MCGLAUGHLIN

FLORIDA, BAPTIST HOME FOR CHILDREN (I). See BAPTIST HOME FOR CHILDREN, JACKSONVILLE.

FLORIDA ASSOCIATIONS (I, III).
I. New Associations. MANATEE SOUTHERN. Organized in 1978 by 19 churches from Southwest Florida Association and two churches from Orange Blossom Association. In 1979, 21 churches reported 547 baptisms, 10,693 members, $2,446,599 total gifts, $407,925 mission gifts, and $7,986,188 property value.
II. Changes in Associations. GREATER ORLANDO. Organized in 1870 as Wekiwa Association, the name was changed to Greater Orlando in 1978.

WEKIWA. Changed name to Greater Orlando Association in 1978.

JAMES R. BEASLEY

FLORIDA BAPTIST CHILDREN'S HOME (I, III). Change and diversification characterized the home, 1969-79. In 1969 T. M. Johns (*q.v.*) retired after 37 years of service to 6,008 children, and the board of trustees elected Roger S. Dorsett to succeed him as superintendent of the home. An ordained minister from Alabama, Dorsett had one year of professional social work training and had served as branch director of the home's facility in Miami, FL.

During Dorsett's three-year tenure, the board grew to 21 members, and the home conducted a long-range study, with professional consultation by Alan Keith-Lucas and Sam Fudge of the Group Care Project, School of Social Work, University of North Carolina. Following this study, several changes were made. First, the home established an additional satellite campus in Tallahassee in 1973 and employed Floyd and Bunette Peeler as the first child care workers. Second, the board approved signing the Civil Rights Compliance Act in Dec., 1971. Third, after the state convention rejected the board's recommended sale of the campus in Lakeland in 1972, extensive renovation of the Lakeland campus was done. Fourth, Walter Delamarter was employed as executive director of the home in Mar., 1974, and branch managers were established on each of the three campuses in Lakeland, Miami, and Tallahassee.

The home gives strong emphasis to multiple services including residential care, foster care, emergency shelter, adoption, and after care. A director of promotion was employed in 1974, and a bimonthly newsletter, *Yours,* was initiated, with a circulation of over 14,000. In 1975 the home began a satellite outpatient office in Pensacola which serves west Florida with referral, family counseling, and public relations services, operating in the office of the Pensacola Bay Association. Other new services included the Emergency Shelter for battered and abused children in Lakeland, caring for more than 175 children per year.

In Nov., 1978, during the Florida Baptist Convention meeting, the home celebrated its 75th anniversary, entertaining more than 2,000 people with dinner on the grounds. In May, 1979, the enlargement of services of the home became possible when the state board of missions approved the use of state funds for purchase of care for services rendered to individual children. The home's annual operating budget in 1969 was $180,000. By 1979 the budget had risen to $1,188,760, and for the past four years the home has operated in the black.

WALTER R. DELAMARTER

FLORIDA BAPTIST FOUNDATION (I, III). Between 1969 and 1979, Gus Johnson continued as administrator. As of Sep. 30, 1979, the foundation held $2,639,685 on behalf of various causes and agencies.

GUS JOHNSON

FLORIDA BAPTIST HISTORICAL SOCIETY (I, III). The 1967 session of the Florida Baptist Convention commissioned the writing of *A History of Florida Baptists* with the state Board of Missions and the society directing the project. Written by E. Earl Joiner, professor of religion at Stetson University, the volume was published in 1972. Rollin S. Armour continued as society curator until 1973 when E. Earl Joiner succeeded him. In 1974 and 1975 the society was reorganized with a new constitution and bylaws approved by the convention.

The society consisted in 1980 of nine rotating directors elected by the convention, a curator and secretary-treasurer elected permanently by the convention, a chairman and vice-chairman elected annually by the directors, and regular members. The first chairman of the reorganized society was Charles Bugg, who was followed by Norman Bennett and Frank H. Thomas, Jr. In 1976 the society began having its annual meeting in May on the campus of Stetson University with a program of speakers and research papers.

E. EARL JOINER

FLORIDA BAPTIST RETIREMENT CENTER (cf. Florida Baptist Retirement Centers, Vol. III). As of Jan., 1980, the center was caring for 73 residents in 14 duplex apartments, a custodial care facility with 30 rooms and apartments, and a nursing facility with a 24-bed capacity.

Along with these resident quarters, the center has on its grounds a manager's home, a seven-room missionary residence, an administrative building containing an arts and crafts department, a small lake, a lakeside pavilion, and a maintenance building.

Applicants to the center must have been residents of Florida and members in good standing of a Baptist church cooperating with the Florida Baptist Convention for at least twelve months prior to making application. Exceptions may be made in case the applicant is an employee of an SBC agency, board, or commission.

William H. Lord, Sr., the present resident manager, began his administration, May 10, 1970. His administration witnessed many changes. Florida Baptist Retirement Centers, Inc., was changed to an agency of the Florida Baptist State Board of Missions and renamed the Florida Baptist Retirement Center. The custodial unit and nursing facility received licenses from the Department of Health and Rehabilitative Services of the state of Florida. A building program was begun and continues.

WILLIAM H. LORD

FLORIDA BAPTIST STATE CONVENTION (I, III).

I. History. Significant program developments occurred in the convention's work in the

1970s. The convention implemented the recommendations of the Study Committee of 15, with Henry Allen Parker as chairman, adopted by the convention's State Board of Missions on July 16, 1968. Many of the creative changes made during the 1970s in the programs of work appeared as suggestions in this committee's report.

The convention established the Director of Associational Missions Program. A change in philosophy of this program involved moving from a district field secretary responsible to the convention's executive secretary-treasurer to an associational program in which the employed vocational leader was directly related to the association. The program provides for financial subsidies from the convention to assist associations as they recruit, employ, and supervise staff workers. In 1967 there were 17 district field secretaries. In 1979 there were 25 full-time and 12 part-time directors of associational missions.

The convention studied and strengthened student work, adopting in Nov., 1970, the report of a special study committee related to the Student Program. Conrad R. Willard was committee chairman. The report established new directions for this program by proposing a new name, Baptist Campus Ministry, a statement of objectives, and a clarification of program emphases and guidelines to implement the report.

The convention implemented a special emphasis planning concept designed to coordinate promotion activities in support of priorities and goals established by the convention. Special emphasis planning is defined as follows: "To provide a cooperative planning process in which selected state convention, associational, and church leaders study needs, determine priorities, set goals and design special activities, projects, and materials to meet priority needs of the churches and denomination."

The convention conducted special mission projects, especially by investing major resources in special mission projects outside the state. This planning provided opportunity for several hundred church leaders to be personally involved in special mission service on foreign and home mission fields.

The major mission project was in the Republic of Korea and was called the Major City Evangelization Project. Preparatory activities included stewardship conferences, church growth institutes, music training projects, home Bible study emphasis, witness training sessions, and target group witnessing. The climax of the three-year project came in the spring of 1980 with central crusades and church revivals conducted in four major metropolitan centers of Pusan, Seoul, Taegue, and Taejon. Kwangju was cancelled because of political unrest. Approximately 250 church, associational, and state leaders participated in the various phases of the project over the three-year period, 1978-80.

Other projects initiated in the 1970s included a working partnership with the Baptist Convention of Pennsylvania-South Jersey, effective Jan. 1, 1979, and the Caribbean Baptist Fellowship, effective Jan. 1, 1980, through Dec. 31, 1981.

The Brotherhood Department sponsored several mission projects in which men were enlisted to meet special needs created by natural disasters in Guatemala, Honduras, Dominican Republic, Brazil, Nicaragua, and Mobile, AL, in the United States.

In 1974, as a part of a program of Bold Advance, the convention established a goal of 200 new churches by 1980. To undergird this effort, which was almost achieved by 1980, three support programs were created:

(1) A Florida Baptist Convention Church Site Committee. This committee is composed of laymen and pastors committed to starting new churches and missions. They have authority and resources to secure church sites in developing areas before they become prohibitively expensive.

(2) Florida Baptist Convention Church Bond Program. This support program helps growing churches provide needed facilities. Since 1971 when the bond program was first offered, 76 churches have used this service, and the issues of the convention's Church Bond Program in Apr., 1980, totaled $12,822,500. No church serviced by the church bond plan has defaulted.

(3) Mission Match-Up Plan. This effort provides a means by which older, established churches in areas not needing new churches may "match-up" with a new church or church-type mission to assist the local sponsoring church if they are not financially strong enough to provide the needed support. The resources will vary in form. They may be financial, but could also be leadership for community surveys, Vacation Bible Schools, music projects, revivals, and most importantly, moral support for small, struggling congregations.

II. Leadership. Harold C. Bennett served as executive secretary-treasurer of the convention from Oct., 1967, to Aug., 1979, when he succeeded Porter W. Routh as executive secretary-treasurer of the Executive Committee, SBC. On Sep. 11, 1979, Dan C. Stringer was elected as the new executive director-treasurer for the Florida Baptist Convention. He had served as executive director-treasurer of the Northwest Baptist Convention, 1971-79.

Other major staff changes also occurred in the 1970s. In 1969 J. Woodrow Fuller became director of the Missions Division, and Keener Pharr became director of the Education Division. B. G. Hickem replaced Oscar Bean as assistant executive-secretary in 1974.

New program leaders in the Education Division included: Robert S. Cook, elected in 1969 as director of the Church Training Department; James E. Frost, who succeeded C. F. Barry in 1970 as director of the Sunday School Department; and Paul R. Bobbitt, who assumed leadership of the Church Music Department in 1970, succeeding W. G. Stroup.

New program leaders in the Missions Division included: William J. Guess, who filled a new position as director of Church Extension in 1977; James A. Ponder, who was elected evangelism secretary in 1970 to succeed Paul A. Meigs; J.

Ray Dobbins, who joined the staff in 1970 to fill the new position as director of the Cooperative Missions Department; Charles F. Ragland, Sr., who succeeded Robert W. Rowell in 1978 as director of the Brotherhood Department; and Vanita Baldwin, who assumed leadership of the Woman's Missionary Union Department in 1977, succeeding Bernice Popham. Carolyn Weatherford who previously filled this position had been selected in 1974 to serve as executive director-treasurer of Woman's Missionary Union, Auxiliary to the SBC.

One other personnel change involved Richard M. Barber, who succeeded Phil Maxwell in 1976 as director of the Florida Baptist Annuity Program.

Presidents of the convention during the 1970s were: Doyle I. Carlton, 1969; A. Douglas Watterson, 1970; W. G. Stracener, 1971; James L. Pleitz, 1972; Joe M. Bamberg, 1973; A. R. Fagan and Virginia R. Parker, 1974; James F. Graves, 1975; John L. Pelham, 1976; Barney B. Burks, Jr., 1977; Cornelius B. Davis, 1978; and N. B. Langford, Jr., 1979.

III. Program and Organization. The major objectives of all state convention program assignments and activity is "to assist the churches in their task of bringing all men to God through Jesus Christ and guiding them in Christian maturity." All program leaders joined in introducing new educational programs and materials for first-time use by the churches in Oct., 1970. New curriculum lines included the Life and Work Series and later a Bible Book Series. These two, plus the Uniform Series, provided three basic curriculum choices for the churches.

Program tasks were clarified and coordinated as part of the changes introduced under the theme, "Shaping the '70's." Churches accepted and implemented these changes with minimum problems and reaction.

The convention created several new program departments and positions in the 1970s. (1) The Cooperative Missions Department relates to language mission work, seminary extension programs, and work with National Baptists, migrants, and the deaf. This new department implemented a new planning and working relationship with the Home Mission Board. (2) A Church Extension office provided leadership in the priority commitment of starting new churches in this growing state. (3) Expanded staff positions provided for new associates in the Evangelism Department and the Sunday School Department. This additional leadership resource was in support of a priority commitment to church growth in the 1970s. (4) Two new Baptist campus ministry positions were established in the Pensacola Bay and Greater Orlando Associations. (5) The organizational structure was adjusted on May 1, 1970, when the Florida Baptist Retirement Center became a regular unit of work of the State Board of Missions with William H. Lord, Sr., succeeding Paul R. Adkins as resident manager in 1970.

IV. Facilities. *Florida Baptist Building, Jacksonville.*—A special committee made a study in

FLORIDA STATISTICAL SUMMARY

FRANK C. RICHARDSON

Year	Associations	Churches	Church Membership	Baptisms	SS Enrollment	VBS Enrollment	CT Enrollment	WMU Enrollment	Brotherhood Enrollment	Ch. Music Enrollment	Mission Gifts	Total Gifts	Value Church Property
1969	47	1,440	638,929	24,141	419,237	160,782	161,379	65,668	24,771	66,880	$ 6,676,469	$ 51,610,980	$228,172,852
1970	47	1,448	647,239	23,008	409,112	163,818	149,519	60,376	23,294	65,748	6,950,470	54,115,088	239,417,774
1971	47	1,468	666,149	28,918	406,608	161,992	121,541	55,933	24,608	68,271	8,914,852	59,876,568	246,281,041
1972	47	1,481	684,747	30,908	414,699	163,595	116,471	54,256	24,204	72,138	10,016,081	67,589,889	274,821,685
1973	47	1,487	708,008	29,041	424,318	161,739	112,228	53,184	24,886	77,603	11,222,051	72,839,199	304,454,888
1974	47	1,494	726,971	29,500	426,262	169,882	109,479	54,260	26,080	80,888	13,166,367	80,554,498	344,739,759
1975	47	1,499	736,531	29,102	446,879	181,054	111,383	56,535	28,053	83,318	14,089,711	87,687,373	382,794,429
1976	47	1,499	747,630	26,080	454,087	171,311	112,481	56,191	28,607	83,460	14,940,350	94,388,814	413,675,547
1977	47	1,511	762,719	25,059	450,088	173,406	110,216	55,495	28,677	84,932	16,485,242	100,889,727	452,025,579
1978	48	1,520	771,196	23,379	438,863	165,784	111,172	53,781	28,356	86,808	17,600,136	113,248,906	483,404,972
1979	48	1,536	786,394	26,403	436,368	161,235	109,708	53,502	28,273	90,509	19,776,702	128,211,197	540,739,500
1980	48	1,550	799,803	30,133	446,513	170,154	113,407	55,313	28,938	91,997	23,518,515	143,940,316	598,816,222

1971-72 concerning the location of the convention's office building. The committee considered alternate locations but recommended that the offices remain in Jacksonville and at the same site. The offices were renovated in 1973. A new Baptist Book Store Building was constructed in 1979 on the block occupied by the convention's office building. The print shop building was removed, and the printing service and equipment were moved to the basement of the Florida Baptist Building.

Lake Yale Baptist Assembly.—The Lake Yale Baptist Assembly program and facilities now provide for an Adult Conference Center, Camp North for girls, and Camp South for boys. Eighty-four additional acres of property adjoining the Lake Yale Baptist Assembly were purchased in 1972 to provide for future expansion. A fellowship building and an additional motel building were completed in 1970. A new conference building, utilized for the first time in 1979 provides for children's work, a media center, additional conference rooms, indoor recreational activities, and a small auditorium. A display area was provided in the lobby of the Conference Building for historical displays of the Florida Baptist Historical Society. During the 1970s, 269,308 persons used the Lake Yale Baptist Assembly facilities during 50 weeks of operation each year.

Blue Springs Baptist Assembly.—In 1974, 126.7 acres of wooded property were purchased for an assembly facility to serve West Florida churches. The new Blue Springs Baptist Assembly facilities will be utilized for the first time in the summer of 1981. This property is located approximately three miles east of Marianna, FL, on Highway 90. The first building phase provides an Adult Conference Center, including a multipurpose building to house an auditorium, conference rooms, kitchen, cafeteria to accommodate 350 persons, and book store facilities. An administration building and three motel units will provide housing for 204 persons. A recreational vehicle park provides 35 hook-ups and other essential facilities. The 23-acre West Florida Baptist Assembly facility in Panama City will continue to be used as a youth camp.

KEENER PHARR

FLORIDA BAPTIST WITNESS (I, III). This paper continues to be published weekly by the five-member, convention-elected *Florida Baptist Witness* Commission. Edgar R. Cooper became editor-manager, Jan. 1, 1971, succeeding William Guy Stracener, who retired after serving 21 years. The paper's first assistant editor-manager, Melvyne D. Mizelle, was elected in 1973.

The circulation increased to 89,000 in 1980. Out of Florida's 1,549 churches, 1,149 are recipients of the *Witness* ministry. A church page service, where churches elect to use the front and back pages for their own local news, was started in 1976. In 1978 a Compugraphic EditWriter was installed, allowing *Witness* staff members to set their own type and prepare

camera-ready copy. The staff also uses a computer terminal for processing subscription lists, bookkeeping, and billing. The *Witness* supports itself through subscriptions and space sold for advertising and promotion. It receives no subsidy from the Florida Baptist Convention.

EDGAR R. COOPER

FORD, SALLIE ROCHESTER (b. Rochester Springs, KY, Oct. 1, 1828; d. St. Louis, MO, Feb. 18, 1910). Woman's Missionary Union leader. Daughter of James Henry and Demoretta Pitts Rochester, she graduated from Georgetown Female Seminary with highest honors (1849). She married Samuel Howard Ford, a Baptist pastor and editor, Mar., 1855. Their children were Rochester Ford, Fanny, Noble, and May.

In 1875-77 she was president of the Baptist Woman's Missionary Society of St. Louis, affiliated with Northern Baptist women. She transferred this experience to Southern Baptist circles in 1883-87 when during the SBC meetings she presided over unofficial meetings of women leading to the organization of WMU. In 1885 she led a successful move to bar men from the women's meetings, in retaliation for the 1885 action of the SBC in refusing to seat women as messengers. Best known for her writings, she was correspondent for the *Louisville Courier.* Her most famous book was *Grace Truman (Love and Principle),* 1857, which espoused Baptist doctrines in a fictionalized way. She is buried in Bellefontaine Cemetery, St. Louis, MO.

CATHERINE B. ALLEN

FOREIGN MISSION BOARD, SBC (I, III). Baker J. Cauthen, chief executive of the board since Jan. 1, 1954, retired, Dec. 31, 1979, after 40 years of service with the Foreign Mission Board (missionary to China, 1939-45; secretary for the Orient, 1945-53; executive secretary, 1954-76; and executive director, 1976-79). When Cauthen announced plans to retire, a 15-member search committee composed of six laypeople (including four women) and nine ministers was appointed in Oct., 1978, to recommend a new executive director. In Aug., 1979, R. Keith Parks was elected to succeed Cauthen effective Jan. 1, 1980.

From Jan. 1, 1970, to Jan. 1, 1980, the FMB appointed 1,270 missionaries, and the number of countries increased from 71 to 94 in which a total of 3,008 missionaries served—an increase of 518 over the 2,490 serving, Jan. 1, 1970. The 94 countries and political entities in which missionaries served were: Angola, Antigua, Argentina, Austria, Bahamas, Bangladesh, Barbados, Belgium, Belize, Benin, Bermuda, Bolivia, Bophuthatswana, Botswana, Brazil, British Virgin Islands (Tortola), Burundi, Cayman Islands, Chile, Colombia, Costa Rica, Dominica, Dominican Republic, Ecuador, El Salvador, Ethiopia, France, Gaza, Germany, Ghana, Greece, Grenada, Guadeloupe, Guam, Guatemala,

Guyana, Haiti, Honduras, Hong Kong, India, Indonesia, Israel, Italy, Ivory Coast, Jamaica, Japan, Jordan, Kenya, Korea, Lebanon, Liberia, Libya, Macao, Malawi, Malaysia, Martinique, Mauritius, Mexico, Morocco, Nicaragua, Niger Republic, Nigeria, Okinawa, Panama, Paraguay, Peru, Philippines, Portugal, Rwanda, Scotland, Senegal, Singapore, South Africa, South West Africa, Spain, Sri Lanka, St. Martin, St. Vincent, Sudan, Surinam, Switzerland, Taiwan, Tanzania, Thailand, Togo, Transkei, Trinidad, Turkey, Uganda, Upper Volta, Uruguay, Venezuela, Yemen, Zambia, Zimbabwe (Rhodesia). China, Laos, Mozambique, Seychelles, St. Martin, Vietnam, and certain countries of Eastern Europe were closed to continuing missionary presence as the decade ended.

In 1970 the Overseas Division proposed a "strategy for the '70s." Missions and missionaries were encouraged, in cooperation with national leaders, to project plans for the next 25 years. This process culminated in the Consultation on Foreign Missions held in Miami Beach, FL, in June, 1975. The results of the conference and the strategy studies were brought together in a paper entitled "Foreign Missions Looks Toward AD 2000" and adopted, Jan. 13, 1976. A second paper entitled "Agenda for the Future" was approved later. The FMB used these papers to project foreign mission work toward the twenty-first century. The plans adopted by the FMB in early 1976 received enthusiastic endorsement by the SBC in June of that year. The FMB launched the foreign missions aspect of Bold Mission Thrust from this base. Subsequently, "a statement of Foreign Mission Board philosophy" was elaborated and approved in 1978.

I. Geographic Areas. For purposes of administration, the FMB divides the world into eight geographical areas, each with an area secretary (director), assisted by field representatives (associates to director). The eight geographic areas are: East Asia, South and Southeast Asia, West Africa, Eastern and Southern Africa, Europe and the Middle East, Middle America and the Caribbean, Eastern South America, and Western South America. In 1976 Hawaii completed a 15-year transition period from a foreign mission field to complete identification with the SBC.

East Asia.—Hong Kong, Japan, Macao, Okinawa, South Korea, and Taiwan comprise East Asia. Although no foreign missionaries are admitted, mainland China continues to be a concern. Recent events indicate some Christian movement within China and heighten anticipation of limited opportunities for Christian involvement. During 1970-72 W. L. Howse, Jr., retired Sunday School Board leader, assisted missions and convention groups in long-range planning. In Sep., 1975, George H. Hays became area secretary, succeeding James D. Belote (*q.v.*). Samuel M. James was named field representative in 1976. In 1975 the Hong Kong

Baptist Convention observed its 40th anniversary.

Work in East Asia focused on evangelism, publications through Baptist Press in Hong Kong (serving over 30 countries), three Baptist hospitals, two Baptist colleges, the Asia Baptist Graduate Theological Seminary, and refugee work in Hong Kong-Macao. The Hong Kong Baptist Convention sent three Chinese missionaries to work among the Chinese in Malaysia-Singapore and Vietnam.

In 1970 East Asia had 371 Southern Baptist missionaries, including 23 journeymen. There were 652 churches with 68,707 members. At the end of 1979, 428 Southern Baptist missionaries were serving, including 42 journeymen. These were cooperating with 980 churches with a composite membership of 95,909.

South and Southeast Asia.—South and Southeast Asia includes Bangladesh, Guam, India, Indonesia, Malaysia, Philippines, Singapore, Sri Lanka, and Thailand. No Southern Baptist missionaries are presently located in Vietnam or Laos, although attempts are made by individuals to maintain unofficial contact with churches there.

In 1970 South and Southeast Asia had a total of 415 Southern Baptist missionaries, including 17 journeymen, cooperating with 271 churches which had 32,147 members. At the end of 1979, 398 Southern Baptist missionaries, including 18 journeymen and 3 special project workers, were cooperating with 745 churches comprised of 5,897 members.

West Africa.—The area of West Africa was created in 1973 when Africa south of the Sahara was divided into two areas: West Africa and Eastern and Southern Africa. H. Cornell Goerner, area secretary since 1957, remained as area secretary for West Africa. Upon his retirement, Dec. 31, 1976, John E. Mills became area secretary, and Billy Lee Bullington became field representative. West Africa includes Benin, Ghana, Ivory Coast, Liberia, Niger Republic, Nigeria, Senegal, Togo, and Upper Volta. Of these, Upper Volta (1971) and Niger Republic (1973) were most recently entered. In 1970, 293 Southern Baptist missionaries, including 14 journeymen and 3 special project workers, were cooperating with 766 churches which had 119,104 members. At the end of the decade, 339 Southern Baptist missionaries, including 26 journeymen and 5 special project workers, were cooperating with 2,882 churches with 310,536 members.

Eastern and Southern Africa.—Eastern and Southern Africa include Angola, Bophuthatswana, Botswana, Burundi, Ethiopia, Mauritius, Kenya, Malawi, Mozambique, Rwanda, South Africa, South West Africa, Tanzania, Transkei, Uganda, Zambia, and Zimbabwe (Rhodesia). The East Africa mission (Kenya and Tanzania) divided on Jan. 1, 1978, into the Kenya and Tanzania missions. The FMB assigned missionaries to Madagascar from 1974 until inability to secure resident visas led to reassignment in 1977. Missionaries entered Mozambique in 1973, but governmental change caused them to withdraw in 1975. Ethiopia (entered 1967) was temporarily evacuated in 1977 for almost a year because of internal political conditions. In 1977 the FMB assigned missionaries for the first time to Rwanda, Seychelles, South Africa, Bophuthatswana, and in 1978 to Mauritius. After a year, work in the Seychelles was abandoned due to governmental pressures. With the murder of missionary Archie Dunaway in Rhodesia in 1978, the full impact of Rhodesia's political situation was felt. Missionaries continued in Rhodesia throughout the period, and the country was renamed Zimbabwe in early 1980. Missionaries were assigned to Transkei in 1979. Although no missionaries are resident in Angola, missionary contact is maintained by missionaries residing in Portugal. Rwanda was entered in 1977 and Burundi in 1979. In late 1979 the FMB voted to enter Sudan.

In 1970 Eastern and Southern Africa had 317 missionaries, including 18 journeymen, cooperating with 528 churches with a total membership of 26,778. At the end of the decade, there were 418 missionaries, including 32 journeymen, cooperating with 1,257 churches which had 88,900 members.

Europe and the Middle East.—Europe and the Middle East include Austria, Belgium, France, Greece, Italy, Portugal, Scotland, Spain, Switzerland, West Germany, Gaza, Israel, Jordan, Lebanon, Libya, Morocco, Turkey, and Yemen. In June, 1976, the FMB added South Asia to the administration of this area to include Bangladesh and India. On Sep. 1, 1979, they were reassigned to the area of South and Southeast Asia.

A conference on Baptist work in the Catholic countries of Europe convened in France in 1972. English-language Baptist churches multiplied and flourished in the area, especially Germany, where there were 23 in 1979. Missionary John W. Merritt serves as executive secretary for the European Baptist Convention, which is composed of representatives from English-language churches. The FMB assigned missionaries to Scotland in 1977, with the encouragement of Scottish Baptists, to work with Americans and Scots involved in the emerging oil industry. An English-language mission was begun in Norway in 1973 with American oil field workers.

In Eastern Europe more than one-half of Europe's 1,300,000 Baptists live in the Socialist countries. The Eastern Europe mission consists of FMB representatives who visit Baptists in Eastern Europe from time to time and correspond with Baptist leaders there. Baptist work in Eastern Europe appears to be growing.

Because Judaism and Islam oppose any overt evangelistic overtures toward their adherents, the work in the Middle East is almost entirely institutional, including health care, publications, and other types of institutional ministries.

In 1970 Europe and the Middle East (excluding India and Bangladesh) had 222 Southern Baptist missionaries, including 13 journeymen, cooperating with 294 churches with a total of 21,039 members. At the end of the decade, there were 295 Southern Baptist missionaries, including 27 journeymen and 3 special project workers, cooperating with 297 churches with a total of 23,353 members.

Eastern South America.—The FMB divided South America into two administrative areas, effective Jan. 1, 1975. These areas are Eastern South America and Western South America. Frank K. Means, area secretary for 23 years (Latin America 1954-68; South America, 1968-75; Eastern South America, 1975-77), retired, Dec. 31, 1977. Thurmon E. Bryant succeeded Means.

Field representatives in Eastern South America during the 1970s included H. Victor Davis, Brazil, 1961-74; Hoke Smith, Jr. (*q.v.*), South field, Latin America, 1962-68, and Spanish South America, 1968-70; Donald R. Kammerdiener, South field, Spanish South America, 1970-75, and Spanish Eastern South America, 1975- ; and Raymond L. Kolb, Brazil, 1974- .

The Latin American Church Development Depth Study Committee made a significant study affecting all of Latin America. Dealing with positive conclusions, negative considerations (of particular importance to the FMB and the missions), and personnel matters, the final report was made in Oct., 1972.

The final report of the Crusade of Americas, made in 1970, showed 30,742 baptisms in Latin America, the largest number of any crusade up to that time. Mass media ministries and production, distribution, and use of Christian literature received preferential budgeting during the decade in Latin America.

At the beginning of the decade, Eastern South America counted 427 Southern Baptist missionaries, including 9 journeymen and 1 special project worker, cooperating with 2,434 churches with a membership of 321,445. At the end of 1979, 456 Southern Baptist missionaries, including 25 journeymen and 1 special project worker, were cooperating with 3,204 churches with a total membership of 479,666.

Western South America.—This area includes Chile and the Bolivarian Republics of Colombia, Venezuela, Peru, Ecuador, and Bolivia. After careful consultation with Brazilian and Canadian Baptists, the FMB voted to begin work in Bolivia, and a couple was appointed in June, 1978. Veteran missionaries, Lamar and Betsy (Watkins) Tribble, transferred from Chile and were the first to arrive on the field in early 1979. The major thrusts in Bolivia are evangelism and literature ministry.

At the beginning of the decade, 210 Southern Baptist missionaries, including 7 journeymen, cooperated with 252 churches with a total membership of 20,703. At the end of 1979, the number had increased to 297 missionaries, including 18 journeymen, cooperating with 414 churches with 32,477 members. Robert Tucker became field representative in 1976.

Middle America and the Caribbean.—This area includes 23 entities, 13 of which were entered during the 1970s: Surinam (1971), Barbados (1972), Dominica (1975), Grenada (1975), Panama (1975), El Salvador (1975), Nicaragua (1976), British Virgin Islands (Tortola) (1976), St. Vincent (1977), Martinique (1977), Cayman Islands (1977), Belize (1977), and St. Martin (1979, discontinued same year). Surinam, South America, and Belize, Central America, though technically not a part of the Caribbean, were assigned to the Caribbean administratively for cultural, political, and language reasons. Established work existed in Costa Rica, Guatemala, Honduras, Mexico, Baptist Spanish Publishing House, Bahamas, Bermuda, Dominican Republic, Trinidad, Leeward Islands, and Windward Islands.

Charles W. Bryan, area secretary since 1968, was assisted by the following field representatives: James D. Crane, Middle America, 1961-70; A. Clark Scanlon, Caribbean, 1968-71, and Middle America, 1971- ; and William W. Graves, Caribbean, 1971- .

Because of proximity to the United States, this area experienced much lay involvement and evangelistic effort from American personnel through special projects. Outreach into French- and Dutch-speaking areas necessitated the creation of suitable Christian literature by the Baptist Spanish Publishing House in El Paso, TX, in addition to the expansion of its Spanish-speaking ministry. English literature for Bible study in the Caribbean was also developed in the area and produced at El Paso. In 1970 Frank W. Patterson, director of the Baptist Spanish Publishing House, was succeeded by Thomas W. Hill, who served until 1977. N. Aldo Broda became the first Latin American director of the publishing house on Nov. 1, 1977. In 1978 a new Spanish hymnal was published and within a month 30,000 were sold. English-language materials were prepared for use in a decentralized approach to ministerial education.

In 1970 Middle America and the Caribbean had 230 Southern Baptist missionaries, including 11 journeymen, cooperating with 567 churches with a total membership of 56,249. At the close of the decade, 379 missionaries, including 27 journeymen and 4 special project workers, cooperated with 1,304 churches with an aggregate membership of 158,581.

II. Programs of Work. The FMB conducts six programs of work: Missionary support, evangelism and church development, schools and student work, publications, hospitals and health care, and benevolent ministries. The program of missionary support addresses the SBC constituency; the remaining programs are centered overseas. The overarching objective of the overseas operations is to share the gospel with every person in the world and to promote the establishment and development of New Testament churches.

Missionary Support.—At the beginning of 1970, 2,490 missionaries were under appointment to 71 countries or separate political entities. At the end of 1979, 3,008 missionaries were under appointment (2,552 career, 226 missionary associates, 215 journeymen, and 15 special project workers), representing a net gain of 518 in the total missionary force. The FMB appointed 2,552 missionaries in the 1970s, bringing the total appointed since 1845 to 6,979. Of the 2,552 appointed during the decade, there were 1,272 career missionaries, 246 missionary associates, 835 journeymen, and 43 special project workers. Reappointments accounted for 156 of the total.

Five missionaries met violent deaths while serving during the decade: Paul (*q.v.*) and Nancy (*q.v.*) (Roper) Potter, 1971, Dominican Republic; Mavis Orisca Pate (*q.v.*), 1972, Gaza; Gladys Genevieve Hopewell (*q.v.*), 1973, Taiwan; and Archie Grover Dunaway, Jr. (*q.v.*), 1978, Rhodesia (Zimbabwe).

In 1970 an annual Thanksgiving retreat was initiated for missionary children who are college freshmen. A universal four-year term of service with one-year furlough was initiated the same year with multiple furlough options offered for shorter terms of service.

In 1971 W. Eugene Grubbs became consultant for laymen overseas, and Truman Smith became consultant for missionary families. William W. Graves became field representative for the Caribbean.

In 1972 the FMB made the field representative plan worldwide. William R. Wakefield became field representative for Southeast Asia and George H. Hays for East Asia. Africa was divided into two administrative areas. H. Cornell Goerner remained the secretary for West Africa, and Davis Lee Saunders became secretary for Eastern and Southern Africa, June 1, 1973.

In 1972 major progress occurred in strengthening the support of missionaries, including adjustments for dollar devaluation, assistance on Social Security taxes, increased allowance for older children, increases in the Margaret Fund for college students, special allowances based on length of service, better insurance coverage, and increased provisions for emeritus missionaries.

In 1973 the FMB assumed total income tax liability of missionaries to foreign governments and provided allowance to assist for furlough transportation needs, and in 1975 made further adjustments in furlough benefits.

In 1975 the FMB divided South America administratively with Frank K. Means retaining Eastern South America and with J. Bryan Brasington becoming secretary for Western South America. John Cheyne became field representative for Eastern Africa and Marion G. Fray for Southern Africa the same year.

In 1975 R. Keith Parks, area secretary for Southeast Asia, succeeded Jesse C. Fletcher as director of the Mission Support Division of the FMB, and William R. Wakefield succeeded Parks as area secretary for Southeast Asia.

Later in 1976, the FMB restructured the Mission Support Division and elected the following to newly created posts: Thomas W. Hill, secretary, Communications Department; William W. Marshall, secretary, Furlough Ministries Department; and William R. O'Brien, secretary, Denominational Coordination Department. Robert L. Stanley became director of news and information service.

In 1977 the FMB authorized four associates for the Overseas Division staff and elected Lewis I. Myers, associate overseas director; Ervin E. Hastey, associate evangelism and church development consultant; John Cheyne, associate consultant for relief ministries; James Cecil, associate consultant for volunteer ministries; and Harold Hurst, associate consultant for health care ministries.

The Mission Service Corps was organized to meet the 1977 SBC challenge of 5,000 self-supporting missions volunteers, serving from one to two years, by 1982. Also, VIM (Volunteer Involvement in Missions) was initiated in cooperation with the Home Mission Board, Brotherhood Commission, and Woman's Missionary Union. The number of Southern Baptist laymen involved in overseas projects increased steadily in the last half of the decade—1975 (1,200), 1976 (1,500), 1977 (2,413), 1978 (28,866), and 1979 (3,793).

The FMB updated its audio equipment and purchased video equipment for a total of approximately $225,000. Continuation of direct mail promotion campaign for *The Commission* brought total paid subscriptions to 40,237.

In 1978 the FMB appointed an all-time high of 350 missionaries for a net gain of 130, for a total of 2,906 at the end of the first full year of Bold Mission Thrust. Resignations of career missionaries were the lowest since 1966. Also in 1978 the FMB completed and dedicated a three-story addition to its office building in Richmond, VA.

At the end of 1979, the FMB staff consisted of 346 employees (47 administrative, 258 full-time, and 41 part-time professional, clerical, and support). During the year, the FMB installed a Univac 90/30 computer, the word processing center processed 3,000,000 lines, and total news and feature releases by News and Information Services reached 808. Paid circulation of *The Commission* reached 41,900 and complimentary copies, 39,821. A total of 1,733,365 missionary education pieces, and 2,600,000 Lottie Moon pamphlets with prayer guides were distributed. A share-the-cost plan was initiated by the Communications Department for certain printed and audiovisual materials.

Total gifts in 1979 reached $74,976,749 with Cooperative Program funds ($30,954,030) and the Lottie Moon Christmas Offering ($36,217,473) providing 89.6 percent of total income. Per capita giving to foreign missions by Southern Baptists in 1979 was $5.60.

Evangelism and Church Development.—The decade began with more than 20 special evangelistic efforts utilizing approximately 1,000 pastors and laypeople as a continuation of the Crusade of the Americas. A special survey of urban missions was conducted in Southeast Asia. Mass media efforts were expanding. More than 4,000 enrolled in radio correspondence courses in Argentina, and apartment ministries were initiated in Korea. New plans for cooperative efforts between missions and conventions, were elaborated in Mexico, Korea, Uruguay, and Trinidad.

In 1972 baptisms more than doubled in Vietnam, and four servicemen's centers received over 300,000 visits in Korea. Ethiopian missionaries conducted a special eight-week Bible teaching program for workers in the Ethiopian Orthodox Church. The Pan American Congress of Baptist men was held in Cali, Colombia, and saw the introduction of Witness Involvement Now (WIN) materials in Spanish.

In 1971 the world mission of reconciliation was projected for 85 countries between 1973 and 1975 under the leadership of Joseph B. Underwood, consultant in evangelism and church development. In 1974 the Baptist Convention of the Dominican Republic elected a woman as president, Baptist women of Korea appointed a home missionary for industrial evangelism, and expanded home mission efforts were reported in Mexico, Venezuela, Ecuador, Brazil, and Rhodesia (Zimbabwe). At least 14 countries had major evangelistic campaigns in 1975, some with the assistance of teams and lay witness people from the United States. The consultant in evangelism and church development initiated plans for major city evangelism. Lay training, stewardship workshops, church music, and religious education emphases were prominent in many areas. Use of mass media increased as a daily radio program in Spanish in prime time was beamed to all of Latin America, and English-language programs were beamed from Swaziland to countries in southern Africa. A three-year pilot project of major city evangelism began in Brazil in the cities of Niteroi and Sao Goncalo in 1976, and intensive efforts to establish preaching points along a newly opened highway in project "Trans Total" occurred simultaneously. In 1977 missionaries working among Indian populations in Guatemala projected a goal of reaching 100,000 in 10 years. Six films were shown on prime time in Costa Rica, and Bible correspondence courses prospered in many areas—3,000 persons enrolled in Benin and 3,000 in Ecuador, and Bible Way Correspondence Course exceeded 10,000 enrollment in Ghana.

In 1977, for the first time, the number of Baptists related to Southern Baptist foreign mission efforts overseas exceeded 1,000,000 (1,071,922). Baptisms were at an all-time high of 98,715. In 90 countries there were 8,533 churches and 10,635 mission points.

Reflecting the impact of Bold Mission Thrust, the Brazil Baptist Convention established a goal of 1,000,000 church members by

1982. A film giving information about Baptists was shown to 5,000,000 in a circuit of 500 theaters in Argentina in 1978. In 1976-77 a special evangelistic thrust among the Giryama tribe of Kenya yielded 185 new churches and 2,825 baptisms, and a similar thrust initiated among the Sukuma people of Tanzania in 1979 reported 2,575 professions of faith in 56 new congregations in the initial eight-week period.

The final year of the decade saw major city evangelistic campaign projections in process in Korea and Brazil (with special help from the Florida and Texas conventions), and 26,601 radio broadcasts, as well as 1,012 television programs aired. Special approaches included a center for urban studies in Kenya, a new community center in Liberia, church growth conferences, evangelism workshops, and WIN schools in several areas.

Schools and Student Work.—The program of schools and student work includes church-related primary and secondary schools, colleges and universities, and theological education institutions ranging from theological institutes on the primary school level through international theological seminaries offering post-graduate study. The program also includes efforts to witness and minister to students on secondary school, college, and university levels. In 1971 a conference on theological education was held in Cali, Colombia. TEE (Theological Education by Extension) was a major thrust of the decade in many areas of the world.

With the advance of education in the developing nations, Baptist-related primary and secondary schools declined numerically, but efforts to evangelize students through centers strategically located near colleges and universities multiplied.

The end of the decade saw 483 missionaries involved in teaching, along with 4,361 nationals. Baptist-sponsored kindergartens numbered 240 with enrollment of 20,908; elementary schools numbered 200 with 45,788 enrolled; secondary schools numbered 50 with 29,037 enrolled; while 9 Baptist colleges enrolled 13,923. Seventy theological seminaries and institutes enrolled 4,934, while 382 seminary extension centers enrolled 6,970. Forty-six student centers manned by 72 missionaries and 41 nationals enrolled 10,719 students in program activities. Osadalor Imasogie was elected in 1979 as the first Nigerian principal of the Nigerian Baptist Seminary, and in 1980, the first European, Ronald Goulding, was elected president of the international seminary in Ruschlikon, Switzerland. Financial problems, because of dramatic dollar devaluation, threatened the existence of Ruschlikon, but a program of austerity, coupled with greater financial participation by European Baptists, gave hope for survival.

Publication Work.—In 1977 N. Aldo Broda became the first Latin American director of the Baptist Spanish Publishing House in El Paso, TX. Another major publication center, Baptist Publishing House (Portuguese) in Rio de Janeiro, Brazil, wrestled with grave financial problems through the early years of the decade but succeeded in stabilizing its ministry and issued a new Portuguese version of the Bible. Other significant advances were made in the publication of Scriptures with the release of a new Chinese version, a Spanish version of *The Living Bible,* and a New Testament in modern Hebrew to which missionary Robert Lindsey made a major contribution. One million New Testaments were distributed in the public schools in the Rio de Janeiro area of Brazil for use in religion classes. Significant advance in music publications saw the release of a new Baptist hymnal in Spanish (1978) containing significant indigenous music, a Chinese Baptist hymnal, a hymnal in a dialect in the Philippines (1972), and music in Indian and African dialects.

Baptists also became involved in general publications in other languages, including Dutch, Lao, Armenian, and various dialects. An international conference on publications work in Kenya in 1978 led to the establishment of International Publication Services in Nairobi for the consolidation of publication efforts in Southern and Eastern Africa. The Jordan Baptist Press was the second largest evangelical publisher in Japan.

In 1973 the Sunday School Board assumed Spanish retail sales in the United States, and in 1979 the future of wholesale distribution of foreign language materials in the country was in process of determination. Innovative efforts to enlarge the utilization of literature in evangelism and church development led to an increased number of bookmobile ministries. In 1977 publications was the theme of the annual Graded Series Foreign Mission Study.

In 1979, 21 publication centers employed 77 missionaries and 508 nationals, published 6,022,016 pieces of 397 periodicals, 3,038,939 volumes of 631 books, 21,635,312 copies of 292 tracts, and utilized 104 book stores and 47 libraries and reading rooms as channels of distribution.

Hospitals and Health Care.—Emerging health care programs in the developing nations, escalating medical costs, and critical personnel needs brought radical changes in the program of "medical missions." An evaluation team did extensive work in evaluating the health programs of the Middle East. Control of many medical institutions passed from the missions to the national conventions or government agencies, although missionaries continued to enjoy freedom to serve in and witness through health care activities. Increasing numbers of health care teams went overseas to serve in short-term projects. The medical receptor program enlisted others in mission-related health care ministries.

In 1970 the program included 21 hospitals and 92 clinics and dispensaries and ministered to 64,508 inpatients and 815,512 outpatients. At the close of the decade, 20 hospitals and 120

FOREIGN MISSION BOARD STAFF

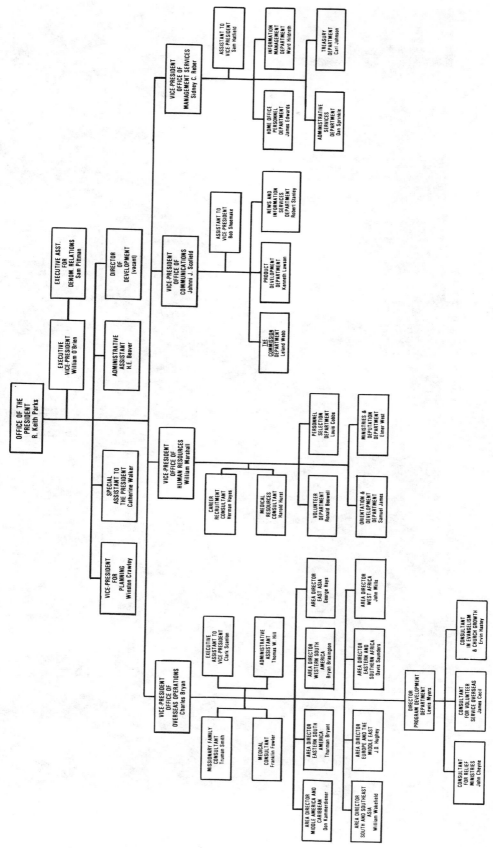

FOREIGN MISSION BOARD (*q.v.*) foyer; world sculpture with peoples of the world murals in background.

clinics treated 92,228 inpatients and 989,296 outpatients. The number of missionary physicians had increased from 47 to 59, and missionary nurses from 77 to 78.

Benevolent Ministries.—This program, defined as social services ministries, includes agriculture, good will and community centers, orphanages, and direct relief work. At the beginning of the decade, 44 missionaries were working in orphanages and good will or community centers. There was limited involvement in agricultural missions and only $104,854 was expended in direct relief. At the close of the decade, 93 missionaries, including 29 agricultural missionaries, were involved in benevolent ministries.

World events altered dramatically the focus of benevolent ministries. While community center-orphanage work experienced a 50 percent increase in missionary personnel, agricultural missions surged forward and world hunger and disaster response ministries funds in 1979 reached $3,090,523 (2,947 percent over 1970). Named as consultant for laymen overseas in 1971, W. Eugene Grubbs received the additional assignment of coordinating relief ministries in 1975. W. L. Smith assisted him from 1975 to 1977, and in 1978 two associate consultants were named, James W. Cecil, for volunteers in missions, and John Cheyne as coordinator of world hunger and disaster relief. Responses to major disasters in Bangladesh, Nicaragua, Honduras, and Guatemala formed a part of the picture in the earlier years of the decade. Heightened awareness to world hunger conditions and refugee problems created by political upheavals dramatically accelerated the financial response of Southern Baptists to this need.

Beginning in 1975, disaster response and hunger relief began to eclipse other phases of benevolent ministries due to the heightened awareness of Southern Baptists to these needs because of several specific national disasters and political upheavals resulting in a multiplicity of refugee crises. Southern Baptists gave $1,673,842 to hunger relief and disaster response in 1975 and $1,646,130 in 1976 in relief funds which were used to minister in 34 countries. In 1978 massive grain distribution occurred in drought-stricken Upper Volta, and extensive ministries were begun with Cambodian and Vietnamese refugees in Thailand. Funds channeled through the FMB for world hunger and disaster response totaled $1,748,000 and were used to minister in 31 countries, but 1979 saw the largest amount contributed to hunger and disaster response ($3,090,523) and the largest single appropriation ($500,000) by the FMB for hunger relief for Cambodian refugees in Thailand.

Contributions.—Total contributions to the FMB from 1845 to 1979 totaled $882,894,760. Of that amount, slightly over one-half ($484,707,239) was given in the 1970s. Expenditures for the decade totaled $501,479,840 of which $432,212,830 (86.19 percent) were operating expenses and $69,267,010 (13.81 percent), capital expenditures. Missionary support accounted for $257,505,443 (55.78 percent) of total expenditures.

New Organizational Structure.—Under the administration of R. Keith Parks, the FMB implemented a new organizational structure in 1980. The FMB changed the title of its chief executive from executive director to president. The head of the elected board, formerly called president, was renamed chairman. The chart accompanying this article describes the new organizational structure and names the executive and management staff.

See also FOREIGN MISSIONS, DIRECTIONS IN.

THOMAS W. HILL

FOREIGN MISSIONARIES, SOUTHERN BAPTIST CONVENTION, 1970-79 (I, III). A total of 2,542 missionaries were appointed in the 1970s. This figure includes career missionaries, missionary associates, journeymen, and special project workers. A total of 6,797 missionaries have been appointed since the beginning of the Foreign Mission Board in 1845.

Included with the name of each missionary below are native state, country or countries of service, and years served in each country. Symbols used are: Missionary Journeyman (J), Missionary Associate (A), and Special Project Worker (SP).

Abell, Betty Kathleen (J); TX; Ivory Coast, 1977-79.

Ables, Jack Mitchell; TX; Ecuador, 1978- .

Ables, Karen Diane Johnston (Mrs. J. M.); MA; Ecuador, 1978- .

Abney, Lynne Louise; WA; Gaza, 1977- .

Acuff, Barbara Jeane (J); MO; Ecuador, 1976-78.

Adams, Carroll Haydon; KY; Liberia, 1974-77.

Adams, Fay Litsey (Mrs. C. H.); KY; Liberia, 1974-77.

Adams, Darrell Wayne; VA; Portugal, 1978- .

Adams, Camille Kaye Adkison (Mrs. D. W.); MI; Portugal, 1978- .

Adams, David Russell (J); TX; Liberia, 1975-77.

Adams, John Hines; GA; Panama, 1977- .

Adams, Martha Jean Morris (Mrs. J. H.); NC; Panama, 1977- .

Adams, Margaret Ann (J); DC; Indonesia, 1972-74.

Adams, Mary Elizabeth (J); TX; Jordan, 1979- .

Aday, Phillip Lynn (J); OK; Bahamas, 1979- .

Aday, Cynthia Harris (Mrs. P. L.) (J); TX; Bahamas, 1979- .

Adian, Virginia Ruth; TX; Kenya, 1973- .

Agron, David Jonathan (J); TN; Cayman Islands, 1979- .

Aldrich, Diane (J); TX; Dominican Republic, 1978- .

Alexander, Carl Allen; AZ; Mexico, 1976- .

Alexander, Josephine Rebecca Holmes (Mrs. C. A.); TX; Mexico, 1976- .

Allard, Joseph Charles; NC; Reappointed; Brazil, 1977- .

Allard, Gloria Ellen Little (Mrs. J. C.); NC; Reappointed; Brazil, 1977- .

Allen, Donna Jean (J); FL; Spain, 1977-79.

Allen, Fred Malcolm; TX; Guyana, 1970- .

Allen, Joy Rocine Watts (Mrs. F. M.); TX; Guyana, 1970- .

Alley, Eddie Ray (J); TX; Austria, 1970-71.

Alley, Betty Louise Allan (Mrs. E. R.) (J); TX; Austria, 1970-71.

Allison, Cathy Lynn (J); WV; Tanzania, 1976-78.

Allred, Cecil Milton, Jr.; TX; Mexico, 1977- .

Allred, Mary Jane Crabb (Mrs. C. M.,Jr.); TX; Mexico, 1977- .

Altizer, Anita Sue (J); VA; Brazil, 1971-73.

Anderson, James Winfred; KY; Reappointed; Philippines, 1978- .

Anderson, Yvonne Williams (Mrs. J. W.); MO; Reappointed; Philippines, 1978- .

Anderson, Phillip Marion; AL; Reappointed; Philippines, 1978- .

Anderson, Martha Brandon (Mrs. P. M.); AL; Reappointed; Philippines, 1978- .

Anderson, Reatta Dene (J); TX; Korea, 1979- .

Anderson, Ronald Ray (J); TN; Liberia, 1973-75.

Anderson, Roxanne (J); AL; Switzerland, 1977-79.

Anderson, William Robert (A); FL; Ghana, 1976- .

Anderson, Betty Mae Brown (Mrs. W. R.) (A); FL; Ghana, 1976- .

Andress, Michael Wayne (J); AZ; Philippines, 1976-78.

Andress, Kristina Sue Herman (Mrs. M. W.) (J); TX; Philippines, 1976-78.

Anthony, John Franklin; AR; Israel, 1973- .

Anthony, Constance June Goble (Mrs. J. F.); IN; Israel, 1973- .

Armstrong, William Hayward; AL; Peru, 1977- .

Armstrong, Sherra Linda Daily (Mrs. W. H.); AL; Peru, 1977- .

Arrington, Charles Anthony (A); SC; Lebanon, 1970-72; 1975-77; Greece, 1972-75.

Arrington, Ottie Elizabeth Ward (Mrs. C. A.) (A); SC; Lebanon, 1970-72; 1975-77; Greece, 1972-75.

Arrant, Edwin Keith (J); TX; Brazil, 1979- .

Ashley, Clinton Matthew; TX; Brazil, 1972-78.

Ashley, Andrea Hustead (Mrs. C. M.); KY; Brazil, 1972-78.

Ashworth, Amelia Jean (J); GA; Argentina, 1977-79.

Atchison, Deborah Ann (J); TX; Brazil, 1979- .

Atkins, Frances (J); OK; French West Indies, 1970-72.

Atkinson, Howard Gene; KY; Colombia, 1979- .

Atkinson, Cora Elizabeth Sweet (Mrs. H. G.); KY; Colombia, 1979- .

Atkinson, Lloyd Hutson; FL; Chile, 1972-77.

Atkinson, Sue Jones (Mrs. L. H.); TX; Chile, 1972-77.

Atkinson, Maria Elena (J); TX; Taiwan, 1973-75.

Austin, James Warren (J); NC; Philippines, 1979- .

Austin, Debra Jo Livingston (Mrs. J. W.) (J); WY; Philippines, 1979- .

Austin, Rhonda Mary (J); AR; Guatemala, 1979- .

Autry, Joe Gene; TX; Korea, 1974- .

Autry, Kathleen McMeekin (Mrs. J. G.); WA; Korea, 1974- .

Babb, Karl David; KY; Mozambique, 1975-77; Philippines, 1977- .

Babb, Susan Marie Saunders (Mrs. K. D.); FL; Mozambique, 1975-77; Philippines, 1977- .

Baer, Stephen Marcus; TX; Botswana, 1979- .

Baer, Rebecca Colleen Routh (Mrs. S. M.); TX; Botswana, 1979- .

Baer, William Edward; PR; Chile, 1978- .

Baer, Teresa Ann Moore (Mrs. W. E.); OH; Chile, 1978- .

Baggett, Anthony Lee; TX; Mexico, 1974- .

Baggett, Zenda Ruth Smith (Mrs. A. L.); TX; Mexico, 1974- .

Bagwell, Emily Caroline (J); SC; Rhodesia, 1970-72.

Baillio, Stephen Emory; LA; Honduras, 1979- .

Baillio, Kala Lane Perkins (Mrs. S. E.); LA; Honduras, 1979- .

Baker, Deborah Ann (J); MD; Japan, 1978- .

Baker, Johnny Justin; LA; Brazil, 1979- .

Baker, Josephine Elizabeth Bains (Mrs. J. J.); LA; Brazil, 1974- .

Baker, Jon Steve (J); Israel; Macao, 1975-77.

Baker, William Lawrence; KY; Ecuador, 1978- .

Baker, Lou Anne Pool (Mrs. W. L.); KY; Ecuador, 1978- .

Baldridge, Gary Lee; TX; Zambia, 1977- .

Baldridge, Barbara Brinkley (Mrs. G. L.); TX; Zambia, 1977- .

Ball, Harry Michael (J); TX; Puerto Rico, 1977-78.

Ballance, Mary Ellen (J); NC; Kenya, 1975-77.

Ballard, Jerrell Rae (A); LA; Colombia, 1972- .

Ballard, Carrie Delores Waler (Mrs. J. R.) (A); LA; Colombia, 1972- .

Ballard, Margie Karen (J); SC; Korea, 1975-77.

Ballard, Ronald Henry; IL; Paraguay, 1976- .

Ballard, Martha Sue Wilson (Mrs. R. H.); AR; Paraguay, 1976- .

Bandy, Rachel Vivian (J); VA; Ghana, 1973-75.

Bane, John Greathouse, III; NC; Italy, 1979- .

Bane, Celia Tolar (Mrs. J. G., III); NC; Italy, 1979- .

Banks, James Glen; OK; French West Indies, 1975-78; Leeward Islands, 1978- .

Banks, Rose Marie Burton (Mrs. J. G.); OK; French West Indies, 1975-78; Leeward Islands, 1978- .

Bannister, James Bruce (J); AL; Zambia, 1976-78.

Barclay, David Anderson; AZ; Indonesia, 1978- .

Barclay, Bonnie Louise Jones (Mrs. D. A.); IN; Indonesia, 1978- .

Barger, Deborah Elaine (J); FL; Dominican Republic, 1974-76.

Barker, Robert B.; MO; Venezuela, 1975- .

Barker, Joyce D. Parrack (Mrs. R. B.); TX; Venezuela, 1975- .

Barnes, Jocelyn Rae (J); CA; Zambia, 1979- .

Barr, Larry Lee (J); VA; Colombia, 1971-72.

Barrentine, Jimmy Lloyd; MS; Paraguay, 1975- .

Barrentine, Joan Winifred Turnage (Mrs. J. L.); MS; Paraguay, 1975- .

Barrett, Herbert Lee; MO; Taiwan, 1971- .

Barrett, Alice Ann Nicoletti (Mrs. H. L.); MO; Taiwan, 1971- .

Barrett, Jerry Wayne; TX; Hong Kong, 1976- .

Barrett, Rebecca Lynn Madison (Mrs. J. W.); NC; Hong Kong, 1976- .

Barrow, Clifton Joe; NC; Kenya, 1977- .

Barrow, Faye Hardy (Mrs. C. J.); NC; Kenya, 1977- .

Barrow, Lydia Ardis (J); GA; Japan, 1975-77.

Barry, Lisa Dru (J); KY; Brazil, 1979- .

Bartels, Richard Alan; MA; Benin, 1979- .

Bartels, Carmela Ruth Underwood (Mrs. R. A.); MO; Benin, 1979- .

Basham, John Stuart (J); VA; Tanzania, 1974-76.

Bashaw, Margaret Erene (J); TX; Kenya, 1974-76.

Bass, Andrea Laine (J); TX; Laos, 1974-75; Macao, 1975-76.

Bass, Raymond Dwight; TN; Kenya, 1977- .

Bass, Joyce Lynn Stevens (Mrs. R. D.); TN; Kenya, 1977- .

Bates, Robert Keith; NC; Chile, 1978- .

Bates, Joyce Nell Sellers (Mrs. R. K.); NC; Chile, 1978- .

Bates, William Richard, Jr. (J); KY; Hong Kong, 1976-78.

Bates, Jane Caley (Mrs. W. R., Jr.) (J); GA; Hong Kong, 1976-78.

Batie, Rodney Eugene; CO; Ivory Coast, 1976- .

Batie, Cynthia Ann McGuirk (Mrs. R. E.); TX; Ivory Coast, 1976- .

Batson, Jabus Dolph; MS; Brazil, 1973-79.

Batson, Ethel Thatcher (Mrs. J. D.); MS; Brazil, 1973-79.

Bauer, Janet Ruth (J); TX; Spain, 1977-79.

Baugh, Robert Franklin (A); KY; Zambia, 1974-78.

Baugh, Blanchie Mathalia Edge (Mrs. R. F.) (A); KY; Zambia, 1974-78.

Baumgardner, Stella Louise (J); KS; Nigeria, 1978- .

Baumgardner, Stephens Linton (A); GA; Brazil, 1978- .

Baumgardner, Frances Castanita Garrett (Mrs. S. L.) (A); AL; Brazil, 1978- .

Baumgardner, Stephens Linton, Jr. (J); FL; Nicaragua, 1978- .

Baumgardner, Paula Kathleen Howard (Mrs. S. L., Jr.) (J); FL; Nicaragua, 1978- .

Beal, Richard Melton; FL; Venezuela, 1978- .

Beal, Martha Sue Lyle (Mrs. R. M.); MS; Venezuela, 1978- .

Beard, Harold Chris (J); LA; Brazil, 1973-75.

Bechtold, Carl William (A); MI; Liberia, 1975-79.

Bechtold, Virginia Lee Simmons (Mrs. C. W.) (A); TX; Liberia, 1975-79.

Beck, Kenneth Howard (A); NJ; Ghana, 1979- .

Beck, Charlotte Mae Todd (Mrs. K. H.) (A); PA; Ghana, 1979- .

Beck, Rosalie (J); TX; Vietnam, 1973-75.

Beckham, William Avery; TX; Thailand, 1974- .

Beckham, Mary Ann Harrison (Mrs. W. A.); TX; Thailand, 1974- .

Bedsole, Rosetta Colleen McIntire (Mrs. J. P.); MO; Ethiopia, 1971- .

Beighle, Dale Edward; KY; Ethiopia, 1975-77; Bophuthatswana, 1977- .

Beighle, Patrica Ann Puckett (Mrs. D. E.); KY; Ethiopia, 1975-77; Bophuthatswana, 1977- .

Benfield, Myron Joseph; IN; Uruguay, 1977- .

Benfield, Jean Alice Gray (Mrs. M. J.); GA; Uruguay, 1977- .

Bennett, Mary Louise (J); AL; Hong Kong, 1971-73.

Bergquist, Stanley Ervin, Jr. (A); PA; Taiwan, 1971- .

Bergquist, Carolyn Elizabeth Glasscock (Mrs. S. E., Jr.) (A); AL; Taiwan, 1971- .

Bethel, Charles Wayne; OH; Leeward Islands, 1978-79; Dominican Republic, 1979- .

Bethel, Jacquelyn Sue Edwards; (Mrs. C. W.); KY; Leeward Islands, 1978-79; Dominican Republic, 1979- .

Bibb, Tollie Marion, Jr.; TX; Ghana, 1974- .

Bibb, Linda Ruth West (Mrs. T. M., Jr.); OK; Ghana, 1974- .

Billings, Connie Juanita (J); TN; Ghana, 1972-72.

Bizzell, Virginia Lynn (J); NC; Nigeria, 1977-79.

Black, Harry Adam (J); TX; Ghana, 1978- .

Black, Ivetta Sue Ring (Mrs. H. A.) (J); AR; Ghana, 1978- .

Blackmon, Dennis Lester; LA; Brazil, 1974- .

Blackmon, Alita Sue Maulden (Mrs. D. L.); LA; Brazil, 1974- .

Blackwell, Anne Leigh (J); VA; Dominican Republic, 1979- .

Blair, Ralph Lee (A); FL; Ecuador, 1974-75.

Blair, Nancy Elnora Sorrow (Mrs. R. L.) (A); GA; Ecuador, 1974-75.

Blakeslee, Lyla K. (J); CO; Philippines, 1970-72.

Blanton, David Michael (J); TX; Ecuador, 1979- .

Blanton, Norma Olivia Dunnaway (Mrs. D. M.) (J); TX; Ecuador, 1979- .

Blanton, Felix Wayne (A); TX; Belize, 1979- .

Blanton, Janie Claire White (Mrs. F. W.) (A); TX; Belize, 1979- .

Bliss, Donald Lee; KS; Kenya, 1973- .

Bliss, Judith Ann Doenges (Mrs. D. L.); OK; Kenya, 1973- .

Bobby, Donna Mae; TN; Chile, 1975- .

Bobo, James Jay; TX; Vietnam, 1974-75; Hong Kong, 1975- .

Bobo, Linda Sue Stansberry (Mrs. J. J.); OK; Vietnam, 1974-75; Hong Kong, 1975- .

Bodenhamer, Ronald Dee; MO; Ethiopia, 1975-77; Kenya, 1977- .

Bodenhamer, Judy Lou Bailey (Mrs. R. D.); MO; Ethiopia, 1975-77; Kenya, 1977- .

Boggs, Samuel Alfred (J); NM; Japan, 1971-73.

Boles, Olin Douglas; TX; Reappointed; Brazil, 1974- .

Boles, Marilyn Miller (Mrs. O. D.); TX; Reappointed; Brazil, 1974- .

Boone, Donald Erwin (J); MS; Kenya, 1971-73.

Boone, Deborah Doolittle (Mrs. D. E.) (J); MS; Kenya, 1971-73.

Boothe, Dwain Holt; OK; Reappointed; France, 1976- .

Boothe, Sylvia DeHart (Mrs. D. H.); OK; France, 1976- .

Bost, Thomas Elton; TX; Japan, 1979- .

Bost, Marylou Wolsey (Mrs. T. E.); TX; Japan, 1979- .

Bostick, Roger McIver, Jr. (A); MS; Rhodesia, 1975-77.

Bostick, Rita Meryl Poe (Mrs. R. M., Jr.) (A); MS; Rhodesia, 1975-77.

Bostick, Ronnie Keith; TX; Zambia, 1972-76; Kenya, 1977- .

Bostick, Sallie Frances Dowdy (Mrs. R. K.); TX; Zambia, 1972-76; Kenya, 1977- .

Boswell, Dennis Gene (J); TN; Rhodesia, 1976-78.

Bowie, Kenneth Wayne; KS; Peru, 1979- .

Bowie, Linda Kay Orton (Mrs. K. W.); KS; Peru, 1979- .

Bowman, Karen Jo (J); TX; Philippines, 1976-78.

Bownds, Bethany Lynn (J); TX; Japan, 1977-79.

Boxley, Robert Moss (J); KY; Botswana, 1970-72.

Boyd, Glenn Thomas; OK; Tanzania, 1971-76; Kenya, 1977- .

Boyd, Paula Jeanine Hart (Mrs. G. T.); LA; Tanzania, 1971-76; Kenya, 1977- .

Boyd, Lester Charles (A); NC; Leeward Islands, 1976– .

Boyd, Fonda Arzelia Bice (Mrs. L. C.) (A); WV; Leeward Islands, 1976– .

Boyd, Shirley Elizabeth (J); AL; Hong Kong, 1973–75.

Boykin, Janie Elvira (J); MS; Liberia, 1979– .

Bozeman, Betty Verell (J); MS; Kenya, 1972–74.

Brackin, John LeRoy; TX; Philippines, 1977– .

Brackin, Lena Anne Lloyd (Mrs. J. L.); KS; Philippines, 1977– .

Bradford, David George (A); TX; Korea, 1975–78.

Bradford, Barbara Sue Keim (Mrs. D. G.) (A); IL; Korea, 1975–78.

Bradley, Donnie Robert; TX; Guatemala, 1977–79.

Bradley, Linda Lou Watts (Mrs. D. R.); TX; Guatemala, 1977–79.

Bradley, Henry Randall; IL; Philippines, 1975– .

Bradley, Claudia Rose Green (Mrs. H. R.); TN; Philippines, 1975– .

Bradley, Robert Alvis, Jr.; AL; Macao, 1978– .

Bradley, Barbara Nell Reeser (Mrs. R. A., Jr.); AL; Macao, 1978– .

Brake, Donald Earl; OK; Paraguay, 1974– .

Brake, Margaret Janice Ray (Mrs. D. E.); KS; Paraguay, 1974– .

Branham, Suzanne (J); TX; Gaza, 1974–76.

Branan, Jack Shortill; GA; Philippines, 1970– .

Branan, Rosanne Oxford (Mrs. J. S.); GA; Philippines, 1970– .

Brandon, Karen Dale; IL; Zambia, 1976– .

Branyon, Jill Beatty (J); SC; Kenya, 1976–78.

Brendle, Timothy Truette; NC; Haiti, 1978– .

Brendle, Ava Lee Abernethy (Mrs. T. T.); NC; Haiti, 1978– .

Brendlinger, Janice Faye (J); MO; Taiwan, 1978– .

Brent, Roy Wilson, Jr.; KY; Kenya, 1972– .

Brent, Diane Lindsey (Mrs. R. W., Jr.); SC; Kenya, 1972– .

Brewster, Phillip James; CA; Philippines, 1976– .

Brewster, Verneda Oretha Sitzes (Mrs. P. J.); MO; Philippines, 1976– .

Bridges, Billie Jean (J); TX; Brazil, 1976–78.

Bridges, Thomas Edward; AL; Brazil, 1978– .

Bridges, Peggy Jo Tomlinson (Mrs. T. E.); AL; Brazil, 1978– .

Bridges, Tilden William; NC; Taiwan, 1977– .

Bridges, Linda Kay McKinnish (Mrs. T. W.); NC; Taiwan, 1977– .

Brisson, Ervin Carson; NC; Israel, 1979– .

Brisson, Louise Ann Davis (Mrs. E. C.); NC; Israel, 1979– .

Brock, Charles Douglas; MO; Philippines, 1970– .

Brock, Dorothy Fern Richardson (Mrs. C. D.); MO; Philippines, 1970– .

Brock, James Robert (J); TX; Tanzania, 1976–78.

Brock, James Vaughn, Jr. (J); NC; Togo, 1979– .

Brooks, Susan Patricia (J); GA; Hong Kong, 1977–79.

Brooks, Timothy Edward (J); WV; Zambia, 1975–77.

Broskie, Danny Lee; VA; Costa Rica, 1976– .

Broskie, Brenda Gaye Shupe (Mrs. D. L.); VA; Costa Rica, 1976– .

Brown, Alvah David; LA; Ivory Coast, 1979– .

Brown, Patricia Irene Westenhover (Mrs. A. D.); LA; Ivory Coast, 1979– .

Brown, Conrad Monroe (J); NC; Malaysia-Singapore, 1976–78.

Brown, Delos Delaney (A); LA; Zambia, 1972– .

Brown, Wanda Anice Smith (Mrs. D. D.) (A); LA; Zambia, 1972– .

Brown, Donald Victor; Germany; Philippines, 1978– .

Brown, Beverley Coralie Stebbins (Mrs. D. V.); MS; Philippines, 1978– .

Brown, Jerel Edward (J); KY; Israel, 1972–74.

Brown, John Marshall (J); AR; Zambia, 1978– .

Brown, Katherine Sue (J); MO; Ghana, 1972–74.

Brown, Raymon LaMon; AL; India, 1979– .

Brown, Patricia Anne Duckett (Mrs. R. L.); AL; India, 1979– .

Brown, Stephen Forrest (J); IL; Vietnam, 1974–75; Indonesia, 1975–76.

Brown, Wayne Eugene; VA; Tanzania, 1975– .

Brown, Carroll Lee Bryant (Mrs. W. E); VA; Tanzania, 1975– .

Bruce, Joe Wayne; MO; Honduras, 1971– .

Bruce, Shirley Swan Plumlee (Mrs. J. W.); AR; Honduras, 1971– .

Bryan, Jo Von; TX; Kenya, 1974– .

Bryan, William Wayne (J); AZ; Togo, 1970–72.

Bryant, Douglas Arnold; GA; Ghana, 1971– .

Bryant, Beverly Ann Bagley (Mrs. D. A.); GA; Ghana, 1971– .

Bryant, Orvell, Jr.; LA; Windward Islands, 1977– .

Bryant, Suzan Rebecca Ward (Mrs. Orvell, Jr.); AR; Windward Islands, 1977– .

Bryant, Thurmon Earl; OK; Reappointed; Brazil, 1975–77.

Bryant, Doris Marie Morris (Mrs. T. E.); TX; Reappointed; Brazil, 1975–77.

Buck, Grant Wayne (A); PA; Israel, 1972– .

Buck, Norma Jeannine Strange (Mrs. G. W.) (A); KY; Israel, 1972– .

Buckingham, Susan Leigh (J); FL; Japan, 1976–78.

Buckland, Gaylon Dale; TX; Honduras, 1978– .

Buckland, Nancy Kaye Nugent (Mrs. G. D.); TN; Honduras, 1978– .

Buice, Waltea Jean (J); VA; Tanzania, 1975–77.

Bullington, Danny Mack (J); AR; Kenya, 1971–73.

Bullington, Jane Carolyn Hollis (Mrs. D. M.) (J); AR; Kenya, 1971–73.

Bumgarner, Kerry Lynn (J); SC; Kenya, 1976–78.

Bunce, Arthur Lloyd; MN; Bangladesh, 1976– .

Bunce, Peggy Lynn Willeford (Mrs. A. L.); OK; Bangladesh, 1976– .

Bunn, Karen Lee (J); TX; Gaza, 1975–77.

Bunn, Terry Eugene (J); NC; Hong Kong, 1973–75.

Burch, Betty Jo (SP); AL; Nigeria, 1978– .

Burch, Gerald Wayne; AL; Japan, 1974– .

Burch, Brenda Gail Bailey (Mrs. G. W.); AL; Japan, 1974– .

Burgess, Linda Lenore (J); MN; Lebanon, 1973–75.

Burgin, Robert Duaine; TX; Reappointed; Korea, 1976– .

Burgin, Sylvia Beth Lester (Mrs. R. D.); TX; Reappointed; Korea, 1976– .

Burke, James Robert; MO; Colombia, 1978– .

Burke, Sharon Lee Kephart (Mrs. J. R.); KS; Colombia, 1978– .

Burkwall, Paul Andrew; MO; Zambia, 1970–73; Nigeria, 1974– .

Burkwall, Faye Irene Stone (Mrs. P. A.); VA; Zambia, 1970–73; Nigeria, 1974– .

Burleson, Blake Wiley (J); TX; Kenya, 1978– .

Burleson, Charles Douglas (J); NC; Cayman Islands, 1977-79.

Burnes, Norman Norwood, III; GA; Israel, 1972-75; Greece, 1975- .

Burnes, Ila Kathryn Batten (Mrs. N. N., III); NC; Israel, 1972-75; Greece, 1975- .

Burnette, Everett Richard; SC; Senegal, 1972- .

Burnette, Dorothy Marie McKeown (Mrs. E. R.); SC; Senegal, 1972- .

Burney, Jerry Doward; TX; Ghana, 1977- .

Burney, Nelda Ruth Bennett (Mrs. J. D.); TX; Ghana, 1977- .

Burns, Horace Franklin (A); OK; Rhodesia, 1973- .

Burns, Annie Elizabeth Rohr (Mrs. H. F.) (A); MO; Rhodesia, 1973- .

Burris, Brenda Kay (J); IL; Guadeloupe, 1978- .

Burrow, Olan Henry; TX; Tanzania, 1976- .

Burrow, Joyce Lynn Ruth (Mrs. O. H.); NM; Tanzania, 1976- .

Bursmeyer, Jacolyn Sue; MO; Chile, 1977- .

Bush, Cyrus William; TN; Korea, 1979- .

Bush, Mary Anne Ramsey (Mrs. C. W.); LA; Korea, 1979- .

Bush, Harry Thurston, Jr.; AL; Indonesia, 1973- .

Bush, Barbara Elva Clement (Mrs. H. T., Jr.); LA; Indonesia, 1973- .

Butler, Catherine Jean (J); TX; Philippines, 1979- .

Butler, John Craig (J); AL; Peru, 1971-73.

Butler, Trent Craver; TX; Switzerland, 1971- .

Butler, Mary Roanna Burnett (Mrs. T. C.); TN; Switzerland, 1971- .

Buttemere, Clive Remond; NY; Costa Rica, 1972- .

Buttemere, Nancy Joanne Fortson (Mrs. C. R.); GA; Costa Rica, 1972- .

Byrd, Robert Glen (J); MD; Kenya, 1977-79.

Cable, Thomas Charles (SP); TX; Windward Islands, 1979- .

Cable, Deanna Leigh Nelson (Mrs. T. C.) (SP); NM; Windward Islands, 1979- .

Cadenhead, Shirley Ann (J); TX; Japan, 1975-77.

Cadle, Betty Lynn; GA; Rhodesia, 1970-77.

Cagle, Mildred Joy Dawson (Mrs. G. W.) (A); AR; Kenya, 1974- .

Calahan, Horace S., Jr. (A); TX; Liberia, 1978- .

Calahan, Mable June Foster (Mrs. H. S., Jr.) (A); TX; Liberia, 1978- .

Caldwell, Cathy Lynn (J); TX; Hong Kong, 1975-77.

Caldwell, Joseph Denzil (J); KY; Taiwan, 1974-76.

Caldwell, Maurice LaRon; AR; Peru, 1971-75.

Caldwell, Martha Baugh (Mrs. M. L.); AR; Peru, 1971-75.

Calhoun, Lois Ethel (A); KY; Jordan, 1970- .

Callis, Fred Daniel, Jr.; NC; Brazil, 1978- .

Callis, Nancy Ruth Bennett (Mrs. F. D., Jr.); NC; Brazil, 1978- .

Camp, Carroll Howard; MS; Uganda, 1979- .

Camp, Mary Cheryl Lever (Mrs. C. H.); SC; Uganda, 1979- .

Campbell, Katrina Lynn (J); TN; Brazil, 1978- .

Campbell, Roderick Lee (J); AL; Malawi, 1973-75.

Canady, Michael Otis; LA; Malawi, 1975-77; 1979- .

Canady, Linda Lucille Patton (Mrs. M. O.); AR; Malawi, 1975-77; 1979- .

Canady, Pride Thomas; NC; Honduras, 1977- .

Canady, Mary Susan Carr (Mrs. P. T.); NC; Honduras, 1977- .

Cannon, Martina Joy (J); KY; Gaza, 1975-77.

Capps, Roger Leon; SC; Malaysia, 1971- .

Capps, Janice Ruth Bell (Mrs. R. L.); AL; Malaysia, 1971- .

Carden, Shirley Ann (J); AR; Peru, 1974- .

Carl, Susan Katherine (J); DC; Yemen/India, 1976-78.

Carlisle, Jason Douglas; TX; Uruguay, 1976- .

Carlisle, Susan Ann Langston (Mrs. J. D.); MS; Uruguay, 1976- .

Carrier, Suzanne (J); CA; Japan, 1973-75.

Carroll, Charles Michael (J); MS; Dominican Republic, 1976-78.

Carter, James Walter; TX; Colombia, 1976- .

Carter, Shirley Tom Sha Lee (Mrs. J. W.); NY; Colombia, 1976- .

Carter, Winslow Lee (J); NC; Kenya, 1973-75.

Casey, Joseph Kenneth (A); SC; Bermuda, 1971-76; Windward Islands, 1976-79.

Casey, Frances Powell (Mrs. J. K.) (A); SC; Bermuda, 1971-76; Windward Islands, 1976-79.

Caster, Linda S. (J); TX; Philippines, 1970-72.

Castlen, James Eudelle; KY; Philippines, 1971- .

Castlen, Shelby Jean Southerland (Mrs. J. E.); VA; Philippines, 1971- .

Cato, Beverly Katherine (J); NC; Colombia, 1975-77.

Caudill, Samuel Patton (J); OK; Kenya, 1971-73.

Causby, Robert Hamrick (J); NC; Liberia, 1975-77.

Cawthon, Frank Douglas, Jr.; CA; Senegal, 1977- .

Cawthon, Sally Ellen Slinkard (Mrs. F. D., Jr.); CA; Senegal, 1977- .

Cearley, Timothy Dane (J); NC; Rhodesia, 1976-78.

Cerda, Gloria Linda (J); TX; Malawi, 1973-74.

Chafin, Herbert Rhea; TX; Honduras, 1978- .

Chafin, Nancy Marie Kelley (Mrs. H. R.); LA; Honduras, 1978- .

Chamberlain, Nancy Ellen (J); MS; Argentina, 1973-75.

Chambless, Virgil Walton, Jr.; GA; Reappointed; Baptist Spanish Publishing House, 1973-77; Chile, 1977- .

Chambless, Lorean Thomas (Mrs. V. W., Jr.); FL; Reappointed; Baptist Spanish Publishing House, 1973-77; Chile, 1977- .

Chandler, James Denver (J); WV; Korea, 1977-79.

Chandler, Mary Ann; AL; Malawi, 1970- .

Cheatwood, Susan Marie (J); AL; Nigeria, 1976-78.

Cherry, John William (A); TX; Zambia, 1971-76; Venezuela, 1976-76.

Cherry, Alma Myra Davis (Mrs. J. W.) (A); TX; Zambia, 1971-76; Venezuela, 1976-76.

Cherry, Rebecca Ann (J); LA; Tanzania, 1970-72.

Cheser, David Wayne (J); KY; Togo, 1972-74.

Cheyne, David Louis (J); TX; Kenya, 1973-75.

Childers, Steven Dale (J); OK; Zambia, 1974-76.

Chipley, Quinton Thomas (J); TN; Kenya, 1979- .

Christy, John Raymond (J); CA; Kenya, 1973-75.

Clark, Allen Whitman, II (J); MO; Tanzania, 1971-73.

Clark, Bruce Alan (J); AL; Iran, 1976-78.

Clark, Diane Elizabeth (J); MD; Jordan, 1979- .

Clark, Hubert Karl, Jr. (J); TN; Kenya, 1976-78.

Clark, Nancy Lee Long (Mrs. H. K., Jr.) (J); VA; Kenya, 1976-78.

Clark, Karren Patricia (J); MO; Hong Kong, 1973-75.

Clark, Stacey Lea (J); LA; Yemen, 1979- .

Clark, Susan Elizabeth (J); TX; Guatemala, 1975-76; Dominican Republic, 1976-77.

Clark, William Bruce; GA; Chile, 1977- .

Clark, Linda Kaye Stevens (Mrs. W. B.); AZ; Chile, 1977- .

Clayton, Kenneth Ray; TN; Spain, 1976-79.

Clayton, Joyce Ann Riddle (Mrs. K. R.); TN; Spain, 1976-79.

Cleary, Thomas Andrew; PA; Austria, 1971- .

Cleary, Sandra Joyce Coffield (Mrs. T. A.); LA; Austria, 1971- .

Cleaver, Constance Merine (J); FL; Argentina, 1974-76.

Clement, Richard Davis; KY; Reappointed; Ecuador, 1974- .

Clement, Barbara Hargrave (Mrs. R. D.); HI; Ecuador, 1974- .

Clements, John LeRoy (J); FL; Bahamas, 1971-72.

Clements, Margaret Rose (J); TX; Peru, 1972-73; Mexico, 1973-74.

Clendenen, Michael Henry; FL; Taiwan, 1974- .

Clendenen, Annette Smith (Mrs. M. H.); KY; Taiwan, 1974- .

Clevenger, Donna Jan (J); TX; Brazil, 1977-79.

Cline, Paul Francis; LA; Botswana, 1979- .

Cline, Sally Ann Boss (Mrs. P. F.); VA; Botswana, 1979- .

Cloninger, Eileen Frances (J); TX; Kenya, 1977-79.

Cluck, Terry Wayne (J); OK; Kenya, 1972-74.

Coad, Norman Lee; MO; Upper Volta, 1972- .

Coad, Beverly Joan Gallegly (Mrs. N. L.); AR; Upper Volta, 1972- .

Cobbs, Brenda Kay Shields (J); IL; Kenya, 1975-77.

Cobbs, Louis Robert, Jr. (J); TX; Kenya, 1975-77.

Codone, Cynthia June (J); FL; Taiwan, 1978- .

Coffey, Gudrin Dorothy (J); Germany; Brazil, 1977-79.

Cohen, Martha Frances Collier (Mrs. C. L.) (A); GA; Taiwan, 1972- .

Coker, Ronald Wayne; NC; Belgium, 1978- .

Coker, Nancy Lee Price (Mrs. R. W.); SC; Belgium, 1978- .

Cole, Harold Virgil (A); OK; Liberia, 1975-76.

Cole, Elva Clarice Ritchie (Mrs. H. V.) (A); TX; Liberia, 1975-76.

Cole, Jerry Wayne; AL; Taiwan, 1979- .

Cole, Sandra Carolyn Northcutt (Mrs. J. W.); AL; Taiwan, 1979- .

Cole, Thomas Lyndal; AL; Argentina, 1971-77.

Cole, Carolyn Barry (Mrs. T. L.); TX; Argentina, 1971-77.

Coleman, Johnnie Lee Victor; OK; Venezuela, 1973- .

Coleman, Sherrie Ann Early (Mrs. J. L. V.); OK; Venezuela, 1973- .

Collins, Charles Anthony; TN; Guatemala, 1976- .

Collins, Jan Elizabeth Hollowell (Mrs. C. A.); TN; Guatemala, 1976- .

Colson, John Virgil (A); GA; Liberia, 1978- .

Colson, Elizabeth Grace Bishop (Mrs. J. V.) (A); MS; Liberia, 1978- .

Colston, Lizbeth Carol (J); GA; Peru, 1979- .

Colville, Patricia Ann (J); Guam; Nigeria, 1979- .

Colvin, James Robert; NC; Japan, 1975- .

Colvin, Martha Ellen Mooney (Mrs. J. R.); VA; Japan, 1975- .

Colvin, Kittie Lou (J); AR; South Africa, 1977-79.

Compton, Bobby Dale; NC; Reappointed; Costa Rica, 1975- .

Compton, Peggy Frances Lowe (Mrs. B. D.); SC; Reappointed; Costa Rica, 1975- .

Congdon, Robert Thomas (J); Nigeria; Thailand, 1975-77.

Conner, Constance Cheryl (J); NM; Venezuela, 1977-79.

Cook, Elwood Eugene, Jr. (J); MO; Ghana, 1974-76.

Cook, Ronald Stephen; Zaire; Kenya, 1978- .

Cook, Barbara Jean Powell (Mrs. R. S.); KY; Kenya, 1978- .

Cook, Thomas Edwin (SP); TX; Gaza, 1978- .

Cook, Bobbie Joyce Cravey (Mrs. T. E.) (SP); TX; Gaza, 1978- .

Cook, William Burton, Jr.; TX; Taiwan, 1974- .

Cook, Karen Ann Powell (Mrs. W. B., Jr.); TX; Taiwan, 1974- .

Cooke, Janet Carolyn (J); CA; Taiwan, 1973-75.

Cooke, Melanie Ann (J); TN; Rhodesia, 1974-76.

Cooper, James Virgil; MS; Korea, 1971- .

Cooper, Amy Lee Gunter (Mrs. J. V.); AL; Korea, 1971- .

Cooper, Leona Chaddick (Mrs. H. B.) (A); LA; Yemen, 1976-78.

Cooper, Marvin Ray; CA; Zambia, 1971-75.

Cooper, Glenda Ferne Southard (Mrs. M. R.); CA; Zambia, 1971-75.

Copeland, Edward Letcher; TN; Colombia, 1974-76; Spain, 1976-77.

Copeland, Linda Hilton (Mrs. E. L.); NC; Colombia, 1974-76; Spain, 1976-77.

Corbin, James Edwin (A); TX; Uganda, 1971-72; 1974; Liberia, 1972-73; Kenya, 1973-74.

Corbin, Johnnie Josephine Isom (Mrs. J. E.) (A); TX; Uganda, 1971-72; 1974; Liberia, 1972-73; Kenya, 1973-74.

Corley, Charles Kendrick (SP); TX; Rhodesia, 1977-78.

Corley, Gayla Loyce Vardeman (Mrs. C. K.) (SP); TX; Rhodesia, 1977-78.

Corley, Olan George (A); OK; Mexico, 1978- .

Corley, Mildred Oneta Garvin (Mrs. O. G.) (A); OK; Mexico, 1978- .

Cornelius, Gerald Ervin, Jr.; TX; Brazil, 1979- .

Cornelius, Blynda Jo Doyle (Mrs. G. E. Jr.); TX; Brazil, 1979- .

Courtney, Donnell Newton; TX; Guatemala, 1970- .

Courtney, Jane Augusta Holtz (Mrs. D. N.); CO; Guatemala, 1970- .

Couts, Bobby Murphey; TN; Benin, 1974- .

Couts, Rebekah Jan Haltom (Mrs. B. M.); OK; Benin, 1974- .

Covington, James Robert (A); KY; Bahamas, 1976- .

Covington, Annie Laurie Burnette (Mrs. J. R.) (A); KY; Bahamas, 1976- .

Covington, Jesse Eugene; AL; Ghana, 1977- .

Covington, Janice Wilson (Mrs. J. E.); AL; Ghana, 1977- .

Cowart, Joseph Mixon; FL; Kenya, 1976- .

Cowart, Susan Lynn Hunt (Mrs. J. M.); MO; Kenya, 1976- .

Cowherd, Charles Philip; VA; Reappointed; Hong Kong, 1973-75.

Cowherd, Margaret Handscombe (Mrs. C. P.); England; Hong Kong, 1973-75.

Cox, James Larry; MS; Ivory Coast, 1975- .

Cox, Cheryl Lee Keathley (Mrs. J. L.); TN; Ivory Coast, 1975- .

Cox, John Russell (J); AL; Liberia, 1978- .

Craig, Howard Lee, III (J); VA; Indonesia, 1978–79; Thailand, 1979– .

Craigmyle, James Phillip; IN; Reappointed; Lebanon, 1978– .

Craigmyle, Doris Jane Rogers (Mrs. J. P.); ME; Reappointed; Lebanon, 1978– .

Crane, Donald Arthur; NJ; Taiwan, 1973–77; Malaysia, 1977– .

Crane, Sandra Elaine Dugger (Mrs. D. A.); FL; Taiwan, 1973–77; Malaysia, 1977– .

Cranford, Janice (J); TX; South Africa, 1979– .

Crawford, Linda Lee; FL; Brazil, 1970– .

Crawford, William Frank, Jr. (J); TN; Brazil, 1979– .

Creecy, Rachel Alice; HI; Hong Kong, 1976– .

Creek, Diana Lynn (J); IL; Brazil, 1978– .

Creighton, Robin (J); LA; Taiwan, 1971–73.

Crissey, Roberta Ann; FL; Brazil, 1974– .

Crittendon, James Edward; SC; Philippines, 1975– .

Crittendon, Trudith Parnice Hall (Mrs. J. E.); SC; Philippines, 1975– .

Crockett, Robert Wayne; TN; Argentina, 1972– .

Crockett, Frances Annette Perkins (Mrs. R. W.); AR; Argentina, 1972– .

Crosby, Paul Franklin; TN; Mexico, 1973–78.

Crosby, Gloria Shambaugh (Mrs. P. F.); MO; Mexico, 1973–78.

Crossley, James David (SP); TN; Rhodesia, 1976–77.

Crossley, Paula Elaine Hude (Mrs. J. D.) (SP); TN; Rhodesia, 1976–77.

Crosslin, Lydia Paulette (J); TN; Brazil, 1976–77.

Crotts, Nancy Gwen; TX; Hong Kong, 1974– .

Croxton, Everett Hubert (A); SC; France, 1974–78.

Croxton, Florence Bereniece Bell (Mrs. E. H.) (A); TX; France, 1974–78.

Cunnyngham, Hal Frank (J); TX; Brazil, 1977–79.

Cunnyngham, Cynthia Kay Dement (Mrs. H. F.) (J); TX; Brazil, 1977–79.

Curlee, Shirley Elizabeth (J); AL; Guatemala, 1972–74.

Curp, William Dale; MO; Ethiopia, 1972–77; Kenya, 1977– .

Curp, Beverly June Stephens (Mrs. W. D.); MO; Ethiopia, 1972–77; Kenya, 1977– .

Daffern, Georgia Elaine (J); TX; Japan, 1973–75.

Dane, Clifford Henry; TX; Brazil, 1972– .

Dane, Peggy Jo Delano (Mrs. C. H.); TX; Brazil, 1972– .

Daniel, Thomas Darrell; NM; Korea, 1978– .

Daniel, Rebecca Sue Bowen (Mrs. T. D.); TX; Korea, 1978– .

Daniel, William Amis (A); NC; Kenya, 1979– .

Daniel, Frances Eugenia Price (Mrs. W. A.) (A); NC; Kenya, 1979– .

Daniels, David Allan; FL; Uruguay, 1979– .

Daniels, Lynda Lee Kjellstrom (Mrs. D. A.); FL; Uruguay, 1979– .

Dannelley, Rebekah Ann (J); TX; Kenya, 1975–77.

Daugherty, Robert Julian (A); TN; Japan, 1973– .

Daugherty, Lillian Myrtle Dabney (Mrs. R. J.) (A); KY; Japan, 1973– .

Daugherty, Shirley Ann (J); OK; Kenya, 1973–75.

Davenport, Sharon L. (J); DC; Argentina, 1970–72.

Davis, Cornelia Evelyn; GA; Kenya, 1973– .

Davis, David Benjamine, Jr. (A); CA; Ghana, 1975–78.

Davis, Patsy Darlene Prince (Mrs. D. B., Jr.) (A); AR; Ghana, 1975–78.

Davis, Donald Lloyd; VA; Uruguay, 1974– .

Davis, Mary Anne Mays (Mrs. D. L.); VA; Uruguay, 1974– .

Davis, Drexel Carter, II; TN; Windward Islands, 1976– .

Davis, Charlotte Rebecca Jones (Mrs. D. C., II); TN; Windward Islands, 1976– .

Davis, Durward Harold (A); FL; Iran, 1975–77; Germany, 1977–77.

Davis, June Hope Roper (Mrs. D. H.) (A); FL; Iran, 1975–77; Germany, 1977–77.

Davis, Elmer Cleveland, Jr. (J); NC; Windward Islands, 1978– .

Davis, Gerald Carson; AL; Philippines, 1975– .

Davis, Glenda Minette Brooks (Mrs. G. C.); MS; Philippines, 1975– .

Davis, Larry Eugene; KS; Nigeria, 1974– .

Davis, Doris Patricia Stavely (Mrs. L. E.); TN; Nigeria, 1974– .

Davis, Leslie Wayne (A); OK; Bahamas, 1975– .

Davis, Eleanor Frances White (Mrs. L. W.) (A); TX; Bahamas, 1975– .

Davis, Patsy Kay; NC; Venezuela, 1977– .

Davis, William Earl; LA; Bolivia, 1978– .

Davis, Judy Virginia Smith (Mrs. W. E.); MS; Bolivia, 1978– .

Day, Fredrick Emerson; LA; Surinam, 1975– .

Day, Janice Louise Byrd (Mrs. F. E.); AL; Surinam, 1975– .

Day, Herbert Jackson; AL; Brazil, 1970– .

Day, Doris Emily Herron (Mrs. H. J.); CA; Brazil, 1970– .

Deaderick, Elbert Thomas, Jr.; TN; Brazil, 1976– .

Deaderick, Billie Cecil Schultz (Mrs. E. T., Jr.); AL; Brazil, 1976– .

Dean, D'Wanna Kay (J); TX; Kenya, 1978– .

Dean, Marjorie Helen; FL; Ivory Coast, 1979– .

Deane, Gary Thomas (J); OH; Guyana, 1971–73.

Debenport, Fred Teller; TX; Taiwan, 1975– .

Debenport, Janie Sue Neese (Mrs. F. T.); TX; Taiwan, 1975– .

DeBerry, Betty Jane (J); KY; Korea, 1970–72.

Deckert, Wayne Benjamin; CA; Japan, 1976– .

Deckert, Kay Ellen Green (Mrs. W. B.); MO; Japan, 1976– .

Deevers, Charles Lee; MS; Ivory Coast, 1974– .

Deevers, Diane Ball Sutherland (Mrs. C. L.); LA; Ivory Coast, 1974– .

Densford, Muriel R. (J); OK; Italy, 1970–72.

Dent, Robert Preston, Jr. (J); MS; Liberia, 1978– .

Deterding, Roy Allen; NB; Venezuela, 1979– .

Deterding, Lisa Lucille London (Mrs. R. A.); NB; Venezuela, 1979– .

Devers, Pamela Jean (J); Bolivia; Colombia, 1978– .

Devore, Samuel Arthur (J); IL; Kenya, 1970–72.

Dick, Margaret Ellen (J); MO; Taiwan, 1976–77.

Dickens, George Dean; AR; Philippines, 1974– .

Dickens, Karr La Voynne Miller (Mrs. G. D.); TX; Philippines, 1974– .

Dickens, Michael Clyde (J); NC; Kenya, 1973–75.

Dickerman, Richard Cary; MO; Macao, 1977– .

Dickerman, Janis Kay Wilson (Mrs. R. C.); IN; Macao, 1977– .

Dietrich, Vernon Lee; TX; Reappointed; Thailand, 1978– .

Dietrich, Dorothy Rolen (Mrs. V. L.); AL; Reappointed; Thailand, 1978– .

Dildy, Walter Robert; TX; Taiwan, 1977– .

Dildy, Jacqueline Alma Hand (Mrs. W. R.); TX; Taiwan, 1977- .

Dillahunty, Donald Freeman (J); MO; Thailand, 1977-79.

Dillman, John Howard; IN; Kenya, 1971- .

Dillman, Kathleen Ann Wisler (Mrs. J. H.); IN; Kenya, 1971- .

Dillworth, Linda Sue; KY; Philippines, 1977- .

Dison, Dale Wilson; AL; Kenya, 1975- .

Dison, Patsy Geraldine Crowder (Mrs. D. W.); AL; Kenya, 1975- .

Dixon, Curtis Leon; OK; Reappointed; Angola, 1974- .

Dixon, Bettye Sue McCown (Mrs. C. L.); OK; Reappointed; Angola, 1974- .

Dobbins, James Dale; OK; Chile, 1979- .

Dobbins, Wanda Jean Carpenter (Mrs. J. D.); KY; Chile, 1979- .

Dockery, Charles Daniel (J); NC; Liberia, 1978- .

Dockins, Deral Eugene; MO; Ecuador, 1975-79.

Dockins, Harriet Elizabeth Wigger (Mrs. D. E.); MO; Ecuador, 1975-79.

Dodson, Dru Alan (J); AR; Israel, 1977-79.

Dodson, Jo Helen Hays (Mrs. D. A.) (J); TX; Israel, 1977-79.

Donaldson, Buck; LA; Reappointed; Kenya, 1978- .

Donaldson, Barbara Hasty (Mrs. Buck); MN; Reappointed; Kenya, 1978- .

Donaldson, Ira Louise; AL; Brazil, 1971- .

Dorriety, Glenda Kay (J); AL; Guam, 1973-75.

Dorris, David Miller; TN; Bangladesh, 1974-76; Reappointed; Israel, 1979- .

Dorris, Wanda Jean Moreland (Mrs. D. M.); KY; Bangladesh, 1974-76; Reappointed; Israel, 1979- .

Dorsey, James Delano; WY; Colombia, 1979- .

Dorsey, Rebecca Savage (Mrs. J. D.); TX; Colombia, 1979- .

Dotson, Lolete Marie; AL; Reappointed; Bophuthatswana, 1977- .

Douglas, Ray Melvin (A); TX; Dominican Republic, 1971- .

Douglas, Mildred Louise Gregson (Mrs. R. M.) (A); TX; Dominican Republic, 1971- .

Dowling, Robert Havener; SC; Peru, 1977-79.

Dowling, Gary Ann Cate (Mrs. R. H.); SC; Peru, 1977-79.

Doyle, Charles Donald; TX; Reappointed; Guatemala, 1979- .

Doyle, Patricia Stone (Mrs. C. D.); NM; Reappointed; Guatemala, 1979- .

Driggers, Marcus Loyd; TX; Chile, 1973- .

Driggers, Ruth Anna Maud Christ (Mrs. M. L.); OK; Chile, 1973- .

DuBard, Rachel Ann (A); MS; Liberia, 1979- .

Dubuisson, Laura Ann (J); MS; Ethiopia, 1971-73.

Duff, Larry (J); IN; Peru, 1979- .

Duff, Nancy Karen Hundley (Mrs. Larry) (J); IN; Peru, 1979- .

Duffield, John Fredrick (J); MO; Ecuador, 1975-77.

Duke, Penny Rolanda (J); VA; Taiwan, 1975-77.

Dunaway, Loyd Nolen; CA; Spain, 1978- .

Dunaway, Elisa Gonzalez (Mrs. L. N.); NM; Spain, 1978- .

Duncan, Cathy Ann (J); GA; Japan, 1979- .

Duncan, Ned Lee; NC; Uruguay, 1973-76.

Duncan, Sandra Carol Rhyne (Mrs. N. L.); TN; Uruguay, 1973-76.

Dunks, Darryle Wayde; TX; Tanzania, 1977-79.

Dunks, Brenda Gail Ford (Mrs. D. W.); TX; Tanzania, 1977-79.

Dunn, Alice Rebecca (J); FL; Japan, 1978- .

Dunn, Herman Wayne (A); NC; Windward Islands, 1979- .

Dunn, Peggy Joanne Hamilton (Mrs. H. W.) (A); NC; Windward Islands, 1979- .

Duvall, Donald Graham; KY; Indonesia, 1972- .

Duvall, Sarah Enfield Eddleman (Mrs. D. G.); Palestine; Indonesia, 1972- .

Duyka, Donna Kathyrn (J); TX; Malawi, 1973; Rhodesia, 1973-75.

Dyches, Obie Dunbar; SC; Chile, 1972- .

Dyches, Doris Virginia Phillips (Mrs. O. D.); SC; Chile, 1972- .

Eades, Terry Lewis (J); MO; Japan, 1975-77.

Early, Paul Davis (A); NC; Bahamas, 1974- .

Early, Lena Elizabeth Allen (Mrs. P. D.) (A); GA; Bahamas, 1974- .

Edmondson, Marilyn Louise (J); NC; Japan, 1979- .

Edwards, James Murray; GA; Mexico, 1974- .

Edwards, Ruth Allen Askew (Mrs. J. M.); GA; Mexico, 1974- .

Edwards, Cheryl Denise (J); TX; Jordan, 1979- .

Edwards, Marsha Anita (J); MO; India, 1976-78.

Edwards, Oma Leitha Jordan (Mrs. Leslie) (A); AL; Gaza, 1976- .

Edwards, Robert Lewis; TX; Colombia, 1972- .

Edwards, Marion Dolores Whitman (Mrs. R. L.); TX; Colombia, 1972- .

Ehrlich, James Cary; TN; Venezuela, 1977- .

Ehrlich, Luana Delores Pollock (Mrs. J. C.); MO; Venezuela, 1977- .

Eitelman, Ray Wesson; TX; Upper Volta, 1974- .

Eitelman, Patsy Irene Walker (Mrs. R. W.); TX; Upper Volta, 1974- .

Elimon, Richard Gregory (J); IL; Philippines, 1973-74.

Elkins, Jennifer Lynn (J); SC; Nigeria, 1970-72.

Eller, Oliver Eugene, Jr.; VA; Jordan, 1974- .

Eller, Marguerite Jane Galloway (Mrs. O. E., Jr.); VA; Jordan, 1974- .

Elliott, Dorothy Marie (A); FL; Japan, 1973- .

Elliott, Larry Thomas; VA; Honduras, 1978- .

Elliott, Donna Jean Dover (Mrs. L. T.); NC; Honduras, 1978- .

Elliott, Mary Eleanor (J); VA; Liberia, 1978- .

Ellis, Constance Lou (J); MS; Korea, 1971-73.

Ellis, Janie Mae (A); NC; Japan, 1977- .

Elmore, Michael Gordon (J); MO; Israel, 1973-75.

Elmore, Cheryl Susanne Bacon (Mrs. M. G.) (J); MO; Israel, 1973-75.

Elsenbrook, Deborah Lynn (J); TX; Liberia, 1975-77.

Englebrecht, Jack Melvin (J); CO; Ghana, 1975-77.

Ennis, Rollie Everett; OK; Tanzania, 1974- .

Ennis, Eva Dell Sanderfer (Mrs. R. E.); AZ; Tanzania, 1974- .

Ertelt, Milton Ernest Howard, Jr.; MI; Malawi, 1974-79; Kenya, 1979- .

Ertelt, Charlotte Ann Huff (Mrs. M. E. H., Jr.); TX; Malawi, 1974-79; Kenya, 1979- .

Erwin, Robert Scott; AL; Brazil, 1970- .

Erwin, Veronica Mae Wheeler (Mrs. R. S.); MS; Brazil, 1970- .

Escalera, Margaret (J); NY; Taiwan, 1974–76.

Estes, Joseph Richard; KY; Reappointed; Spain, 1976–77.

Estes, Helen Trout (Mrs. J. R.); TN; Reappointed; Spain, 1976–77.

Estes, Vickie Janet (J); NC; Hong Kong, 1973–75.

Ethredge, Walter Jerome; GA; Togo, 1976– .

Ethredge, Joann Bertice Davis (Mrs. W. J.); GA; Togo, 1976– .

Eudy, Garry Edgar; AL; Panama, 1978– .

Eudy, Mary Kathryn Scogin (Mrs. G. E.); AL; Panama, 1978– .

Evans, Orlynn Reece; KS; Liberia, 1970–78.

Evans, Evelyn Gatson (Mrs. O. R.); MO; Liberia, 1970–78.

Evans, Richard David; CA; India, 1975–75.

Evans, Virginia L. Coker (Mrs. R. D.); OK; India, 1975–75.

Everhart, Jackie Dean; OK; India, 1972–73; Korea, 1974– .

Everhart, Sharon Janelle Singer (Mrs. J. D.); OK; India, 1972–73; Korea, 1974– .

Faile, Cherry Edith (J); Nigeria; Yemen, 1978– .

Faile, George Marion (J); GA; Korea, 1972–74.

Fairchild, Bernard Lee; MT; Jordan, 1979– .

Fairchild, Annette Louise Oma (Mrs. B. L.); MT; Jordan, 1979– .

Fallaw, Billy Keith; SC; Brazil, 1970– .

Fallaw, Henrietta Ann Monteith (Mrs. B. K.); SC; Brazil, 1970– .

Falwell, Reuben Hale, Jr. (A); KY; Hong Kong, 1970– .

Falwell, Catherine Rowena Gunter (Mrs. R. H., Jr.) (A); MS; Hong Kong, 1970– .

Farrell, Rhonda Ann (J); CA; Colombia, 1976; Mexico, 1976–78.

Farris, Edward James; MO; Brazil, 1975– .

Farris, Roberta Kay Ott (Mrs. E. J.); KS; Brazil, 1975– .

Fast, Genita Gail (J); OK; Gaza, 1973–75.

Faulkner, John Herschel; AL; Rhodesia, 1970– .

Faulkner, Patricia Anne Williams (Mrs. J. H.); AL; Rhodesia, 1970– .

Faulkner, Rebecca June (J); TN; Jordan, 1977–79.

Ferguson, William Griffin (A); AR; Brazil, 1978– .

Ferguson, Betty Jane Sullivan (Mrs. W. G.) (A); IL; Brazil, 1978– .

Ferrington, Darryl Kirk (J); LA; Japan, 1975–77.

Ferrington, Mary Catherine Sydes (Mrs. D. K.) (J); LA; Japan, 1975–77.

Fewell, William Roy (J); TX; France, 1971–73.

Fewell, Sheila Dore (Mrs. W. R.) (J); TX; France, 1971–73.

Findley, Fred Holliman, Jr.; AL; Bangladesh, 1979– .

Findley, Kalliope Kathryne Manis (Mrs. F. H., Jr.); AL; Bangladesh, 1979– .

Fink, Mary Ida Winecoff (Mrs. T. F.) (A); NC; Jordan, 1979– .

Finnell, David Lynn; KY; Malaysia, 1978– .

Finnell, Linda Ruth Lipscomb (Mrs. D. L.); MS; Malaysia, 1978– .

Firesheets, Lela Elizabeth (J); LA; Zambia, 1972–74.

Fish, Lisa Jean (J); MO; Spain, 1979– .

Fisher, Charles Lonell; NC; Philippines, 1978– .

Fisher, Roberta Mae Johnson (Mrs. C. L.); CA; Philippines, 1978– .

Fleming, Connie Marie Ellard (Mrs. Phillip) (J); MS; Japan, 1974–76.

Fleming, Grace Courtney (J); NY; Argentina, 1977–78.

Fletcher, James Palmer, Jr.; DC; Okinawa, 1974– .

Fletcher, Donna Lee McDonald (Mrs. J. P., Jr.); TN; Okinawa, 1974– .

Fletcher, Woodrow Elmer; AR; Peru, 1975– .

Fletcher, Sylvia Jean Howard (Mrs. W. E.); OK; Peru, 1975– .

Flood, Joyce Ann (J); MO; Guatemala, 1971–73.

Florence, Frank Tillman, Jr. (A); KY; Colombia, 1970–73.

Florence, Leila Elizabeth Vater (Mrs. F. T.) (A); KY; Colombia, 1970–73.

Floyd, Erma Faye (J); MO; Indonesia, 1971–73.

Forbes, William Stanley (J); FL; Kenya, 1976–78.

Ford, David Allan; MO; Argentina, 1978– .

Ford, Janene Marie Wilson (Mrs. D. A.); AR; Argentina, 1978– .

Ford, Jack Wilkes (A); TX; Gaza, 1977– .

Ford, Charlotte Elizabeth Marr (Mrs. J. W.) (A); FL; Gaza, 1977– .

Foreman, Jo Anne; OH; Honduras, 1977– .

Forman, Cathy Sue (J); KY; Gaza, 1974–76.

Foster, Wilburn Furn, Jr. (A); TX; Korea, 1975–76; Venezuela, 1978–79.

Foster, Doris Ann Gummelt (Mrs. W. F., Jr.) (A); TX; Korea, 1975–76; Venezuela, 1978–79.

Foster, William Edwin, Jr. (J); SC; Okinawa, 1979– .

Fox, Richard Allen; TN; Indonesia, 1979– .

Fox, Joan Elaine Storrs (Mrs. R. A.); TN; Indonesia, 1979– .

Fox, Stephen Lee (J); CO; Hong Kong/Macao, 1977–79.

Frailey, Homer Valjean; WY; Morocco, 1978– .

Frailey, Mary Frances Walker (Mrs. H. V.); MS; Morocco, 1978– .

Franks, Jewel Nolan (A); AR; South Africa, 1978– .

Franks, Jeanne Sheridan (Mrs. J. N.) (A); OK; South Africa, 1978– .

Frazier, Jerry Allen (J); KS; Japan, 1976–78.

Frazier, William Donaldson; TN; Reappointed; Nigeria, 1979– .

Frazier, Ina Sandidge (Mrs. W. D.); TN; Reappointed; Nigeria, 1979– .

Freeman, Linda Joy (J); WA; Ecuador, 1979– .

French, Cheryl Kay (J); OH; Tanzania, 1978– .

French, Mary Jo Ann; KY; Peru, 1973– .

Frost, Patricia Jane; AR; Jordan, 1978– .

Fudge, Billie Frank; OK; Korea, 1973– .

Fudge, Peggy Ruth Webster (Mrs. B. F.); OK; Korea, 1973– .

Fulbright, Ellis Grady; NC; Zambia, 1974– .

Fulbright, Ruby Ann Jones (Mrs. E. G.); NC; Zambia, 1974– .

Fulks, Paul Leon, Jr. (J); TX; Germany, 1978–79.

Fulton, Rhonda Gaye (J); TX; Ghana, 1976–78.

Fuqua, Vivian A. (J); MS; Honduras, 1970–72.

Furlow, Thomas Langford (J); AL; Liberia, 1976–77.

Futch, Deborah Lynn (J); TX; Argentina, 1975–77.

Futrell, Russell Wayne (J); LA; Lebanon, 1978– .

Gaddis, William Rees, Jr.; TX; Indonesia, 1974– .

Gaddis, Linda Kay Nickell (Mrs. W. R., Jr.); OK; Indonesia, 1974– .

Gadway, Ann Irene (J); WA; Paraguay, 1979– .

Gaines, Anita Valrie (J); TX; Chile, 1976–78.

Gaines, Jane Ellen; AL; Reappointed; Nigeria, 1977– .

Gammon, William Clarence (J); VA; Botswana, 1979– .

Gannon, Kerry Charles (J); CA; Kenya, 1979– .

Gardner, Charles Kenneth; NC; Taiwan, 1974– .

Gardner, Betty Ruth Little (Mrs. C. K.); NC; Taiwan, 1974– .

Gardner, Donald Duane; TX; Hong Kong, 1979– .

Gardner, Edna Denise (J); CA; Colombia, 1975; Venezuela, 1975–77.

Gardner, Pamela Anne (J); VA; Paraguay, 1977–79.

Garner, Linda Faye (SP); TX; India, 1973–76.

Garner, Sharon Lee (J); MD; Indonesia, 1971–73.

Garrett, Alita Beth (J); NM; Macao, 1979– .

Garrett, Robert Irving, Jr.; TX; Argentina, 1979– .

Garrett, Nelda Jane Huff (Mrs. R. I., Jr.); TX; Argentina, 1979– .

Gary, Alvin Lynn; TX; French West Indies, 1972– .

Gary, Judy Earlene Bergstrom (Mrs. A. L.); NM; French West Indies, 1972– .

Gaskin, Raymond Kenneth; FL; Dahomey, 1973–73.

Gaskin, Jewell Horton (Mrs. R. K.); FL; Dahomey, 1973–73.

Gaston, Minnie Alice (A); WV; Surinam, 1978– .

Gates, Linda Beth (J); SC; Guadaloupe, 1973–75.

Gates, Michael David (J); LA; Philippines, 1973–75.

Gatewood, Jack Dale (J); OK; Brazil, 1974–76.

Gaunt, Gary Allen (J); MO; Rhodesia, 1977–78; Malawi, 1978–79.

Gay, Larry Nelson (J); AL; Venezuela, 1977–79.

Gay, Susan Frances Tribble, (Mrs. L. N.) (J); AL; Venezuela, 1977–79.

Geiger, Robert Edwards (A); CA; Jordan, 1976–78.

Geiger, Karla Fae McClendon (Mrs. R. E.) (A); AR; Jordan, 1976–78.

Gellerstedt, John Robert (J); GA; Japan, 1978– .

Gera, George Michael; NY; French West Indies, 1977– .

Gera, Sheryl Ann Carter (Mrs. G. M.); DC; French West Indies, 1977– .

Gibson, Fred Meyer (A); AL; Singapore, 1977– .

Gibson, Mary Ella Bowers (Mrs. F. M.) (A); TN; Singapore, 1977– .

Gierhart, Robert Dale; CO; Japan, 1978– .

Gierhart, Gail Chiemi Morihara (Mrs. R. D.); HI; Japan, 1978– .

Gilger, Steven Mark (J); TX; Ghana, 1978– .

Gilger, Nita Jean Hyden (Mrs. S. M.) (J); TX; Ghana, 1978– .

Gillchrest, Beverly Jean (J); OR; Venezuela, 1971–73.

Gilliland, Karen Lynn (J); OK; Colombia, 1973–75.

Gipson, Joanna Lee (J); TX; Guatemala, 1977–79.

Girard, William Meshew; CA; Korea, 1978– .

Girard, Charlotte Miriah Rawls (Mrs. W. M.); AL; Korea, 1978– .

Glascock, Patricia Carol (J); MD; Tanzania, 1978– .

Glass, Kenneth Denton (A); AL; Philippines, 1971–74.

Glass, Cona Amodean Booher (Mrs. K. D.) (A); OK; Philippines, 1971–74.

Glaze, Betty Ann (J); LA; Senegal, 1976–77; Ghana, 1977–78.

Glenn, Charles Kenneth; GA; Germany, 1970–75; 1979– ; Liberia, 1975–76; Iran, 1977–79.

Glenn, Beth Boroughs (Mrs. C. K.); SC; Germany, 1970–75; 1979– ; Liberia, 1975–76; Iran, 1977–79.

Glenn, Don Tyrone; AL; Togo, 1976– .

Glenn, Joy Ada Williams (Mrs. D. T.); AL; Togo, 1976– .

Glenn, George Michael; CO; Venezuela, 1978– .

Glenn, Rebecca Sue Ratliff (Mrs. G. M.); KY; Venezuela, 1978– .

Goad, Kenneth Lee; TX; Vietnam, 1972–75; Philippines, 1975–78.

Goad, Elizabeth Scott (Mrs. K. L.); TX; Vietnam, 1972–75; Philippines, 1975–78.

Goff, William Edward; TX; Venezuela, 1971– .

Goff, Emilee Griffith (Mrs. W. E.); TX; Venezuela, 1971– .

Golmon, Robert Truett; MS; Malaysia, 1971–77; Philippines, 1977– .

Golmon, Angelyn Deaton (Mrs. R. T.); TN; Malaysia, 1971–77; Philippines, 1977– .

Gonzales, Michael Anthony; TX; Spain, 1976– .

Gonzales, Dalia Marroquin (Mrs. M. A.); TX; Spain, 1976– .

Gooch, David Lee (J); TN; Hong Kong/Macao, 1970–72.

Goodgame, Richard Wilder; TN; Uganda, 1979– .

Goodgame, Susan Boone (Mrs. R. W.); TX; Uganda, 1979– .

Goodman, Thomas Kime (A); TX; Nigeria, 1973–77.

Goodman, Georgia Dell Pendley (Mrs. T. K.) (A); TX; Nigeria, 1973–77.

Goodwin, Jerry Dan (J); TX; Hong Kong/Macao, 1970–71.

Goodwin, Samuel Dennis (J); AL; Korea, 1973–75.

Gopffarth, William; TX; Philippines, 1974– .

Gopffarth, Ruby Darlene Mitchell (Mrs. William); TX; Philippines, 1974– .

Gordon, Vickie Lynn (J); NC; Malawi, 1972–74.

Graham, Cornelia Ruth (J); KY; Tanzania, 1976–78.

Graham, Donald William; TN; Peru, 1970–72.

Graham, Ramona Jean Harrell (Mrs. D. W.); AL; Peru, 1970–72.

Grammier, Mary E. (J); TX; Thailand, 1970–72.

Granberry, Diana Lee (J); TX; Venezuela, 1973–75.

Grant, Connie Ann (J); FL; Brazil, 1979– .

Graves, Charles Dudley (J); AL; Italy, 1972–74.

Graves, James Frederick, Jr. (SP); KY; Ghana, 1976–76.

Graves, Alecia Diane Franklin (Mrs. J. F., Jr.) (SP); SC; Ghana, 1976–76.

Gray, Elton Pierce (A); TN; Okinawa, 1970– .

Gray, Dorothy Marie Eavenson (Mrs. E. P.) (A); MS; Okinawa, 1970– .

Gray, Harold Edward (J); AL; Ethiopia, 1975–76; Kenya, 1976–77.

Gray, John Adam; PA; Upper Volta, 1975– .

Gray, Joanne Mary Garlow (Mrs. J. A.); India; Upper Volta, 1975– .

Gray, Patricia Jean (J); IN; Switzerland, 1979– .

Green, James Edwin (A); OK; Kenya, 1976– .

Green, Ruth Ann Hill (Mrs. J. E.) (A); OK; Kenya, 1976– .

Green, James Henry; LA; Reappointed; Panama, 1975– .

Green, Barbara Hanscom (Mrs. J. H.); IL; Reappointed; Panama, 1975– .

Green, John George (A); AL; Korea, 1979– .

Green, Mary Edna Burke (Mrs. J. G.) (A); AL; Korea, 1979– .

Green, Ray Franklin (A); AL; Taiwan, 1978– .

Green, Grace Virginia Graben (Mrs. R. F.) (A); AL; Taiwan, 1978– .

Greer, Gary Michael; OH; Gaza, 1978– .

Greer, Frances Elaine Fleming (Mrs. G. M.); SC; Gaza, 1978– .

Greer, Felix Vardaman, Jr.;
LA; Liberia, 1979- .

Greer, Frances Waldine
Brummett (Mrs. F. V., Jr.);
MS; Liberia, 1979- .

Gregory, Mary Catherine (J);
MO; Hong Kong, 1975-77.

Gresham, Lamar Wayne; GA;
Philippines, 1970- .

Gresham, Betty Lucretia
Aultman (Mrs. L. W.); GA;
Philippines, 1970- .

Griffin, Stephen Dale (J); FL;
Zambia, 1973-75.

Griffith, Mary Frances (J); MO;
Taiwan, 1977-79.

Grindstaff, Jackie Carol (J); TN;
Spain, 1978- .

Grohman, Tyrrel Christopher
(J); TX; Dominican Republic,
1978- .

Grohman, Alicia Kaye Smith
(Mrs. T. C.) (J); TX;
Dominican Republic,
1978- .

Grosdidier, Glen Leroy; TX;
Philippines, 1973- .

Grosdidier, Ruth Elizabeth
Trahan (Mrs. G. L.); TX;
Philippines, 1973- .

Groseclose, Leslie David; WV;
Israel, 1976- .

Grossman, Paul Henry; IN;
Reappointed; Senegal,
1977- .

Grossman, Peggy Chamberlin
(Mrs. P. H.); KY;
Reappointed; Senegal,
1977- .

Grumbles, Mark Kevin (J); VA;
Paraguay, 1975-77.

Gruver, Daniel David Isaiah
(A); MO; Panama, 1975-75.

Gruver, Jane Arnetta Miller
(Mrs. D. D. I.) (A); AR;
Panama, 1975-75.

Gryseels, Diane E. (J); TX;
Vietnam, 1970-72.

Guest, Ronda Lou (J); AL;
Mexico, 1971-73.

Guest, Sharon Sue (J); AL;
Brazil, 1973-75.

Gunn, Shirley Ann; NC;
Nigeria, 1975- .

Gurney, Julius, III (J); NM;
Colombia, 1979- .

Gustman, Ronald Preston; WA;
Zambia, 1979- .

Gustman, Shirley Anita
Mohundro (Mrs. R. P.); TN;
Zambia, 1979- .

Guyton, Reba Ann (J); GA;
Korea, 1976-78.

Gwathmey, Ellen Temple (J);
VA; Japan, 1972-74.

Haga, Connie Ann (J); GA;
Yemen, 1978- .

Hagood, Charles David; AL;
Chile, 1978- .

Hagood, Rebecca Jean Adams
(Mrs. C. D.); TX; Chile,
1978- .

Hale, George Cecil; GA; Peru,
1978- .

Hale, Mary Suzanne McQuade
(Mrs. G. C.); CA; Peru,
1978- .

Hall, Carl Ray; AR; Kenya,
1970- .

Hall, Alice Geraldine Wright
(Mrs. C. R.); AR; Kenya,
1970- .

Hall, Cynthia Karen; TX;
Brazil, 1979- .

Hall, Diana Louise; AL;
Colombia, 1973- .

Hall, Nancy Annette; VA;
Jordan, 1973-77; Gaza,
1977- .

Hall, Robert Louis, Jr. (J); TN;
Kenya, 1972-74.

Hall, Alice Suzanne Taylor
(Mrs. R. L., Jr.) (J); TN;
Kenya, 1972-74.

Hall, Thoma Jan (J); AL;
Taiwan, 1975-77.

Halsell, Thomas Earle, Jr.; IN;
Senegal, 1976- .

Halsell, Frances Marion
Marchiando (Mrs. T. E., Jr.);
TX; Senegal, 1976- .

Ham, Nina Faye (J); AL;
Paraguay, 1979- .

Hampsher, Harry Frank (A);
PA; Portugal, 1977- .

Hampsher, Martha Florence
Leob (Mrs. H. F.) (A); PA;
Portugal, 1977- .

Hampton, Charles Alvis (A);
AR; Ethiopia, 1976-77; South
Africa, 1977- .

Hampton, Evelyn Marie Harden
(Mrs. C. A.) (A); AR;
Ethiopia, 1976-77; South
Africa, 1977- .

Hancock, Harold Ray; AL;
Korea, 1970- .

Hancock, Mary Helen Lee
(Mrs. H. R.); AL; Korea,
1970- .

Hancox, Jack Donald; TN;
Reappointed; Haiti, 1978- .

Hancox, Doris Hughes White
(Mrs. J. D.); TN;
Reappointed; Haiti, 1978- .

Haney, David Warner (A); TX;
Indonesia, 1974-78.

Haney, Julia Jenett Brown (Mrs.
D. W.) (A); TX; Indonesia,
1974-78.

Hankins, Jerry Ronald (J); AL;
Japan, 1975-77.

Hannah, Glenda Joyce (J); NC;
Mexico, 1974-76.

Hardeman, George Walton, III;
SC; Guatemala, 1971- .

Hardeman, Helen Lynn Dalton
(Mrs. G. W., III); GA;
Guatemala, 1971- .

Hardie, Charles Curtis; AL;
Taiwan, 1974- .

Hardie, Phyllis Jean Garner
(Mrs. C. C.); GA; Taiwan,
1974- .

Hardin, Carol Lee (J); FL;
Bangladesh, 1976-78.

Hardin, Doylene (J); TX;
Mexico, 1979- .

Hardin, Jennifer (J); LA;
Taiwan, 1976-78.

Hare, Stanley Horace (J); NC;
Liberia, 1979- .

Harless, James Clyde; AL;
Colombia, 1970- .

Harless, Jean Kay Hairston
(Mrs. J. C.); AL; Colombia,
1970- .

Harmon, Peggie Emmaline; NC;
Brazil, 1973- .

Harms, William David; CT;
Honduras, 1972- .

Harms, Billie Joyce Harrison
(Mrs. W. D.); IN; Honduras,
1972- .

Harnage, Elizabeth Irene (J);
FL; Mexico, 1972-73.

Harner, Dean Frederick; FL;
Brazil, 1971- .

Harner, Shirley Kay Butler
(Mrs. D. F.); IL; Brazil,
1971- .

Harper, Charles Lee (J);
Paraguay, 1979- .

Harper, Oliver Hunt; FL;
Indonesia, 1970- .

Harper, Virginia Louise Nethery
(Mrs. O. H.); AL; Indonesia,
1970- .

Harper, Richard Lynn; TX;
Argentina, 1977- .

Harper, Kathy Loyce Wylie
(Mrs. R. L.); TX; Argentina,
1977- .

Harper, Stanley Lawrence (J);
MS; Rhodesia, 1975-77.

Harper, William Robert (J);
Paraguay; Venezuela,
1975-77.

Harrell, Norman Lynn; TX;
Portugal, 1971- .

Harrell, Gunita Lois Musick
(Mrs. N. L.); TX; Portugal,
1971- .

Harrington, Judith Inez (J);
TX; Rhodesia, 1971-73.

Harris, Carolyn Knight (J); VA;
Bophuthatswana, 1978- .

Harris, Denise Bernice (J); TN;
Botswana, 1979- .

Harris, James Gordon, III; LA;
Philippines, 1970-75.

Harris, Joyce Behm (Mrs. J. G.,
III); IN; Philippines, 1970-75.

Harris, Jerry Leslie; NM;
Windward Islands, 1975- .

Harris, Ruth Ann Barnes (Mrs.
J. L.); OK; Windward
Islands, 1975- .

Harris, Marjorie Jane (J); NC;
Taiwan, 1974-76.

Harris, Marlin Jefferson (J);
AL; Bangladesh, 1975-77.

Harris, Mary Anne (J); GA;
Jordan, 1979- .

Harris, Ruth Ladd (Mrs. R.
L.); FL; Bermuda, 1978- .

Harrison, Rebecca Ann (J); GA;
Jordan, 1978- .

Hart, Donald Gary; AL;
Venezuela, 1978- .

Hart, Patricia Ann Creel (Mrs. D. G.); AL; Venezuela, 1978- .

Harthcock, Edward Gary (A); MS; Leeward Islands, 1975- .

Harthcock, Evelyn Dorothy White (Mrs. E. G.) (A); NC; Leeward Islands, 1975- .

Harvey, Jimmie Lewis; TX; Indonesia, 1972-79.

Harvey, Roma Elaine Kelsey (Mrs. J. L.); MO; Indonesia, 1972-79.

Hasenmyer, Wayne Leon; IN; Japan, 1971-79.

Hasenmyer, Linda Lee DeMar (Mrs. W. L.); KY; Japan, 1971-79.

Hatcher, Marilyn Marie (J); MO; India, 1970-72.

Hausler, James Darrell; OK; Paraguay, 1974- .

Hausler, Gloria Jean Young (Mrs. J. D.); TX; Paraguay, 1974- .

Hawkins, Charles Elery; GA; Philippines, 1975- .

Hawkins, Bette Ann White (Mrs. C. E.); IL; Philippines, 1975- .

Hawkins, Roy Dean; AR; Venezuela, 1973- .

Hawkins, Judith Ellen Palmer (Mrs. R. D.); OK; Venezuela, 1973- .

Hayes, David Lyle (J); MI; Ghana, 1977-79.

Hayes, Ralph William; TX; Mexico, 1974- .

Hayes, Judith Faye Endel (Mrs. R. W.); TX; Mexico, 1974- .

Hayes, Tome Ray; LA; Lebanon, 1974-78.

Hayes, Gayle Ann Burton (Mrs. T. R.); OK; Lebanon, 1974-78.

Haylock, Arthur Ray; FL; Reappointed; Dominican Republic, 1970- .

Haylock, Martha Gean Higdon (Mrs. A. R.); AL; Reappointed; Dominican Republic, 1970- .

Haylock, Janet Lee (J); FL; Mexico, 1979- .

Hays, Ida Mae; MO; Brazil, 1971- .

Haywood, Kenneth Price (SP); KY; Ghana, 1979- .

Haywood, Laney Carroll Jordan (Mrs. K. P.) (SP); KY; Ghana, 1979- .

Hazzard, Robert Dean; IN; Indonesia, 1975-79; Philippines, 1979- .

Hazzard, Anna Kay Grove (Mrs. R. D.); PA; Indonesia, 1975-79; Philippines, 1979- .

Hearon, Thomas Eldon (J); LA; Argentina, 1973-75.

Hebb, John Walter, Jr.; WV; Mexico, 1976- .

Hebb, Pauline Rebecca Hansen (Mrs. J. W., Jr.); FL; Mexico, 1976- .

Heflin, Billie Kay (J); AL; Leeward Islands, 1979- .

Helton, David Arthur; MO; Mexico, 1975- .

Helton, Mary Jan Rodgers (Mrs. D. A.); MO; Mexico, 1975- .

Helton, Yvonne Erma; KS; Guatemala, 1975- .

Henderson, Ronald David (J); OK; Austria, 1972-74.

Henderson, Sandra Gay (J); TX; Rhodesia, 1970-72.

Henderson, Susan Kay (J); VA; Colombia, 1973-75.

Hendricks, Melinda Jo (J); AR; Paraguay, 1979- .

Hendrickson, Francis Harry (A); PA; Kenya, 1977- .

Hendrickson, Phyllis Mary Martin (Mrs. F. H.) (A); NB; Kenya, 1977- .

Henry, Larry William; CO; Spain, 1975- .

Henry, Marilyn Virgie Alford (Mrs. L. W.); NM; Spain, 1975- .

Hepp, Patrick Alan (J); KY; Bangladesh, 1976-78.

Herbert, Janet Susan (J); AL; Bahamas, 1978- .

Herman, Michael Dennis; NC; Colombia, 1978- .

Herman, Betsy Love Newton (Mrs. M. D.); NC; Colombia, 1978- .

Hernandez, Melba (J); TX; Mexico, 1974-76.

Herrin, Debra Jane (J); NC; Philippines, 1976-78.

Herrington, Russell Arnette; MS; Costa Rica, 1973- .

Herrington, Brenda Annette Horton (Mrs. R. A.); GA; Costa Rica, 1973- .

Heskett, John Phillips (A); AR; Mexico, 1977-77.

Heskett, Lorene Genevieve Burton (Mrs. J. P.) (A); MO; Mexico, 1977-77.

Hester, Jenifred Ann; TX; Colombia, 1973- .

Hickey, Robert Deon (J); IL; Rhodesia, 1970-72.

Hickey, Vicki D. Stowers (Mrs. R. D.) (J); IL; Rhodesia, 1970-72.

Hickman, Karen Jo (J); KS; Colombia, 1979- .

Hicks, Gordon Scott (J); OK; Venezuela, 1979- .

Hicks, Margaret Lue (J); MS; Yemen/India, 1976-78.

Hicks, Pamela Lu (J); TX; Peru, 1977-79.

Hicks, Raymond Curtis; MI; Israel, 1978- .

Hicks, Beverly Ann Miller (Mrs. R. C.); KY; Israel, 1978- .

Hicks, Steven Patrick; LA; Mexico, 1973- .

Hicks, Minnie Katheryn Greer (Mrs. S. P.); MS; Mexico, 1973- .

Highfill, Donald Bryan; OK; Brazil, 1973- .

Highfill, Erma Ann Hawkins (Mrs. D. B.); MO; Brazil, 1973- .

Hightower, Veldee Arnold; SC; Zambia, 1979- .

Hightower, Sharon Peggy Dean (Mrs. V. A.); GA; Zambia, 1979- .

Hilbun, William Marvin, Jr. (SP); MS; Nigeria, 1971-72.

Hilbun, Lucy Claire Ewing (Mrs. W. M., Jr.) (SP); MS; Nigeria, 1971-72.

Hill, Daniel Robert; GA; Bangladesh, 1973- .

Hill, Delores Olivia Wilson (Mrs. D. R.); TX; Bangladesh, 1973- .

Hill, Georgia Carolyn; CA; Brazil, 1978- .

Hill, James Allen; AL; Philippines, 1975- .

Hill, Emily Elizabeth Gordon (Mrs. J. A.); NC; Philippines, 1975- .

Hill, John Albert (A); AL; Portugal, 1978- .

Hill, Evelyne Marie Campbell (Mrs. J. A.) (A); KY; Portugal, 1978- .

Hill, Margaret Elizabeth (J); GA; Rhodesia, 1976-78.

Hill, Minnie Gail; AL; India, 1978- .

Hill, Otis Monroe; SC; Colombia, 1973-79.

Hill, Marjorie Wynn Blackwell, (Mrs. O. M.); SC; Colombia, 1973-79.

Hill, Rebecca Susan (J); VA; Peru, 1974-76.

Hill, Ronald Elmer; TX; Liberia, 1974- .

Hill, Sharon Lynn Naylor (Mrs. R. E.); OK; Liberia, 1974- .

Hinderer, Linda Kay (J); KS; Hong Kong, 1976-78.

Hines, James Frank (J); OK; Ghana, 1972-74.

Hines, John Brantley (A); GA; Trinidad, 1971-71.

Hines, Margaret Lela Louise Leek (Mrs. J. B.) (A); MO; Trinidad, 1971-71.

Hinton, Kenneth Clayton; AL; Indonesia, 1977- .

Hinton, Thomas Russell (J); NC; Tanzania, 1978- .

Hinton, Kim Maria Allen (Mrs. T. R.) (J); NC; Tanzania, 1978- .

Hite, Raymond Harmon; VA; Ghana, 1974-77.

Hite, Vivian Gail Hargrove (Mrs. R. H.); MO; Ghana, 1974-77.

Hitt, William Lee; TX; Thailand, 1975– .

Hitt, Kaaren Lee Hammock (Mrs. W. L.); TX; Thailand, 1975– .

Ho, Frances Chui Yiu (J); China; Vietnam, 1971–73.

Hoaldridge, Vernon Marti, Jr.; TX; Israel, 1971– .

Hoaldridge, Judy Ann Farmer (Mrs. V. M., Jr.); TX; Israel, 1971– .

Hodges, Albert Roy; TX; Upper Volta, 1978– .

Hodges, Karen Sue Atwood (Mrs. A. R.); AR; Upper Volta, 1978– .

Hodges, David William; MO; Brazil, 1979– .

Hodges, Ramona Gay Miller (Mrs. D. W.); CO; Brazil, 1979– .

Hoffman, Deborah Jean (J); TX; Nigeria, 1976; Rhodesia, 1976–77.

Hoffman, Michaelee Marie (J); TX; Brazil, 1974–76.

Hogstrom, Minda Irene (J); LA; Gaza, 1976–78.

Holcomb, Sandra Jeanne (J); OK; Colombia, 1970–72.

Holden, Gregory Brian; NC; Philippines, 1978– .

Holden, Wanda Joan Durham (Mrs. G. B.); GA; Philippines, 1978– .

Holder, George Richard; OK; Colombia, 1973–76.

Holder, Sharon Rogene Hubbard (Mrs. G. R.); TX; Colombia, 1973–76.

Holder, Richard Albertus; TN; Paraguay, 1976– .

Holder, Carolyn Grace Pederson (Mrs. R. A.); TX; Paraguay, 1976– .

Holder, Vivian Dell; LA; Reappointed; Liberia, 1979– .

Hollamon, William Earl, Jr. (J); NC; Kenya, 1979– .

Holland, Eleanor Lois (J); GA; Japan, 1971–73.

Holland, James Vernon; TX; Angola, 1974–76; Botswana, 1976–77; Mexico, 1977– .

Holland, Carolyn Gene Roach (Mrs. J. V.); TX; Angola, 1974–76; Botswana, 1976–77; Mexico, 1977– .

Holland, Sue Ann (J); OH; Yemen, 1979– .

Hollaway, Ralph William; AR; Japan, 1972–76; Morocco, 1978– .

Hollaway, Linda Frances Louton (Mrs. R. W.); FL; Japan, 1972–76; Morocco, 1978– .

Hollenbaugh, Wayne Carl (J); VA; Liberia, 1976–78.

Holmes, Dorothy Ann (J); Canada; Argentina, 1979– .

Holt, Gerald Howard, Jr.; NM; Colombia, 1973– .

Holt, Marcie Virginia Roman (Mrs. G. H., Jr.); IL; Colombia, 1973– .

Holt, Katherine Hull (J); TN; Japan, 1970–72.

Holt, Ted Howard (J); TN; Mexico, 1979– .

Holt, William Rex, Jr.; AR; Togo, 1975– .

Holt, Sharon Kay Puckett (Mrs. W. R., Jr.); AR; Togo, 1975– .

Holth, William Judson (SP); FL; Windward Islands, 1978–79.

Holth, Barbara Anne Delchamps (Mrs. W. J.) (SP); WV; Windward Islands, 1978–79.

Honeycutt, Dwight Alec; AL; Colombia, 1977– .

Honeycutt, Ruth Patricia Bateman (Mrs. D. A.); GA; Colombia, 1977– .

Hood, Bobby Terrell; MS; Argentina, 1971–75.

Hood, Della Sue Bates (Mrs. B. T.); AL; Argentina, 1971–75.

Hook, Charles Rogers (A); SC; Windward Islands, 1979– .

Hook, Martha Anne Rush (Mrs. C. R.) (A); SC; Windward Islands, 1979– .

Hopkins, Patricia Sue (J); KY; Philippines, 1972–74.

Hopper, Karen Lynn; WA; Philippines, 1974– .

Horn, Richard Noel; TX; Japan, 1972– .

Horn, Joan Kay Ezell (Mrs. R. N.); NM; Japan, 1972– .

Horn, Susan Gail (J); VA; India, 1977–79.

Horne, Raymond Dwight; GA; Togo, 1976– .

Horne, Janice Gaye Cochran (Mrs. R. D.); GA; Togo, 1976– .

Horner, Robert William, III; AL; Chile, 1977– .

Horner, Mary Margaret Pruitt (Mrs. R. W., III); AL; Chile, 1977– .

Hortin, Mary Jane (J); IN; Japan, 1975–77.

Horton, James Edwin; OK; Kenya, 1973– .

Horton, Mary Frances Gale (Mrs. J. E.); OK; Kenya, 1973– .

Hoskins, Martha Sue (J); VA; Brazil, 1979– .

Hostetler, Harold Rutherford, Jr.; SD; Panama, 1979– .

Hostetler, Brenda Skelton (Mrs. H. R., Jr.); VA; Panama, 1979– .

House, Janice Marie (J); TN; Japan, 1975–77.

Houser, James Stacy; CA; Tanzania, 1979– .

Houser, Sheila Ann Graham (Mrs. J. S.); Lebanon; Tanzania, 1979– .

Housley, Doris Elaine (J); GA; Vietnam, 1970–72.

Houston, Carl William (A); SC; Malawi, 1978– .

Houston, Doris Gertrude Bivens (Mrs. C. W.) (A); SC; Malawi, 1978– .

Houston, Susan Marie (J); MO; Argentina, 1973–75.

Houts, Laura Carolyn; IA; Ghana, 1976– .

Howard, Robin Ann (J); TN; Bophuthatswana, 1978– .

Howell, Charles Herbert; NC; Peru, 1978– .

Howell, Judith Gail O'Ferrell (Mrs. C. H.); NC; Peru, 1978– .

Hubbard, Jerry Anderson; MO; Zambia, 1973– .

Hubbard, Dorothy Louise Smart (Mrs. J. A.); TX; Zambia, 1973– .

Hudson, Cheryl Lynn (J); MO; Taiwan, 1975–77.

Hudson, Doris Alma Lee (Mrs. E. T.) (SP); LA; Jordan, 1979– .

Hudson, Michael Dennis; MI; Bahamas, 1978– .

Hudson, Gloria Durrett (Mrs. M. D.); KY; Bahamas, 1978– .

Huesing, Gretchen Anita (J); TX; Colombia, 1973–75.

Huey, Jimmy Mac (J); TX; Philippines, 1974–76.

Huey, Sylvia Ann Schimek (Mrs. J. M) (J); TX; Philippines, 1974–76.

Huffman, Cindra Gayle (J); FL; India, 1971–73.

Huffman, Marilyn Kaye (J); KY; Japan, 1976–78.

Hughes, Edna Reid (J); KY; Ethiopia, 1971–73.

Hughes, Juanita Parrott (Mrs. T. W.); LA; Nigeria, 1973–77.

Hughes, Larry Vernon (J); OK; Malawi, 1970–72.

Hughes, Mary Lois (J); SD; Brazil, 1977–79.

Hughes, Robert Don; CA; Nigeria, 1979– .

Hughes, Teresia Gail Wallace (Mrs. R. D.); AL; Nigeria, 1979– .

Hughes, Stanley LeRoy (J); TX; Hong Kong, 1974–76.

Hughes, Jean Elaine Leverett (Mrs. S. L.) (J); TX; Hong Kong, 1974–76.

Hulet, Clayton Keith; OK; Brazil, 1973– .

Hulet, Jerrie Leta Bell (Mrs. C. K.); OK; Brazil, 1973– .

Hull, Michael John; CA; Mexico, 1978– .

Hull, Bonnie Lucille Eby (Mrs. M. J.); MI; Mexico, 1978– .

Humble, David Earl; AR; Japan, 1979– .

Humphrey, Raymond David (A); AR; Zambia, 1971–75.

Humphrey, Betty Lou Hutchins
(Mrs. R. D.) (A); AR;
Zambia, 1971–75.

Huneycutt, Thomas Alfred; NC;
Austria, 1977– .

Huneycutt, Sandra Gayle Argo
(Mrs. T. A.); NC; Austria,
1977– .

Hunt, Margaret Ann (J); TX;
India, 1972–74.

Hunt, Ronald Wayne; CA;
Liberia, 1973–79.

Hunt, Anita Kaye Coleman
(Mrs. R. W.); OK; Liberia,
1973–79.

Hunt, Susan Lynn (J); MO;
Malawi, 1972–74.

Hunter, Robert Cordell (A); SC;
Tanzania, 1978– .

Hunger, Barbara Anne Barnes
(Mrs. R. C.) (A); NC;
Tanzania, 1978– .

Hunter, William Hal (A); FL;
Japan, 1975–77.

Hunter, Esther Lena Strange
(Mrs. W. H.) (A); FL; Japan,
1975–77.

Hurst, Cynthia Kay (J); CA;
Mexico, 1979– .

Hutson, Cheryl Jan (J); IL;
Kenya, 1976–78.

Hyde, William Paul; IA;
Philippines, 1978– .

Hyde, Garlinda Sue Gage (Mrs.
W. P.); IA; Philippines,
1978– .

Isbell, Marcia Faye (J); GA;
Hong Kong, 1972–74.

Jackson, Cynthia Verlene (J);
OK; Chile, 1976–78.

Jackson, Thomas Eugene (J);
TN; Ghana, 1977–78.

Jackson, Thomas Teague; FL;
Korea, 1971– .

Jackson, Betty Barbara Swartz
(Mrs. T. T.); MO; Korea,
1971– .

Jacobs, Robert Raymond (J);
OK; Colombia, 1970–72.

Jacobson, David John; MN;
Costa Rica, 1974–79.

Jacobson, Janice Marie Bloomer
(Mrs. D. J.); OH; Costa
Rica, 1974–79.

Jacques, George Chester; AZ;
Taiwan, 1976– .

Jacques, Charlene Frances
McNamara (Mrs. G. C.);
CA; Taiwan, 1976– .

James, Sharon Elizabeth (J);
VA; Dominican Republic,
1974–76.

Jenkins, Orville Boyd; OK;
Kenya, 1975– .

Jenkins, Edith Marie McSwain
(Mrs. O. B.); AR; Kenya,
1975– .

Jennings, Alta Grace (J); LA;
Zambia, 1970–72.

Jennings, Lois Ann Drury (Mrs.
W. J.); AL; Brazil, 1973– .

Jernigan, Clarence Archibald
(SP); TX; Gaza, 1974–76.

Jernigan, Kathryn Elaine
English (Mrs. C. A.) (SP);
TX; Gaza, 1974–76.

Johnson, Craig Allen; NM;
Mexico, 1979– .

Johnson, Brenda Diane Sealock
(Mrs. C. A.); GA; Mexico,
1979– .

Johnson, Daniel LaFloy (J); MS;
Bangladesh, 1979– .

Johnson, Dixie Dianne (J); KY;
Brazil, 1971–73.

Johnson, Donald Edwin; NJ;
Peru, 1979– .

Johnson, Linda Sue McNabb
(Mrs. D. E.); FL; Peru,
1979– .

Johnson, Donald Ray; MO;
Brazil, 1976– .

Johnson, Bethele Walker (Mrs.
D. R.); MO; Brazil, 1976– .

Johnson, Gay Lynn (J); TX;
Kenya, 1976–78.

Johnson, Gerald Dwight (J);
AR; Morocco, 1978–79;
Kenya, 1979– .

Johnson, Debbie Kay Wilson
(Mrs. G. D.) (J); AR;
Morocco, 1978–79; Kenya,
1979– .

Johnson, Janice Kay (J); DC;
Nigeria, 1977–79.

Johnson, Kimble Wade (J); MS;
Kenya, 1977–79.

Johnson, Leon Raymond (J);
AR; Tanzania, 1970–72.

Johnson, Robert Edward; VA;
Brazil, 1979– .

Johnson, Celia Claycomb (Mrs.
R. E.); TX; Brazil, 1979– .

Johnson, Wilson, III (J); VA;
Japan, 1978– .

Johnson, Anne Rowland Swann
(Mrs. Wilson, III) (J); VA;
Japan, 1978– .

Jolly, Lawson Elmer, Jr.; GA;
Costa Rica, 1970–72.

Jolly, Judith Lee Richbourg
(Mrs. L. E., Jr.); FL; Costa
Rica, 1970–72.

Jones, Barbara Ann (J); CA;
Philippines, 1978– .

Jones, Barbara Frances (J); NV;
Brazil, 1971–73.

Jones, Brenda Paige (J); AL;
Kenya, 1973–75.

Jones, Coy Walter, Jr.; GA;
Indonesia, 1975–78;
Philippines, 1978–79.

Jones, Theresa Diane Stephens
(Mrs. C. W., Jr.); GA;
Indonesia, 1975–78;
Philippines, 1978–79.

Jones, Doy Lee (A); AR;
Ecuador, 1977– .

Jones, Betty June Matts (Mrs.
D. L.) (A); OK; Ecuador,
1977– .

Jones, Jerry Ann (J); AR;
Tanzania, 1974–76.

Jones, Jerry Dale (J); NM;
Austria, 1970–72.

Jones, Joseph Randall; KY;
Paraguay, 1972–74.

Jones, Lawanna Kay Cain (Mrs.
J. R.); KY; Paraguay,
1972–74.

Jones, Michael Lloyd (J); CA;
Kenya, 1979– .

Jones, Pamela Sue Holloway
(Mrs. M. L.) (J); MO;
Kenya, 1979– .

Jones, Nancy Carol (J); TN;
Hong Kong, 1970–72.

Jones, Robert Edward (J); NC;
Honduras, 1977–79.

Jordan, Frances Ellen (J); TX;
Hong Kong, 1975–77.

Joslin, Alice Babbette (J); MO;
Kenya, 1973–75.

Joslin, Ruth Ann (J); MO;
Hong Kong, 1977–79.

Joule, Gail Parkison; OK;
Paraguay, 1971– .

Joule, Jerry Dona Divine (Mrs.
G. P.); OK; Paraguay,
1971– .

Joye, Raymond Dewey; SC;
Nigeria, 1971–77.

Joye, Margaret Oakes (Mrs. R.
D.); SC; Nigeria, 1971–77.

Kammerdiener, David Daniel
(J); OK; Uruguay, 1979– .

Kannon, Jerre Lynne (SP); GA;
Gaza, 1978–79.

Karr, John Paul (J); AL; Israel,
1979– .

Keathley, Monica Sue; MO;
Upper Volta, 1977– .

Keaton, Larry Neil; OH; Spain,
1973–76.

Keaton, Kitty Deborah Ray
(Mrs. L. N.); KY; Spain,
1973–76.

Keck, Dianne Lee (J); NC;
Japan, 1973–75.

Keller, Harriet Vivian (J); KY;
Lebanon, 1973–75.

Keller, Howard Wayne; LA;
Brazil, 1978– .

Keller, Linda Emma Richard
(Mrs. H. W.); LA; Brazil,
1978– .

Keller, Marsha Leigh (J); AL;
Argentina, 1974–76.

Kelley, David Neal (J); TX;
Ecuador, 1973–75.

Kellum, Douglas Lewis (J); MS;
Vietnam, 1972–74.

Kellum, James Lewis, Jr.; MS;
Vietnam, 1971–76;
Philippines, 1976– .

Kellum, Iva Paulette Wolfe
(Mrs. J. L., Jr.); MS;
Vietnam, 1971–76;
Philippines, 1976– .

Kelly, Emily Anne (J); AL;
Philippines, 1977–79.

Kelly, Noel Michael (J); TX;
Indonesia, 1971–73.

Kelly, Susan Diane Houghton
(Mrs. N. M.) (J); TX;
Indonesia, 1971–73.

Kendall, Floyd Kay; OK;
Thailand, 1978– .

Kendall, Jeanette Marie Hiskey (Mrs. F. K.); MO; Thailand, 1978- .

Kendrick, Karen Ann (J); AL; Kenya, 1978; Thailand, 1978- .

Kent, William Thomas; LA; Paraguay, 1974- .

Kent, Judith Claire Preddy (Mrs. W. T.); LA; Paraguay, 1974- .

Keown, Sherrill Ann (J); AL; Korea, 1974–76.

Key, Michael Herbert; TX; Togo, 1972- .

Key, Marsha Hall (Mrs. M. H.); TX; Togo, 1972- .

Keyes, Donna Lynne (J); MS; Brazil, 1973–75.

Kidd, Sanford Maxey, Jr.; VA; Kenya, 1974–75.

Kidd, Charlotte Sue Monk (Mrs. S. M., Jr.); GA; Kenya, 1974–75.

Kight, Carolyn (J); GA; Uganda, 1971–73.

Killian, Kathy Sue (J); NC; Israel, 1979- .

Kimberling, Beth Elaine (J); MO; Ecuador, 1977–79.

Kinchen, George Henry, Jr. (A); GA; Botswana, 1977- .

Kinchen, Sandra Martrelle Hicks (Mrs. G. H., Jr.) (A); GA; Botswana, 1977- .

King, Calvin Henry (J); GA; Ghana, 1976–78.

King, Melissa Kay (J); TX; Hong Kong, 1979- .

Kinnison, Jack William, Jr.; TX; Laos, 1972–75; Thailand, 1975- .

Kinnison, Ruth Lynnette Penuel (Mrs. J. W., Jr.); AL; Laos, 1972–75; Thailand, 1975- .

Kirby, Nathaniel Benjamin; AR; Venezuela, 1978- .

Kirby, Charlotte Halbert (Mrs. N. B.); AR; Venezuela, 1978- .

Kirkpatrick, Thomas Desmond; CA; Lebanon, 1972–73; Bangladesh, 1973- .

Kirkpatrick, Beverly June Wynn (Mrs. T. D.); OK; Lebanon, 1972–73; Bangladesh, 1973- .

Kirkpatrick, Vance Crawford; LA; Kenya, 1971- .

Kirkpatrick, Cherry Dance Pratt (Mrs. V. C.); LA; Kenya, 1971- .

Kirkwood, Virginia Ann (J); MD; Japan, 1979- .

Kitts, Iva Nell (J); NC; Japan, 1977–79.

Klein, Elizabeth Susan (J); CO; Tanzania, 1972–74.

Kliewer, Matthew Dean (J); OK; Philippines, 1977–79.

Kluck, Sharon Dianne (J); TX; Brazil, 1973–75.

Knight, Charles Gray; AL; Benin, 1978- .

Knight, Sharon Sizemore (Mrs. C. G.); AL; Benin, 1978- .

Koehn, William Edwin; KS; Yemen, 1974- .

Koehn, Martha Sue Elizabeth Walker (Mrs. W. E.); KS; Yemen, 1974- .

Koenig, Jodi Bernice (J); NY; Macao, 1979- .

Krueger, Walter Adam (J); MO; Botswana, 1979- .

Krueger, Cynthia Clarke (Mrs. W. A.) (J); TX; Botswana, 1979- .

Lace, Catherine Diane (J); PA; Thailand, 1974–76.

Lachina, Vincent Joseph (J); TN; Kenya, 1970–72.

Ladd, Fred Clinton (A); OK; Philippines, 1975–78.

Ladd, Sabra Marie Russell (Mrs. F. C.) (A); OK; Philippines, 1975–78.

Laffoon, Robert Glenn; MO; Reappointed; Tanzania, 1973–77.

Laffoon, Hannah Baker (Mrs. R. G.); MO; Reappointed; Tanzania, 1973–77.

Laird, James William; TX; Venezuela, 1977- .

Laird, Pamela Kaye Ingersoll (Mrs. J. W.); TX; Venezuela, 1977- .

Lamm, Wilma June (J); SC; Brazil, 1978- .

Land, Floyd Mitchell; TX; Togo, 1975–79; Ivory Coast, 1979- .

Land, Vivian Lea Shook (Mrs. F. M.); TX; Togo, 1975–79; Ivory Coast, 1979- .

Landers, John Monroe, Sr.; OK; Brazil, 1971- .

Landers, Sharon Sue Bamberry (Mrs. J. M., Sr.); KS; Brazil, 1971- .

Lane, Evelyn Ruth (J); NC; Rhodesia, 1976–78.

Lane, Joy Aileene (J); TX; Taiwan, 1979- .

Lane, Patricia Ruth (J); KS; Israel, 1977–79.

Langley, Edward Philip; TX; Rhodesia, 1971–79; Togo, 1979- .

Langley, Judy Mae Smith (Mrs. E. P.); TX; Rhodesia, 1971–79; Togo, 1979- .

Lanier, Carol Bomer (J); TN; Zambia, 1979- .

Lansford, Notie Harold, Jr. (J); TX; Kenya, 1976–78.

Laramore, John Ernest; GA; Guatemala, 1970–78.

Laramore, Nancy Sparks Roach (Mrs. J. E.); GA; Guatemala, 1970–78.

Larkin, Alicia Ellen (J); NJ; Spain, 1977–78.

Lascelles, Anita Ruth (J); TX; Paraguay, 1979- .

Lassiter, James Harold; OK; Vietnam, 1973–75; Ivory Coast, 1975- .

Lassiter, Barbara Anne Lindsey (Mrs. J. H.); Israel; Vietnam, 1973–75; Ivory Coast, 1975.

Latham, Tony Glenn; TN; Philippines, 1975- .

Latham, Kathy Frances Jennings (Mrs. T. G.); MS; Philippines, 1975- .

Lathrop, Felix Keith; FL; Liberia, 1976- .

Lathrop, Roxyanne Gail King (Mrs. F. K); FL; Liberia, 1976- .

Law, Thomas Lee, III; TX; Paraguay, 1978- .

Law, Linda Louise Roberts (Mrs. T. L., III); NC; Paraguay, 1978- .

Lawrence, Linda Sue (J); NC; Mexico, 1976–78.

Lawson, Barbara Eileen; VA; Indonesia, 1974–78.

Lawson, David Paul (J); TN; Kenya, 1976–78.

Layton, Bradley Ward; KS; Ecuador, 1978- .

Layton, Carol Ann Knight (Mrs. B. W.); TX; Ecuador, 1978- .

Leagans, Cecil Ellis, Jr.; NC; Colombia, 1978- .

Leagans, Julia Halbert (Mrs. C. E., Jr.); AR; Colombia, 1978- .

Leard, Annice Ellen (J); GA; Costa Rica, 1977–79.

Lee, David Armin; TX; Peru, 1978- .

Lee, Sandra Lyn Malloy (Mrs. D. A.); TX; Peru, 1978- .

Lee, Juniorous Archibald; AR; India, 1976- .

Lee, Carolyn Sue Stewart (Mrs. J. A.); AR; India, 1976- .

Lee, Larry Horace; AL; Windward Islands, 1979- .

Lee, Wanda Gail Seay (Mrs. L. H.); AL; Windward Islands, 1979- .

Lee, Paul Douglas, Jr.; MS; Spain, 1975- .

Lee, Brenda Anne Haggard (Mrs. P. D., Jr.); MS; Spain, 1975- .

Lee, Stan Ronald; SC; Rwanda, 1978- .

Lee, Beverly Marlene Long (Mrs. S. R.); SC; Rwanda, 1978- .

Leggett, John Lonzo (J); GA; Togo, 1972–74.

Lemaster, Richard Franklin, Jr.; MD; Benin, 1977- .

Lemaster, Joyce Ann Flood (Mrs. R. F., Jr.); MO; Benin, 1977- .

Lemoine, Byron Francis, III (J); LA; Israel, 1974–76.

Lewis, Roger Allan; TX; Colombia, 1975- .

Lewis, Carole Anne Saucier (Mrs. R. A.); TX; Colombia, 1975– .

Lidholm, Elaine Joy (J); MO; Kenya, 1972–74.

Linderman, John Broadus, Jr. (J); SC; Austria, 1978– .

Lindwall, David Erik (J); CA; Martinique, 1978– .

Linebarger, Gary Douglas; MO; Taiwan, 1973– .

Linebarger, Elizabeth Inez Erwin (Mrs. G. D.); NM; Taiwan, 1973– .

Linton, Kimberly Ann (J); TX; Brazil, 1979– .

Lochala, Richard Mark (J); AR; Philippines, 1978– .

Lochridge, James Thaddeaus; GA; Reappointed; Philippines, 1973– .

Lochridge, Mary Frances Manuel (Mrs. J. T.); NC; Reappointed; Philippines, 1973– .

Locke, Charles Kenneth (A); TX; Hong Kong, 1970–76.

Locke, Lou Ann Lewis (Mrs. C. K.) (A); NC; Hong Kong, 1970–76.

Lockhart, Mary Guy (J); MS; Rhodesia, 1972–74.

Long, Charles Percy; MS; Belgium, 1972–79.

Long, Sandra Sue Young (Mrs. C. P.); AR; Belgium, 1972–79.

Long, David Clifton; NC; Brazil, 1978– .

Long, Sue Renee Shamburger (Mrs. D. C.); TX; Brazil, 1978– .

Long, James Shannon; SC; Chile, 1972–75; 1978– .

Long, Miriam Loraine Patterson (Mrs. J. S.); SC; Chile, 1972–75; 1978– .

Longan, Marcia Lee (J); TX; Rhodesia, 1975–77.

Loo, Larry Yau Sing (A); HI; Tanzania, 1976– .

Loo, Sydney May Lee (Mrs. Larry) (A); HI; Tanzania, 1976– .

Looney, Anna Mae (J); OK; India, 1974–76.

Lotz, Karen Sue (J); TX; Brazil, 1974–76.

Lovegren, Mary Lee (J); Palestine; Nigeria, 1977–79.

Lumpkin, Cynthia Jane (J); TN; Ethiopia, 1975–77.

Maddox, Nancy Apple (J); IA; Nigeria, 1976–78.

Madon, Jacquelyn Alice (J); GA; Guatemala, 1975–77.

Magee, Bobby Gerald; MS; Chile, 1970–74; Colombia, 1974– .

Magee, Dolores Janette Bradley (Mrs. B. G.); MS; Chile, 1970–74; Colombia, 1974– .

Mandaville, Brice David (J); CA; Kenya, 1979– .

Maness, Wayne Edwin; MO; Philippines, 1971– .

Maness, Margaret Jeanne Swope (Mrs. W. E.); MO; Philippines, 1971– .

Manferd, Elliott; AL; Chile, 1975– .

Manferd, Rebecca Josephine Johnson (Mrs. Elliott); TX; Chile, 1975– .

Mangrum, Mary Elizabeth (J); TN; Costa Rica, 1974–76.

Mann, Lloyd Wesley; OK; Dominican Republic, 1971–79; Mexico, 1979– .

Mann, Wilma Mirela Mendoza (Mrs. L. W.); Costa Rica; Dominican Republic, 1971–79; Mexico, 1979– .

Mann, Nathaniel Edward; GA; Brazil, 1978– .

Mann, Gail Dixon (Mrs. N. E.); GA; Brazil, 1978– .

Mansker, Janis Lea (J); MO; Nigeria, 1979– .

Mantooth, Robert Donald; GA; Israel, 1973– .

Mantooth, Suzanne Chase Fitts (Mrs. R. D.); TN; Israel, 1973– .

Manuel, Ralph Eugene; OK; Brazil, 1979– .

Manuel, Donna Marie Acker (Mrs. R. E.); WI; Brazil, 1979– .

Marble, Elmo Russell (A); UT; Ecuador, 1971–75.

Marble, Floy Elizabeth Jacob (Mrs. E. R.) (A); China; Ecuador, 1971–75.

Marchiando, Frances Marion (J); TX; Ecuador, 1972–73.

Marlowe, Tommy Herold; LA; Togo, 1973–75.

Marlowe, Charlotte Flanagan (Mrs. T. H.); LA; Togo, 1973–75.

Maroney, Jimmy Kent; TX; Ghana, 1970–73; Ethiopia, 1973–78; Kenya, 1978– .

Maroney, Frances Kay Farmer (Mrs. J. K.); TX; Ghana, 1970–73; Ethiopia, 1973–78; Kenya, 1978– .

Martin, John Albert (J); AL; Hong Kong, 1979– .

Martin, Robert Jackson (A); NC; Liberia, 1978– .

Martin, Nancy Carolyn Palmer (Mrs. R. J.) (A); FL; Liberia, 1978– .

Martin, Theresa Ann (J); VA; Colombia, 1976; Mexico, 1976–78.

Martzen, Ernest Hinds; CA; Philippines, 1979– .

Martzen, Sandra Ellen Mancebo (Mrs. E. H.); CA; Philippines, 1979– .

Mashburn, Mary Margaret (J); NC; Venezuela, 1974–76.

Mashburn, Telfair James, III (J); AL; Israel, 1971–73.

Mason, Melba June; FL; Tanzania, 1971– .

Mason, William Cordell; AL; Tanzania, 1971–74; India, 1974–78.

Mason, Mona Dell Holloway (Mrs. W. C.); LA; Tanzania, 1971–74; India, 1974–78.

Mathis, James Franklin (J); NM; Ethiopia, 1973–75.

Mawk, Thomas Dean (J); MS; Brazil, 1976–78.

May, William Robert; AL; Brazil, 1978– .

May, Marilyn Doylene Jewell (Mrs. W. R.); VA; Brazil, 1978– .

Mayhall, Janet Marie (J); Nigeria; Brazil, 1976–78.

McAlister, Martha Ann; NC; Tanzania, 1978– .

McAninch, Ernest Gerard; GA; El Salvador, 1979– .

McAninch, Lee Ann Brittain (Mrs. E. G.); IL; El Salvador, 1979– .

McAtee, James Edward; MS; Indonesia, 1971– .

McAtee, Carolyn Lenora Mahaffey (Mrs. J. E.); MS; Indonesia, 1971– .

McAtee, Jerry Wade; SC; Jordan, 1976– .

McAtee, Frances Lorraine Easley (Mrs. J. W.); KY; Jordan, 1976– .

McBride, Juanita Loyce; TN; Gaza, 1978– .

McCalister, Joyce Dale (J); IN; Senegal, 1976–77.

McCall, William Earnest; TN; Togo, 1975– .

McCann, Rodney Edward (J); LA; Belgium, 1972–74.

McClung, Donald Len (J); GA; Kenya, 1977–79.

McClure, Carolyn Ruth (J); MO; Philippines, 1979– .

McConnell, Ruth Anne (J); KY; Yemen, 1977–79.

McCormick, David Morrison; IL; Hong Kong, 1974– .

McCormick, Deana Martyne Wear (Mrs. D. M.); CA; Hong Kong, 1974– .

McCoy, Gary Wayne; MO; Korea, 1974– .

McCoy, Mary Nell Swope (Mrs. G. W.); MO; Korea, 1974– .

McCoy, John Franklin, Jr.; GA; Nigeria, 1971–78.

McCoy, Barbara Irene Taylor (Mrs. J. F., Jr.); SC; Nigeria, 1971–78.

McCoy, Larry Rhyne; NC; Panama, 1977– .

McCoy, Charlot Lorene Fox (Mrs. L. R.); NC; Panama, 1977– .

McCullough, John Edward (J); AL; Tanzania, 1972–74.

McCustion, Debra Ann (J); AR; Liberia, 1977–79.

McDade, Richard Warren; TN; Colombia, 1976– .

McDade, Barbara Ann Bennett (Mrs. R. W.); TN; Colombia, 1976– .

McDaniel, Major Cyrus, Jr. (A); MS; Korea, 1973– .

McDaniel, June Evelyn Vineyard (Mrs. M. C., Jr.) (A); MS; Korea, 1973– .

McDaniel, Phyllis Esther (J); GA; Liberia, 1973–75.

McDonald, Grant Charles; PA; Colombia, 1977– .

McDonald, Elmire Aine Mende (Mrs. G. C.); MD; Colombia, 1977– .

McDonnough, Vallie Merle (A); IL; Philippines, 1970–71.

McDonnough, Helen Louise Hildebrandt (Mrs. V. M.) (A); IL; Philippines, 1970–71.

McDowell, Janet Lee (J); MO; Tanzania, 1977–79.

McEachern, Robert Thomas, Jr.; AZ; Korea, 1973– .

McEachern, Judy Gail Iglehart (Mrs. R. T., Jr.); TX; Korea, 1973– .

McEachin, Thomas Miller; GA; Taiwan, 1974– .

McEachin, Mary Blair Parrish (Mrs. T. M.); FL; Taiwan, 1974– .

McEntire, Dennis Pierce; VA; Paraguay, 1970– .

McEntire, Nancy Jean Reynolds (Mrs. D. P.); VA; Paraguay, 1970– .

McFadden, John Wilbur, Jr.; LA; Nigeria, 1972– .

McFadden, Floyd Alice McPhail (Mrs. J. W., Jr.); OK; Nigeria, 1972– .

McFadden, Roy Patton; SC; Dominican Republic, 1979– .

McFadden, Sue Whitmire (Mrs. R. P.); AL; Dominican Republic, 1979– .

McFerron, Jerry Don (J); TX; Japan, 1979– .

McGaha, Susan Annette (J); NC; Philippines, 1978– .

McGee, Cynthia Love; TN; Chile, 1977– .

McGill, Albert Oliver; AL; Panama, 1976–77.

McGill, Suzanne Price (Mrs. A. O.); AL; Panama, 1976–77.

McGlone, Gregory Scott (J); WV; Venezuela, 1975–77.

McKenzie, Carole Ellen (J); TN; Nigeria, 1979– .

McKinney, Jack Wallace, Jr.; OK; Zambia, 1978– .

McKinney, Gayle Easley (Mrs. J. W., Jr.); TX; Zambia, 1978– .

McKinnon, Darlene Ann (J); MD; Ghana, 1971–73.

McLean, Naomi Lee (SP); SC; Gaza, 1975–78.

McMannis, Everett Leo (J); KY; Botswana, 1972–74.

McMannis, Linda Grace Rice (Mrs. E. L.) (J); OH; Botswana, 1972–74.

McMichael, Juanita Anne (J); VA; Mexico, 1970–72.

McNair, John Louis; MS; India, 1974–76; Spain, 1976– .

McNair, Sarah Kathleen Lee (Mrs. J. L.); MS; India, 1974–76; Spain, 1976– .

McNeely, Donald Edward (A); TX; Zambia, 1976– .

McNeely, Clara Helen Trayler (Mrs. D. E.) (A); TX; Zambia, 1976– .

McNeil, Winston William; FL; Colombia, 1973–77.

McNeil, Patricia Naish (Mrs. W. W.); AL; Colombia, 1973–77.

McPherson, James Earl; TX; Lebanon, 1973–76; Jordan, 1976–77; Gaza, 1977– .

McPherson, Sharon Janet Hanson (Mrs. J. E.); AR; Lebanon, 1973–76; Jordan, 1976–77; Gaza, 1977– .

McPherson, John Thomas (J); TN; Zambia, 1971–73.

McQueen, Marcia Jayne (J); NC; Panama, 1979– .

McTyre, John Andrew (J); GA; Austria, 1979– .

Meacham, Harold Eugene; KS; Malawi, 1974–79; Transkei, 1979– .

Meacham, Cordelia Lavonne Thompson (Mrs. H. E.); TX; Malawi, 1974–79; Transkei, 1979– .

Meador, Clyde Davis, Jr.; AR; Indonesia, 1974– .

Meador, Lola Elaine Grisham (Mrs. C. D., Jr.); TX; Indonesia, 1974– .

Meador, Paula Wynn (J); TN; Paraguay, 1977–79.

Meadors, Paul Daniel (J); WV; Israel, 1975–77.

Meadows, Michael Gaston; TX; Japan, 1975– .

Meadows, Jane Catherine Carpenter (Mrs. M. G.); TX; Japan, 1975– .

Meares, Cathy Jan (J); TX; Ecuador, 1974–76.

Medley, Anne Wynelle (J); TX; Botswana, 1976–78.

Meister, Leland Austin (J); TX; Yemen, 1971–73.

Meister, Mildred Virginia Basden (Mrs. L. A.) (J); TX; Yemen, 1971–73.

Menzies, Marina Eileen; CA; Honduras, 1974– .

Merck, Daniel Edward (A); AL; Thailand, 1978– .

Merck, Barbara Jean Holt (Mrs. D. E.) (A); FL; Thailand, 1978– .

Meredith, Brenda Jeannette (J); MO; Guatemala, 1971–73.

Meredith, Sue Ann (J); OH; Peru, 1972–74.

Messer, Isaac Daniel; SC; Uruguay, 1977– .

Messer, Lois Ann Phillips (Mrs. I. D.); SC; Uruguay, 1977– .

Michael, Margaret Jane (J); MO; Taiwan, 1971–73.

Michel, Kenneth Lee (J); TX; Scotland, 1979– .

Milam, Beverly Ann (J); MA; Yemen, 1978– .

Milby, Joanna Rae (J); KY; Brazil, 1972–74.

Miles, Donna Tress (J); GA; Angola, 1974–76; Rhodesia, 1976-76.

Miller, David Stanley (J); AR; Guatemala, 1978– .

Miller, Edward Lee; TX; Zambia, 1978– .

Miller, Linda Ann Brewer (Mrs. E. L.); TX; Zambia, 1978– .

Miller, Gary Don (J); TX; Tanzania, 1972–74.

Miller, James, Jr.; SC; Ecuador, 1977– .

Miller, Sarah Hilda Herndon (Mrs. James, Jr.); NC; Ecuador, 1977– .

Miller, Randy Charles (J); MI; Ecuador, 1976–78.

Miller, Ronald James; OK; Malawi, 1978– .

Miller, Delinda Ann Sneed (Mrs. R. J.); TX; Malawi, 1978– .

Miller, Sheila Belinda (J); AR; Brazil, 1975–77.

Milligan, Gerald Haskell; OK; Gaza, 1976– .

Milligan, Arylis Jean Rayburn (Mrs. G. H.); OK; Gaza, 1976– .

Mincey, Elizabeth Annette (J); NC; Nigeria, 1977–79.

Minter, Shirley Mae (J); VA; Honduras, 1977–77.

Mitchell, Donna Gail (J); MI; Honduras, 1971–73.

Mitchell, Harold Edward; AR; Tanzania, 1976– .

Mitchell, Frances Rene Boschetti (Mrs. H. E.); AR; Tanzania, 1976– .

Mitchell, Margaret Ann (J); AR; Argentina, 1970–72.

Mixson, Daniel James (J); FL; Indonesia, 1972–74.

Mobley, Gregory (J); KY; Nigeria, 1979– .

Moffett, Elzie Serwood, Jr.; LA; Japan, 1976– .

Moffett, Margaret Jane Denton (Mrs. E. S., Jr.); TX; Japan, 1976– .

Mohn, Nancy Elizabeth (J); Germany; Brazil, 1975–77.

Mohundro, Shirley Anita (J); TN; Kenya, 1971–73.

Monroe, John Wayne; TX;
Rhodesia, 1971– .
Monroe, Mary Etta Anthony
(Mrs. J. W.); TX; Rhodesia,
1971– .
Montgomery, Billy Lloyd; TX;
Ghana, 1975– .
Montgomery, Sandra Kay Stone
(Mrs. B. L.); AR; Ghana,
1975– .
Moore, Billy Bob; AR;
Reappointed; Trinidad,
1975–77.
Moore, Aletha Lane (Mrs. B.
B.); TX; Reappointed;
Trinidad, 1975–77.
Moore, Eugene Alman; SC;
Tanzania, 1970– .
Moore, Laura Marie Agnew
(Mrs. E. A.); SC; Tanzania,
1970– .
Moore, James Stanley; OK;
Brazil, 1978– .
Moore, Mary Ann Tobey (Mrs.
J. S.); CA; Brazil, 1978– .
Moran, Douglas Raymond (J);
KY; Japan, 1977–79.
Morgan, Christine (J); KY;
Japan, 1971–73.
Morgan, Judith Ann (J); TN;
Brazil, 1974–76.
Morgan, Quinn Pett, Jr.; LA;
Rhodesia, 1976– .
Morgan, Martha Lynn Perry
(Mrs. Q. P., Jr.); NJ;
Rhodesia, 1976– .
Morris, Barry Noland (J); FL;
Thailand, 1973–75.
Morris, Ann Marie Downing
(Mrs. B. N.) (J); TN;
Thailand, 1973–75.
Morris, Daniel Platt (J); MS;
Hong Kong, 1978– .
Morris, Laura Marie (J); HI;
Chile, 1978– .
Morris, Robert Eugene, Jr. (J);
IA; Nigeria, 1978– .
Morris, Valerie Jean (J); IN;
Uruguay, 1975–77.
Morton, Kathy Dianne (J); TN;
Peru, 1972–74.
Mosby, William James (A);
MO; Yemen, 1977–79.
Mosby, Jo Ann Savage (Mrs.
W. J.) (A); KS; Yemen,
1977–79.
Moseley, William DeWitt; FL;
Brazil, 1971–76; 1978– .
Moseley, Barbara Ann Cooke
(Mrs. W. D.); MS; Brazil,
1971–76; 1978– .
Mote, Darrel Wayne (J); OK;
Philippines, 1972–74.
Moye, Jerry Elmer Lee; IL;
Hong Kong, 1972– .
Moye, Emma Ruth Holland
(Mrs. J. E. L.); SC; Hong
Kong, 1972– .
Moyer, John Robert (J); FL;
Surinam, 1975–77.
Moyer, Carol Elaine Chitty
(Mrs. J. R.) (J); FL;
Surinam, 1975–77.

Mullican, Kenneth Reed, Jr.;
TX; Gaza, 1970–76.
Mullican, Lenore Lindsey (Mrs.
K. R., Jr.); NJ; Gaza,
1970–76.
Mullinax, Marc Stephen (J);
NC; Korea, 1979– .
Murphy, Michael Carl; TX;
Guatemala, 1976– .
Murphy, Beatrice Jean Moore
(Mrs. M. C.); TX;
Guatemala, 1976– .
Muskrat, James Bruce; OK;
Argentina, 1977– .
Muskrat, Nancy Jean Woods
(Mrs. J. B.); MO; Argentina,
1977– .
Myers, Martha Crystal; AL;
Yemen, 1977– .

Nabors, Thomas Claude; MS;
Gaza, 1971–77; Israel,
1977– .
Nabors, Marilyn Jo Swift (Mrs.
T. C.); MO; Gaza, 1971–77;
Israel, 1977– .
Nakanishi, Stanley Jay (J);
Japan; Japan, 1979– .
Naylor, Rebekah Ann; AR;
India, 1973– .
Nealy, Walter Barry; LA;
Brazil, 1976– .
Nealy, Donna Lynn Dennis
(Mrs. W. B.); TX; Brazil,
1976– .
Neese, Eddie Ray; TX;
Indonesia, 1977– .
Neese, Judith Irene Pulis (Mrs.
E. R.); WY; Indonesia,
1977– .
Neighbour, Ralph Webster, Jr.
(A); MI; Singapore, 1974–77.
Neighbour, Ruth Elaine
Johnston (Mrs. R. W., Jr.)
(A); MN; Singapore, 1974–77.
Nelson, Ann Elizabeth (J); TX;
Windward Islands, 1977–79.
Nelson, James Hugo; AR;
Ethiopia, 1970–77.
Nelson, Roberta Martina Bos
(Mrs. J. H.); WA; Ethiopia,
1970–77.
Nelson, Linda Ann (J); AL;
Venezuela, 1971–73.
New, Benny Lynn; TX;
Taiwan, 1970– .
New, Patsy Darlene Compton
(Mrs. B. L.); TX; Taiwan,
1970– .
Newell, Neal Curtis, Jr. (J); AL;
Japan, 1971–73.
Newman, Linda Diane (J); TX;
Colombia, 1972–74.
Newman, Van Gene; AL; Chile,
1975– .
Newman, Ira Dean Harris (Mrs.
V. G.); AL; Chile, 1975– .
Newton, Thomas Michael; LA;
Korea, 1973– .
Newton, Wanda Dedeaux (Mrs.
T. M.); MS; Korea, 1973– .
Niager, Karen Elaine (J); GA;
India, 1979– .

Nichols, Julia Carolyn (J); TX;
Mexico, 1976–78.
Nichols, Malcolm Grant (A);
TN; Korea, 1977– .
Nichols, Marilyn Jean Lee (Mrs.
M. G.) (A); MS; Korea,
1977– .
Nichols, Rebecca Lynn (J); KY;
Argentina, 1976–78.
Nicholson, William Ward; TX;
Nigeria, 1973– .
Nicholson, Lou Ann Carrington
(Mrs. W. W.); TX; Nigeria,
1973– .
Noble, John Charles (J); KS;
Zambia, 1977–79.
Noffsinger, Carolyn Ann (J);
KY; Liberia, 1970–72.
Noles, Jana LaRue (J); AR;
Liberia, 1977–79.
Norfleet, Michael Roy; CA;
Taiwan, 1974– .
Norfleet, Alma Kay Walker
(Mrs. M. R.); TX; Taiwan,
1974– .
Norman, Debra Ann (J); IN;
Kenya, 1976–78.
Norman, Victor Dawson; AL;
Colombia, 1979– .
Norman, Kathy Jo Kuykendall
(Mrs. V. D.); AL; Colombia,
1979– .
Norton, John Edward; AL;
Japan, 1977– .
Norton, Nancy Janell Turner
(Mrs. J. E.); FL; Japan,
1977– .
Norville, Buddy Vance; TX;
Ivory Coast, 1974–78; Liberia,
1979– .
Norville, Brenda Conwell (Mrs.
B. V.); TX; Ivory Coast,
1974–78; Liberia, 1979– .
Norwood, John Vickers; TX;
Indonesia, 1972– .
Norwood, Diana Maurice Crane
(Mrs. J. V.); OK; Indonesia,
1972– .

O'Conner, Louis, Jr.; AL;
Reappointed; Bangladesh,
1975–77; Korea, 1977– .
O'Conner, Barbara Crumbley
(Mrs. Louis, Jr.); OH;
Reappointed; Bangladesh,
1975–77; Korea, 1977– .
O'Dell, Daniel Raymond; VA;
French West Indies, 1976– .
O'Dell, Janet Theresa Hester
(Mrs. D. R.); IL; French
West Indies, 1976– .
Odle, Raymond Lee (A); IL;
Yemen, 1974–79.
Odle, Mildred Ila Peebles (Mrs.
R. L.) (A); IL; Yemen,
1974–79.
Okazaki, Mark Hitoshi (J); HI;
Korea, 1979– .
Oldham, Larry Eugene; NC;
Dominican Republic,
1977– .
Oldham, Elizabeth Ann
McCarthy (Mrs. L. E.); NC;
Dominican Republic,
1977– .

Oliver, Billy Louis; TX; Yemen, 1975-79; Uganda, 1979- .

Oliver, Janice Kay McCain (Mrs. B. L.); TX; Yemen, 1975-79; Uganda, 1979- .

Olmstead, Pennie Lynn; KS; Brazil, 1979- .

Orange, Charles Victor; KY; Tanzania, 1977- .

Orange, Cheri Lynn Wilson (Mrs. C. V.); CA; Tanzania, 1977- .

Ortis, Karl Robert (J); LA; Macao, 1979- .

Osborne, Darrell Franklin (A); Canada; Nigeria, 1974- .

Osborne, Dorothy Margaret Scott (Mrs. D. F.) (A); Canada; Nigeria, 1974- .

Overstreet, Donald Gene; CA; Windward Islands, 1976- .

Overstreet, Maudie Carol Greenwalt (Mrs. D. G.); TX; Windward Islands, 1976- .

Overton, Philip Randal (A); IL; Panama, 1974-76; Yemen, 1976-78; Windward Islands, 1978- .

Overton, Ellen Sue Sevier (Mrs. P. R.) (A); LA; Panama, 1974-76; Yemen, 1976-78; Windward Islands, 1978- .

Owen, Herbert Michael; AL; Guatemala, 1975- .

Owen, Sarah Kathryn Strozier (Mrs. H. M.); GA; Guatemala, 1975- .

Owen, Ricky Brent (J); TX; Tanzania, 1977-79.

Owens, Larry Wayne (J); NC; Venezuela, 1979- .

Owings, Timothy Lawrence; FL; Brazil, 1979- .

Owings, Kathleen Lynn Pignato (Mrs. T. L.); WV; Brazil, 1979- .

Packwood, James Sidney; OK; Ecuador, 1978- .

Packwood, Karon Dawn Haygood (Mrs. J. S.); TX; Ecuador, 1978- .

Page, Naomi; TX; Panama, 1974-75.

Page, Robert Jo; SC; Philippines, 1971-78; Thailand, 1978- .

Page, Judith Lyn Germaux (Mrs. R. J.); PA; Philippines, 1971-78; Thailand, 1978- .

Palmer, Dennis Lee (A); IL; Taiwan, 1978- .

Palmer, Patricia Ann Murphy (Mrs. D. L.) (A); OH; Taiwan, 1978- .

Palmer, Phillip Burl; TX; Gaza, 1978- .

Palmer, Laura Elayne Russell (Mrs. P. B.); TX; Gaza, 1978- .

Panjic, Annie Lucile (J); AL; Hong Kong, 1972-73.

Pannell, Randall Jack; TX; Argentina, 1979- .

Pannell, Janet Patricia Davies (Mrs. R. J.); TX; Argentina, 1979- .

Panter, Danny Michael; MS; Togo, 1976- .

Panter, Elizabeth Ann Wallace (Mrs. D. M.); MS; Togo, 1976- .

Paris, Sue Jane (J); IN; Argentina, 1975-77.

Park, David Michael; TX; Philippines, 1975- .

Park, Mary Lois McClintock (Mrs. D. M.); TX; Philippines, 1975- .

Park, James Aaron; KY; Liberia, 1972- .

Park, Olive Jane Parsons (Mrs. J. A.); KY; Liberia, 1972- .

Parker, Pamela Jean Kelley (Mrs. R. R., Jr.); SC; Rhodesia, 1971- .

Parker, David Gaynor; GA; Zambia, 1978- .

Parker, Carol Yvonne Brannan (Mrs. D. G.); VA; Zambia, 1978- .

Parker, Janice Sue (J); TN; Japan, 1976-78.

Parker, Marilyn Jean (J); TX; Argentina, 1971-72.

Parrish, Betty Pauline; FL; Chile, 1974- .

Parsons, John Lee (J); TN; Vietnam, 1974-75.

Partin, Duane Bivins; GA; Brazil, 1972-79.

Partin, Helen de Alva Roberts (Mrs. D. B.); TN; Brazil, 1972-79.

Pate, Carl Richard; CA; Taiwan, 1976-78.

Pate, Peggy Ann Segui (Mrs. C. R.); SC; Taiwan, 1976-78.

Patterson, Carol Anne (J); FL; Guam, 1976-78.

Patterson, Floyd Elias; IL; Ecuador, 1973- .

Patterson, Carole Ann Kaemper (Mrs. F. E.); IL; Ecuador, 1973- .

Patterson, Margaret Anne (J); NC; Brazil, 1973-75.

Patterson, Mary Lucile (J); SC; Korea, 1978- .

Payne, Van Chancy (J); MS; Kenya, 1975-77.

Payne, Mary Gwendolyn Gullage (Mrs. V. C.) (J); MS; Kenya, 1975-77.

Pearce, Dorothy Ann; SC; Paraguay, 1973- .

Peddicord, Sharon Gail; DC; Brazil, 1977- .

Pegram, Linda Jo (J); WV; Vietnam, 1972-74.

Pegram, Norma Jean (J); WV; Taiwan, 1973-75.

Pendley, Frances Hill Read (Mrs. L. C.) (A); KY; Yemen, 1973- .

Pennington, Anna Ruth; VA; Brazil, 1976- .

Pennington, James Barry (J); MO; Israel, 1979- .

Pennington, Mark Sowell (J); TN; Kenya, 1978- .

Pentz, Gloria Louise (J); MA; Japan, 1979- .

Perez, Rebecca Anne (J); NM; Tanzania, 1975-76.

Perimon, Edwin Oliver (A); TX; Trinidad, 1976- .

Perimon, Joyce Clifton (Mrs. E. O.) (A); OK; Trinidad, 1976- .

Perkins, Joe Dan; TX; Ghana, 1977- .

Perkins, Jo Liane Sanders (Mrs. J. D.); TX; Ghana, 1977- .

Perkins, John Luther; AL; France, 1978- .

Perkins, Sarah Elizabeth Grant (Mrs. J. L.); MS; France, 1978- .

Permenter, Debra Susan (J); TX; Korea, 1978- .

Perrill, Jerald Wilson; KS; Laos, 1970-75; Thailand, 1975- .

Perrill, Jimmie Elaine Fortenberry (Mrs. J. W.); MS; Laos, 1970-75; Thailand, 1975- .

Perry, Annette; AR; Senegal, 1975-78.

Perry, Delores Kay (J); TX; Panama, 1975-77.

Perry, Martha Lynn (J); NJ; Rhodesia, 1972-74.

Perry, Rheta (SP); GA; Gaza, 1977-79.

Perry, Robert Lee; MO; Mexico, 1973- .

Perry, Nancy Boone Whitlow (Mrs. R. L.); MO; Mexico, 1973- .

Peterson, Arnold Allen; IA; Korea, 1973- .

Peterson, Barbara Dee Warren (Mrs. A. A.); MO; Korea, 1973- .

Peterson, Dale Wood (J); TX; Israel, 1977-79.

Peterson, Kenneth Dean (J); IA; Togo, 1971-73.

Peterson, Penny Lynn (J); France; Argentina, 1975-76.

Petrus, Bonita Godwin (J); MD; Switzerland, 1976-78.

Petty, Benny Lee; TN; Hong Kong, 1978- .

Petty, Maria Atkinson (Mrs. B. L.); TX; Hong Kong, 1978- .

Phifer, Dudley Ayers; TX; Malawi, 1974-79; Transkei, 1979- .

Phifer, Rebecca Ruth Reagan (Mrs. D. A.); TX; Malawi, 1974-79; Transkei, 1979- .

Phillips, Bill Edd; TX; Zambia, 1978- .

Phillips, Mary Dean Terry (Mrs. B. E.); TX; Zambia, 1978- .

Phillips, Gene Allen; KY; France, 1973- .

Foreign Missionaries

2230

Phillips, Jacqueline Margaret
Freeman (Mrs. G. A.); SC;
France, 1973- .
Phillips, Larry Dean; TX; Hong
Kong, 1975- .
Phillips, Charlotte Anne
Trapman (Mrs. L. D.); IL;
Hong Kong, 1975- .
Phillips, Linda Edythe; CA;
Taiwan, 1975- .
Phillips, Robert Harvey (J); TX;
Okinawa, 1974-76.
Philpot, William Bradford (J);
AL; Kenya, 1975-77.
Phipps, Russell Carl (J); OK;
Zambia, 1973-75.
Phipps, Lee Ann Teal (Mrs. R.
C.) (J); OK; Zambia,
1973-75.
Pickle, William Stewart; TN;
Ecuador, 1974- .
Pickle, Clara Louise Smith
(Mrs. W. S.); NY; Ecuador,
1974- .
Pickler, Karen Estelle (J); NC;
Japan, 1979- .
Pierce, Joyce Marie (J); MO;
Italy, 1970-72.
Pinkston, Homer David (A);
OK; Thailand, 1971-76.
Pinkston, Carma Darlee Barlow
(Mrs. H. D.) (A); OR;
Thailand, 1971-76.
Pinson, Merilyn Sue; WV;
Upper Volta, 1974-77.
Pipkin, Harry Wayne; TX;
Switzerland, 1978- .
Pipkin, Arlene Law Schenk
(Mrs. H. W.); MA;
Switzerland, 1978- .
Pirkle, Donald Enoch; GA;
Gaza, 1977- .
Pirkle, Patricia Anne Ard (Mrs.
D. E.); MS; Gaza, 1977- .
Pirtle, Ronald Clayton; CA;
Yemen, 1973- .
Pirtle, Susan Elizabeth Allen
(Mrs. R. C.); GA; Yemen,
1973- .
Pitts, James Jefferson, Jr. (J);
SC; Korea, 1978- .
Poe, Martha Elizabeth (J); VA;
Peru, 1975-77.
Polglase, Jeffrey Kenneth (J);
Japan; Zambia, 1979- .
Pope, William Leonard; AL;
French West Indies, 1975-78;
Bahamas, 1979- .
Pope, Ada Ruth Asher (Mrs. W.
L.); KY; French West Indies,
1975-78; Bahamas, 1979- .
Porter, Anthony Morris (J); TX;
Kenya, 1976-78.
Porter, Colleen Louise (J); TX;
Dominican Republic,
1976-78.
Porter, Janice Nell (J); TX;
Angola, 1975-76; Botswana,
1976-77; South Africa,
1977-77.
Porterfield, Carolyn Marie (J);
CO; Japan, 1977-79.
Potter, Edith Nell; TN;
Colombia, 1976-79.

Pounders, Thomas Jefferson, III
(J); AR; Japan, 1979- .
Powell, Billy Vern; OK;
Venezuela, 1977- .
Powell, Norma Faye Patrick
(Mrs. B. V.); OK; Venezuela,
1977- .
Powell, John Randall (J); LA;
Liberia, 1975-77.
Powers, Emmett Eugene; TN;
Argentina, 1979- .
Powers, Virginia Katherine
Morris (Mrs. E. E.); DC;
Argentina, 1979- .
Powers, James Wendell (A);
KY; Taiwan, 1974- .
Powers, Laquita Joy Inmon
(Mrs. J. W.) (A); MS;
Taiwan, 1974- .
Powers, William McMillan (J);
KY; Israel, 1970-72.
P'Pool, Rebecca Lynn; NM;
Japan, 1977- .
Prater, Rosemary Kay (J); KS;
Peru, 1971-73.
Price, David Stuart (J); LA;
Kenya, 1978- .
Price, Levi Weldon, Jr.; TX;
Mexico, 1976- .
Price, Luethyl Dawkins (Mrs. L.
W., Jr.); LA; Mexico,
1976- .
Price, Thera Jean (J); MO;
Senegal, 1973-75.
Prickett, Anna Lynn (J); MS;
Yemen, 1971-72; Gaza,
1972-73.
Pruitt, Carla Jane (J); MO;
Japan, 1974-76.
Purcell, Wandena Ann (J); NM;
Rhodesia, 1975-77.
Purtle, Charles Edward; AR;
Dominican Republic,
1973- .
Purtle, Priscilla Jane Altom
(Mrs. C. E.); TX; Dominican
Republic, 1973- .
Putnam, Alan Blair (J); NC;
Belgium, 1975-77.
Putnam, William Albert (J);
AR; Philippines, 1979- .

Quarles, Samilee (J); TX;
Kenya, 1975-77.
Quimby, Hybart Reginald; FL;
Spain, 1979- .
Quimby, Karen Jo King (Mrs.
H. R.); TX; Spain, 1979- .

Raguse, Betty Jean (J); MN;
Nigeria, 1978- .
Rains, Randall Marc (J); TN;
Rwanda, 1977-78; Kenya,
1978- .
Rains, Betty Gail Cope (Mrs. R.
M.) (J); AL; Rwanda,
1977-78; Kenya, 1978- .
Ramsey, John Thomas; TX;
Brazil, 1978- .
Ramsey, Carolyn Ann Magee
(Mrs. J. T.); TX; Brazil,
1978- .
Ramsey, Mary Anne (J); LA;
Korea, 1972-74.

Randall, Maurice Lee; GA;
Rhodesia, 1971- .
Randall, Shirley Irene Jackson
(Mrs. M. L.); WA; Rhodesia,
1971- .
Rankin, Jerry Allen; MS;
Indonesia, 1970- .
Rankin, Bobbye Ann Simmons
(Mrs. J. A.); AL; Indonesia,
1970- .
Ray, Charles Augustus (A); TX;
Malaysia, 1971-72; Thailand,
1972-77; Japan, 1977- .
Ray, Mary Elizabeth Gilbert
(Mrs. C. A.) (A); MS;
Malaysia, 1971-72; Thailand,
1972-77; Japan, 1977- .
Ray, Cheryl Lynne; OK;
Zambia, 1972-77.
Ray, John William (J); MS;
Taiwan, 1973-75.
Rayborn, Timothy Dwain (J);
MS; Guam, 1971-73.
Rayborn, Nancy Carroll Goff
(Mrs. T. D.) (J); MS; Guam,
1971-73.
Rayburn, Harold Douglas; AL;
Mexico, 1979- .
Rayburn, Wanda Martin (Mrs.
H. D.); AL; Mexico,
1979- .
Rayford, Richard Drexel (J);
NC; Austria, 1976-78.
Red, Douglas Lee (J); PA;
Taiwan, 1978- .
Red, Kathryn Jean Waltz (Mrs.
D. L.) (J); NY; Taiwan,
1978- .
Reed, Don Wayne; TX; Peru,
1971-76.
Reed, Wanda June Stephens
(Mrs. D. W.); AR; Peru,
1971-76.
Reed, Karen Ann (J); TX;
Dominican Republic,
1975-77.
Reed, Polly Ann (J); TX;
Colombia, 1974-76.
Reeder, Michael Gene; KS;
Colombia, 1978- .
Reeder, Stephanie Miller (Mrs.
M. G.); OK; Colombia,
1978- .
Rees, Carl Marion, Jr.; MO;
Honduras, 1978- .
Rees, Martha Marie French
(Mrs. C. M., Jr.); CA;
Honduras, 1978- .
Rees, Evan Thomas (J); OH;
Kenya, 1979- .
Reeves, Gerald Boyd; GA;
French West Indies, 1979- .
Reeves, Shirley Maxine Day
(Mrs. G. B.); GA; French
West Indies, 1979- .
Reeves, Linda Joyce (J);
Venezuela; Argentina,
1972-74.
Reeves, Robert Francis; IL;
Trinidad, 1973-75.
Reeves, Beverly Ann Miller
(Mrs. R. F.); IL; Trinidad,
1973-75.

Remington, Aaron Miller; AR;
Portugal, 1977- .
Remington, Mary Beth Unger
(Mrs. A. M.); MO; Portugal,
1977- .
Resseguie, Sharon Elaine (J);
PA; Liberia, 1971-73.
Rexrode, Annie Ruth Boldger
(Mrs. M. B.) (A); TN; Israel,
1977- .
Reynolds, Charles Edward (J);
NC; Austria, 1977-79.
Reynolds, Loretta Joan (J); AL;
Leeward Islands, 1978- .
Reynolds, William Raymond
(A); TN; Belgium, 1972- .
Reynolds, Helen Elizabeth
Moses (Mrs. W. R.) (A); FL;
Belgium, 1972- .
Reynolds, Woodrow Ronnie;
WV; Argentina, 1975- .
Reynolds, Glenda Carol Arton
(Mrs. W. R.); NC;
Argentina, 1975- .
Rhoads, Paul Allen; AR; Korea,
1973- .
Rhoads, Lana Sue LeGrand
(Mrs. P. A.); MO; Korea,
1973- .
Rice, Donald Lee; CA;
Tanzania, 1979- .
Rice, Julia Carroll (Mrs. D. L.);
LA; Tanzania, 1979- .
Rice, James Lawon; FL;
Uganda, 1974- .
Rice, Linda Clarkson (Mrs. J.
L.); VA; Uganda, 1974- .
Richards, Judith Claire (J); NY;
Taiwan, 1973-75.
Richardson, Beverly Jane; MO;
Jordan, 1975- .
Richardson, Dean Edward (A);
TX; Ghana, 1973-79.
Richardson, Joyce Erline Wade
(Mrs. D. E.) (A); TX;
Ghana, 1973-79.
Richardson, James Muse; VA;
Kenya, 1976- .
Richardson, Marcia Lynne
Jones (Mrs. J. M.); MO;
Kenya, 1976- ..
Richardson, Shelley Phipps; LA;
Philippines, 1970-72.
Richardson, Patricia Joy Carter
(Mrs. S. P.); TN; Philippines,
1970-72.
Richerson, Toni Gail (J); TX;
Japan, 1977-79.
Richmond, Suzanne E'Laine (J);
TX; Nigeria, 1977-78.
Rickaway, Albert Lee, Jr. (J);
TX; Argentina, 1979- .
Rickaway, Linnell Faith Byrd
(Mrs. A. L., Jr.) (J); MT;
Argentina, 1979- .
Ringer, Douglas George; OK;
Laos, 1972-75; Thailand,
1975- .
Ringer, Brenda Nell Barnes
(Mrs. D. G.); OK; Laos,
1972-75; Thailand, 1975- .
Ritger, Robin Elizabeth (J);
TX; India, 1972-74.

Rivers, Barbara Lynn (J); TX;
Guatemala, 1978- .
Roach, Gene Ray; NM;
Tanzania, 1979- .
Roach, Jane Carolyn
McClendon (Mrs. G. R.);
AL; Tanzania, 1979- .
Roaten, Paul Eric; MS;
Uruguay, 1970- .
Roaten, Betty Lou Marbury
(Mrs. P. E.); TN; Uruguay,
1970- .
Robbins, Patricia Ann (J); NC;
Japan, 1976-78.
Roberson, Carolyn; TX;
Rhodesia, 1972-78;
Bophuthatswana, 1978- .
Roberts, Clara Bell (J); TX;
Liberia, 1972-74.
Roberts, Clyde Nakomas; FL;
Mexico, 1970- .
Roberts, Roxie Elizabeth Pitts
(Mrs. C. N.); FL; Mexico,
1970- .
Roberts, David Harrill; FL;
Zambia, 1973-75; Kenya,
1976-76.
Roberts, Madonna Jean
Richards (Mrs. D. H.); IN;
Zambia, 1973-75; Kenya,
1976-76.
Roberts, Edwin Donald, Jr. (J);
AL; Gaza, 1970-72.
Roberts, Judith Florence (J);
NY; Colombia, 1975-77.
Roberts, Rita Willien; SC;
Brazil, 1971- .
Roberts, Robert Vincent; FL;
Panama, 1975- .
Roberts, Brenda Sue Knight
(Mrs. R. V.); FL; Panama,
1975- .
Roberts, William Preston; AL;
Japan, 1971- .
Roberts, Patricia Ann Barr
(Mrs. W. P.); MS; Japan,
1971- .
Robertson, Homer Doyne; AR;
Peru, 1979- .
Robertson, Martha Ann Mathis
(Mrs. H. D.); MS; Peru,
1979- .
Robertson, Jerry Ray; KY;
Ivory Coast, 1977- .
Robertson, Carol Ann Johnson
(Mrs. J. R.); LA; Ivory
Coast, 1977- .
Robertson, Judith Ann; AR;
Taiwan, 1974- .
Robertson, Kenneth George;
AR; Senegal, 1976- .
Robertson, Margaret Anne
Howard (Mrs. K. G.); AR;
Senegal, 1976- .
Robertson, Leonard Gene, Jr.
(J); AL; Kenya, 1979- .
Robinson, Charles Barry (J);
GA; Liberia, 1975-77.
Robinson, Frances Charlene (J);
TN; Japan, 1974-76.
Robinson, Mikel Francis (J);
MO; Ghana, 1974-76.
Robuck, Thomas Durward; TX;
Brazil, 1974- .

Robuck, Elizabeth Sue Jones
(Mrs. T. D.); TX; Brazil,
1974- .
Rodgers, Kathryn Louise (J);
TN; Taiwan, 1974-76.
Rodgers, Lloyd Walter (J); TX;
Singapore, 1979- .
Rogers, Joan Marie (J); NC;
Korea, 1975-77.
Roller, Helen (A); CA;
Rhodesia, 1971-76.
Romanstine, Stanley Eugene, Jr.
(J); SC; Israel, 1977-79.
Romanstine, Susan Elaine
Greene (Mrs. S. E., Jr.) (J);
TN; Israel, 1977-79.
Roper, Harriet Elizabeth (J);
TX; Mexico, 1974-76.
Rorabaugh, Dan Elmer; CA;
Tanzania, 1977- .
Rorabaugh, Peggy Dale Burson
(Mrs. D. E.); KS; Tanzania,
1977- .
Rosell, Rebeca (J); Cuba; Peru,
1975-77.
Ross, John Bennett, V (SP); IL;
Windward Islands, 1979- .
Ross, Clara Lisa De Loach
(Mrs. J. B., V) (SP); TX;
Windward Islands, 1979- .
Ross, Joyce Marie (J); MO;
Trinidad, 1970-72.
Ross, Paul Vaughn; ID; Kenya,
1975- .
Ross, Ruby Johnene Hamby
(Mrs. P. V.); TX; Kenya,
1975- .
Roumillat, Janice Marie (J); SC;
Guatemala, 1973-75.
Routledge, Dan Clayton; MO;
Ivory Coast, 1973- .
Routledge, Beth Ann Thompson
(Mrs. D. C.); OK; Ivory
Coast, 1973- .
Rowell, Albert Brent (J); TN;
Bangladesh, 1978- .
Rowland, Wade Russell; NC;
Reappointed; India, 1974-78.
Rowland, Betty Jean Ausborn
(Mrs. W. R.); AL;
Reappointed; India, 1974-78.
Ruble, Wade Eugene; VA;
Indonesia, 1971- .
Ruble, Peggy Comer (Mrs. W.
E.); GA; Indonesia, 1971- .
Rucker, Roger Wayne; TX;
Lebanon, 1979- .
Rucker, Linda Sue Sovall (Mrs.
R. W.); KY; Lebanon,
1979- .
Rupp, Daniel Henry; IN;
Colombia, 1974- .
Rupp, Linda Diane Boyd (Mrs.
D. H.); TX; Colombia,
1974- .
Rush, Marilyn Kay (J); OK;
Thailand, 1973-75.
Russell, Judy Elaine (J); AZ;
Brazil, 1974-76.
Russell, Peggy Ruth; LA;
Liberia, 1976- .
Rymal, John Lawrence; TX;
Ghana, 1979- .

Sacco, Mack Louis; IL;
Lebanon, 1970–76; 1978– ;
France, 1976–77.

Sacco, Linda Faye Bennett
(Mrs. M. L.); OK; Lebanon,
1970–76; 1978– ; France,
1976–77.

Sams, Lois Ann (J); TN;
Philippines, 1977–79.

Sanders, Susan Janice (J); AR;
Indonesia, 1974–76.

Sanders, Teresa Ann (J); OK;
Kenya, 1975–77.

Sands, Charles Dorrance, III;
FL; Korea, 1970– .

Sands, Elizabeth Kay Leedy
(Mrs. C. D., III); OH;
Korea, 1970– .

Sanford, Fred Haywood; FL;
Benin, 1974–79; Ivory Coast,
1979– .

Sanford, Patricia Gale Lark
(Mrs. F. H.); SC; Benin,
1974–79; Ivory Coast,
1979– .

Sarrett, Steven Mitchell (J); AR;
Peru, 1979– .

Sarver, Calvin Y.; CA; Ghana,
1975– .

Sarver, Claudia Marie Herndon
(Mrs. C. Y.); CA; Ghana,
1975– .

Sasser, Thomas Lynn; TX;
Chile, 1975–77.

Sasser, Sandra Sue Talley (Mrs.
T. L.); LA; Chile, 1975–77.

Saunders, John Alvan Lee II (J);
Nigeria; Kenya, 1976–78.

Savage, Roy Eldredge, Jr.; TX;
Ivory Coast, 1971–74.

Savage, Kay Donna Cargill
(Mrs. R. E., Jr.); TX; Ivory
Coast, 1971–74.

Sawyer, Danny Ray; MO;
Nigeria, 1977– .

Sawyer, Kathleen Bonnie Modak
(Mrs. D. R.); OH; Nigeria,
1977– .

Sawyer, Mary Camille (J); AR;
Japan, 1974–76.

Scales, George Larry; AL;
Tanzania, 1979– .

Scales, Sandra Joan Green (Mrs.
G. L.); AL; Tanzania,
1979– .

Schaffner, Karen June (J); TX;
Ghana, 1974–76.

Schellenberg, Daniel; Kenya;
Kenya, 1973– .

Schellenberg, Catherine Boone
(Mrs. Daniel); TX; Kenya,
1973– .

Schmidt, Joe Mack (J); TX;
Costa Rica, 1974–76.

Schmidt, Rebecca Sue (J); FL;
Tanzania, 1973–75.

Schmulbach, Karen Lee (J);
MS; Macao, 1979– .

Schooling, Raymond Carl (J);
MO; Cayman Islands,
1975–77.

Schulz, Clyde Emil, Jr. (J); LA;
Brazil, 1976–78.

Scott, Deborah Lynn (J); VA;
Dominican Republic,
1977–79.

Scott, Freddie Rae; TX;
Reappointed; Philippines,
1977– .

Scott, Mary Yvonne Fenton
(Mrs. F. R.); OK;
Reappointed; Philippines,
1977– .

Searcy, Theron Michael; GA;
Bahamas, 1976– .

Searcy, Charlotte Garbett (Mrs.
T. M.); GA; Bahamas,
1976– .

Seelig, Timothy Garrett (J); TX;
Austria, 1974–76.

Seelig, Vicki Jean Standefer
(Mrs. T. G.) (J); TX;
Austria, 1974–76.

Segars, Edwin Robert (A); SC;
Thailand, 1977–79; Senegal,
1979– .

Segars, Dorothy Lena Patterson
(Mrs. E. R.) (A); SC;
Thailand, 1977–79; Senegal,
1979– .

Selle, Margaret Lounelle (A);
NC; Taiwan, 1973– .

Sellers, Robert Preston; FL;
Indonesia, 1975– .

Sellers, Janie Day Tyler (Mrs.
R. P.); OK; Indonesia,
1975– .

Sergeant, William Lyle; IA;
Korea, 1970–76; Taiwan,
1976– .

Sergeant, LaVeta Mae Pierce
(Mrs. W. L.); KS; Korea,
1970–76; Taiwan, 1976– .

Sewell, Donald Eugene; TX;
Mexico, 1978– .

Sewell, Rebecca Graves (Mrs.
D. E.); FL; Mexico, 1978– .

Sharp, Jeffrey Robert; NY;
Hong Kong, 1979– .

Sharp, Constance Elizabeth
Booth (Mrs. J. R.); KY;
Hong Kong, 1979– .

Shaver, Wendy Lee (J); DC;
Japan, 1978– .

Shaw, Timothy John (J); CA;
Zambia, 1970–71.

Shearer, Ronald Ray (J); TN;
Zambia, 1970–72.

Shehane, Robert Wayne; TX;
French West Indies, 1973– .

Shehane, Carel Jane Harrison
(Mrs. R. W.); TX; French
West Indies, 1973– .

Shelly, James Calvin, Jr.; GA;
Brazil, 1971–75.

Shelly, Patsy Leona McAliley
(Mrs. J. C., Jr.); GA; Brazil,
1971–75.

Shelton, Paul Leslie (J);
Uruguay; Spain, 1976–78.

Shelton, Rexann (J); TX;
Japan, 1973–74.

Shepard, Samuel Groover (A);
Brazil; Portugal, 1975– .

Shepard, Charlotte Green (Mrs.
S. G.) (A); Nigeria; Portugal,
1975– .

Sheppard, Rex Gerald (J); TX;
Kenya, 1972–74.

Sherer, Robert Hollis; IL;
Japan, 1971– .

Sherer, Claudia Beth Kruer
(Mrs. R. H.); MO; Japan,
1971– .

Sheriff, Everett Paul; TX;
Philippines, 1979– .

Sheriff, Lucille Elaine Adcock
(Mrs. E. P.); OK;
Philippines, 1979– .

Sherman, Dorothy Eugenia (J);
GA; Japan, 1979– .

Sherouse, John Neil, Jr. (J); FL;
Japan, 1974–76.

Sherouse, Marsha Louise
Mathews (Mrs. J. N., Jr.) (J);
FL; Japan, 1974–76.

Shirley, Kenneth Marvin (J);
SC; Liberia, 1975–77.

Shockley, Michael Malone; MO;
Ghana, 1975– .

Shockley, Joan Darlene Short
(Mrs. M. M.); CO; Ghana,
1975– .

Short, Morene Tyson (Mrs. J.
T.) (A); TX; Tanzania,
1979– .

Shotts, D'Anna Kay (J); IN;
Nigeria, 1979– .

Shows, Pamela Wynn (J); SC;
Japan, 1978– .

Shurling, Rebecca Jane (J); FL;
Korea, 1972–74.

Sibley, Ernest Albert; TX;
Malawi, 1972– .

Sibley, Auttie Lou Aston (Mrs.
E. A.); TX; Malawi,
1972– .

Siebenmann, Paul Charles; TX;
Dominican Republic,
1972– .

Siebenmann, Peggy Sue Beckett
(Mrs. P. C.); TX; Dominican
Republic, 1972– .

Simmons, Bobby Eugene (A);
MS; Hong Kong, 1974–76;
Philippines, 1976– .

Simmons, Mary Lou Johnson
(Mrs. B. E.) (A); MS; Hong
Kong, 1974–76; Philippines,
1976– .

Simmons, Cornelia Beatrice
Brasington (Mrs. G. C.) (A);
SC; Yemen, 1975–79.

Simmons, James Melvin; MI;
Okinawa, 1977– .

Simmons, Marilyn Camille
Bishop (Mrs. J. M.); AR;
Okinawa, 1977– .

Simmons, Othar Errol; LA;
Spain, 1974– .

Simmons, Mary Joyce Ishee
(Mrs. O. E.); MS; Spain,
1974– .

Simon, Jerry Glynn; LA;
Uganda, 1970–74; Taiwan,
1974–77.

Simon, Carol Elizabeth Martin
(Mrs. J. G.); MS; Uganda,
1970–74; Taiwan, 1974–77.

Simpkins, George James, IV;
AL; Argentina, 1979– .

Simpkins, Jackie Green (Mrs. G. J., IV); MS; Argentina, 1979- .

Simrell, William Douglas; AL; Ivory Coast, 1976- .

Simrell, Paula Ann Gotcher (Mrs. W. D.); MS; Ivory Coast, 1976- .

Sims, Robert Willis; AL; Ghana, 1973- .

Sims, Rose Sherrod McCrow (Mrs. R. W.); MS; Ghana, 1973- .

Singleton, Jonathan; MS; Windward Islands, 1979- .

Singleton, La Homa Dean Martin (Mrs. Jonathan); MO; Windward Islands, 1979- .

Sivage, Vernon Wiley; TX; Rwanda, 1978- .

Sivage, Sandra Caldwell (Mrs. V. W.); TX; Rwanda, 1978- .

Sliger, Gloria Anne; GA; Rhodesia, 1977- .

Sloan, Charles Buford (J); GA; Kenya, 1974-76.

Slusher, Ida Louise (J); KY; Gaza, 1979- .

Smallwood, Karen Janell (J); KY; Colombia, 1976; Philippines, 1976-78.

Smedley, Gloria Eileen (J); CO; Colombia, 1974-76.

Smith, Albert Gene; TX; Ghana, 1977- .

Smith, Janice Sue Hanson (Mrs. A. G.); TX; Ghana, 1977- .

Smith, Barbara Jo (J); MS; Nigeria, 1976; Tanzania, 1976-78.

Smith, Betty Ann; MD; Brazil, 1973- .

Smith, Beverly Jean (SP); MS; Tanzania, 1977-78.

Smith, Carson Henry (J); DC; Senegal, 1975-77.

Smith, Catherine Susan (J); GA; Honduras, 1979- .

Smith, Donna Louise (J); OK; Peru, 1976-78.

Smith, Douglas Glen (J); OK; Hong Kong/Macao, 1970-72.

Smith, Frieda Gaye Cummins (Mrs. D. G.) (J); NM; Hong Kong/Macao, 1970-72.

Smith, Edward Lee; AR; Botswana, 1971- .

Smith, Dorothy Charlene Clements (Mrs. E. L.); AR; Botswana, 1971- .

Smith, Gordon Louis (J); KY; Kenya, 1977-79.

Smith, Minda Ann Lance (Mrs. G. L.) (J); KY; Kenya, 1977-79.

Smith, James Allen (J); VA; Germany, 1976-78.

Smith, Jesse Allen; SC; Reappointed; Philippines, 1978- .

Smith, Mary Frances Barnette (Mrs. J. A.); SC; Reappointed; Philippines, 1978- .

Smith, John Williams (A); NC; Tanzania, 1977- .

Smith, Mary Christine Smith (Mrs. J. W.) (A); NC; Tanzania, 1977- .

Smith, Nancy Jean (J); GA; Jordan, 1976-78.

Smith, Paul Stephen (J); TN; Uganda, 1970-70.

Smith, Avis Lorene Hemenway (Mrs. P. S.) (J); TN; Uganda, 1970-70.

Smith, Peggy Jo (J); IN; Korea, 1974-76.

Smith, Rebecca (J); TX; Taiwan, 1976-78.

Smith, Richard Linn (J); MO; Angola, 1975-76; Rhodesia, 1976-77.

Smith, Rita Anne; FL; Liberia, 1978- .

Smith, Stanley Keith (J); MO; Indonesia, 1971-73.

Smith, Stanly Barnette; SC; Philippines, 1979- .

Smith, Dorothy Piper (Mrs. S. B.); WI; Philippines, 1979- .

Smith, Thomas Lee; NC; Liberia, 1978- .

Smith, Shirley Fay Canada (Mrs. T. L.); WV; Liberia, 1978- .

Smith, Wade Hamil; AL; Reappointed; Brazil, 1972- .

Smith, Shirley Ann Cook (Mrs. W. H.); AL; Reappointed; Brazil, 1972- .

Smith, William Weldon, Jr.; VA; Thailand, 1974- .

Smith, Susan Jaynell Allen (Mrs. W. W., Jr.); TX; Thailand, 1974- .

Smithen, Elbert Lee, Jr. (A); NM; Peru, 1978- .

Smithen, Winifred Jo Clary (Mrs. E. L., Jr.) (A); TX; Peru, 1978- .

Smoot, Juanita Louise (J); WA; Brazil, 1978- .

Smothers, Charles Edward; TN; Paraguay, 1972- .

Smothers, Dicie Eulene Wells (Mrs. C. E.); FL; Paraguay, 1972- .

Snell, Donald Borland; AL; Trinidad, 1973-79; Dominica, 1979- .

Snell, Nancy Ida Batchelor (Mrs. D. B.); NY; Trinidad, 1973-79; Dominica, 1979- .

Sorrells, Fred Hilton (J); TX; Kenya, 1974-76.

Soule, Cynthia Ann (J); GA; Honduras, 1977-79.

South, Daniel Roy; TN; Chile, 1976- .

South, Cheryl Louise Davis (Mrs. D. R.); AR; Chile, 1976- .

Sowder, Michael Joe (J); TX; Iran, 1978-79; Scotland, 1979- .

Spann, Carry Edward; AR; Brazil, 1971-76.

Spann, Edith Jan Tillinghast (Mrs. C. E.); TX; Brazil, 1971-76.

Spann, Jimmie Durr; TX; Reappointed; Uruguay, 1975- .

Spann, Norma Jean Sparks (Mrs. J. D.); TX; Reappointed; Uruguay, 1975- .

Speegle, Bobby Chunn (A); AL; Liberia, 1975-79.

Speegle, Mary Sue Prince (Mrs. B. C.) (A); AL; Liberia, 1975-78.

Spence, Jacquelyn Kay (J); WY; Brazil, 1971-72.

Spence, Verna Ruth (A); AR; Lebanon, 1978- .

Spiegel, David James; IL; Brazil, 1979- .

Spiegel, Laura Anne Berry (Mrs. D. J.); Brazil; Brazil, 1979- .

Spires, Jerry Douglas; AR; Malawi, 1977- .

Spires, Joyce Christine Milner (Mrs. J. D.); MS; Malawi, 1977- .

Spivey, Julie Dean (J); DC; Jordan, 1976-78.

Springate, Ronald Jay; MO; Colombia, 1978- .

Springate, Linda Shrimpton (Mrs. R. J.); MO; Colombia, 1978- .

Sprinkle, Randy Leon; MO; Ethiopia, 1975- .

Sprinkle, Nancy Elizabeth Phillips (Mrs. R. L.); MO; Ethiopia, 1975- .

Squyres, Jerry Willie; LA; Taiwan, 1973-76.

Squyres, Carol Fran Stephenson (Mrs. J. W.); LA; Taiwan, 1973-76.

St. Amant, Clyde Penrose (A); LA; Switzerland, 1971-77.

St. Amant, Jessie Louise Davis (Mrs. C. P.) (A); TN; Switzerland, 1971-77.

Stainer, Ethne Ada (A); Australia; Yemen, 1978- .

Stallworth, Thomas Craig; FL; Austria, 1979- .

Stallworth, Brenda Gay Mixson (Mrs. T. C.); FL; Austria, 1979- .

Stancil, Wilburn Thomas; TN; Argentina, 1979- .

Stancil, Patricia Ann Adee (Mrs. W. T.); MO; Argentina, 1979- .

Stanford, James Alfred (A); NC; Costa Rica, 1977-78.

Stanford, Carolyn Alice Flynt (Mrs. J. A.) (A); FL; Costa Rica, 1977-78.

Stanley, Daniel Lewis (J); VA; Ghana, 1979- .

Stanley, John Leslie (J); AL; Kenya, 1979- .

Stanley, Kathy Gale Cleveland (Mrs. J. L.) (J); LA; Kenya, 1979- .

Stanley, William Robert (J); MO; Kenya, 1976–78.

Stanton, Ted Oscar; AR; Argentina, 1976– .

Stanton, Mary Frances Ridgell (Mrs. T. O.); AR; Argentina, 1976– .

Stapleton, Trenta Elaine (J); GA; Venezuela, 1974–76.

Starkey, Thomas McCue; MN; Benin, 1978– .

Starkey, Pamela Russell (Mrs. T. M.); MS; Benin, 1978– .

Staton, Raymond Clifford, Jr.; NC; Ethiopia, 1973–77; Tanzania, 1978– .

Staton, Myrtie Philecta Clarke (Mrs. R. C., Jr.); NC; Ethiopia, 1973–77; Tanzania, 1978– .

Steeger, William Paul; NY; Ethiopia, 1976–77; Seychelles, 1977–78; South Africa, 1979– .

Steeger, Martha Susan Bowman (Mrs. W. P.); AL; Ethiopia, 1976–77; Seychelles, 1977–78; South Africa, 1979– .

Steele, Craige Allen; NC; Brazil, 1975– .

Steele, Ellen May Barlow (Mrs. C. A.); NC; Brazil, 1975– .

Steele, Edward Lee; OK; Nicaragua, 1978– .

Steele, Kathryn Randquist (Mrs. E. L.); OK; Nicaragua, 1978– .

Stella, Anthony, Jr.; FL; Reappointed; Korea, 1978– .

Stella, Mary Sommerkamp (Mrs. Anthony, Jr.); FL; Reappointed; Korea, 1978– .

Stephens, Bobby Herbert; TX; Ethiopia, 1975–79.

Stephens, Donna Gay Kirk (Mrs. B. H.); TX; Ethiopia, 1975–79.

Stephens, Kenneth Harold; TX; Dominican Republic, 1975– .

Stephens, Nancy Jean Carlton (Mrs. K. H.); IL; Dominican Republic, 1975– .

Stephens, Martha Viola (J); NM; Mexico, 1972–74.

Stephenson, James Lamar (J); MS; Kenya, 1972–74.

Stevens, Archie Poe; SC; Brazil, 1978– .

Stevens, Anna Joyce Oliver (Mrs. A. P.); TX; Brazil, 1978– .

Stevens, David Eugene (J); MO; Kenya, 1975–77.

Stevens, Paul Lorance (J); KS; Malaysia/Singapore, 1974–76.

Stevens, Tom Matthew (J); OK; Ghana, 1974–76.

Stewart, Emily Dawn (J); VA; Korea, 1970–72.

Stewart, Larry Alan (J); AL; Ghana, 1971–73.

Stewart, Mary Joan; MS; Ecuador, 1972–78; Baptist Spanish Publishing House, 1978– .

Stickney, Allen Newell; TX; Kenya, 1970–75; 1978– .

Stickney, Alice Faye Miles (Mrs. A. N.); TX; Kenya, 1970–75; 1978– .

Stillman, Peter Alan (J); NC; Japan, 1977–79.

Stillman, Jennie Lee Jennings (Mrs. P. A.) (J); TN; Japan, 1977–79.

Stilwell, Rodney Dale (J); NC; Uruguay, 1978– .

Stokeld, Susan Elaine (J); LA; Philippines, 1970–72.

Stone, Gary Trenton (J); SC; Ecuador, 1979– .

Stone, Lily Ellen Pascoe (Mrs. G. T.) (J); SC; Ecuador, 1979– .

Stooksbury, Patricia Sue; TN; Costa Rica, 1976– .

Straub, Ronda Kaye (J); KY; Chile, 1977–79.

Strength, Teresa Ann (J); AL; Brazil, 1974–76.

Strickland, Mary Jenell (J); NC; Taiwan, 1970–72.

Strickland, Nancy Seaborn; GA; Upper Volta, 1978– .

Strickland, Stanley Lee (SP); OK; Ghana, 1979– .

Strickland, Mary Alice Durnal (Mrs. S. L.) (SP); LA; Ghana, 1979– .

Stroope, Michael Wayne; TX; Sri Lanka, 1977– .

Stroope, Virginia Kay George (Mrs. M. W.); TX; Sri Lanka, 1977– .

Styers, Donna Louise; TN; Chile, 1979– .

Sugg, Robert Perkins, Jr.; MS; Taiwan, 1977– .

Sugg, Nan Hollingsworth Gregory (Mrs. R. P., Jr.); MS; Taiwan, 1977– .

Sullivan, Geri Lea (J); MS; India, 1970–72.

Sullivan, Martha Ann (J); CO; Taiwan, 1977–79.

Sullivan, Mary Douglas (J); TN; Argentina, 1970–72.

Sumerlin, Janis Ann; TX; Brazil, 1979– .

Summerall, Richard Virgil (J); TX; Colombia, 1974–76.

Summers, Mary Lois; TX; Brazil, 1977– .

Sumrall, Tom Dan (A); TX; Brazil, 1977– .

Sumrall, Dorothy Jane Nickey (Mrs. T. D.) (A); MS; Brazil, 1977– .

Sutley, Teresa Louise (J); OK; Rhodesia, 1973–75.

Sutton, Albert Clinton, Jr.; FL; Angola, 1973–76; Botswana, 1976–77; Brazil, 1978– .

Sutton, Eleanor Virginia Cox (Mrs. A. C., Jr.); TN; Angola, 1973–76; Botswana, 1976–77; Brazil, 1978– .

Sutton, Mark Allen; AR; France, 1975– .

Sutton, Dorothy Susan Hill (Mrs. M. A.); LA; France, 1975– .

Swan, William Russell; AR; Philippines, 1975–76; Hong Kong, 1976– .

Swan, Janet Ruth Morgan (Mrs. W. R.); OK; Philippines, 1975–76; Hong Kong, 1976– .

Swann, Roger Lamar; TN; Tanzania, 1978– .

Swann, Beverly Kay Wales (Mrs. R. L.); FL; Tanzania, 1978– .

Swiney, Kathleen Joyce (J); TX; Colombia, 1974–75.

Sylvester, John Albert, Jr. (J); AL; Hong Kong/Macao, 1970–72.

Synco, Cornelia Elizabeth (SP); AL; Gaza, 1977–79.

Tackett, Tonita Noreen; OH; Brazil, 1979– .

Tallman, Gary Robert (A); WY; Rhodesia, 1976–78; South Africa, 1978– .

Tallman, Elizabeth Joann Griffith (Mrs. G. R.) (A); IA; Rhodesia, 1976–78; South Africa, 1978– .

Tamashiro, Linda Harue (J); HI; Honduras, 1974–76.

Tapp, Chester Garland, Jr.; GA; Gaza, 1979– .

Tapp, Judith Ann Emory (Mrs. C. G., Jr.); FL; Gaza, 1979– .

Tarpley, John Leeman; TN; Nigeria, 1977– .

Tarpley, Margaret Anne Johnson (Mrs. J. L.); TN; Nigeria, 1977– .

Tarry, Rebecca Jane (J); KY; Hong Kong, 1971–73.

Tatom, John Henry; OK; Indonesia, 1970–75; 1976– ; Thailand, 1975–76.

Tatum, Wilson Ray; TX; Lebanon, 1973–76; Yemen, 1976–78; Jordan, 1978– .

Tatum, Cheryl Anne Green (Mrs. W. R.); TX; Lebanon, 1973–76; Yemen, 1976–78; Jordan, 1978– .

Taylor, Edward Lynn, Jr.; MS; Brazil, 1979– .

Taylor, Nita Joan Kaler (Mrs. E. L., Jr.); KY; Brazil, 1979– .

Taylor, John Harold (A); IA; Kenya, 1976– .

Taylor, Virginia Marie Dobbs (Mrs. J. H.) (A); OK; Kenya, 1976– .

Taylor, Pamela Kay (J); TN; Brazil, 1972–74.

Taylor, Vi Marie Buster (Mrs. T. W.) (A); TX; Hong Kong, 1977- .

Teague, Patricia Jean McSwain (Mrs. G. F.) (A); NC; Jordan, 1976-78; Gaza, 1978- .

Teel, James Howard; AL; Reappointed; Bangladesh, 1979- .

Teel, Clara Maxine Yeager (Mrs. J. H.); AL; Reappointed; Bangladesh, 1979- .

Temple, Susan (J); TX; Kenya, 1979- .

Tenney, Claudia Rae (J); OH; Brazil, 1978- .

Terrell, Stephen Max (J); IN; Ethiopia, 1973-74.

Terry, Jerold Murphy; IL; Laos, 1970-75; Thailand, 1975-78; Sri Lanka, 1978-79.

Terry, Linda Lou Oakes (Mrs. J. M.); TX; Laos, 1970-75; Thailand, 1975-78; Sri Lanka, 1978-79.

Terry, John Mark; AR; Philippines, 1975- .

Terry, Barbara Ellen Whittle (Mrs. J. M.); TX; Philippines, 1975- .

Tesseneer, Susan Wyman (J); KY; Brazil, 1972-74.

Testerman, Dennis Eugene (J); VA; Nigeria, 1978- .

Thomas, Charles Frank; GA; Upper Volta, 1974-78; France, 1978- .

Thomas, Kathie Norvell Brown (Mrs. C. F.); KY; Upper Volta, 1974-78; France, 1978- .

Thomas, Larry Scott; TX; Tanzania, 1977- .

Thomas, Gayle Delight Bryan (Mrs. L. S.); TX; Tanzania, 1977- .

Thomas, Phyllis Dianne; NC; Chile, 1976- .

Thomas, Rebecca Sue (J); KY; Uruguay, 1977-79.

Thomas, Sarah Grace Stephens (Mrs. C. E., Jr.) (A); AL; Yemen, 1979- .

Thomason, Ann Elizabeth; LA; Taiwan, 1973- .

Thomaston, William Harold (A); AL; Nigeria, 1976- .

Thomaston, Martha Joyce Brooks (Mrs. W. H.) (A); GA; Nigeria, 1976- .

Thompson, Colleen (J); TX; Windward Islands, 1979- .

Thompson, Jess Boyd, Jr.; TX; Ghana, 1976- .

Thompson, Jesse Glen; TX; Philippines, 1975- .

Thompson, Marvella Kay Upton (Mrs. J. G.); TX; Philippines, 1975- .

Thompson, Thurman Bradley; TX; Mexico, 1974-78.

Thompson, Patricia Ann Bennett (Mrs. T. B.); AR; Mexico, 1974-78.

Thomsen, Gayla Annette (J); OK; Kenya, 1976-78.

Tilley, James Milton; TX; Brazil, 1977- .

Tilley, Thelma Fay Croom (Mrs. J. M.); TX; Brazil, 1977- .

Tillinghast, Jon Dalton; OK; Yemen, 1971-79.

Tillinghast, Alice Marie Gaidaroff (Mrs. J. D.); OK; Yemen, 1971-79.

Tobey, Manley William, III (J); MD; Thailand, 1978- .

Tobias, Nolan Conrad; MN; Costa Rica, 1976-79; Bahamas, 1979- .

Tobias, Carolyn Kay Leedy (Mrs. N. C.); MO; Costa Rica, 1976-79; Bahamas, 1979- .

Todd, Linda Sue (J); TN; Brazil, 1978- .

Todd, Naomi Louise (J); FL; Japan, 1978- .

Tom, Daniel (J); HI; Taiwan, 1971-73.

Tomlinson, Ben David (J); CA; Colombia, 1977-79.

Tomlinson, Marissa Mata (Mrs. B. D.) (J); IL; Colombia, 1977-79.

Tope, Charles Alvin; MO; Reappointed; Kenya, 1971-75.

Tope, LaVerne Warnecke (Mrs. C. A.); MO; Reappointed; Kenya, 1971-75.

Toro, Radames, Jr. (J); PR; Thailand, 1975-77.

Touchton, Patricia Anne (J); FL; Peru, 1973-75.

Townsend, John Mayes; TX; Brazil, 1979- .

Townsend, Sharon Dianne Kluck (Mrs. J. M.); TX; Brazil, 1979- .

Townsend, Thomas Craig; TN; Indonesia, 1975-75.

Townsend, Nancy Elaine Winters (Mrs. T. C.); CA; Indonesia, 1975-75.

Trail, Randy Clyde (J); TX; Liberia, 1977-79.

Travis, David Orion; OK; India, 1979- .

Travis, Glenda Gayle Cleveland (Mrs. D. O.); OK; India, 1979- .

Tressler, Penny Kay (J); ME; Venezuela, 1979- .

Truitt, William David; NY; Mexico, 1975- .

Truitt, Paula Sue Pevy (Mrs. W. D.); LA; Mexico, 1975- .

Tucker, Robert Lee (J); TN; Kenya, 1975-77.

Tucker, Roy Nelson; GA; Mexico, 1973-74.

Tucker, Carol Ann Barnette (Mrs. R. N.); GA; Mexico, 1973-74.

Tunnell, Gene Vaughan; MO; Vietnam, 1971-77; Honduras, 1977-78.

Tunnell, Priscilla Charlene Jones (Mrs. G. V.); GA; Vietnam, 1971-77; Honduras, 1977-78.

Turnbull, Thomas Dean (J); IL; Spain, 1976-78.

Turner, Cecil Edwin, Jr. (J); TX; Okinawa, 1972-74.

Turner, Lonnie; KY; Zambia, 1976- .

Turner, Frances Irene Howard (Mrs. Lonnie); KY; Zambia, 1976- .

Turner, Sammy Gene; AR; Kenya, 1970-78.

Turner, Bonnie Anne Sherman (Mrs. S. G.); OH; Kenya, 1970-78.

Turpin, Connie Corinne (J); NC; Brazil, 1976-78.

Tuttle, Robert Neil; NC; Japan, 1977- .

Tuttle, Susan Marie Spencer (Mrs. R. N.); KS; Japan, 1977- .

Twiford, Bobby Lee (A); VA; Rhodesia, 1974-78.

Twiford, Joahn Berryman (Mrs. B. L.) (A); VA; Rhodesia, 1974-78.

Tye, James Edward; OK; Ecuador, 1970- .

Tye, Shirley Ann Bynum (Mrs. J. E.); NM; Ecuador, 1970- .

Tyler, Phyllis Jane (J); TX; Vietnam, 1972-74.

Tyson, Beverly Kaye (J); AR; Brazil, 1978- .

Ullom, Robert Lynn; WV; Japan, 1978- .

Ullom, Maureen Powell (Mrs. R. L.); GA; Japan, 1978- .

Umberger, John Wendell (J); KY; Tanzania, 1976-78.

Umberger, Elizabeth Suzanne Fletcher (Mrs. J. W.) (J); GA; Tanzania, 1976-78.

Upshaw, David Franklin (J); VA; Kenya, 1974-76.

Upton, Samuel Tommy; MO; Malawi, 1971- .

Upton, Milda Marlyn Sconce (Mrs. S. T.); IL; Malawi, 1971- .

Valerius, Carol Ann (J); TX; Brazil, 1977-79.

Vance, Mary Pamela (J); TX; Switzerland, 1978- .

VandenHengel, George John, Jr.; PA; Argentina, 1979- .

VandenHengel, Marilyn Harris (Mrs. G. J., Jr.); VA; Argentina, 1979- .

VanDevender, William Douglas (J); TX; Vietnam, 1970-72.

Vandiver, Roy Alvin; TX; Ivory Coast, 1976- .

Vandiver, Connie Lee Gaultney (Mrs. R. A.); AL; Ivory Coast, 1976- .

Vasquez, Joe Sandoval; TX; Spain, 1975-77.

Vassar, Thomas Eli, Jr.; SC; Venezuela, 1977- .

Vassar, Margaret Ann Mathis (Mrs. T. E., Jr.); SC; Venezuela, 1977- .

Vaught, Betty Mae (A); OK; Hong Kong, 1970- .

Veal, Pamela Ann (J); TX; Mexico, 1970-72.

Venegas, Rafael Adrian; PR; Mexico, 1979- . .

Venegas, Mary Dale Clifton (Mrs. R. A.); AL; Mexico, 1979- .

Verm, Ray Alan; TX; Paraguay, 1976-79.

Verm, Justina Jane Leonard (Mrs. R. A.); TX; Paraguay, 1976-79.

Vessey, Susan Raylene (J); France; Japan, 1977-79.

Vestal, Patricia Elizabeth (J); AR; Brazil, 1976-78.

Vick, David Lee; AR; Argentina, 1978- .

Vick, Barbara Caston (Mrs. D. L.); LA; Argentina, 1978- .

Viertel, Weldon Ernest; TX; Reappointed; Barbados, 1970-72; Baptist Spanish Publishing House, 1972- .

Viertel, Mary Joyce Garrett (Mrs. W. E.); TX; Reappointed; Barbados, 1970-72; Baptist Spanish Publishing House, 1972- .

Viser, William Coke; TN; Brazil, 1978- .

Viser, Susan Kay Sims (Mrs. W. C.); AR; Brazil, 1978- .

Viverette, Charles Raymond, Jr. (J); TX; Jordan, 1978- .

Von Kanel, Randall Lewis (J); MS; Cayman Islands, 1978- .

Waddill, Thomas Albert; VA; Zambia, 1972- .

Waddill, Blanche Lucille Howard (Mrs. T. A.); NC; Zambia, 1972- .

Wade, George Thomas, Jr.; GA; Kenya, 1976-78; Botswana, 1979- .

Wade, Diana Sue Wolfe (Mrs. G. T., Jr.); OK; Kenya, 1976-78; Botswana, 1979- .

Wakefield, Larry Wayne; TN; Mexico, 1978- .

Wakefield, Peggy Ann Wright (Mrs. L. W.); KY; Mexico, 1978- .

Waldrop, Leo Eugene; TX; Surinam, 1971- .

Waldrop, Margaret LaVinia West (Mrs. L. E.); TX; Surinam, 1971- .

Wales, Beverly Kay (J); FL; Honduras, 1972-74.

Walker, Carlton Eugene, Jr. (J); VA; Taiwan, 1976-78.

Walker, James Charles; AL; Reappointed; Malawi, 1978- .

Walker, Charlotte Jean Fulton (Mrs. J. C.); AL; Reappointed; Malawi, 1978- .

Walker, Karen Denise (J); TX; Nigeria, 1977-79.

Walker, Michael Paul; IL; Ghana, 1979- .

Walker, Wanda Gale Wells (Mrs. M. P.); MA; Ghana, 1979- .

Walker, Richard Edward; TX; Reappointed; Brazil, 1975-77.

Walker, Beatrice Rodgers (Mrs. R. E.); AR; Reappointed; Brazil, 1975-77.

Walker, Toby Ray; OK; Argentina, 1972- .

Walker, Janet Laura Stephenson (Mrs. T. R.); OK; Argentina, 1972- .

Wall, Deborah Lee (J); GA; Korea, 1974-76.

Wallace, Barbara Jane (J); VA; Leeward Islands, 1976; French West Indies, 1977-78.

Wallace, David Ray; MO; Kenya, 1972- .

Wallace, Shary Ann Samuel (Mrs. D. R.); TX; Kenya, 1972- .

Wallace, Jolyne Elizabeth (A); TX; Gaza, 1974 .

Wallace, Karl Wesley; MS; Peru, 1978- .

Wallace, Peggy Susan Vaughn (Mrs. K. W.); MS; Peru, 1978- .

Ward, Demming Morton (SP); SC; India, 1977- .

Ward, Susan Clio Holloway (Mrs. D. M.) (SP); NC; India, 1977- .

Ward, John Douglas (J); Brazil; Belgium, 1977-79.

Ward, Mary Lynda (J); AL; Korea, 1977-79.

Ware, James Cullen; LA; Reappointed; Colombia, 1971-77.

Ware, Susan Goodwin (Mrs. J. C.); LA; Reappointed; Colombia, 1971-77.

Warren, Jack Douglas (J); TX; Brazil, 1973-75.

Warren, Ronald William (J); TN; Ghana, 1976-78.

Warrington, John Thomas; MS; Costa Rica, 1976- .

Warrington, Sandra Ellen Dill (Mrs. J. T.); MS; Costa Rica, 1976- .

Warth, Russell Lee (J); MI; Thailand, 1975-77.

Wasson, Lynda Anne (SP); AR; Gaza, 1978-79.

Watson, Carlotta Ann (J); SC; Gaza, 1979- .

Watson, James Delane; TX; Mexico, 1971-79; Panama, 1979- .

Watson, Margey Ruth Stohler (Mrs. J. D.); TX; Mexico, 1971-79; Panama, 1979- .

Watts, Harriet Elaine (J); TX; Tanzania, 1972-74.

Watts, Judy Lynne (J); AL; Korea, 1979- .

Watts, Reuben Victor (A); NC; Bophuthatswana, 1979- .

Watts, Mildred Jane Andrews (Mrs. R. V.) (A); VA; Bophuthatswana, 1979- .

Waugh, Phillip Harvey (J); NC; Taiwan, 1978- .

Waugh, Cynthia Drake (Mrs. P. H.) (J); IN; Taiwan, 1978- .

Weatherman, Leo Edward (A); IA; Brazil, 1978- .

Weatherman, Dorothy Mae Hiler (Mrs. L. E.) (A); AR; Brazil, 1978- .

Weaver, Cynthia Marie; TN; Taiwan, 1979- .

Webb, John Darrell (J); GA; Brazil, 1979- .

Webb, Lehman Franklin (A); AR; Singapore, 1970-77.

Webb, Nettie Virginia Bryant (Mrs. L. F.) (A); AR; Singapore, 1970-77.

Webster, Steven Lee (J); VA; France, 1978- .

Weems, Marion Lee (J); TN; Vietnam, 1970-72.

Welborn, Barbara Anne (J); SC; Korea, 1973-75.

Welborn, Cathryn Sue (J); OK; Dominican Republic, 1976-78.

Welch, Virginia Ann (J); VA; Zambia, 1977-79.

Wellmon, Wayne Kenneth (A); NC; Windward Islands, 1978- .

Wellmon, Sylvia Allen Polk (Mrs. W. K.) (A); NC; Windward Islands, 1978- .

West, Morris Ray; TX; Chile, 1977- .

West, Elizabeth Cox (Mrs. M. R.); TX; Chile, 1977- .

West, Ronald Eual; AR; Taiwan, 1978- .

West, Elinda Faye Tidwell (Mrs. R. E.); AR; Taiwan, 1978- .

West, Vernal Ray; OK; Kenya, 1971- .

West, Patsy Ann Ingram (Mrs. V. R.); OK; Kenya, 1971- .

Westbrook, Charles Norris; SC; Japan, 1978- .

Westbrook, Jane Derrick (Mrs. C. N.); SC; Japan, 1978- .

Westfall, Sandra Alane (J); MO; Japan, 1971-73.

Wharton, Dwight Albert (J); AR; Zambia, 1979- .

Wheeler, Harold Loyd (A); TX; Brazil, 1976- .

Wheeler, Gloria Beatrice Bell (Mrs. H. L.) (A); TX; Brazil, 1976- .

Whitaker, Carol Lee (J); IA; Japan, 1974-76.

White, Elmer Elwood (A); NM; Colombia, 1979- .

White, Lavona Kay Garrison (Mrs. E. E.) (A); TX; Colombia, 1979- .

White, Jerry Beason; MS; Korea, 1974- .

White, Glenda Rae Nix (Mrs. J. B.); MS; Korea, 1974- .

White, Joseph Phil (SP); AL; India, 1978- .

White, Leon Solomon; AL; Argentina, 1970- .

White, Sarah Lou Tyler (Mrs. L. S.); AL; Argentina, 1970- .

White, Lynda Jean; VA; Yemen, 1974-79.

White, Lynn Ashley (J); TN; Liberia, 1978- .

White, Robert Charles (J); GA; Botswana, 1977-79.

White, Shelby Randell (J); KY; Hong Kong, 1979- .

Whitler, Rachel Ann (J); KY; Philippines, 1978- .

Wickes, Dorothy Elizabeth Jeffries (Mrs. H. W.) (A); IN; Gaza, 1976- .

Wigger, Larry David; MO; Reappointed; Indonesia, 1976- .

Wigger, Barbara Jean Jett (Mrs. L. D.); MO; Reappointed; Indonesia, 1976- .

Wilburn, Janet Merle; OK; Argentina, 1979- .

Wilkens, Edy Louise (J); TX; Guatemala, 1973-75.

Wilkinson, Christopher Wayne (J); FL; Liberia, 1979- .

Wilkinson, Gwendle Van Smith (Mrs. C. W.) (J); TN; Liberia, 1979- .

Williams, Brenda Merle (J); MO; Brazil, 1972-74.

Williams, Cecil Broward (A); FL; Tanzania, 1979- .

Williams, Aline Veryl Weber (Mrs. C. B.) (A); FL; Tanzania, 1979- .

Williams, Donald Marvin; CA; France, 1978- .

Williams, Peggy Jean Hughes (Mrs. D. M.); TX; France, 1978- .

Williams, Donna Lynn (J); OK; Mexico, 1977-79.

Williams, Fred Leon (A); AR; Brazil, 1971-79.

Williams, Geraldine Helen Washington (Mrs. F. L.) (A); OK; Brazil, 1971-79.

Williams, James Archie, Jr.; GA; Eastern Europe, 1976- .

Williams, Nada Horak (Mrs. J. A., Jr.); Yugoslavia; Eastern Europe, 1976- .

Williams, Joey Herbert; NM; Jordan, 1971-74; Rhodesia, 1974- .

Williams, Sylvia Evelyn Lawrence (Mrs. J. H.); NJ; Jordan, 1971-74; Rhodesia, 1974- .

Williams, John Luther; VA; Brazil, 1974- .

Williams, Loretta Lee Clinton (Mrs. J. L.); AL; Brazil, 1974- .

Williams, Keith Harris; MO; Philippines, 1979- .

Williams, Suzanne Baird (Mrs. K. H.); OK; Philippines, 1979- .

Williams, Mary Ruth (J); TX; Philippines, 1972-74.

Williams, Michael Edward; LA; Honduras, 1976-79.

Williams, Deborah Ramona Simmons (Mrs. M. E.); TX; Honduras, 1976-79.

Williams, Robert Alexander, Jr.; TN; Honduras, 1970- .

Williams, Olivia Eugenia Burrell (Mrs. R. A., Jr.); GA; Honduras, 1970- .

Williams, Sue Ann (J); MO; Nigeria, 1971; Rhodesia, 1971-73.

Williams, Tommie Andrew (J); GA; Israel, 1978- .

Williams, Van Wagner, III; MS; India, 1974- .

Williams, Sarah Kathryn McGlamery (Mrs. V. W., III); TX; India, 1974- .

Williams, William David, Jr.; Germany; Colombia, 1977-79.

Williams, Cathy Elaine Northcutt (Mrs. W. D., Jr.); GA; Colombia, 1977-79.

Williamson, Robert Ellis; AL; Rhodesia, 1975-79; Bophuthatswana, 1979- .

Williamson, Vicki Darlene Davis (Mrs. R. E.); AL; Rhodesia, 1975-79; Bophuthatswana, 1979- .

Willis, James Russell, II (J); CO; Ethiopia, 1974-76.

Willis, Joy Eileen (J); NM; Argentina, 1971-73.

Wilson, Charles Edward (J); AL; Spain, 1974-76.

Wilson, Gene O'Neil; SC; Reappointed; Brazil, 1976- .

Wilson, Angelle Kenney (Mrs. G. O.); GA; Reappointed; Brazil, 1976- .

Wilson, George Raymond, Jr.; OK; Reappointed; Hong Kong, 1978- .

Wilson, Elizabeth Schreiber (Mrs. G. R., Jr.); FL; Reappointed; Hong Kong, 1978- .

Wilson, Glenice (J); TX; Kenya, 1977-79.

Wilson, James David; TX; Colombia, 1978- .

Wilson, Sue Ella Copple (Mrs. J. D.); TX; Colombia, 1978- .

Wilson, James Henry (J); TX; Okinawa, 1970-72.

Wilson, Jere Allan; GA; Brazil, 1973-77.

Wilson, Joyce Ann Braswell (Mrs. J. A.); IL; Brazil, 1973-77.

Wilson, Linda Faye (J); KY; Costa Rica, 1971-73.

Wilson, Mary Linda (J); GA; Ivory Coast, 1978- .

Wilson, Michael Stanley; OK; Togo, 1977- .

Wilson, Vera Beth Phillips (Mrs. M. S.); OK; Togo, 1977- .

Wilson, Patricia Anne (J); TX; Korea, 1978- .

Wilson, Ronald Bruce; SC; Dominican Republic, 1976- .

Wilson, Janice Sue Hinson (Mrs. R. B.); SC; Dominican Republic, 1976- .

Windus, Anna Kay (J); NY; Mexico, 1978- .

Winstead, Ronnie Gilbert; AR; Taiwan, 1971- .

Winstead, Ina Mae Jones (Mrs. R. G.); MO; Taiwan, 1971- .

Wise, Betty Carla (J); TN; Paraguay, 1975-77.

Witherspoon, John Allen; MO; Argentina, 1970- .

Witherspoon, Linda Louise Eagleson (Mrs. J. A.); KS; Argentina, 1970- .

Witten, Larry Franklin (J); KY; Ethiopia, 1976; Malawi, 1977-78.

Wohler, Cynthia Jean (J); MN; Korea, 1977-79.

Wolf, James Michael; OK; Taiwan, 1971- .

Wolf, Patricia Adeline Pickle (Mrs. J. M.); WI; Taiwan, 1971- .

Womack, Milton Onard; OK; Singapore, 1975-76; Hong Kong, 1976- .

Womack, Mary Anne Clark (Mrs. M. O.); SC; Singapore, 1975-76; Hong Kong, 1976- .

Womack, William Lloyd, Sr. (A); MO; Guyana, 1971-72; Leeward Islands, 1972- .

Womack, Elba Walker (Mrs. W. L., Sr.) (A); MO; Guyana, 1971-72; Leeward Islands, 1972- .

Woodcock, Diane Gwen (J); VA; Macao, 1977-79.

Woods, Elmon Lloyd (A); TX; Rhodesia, 1976-78; Liberia, 1979- .

Woods, Joann Cannon (Mrs. E. L.) (A); TX; Rhodesia, 1976–78; Liberia, 1979– .

Woods, Tony Ray; TX; Japan, 1978– .

Woods, Marsha Glee Smith (Mrs. T. R.); CO; Japan, 1978– .

Woolwine, Sylvia Lynn (J); TN; Nigeria, 1976–78.

Wootton, James Leonard (A); IL; Korea, 1970– .

Wootton, Mary Lou Teegarden (Mrs. J. L.) (A); IL; Korea, 1970– .

Workman, Gerald Monroe, Jr.; TX; Malawi, 1970– .

Workman, Barbara Ann Fetters (Mrs. G. M., Jr.); TX; Malawi, 1970– .

Worthington, Anne Earle (J); MD; Brazil, 1975–77.

Wright, Andrew Charles (J); WA; Vietnam, 1972–74.

Wright, Charles Thomas (J); GA; Thailand, 1979– .

Wright, Elizabeth Palmer (J); VA; India, 1979– .

Wright, Gerald David; TX; Nigeria, 1979– .

Wright, Kathren Brenda Scruggs (Mrs. G. D.); TX; Nigeria, 1979– .

Wright, Jo Anna (J); LA; Gaza, 1971–73.

Wright, John Rowland, Jr. (J); VA; Ghana, 1977–79.

Wright, Marvin Roger; DE; France, 1979– .

Wright, Linda Ann Wilson (Mrs. M. R.); DE; France, 1979– .

Wyckoff, Arthur Robert; NJ; Brazil, 1976– .

Wyckoff, Shirley May Tysen (Mrs. A. R.); NY; Brazil, 1976– .

Wylie, Ted David; OK; Philippines, 1976–77.

Wylie, Dawn Ella Kircher (Mrs. T. D.); KS; Philippines, 1976–77.

Yagi, Dickson Kazuo; HI; Japan, 1971– .

Yagi, Ellen Ogawa (Mrs. D. K.); CA; Japan, 1971– .

Yarbrough, Sarah Diane (J); AL; India, 1974–76.

Yarbrough, Teddy Everett; AL; Guatemala, 1972– .

Yarbrough, Glenda Frances Mixon (Mrs. T. E.); FL; Guatemala, 1972– .

Yeakey, Kerry Clay (J); MS; Indonesia, 1974–76.

Yoder, Larry Carl; PA; Belgium, 1971–76.

Yoder, Laurabelle Evelyn Barr (Mrs. L. C.); KY; Belgium, 1971–76.

Yon, Jo Anne (J); VA; Peru, 1978– .

York, Ted Elden (J); NC; Liberia, 1974–76.

Young, Brenda Gayle (J); TX; Upper Volta, 1978– .

Young, David Ray; OK; Austria, 1979– .

Young, Gail Elizabeth Longino (Mrs. D. R.); MS; Austria, 1979– .

Young, David Vern; TX; Yemen, 1978– .

Young, Neta Ann Hendricks (Mrs. D. V.); CA; Yemen, 1978– .

Young, Hilmon Earl (A); VA; Ghana, 1977–78.

Young, Inez Napier (Mrs. H. E.) (A); VA; Ghana, 1977–78.

Young, Jack Newberry; MO; Reappointed; Brazil, 1977– .

Young, Betty Jean DeVore (Mrs. J. N.); TX; Reappointed; Brazil, 1977– .

Young, Joe Vernon (J); KY; Liberia, 1979– .

Young, Kathy Emily (J); TN; Tanzania, 1974–76.

Zuckero, Florence Elizabeth (J); TX; Tanzania, 1976–78.

DOROTHY OWEN

FOREIGN MISSIONS, DIRECTIONS IN. *Foreign Mission Board Members.*—FMB

members evinced a desire to become more involved in the work of foreign missions. In 1975 the board pointed out to the SBC Executive Committee "the great importance of the work of local members of the board and our hope that their number will not be substantially reduced or eliminated." Nevertheless, in 1977 SBC action reduced the number of local board members from 18 to 12.

The FMB stoutly resisted the suggestion of the Committee of Fifteen that the SBC Executive Committee draw up a strategy for home and foreign missions. The result was a crisis situation in which the role of agency boards' trustees was first questioned and then reaffirmed; and the two mission boards were instructed, in due course, to formulate strategies for the future. Bold Mission Thrust was the ultimate outcome.

The Administrative Committee, on Feb. 10, 1976, reaffirmed the FMB's "long-standing position of non-involvement of its missionary representatives in political affairs." The committee took this action in response to irresponsible charges made in the public press and otherwise that missionaries were agents of the Central Intelligence Agency.

Administration.—The FMB increased the number of overseas fields from 71 to 94 and, as the work enlarged, created new administrative areas by dividing existing areas. These and other developments necessitated staff adjustments and additions. The field representative plan, which originated in Latin America, was made operational worldwide. Mission support projects, aimed at making missions more real and needs more specific, were directed more pointedly at individuals, churches, associations, state conventions, and institutions.

Financially, the FMB and its operations enjoyed unprecedented support from the churches in terms of actual amounts given for foreign missions. Receipts from the Cooperative Program, Lottie Moon Christmas Offering, and other sources increased significantly. The percentage of total Cooperative Program receipts for SBC causes which the FMB received, however, tended to diminish. If income increased, so did the needs. Money was never adequate to meet them. Expansion into new countries and new ministries made larger budgets not only unavoidable but highly imperative. Soaring inflation at home and overseas and other problems created hardships. Devaluation of the United States dollar caused special pressure on FMB funds.

Staff: Missionary and Home Office.—The missionary staff increased from 2,490 at the end of 1969 to 3,008 at the end of 1979. The growth rate in short-term categories was proportionately greater than in the career category. Personnel losses, though regrettable, seemed unavoidable. The Mission Service Corps, established by SBC action in 1977, hoped to involve 5,000 Southern Baptists in one- to two-year missionary assignments, either in the United States or overseas.

Multiplied opportunities existed for reinforcing mission efforts through a variety of volunteer short-term projects, and through involvement of non-missionary personnel living overseas. Missionary roles changed somewhat toward a helping stance and further changes were predicted. Women missionaries assumed enlarged responsibilities, with better-defined types of missionary service.

The FMB explored ways to make furloughs more meaningful, recognized and emphasized board responsibility for furlough time, and promoted in-service training to upgrade or sharpen missionary skills. Innovations for missionary children included one trip back to the field at board expense for those in college. Services honoring retiring missionaries and home office staff members became a regular agenda item for the annual board meeting.

Overseas Ministries.—Evangelism and church development continued to be the central thrusts of missionary labors. The FMB attempted new approaches. Correspondence courses were used as media for Christian witness and growth and as follow-up for broadcasts and evangelistic campaigns. The population movement from rural to urban areas led to experimentation to find new ways of reaching and ministering to the masses in the cities. Statistical reports from the FMB to the SBC reflected heightened or awakened interest in radio and television, student centers, book stores, library-reading rooms, and the number of missionaries involved in agricultural work.

Theological Education by Extension, while not an exact substitute for training in residence, was used more and more to assist students unable to spend several years in a theological training center.

Traditionally, Southern Baptists have tended to keep publications and radio and television separate and distinct. This past decade, however, witnessed a recognition of their relatedness, as well as the desirability of carefully coordinating all mass media efforts for maximum impact.

The FMB augmented "curative medicine" in medical missions with "preventive medicine." The health care team, as a consequence, was amplified to include new members.

FRANK K. MEANS

FORK UNION MILITARY ACADEMY (I, III). In 1973 Fork Union celebrated its 75th anniversary. A new infirmary, named for Julian H. Yeatman, academy physician for 49 years, was constructed in 1978. In the 1978-79 session, 662 students from 31 states and 20 foreign countries were enrolled. There were 84 high school graduates in 1979, and 82 received postgraduate high school certificates. Total assets on June 30,

1979, were $6,923,682. Kenneth T. Whitescarver has served as president since 1968.

A. PAUL THOMPSON

FORMOSA, MISSION IN (I). See Taiwan (Formosa), Mission in.

FOUNDATION EXECUTIVES, THE ASSOCIATION OF BAPTIST. See Association of Baptist Foundation Executives.

FOUNTAIN, DAVID C. (b. New York State, 1843; d. Washington, DC, June 9, 1920). Prominent layman and church founder. He and his wife Josephine had three children: Clarence, Winifred, and Elizabeth. After serving in the New York Infantry during the Civil War, Fountain came to Washington to fill an appointment in the federal government. He worked also as a public-school teacher and assistant postmaster, serving in the latter position until his death. Joining Second Baptist Church in 1873, he served as deacon, trustee, and Sunday School superintendent. Fountain assisted in the early days of Capitol Hill Sunday School which led to the establishment of Metropolitan Baptist Church, now Capitol Hill-Metropolitan Church, in 1879.

Fountain then led in establishing a Sunday School near Uniontown, DC, which resulted in the formation of the Anacostia Baptist Church, now First Baptist of Friendly, MD, in 1884. In 1891 he organized a Sunday School which in 1895 became the East Washington Heights Baptist Church. He served these churches as Sunday School superintendent, church treasurer, and deacon.

In 1908 Fountain began a Sunday School which became Randle Highlands Mission. It is now the Fountain Memorial Baptist Church. He is buried in the Congressional Cemetery in the District of Columbia.

FRANCES BECK

FRANCE, MISSION IN (III). In 1979 the French Baptist Federation had 3,000 members in 88 churches and preaching points. About 1,500 other Baptists were in France, most of them unrelated to the European Baptist Federation or the Baptist World Alliance. The Federation has a small pastoral school, a radio recording studio, and a youth hostel, all under one roof in Paris. A children's home is north of Paris. In 1979 eight Southern Baptist missionary couples and a journeyman were serving in France. Five of the couples were in pioneer evangelism, seeking to establish and build up churches in cities where Baptists were unknown. A new church in Bordeaux has resulted from this missionary effort.

J. D. HUGHEY

FREE WILL BAPTISTS, NATIONAL ASSOCIATION OF (I, III). The National Association of Free Will Baptists grew 28 percent in the 1970s with a membership surge from 181,136 to 231,167. The group organized 274 new churches and ended the decade with 2,437 churches in 41 states. The movement observed its 250th anniversary in 1977.

Three landmark decisions concerning other denominations, higher education, and literature publication influenced the movement. The NAFWB terminated its 26-year affiliation with the National Association of Evangelicals in 1972. In 1977 Free Will Baptist Bible College, Nashville, TN, which awarded 574 bachelor's degrees in the 1970s, was instructed to develop a graduate program for Free Will Baptist students. The school previously received an A rating from the University of Tennessee and certification for teacher training in elementary education. In 1978 the Church Training Service Department and the Sunday School Department merged into the Sunday School and Church Training Department, placing all curriculum materials under one board and general director.

Leadership changes occurred in six of eight national departments, leaving only the Sunday School Department and the Retirement and Insurance Department with uninterrupted leadership. The decade's major publishing effort was the publication of *Who's Who Among Free Will Baptists* (1978), 493 pages of biographies and encyclopedic denominational information.

Missions and education benefited as per capita giving rose 164 percent from $61.83 to $163.52 and the Home Missions Department, Foreign Missions Department, and FWBBC tripled their budgets. Home missions increased from 30 missionaries and a $200,000 budget in 1970 to 96 missionaries and a $987,564 budget in 1979; foreign missions from a $640,000 budget and 73 missionaries to a $1,800,000 budget and 98 missionaries; and the FWBBC from a $635,000 budget and 480 students to a $1,700,000 budget and 614 students.

JACK WILLIAMS

FREEDOM, BAPTISTS FOR. See BAPTISTS FOR FREEDOM.

FREEMAN, JOHN DELONG (b. Allene, AR, Feb. 25, 1884; d. Nashville, TN, Oct. 11, 1974). Pastor, editor, and denominational executive. The son of John D. Freeman and Mary Mecha Mills, farmers, he attended the University of Arkansas (B.A., 1910), Duke University (M.A., 1913), and The Southern Baptist Theological Seminary (Th.M., 1916). He married Landis Barton, Oct. 9, 1918. They had two daughters, Georgia Mae and Lucy Catherine.

Ordained by First Baptist Church, Conway, AR, May 31, 1914, Freeman was pastor in Louisville, KY; Springfield, KY; and Nashville, TN. He also served as missionary in southwest Arkansas, 1916-18. He became editor of the *Baptist and Reflector*, Tennessee Baptist state paper, in 1925, holding that position until July 1, 1933, when he became executive secretary of the Tennessee Baptist Convention.

Freeman led in the organization of the Tennessee Baptist Foundation in 1938 and was its first executive secretary, while serving as the Tennessee Convention's executive secretary. He resigned both positions in Nov., 1942, to become editor of the *Western Recorder,* Kentucky Baptist state paper. In 1946 he joined the staff of the Home Mission Board, serving as secretary of the Rural Church Department until his retirement in 1951. He is buried in Mt. Olivet Cemetery, Nashville, TN.

ALVIN C. SHACKLEFORD

FRENCH WEST INDIES, MISSION IN (III). In May, 1978, the mission began functioning as two stations, one each on Guadeloupe and Martinique. Three families and one journeyman are assigned to Guadeloupe, serving four churches and one mission point with an approximate resident membership of 76 and an average Sunday School attendance of 142. Some sects are strong and others are gaining influence as Baptists and one other evangelical group seek to present the claims of Christ to a materialistic society.

Baptist witness on Martinique began over three decades ago with non-Southern Baptist groups. One strong church is led by a pastor from France. The first Southern Baptist missionary couple moved to Martinique in 1978 and began worship services in their home. The first baptism was in 1979. Shortly after the arrival of a second missionary couple in 1979, a small house was secured in a public housing development, and the Good Shepherd Mission was begun.

DANIEL R. O'DELL and GEORGE M. GERA

FRUITLAND BAPTIST BIBLE INSTITUTE (I). Owned and operated by the Baptist State Convention of North Carolina, the Fruitland Baptist Bible Institute offers ministerial education for persons unable to attend college or seminary. In addition to courses in the biblical, theological, historical, and practical areas of ministerial training, the curriculum includes basic adult education courses for the 200 students who attend the school. From its beginning, the institute has offered a diploma program for its 1,200-plus alumni. Some of these graduates have continued their education at a college or seminary. Many of them serve effectively as ministers throughout the SBC.

See also BIBLE INSTITUTE, THE, VOL. III.

KAY M. HUGGINS

FUNDAMENTAL BAPTIST FELLOWSHIP, THE (I). See WORLD BAPTIST FELLOWSHIP.

FURMAN UNIVERSITY (I, III). During the last six years of the administration of President Gordon Williams Blackwell, 1970-76, Furman continued to strengthen its academic program. In 1971, in cooperation with Clemson University, Furman established a Master of Business Administration program. The university set up a Division of Continuing Education in 1973. Phi Beta Kappa granted the university a chapter in the same year.

Blackwell established a development office, reorganized and expanded the business affairs office, and reorganized the administrative structure of the student affairs office. In an effort to involve a larger segment of the university in decision making and planning, he set up an office of institutional planning and research and established a management planning program. To assure continuing communication with South Carolina Baptists, he appointed an assistant to the president for denominational relations.

Development of the campus continued with the construction of a physical activities center, 1973, and a music building, 1975. The installation of an advanced computer in 1976 greatly increased the computer center's data processing and computing capabilities. Construction continued in 1977 with the enclosure of a portion of the library patio, creating space for 50,000 volumes and 42 study carrels. In 1978 a second greenhouse and new learning resource centers for biology, computer science, and mathematics were constructed.

In 1975-76 Furman celebrated its 150th anniversary. Following the retirement of Blackwell in 1976, John E. Johns, former president of Stetson University, became the ninth president of Furman.

Beginning in the mid-1970s, four grants made possible an extensive faculty development program: the Kellogg Foundation, 1975, a three-year grant to improve faculty planning and encourage faculty to introduce new courses, revise old ones, and devise new instructional techniques; the Lilly Foundation, 1978, a grant to improve the teaching of new faculty; the Mellon Foundation, 1978, a three-year grant for the professional growth of mid-career faculty; and the National Endowment for the Humanities, 1979, a challenge grant to upgrade and advance instruction in the humanities.

Under Johns, denominational relations have been strengthened. The university established a program to assist students interested in church-related careers. A special committee appointed to study the nine institutions and agencies supported by the South Carolina Baptist Convention published a report acknowledging Furman's fiscal responsibility and reputation for academic excellence.

On July 22, 1980, Furman broke ground for an infirmary and announced plans for a three-year $30,000,000 fund-raising campaign. Money raised will go toward building construction and renovation, faculty support, student and program development, endowment, and current operations.

In the fall of 1979, enrollment included 2,363 undergraduates; 372 graduate students, including 190 in the Clemson-Furman M.B.A. program; and 335 students in the Division of Continuing Education. Eighty-four percent of the 145 full-time faculty members held earned doctorates. Total assets in May, 1979, were $66,349,000; endowment was $19,614,000; and income from endowment was $1,780,000.

MARGUERITE HAYS

FUSON, WILLIAM ALBERT (b. Wakefield, IL, Sep. 24, 1869; d. Terre Haute, IN, Feb. 16, 1963). Pastor, home missionary, state evangelist, and associational missionary. The son of Abigail Lemmon and William M. Fuson, a minister, he married Laura Carter, Mar. 5, 1890. They had five children: Sarah, Robert, Thomas, Evelyn, and Roxie. Ordained in 1892, Fuson served as a minister for more than 70 years, leading 24 churches and organizing several new churches. Affectionately called "Bill the Baptist," Fuson often debated ministers of other denominations on doctrinal points. He helped organize the Illinois Baptist State Association in 1907 and served as moderator in 1913-14. He is buried in Washington Street Cemetery, Casey, IL.

JIM NORMAN

G

GAMBLING (I). The deliberate wagering of valuable considerations upon events which lie mostly in the realm of chance or luck. Estimates of the amount gambled annually in the United States often exceed $50,000,000,000.

State legalized gambling has grown in recent years. Many states have legalized bingo, casino gambling, lotteries, and off-track betting. Numerous studies have pointed out the problems associated with legalized gambling: (1) gambling fails to produce significant revenues; (2) the poor are most victimized by legalized gambling; and (3) gambling continues to be a large source of income for organized crime.

With regard to SBC action in the 1970s, only the messengers to the 1977 Convention addressed the issue of gambling. A general resolution on Christian morality stated, "We express vigorous opposition to gambling in all its forms, and especially to the efforts of the gambling industry to legalize gambling by state and national laws; . . . and . . . we commend members of our legislatures and of Congress who take a stand against the evils of legalized gambling and support them in their defense of public morality."

PHIL STRICKLAND

GARDNER, DAVID MARSHALL (b. Milan, TN, Nov. 12, 1886; d. Dallas, TX, Oct. 25, 1972). Pastor and editor. Son of Jesse Franklin and Catherine Cordelia (West) Gardner, sharecroppers, he was a graduate of Baylor University (1912) and Southwestern Baptist Theological Seminary (1914). He married Sadie Ray Woodward of Clarendon, TX, May 19, 1915. They had three children: Sadie, David, Jr., and Edith. He served as pastor of Baptist churches at Clarendon, TX, 1915-16, and Memphis, TX, 1917-20; Ensley Church, Birmingham, AL, 1920-29; First Church, St. Petersburg, FL, 1929-44. He was author of *A Rainbow for Every Cloud* (1935), *Radiant Realities* (1938), and *Pictures of Salvation* (1939).

Named editor of the *Baptist Standard* of Texas in 1944, he established a reputation for bold editorials. He was a strong opponent of church union. He also encouraged Texas Baptists to accept the 1954 Supreme Court desegregation decision. Gardner's 10-year editorship of the *Standard* was characterized by steady circulation growth—from 110,000 to 281,000. With assets of $1,000,000, the paper moved to its own building on the edge of the central business district of Dallas. He is buried in Hillcrest Mausoleum, Dallas, TX.

JOHN J. HURT

GARDNER, JOSEPH WATT (b. Melbourne, AR, Oct. 30, 1884; d. Austin, TX, June, 1975). Missionary to the deaf. Converted at the age of 10, he graduated from the University of Arkansas (B.A., 1906) and The Southern Baptist Theological Seminary (Th.M., 1914). He married Iva Cox, Oct. 3, 1914. Under appointment by the Home Mission Board, he traveled throughout the South preaching to the deaf and speaking to churches about deaf work. He is buried at Austin, TX.

CARTER E. BEARDEN

GARDNER-WEBB COLLEGE (I, III). Elevated to four-year status in 1969, the college was accredited by the Southern Association of Colleges and Schools in 1971. A member of the North Carolina Association of Colleges and Universities and accredited by the National League of Nursing, the National Association of Schools of Music, and the North Carolina Board of Higher Education, the college awards A.A., B.A., B.S., and M.A. degrees. On a 1200-acre campus with 30 buildings and an 80-member faculty, the college conducts a day program, an evening college, a summer school, and a graduate program for 1,500 students. E. Eugene Poston resigned as president in 1976 and was succeeded by Craven Williams. The total assets of the college in 1980 were $17,250,000.

CRAVEN WILLIAMS

GARRISON, GEORGE FRANK (b. Greenville, GA, Sep. 27, 1898; d. Atlanta, GA, Jan. 11, 1981). Home missions administrator. The son of John Thomas Garrison, farmer-merchant, and Sallie Culpepper Garrison, he was a graduate of Locust Grove Institute, Locust Grove, GA (1918), and attended Mercer University for one year. He married Gladys Simmons of Macon, GA, Dec. 22, 1920. They had one son, George Frank Garrison, Jr.

Elected to the board of directors of the Home Mission Board, SBC, in 1930, he served as recording secretary, 1931-44, and as president, 1944-53. Garrison, an insurance agent, joined the HMB staff in 1953 as assistant executive secretary-treasurer and superintendent of church loan funds. He was recognized in 1962 for his involvement in the acquisition of a three-story office building, later enlarged to eight stories, when the 161 Spring Street structure was named the Lawrence-Garrison Building.

During his 12-year guidance of the church loans operation, the corpus of the board's loan funds multiplied more than four times. During this period, he gave primary attention to the board's business and financial concerns. Upon his retirement in 1965, the church loans operation and the general business concerns of the HMB were separated.

Other service included: Member, SBC Inter-Agency Council; moderator, Atlanta Baptist Association; and member, SBC Committee on Denominational Calendar. He is buried in Westview Cemetery, Atlanta, GA.

RUTH MCKINNEY

GARROTT, WILLIAM MAXFIELD (b. Batesville, AR, June 20, 1910; d. Winston-Salem, NC, June 25, 1974). Foreign missionary. The son of E. P. J. Garrott and Eula Maxfield, a pastoral family, he attended Hendrix College (B.A., 1929), The Southern Baptist Theological Seminary (Th.M., 1932; Ph.D., 1934), and Union Theological Seminary. He married Dorothy Shepard Carver, Dec. 29, 1938. Their children were Elizabeth, William, Dorothy, and Jackson. Appointed by the Foreign Mission Board, Apr. 19, 1934, he served in Japan, 1934-41 and 1947-74. The last Southern Baptist missionary remaining in Japan in 1941, he was interned and repatriated, 1942. Garrott was assigned to Hawaii, 1946-47, until he could return to Japan. He served as professor and president of Seinan Gakuin University, 1948-52. He is buried at Kitakyushu, Japan.

FRANK K. MEANS

GAVELS, SOUTHERN BAPTIST CONVENTION (I). Woman's Missionary Union of the SBC presented two gavels of historical significance and special interest to the Convention at its 1981 meeting in Los Angeles, CA. Christine Burton Gregory, WMU president, presented the gavels to Bailey E. Smith, SBC president, with the expressed hope that the gavels would be "a reminder to Convention presidents and Convention messengers that the important business of the Convention is missions."

The Lottie Moon Gavel, named for this famous missionary, was made of wild cherry wood from a tree cut at Viewmont, birthplace of Lottie (Charlotte) Moon (*q.v.* II) near Scottsville, VA.

The Annie Armstrong Gavel, named for this founder and early leader of WMU, was made from a stair railing post at the Eutaw Place Baptist Church in Baltimore, MD (now known as Woodbrook Baptist Church), which Annie Walker Armstrong (*q.v.* I) helped to organize in 1871 and in which she served for over 30 years.

LYNN E. MAY, JR.

GAZA, MISSION IN (I, III). Gaza, ruled by Israel, had one small Baptist church (Arabic- and English-speaking) on the Baptist hospital compound in 1980. The compound served as the center for the work of 32 missionaries in this country. For 26 years missionaries have ministered in this 60-bed hospital. Seventy-six students were studying nursing in the School of Health Sciences, one of three institutions in Gaza which offer specialized educational opportunities. The library located on a Gaza thoroughfare was also providing an effective ministry.

ELISE NANCE BRIDGES

GENERAL ASSOCIATION OF GENERAL BAPTISTS. See GENERAL BAPTISTS, GENERAL ASSOCIATION OF.

GENERAL ASSOCIATION OF REGULAR BAPTIST CHURCHES. See REGULAR BAPTIST CHURCHES, GENERAL ASSOCIATION OF.

GENERAL ASSOCIATION OF SEPARATE BAPTISTS IN CHRIST. See SEPARATE BAPTISTS IN CHRIST, GENERAL ASSOCIATION OF.

GENERAL BAPTISTS, GENERAL ASSOCIATION OF (I). In the late 1970s the General Association reported 72,764 members in 837 churches in 16 states. Its major strength is in the Midwest, and its headquarters are in Poplar Bluff, MO. In 1980 the denomination completed its world headquarters building, which houses various denominational ministries, such as departments of Christian Education and Publications, Women's Missions, Evangelism, Stewardship, and Nursing Home Ministries. The denomination also sponsors home and foreign missions.

The denominational paper is the *General Baptist Messenger,* edited by Wayne Faust. General Baptists also sponsor Oakland City College, which won accreditation in 1978. The basic budget of the denomination increased 160 percent during the 1970s, reaching the $1,000,000 mark for the first time. During the decade the denomination planted about 100 churches through its home mission program and planted 75 new churches in Jamaica and the Philippines through foreign mission efforts. The General Association opened new book stores, initiated an area consultant service, and developed a new thrust in youth ministries.

See also GENERAL BAPTISTS, Vol. I.

WAYNE FOUST

GEORGETOWN COLLEGE (I, III). The 1970s began with the announcement that five new dormitories would be built at a cost of $1,361,000. The project was included in the developing residence park area of the campus which eventually included 12 dormitories.

In Sep., 1972, the Kresge Foundation of Birmingham, MI, awarded a $50,000 challenge grant to Georgetown to apply towards the renovation of Giddings Hall, the projected administrative center of the campus. Two months later, the James Graham Brown Foundation of Louisville, KY, made a grant of $300,000 to help fund the renovation. May 17, 1973, was a day of dedication as Flowers Hall for women was named in honor of the S. H. Flowers of Middlesboro, KY. In Sep., 1973, construction began on the first building of a proposed fine arts complex. A drama classroom building was constructed on the west side of the science center.

A number of major gifts continued to come to Georgetown in the 1970s to be used for four-year scholarships. In 1976 the Brown Foundation announced the awarding of $100,000 to be used for scholarships. Later in 1976, an additional $100,000 was presented to the college by this foundation, bringing to $250,000 the total this organization had awarded to the college for scholarships in recent years.

In Oct., 1976, Pierce Hall, a dormitory for women, was dedicated in memory of the parents of W. Vinson Pierce, an alumnus and longtime trustee. The George Matt Asher, Jr., Science Center, named in memory of another alumnus and trustee, was dedicated, Oct. 21, 1977.

During that same month, Robert L. Mills announced his retirement as president, a position he had held since 1959. As Georgetown's 20th president, Mills served in that position longer than any other person. Major improvements in campus facilities characterized his administration.

The 1978-79 academic year was dedicated to the observance of the sesquicentennial anniversary of the college. An 11-member committee headed by Ruth Heizer, associate professor of philosophy, planned and coordinated the events. The year-long schedule of activities began with a congratulatory telegram to Georgetown College from President Jimmy Carter.

Two publications relating to the sesquicentennial were printed that year. *A Sesquicentennial*

History of Georgetown College, a commemorative brochure by Carl Fields, was mailed to alumni and other friends. A more comprehensive work, the 210-page *History of Georgetown College* by Robert Snyder, was released at commencement.

Adding to the eventful sesquicentennial year was the election of Ben M. Elrod as Georgetown's 21st president in June, 1979. He announced the start of a major capital campaign to raise funds for endowment and building needs. The goal was set at $4,000,000. A challenge goal of an additional $2,500,000 was adopted to provide the funds needed for a new health, physical education, and recreation building. In the early stages of the campaign, the James Graham Brown Foundation pledged a gift of $1,000,000, providing the college could raise $2,000,000 in matching funds.

In 1979-80 Georgetown had a student enrollment of 1,210, with faculty and staff members numbering 217. The library contained 120,601 volumes. The value of buildings and grounds was estimated at $11,000,000. The total operating budget was $5,200,000, and endowment funds amounted to $3,600,000.

ROBIN OLDHAM

GEORGIA, BAPTIST CONVENTION OF THE STATE OF (II, III). The Georgia Baptist Convention experienced one of its most significant periods between 1970 and 1980. In 1979 total Cooperative Program receipts were $12,739,512.

I. Executive Committee. During this period, the Executive Committee acquired a new assembly operation, Norman Baptist Assembly, Norman Park, and a $20,000,000 building at the Georgia Baptist Medical Center (Baptist Towers) was completed. The Executive Committee, through its Program of State Missions, erected four new Baptist Student Centers and remodeled two others.

New Baptist student facilities dedicated include a Baptist Student Center at the Georgia Institute of Technology, Atlanta, dedicated in 1970; a center at West Georgia College in Carrollton, dedicated in 1973; a center at Armstrong Junior College, Savannah, dedicated in 1976; and a center at Georgia Southwestern College, Americus, dedicated in 1978.

The Baptist Student Center building for Georgia College at Milledgeville was purchased in 1971 and was remodeled completely and dedicated in 1979. In 1973 facilities were developed on property owned by the Executive Committee for use by Baptist students at Abraham Baldwin Agricultural College in Tifton. In 1978 land near the college was acquired by the Executive Committee, and facilities were placed on the newly-acquired land in 1978. Also in 1978, property used formerly as a church was purchased by the Executive Committee for a Baptist Student Center at South Georgia College, Douglas.

In 1970 the convention authorized establishment of a Church-Minister Relations Service.

Roy W. Hinchey was elected secretary of this department of work in the Program of State Missions by the Executive Committee in Sep., 1971, to begin work, Nov. 1, 1971. Hinchey retired in 1975, and was succeeded by W. Howard Ethington.

In 1974 The Georgia Baptist Program of Extension Education was transferred to the Education Division of the Program of State Missions, and since that time has functioned as the Education Extension Program, a department of the Program of State Missions. Billy H. Adams was elected first secretary of this department. From 1949 until 1974, the Extension Program had been operated by Mercer University and funded through the State Missions Program of the convention.

The convention, in 1969, requested the Georgia Baptist Hospital Commission to consider the possibility of expanding the program to include a counseling ministry to pastors. This ministry became effective, Sep. 1, 1970, based upon a funding agreement worked out between the Hospital Commission and the Administration Committee of the Executive Committee. This ministry continues to function.

A fourth Capital Improvements and Endowment Program was approved by the convention at its 1970 session, and a fifth became effective in 1976.

Norman College discontinued operation in June, 1971. The Executive Committee assumed responsibility for assets and liabilities of the college and the property and authorized its use as the Norman Baptist Assembly. This was the second major assembly to be operated by the Executive Committee within the Program of State Missions. Georgia Baptist Assembly, Toccoa, has been in operation since 1963.

In 1971 trustees of Atlanta Baptist College (Mercer University in Atlanta) voted to sell to the convention's Executive Committee 25 acres of college-owned land for use for relocating the convention's administrative offices. The Executive Committee purchased the property and authorized the Administration Committee and the executive secretary to proceed with plans for a new Georgia Baptist Center to house institution and agency offices of the convention and administrative offices of the Executive Committee. In Nov., 1975, the Executive Committee occupied a new Georgia Baptist Convention Center at 2930 Flowers Road, South, Atlanta, constructed at a contract price of $5,600,000. This was the first new facility constructed by the Executive Committee for its own use since the convention was organized in 1822. Offices for the Program of State Missions are in the Baptist Center also.

II. Program of State Missions. The Executive Committee voted in Mar., 1973, to reorganize the staff of the Program of State Missions upon the basis of the division system. Action taken by the Executive Committee was based upon recommendations of the Administration Committee of the Executive Committee follow-

Top, right: GEORGIA BAPTIST ASSEMBLY, Dining Room, Toccoa; *Top, left:* NORMAN BAPTIST ASSEMBLY, Brand Hall, Norman Park; *Bottom, right:* BAPTIST VILLAGE (*q.v.*), Chapel, Waycross; *Center, right:* PACES FERRY TOWERS, Atlanta; *Center, left:* MERCER UNIVERSITY (*q.v.*), Physical Education Building, Atlanta; *Bottom, left:* GEORGIA BAPTIST MEDICAL CENTER (*q.v.*), Towers Building, Atlanta.

Above: GEORGIA BAPTIST CENTER, Atlanta, houses offices of the Georgia Baptist Convention. GEORGIA BAPTIST STUDENT CENTERS. *Below, left:* Armstrong Baptist Center, Savannah; *Below, right:* Baptist Center, Georgia College, Milledgeville; *Lower, left:* Baptist Center, Georgia Southwestern, Americus; *Lower, right:* West Georgia Baptist Center, Carrollton.

ing a five-year study. Reasons cited for the change to the division system were: (1) Growth in the volume of work, which required additional personnel, (2) the development of established programs and the addition of new ministries in recent years, (3) changes in the structures in the SBC, associations, and church organizations, requiring changes in state convention organizations for more effective promotion, (4) successful experience in some of the larger state conventions affiliated with the SBC in the use of this system of organization and administration.

Evangelism and Missions Division.—Ernest J. Kelley, an administrative assistant to the executive secretary, was named director of this division. Kelley resigned in 1978 to assume a position with the Home Mission Board, SBC. Henry K. Neal was named director.

Neal had been director of the Department of Metropolitan Missions which was created upon convention authorization in 1972, and which was activated as a department on Aug. 1, 1973. This division was renamed the Department of Urban Missions, and upon Neal's election as division director, William I. Long, an associate in the Evangelism Department, was elected secretary of the Urban Missions Department.

Also in the Evangelism and Missions Division, a program of Special Missions Ministries was changed to department level in 1979, with Archie H. Mayo, who had headed the program ministry, as department secretary. A Language Missions Program within this division was begun in 1977 with Jerry K. Baker as program leader. Edward R. Davie became the first black department secretary in 1979 upon the retirement of Earle F. Stirewalt as secretary of the Program of Work with Black Baptists.

Church Services and Materials Division.—Julian T. Pipkin, longtime secretary of the Sunday School Department, was elected to head this division. A. Jerrell Pritchett, an associate in the Sunday School Department, was elected secretary of the Sunday School Department. Pritchett resigned in early 1980.

Education Division.—Aubrey L. Hawkins is division director. Hawkins had served from 1952 to 1973 as secretary of the Department of Student Work. D. Eugene Briscoe, an associate in the Department of Student Work, was elected department secretary. The Education Extension Program was placed within this division in 1974.

Administrative Division.—The executive secretary heads this division. In the division system of organization the position of administrative assistant to the executive secretary was created. Bernard D. King, longtime secretary of the Brotherhood Department of the convention, was elected to this position. King was succeeded as Brotherhood secretary in 1973 by R. Eugene Dailey, who had been an associate in the Sunday School Department.

James A. Lester, who had served, 1957-68, as secretary of public relations, and from 1968 to 1974 as editor of the *Baptist and Reflector,* news journal of the Tennessee Baptist Convention, again became director of public relations for the convention in Aug., 1974, and upon occupancy of the new Baptist Center was named manager of the Baptist Center in addition to responsibilities as head of the Department of Public Relations.

When the Executive Committee assumed responsibility for Norman College and voted to authorize establishment of an assembly, Garnie A. Brand, who had served as a vice-president of Norman after leaving the State Missions Program in 1969, was elected manager of the Norman Baptist Assembly. Brand retired in 1979, and was succeeded by Paul A. Peace, who had been assistant manager, and prior to that an associate secretary in the Department of Church Training.

During the period, 1969-80, growth at Georgia Baptist Assembly property at Toccoa continued until approximately $3,000,000 had been invested in land, equipment, and new buildings. Clifton A. Forrester resigned as manager of the assembly in 1972, and was succeeded by Harold L. Sangster.

In 1972 the convention marked the 150th anniversary of its founding, June 29, 1822, with ceremonies at Powelton Baptist Church, site of the 1822 founding, and at the annual session of the convention in Savannah.

During 1972 *A History of the Georgia Baptist Convention, 1822-1972,* by James Adams Lester, was published in conjunction with the sesquicentennial year, as was a history of *The Christian Index,* Georgia Baptist news magazine, entitled *An Old Friend with New Credentials,* by *Index* editor Jack U. Harwell.

In 1977 the Executive Committee voted to establish a sister state relationship with the Baptist State Convention of New York. This has been implemented by assistance from the Georgia Baptist Convention to the sister convention in New York since that time.

III. Capital Improvements and Endowment Program. The convention approved a Capital Improvements and Endowment Program in 1970, the fourth program of its type since 1955. While continuing provision for capital improvement projects and endowment, a new feature was introduced by the establishment of a scholarship endowment fund to be administered by the Georgia Baptist Foundation for the benefit of students from cooperative Georgia Baptist churches attending one of the Georgia Baptist colleges. The total amount of the fourth program was $11,625,000 (not including goals of the Georgia Baptist Foundation), of which $6,475,000 was to be funded through the Cooperative Program.

A fifth Capital Improvements and Endowment Program was approved by the convention in 1976 and became operative in 1977, upon completion of the earlier program. The goal for the fifth program was $13,350,000 with $8,000,000 to be provided from Cooperative Program budget receipts over a six-year period ending in 1982.

GEORGIA STATISTICAL SUMMARY

Year	Associations	Churches	Church Membership	Baptisms	SS Enrollment	VBS Enrollment	CT Enrollment	WMU Enrollment	Brotherhood Enrollment	Ch. Music Enrollment	Mission Gifts	Total Gifts	Value Church Property
1969	93	2,998	1,007,400	27,886	617,124	298,440	214,580	119,054	47,645	96,109	$10,948,173	$ 72,998,486	$357,328,626
1970	93	2,974	1,007,856	28,458	600,239	271,206	204,177	112,372	47,168	98,178	10,745,665	76,103,542	376,873,018
1971	93	2,952	1,018,052	30,076	585,050	272,725	172,166	107,024	49,958	98,879	11,270,175	83,517,369	399,213,931
1972	93	2,936	1,033,299	33,107	584,964	261,347	170,622	104,709	50,963	107,884	13,453,907	91,237,636	429,341,786
1973	92	2,934	1,040,643	29,694	575,448	267,740	160,754	102,331	52,102	114,391	15,271,610	103,389,259	472,803,803
1974	92	2,917	1,052,172	30,135	579,773	263,866	157,773	106,045	51,033	122,494	16,836,570	113,932,689	524,803,016
1975	92	2,924	1,070,687	31,762	587,736	263,855	158,254	106,739	54,099	129,752	16,595,596	124,096,349	579,894,883
1976	92	2,956	1,085,109	28,650	603,399	265,328	154,966	109,702	54,358	130,737	19,238,862	137,625,497	630,762,625
1977	92	2,947	1,091,878	25,875	601,081	263,275	150,530	109,162	54,022	131,453	25,127,108	151,009,071	691,723,729
1978	92	2,954	1,098,523	24,585	594,093	263,610	148,759	107,002	52,951	132,607	22,454,248	168,186,000	766,169,228
1979	92	2,958	1,097,607	26,228	589,477	257,931	144,379	106,919	54,324	134,689	27,339,970	164,753,430	835,108,985
1980	92	2,972	1,124,280	30,417	594,075	271,907	144,348	107,288	55,772	140,579	32,125,447	180,566,001	922,808,535

MARY HELEN JOHNSON (MRS. JACK MILTON) GOODWIN

This fifth program, as with the others, was a matching program with the convention responsible for raising monies and each institution responsible for raising an amount equal to that to be made available by the convention. The matching regulation does not apply to allocations for Baptist Student Center projects, Georgia Baptist Assembly, Norman Baptist Assembly, and other areas of state mission work for which only one special offering appeal is made annually.

The idea of a Capital Improvements and later a Capital Improvements and Endowment Program was projected on the concept that the institutions match funds available to the Cooperative Program to be raised from individual friends, alumni foundations, corporations, and other groups, and not from offerings of the churches or promoted through denominational organizations.

Through 1979 a total of $4,895,354 was available and applied on the Capital Improvements and Endowment Program of 1976.

Since inception of the program in 1955, including the matching provisions of the program, approximately $50,000,000 has been raised for capital improvements and endowment of Georgia Baptist institutions.

JAMES A. LESTER and SEARCY S. GARRISON

GEORGIA ASSOCIATIONS (I,III).

I. New Associations. ETOWAH. Organized Jan. 10, 1961, at Jasper First Church by 13 churches in Cherokee County and 3 in Pickens County. The 16 churches withdrew from Marble Valley, Noonday, and Hightower Associations. In 1979, 16 churches and 7 missions reported 98 baptisms, 4,986 members, $617,353 total receipts, $122,791 mission gifts, and $3,639,000 property value.

II. Changes in Associations. SOUTH RIVER. Composed of 13 churches in DeKalb, Clayton, and Henry Counties, the South River Association voted in Sep., 1963, to withdraw from the Georgia Baptist Convention and the Southern Baptist Convention.

MARBLE VALLEY. Disbanded Jan. 10, 1961, for its churches to join the Etowah Association.

CHARLES O. WALKER

GEORGIA BAPTIST CHILDREN'S HOME, INC. (I, III). Ten years of growth and change have resulted in new programs, new buildings, and new concepts in service to troubled children and their families by the Georgia Baptist Children's Home, Inc.

A multiservice ministry now cares for more than 800 boys and girls each year. In addition to residential care on the home's three campuses, foster homes and family assistance through counseling and family aid have become an important part of the total program of care.

Satellite offices in several metropolitan areas of Georgia are used by family service workers to assist families before, during, and after a child is being cared for by Georgia Baptist Children's

Home. Families share in setting goals for education, problem solving, and home adjustment as the total growth plan for the youth is developed.

Campuses are located at Baxley, Meansville, and Palmetto, with a central office at 2930 Flowers Road, South, Atlanta. Following the death of John C. Warr, June 9, 1969, Clarence F. Sessions served as acting administrator until O. Leonard Pedigo was named administrator, Apr. 1, 1970. Superintendents are A. W. Coleman, Baxley; Ancil Baird, Meansville; David H. McGowan, Palmetto; and Jim Cole, Augusta. The Augusta ministry will be developed during the first part of the 1980s to care for developmentally disadvantaged persons.

O. LEONARD PEDIGO, JR.

GEORGIA BAPTIST FOUNDATION (I, III). From Sep., 1969, to June, 1980, the principal of trust funds held by the Georgia Baptist Foundation grew from about $10,000,000 to approximately $25,000,000. The increase came from gifts, life income trusts, wills, the Cooperative Program, and endowment transfer from a Baptist institution to this agency for investment. The will of Edward Seitzinger provided the largest testamentary gift ever received directly. The biggest single irrevocable commitment came through the Georgia Baptist Convention from the Warren Sewell estate. Harry V. Smith, Sr., retired as executive secretary, Dec. 31, 1970, and was succeeded by Charles C. Duncan. In 1972 the rotation system for foundation trustees was instituted, and their number was increased to 10.

CHARLES C. DUNCAN

GEORGIA BAPTIST HISTORICAL SOCIETY (III). Presidents during the last 10 years were Charles O. Walker, 1970-72, 1978-79; Robert G. Gardner, 1972-74, 1975-77; J. R. Huddlestun, 1975-76; P. Harris Anderson, elected and died in 1977; Betty Sanders Snyder, 1977-78; and Thomas D. Austin, 1979- . The society published *Obituaries Published by the Christian Index, 1822-1875* (1972), *Marriages Published by the Christian Index, 1828-1855* (1974), and volumes 2 through 7 of *Viewpoints, Georgia Baptist History*.

In recent years 200 church minutes on microfilm and other minutes from black Missionary, black Primitive, white Primitive, and white Freewill associations were added to the collection. Indexes of *The Christian Index* include ordinations to date, obituaries and pictures to 1970, marriage records to 1960, and miscellaneous data on pastors, churches, and other subjects. Mary Overby continues as curator of the collection. The society has a two-day spring meeting and a breakfast during the annual sessions of the Georgia Baptist Convention.

CHARLES O. WALKER

GEORGIA BAPTIST HOMES, INC. (cf. Peachtree-on-Peachtree Inn, Vol. III). Georgia Baptist Homes, Inc., formed in 1979, operates three retirement residences. C. L. Leopard is administrator. Peachtree-on-Peachtree Inn in Atlanta is a high-rise building for 150 occupants, offering worship services, recreational activities, furnished rooms, maid service, three meals a day, and convenient shopping.

In 1977 the Georgia Baptist Convention expanded its ministry to the elderly through the purchase of Paces Ferry Tower and Court Apartments in Atlanta, providing for 240 residents. Facilities include a studio, one- and two-bedroom apartments, a restaurant, and a chapel. Plans call for immediate expansion with a high-rise residential building to replace the Court Apartments.

Harvest Heights Baptist Home, a 25-apartment complex located in Decatur, opened in 1980 as a result of the 1978 gift of 10 acres of land, church building, and all assets of Harvest Heights Baptist Church. Plans call for certification to provide intermediate and skilled nursing care for 144 residents, at which time the facility will be expanded by the addition of the Georgia Baptist Nursing Center.

JAMES C. BRYANT

GEORGIA BAPTIST MEDICAL CENTER (cf. Georgia Baptist Hospital, Vol. I). This modern hospital and medical center cared for 20,000 patients with 125,000 patient days during 1979. Owned by the Georgia Baptist Convention, the center is operated by a nine-member commission, elected by the convention's executive committee. In 1980 the Georgia Baptist Health Care System was activated. This is a system of satellite health care facilities which extends services of the medical center in Atlanta to communities in the state. The center now identifies itself as a comprehensive, multi-disciplinary, family-oriented, tertiary medical center. The hospital also has a community hospital ontology program in cooperation with the National Cancer Institute.

The Baptist Professional Building, a part of the medical center complex, was paid for in 1969. A Nurses' Education Building was completed in 1959. The Nurses' Dormitory, a high-rise facility above the education building, was completed in 1963. In 1965 the School of Nursing Activities Building was completed and occupied. A cooperative arrangement between the School of Nursing and Tift College provides degree opportunities for the student nurses. The School of Nursing had 405 students in 1980. The Baptist Tower, a complete new hospital facility, was completed Dec. 11, 1974, at a cost of $18,026,497. This brought the number of buildings in the medical center complex to 11.

In 1980 agreement was reached for the purchase of Watkins Memorial Hospital and Gilmer County Nursing Home from Gilmer County Health Authority. These facilities were added to the Georgia Baptist Medical Center operations. In the extensive hospital complex, a parking building was constructed along with two additions to the parking garage, the latest in

1970. This brought the total invested in parking facilities to more than $2,000,000. In Mar., 1974, the Baptist Professional Building East was completed at a cost of almost $3,000,000. The radiation therapy facility for the medical center is located in this building.

Robert L. Zwald became administrator on Jan. 19, 1979. He succeeded Edwin B. Peel, who became director of development. Peel retired in June, 1979, after 32 years as hospital administrator and director of development.

SEARCY S. GARRISON

GEORGIA BAPTIST VILLAGE FOR THE AGED (I). See BAPTIST VILLAGE, INC.

GERMAN BAPTISTS IN NORTH AMERICA. See CANADIAN BAPTISTS; NORTH AMERICAN BAPTIST CONFERENCE.

GERMANY, MISSION IN (cf. Germany, West, Mission in, Vol. III). Since 1969 the Baptists of Western and Eastern Germany have had separate organizations. In 1979 the one in the Federal Republic of Germany (west) included 72,000 church members, and the one in the Democratic Republic of Germany, 21,000. Southern Baptist financial assistance to the Baptists of the Federal Republic was no longer needed except for joint projects such as ministry to Yugoslav laborers and to immigrants from Russia. Only limited contacts existed with Baptists of the Democratic Republic, but in 1979 help was given for building a church in East Berlin. Southern Baptist missionaries in the Federal Republic were working mainly with English-language Baptist churches, which in 1979 numbered 23 with 2,451 members. Four missionaries were pastors of English-language churches, and another missionary, John W. Merritt, was executive secretary of the European Baptist Convention (English language).

J. D. HUGHEY

GHANA, MISSION IN (III; cf. Gold Coast, Mission in, Vol. I). Steady progress in developing indigenous churches has followed Ghana's expulsion of Nigerians, who began Baptist work in 1969. By the end of 1979 churches and preaching stations numbered 90 with a membership of 4,000. New programs of work included Theological Education by Extension, a public health program, dentistry, a radio-television ministry, literacy, a reorganized publications center, a music ministry, a training center for rural leaders, and agricultural evangelism. Missionaries numbered 69 working in six stations. In 1979 the Ghana Baptist Convention adopted an enlarged program of work and a larger budget. Bill Bullington, field representative for West Africa, was living in Accra, the capital city.

JOHN E. MILLS

GIBSON, JOHN GLENN (b. Morgan County, AL, Mar. 29, 1832; d. Atlanta, GA, Feb. 15, 1900). Second corresponding secretary of the State Mission Board of the Georgia Baptist Convention. Son of the Jonathan Gibsons, he went to live with his grandmother on a farm in Oglethorpe County, GA, following his mother's death when he was a young child. Converted in 1850, he joined the Millstone Church. He studied law in the years before the Civil War but did not seek a license to practice. He entered the Confederate Army as captain of a company of artillery.

Upon his release from the Army, he yielded to the call to preach and was ordained in Nov., 1865. He preached and practiced law, being judge of Oglethorpe County Georgia Court for two years, 1867-69.

His influence extended to churches throughout the state. When the Georgia Baptist Convention met in Gainesville, GA, in 1877, Gibson was appointed to preach on the second day. This was the first convention that he attended, and his message was acclaimed as one of the greatest delivered. Asked to serve as corresponding secretary, he declined. Meeting in Hawkinsville in 1891, the convention again elected him as corresponding secretary. He accepted and served until 1899 when he declined reelection because of ill health. Twice married, his second wife was Mary Hartsfield, a sister of his first wife. They had no children. He is buried in Clark Cemetery, Lexington, GA.

R. L. DUKE

GIBSON, OSCAR LEE (b. Winchester, KS, May 2, 1887; d. Stillwater, OK, July 13, 1978). Pastor. The son of W. H. and Mary Gibson, he married Ora Rachel McHargue in Tyrone, OK, Sep. 7, 1911. They had six children: Henrietta, Oscar Lee, Jr., William, Pauline, Mary, and Hugh. He attended Oklahoma Baptist College (B.A., 1911), and The Southern Baptist Theological Seminary (Th.M., 1915; Th.D., 1916). His pastorates included Henessey and Yukon, OK, First, Fayetteville, AR, and First, Stillwater, OK, 1927-40. He was hospital chaplain at Perry, OK, 1954-56, and Stillwater, 1954-62. He also served on the boards of Oklahoma's state convention and Oklahoma Baptist University. Gibson is buried in Fairlawn Cemetery, Stillwater, OK.

J. M. GASKIN

GINSBURG, SOLOMON L. (b. Suwalki, Poland, Aug. 6, 1867; d. Sao Paulo, Brazil, Mar. 31, 1927). Foreign missionary. Disowned by his Jewish parents when he became a Christian, he attended Regions Beyond Missionary Training College, London. He married Amelia Caroline Bishop, Apr., 1892. Following her death, he married Emma Morton, Aug. 1, 1893. They had eight children: Arville, Brazilia, Claire, Robert, Estelle, Henrietta, Louis, and Emily.

Ginsburg was not a Baptist when he first went to Brazil as a missionary, 1890. He debated Baptists on baptism, then submitted to immersion in 1891 and sought to convince earlier converts whom he had sprinkled. Appointed to Brazil by the Foreign Mission Board, SBC, in 1892, he served in Campos, Pernambuco, Nictheroy (Niteroi), and Bahia, traveling extensively throughout Brazil. He and Erik A. Nelson (q.v. II) organized the first Baptist church in the Amazon Valley, Belem, 1897. He was corresponding secretary, Brazilian Baptist Home Mission Board, and staff member, Carroll Memorial Publishing House, Rio. He is buried in the English Cemetery, Sao Paulo.

FRANK K. MEANS

GIRLS IN ACTION (III). Since 1970 the Woman's Missionary Union, SBC, organization for girls ages 6 through 11 or grades 1 through 6. Materials for weekly mission study meetings are provided to Girls in Action leaders in a quarterly magazine called *Aware*. *Discovery* is a member monthly magazine containing stories, games, puzzles, and pictures correlated with the corresponding unit of study in *Aware*.

Missions Adventures, an individual achievement plan, provides a way for members to learn more about missions on their own. The three adventures contain activities in different categories. The revised plan, beginning in 1981, offers six adventures. The activities of day camping provide opportunities for teaching missions in an outdoor setting.

In 1979 there were 20,170 Girls in Action organizations with a total membership of 202,879.

JIMMYE WINTER

GIVING TRENDS IN THE 1970s. Southern Baptists believe that Christian giving is vital to individual spiritual development and to a church's fulfillment of its mission. During the 1970s, many concerns were expressed about giving because of new stewardship studies and uncertain economic and world conditions.

In determining trends, countless variables must be considered. Statistics must eventually be interpreted in light of regional and national events, denominational emphases, and local church factors. It is possible, however, to chart progress or decline in giving through the churches both in actual dollars and percentage change. The following information forms a basis for examining the giving response through SBC churches. Statistics were compiled from the uniform church letters completed by Southern Baptist churches.

I. Facts About Giving During the 1970s

	1970	1979	Percentage Change
Total Receipts	$892,255,918	$2,222,082,159	+149.0
(Total gifts plus all other receipts)			
Total Gifts	$857,098,689	$2,085,955,800	+143.4
(Tithes, offerings, and special gifts)			
Total Mission Expenditures	$138,500,883	$ 356,207,790	+157.2
(Cooperative Program, associational missions, special mission offerings, church sponsored mission expenditures, and other designated mission expenditures)			
Reported Tithers	1,323,403	1,566,459	+18.4
Total Church Membership	11,629,880	13,379,073	+15.0
Resident Church Membership	8,451,769	9,604,482	+13.6

During the 10-year period, 1,245 new churches were organized, making 35,605 churches. There are presently 34 state conventions with three of these being formed in the 1970s.

Inflation has been the most pressing and difficult economic concern. The inflation increase for 1970-79 was nearly 87 percent. This produced higher personal incomes but also greatly accelerated costs. Churches have been affected accordingly. While increased income because of inflation has value, it also has deceptive qualities. If an adjustment is made for inflation, Southern Baptists giving increased by 30 percent as compared to the 143 percent increase recorded on total gifts.

Individual per capita giving, based on total gifts and resident church membership, changed as follows:

1970: $101.41   1979: $217.18

Using an average Sunday School attendance (half of the reported Sunday School enrollment) and adjusting for inflation, the annual per person budget offerings in 1970 were $235.13; and in 1979 they were $305.02, a 29 percent increase. In 1970, 15.7 percent of the resident membership were reported as giving at least a tithe of their income through their church. In 1979, 16.3 percent of the resident membership were reported as tithers.

II. Promotional Emphases Affecting Giving. *National Stewardship Seminars.* —Three historic seminars on stewardship and mission support were conducted in 1971 (Glorieta), 1975 (Lake Yale, Florida), and 1976 (Ridgecrest). Participants represented a cross section of pastors, state convention personnel, directors of missions, and SBC agency representatives. The seminars broadened their view of and appreciation for biblical stewardship. Christian giving was set in the context of a distinctly Christian life-style that reflected an acknowledgment of God's ownership and a commitment to the lordship of Christ and the mission of his church.

New Stewardship and Mission Support Materials. —An increasing volume of materials on stewardship, both at the practical and theological levels, appeared during the decade. Included was a series of new church study course books on stewardship. Books published were: *The Spirit-Filled Steward* (1974), Charles M. McKay; *Living the Responsible Life* (1974), Cecil A. Ray; *Living and Giving* (1974), Marietta P. Howington; *Bread: Living with It/Making It/Sharing It* (1975), Nathan Stone; *What the Bible Says About Stewardship* (1976), A. R. Fagan; *God Has Done His Part. . .* (1977), Carolyn Weatherford; and *Witness to the World* (1979), Porter W. Routh.

Updated stewardship materials and new resources emphasizing year-round giving, the church stewardship committee, and budget development and promotion programs appeared. Church leaders were also exposed to a greater volume of stewardship articles through SBC periodicals.

Promotional Plans and Strategies. —Associational Stewardship Decision Nights were conducted widely, 1973-76. These meetings of key church leaders majored on a challenge to the churches regarding their local, associational, and world mission ministries. An explanation of available budget programs was given, and participants met by church groups to analyze their needs and desires for giving goals and budget emphases.

"Operation One" was an emphasis on the financial support of missions during the years 1973-75. Its intent was to revitalize within Baptists the claim of Christ to teach and witness to the whole world.

One of the most significant plans during the decade was the 50th anniversary of the Cooperative Program in 1975. One of the highlights of the celebration was a Cooperative Program Prayer Breakfast held on May 13, 1975. The breakfast, which attracted many agency executives, state Baptist convention leaders, and other church members, was held in the old Ellis Auditorium, now part of Cook Convention Center, in Memphis, TN, where Southern Baptists started the Cooperative Program on May 13, 1925.

As a climax to the breakfast, Porter Routh, executive secretary-treasurer of the Executive Committee, SBC, lit a Cooperative Program torch which more than 2,150 Southern Baptist Royal Ambassadors carried from Memphis to Miami Beach, FL, where the 1975 SBC meeting was held—a distance of 1,468 miles. The flame of the torch represented the light of God's word to the world. The last runner carried the torch into the convention center to begin the 1975 SBC meeting. Other highlights included:

1. A special Cooperative Program film, entitled *Rope of Sand.*

2. Thousands of Southern Baptists signing a "Declaration of Cooperation," signifying renewed commitment to mission support through the Cooperative Program.

3. A Woman's Missionary Union creative arts contest on both the state and national level.

4. Cooperative Program birthday parties and rallies in state conventions and during the SBC.

5. Stewardship development and Cooperative Program promotion materials designed especially for the support of the anniversary celebration and to call for increased giving for missions support.

6. A series of 12 Cooperative Program ads related to the ministries of the agencies of the Convention. These ads were placed in every state Baptist paper. The theme of the ads was "The Cooperative Program—the *Means* to the *Way* for 50 years."

While noting with gratitude the growth in giving during the decade, Southern Baptists recognize that greater growth must be realized in the next decade in order to support local church ministries adequately and to provide necessary funds for Bold Mission Thrust. Biblical giving was one of the pressing concerns identified in the Impact 80's Emphasis Plan adopted by the SBC in 1975.

See also COOPERATIVE PROGRAM; STEWARDSHIP SEMINARS, NATIONAL.

ERNEST D. STANDERFER and MICHAEL L. SPEER

GLASS, JESSIE LIGEN PETTIGREW (b. Tazewell County, VA, Apr. 7, 1877; d. Fort Worth, TX, Oct. 14, 1962). Foreign missionary. The daughter of Sallie Pettigrew and Thomas Pettigrew, a mill worker, she received her nursing degree from Touro Infirmary in Louisiana in 1899. The first registered nurse appointed by the Foreign Mission Board, Aug. 5, 1901, she served in Hwangshien, Shantung, China. Interned early in World War II, she was repatriated in 1943. She married Wiley Blount Glass (*q.v.* III), Mar. 16, 1916. They had two children, Gertrude and Bryan. She is buried in Laurel Land Cemetery, Fort Worth, TX.

FRANK K. MEANS

GLEN DALE CHILDREN'S HOME (I, III). In 1974 Harold Holderman became the 20th superintendent of Glen Dale Children's Home in Kentucky. During its 65 years of operation, Glen Dale has cared for over 2,600 children and young people. The original investment of $3,500 in 16 acres has grown to more than $1,629,363 in total assets.

In 1976 the Kentucky Baptist Board of Child Care adopted a 10-year long-range plan designed to ensure a relevant and updated program. Record-setting Thanksgiving offerings continue to be a strong part of the support of the home. In 1978 the board of directors, in keeping with the long-range plan, voted to begin updating the buildings on the campus. New family-style cottages were scheduled to be erected beginning in the fall of 1980. The new cottages will take advantage of the latest in dining and solar energy techniques. Gardner Hall will remain as the administration building, and it will be renovated after the cottages are completed.

WILLIAM E. AMOS

GLORIETA BAPTIST CONFERENCE CENTER (cf. Glorieta Baptist Assembly, Vols. I, III). The Sunday School Board has continued to develop the Glorieta facility and to assure increased use on a sound basis. Beginning in 1970, the total operating cost of the assembly, including auditorium, conference, and exhibit space, was placed on a cost-recovery basis from charges to guests. Glorieta Assembly became a part of the newly created Assemblies Division of the SSB, Oct. 1, 1971. In July, 1972, the name changed to Glorieta Baptist Conference Center to support the concept of a year-round center operated for training, worship, denominational fellowship, evangelism, retreats, and spiritual growth.

Major changes since 1969 include renovation of Oklahoma Hall, 1970, adding heat to and renovation of the small auditorium, 1971, development of the day camp, 1972, placing telephone and electrical lines underground, 1974, new waste water treatment plant, 1979, and Aspen Auditorium, 1980. Most other housing and conference space has been upgraded for winter programs.

Approximately 52,000 guests participated in 228,000 days of conferences during 1978-79. Summer conferences accounted for 158,000 guest days, and fall-winter-spring conferences for 70,000. On Oct. 1, 1973, Larry Haslam became manager, succeeding Mark Short, Jr., who had served since 1966.

ROBERT M. TURNER

GLOSSOLALIA. See CHARISMATIC MOVE-MENT AND SOUTHERN BAPTISTS.

GOLD COAST, MISSION IN (I). See GHANA, MISSION IN.

GOLDEN GATE BAPTIST THEOLOGI-CAL SEMINARY (I, III). The 1970s were years of unprecedented growth and development for Golden Gate Seminary. Student enrollment grew from 366 in 1969-70 to 716 in 1979-80, a 98 percent increase. The seminary began new academic programs and off-campus centers and received accreditation from the Western Association of Schools and Colleges, 1971. Additional facilities were constructed, and new faculty and staff personnel were employed.

Academic Programs.—The Doctor of Ministry degree, introduced in 1972, received full accreditation in 1978 from the Association of Theological Schools. A faculty member was appointed director of the D.Min. program in 1979. In 1980 the option of an ethnic emphasis was added to the D.Min. program. In 1979 the Master of Theology degree was reinstated. In 1974 the Master of Church Music degree was resumed with a revised curriculum and additional faculty. In support of a growing music program, generous donors gave a Baldwin grand piano, a three-manual Allen Digital Computer organ, a harpsichord, a piano lab, and handbells. In 1979 the trustees approved the application procedure for full accreditation by the National Association of Schools of Music.

In 1978 Golden Gate significantly expanded its continuing education program to assist pastors and church staff to update their education, and in 1979 appointed a faculty member to direct the program.

During the decade, the seminary began several off-campus programs: The Southern California Center, started in Garden Grove in 1973; the Phoenix, AZ, Center in 1977; and the Northwest Center, Portland, OR, in 1980. Some courses and seminars were also offered in other cities, including Salt Lake City, UT, and Seattle, WA. Credit courses at all sites were applicable to the M.Div. and M.R.E. degrees and the diplomas in theology and religious education. At the Evening Star Baptist Church in Los Angeles, a special diploma program was instituted for black pastors.

During the 1970s Golden Gate placed new emphasis on evangelism by adding a faculty member to teach in this area, and gave new priority to supervised ministry (field education). All students were required to participate in

some form of ministry under supervision as a part of their educational programs.

The seminary made use of visiting professors and adjunct personnel, especially in the four-week terms, to enrich the curriculum through specialized electives focusing on their respective areas of experience and knowledge. New provision was made for an evening school program designed to prepare wives of students for their responsibility in ministry.

In 1977 the quarter plan was replaced by the semester system, with a four-week term in January and in the summer. By 1981 two four-week terms comprised summer school.

Lectureships and Endowed Chairs.—In 1969 Golden Gate inaugurated the H. I. Hester Lectureship on Preaching with Theodore F. Adams (*q.v.*) as lecturer. In 1971 the Derward W. Deere (*q.v.* III) Lectureship on Biblical Studies was instituted to honor the long-time professor of Old Testament. The first lectures were delivered by Wayne E. Ward, professor of theology at Southern Baptist Theological Seminary.

The trustees authorized the creation of three endowed chairs: (1) The E. Hermond Westmoreland (*q.v.*) Chair of Evangelism was established in 1978 to honor a former trustee and chairman of the committee which selected the Strawberry Point campus in the 1950s. (2) The Baker James Cauthen Chair of World Missions was approved by trustees in 1977 to highlight the cause of missions and honor the executive director of the Foreign Mission Board, 1954-79. (3) The William A. Carleton (*q.v.*) Chair of Church History was authorized by the trustees in 1980 to honor the former academic dean and professor of church history, 1953-70.

In 1979 G. William Schweer was named E. Hermond Westermoreland Professor of Evangelism.

Personnel.—In 1977 Harold K. Graves retired after serving for 25 years as president of Golden Gate. Appropriate recognition was given to his distinguished leadership, especially in obtaining and building the present campus in Mill Valley. He was designated president emeritus by the trustees, and the administration building was named for him. The Harold K. Graves Scholarship Fund was established to provide financial assistance for outstanding first-year students.

The trustees set up the Harold K. Graves Award to honor those who had given outstanding service to Golden Gate and named Graves the first recipient. Subsequently, it was presented to Guy W. Rutland, Jr., William A. Carleton, and Floyd D. Golden. The award is made annually.

In the summer of 1977, the trustees elected as president William M. Pinson, Jr., pastor of the First Baptist Church, Wichita Falls, TX, and former professor of Christian ethics at Southwestern Baptist Theological Seminary. His inauguration was held in Apr., 1978.

On the retirement of William A. Carleton in 1970, the trustees elected Elmer L. Gray academic dean. After serving for four years, he became editor of the *California Southern Baptist.* He was succeeded in 1976 by W. Morgan Patterson, David T. Porter Professor of Church History and director of graduate studies at Southern Seminary.

Nobel D. Brown served as dean of students, 1974-79, and was succeeded by Robert L. Cannon in 1980.

Faculty members in order of election since 1970 were: J. Kenneth Eakins (1970-), Old Testament, archaeology; Gordon L. Green (1970-72), preaching; John P. Johnson (1972-76), church music; Paul W. Turner (1972-80), ministry; John H. Parrott (1973-79), preaching; F. Daniel Boling, Jr. (1973-), religious education; Max D. Lyall (1974-), church music; Nobel D. Brown (1974-79), dean of students; Robert L. Cate (1975-), Old Testament; G. William Schweer (1975-), evangelism; W. Morgan Patterson (1976-), academic dean, church history; Naymond H. Keathley (1976-), New Testament; D. Glenn Saul (1976-), ethics; Ronald D. Bostic (1977-78), church music; David N. Roberts (1977-78), church history; William M. Pinson, Jr. (1977-), president; Jerry M. Stubblefield (1977-), religious education; William L. Hendricks (1977-), theology and philosophy of religion; Samuel Y. C. Tang (1978-), Old Testament; S. Alfred Washburn (1978-), church music; Cecil R. White (1979-), librarian; H. Craig Singleton (1980-), church music; Elsie M. McCall (1980-), religious education; and Doran C. McCarty (1980-), ministry.

Faculty members who retired during the decade were: J. Winston Pearce (1961-70), preaching; Carlyle Bennett (1953-72), church music; Elma Bennett (1953-72), church music; Jack W. Manning (1950-76), church history; C. Arthur Insko (1950-76), ethics; Fred L. Fisher (1952-76), New Testament; Geil Davis (1957-78), religious education; and Orine H. Suffern (1954-80), church music.

In 1976 the Sunday School Board, SBC, initiated a proposal to the six SBC seminaries to underwrite the cost of an additional faculty position in the area of religious education. This faculty member would serve as liaison between the seminary and the SSB in their mutual educational interests. Jerry M. Stubblefield was elected to this position in 1977.

Visiting professors of missions during the 1970s included Buford Lee Nichols, Finlay Graham, Ted Lindwall, Gordon Robinson, A. L. Gillespie, Richard T. Plampin, Rudolph M. Wood, H. Cornell Goerner, and Roger L. Capps. Baker James Cauthen served as Distinguished Professor of World Missions in 1980-81.

Visiting professors in other fields included J. P. Allen (preaching and worship), Penrose St. Amant (church history), Joe Davis Heacock (religious education), Robert J. Hastings (religious education), Samuel Y. C. Tang (Old Testament and Chinese Studies), and Bobby D. Compton (church history).

Facilities.—In 1971 a pedestrian bridge was constructed through the generosity of Guy W. Rutland, Jr., to provide easy access to the student center from the dormitories. In 1973 six three-bedroom apartments for students were finished. A residence for visiting professors of missions, made possible through a gift from Violet Embry Platt, was dedicated in 1974. Tichenor Village, composed of 24 one-bedroom apartments, was completed in 1977.

In 1978 the SBC allocated $4,297,000 in capital funds to be received over a five-year period for construction of a library building, classrooms and offices, student housing, and a child care facility. In 1980 work on the new library began with completion anticipated in 1981. Plans called for 37,800 square feet of floor space, 20 reading areas, 120 student carrels, rooms with audiovisual recording capacity, group study rooms, seating space for more than 300 persons, a television studio, a more serviceable technical services area, and compact storage areas. The total projected cost of the library program was $4,285,000. The library collection has continued to increase with 98,113 volumes reported in 1980.

Trustees.—The following persons served as chairmen of the trustees during 1970-80: Ernest P. Guy, 1968-71; H. J. Flanders, Jr., 1971-76; Charles A. Carter, 1976-79; Guy W. Rutland, Jr., 1979-80; and E. Glen Paden, 1980- . In the late 1970s three women were elected to the trustees: Bettye Cothen, Mildred Carlton, and Barbara Floyd.

Miscellaneous.—Golden Gate sponsored numerous activities and creative projects, 1970-80. Especially noteworthy were the church growth conferences, family enrichment programs, China Mission Institute, programs for ethnic and minority groups, Urban Training Event, "live-in" courses, lecture-dialogues, a puppet ministry, and plans for a world mission center. In 1979 a faculty member was appointed as director of the proposed center.

In 1977 the trustees adopted and the faculty subscribed to the Baptist Faith and Message approved by the SBC in 1963. It replaced the 1925 SBC statement. A special signing ceremony held in Nov., 1977, at which Herschel H. Hobbs, SBC president in 1963 and chairman of the committee which drafted the statement, spoke.

In 1974 the trustees appointed a Long-Range Planning Committee to review objectives and programs of the seminary. A survey conducted among alumni, students, faculty, church staff, and denominational leaders resulted in a valuable report in 1976 which the faculty and administration then used to bring about improvements in academic programs and emphases.

In the area of development the seminary put forth determined efforts during the decade to increase endowment, especially for the chairs of evangelism, missions, and church history, and for the new library.

In developing its programs and extending its

KANSAS-NEBRASKA CONVENTION OF SOUTHERN BAPTISTS (*q.v.*) BUILDING, Topeka, KS. Completed in 1977. Provides offices for convention staff.

GOLDEN GATE BAPTIST THEOLOGICAL SEMINARY (*q.v.*), Mill Valley, CA. Cresting the Strawberry Point peninsula, the campus commands a sweeping view of San Francisco Bay and the city of San Francisco.

GOLDEN GATE BAPTIST THEOLOGICAL SEMINARY (*q.v.*), Mill Valley, CA. New library. This $4.3 million facility, completed in 1981, houses more than 100,000 volumes, includes a recording and television studio, and seats 316 persons. The structure is the first major building constructed on the campus since 1959.

ministry of theological education in the 1970s, Golden Gate sought to focus its special responsibility to the churches and state conventions in the western region of the United States and to discharge its part in the effort of Bold Mission Thrust. As a consequence, there was a strong emphasis on missions, evangelism, church planting, and church growth. Furthermore, Golden Gate alumni have increasingly taken positions of leadership in churches, state conventions, and missions.

W. MORGAN PATTERSON and HAROLD K. GRAVES

GOLDEN GATE BAPTIST THEOLOGICAL SEMINARY, NORTHWEST CENTER OF.

An off-campus training center operated by Golden Gate Baptist Theological Seminary in Portland, OR, since the fall of 1980. Planning began in 1978 with the objective of providing seminary-level educational opportunities for pastors and other church leaders in the Northwest. Courses are offered leading to Master of Divinity and Master of Religious Education degrees, as well as diploma programs for noncollege graduates.

Launched with the enthusiastic support and cooperation of the Northwest Baptist Convention, the center is located in the Baptist Building where newly renovated classrooms and offices are provided. Ernest J. Loessner became the center's first director. He, Clayton K. Harrop, and Wayne McDill served as the first faculty. The Northwest Convention designated the 1979 Sylvia Wilson State Missions Offering for the development of the center.

HERB HOLLINGER and W. MORGAN PATTERSON

GOLDEN GATE BAPTIST THEOLOGICAL SEMINARY, SOUTHERN CALIFORNIA CENTER OF.

An off-campus training center operated by Golden Gate Baptist Theological Seminary in Los Angeles since 1973. Calls from southern California for seminary-level courses to be offered in that area as early as 1964 eventually prompted study to determine need and interest. With the cooperation of the directors of missions for Southern Baptist associations in the Los Angeles area, a site was selected. The seminary leased office and classroom space in Garden Grove, Orange County, and elected John Parrott as director and professor of preaching for the center. The Mill Valley campus provided a basic library of 1500 volumes with reserve books provided for each course.

Classes began in Sep., 1973, with two professors from Mill Valley assisting Parrott. Thirty-five students enrolled, including 12 for the D.Min. program. Enrollment varied from year to year, reaching beyond 50 in degree program studies. Many students, beginning their work there, completed degrees on the Mill Valley campus.

Since 1976, Fred L. Fisher, retired professor of New Testament at Golden Gate, has been the resident director and professor. Other faculty members commute from Mill Valley, and adjunct teachers are engaged as needed. In addi-

tion to degree level work, diploma studies are offered to noncollege graduates. Such studies have been especially helpful to black pastors.

HAROLD K. GRAVES

GOVERNMENT INTERVENTION AND THE CHURCHES.

Baptist concerns in public affairs arise out of a particular understanding of the church and the state: the concept of a free church and a free or secular state. By a free church Baptists have meant a church free of political alliances, sanction, or support, subject only to the lordship of Christ, and comprised only of believers voluntarily committed to Christ. By a secular state, Baptists have meant a limited state, limited to this age or *seculum,* in which the people have excluded civil authority from religious affairs.

During the 1970s a recurring pattern of United States church-state relations has been government intervention in the life of the churches. Government intervention in religion has actually become the dominant trend in church-state relations. While not new to the American scene, it has become in recent years the most crucial single issue facing the churches in public affairs and in the relationship of the churches to government. Unfortunately, the problem is far from resolution. It will probably continue to plague the churches in the coming decade.

The increasing intrusion on the part of government into the life of the churches constitutes a mounting crisis in American church-state relations. It is a serious threat to the prophetic role of religion and to the constitutional guarantee of "a free exercise of religion." The problem appears particularly acute to those groups such as Baptists who have sought to maintain the institutional separation of church and state and the prophetic role of religion in the body politic. Their goal has been to maintain their prophetic role without accountability to government or political advantage or disadvantage to the churches in carrying out their mission in public affairs.

Nowhere is this trend more evident than in the passing of government regulations that bear directly on churches, church agencies, and church institutions. These rulings and legislation have profound implications both with regard to the relationship of these church agencies and institutions to government and to the churches to whom these agencies and institutions have traditionally belonged.

The Internal Revenue Service is continuing to issue rulings which make tax exemption for the churches conditioned upon the noninvolvement of the churches in public affairs, financial accountability of the churches to government, nondissemination of information regarding voting records of members of Congress, and church compliance with government guidelines for employment and enrollment in church institutions.

Although without statutory authorization, the Department of Labor and the Internal Revenue Service have issued rulings dissecting churches from church institutions—even when those institutions are owned, operated, and maintained by the churches themselves. Even more significantly, government rulings have presumed to define the mission of the church and the nature of religion by ruling which activities of the churches are "religious" and which are not. Such initiatives on the part of government are viewed with grave alarm by the churches.

The special place given to religion in the First Amendment is increasingly threatened by government intervention in church affairs and the trend of government to ignore the special place accorded to religion in the Constitution. The tendency in government is not to make any distinction between a church or church agency and a nonsectarian charity or enterprise.

The institutional independence of church and state is essential to the free exercise of religion and thereby to the authentic mission of the church and society and in the life of the nation. This independence or nonentanglement of church and state makes possible true interaction between church and state in public affairs.

JAMES E. WOOD, JR.

GRADED SERIES CONFERENCE (cf. Missionary Education Council, Vol. II; Mission Education Promotion Conference, Vol. III). Two conferences of Foreign Mission Board, Home Mission Board, Brotherhood, and Woman's Missionary Union, SBC, personnel which plan and promote the respective annual mission study books and related materials. This function was formerly a part of the Missions Education and Promotion Conference (MEPC) which did broad missions education planning and coordinating. In the early 1970s because of shift in agency personnel, many activities of MEPC were curtailed. Left only with planning and promoting annual foreign and home mission studies, the organization changed its name to Foreign Mission and Home Mission Graded Series Conferences.

An action taken by the conference in 1979 changed Graded Series to Annual Mission Study; therefore, the conferences are called Annual Foreign Mission Study and Annual Home Mission Study Conference.

JUNE WHITLOW

GRAND CANYON COLLEGE (I). With a 1980 enrollment of 1,200, Grand Canyon is accredited by North Central Association. The budget grew to $3,200,000 for 1979. Assets exceed $6,000,000. Bill R. Williams became president in 1978. Previous presidents since the 1950s were Eugene N. Patterson, 1959-65; Charles L. McKay (acting president), 1965-66; Arthur K. Tyson, 1966-72; William R. Hintze, 1973-77; and Dillard Whitis (acting president), 1977-78.

The curriculum is liberal arts, featuring 23 majors and 35 minors. Artist-in-residence programs exist in both art and music. The graduating class of 1979 was a record 210. Approximately 80 percent of the students are from Arizona, and about 20 percent of the students live on campus.

In addition to the original bungalow-style buildings constructed in 1951, there are several permanent buildings: Antelope Gym, 1957; Fleming Library, 1957 and 1963; Cooke Health Center, 1961; Bright Angel Hall, 1961; Kaibab Hall, 1963 and 1966; Ethington Theater, 1975; and Tell Energy/Science Building, 1976.

The college has an outstanding intercollegiate sports program, boasting numerous district and area titles in baseball and basketball, plus two NAIA national titles in basketball, 1975 and 1978, and the 1980 NAIA national collegiate baseball championship.

PAUL BARNES

GRANT, JAMES RICHARD (b. Dover, AR, Mar. 16, 1880; d. Little Rock, AR, Nov. 4, 1951). Educator. Son of Daniel Richard and Mary Elizabeth (Aikins) Grant, farmers, he attended the University of Arkansas (B.A., 1908), the University of Chicago (M.A., 1914), and Peabody College (Ph.D., 1925). He married Gracey Sowers of Monticello in 1910, and they had five children: Bertie, James R., George S., Grace, and Daniel R. He was professor of education at the University of Arkansas, 1912-20; Arkansas state supervisor of rural education, 1920-26; president of Arkansas Tech, 1926-31; and president of Ouachita Baptist College, 1933-49.

During his presidency, Ouachita survived the critical period of the Great Depression, attained accreditation by the North Central Association, and grew from an enrollment of 236 to 897. Among his books are *Acquiring Skill in Teaching* (1922) and *The Life of Thomas C. McRae* (1932). He is buried in Roselawn Memorial Park, Little Rock, AR.

DANIEL R. GRANT

GRAVES, ANN JANE BAKER (b. near Baltimore, MD, Dec. 30, 1804; d. Baltimore, MD, Jan. 18, 1878). Leader of first general meeting of Southern Baptist women. Daughter of Jane Baker and Judge William Baker, she married John James Graves, a physician. They had seven children: Rosewell (q.v. I), William, John, Harry, Annie, Lillie, and Martha. In 1867 she organized a Baptist female prayer meeting in Baltimore for support of native Bible women in Canton, China, where her son Rosewell served as a missionary.

During the SBC meeting in Baltimore, May, 1868, she called Baptist women to a meeting in the basement of the First Baptist Church. She urged them to pray and to return to their churches to raise money to support native Bible women in China. This apparently was the first general meeting of Baptist women in the SBC. In Oct., 1871, Woman's Mission to Woman was organized in Baltimore with Graves as corresponding secretary. She is buried in Loudon Park Cemetery, Baltimore, MD.

DORIS DEVAULT

GREECE, MISSION IN. In 1972 Southern Baptist mission work developed in Greece through laymen (English-speaking) who wanted to worship, have access to religious education, and witness. Clyde R. Campbell served as the first pastor of the Trinity Baptist Church in Athens. In 1980 a missionary couple was ministering to this active fellowship, composed mainly of military personnel and civilian company employees. The church maintains a fraternal relationship with the Greek Baptist Church in Athens. The missionary pastor was traveling once a month to conduct services and Bible studies for a group of Americans near Xanthi in Northern Greece.

ELISE NANCE BRIDGES

GREENE, ADRIAN TOY, JR. (b. Pacolet, SC, Jan. 25, 1920; d. Columbia, SC, Mar. 18, 1974). Minister, writer, and denominational leader. The son of Adrian Toy, an accountant, and Keturah (Hamrick) Greene, he graduated from Wofford College (B.A., 1941) and The Southern Baptist Theological Seminary (Th.M., 1944). He married Kathryn (Abee) Greene, Sep. 24, 1946. They had four children: Kathryn, Adrian, Edith, and Margaret. Greene served as Royal Ambassador secretary for the Kentucky Baptist Convention during his seminary student days. Following graduation, he served as Royal Ambassador secretary for North and South Carolina Baptists. His pastorates included: New Hope Church, Cross Anchor, SC; Lucas Avenue Church, Laurens, SC; and Sunset Park Church, Wilmington, NC. He also served as associational superintendent of missions in the Cabarrus Association, Concord, NC.

In 1963 Greene became the first director of the Missions Department of the South Carolina Baptist Convention. In 1970 he was elected assistant general secretary-treasurer of the convention's General Board, a position he held until his death. Noted for his unusual ability to promote missions through human interest stories, he also wrote articles for many religious publications. He is buried in Oakwood Cemetery, Hickory, NC.

THOMAS J. BRANNON

GREER, ISAAC GARFIELD (b. Watauga County, NC, Dec. 5, 1881; d. Chapel Hill, NC, Nov. 24, 1967). State Baptist leader. Son of Phillip and Mary Greer, farmers, he married Willie Spainhour in 1916. They had two children, I. G., Jr., and Joseph. Following the death of his first wife, he married Hattie O'Briant in 1963. A graduate of the University of North Carolina (A.B.), he received the LL.D. degree from Wake Forest College in 1942.

Named general superintendent of the Baptist Children's Homes of North Carolina in 1932,

Greer served in this position until 1948. He was executive vice-president of the North Carolina Business Foundation, 1948-56. He served also as president of the Baptist State Convention of North Carolina, 1943, and the Southern Appalachian Historical Association. Greer was noted for his interpretation of ballads and folk songs of the Appalachian Mountains. He is buried in Chapel Hill Cemetery, Orange County, NC.

W. R. WAGONER

GRENADA, MISSION IN. Grenada is one of the Windward Islands lying about 150 miles north of Venezuela. It is an independent state of the British Commonwealth. Tourism and agriculture are the main streams of the economy for this nation of 110,000 in 133 square miles. Baptist work began on Aug. 9, 1975, with the arrival of one general evangelist. Membership in six fellowships is 177. Six Southern Baptist missionaries served in 1979. Ministries included evangelism, dental work, prison services, social work, and education. The mission emphasized involving nationals in general support and involvement in the total program. Two Grenadian Baptists were attending the Barbados Baptist Theological College.

W. KENNETH WELLMON

GRICE, HOMER LAMAR (b. Citra, FL, Apr. 12, 1883; d. Nashville, TN, May 17, 1974). Denominational leader. Son of Albert and Sarah Lee (Bennett) Grice, he married Ethel Harrison in Birmingham, AL, Aug. 21, 1912. A graduate of Mercer University (1912) and George Peabody College (M.A., 1929), Grice taught in Alabama public schools and worked for seven years with the United States Railway Postal Service. From 1913 to 1915, he was professor of English literature at Ouachita Baptist College. He was pastor of First Baptist Church, Washington, GA, 1915-24, where he conducted some of the first Vacation Bible Schools.

In Sep., 1924, Grice became the first secretary of the Vacation Bible School Department at the Sunday School Board, Nashville, where he served until retirement, Jan. 1, 1953. He promoted VBS for Southern Baptists, edited all VBS materials, and wrote about 45 children's books. He is buried in Woodlawn Cemetery, Nashville, TN.

See also VACATION BIBLE SCHOOL, VOL. II.

CHARLES F. TREADWAY

GRIFFIN, JASPER HARRISON (b. Bartow, FL, July 13, 1883; d. DeLand, FL, Sep. 23, 1976). Pastor and denominational leader. Son of James Griffin and Georgia (Cook) Griffin, farmers, he attended Summerlin Institute, Bartow, FL; Columbia College, Lake City, FL; Stetson University (M.A., 1927; D.D., 1931); and the University of Chicago. While a student in Chicago, he became pastor of the Auburn Park Baptist Church in the Greater Chicago area.

In 1918 Griffin married Cleo Dale Latimer of Ozark, AL. They had two sons, Harrison Dale and Huber Harrison. He served as pastor of the First Baptist Church, Winter Haven, FL, 1918-38. In 1931 Griffin traveled three months throughout Florida raising money to help lift the debt of the Florida Baptist Children's Home in Arcadia. He served as secretary of the Brotherhood Department of the Florida Baptist Convention, 1938-45, and later as secretary of the convention's Department of Christian Education, 1945-52.

After retirement from denominational service in 1952, Griffin continued to live in DeLand where he maintained close ties with and gave strong support to Stetson University. He served as interim pastor in churches in many cities in Florida, including New Smyrna, St. Augustine, Eau Gallie, and Lake Placid. He is buried in Oakdale Cemetery, DeLand, FL.

FRANK H. THOMAS, JR.

GROWTH OF SOUTHERN BAPTISTS (I, III). See SOUTHERN BAPTISTS, GROWTH OF.

GUADELOUPE, MISSION IN. See FRENCH WEST INDIES, MISSION IN.

GUAM, MISSION IN (III). The Tamuning Mission was organized as Tamuning Baptist Church in 1970. Student work began at the University of Guam in 1972 and is called "Student Bible Fellowship." A student center was constructed in 1974 near the university campus. In 1980 four missionary couples were serving on Guam. Personnel of the journeyman program have assisted in the work since 1971.

MARTHA ELLEN MARLER

GUATEMALA, MISSION IN (III; cf. Guatemala-Honduras, Mission in, Vol. I). The Guatemala Baptist Convention consists of 67 churches with 125 missions reporting 6,454 members. During the 1970s administration of the bookstore, the two theological schools, and all aid to churches was passed from the mission to the convention. Work among the K'ekchi Indians grew from one church in 1970 to 13 churches, 51 missions, and a membership of 2,074. Following the 1976 earthquake, Southern Baptists helped rebuild 16 church buildings, aided 400 Baptist families in replacing their homes, and rebuilt 333 houses, 3 schools, and 1 health center. Approximately 750 Baptist volunteers came to Guatemala to help in relief and evangelism. In 1979, 25 career missionaries and six short-term personnel were serving in the country.

A. CLARK SCANLON

GULFSHORE BAPTIST ASSEMBLY (cf. Gulfshore and Kittiwake Assemblies, Vol. III). On Aug. 17, 1969, hurricane Camille either flattened or ruined every building, except one, at Gulfshore Assembly. During the 1969 meeting of the Mississippi Baptist Convention, an Assembly Study Committee was appointed, with Beverly Tinnin as chairman. This committee recommended in Nov., 1971, that the assembly be rebuilt on the same site, alongside the Bay of St. Louis.

A second Assembly Study Committee, Estus Mason, chairman, recommended in 1972 that an assembly capital needs program be included in the convention budget, and that a capital funds campaign be launched. Beverly Tinnin was chairman of the steering committee appointed to implement action on the rebuilding.

David Grant, then president of the state convention, was elected general chairman of a "Restore Gulfshore" fund-raising campaign. He and at least 400 pastors, denominational workers, and laymen sought to raise $1,250,000 in two years, 1973-74. Many Mississippi Baptist churches voted to give two percent of their budgets for three years. At the 1974 convention, Grant announced that money and commitments totaled $1,346,984. Messengers to the convention voted to go ahead with construction, though the estimated cost had risen to $3,500,000.

The convention board in May, 1976, awarded the restoration contract to Roy Anderson, Inc., of Gulfport, on recommendation of the Gulfshore Restoration Committee, Brooks Wester, chairman. Anderson's bid of $3,750,000 was for hurricane-proof construction.

Ground breaking for the three-story main building was held, July 1, 1976. The old gymnasium, left standing after hurricane Camille, was to be remodeled for use as an auditorium. However, it burned in Sep., 1976. Afterward, a new auditorium was built on its foundations. New Gulfshore buildings were designed by the architectural firms, Caudill, Rowlett, and Scott of Houston, TX, and Slaughter, Smith, and Allred of Pascagoula, MS.

The convention board appointed Frank Simmons as director of assembly operations and Freddie Cook, Jr., as supervisor of buildings and grounds maintenance.

Gulfshore Assembly's new facilities were dedicated on May 5, 1978. James L. Sullivan, a Mississippi native and retired president of the Sunday School Board, SBC, who had spoken at the first Gulfshore dedication, July 22, 1960, was the speaker. Others on the program included W. Douglas Hudgins, executive secretary, state convention board, 1969-73, and Earl Kelly, executive secretary, convention board, 1973- . Mississippi's Singing Churchmen presented special music. At the dedication service the main building was named the Chester L. Quarles (*q.v.* III) Administration Building in memory of Quarles, executive secretary when Mississippi Baptists secured the assembly property. This building includes two wings for sleeping accommodations and a center section for offices, cafeteria, book store, laundry, infirmary, and classrooms.

During 1978, the first year of operation since 1969, Gulfshore provided for 4,181 registered summer guests. Twenty-three conferences were conducted by departments of the convention board. The assembly provided for 8,656 registered guests, Sep. 1, 1978-Aug. 31, 1979. Individual church and retreat groups also used the conference center.

ANNE WASHBURN MCWILLIAMS

GUYANA, MISSION IN (III). By 1970 six career missionary couples served in Guyana. Since 1975, the missionary force has been reduced to one couple, due to government restrictions. Emigration from Guyana caused a loss of pastors and key church leaders, resulting in a membership drop to 800 in 10 churches and 10 missions and a reduction in some programs of work. The Baptist Cooperative Convention of Guyana was organized in 1973, and all mission work is carried out through the convention. Missionaries work directly with national leadership in such areas as evangelism, theological and lay leadership training, mass media, Christian education, social ministries, and camping.

CHARLES LOVE

GWALTNEY, LUTHER RICE (b. Isle of Wight County, VA, Nov. 10, 1830; d. Rome, GA, July 18, 1910). Pastor and educator. The son, grandson, and great-grandson of Baptist preachers, Gwaltney was educated at Columbian College, Washington, DC (B.A., 1853; M.A., 1857). He was pastor of churches at Greenville, NC, 1855-57; Edgefield, SC, 1858-68, 1893-1901; Rome, GA, 1869-76; and Athens, GA, 1890-93.

While pastor in Rome, Gwaltney led in founding Cherokee Baptist Female College, forerunner of Shorter College. He acted as president, 1873, 1875-76, and served as professor of moral and mental philosophy, 1873-76. Early in 1876 he proposed that Alfred Shorter (q.v. I) rebuild and endow the institution. From 1876 to 1882 Gwaltney was president of Judson Female Institute, Marion, AL. In 1882 at the request of Alfred Shorter, he returned to Rome and the college to become president, 1882-90, and later associate president, 1890-91. He also served as professor of moral and mental philosophy, 1882-91. After his final pastorate he came back to Shorter as chaplain and professor of Christian morals, 1901-10.

Gwaltney was married twice—to Louisa Davidson, who died leaving two children, and to Sophia B. Lipscomb, who bore seven children. He is buried in Myrtle Hill Cemetery, Rome, GA.

ROBERT GARDNER

GWATHMEY, ABBY MURRAY MANLY (b. Tuscaloosa, AL, Sep. 12, 1839; d. Richmond, VA, Dec. 18, 1917). Woman's Missionary Union leader. The daughter of Basil Manly, Sr. (q.v. II), and Sarah (Rudulph) Manly, she graduated from Richmond Female Institute in 1856 and married William Henry Gwathmey, Dec. 7, 1858. They had nine children: Ann, Basil Manly, Helen, Sarah, Richard, Charlotte, Abby, Mariah, and Alberta. She served as chairman of the Virginia Central Committee, 1893-97, and for one year, 1894-95, as president of the WMU, SBC, when the Week of Self Denial and Thank Offering (later Annie Armstrong Offering) was instituted. She is buried in Hollywood Cemetery, Richmond, VA.

DORIS DEVAULT

H

HACKLEY, WOODFORD BROADUS (b. Culpeper County, VA, Aug. 2, 1894; d. Richmond, VA, Sep. 24, 1978). Educator and Baptist historian. Son of Walter Edgar and Marion Alice (Wood) Hackley, farmers, he graduated from the University of Virginia (A.B., 1914), Northwestern University (M.A., 1916), and Harvard University (M.A., 1917). He also studied at Johns Hopkins University, Columbia University, and the University of Berlin. He was principal of Jefferson High School, Culpeper County, VA, 1920-24, and professor of ancient languages, University of Richmond, 1924-62.

Hackley became secretary of the Virginia Baptist Historical Society in 1954 and treasurer in 1962. He continued in these positions through 1974, serving also as curator of the society's collection. In 1962 he initiated publication of *The Virginia Baptist Register,* which he edited through 1971. In 1972 he published *Faces on the Wall.* A recognized authority on Baptist history, he did extensive research and wrote numerous articles. From 1960 to 1968, he served as Virginia member of the Historical Commission, SBC. He married Betty Blair, Sep. 21, 1927. He is buried in Jeffersonton Baptist Church cemetery, Culpeper County, VA.

JOHN S. MOORE

HAGLER, OTTIS JOHN (b. Concord, NC, June 4, 1908; d. Raleigh, NC, May 11, 1979). State convention leader. Son of Sebe Blair and Laura Elizabeth (Shelton) Hagler, merchants, he married Wilma Louise Agee, July 15, 1931. They had one son, John. A graduate of Wake Forest College (B.A., 1932), Hagler attended Southwestern Baptist Seminary. He served as secretary of the Stewardship Department and the Annuity Plans Department of the North Carolina Baptist State Convention, 1956-60. Elected secretary of stewardship promotion for the state in 1960, he was named director of the Division of Stewardship Promotion and Editorial Service in 1962. He retired in 1970.

Before joining the North Carolina Convention staff, he served as pastor of three churches in North Carolina and Florida. From 1942 to 1946, he was chaplain at Veteran's Administration Hospital at Oteen, NC, in cooperation with the North Carolina Convention. He is buried in Sharon Memorial Cemetery, Charlotte.

CHARLES RAY RICHARDSON

HAITI, MISSION IN. Baptist work began in Haiti in 1823 under Thomas Paul, an American black. English and Jamaican Baptists also assisted in the beginning. In 1964 the Convention Baptiste D'Haiti (CBH) was formed with the aid of the American Baptist Convention, which had worked in Haiti since 1923. In 1980 the CBH counted 42,000 members in 86 churches and 800 preaching stations. Four other major Baptist groups were also present. Upon invitation of the CBH, the first SBC missionary couple arrived in 1978. A second couple came in 1980. Development and education are the assigned areas of work.

JACK D. HANCOX

HALE, ELDON WESLEY (b. Washington County, MO, June 12, 1918; d. Norman, OK, Oct. 25, 1978). Area missionary. Licensed to preach, Nov. 28, 1943, by Oak Grove Baptist Church, Fletcher, MO, he was ordained to the ministry, Oct. 7, 1945, by Liberty Church, Belgrade, MO. He was a graduate of William Jewell College (1950). He married Mary Dee Russell, Aug. 30, 1942. They had two children, Sandra and Bennie.

Hale's first pastorate was Liberty Church, Belgrade, MO. In 1951 he was working for the United States government when he was transferred to Michigan. His first church in that state was Solid Rock Church, Lansing, 1953. He served on the executive committee of the Motor Cities Baptist Association, 1955-57. In 1955 he became pastor of First Church, Berrien Springs. In 1961 he accepted the call of First Church, Gwinn, and was appointed by the

Home Mission Board and the state convention as pastoral missionary for Upper Peninsula Association. He devoted full time to the associational work as area director of missions after 1963. Under Hale's leadership the association grew from two churches and two church-type missions to eight churches and two church-type missions.

HOWARD CLARK

HALF MOON BLUFF CHURCH (LA) REPLICA. In 1978 Washington Association, aided by the Louisiana Baptist Convention, built a replica of the state's first Baptist church (founded Oct. 12, 1812) by the Bogue Chitto River five miles from Franklinton. Located on the Washington Parish fairgrounds, the replica is opened during the annual fair. Baptists provide singing, displays of artifacts, and hospitality.

JOHN H. ROBSON

HALL, DICK HOUSTON, JR. (b. New Albany, MS, Feb. 27, 1898; d. Gainesville, GA, Dec. 17, 1978). Pastor. The son of Corrie and Dick Hall, Sr., a lumber dealer, he attended Mississippi College (B.S., 1919), The Southern Baptist Theological Seminary (Th.M., 1924; Th.D., 1937), and the University of Louisville (M.A., 1925). He married Lora Neece Miller in 1923. They had four children: Dick, III, Marmon, Judy, and Evelyn. Following her death, he married Juaneese Martin of Gainesville, GA, Oct., 1972.

Hall was a pastor in Nelson County, KY; Erlanger, KY; Miami and DeLand, FL; and from 1940 to 1965 was at First Baptist Church, Decatur, GA. He served also as a trustee of Southern Seminary and as a member of the Foreign Mission Board, Home Mission Board, Baptist Joint Committee on Public Affairs, and Southern Baptist Foundation. He served as chairman of the Chaplains' Commission, SBC, under the aegis of the Home Mission Board.

In 1962-63 Hall was secretary of the SBC committee which wrote the revised Baptist Faith and Message statement. In the Georgia Baptist Convention, he was convention president, 1960-61; chairman of Baptist Village trustees; *Christian Index* board chairman, and Hospital Commission vice-chairman. He was vice-president of Atlanta Baptist College, 1965-68. He resigned in public protest when the school accepted federal funds. He is buried in the New Albany, MS, cemetery.

JACK U. HARWELL

HALLOCK, EDGAR FRANCIS (b. Havensville, KS, Sep. 22, 1888; d. Norman, OK, June 9, 1978). Pastor. The son of Henry Stephen and Eliza Ann Martin Hallock, he was a graduate of Ottawa University (Kansas) and Rochester Theological Seminary. He married Vera Elizabeth Day, June 28, 1915. Their children were Edgar, Jr., Roger W., Ardelle, Vera, Elizabeth, and Ann. He was pastor of First Churches, Pittsburg, KS, 1917-21, Nowata,

OK, 1921-22; and Norman, OK, 1923-69. Hallock was a pioneer in Baptist Student Union work in Oklahoma, beginning in 1924, and was president of the state convention in 1953. He was awarded the distinguished service citation by the University of Oklahoma in 1968. He is buried in the I.O.O.F. cemetery at Norman, OK.

J. M. GASKIN

HANNIBAL-LAGRANGE COLLEGE (I; cf. Missouri Baptist College, Vol. III). In 1967 Hannibal-LaGrange joined the newly established Missouri Baptist College of St. Louis, MO, to form a dual campus school. In 1973 the Executive Board of the Missouri Baptist Convention, with the mutual consent of both campuses, voted to separate the two facilities, thus reestablishing Hannibal-LaGrange as a coeducational liberal arts junior college.

L. A. Foster retired in 1970 after serving as president for 20 years, and Frank Kellogg was elected to fill the vacancy. Kellogg resigned in May, 1973, to give his full time to the college in St. Louis. Hannibal-LaGrange then named Gerald E. Martin of Memphis, TN, president. Martin was inaugurated as the 12th president, on Oct. 1, 1974.

One of a number of changes to be made was the creation of the new Division of Continuing Education which became the fourth classification of courses currently being offered. Classes are held at night, both on campus and at extension centers. In addition to these regular college courses, occasional special-interest classes and seminars have been arranged which are not designed for college credit but are offered as a service to the community.

Another change has been the addition of the degree of Associate in Applied Science (A.A.S.). Hannibal-LaGrange also offers a limited number of bachelor's degrees, all of which are related to the general field of religion. They include theology, religious education, and church music. All are accredited by the North Central Association of Colleges and Schools. These programs are designed especially for students who are interested in church-related vocations either on a part-time or a full-time basis.

Administrative and faculty personnel now number 59. Student enrollment averages well above 400 per semester. The fall, 1979, enrollment was 416.

Under the revised charter, the board of trustees consists of 25 members, each of whom is nominated and elected by the Missouri Baptist Convention.

Recent modifications include the modernization of the school cafeteria to a capacity of 300, the creation of the college art center, and the partial air conditioning of dormitories as well as the library. The college union and the college bookstore have been relocated and improved. A library built in the 1960s houses more than 24,000 volumes.

L. A. FOSTER

HARDIN-SIMMONS UNIVERSITY. Owned by the Baptist General Convention of Texas, Hardin-Simmons concluded the 1970s with a 30-year record enrollment of 1,839. Jesse C. Fletcher became the 12th president in 1977, succeeding Elwin Skiles, whose presidency was the second longest in the university's history, 1966-77. Under Fletcher's direction, a new academic organization was instituted, including a core curriculum in the College of Arts and Sciences and professional schools of music, education, business and finance, and nursing. An increasingly well-qualified faculty was attracted to the school as the percentage of faculty with terminal degrees increased from 50 to 75.

The Profile for Progress campaign, begun by President Skiles in 1968, had its initial appeal for funds in 1973. The $7,500,000 raised funded the $2,400,000 Richardson Library, five other major new buildings, and the remodeling of eight others. The campaign also endowed a faculty enrichment fund in excess of $1,000,000 and provided the initial $1,000,000 for the $3,500,000 Mabee Physical Education-Health-Athletic complex. The permanent endowment fund doubled in the 1970s to more than $11,000,000.

CRAIG BIRD

HARDING, EARL OTHA (b. Johnson County, MO, May 17, 1912; d. Jefferson City, MO, Aug. 12, 1973). Son of Edwin and Elizabeth Thomas Harding, farmers, he was a graduate of Central Missouri State University (B.A., B.S.) and Central Baptist Theological Seminary (Th.D.). He married Alice Cole, Dec. 17, 1937. They had one son, James Earl Harding.

Harding served churches in Missouri for 22 years; in addition to student pastorates, he served the First Baptist Churches of Lee's Summitt, Warrensburg, and Joplin. During his pastoral ministry, he was active in the affairs of the Missouri Baptist Convention, serving as a member of the executive board, 1945-51, and as convention recording secretary, 1946-53. He also served as a member of the SBC Historical Commission; the Public Relations Advisory Committee of the Executive Committee, SBC; the board of directors of Midwestern Baptist Theological Seminary; the SBC Inter-Agency Council; the governor's task force on the role of private higher education in Missouri, 1970; and as Honorary Chaplain of the United States House of Representatives, Nov., 1971. Harding was also active in Americans United for Separation of Church and State.

Harding assumed the post of executive secretary of the Missouri Baptist Convention in 1954, serving for nearly 20 years. His interest in world missions moved him to visit 79 countries. He also stayed in contact with missions in Missouri and Iowa. Under his leadership, Windemere Baptist Assembly was purchased and developed. The chapel there is named for him. Also the new Baptist Building for Missouri was built in 1970 and occupied in 1971. His interests outside his work included antiques and music. He was an accomplished organist. Harding is buried in the Warrensburg, MO, cemetery.

H. L. MCCLANAHAN

HARGRAVE MILITARY ACADEMY (I, III). In the 1979-80 session, 353 students enrolled. Twenty-five of these were coed day students. During this session the school had 34 full-time teachers. In the spring of 1980, 41 students graduated with diplomas. The summer session in 1980 had an enrollment of about 125. Grades 6 through 12 plus one year of postgraduate study are offered. The regular session can accommodate up to 400 cadets. The final payment on all building notes was made in Jan., 1978, and the school became debt free for the first time since 1950. Total assets on May 31, 1979, were $4,305,113. Total income for the year ending May 31, 1979, was $1,577,728. Vernon T. Lankford succeeded Joseph H. Cosby as president on July 1, 1970.

VERNON T. LANKFORD

HARRELL, WILLIAM ASA, JR. (b. Grandview, TX, Mar. 14, 1903; d. Nashville, TN, Feb. 26, 1971). Church architecture administrator. Son of William Harrell, merchant-farmer, and Ora Katherine (Smyth) Harrell, he married Mary Louise Jarrell, Dec. 16, 1928. They had one daughter, Susan. After studying at Baylor University and George Peabody College, he worked with the Alvarado Baptist Association in Texas and the Baptist General Convention of Texas, 1923-26. He joined the Sunday School Board, Nashville, working in the Sunday School and Training Union Departments until 1940; then he served as secretary of the Church Architecture Department until his death. He is buried in Woodlawn Cemetery, Nashville, TN.

ROWLAND E. CROWDER

HARRIS, JAMES GORDON (b. Little Rock, AR, Oct. 27, 1913; d. Fort Worth, TX, July 31, 1977). Pastor. The son of James Gordon Harris, a minister, and Ellen McManaway Harris, he was a graduate of Louisiana Baptist College (B.A., 1935) and Southwestern Baptist Theological Seminary (Th.M.; M.R.E., 1939). He married Tunis Johns, Jan. 10, 1939. They had three children: Jane, John, and Gordon.

From 1940 to 1954, Harris served as pastor of churches in Louisiana, Alabama, and Arkansas. He served University Baptist Church, Fort Worth, TX, 1954-77. He was chairman of the Texas Baptist Executive Board, 1969-71; first vice-president of the SBC, 1973-74; and president of the Baptist General Convention of Texas, 1975-77. He served as a trustee of Baylor University, the Foreign Mission Board, and the SBC Christian Life Commission. He is buried in Greenwood Cemetery, Fort Worth, TX.

ROSALIE BECK

HARRISON-CHILHOWEE BAPTIST ACADEMY (I, III). The decade, 1970-80, was one of innovation and change. Hubert B. Smothers succeeded Charles C. Lemons as the fourth president in Oct., 1970. The programs and staff grew to include a college preparatory program for the deaf, an art department, an art gallery, a Bible school, a child development center, driver education, a counselor, a supervisor of property, a deaf program coordinator, a public relations coordinator, a director of development, and a student recruiter.

During the decade, Chilhowee established a founder's day; received the Seymour Elementary School building as a gift; received accreditation by the Southern Association of Colleges and Schools; formed the Oscar and Victoria Woody Trust Fund and named Woody Auditorium in their honor; and created the Corrie ten Boom Freedom Scholarship during Corrie ten Boom's visit as commencement speaker. In 1980 the academy celebrated its 100th anniversary and engaged in an advancement campaign to kick off its second 100 years.

HUBERT BON SMOTHERS

HARTSFIELD, GREEN W. (b. Muscogee County, GA, Dec. 14, 1833; d. Arcadia, LA, May 22, 1896). Pioneer leader. The son of Andy and Ghasky Hartsfield, he settled near Shreveport, LA, in 1849. He joined Providence Church, 1851, and was ordained there, 1859. Educated at Mt. Lebanon University, 1860-63, he married Eunice Brown, May 1, 1862. Their children were Nora, Mary, George, Lillian, and Edna. He was pastor of Mansfield Church, 1866-76, 1882-87; Arcadia Church, 1888-96; and from these centers served some 20 additional congregations.

Clerk of Grand Cane Association 22 years and of the Louisiana Baptist Convention 18 years, Hartsfield held numerous additional denominational offices. He contributed to Baptist papers and was influential in establishing a Baptist newspaper for Louisiana, a forerunner of the *Baptist Message*. He was a leader in Sunday Schools, work with black Baptists, temperance movements, and agricultural and literary activities. He is buried in the Arcadia, LA, cemetery.

WILLIAM A. POE

HARTWELL, JESSE (b. Buckland, MA, May 2, 1795; d. Mt. Lebanon, LA, Sep. 16, 1859). Pastor and educator. The son of Jesse Hartwell, a minister, and Jerusha Hartwell, he studied for the ministry at Brown University (A.B., 1819) and served as pastor of Second Baptist Church, Providence, RI (1819-22), during which time he married Maria Thayer. She bore one child and died. In search of healthful climate, he moved to Charleston, SC, establishing a lasting friendship with Richard Furman (*q.v.* I). In May, 1824, he married Margaret Forman Brodie. They had two sons, including J. Boardman Hartwell, longtime missionary to China, and three daughters.

Hartwell was pastor of four South Carolina churches and a founding professor of Furman Academy and Theological Institution. As agent of the Triennial Convention, he moved to Alabama and served churches in Carlowville and Montgomery. He taught at Howard College, 1844-48, attending the Augusta, GA, convention which formed the SBC. He was president of the Domestic (Home) Mission Board, 1845-49. Subsequently he was principal of Camden, AR, Female Institute and president of Mt. Lebanon University, LA. He is buried in the Mt. Lebanon, LA, cemetery.

LEE N. ALLEN

HARVEY, P. CASPAR (b. Gallatin, MO, Nov. 25, 1889; d. Liberty, MO, May 28, 1975). Educator. Son of Wesley and Cora (Casper) Harvey, missionaries, he attended William Jewell College (A.B., 1910; A.M., 1911), Kansas City School of Law, and the University of Chicago. He married Victoria Adelaide Unrah, June 11, 1919. They had no children.

Harvey spent most of his career, 1910-58, at William Jewell College, serving as professor of English composition, director of public relations, director of forensics, and managing editor of the college alumni bulletin. His students won high honors in debate and oratorical contests. He coached the United States team which represented all colleges and universities of the nation· in international intercollegiate debates in Great Britain, 1939. A member of the Second Baptist Church of Liberty and the Liberty Rotary Club, he retired in 1958. He is buried in Fairview Cemetery, Liberty, MO.

H. I. HESTER

HASKINS, THOMAS PAUL (b. Weakley County, TN, Mar. 2, 1891; d. Hugo, OK, Dec. 18, 1976). Pastor. The son of Will and Rosa Haskins, farmers, he attended Hall-Moody College, Martin, TN, and Southwestern Baptist Theological Seminary. He married Lois Maple Baker, Nov. 28, 1911. They had four children: Ruth, Dathel, Truitt, and Thomas. He served as a pastor in Tennessee, Missouri, and Oklahoma; assistant executive secretary, Baptist General Convention of Oklahoma, 1935-48; state evangelist, 1951-57; Baptist Memorial Hospital chaplain, Oklahoma City, 1958-66; and assistant pastor, First Church, Enid, 1967-72. He is buried at Enid, OK.

ROBERT EUGENE HASKINS

HASTINGS, LUTHER THOMAS (b. Bedford County, TN, July 23, 1884; d. Monroe, LA, Feb. 15, 1978). Pastor and educator. Educated at Union University, Jackson, TN, and Southwestern Baptist Theological Seminary, his pastorates included Central Church, Jacksonville, TX, 1917-19; Coliseum Place, New Orleans, 1920-25; and First Baptist, Monroe, LA, 1925-49. In 1913 he married Cora Brownlow. They had one son, Brownlow. Hastings served as president of the Louisiana Baptist Convention, 1939-40, and as evangelist in Louisiana and Texas. Upon retiring from the pastorate, he taught at Clear Creek Baptist School, Pineville, KY, for nine years. He is buried in Memorial Park, Monroe, LA.

JAMES T. HORTON

HATHAWAY, MAUDE WALL (b. near Anna, IL, Aug. 4, 1884; d. Murphysboro, IL, Dec. 4, 1978). Good will center missionary and denominational leader. Daughter of Anna Wright Wall and James Byrd Wall, farmers, she earned a teacher's certificate from the College of Music and Expression in Chicago, IL, in 1907 and was graduated from the Woman's Missionary Union Training School, Louisville, KY (B.M.T., 1918). In 1909 she married Frank B. Southall. They had one daughter, Louise. After his death she married John Hathaway, Dec. 25, 1922.

She was a missionary for the good will center in Harrisburg, IL, 1918-22, and for a few months in 1922 acted as WMU corresponding secretary. The Illinois WMU elected her state president in 1927 and 1928. Hathaway served as a state approved Sunday School worker, 1928-33.

She became executive secretary of Illinois WMU in 1933 and served until 1950, except for the years 1943 and 1944 when she was field missionary. While in office she wrote *Soul Winning in Your Community* and *There Stood By* (1948). She retired in 1950, returning to the office as interim for several months in 1954-55. During retirement she lived in Carbondale and Cairo, IL. She is buried in Rose Hill Cemetery near Marion, IL.

HELEN SINCLAIR

HAWAII, MISSION IN (I, III). At the beginning of the 1970s, eight foreign missionaries were still on loan to the Hawaii work, and the Foreign Mission Board still provided a small amount for the Hawaii Baptist Convention budget. Assistance for the convention budget ended with the 1974 budget year. No foreign missionaries were assigned to Hawaii beyond 1977.

See also HAWAII BAPTIST CONVENTION.

WINSTON CRAWLEY

HAWAII ASSOCIATIONS (III). During the 1970s, no new associations were organized in Hawaii. The six associations affiliated with the Hawaii Baptist Convention in 1970 continued their work throughout the decade.

LYNN E. MAY, JR.

HAWAII BAPTIST ACADEMY. Hawaii Baptist Academy offers a quality Christian education for approximately 800 students from all cultural and religious backgrounds in kindergarten through 12th grade. The total educational experience at the academy is aimed toward developing the best in each student intellectually, socially, physically, and spiritually through a personal faith in Jesus Christ. The community recognizes the academy as an outstanding academic institution, and selection to attend is eagerly sought and considered an honor.

The Western Association of Schools and Colleges has accredited the academy, which is also a member of the Association of Southern Baptist Colleges and Schools. Stanley A. Sagert has been president of the academy since 1970.

In addition to a curriculum designed to prepare students for higher education, the academy provides a full program of student government and club, social, and sports activities. Bible is taught at every grade level, and the Christian way of life is presented as the highest goal. Christian students are trained to lead out in their churches and on campus in chapel programs, Bible study groups, class camps, and special religious emphasis weeks.

In 1973 the academy began an ongoing capital program among parents, Baptists, and friends from Hawaii and the mainland to develop the junior-senior high school campus at 2429 Pali Highway in Honolulu. During the same year, Dan H. Kong, then pastor of Olivet Baptist Church, joined the academy to help raise support on the mainland. In 1975 the secondary division moved into a new four-story classroom building. In 1980 efforts were being made to secure donations to begin the multipurpose building which was removed from original construction plans because of inflation and insufficient funds. This building will complete the basic physical plant necessary to maintain the school's educational standards.

The elementary school continues to be operated at the 1225 Nehoa Street location in Honolulu, with an extension of grades one through four meeting in classrooms of the First Baptist Church of Nanakuli on Oahu.

STANLEY SAGERT

HAWAII BAPTIST CONVENTION (I, III). The Hawaii Baptist Convention offices moved from 1225 Nehoa Street, Jan., 1971, to property owned by the convention at 2042 Vancouver Drive. The Baptist Student Center and convention offices share the space. The convention increased in the 1970s from 30 churches with 9,554 members to 39 churches and 18 mission and language congregations with 11,110 members. Malcolm Stuart, a foreign missionary and director of missions, resigned to go on furlough. Sam Choy was elected, June, 1976, as director of missions. The convention opened work in American Samoa in Aug., 1977, with the sending of Ray and Lena Viliamu as joint missionaries of the convention and the Home Mission Board, SBC. The Viliamus started the Happy Valley Baptist Church in Pago Pago. This church has begun work in Western Samoa.

Visitors to Hawaii comprise one of the major industries. There were over 4,000,000 visitors in 1979. The convention churches minister to the visitors at their services and by having chapel services at several hotels. Veryl Henderson was named resort missionary, Jan., 1979, to help with this and other phases of the ministry.

HAWAII STATISTICAL SUMMARY

Year	Associations	Churches	Church Membership	Baptisms	SS Enrollment	VBS Enrollment	CT Enrollment	WMU Enrollment	Brotherhood Enrollment	Ch. Music Enrollment	Mission Gifts	Total Gifts	Value Church Property
1969	6	29	9,474	503	9,144	3,648	2,313	1,078	531	882	$123,860	$1,097,494	$ 6,712,083
1970	6	31	9,124	363	8,261	3,278	2,052	1,074	348	769	139,143	1,133,787	7,689,010
1971	6	32	9,452	389	7,580	3,081	1,713	993	267	873	172,694	1,269,217	7,592,045
1972	6	32	9,572	498	7,274	2,827	1,506	890	165	957	208,377	1,405,253	7,668,574
1973	6	32	10,173	535	6,854	3,615	1,373	876	260	961	264,687	1,089,647	8,303,404
1974	6	33	10,557	586	7,011	3,142	1,077	932	397	1,068	319,232	1,193,879	9,494,350
1975	6	35	11,030	639	7,436	3,171	1,130	1,060	371	1,170	305,805	1,407,464	10,664,285
1976	6	36	11,682	630	7,595	3,238	1,106	1,038	323	1,096	390,596	1,646,077	11,768,410
1977	6	37	11,969	540	7,655	3,610	1,107	872	253	1,150	354,288	1,730,058	14,995,431
1978	6	38	11,350	654	7,549	3,382	1,164	903	315	1,167	342,649	1,733,741	15,020,725
1979	6	38	10,978	516	7,697	3,485	1,336	877	261	1,233	390,922	2,028,903	16,984,136
1980	6	39	11,346	787	8,054	3,180	1,300	875	204	1,352	595,306	2,387,132	19,853,890

SUSAN ROWE

Baptist Student Centers.—Larry Thomas was succeeded by Lloyd Cornell in 1972 and Nelson O. Hayashida in 1976 as state student director and associate director of cooperative church development. Josephine Harris retired in 1973 as director of the Hilo center; Leon Johnson began as director in 1980.

Puu Kahea Baptist Assembly.—Rudolph E. Peterson retired in May, 1971, after 21 years as manager. The assembly is being upgraded with new cottages and a manager's residence. In 1980 the manager was R. Lloyd Priddy, Jr.

The Hawaii Baptist.—Edmond R. Walker served as editor of this monthly paper for 15 years. Sue Nishikawa, who was associate editor, 1970-79, was elected editor, Feb., 1979. She served until 1980. The paper is mailed to every Baptist family in Hawaii Baptist churches.

Woman's Missionary Union.—The Woman's Missionary Union of the convention was organized in Aug., 1944. The representatives of the four churches attending the meeting elected Maude B. Dozier as president. Sue Saito was elected executive secretary in 1954. The title was later changed to WMU director.

When the convention restructured its administrative services, the WMU became a department of the Cooperative Church Development Division. In 1976 it was transferred to the Cooperative Missions Division, with Sue (Saito) Nishikawa serving as WMU department director and division associate director.

The WMU initiates state offering goals for foreign, home, and state missions and suggests allocations for the state missions offering. The goals and allocations are approved by the state executive board.

EDMOND WALKER and SUE NISHIKAWA

HAYES, JAMES MADISON, SR. (b. Wilkes County, NC, Apr. 12, 1892; d. Winston-Salem, NC, Apr. 14, 1978). Founder of North Carolina Baptist Homes for the Aging. Son of John and Sara Hayes, farmers, he married Aline Clifford Pace, June 16, 1918. They had three children. Hayes attended Wake Forest College (B.A., 1917) and received his law license in 1921. He practiced law briefly in Wilkes County before entering the ministry. Ordained Apr. 23, 1922, he received a degree in theology from Southern Baptist Theological Seminary in 1924. Hayes held pastorates in Elkin, NC; Lexington, NC; and Beckley, WV, before going to Winston-Salem in 1939 as pastor of North Winston Baptist Church.

In 1951 he was named general superintendent of the proposed North Carolina Baptist Homes for the Aging. For the next nine years he led North Carolina Baptists in their ministry to the aging. Little money was available for the venture, which he later referred to as "an undertaking of faith." By 1960, when he retired, three homes and a skilled nursing facility had been established. After he retired, Hayes practiced law in Winston-Salem. He published a *History and Memoirs of North Carolina Baptist Founding and*

First Decade (1950-60) Homes for Aging (1972). He is buried in Forsyth Memorial Park, Winston-Salem, NC.

ELIZABETH BRANTLEY

HAYS, LAWRENCE BROOKS (b. London, AR, Aug. 9, 1898; d. Chevy Chase, MD, Oct. 12, 1981). Lawyer, political leader, and Southern Baptist Convention president. He was the only son of Steele and Sallie (Butler) Hays, a lawyer and teacher, respectively. The family lived in Atkins, AR, until 1903, when they moved to Russellville, AR. Hays received his primary and secondary education in Russellville. A graduate of the University of Arkansas in Fayetteville (A.B., 1919) and George Washington University Law School (L.L.B., 1922), Hays received the honorary L.L.D. degree both from Mercer University (1957) and William Jewell College (1958). He married Marion Prather, Feb. 2, 1922. They had two children, Betty Brooks (Bell) and Marion Steele.

Hays practiced law in Russellville, 1923-25, served as assistant attorney general of Arkansas, 1925-27, was defeated for governor of Arkansas on a reform platform in 1928 and 1930, and practiced law in Little Rock, AR, 1928-34. Elected a member of the Democratic National Committee, 1932-39, he was defeated for the Arkansas fifth district congressional seat in a special election in 1933. He served as director of the National Recovery Administration (NRA) for Arkansas, 1934-35; as regional attorney (Little Rock) for the United States Department of Agriculture, 1935-41; as assistant director of Rural Rehabilitation, 1941-42; and as member of the United States House of Representatives from the fifth district of Arkansas, 1943-59. Remembered for his involvement in the cause of civil rights, foreign affairs, and human justice, Hays worked consistently to help the poor and disadvantaged both as a public official and a private citizen.

After opposing the views of then Arkansas Governor Orval Faubus during the 1958 Little Rock school desegregation crisis, Hays was defeated for his seat by an avowed segregationist. He served as a special adviser to President Dwight D. Eisenhower, who appointed him to the board of the Tennessee Valley Authority, 1959-61. Hays was assistant secretary of state for congressional relations and later was special presidential assistant, 1961-63, under President John F. Kennedy. Hays also served as special presidential assistant under President Lyndon B. Johnson, 1963-64.

Hays served on the faculties of Rutgers University, the University of Massachusetts, and North Carolina State University. He was first director of the Ecumenical Institute at Wake Forest University, 1969-74. He also served as chairman of the North Carolina Human Relations Commission.

Ordained a deacon by First Baptist, Russellville, in 1923, he served in numerous local church and denominational responsibilities. He was both a Sunday School teacher of a men's class at Second Baptist, Little Rock, and general superintendent of the Sunday School. He served as chairman of the Rural Church Committee for the Arkansas Baptist State Convention, 1928-29; trustee of Arkansas Baptist Hospital, 1933-35; second vice-president of the SBC, 1951; member Social Service Commission, SBC, 1948-54; member of the Christian Life Commission, SBC, 1955-60, and chairman, 1955-57; and president of the SBC, 1957-59.

Hays was active in numerous organizations, serving as a member of the governing boards of George Peabody College and George Washington University, Boy Scouts of America, National Conference of Christians and Jews, Lions Club, and others.

Hays wrote numerous books, including *The Baptist Way of Life* with John E. Steely (1963, revised 1981), *A Hotbed of Tranquility* (1968), *Politics is My Parish* (1981), *A Southern Moderate Speaks* (1959), and *This World: A Christian's Workshop* (1958). He is buried in Russellville, AR.

A. RONALD TONKS

HEATHEN HELPER, THE. A missions paper published in Louisville, KY, beginning, Nov., 1882, by the Central Committee of Kentucky Women's Missionary Societies. Agnes Osborne, corresponding secretary of the Central Committee, was the editor. Begun in response to requests from the growing number of societies for printed matter, the paper provided reports, news items, missionary letters, and editorials. Osborne invited the other 13 state central committees to have contributing "editresses." They were the editorial staff, and the eight-page illustrated paper became the official organ of women's societies throughout the South. The last issue was apparently printed in July, 1888.

BOBBIE SORRILL

HEMPHILL, FRITZ DEAN (b. Rutherford County, NC, Sep. 4, 1904; d. Hickory, NC, Nov. 8, 1978). Pastor and educator. Son of the George Hemphills, farmers, he attended Wingate College (A.A.) and Wake Forest University (B.A., 1935). He was a leader in organizing churches and developing Sunday Schools throughout North Carolina, working extensively in Sunday School enlargement campaigns. From 1948 to 1960, while serving as pastor of West Hickory Church, he promoted and directed the Central Training School in Hickory, one of the largest of its kind in the SBC. Hemphill also served on the North Carolina Convention's general board, 1951-55, serving as vice-chairman for one year. A member of the board of trustees of Wake Forest University, he also served as director of Fruitland Baptist Bible Institute and Camp.

Hemphill married Rose Johnson on Apr. 11, 1929. They had four children: George, Eschol, Robert, and James. He is buried in Oakwood Cemetery, Hickory, NC.

KAY M. HUGGINS

HENDRICK MEDICAL CENTER (cf. Hendrick Memorial Hospital, Vols. II, III). In the fiscal year 1978-79, the hospital reported 464 beds, 19,132 inpatients, 20,154 outpatients, patient income of $24,909,123, and donations from the Baptist General Convention of Texas totaling $193,190. Total asset value was over $28,000,000. Recent additions to the medical facility included a seven-story wing and a regional trauma center constructed through the efforts of a donor campaign. This drive raised more than $4,000,000 of a $12,000,000 goal. The medical center has 1,300 employees and 150 members on its medical staff.

JENNIFER M. DACY

HENRY, DOLAN EDWARD (b. Putnam County, TN, Dec. 20, 1923; d. Camp Hill, PA, Feb. 28, 1970). Pastor and superintendent of missions. Son of Joseph H. and Maggie L. Henry, he attended Carson-Newman College (B.S., 1953) and Southwestern Baptist Theological Seminary (B.D., 1957). He married Margaret Ruth Hill, Jan. 20, 1946. They had three children. After serving for several years as pastor of churches in Tennessee, Texas, Ohio, and Pennsylvania, he was named superintendent of missions of Keystone Baptist Association, Harrisburg, PA, in 1965. He served in this position until his death. He assisted in the formation of the Baptist Convention of Pennsylvania-South Jersey. He is buried in the Gettysburg, PA, National Cemetery.

RUTH HENRY

HERRING, BENJAMIN OSCAR (b. Bardwell, TX, Jan. 27, 1889; d. Waco, TX, July 22, 1973). Pastor, teacher, and school administrator. Son of Stephen A. and Martha Loveless Herring, he was a graduate of Baylor University (B.A., 1923; M.A., 1927) and The Southern Baptist Theological Seminary (Th.M., 1919; Ph.D., 1929). He married Bertha Elizabeth Shiplet, Oct. 20, 1909. They had two sons. Following her death, he married Dora Mae Perry, July 2, 1955.

He served as pastor of churches in Kentucky and Texas for 29 years. He was professor of Bible at Baylor University, 1924-45, and president of Golden Gate Baptist Theological Seminary, 1946-52, and Grand Canyon College, 1952-54. He then taught at Howard Payne College until retirement. He wrote *Studies in the Prophets* (1944).

HAROLD K. GRAVES

HERRING, RALPH ALDERMAN (b. Pender County, NC, Aug. 18, 1901; d. Charlotte, NC, July 2, 1972). Pastor, denominational leader, and writer. The son of missionaries David Wells and Alice Rea Herring, he lived in China until age 12. He attended Buie's Creek Academy (now Campbell College), Wake Forest College (B.A., 1921), and The Southern Baptist Theological Seminary (Th.M., 1925; Th.D., 1929). He married Willeen Tull, Aug. 5,

1925. They had four children: Ralph, David, Jackson, and Margaret.

His pastorates were in Crestwood, KY, 1924-29; First Church, Ashland, KY, 1929-36; and First Church, Winston-Salem, NC, 1936-61. During 1961-68, Herring was director of the Seminary Extension Department of the Southern Baptist seminaries. Other positions of denominational leadership included president, North Carolina Baptist Convention, 1943-44, 1944-45; second vice-president of the SBC, 1937-38; a member of the Foreign Mission Board; and trustee of Southern Seminary, Wake Forest College, Campbell College, and Southeastern Baptist Theological Seminary.

Herring wrote four books: *Studies in Philippians* (1952), *The Cycle of Prayer* (1966), *The Profile of Christian Experience* (1968), and *God Being My Helper* (1955).

RAYMOND M. RIGDON

HESTER, CAROLYNE LOUISE GEER (b. Anderson, SC, Sep. 19, 1899; d. Kansas City, MO, Oct. 14, 1976). College staff member. The daughter of Levi and Mildred Geer, farmers, she attended Anderson College (A.B.). She entered Woman's Missionary Union Training School, Louisville, KY, in 1919, and together with her husband, H. I. Hester, whom she married, Nov. 1, 1921, planned missionary service in Brazil. Ill health prevented this. After two years of teaching at Furman University, the Hesters moved to Liberty, MO, where Hester chaired the department of Bible at William Jewell College. Carolyne served as hostess in Melrose Hall, residence building for women from 1927-43. A nurse's aide during World War II, she also held active membership in local women's organizations. She is buried in Memorial Cemetery, Liberty, MO.

DORIS D. HOWELL

HESTER, H. I., LECTURESHIP ON PREACHING. See PREACHING, H. I. HESTER LECTURESHIP ON.

HICKERSON, CLYDE VERNON (b. Remington, VA, Apr. 19, 1898; d. Richmond, VA, Nov. 29, 1977). Pastor and denominational leader. The son of John B. and Florence (Brown) Hickerson, he graduated from the University of Richmond (B.A., 1920) and The Southern Baptist Theological Seminary (Th.M., 1923). He studied further at the University of Louisville and received a D.D. from the University of Richmond in 1946. Hickerson married Amy Compere, Oct. 23, 1923. They had four daughters: Amy, Sue, Elizabeth, and Louise. His pastorates were First Church, Russellville, AR, 1922-34; First Church, Hot Springs, AR, 1934-38; Baptist Temple, San Antonio, TX, 1938-44; and Northminster Church, Richmond, VA, 1944-65, emeritus, 1965-77.

Recognized for strong pastoral leadership, in 1951 he served as chairman of a preaching mission to Japan sponsored by the Foreign Mission

Board, SBC. He served on the SBC Executive Committee and on the Foreign Mission Board, 1945-52. Also he was a trustee of *The Religious Herald,* 1959-69, and the University of Richmond, 1956-70, emeritus, 1970-77. He authored three books: *The Home of the Master* (1938), *Respectable Sinners* (1939), and *The Twofold Power of the Gospel* (1942). He is buried in Greenwood Memorial Gardens, Richmond, VA.

FREDERICK J. ANDERSON

HIGH PLAINS BAPTIST HOSPITAL (III). The hospital was valued in 1980 at over $22,000,000. At that time, it was licensed for 304 beds and could accommodate over 400. Special areas of care were the Bivins Rehabilitation Unit, the Obstetrics-Gynecology Department, Opthalmology Department, and the One-day Surgery Unit. Operating under the auspices of the Baptist General Convention of Texas, Baptist Hospital was the first health-care facility in Amarillo to offer clinical pastoral care. T. H. Holloway, Jr., is administrator.

SHELLY SMITH

HIGHER EDUCATION, TRENDS AMONG BAPTISTS IN. Accreditation was the major emphasis in higher education among Southern Baptists in the early 1970s. By 1972 all colleges supported by Baptist state conventions were members of their regional accrediting associations.

Several colleges made significant changes in service offered. Bluefield, Missouri Baptist, and Wingate Colleges changed from two to four-year schools in the 1970s. Hannibal-LaGrange was accredited to offer four-year programs in church vocations. Virginia Intermont became both a four-year school and coeducational. Two other women's colleges, Averett and Mary Hardin-Baylor, also accepted men students. Norman College closed in 1970, and the University of Corpus Christi ceased operation as a Baptist institution in 1972.

Many Baptist institutions initiated programs in adult education or lifelong learning. Some of these were evening programs and were projected as community service projects. Other programs leading to a degree such as the Bachelor of General Studies were offered. Requirements for basic curriculum were usually relaxed for the applicant for the new degree while minimum age limits were set.

Identification by the Baptist Education Study Task of the needs for closer denominational ties and better communication led Southern Baptist institutions of higher education to enter a period emphasizing the uniqueness of their Christian purpose and commitments. Under the leadership of Benjamin Coleman Fisher, executive director-treasurer of the Education Commission, SBC, college leaders held extensive conferences with denominational leaders concerning closer ties between mission agencies and the colleges and conducted the National Colloquium on Christian Education at Williamsburg, VA, in 1976.

As a result of the colloquium, Earl J. Mc-Grath, executive director, Program of Liberal Studies of the University of Arizona, conducted a study published as *Study of Southern Baptist Colleges and Universities, 1976-77.* The report revealed that in the decade ending in 1975, enrollment in Southern Baptist colleges and universities had increased by 31 percent. The rating of schools by the faculty and staff at Southern Baptist colleges was found to be high, compared to other independent institutions. The schools studied were concerned for learning and were judged surprisingly innovative.

Financial data gathered by John Minter Associates and published in the McGrath study showed Southern Baptist colleges and universities slightly stronger financially than independent higher education institutions nationwide. The Baptist schools owned a larger portion of the assets at their disposal and were increasing in endowment assets more rapidly than the national sample. Minter expressed caution concerning fiscal strength because of the receipt of a high proportion of revenue from current giving, heavy dependence on current income including tuition, growth of liabilities, and the fact that a few institutions were experiencing financial stress.

A major conclusion of the McGrath study was that Baptist schools needed clear statements of Christian purpose and they needed to do a good job of communicating this purpose to Southern Baptists.

Concern for governance grew with the focus on purpose. The responsibility of trustees both to the institution and the denomination was emphasized through publications and training sessions. Denominational participation also became a major consideration in the choice of chief administrative officers for a majority of the institutions.

Concern for the purpose of Baptist institutions was emphasized in a year-long debate in 1979. The ultimate decision made that year by the North Carolina Baptist State Convention and Wake Forest University was to move to a "covenant" relationship between the university and the state convention.

The general study of purpose resulted, also, in the National Conference on Bold Christian Education and Bold Missions sponsored by the Association of Southern Baptist Colleges and Schools and the Education Commission, SBC, in 1979. The association also participated with representatives from 22 other Christian denominations in the two sessions of the National Congress on Church-Related Colleges and Universities. Faculty members and administrators from 600 church-related colleges and universities, along with leaders from each of the denominations, met in South Bend, IN, in June, 1979, and in Washington, DC, in Feb., 1980. During the meeting they discussed and reaffirmed the role and value of the church-related college. Southern Baptist educators gave significant leadership in this movement.

An increasing number of Southern Baptist colleges and universities in the last two decades have become significantly more dependent on state and federal student aid programs for scholarship assistance. Most have made clear distinctions between student aid grants and grants made directly to the schools. The legal distinction between the two forms of aid was still in question in 1980.

As more church-related schools have accepted student aid funds from governmental groups, the number of national educational organizations attempting to influence the distribution of funds and the regulatory requirements has increased. This trend has led Southern Baptist schools to be involved in more national movements and organizations and to join with other denominations in the cause of promoting church-related higher education.

ARTHUR L. WALKER, JR.

HIGHLAND LAKES BAPTIST CENTER. A 396-acre retreat center, 25 miles southwest of Indianapolis, IN, owned and operated by the State Convention of Baptists in Indiana, and begun in 1967. Development for year-round use is under the direction of O. Thomas Woods, director of Brotherhood and Camp Development for the convention, with one full-time employee, Oliver Daniels. Volunteers from Indiana churches, state staff families, missionary families, Campers on Mission, and church and student groups from Alabama, Florida, Georgia, Mississippi, Missouri, North Carolina, South Carolina, and Texas have assisted. Christian Service Corps volunteer Eugene Readinger, forester, supported by First Baptist Church, Baton Rouge, LA, renders valuable service.

Development thus far includes maintenance and storage buildings, six dormitories, a temporary auditorium, a temporary lodge with food facilities, a rustic area building, tent camping area, a prayer garden, roads, underground utilities, and a modern sewer system. Financing is provided through Broadway Bond Issues, state mission offerings, and the Life Touching Contributor Plan, adopted in 1978. The LTC plan sought 2,500 contributors to pledge an amount above regular church gifts, to be given over a three-year period. Use includes camps, retreats, and training for family, church, associational, and state groups. Future development plans include a main lodge, recreational facilities, and two lakes.

MRS. E. HARMON MOORE

HILLCREST BAPTIST HOSPITAL (III; cf. Hillcrest Memorial Hospital, Vol. III). In 1979 the bed capacity was 368, and assets totaled $31,000,000. Facilities in addition to the hospital buildings included a 525-space parking garage, a 10-story medical office building, and the Fentress Cancer Center. A five-story administration-education building was scheduled to be completed in 1981. The hospital, operated by the Baptist General Convention of Texas, receives financial assistance through the Cooperative Program. Friends of the hospital help with gifts through the Department of Development. Alton Pearson, president, has been associated with the hospital since 1953, with the exception of two years.

CURTIS HOLLAND

HINTZE, WILLIAM ROBERT (b. El Paso, TX, July 10, 1925; d. Phoenix, AZ, Nov. 17, 1977). Missionary and educator. Son of Pearl and Charles Hintze, a steelworker, he attended the Texas College of Mines (B.S., 1950). He married Barbara Ruth Laughman, Sep. 12, 1952. They had four children: William, Jr., Robin, Fred, and Richard. Hintze rose through the ranks at Bell Telephone Company to become director of personnel for all company operations in the Southwest.

Responding to a call to the ministry, he attended Southwestern Baptist Theological Seminary (Th.M., 1958; Th.D., 1966). Appointed a missionary to Ecuador in 1960, he served as professor of theology in the Baptist seminary. He returned to the United States in 1972 to become professor of religion at Grand Canyon College, succeeding to the presidency in 1972.

JOE CAUSEY

HISTORICAL COMMISSION, SBC (I, III). Continuing its assignment as the history agency of the SBC, the commission expanded its services and ministry to the denomination. In 1970 a comprehensive restudy of the relationship between the Sunday School Board, SBC, and the commission was completed. The commission continued to be housed in the SSB building at 127 Ninth Avenue, North, Nashville, TN. Charges for office space, library space, and library services, and the procedure for handling the library materials of the commission by the staff of the jointly operated Dargan-Carver Library were revised to the mutual satisfaction of both agencies.

Davis Collier Woolley (q.v. III) served as executive secretary of the commission until his death, Jan. 15, 1971. Lynn Edward May, Jr., research director, 1956-71, was elected to succeed Woolley as executive director, Apr. 19, 1971. The commission employed Alfred Ronald Tonks as research director, Jan. 1, 1972, and changed his title to assistant executive director in 1973. As part of its 20th anniversary, the commission published a history of its work entitled *Southern Baptists and Their History* (1971), by Hubert Inman Hester.

A special consultation conducted by the commission, Apr. 17-18, 1972, provided guidance to the agency in planning for the 1970s. Programs projected included additional staff support in the area of editorial services, expansion of oral history, and development of a Baptist indexing program, as well as enlargement of the resources of the commission's library.

During the decade the commission expanded its service to churches and the denomination through conducting history workshops to train participants in collecting and preserving materials, writing history, and communicating Baptist heritage. In cooperation with state and associational leaders, the commission staff conducted a series of one to four such workshops in 20 states between 1976 and 1980. Following extensive promotion by the commission, the number of churches reporting history committees increased dramatically to a total of 6,919 in 1978. Encouragement was given to Convention agencies to keep accurate and comprehensive records and to preserve relevant and significant primary source materials. The SBC meeting in Los Angeles in 1981 designated the commission as the central depository for non-active archives of the SBC, its agencies, and its officers. Major collections of personal papers of two former SBC presidents were added to the manuscript holdings of the commission during the decade.

The commission enlarged its oral history program through a Convention-wide oral history workshop in Sep., 1973, several state oral history workshops, conferences with SBC agencies, and the collection of the oral memoirs of living, former SBC presidents. Memoirs collected by the commission during the decade included those of Louie D. Newton, R. G. Lee (q.v.), J. D. Grey, Brooks Hays (q.v.), Herschel H. Hobbs, and K. Owen White. Encouragement and assistance were also given to newer state conventions to promote the collecting of oral memoirs of their living pioneers.

In 1974 the commission, in cooperation with several state and SBC agencies, developed an innovative computer system for information storage and retrieval which came to be known as the Baptist Information Retrieval System (BIRS). The system has produced annual indexes to Baptist state papers in Alabama, Kentucky, North Carolina, and Texas, as well as to 48 additional periodicals through the *Southern Baptist Periodical Index*. BIRS also provides bibliographical computer printouts in response to individual search requests.

To help the Baptist past become a present resource to enrich the life and work of the churches and denomination, the commission developed new materials and expanded its promotional activities. On Nov. 26, 1973, the commission expanded its professional staff by employing Charles William Deweese as assistant director of editorial and research services. His title was changed to director of editorial services in 1976.

The commission coordinated the SBC denominational emphasis "We Hold These Truths" as a part of the bicentennial celebration of the United States in 1976. "Let Christ's Freedom Ring" was the special theme of the church emphasis program developed by the Historical Commission in conjunction with the Baptist Joint Committee on Public Affairs and the Christian Life Commission. The Historical Commission also conducted a conference on Baptists and the Bicentennial, helped develop a Bicentennial Resource Kit, and published and distributed over 21,000 copies of a pamphlet, "Suggestions for Baptist Participation in the USA Bicentennial." History writing contests sponsored by the commission in 1970 and 1976 stimulated the writing of articles and books in Baptist studies.

To promote interest in and study of the Baptist heritage, the commission sent guidelines and support materials to more than 25,000 church leaders to assist in conducting an annual Baptist Heritage Emphasis. "Worth Remembering," an audiovisual presentation produced in 1978 on the work of the commission, has been circulated broadly among the churches and has significantly increased the demand for the commission's materials and services. Throughout the decade programs of the agency's annual meeting focused on historical aspects of themes of current interest to Baptists such as Baptist thought, Baptist polity, and black Southern Baptist heritage.

In order to communicate Baptist heritage more effectively, the commission in 1979 developed "The Baptist Heritage Series" of 10 pamphlets, each of which focused on a key part of the Baptist story. By mid-1981 over 1,100,000 copies had been sold. In 1975 the content of *Baptist History and Heritage* assumed a thematic approach and the annual Norman W. Cox (*q.v.* III) Award for the best article published by the commission was inaugurated. Quarterly circulation of this journal was over 2,000 in 1980. The ongoing circulation of the most popular thematic issue, "The Role of Women in Baptist History," has exceeded 5,000. The commission also provided copy for the "Historical Perspectives" section of three issues of *The Quarterly Review* throughout the decade.

The commission continued to expand the resources of its library. The 11,140,000 pages of Baptistiana on microfilm in 1980 represented an increase of 2,303,388 pages during the decade. These materials plus the commission's 17,537 books, 67,800 state and associational annuals, 8,740 loose and bound volumes of periodicals, and thousands of pamphlets, recordings, photographs, and extensive manuscript collections were valued at $315,182 in 1980. Through research projects conducted by its staff, the commission provided historical data for agencies, conventions, associations, churches, and individuals.

During the decade the commission cooperated in several inter-agency projects including serving as a sponsor of the convocation, "Women in Church-Related Vocations."

At the close of the decade a Long-range Planning Committee "to study the ministry of the Historical Commission for the remainder of the twentieth century" was appointed. On Apr. 20, 1981, the commission approved far-reaching recommendations of this committee. The recommendations expressed in detail the commission's commitment to serve Southern Baptists by (1) intensifying and expanding its role as interpreter of Southern Baptist heritage and life; (2) developing a library containing all necessary materials and adequate physical facilities to become a

world center for Baptist studies; and (3) continuing to produce and distribute materials for the study of Baptist heritage and life.

See also Baptist Information Retrieval System (birs); Microfilm, Major Baptist Collections of the Historical Commission, SBC; Oral History Among Southern Baptists.

A. RONALD TONKS

HISTORIOGRAPHY, ANABAPTIST. See Anabaptist Historiography.

HISTORIOGRAPHY, BAPTIST (I, III). The publication of a variety of materials related to Baptist history marked the 1970s. Most conspicuous were state Baptist histories, local church histories, titles dealing with the bicentennial theme, biographies, and reprints of classical items.

In the decade begun in 1970 Baptists in no less than 17 state conventions had their story published under various titles: Alaska (1971), by N. R. Hunke; Arkansas (1979), by E. G. Hinson; California (1978), by E. L. Gray; Florida (1972), by E. E. Joiner; Georgia (1972), by J. A. Lester; Illinois (1976), by R. J. Hastings; Indiana (1973), by A. R. Tonks; Kentucky (1975), by L. T. Crismon; Louisiana (1973), by G. L. Greene; Mississippi (1971), by R. A. McLemore; Northern Plains Convention (1978), by Nicy Murphy; Ohio (1979), by L. H. Moore; Oregon (1970), by A. W. Wardin, Jr.; South Carolina (1971), by L. L. Owens; Tennessee (1974), by W. F. Kendall; Texas (1970), by R. A. Baker; Virginia (1973), by R. E. Alley, and another by J. S. Moore and W. L. Lumpkin.

Representative of comprehensive accounts of historic local churches are: First Baptist Church, Nashville, TN (1970), by L. E. May, Jr.; First Church, Beaumont, TX (1972), by W. R. Estep; First Church, Jackson, MS (1976), by R. A. (*q.v.*) and N. P. (*q.v.*) McLemore; South Main Church, Houston, TX (1978), by A. and W. Yost; and First Church, Montgomery, AL (1979), by L. N. Allen. In most cases the churches engaged a professional historian to undertake the task.

The major volume treating the United States bicentennial theme in its relation to Baptists was *Baptists and the American Experience* (1976), edited by J. E. Wood, Jr., composed of 20 papers delivered at the Baptist National Bicentennial Convocation in Washington, DC, in Jan., 1976.

Biographical subjects of special interest include: Isaac Backus (*q.v.* I) (his diary published in three vols., 1979), ed. by W. G. McLoughlin; Lott Carey (1978), by L. Fitts; William Carey (1978, *q.v.* I), by M. Drewery; Baker James Cauthen (1977), by J. C. Fletcher; Morgan Edwards (1980, *q.v.* III), by T. R. McKibbens, Jr., and K. L. Smith; Obadiah Holmes (1978, *q.v.* I), by E. S. Gaustad; the family of Adoniram Judson (1980, *q.v.* I), by J. J. Brumberg; William Knibb (1973), by Philip Wright; Helen Barrett Montgomery (1972), by L. A. Cattan;

Holcomb, Thomas Luther

and Lottie Moon (1980, *q.v.* II), by C. B. Allen.

A few volumes deal with Baptists from the perspective of the denomination: *The Baptists in America* (1979), by O. K. and M. M. Armstrong, a popular study of Baptists and a revision of their *The Indomitable Baptists* (1967); *Baptist Atlas* (1980), by A. W. Wardin, Jr.; and *The Southern Baptist Convention and Its People, 1607-1972* (1972), by R. A. Baker.

Several monographs of particular significance from the period should be noted: *Women in Baptist Life* (1979), by H. L. McBeth; *Shapers of Baptist Thought* (1972), by J. E. Tull; *Not a Silent People: Controversies That Have Shaped Southern Baptists* (1972), by W. B. Shurden; and a trilogy by J. W. Burton (*q.v.*) on Southern Baptist development in the 19th century: *Road to Augusta* (1976), *Road to Recovery* (1977), and *Road to Nashville* (1977). Dealing with social concerns are: *Churches in Cultural Captivity: A History of the Social Attitudes of Southern Baptists* (1972), by J. L. Eighmy; and *Social Ethics Among Southern Baptists, 1917-1969* (1973), by G. D. Kelsey.

In the 1970s the reprinting of Baptist classics flourished. Scores of out-of-print, indispensable sources were made available, such as the writings of John Asplund (*q.v.* III), Isaac Backus, Thomas Crosby (*q.v.* I), Morgan Edwards, John Leland (*q.v.* II), William Sprague, and many others. Graduate theses and dissertations on Baptist subjects are available as microfilm and/or books through University Microfilms, International, Arno Press, and other resources.

In 1976 E. C. Starr completed his massive bibliographical compilation, *A Baptist Bibliography,* with the publication of volume 25.

BIBLIOGRAPHY: Robert G. Gardner, "Baptist Reprints," *Baptist History and Heritage* (Jan., 1980).

W. MORGAN PATTERSON

HITE, BOB (b. Montgomery County, IA, Aug. 31, 1913; d. Smyrna, GA, Oct. 19, 1979). Pastor and evangelist. Married to Frances Trenette Busse, June 24, 1938, he was a graduate of Texas Wesleyan College (B.A.) and Southwestern Baptist Theological Seminary (B.D.). He served 19 years as pastor of churches in Washington, Texas, and Georgia and as editor of the *Pacific Coast Baptist* (*Northwest Baptist Witness,* 1947-50), official journal of the Northwest Baptist Convention. He is buried in Georgia Memorial Park, Smyrna, GA.

ROLAND HOOD

HITE, MARY EVA (b. Lexington County, SC, Feb. 29, 1888; d. Batesburg, SC, Sep. 29, 1977). Educator and activist on behalf of the aging. Daughter of William Stanmore Hite, a postmaster, and Ella (Prater) Hite, she graduated from Winthrop College (B.A., 1908) and the University of South Carolina (M.A., 1943). She was instrumental in instituting the South Carolina teacher retirement system. Hite chaired the South Carolina Legislative Committee on Aging in 1960 and was a delegate to the White House Conference on Aging in 1961. She

helped create and direct senior adult clubs in her hometown, winning the Outstanding Older South Carolinian Award in 1973. Hite is buried in the Batesburg, SC, cemetery.

MARION ALDREDGE

HODGES, JESSE WILSON (b. Thackerville, OK, Apr. 4, 1882; d. Oklahoma City, OK, June 13, 1971). Pastor. Ordained in 1914, he attended Hardin-Simmons University (B.A., 1917), the University of Texas (M.A., 1920), and The Southern Baptist Theological Seminary (Th.M., 1921). He married Myra Jane Barnes in May, 1919. They had seven children: Frances, Julius, Martha, James, Mary, Ruth, and Dan. Oklahoma pastorates included First, Vinita, 1920-23; First, Okemah, 1923-34; and First, El Reno, 1934-54. He was associate pastor of First, Oklahoma City, 1956-68. He is buried at El Reno, OK.

J. M. GASKIN

HOLCOMB, THOMAS LUTHER (b. Purvis, MS, Dec. 22, 1882; d. Dallas, TX, Sep. 13, 1972). Denominational executive and pastor. The son of William B. Holcomb, a Mississippi Baptist minister, and Ada Broom Holcomb, he attended Mississippi College (B.S., 1904) and The Southern Baptist Theological Seminary (Theology Graduate Certificate, 1908). Honorary doctoral degrees were conferred upon him by Mississippi College, Howard Payne College, and Mercer University. Ordained in 1904, he married Willie Jenkins of Durant, MS, May 8, 1910. They had two children, Luther and Louise.

Holcomb served as pastor in Durant, Yazoo City, Pontotoc, and Columbus, MS, prior to 1918. During World War I he served as religious director for the YMCA in France. In 1919 he returned to Columbus as pastor until 1921. He was pastor of First Baptist Church, Sherman, TX, 1921-28, and served as executive secretary of the Baptist General Convention of Texas, 1928-29. He was pastor of First Baptist Church, Oklahoma City, OK, 1929-35.

In June, 1935, he became executive secretary-treasurer of the Sunday School Board. Upon his retirement in 1953, the board's annual budget had grown from $1,700,000 to more than $12,000,000. During his tenure, a comprehensive church music education program was begun, a 12-story administration building was completed, Ridgecrest Baptist Assembly was expanded, and a second Convention-wide summer assembly was established at Glorieta, NM.

The day following his retirement from the board, he became executive secretary of the Southern Baptist Foundation. In 1959 he retired again, becoming associate pastor of Lakewood Baptist Church, Dallas, TX.

Following the death of his first wife, Holcomb married Eunice King of Sherman, TX. He is buried at Durant, MS.

CHARLES WILLIS

HOLLON, ELLIS WING, JR. (b. Little Rock, AR, Sep. 1, 1932; d. Raleigh, NC, Apr. 8, 1979). Pastor and teacher. Son of Grace Holderfield and Ellis Wing Hollon, a construction foreman, he attended Ouachita Baptist University (B.A., 1954), Duke University (M.S., 1960), Southeastern Baptist Theological Seminary (B.D., 1959; Th.M., 1961), and Emory University (Ph.D., 1966). He married Gurtha DePriest, Aug. 24, 1952. They had one daughter, Faye.

Early in his career Hollon served as pastor of churches in Arkansas and North Carolina. From 1962 to 1967, he taught successively at Georgia State College, Mobile College, and Middle Tennessee State University. In 1967 he joined the faculty of Southeastern Seminary, where he taught philosophy of religion for 12 years. A contributor to Volume III of the *Encyclopedia of Southern Baptists*, he was a prodigious reader and the author of papers in several religious and scholarly journals. Hollon is buried in the seminary cemetery at Wake Forest, NC.

JAMES E. TULL

HOLMAN BIBLE PUBLISHING COMPANY. America's oldest Bible publisher, the A. J. Holman Company, Inc., traces its existence back to Christopher Sower, publisher of the first European-language Bible in America (German, Luther's translation) in Pennsylvania in 1743. Andrew Jackson Holman joined the successor to Sower in 1839 and in 1869 absorbed that company and formed the A. J. Holman Company, which incorporated in 1912. The company became a subsidiary of J. B. Lippincott in 1961 and of Harper and Row in 1978.

Holman introduced new features such as self-pronunciation, 1892; the first American hand Bible, 1892; verse references, 1942; and the only modern-language translation from the Peshitta (Lamsa), 1957.

The Sunday School Board bought the assets of Holman on Apr. 30, 1979, for $2,100,000. The board continues the Holman name, a mark of quality in Bibles, and publishes under that name the KJV, RSV, Darby, Lamsa, and New American Standard translations and a few Bible reference books. The *Master Study Bible New American Standard Edition* (1981) is one of the most complete study Bibles ever published.

JAMES W. CLARK

HOLMES, REID THOMAS (b. Wildwood, NJ, Mar. 25, 1918; d. Winston-Salem, NC, Nov. 2, 1976). Hospital executive. Son of Thomas Holmes, automobile salesman, and Effie Holmes, homemaker, he attended Duke University (A.B., 1939; certificate in hospital administration, 1940). He served as assistant to the superintendent of Duke Hospital, 1940-41, and as assistant superintendent of the same institution, 1941-45. He became adminstrator of North Carolina Baptist Hospital in 1945 and continued in this position until his retirement in 1974.

During Holmes' administration, the hospital grew from a 300-bed general hospital to a 650-bed referral and teaching hospital. Among other achievements, it purchased the first cobalt therapy machine for the treatment of cancer in North Carolina; developed one of the first hospital minimal care units in the nation; and began one of the first schools of pastoral care in the South. Holmes was president of the North Carolina Hospital Association in 1949. He was a deacon and trustee of First Baptist Church, Winston-Salem.

Holmes married Betty Pollard of Durham, NC, Sep. 19, 1941. They had two children, Lynn Holmes Trotter and Reid Thomas Holmes, Jr. He is buried in Forsyth Memorial Gardens, Winston-Salem, NC.

CALVIN KNIGHT

HOME BIBLE STUDY. Home Bible Study, begun in Oct., 1978, is a project sponsored by the Sunday School Board to provide and promote regular and systematic Bible study in the home. The project uses broadcast media and printed curriculum material. *At Home with the Bible*, National Religious Broadcasters Award of Merit winner for 1980, is a weekly television-radio broadcast aired on various television and radio stations throughout the nation and produced in cooperation with the Radio and Television Commission.

Printed Bible correspondence material is made available monthly through the *Home Bible Study Guide*, which uses a programmed instruction format that allows the user to respond actively to the study material. Participants in Home Bible Study are encouraged to complete a review test contained in each monthly *Guide*. In the first year more than 100,000 persons enrolled in the Bible correspondence course using the *Home Bible Study Guide*.

Initial financial support for Home Bible Study came from priority funds of the SSB. Long-range plans call for the project to be self-supporting through contributions from persons who participate in the study. No Cooperative Program funds support Home Bible Study.

See also RADIO-TELEVISION BIBLE CORRESPONDENCE COURSE.

ROBERT G. FULBRIGHT

HOME MISSION BOARD, DIVISION OF PERSONNEL. With the reorganization of the Home Mission Board staff, effective Jan. 1, 1971, the Division of Personnel was formed with Glendon McCullough as director. The division included the Department of Missionary Personnel, the Office of Personnel Development, and the Office of Personnel Employment, thus combining all facets of personnel—headquarters and field. E. Warren Woolf became division director, Jan. 1, 1972.

Don Rhymes directs the Department of Missionary Personnel with Jerry L. Scruggs, Jerry B. Graham, and C. Irvin Dawson as associate directors. This department screens all candi-

HOME MISSION BOARD (*q.v.*) BUILDING, Atlanta, GA. Built in 1967, occupied in 1968, and leased until purchased in 1972. The seven-story structure contains 90,000 square feet.

WOMAN'S MISSIONARY UNION (q.v.) TRAINING SCHOOL, Louisville, KY. Completed in 1917 at 334 East Broadway, this fifteenth-century Gothic structure known as the "House Beautiful" was the home of the school until 1941 when the school moved to 2801 Lexington Road. In 1951 the property was sold to WAVE Studios for $160,000.

dates for missionary, missionary associate, US-2, church pastoral assistance, and language pastoral assistance. The department staff recruits at all Southern Baptist seminaries and gives special emphasis to the enlistment of experienced pastors for home mission service.

Charles B. Hancock directs the work of Personnel Development with K. Lynn Wright as the assistant director. In addition to psychological evaluations of all candidates, they provide a ministry of mental and emotional health to HMB personnel.

Personnel Employment, under the direction of Katherine G. Roberson, recruits and employs all support personnel in the headquarters office. In addition to administering the work of these areas, the division director also handles compensation administration and in-service training.

WARREN WOOLF

HOME MISSION BOARD, SBC (I, III). *Context for Mission Strategy.*—The Home Mission Board entered the 1970s wrestling with many of the old problems of the 1960s: Civil rights, the Vietnam war, an economic slowdown, crime, violence, and drugs. More than 80,000,000 persons were not identified with any religious group. While Southern Baptists had been channeling energy and resources to the northern and western sections of the nation in a continuation of their pioneer movement, the population was shifting to the Sunbelt. The ethnic segments, especially Spanish, blacks, and Indo-Chinese, were growing rapidly by birthrate and immigration.

The Jesus Movement exploded in the first years of the decade, signaling a new emphasis on man's search for meaning that would usher in the charismatic, the cultic, the mystical, and the electric church. Southern Baptists were especially sensitive to many of these changes, and in its 1976 report to the SBC the HMB described 1971-75 as "the best five-year period in evangelism our denomination has ever known." Baptisms exceeded 400,000 each of those years, and Southern Baptists widened their lead over the United Methodists as the largest Protestant denomination in the nation. Progress in race relations seemed to warrant the discontinuance in 1971 of the board's "Crisis Committee" appointed in 1968 when the SBC approved the "Statement Concerning the Crisis in Our Nation" and assigned leadership to the HMB.

In 1973, while relieved with the war's end, the nation sought to assess failure in Vietnam; and a crisis of leadership upset the populace with the exposures of presidential misdeeds in the Watergate scandal, eventually resulting in the resignation of President Richard Nixon. Meanwhile, other world concerns surfaced or intensified: Energy, hunger, nuclear proliferation, and the civil rights of women, Indians, and Spanish-speaking Americans. Evangelical Christians found their numbers increasing and their influence stronger. Jimmy Carter, a Southern Baptist from Georgia, was even elected President in 1976.

Such was the context in which the HMB would forge for the first time a national, comprehensive mission strategy. The 1960s had set the stage as Southern Baptist churches were established in all states, even spilling over into Canada. The agency had established with the 32 state Baptist conventions cooperative agreements that welded the mission force and the state efforts into compatible units. More than two-thirds of the 2,235 missionaries were jointly employed by the board and one of the states. In 1970 the agency dropped the use of the term "pioneer" to designate an organizational unit existing to serve those areas entered by Southern Baptists after 1941, and in its place created the Department of Church Extension, reflecting a concern of the entire nation for starting new work.

For a decade the agency had been seeking the "single uniform mission program" it had been instructed in 1959 by the SBC to develop. In 1970 the agency reported to the SBC through its 12 assigned programs, reflecting 12 programs, not one, despite attempts in the past to rally under such emphases as the 30,000 Movement, Project 500, and Extend Now. Meanwhile, the role of the agency was shifting. Arthur B. Rutledge (*q.v.*), executive director, often reported on the newer catalytic concept, namely, "to help churches discover needs and provide ministries to meet those needs without financial assistance or denominational missionary personnel." In keeping with this concept the staff in Atlanta would nearly double. The agency would also undergo three major reorganizations and many minor ones.

Reorganizations.—The first reorganization opened the decade as the agency's scattered divisions were gathered into three sections: Planning and Coordination, Program Implementation, and Program Services. The move sought to improve administration, planning, and coordination. Then in 1975, responding to a desire by some within the SBC for a greater emphasis on evangelism and a separate evangelism commission, the board created a fourth section on Evangelism, and the SBC approved two additional evangelism programs. The final reorganization of the decade came in 1979 when the departments of Church Extension and Language Missions, both with major shares of the agency's budget and personnel, became divisions within the Missions Section.

The Planning and Coordination Section, later shortened to Planning Section, had been built on a department that once spent its time on door-to-door and telephone surveys, but in 1970 among its assignments was the utilization of national data resources for in-depth studies of all geographic areas. Out of this came two tools for a national strategy, the church index and the evangelism index, to aid in the ranking of areas of greatest mission need. The Planning and Coordination Section also elevated cooperative agreements with the states to a more refined and inclusive level through the appointment of regional coordinators to work closely with each state. Another national strategy tool to emerge was the Long-Range Planning Base by which the states and the board projected their work. At this point, coordinators, without specific program assignments, consulted with state convention staffs on intermediate and long-range planning.

In 1980 the HMB directors changed the titles of the board's officers and top staff members. The executive director-treasurer became president and chief financial officer. Directors of the board's four sections were renamed vice-presidents for their respective sections. The head of the elected board, formerly called president, was renamed chairman.

Bold Mission Thrust Planning and Implementation.—The HMB in 1974 could thus be seen as an organization waiting for a focus. The denomination was now national, the states and the board were unified, a new planning ability existed, and the agency had reorganized for more effective administration and planning. In that year the board articulated its planned portion of the denomination's coming emphasis on Bold Mission, and the board's theme would be Bold Mission Thrust with two objectives:

- Let every person in our land have an opportunity to hear and accept the gospel of Jesus Christ!
- Let every person in our land have an opportunity to share in the witness and ministry of a New Testament fellowship of believers!

With the statement of those objectives, formulation of a national missions strategy had begun. In 1975 Bold Mission Thrust was projected to involve "every church, every association, every state convention, every individual." Gerald Palmer, who recently had been elevated to direct the Missions Section, and Bill Hogue, director of the new Evangelism Section, led in the articulation of the new national strategy and in the enlistment of all Southern Baptist mission units in developing their own goals and objectives. Leonard Irwin, director of the Planning Section, provided such information through detailed computer studies on every county in the nation, focusing on needs for evangelization and new churches.

In four broad areas, targets of concern were identified to receive priority in the allocating of budget and personnel:

1. *Counties without an effective evangelistic witness.* Over 600 counties in the United States did not have a Southern Baptist congregation.

2. *Key cities.* The objective was to evaluate the needs of certain key cities and to correlate the planning and use of the mission resources.

3. *Cultural and life-style groups.* The objective was to identify ethnic groups, the poor, apartment or mobile home residents, and subculture groups in each county and community and to correlate planning and allocation of resources.

4. *Transitional communities with churches in crisis.* The objective was to identify churches whose witness had been weakened or was being lost and to assure continuation of a strengthened congregational witness.

The Services Section, under the direction of Robert Bingham, geared up for personnel, business, and communication support.

Bold Mission Thrust, carefully orchestrated by the board to involve every program of the agency and every unit of the denomination, so captured the imagination of all Southern Baptists that the denomination dropped other designations of "Bold Mission" and received permission from the HMB to use "Bold Mission Thrust" as the comprehensive term for the denomination's emphasis.

In his final report to the board's directors in Oct., 1976, Arthur B. Rutledge included the following:

Our planning experiences of the past six years have served the Board well in the preparatory stages of Bold Mission Thrust. . . .

We are meeting with a hearty response on the part of leadership groups. . . . Our staff has met with state convention missions and evangelism directors (jointly once, for the first time in history . . .), state convention executive secretaries, state paper editors, associational directors of missions and other associational officers. We have conferred fully with program leaders of other SBC agencies. The Bold Mission Thrust was the all encompassing theme at both Glorieta and Ridgecrest home missions conferences. . . .

Without exception we have met with a high level of enthusiasm and optimism. . . . Our staff is geared up in such a way that every program and every service . . . can "plug in." . . . Bold Mission Thrust (is) in the number one spot in all of our planning.

William G. Tanner succeeded Rutledge, Jan. 1, 1977, and he immediately announced his enthusiastic support of Bold Mission Thrust. He reported the following to the SBC that year: "The year 1976 was given to preparation for and creation of awareness of the Bold Mission Thrust emphasis. . . . In budget planning, high priority is given to the agency's emphasis. The 1977 budget includes some of the earlier projects of Bold Mission Thrust, but in the current process of planning (the) 1978 budget, a large section of this budget is allocated to missionary positions, projects, and events related to the emphasis."

Closing his report to the Convention, Tanner highlighted the increasing use of volunteers: "The plans for implementing Bold Mission Thrust call for a high level of volunteer action for two reasons: (1) There are thousands of Southern Baptists who want to become personally involved in missions and (2) it will be impossible to employ the number of missionaries needed." As if to underscore his words, the Department of Special Missions Ministries reported approximately 14,000 volunteers assigned for home mission work in 1976.

At the 1977 SBC, Jimmy Carter, United States President, excited Southern Baptists in a televised message when he challenged them to double their mission force by adding 5,000 volunteers by 1982 to serve one or two years in the USA or overseas to reach the objectives of the denomination's Bold Mission Thrust.

By December the SBC had created an office

for Mission Service Corps, as the emphasis was named, to coordinate volunteers for both the home and foreign mission agencies. The HMB had named a coordinator and before the year closed, five volunteers were under appointment.

The board reported to the SBC in 1980 that it had appointed only 319 Mission Service Corps volunteers, and the Foreign Mission Board reported even fewer. While the effort did not immediately realize its lofty goals of enlisting the 5,000 for one or two years' service (financed primarily by the volunteers, their families, or their churches), the massive information effort which accompanied the emphasis produced rather startling results. The Special Missions Ministries Department reported the assignment in 1979 of more than 30,000 volunteers for short- and long-term mission projects. Programs using volunteers in evangelism, Christian social ministries, language missions, and others also reported an explosion in the number responding.

Near the close of 1977, William Tanner had written, "Bold Mission Thrust has proven to be a significant test of the capacity of Southern Baptists to work together in mounting a major missions and evangelism thrust in the United States. Each state convention has developed its own bold mission planning. This is why you hear such terms as Bold Advance in Florida, North Central States Mission Thrust in the seven states in the central part of the United States, Good News Texas, Sharing Christ in Bold Mission in Arizona, Horizons Hawaii—Stronger Churches in Bold Mission, Advance '77-'79 in Maryland, and Bold Horizons in Louisiana.''

As Bold Mission Thrust was implemented as the national missions strategy, some correctives in emphasis occurred. Most noticeable was the effort not to lose "ministry to persons" in the emphasis on evangelizing and congregationalizing. In his 1979 report to the board's directors, Tanner said, "Ministry to persons will continue to be a major concern of the HMB." Earlier he had written, "We are committed to BMT's unwritten but equally vital goal of ministry. For us, ministry will never be the missing element in Bold Mission Thrust.''

Territorial Realignments.—The decade also witnessed territory realignments for the HMB. At the close of 1974, the board terminated its assistance to mission work in Panama and the Canal Zone, transferring direction to the FMB and gradually withdrawing all financial assistance. After the nearly 70 years of home mission work there, there were 42 churches with 6,600 members. The board owned property valued in excess of $1,000,000. In 1976 the HMB joined the Hawaii Baptist Convention in sending the first Southern Baptist missionaries to American Samoa, and studies were made toward work in other American territories in Micronesia.

Disaster and Refugee Relief.—An organized method of responding to disasters within the United States began in 1969 as the agency completed arrangements with the American Red Cross. During the decade funds were allocated by the board for disaster relief through the Christian Social Ministries Department. In cooperation with the Brotherhood Commission and various state Baptist conventions, the denomination was able to respond immediately with funds, personnel, and other assistance in a significant number of disasters.

While the agency had a history of responding to the needs of refugees coming to the United States, a new challenge presented itself in 1973 and 1974 at the close of the Vietnam war. Again Southern Baptists responded, led by the HMB which added personnel to its office of immigration and refugee service, placed mission personnel in refugee camps, and aided Southern Baptists in resettling more than 3,000 Vietnamese in 1974, 1975, and 1976. Later, the denomination was called to respond to the needs of refugees fleeing Cambodia and Laos, as Tanner challenged the churches again to meet massive human need.

At the decade's close, the HMB staff had grown from 90 to 103, supported by more than 200 other personnel. The number of missionaries had increased from 2,235 to 2,922. The annual budget had been raised from $13,000,000 to more than $33,800,000.

Closing the decade, Tanner said, "As the implementation stage of Bold Mission Thrust is begun, it appears that an 'imperative of immediacy' concerning world evangelization must become the paramount priority. Our world stands today in perhaps the most precarious position politically that it has faced in the last three decades. Global brinkmanship and world survival have rapidly moved to the 'front of the line.' Consequently, we must maintain as a denomination a sense of urgency about our redemptive mission to America and to the world. Certainly the moment is ours. The decade of the eighties could be labeled the most pivotal decade in the history of our nation."

See also ASSOCIATIONAL ADMINISTRATION SERVICE, HMB PROGRAM OF; BLACK CHURCH RELATIONS, HMB PROGRAM OF; CHAPLAINCY MINISTRIES, HMB PROGRAM OF; CHURCH EXTENSION, HMB PROGRAM OF; CHURCH LOANS, HMB PROGRAM OF; CHRISTIAN SOCIAL MINISTRIES, HMB PROGRAM OF; EVANGELISM, HMB PROGRAMS OF; HMB, DIVISION OF PERSONNEL; HOME MISSIONS, DIRECTIONS IN; INTERFAITH WITNESS, HMB PROGRAM OF; LANGUAGE MISSIONS, HMB PROGRAM OF; METROPOLITAN MISSIONS, HMB PROGRAM OF; MISSION SERVICE CORPS; RESEARCH, HMB DIVISION OF; RURAL-URBAN MISSIONS, HMB PROGRAM OF; SPECIAL MISSION MINISTRIES, HMB DEPARTMENT OF.

                                              WALKER L. KNIGHT

HOME MISSIONS, DIRECTIONS IN.

I. Evangelism. Directions in evangelism grow out of the first priority of the Home Mission Board, evangelism strategy. This Bold Mission Thrust priority is "To commit the entire organization to the task of evangelizing, providing leadership, and allocating resources to assist every facet of Southern Baptist life so each member will be challenged, motivated, and equipped to engage in personal evangelism so that increased numbers of persons will respond.''

Expressed simply, evangelism is the first priority of the HMB. All programs, personnel, and projects are grounded in this priority. The board of directors and the administration of the HMB have charged the Evangelism Section with leading the way in the implementation of this objective.

The Evangelism Section has the role of leadership in evangelism for the SBC and is the equipper of all programs and personnel for the work of evangelism. Relationships are necessary to accomplish this goal.

The Evangelism Section has working relationships with HMB programs, associations, the Sunday School Board, Woman's Missionary Union, Brotherhood, the Foreign Mission Board, the Radio and Television Commission, and seminaries.

To measure success in evangelism, the Evangelism Section has set five major goals: (1) To lead churches to increase baptisms, (2) to lead Southern Baptists to make special efforts to reach adults, (3) to motivate lay people to engage in personal evangelism, (4) to challenge staff missionary personnel to increase professions of faith, and (5) to encourage every church to conduct annually at least one evangelistic event.

Conceptually, evangelism is designed to be simplified, with concentration on practical application; communicative, with clear and easily understood channels of information; and implementive, with adequate resources and assistance to accomplish the goals.

Program. —The three programs of the Evangelism Section of the HMB charged with implementing these goals are Evangelism Development, Mass Evangelism, and Personal Evangelism. Southern Baptist evangelism strategy originates in the Evangelism Section and moves out to the states, associations, and individual churches.

The Evangelism Section provides leadership and resources to fulfill the five goals listed earlier. This task includes preparation, training, and follow-up. In assisting churches in the planning stages, the Evangelism Section recommends a correlated evangelistic effort, including prayer for spiritual awakening, prospect discovery, Sunday School enlargement, witness training, and revival meeting. A correlated evangelistic effort has proven to be more effective than single, isolated events.

Preparation involves creating a spiritual climate for revival. A person's or church's relationship to God is the basis of any evangelistic success. Spiritual awakening, through prayer and revival, moves the church toward active concern for people. Basic to any successful evangelistic effort are training and follow-up.

The Evangelism Section offers personnel and resources for both.

Strategy resources include printed materials in basic preparation, such as, ''Growing an Evangelistic Church''; in training, such as, Lay Evangelism School training and TELL Witness Training; and in follow-up, such as a *Counselor Guide* and various tracts, including ''Your New Life,'' ''A New Dimension,'' ''Life Commitment,'' and ''Toward Christian Maturity.'' Technological materials in video or film, media, and cassette tapes are also available resources.

Personnel. —The purpose of evangelism personnel is to be interpreters, resource persons, and equippers of the strategy. Personnel are facilitators of programs. Each department at the HMB will eventually have a minimum of two staff persons in order to satisfy the criteria of its existence and HMB policy.

Five full-time national consultants consult, interpret, provide resources, and equip in their specialized fields. At present, the five national consultants work with ethnics, blacks, women, youth, children, and young parents. In the future, several other areas of specialized work may highlight the need for more consultants. Possibilities include regional consultants, specific language consultants, and part-time consultants in crusade revival evangelism, in witness training, and on seminary campuses.

The Evangelism Section will make an effort to place an evangelism director in each state and to support states which need a second staff person. The HMB also supports evangelism missions personnel.

Projects. —Evangelism projects are considered on the basis of merit and priority concerns. As programs and strategies develop, projects are to accomplish the strategy. Priority one, evangelizing, is the Evangelism Section's way of implementing Bold Mission Thrust. Evangelism will move forward in an unwavering commitment to Bold Mission Thrust.

C. B. HOGUE

II. Missions. The Missions Section is responsible for implementing 10 programs assigned to the HMB by the SBC. In 1980 over 2,900 missions personnel, all of whom receive all or some financial provision from the board, were related to this section. In addition, over 1,400 student summer missionaries and 200 other persons were receiving short-term assistance for missionary assignments. In 1979 the section office channeled more than 30,000 persons to volunteer assignments and has under HMB endorsement more than 1,200 chaplains.

Under the leadership of William G. Tanner, executive director, the board developed a comprehensive statement of strategy called Target: AD 2000. This plan, in effect, sets the direction for missions on the part of the HMB.

The Missions Section and its related organizations have evangelism as a basic commitment. Special emphasis will be given to training missionary personnel in witnessing skills. When the board provides assistance to associations and churches, it will expect that emphasis will be given to evangelism by these units of Southern Baptist life.

"Congregationalizing" (a term coined to define the emphasis of giving everyone an opportunity to share in the witness and ministry of a New Testament fellowship of believers) expresses one of the major emphases of the HMB. Procedures are being developed to accelerate the progress toward self-support and strong local identity of new churches. The goal of a total of 50,000 Southern Baptist churches by the year 2000 appears to be achievable in the light of more than 1,000 church-type missions being established during 1979. At the same time, the rate of losses of churches as a result of changing communities and of losses through individual movements means that Southern Baptists face a significant challenge.

The HMB will continue to appoint, support, and accept an adequate number of missions personnel to serve in their vital role in accomplishing the purpose of home missions. The nature of the work of missionaries has gradually shifted from that of being primarily related to local fields to that of catalytic-type missionaries who provide leadership to churches and associations as well as volunteers in order to accomplish the purposes of missions. The actual number of volunteers in the years ahead will depend on the financial generosity of churches and the denominational priorities.

The 1980s have been called the decade of the volunteer. Building on the responses of the 1970s, the HMB will seek to facilitate the use of volunteers in a cooperative effort with state conventions and associations. A computer system (initially called VIM Process in which the name and skills of volunteers are matched with the service opportunities) is proving to be valuable in assisting in the assignment and use of volunteers. Of crucial concern is the need for better supervision. A process for training persons in the supervision of volunteers has been initiated and will be implemented.

The mission work of the board gives major attention to geographical frontiers of the nation. Most areas of the nation are part of the state conventions. Plans are being developed for organizing state conventions in New England, Iowa, and Minnesota and Wisconsin by 1985. It is expected that Puerto Rico will become a state convention at a future time.

In 1980, 540 counties in the nation were without a Southern Baptist congregation. The drastic shifting of populations into the Sunbelt areas and the development of energy corridors in the West indicate that the geographical concept of frontiers is not dead.

However, the word *frontier,* as used by the HMB, includes many other frontiers which are reflected by differences in social, economic, religious, and cultural backgrounds. Increased immigration, including the expanding numbers of refugees, continues to enlarge the responsibility of language missions work. The social setting of the aging, divorced persons, and children in one-parent families, challenges Southern Baptists to respond with effective ministries. Special attention must be given to the churches in transitional communities in order to maintain the present witness or to reestablish a Southern Baptist witness where churches have moved away from these critical areas of need.

The HMB continues to recognize the indigenous nature of Baptist work. This means constantly shifting the load of financial responsibility to state conventions, associations, and churches in order to release funds for new work.

The term "ministries" expresses the continuing concern of Southern Baptists for the needs of persons whether these needs are spiritual, physical, social, economical, or emotional. Special emphasis will be given to encourage the local churches to provide the ministries with the HMB assisting a church or group of churches to carry out these responsibilities.

GERALD PALMER

III. Associational Missions. Associational missions are specific ways in which the association fulfills its mission, supporting the mission of the church. The current working definition, derived from this concept, states that an association is a fellowship of churches on mission in their setting.

The association is a structure by which churches achieve certain elements of their mission cooperatively. As the primary unit of cooperation beyond the local congregation, the association helps the church confront its mission in its immediate area.

Associational missions involves those acts of mission which require more resources than a single local church can provide. The association finds expression of love, care, and purpose from within through prayer, study of its context, and identification of needs, opportunities, and resources. Through using good principles of planning, it finds the best ways to facilitate local church work and to take initiative in discipling men and women in Christ.

Denominational agencies and state conventions fulfill their mission by assisting local churches. Through proper planning and relationships, denominational programs and emphases become means by which the association can be assisted in fulfilling its mission. Three representative examples of this kind of cooperation are literacy missions, simultaneous revival meetings, and coordinated program planning emphases, such as Bold Mission Thrust.

JAMES NELSON

IV. Missions Ministries. The HMB created the Missions Ministries Division in 1971 to group together 5 of the 10 programs previously included in the former Division of Missions. The Mission Ministries Division initially included the departments of Christian Social Ministries, Church Extension, Language Missions,

Cooperative Ministries with National Baptists, Interfaith Witness, and Special Mission Ministries. The division gave special attention to strategies for establishing new churches and to ministering and witnessing across frontiers of religious, ethnic, racial, cultural, and social opportunities. In 1979 Language and Church Extension were restructured as separate divisions.

A growing pluralism in American life-styles, cultures, religions, and ethnicity created an enlarged challenge for missions ministry. Home missionaries became equippers as well as practitioners in their various places of ministry. Thousands of volunteers were enlisted for training in such ministries as weekday ministries, alcohol and drug abuse, family counseling, the blind, disaster relief, literacy, witness to other faiths, black Baptist relationships and development, lay teams for church builders, resort, recreation, music, puppetry, Bible classes in unchurched areas, US-2, Christian Service Corps, summer missions, innovators, semester missions, campers on missions, inner city, mission centers, and rescue missions.

Special liaison with Woman's Missionary Union and Brotherhood has been established to facilitate their implementation of many of these ministries in their mission action programs.

M. WENDELL BELEW

V. Planning. The HMB has long realized that faith and facts must be joined for an effective mission strategy to be developed. Under the leadership of Arthur B. Rutledge (q.v.), executive secretary, a committee of the board developed long-range objectives and goals up to 1977 and defined 14 basic mission guidelines. The committee report was adopted as Direction '77 in 1967. The report was updated in 1974 and adopted as Direction '79.

William G. Tanner, newly elected executive director, directed the Planning Section in 1977 to provide guidance in the development of a long-range plan which was then completed and adopted by the board as Target AD 2000 in 1978. The plans include a theological base, a statement of purpose of the HMB, and projected trends and objectives up to the year 2000. A mid-range plan Direction '82 was adopted, Oct., 1979, which serves as a bridge between the long-range and the annual operating plan and includes the HMB response to the SBC emphasis, Bold Mission Thrust.

LEONARD IRWIN

VI. Volunteerism. This is a movement of laypersons (and other nonprofessional missionaries such as pastors and other church staff members) who take an active and personal involvement in meeting mission needs. Volunteers serve as individuals, couples, families, and groups with ages ranging from high school through retired adults. Volunteers give a few days, a week, a month, a year, or a lifetime in filling mission needs that cannot be met by career personnel alone. Volunteers provide most or all of their expenses. This movement personalizes missions, increases missions awareness, and extends mission work. Between 20,000 and 30,000 persons served voluntarily each year during the 1970s. The Special Mission Ministries Department relates to most volunteers in home missions.

MICHAEL D. ROBERTSON

HONDURAS, MISSION IN (III; cf. Guatemala-Honduras, Mission in, Vol. I). During the 1970s missionaries engaged in evangelism and church development, disaster and hunger relief, rural medical work, leadership and ministerial training, and literature evangelism. Missionaries aided victims of hurricane Fifi in Honduras, earthquakes in Nicaragua and Guatemala, and the civil war in Nicaragua. Baptists strengthened their literature ministry through construction of a bookstore-deposit building in Tegucigalpa, resulting in a 40 percent sales increase in 1979. During 1979 medical personnel treated 2,721 patients. Convention leadership assumed the direction of the theological institute, management of the bookstore, and leadership in a national evangelistic thrust. Hundreds of conversions occurred, and 6,000 Bibles were distributed. Baptists began the 1980s with 31 churches, 38 pastors, 55 preaching points, 2,374 members, and 30 missionaries.

A. CLARK SCANLON

HONG KONG-MACAO, MISSION IN (I, III). Baptist Press published a new Baptist hymnal in Chinese in 1973 and celebrated the 80th anniversary of the press in 1979. David Y. K. Wong, prominent architect and Baptist layman in Hong Kong, was the first Oriental to be elected president of Baptist World Alliance, 1975. Pui Ching School celebrated its 90th anniversary in Nov., 1979. A Baptist communications center was established with facilities for radio program production and broadcasting in Hong Kong and mainland China. A major cities evangelization program conducted during 1977-78 resulted in significant increases in baptisms and church membership. The Langford-Smith Medical Group was established in Hong Kong, and the Hope Medical Clinic in Macao. Seventy-one missionaries, including eight journeymen, served at the end of the 1970s.

GEORGE H. HAYS

HOOK, GEORGE DOWNS (b. Ft. Collins, CO, Dec. 3, 1916; d. Leupp, AZ, Feb. 12, 1971). Missionary to the Indians. The son of Jan Hook and Zora Hook, a jeweler, he married Margaret Sartwell, June 18, 1939. They had four children: Robert, Genevieve, Betty, and Dorothy. He attended Westmont College (A.B., 1944) and Central Baptist Seminary (Th.M., 1949). Although not Indian, Hook learned Navajo and taught Indians to read it. He is buried at Winslow, AZ.

B. FRANK BELVIN

HOPKINS, JULIAN SETZER (b. Ashe County, NC, Aug. 11, 1901; d. Wilkesboro, NC, Jan. 27, 1979). Pastor and evangelism secretary. The son of George and Fannie Hopkins, he was a graduate of Wake Forest College (1920) and Southern Baptist Theological Seminary (Th.B., 1936). On July 14, 1927, he married Elizabeth Stewart MacGuire Daniel. They had two children, Robert and Elizabeth. Hopkins served as pastor of Eller Memorial Church, Greensboro, NC, 1930-36; Ephesus and Providence churches, Winchester, KY, 1936-38; First Church, Waynesville, NC, 1938-40; Green Street Church, High Point, NC, 1940-49; and First Church, Suffolk, VA, 1949-56.

Hopkins had a deep and lasting commitment to evangelism and church growth. In 1956 he became secretary of evangelism for North Carolina Baptists. Remaining at this position until 1969, he was largely responsible for the creation of the Division of Evangelism and, later, the establishment of the chair of evangelism at Southeastern Baptist Theological Seminary. He is buried in Raleigh Memorial Park, Raleigh, NC.

W. W. FINLATOR

HOSPITAL COMMISSION OF KENTUCKY BAPTISTS (I). See BAPTIST HOSPITALS, INC.

HOSPITALS, LOUISIANA. See LOUISIANA HOSPITALS.

HOSPITALS, OKLAHOMA. From 1916 to 1978, the Baptist General Convention of Oklahoma operated the following hospitals: Oklahoma Baptist at Muskogee, 1916-62; Miami Baptist at Miami, 1917-78; Southwest Baptist at Mangum, 1949-65; Perry Memorial at Perry, 1951-74; Stillwater Municipal at Stillwater, 1952-69; Bass Memorial at Enid (formerly Enid General), 1953-78; Bristow Memorial at Bristow, 1954-75; Grand Valley at Pryor, 1954-75; Cordell Memorial at Cordell, 1956-75; Baptist Medical Center of Oklahoma in Oklahoma City (formerly Baptist Memorial), 1959-78; Sayre Memorial at Sayre, 1961-75; and Grove General at Grove, 1963-78. The hospitals at Muskogee, Miami, Mangum, Enid, and Grove and Baptist Medical Center were owned and operated by the convention. The others were operated on lease agreements.

Due to increasing government intervention in hospital administration, the convention felt some operating changes were needed. In 1975 a group of Baptist laymen organized the Oklahoma Health Care Corporation, and the convention transferred the leased hospitals to this group. The Baptist Medical Center, Inc., was formed in 1977, and the convention transferred the Baptist Medical Center of Oklahoma property to this corporation. A few months later the convention transferred the hospitals at Miami, Enid, and Grove to the Oklahoma Health Care Corporation. The convention maintains a Bap-

tist chaplaincy program in each hospital transferred to Oklahoma Health Care Corporation and to Baptist Medical Center, Inc.

JOE L. INGRAM

HOUGH, RAYMOND FRANKLIN, SR. (b. Brief, NC, Sep. 27, 1890; d. Salem, VA, June 17, 1977). Children's home superintendent and Virginia Baptist lay leader. Son of William Amos and Vera (McManus) Hough, farmers, he was a graduate of Wake Forest College (B.A., 1916) and received honorary degrees from Roanoke College (LL.B., 1942) and the University of Richmond (LL.D., 1954). He served as superintendent, Sylva Collegiate Institute, Sylva, NC, 1919-24; superintendent, Kennedy Home, eastern division of North Carolina Baptist Children's Homes, Kinston, NC, 1924-28; and superintendent, Virginia Baptist Children's Home, Salem, VA, 1928-56.

Hough married Elma Johnson, June, 1917. They had two sons, Raymond Franklin, Jr., and Mac Johnson. He served on the Virginia Baptist Board of Missions and Education and was president of the Baptist General Association of Virginia in 1946 and 1954. He served on the boards of Virginia Intermont College, Hargrave Military Academy, Virginia Baptist Homes, and the Home Mission Board, SBC. Retiring on Dec. 31, 1956, he was succeeded by his son, R. Franklin Hough, Jr., as director of the Virginia Baptist Children's Home. He is buried in Sherwood Memorial Park, Salem, VA.

JOHN S. MOORE

HOUSTON BAPTIST UNIVERSITY (cf. Houston Baptist College, Vol. III). Changing from a college to a university in 1973, the institution in 1980 offered programs in Christianity, business, nursing, science, premedicine, and education. Under its first and only president, William H. Hinton, the university grew from a freshman class of 196 students in 1963, on a 200-acre campus comprised of seven buildings with assets totaling just under $9,000,000, to an enrollment in the 1979-80 academic year of 2,005 students, including approximately 200 graduate students in business, nursing, and education. The campus now has 18 buildings, with total assets nearing $28,000,000. The university's endowment is $13,000,000. Alumni total 2,300.

KIRK LEWIS

HOWARD COLLEGE EXTENSION DIVISION (III; cf. Extension Centers, Baptist College, Vol. I). George H. Jackson became director of Howard College Extension Division in 1969 after a year as associate director. Under his leadership several changes occurred. An institute program employing professional educators and offering college credit was established throughout Alabama. Local church centers, with the same standards and curriculum as in regular centers, encourage laypersons in serious Bible study. The Extension Division cooperates with junior colleges in offering Bible survey and methods courses. The average annual enrollment in the 1970s exceeded 2,000. Since its founding in 1947, 28,000 different people have enrolled in the Extension Division.

GEORGE H. JACKSON

HOWARD PAYNE UNIVERSITY (cf. Howard Payne College, Vols. I, III). Founded in 1889 as Howard Payne College, the institution became Howard Payne University in 1974. Assets of the four-year liberal arts university total over $20,000,000. Ralph A. Phelps, Jr., was appointed president in Mar., 1980, succeeding Roger L. Brooks. On the main campus near downtown Brownwood, TX, are classroom facilities, the Walker Memorial Library, and residence halls. The J. Howard Hodge Memorial Bell Towers have been erected as the first phase of the Institute of Christianity complex. This complex offers training for students in Christian service.

Less than one-half mile south of the main campus is the Douglas MacArthur Academy of Freedom which offers an honors program in the social sciences and houses memorabilia of the late general. Howard Payne belongs to both the National Association of Intercollegiate Athletics and the Lone Star Conference.

DON JACKSON

HOWELL, BROOKSIE KELLY (b. Gold Dust, TN, Feb. 4, 1888; d. Dallas, TX, June 15, 1975). Woman's Missionary Union leader. The daughter of James and Amy Kelly, plantation owners, she married William Clem Howell, Dec. 22, 1915. They adopted a daughter, Anne Elizabeth. She served as associational young people's leader, Crockett Association, TN, 1930-33; an officer of Tennessee WMU, acting as young people's leader in West Tennessee, 1934-35; dormitory hostess, Union University, 1936; housemother, Baylor University, 1938-42; and young people's leader, Bellevue Baptist Church, Memphis, TN, 1942-44. She became executive secretary, California WMU, Dec., 1944, serving until Aug., 1952.

Upon retirement, Howell established a memorial fund for California state missions before returning to Alamo, where she was active in world missions conferences for the Home Mission Board, 1952-73. She is buried at Alamo, TN.

POLLY A. MCNABB

HOWELL, CARL ALONZO (b. Wilkes County, NC, Dec. 15, 1901; d. Leesburg, FL, Dec. 8, 1978). Pastor. The son of John Howell, farmer, and Mattie Howell, teacher, he attended Carson-Newman College (B.A.) and Southern Baptist Theological Seminary (B.D., 1929). Ordained by the First Baptist Church, Jefferson City, TN, he married Gladys Fulton, Dec. 28, 1919. They had three children: John, Anne, and Carol. Howell served as pastor of churches in Dayton, TN; Eustis and Leesburg, FL; and Chattanooga, TN, 1928-45.

In 1945 Howell began a long ministry at Murray Hill Church, Jacksonville, FL. Under his leadership the church became a leading force in mission activity. Eleven missions were established, and 20 young men were licensed to preach, including Howell's son, John. Howell served as president of the Florida Baptist Convention, 1958-59. He was trustee at Baptist Hospital, Jacksonville, 1958-70. He is buried in Hillcrest Memorial Gardens, Leesburg, FL.

PAUL E. WRENN, JR.

HOWELL, JOHN EDMUND (b. Lynchburg, VA, July 12, 1933; d. Louisville, KY, Sep. 4, 1979). Pastor. The son of Carl Alonzo Howell, a Baptist minister, and Gladys Fulton Howell, he graduated with honors from Stetson University (B.A., 1955). He also attended Yale University Divinity School (B.D., 1959) and Duke University (Ph.D., 1963), where his dissertation in American historical theology on Horace Bushnell won a publication prize. He married Betty Jean Henderson of Tallahassee, FL, Aug. 3, 1956. They had five children: Leslie, John, Philip, Emily, and Daniel.

Howell served four pastorates: First Church, DeLand, FL; Northside Drive Church, Atlanta, GA; First Church, Washington, DC; and Crescent Hill Church, Louisville, KY. He was a trustee of Southeastern Baptist Theological Seminary, secretary of the seminary's board, and a member of the board's executive committee. He was visiting professor of pastoral studies at Southern Baptist Theological Seminary. Stetson University granted him a Distinguished Alumnus Award in 1973. Howell led the first retreats for Protestant military chaplains in the Vietnamese conflict. He was decorated with the Four Chaplains Silver Medallion for this service. Howell is buried in Cave Hill Cemetery, Louisville, KY.

JOHN EWING ROBERTS

HOWSE, WILLIAM LEWIS, JR. (b. Fayetteville, TN, Feb. 26, 1905; d. Locust Dale VA, Dec. 27, 1977). Educator and denominational leader. Son of Emma Howse and William Lewis, Sr., a minister, he attended Union University (1926), Baylor University (M.A., 1932), and Southwestern Baptist Theological Seminary (M.R.E., 1934; D.R.E., 1937). He married Genevieve Morgan of Fort Worth, TX, Oct. 28, 1930. They had one son, William Lewis, III.

While instructor, then professor, at Southwestern Seminary, 1932-54, he served as educational director at Broadway Baptist Church, Fort Worth, 1935-45. During his tenure at Southwestern, he also served Polytechnic Church and University Church, Fort Worth, and First Church, Dallas. From 1954 until retirement in 1971, he was director of the Education Division of the Sunday School Board, SBC. During this time, he led in strengthening educational programs and in efforts of program correlation and coordination.

Howse served as an officer for various denominational and state organizations related to educational work. He also authored several books and pamphlets. In 1971 he became a consultant for the Foreign Mission Board, serving in East Asia, Middle America, the Caribbean, and finally in Richmond, VA, for the board's Mission Support Division until his death. He is buried at Dallas, TX.

MORTON F. ROSE

HUBBARD, WALKER CLARENCE (b. Alba, AL, June 24, 1902; d. Portales, NM, Sep. 24, 1977). Children's home and boys' ranch superintendent. Son of Franklin Hubbard, a grocer, and Lily Kirk Hubbard, a teacher, he moved to Afton, OK, at the age of two and was converted and baptized at the age of 12. He attended Oklahoma Baptist University (B.S., 1932), and Kansas State Teachers College (M.S., 1934). He married Dorothy Dana Davison, May 1, 1926. After the death of their infant son, Kenneth, they adopted four children: Marvin Dale, Lee, Allen Dale, and Bessie Marie.

Hubbard taught and coached in Oklahoma and New Mexico before his appointment as superintendent, Baptist Children's Home, Portales, NM, in 1937. The superintendency of the New Mexico Boys' Ranch near Belen was added to his duties in 1954. He served on the National Conference on Youth, was a Rotarian, was listed in *Who's Who in American Colleges* and *Who's Who in New Mexico,* and was a 40-year member of the First Baptist Church, Portales, NM. He retired from the children's home and boys' ranch in 1971. He is buried in Portales Memorial Cemetery, Portales, NM.

JOHN W. RANSDELL

HUGGINS, MALOY ALTON (b. Marion County, SC, Oct. 5, 1890; d. Raleigh, NC, Apr. 11, 1971). State convention executive. The son of Alice (Lundy) and Alexander Huggins, a merchant, he attended Wake Forest College (B.A., M.A.) and the University of North Carolina (M.A.). On July 13, 1918, he married Katherine Elizabeth Morris. They had two daughters, Minnie and Katherine.

Huggins taught Greek and Latin at Union University, Jackson, TN, for several years until he returned to eastern North Carolina to serve as teacher and principal in the public schools. Later he became professor at Meredith College in Raleigh. He was the author of several books and articles, most of them dealing with Baptist history. His best-known work was *A History of North Carolina Baptists, 1727-1932* (1967).

Huggins served for 27 years as general secretary-treasurer of the Baptist State Convention of North Carolina, 1932-59. Mission offerings increased from $480,484 to $5,912,101 during his tenure, and the number of churches increased from 2,374 to 3,307. His tenure was also a period of growth for Baptist colleges and social service institutions in North Carolina. Bowman Gray School of Medicine was created, and Wake Forest College moved to Winston-Salem,

NC, and became a university. Boiling Springs Academy became Gardner-Webb Junior College, Fruitland Bible Institute was established, and after World War II, Chowan reopened as a junior college. Huggins is buried in Montlawn Cemetery, Raleigh, NC.

BEN C. FISHER

HUMAN RIGHTS, DECLARATION OF. See DECLARATION OF HUMAN RIGHTS.

HUMAN RIGHTS AND INTERNATIONAL AFFAIRS. Human rights in international affairs did not find legal expression until after World War II. There was no generally accepted postulate of international law obligating nations to guarantee religious liberty prior to the United Nations Declaration of Human Rights, adopted Dec. 10, 1948.

The preamble to the U.N. declaration declares that "recognition of the inherent dignity and of the equal and inalienable rights of all members of the human family is the foundation of freedom, justice and peace in the world." Ironically, the very century which has experienced the emergence of such a universal declaration has, at the same time, witnessed repeated and ruthless acts of suppression of human rights by a wide range of governments, both on the left and the right.

Concern for human rights became during the 1970s the most significant single development in international affairs. Through the historic Helsinki Final Act of 1975, signed by 35 states of Europe and North America, for the first time human rights were made an integral part of international agreement and basic to the "principles guiding relations between particular states." In an altogether unparalleled manner, the issue of human rights became a major factor in international relations and a mounting civil and political issue in national and international affairs. It is readily acknowledged by most experts as one of the key problems facing mankind in the remaining decades of this century. Respect for human rights, the House Committee on Foreign Relations declared, "is fundamental to our national tradition" and deserves far higher priority in the country's foreign policy as "both morally imperative and practically necessary."

Baptist concerns for human rights found expression in various denominational structures as well as in official pronouncements of national and international bodies of Baptists. The Baptist World Alliance Congresses of 1970, 1975, and 1980 adopted official statements in support of human rights throughout the world. A "Manifesto" adopted by the Twelfth BWA Congress of 1970 affirmed that Baptists "seek equal civil rights for all men and women and support the responsible use of these rights by all. . . . We will strive to conquer racism, achieve brotherhood, alleviate poverty, abolish hunger, and support morally sound population objectives." The BWA Congress of 1975 affirmed the principles set forth in the U.N. Universal Declaration of Human Rights. In the following year the BWA endorsed the promotion of the U.N. Human Rights Day among Baptists throughout the world.

In North America, particular attention was given to human rights in international affairs through the Baptist Joint Committee on Public Affairs, which was brought into being primarily out of human rights concerns. The Joint Committee commended President Jimmy Carter for his commitment to the implementation of human rights in United States foreign policy and, in 1977, reiterated its strong support for human rights throughout the world. The same year the SBC adopted a resolution supporting human rights, as it had done in 1963 and 1965. In 1979 the Joint Committee urged Senate ratification of the pending U.N. conventions and covenants on human rights, along with the American Convention on Human Rights.

BIBLIOGRAPHY: J. W. Baker, ed., *The Church, the State, and Human Rights* (1980).

JAMES E. WOOD, JR.

HUNGER, WORLD. The plight of starving people has always concerned sensitive Southern Baptists. The missionary Lottie Moon (*q.v.* III) actually gave up her life because she refused to eat when her Chinese friends were starving.

Only in the mid-1970s, when a worldwide food shortage aroused great popular concern, did Southern Baptists develop an organized denominational response to hunger and begin to attack its structural causes. In 1974 and 1975 the Foreign Mission Board experienced a dramatic, unsolicited increase in gifts for hunger. This new level of giving enabled the FMB to be involved both in short-term emergency relief and in long-term efforts to help the hungry help themselves.

This new interest yielded other results as well. In 1975 the Christian Life Commission called wide attention to hunger by means of a mailing to every Southern Baptist church. The CLC also began vigorous efforts to keep Southern Baptists informed about the moral dimension of the hunger problem and related public policy issues. By 1976 Southern Baptist periodicals were showing a marked increase in attention to the injustice of hunger. Also in that year, representatives of SBC agencies with program assignments related to hunger began meeting together to coordinate their efforts. This group soon initiated a proposal that World Hunger Day be placed on the denominational calendar on the first Wednesday in August each year.

Ultimately approved by the SBC, the first World Hunger Day was observed in 1978. This special day, later moved to the second Sunday in October, continues as an educational emphasis which is promoted by the CLC and other interested SBC agencies.

In Nov., 1978, a Convention-wide Convocation on World Hunger was held at Ridgecrest. Receiving wide attention in the denominational press and occurring in the same year as the first World Hunger Day, the convocation helped to establish hunger as a major item on the agenda of Southern Baptists.

Popular concern about hunger continued to increase. In 1979 the Home Mission Board voted to employ a consultant on domestic hunger, and a CLC staff member testified before the United States Presidential Commission on World Hunger. By 1980 annual hunger and relief offerings given by Southern Baptists totaled over $3,000,000, and resolutions on world hunger had been passed by the SBC every year since the mid-1970s.

Compared to some other major denominations, Southern Baptist hunger offerings are still low and denominational staff involvement is minimal. Progress, however, has been extremely rapid, and there can be no doubt that thousands of people have been saved from starvation because of the concern of Southern Baptists.

See also POVERTY, VOL. III.

W. DAVID SAPP

HYMN WRITERS, BAPTIST (I, III). The writing of new hymn texts and hymn tunes by Baptists continued in the 1970s. *Baptist Hymnal* (1975 ed.) provided an outlet for a number of new texts and tunes, some of which had appeared first in the previous decade.

Authors.—Richard D. Baker, "I Have Heard the Voice of Jesus"; Mark Blankenship, "As We Gather Around the Table of Our Lord"; Bill Cates, "Do You Really Care"; Betty Jo Corum (*q.v.* III), "Peace in Our Time, O Lord"; Harry Eskew, trans., "Lord, You Bid Us Ever"; Thomas A. Jackson, "We Are Called to be God's People"; Kurt Kaiser, "Pass It On"; Thomas B. McDormand, "Where Can We Find Thee, Lord, So Near"; Edwin McNeely, "New Life for You"; W. Elmo Mercer, "The Time Is Now, the Lord Is Here"; William R. O'Brien, "The Cattle on a Thousand Hills Are His"; J. Edwin Orr, "Search Me, O God"; Ernest A. Payne, "Lord, Who Dost Give to Thy Church for Its Healing"; W. E. Penn (*q.v.* II), "There Is a Rock in a Weary Land"; Milburn Price, "O Lord, Who Came to Earth to Show"; William J. Reynolds, "Share His Love"; Thad Roberts, Jr., "God of Earth and Outer Space."

Composers.—Richard D. Baker, "Loriann"; Mark Blankenship, "North Phoenix"; A. L. Butler, "Ada"; Bill Cates, "Cates"; James D. Cram, "Hunter's Glen"; Kurt Kaiser, "Pass It On"; W. Elmo Mercer, "Benson"; William R. O'Brien, "Jalan"; W. E. Penn, "Sheltering Rock"; Milburn Price, "Pax Iam"; William J. Reynolds, "Sullivan"; Don Riddle, "Liberty"; Frederick J. Work, and John W. Work, Jr., "Were You There"; John W. Work, III, "Go Tell It."

WILLIAM J. REYNOLDS

HYMNALS, BAPTIST (I, III). Nineteen years after the 1956 *Baptist Hymnal*, a new hymnal was published for Southern Baptist churches. The Church Music Department of the Sunday School Board, SBC, initiated this project in 1972. A 68-member hymnal committee was appointed including pastors, theologians, ministers of music, state music secretaries, professional musicians, concert artists, religious educators, organists, college and seminary music faculty, evangelistic singers, denominational agency personnel, and others.

A research survey of current hymn-singing practices in SBC churches brought unusual insight to the committee. To replace hymns no longer widely used in the churches, the committee searched many sources of Christian song, including older traditions, contemporary songs of the gospel, and new songs.

The hymnal reflects the biblical emphasis of Baptist tradition. Hymn texts were critically examined for theological accuracy and doctrinal soundness. A wide variety of tunes reflected a basic concern for musical values.

The organization of the hymnal reflects a God-centered rationale. The hymns are arranged logically and sequentially in four sections: God, God Speaks, God's Work, and God's People. The balance and proportion in these major divisions provide material for congregational singing in the life of the church—worship, fellowship, witness, evangelism, and missions—and the many experiences of the Christian life.

Baptist Hymnal (1975 ed.) was premiered on Mar. 13, 1975, at PraiSing with 10,000 people singing from its pages for the first time. By the end of 1980, approximately 4,000,000 copies had been distributed, reflecting its acceptance by the churches.

New Songs of Praise (in Chinese) was published in Hong Kong for Baptist churches in 1973. *Himnario Bautista* (in Spanish) was published by the Casa Bautista de Publicationes, El Paso, TX, in 1978. *Cantor Cristao* (in Portuguese) was published in Rio de Janeiro in 1978. These three hymnals included many indigenous hymns and tunes, reflecting a slowly diminishing reliance on imported hymns and gospel songs from Western culture and the increasing influence of music missionaries.

See also PraiSing, Music in Missions.

WILLIAM J. REYNOLDS

HYMNODY, SHAPE-NOTE. See Shape-Note Hymnody.

I

IDAHO, SOUTHERN BAPTISTS IN. See Utah-Idaho Southern Baptist Convention.

ILLINOIS, BAPTIST FOUNDATION OF (III). The foundation adopted a new constitution in 1969 and became similar to a department of work with only figurehead corporate officers being elected. Arthur E. Farmer, director of the Special Ministries Division of the Illinois Baptist State Association, directed the foundation beginning in 1972. The work was reassigned to James B. Doom, director of the Stewardship Department, in 1979. The assets of the foundation as of Dec. 31, 1979, were $79,534.

JAMES DOOM

ILLINOIS, BAPTIST MISSIONARY CONVENTION OF. Originally Baptist Gospel Missionary Convention (BMC), organized in Patterson, IL, Feb. 24, 1904, to support Joseph K. David, of Syria (now Lebanon), in a mission among his people. Eventually this organization sponsored missionaries in three Middle Eastern nations, turning its work over to the Foreign Mission Board, SBC, in 1919.

The primary leader of this organization was Joseph O. Raines (*q.v.* II), pastor in the Sandy Creek Association. Churches in Apple Creek, Bay Creek, Carrollton, and Macoupin Associations joined in support. It became the official missionary organization of the Illinois Baptist State Association when this group was organized in 1907. *The Primitive Missionary* was its promotional organ until 1905, when that paper merged with *The Illinois Baptist*.

The first foreign field entered was Syria. Joseph K. and Naomi Ruth David arrived there in Apr., 1904. A church was organized in Rasheya. After J. K. David's death in 1909, the work was carried on by his brother, N. K. David, and Fadlow Bausby, who became the leader of Baptist work in Lebanon.

The second field entered was Persia, now Iran. John Isaac, in 1908, and Yonan H. Shabaz, in 1911, both Assyrians, became missionaries. Isaac began a mission on Urmia Plain in 1909. Shabaz, adopting Baptist views, had traveled to London to have Charles Haddon Spurgeon (*q.v.* II) baptize him. Finding Spurgeon dead, he traveled to New York for baptism by Robert Stuart McArthur, pastor of Calvary Baptist Church, later Baptist World Alliance president. After training at Columbia University, Shabaz returned to establish mission support by the Baptist Persian Committee. The BMC adopted the work in 1911. Absolum George, trained at Baylor University and Southwestern Baptist Theological Seminary, also went to Persia in 1913.

The third field entered was Galilee. Shukrie Mosa, a Galilean, wanted to return to Nazareth as a missionary. Appointed in 1910, he worked until World War I. Drafted into the Persian army, he returned to give the Nazareth Church a good foundation.

The work of the BMC was disrupted by World War I. The Persian work was never reopened. John Isaac was martyred by Moslem Kurds in 1918. The Foreign Mission Board took over the remaining missions in 1919.

BIBLIOGRAPHY: Charles L. Chaney, "A History of the Baptist Missionary Convention of Illinois, 1904-1919," (unpublished Th.M. thesis, The Southern Baptist Theological Seminary, 1960).

CHARLES L. CHANEY

ILLINOIS, BLACK AND ETHNIC CHURCH GROWTH IN. An intensive effort was begun in 1973 to mobilize churches of the Illinois Baptist State Association to extend their ministry and witness to all people and places in the state. The effort had a dramatic effect on the multiplication of black and ethnic Southern Baptist churches in the state.

During the 1960s, only three black churches were affiliated with IBSA. During the 1970s, 36 affiliated. By 1980, 47 black churches associated with IBSA, 10 in Metro-East Association and 28 in Chicago Metro Association. Bill Affolter and Don Sharp served as coordinators for black churches in those associations.

The strategy for black church growth has been to cooperate with National Baptists wherever possible and to acquaint unaligned black pastors and churches with program helps and resources available through the various agencies. New work has been started in black communities using fully supported black church planters.

In 1965 the IBSA counted four ethnic churches and missions. In 1980 there were 40. This growth was made possible in part by a large increase in support for this work—from $24,940 in 1965 to $294,800 in 1980. In 1975 the Department of Brotherhood and Language Missions was created, and James Edward Godsoe was named director. Marvin O. Berry, Frank Medina, Tim C. Terry, and Peter Kung provided on-the-field leadership as catalytic missionaries.

Most ethnic churches in Illinois have grown out of direct evangelism and discipling done by mission pastors and fully and partially supported church planters.

Long-range strategy calls for 100 black churches, 100 ethnic congregations, and 65 churches with deaf ministries by 1985.

JAMES E. GODSOE

ILLINOIS ASSOCIATIONS (I, III).
I. New Associations. NORTH CENTRAL. Organized with four churches during 1971: Bethel, Princeton; Calvary, Streator; Harmony, Ottawa; and Northbrook, Mendota. These churches that year reported 283 resident members, $38,087 total gifts, and $1,883 mission gifts. It disbanded in 1977 and the three remaining churches united with Three Rivers Association.

QUAD CITIES AREA. Organized in 1979 by seven churches from Sinnissippi: Calvary, East Moline; Coal Valley; First, Greenrock; Joy; Kennedy Drive, Moline; Memorial, Milan; and Peoples Missionary, Rock Island. In 1980 seven churches and one mission reported 46 baptisms, 835 members, $176,447 total gifts, and $33,482 mission gifts.

II. Changes in Associations. CENTRAL. Name changed from Sangamon Valley in 1972.

CHICAGO METRO. Name changed from Metropolitan Chicago in 1972.

EAST ST. LOUIS. Name changed to Metro East in 1971.

GREATER WABASH. Name changed from Mt. Erie in 1975.

ILLINOIS VALLEY. Merged with Metro Peoria in 1976. Area consisted of 11 full counties and parts of three others.

METRO EAST. Name changed from East St. Louis in 1971.

METROPOLITAN CHICAGO. Name changed to Chicago Metro in 1972. There were 117 units of work by 1979.

MT. ERIE. Name changed to Greater Wabash in 1975.

SANGAMON VALLEY. Name changed to Central in 1972. Decatur is the hub of the association.

HAROLD E. CAMERON

ILLINOIS BAPTIST, THE (I, III).
Weekly newspaper of the Illinois Baptist State Association. Robert J. Hastings continues as editor. The paper was moved in 1971 to Springfield, where the state association has its headquarters. Until 1968, the paper was available by individual subscriptions or the church budget plan. On Jan. 1, 1968, the paper was placed in the state Cooperative Program budget, providing subscriptions for all members of Southern Baptist churches in Illinois. The 1980 circulation was about 46,000.

ROBERT J. HASTINGS

ILLINOIS BAPTIST CHILDREN'S HOME, THE (I, III). A total of 95 children and youth can be served at any one time in 42 residential care beds, 8 group home beds, 15 foster home placements, 15 adoptive home placements, 10 maternity home beds, and 5 independent living placements. The primary campus near Carmi consists of three family-style cottages, two farm cottages, and an administration building surrounded by 850 acres of farmland. The maternity home is four miles from this complex, while the group home is 80 miles away at Carbondale.

Theron Hartis King was the last superintendent of the home, 1963-71. At his retirement, the Illinois Baptist State Association was reorganized and the home became a department within the division of special ministries under the supervision of Arthur Emmitt Farmer. At Farmer's retirement in 1979, Prince Edward Claybrook became the second director of Special Ministries of the IBSA responsible for the child care operation.

During King's administration, a modern social services department was organized, the physical facilities were upgraded, and a successful endowment fund program was begun. Farmer's administration was marked by the building of two farm group homes to utilize the farm facilities in a work training program for adolescent boys, and by the organizing of a new maternity home serving unwed mothers and a related adoption program.

During the 1970s, Gordon Len Lantrip was in charge of the residential care services, and Leon Elvis Talley was director of social services.

GORDON LANTRIP

ILLINOIS BAPTIST HISTORICAL COMMITTEE (III). The committee continues its service of procuring and preserving historical materials. Recent accomplishments include publication of the *History of New Design Baptist Historical Cemetery* by L. L. Leininger (1970), and restoration of the cemetery; relocation of the Baptist historical library from Carbondale to Springfield in 1973; a new history of Illinois Baptists, commissioned in 1973, entitled *We Were There* (1976), an oral history of Illinois Baptists, by Robert J. Hastings; and a historical tour of Baptist sites, held originally in 1978 and repeated in 1979. Tour directors were Bill Fox, chairman, and Noel M. Taylor, former state executive secretary.

BILL FOX

ILLINOIS BAPTIST RETREATS, ASSEMBLIES, AND CAMPSITES. During the 1970s Illinois Baptists upgraded their retreats, assemblies, and campsites. Lake Sallateeska encampment now offers accommodations for approximately 300 persons. This camp was developed from a summer youth facility into a year-round retreat site. Improvements made during the decade include a new sewage and bath facility with two bath houses, 1977, winterization and renovation of the dining room and cabins, 1976-77, renovation of the auditorium, 1978, and the addition of three lodges and a nurses' station, 1979. Illinois Baptists also own a campsite near Streator. A long-range development program has been adopted and is being implemented.

ARTHUR FARMER

ILLINOIS BAPTIST STATE ASSOCIATION (I, III).
   I. History. The 1970s were years of consolidation and adjustments for the Illinois Baptist State Association (IBSA). Three major decisions made at the end of the preceding decade cast the direction of work for the immediate future: the selection of James Hillman Smith as the executive secretary, the adoption of a new constitution with its executive system, and the move of state offices to Springfield.

Smith's selection in 1967 was in harmony with the total movement of IBSA toward efficiency in operation and its vision of all Illinois as a valid mission field for Southern Baptists. Smith had received early theological training from Moody Bible Institute in Chicago. His work during the 1970s reflected an awareness of the urban situation along with a sensitivity to the rural setting of much of Illinois. The new constitution, adopted in 1969, provided the vehicle for reshaping the way of doing things and clarifying the mission task of the state association.

The final component in refocusing the vision of IBSA came in Aug., 1971, as the Springfield offices opened. The dedication of the new building, built without any expenditure of mission money, took place Nov. 11 at the annual session. By 1972 the major job roles, as specified by the constitution, were filled. A stewardship emphasis held in 1972 not only sought to increase individual and church gifts to the Cooperative Program but also changed the ratio of mission dollars going outside the state from 38 percent to 41 percent by 1975.

During the early part of the decade, Southern Baptists began to lead out in setting the moral tone of the state. A strong stand against state aid to parochial schools and opposition to the state lottery gave Baptists focal points around which to rally. In 1973 the association allocated expenses for an unofficial lobby for IBSA in the Illinois General Assembly.

Recognizing that in 1973 there were still over 400 geographical areas in need of Baptist witness, IBSA launched in 1974 "Extend Now to All of Illinois," a program led by new church extension director Charles Leonard Chaney. Its purpose was to identify areas of need for new churches, encourage awareness of the need, and work to undergird new work in these areas. The goal set for Cooperative Program giving was $2,000,000 by 1976. As the state association grew in effectiveness, long-range planning brought about an orderly movement toward the objective of the association. One aspect of this planning projected that the 1979 budget for special ministries should no more than equal that of Church Development or Church Extension.

Though 1975 saw the exposure of the misappropriation of funds at the Carmi Children's Home, Illinois Baptists moved forward in a wide variety of new projects. "North Central States Mission Thrust" sought to double the number of churches in the north central United States by 1990. "PraiSing '75" brought together musicians from all over the SBC in an outburst of praise. New workers in Baptist Student Ministries, Christian Social Ministries, and among internationals expanded the scope of the ministry. Enlistment of black churches became a state priority. To facilitate these new areas of emphasis, a cooperative agreement with associations in which new workers were assigned enabled supervision of these workers by the local associations.

The state association undertook a bold new initiative in 1976 with a four-year plan for launching new churches in Illinois. The "Million Dollar Offering for New Churches" pumped funds into areas of direct need, enabling evangelical witness where none had been present previously. As the nation celebrated its bicentennial, Baptists in Illinois shared their heritage of solidity with that freedom in a July 4 and 5 freedom rally at the state fairgrounds.

Throughout the 1970s, the state association placed new emphasis upon equipping the people of God. Family ministry, the minister and his family, preaching, lay renewal, and training enriched Illinois churches and individuals. As demand for equipping programs grew, the state association established an adult equipping center at Springfield. This center serves as a meeting place for the Boyce Bible School Center, begun in 1978, and family life and spiritual enrichment activities. Other equipping conferences also make use of these facilities.

James H. Smith resigned to become executive director of the Brotherhood Commission, SBC, in 1979. The following year, Illinois Baptists elected Ernest E. Mosley, of the Church Administration Department, Sunday School Board, SBC, as executive director of the state association. The 1970s saw the retirement of several Baptist leaders from Illinois: George Edward Wheeler, Harrison C. Croslin, Jr., and Arthur Emmitt Farmer. These men represented vision, dedication, and stability for the association in a time of transition.

LEE GALLMAN, JR.

Illinois Baptist Building. —On recommendation of a committee appointed in 1966 to study moving state offices from Carbondale, the IBSA in 1969 voted to relocate its offices in Springfield and erect a new building there on property costing $150,000. The board of directors elected a building committee: Archie Brown, chairman; Raymond Taylor, Maurice Swinford, Norman Watson, Charles Boling, Myron Dillow, Everett Lemay, G. Pat Robinson, David Williams, and Robert M. Thompson. The board employed Terry and Henderson, Architects, to design the new building and L. D. Lawrence Construction Company to build it. In Aug., 1971, the IBSA moved its offices from Carbondale to Springfield. The board held its first meeting in the new office building two weeks later. On Nov. 11, 1971, during its annual meeting, the IBSA dedicated the new Illinois Baptist Building.

ARCHIE E. BROWN

Organizational Structure. —Work of the IBSA is done by a carefully structured executive system,

headed by the executive director. The board of directors, elected by the state association in annual meeting, employs the director, assigns tasks, recommends budget, and establishes role specifications for all executive personnel. The board sets policy and monitors the work of the executive system.

The executive system includes three subsystems: (1) The management system is a chain of command from the executive director to division directors to department directors and associate department directors. Each person is accountable to his or her manager for performance of assigned responsibilities. (2) The appeal system inverts the chain to allow a decision to be appealed to successive higher authority, with the board as the ultimate level. This is to allow recourse for any person unfairly treated. Participation is encouraged by policy but not widely used in actual practice. (3) The representative system is a horizontal relationship between all persons on any one level, allowing united strength on similar concerns.

The organization was established in the state association constitution of 1969. It was fully implemented with the division directors employed by 1972. The experience of working with the system led to modification by the board in 1977 and 1978, but the basic structure continued as the organizational pattern through 1979.

KEITH W. STANFORD

II. Program of Work. *Church Development Division.* —This division assists in developing Baptist churches. The IBSA reported 910 churches in 1979. Originally the division consisted of five departments: Sunday School, Church Training, Baptist Student Union, Evangelism, and Church Music. Ronald Sinclair Lewis, the first director, 1972-77, led the department in launching a summer training conference, "Gloricrest," for all church workers and in beginning Illinois College of Christian Training. Maurice Lysle Swinford became director of this division in 1978. In 1980 the IBSA board approved the division's proposed strategy for growth which focused on increasing Sunday School enrollment, Christian training, and evangelism.

MAURICE SWINFORD

Church Extension Division. —This division (CED), which assists churches in ministries beyond themselves, originally consisted of four departments: Missions, Stewardship, Woman's Missionary Union, and Brotherhood. Charles Leonard Chaney became first director in 1972. In June, 1975, the Brotherhood Department became Language Missions and Brotherhood Department. This department divided into Departments of Language Missions and Lay Mobilization in 1978. Stewardship was moved to the Administrative Division and Student Ministries transferred to CED in Mar., 1978. Major division projects were: "Extend Now to

All of Illinois, 1973-76,'' an effort to begin 100 new churches in three years; "Bold Mission—Illinois, 1978-80,'' an effort to call churches to bold praying, growing, going, and giving; and "Million Dollar Offering for New Churches, 1977-80.''

CHARLES L. CHANEY

Church Music.—Roderick D. Latta, state music secretary, 1967-77, was succeeded by Carl Wayne Sheppard, July 1, 1977. The Singing Illinoisans, a statewide choral organization organized in 1971, and the IBSA Orchestra performed for the 1980 meetings of the SBC and the Southern Baptist Church Music Conference in St. Louis, MO. This choral group participated in a foreign mission tour to Ecuador in 1979. In 1977 a new choral organization was formed, The Singing Churchmen of Illinois, composed of full-time ministers of music.

In 1979 the churches reported 675 elected music directors (50 full-time ministers of music) and a music program enrollment of 19,992.

CARL W. SHEPPARD

Evangelism.—As a part of the Church Development Division, this department is responsible for helping churches grow through evangelism training and development. Several directors served the department in the 1970s: James Alton Ponder, 1967-70; Russell Gene Richardson, 1972-74; Kenneth Eldon Carter, 1974-76; and John Waymon Somers, 1977-79. Richardson was renamed director in 1980. The position of evangelism intern, added in 1975, was changed to associate status in 1978.

Significant evangelism accomplishments included the pilot project for Lay Evangelism Schools in Chicago, 1971; a record high of 9,284 baptisms in 1972; the first state conference on child conversion in 1974; and 60 percent of IBSA churches participating in simultaneous revivals in the ''Year of Evangelism,'' Apr., 1979. A 9.8 percent increase in baptisms was recorded in 1979, reversing a seven-year period of decline.

RUSSELL G. RICHARDSON

Language Missions.—Language Missions was included in the Missions Department, 1970-74. The IBSA created the Department of Brotherhood and Language Missions in 1975. James Edward Godsoe served as director of both areas of work until Jan., 1978, when Brotherhood work was incorporated into the Department of Lay Mobilization.

To achieve a goal of 100 language churches and missions and 65 churches with ministries to the deaf by 1985, Marvin Owen Berry, Francisco Armando Medina, Timothy Calhoun Terry, and Peter Chung-Hong Kung were employed as catalytic missionaries to provide on-the-field leadership. Robert Marshall Landes was employed as director of Deaf Ministries in June, 1980. The Million Dollar Offering for New Churches helped make possible the open-ing of new language churches. At the end of the 1970s, there were 41 active language congregations in the state.

JAMES E. GODSOE

Lay Mobilization.—This department, formed in 1978, assists churches in growing men and boys toward spiritual maturity, in discovering their spiritual gifts, and in equipping them for the essential ministries of a church: prayer, evangelism, stewardship, community ministries, and direct mission involvement. Men are challenged to involvement through the personal disciplines of daily prayer, self-initiated Bible study, Scripture memory, giving, and life-style witnessing.

Activities include leadership training, retreats, annual camps, Royal Ambassador Congress, state RA track meet, and national RA congresses. Christian discipleship seminars began in 1980, and annual prayer and discipleship conferences have trained leaders in equipping men for ministry. A statewide network of key Baptist men has begun to mobilize men for disaster relief and reconstruction, life ministry teams, and lay witnessing. Robert Homer Stuckey, missionary to Indonesia, 1962-77, became first department director, Feb. 1, 1978.

ROBERT H. STUCKEY

Leadership Training.—Bluford Monroe Sloan resigned as Church Training director in Sep., 1969. His responsibilities had included Church Training, Church Recreation, Church Administration, and Church Library. Don Eugene Dillow became Church Training director, Feb. 16, 1970, with responsibility for Church Training, Church Administration, Family Life, and Vocational Guidance. In 1974 the Baptist Counseling Service was created, and the department name was changed to Church Administration and Training Department with five service areas: Church Administration, Pastoral Ministries, Family Life, Vocational Guidance, and Church Training. This department was divided in 1977 to form the Leadership Training Department and the Office of Church-Minister Relations. Leadership Training was assigned Church Training, Illinois College of Christian Training, Boyce Bible Center, and Conference Center coordination. Rick Edward Heironimus became Leadership Training director in 1978. Church Library was reassigned to this department in 1979.

RICK E. HEIRONIMUS

Missions.—In 1970 James Edward Godsoe, Kenneth Wayne Neibel, and Marvin Owen Berry were area missionaries; Walter William Mihlfeld, rural missionary; Herbert Fay Hughes, Christian Social Ministries (CSM) director, East St. Louis; and the IBSA had two pastoral missionaries. In 1973 all communities beyond 500 population needing new churches were identified. Harold Dean Preutt became CSM director, Rock Island. Associational church extension directors were employed: Louie Dan Patrick, Lake County Association; and Charles Wesley Cress, Jr., Fox Valley Association. Thomas Edward Adams replaced Cress in 1978. Mihlfeld retired as Southern Illinois rural urban director in 1979. James Eugene Norman was an area rural urban director. Marvin Peters became area church extension director for North Central Illinois in 1980.

Work with blacks has been led by Larry Duane Carter and William Pryor Affolter in Metro-East St. Louis, and Donald Lee Sharp became liaison with black churches in Chicago Metro Association.

The following were appointed Church Extension directors: Larry Duane Carter, Illinois, 1977; Roy Dean Hill, Three Rivers Association, 1978; and Marvin Peters, Northern Illinois, and John Paul Holsey, Chicago Metro Association, 1980.

In 1979 there were 34 associations served by 27 directors of missions. During the decade 131 new churches were constituted.

HAROLD EDWARD CAMERON

Office of Church-Minister Relations.—The IBSA board of directors approved the establishment of a Church Staff Information Service in 1971. Considering that the timing was inappropriate to implement such a program, James H. Smith, executive director, did not recommend to the board until Sep. 13, 1977, that the service be implemented under the name of the Office of Church-Minister Relations.

The response of the churches and ministers during that first year indicated that the timing was right because 136 churches requested assistance, and 486 ministers placed their biographical forms on file with the Office of Church-Minister Relations.

DON E. DILLON

Special Ministries Division.—This division aids the churches in related ministries, originally including child care, college room and board facilities, retreat facilities, Baptist Foundation, church building planning, and financing.

Arthur Emmitt Farmer, first director from Oct., 1971, until retirement in May, 1979, was succeeded in Oct., 1979, by Prince Edward Claybrook.

In Mar., 1978, church architecture was reassigned to the Sunday School Department in the Church Development Division, and the Baptist Foundation and Broadway Bond programs were reassigned to the Stewardship Department in the Administrative Division. Unwed mother and adoption ministries were added in Mar., 1978, and ministry to senior adults was added in Sep., 1979.

PRINCE EDWARD CLAYBROOK

Stewardship Department.—Harrison C. Croslin, Jr., retired in 1978 after 16 years as director of the Stewardship Department. The depart-

ment cooperated with the Stewardship Commission, SBC, in a statewide Committed to Care Program to raise the income level of churches during 1972. Operation One, promoted 1973-75, resulted in a Cooperative Program increase of 49.5 percent. The IBSA moved from a 37-63 percent SBC-state division of Cooperative Program funds in 1973 to a 41-59 percent division in 1977.

The department was transferred from the Church Extension Division to the Administrative Division, Mar. 7, 1978, to make the IBSA executive secretary "more directly responsible for the income through Cooperative Program promotion." James B. Doom became department director, Sep. 11, 1978. The Baptist Foundation, which had been in the Special Ministries Division since 1972, was reassigned to the Stewardship Department in 1979. That year church bond programs were also assigned to this department. As of Jan. 1, 1980, a total of $26,131,200 in convention-backed bonds had been issued.

JAMES B. DOOM

Student Ministries.—Robert Eugene Blattner continues in the position of state director. New campus directors have been Winston Franklin Cofer, who began his ministry in Chicago in Feb., 1976; Eleanor Louise Harper, who resigned from the University of Illinois in May, 1976; William Steven Butler at Illinois State University since Aug., 1976; Harrel Harvey Morgan at University of Illinois beginning in Aug., 1977; Mark Alan Frakes who began in the Metro-East Edwardsville areas in 1978; and Sylvan Henry Knobloch, who started at Eastern Illinois University in 1979. The Student Center in Champaign, housing a men's dormitory, was sold in Feb., 1974, and a large house was purchased for a Student Center in Sep., 1975. Baptist Student Union groups have increased. More students have been involved in summer missions. Associations have become involved in supporting Student Ministries.

ROBERT E. BLATTNER

Sunday School.—A program of enlisting and training volunteer consultants was begun in 1970 as a means of promoting and developing Sunday School work. In 1971 churches began reporting using Backyard Bible Clubs. Twelve churches in three associations reported enrolling 2,500 children with 250 professions of faith. A week of summer training for church Sunday School workers was held in Illinois for the first time at East Bay Camp near Bloomington, July 30-Aug. 3, 1973. Don Eugene Herman resigned as associate director in 1971. John Wesley Perkins, Jr., director of the Sunday School Department, 1968-74, was succeeded by Billy Donald Allen in Jan., 1975. Allen resigned in 1977. David E. Laird became director in Aug., 1977. William Leon Crider was employed as associate director in 1979.

DAVID E. LAIRD

ILLINOIS STATISTICAL SUMMARY

Year	Associations	Churches	Church Membership	Baptisms	SS Enrollment	VBS Enrollment	CT Enrollment	WMU Enrollment	Brotherhood Enrollment	Ch. Music Enrollment	Mission Gifts	Total Gifts	Value Church Property
1969	34	899	188,697	7,908	138,998	70,549	46,157	21,860	6,749	14,801	$2,028,394	$13,994,833	$ 61,646,114
1970	34	901	191,359	7,628	136,599	63,356	44,885	20,507	6,434	14,701	2,121,144	14,402,418	67,234,899
1971	35	894	193,974	7,613	133,715	66,474	35,885	18,527	6,710	14,158	2,377,137	16,001,088	69,437,316
1972	35	889	199,016	9,073	135,661	74,833	34,890	17,310	6,611	15,577	2,603,141	17,481,691	73,347,798
1973	35	888	201,753	7,941	135,844	69,821	31,839	16,091	6,401	16,073	2,766,522	18,051,917	78,868,562
1974	35	878	204,014	7,620	131,036	63,506	28,090	16,090	6,137	16,535	3,099,822	19,808,356	86,161,222
1975	35	881	206,912	7,985	131,270	70,458	25,653	16,207	6,134	17,218	3,441,716	22,437,733	95,355,170
1976	34	890	209,564	7,503	135,153	62,314	23,688	17,177	6,284	18,042	3,973,970	24,583,931	104,873,389
1977	33	891	214,099	6,797	136,303	63,012	21,523	16,703	5,647	18,101	4,432,265	26,793,753	115,970,873
1978	33	889	215,989	6,459	131,962	59,595	21,156	16,727	5,325	18,572	4,811,775	28,883,038	133,488,222
1979	33	890	219,145	6,625	129,297	59,151	18,831	15,787	4,891	19,992	5,360,013	31,484,913	148,239,689
1980	34	908	223,177	8,081	131,850	63,766	18,973	16,366	5,987	21,559	6,048,941	34,952,052	167,197,003

BETTY R. WALKER

Woman's Missionary Union.—Two significant emphases affected Illinois WMU in the 1970s. WMU moved into the Grouping-Grading Plan. Volunteer consultants who assisted in training leadership accepted responsibility for promotion of age level organizations.

Helen Stuart Sinclair continued as director, completing her 25th year in Feb., 1980. Russell Fay Drinnen, Young Woman's Auxiliary-Sunbeam Band director, became assistant director with convention reorganization and the resignation of Evelyn Louise Tully in 1969. In Jan., 1971, Helen Gore Williams became WMU associate, serving until she transferred to Church Extension secretary, Feb., 1974. On Sep. 1, 1974, Tully, former Girls in Action director, resigned as Acteens consultant for WMU, Birmingham, to return as Illinois associate. Presidents serving in the decade were: Ruth Claybourne, 1970-73; Mary Ridings, 1973-76; Mickey Patrick, 1976-80; and Ann Branon, 1980- .

BIBLIOGRAPHY: Robert J. Hastings, *We Were There: An Oral History of the Illinois Baptist State Association, 1907-1976* (1976).

ILLINOIS BAPTIST STUDENT CENTER, CARBONDALE.

From Nov., 1967, to July, 1972, Robert C. Fuson, Jr., James Lyles, and Monty Knight served as directors of the Baptist Student Center. The present director, Larry Shacklee, has served since Aug., 1972. The center provides a Baptist Student Union, college credit Bible classes, seminary extension classes, noncredit devotional Bible classes, music instruction, fine arts teams, and youth-led revival teams. A strong emphasis is placed on maintaining a dormitory community life-style that is distinctively Christian.

LARRY SHACKLEE

INDIA, MISSION IN (III).

Southern Baptist mission work centers in Bangalore. In 1973 the 80-bed Bangalore Baptist Hospital opened. The Senter Cawthen Crook Christian Student Center operates an active program. The Karnataka Baptist Sabhegala Samaikya, a state Baptist Convention, organized in 1976. The mission has an educational thrust with three missionaries assigned as professors to seminaries and one to the University of Agricultural Sciences, Bangalore.

REBEKAH A. NAYLOR

INDIAN BAPTISTS, OKLAHOMA.

Among the 135,000 Indians representing 67 tribes in Oklahoma, there are five Baptist associations with about 400 churches and missions. Membership in 1979 was 15,390. Indian missions work is directed by the state convention's Department of Cooperative Missions.

J. M. GASKIN

INDIAN OCEAN ISLANDS, MISSION IN.

See MAURITIUS, MISSION IN.

INDIANA, BAPTIST FOUNDATION
OF. A subsidiary of the State Convention of Baptists in Indiana authorized in 1967 and incorporated in 1972. Memorial funds producing scholarships for church vocational persons have been established, and the first will benefiting the foundation has been probated. E. Harmon Moore served as the foundation's treasurer-director. Foundation assets totaled $39,250 in 1980.

E. HARMON MOORE

INDIANA, STATE CONVENTION OF BAPTISTS IN (III).
I. History. *Growth.*—Emphasis on church extension, through budgeting and personnel, resulted in an increase in church membership and in the number of churches affiliated with the State Convention of Baptists in Indiana from 1969 to 1979. Church membership increased 48.1 percent, from 50,511 to 74,800. The number of churches grew from 230 to 276, a 20 percent gain.

Cooperative Program.—The principal support of the convention budget comes from Cooperative Program funds from the churches. Other income sources include: Home Mission Board, Sunday School Board, *Indiana Baptist* subscriptions and advertising, associational missions agreements, building tenant utilities, and Highland Lakes Baptist Center fees. Gifts from churches rose from $4,114,700 in 1969 to $11,158,634 in 1979, a 187 percent increase. In 1958 the churches shared $70,149 through the Cooperative Program; in 1979 gifts reached $980,039. The convention has never shared less than 25 percent for SBC causes. The 1980 percentages were 31.5 percent for the SBC and 68.5 percent for state causes.

Highland Lakes Baptist Center.—The convention issued two series of bonds for purchasing additional land for the center, an assembly ground near Monrovia, IN. Construction proceeded according to a master plan as funds from previous bond issues and state mission offerings were available.

Meetings.—A 1976 special convention, called to consider a capital funds drive for financing construction of the center, requested the executive committee of the executive board and Highland Lakes Development Committee to find an alternate plan of financing and present it to the convention in 1977. The plan, Life Touching Contributors, was adopted, Nov., 1977.

The annual convention, composed of from 2 to 10 messengers from each church, provides fellowship, adopts a budget, elects officers and executive board members, and considers any business presented. Past presidents were: John Dorough, 1968-70; O. Thomas Woods, 1970-72; B. T. Scrivner, 1972-74; Leamon Blalock, 1974-76; Don Moore, 1976-78; and Robert Nall, 1978-80.

Executive Board.—The executive board of 30 members controls projects funded by the convention budget and elects personnel. It has charge of convention business, *ad interim*, reporting to the convention annually. Upon the resignation of L. E. Lawson, director of Brotherhood and Evangelism in 1973, the board created a Department of Stewardship and Evangelism by realigning responsibilities of department directors, and added Camp Development to Brotherhood, forming a new committee of the board. O. Thomas Woods came as Brotherhood/camp director, and Thomas E. Halsell as director for Stewardship and Evangelism. A constitutional change stipulated that the convention, rather than the board, elect board officers and that the tenure of members be limited to one three-year term, or no more than five years. Chairmen were: O. Thomas Woods, 1967-70; Leamon Blalock, 1970-74; James Brewer, 1974-75; B. T. Scrivner, 1975-77; Thomas Moncrief, 1977-78; Don Moore, 1977-79; and Glen Flowers, 1979-80.

Policy for Beginning New Institutions.—Long-range Planning Committee recommendations, adopted by the convention in 1969, set up guidelines for beginning hospitals, schools, colleges, child care facilities, and homes for the aging. Guidelines require a church membership of 300,000 and/or 1,000 churches; an affirmative vote in two consecutive conventions, one if the executive board initiates the project; and continuation and strengthening of services and projects already under way, as funds and personnel permit.

Anniversaries.—On its 15th anniversary, the convention published a history, *Sunrise On the Wabash,* by A. Ronald Tonks, assistant executive director of the Historical Commission, SBC. The 15th convention met at the Indian Heights Baptist Church, Kokomo. Tom Ed Moore, son of E. Harmon Moore, composed and directed two anthems for the occasion. Noel M. Taylor, executive secretary of the Illinois Baptist State Association when the Indiana Convention was organized, was guest speaker. E. Harmon Moore brought the anniversary message. A reception in honor of the 15th anniversary of Moore's service with the convention and an autograph party for A. Ronald Tonks followed the evening meeting.

Observance of the 20th anniversary at Northeast Park Baptist Church, Evansville, featured a five-minute vignette in each session, showing facets of growth, and a slide presentation depicting persons and events of the 20 years.

Embezzlement.—The 1972 audit of the treasurer's books showed a discrepancy and cash records missing. Allegedly, a trusted bookkeeper had embezzled funds. The exact loss, partially covered by insurance, could not be ascertained. A civil court case failed to produce a conviction, or further assets, and the case was closed.

Administration.—At the Nov., 1979, board meeting, E. Harmon Moore, executive director, announced his retirement, effective Jan. 1, 1981. Charged with finding a successor for Moore, the executive committee recommended

R. V. Haygood, associate director, to the board, Feb., 1980. He was elected.

Haygood is responsible for administering the budget and managing the physical facilities owned by the convention. He directs the Baptist Foundation and supervises seven departments of work, leads in budget planning and calendar coordination with department directors, submits plans to the executive committee and the executive board for approval, and supervises their implementation.

MRS. E. W. SPRINGS

II. Program of Work. *Sunday School, Church Music, and Building Consultant.*—Lew Reynolds, director since 1967, emphasized starting Sunday Schools, Bible study groups, Backyard Bible Clubs, and church and mission Vacation Bible Schools. Other promotion included leadership conferences, curriculum clinics, ACTION program, Spiral Growth Plan, and INDY 5000, a special effort to enroll 5,000 in Bible study in 1973-74.

Reynolds conducts annual associational music and choral clinics and provides information and counsel for church building planning.

Church Training, Baptist Student Ministries, Church Administration, and Supporting Services.—Directors have been Eldon Boone, 1969-70, and Don Herman, 1971- . Herman conducted leadership conferences, pastor-director training sessions, and the annual youth rally with Bible drill and speakers' tournament to strengthen Church Training.

The 1,000th Baptist Student Union in the nation began on Indiana University-Kokomo campus in 1976. There are BSU organizations on 26 campuses in the state. Financial aid, in the form of scholarships, provides directors for most campuses. Other campuses have volunteers. Other state BSU's have contributed to the support of directors. The convention owns a building on the Purdue campus, West Lafayette. Associations provide buildings on campuses at Indiana State, Terre Haute; Ball State, Muncie; and Indiana University, Bloomington.

Herman promoted church growth seminars to assist church staffs. Support ministries are church recreation, media, and family ministries.

Woman's Missionary Union.—Margaret Gillaspie has been director since 1968. WMU, functioning as a department with a committee on the executive board, promotes a week of prayer for state missions each September, home and foreign mission offerings annually, Girls in Action and Acteen camps, leadership training, and prayer retreats. A promotion committee, composed of officers and members at large, meets annually to plan the work. "Hoosier Helper" continues as a semiyearly promotional publication.

Indiana WMU participated in North Central Mission Thrust Prayer-Partner project promoted by WMU, SBC, and Share-a-Leader training project with Georgia WMU in 1978.

The 20th anniversary convention recognized Gillaspie and past presidents, including Sadie Griffin, 1969-72; Doris Kissel, 1972-76; and Cleo Cox, 1976-80.

MRS. E. HARMON MOORE

Brotherhood and Camp Development.—O. Thomas Woods, director since 1973, seeks to involve men and boys in missions through programs, prayer, and mission activities. Special projects include Baptist Men's convention and retreats, Royal Ambassador congress and camps, lay renewal, and state regional disaster teams. Woods coordinates volunteer labor and other projects involved in providing facilities at Highland Lakes Baptist Center.

GLEN FLOWERS

Missions.—R. V. Haygood served as director, 1969-80. Beginning missions, cooperation with black Baptists, Christian Social Ministries, Language Missions, Interfaith Witness, Chaplaincy, and Special Ministries are activities of the Missions Department. C. E. Wiley serves as state missionary. Virgil Clark, Jess Cooke, Randall Jones, Dale Maddux, Kenneth Neibel, Allan Pollock, George Senter, Robert Wiley, and James Fuller are directors of missions. Transferring elsewhere were Lyndon Collings, Dale Dozier, Robert Holland, Presley Morris, John Pate, Charles Smith, Gene Lake, Thomas Sykes, and Lowell Wright. Jess Dittmar retired.

Conferences on "Churches in Racially Changing Communities," monetary aid for pastors attending Ridgecrest Conference Center, and a scholarship for a black pastor are efforts to strengthen relationships with black Baptists. Northwest Baptist Association employs a part-time director of cooperative ministries, James Butler, for aiding black churches. Four black churches affiliate with the state convention.

In 1978 Christian Social Ministries director Michael Flannery replaced Marshall Moore, who had served in Indianapolis since 1970. Upon the retirement of Don Weeks from the Gary Baptist Center in Jan., 1979, it closed, making way for a municipal convention center, and Robert Pollan became CSM director in the Northwest Association that same year.

Working with the Spanish-speaking population of the Gary-Hammond area were language missionaries Gary Carpenter, 1968-69, and Leland Warren, 1969-73. Cass Vincent, 1973-78, made contacts with Slovak groups. Under his ministry the Seaman's Center, Port of Indiana, opened with the cooperation of the governor's office and Northwest Baptist Association. This association, aided by the Home Mission Board, constructed a building for the center on port property. Churches furnish supplies and host the officers and seamen.

The Missions Department provides information to alert pastors and churches concerning opportunities for chaplaincy in industrial, penal, and health facilities, and provides training sessions for dealing with cults.

INDIANA STATISTICAL SUMMARY

Year	Associations	Churches	Church Membership	Baptisms	SS Enrollment	VBS Enrollment	CT Enrollment	WMU Enrollment	Brotherhood Enrollment	Ch. Music Enrollment	Mission Gifts	Total Gifts	Value Church Property
1969	14	219	50,234	3,034	43,378	28,388	13,963	6,225	1,983	3,964	$ 430,365	$ 4,132,821	$16,816,302
1970	14	226	53,153	3,074	41,787	25,136	12,602	5,748	2,145	4,392	478,667	4,387,407	17,954,244
1971	15	226	55,789	4,056	42,486	25,650	11,514	5,422	2,642	4,976	678,137	4,874,975	18,616,810
1972	14	232	59,234	4,150	45,026	28,627	11,578	5,882	2,544	5,327	785,266	5,611,190	20,670,504
1973	14	242	61,369	4,281	46,408	30,161	10,877	5,516	2,481	6,108	897,786	6,096,765	22,982,221
1974	14	249	65,553	3,902	47,847	32,686	10,565	5,664	2,470	6,383	1,050,474	6,633,955	28,803,438
1975	14	248	66,456	4,249	48,919	33,341	9,593	6,175	2,981	6,566	1,073,089	7,179,275	32,733,428
1976	14	250	68,999	3,798	53,055	27,934	10,052	6,433	3,136	6,529	1,224,457	8,195,495	37,632,284
1977	14	255	70,909	2,947	50,827	28,679	9,599	6,280	3,150	6,468	1,307,371	8,919,880	40,630,258
1978	14	264	72,941	2,750	48,514	27,584	9,183	6,207	3,125	6,329	1,478,365	9,922,228	47,224,249
1979	14	269	74,800	3,125	48,778	27,498	9,498	6,110	3,111	7,084	1,679,722	11,240,480	51,476,164
1980	14	272	76,852	3,783	50,380	26,033	10,575	4,996	2,451	7,647	1,899,472	11,820,287	56,071,276

E. HARMON MOORE

Resort Ministries director B. T. Scrivner conducts worship services in state parks, ministering to individuals as the need arises. The convention provides a van for The Southern Baptist Theological Seminary students to commute weekly to serve in Indiana churches. The state president appointed a prayer committee in 1977 to plan and promote a statewide prayer emphasis. Park Avenue Baptist Church, Titusville, FL, Peter Lord, pastor, contributed finances and encouragement. Churches, associations, and the state conducted prayer retreats.

Mission volunteers include Christian Service Corps, Campers on Mission, BSU, church groups, summer student missionaries, and seminarians.

North Central Mission Thrust motivated an awareness of need in Indiana, resulting in a special link with the Arkansas Baptist Convention. Mission sponsorship and ministers for special occasions benefit Indiana churches.

Stewardship and Evangelism.—Directors have been Thomas E. Halsell, 1973-79, and James W. Abernathy, 1980- . Associational clinics promote stewardship development and training for church leaders. The state Evangelism Conference fosters a spirit of evangelism among pastors. As part of North Central Mission Thrust, Halsell promoted simultaneous revivals in Good News, Indiana, 1979. All associations participated, resulting in over 1,000 conversions and 700 additions to churches. A Bold Mission linkup with the Arkansas Baptist Convention provided 110 preachers and music directors for this effort.

Communications, Editorial Services, Christian Life Committee, and Public Relations.—Editors of the *Indiana Baptist,* the convention's official paper for Baptist news and communication, have been Alvin C. Shackleford, 1965-76, and Gene Medaris, 1977-81. The Christian Life committee functions to assist the convention and churches in Christian response to ethical, moral, and legislative matters.

Report of Long-range Planning Committee.—The board adopted recommendations by a committee, appointed by the chairman, for objectives and goals for the 1980s: an emphasis on prayer, renewed commitment to the goals of North Central Mission Thrust, additional staff services as needed and funds permit, emphasis on stewardship development, completion of Highland Lakes Baptist Center, motivation for church growth, and correlated planning with associations and churches.

BIBLIOGRAPHY: A. Ronald Tonks, *Sunrise on the Wabash: A Short History of Indiana Southern Baptists* (1973).

E. HARMON MOORE

INDIANA ASSOCIATIONS (III).

I. New Associations. NORTHWEST. Organized in Nov., 1971, with 43 churches by merging Lake Michigan and Northern Indiana Associations. In 1979, 36 churches reported 282 baptisms, 12,282 members, $1,843,323 total gifts, $108,974 mission gifts, and $7,433,500 property value.

WEST CENTRAL. Organized in Nov., 1970, at First Southern Baptist Church, Terre Haute, with seven churches from Central Association. In 1979 eight churches reported 76 baptisms, 1,222 members, $264,446 total gifts, $20,897 mission gifts, and $639,000 property value.

II. Changes in Associations. LAKE MICHIGAN. Organized in 1955, this association merged with Northern Indiana to form Northwest Association in 1971.

NORTHERN INDIANA. Organized in 1958, this association merged with Lake Michigan to form Northwest Association in 1971.

E. HARMON MOORE

INDIANA BAPTIST (III). Weekly news journal of Indiana Baptists. The circulation increased from 6,018 in 1969 to 9,680 in 1980. The newspaper changed from magazine to tabloid size in 1969. Alvin C. Shackleford, who resigned as editor in 1976 to become editor of the *Baptist and Reflector,* was succeeded by Gene Medaris in 1977. Medaris resigned in 1981.

GLEN FLOWERS

INDONESIA, MISSION IN (I, III). The Indonesian Baptist Union was formed in 1971. That same year, amid spiritual revival, the missionaries voted striking changes in their approach. Field evangelists became itinerant church planters, rather than supervisors of subsidy for congregations and pastors. Seminary education expanded through extension centers. Disagreements caused considerable friction between missionaries and Indonesian Baptist leaders, but the end of the decade saw renewed cooperation. During the 1970s Indonesians became directors of several Baptist institutions. The Immanuel Hospital opened in Bukittinggi, a strongly Muslim area of Sumatra. Opposition to Baptist presence there resulted in an attempted bombing in 1976. Increased Muslim resistance, with tightened visa restrictions, reduced the number of missionaries from 123 in 1972 to 101 in 1980. Seminary students, including extension, totaled 400. Three hundred churches and missions had 14,625 members. An indigenous denomination on the islands of Sulawesi, Halmahera, and Kalimantan officially became Baptist, adding several thousand members.

WILLIAM N. MCELRATH

INERRANCY. The use of the term *inerrancy* in relation to the Scriptures is a current matter of interest among Southern Baptists. The Baptist Faith and Message reads, "The Holy Bible . . . has . . . truth, without any mixture of error, for its matter." Repeated refusals to change the wording indicate Southern Baptists' acceptance of this statement. The word *inerrant* does not appear in the Bible. Perhaps the statement closest to its meaning is 2 Timothy 3:16a, which literally says, "Every single part of Scripture is God-breathed." Inerrancy refers, according to some, to the original autographs whose existence is unknown. To others, it refers to the truth of Scripture contained in any translation. Inerrancy is accepted by faith, not sight.

See also BAPTIST FAITH AND MESSAGE FELLOWSHIP, THE; BIBLE, CONTROVERSIES ABOUT THE; CONSERVATIVE THEOLOGY, RESURGENCE OF.

HERSCHEL H. HOBBS

INFORMATION RETRIEVAL SYSTEM, BAPTIST. See BAPTIST INFORMATION RETRIEVAL SYSTEM.

INGLE, CLIFFORD (b. Howard, KS, Jan. 15, 1915; d. Kansas City, MO, Apr. 17, 1977). Educator and minister. Son of Jess Newton, a railroad employee, and Martha Ellen (Gadbury) Ingle, he was a graduate of Southwest Baptist College (A.A., 1936), William Jewell College (B.A., 1938), and Southwestern Baptist Theological Seminary (B.D., 1947; M.R.E., 1948; D.R.E./Ed.D., 1952-1973). He served as student pastor of churches in Missouri and Texas, 1934-41, Army chaplain, 1942-46, pastor of Walnut Creek Baptist Church, Fort Worth, TX, 1949-51, teacher-director of the Baptist Student Center, 1951-59, and professor of philosophy and ethics, 1957-59, at Southwest Missouri State University, and first professor of religious education and church administration at Midwestern Baptist Theological Seminary, 1959-77.

Ingle wrote *The Military Chaplain as a Counselor* (1953) and edited *Children and Conversion* (1970). On June 17, 1941, he married Theda Celeste Smith of Wichita Falls, TX. They had two sons, John Barry and Thomas Lynn. He is buried in White Chapel Memorial Gardens, Kansas City, MO.

G. HUGH WAMBLE

INGRAHAM, HAROLD EDWARD (b. Hagen, GA, Feb. 24, 1898; d. Nashville, TN, Feb. 6, 1975). Denominational worker. Son of Jarvis Ingraham, a schoolteacher, and Georgia (Stroberg) Ingraham, he attended public schools in Jacksonville, FL, George Peabody College, Nashville, and The Southern Baptist Theological Seminary (Th.G., 1935). Stetson University, Deland, FL, honored him with the D.C.E. degree in 1953. He married Sybil Ley, July 18, 1924. They had three children: Marcia, Anna, and Frank.

Before joining the Sunday School Board staff in 1922, he was clerk, Southern Express Company and Atlantic Coast Line Railroad, life insurance salesman, and educational director for his home church, Main Street Baptist, Jacksonville. Ingraham retired from the SSB in 1966, having served as associate secretary and secretary of the Sunday School Administration Department, Sunday School administrator, business manager, and director, Service Division. He is buried in Woodlawn Cemetery, Nashville, TN.

HUBERT BON SMOTHERS

INLOW YOUTH CAMP (I, III). Located in the Manzano Mountains, 60 miles southeast of Albuquerque, this camp has land, buildings, and equipment valued at more than $250,000. Camping is limited to summer only, since the facilities are often inaccessible during the winter months. Maximum capacity is 400.

The convention business manager, in cooperation with the resident manager, is responsible for the operation, maintenance, and development of the camp. Program activities for convention camps are planned by the division or sponsoring organization. Camps for boys, girls, coeducational music groups, family camps for Indians and Spanish, camps for deaf and delinquent youth, church family groups, and youth retreats are welcomed.

During the 1970s, Heritage Chapel was built, the forest road was graveled to make access possible during the rainy seasons, concrete sidewalks were placed in strategic places, and Aspen Cabin was completed. The kitchen was remodeled with new cabinets, counters, stoves, dishwasher, ice machine, and a second walk-in refrigerator was added. A three-bedroom, modern residence for the manager was also constructed, with an independent water system and modern sewage treatment plant.

A total of 18,056 persons attended camp, 1970-79, with 3,139 decisions registered. Most of these were professions of faith in Christ, but many volunteered for full-time Christian service.

THEODORE K. ROBERTS

INSPIRATION, THEORY OF. Inspiration (Latin, *inspiro,* to breathe in) denotes the Holy Spirit's action upon people, enabling them to write God's revelation of himself, his will, and purpose (cf. 2 Pet. 1:21; 2 Tim. 3:16). Southern Baptists largely reject the view of a heightening of man's natural powers. Generally they hold to the verbal plenary theory or the dynamic theory. The former sees the Spirit as inspiring the very words of Scripture, but usually denies the dictation concept. The latter holds that the Spirit inspired the writers and guarded them from error, allowing them to choose the words. Both see the writers' personalities in their particular work. They also agree that the product is the divinely inspired Word of God.

See also INSPIRATION, Vol. I; INSPIRATION OF THE SCRIPTURES, Vol. I.

HERSCHEL H. HOBBS

INTER-AGENCY COUNCIL (I, III). From 1958 until 1976, the Inter-Agency Council membership included heads of agencies, representatives of the boards of agencies, chief assistants to the heads of agencies, and designated program leaders. In 1976 the IAC was reorganized to include only the heads of agencies. Two auxiliary groups are directly responsible to the IAC: The Coordinating Committee and the Forum.

Membership of the Coordinating Committee varies in number from year to year. In 1980 it had 88 members. Organized into subcommittees and work groups, the committee meets two or three times annually in two-day meetings and conducts studies and conferences on various program interests. The forum, which meets annually to discuss major concerns of Southern Baptists, consists of combined IAC and Coordinating Committee memberships. The IAC meets once annually and on call to discuss questions of inter-agency concern, elects its own officers, and approves all officers nominated by the Coordinating Committee. SBC Bylaw 25 controls IAC work.

ALBERT MCCLELLAN

INTERFAITH WITNESS, HOME MISSION BOARD PROGRAM OF (cf. Nonevangelicals, Home Mission Board Program of Work Related to, Vol. III). The name of the Department of Work Related to Nonevangelicals changed to Interfaith Witness in 1970, and by 1980 the focus broadened to include other Protestants.

The objective of assisting Baptists to witness effectively to persons of other faiths is implemented through research and a variety of materials, conferences, and program suggestions. The department has sponsored dialogues with Buddhists, Jews, Muslims, Orthodox, Roman Catholics, the Reorganized Church of Jesus Christ of Latter Day Saints, and Lutherans (with North American Baptist Fellowship).

Department directors have been Joseph R. Estes, 1966-70; M. Thomas Starkes, 1970-74; and Glenn A. Igleheart, 1975- .

Other staff positions at the HMB have been held by William Burke (*q.v.*), 1966-69; Starkes, 1967-70; Kate Ellen Gruver, 1973-77; Peter Chen, 1978- ; C. B. Hastings, 1970- ; Gary H. Leazer, 1979- ; and William B. Mitchell, 1966-77, who also served as acting director in 1975.

Four regional missionary-directors promote the work in multistate sections of the country. Persons serving in this capacity have included Igleheart, 1968-75; A. Jase Jones, 1969-78; William R. McLin, 1968-79; Lloyd N. Whyte, 1970- ; George J. Sheridan, 1975- ; Maurice Smith, 1979- ; and A. L. McDaniel, Jr., 1980- . Chris D. Elkins served, 1977-79, as a consultant on the Unification Church.

GLENN A. IGLEHEART

INTERNATIONAL BULLETIN OF MISSIONARY RESEARCH. Published quarterly since 1977 by the Overseas Ministries Study Center, Ventnor, NJ, this has the largest circulation of all scholarly journals for mission studies. Established in 1950 as the *Occasional Bulletin* from the Missionary Research Library in New York City, it was joined by the *Gospel in Context* journal in 1980, and received its present name in 1981. The journal features scholarly articles on mission theology, history, and anthropology, and deals with a wide range of issues and concerns for persons involved in missionary work and study. It includes book reviews, policy statements from mission agencies, bibliographies, and checklists of journals and dissertations.

GERALD H. ANDERSON

INTERNATIONAL STUDENT MINISTRY. The name applied to most programs of ministry and witness to college and university students from other countries who are studying in the United States. The work focuses on students themselves but also includes family members who are with them. Nationally the responsibility for the work is assigned to the Sunday School Board through National Student Ministries, with some involvement of the Home and Foreign Mission Boards, Woman's Missionary Union, and the Brotherhood Commission.

Locally, the director of Baptist student ministries takes initiative for the work and develops special programs on campus, as well as through the churches. These programs include host families, teaching conversational English, and programs for international wives and children. Regional activities include state international student conferences and Christian international student conferences.

Friendship international houses, coordinated through National Student Ministries, host international students for 10 to 12 days during the Christmas holidays. In cooperation with the American Bible Society, Bibles are distributed to international students in their own language. In 1979 there were 263,938 international students on American campuses.

CHARLES M. ROSELLE

IOWA SOUTHERN BAPTIST FELLOWSHIP. The first Southern Baptist church in Iowa was organized near Anamosa on June 12, 1954. The Missouri Baptist Convention through Bruce Maples of the state staff, Harry B. Eates, and Everett Bryant furnished leadership.

Chapels were planted in Lineville and Ottumwa during 1955-56. Leadership included First Baptist Church, Princeton, MO; Harry Clifton; Clarence Dowell; First Baptist Church, Jefferson City, MO; and Earl O. Harding (q.v.), executive secretary of the Missouri Baptist Convention.

In 1956 North Grand River Association in Missouri allowed their missionary, Avery Wooderson, to spend one week a month working in Iowa. From 1960 until 1968 Wooderson served as superintendent of Iowa missions. Sixteen new churches and chapels resulted from his leadership.

The Iowa Southern Baptist Association was organized, Apr. 17, 1965, at the First Baptist Church, Winterset. Clarence Dowell was moderator; Wesley Lindsay, assistant moderator; Roy Davis, clerk-historian; and H. A. Lindberg, treasurer.

The Iowa Southern Baptist Fellowship was organized, Dec. 1, 1972, at Trinity Church, Des Moines, with David Holden, president; Elmer Hatfield, vice-president; John Hamilton, secretary; and James Potter, treasurer.

Home missionary David T. Bunch served as area and state director of missions, 1968-78. During that time the number of churches grew from 29 to 57, membership from 3,669 to 8,095, mission gifts from $63,111 to $198,004, and total gifts from $525,017 to $1,571,488.

Four associations were formed in 1975: North Central at Calvary Church, Marshalltown; South Central at Calvary Church, Leon; Eastern, now known as Great Rivers, at First Church, Bettendorf; and Western at Pioneer Church, Denison.

A. Wilson Parker became executive director of the Iowa Fellowship in 1979. His staff includes church development director Mike McCrocklin, language catalytic missionary Michael Roberts, Christian social ministries director Greg Whitetree, and three associational directors of missions: David Holden for Great Rivers, Lowell Houts for North Central, and Richard S. Lamborn for Western and South Central.

RICHARD S. LAMBORN and LOIS MOELLER LAMBORN

IRAN, MISSION IN (III). Mission work in Iran was temporarily suspended in 1979 due to the unsettled political situation. Four English-language Baptist fellowships were active in Tehran, Ahwaz, Isfahan, and Shiraz until 1978-79, when most American businessmen felt it wise to leave the country. Records show a total of 37 baptisms in 1978. The first Baptist church in Tehran was organized in 1973. The other groups functioned as affiliated missions.

ELISE NANCE BRIDGES

ISRAEL, MISSION IN (I, III). In 1980, 40 missionaries were engaged in various types of Christian service throughout Israel. At Petah Tigva the Baptist Village served as a conference center. A well-established school and church were located in Nazareth. In Haifa a Christian service training center was reactivated in 1979. Book stores operated in Jerusalem and Tel Aviv (in conjunction with an arts and crafts center). Missionaries were working in 6 churches, 16 preaching points, and 3 community and kindergarten centers.

ELISE NANCE BRIDGES

ITALY, MISSION IN (I, III). Italian Baptists have assumed responsibility for most denominational work, supported by the present group of 16 missionaries. The 1979 records listed 4,350 Baptists and an increase in baptisms. Thirteen students were enrolled in seminaries. An extensive expansion of radio broadcasting led to the establishment of a mass media center in Rome, where missionaries also worked in the Betania Center and English-language church. The publications center there was closed in 1978. The Filadelfia Center in Rivoli sponsored a mobile evangelistic unit, education by extension, a linguistic institute, and classes in theology. Missionaries also served in other pastoral support ministries.

ELISE NANCE BRIDGES

IVORY COAST, MISSION IN (III). Since 1970 when eight missionaries were assigned to the capital, Abidjan, missionaries, now totaling 28, have entered Bouake, Daloa, and San Pedro. The emphasis on church planting and growth has produced 52 churches and preaching points with a membership of 3,032 in 1979. Contributing to this growth were social minis-tries, a music ministry, agricultural-evangelism, Theological Education by Extension, a Bible correspondence school, and a flourishing dental center. Abidjan was also the location for publi-cation and media ministries, which served all of French-speaking West Africa. A new building serving these ministries was dedicated in 1979. Associational work for Nigerians living in Ivory Coast was reactivated, and a new association for French-speaking language churches was begun.

JOHN E. MILLS

J

JACKSON, MARQUIS DEWITT (b. Wauchula, FL, Jan. 22, 1898; d. Jacksonville, FL, Jan. 1, 1978). Pastor. Son of William Edgar Jackson and Rosetta Bethea Jackson, farmers, he attended Baptist Bible Institute (now New Orleans Baptist Theological Seminary), Stetson Academy, and the University of Florida. On June 9, 1918, he married Theressa Katherine Fredericks. They had three children: Orville, Etoile, and Evelyn.

Jackson served churches in several Florida cities, including Callahan, Jacksonville, Seville, Fort Meade, Gainesville, Davenport, LaBelle, Nocatee, Greenville, Orlando, Longwood, and Edgewater. In 1931 he left the pastorate to care for his widowed mother and younger brothers. Later he returned to the pastorate and contin-ued until his retirement in 1965. He served as recording secretary of the Florida Baptist Con-vention, 1940-65. On his retirement, the Florida Baptist Convention *Annual* was dedicated to him.

EVELYN J. PAGE

JACOBS, ROXIE MARIE (b. Sweetwater, TN, Aug. 9, 1894; d. Sweetwater, TN, July 14, 1979). State convention worker. The daughter of ·Jefferson Pryor and Mary Sands Jacobs, farmers, she was educated at Christianburg, TN, Grammar School; Monroe County, TN, High School; and Carson-Newman College (B.A., 1915). Carson-Newman recognized her with the Distinguished Alumni Award in 1970. In 1920, Jacobs began working with the Tennes-see Baptist Convention as bookkeeper and assis-tant editor of the *Baptist and Reflector*. In 1923, she became Baptist Young People's Union Junior-Intermediate leader. She worked with such state convention leaders as W. D. Hudgins (*q.v.*), William H. Preston, Henry Rogers, and Charles L. Norton during the more than 34 years that she served Tennessee Baptists. She is buried in Christianburg Baptist Church ceme-tery.

JOHNNIE HALL

JAMAICA, MISSION IN (I, III). Dottson and Betty (Frink) Mills served as representa-tives to the Jamaica Baptist Union from 1963 to 1975. Daniel and Betty Alice (Cowan) Carroll served as religious education specialists, 1970-73. The Caribbean Bible Lessons editorial office opened in Kingston in 1975, with Clifford and Helen (Ashford) Graham serving as the first editorial administrators. In 1976 Morris and Joyce (Hickman) Wright transferred from Japan to assume duties due to Graham's illness. Raymond Anglin was appointed by the union in 1976 to serve as Christian education coordina-tor. Heckford and Herma Sharpe were ap-pointed by the union to Grenada in 1977. They serve as partners with Southern Baptist mission-aries there.

MORRIS J. WRIGHT

JAMES, EWING STANFORD (b. Butler, OK, Mar. 1, 1900; d. Dallas, TX, Apr. 26, 1976). Editor and denominational leader. Son of Albert D. James, teacher-farmer, and Soph-ronia Turner James, he married Opal Clark, Leedey, OK, Sep. 1, 1925. Their children were Mrs. Leroy Daniel, Mrs. Shirley Young, Billy, and Jo Anne.

James spent his early years working on farms and in oil fields and teaching until age 21 when he made a profession of faith, Butler, OK. He soon decided "God wanted all I had" and mixed preaching with public school teaching while attending Southwestern Technological College in Oklahoma (A.B., 1926). His first full-time pastorate was First Church, Liberal,

KS, 1928-30. He resigned for theological study but en route to Southwestern Baptist Theological Seminary, he stopped at Cisco, TX, visited the pastorless First Baptist Church, was invited to preach, and was quickly called as pastor. He served this church seven years and then 17 years, 1930-54, at First Church, Vernon, TX.

Elected editor of the *Baptist Standard,* 1954, he soon became known for his orthodox theology, his commitment to separation of church and state, and his criticism of Baptist agencies when he believed they were wrong. He wielded profound influence as an editor. He served as second vice-president of the SBC, 1961-62.

James lacked a formal theological education but compensated by constant study and wide reading. He received the D.D. degree from Howard Payne College, 1936, and Hardin-Simmons University, 1945. When he retired, Nov. 1, 1966, the *Standard* circulation had increased during his 12-year editorship from 281,000 to 368,000, and it had assets of $1,184,000. He is buried in the Vernon, TX, cemetery.

JOHN J. HURT

JANES, HORACE LEE (b. Paris, TN, Mar. 23, 1896; d. Tulsa, OK, Sep. 24, 1972). The son of Edward Wesley and Lillie Westcott Janes, he married Rubye Mae Cooper, Sep. 10, 1916. They had three children: Dathel, Edwina, and Arline. He attended Hall-Moody Institute and Union University in Tennessee before moving to Oklahoma in 1922. His service included pastorates at Texhoma, Cordell, Hobart, Henryetta, and Elk City, all in Oklahoma. In 1954 he began a 14-year tenure with Oklahoma's Baptist Foundation, retiring in 1962. He is buried in Memorial Park Cemetery, Edmond, OK.

J. M. GASKIN

JANIES, AMADIE (b. Richard, LA, July 4, 1897; d. Eunice, LA, Dec. 9, 1972). Pastor and French missionary. Son of Jerome Janies and Slavie Cormier, farmers, he married Amanda Sonier on Dec. 26, 1917. They had five children: Carrley, Lovinie, Verna, Eldine, and LeRoy. Converted from Roman Catholicism as a young adult, he was educated at Acadia Baptist Academy. He served as pastor at Church Point, Evangeline, Crowley French Mission, Lejeune Memorial, Mamou, and Chataignier, all in Louisiana. He served as a French missionary for the Evangeline Association when Baptist work was started in several south Louisiana towns. He is buried in Mt. Calvary Cemetery, Eunice, LA.

CHARLES R. EDWARDS

JAPAN, MISSION IN (I, III). A five-year effort from 1972 to 1977 enabled the Japan Baptist Convention to achieve a self-supporting operating budget. Self-support gave the convention more confidence and a sense of urgency in evangelistic outreach. The mission adopted and initiated a goal-oriented plan of organization and operation with a program base design. An exchange program between Seinan University and Baylor University began in 1972. Jordan Press exceeded $3,000,000 in annual sales as the second largest Christian publishing company in Japan. The decade ended with 180 churches, 75 preaching points, and a membership of 25,485. At the end of 1979, 154 missionaries were under appointment, including 17 journeymen.

GEORGE H. HAYS

JENKINS, JAMES LINEBERRY (b. Stanly County, NC, July 16, 1883; d. Boiling Springs, NC, Mar. 21, 1973). Minister and educator. Son of Lewis and Elizabeth (Littleton) Jenkins, farmers, he married Kate Watson, Jan. 2, 1918. They had four children. An alumnus of Wake Forest College (B.A., 1910), he attended The Southern Baptist Theological Seminary. He served the North Carolina Baptist State Convention for two years as an evangelist. He served as pastor in Parkton, NC; Umatilla, FL; and Boiling Springs, NC, 1927-52.

Jenkins was professor of religion, 1930-45, and president, 1932-35, of Boiling Springs Junior College. He also served as a teacher and counselor at Fruitland Bible Institute for nearly 20 years and as president of the North Carolina Baptist Pastors' Conference. He is buried in Spring Hill Cemetery near Wagram, NC.

JAY JENKINS

JESUS CHRIST, TEACHING OF. Also referred to as proclamation of Jesus and in the early church as "words of the Lord." Certain radical scholars, preeminently Rudolf Bultmann, have taken the position that very little of the actual words of Jesus can be recovered. Other scholars, however, such as T. W. Manson and Joachim Jeremias, have resolutely resisted such an unwarranted conclusion. Critical scholars, as Norman Perrin, have established three criteria for authenticity (dissimilarity, coherence, and multiple attestation). Birger Gerhardsson has raised the significant possibility that the disciples "listened" like the students of rabbis.

The core of the Lord's words clearly centers in the eschatological announcement of the coming Kingdom of God (Mark 1:15). The idea is present in the Old Testament (as Dan. 4:34). This reign of God refers to the will of God on earth, as in the memorable parallelism in the Lord's Prayer (Matt. 6:10). Through the parables Jesus spoke of the rule of God through metaphors of God (king, father, and householder). Jesus portrayed the Kingdom as both catastrophic in import and gracious in character. Both faith and repentance were expected. The Kingdom was already fulfilled (Luke 11:20) but not yet fulfilled completely (Mark 14:25).

The teachings merit a major place in Christian theology, because of their stress on sovereignty and radical discipleship.

See also JESUS CHRIST, Vol. I.

PETER RHEA JONES

JOHENNING BAPTIST CENTER. See DISTRICT OF COLUMBIA BAPTIST CONVENTION.

JOHNS, THOMAS MAXWELL (b. Headland, AL, Sep. 22, 1898; d. Greenville, SC, Oct. 29, 1977). State children's home executive. Son of John and Ella (Horn) Johns, farmers, he attended Troy Normal School, Troy, AL, and the University of Florida. Johns married Susie Elizabeth Spires on Feb. 12, 1921. They had one son, John Edwin. He taught history in central Florida schools for 10 years before becoming superintendent of Florida Baptist Children's Home in 1932. During his 37 years of ministry, Johns cared for 6,008 children.

He and his wife led the home as it moved from Arcadia to Lakeland in 1945 and built an extensive campus of 15 buildings for the care of dependent and neglected children. During the 1950s a vocational training program was established along with casework services, foster care, and family-style cottages. Johns led the way in decentralizing services with the establishment of a 36-bed home for children in Miami, FL, in 1958.

He was past president and a charter member of the Florida Group Child Care Association, which pioneered licensing standards for child care in Florida. Johns was also a past president of the Southern Baptist Child Care Executives Association. He was elected president of the Florida Baptist Convention in 1965. He is buried in Memorial Gardens, Lakeland, FL.

WALTER R. DELAMARTER

JOHNSON, CHARLES D. (b. Banner, MS, May 27, 1888; d. Monticello, AR, Oct. 19, 1977). Educator. Son of Charles Albert Johnson, a physician, and Evangeline Howell Johnson, he married Calude Jaudon Eager of Belton, TX, Nov. 26, 1913. They had one child, Charles.

Johnson attended Mississippi College (A.B., 1910; A.M., 1916; L.L.D., 1950), State University of Iowa (Ph.D., 1921), and Mercer University (Litt.D., 1953). His career from 1916 to 1962 included positions as professor, department chairman, dean, and president at Ouachita Baptist College, Arkansas Agricultural and Mechanical College, Blue Mountain College, and Baylor University. He established and edited publications and founded college departments, professional and scholastic fraternities, social clubs, and southwide literary organizations. Major contributions to the SBC were his service as chairman of the Education Commission, 1932-53, and his book, *Higher Education of Southern Baptists* (1955). He is buried in Oakland Cemetery, Monticello, AR.

DENNIS M. DODSON

JOHNSTON, GLADYS ATKINSON (b. Spartanburg, SC, Mar. 24, 1901; d. Honea Path, SC, July 17, 1967). Philanthropist. The daughter of Minnie Atkinson and Edward Atkinson, railroad worker, she attended Anderson Junior College (B.A., 1924). She married Olin D. Johnston (*q.v.* III), Dec. 27, 1924. They had three children: Olin D., Jr., Sallie, and Gladys. Her husband was governor of South Carolina, 1935-39, 1942-44, and United States senator, 1944-63. A trustee of Anderson Junior College, she gave $250,000 to the college to build a library as a memorial to her husband. She is buried at Honea Path, SC.

JOHN HUSS

JONES, JOSEPHINE PROCTOR (b. Lancaster, KY, Sep. 4, 1902; d. Jacksonville, FL, Dec. 3, 1974). Woman's Missionary Union leader. Daughter of Joseph and Susan Pittman Jones, farmers, she grew up in Danville, KY, attending Center College, Danville (A.B., 1925), and WMU Training School (M.R.E., 1927). She devoted her life to missions education through WMU as an employed WMU director, Birmingham (AL) Baptist Association, 1927-29; Young People's secretary, Kentucky WMU, 1929-42; executive secretary, WMU, Illinois Baptist State Association, 1943-44; and executive secretary, Florida WMU, 1944-67.

Jones was sensitive to the needs of all people, particularly foreign-born and black Americans. She began an interracial dialogue between herself and the presidents of the women's missions organizations of the three black conventions that were active in Florida during the 1960s when racial tension was at its height. This dialogue resulted in a conference on missions and fellowship.

She was one of four writers of the first *Round Table Group Guide* and wrote articles for various WMU publications. The Josephine P. Jones Chapel at Camp North, Lake Yale Baptist Assembly, and the Josephine Proctor Jones Memorial Scholarship established at Southern Baptist Theological Seminary continue to influence missions education. She is buried in Brookside Cemetery, Campbellsville, KY.

ELIZABETH PAINTER and VANITA BALDWIN

JONES, ROBERT STANLEY (b. Murray, KY, Feb. 11, 1889; d. Murray, KY, May 19, 1960). Director of annuity investments. The son of L. Clint and Delilah T. (Rogers) Jones, he was converted at age 12. He graduated from Baylor University (A.B.) and Southwestern Baptist Theological Seminary (Th.B., M.R.E.). He married Mary Ruth Bowden of Memphis, TN, July 21, 1920. Their children were Kathleen and Mary Ruth. In Aug., 1920, the couple went to Brazil as missionaries. Bronchial pneumonia forced him to retire from the mission field in 1930.

Jones became associate secretary, Foreign Mission Board, SBC, in 1933. The Relief and Annuity Board, SBC, employed him in 1943 as associate secretary to direct its relief ministry. In 1954 this agency appointed him acting treasurer-investment director. Later when a treasurer was named, Jones continued as director of investments until he retired in 1958. He is buried in the cemetery of First Baptist Church, Murray, KY.

LARRY CRISMAN

JORDAN, MISSION IN (I, III). During the 1970s Baptists intensified their witness in Amman, the capital city. A Baptist elementary school opened in 1974. Property was bought for a Baptist center, which included a church and offices for the Baptist convention and the mission. The book store continued its ministry of literature distribution and evangelism. In the village of Ajloun, where Baptist work began, the hospital reduced its beds from 50 to 30, and many of the more serious cases were referred to new government hospitals. The school of nursing was discontinued because of the lack of qualified students. The girls' school continued its work. In 1979 the eight Baptist churches of Jordan had 318 members and 51 baptisms. Thirty-two missionaries were working in the institutions and churches.

J. D. HUGHEY

JOURNAL OF CHURCH AND STATE. A scholarly journal concerned with the subject of church and state, published by J. M. Dawson Studies in Church and State, Baylor University, Waco, TX. Founded Nov., 1959, as *A Journal of Church and State,* a semiannual publication, and expanded to three issues per year in 1964, its title changed to *Journal of Church and State* in Feb., 1970. The journal includes articles and other materials related to religious liberty and church and state. A regular nation-by-nation compilation of religious liberty and church-state occurrences was added in May, 1960, and a list of "Recent Doctoral Dissertations in Church and State" became a standard feature in June, 1965. James E. Wood, Jr. (1959-73,1980-   ), and James Leo Garrett, Jr. (1774-79), have served as editors.

EDWARD N. CURTIS

JUDSON COLLEGE (I, III). The purpose of Judson College, an Alabama Baptist senior liberal arts college for women, remains essentially

the same as it was when established in 1838—to provide a quality education in a Christian atmosphere. Academic features include a two-year, 10-month baccalaureate degree program, professional internships, ROTC in cooperation with Marion Military Institute, and the first air traffic control specialist program requested of a women's college by the Federal Aeronautics Administration. The latest academic innovation is a minor in Christian missions.

The campus includes buildings of Williamsburg type architecture, stables, and a lake. The newest structure is the Bessie Mills Mead Hall Home Economics Building (1978). Norman H. McCrummen became president in 1970. A native of Montgomery, he was educated at Mercer University and The Southern Baptist Theological Seminary and held pastorates in Alabama.

NORMAN H. McCRUMMEN

JUDSON COLLEGE (Elgin, IL). Founded in 1963, this Christian, liberal arts college with studies leading to a bachelor of arts degree, uses a trimester calendar. Close to 500 students attend classes on the 75-acre campus in Elgin, a city of 62,000, located 40 miles west of Chicago.

Division majors are Christian religion and philosophy, communication arts, fine arts, science-mathematics, human relations, and human institutions. Special vocationally oriented programs exist in business administration, communications, computer programming, human services, laboratory technique, and paraministerial services, as well as a teacher education sequence in elementary, secondary, art, music, and physical education.

Extracurricular programs include intramural and intercollegiate sports, newspaper and yearbook, student government, music and drama, and community service. Chapel is held three days a week with required attendance. The college prohibits smoking, dancing, alcoholic beverages, and illegal drugs. Faculty and administrators have all professed Christ as Lord and Savior.

The college cooperates with Southern Baptists and other Baptist groups.

H. EVERETT ANTHONY

K

KANSAS ASSOCIATIONS (I, III). See Kansas-Nebraska Associations.

KANSAS CONVENTION OF SOUTHERN BAPTISTS (I, III). See Kansas-Nebraska Convention of Southern Baptists.

KANSAS-NEBRASKA ASSOCIATIONAL CAMPS. At least five associations in the Kansas-Nebraska Convention of Southern Baptists have owned and operated their own camps. They are Tri-County, Sedgwick, Twin Valley, Blue Stem, and Central.

Tri-County Baptist Camp. The first associational camp in Kansas was purchased by Tri-County Baptist Association. In 1960 the association bought 80 acres located on State Highway 103, two miles west of Weir, KS, at a cost of $1,200. On Aug. 11, 1960, the executive board of the association adopted ground plans, including a plat of lots and utility lines.

Approval was given at the 1961 meeting of the association for a tabernacle to be built, and to proceed with fencing, water, and sewerage work. A frame dining hall was built in 1962 with a loan secured from the Church Loan Association of Kansas Southern Baptists. The first camps were held that summer. In subsequent years a brick and metal dining hall was constructed.

In 1980, 10 churches owned cabins at the camp. The camp has sleeping facilities for 120 persons. The camp and association are debt free. James Shope, director of missions, serves as camp manager.

Shiloh Baptist Assembly. In the 1962 annual meeting of Sedgwick Baptist Association, an assembly committee reported that "about 50 acres of beautiful, wooded area on the north bank of the Arkansas River" was available for associational assembly grounds. The annual associational missions offering in 1963 was taken for development of the assembly grounds. This, along with an initial offering of $2,500 and a bank loan of $7,500, was used to purchase the land.

Sixty different groups used the assembly grounds in 1964. Receipts that year were in excess of $3,000. A contract was let that year for $47,000 to build the first building on the grounds. Two cabins and a swimming area were constructed in 1968. A total of 1,155 persons from 49 different groups used the facilities in 1969.

The board of directors reported major remodeling under way in 1979 at a cost of more than $26,500. While the assembly is now known as Shiloh Baptist Assembly, it was called the Russell Conference Center before 1970. Ray Emery is chairman of the board of directors.

Camp Mitchell. Central Baptist Association purchased the old Mitchell School directly across the street from Mitchell Baptist Chapel for use as a camp. The property, consisting of 4.2 acres, was bought for $1,000. This provided a gym, restrooms, showers, kitchen, and five classrooms. Records indicate that camps as large as 100 persons used the facilities the first year it was opened in 1969. Mitchell Chapel gave permission to use their building for worship services.

Extensive remodeling was undertaken in 1974. The cost was only $3,000 as much of the labor was volunteer. The 1974 report to the association referred to a study of the feasibility of continued ownership and use of the camp. During the 1975 annual meeting of the association, the camp was sold for $2,500.

Virgil Baptist Assembly. Twin Valley Association scheduled Royal Ambassador, Girls' Auxiliary, and youth camps at Cedar Bluff Camp, located north of Coffeyville, for the summer of 1970. However, in the February meeting of the executive board, the association joined with Blue Stem Association in accepting as a gift the Virgil School at Virgil, KS.

The camp consists of a three-story brick school building. The building is equipped with steam heat and can be used any time of the year. Sleeping facilities can accommodate 100 campers comfortably. This building is officially known as Locke Hall in honor of Gerald Locke, director of missions at the time the assembly was acquired.

The brick gym on the assembly is usable, but needs work. In 1973 a loan of $6,200 was obtained and a swimming pool was constructed. The loan has since been paid off. The assembly has ample room for a ball field, archery range, and a playground area.

The facilities are used at least four weeks each year by the camps of the associations. In 1976, 679 campers used the facilities. They are also used by several churches in the association and by outside church groups.

The assembly is governed by a board consisting of the moderator, missionary, and three members of the missions committees of Blue Stem and Twin Valley Associations. Gerald Locke, director of missions, serves as camp manager.

JAMES H. SHOPE

KANSAS-NEBRASKA ASSOCIATIONS (cf. Kansas Associations, Vols. I, III).

I. New Associations. Western Kansas.

Formed Oct. 1, 1970, by combining Southern Plains and part of High Plains Associations. High Plains churches joining Western Kansas were First of St. Francis, First of Oberlin, First Southern of Goodland, and Southern Baptist Chapel of Colby. Six other churches from High Plains joined Central Association: First Southern of Hays, First Southern of Hill City, Trinity of Hoisington, First Southern of Plainville, First Southern of Russell, and First of Wakeeny. In 1979, 14 churches reported 313 baptisms, 2,924 members, $508,585 total gifts, $60,049 mission gifts, and $3,307,532 property value.

II. Changes in Associations. HIGH PLAINS. Organized in 1954, the association disbanded in 1970. Six of its churches joined Central Association. Four helped form Western Kansas Association.

SOUTHERN PLAINS. Organized in 1954, the association disbanded to form Western Kansas Association in 1970.

See also KANSAS-NEBRASKA ASSOCIATIONAL CAMPS.

ROBERT E. SMITH and JAMES SHOPE

KANSAS-NEBRASKA BAPTIST STUDENT WORK. Kansas-Nebraska Baptists had student work on 11 college campuses in 1969. There were no employed campus directors. Harold Inman, state director of campus ministry, worked with the volunteer directors, including C. F. Craighead at Coffeyville Junior College, Steve Timken at Fort Hays State College, Bill Long at Garden City Junior College, Dallas Roark at Kansas State Teachers College at Emporia, Jim Martin at Omaha University, Fred Gibson at Ottawa University, and Yvonne Keefer at Kansas University at Lawrence.

Floyd Smith became full-time director at Emporia State University in 1974 following the service of volunteers Dallas Roark, 1968-73, and Larry Duncan, 1973-74. Linda Blain became associate there in 1976.

Yvonne Keefer has been director at the University of Kansas in Lawrence since 1969. Associates ministering to internationals have been Lana Church, 1973, Kent Gee, 1973-74, and Ben Broome, 1974-80. Luther Alexander was named associate there in 1978.

John Bolin served as part-time director at Kansas State University in Manhattan from the mid-1960s to 1973. Bob Anderson was named associate in 1972 and became the director in 1973. Judy Smith served as an associate, 1974-79.

Lana Church directed student work in the Kansas City schools, 1973-76. Jon Sapp became director at Washburn University of Topeka in 1977. Volunteers served Wichita State University until Jim Herron was employed in 1978. Brett Yohn became director at the University of Nebraska in 1972. Pam Nelson became an associate there in 1976. Norman Clampitt served the Omaha metropolitan area, 1975-79, and Ray Crawford came to direct the work in 1978.

R. Rex Lindsey succeeded Harold Inman as state director of campus ministry in 1971. Bob Anderson and Brett Yohn became associates for Kansas and Nebraska, respectively, in 1978. The executive secretary for the work is Yvonne Keefer of Lawrence. In 1979 all except two of the four-year institutions in the two-state area with more than 5,000 enrolled had one or more campus ministers.

YVONNE KEEFER

KANSAS-NEBRASKA CONVENTION OF SOUTHERN BAPTISTS (cf. Kansas Convention of Southern Baptists, Vols. I, III).

I. History. Official action to change the name of the convention to the Kansas-Nebraska Convention of Southern Baptists was initiated in 1972 and approved, Nov. 7, 1973.

In Aug., 1969, the Kansas Securities Commission had placed the convention under a five-member board of managers. The board of managers reported that the convention needed to raise $1,600,000 to underwrite the deficit of the Church Loan Association. A program called "Strengthen Our Witness" was started to raise the necessary funds. The Stewardship Commission, SBC, gave assistance. Raising the needed monies involved selling the state office building in Wichita, KS, and receiving financial help from the Home Mission Board. Conventions in other states pledged $489,675. In a five-year period they gave $268,500 to the program. Churches within the state convention pledged $672,109. In a five-year period they gave $517,400. Stronger churches gave additional money to churches within the convention which were delinquent with their payments. During the period regular gifts through the Cooperative Program increased annually.

On Dec. 31, 1973, Church Loan Association bonds and coupons were called for payment. Assets and liabilities were transferred to the state convention. Loan payments from the churches are being handled through the Kansas (later Kansas-Nebraska) Southern Baptist Foundation.

In 1974 the convention staff requested a HMB study concerning the constituency of the two-state convention.

The study revealed that the bulk of the convention's membership (92 percent of the resident members and 82.3 percent of the churches) was located within a 150-mile radius of Topeka, KS. Authorization was given in the 1974 convention to begin the process of moving the state convention offices to Topeka.

The 1975 convention authorized a $400,000 loan, and launched a program called "Debt Free in Three" to raise $520,000. A contract was let by the Executive Board of the convention in Apr., 1976, to build a new Baptist building in Topeka. Ground-breaking ceremonies were held May 14, 1976, at 5410 West 7th Street in Topeka. More than $100,000 was pledged through the campaign. However, only about $84,000 was finally realized.

The convention entered the new building in Aug., 1977. The building was dedicated Nov. 8, in connection with the 32nd annual meeting of the convention.

James C. (Pat) McDaniel resigned as executive director of the convention, July 31, 1977, to accept a position with the Annuity Board, SBC, and was succeeded by Richard Rex Lindsay, state missions director, who was elected in the 1977 annual convention.

II. Program of Work. The convention's Executive Board has 36 members. At least three of the 12 members elected annually must be other than pastors. No salaried employee of the convention or any of its agencies is eligible to serve on the board.

The Executive Board has an executive committee of eight persons plus the elected officers. Four members are elected annually for a two-year term. The committee functions as the Personnel and the Finance Committees of the convention.

Other committees of the Executive Board include Missions, Student Work, and Brotherhood. The Missions Committee has nine members from the Executive Board with directors of missions serving as ex-officio members. The Brotherhood Committee is composed of the elected director from each association and is responsible to the Executive Board.

The convention first elected a Historical Commission in 1971. Two members are elected annually by the convention. The commission reports to the convention annually. A Historical Society was started in 1975. The society was authorized to publish, "at least annually," a paper called "The Kansas-Nebraska Baptist Story." The first issue was printed in 1976.

Areas of responsibility and ministry within the convention are as follows: The executive director, R. Rex Lindsay, works in the areas of Administration, Stewardship, and Campus Ministries. Harry R. Taylor, director of the Church Music Department, also works in Church Administration and Church Recreation. Harold Inman, director of the Church Teaching Department, works with Sunday School, Church Training, and Church Architecture. Dewey Hickey, director of Church Extension, works with the Brotherhood as well as with pastor-directors, pastors receiving pastoral aid, and language missionaries. John F. Hopkins, field consultant in Christian Social Ministries, also serves as editor of the *Baptist Digest*. Viola Webb, director of Woman's Missionary Union, works with media centers and with internationals. Harold L. Conley serves as director of stewardship as well as business administrator-comptroller for the convention and of the Baptist Foundation. Rennie Berry, director of evangelism, also serves in the area of Family Ministries. Terry McIlvain serves as evangelism intern in the area of Youth Evangelism. Deliberate effort is made to keep the state staff small in order to provide more field missionaries and services. Major emphasis during this decade has been on persons rather than on property and buildings.

Associational Missions. — The state convention, with assistance from the HMB, supplements the salaries of 10 directors of missions who function in 12 associations in the two-state area. These directors are employed by their respective associations. The associations set the salaries and job descriptions.

Directors of missions function with the executive director in planning, setting goals and directions, and evaluating programs of action. They function with the Missions Committee of the Executive Board in setting mission strategy, budgets, and activities.

Language Missions. — In 1970 three Spanish pastors served in the convention. Language Missions was also involved in an Indian ministry at Haskell Institute in Lawrence, KS, with Sam Morris as director. Donald Otwell ministered to the deaf in Kansas City, KS. Pat Heriford directed that work in 1979. The Language Mission Department in the 1970s assisted churches in beginning eight new Spanish missions of which six survived as churches or church-type missions. In 1978 the first Asian mission was begun. Moon Gong Hong is pastor of the Korean Baptist Church of Central Kansas in Junction City.

Christian Social Ministries. — Three mission centers were in operation at the beginning of the 1970s: Omaha Baptist Center, Omaha, NB, the Duane McCormicks, directors; Pine Ridge Baptist Center, Topeka, the Charles Rankins, directors; and Good Neighbor Center, Wichita, Dorothy Milam, director. The Youth and Family Services ministry was active in Topeka, Kaw Valley Baptist Association, John Cromer, director; Kansas City Baptist Association, John Hopkins, director; and Sedgwick Association, Harry Moratto, director. C. H. Rankin died, July 8, 1972, and Eugene Kreiger moved to Topeka to direct the Pine Ridge Center until his resignation in 1978. The Larry Erwins became directors of the Pine Ridge Center in 1979. Dorothy Milam resigned in 1976, and the Good Neighbor Center in Wichita came under the direction of Cheryl Sorrels. John Hopkins resigned in 1974 as director of Youth and Family Services for the Kansas Baptist Association, to become area consultant in Christian Social Ministries for the convention. Robert T. Mills, who earlier functioned in an intern program with the association and Midwestern Baptist Theological Seminary, became director of Christian Social Ministries in that association. He resigned in Feb., 1979, to become pastor of First Baptist Church of Bethel, Kansas City, KS. Les Arnold was employed in Aug., 1979, as Mission Action/Ministries associate. Steve Aycock, in 1977, became the associate director for Mission Action for the Western Kansas Association, a newly created position.

Woman's Missionary Union. — The WMU work of the convention has been led by Viola W. Webb since July, 1957. Norma Briggs served as

KANSAS-NEBRASKA STATISTICAL SUMMARY

Year	Associations	Churches	Church Membership	Baptisms	SS Enrollment	VBS Enrollment	CT Enrollment	WMU Enrollment	Brotherhood Enrollment	Ch. Music Enrollment	Mission Gifts	Total Gifts	Value Church Property
1969	13	198	53,210	2,403	40,536	20,053	18,303	6,968	2,373	4,987	$ 555,664	$ 4,495,614	$19,631,134
1970	13	200	54,779	2,393	39,211	21,691	17,630	6,560	1,867	5,276	648,395	4,693,040	20,291,959
1971	13	200	55,497	2,671	37,967	21,480	14,297	6,263	2,062	5,405	847,777	4,919,635	20,616,640
1972	13	198	57,666	3,105	38,519	21,914	13,703	6,021	2,016	5,932	867,760	5,303,752	21,361,997
1973	13	200	59,366	2,726	40,641	23,654	12,773	5,816	2,267	5,716	1,003,571	5,749,738	23,364,968
1974	13	204	61,246	2,850	39,579	22,695	12,023	5,438	2,172	5,510	1,015,343	6,601,027	25,877,892
1975	13	208	62,348	2,625	38,711	22,567	11,112	5,462	1,964	6,343	1,187,508	7,433,174	29,574,140
1976	12	210	64,194	2,653	41,975	19,821	11,582	5,375	2,086	6,614	1,416,552	8,582,742	34,977,618
1977	12	208	64,541	2,284	41,497	19,281	10,631	5,144	1,979	6,866	1,476,939	9,200,008	38,563,619
1978	12	213	66,263	2,260	40,942	19,262	10,952	5,071	2,040	6,999	1,655,461	10,348,423	44,049,649
1979	12	211	68,035	2,552	40,221	20,011	10,320	5,149	1,891	7,080	1,774,944	11,577,062	49,790,358
1980	12	219	69,584	3,021	41,909	19,097	10,478	5,278	2,062	7,378	2,106,921	13,619,105	54,943,818

state president, 1969-71. There were 6,844 persons enrolled in 1969. Mission offerings that year were $48,842 for the Lottie Moon Christmas Offering, $5,599 for the state mission offering, and $2,950 for Strengthen Our Witness Offerings.

The 25th Anniversary of WMU in the state convention was observed in 1971. Opal Bates was elected president of the state organization. She served until 1976.

The first statewide Acteens retreat was held in 1972 in the Immanuel Baptist Church of Wichita with 300 girls attending. Several Acteens from the state convention churches attended the first National Acteens Conference held at Glorieta in 1972.

Maxine Barber served as WMU president, 1976-78. Renoma Foster succeeded her in 1979. Enrollment in mission organizations totaled 5,135 in 1979. Mission offerings in 1979 were $155,658 for Lottie Moon Christmas Offering, $93,523 for Annie Armstrong Easter Offering, and $44,809 for state missions.

Baptist Digest.—The official publication of the convention is the *Baptist Digest*. James C. (Pat) McDaniel served as managing editor along with his duties as executive director of the convention until Nov. 1, 1973. Lynn P. Clayton became editor in Nov., 1973, and served until July 15, 1978. He resigned to become editor of the *Baptist Message*, the Louisiana Baptist newspaper. John Hopkins, who was already serving the convention in Christian Social Ministries and Brotherhood, became editor, July 22, 1978. Derek Taylor is associate editor in charge of production. Brenda Hall serves as editorial associate. The present circulation is 7,200.

DEWEY HICKEY and JAMES SHOPE

KANSAS-NEBRASKA SOUTHERN BAPTIST FOUNDATION. A nine-member board of directors operates the foundation. In 1970 the foundation's assets totaled $89,377, of which $66,335 were in land, buildings, and church bonds. Loans to churches totaled $9,864, of which the audit listed $4,580 as doubtful. The Revolving Building Loan Fund balance was $21,808. J. R. (Dick) Glenn, a board member, was chosen by the board to serve as executive secretary in 1970 and 1971.

In 1972 a study committee was chosen to make recommendations on the future of the foundation. The committee consisted of three members of the foundation board, three members of the convention executive board, with the president of the convention, H. E. Alsup, and the executive director of the convention, Pat McDaniel, as ex-officio members. The committee recommended that the foundation be continued but that changes be made. The Articles of Incorporation and Bylaws were revised, with provision for selecting an executive director. Instead of starting a new staff position, Pat McDaniel became executive director of the foundation. W. Robert Powell, administrative assistant of the convention, took the same position with the foundation.

ANITA WILSON

In 1974 "Nebraska" was added to the convention name. Known as the Kansas Southern Baptist Foundation since 1949, the foundation became Kansas-Nebraska Southern Baptist Foundation. The assets of the foundation had grown to $137,184.

The convention voted to call in all the bonds of the Church Loan Association, Dec. 31, 1973. This purchase was financed by gifts from churches, other conventions, the Kansas Convention, and loans. As the churches paid off their debts to the Kansas-Nebraska Convention, those funds were to be transferred to the foundation to be added to the Revolving Building Loan Fund. The foundation began receiving these funds in 1975. The assets of the foundation totaled $588,220, Dec. 31, 1975.

On July 31, 1977, Pat McDaniel and W. Robert Powell resigned their convention and foundation positions. In Oct., 1977, R. Rex Lindsey became executive director of the foundation. In Dec., 1977, Harold Conley became business administrator comptroller for the foundation.

The assets of the Church Loan Association continued to be transferred to the foundation as churches paid off their loans. Since the association made no new loans, the amount of funds coming to the foundation began to decline. The growth assets of the foundation were: 1976, $1,109,964; 1977, $1,466,726; 1978, $1,587,091; and 1979, $1,768,300.

The foundation has grown to be a powerful mission force in the convention. Of its $1,768,300 in assets in 1979, $1,475,232 were in its Revolving Building Loan Fund to help churches that could not secure commercial loans for building purposes. The interest from these loans is used in missions in Kansas-Nebraska. The foundation gave $105,019 to missions work in 1979.

See also KANSAS CONVENTION OF SOUTHERN BAPTISTS, VOLS. I, III.

DOYLE SMITH

KEITH, GLADYS (b. near Kilmichael, MS, Feb. 1, 1905; d. Kilmichael, MS, Aug. 19, 1970). Home missionary. Daughter of William Henry and Molly (Grantham) Keith, farmers, she attended Blue Mountain College (1925-28) and Baptist Bible Institute (B.R.E., 1944). She taught school in Mississippi for six years. In 1935 she went to work at Rachel Sims Mission in New Orleans, LA, and was appointed as a missionary by the Home Mission Board the following year. During her years of service, 1936-60, a new building was erected for Rachel Sims Mission, three other mission centers were developed, and a Baptist church was organized on the riverfront. After retirement, Keith lived in Mississippi. She is buried in the cemetery of the Kilmichael, MS, Baptist Church.

ELLA KELLER

KENTUCKY, GENERAL ASSOCIATION OF BAPTISTS IN (I). See KENTUCKY BAPTIST CONVENTION.

KENTUCKY ASSOCIATIONS (I, III).

I. New Associations. GRAYSON COUNTY: Organized in Dec., 1969, by the following Twin Lakes Association churches: Caneyville, Clarkson, Leitchfield First, and Holly. Goshen Association churches Little Clifty, Pleasant Run, and Shrewsbury joined Grayson County in 1972. In 1975 Goshen Association churches Liberty and New Hope joined this fellowship. In 1980 nine churches reported 28 baptisms, 2,100 members, $268,462 total gifts, and $69,041 mission gifts.

II. Changes in Associations. TWIN LAKES: Organized in 1962, it was dissolved in 1969 when its churches organized Grayson County Association.

·A. B. COLVIN

KENTUCKY BAPTIST BOARD OF CHILD CARE (III). The Pine Crest Children's Home in Morehead, KY, closed in 1972 due to the changing needs over the state. The board presently operates the two remaining homes, Spring Meadows and Glen Dale, and regional offices in Louisville, Lexington, and Madisonville to process applications for service. It also provides a statewide network of foster homes and a residence for unwed mothers in Louisville, opened in 1976. Corresponding with that ministry was the reopening of the adoption program, which had been closed in 1972, to place infants with appropriate families in Kentucky. Following the retirement of C. Ford Deusner as the second general superintendent of the agency, William E. Amos succeeded him in 1972.

WILLIAM E. AMOS

KENTUCKY BAPTIST CONVENTION (III; cf. Kentucky, General Association of Baptists in, Vol. I).

I. Expansion and Development. As Kentucky Baptists entered the 1970s, the main focus was upon the completion of sufficient facilities at Cedarmore Assembly. The convention was faced with about $500,000 residual financial obligations carried over from the closing of Kentucky Southern College in 1969. This was paid off in 1974.

In the spring of 1972, a number of improvements were made at Cedarmore. These included reconstruction of the dam on the lake, building of new facilities like the faculty and administration building at Cedar Crest, new facilities at the youth camp section, and a new dining room at Camp RABRO for boys. These improvements and additions, costing about $568,000, were paid off by the middle of the decade. A debt on the Baptist Building (constructed in 1957) of $95,000 was paid off in July, 1977.

On Feb. 25, 1972, Franklin Owen, pastor of Calvary Baptist Church, Lexington, KY, was named executive secretary-treasurer elect. He worked jointly with Harold Sanders from June 1 until his retirement, Aug. 31, 1972.

Cooperative Program receipts in the fiscal

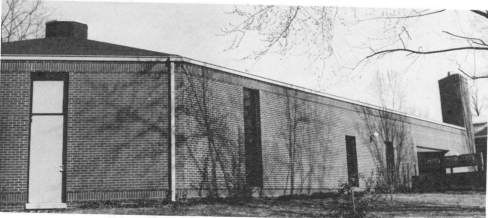

KENTUCKY BAPTIST STUDENT CENTERS. *Top:* Baptist Student Center, Northern Kentucky University, Highland Heights (purchased in 1974); *Center:* Baptist Student Center, University of Louisville (completed in 1974); *Bottom:* Baptist Student Center, University of Kentucky, Lexington (completed in 1978).

KENTUCKY BAPTIST CONVENTION (*q.v.*) BUILDING, Middletown. Enlarged in 1979, the 48,000-square foot structure houses offices of the convention staff, the state WMU, and the *Western Recorder.*

year Sep. 1, 1968, through Aug. 31, 1969, were $3,675,875. Receipts for the same general Cooperative Program fund in the fiscal year ending Aug. 31, 1979, were $8,577,206. This increase was continuing to accelerate as Kentucky Baptists entered the 1980s.

In 1974 the Executive Board purchased four acres east of the Baptist Building from the Board of Child Care. In 1979 two additional acres west of the building were purchased, completing an appropriate setting for the state convention offices.

In 1979 a new Baptist Building addition was completed. Three large office suites, five spacious committee rooms, an adequate chapel, and meeting room were created. All of the old building was refurbished. Adequate parking facilities were added. The cost of approximately $1,500,000 was paid partially from accumulated funds with the balance borrowed from the convention's own mission reserve funds.

During the decade, an Executive Board study resulted in the board's reorganization in a manner to work more closely with the board's division staff plan. The new committee structure matched the three staff divisions: Business and Finance, Church Services, and Missions. A Nominating and Program Evaluating Committee and a Committee on Agencies, to relate with agency heads, completed the structure except for the Administrative Committee which consists of the chairman of the five standing committees plus six members chosen by the Executive Board at large.

A new salary administration and wage program was adopted in 1979. This system further standardized remuneration, including provisions for objectifying modest individual merit wage increases in addition to overall cost-of-living adjustments.

II. Church Services Division. In 1972 a division committee was established to coordinate the work of the state departments that have organizations in the churches. Roy Boatwright, Sunday School director, served as chairman the first year, with James Whaley, Church Training director, serving as chairman the second year. In 1974, at the state convention in Paducah, the division concept was further implemented with Whaley elected as division coordinator. The division included these departments: Brotherhood, Camps and Assembly, Music, Church Training, Student Work, and Sunday School.

In 1974 the positions of preschool worker in the Sunday School Department and an associate in the Church Training Department were discontinued. At the same time, two positions, preschool/children's consultant and youth consultant, were added to the staff of the Church Services Division. These two staff members work primarily with the Sunday School and Church Training Departments. During the 1970s, the preschool and children's consultant was Betty Allnatt to 1975; Polly Hargis Dillard has served since 1977. John Carney served as

youth consultant, 1974-75, with Wanda Carpenter Dobbins serving, 1975-79.

Brotherhood Department.—Forrest R. Sawyer, who became director of the department in 1954, and Calvin Fields, who became the associate in the department in 1966, continue in these places of service. From 1970 to 1979, the number of churches with Brotherhood work increased from 617 to 701. In the latter part of this period, there was a substantial increase in men and boys involved in mission projects.

Camps and Assembly Department.—In 1971 Marvin Byrdwell retired as manager of Cedarmore Baptist Assembly. Arlis Hinson was elected to that position, serving until Apr., 1977. The assistant manager, Frank Heberlein, was elected director of the Camps and Assembly Department, holding that position until Mar., 1979. Upon the retirement of Heberlein, Marshall Phillips was elected as director of the department, which includes the management of Cedarmore.

Two swimming pools have been added since 1970, one at the boys' camp (Camp RABRO) and the other at the girls' camp (Cedar Crest). Recreation facilities have been improved. The latest addition is a nine-hole frisbee golf course, completed in 1979.

The organizational structure was changed in 1976, from being directed by the Kentucky Baptist Convention's Executive Board Assembly and Camps Committee to a department in the Church Services Division.

Church Music Department.—During the 1970s, music ministry enrollment in Kentucky Baptist churches grew from 44,273 in 1969 to 67,728 in 1979. The Kentucky Baptist Chorale, a ministers of music chorus formed in 1965, began concerts in the 1970s, highlighted by a European mission tour in May, 1979. The department is now sending summer music field workers to regional and associational camps, resulting in over 1,000 children studying music for a five-day period in each camp. Oct., 1973, marked the beginning of associational shoptalks, conferences for music directors, and other church music leaders. In 1979 a total of 1,059 attended from 501 churches in 58 associations. In May, 1977, Donald A. Spencer was employed as an associate. Eugene Francis Quinn continues as director.

Church Training Department.—James Whaley served as secretary-director, 1953-74. In 1974 he became the Church Services Division coordinator. Vernon Cole, associate since Aug., 1969, was elected director in May, 1975. The department has continued the basic Church Training program of the SBC. In addition, the department has become multiple ministry in its function. Church Administration was transferred to Church Training with the death of G. R. Pendergraph (*q.v.*) in 1972. Church Media-Library Services was transferred to Church Training in Jan., 1975. Herbert Jukes served as associate, 1975-77. Michael King became associate in Jan., 1978.

Student Work Department.—In 1972 James Chester Durham, who had served as secretary of the Baptist Student Department since 1941, became assistant to the KBC executive secretary. In 1973 Donald Lynn Blaylock was elected department director. In 1979 there were 42 campuses in the state served by 15 campus ministers, 11 seminary interns, 1 part-time and 15 volunteer directors. Between 1970 and 1980, two people served as associates in the department, John David Book, 1975-78, with Ralph Hopkins beginning service in 1980.

New student centers completed during the decade include the University of Louisville, 1974, and the University of Kentucky, 1978. In 1979 construction was begun on a new center at Murray State University. A center has also been secured at Northern Kentucky University with new or additional property purchased by Northern Kentucky, Western Kentucky, Murray State, and Eastern Kentucky Universities.

Sunday School Department.—In 1976 Roy Boatwright retired after 24 years of service as director. Fred Halbrooks, associate in the department and former missionary to Brazil, was elected director. During the 1970s, associates in the department included Frank Smith, 1970-73; Fred Halbrooks, 1974, becoming director in 1976; Jim Rennell, 1977-79; and Tom Huls, 1978 to the present.

III. Missions Division. In Nov., 1974, the Executive Board named A. B. Colvin of the Direct Missions Department assistant to the executive secretary-treasurer. His responsibility was to correlate the work of the missions-related departments: Direct Missions, Evangelism, Brotherhood, and Interracial Cooperation (Brotherhood was later moved to the Church Services Division and Stewardship-Promotion was moved to Missions Division). This arrangement has greatly facilitated the cooperative work of these departments and strengthened the supervision of the executive secretary-treasurer. The Church-Minister Service function has been performed directly by Colvin.

Church-Minister Services.—In the annual meeting of the convention in 1972, the Executive Board was instructed to implement the establishment of a service to place pulpit committees in touch with pastors, staff members, and denominational workers, and such people in touch with committees. On May 8, 1974, the Executive Board voted that the executive secretary-treasurer and the director of Direct Missions, A. B. Colvin, "be responsible for implementing a church-minister service." The service was to be based on the principles of Holy Spirit leadership, advice of experienced people, response to requests for assistance, confidentiality and the spirit of reconciliation, and prayerful assistance. During the 1970s, thousands of individuals and hundreds of churches and agencies have been assisted by this service. When Colvin moved from the Direct Missions Department to the Missions Division, this function was moved with him.

Cooperative Ministries: Christian Life Department.—This department, established in 1966, was served by Herman Ihley (*q.v.* III), secretary from Mar. 1, 1967, until his death, Apr. 15, 1970. The Herman Ihley Memorial Scholarship Fund was authorized by the Executive Board in 1970. With a goal of $50,000, almost $43,000 was in trust by 1979. Income from this fund is used to assist worthy ministerial students of any race. Also in cooperation with the Home Mission Board, scholarships are provided for qualified black students in colleges and seminary.

At the May 3, 1971, Executive Board meeting, William H. Rogers was elected to succeed Ihley. He assumed his duties, Aug. 1, 1971. Rogers works with the Kentucky Baptist Convention and the General Association of Baptists in Kentucky, has staff responsibility for the concerns of the Christian Life Committee, is involved with concerns of the Department of Interfaith Witness of the Home Mission Board, and serves on the board for the Kentucky Interfaith Aging Project.

The Interracial Department was reorganized in the spring of 1974 and given a new title, Cooperative Ministries: Christian Life, along with additional responsibilities.

In cooperation with the Kentucky Baptist Board of Child Care, conferences relating to ministry to families were begun in 1975 with Swan Haworth as resource person. This has become an annual conference to help pastors and leaders deal with family concerns.

Direct Missions Department.—The 1970s were characterized by several changes in the Direct Missions Department. In 1971 a wage program for missionaries employed under the supervision of the Department was adopted by the KBC and implemented in 1972. On Jan. 1, 1975, A. B. Colvin, director of the Missions Department since 1958, became head of the Missions Division and an assistant to the executive secretary-treasurer. At the same time, Robert C. Jones, associate director and director of mountain missions since 1968, became director of the department. In June, 1977, I. Houston Lanier, director of missions in Laurel River Association, became director of mountain missions and an associate in the department.

During the 1970s many associations became deeply involved in long-range planning for the first time. Language missions received a strong emphasis. Work was conducted with Koreans, Chinese, Spanish, Laotian, and the deaf. In 1980 there were 48 directors of associational missions, 5 county missionaries, 23 local missionaries, 4 communities missionaries, 3 in-service guidance directors, 8 Christian social ministries directors, 3 language missionaries, and 17 special workers throughout Kentucky.

Evangelism Department.—Thomas Hicks Shelton, secretary of the department, led in a vigorous program of evangelism and helped plan and implement the work during the Crusade of the Americas. He retired at the end of 1976. Jay Brown, pastor of Farmdale Baptist Church,

Louisville, became director, Apr. 1, 1977. He led over 100 Kentucky Baptist pastors to participate in a simultaneous revival in Ohio churches during his first year. Area evangelism conferences have been started in 10 areas of the state to promote evangelism. An annual state youth evangelism conference was initiated in 1979. The work of interfaith witness was added to the department in 1977. New conferences have been added to acquaint church leaders with personal and mass evangelism methods. A seminar, Growing an Evangelistic Church in Kentucky, is being held annually to assist pastors with a strategy for this special emphasis.

Stewardship-Promotion Department.—The public relations work of this department has grown over the years so that it now develops public relation programs, including news releases, layout for brochures, posters, booklets, and other material for the Kentucky Baptist Convention.

Since 1972, the department has been responsible for the tract ministry. Churches and associations in Kentucky use more than a million tracts and leaflets each year. An audiovisual library of 16mm films, filmstrips, and slides is provided and serviced.

The director, Jesse Stricker, now serves as liaison with the five educational institutions and the Agencies Committee of the Executive Board. This includes servicing a growing matching funds scholarship program which was begun May 2, 1972, for the three senior colleges.

IV. Business Division. The Annuity, Business, and Foundation Departments were organized into the Business Division in May, 1975. J. Chester Durham served as the coordinator until his death, Sep. 8, 1975. Barry Allen, business manager, was elected as assistant to the executive secretary-treasurer and director of the Business Division, Jan. 1, 1977.

Business Department.—The 1970s brought several changes in the operation of this department. Garnett B. Morton retired, June 30, 1975, after 23 years as business manager. Barry G. Allen, assistant since Aug. 1, 1973, succeeded him. Douglas Hays, assistant accountant since Mar. 15, 1967, became accountant and data processing supervisor. John Pate, former Brotherhood Commission employee, was employed as general purpose room supervisor. During the decade, all accounting, reporting, and address files were converted to a computer system, a new salary administration plan was developed, and a records management system was implemented.

Annuity Department.—Arthur W. Walker retired as director, Apr. 1, 1972, and was succeeded by Byrd R. Ison. During the decade, the annuity program grew rapidly as more and more churches responded to the 10 percent formula of total compensation. Approximately two-thirds of the 2,200 churches were in some part of the annuity program. The department works with the Stewardship and Foundation

KENTUCKY STATISTICAL SUMMARY

Year	Associations	Churches	Church Membership	Baptisms	SS Enrollment	VBS Enrollment	CT Enrollment	WMU Enrollment	Brotherhood Enrollment	Ch. Music Enrollment	Mission Gifts	Total Gifts	Value Church Property
1969	80	2,192	666,836	19,447	385,157	189,062	100,052	59,524	16,377	44,273	$ 6,317,509	$ 39,638,212	$189,203,318
1970	80	2,194	670,631	17,504	376,953	171,476	95,161	54,079	16,089	44,387	6,611,781	41,220,646	193,251,849
1971	80	2,197	673,466	18,832	363,758	167,268	76,077	51,383	16,741	45,839	7,325,660	44,025,359	200,748,866
1972	80	2,201	684,246	22,084	364,200	170,870	71,328	51,428	17,095	50,376	7,833,021	47,658,277	215,918,031
1973	80	2,205	690,792	22,267	362,728	176,348	68,040	50,681	18,604	55,025	8,680,448	51,144,007	235,677,567
1974	80	2,201	697,685	20,978	362,849	181,762	64,631	51,677	18,093	56,971	9,789,390	55,653,240	258,092,957
1975	80	2,201	708,909	21,075	367,550	186,531	63,539	52,953	17,422	58,866	10,787,666	63,017,373	291,023,397
1976	80	2,195	715,469	19,353	370,104	176,082	60,621	52,458	17,881	59,436	11,651,407	69,348,627	321,915,320
1977	80	2,200	720,358	16,645	368,214	173,322	58,465	49,943	16,398	59,372	13,205,158	75,399,319	347,395,683
1978	80	2,206	724,342	15,861	365,790	173,334	59,183	48,968	16,549	62,724	13,983,703	83,522,621	385,652,320
1979	80	2,206	730,405	17,898	362,130	184,864	61,055	50,120	17,518	68,373	15,573,553	91,785,053	427,726,138
1980	80	2,204	738,126	21,148	366,254	190,705	62,823	52,310	19,695	74,677	17,289,092	101,211,359	472,639,331

LEO T. CRISMON

Departments in conferences on total steward-ship commitment.

Foundation Department.—The department con-tinues its relationship to and support of the KBC. The charter of the foundation was changed, Dec. 29, 1970, to include churches among the institutions they serve. The assets managed by the foundation on Aug. 31, 1979, were $9,282,000. Grady Randolph has been director of this department since Mar. 1, 1969.

Bibliography: Leo T. Crismon (ed.), *Baptists in Ken-tucky, 1776-1976* (1975).

FRANKLIN OWEN

KENTUCKY BAPTIST FOUNDATION (II, III). Grady L. Randolph has served as exec-utive secretary since 1969. Assets in 1980 totaled $9,200,000. As a department of the Kentucky Baptist Convention, the foundation operates under the direction of a nine-member board of directors.

GRADY L. RANDOLPH

KENTUCKY BAPTIST HERITAGE, THE. The publication of the Kentucky Baptist Historical Society, begun in 1971, with one to three issues a year (no issues published in 1973 and 1974), related to Kentucky Baptist histori-cal resources. The Kentucky Baptist Historical Commission, created in 1966, became a joint publisher in 1972. Editors have been Wendell H. Rone, Sr., James E. Taulman, Ira (Jack) Birdwhistell, and Earl C. Goins.

LEO T. CRISMON

KENTUCKY BAPTIST HISTORICAL COMMISSION (III). The commission holds annual meetings in different parts of the state. Reports appear in the Kentucky Baptist Con-vention *Annual.* The commission sponsored the production of portraits of 15 former general secretaries of the General Association of Bap-tists in Kentucky (now the Kentucky Baptist Convention). A publication, *Kentucky Baptist Heritage,* has been published jointly with the Kentucky Baptist Historical Society since Jan., 1971. Markers have been placed at historic Bap-tist sites. On Apr. 19, 1976, at Harrodsburg, the commission had part in observing the 200th anniversary of the first Baptist preaching in Kentucky by Thomas Tinsley and William Hickman (*q.v.* I) in Apr., 1776. Indexing of the *Western Recorder* by the Baptist Information Retrieval System has been pursued since 1976.

See also KENTUCKY BAPTIST HISTORICAL SOCIETY.

LEO T. CRISMON

KENTUCKY BAPTIST HISTORICAL SOCIETY (I). The society, with headquarters at the Kentucky Baptist Building, Middletown, since 1957, began the publication of *Kentucky Baptist Heritage* in Jan., 1971 (jointly with the Kentucky Baptist Historical Commission since 1972). Annual meetings are held in historic areas over the state. Yearly reports appear in the Kentucky Baptist Convention *Annual.* The suggestion of the society in 1955 to recognize two centuries of Baptist life and work in Ken-tucky culminated in the publication of *Baptists in Kentucky, 1776-1976: A Bicentennial Volume* (1975) and in the bicentennial celebration at Harrods-burg, Apr. 19, 1976, a dual celebration of Bap-tist and national beginnings.

See also KENTUCKY BAPTIST HISTORICAL COMMISSION.

LEO T. CRISMON

KENYA, MISSION IN (cf. East Africa, Mission in, Vol. III). During the 1970s, mis-sionaries shared responsibility for development with the Kenya Baptist Convention, organized in 1971. Bible schools began at Kisumu in 1971 and Kitale in 1973, and Theological Education by Extension began in 1974. The assembly at Limuru became a center for national and inter-national conferences and provided facilities for a language school, Bible correspondence school, agricultural work, and vocational education. Student ministries on Nairobi's college cam-puses began in 1972. In 1977 the music ministry expanded. An evangelistic thrust in 1976-77 among the Giryama tribe emphasized starting churches quickly, with extensive follow-up and training later. During the thrust 185 congrega-tions were started, and almost 3,000 people were baptized. Separate mission organizations in Kenya and Tanzania took form in 1978. As the decade ended, 120 missionaries served in more than 15 localities, and 450 churches re-ported 22,300 members.

JOY NEAL

KEY '73. An evangelism project with its pri-mary thrust in 1973 which involved evangelicals from 70 denominations. Forty-two churchmen, including Southern Baptists C. E. Autrey, John Havlik, and Alistair Walker, in a meeting chaired by Billy Graham, launched the project in 1967. The project title related to the site of the first meeting near the Key Bridge in Washing-ton, DC. Southern Baptists in 1968 approved a statement encouraging Baptists "to share evangelistic concerns and insights with all Chris-tian groups," and gave leadership to the Home Mission Board. Kenneth Chafin, HMB evange-lism director, served on the executive committee, 1970-72. The project aired three television spe-cials and distributed 50,000,000 Bibles. In 1973 some denominations reported unusual evangelis-tic success.

BIBLIOGRAPHY: T. A. Raedeke, *Yesterday, Today and Forever* (1974).

JOHN F. HAVLIK

KIAMICHI BAPTIST ASSEMBLY (III; cf. Kiamichi Assembly, Vol. II). Oklahoma conference center. The period 1969-80 was one of rebuilding and expansion. A significant change was the replacement of the original tab-ernacle with a larger steel structure costing more than $75,000. Another change was larger at-

2307 Kittles, Grace Evans

tendance at the preteen and youth camps. In 1969 attendance at the preteen camp was 480, the youth camp 1,055. In 1979 camps recorded 908 in the preteen assembly and 1,205 in the youth assembly. Budgets for the period also reflected growth. The 1969 budget was $13,156, while the budget adopted for 1980 was $44,220.

ROBERT S. JACKSON

KING, CHARLES NEWTON (b. West Point, MS, Feb. 2, 1896; d. Lexington, KY, Feb. 28, 1975). Pastor. The son of Ella Thornton, he attended Fisk University (A.B.) and the University of Cincinnati (M.Ed.). For 24 years he served as pastor of Corinthian Baptist Church, Frankfort, KY. In 1974 he became the first black elected to a national office of the SBC, when he was elected second vice-president. He also served as second vice-president, 1971-72, and as a member of the executive board of the Kentucky Baptist Convention. King was honored as the outstanding clergyman in Franklin County, KY, in 1969. He was married first to Helen Walker of Cincinnati and later to Ella Scott of Paris, KY. He is buried at Frankfort, KY.

ROBERT J. O'BRIEN

KING, MARTIN LUTHER, JR. (b. Atlanta, GA, Jan. 15, 1929; d. Memphis, TN, Apr. 4, 1968). Civil rights leader and pastor. Son of Martin Luther King, Sr., and Alberta Williams King, he attended Morehouse College (B.A., 1948), Crozer Theological Seminary (B.D., 1951), and Boston University (Ph.D., 1955). On June 18, 1953, he married Coretta Scott. Their children were Yolanda, Martin, III, Dexter, and Bernice. He served as pastor of Dexter Avenue Baptist Church, Montgomery, AL, 1954-60, leading a successful movement to desegregate public transportation. He was co-pastor of Ebenezer Baptist Church, Atlanta, GA, 1960-68.

As president of the Southern Christian Leadership Conference from 1957 until his death, he became internationally known for his philosophy of nonviolent resistance as a civil rights leader. He received more than 300 awards, including the Nobel Peace Prize in 1964. His body is entombed at the Martin Luther King Center for Social Change, Atlanta, GA.

SIDNEY SMITH

KING, SPENCER BIDWELL, JR. (b. Birmingham, AL, Feb. 19, 1904; d. Atlanta, GA, Dec. 14, 1977). Historian. The son of Lizzie Emma Dodson and Spencer Bidwell King, Sr. (q.v. II), a prominent Baptist minister, he attended Mercer University (B.A., 1929), Peabody College (M.A., 1936), and the University of North Carolina (Ph.D., 1950). After teaching at Fruitland Institute, 1930-33, and Mars Hill College, 1933-46, in North Carolina, he spent the most significant part of his career at Mercer University. In the history department he was associate professor, 1946-48, professor,

1948-73, chairman, 1946-70, and professor emeritus, 1973-77.

King's specialty was Georgia history. He was author or editor of seven volumes, including *Georgia Voices: A Documentary History to 1872* (1966). In addition, he contributed numerous articles and book reviews to three encyclopedias, several scholarly journals, and the Macon newspaper.

Concerned also with preserving and writing Baptist history, King was on the Historical Commission, SBC, 1966-73; on the Georgia Baptist History Committee, 1954-76; and served as president of the Southern Baptist Historical Society, 1971.

On Dec. 26, 1934, he married Caroline Janet Paul. They had three children: Spencer Bidwell, III, Janet, and Margaret. He is buried in Oak Grove Cemetery, Americus, GA.

ROBERT GARDNER

KIRKLAND, PAUL GILBERT (b. Urbana, IL, Feb. 24, 1912; d. Louisville, KY, Aug. 7, 1979). Fund raiser and financial consultant. The son of Nancy Kirkland and Robert Kirkland, a traveling evangelist, he attended the University of Illinois and The Southern Baptist Theological Seminary (Th.B., 1951). On Aug. 20, 1931, he married Betty Reed. They had four children: Mary, Bobbie, Gil, and Ray. After pastorates in Illinois, Arkansas, Tennessee, and Kentucky, he served as a church fund raiser and financial counselor. In 1964 he became the first executive director of the Southern Seminary Foundation, serving until his retirement in 1977. He is buried in Cave Hill Cemetery, Louisville, KY.

JOHN JOSEPH OWENS

KITTLES, GRACE EVANS (b. near Captola, GA, Feb. 23, 1883; d. Sylvania, GA, July 9, 1970). Woman's Missionary Union leader. Daughter of James Hezekiah and Therissa Zeigler Evans, she attended Cox College (B.A.). She married Peter Randolph Kittles, a banker, in 1903 and moved to Sylvania.

Active in leadership of Royal Ambassadors, she was an RA counselor at First Baptist Church, Sylvania, for more than 20 years, beginning in 1919, and later was counselor at state RA conclaves and hostess for other Georgia WMU youth events. She served as Georgia WMU president and WMU, SBC, vice-president, 1942-47.

During her presidency, Glendon McCullough (q.v. III) became the first Georgia RA secretary, WMU-sponsored youth missions tours were begun, and women contributed $100,000 to rebuild Warren Memorial Hospital in China. In 1946 she led in the acquisition of property for building WMU-owned Camp Pinnacle and was camp hostess for 10 years. For several years she was hostess for the WMU Training School, Louisville, KY. In her eighties, she was pianist and children's teacher for Sylvania Mission, which became Memorial Baptist Church. She is buried in the city cemetery at Sylvania, GA.

DOROTHY PRYOR

KLAUPIKS, ADOLFS (b. Novogorod, Russia, Mar. 10, 1900; d. Applebachsville, PA, Mar. 27, 1979). Latvian Baptist leader and relief coordinator for the Baptist World Alliance. The son of Janis and Katrine Klaupiks, he was educated at Latvian Baptist Seminary, Riga (1925-29), Newton Theological Institute, Newton Centre, MA (1929-32), and the University of Boston (1930-32). He married Rasma Brekters, Jan. 16, 1933. Pastor of churches at Petersburg, Russia, 1922-25, and Jelgava, Latvia, 1927-29, he was also editor of *Kristga Balss* and director of publications, Latvian Baptist Union; general secretary of Latvian Baptist Union; field representative of BWA, 1947-50; and coordinator of Baptist World relief, 1950-68. He was responsible for settling 12,000 European refugees in North America, South America, Asia, and Australia after World War II. He is buried in Applebachsville Cemetery, Bucks County, PA.

C. E. BRYANT

KOINONIA MINISTRIES. Housing and education ministry of Koinonia Farms, Americus, GA. Founded by Clarence Jordan (*q.v.* III) in 1942, Koinonia provides low-cost housing for the poor through a program called the Fund for Humanity. Energy-efficient homes are sold for the cost of materials. No interest is charged, and payments are scaled to income. This ministry has reached from Sumter County, where about 85 homes are built each year, to Zaire, Uganda, and Guatemala. The organization's educational ministries include a nursery and a child development center for preschoolers, tutoring programs for school-age children, and a summer program featuring crafts, Bible school, travel, and swimming instruction.

PAUL D. SIMMONS

KOREA, MISSION IN SOUTH (III; cf. Korea, Mission in, Vol. II). In 1979 churches totaled 662 with nearly 30,000 members, and the missionary staff was 85. Wallace Memorial Baptist Hospital elected its first Korean administrator, increased its bed capacity to 210, attained full self-support, inaugurated its first mobile clinic, and continued an aggressive evangelistic outreach. The seminary gained government accreditation, had an enrollment of 611 on its Taejon and Seoul campuses, and elected its first Korean president. The Church Development Board provided curriculum materials, training, book store outlets, and an assembly ground, and elected its first Korean director. The Foreign Mission Board and the Florida Baptist Convention cooperated with the Korea mission and convention in a three-year major cities evangelization program which strengthened the churches.

GEORGE H. HAYS

L

LA HORA BAUTISTA (THE BAPTIST HOUR). The Radio and Television Commission, SBC, desiring to share the gospel with Hispanics in the United States, Mexico, Central and South America, aired "La Hora Bautista," 1958-64. Radio speakers were Lloyd Corder, Leobardo Estrada, and Hugo Ruiz. This program became *"Momentos de Meditación,"* ("Moments of Meditation").

LEOBARDO ESTRADA

LAKE PLACID BAPTIST MINISTRIES. See NEW YORK RESORT MINISTRIES.

LAMB, WILLIAM HOBART (b. Red Ash, TN, Mar. 19, 1910; d. Knoxville, TN, Jan. 13, 1977). Pastor and associational leader. Son of Alafair and Thomas Lamb, miners, he married Louise Davenport, Jan. 1, 1933. They had three children: Thomas, Gail, and Lonnie. He served churches in Tennessee and Kentucky until moving to Indianapolis, May, 1955. He started a mission which became Marwood Baptist Church, Indianapolis, and led it to sponsor other missions. Lamb was a vice-president, Regional Fellowship of Indiana Southern Baptists, 1956, an organization which predated the state convention. He is buried in Woodlawn Cemetery, LaFollette, TN.

E. HARMON MOORE

LAMBDIN, INA SMITH (b. Knoxville, TN, Feb. 20, 1895; d. Nashville, TN, May 13, 1975). Denominational leader. Daughter of William W. Smith, iron mill worker, and Mary Elizabeth (Chitwood) Smith, she graduated from Tennessee College (A.B.) and George Peabody College (M.A.). She married Jerry E. Lambdin (*q.v.* III), Dec. 17, 1919. She served as Junior-Intermediate leader, Alabama Baptist Convention, and paid Training Union worker, First Baptist Church, Nashville, TN, before becoming editor of Junior and Intermediate Training Union quarterlies at the Sunday

School Board, 1938-60. She is buried in Wood-lawn Cemetery, Nashville, TN.

PHILIP B. HARRIS

LANGUAGE MISSIONS, HOME MIS-SION BOARD PROGRAM OF (III). During the 1970s, approximately 10 percent of the churches related to the SBC were comprised of ethnic Americans other than blacks. By the end of the decade, 74 ethnic groups, including internationals, refugees, and immigrants, and 55 American Indian tribes were studying the Bible in 70 languages and numerous dialects. About 1,400 Hispanic, 360 American Indian, 370 Asian, 30 Caribbean, 50 European, and 15 Arabic congregations and over 450 churches ministered among internationals and 700 among the deaf, as well as among seaport and diplomatic personnel.

During the 1970s the Home Mission Board encouraged SBC agencies to assist language-culture congregations and to produce language materials. The Woman's Missionary Union, Sunday School Board, Brotherhood Commission, Seminary Extension Department, and Baptist Press have organizational units designed to meet the needs of ethnic Americans. The Annuity Board and Stewardship Commission provide language materials. The Historical, Education, and Radio and TV commissions continue to undergird language missions.

Ethnic persons serve on boards and commissions. The HMB was the first agency to elect an ethnic person to lead an agency program. Other agencies, state conventions, and associations have since elected language-culture persons to their staffs. In 1971 Oscar Romo succeeded Gerald Palmer as director of the HMB's language missions program.

OSCAR ROMO

LANGUAGE PUBLISHING. The first Baptist Spanish periodical in the United States, *El Bautista Mexicano,* appeared in 1939. Published by the Texas Baptist Mexican Convention, it became an all-purpose magazine for Hispanic Baptists. The Baptist Spanish Publishing House published and distributed Spanish language materials until 1980, when the Sunday School Board, SBC, assumed these responsibilities for the USA. The SSB began publishing dated language materials in 1964. In Jan., 1980, a language unit was established to prepare materials, beginning with Spanish, with planned expansion to Vietnamese, Korean, Chinese, and other languages.

Nuestra Tarea, the first SBC missions magazine in Spanish, appeared in 1955. Woman's Missionary Union, assisted by the Home Mission Board, publishes *Nuestra Tarea* and other works in Spanish. Other SBC entities also publishing language materials include the HMB (many languages), the Brotherhood Commission (Spanish, Chinese, and Korean since 1978), the Annuity Board (Spanish, Arabic, Laotian, and Vietnamese), and many state con-ventions (various languages). Other language publishing includes Hungarian materials, Spanish periodicals (*La Voz Bautista,* FL, and *El Misionero Bautista,* NM), and newsletters in Korean (*Kyohwui Sungchangjee,* TX), Vietnamese (*The Light,* CA), and Chinese (*News Letter,* CA). Language publishing in the SBC is growing rapidly.

ALCIDES GUAJARDO

LANSDELL, RINALDO ADDISON (b. Wrightsboro, GA, June 4, 1875; d. Hephzibah, GA, Feb. 3, 1937). Minister and educator. Son of Edwin Erwin and Anna Augusta Cody Lansdell, he was educated at Mercer University (A.B., 1901) and Southern Baptist Theological Seminary (Th.M., 1904). Lansdell married Ruth Sanders Kilpatrick, Jan. 29, 1902. They had seven children: Cyrus, Anna, Ruth, Lillian, Emily, Rinaldo, Jr., and Joseph.

He was pastor of First Baptist Church, Laramie, WY, 1905-09, and associate pastor of Immanuel Baptist Church, Salt Lake City, UT, 1909-10. He returned to Georgia in 1910 to serve as financial secretary and field representative of Bessie Tift College (now Tift College). In 1913 he joined the SBC Foreign Mission Board as field secretary and fund raiser. He was also financial secretary for the University of Richmond. Lansdell was a leader in the founding of Bluefield College and, in Aug., 1920, he became the first president of that junior college for men. He is buried in the Hephzibah, GA, cemetery.

H. EUGENE MCLEOD

LAOS, MISSION IN. The "house church" approach to worship and evangelism received primary attention from the beginning of the work in Mar., 1971. Scripture distribution, film evangelism, and student ministries also introduced the ethnic Laotians, Buddhist people, to the gospel. Nine Baptist missionaries, along with other foreigners, were asked to leave Laos in mid-1975. The new Communist government desired time to reeducate its people without outside influence. In 1980 Laotian people were continuing to flee their homeland for refuge in neighboring Thailand and other friendly nations.

J. MURPHY TERRY

LAWRENCE, UNA ROBERTS (b. Gainesville, AR, Aug. 6, 1893; d. Jacksonville, AR, Jan. 13, 1972). Leader and writer for Woman's Missionary Union and Home Mission Board. The only daughter of Hulett Wayman Roberts, a schoolteacher, and Mary Moffitt Roberts, she graduated from Central College in 1918 and the WMU Training School in 1919. She married railroad employee Irwin Lawrence, Feb. 25, 1921.

In Arkansas she was state Sunbeam Band leader, 1915, and young people's secretary, WMU, 1920-26. She was HMB mission study editor, 1926-47. During this time she served as personal service chairman, 1929-32, and mission study chairman, 1930-47, of WMU, SBC; wrote extensively for WMU periodicals; and initiated the "Missionary Round Table." Her numerous books include *The King's Own* (1920), *The Life of Lottie Moon* (1927), *Pioneer Women* (1929), and *The Word of Their Testimony* (1932). She is buried in the Mount Moriah Cemetery, Kansas City, MO.

DORIS DEVAULT

LAWTON, SAMUEL MILLER (b. Estill, SC, Nov. 12, 1899; d. Ridgecrest, NC, Nov. 3, 1971). Educator. He was blind from birth. His parents were Sarah Miller and Thomas Lawton, an insurance executive. He graduated from Furman University (B.A., 1920), Southern Baptist Theological Seminary (Th.G., 1922), and Peabody College (M.A., 1927; Ph.D., 1939). Married in 1924 to Alice Stockton of Decatur, AL, they had two children, Mary and Frank. While teaching at North Greenville Baptist Academy, Tigerville, SC, he was instrumental in the academy's transition to a junior college in 1934. He left the college in 1942, spending the remainder of his life as chaplain at South Carolina School for the Deaf and Blind, Spartanburg, SC. He is buried at Ridgecrest, NC.

DON KIRKLAND

LAY EVANGELISM SCHOOL. A Home Mission Board project developed in 1970 to train laypersons to witness. The project involves enlisting, motivating, and equipping Christians to share their faith and to bring persons to faith in Jesus. The strategy of the lay evangelism school is focused in the local congregation.

In early 1970, the Evangelism Division of the HMB brought together more than 40 persons to consider the task of training the laity to witness. Kenneth Chafin, then director of the division, explained, "For years we have underestimated the layman's potential for evangelism, keeping us from utilizing his insight, interest, and ability to reach the lost. We have failed to recognize his need for specific training to develop his skills, thus creating a real vacuum in the churches."

According to Jack Stanton, then lay witness director for the HMB, "The staff and task force determined to develop the training in the 'laboratory' of the local church." After the staff researched every type of witness training available, 13 original "laboratory" schools were held in Atlanta, GA, churches in 1970 and 1971 to develop and test various training methods. In 1971 a national strategy was launched in three key cities—Chicago, IL, in April and Houston, TX, and Los Angeles, CA, in May.

Using the feedback of the original task force of 40 persons, the Evangelism Department at the HMB developed materials for lay evangelism leadership. Other materials for use in the schools by trainees were developed by the Church Training Department of the Sunday School Board. These original materials served the churches until 1979 when new materials were produced.

Training the laity to witness became a per-

manent priority of the SBC in 1975 at the Miami, FL, Convention through creation of a program of personal evangelism. Continued emphasis and update on lay evangelism schools became a part of this program.

The two task objectives for every person participating in a lay evangelism school are: (1) To be able to share a personal testimony about Christ with a non-Christian, and (2) to be able to communicate clearly the truth of the gospel about Christ to a non-Christian.

The two spiritual objectives for every person participating in a lay evangelism school are: (1) To experience daily a full and meaningful Christian life, and (2) to make witnessing a part of the daily life-style in Jesus Christ.

The lay evangelism school involves three months of preparation, one week of intensive training, and three months of continued training.

Between 1970 and 1977, more than 750,000 Southern Baptists were trained through lay evangelism schools. Through 1977, estimates show that at least 18,000 Southern Baptist churches conducted at least one lay evangelism school. Hundreds of churches in Europe, New Zealand, Latin America, and India have participated in lay evangelism schools.

See also EVANGELISM, HOME MISSION BOARD PROGRAMS OF.

JOHN F. HAVLIK

LAY RENEWAL. Lay Renewal is a strategy jointly promoted by the Home Mission Board and the Brotherhood Commission since 1973. The overall strategy, called "A Journey into Lifestyle Evangelism and Ministry," is a church-centered process of weekend events (the Lay Renewal Weekend and the Ministry Evangelism Weekend), continuing small group activities after each weekend, and lay ministry and evangelism programs. The emphasis helps churches and individual believers develop their strategies of a life-style of evangelism and ministry. National leaders are Reid Hardin, HMB, and David Haney, Brotherhood Commission. About 500 Southern Baptist churches take part in this program each year.

DAVID HANEY

LAY UTILIZATION STUDY. At its Sep., 1969, meeting, the SBC Executive Committee appointed a Lay Utilization Study Committee to study the potential of Baptist men in church and denominational life. This committee sponsored a consultation in Nashville, TN, on Dec. 3-5, 1970, involving about 300 laymen, pastors, and denominational workers. Owen Cooper, later president of the Convention, 1972-74, served as chairman. Six areas of concern to Baptist laymen were considered: Evangelism, missions, the community, the local church, the denomination, and lay-pastor relationships.

The committee addressed its findings in the six study areas to laymen, churches, pastors, associations, and conventions in a 42-page book entitled *Listen! A Message From Baptist Laymen for*

Laymen, Pastors, Churches, and Denominational Leaders (1971). Key findings were:

1. Laymen of the Southern Baptist Convention are underutilized in the churches and in the Convention.

2. Programs for Southern Baptist laymen are fragmented, uncoordinated, and so varied that their effectiveness is lost.

3. Lay programs are too often carried over from a former generation rather than designed for the modern age. They are frequently inadequate in scope, insufficient in challenge, and ineffective in impact.

4. Southern Baptists should develop more programs and more effective programs for the fuller utilization of laymen.

ALBERT MCCLELLAN

LAYMEN'S CORPORATIONS, OKLAHOMA. The Baptist Laymen's Corporations of Oklahoma City and Tulsa, representing churches in their respective areas, have as their purpose the development, promotion, and operation of religious, charitable, educational, and benevolent endeavors, particularly those performed by the Baptist General Convention of Oklahoma. Election of directors is approved and confirmed by the convention.

The first project of the Baptist Laymen's Corporation of Oklahoma City was construction of the Doctors Medical Building near Baptist Medical Center, Oklahoma City. In Sep., 1963, the corporation began construction of what is now known as Baptist Retirement Center, Oklahoma City. The complex, which has been operated by the corporation since it opened in 1965, consists of a 114-bed nursing home (Lackey Manor), 136 apartment units, and 3 private dwellings. Don Donalson has been administrator since 1970.

The Baptist Laymen's Corporation of Tulsa was incorporated on Sep. 28, 1979. Its primary responsibility is the operation of the Tulsa Baptist Retirement Center at Owasso consisting of 96 apartment units. The present director is Monroe Palmer.

JOE L. INGRAM

LEACH, MILTON SHARP, SR. (b. Weatherford, TX, July 11, 1905; d. Kingsville, TX, Aug. 12, 1965). Home missionary. He grew up in Buckner Baptist Children's Home, Dallas, where he was converted and baptized by R. C. Buckner (*q.v.* I). He graduated from Wayland College, Howard Payne College, Southwestern Baptist Theological Seminary (Th.M.), and Pikes Peak Bible Seminary in Colorado (Th.D.). Ordained in 1923, Leach served as pastor of Anglo and Spanish churches until his appointment, Oct. 1, 1944, to minister to Latin Americans in Texas and New Mexico. In 1950 he became promotional secretary of the Spanish-American Baptist Convention of New Mexico. He married Eunice Marie Barrett of Plainfield, TX, May 25, 1925. They had four children: Milton S., Jr., Charles Seth, Dorothy, and Hattie.

KATE ELLEN GRUVER

LEADERSHIP (III). See CHURCH ADMINISTRATION.

LEADERSHIP CHANGES, SOUTHERN BAPTIST CONVENTION. See SOUTHERN BAPTIST CONVENTION LEADERSHIP CHANGES.

LEBANON, MISSION IN (II, III). During much of the 1970s, Lebanon reeled from civil war between its citizens of two cultures, Christian and Muslim. Baptist work continued during the troubled times with only brief interruptions. While Muslims and Christians not far away were killing each other, Muslim and Christian children in the Beirut Baptist School walked arm in arm through the corridors. In 1979 there were 475 Baptists in 12 churches. Twenty-five missionaries were assigned to Lebanon. Three international institutions, the Mass Media Center, the Arab Baptist Publications office, and the Arab Baptist Theological Seminary, increased the possibility of close cooperation by adopting the same address.

J. D. HUGHEY

LEE, MAURICE JOHN (b. Belle Isle, LA, Sep. 21, 1906; d. Guymon, OK, Apr. 11, 1977). Pastor. The son of Clarence and Clara Lee, he married Beatrice Neoma Robertson, June 13, 1935, at Welsh, LA. They had three sons: James W., Thomas R., and William W. Educated at Acadia Academy, Louisiana College, and New Orleans Baptist Theological Seminary, he was pastor of churches in Louisiana and Texas. His last pastorate was at First Church, Guymon, OK, where he retired as pastor-emeritus in 1971.

Lee served on the Home Mission Board, SBC, and the Historical Commission of the Oklahoma Convention; as president of the Baptist General Convention of Oklahoma, 1962-63; as a member of the convention board, 1963-67; and as a trustee of Oklahoma Baptist University. He was author of three books: *Notes on Revelation, Studies in the Christian Experience,* and *Bible Briefs of Baptist Beliefs.* He is buried in Elmhurst Cemetery, Guymon, OK.

J. M. GASKIN

LEE, PERCY ALAN (b. Melita, Manitoba, Canada, Dec. 25, 1899; d. Surrey, British Columbia, Canada, June 5, 1976). Merchant and Baptist leader. The son of George and Catherine Lee, farmers, Lee married Marion Colpitts, July 14, 1928. They had one daughter, Catherine. He served as president, Convention of Regular Baptists of British Columbia, 1945-50, and member of the Board of Governors, Northwest Baptist Bible College, 1945-53. In 1953 the Lees sought help from Oregon-Washington Southern Baptists in starting Kings Road Baptist Church of North Vancouver, British Columbia, the first Southern Baptist church actually begun by Southern Baptists in Canada. Lee became first treasurer of Capilano Association, Oct. 9, 1955. He is buried in Valley View Memorial Gardens, Surrey, British Columbia.

LEE, ROBERT GREENE (b. Fort Mill, SC, Nov. 11, 1886; d. Memphis, TN, July 20, 1978). Pastor, author, and denominational leader. Son of David Ayers, farmer, and Elizabeth Bennett Lee, homemaker, he attended Furman University (B.A., 1913) after working on the Panama Canal construction project to earn school money. He was awarded 11 honorary doctorates. One of six brothers and two sisters, he was baptized, Aug. 5, 1898, into the Fort Mill, SC, Baptist Church. The same congregation ordained him to the gospel ministry, Apr. 3, 1910.

Lee served as pastor of Red Bank Church, Saluda, SC, 1917; First Baptist, Edgefield, SC, 1918-20; First Baptist, Chester, SC, 1920-21; First Baptist, New Orleans, LA, 1922-25; Citadel Square, Charleston, SC, 1925-27; and Bellevue, Memphis, TN, 1927-60. During his 32 years as pastor of Bellevue, the membership grew from 1,739 to 9,469. Additions totaled 24,071, and baptisms numbered 7,649.

Lee was married to Bula Gentry on Nov. 26, 1913, in Greenville, SC. They had one daughter, Bula Gentry Lee King.

Lee prepared 50 books of sermons. Elected president of the Tennessee Baptist Convention four times in the 1930s, he served as president of the SBC for three terms, 1948-51. In great demand as a preacher and speaker, he traveled in every state of the USA and to many foreign countries as guest speaker in Bible conferences, assemblies, and as a revivalist in churches. He delivered his famous sermon, "Payday Someday," 1,275 times. It was also filmed and made into a sacred opera. Numerous memorials have been erected in his honor. These include the Lee Auditorium and the Lee Memorial Garden and Memento House at Bellevue Baptist Church, Memphis; Lee Chapel, Baptist Bible Institute, Graceland, FL; and Lee Memorial Library Room, New Orleans, LA.

Two biographies about Lee have been written—*Robert G. Lee, A Chosen Vessel,* by E. Schyler English (1949) and *Robert Greene Lee, The Authorized Biography,* by John Ervin Huss (1967). He is buried in Forest Hill Cemetery, Memphis.

LEEWARD ISLANDS, MISSION IN. See ANTIGUA, MISSION IN; ST. KITTS, MISSION IN; TORTOLA, MISSION IN.

LEWIS, WALTER OLIVER (b. Stanbury, MO, Feb. 22, 1877; d. Washington, DC, May 28, 1965). Baptist World Alliance leader. He was educated at William Jewell College, Southern Baptist Theological Seminary, and the Universities of Berlin, Erlangen, Halle, and Leipzig in Germany. Ordained in 1897, he served pastorates in St. Louis, then in St. Joseph, where he married Jessie Thompson. They had two sons, Frank D. and Robert E. He

was professor of philosophy at William Jewell College, 1910-22, except for a period as a chaplain to American troops in Europe in World War I. Lewis was representative of the American Baptist Foreign Mission Society in Europe, 1922-39.

Lewis was elected general secretary of the BWA in 1939. At that time its headquarters were in London. In 1940 he helped move the Alliance headquarters to Washington, DC, because of wartime bombing in London, but repeatedly traveled the dangerous Atlantic to preserve communications between Baptists of Europe and America. He signed papers for purchase of the BWA headquarters building at 1628 Sixteenth St., NW, Washington, DC, Dec., 1947. When Arnold T. Ohrn was elected general secretary of the BWA in 1948, Lewis voluntarily returned to Europe as BWA associate secretary, directing Baptist relief work across the ravaged continent.

LIBERATION THEOLOGY. Luke reported that in the presence of the people who knew him best, the inhabitants of Nazareth, Jesus identified himself as the one anticipated by the prophet Isaiah (4:18-19). This and other biblical accounts relate the acts of God which liberate people from bondage and which alleviate suffering. If God has been detected most clearly in the past addressing authentic needs of humanity, then the true seeker is most likely to discover the present activity of God in ministry to meet authentic human need.

How ought one to minister to those with serious deprivation? The task is one of evangelism, carrying the message of salvation to those in deprivation. The message, however, is only the beginning of evangelism. The call of liberation theologians is to qualitative evangelism as well as quantitative evangelism. To bring a message of hope for deprived individuals is insufficient without also enabling them to overcome deprivation so that hope can become a reality.

Qualitative evangelism addresses the whole person. One shares the gospel message of the Bible, and then one attends to respondents by helping them discover an authentic life-style fulfilling their creative potential. Enabling is the completion of preaching. The idea of enabling avoids the problem of paternalism. Spiritual and social assistance can seek to remake persons (and nations) on the basis of an externally imposed model which can become a tool of exploitation. Enabling on the other hand speaks of the gradual unfolding of true selfhood in freedom.

The gospel message itself may be simple, but the enabling work of evangelism is quite complex. Oppression and deprivation complicate the task immensely. How to enable depends upon the context of the respondent. Authentic enablement may require tools of psychology, sociology, economics, vocational counseling, medical assistance, and other forms of help, as well as religious instruction. The most difficult problem of all, which will require the solidarity of committed believers, is the task of changing oppressive institutions—governmental and religious.

Traditional theology sometimes does not address itself to the task of qualitative evangelism. In the past theological writings have focused on devotional instruction or on systematic formulation of doctrine to establish orthodox norms for the church. Liberation theology suggests a different methodology.

Within a concrete situation of need, one must engage in pastoral ministry to alleviate suffering. In the concrete situation of struggling to bring relief to the oppressed, one begins to grasp the reality of the situation and the realistic needs of those to whom one seeks to minister. In reflection one begins to discern the liberating Spirit of God at work. This leads to exegetical reflection appropriate for the given context. Additionally, one is led to holistic reflection which seeks input from all disciplines and helping professions. Such reflection then leads to concrete planning for returning to the original situation better prepared to participate with the liberating Spirit of God already at work.

What results from this methodology is a growing ability to enable the poor to change themselves and their circumstances. The task of the theologian (and for that matter, all Christians) becomes not so much a task of right-knowing (orthodoxy) as much as a task of right-doing (orthopraxy). Right-doing is more difficult to define and is impossible to universalize because right-doing does not exist apart from a ministry context. One is not left without guidance, however, because one discovers the norm for right-doing contextually through biblical studies.

Liberation theology is oriented toward this-worldly activity rather than other-worldly concerns. Why this is so can be discerned by examining the history of the current movement. Several generations of Christian missionaries tried to evangelize China during the past 200 years with nominal success. Suddenly in one generation a European philosopher named Marx changed China. Less dramatically perhaps, but with remarkable effectiveness, Marxism has been embraced by increasing numbers of economically deprived persons around the world. They have received it as good news and as the herald of hope for a new day. Within traditional strongholds of Catholicism, especially Latin America, sensitive priests began to ask why. Their answer was that traditional Catholicism had become a part of the status quo and no longer really expected the gospel to solve the serious deprivation of the masses in the Third World.

The situation appeared to be approaching a crisis wherein the church had to abdicate to the oncoming onslaught of Marxism hoping to co-exist as a remnant or to rediscover a realistic vision of the kingdom of God as a this-worldly goal for humanity. Gustavo Gutierrez crystalized the basic issue in his now classic work, *A Theology of Liberation* (1973), in asking about the relationship of salvation to the historical process of the liberation of man. For the liberation movement the answer is that both individual and corporate salvation find expression as the historical process of liberation. That creation relates to history, that the revelation of God is the record of God's saving activities in history, and that the preaching of Jesus embraced a kingdom of God which radically reshaped the social structures of this world all point the liberation theologians to the belief that God's kingdom will include history.

If this is so, then history is changeable and Christians are called to effect that change empowered by the Spirit of God. Further, fellow human beings become important allies whether or not they embrace specific Christian doctrines because they too are makers of history. A solidarity of humanity is envisioned because of the common goal of this world giving birth to a better world, namely, the kingdom of God.

Most Southern Baptists can affirm the pastoral commitment of liberation theology but will have difficulty affirming the idea of salvation in history envisioned by liberation theology. Although many Southern Baptists will be concerned about the overt political activities of liberation theologians, they may underestimate the attractiveness of Marxism to the deprived masses of the world. To point out that the practice of Marxism in society has achieved far less than the promised dream may be inadequate, especially if one is advocating a church whose practice has achieved far less than the envisioned kingdom of God. The challenge of Marxism will not be met by theory alone, it must be met through praxis—through authentic ministry (see Matt. 25:35-36, 40).

BIBLIOGRAPHY: J. M. Bonino, *Sharing Theology in a Revolutionary Situation* (1975). R. M. Brown, *Theology in a New Key* (1978). E. Dussel, *History and the Theology of Liberation* (1976). R. Gibellini, ed., *Frontiers of Theology in Latin America* (1979). D. Migliore, *Called to Freedom* (1980). S. Ogden, *Faith and Freedom: Toward a Theology of Liberation* (1979). J. L. Segundo, *The Hidden Motives of Pastoral Action* (1978); *The Liberation of Theology* (1976). J. Sobrino, *Christology at the Crossroads* (1978). J. Topel, *The Way to Peace; Liberation Through the Bible* (1979).

F. WILLIAM RATLIFF

LIBERIA, MISSION IN (II, III). William R. Tolbert, Jr., Baptist pastor and president of the Liberia Baptist Missionary and Educational Convention, was inaugurated president of the nation, July 23, 1971, giving new prominence to Baptists. The long-range impact of Tolbert's assassination in early 1980 is not yet known. The mission adopted a strategy of work calling for evangelistic missionaries in every part of the country, and by 1979 had stations in Monrovia, Buchanan, Greenville, Yekepa, Voinjama, and Mano River. Ricks Institute strengthened its high school programs under an African principal and added junior college work. Journeymen taught Bible courses in government schools in Yekepa and Voinjama. At Ricks a program of work with men and boys was begun. Possibly the major accomplishments of the decade were the formation of the Liberia Baptist Seminary in 1976 and graduation of the first class in 1979. In 1979 missionaries numbered 53.

JOHN E. MILLS

LIBRARY, CHURCH (II, III). The purpose of the Program of Church Library Development is to develop services and materials for use by Southern Baptist churches, associations, and state conventions in establishing, conducting, enlarging, and improving church library services. These services include providing and promoting the use of printed and audiovisual media and consulting with church leaders and members in the use of media. The task of the program is to educate persons in the use of media and to provide media and media services to support the church in the achievement of its mission.

In Aug., 1978, Wayne E. Todd retired as secretary of the Church Library Department; in June, 1979, Mancil Ezell became secretary. In May, 1979, Choice Creations Tracts were introduced—50 titles designed for use in outreach and ministry. Six titles are produced in Spanish. By May, 1980, the number of registered church media libraries reached 24,347 with 1,010 associations organized for church media library promotion. The Sunday School Board changed the name of the Church Library Department to the Church Media Library Department in 1980.

The department assists in the continuing development and operation of curriculum labs in Southern Baptist seminaries and colleges, provides training opportunities for library workers at Ridgecrest and Glorieta, conducts seminars in the Church Program Training Center, and sponsors church, association, and state convention library events.

MANCIL EZELL

LIBYA, MISSION IN (III). In spite of political changes, the English-language Baptist church of Tripoli, which was organized in 1962, continued its ministry to Americans and other foreigners. The missionary couple appointed to Libya in 1965 are still there. Direct evangelism among Muslims is forbidden.

J. D. HUGHEY

LICENSING OF MINISTERS. See MINISTERS, LICENSING OF.

LIGHT. A bimonthly publication of the Christian Life Commission, SBC, first published in May, 1948, by the commission's forerunner, the Social Service Commission. The Christian Life Commission continued the publication on an occasional basis until placed on a regular schedule in 1978 with William M. Tillman, Jr., as managing editor. The commission provides the publication free to pastors, other church staff persons, denominational workers, students, and other persons who have a special interest in applied Christianity.

WILLIAM M. TILLMAN, JR.

LITTLEFORD, WARREN (b. Aurora, IL, Nov. 19, 1926; d. Minneapolis, MN, Sep. 10, 1973). Pastor, pioneer missionary, and denominational leader. Son of Berniece and Warren Littleford, Sr., he was educated at Southern Illinois University (B.A., 1952) and Southwestern Baptist Theological Seminary (B.D., 1956). He married Anda Sawyer, June 30, 1949. They had five children: Laura Sue, Warren Ray, John Lee, Stanley David, and Prisca Ann.

While a student at SIU, he served as a Baptist Student Union summer missionary to Hawaii in 1951. In 1956 he accepted a call to Minnesota from families interested in organizing a church. Later this organization became the Southtown Baptist Church, Minneapolis, the first SBC church in Minnesota. When the Northland Baptist Association was organized in 1966, he was chosen as superintendent of missions. During his eight years as superintendent, he began summer mission work, opened channels of communication with other denominations, extended the witness of Baptists to language groups, and guided the inauguration and implementation of a vigorous associational program, while remaining a vibrant personal witness and an unusually effective preacher. After serving nearly 17 years in the pioneer area, there were 46 Southern Baptist churches with 2,000 members in the state. He is buried in Lakewood Cemetery, Minneapolis, MN.

MYRON D. DILLOW

LITTLEJOHN, CARRIE UARDA (b. Spartanburg, SC, May 3, 1890; d. Asheville, NC, Jan. 9, 1980). Educator. Daughter of Aaron David Littlejohn, a farmer, and Hattie Rountree Littlejohn, she attended Converse College, Woman's Missionary Union Training School (1915), Hartford School of Religious Education (B.R.E., 1930) and Northwestern University (M.S., 1934). She studied also at the University of Chicago and George Washington University. She received an honorary doctorate, June 6, 1944, from Georgetown College in Kentucky.

Littlejohn joined the faculty of WMU Training School, Louisville, KY, in 1921 as director of its goodwill center. She served as associate principal, 1925-30, and principal, 1930-48. The office was renamed president in 1948. Serving in this capacity until 1951, she was cited for her "open vision, clear thinking, and hard work."

During her administration the training school moved toward an expanding curriculum, higher educational standards, better library facilities, and enrollment of more day students and wives of seminary students. In 1941 the school moved to a new location on Lexington Road in Louisville.

Littlejohn was author of *History of Carver School of Missions and Social Work* (1958). She is buried in Cedar Springs Cemetery near Spartanburg, SC.

DORIS DEVAULT

LOGO, SOUTHERN BAPTIST CONVENTION. See SOUTHERN BAPTIST CONVENTION LOGO.

LOPEZ MUNOZ, AUGUSTIN ERNESTO (b. Cardenas, Cuba, Nov. 11, 1904; d. Miami, FL, Oct. 17, 1979). Cuban pastor and educator. Ordained to the ministry in 1928, Lopez served as pastor of several Baptist churches in Cuba. He was educated in the Baptist Theological Seminary of Western Cuba, which he later served as president. His leadership ability became a stabilizing force during the 1960s when many Baptist leaders were imprisoned by the Castro government. Upon retirement, he moved to the USA, where he continued his ministry among Spanish-speaking churches.

J. DAVID FITE

LOTT CAREY BAPTIST FOREIGN MISSION CONVENTION (II, III). Support comes mainly from churches on the eastern seaboard of the United States. These churches hold membership in one of the National Baptist conventions. With a minimum of overhead, this convention boasts of sending 87 percent of its income to mission stations in India, Guyana, Nigeria, Zaire, South Africa, Haiti, and Liberia. The only objective of this convention is foreign missions, with emphasis on evangelism, medicine, and industrial training. Wendell C. Somerville is executive director.

EMMANUEL L. MCCALL

LOTT, THEODORE FRANKLIN (b. Sumrall, KS, Aug. 20, 1910; d. Fort Worth, TX, Apr. 22, 1978). Pastor and broadcast producer. The son of William Jefferson Lott, a minister, and Lonie Smith Lott, he attended Jones County Junior College, Ellisville, MS (A.A.), Mississippi Southern College, and Sam Houston State College (B.A.). He married Marie Leverkuhn, June 13, 1938. They had one daughter, Marilyn Candace. He was pastor of several Texas churches before retiring in 1951 because of failing health. He was co-owner and operator of radio station KSAM, Huntsville, TX, 1951-55. In 1955 he was named director of radio production for the SBC Radio and Television Commission.

In addition to producing several weekly radio programs, Lott served as announcer for "The Baptist Hour," 1955-65. He pioneered in foreign language radio production with "La Hora Bautista," the Spanish version of "The Baptist Hour," in 1958. He helped to develop "Master Control" in 1959, widely recognized for its innovative approach to religious programming. In 1965 Lott was named director of educational services. In this work he pioneered in helping churches produce quality radio and television programs. He is buried in Greenwood Memorial Park, Fort Worth, TX.

JERRY PILLOW

LOTTIE MOON CHRISTMAS OFFERING. See WEEK OF PRAYER FOR FOREIGN MISSIONS AND LOTTIE MOON CHRISTMAS OFFERING.

LOUISIANA, BEL FEDERAL CREDIT UNION OF. Chartered on Mar. 28, 1975, this organization's membership is limited to employees of Louisiana Baptist churches, the Louisiana Baptist Convention, its institutions and agencies, and the immediate families of all these employees. The first officers were James F. Cole, president; H. Wesley Bowman, secretary; and J. D. Cheatham, treasurer. By Dec. 31, 1979, membership was 579, and assets totaled $432,366.

J. D. CHEATHAM

LOUISIANA ASSEMBLIES: STATE, ASSOCIATIONAL, AND REGIONAL (cf. Louisiana Baptist Encampment, Vol. II; Louisiana Baptist Encampments and Assemblies, Vol. III). Clara Springs Encampment, Dry Creek Baptist Assembly, and Tall Timbers continue full programs of operation. Mandeville Encampment, Sligo Assembly, Friendship Encampment, and Camp Stallion no longer exist.

Acadian Baptist Center began in 1976 on property and facilities of the former Acadia Academy leased to six south Louisiana associations. With facilities for year-round accommodations, an active program is maintained.

Bundick Lake Retreat Center, opened near DeRidder in 1977, and owned and operated by First Baptist Church, DeRidder, is available to other groups. It features both motel- and dormitory-type accommodations, well-equipped classrooms, a recreational building, and dining facilities.

Camp Bethany at Bethany, opened June 1, 1980, is owned and operated by Northwest Louisiana Association. It can accommodate 240 for conferences, dining, recreation, and overnight stay.

Camp Living Waters was developed in 1979 on property near Loranger following the sale of Southeast Assembly property of Mandeville. It is a ministry of southeast Louisiana associations and provides a variety of events throughout the year.

Harris Baptist Assembly, an associational camp near Minden, has recently been remodeled, facilities have been upgraded, and a manager has been employed.

Judson Baptist Retreat Center, owned and operated by Judson Association, was opened in Oct., 1979, near Jackson, and can accommodate 80 people.

Louisiana Baptist Conference Center is being developed seven miles west of Alexandria on 671 acres purchased by the Louisiana Baptist Convention in 1975. This tract, located at the point where the western hills of Louisiana begin, is surrounded and protected by Kisatchie National Forest. The intention of the Executive Board is to develop a center for the training and education of church staff and lay persons and to provide facilities to aid in the renewal of believers.

JOHN G. ALLEY

LOUISIANA ASSOCIATIONS (II, III).

I. New Associations. NORTHEAST. Organized Oct. 12, 1977, at First Church, West Monroe, when 18 Trenton Association churches merged with Ouachita Parish Association. In 1979, 40 churches reported 674 baptisms, 32,683 members, $7,344,129 total receipts, and $803,078 mission gifts.

TWO RIVERS. Organized Oct. 15, 1979, when Amite River and Tangipahoa Associations merged. In 1979, 25 churches in the newly formed association located in St. Helena and Tangipahoa parishes reported 142 baptisms, 7,254 members, $1,089,152 total receipts, and $170,944 mission gifts.

WEBSTER-CLAIBORNE. Organized Oct. 21, 1976, when plans for merger of Webster and Liberty Associations, located in Webster and Claiborne parishes, were finalized. In 1979, 41 churches reported 297 baptisms, 15,312 members, $2,853,037 total receipts, and $473,629 mission gifts.

II. Changes in Associations. AMITE RIVER. Organized in 1910, it merged in 1979 with Tangipahoa Association to form Two Rivers.

LIBERTY. Organized in 1895, it merged with Webster Association to form Webster-Claiborne in 1975.

OUACHITA PARISH. Organized in 1945, it dissolved to join with 18 Trenton Association churches to form Northeast Association in 1977.

TANGIPAHOA. Organized in 1905, it merged with Amite River Association to form Two Rivers in 1979.

TRENTON. Organized in 1953, 18 of its churches joined with Ouachita Parish Association to form Northeast in 1977. Four churches remained in Trenton Association.

WEBSTER. Organized in 1922, it merged with Liberty Association to form Webster-Claiborne in 1975.

MELBA B. VODA

LOUISIANA BAPTIST CHILDREN'S HOME (II, III).

Wade B. East, who became superintendent-treasurer in 1962, continued in that capacity throughout the 1970s. During the 1970s the following were constructed: eight cottages replacing older buildings, the Frank C. Sheppard Infirmary, the Helen and Wilbur Humphries Staff Cottage, the Rucker-Austin Center (a multipurpose building), and a swimming pool.

In 1980 the campus totaled 110 acres. Capital assets in 1979 were $5,780,601 with no capital indebtedness. The Cooperative Program allocation for 1980 was $413,000. Additional income is derived from endowment, individual gifts, wills, memorials, and the annual fall food roundup. In 1979, 130 children received institutional care at the home. A foster-care ministry began in 1964. From 300 to 350 children, in addition to those in institutional care, receive annual assistance.

EARL D. MERCER

LOUISIANA BAPTIST CONVENTION (II, III).

I. History. Interest in Baptist history intensified in the 1970s with anniversary celebrations. The convention commemorated its 125th anniversary in 1973 and the 75th anniversary of the Louisiana Children's Home in 1974. A library-archives facility was developed in the Baptist Building in 1971. Convention historian Glen Lee Greene wrote a new history of Louisiana Baptists, *House Upon A Rock* (1973), and the *Louisiana Baptist Historical Atlas* (1975). A replica of the original Half Moon Bluff Church building was constructed during 1978 on Washington Parish Fairgrounds as a joint project of Washington Association and the state convention. Encouraged by the Louisiana Baptist History Committee, chaired by William A. Poe, the Louisiana Baptist Historical Society was reorganized in 1978.

Church Growth, Baptisms, and Stewardship. — Church membership in the 1970s increased from 453,557 to 524,566. In 1979 churches totaled 1,309 and missions 51. Baptisms totaled 148,146 during the decade. Stewardship gains showed a steady increase in church offering plate dollars from $40,455,282 to $99,250,921. Cooperative Program receipts for world missions increased from $3,727,188 to $9,239,780. Gifts for Southern Baptist causes, adding Cooperative Program to designated gifts—including Lottie Moon and Annie Armstrong offerings—rose from $1,951,066 to $5,286,213. Physical assets of the churches and convention agencies grew from $205,256,083 to $436,291,593.

State Missions Services. — Staff reorganization in 1976 resulted in the following: Office of Executive Director, Robert L. Lee; Office of Executive Assistant, Truman Kerr; Office of Business and Personnel Manager, Wesley Bowman; Office of Evangelism Promotion, Leonard Sanderson; Office of Stewardship Promotion, Grady Welch; Church Programs Division, Charles Lowry; Baptist Student Work Division, Udell Smith; Missions Division, Don Mabry; Church/Minister Relations Division, Glen Edwards. Related departments report to division and office directors. The Church/Minister Relations Division was set up in 1978 for counseling ministers and church committees. The convention had approved the program in 1973 following the study of a committee chaired by John S. Harris. Office and division directors of the state board became a task force program planning and management team chaired by executive assistant Truman Kerr and reporting to the executive director.

The convention purchased new properties during the 1970s. A former medical clinic adjoining the Baptist Building was bought and furnished for $319,012 to house offices of the Church/Minister Relations Division. In 1975 the convention secured 673 acres eight miles

FIRST BAPTIST CHURCH, Mansfield, LA. Dedicated on Dec. 7, 1980. *Top:* Front view of sanctuary. *Center:* Interior view of sanctuary. *Bottom:* Rear view of sanctuary.

LOUISIANA BAPTIST CONVENTION (*q.v.*), CENTER FOR MINISTRY, Alexandria. Formerly a medical clinic, it houses the Church/Minister Relations Division.

NORTHEAST LOUISIANA BAPTIST ASSOCIATION Office Building, Monroe. Acquired and renovated in 1979.

southwest of Alexandria from Joyce Brewer for $334,816 to be developed as a state conference center. Feasibility studies of a committee chaired by John G. Alley concluded with recommendations that it be developed. Approved by convention action, a committee was appointed to develop plans and funding procedures. Mark Short, former manager at Glorieta Baptist Conference Center, employed as associate director of Church Programs Division in 1979, was asked to serve as counselor to the committee.

The convention sold Mandeville assembly property to the state in 1978 for $400,000; $300,000 was transferred to local trustees for development of another encampment at a new site.

Staff personnel assisted churches in promoting evangelism and the growth of churches and missions. The convention projected bold goals annually and adopted the SBC Bold Mission Thrust emphasis to share the gospel with every person on earth by A.D. 2000. Renewal and new church program plans developed the work of Sunday School and Church Training to motivate lay witnessing, enlistment, and Christian family life. Sixteen directors of missions in the state worked closely with the state missions staff to serve church needs and associations in promoting mission causes.

Baptist Student Work on campuses was marked by center development and transfer of center ownership to the executive board.

Increased use of visual communications encouraged installation of a soundproof studio in the Baptist Building for productions of the staff and church groups. An electronic message center was installed atop the building to beam Scripture thoughts to the public. The 1976 payment of a mortgage on the Baptist Building was celebrated with a dinner attended by convention and community leaders.

Two overseas crusades directed by Leonard Sanderson enlisted pastors, musicians, and laypersons. Extraordinary results in Korea in 1970 inspired an evangelistic thrust among churches in Louisiana. The 20-city evangelistic crusade resulted in 19,788 professions of faith. Lay witnessing schools were held in Liberia during 1977.

Missions involvement engaged cosponsoring churches for new missions and churches. Cooperative Missions enlarged to include ongoing language missions, French radio broadcasts, deaf missions, ethnic and refugee missions, resort ministries, offshore ministries, seamen's ministries, and interfaith witness. Woman's Missionary Union, working with the Missions Division headed by Kathryn Carpenter and Don Mabry, effected missions expansion.

A joint session of two black conventions with the Louisiana Convention in Lake Charles in 1975 encouraged work with National Baptists. The convention presented $1,500 to E. A. Henry, president of Union Baptist Theological Seminary, New Orleans, for a building program. In 1978, $2,000 went to B. F. Martin,

president of United Theological Seminary, Monroe, for a building.

Special relief projects among churches raised funds for the hungry in depressed countries and for refugees fleeing oppression. Churches were encouraged to receive sponsored refugee families. A disaster relief program was inaugurated under the management of the Men and Boys Department. A large van was purchased and equipped to serve meals and render emergency assistance during disasters. Churches were encouraged to receive donations for a new chapel at Angola prison.

Institutions and Agencies.—Convention-elected trustees own and operate Louisiana College, Louisiana Children's Home, Arcadia Baptist Home, Louisiana Baptist Foundation, and the *Baptist Message.*

Hospital sponsorship terminated with the release and transfer of ownership to trustees: Alexandria Baptist Hospital was released by convention action in 1970, as was Beauregard Memorial of DeRidder in 1975. Transfer was requested by hospital boards in order to secure government low interest loans for expansion.

The convention closed Acadia Academy in 1973 due to decline in enrollment and deficit budgeting. Properties were transferred to the executive board, which leased them to a local Baptist group.

Leadership Changes.—Veteran pastors of prominent churches who retired included R. Houston Smith, First Church, Pineville, 1972; J. D. Grey, First Church, New Orleans, 1972; James W. Middleton, First Church, Shreveport, 1974; James T. Horton, First Church, Monroe, 1975; James W. Taylor, Highland Church, Shreveport, 1978; and George A. Ritchey, First Church, Mansfield, 1973, who accepted a part-time position in the Church/Minister Relations Division.

Death claimed J. Norris Palmer (*q.v.*). Scott L. Tatum resigned Broadmoor Church, Shreveport, 1974, to accept a professorship at Southwestern Baptist Theological Seminary.

Louisiana College president G. Earl Guinn retired in 1974 and accepted a professorship at Southern Baptist Theological Seminary. Robert L. Lynn of Oklahoma succeeded him as president in 1975. *Baptist Message* editor James F. Cole resigned in 1977 to become alumni director at Baylor University. Lynn P. Clayton was elected editor in 1978. Arcadia Baptist Home administrator Raymond Gaudet resigned in 1975, and L. T. Stringer was elected to succeed him.

W. L. Sewell retired as associate executive director in 1977 and was succeeded by James E. Carter as executive assistant. Carter resigned in 1978 to become pastor of University Church, Fort Worth, TX. Truman Kerr was elected executive assistant in 1978. Convention public relations director John W. Green died in 1978. Other staff retiring were Leo Marler, 1970; J. L. Pollard, 1971; J. D. Scott, 1971; Carl E. Conrad, 1976; and T. L. Pfeifer, 1976. Retiring directors of missions were St. Clair Bower,

1971; H. T. Sullivan, 1973; T. W. Leachman, 1975; A. L. New, 1975; Mercer C. Irwin, 1976; Arnold Nelson, 1977; and Luther B. Hall, 1977.

Veteran French preachers L. C. Smith *(q.v.)*, Lawrence Thibodeaux *(q.v.)*, Amadie Janies *(q.v.)*, A. D. Martin *(q.v.)*, Eugene Broussard *(q.v.)*, and twin brothers, Adea *(q.v.)* and Johnny Vidrine *(q.v.)*, died during the 1970s.

ROBERT E. LEE

II. Program of Work. CONVENTION COMMITTEES. The convention conducts its work through eight standing committees, boards of trustees for five agencies and institutions, and the executive board. The standing committees have the following responsibilities: *Committees*—nominates membership of standing and special convention committees; *Nominating*—nominates members of boards; *Order of Business*—plans and recommends agenda for annual convention; *Credentials*—supervises registration and accreditation of messengers to the convention; *Resolutions*—recommends action on resolutions; *Arrangements*—prepares physical arrangements for the messengers during convention; *Public Affairs*—recommends statements on public issues and speaks for the convention when so authorized; and *History*—encourages development and preservation of historical materials.

EXECUTIVE BOARD. The convention assigns its work between annual sessions to the executive board. Members of the board are elected from each area of the state to represent the convention in that area. Five standing committees serve in an advisory role to the executive board: *Nominating*—recommends executive board members and the chairmen pro tem of standing committees; *Program*—reviews, appraises, and coordinates total convention program, budget goals, and allocations; *Operating*—recommends organization and policies for state missions services and recommends budget allocations for these services to the program committee; *Denominational Cooperation*—assists the executive board in relating to SBC programs; and *Executive*—advises the board in areas specifically assigned by the convention or where no assignment is designated to other committees.

An auxiliary operation committee, the Executive Board-Woman's Missionary Union Program Coordination Committee, is to foster increased cooperation in planning and carrying out mission programs.

The executive board staff for state missions services is organized in four major divisions (Missions, Church Programs, Student Work, and Church/Minister Relations) and two promotional offices (Evangelism and Stewardship).

STATE MISSIONS SERVICES. *Administration.*—Administering the work of state missions services are Robert L. Lee, executive director, Truman Kerr, executive assistant, and Wesley Bowman, business and personnel manager. Berniece Camp is administrative assistant to Lee, and Melba Voda is executive office assistant. Chief accountant and assistant business manager is William C. Widman.

Evangelism Promotion.—Leonard Sanderson is director of the Evangelism Promotion Office. Calvin Cantrell is associate. They promote and coordinate evangelistic emphases and endeavors in churches and associations, statewide evangelism conferences and seminars, and lay renewal projects. This office is functionally related to all state missions services divisions and departments to keep them aware of and committed to winning persons to Jesus Christ and developing them in witnessing.

Stewardship Promotion.—Grady Welch as director of the Stewardship Promotion Office is responsible for promoting giving by the churches through the Cooperative Program and giving by members through their church with the tithe as a minimum standard. Assistance to Louisiana churches in Together We Build campaigns is also provided. This office is functionally related to all state missions services divisions and departments to encourage their participation in emphasizing stewardship and Cooperative Program support.

Church Programs.—Charles Lowry directs the Church Programs Division. Associate director and church growth consultant is Mark Short, Jr. Departments within this division and their directors are: Sunday School, Beau Colle; Church Training, Kenneth Mooney; Church Music, Carroll Lowe; and Church Administration and Church Architecture, Earl Sandifer. Age-group consultants are Helen May, youth, and Evelyn Henderson, preschool. Three part-time consultants assist in the music area: Nancy Spears, graded choirs; Teresa Thomason, keyboard; and R. E. Thompson, handbells.

Each of the departments within this division relates to existing programs in the churches and gives assistance in planning, developing leadership, and improving effectiveness. Guidance is provided through conferences, seminars, clinics, workshops, personal consultation, and distribution of printed material.

Additional areas of work within the churches for which this division gives help include church recreation, drama, media centers (libraries), kindergarten, children's worship, single adults, senior adults, work with mentally retarded, Bible memory for children, Bible usage drills for younger youth, speaker's tournaments for older youth, and family ministry.

Church/Minister Relations.—The newest division is Church/Minister Relations, directed by Glen Edwards. The division offers personal and family counseling, information services to pastor search and personnel committees, a ministry to retirees, continuing education through conferences, seminars, and seminary extension courses, and annuity/retirement guidance to churches and church staff personnel. George Higgins is director of the Information Services and Continuing Education Departments. Sam Reeves and George Ritchey serve as ministers to retired preachers, staff members, and denominational employees. Lucian Conway is consultant in annuity/retirement benefits planning. The division is housed in a separate building near the Baptist Building and is connected to it by walkway and driveway. A large conference room is included.

Student Work.—Under the direction of Udell Smith, the Student Work Division seeks to minister to college campuses and to involve students in mission service and support. Specialized ministry includes international students and nursing students, Julie Peacock, director; and high school students, Bob Walden, director.

Student centers owned or leased by the convention are located in Baton Rouge, Lafayette, Lake Charles, Hammond, Monroe, Natchitoches, New Orleans (2), Ruston, Shreveport (2), Alexandria, Thibodaux, and Eunice. Student offices at Louisiana College are in the student union building.

Campus Baptist Student Union directors are: Myra Gulledge, Northwestern; Carl Smith, Louisiana State University, Shreveport; Lynn Hawkins, Louisiana Tech; Sam Sanford, Northeast; Willard Johnson, LSU, Alexandria; Tom Lutner, McNeese; Wally Goodman, Jr., University of Southwestern Louisiana; Frank Horton, LSU, Baton Rouge; T. V. Owens, Southeastern; Gerald Stovall, University of New Orleans; Tom Cobb, Nicholls; Raymond Crawford, Tulane and New Orleans Medical Schools; Charles Harvey, Jr., LSU, Eunice; John Moore, Louisiana College; Cleatice Sipes, Centenary, LSU Medical, Northwestern Nursing, and Bossier Community College.

Missions.—The Missions Division, of which Don Mabry is director, is the largest program of the executive board in both budget and personnel. Within this division are four departments of work in addition to 16 directors of missions who work with the associations.

The Cooperative Missions Department director is Leon Hyatt, Jr. Associates and areas of responsibility are: Larry Barnett—deaf missions, volunteer missions, and interfaith witness; Jimmy Brossette—resort missions, offshore missions, and churches in transition; Rafael Melian—ethnic missions, refugees, and immigrant ministries; and Elie Woerner—French missions and French radio broadcasts.

The Baptist Men and Boys Department director is John T. Winters. Cal Jones is associate. This department trains leadership to involve men and boys in missions education and mission action. Custodian of the disaster relief van owned by the convention, it enlists, trains, and mobilizes crews for operating the van in areas struck by disaster. It also provides involvement in mission projects and conducts summer camps for boys.

The Work with National Baptists Department director is Harvey W. Hoffman, Jr. Fifteen regional missionaries and consultants assist the implementation of this department's work. The department is responsible for assisting black church leaders, exploring areas where new black Baptist missions and churches are needed, providing scholarships for black students, and helping maintain a cooperative spirit between black churches and the work of Louisiana Baptists.

Directors of missions give leadership to one or more associations within the state. They are: Walter Barnard, Lee Dickson, J. I. Funderburk, John Gilbert, Charles Haley, Jerry Edmondson, Charles Harlon, Koy Lee Haywood, Nolan Johnston, Raymond Jones, T. H. Mercer, Wallace Primeaux, George Roberts, Arthur Rockett, W. D. Stogner, and Milton Williams. Associational missions associates are: Ralph Turner, H. J. Rushing, Bill Summer, Miguel Olmedo, Hugh Foster, James Nichols, and Vernon Chevallier.

Woman's Missionary Union is not technically a department of the Missions Division but is a vital auxiliary to that work. Kathryn Carpenter is director-treasurer, Frances Grafton is director of Baptist Women/Baptist Young Women, and Margaret Parson is director of Girls in Action and Acteens. This auxiliary trains leadership to involve women, girls, and children in mission education and mission action. It also conducts summer camps for girls at the WMU owned and operated Camp Tall Timbers.

Support Services.—Four in-building departments give support services to the programs of work outlined above. The Public Relations director is Dick Davis. The director of Art/Media Services is Don Sampson, and John Lehmann is Media Production consultant. Ken Nichols is manager of Purchasing and Printing, and Clarence Kennedy is building superintendent.

COSPONSORING CHURCH PROGRAM. In 1977 the Cooperative Missions Department instituted the use of cosponsoring churches to strengthen Louisiana missions. Most existing mission work was in the southern area of the state, whereas most of the stronger churches were in the northern portion. Churches in the northern region were invited to assist in sponsorship of mission churches. A cosponsoring church works through the sponsoring church and performs four functions: (1) Provides a monthly supplement for its mission church; (2) invites the mission pastor to the cosponsoring church yearly; (3) allows its pastor to participate in the work of the mission church each year; and (4) sends a group of its members to participate in an activity of the field of its misssion church at least once each year.

By Apr., 1980, 73 churches were participating and providing $8,516 per month for mission churches. Personal and financial involvement of cosponsoring churches released new energy which has resulted in significant expansion of mission activity throughout the state.

CHURCH SITE CORPORATION. The 1979 Louisiana Baptist Convention approved the establishment of a Church Site Corporation as a wholly-owned, nonprofit, subsidiary corporation of the convention's executive board. The purpose of this corporation is to assist in the acquisition of church sites for new Louisiana Baptist churches and missions. Funds derive from donations, bequests, allocations from the Georgia Barnette State Missions Offering and

LOUISIANA STATISTICAL SUMMARY

Year	Associations	Churches	Church Membership	Baptisms	SS Enrollment	VBS Enrollment	CT Enrollment	WMU Enrollment	Brotherhood Enrollment	Ch. Music Enrollment	Mission Gifts	Total Gifts	Value Church Property
1969	53	1,312	470,269	14,813	283,883	179,790	143,573	44,612	14,874	44,337	$ 6,198,886	$ 36,168,077	$173,557,620
1970	51	1,309	474,474	14,524	275,455	139,590	137,217	40,065	13,569	43,247	5,841,986	37,226,500	176,607,043
1971	51	1,310	482,580	16,494	270,658	136,158	119,319	35,847	14,756	44,157	6,474,451	40,670,583	183,732,756
1972	51	1,309	489,727	17,527	269,813	124,927	116,893	36,144	14,062	48,145	7,073,140	44,312,134	183,230,714
1973	51	1,314	495,746	15,831	273,169	126,461	112,705	35,166	14,815	50,675	7,980,813	46,470,400	191,762,416
1974	51	1,314	501,903	14,973	271,340	132,308	107,451	35,749	14,409	53,060	8,633,745	50,902,187	210,434,464
1975	51	1,309	506,801	14,578	272,292	135,782	106,417	36,432	14,731	54,356	9,183,811	56,970,036	234,768,603
1976	50	1,307	514,594	13,578	285,756	125,778	104,486	36,313	13,718	55,551	10,620,523	64,320,285	258,006,196
1977	50	1,311	520,735	11,996	284,762	127,696	99,803	35,801	14,114	55,401	11,681,030	71,408,714	290,156,699
1978	50	1,310	519,555	12,896	284,065	125,871	98,196	33,973	13,744	58,142	13,689,780	80,784,789	329,978,554
1979	49	1,316	526,557	14,413	289,707	131,245	95,749	34,276	13,661	59,975	15,974,670	91,912,490	385,905,021
1980	49	1,320	536,197	16,206	297,425	135,558	97,946	34,968	14,054	62,921	17,667,149	103,521,632	446,034,959

BERNIECE CAMP

the Cooperative Program, interest income, and profits from property dealings.

Officers of the corporation are: Joe Lovelady, president, a New Orleans pastor; Gay Juban, vice-president, Baton Rouge layman; and Robert L. Lee, recording secretary, convention executive director.

ROBERT L. LEE, LEON HYATT, JR.
and TRUMAN C. KERR

LOUISIANA BAPTIST FOUNDATION (II, III). On Dec. 31, 1979, assets managed by the foundation totaled $6,732,166. Income disbursements to all beneficiaries from the beginning of the foundation in 1944 through 1979 amounted to $5,340,814. The foundation's charter was amended in Nov., 1975, to authorize it to manage funds for Baptist churches cooperating with the Louisiana Baptist Convention. Subsequently, First Church in Baton Rouge placed over $42,000 with the foundation, and First Church, Shreveport, placed over $500,000 in its trust.

W. B. "Monty" Townsend was employed in Sep., 1978, as administrative assistant. His responsibilities included directing the investment program, revising investment policies, and supervising the transfer of accounting procedures to computerization.

The foundation has continued to utilize television in promoting Christian stewardship of estates. From 1970 through 1979, information and assistance were provided for completion of 915 wills, including $6,862,000 designated for Baptist causes. In Dec., 1979, the foundation changed from the book value method of accounting for pool investments to the market value method.

HERSCHEL C. PETTUS

LOUISIANA BAPTIST HISTORICAL SOCIETY. After being launched on July 2, 1960, the society was reorganized periodically, most recently in July, 1978, following eras of inactivity. In its meeting on Dec. 2, 1978, the society celebrated the 130th anniversary of the Louisiana Baptist Convention. Eugene Spruell was president in 1980.

EUGENE SPRUELL

LOUISIANA BAPTIST MANOR. A ministry to the senior adult community conducted by Colorado Baptist Manor, Inc., Louisiana Baptist Manor is a 10-story apartment building located in Denver, CO. It was purchased at a cost of $1,235,000 in 1978, $300,000 of which was provided by the Colorado Baptist Foundation. The property was appraised at $2,080,000 in 1980.

The manor has approximately 45 buffet apartments, 45 one-bedroom apartments, and 10 two-bedroom apartments. The project is operated as a nonprofit ministry. Two live-in couples serve as on-the-grounds managers, and W. H. (Tony) Anthony serves as general manager for the manor corporation. Bill Landers is

LOUISIANA COLLEGE (*q.v.*), Pineville. Guinn Auditorium and Religious Education Center, opened in 1973. Serves as the worship center for students and hosts local community events.

LOUISIANA BAPTIST CHILDREN'S HOME (*q.v.*), Monroe. *Top, left:* Feazel Cottage, dedicated in 1977. *Bottom, left:* Helen and Wilbur Humphries Staff Cottage, dedicated in 1978. *Top, right:* Frank C. Sheppard Infirmary, dedicated in 1972. *Bottom, right:* Rucker-Austin Center, a multipurpose building, dedicated in 1980.

president. The 100-unit manor is within walking distance of services the residents might need. Weekly spiritual activities are carried on by participating Southern Baptist church groups.

BILL LANDERS

LOUISIANA BAPTIST ORAL HISTORY. The assembling of recordings of Louisiana Baptist history was begun in 1976 by John W. Green, director, Public Relations, Louisiana Baptist Convention. In 1978 the Historical Commission, SBC, staff conducted an oral history workshop in Alexandria. One object of the state convention's program has been to make tapes documenting early mission activity of the convention.

The series of recordings describes the establishment of missions and pioneer churches in French Louisiana. The tape recorded memoirs of St. Clair Bower relate more than a half century of mission progress along the Old Spanish Trail. Other recorded materials deal with the early days of denominational institutions: Louisiana College, Louisiana Baptist Children's Home, and Baptist Bible Institute (New Orleans Baptist Theological Seminary). Some associational history has been recorded. Responsibility for continuing these tapes is under the direction of the convention's Church/Minister Relations Division.

GEORGE A. RITCHEY

LOUISIANA BAPTISTS AND SOCIAL ISSUES. The 1970s focused on several key moral issues for Louisiana Baptists, as for the nation: abortion, child abuse, homosexuality, pornography, and television programming abuse. In convention, messengers called for preventive counseling in would-be abortion cases so that alternative measures could be recommended. Churches were called upon to deal positively with awareness and prevention of the problem of child abuse, working redemptively with abusive parents. The convention took a forgiving stance toward the homosexual but defined homosexuality as "unnatural, offensive, and totally contrary to the teaching of God's word." The recurring position on pornography and the violence, profanity, and sensuality of television programming was a call to active crusading against such exploitation by the media. In convention action, messengers deplored the media rating systems, increasing amounts of obscene mail, and the apathy of individuals about monitoring their own viewing and reading.

Governmental concerns became moral issues, beginning with a resolution opposing the Prayer Amendment and commending Louisiana Baptists who wrote legislators requesting its defeat and those legislators who voted against it. Good citizenship was stressed in the midst of an expensive and morally questionable election period. Baptists were urged to follow Christian principles in voting and in any part of the election process. An appeal for prayer support for

President Jimmy Carter deplored terrorism and called for peaceful solutions in obtaining the release of the hostages in Iran. At the same time, the President was commended for setting the White House Conference on Families, which hopefully would underline the strengths of the family and its biblical basis.

Since mid-decade, Christian response to victims of natural disasters has been formalized through a disaster relief ministry and a ham radio ministry.

SARAH FRANCES ANDERS

LOUISIANA COLLEGE (I, III). The 1970s saw continued expansion and improvement of the physical plant. Completion of Guinn Auditorium and Religious Education Center in 1973 provided a 2,000-seat facility for campus, community, and denominational use. The Gladys Tatum West Pipe Organ, donated by the H. O. West family of Minden, LA, is one of the largest built in America in recent times. Bolton Chapel, with a smaller pipe organ and seating 300, is located on the lower level of this building. It houses the Department of Religion, Philosophy, and Classical Languages. In 1978 the first phase of the Stephen M. and Jewel C. English Student Village opened for occupancy with 40 women and 52 men. The apartments were largely funded by a $500,000 gift from the children of the couple whose name the building bears. These apartments for singles provide an innovative option to traditional housing.

The Billy Allgood Baseball Field in 1970 and the Parrish Fuller Fitness Trail in 1979 were additions to physical fitness facilities. In 1980 major interior renovation was begun on Alexandria Hall, whose first floor is the center of administration. The spring of 1980 also saw the Morgan W. Walker Student Center undergoing extensive renovation.

In response to needs made more apparent through a self-study, a dramatic expansion of student development programs characterized the 1970s. Under the leadership of Edward L. Heath, vice-president for student development, a staff of professionals in the area of student life was assembled to direct counseling, housing, student activities, and orientation.

Renewal of accreditation by the Southern Association of Colleges and Schools marked the beginning of the decade. In the 1970s the number of full-time faculty in the Music Department with doctorates increased from one to four. Other departments of the college reported similar progress.

A change of administration occurred in mid-decade when, after a tenure of 23 years, G. Earl Guinn resigned as president to join the faculty of Southern Baptist Theological Seminary. Robert L. Lynn, vice-president of administration at Oklahoma Baptist University, became the new president in 1975. Under Lynn's administration other milestones were realized in the implementation of a new central curriculum in 1977, built around a sequence of values courses. The college adopted "Focus on Quality" as the theme of a three-year emphasis in conjunction with the 75th anniversary of the institution in 1981.

Financial support is derived not only from tuition and a generous share of the Louisiana Convention budget, but also from the gifts of friends in the community and beyond. The largest single gift in the history of the college, more than $670,000, was received in Feb., 1980, from the families of three brothers, Herman, Andrew, and C. O. Walker, who reside at Taylor and Minden, LA. Near the end of the decade a fund-raising campaign realized $1,330,000 in cash and pledges from the citizens of the Alexandria-Pineville community where the college is located.

The 1970s were a decade of growth in which enrollment increased by half while dormitory students doubled in number, a clear indication of the increasing residential nature of the college. Cumulative enrollment for the 1979-80 session was 1,715. Prior to the 1980 commencement the college had conferred a total of 6,229 degrees.

LANDRUM SALLEY

LOUISIANA HOSPITALS. Louisiana Baptist Convention hospital services began in 1916 with the acceptance of a small hospital in Alexandria. Baton Rouge General was second in 1944. Beauregard Memorial, DeRidder, was constructed in 1947, and Homer Memorial was a lease operation beginning in 1949. Costly facilities and operations, coupled with convention policy of refusing federal funds, led to the release of all four. By convention vote Homer was released in 1967, Baton Rouge in 1969, Alexandria in 1970, and DeRidder in 1974. The release of DeRidder carried a recommendation to use hospital allocations for direct missions and special needs. Hospital ministries are conducted through local pastoral care, including the use of laypersons.

See also LOUISIANA BAPTIST CONVENTION, Vols. II, III.

CARL A. HUDSON

LOUISVILLE BAPTIST HOSPITALS, THE (cf. Kentucky Baptist Hospital, Vols. I, III). This institution is composed of two hospitals, Highlands Baptist Hospital (formerly Kentucky Baptist Hospital, 1924-78), and Baptist Hospital East (opened 1975). Highlands Hospital has 276 patient beds, including a 60-bed psychiatric unit, a 19-bed physical rehabilitation unit, a 28-bed oncology unit, and a cardiac rehabilitation unit. Baptist Hospital East has 253 patient beds, including medical surgical units, a maternity unit, a doctors' building, and an intensive care unit. A fully accredited two-year School of Nursing is a part of the Louisville Baptist Hospitals. The hospitals are affiliated with a School of Radiologic Technology based at Bellarmine College. The Louisville Baptist Hospitals have an accredited program in clinical pastoral education and an accredited Pastoral Counseling Center.

In 1974 the Louisville Baptist Hospitals took over the clinic maintained on the campus of Southern Baptist Theological Seminary and changed the name to the H. Hart Hagan Clinic. The purpose of the clinic is to provide primary/ambulatory services to the students and faculty of the seminary. Part-time physician coverage is available. Nurse coverage is provided for initial screening and minor treatment.

In 1979 Highlands Baptist Hospital and St. Anthony Hospital formed the Highlands Medical Center to maximize sharing of services. A skyway was constructed to join the hospitals and provide for easy movement of patients between hospitals. In 1980 there were plans for a doctors' building.

The executive vice-president of the Louisville Baptist Hospitals is Ben R. Brewer. The Louisville Baptist Hospitals are a part of Baptist Hospitals, Inc.

BEN R. BREWER

LOWTHER, ALBERT LEE (b. Pauls Valley, OK, Sep. 14, 1902; d. Oklahoma City, OK, Oct. 29, 1978). Pastor and missions director. The son of Henry Hamilton and Rena McMahan Lowther, he attended Oklahoma Baptist University (B.A., 1934). After serving pastorates at Davenport, Bowlegs, Oilton, and Seminole, OK, he became director of missions for Tulsa-Rogers Association, 1943-49, and then for Capital Association, Oklahoma County, 1949-71. In 1949 he married Jessie Keyes. They had four children.

J. M. GASKIN

LURTZ, JON WADE (b. Detroit, MI, Jan. 21, 1920; d. Oklahoma City, OK, Dec. 15, 1972). Pioneer area missionary. The son of George and Susannah Lurtz, farmers, he attended Oklahoma Baptist University (B.A., 1958), Midwestern Baptist Theological Seminary (1959), and Southwestern Baptist Theological Seminary (B.D., 1961). He married Vergie Jones, June, 1946. They had six children: Donna, Deborah, Darla, Dianne, Jon, Jr., and Timothy.

Lurtz served as pastor of First Southern Baptist Church, Garden City, KS, 1961-64. He was appointed by the Home Mission Board in July, 1961, to serve as pastoral missionary in Garden City. When he began to serve in Southern Plains Association, Jan., 1965, only five churches and one mission existed. In 1972 the association had 12 churches and 10 missions. In Oct., 1970, he began to serve in High Plains Baptist Association as well. These two associations contained the western counties of Kansas from its northern to southern borders. Lurtz is buried in Resthaven Cemetery, Oklahoma City, OK.

JAMES H. SHOPE

LUTHER RICE SEMINARY (III). Reorganized in 1979 into a Bible College Division and a Graduate Division, the seminary has a

23-member faculty (16 full-time) and offers training at the undergraduate, first-professional, graduate, and nondegree levels. Of the 1,569 students enrolled in 1980, 1,422 were in the external (off-campus) program. Robert G. Witty continued to serve as president. Gene M. Williams was named president-elect in 1981.

DANIEL H. HOLCOMB

LYNE, MARY NELLE (b. Russellville, KY, May 6, 1883; d. Bowling Green, KY, Nov. 27, 1969). State Woman's Missionary Union leader. Daughter of Selden Lyne, a banker, and Bettie Lyne, homemaker, she was educated at Logan College, Russellville, KY (A.B.), WMU Training School, Louisville, KY (B.M.T., 1917), and Columbia University (M.A.). After serving as principal of Cantonese Girls' School, Shanghai, China, 1917-27, she was acting Alabama WMU executive secretary, 1934-41; missions education teacher, WMU Training School, 1941-46; and missionary to the Chinese in Berkeley, CA, and Phoenix, AZ, 1946-51. She is buried at Russellville, KY.

KATHRYN JASPER

M

MACAO, MISSION IN. See HONG KONG-MACAO, MISSION IN.

MADDOX, W. GORDON (b. Campbell County, KY, Jan. 29, 1897; d. Dallas, TX, Sep. 13, 1977). Physician and Baptist layman. Son of William Edward and Jennie Keturah (Byrd) Maddox, farmers, Maddox married Ruth Mitchell, Aug. 25, 1921. They had three children: W. G., Jr., D. L., and Dorothy Jane. After receiving a pharmacy degree (Ph.G.) from the University of Texas and a medical degree (M.D.) from Baylor University, Maddox combined a 28-year teaching career at Baylor School of Medicine with a 25-year medical practice in Dallas, a 14-year family practice in Denton, TX, and a 13-year ministry as seminary physician at Southwestern Baptist Theological Seminary.

Maddox was one of the first physicians to do research on nicotine and to speak against the use of tobacco. He served as the personal physician for George W. Truett (q.v. II) and worked in a tuberculosis mission hospital in Tanzania, 1962-63. He is buried in Restland Memorial Park, Dallas, TX.

TOM NETTLES

MAINE, SOUTHERN BAPTISTS IN. See MARYLAND, BAPTIST CONVENTION OF; NEW ENGLAND, BAPTIST GENERAL ASSOCIATION OF.

MAJOR, ROBERT WESLEY (b. Greenwood, SC, Jan. 26, 1915; d. Charleston, SC, May 1, 1979). Minister and denominational leader. The son of David Major, a policeman, and Maggie (Morrison) Major, he attended Erskine College (B.A., 1937) and The Southern Baptist Theological Seminary (Th.M., 1944). He married Bess Denton, June 10, 1939. They had two sons, John Timothy and David Robert. Pastor for 29 years at Ashley River Church, Charleston, SC, he served as president of the South Carolina Baptist Convention in 1965. He was also a member of the Home Mission Board. He is buried at Charleston, SC.

FLYNN T. HARRELL

MALAWI, MISSION IN (III). Missionaries in Malawi emphasize the training and equipping of African leaders. In 1980 leadership training was occurring on three levels—local, extension, and a Bible school in Lilongwe—with some pastors getting advanced training in neighboring countries. Cassette tapes and an audiovisual library based in Blantyre undergirded this emphasis. Bible Way Correspondence School and publication ministries based in Lilongwe were aiding in evangelistic outreach. Gerald Workman, Africa's first full-time music missionary, and his wife Barbara (Fetters) arrived in Malawi in 1971. Agricultural and social ministries assisted in meeting human need. Blantyre's English-language church ministered to the university and international communities. In 1977 missionaries and convention leaders began planning for a nationwide stewardship and evangelistic campaign for 1980-81. Missionary activity expanded in the 1970s to include Balaka and Mzuzu. At the end of 1979, the 29 missionaries worked with almost 12,000 Malawi Baptists in 185 churches.

JOY NEAL

MALAYSIA-SINGAPORE, MISSION IN (III; cf. Malaya, Mission in, Vol II). Missionaries entered the East Malaysia states of Sabah in 1964 and Sarawak in 1970 but were later denied work permits. Thus, no Southern Baptist missionaries have lived in these states since

1973 and 1978, respectively. Missionaries work in cooperation with the Malaysia Baptist Convention, the Singapore Baptist Convention, and area associations. An urban evangelism strategy was begun in 1975 in Singapore to reach the masses in high-rise apartments. Baptists have work in every state of Malaysia. In Jan., 1980, 38 missionaries were in this mission (including eight associates and one journeyman).

RUSSELL A. MORRIS

MARGARET FUND (II, III). In 1961 the administration of this scholarship fund for children of missionaries was transferred from the Woman's Missionary Union, SBC, to the Foreign and Home Mission Boards. By 1980 a FMB budget allocation of $800,000 assisted about 600 recipients, and $165,000 from the HMB went to about 200 students, bringing the total amount of assistance provided since 1916 to more than $9,000,000. Special endowments within the Margaret Fund provide for the annual Elizabeth Lowndes Scholarship and make possible a gift of $100 to each former fund recipient appointed as a career missionary or $50 to each who becomes a missionary associate, journeyman, or US-2 appointee. The Burney Gifts have been discontinued. In June, 1980, the Mary B. Rhodes Medical Scholarship became an interest free loan, canceled if appointed.

DORIS DEVAULT

MARKHAM, OSCAR CLYDE (b. near Pulaski, TN, Oct. 27, 1900; d. near Dover, TN, Oct. 27, 1976). Pastor and Bible college administrator. A graduate of Union University (B.A., 1938), he married Bonnie Paysinger, Mar. 8, 1925. They had one son, Charles Edwin. After Bonnie's death he married Annie C. Parrish, Feb. 15, 1957. Ordained in Pulaski, TN, Aug. 25, 1929, he served pastorates in Tennessee and Kentucky; was clerk of West Kentucky Association, 1949-55; and member of the Kentucky Baptist Historical Commission, 1972-76. He edited *The Baptist Herald* of Mid-Continent Baptist Bible College and served this school as teacher, dean, registrar, and president, 1949-76. He is buried at Clinton, KY.

LEO T. CRISMON

MARLER, JAMES DAVID (b. Wattsville, SC, Dec. 13, 1909; d. Phoenix, AZ, May 27, 1973). Pastor, Army chaplain, and denominational officer. The son of Janice and Clayton Marler, he graduated from Wingate College (1936) and New Orleans Baptist Theological Seminary. He married Ruth Cooper, Nov. 25, 1931. Their children were Delphia and David. Ordained by Lucas Avenue Baptist Church, Laurens, SC, Sep. 8, 1929, he served 20 years as a chaplain in the United States Army, retiring as a lieutenant colonel. He was a pastor in North Carolina prior to Army service and in Arizona following his military career. He served two terms as president of the Arizona Conven-

tion, 1968-70. Marler is buried in the Coolidge Cemetery, Coolidge, AZ.

JOE CAUSEY

MARNEY, LEONARD CARLYLE (b. Harriman, TN, July 8, 1916; d. Lake Junaluska, NC, July 3, 1978). Pastor, teacher, and theologian. The son of Sarah Marney and John Marney, a manufacturing plant foreman, he graduated from Carson-Newman College (B.A.) and The Southern Baptist Theological Seminary (Th.M., 1943, Th.D., 1946). On June 20, 1940, he married Elizabeth Christopher. Their children were Christopher and Susan. After brief pastorates in Beaver Dam and Paducah, KY, he began a 10-year ministry at First Baptist Church, Austin, TX, 1948-58. He also served as professor of Christian ethics at Austin Presbyterian Seminary. From Austin he went to Charlotte, NC, as senior minister of Myers Park Baptist Church, 1958-67, resigning to establish Interpreters' House, an ecumenical center for study and renewal, for clergy and laity, at Lambuth Inn, Lake Junaluska, NC.

He was invited for lectureships and preaching on many campuses: Princeton, Harvard, Yale, Union, Vanderbilt, Colgate-Rochester, Andover-Newton, and many others. He received honorary degrees from the University of Glasgow, Scotland, Wake Forest University, Johnson C. Smith University, and Kalamazoo College.

In addition to his service on commissions of the Baptist World Alliance, Marney was a member of the National Advisory Commission on Rural Poverty and vice-president-at-large of the National Council of Churches. He served as a trustee for *The Christian Century* and as an editorial board member of *Religion in Life*. He was the author of a dozen books. He is buried in Evergreen Cemetery, Charlotte, NC.

CLAUDE BROACH

MARRIAGE AND FAMILY. See PASTORAL CARE.

MARS HILL COLLEGE (II, III). A four-year, coeducational Baptist college at Mars Hill, NC, with a 1979-80 enrollment of 1,940 and a staff of over 200. Fred B. Bentley continues as president. The campus includes 180 acres and 29 buildings, valued at $20,000,000. The endowment is $6,000,000. Fully accredited, Mars Hill has developed several new emphases over the past six years.

The competence-based curriculum is a pioneer model within the nation. Area pastors, church workers, and students use the Center for Christian Education Ministries, a facility housing numerous Baptist materials. Its director conducts seminars and workshops throughout western North Carolina. The Rural Life Demonstration Center, on a nearby 1,000-acre farm, is a laboratory for studying conservation and learning the values and heritage of home and family life.

FRED B. BENTLEY

MARTIN, OLIVE BRUNSON (b. Hampton, VA, Aug. 5, 1893; d. Norfolk, VA, June 15, 1972). Woman's Missionary Union leader. Daughter of Anne Wood Brunson and John Thomas Brunson, a cabinetmaker, she married George R. Martin of Norfolk, VA, Sep. 5, 1912. They had no children. She served as WMU president for Virginia, 1926-31, 1934-46. Under her leadership, summer camps for youth flourished, goodwill centers opened, interracial work began, and Virginia WMU organizations increased from 2,784 to 4,228.

Martin served as first stewardship chairman, WMU, SBC, 1929-33, and as president, 1945-56. Her 11 years of leadership were marked by steady growth. Local organizations increased from 41,227 to 79,101 and membership from 739,360 to 1,345,153. The Lottie Moon Christmas Offering almost quadrupled, and the Annie Armstrong Offering more than doubled. She led in the enlargement of the Birmingham headquarters staff and purchase of a new building; the erection of a WMU Training School (Armstrong Memorial) in Rome, Italy; and the initial planning for transfer of Royal Ambassadors to the Brotherhood Commission, SBC.

In 1947 she was elected to the Executive Committee of the Baptist World Alliance. From 1948 to 1960, she served as chairman of the Women's Department, BWA. She was instrumental in organizing continental unions within this organization. She is buried in Forest Lawn Cemetery, Norfolk, VA.

DORIS DEVAULT

MARTINIQUE, MISSION IN. See FRENCH WEST INDIES, MISSION IN.

MARY HARDIN-BAYLOR, THE UNIVERSITY OF (cf. Mary Hardin-Baylor College, II, III). This institution began the 1970s as the oldest women's college west of the Mississippi and ended the decade as a coeducational university. It became coeducational in 1971, and by 1975 the student population was 60 percent female and 40 percent male. University status was attained in 1978. A $6,000,000 capital campaign made possible the new Sanderford Administrative Complex, Clements Advancement Building, and complete renovation of the Presser Fine Arts Building. A new classroom building is being planned.

Bobby E. Parker succeeded William B. Tanner as president in 1971. In 1973 the Mabee Student Center was dedicated. Enrollment was nearing the optimum of 1,200 in 1980. The B.S. in Nursing degree leads the field of graduates, followed by bachelor's degrees in science, education, business, art, music, religion, languages, psychology, and sociology.

BOBBY E. PARKER

MARYLAND, BAPTIST CONVENTION OF (III; cf. Maryland Baptist Union Association, Vol. II).

I. History. Among items making the Baptist Convention of Maryland (BCM) unique in 1969 and 1970 was its participation in forming two new state conventions. Both had been administratively related to the BCM as fellowships prior to their convention status.

New York.—The founding of the first Southern Baptist congregation, LaSalle Baptist, Niagara Falls, came in the summer of 1954. In 1958 churches in New York, Upper New Jersey, and Connecticut under the administrative leadership of the BCM formed a "fellowship" as a means of developing a state convention. The fellowship was the guiding body toward construction of the convention. The organization of the Baptist Convention of New York took place on Sep. 25-26, 1969, at Central Church, Syracuse. When organized as the 31st state convention of the SBC, New York Southern Baptists had 5 associations, 70 churches, 27 chapels, and 10,139 members. Largest of the associations was the Metropolitan New York Association which had 43 churches, 15 chapels, and 7,000 members. Paul S. James became the first executive director. The BCM offered structures and services of an established convention and received freshness and challenge inherent in new work.

Pennsylvania-South Jersey.—One hundred and sixty-five messengers and 85 visitors were present for the constitution of the Baptist Convention of Pennsylvania-South Jersey as the 32nd state convention for Southern Baptists held in the Country and Town Baptist Church, Camp Hill, PA, Oct. 2-3, 1970. Embracing all of Pennsylvania and approximately half of New Jersey, the new convention ministers to some of America's. largest cities. The convention organized with 8,520 members in 60 churches and 30 missions, and approved a total operating budget of $120,500, calling for $96,000 in Cooperative Program receipts from churches. The new convention approved 20 percent of all undesignated income for world mission causes, elected Joseph M. Waltz (*q.v.*) as its first executive secretary, and in 1972 hosted the SBC meeting in Philadelphia.

New Town: Columbia.—A new city to be named Columbia was announced in 1963 when the Rouse Company revealed the purchase of 14,000 acres of land in Howard County, MD, for the purpose of building a new kind of planned city. Construction began in 1966, and the first residents moved in during 1967. Columbia is a city planned for 110,000 people. The city consists of seven villages that will house 15,000 persons each. Neighborhoods containing from 800 to 1,200 families each exist in the villages.

In 1964 various religious groups began grappling with the problem of how to develop churches in Columbia. All church buildings had to be erected at the hub of each village where the shopping center and other facilities were located. After considerable study, the groups (which called themselves the Columbia Cooperative Ministry) came up with the idea of the Interfaith Center, a building whose facilities the 13 major Protestant denominations could share. Shared finances, administration, program mission, and staff for the common facilities relieve the total amount of funds tied up in real estate and free more of the bodies' resources for engagement in mission, and free the time and energies of members of these religious bodies usually spent in maintaining buildings for mission purposes.

In 1968, 16 Baptist leaders in Maryland met at the Baptist Building in Lutherville to discuss the concept of the new city of Columbia and the prospects of introducing Southern Baptist religious activities into the new city. Seven Southern Baptist churches representing three different Southern Baptist associations in Maryland soon sponsored the organization of the Columbia Missions Committee. In 1970 James Hamblen became the first director of Southern Baptist activities in Columbia. Hamblen also served as the Home Mission Board staff consultant for "new planned cities" for the SBC.

In 1970 six family units began meeting on Wednesday evenings in the facilities of the First Presbyterian Church of Howard County. Three years after the meeting, more than 40 people became charter members of the Columbia Baptist Fellowship. The fellowship continued to grow and moved into the newly constructed Oakland Mills Religious Facility—"The Meeting House"—in Apr., 1975. Here the Columbia Baptist Fellowship shares facilities with Jewish, Roman Catholic, Lutheran, and Brethren congregations. The architectural design of the building followed the principle of sharing a common baptistry; a common entrance court and foyer became the physical expression of interfaith cooperation. A major requirement that the building be receptive to all faiths led to the avoidance of obvious symbolism associated with specific sects.

Columbia Baptist Fellowship is the leading Protestant group in Columbia. The fellowship has Bible study, church music, missions, deaf ministry, resources for family growth, ministry to senior citizens, and Backyard Bible Schools. The fellowship sponsors two missions. Southern Baptists expect to have a minimum of four to as many as seven fellowships in Columbia.

Association/State Convention Cooperative Agreement.—The BCM was apparently the first state convention to effect a working cooperative agreement with every association in the convention. General principles included the following:

(1) The association and the state convention shall cooperate in a plan of work and financial support of personnel and programs jointly related to both agencies. This agreement does not imply that the only contact between state convention and churches in the association shall be through the same office, but lays down principles for planning and calendaring of work and jointly supporting personnel and programs. In this agreement, both parties pledge themselves to open lines of communication and to clear understanding by all state staff and by the executive committee and program leaders of the association.

(2) The plan of work shall be cooperatively developed by appropriate representatives of both bodies in accord with the policies of the association and state convention. In the event the policies of the bodies differ, the plan shall state a written policy to be followed.

(3) Financial support for personnel and the plan of work shall be agreed upon in an annual cooperative conference. Plans made in the annual conference will not be limited to a one-year period. Associational leaders may avail themselves of projections and long-range plans of state convention staff as desired. Generally, financial support provided by the state convention shall consist of underwriting salaries and allowances of personnel, but may include participation in programs and projects.

(4) General administration and promotion of the plan of work shall be by association. The association is expected to take the initiative in planning, conducting, and evaluating its own programs. The state convention shall assist in promoting programs in the association where applicable and shall administer those programs for which it is primarily responsible in the association, such as Baptist Student Unions.

(5) Changes in plan and budget may be recommended by either agency. The association shall be given as much advance knowledge as possible regarding change in state convention support designated for salary and other benefits. Recommended changes shall mainly be made in cooperative planning conferences held annually. Official action involving the cooperative plan and budget shall be taken by both agencies according to their regular procedures. Some state convention action may be subject to concurrence by the HMB. Action shall not be implemented until both agencies have finally approved the recommendation.

(6) Allocation of funds by the state convention shall be made monthly upon receipt of appropriate reports.

Bold Mission Thrust—In keeping with SBC objectives to give every person an opportunity to hear and accept the gospel, and for all people to have an opportunity to worship with fellow believers, the BCM in 1976 established three priority concerns that implement and encompass "Bold Missions."

(1) Equipping Saints for Mission, Ministry, and Service. The objective is to assist each church in the BCM in creating a spiritual climate for Christian growth and fellowship and equipping Christians for witness, ministry, and service.

(2) Local Congregational Extension. The objective is to assist each church in the BCM in understanding the basic nature and mission of the church and expressing God's concern for persons by extending the witness of their church into new areas of the community and association.

(3) World Mission Support. Objectives are to assist each church in the BCM in understanding the biblical basis for missions and in leading Christians to support world missions through prayer, the Cooperative Program, special mission offerings, and life commitment to the end

that the people of our world may have the opportunity to hear the gospel and share in God's redeeming grace.

Southern Baptists focused on Baltimore Baptist Association as a pilot for BMT in 1976. A survey, later made of Baltimore churches to determine the rank and file appraisal of the emphasis, showed a 27 percent increase in average weekly Sunday School attendance since 1976. Fifty-three percent bolstered their tithe and offering receipts, while 41 percent had increased baptisms.

More than a third of the Baltimore churches reported making greater efforts in touching more lives in a redemptive way than in recent memory. The method of BMT in Maryland provided the motivation for a number of churches to carry out the task of evangelizing and ministering more effectively in their own communities. This involved a fourfold emphasis: (1) BMT provided a process for the churches to utilize in determining their own communities; (2) BMT provided special encouragement and survival tactics for churches in declining neighborhoods; (3) BMT helped prompt churches to reach persons of cultural, ethnic, and racial backgrounds different from that of the majority of the church's members; and (4) BMT sparked some churches to engage in intensive mission ministries to hurting persons in their own communities. BMT also awakened concern within some churches for the needs of persons not adequately churched in communities beyond their own fields of responsibility. Maryland Baptists set BMT goals for 1977-79 which would stretch their faith to believe God could do great things through ordinary people who were obedient to him.

II. Programs of Work. *Church Development.*—The 1970s were years of change, consolidation, cooperation, and challenge. Beginning the decade, departments of work represented every major church program of work, but little attempt existed to provide basic coordination of programs planned at the state or associational levels. The staff had expanded during the 1960s and continued into the new decade.

Charles R. Barnes became Sunday School secretary in Mar., 1970, succeeding John Tubbs, who had served for 10 previous years. In 1973 a major restructuring occurred in the entire State Mission Board's programs of work through establishing three major divisions of work: Church Development, Cooperative Missions, and Business Services. Woman's Missionary Union continued to function as an auxiliary, but was administered as a department of work. Charles R. Barnes headed Church Development. Sam High, who served as Church Training director, retired early due to failing health. James Osborn became Church Training director. Mary Kathryn Black became the first youth/adult director in the Church Development Department in 1973. She resigned to accept a position with the Sunday School Board, SBC, in Dec., 1977. Fred White, evangelism and Sunday School consultant, resigned to become director of the Direct Evangelism Department of the

HMB in Dec., 1978. Jack Parrott became director of Evangelism and Church Administration in May, 1979. Curtis Griffis became first director of religious education for the Baptist General Association of New England in 1973, serving until 1978. Al Riddley became the director of this work in Jan., 1979.

Cooperative Missions.—The Cooperative Missions Department is engaged in planning, coordinating, and administering a comprehensive program of mission outreach and ministry in the territory served by the BCM. In 1972, in a change in the organizational structure of the BCM, the Missions Department became designated the Department of Cooperative Missions, with responsibility for mission administration, Brotherhood, evangelism, stewardship promotion, church administration, and student ministries. E. Milford Howell had served as director of the Missions Department. Upon his resignation, John E. Saunders became director of the new Department of Cooperative Missions.

For years the HMB and the BCM have cooperated in certain areas of mission outreach and ministry within the convention territory. The HMB provides financial help and some field services; the Department of Cooperative Missions has administrative responsibilities for the work.

A significant new direction of mission outreach took place in 1973, with the addition of a director of language missions within the department. James N. Lewis served in this capacity until 1975, when Minor Davidson became director of language missions. By the end of the decade, 16 ethnic congregations were established and 15 churches were maintaining ministries with the deaf.

In 1976 the student ministries section of the Cooperative Missions Department became a separate department in the convention's organizational structure.

In 1977 Neil E. Wilson became director of Brotherhood, Skycroft, and Stewardship within the department. George W. Bullard, Jr., joined the staff in Jan., 1977, as consultant to churches in transition. This was a two-year intern program jointly sponsored with the HMB.

Through the 1970s, every phase of mission work was strengthened, and many areas of special mission ministries were entered.

Ministries in Higher Education.—The 1970s were years of change and growth for student work in the BCM. When the state mission board reorganized the convention staff in 1972, it placed the Student Department in the Cooperative Missions Department. William E. Bolin followed Keith H. Harris as director of the department in 1973. Further reorganization took place following a lengthy study of student work in Maryland. In 1976 all of the convention work relating to higher education was grouped together to form a new department—Ministries in Higher Education (MHE). The new department became responsible for Baptist student work, church-student work, religious studies, seminary extension, and ministerial student aid.

The state mission board reorganized itself in

LARRY E. HIGH

MARYLAND STATISTICAL SUMMARY

Year	Associations	Churches	Church Membership	Baptisms	SS Enrollment	VBS Enrollment	CT Enrollment	WMU Enrollment	Brotherhood Enrollment	Ch. Music Enrollment	Mission Gifts	Total Gifts	Value Church Property
1969	20	322	92,303	4,768	77,119	45,554	23,592	13,409	4,338	8,824	$1,309,266	$ 9,250,150	$ 39,648,295
1970	16	278	87,876	4,126	68,593	39,527	18,894	10,690	3,727	7,886	1,255,902	8,761,763	39,890,567
1971	14	252	84,281	3,946	60,876	32,854	12,516	9,124	3,440	7,305	1,431,898	9,342,096	44,815,003
1972	14	254	86,442	4,547	62,467	38,513	11,650	9,582	3,840	8,566	1,618,219	9,870,462	47,030,051
1973	15	254	89,040	4,981	63,812	34,107	11,715	9,568	3,652	9,633	1,657,423	10,100,395	51,472,663
1974	15	264	92,663	4,579	63,775	31,384	10,945	10,087	3,556	10,048	1,913,058	10,902,040	60,297,042
1975	15	267	95,224	4,357	63,206	43,372	10,639	9,896	3,919	9,887	2,123,929	12,161,841	71,033,874
1976	15	279	98,573	4,088	65,123	35,290	10,280	9,698	3,661	9,705	2,302,025	13,591,029	77,288,949
1977	15	281	100,126	3,559	66,002	35,566	9,686	9,404	3,489	9,772	2,524,951	14,933,855	88,926,949
1978	16	287	100,169	3,588	63,600	32,494	10,607	8,879	4,011	10,332	2,845,604	16,349,454	97,515,784
1979	16	295	102,412	3,900	63,473	33,810	9,299	8,808	3,613	10,445	3,083,435	18,286,110	105,814,050
1980	16	295	104,404	4,750	64,574	33,929	10,544	8,979	3,472	10,981	3,741,096	19,836,144	117,970,533

1979, creating new committees which related to the four major departments of work. The Christian Higher Education Committee was given the key function of assisting the director-coordinator of MHE, with evaluation and program development for all areas of work assigned to the department.

A New England-wide program of student ministries was initiated in 1973. The work in Greater Boston, directed by Mack I. Taylor, 1942-75, provided the base for the expansion of work. In 1975 The Southern Baptist Theological Seminary campus ministry intern, Susan Sprague, paved the way for the first full-time Baptist campus minister at Yale University, Charles J. Scalise. As the work continued to develop through the utilization of volunteer directors, seminary interns, and US-2 workers, Scalise was given the additional responsibility of acting state director of Baptist Student Ministries in New England in 1978.

The first full-time Baptist campus minister for work in the Baltimore Association was hired in 1976. He worked for one year in a part-time capacity before his position was fully funded. Stanley Hendricks, a Baltimore city school vice-principal, initiated work at predominantly black Morgan State University. The work grew to be the largest religious organization at the school, demanding more time and effort than a volunteer could give it. In 1976 the HMB appointed Nathaniel Milton as US-2 student worker at the university. The work continues as a significant expression of interracial and interdenominational cooperation.

At the beginning of the 1970s, Maryland Baptists had a ministry to students on 12 campuses; at the close of the decade they ministered on 27 campuses. The total BCM budget for student work was $38,045 in 1970 and $98,901 in 1979.

See also NEW ENGLAND, BAPTIST GENERAL ASSOCIATION OF; NEW YORK, BAPTIST CONVENTION OF; PENNSYLVANIA-SOUTH JERSEY, BAPTIST CONVENTION OF.

ROY GRESHAM, CHARLES BARNES
MINOR DAVIDSON, WILLIAM E. BOLIN

MARYLAND, BAPTIST FOUNDATION OF (III). The 1970s saw growth in the use of the foundation's services by churches of the Baptist Convention of Maryland. Baptists placed property, scholarship funds, and bequests from wills with the foundation. The largest of the trust accounts continues to be that of the Baptist Convention of Maryland. The foundation as of Dec. 31, 1979, managed trust funds of the convention with market values in excess of $1,000,000. Home, foreign, and state mission endeavors continue to be beneficiaries of the income derived from the invested funds of the foundation. Gilbert E. South continues as executive secretary.

GILBERT E. SOUTH

MARYLAND, INC., BAPTIST CHILDREN'S AID SOCIETY OF (cf. Children's Aid Society, Maryland Baptist, Vol. I; Baptist

Children's Aid Society, Vol. III). The purpose of this corporation as stated in present by-laws is "the supplemental care of children under 18 years of age who regularly attend Sunday School in Baptist Convention of Maryland churches after needs have been established by the executive secretary and to love, support and encourage these children to become responsible Christian adults." The board of trustees has the power to use such methods to accomplish its purpose as in its judgment may seem wise and necessary.

Carolyn Henderson, a former executive secretary, 1936-49, died in 1972. She was succeeded by Thelma H. Culbreth. Thelma Keller retired in 1976 after 15 years of service as office secretary. Rowland Ness (*q.v.*) served as president of the trustees from 1954 until his death in 1977. He was succeeded by Orville D. Tarner, Baltimore accountant, who served until 1979. Robert Moore, pastor, Greenridge Baptist Church, Greenridge, MD, was elected president in 1979.

Service is being given 51 children representing 17 families. The society supplements food budgets, provides clothing, secures medication, pays summer camp fees, and counsels parents and children. The 1979 budget was $45,000, met by income from investments, gifts from individuals and churches, and the Cooperative Program.

MARGARET COOPER

MARYLAND, INC., THE BAPTIST CHURCH EXTENSION SOCIETY OF. An agency of the Baptist Convention of Maryland charged with assisting churches in the development of churches, Sunday School facilities, and other projects sponsored by Maryland Baptists. The society extends financial assistance through three types of funding: a general fund, a guarantor fund, and a revolving fund.

The general fund consists principally of Cooperative Program allocations from the state convention. Trustees of the society use this fund to make gifts to churches when there is little likelihood the churches will be able to repay the advances. The guarantor fund comprises monies received by the society from church bond issues where the society acts as a guarantor for these bonds. The revolving fund is the society's loan fund. This money has accumulated through gifts, bequests, and interest earned on loans to churches.

In 1970 loans totaling $11,192 were made by the society to Maryland Baptist churches. Gifts to churches that year totaled $7,800. By 1979 the society had expanded its service to the point where mortgage loans totaling $29,000 were made and guarantees were issued on two bond programs. The 1979 records also revealed that the society had a liability on church bonds amounting to $900,000. This liability was secured by real estate valued in excess of $5,500,000. Alan H. Stocksdale, a Baptist attorney in Baltimore, is president of the society.

ALAN H. STOCKSDALE

MARYLAND, INC., THE BAPTIST HOME OF (FOR AGED) (II, III). Completion in 1970 of the Willoughby McCormick Wing at Rainbow Hall, under the presidency of S. Arthur Eppley, essentially doubled accommodations at the Baptist Home of Maryland, increasing total capacity to 64. Construction of ranch-style houses for the administrator and resident minister occurred during the tenure of Stephen G. Heaver, president, May, 1971, through Oct., 1972.

In the remainder of the decade the presidency of William D. Hillis, Johns Hopkins Hospital physician, centered upon concerted efforts to establish closer ties between the home and churches comprising the state convention. Open circulation of information regarding every aspect of the institution's operations principally attained this goal.

Relocation of the infirmary to the McCormick wing in 1976 effected substantial modernization and enlargement of health care facilities. Repartitioning of existing space created three additional private rooms.

Following a convention-wide appeal to raise $78,000 during a 1976 Thanksgiving offering, contributions exceeded $81,000, reversing the decade's trend toward progressive deficit spending. Continued patterns of increased giving and bequests thereafter overcame extraordinary increases in operational costs, arising from the markedly inflationary economy, ballooning health care costs, and government regulation.

Expanded operational expenditures during the decade, rising from $167,669 in 1970 to $509,300 in 1979, reflected the degree of growth and improving quality of care experienced. Direct Cooperative Program support from the state convention increased from $17,000 in 1970 to a high of $30,000 in 1978. Fees paid by residents provided most of the income (61.2 percent in 1979) covering operational costs.

WILLIAM D. HILLIS

MARYLAND ASSOCIATIONS (II, III).
I. New Associations. HOWARD. Organized on Oct. 29, 1973. Under the leadership of James Hamblen, resource consultant in new town planning for the Home Mission Board, seven churches separated themselves from the three surrounding associations to begin identifying with Howard County, Md. The planned community, Columbia, changed Howard County from basically rural to commuter oriented for Baltimore and Washington, DC. Only two Southern Baptist churches existed in the county before 1960. Five churches were started in the next 13 years to minister to the fast growing population. In 1980 eight churches reported 186 baptisms, 2,577 members, $729,610 total gifts, $98,481 mission gifts, and $4,794,500 property value.

II. Changes in Associations. DELAWARE.

Until 1957, the Baptist Convention of Maryland was comprised only of churches in Maryland. With the entrance of the Manhattan Baptist Chapel in New York City into the convention in 1957 and the subsequent growth of Southern Baptist work in the Northeast, the Maryland Convention included 11 states by 1960. In the 1970s the pattern reversed. The formation of the New York and the Pennsylvania-South Jersey Conventions necessitated the BCM adjusting geographical boundaries. Delaware has become the prime concern of the state convention outside geographical Maryland. The entire state of Delaware is one association, with offices in Dover and a full-time director of missions. Delaware is treated as an association in programming rather than as a state. In 1979 nine churches and two missions reported 101 baptisms, 3,492 members, $645,667 total gifts, $79,313 mission gifts, and $3,792,500 property value.

MICHAEL COX and ROY GRESHAM

MARYLAND BAPTIST, THE. (II, III). Official news journal of the Baptist Convention of Maryland. R. Gene Puckett resigned as editor in 1979, following 13 years at the post, to become executive director of Americans United for Separation of Church and State. Larry E. High, associate editor, was named acting editor. On Oct. 1, 1979, High was elected editor of the publication. The circulation on Dec. 31, 1979, was 17,462.

On Jan. 21, 1971, *The Maryland Baptist* began publication of *The New England Baptist* and the *Penn-Jersey Baptist*. The New England paper, a monthly, served Southern Baptists in the six New England states which were affiliated with the Baptist Convention of Maryland. *The New England Baptist* was published from the offices of *The Maryland Baptist* throughout the 1970s. The *Penn-Jersey Baptist,* also a monthly, was published for the Baptist Convention of Pennsylvania-South Jersey and mailed to church members in Southern Baptist congregations within the geographical boundaries of the Penn-Jersey Convention.

In July, 1979, responsibility for publishing the *Penn-Jersey Baptist* was transferred to the state convention staff in Harrisburg, PA.

See also PENN-JERSEY BAPTIST.

LARRY E. HIGH

MARYLAND CONFERENCE, RETREAT, CAMPING CENTER—SKYCROFT. Conference center of the Baptist Convention of Maryland, located in Frederick County, MD, atop South Mountain near Middletown.

In its 1915 annual meeting, the Maryland Baptist Union Association (now the Baptist Convention of Maryland) appointed a committee "to look into the feasibility of establishing in Maryland, under Baptist direction, a summer encampment." Between then and 1968, a variety of rented facilities for a summer encampment were used. These included Camp Wo-Me-

To in Rocks, MD, owned and operated by Maryland Woman's Missionary Union.

In May, 1971, the convention's state mission board authorized the executive committee to recommend "a site . . . central in the state, and to obtain tentative plans for the development of a conference-retreat-camping center, which will meet the overall program requirements of the convention and its affiliated churches." At the Nov., 1971, annual state convention, a standing committee of the state mission board was created. In Oct., 1972, the property in Frederick County was acquired. Within a few months an architect was engaged to develop a comprehensive site plan.

From its beginning Skycroft was developed through the efforts of the Baptist laymen of Maryland. In 1973-74, even in its undeveloped state, it provided activities for dozens of Maryland church groups and hundreds of individuals. Several groups worked at Skycroft during their free time to make the center usable for picnics, hiking, day retreats, and limited overnight camping. Trails and future building sites were cleared by volunteers. Convention employees James Allcock and John Saunders coordinated the work at the Maryland Baptist Building.

At the 1974 annual meeting of the state convention, plans were approved to begin construction on phase one of the Skycroft project. This included a water sewage system, gravel roads and walks, an electrical system, a conference center and dining hall complex, and three retreat lodges with lounges, kitchenettes, and appropriate furnishings.

Groundbreaking ceremonies were held, Apr. 3, 1976. By May, 1977, the two lodges and the dining hall and conference complex were under roof. Volunteers completed the interior painting, and plans were made to lay the carpet and complete the transfer of furnishings. These two lodges had a capacity of 120 people. The dining hall and conference center would care for 150.

In Feb., 1979, phase one of the building campaign at Skycroft ended. In June, 1979, in anticipation of the next phase of development, the state mission board started placing in escrow the money received for the "Mountain for the Master Campaign" to be designated for the second phase of development. As the 1970s drew to an end, Maryland Baptists were contributing approximately $3,000 per month towards the Skycroft development drive.

LINDA MILES

MASSACHUSETTS, SOUTHERN BAPTISTS IN. See MARYLAND, BAPTIST CONVENTION OF; NEW ENGLAND, BAPTIST GENERAL ASSOCIATION OF.

MATTHEWS, MILDRED (b. Morrilton, AR, Sep. 28, 1890; d. Jonesboro, AR, Oct. 25, 1964). Missionary. Daughter of Robert and Amma (Hawkins) Matthews, she attended State Teachers College, Conway, AR, and Woman's Missionary Union Training School,

Louisville, KY, graduating in 1919. Appointed to Cuba by the Home Mission Board in 1920, she served 35 years as teacher, city missionary, author, worker in church organizations, and West Cuba WMU president and secretary. She also assisted in organizing the Columbian WMU, 1950. She is buried in Westlawn Cemetery, Jonesboro, AR.

DOLLIE E. HIETT

MAURITIUS, MISSION IN. Home to 900,000 people, the island of Mauritius in the Indian Ocean became an independent nation in 1968. Southern Baptist witness there began in Sep., 1978, when Norman and Jean (Powell) Wood transferred from Zambia. The initial invitation came from a small Chinese Christian fellowship. The Woods witnessed to the Chinese, in individual and small group Bible studies, and to groups of young people. In 1980 plans for continuation and expansion of work in Mauritius centered in using volunteers who can fill specific needs identified by government agencies.

JOY NEAL

MAY, MAE LEE JENKINS (b. Madison County, MS, Apr. 8, 1914; d. Madison, MS, July 1, 1976). State Woman's Missionary Union leader. Daughter of Joseph E. and Ruth Henderson Jenkins, farmers, she was valedictorian at Madison-Ridgeland High School in Madison, MS. She attended Belhaven College, Jackson, MS (B.A., 1936). After teaching high school in Magee and Carthage, MS, 1936-38, she married William Vernon May, of Mendenhall, MS, on May 8, 1938. They had two sons, William Vernon, Jr., and Joseph Simeon.

May served as Mississippi director of WMU, 1969-74, and vice-president of SBC WMU for the same period. During her administration of Mississippi WMU, three significant events occurred: (1) Retirement of Edwina Robinson, executive secretary, May, 1, 1971, and election of Marjean Patterson as her successor; (2) restoration of two of the principal buildings at Camp Garaywa destroyed by fire, Sep. 21, 1970; and (3) purchase of 9.6 acres of land for a buffer zone between Camp Garaywa and new subdivisions.

As a memorial to her, a plaque and Bible were placed in one of the prayer rooms at Mississippi Baptist Medical Center, Jackson, MS, by the WMU at First Baptist Church, Louisville, MS. She is buried in Jessamine Cemetery, Ridgeland, MS.

C. B. HAMLET, III

MAYO, SAM TILLMAN (b. Geneva, GA, Mar. 3, 1896; d. Montezuma, GA, Mar. 5, 1957). Home Missionary. A graduate of Howard College (Samford), he attended The Southern Baptist Theological Seminary. He married Hazel Clemont Hunt, Dec. 29, 1925. He served as superintendent of Baptist Children's Home in Missouri, as pastor, and for several years in rural

evangelism. The Home Mission Board appointed the Mayos, Jan. 1, 1948, as the first Southern Baptist missionary couple to work with migrants. They wrote the book, *The Trail of Itchin' Feet* (1957).

JEWELL BEALL

McCALL, GEORGE ROBERT (b. Screven County, GA, Feb. 17, 1829; d. Macon, GA, Oct. 6, 1895). Georgia pastor. The son of Caroline (Griner) McCall and Moses N. McCall, a Baptist minister, he graduated from Mercer University (1853). Ordained to the ministry at Middleground Baptist Church, Sep. 24, 1854, he was called in Oct., 1854, to Richland Church, Twiggs County, which he served 25 years. Other churches served were Stone Creek and Beech Spring, Twiggs County; Hayneville and New Providence, Houston County; Evergreen, Blue Spring, Antioch, and Corinth, Pulaski County; Hawkinsville, Cochran, Griffin, Jeffersonville, Swainsboro, and Louisville.

Moderator of Ebenezer Association, 1868-81, McCall preached the introductory sermon for that body seven times, and the missionary sermon 13 times. He was clerk of the Georgia Baptist Convention for 27 years, 1869-95, and secretary of the SBC two years, 1874-75. He served Mercer University as trustee secretary, 1876-92, and treasurer, 1878-92, and as financial agent and professor of theology for shorter periods. He served also on the committee of the Georgia Baptist Convention, 1870, on the relocation of Mercer. He is buried at Hawkinsville, GA.

W. J. CARSWELL

McCALL, JOHN WILLIAM, SR. (b. Star, MS, June 24, 1885; d. Nairobi, Kenya, Apr. 12, 1976). Attorney and lay leader. The son of farming parents, James Mansel and Roseanna Singletary McCall, he was a law graduate of the University of Mississippi (L.L.B., 1911). He married Lizette Kimbrough, June, 1912. They had five children: Duke, John, Charles, Katrina, and Lizette. An attorney and juvenile court judge in Memphis, TN, he served on the Brotherhood Commission, SBC, as a trustee for 42 years, retiring as chairman in 1964. Predeceased by his wife, McCall was living on the mission field with his missionary daughter, Lizette Bethea, when he died. He is buried in St. Peter's Cemetery, Oxford, MS.

ROY JENNINGS

McCASLAND, PAUL ALEXANDER (b. Hunt County, TX, July 10, 1902; d. Portland, OR, Aug. 28, 1957). Pastor and evangelist. Son of John and Mary McCasland, farmers, he married Bettie Watson, Aug. 29, 1928. They had three children: John, Carroll, and Marilyn. A graduate of Howard Payne College (B.A.) and Southwestern Baptist Theological Seminary (Th.M., M.R.E.), he was pastor for 11 years in Herrin, IL. On June 1, 1951, he became secretary of evangelism and brotherhood of the Northwest Baptist Convention, serving until his death. He is buried in Lincoln Memorial Park, Portland, OR.

ROLAND HOOD

McCAUL, THOMAS VADEN (b. Charles City County, VA, Nov. 25, 1878; d. Gainesville, FL, Nov. 18, 1972). Pastor and denominational leader. Son of William W. and Indianna (Bowles) McCaul, farmers, he was educated at Richmond College (B.A., 1902), The Southern Baptist Theological Seminary (Th.M., 1905), and the University of Virginia (M.A., 1908). Honorary doctorates were conferred upon him by Richmond College (D.D., 1925) and Stetson University (D.D., 1941). He married Waldine Beard Searce, July 29, 1908. They had one child, Thomas V., Jr.

McCaul served as pastor of churches in Virginia and South Carolina before becoming pastor of the First Baptist Church, Gainesville, FL, in May, 1922. He served the church for 27 years and upon retirement in 1949 was elected minister emeritus. Active in denominational and community affairs, he held many local, state, and national offices, including vice-president, 1932; and president, 1938-39, of the Florida Baptist Convention; vice-president of the SBC, 1947; trustee of Southern Seminary; and charter member and second president of the Gainesville Kiwanis Club. One of the 12 founders of the national social fraternity, Sigma Phi Epsilon, McCaul served as national chaplain of the group for 30 years. He authored numerous articles for denominational publications and composed several pieces of music, including a "Centennial Hymn" for First Baptist Church, Gainesville (1970).

McCaul is buried at Gainesville, FL.

JAMES R. BEASLEY

McCLELLAN, JOHN LITTLE (b. Sheridan, AR, Feb. 25, 1895; d. Little Rock, AR, Nov. 28, 1977). United States Senator from Arkansas. Son of Isaac Scott McClellan, a lawyer, and Belle Sudduth McClellan, he married Norma Myers Cheatham, Nov. 10, 1937. They had five children: Max, John L., Jr., James, Doris, and Mary Alice. He was admitted to the Arkansas Bar at age 17 by a special act of the Arkansas Legislature, becoming the youngest lawyer in the USA. Self-educated, he served two terms in the United States House of Representatives, 1935-38, from Arkansas' sixth Congressional District. Elected to the United States Senate in 1942, he served until his death in 1977.

McClellan rose to national prominence as chairman of the Senate Permanent Subcommittee on Investigations, 1955-73. He conducted 106 separate hearings on organized crime, labor racketeering, and other abuses in business and government. He served also as chairman of the Senate Government Operations Committee for 22 years before becoming chairman of the Senate Appropriations Committee in 1972. He is buried in Roselawn Memorial Park, Little Rock, AR.

ROBERT LARKAN SNIDER

McCULLOUGH, WARD GLENDON (b. Griffin, GA, Sep. 9, 1921; d. Memphis, TN, Aug. 23, 1978). Brotherhood and home missions executive and pastor. Son of Thomas Ward and Fannie Belle (Roebuck) McCullough, he graduated from Brewton-Parker Junior College, Mt. Vernon, GA (1940) and Baylor University (B.A., 1945). He married Ernestine Kesler, May 21, 1955, who died in 1969. They had four children: Katherine, Kenneth, Elizabeth, and Deborah. On Apr. 11, 1974, McCullough married Marjorie Jones, a foreign missionary and former Girls Auxiliary director for Woman's Missionary Union.

Following graduation from Brewton-Parker, McCullough served as pastor of First Baptist Church, Hazelhurst, GA. For 10 years beginning in 1945, he was the Royal Ambassador secretary for the Georgia Baptist Convention. After four years as associate pastor of Druid Hills Baptist Church, Atlanta, McCullough joined the Home Mission Board as secretary of the Personnel Department in 1959. On Jan. 1, 1971, he became director of the Division of Personnel at the board and on Nov. 1, 1971, accepted a call as executive director of the Brotherhood Commission, Memphis, TN, a position he held until his death in a traffic accident.

During almost eight years as chief administrative officer, McCullough sought to motivate the laity in witnessing, ministry, and decision making. Only two months before his death, he achieved part of his dream by bringing together 3,000 Southern Baptist lay leaders in 16 vocations for ministry discussions, with the President of the United States providing the challenge. He is buried in Arlington Cemetery, Atlanta, GA.

See also BROTHERHOOD COMMISSION, SBC.

ROY JENNINGS

McDANIEL STATEMENT, THE. An antievolution statement adopted by the SBC in 1926. George W. McDaniel (*q.v.* II), SBC president, ended his address to the 1926 Convention with the words, "This Convention accepts Genesis as teaching that man was the special creation of God, and rejects every theory, evolution or other, which teaches that man originated in, or came by way of, a lower animal ancestry." The 1926 Convention requested SBC agencies to give evidence of their acceptance of the McDaniel Statement. This request precipitated several other controversies in Baptist life.

DAVID W. DOWNS

McDOWELL, EDWARD ALLISON, JR. (b. Mitford, SC, Aug. 20, 1898; d. Atlanta, GA, Aug. 25, 1975). Seminary teacher. Son of Edward and Eva (Scott) McDowell, he graduated from Furman University (A.B., 1919). He was a newspaper reporter, 1919-22, and private secretary to the governor of South Carolina, 1923-25, before enrolling in The Southern Baptist Theological Seminary (Th.M., 1928; Ph.D., 1931). McDowell served as fellow in New Testament

Greek under A. T. Robertson, 1928-31. In 1925 he married Doris Price of Columbia, SC. Their two children were Edward, III, and Elizabeth.

Following pastorates at Vinton, VA, Baptist Church and First Baptist Church, Union, SC, he was elected in 1935 to the faculty of Southern Seminary, where he taught for 17 years. In 1952 he became professor of New Testament Interpretation at Southeastern Baptist Theological Seminary, a post he held until his retirement in 1964.

McDowell was a member of the Society of Biblical Literature and Exegesis, a charter member of the Board of Directors and Life Fellow of the Southern Regional Council, chairman of the executive committee of the North Carolina Council on Human Relations, member of a special SBC Committee on Race Relations, and member of the board of trustees of the American Baptist Theological Seminary.

The author of three major books—*Son of Man and Suffering Servant* (1944), later entitled *Jesus and His Cross; A Source Book of Interbiblical History* (1948), with W. Hersey Davis; and *The Meaning and Message of the Book of Revelation* (1951)—McDowell also wrote the commentaries on the Johannine epistles in *The Broadman Bible Commentary.* He composed the text of "The Seminary Hymn" of Southeastern Seminary. McDowell is buried in the cemetery of Southeastern Seminary in Wake Forest, NC.

DONALD E. COOK

McGLON, CHARLES ADDIS (b. New Smyrna Beach, FL, June 27, 1910; d. Louisville, KY, Dec. 17, 1974). Professor of speech and mass media. Son of Charles Robert and Florence McDonald McGlon, farmers, he graduated from the University of Florida (B.A., 1936; M.A., 1939) and Columbia University (Ph.D., 1951). He married Jessie M. Lowe of Daytona Beach, FL, Sep. 27, 1933. They had two children, Ellen and Kenneth Allen. He taught speech and drama at Peabody College, Nashville, TN, 1940-43, and speech, religious drama, and mass media at The Southern Baptist Theological Seminary, Louisville, KY, 1943-74. He is buried in Cave Hill Cemetery, Louisville.

JESSIE M. MCGLON

McIVER, JOHN ARCHIE (b. Lee County, TX, Nov. 5, 1885; d. Bartlesville, OK, Dec. 1, 1976). Pastor and denominational worker. The son of John McIver, Sr., a farmer, he attended Baylor University (B.A., M.A.) and Southwestern Baptist Theological Seminary (Th.M., 1922). He married Annie Moon Robertson, May 25, 1921. Their children were Melba, Annie, Mary, and Ray. Following her death, he married Edith Breece, Nov. 11, 1967. He served as pastor of several churches in Texas and North Carolina. He served also for seven years as a district missionary in Texas and for 12 years on the staff of Southwestern Seminary. He is buried at Fort Worth, TX.

FELIX M. GRESHAM

McKAY, FANA RUTH (b. Morton, MS, Feb. 6, 1908; d. Riverside, CA, Dec. 7, 1975). Teacher and writer. The daughter of Henry and Ruby Measells, plantation owners, she married Charles L. McKay, Apr. 14, 1928. Their children were Ruth and June. She attended Mississippi College (B.A., 1937). She served as president of the Arizona Southern Baptist Pastors' Wives Association in 1967. An elementary school teacher, she was also a lesson writer for the Sunday School Board. She is buried in Memory Lawn Memorial Park and Chapel Mausoleum, Phoenix, AZ.

JOE CAUSEY

McKAY, M. RAY (b. Jefferson County, MO, July 28, 1896; d. Durham, NC, July 4, 1977). Pastor, teacher, and denominational leader. Son of John Price McKay, a Baptist minister, and Lula McKay, he was a graduate of Shurtleff College (B.Phil., 1922) and The Southern Baptist Theological Seminary (Th.M., 1926; Th.D. 1928). He did postdoctoral studies at the University of Chicago, Garrett Biblical Institute, and the University of Edinburgh. He married Mary Favoright, July 26, 1926. Their children were Rosemary and David Ray. He served as pastor of First Baptist Church, Aurora, IL, 1924-38; First Church, Topeka, KS, 1938-44; and Second Church, Little Rock, AR, 1944-52.

In 1952 McKay joined the faculty of Southeastern Baptist Theological Seminary in the second year of the seminary's existence. He became the first professor of preaching, a post he occupied from 1952 until retirement in 1964, at which time he became professor-emeritus. As a member of the Foreign Mission Board, SBC, McKay went on a worldwide tour in 1951, preaching in evangelistic meetings at numerous mission points. Always in demand as a speaker, he served 15 churches as interim pastor and conducted many revival meetings. During retirement years, the McKays lived in Raleigh, NC, where they were active members of Hayes Barton Baptist Church. He is buried in the cemetery of Southeastern Seminary, Wake Forest, NC.

THOMAS A. BLAND

McLELLAND, JAMES FRED (b. Meridian, MS, May 21, 1903; d. Pineville, LA, Nov. 19, 1971). Pastor. Son of the William McLellands, farmers, he was educated at Hattiesburg, MS, High School, Mississippi College, and Baptist Bible Institute (now New Orleans Baptist Theological Seminary). He married Frances Tool in 1923. They had two children, a daughter and a son.

McLelland was selected rural pastor of the year in 1939 by *Progressive Farmer* magazine and the Sears Roebuck Foundation. Ordained by First Baptist Church, Hattiesburg, in 1927, he was pastor of Enon Baptist Church, Franklinton, LA, 1934-41. He served as director of rural church enlistment and evangelism for the Louisiana Baptist Convention, 1941-53. Returning to the pastorate, he organized and served as first pastor of Horseshoe Drive Church, Alexandria, LA. His last pastorate was First Baptist, Lake Arthur, LA, 1965-66. He and his wife are buried at Pineville, LA.

J. D. SCOTT

McLEMORE, NANNIE PITTS (b. Harvest, AL, Sep. 21, 1900; d. Jackson, MS, Jan. 24, 1980). Educator and author. Daughter of James Ervin and Lola Sanderson Pitts, farmers, she attended Athens College, Athens, AL (A.B., 1921). After teaching in high schools in Northport, Escambia County, and Monrovia, AL, 1921-25, she married Richard Aubrey McLemore (q.v.), June 2, 1927. They had one son, Harry Kimbrell. She studied at Peabody College, Nashville, TN (M.A., 1927), and did further graduate studies at Vanderbilt University while her husband completed his graduate work.

McLemore taught at McComb, MS, High School, 1925-27, Jones Junior College, 1927-30, and Perry County, AL, High School, 1936-37. In addition to her active roles as a mother and the wife of a college administrator and president, she was a member of the Mississippi Historical Society, serving on its board of directors and as its president, 1973-74. She was the Mississippi division president of the American Association of University Women, 1950-52, and was a member of the Mississippi Genealogical Society. She served as acting executive secretary-treasurer of the Mississippi Baptist Historical Commission, 1976-80.

With her husband, she coauthored *Outline of Mississippi History* (1941), *Mississippi Through Four Centuries* (1944), *The Mississippi Story* (1959), *A History of First Baptist Church, Jackson, Mississippi* (1975), and *A History of Mississippi College* (1979). She was a contributing author to *A History of Mississippi* (1973). She is buried in Highland Cemetery, Hattiesburg, MS.

WALTER HOWELL

McLEMORE, RICHARD AUBREY (b. Perry County, MS, June 6, 1903; d. Jackson, MS, Sep. 1, 1976). Educator and historian. Son of Hezekiah and Tabitha (Small) McLemore, both teachers, he graduated from Mississippi College (A.B., 1923), Peabody College (M.A., 1926), and Vanderbilt University (Ph.D., 1933). He married Nannie Pitts (q.v.), June 2, 1927. They had one son, Harry Kimbrell.

After serving as professor and administrator at Jones Junior College and Judson College, McLemore became professor of history at Mississippi Southern College in 1938. In 1945 he became dean and served as acting president in 1955. In 1957 he became president of Mississippi College and served until 1968. He was director of the Mississippi Department of Archives and History, 1969-73, and served as executive secretary-treasurer of the Mississippi Baptist Historical Commission, 1968-76.

A member of the American, Southern, and Mississippi Historical Associations, McLemore was executive director of the Mississippi American Revolution Bicentennial Commission. He was the Mississippi member of the Historical Commission, SBC, 1970-76. He wrote (with others) several texts on American history, including *Fundamentals of Citizenship* (1950), *Our Nation's Story* (1954), and *A High School History for Modern America* (1966). McLemore wrote *Franco-American Diplomatic Relations, 1816-1836* (1940) and *A History of Mississippi Baptists* (1970). He was the editor of *A History of Mississippi* (1973). He and Nannie McLemore coauthored several texts on Mississippi history, as well as *A History of First Baptist Church, Jackson, Mississippi* (1975) and *A History of Mississippi College* (1979).

He is buried in Highland Cemetery, Hattiesburg, MS.

WALTER HOWELL

MEDEARIS, THOMAS WHITTIER (b. Columbus, IN, Apr. 11, 1889; d. Pasadena, CA, July 7, 1970). State Baptist executive. Son of Thomas Whittier and Susan Carns Medearis, farmers, he grew up in Illinois, where he was licensed and ordained to preach at the age of 19. After moving to Missouri, he married Mary E. Miller of Sarcoxie, Jan. 13, 1913. Their children were Roger, Miller, Dorothy Lou, and Marian. He graduated from Southwest Baptist College (A.A.) and William Jewell College (B.A.), later attending Central Baptist Seminary (B.D.), Kansas City, KS.

Medearis served as pastor of the First Baptist churches of Lamar, Fayette, and Bolivar, MO, and Bristow and Miami, OK. For three years he was head of the Bible Department of Southwest Baptist College. On July 1, 1942, he became general superintendent of missions for the Missouri Baptist General Association. In 1945 the association purchased *The Word and Way* which has been, since Jan. 1, 1946, the official Missouri Baptist journal. During his tenure the state offices were moved from Kansas City to Jefferson City in 1948. He retired on June 30, 1954. He is buried in Park Cemetery, Carthage, MO.

THOMAS W. NELSON

MEDICAL-DENTAL FELLOWSHIP, BAPTIST. See BAPTIST MEDICAL-DENTAL FELLOWSHIP.

MELTON, HENRY MARTIN (b. Dawson, GA, Aug. 27, 1888; d. Arlington, GA, Sep. 6, 1969). Pastor. The son of Benjamin and Laura (Turner) Melton, farmers, he attended Mercer University (B.A., 1909) and The Southern Baptist Theological Seminary (B.D., 1916). He married Mary Margaret Layman, June 14, 1916. They had three children: Mary, Laura, and Buckner.

Melton served as pastor of Arlington, Bluffton, Benevolence, and Norman Park Churches, all in Georgia. He also helped establish Bluffton

Assembly and served as first manager of Rockbridge Assembly, Franklin, GA, 1961. The first associational missionary in Georgia, he served Western Association, 1950-61, and Colquitt County Association, 1936-50. He also served as vice-president of the Georgia Baptist Convention, 1949. Melton is buried in Oak Grove Cemetery, Arlington, GA.

HENRY K. NEAL

MEMORIAL BAPTIST HOSPITAL SYSTEM, HOUSTON (cf. Memorial Hospital, Houston, Vol. I; Memorial Baptist Hospital, Houston, Vol. III). On Sep. 11, 1970, the trustees of Memorial Baptist Hospital of Houston requested that the executive board of the Baptist General Convention of Texas recommend that the convention "divest itself of all ownership, control, responsibility and/or authority over the Memorial Baptist Hospital of Houston . . . transferring this responsibility to an independent, non-profit organization." The trustees wanted to build an additional physical plant. This project would require major loans and federal and community support exceeding convention regulations. The convention's executive board referred the request to the convention without recommendation.

The convention, meeting in Houston, Oct. 26-28, 1971, passed a resolution separating the Houston hospital system from the convention by a vote of 907 to 352. The hospital system became a nonsectarian, Christian institution on Jan. 1, 1972. Its new charter required that at least 25 percent of the membership of the trustees be Baptists.

EDWARD N. CURTIS

MEMORIAL HOSPITAL, BAPTIST, GADSDEN (II, III). See BAPTIST MEDICAL CENTER, GADSDEN.

MEMORIAL HOSPITAL, BAPTIST, MEMPHIS (II, III). Expansion since 1965 has brought the bed capacity to 2,055. The hospital's plant, auxiliary services, and land have an asset value of approximately $250,000,000. About half of the hospital's patients come from outside Memphis and Shelby County. In 1979 the annual admission of patients was at the rate of 59,403, and total patient days were at the rate of 533,015. Outpatient visits of all kinds were at the annual rate of approximately 348,000. The medical staff of the hospital consists of 932 physicians, most of whom are medical specialists. The hospital offers medical education programs including internships and medical residencies in internal medicine, general surgery, neurosurgery, pediatrics, obstetrics-gynecology, radiology, orthopedics, and pathology.

The 1980 budget of the hospital was $155,000,000. The hospital employs about 5,250 persons on a full-time basis and 300 on a part-time basis. Licensed by the state of Tennessee, it is fully accredited by the Joint Commission on Accreditation of Hospitals.

FRANK S. GRONER

MEMORIAL HOSPITAL, BAPTIST, SAN ANTONIO (II, III). See BAPTIST MEMORIAL HOSPITAL SYSTEM, SAN ANTONIO.

MEMORIAL HOSPITAL (MO), BAPTIST. See BAPTIST MEMORIAL HOSPITAL.

MERCER, SILAS (b. near Currituck Bay, NC, Feb. 25, 1745; d. Wilkes County, GA, Aug. 1, 1796). Colonial Georgia Baptist leader. Educated at home and reared in the Church of England, he was converted to the Baptist cause when he began to read the Scriptures to disprove the arguments of the Baptist "dissenters." He moved to Wilkes County, GA, Dec. 7, 1773, with his wife, Dorcas, and children, Jesse (q.v. II) and Ann. Later children were Daniel, Moriah, Mourning, Hermon, and Joshua.

Mercer was baptized at age 30 into the fellowship of the Kiokee Church, the oldest Baptist congregation in Georgia. He devoted himself to the revolutionary cause, becoming one of the six Georgia Baptist chaplains in the colonial forces. While fleeing to North Carolina, Mercer encouraged the Colonial forces at the Battle of Burke County Jail, Jan. 27, 1779. This battle gave the Americans their first success on Georgia soil.

During his six years in North Carolina, he preached nearly every day, returning to Georgia in 1783 with the rank of major. He participated in the founding of the first Baptist association in the state, the Georgia Association, on Oct. 11, 1784, and later served as its moderator. He wrote a "Remonstrance" for the association to the state legislature against a bill which would require public support for religious denominations.

Mercer founded the Phillips' Mill Church in Wilkes (now Taliaferro) County on May 7, 1785, and the Wheatley's Mill Church (later called Bethesda, located in Greene County) in the same year and served as their pastor until his death. On July 1, 1786, he organized the Powell's Creek Church (later called Powelton), and in 1788 he founded the Hutton's Fork Church (now Sardis). He assisted in the beginnings of Clark's Station Church and Liberty (now Big Creek) Church.

Mercer was convinced of the importance of education by Richard Furman (q.v. I) and founded the Salem Academy in his home in 1793. He was author of *Tyranny Exposed, And True Liberty Discovered* (1807). He is buried in Phillips' Mill Church cemetery, Taliaferro County, GA.

J. R. HUDDLESTON

MERCER UNIVERSITY (II, III). Raleigh Kirby Godsey, former dean of the College of Liberal Arts and executive vice-president, was named president on July 1, 1979, succeeding Rufus Carrollton Harris, who became chancellor of the university.

The 1970s saw major growth in many areas of the university. The student body grew from 1,955 in 1969 to 4,525 in 1979-80, a record enrollment. Operating expenses increased from

$5,700,000 in 1969-70 to $22,090,439 in 1979-80. The faculty grew from 110 to 265 in the same period.

Major events of this period included the merger of the Atlanta Baptist College, becoming Mercer University in Atlanta in 1972; the beginning of a School of Business and Economics in 1978; and the move of the Walter F. George School of Law to new 90,000-square feet facilities in 1979. New construction included the Ida B. Patterson Infirmary in 1975, the I. M. Sheffield, Jr., Physical Education Building at Mercer University in Atlanta in 1979, and the modern pharmaceutical facility of the Southern School of Pharmacy in 1972. This building is a multidisciplinary, family-centered, comprehensive center, offering extensive services to the public. The school has gained nationwide recognition for its program to educate the public on drug abuse. The Administration Building, built between 1871 and 1874, located in Macon, and designated a historic shrine, was completely remodeled in 1979.

The launching of a medical school became a reality with groundbreaking for the new facility in May, 1980. This school is designed for the education of primary physicians who will locate in the underserved areas of Georgia. The first class was to matriculate in 1981.

Plans are now under way for the sesquicentennial celebration of the university in 1983.

ALLEN B. COMISH

MEREDITH COLLEGE (II, III). John Edgar Weems became the sixth president, Jan. 1, 1972. Enrollment increased in the 1970s from 1,159 to 1,550; the full-time faculty from 58 (39.7 percent with doctorates) to 72 (56.9 percent with doctorates); endowment from $1,450,000 to $5,825,477; and the campus by two academic buildings, two residence halls, a president's residence, and a college and continuing education center. Meredith added programs in cooperative education, study abroad, and continuing education. To the Bachelor of Arts it added the Bachelor of Science and the Bachelor of Music degrees.

Support from the Baptist State Convention of North Carolina totaled $470,377 in 1979. Also in 1979, Meredith's trustees approved a seven-year drive to raise $20,000,000 for endowment, programs, and construction.

CAROLYN C. ROBINSON

MERRITT, JAMES WHITE (b. Johnstonville, GA, Dec. 29, 1886; d. Gainesville, GA., June 17, 1972). State Baptist leader. Son of Bozeman Merritt, schoolteacher, and Martha (White) Merritt, he was converted and baptized in the First Baptist Church, Gainesville, GA, Apr. 18, 1898. He attended Gainesville public schools but received no other formal education. He married Zillah Johnson, Oct. 3, 1916. They had two children, James White, Jr., and Zillah Johnson.

He served Georgia and Southern Baptists as a lay volunteer and as an elected leader, beginning with his election in 1917 as president of Georgia Baptist Young People's Union. He served with the Georgia Baptist program of state missions as field secretary for Sunday School work, 1920-25. In this position he laid the foundations for Vacation Bible Schools and led the organized Sunday School toward a vital Bible teaching ministry of the churches.

Merritt served as business manager of *The Christian Index,* 1925-30, and in 1930 became executive secretary-treasurer for the executive committee, Georgia Baptist Convention. He served in this position until his retirement, Dec., 1954. He also served as recording secretary for the SBC, 1954-64. He is buried at Gainesville, GA.

BERNARD D. KING

METROPOLITAN MISSIONS, HOME MISSION BOARD PROGRAM OF (III; cf. City Missions, Vol. I). E. Warren Rust *(q.v.)* assumed leadership of the Metropolitan Missions Department in 1971. In June, 1975, Don Hammer became associate director. The two formed a team to assist churches, associations, and state conventions in identifying needs, discovering resources, and recommending strategies related to Southern Baptist work in urban communities of 50,000 and above.

The two men reversed leadership roles due to Rust's health in 1978. Rust's death in Apr., 1979, led to departmental reorganization and a new emphasis on PACT (Project: Assistance for Churches in Transition). Jere Allen was named associate director, Sep. 1, 1979. David Beal, national consultant in multifamily housing, was added to the staff in Apr., 1980.

DON HAMMER

MEXICAN BAPTIST BIBLE INSTITUTE (III). The institute continues a program of theological education with courses offered in Spanish. It operates under the Missions Division, Baptist General Convention of Texas. Its second president, H. B. Ramsour, Jr., retired in 1976 and was succeeded by Daniel J. Rivera. Accreditation is being sought through the American Association of Bible Colleges.

The purpose of the school is to train Hispanics for church-related vocations. Present property on the southern edge of San Antonio, TX, consists of eight debt-free buildings. A long-range program includes plans for nine additional buildings and the enrollment of 450 students by 1988. A satellite program has centers in nine cities over the state with plans for a total of 12 by 1981.

ERNEST E. ATKINSON

MEXICAN BAPTIST CONVENTION OF TEXAS (II). The Mexican Baptist Convention voted in 1961 to try an agreement of unification for three years before making a final decision on whether to become a part of the Baptist General Convention of Texas. In 1964, in Lubbock, TX,

WINGATE COLLEGE (*q.v.*), Wingate, NC. Dickson-Palmer Center, completed in 1977, provides more than 30,000 square feet of leisure space for students.

MEREDITH COLLEGE (*q.v.*), Raleigh, NC. Christina Brown and Seby B. Jones Chapel. A 13,000-square-foot structure, seating 307, scheduled for completion in fall of 1982 at a projected cost of $1,100,000.

the Mexican Baptist Convention voted to become the Mexican Baptist Departmental Convention of Texas. During the 1974 annual meeting in Houston, the term "Departmental" was dropped and the Mexican Baptist Convention of Texas became an integral part of the Baptist General Convention of Texas.

In 1980 more than 550 Spanish-speaking congregations with about 40,000 members were affiliated with the Mexican Baptist Convention and the Baptist General Convention of Texas. Under the unification agreement, the Mexican Baptist Convention officers meet annually with their counterpart Baptist executive board personnel for input on program and budget proposals. Officers and personnel work together in the promotion of all Texas and SBC programs. The president of the Mexican Baptist Convention is an ex-officio member of the executive board of the Baptist General Convention of Texas.

In 1974 *La Hora de Proclamatión* (The Hour of Proclamation) a Spanish radio program, was launched with Carlos Paredes as announcer, Bob Russell as recording engineer, and Leobardo C. Estrada as speaker. Special television programs are produced in San Antonio. The Mary Hill Davis State Missions Offering funds this ministry.

See also BAPTIST CHILDREN'S HOME AT SAN ANTONIO; MEXICAN BAPTIST BIBLE INSTITUTE; NUESTRA TAREA; RIO GRANDE RIVER MINISTRY; TEXAS, BAPTIST GENERAL CONVENTION OF; VALLEY BAPTIST ACADEMY.

LEOBARDO C. ESTRADA

MEXICO, MISSION IN (II, III). In the 1970s the Mexico mission made progress in integrating and broadening its ministries, including medical, theological education, literature, radio, television, student centers and homes, agriculture, and field evangelism. Baptists of Mexico sent out their first foreign missionary couple to Honduras in 1979. By 1980 Southern Baptist career missionaries in Mexico totaled 89. Hundreds of Southern Baptist volunteers came each year to share testimonies through music, carpentry, arts, and preaching. There were 410 churches with 37,000 members in 1979. Mexican Baptists' financial contributions more than kept pace with inflation.

JAMES PHILPOT

MICHIGAN, BAPTIST STATE CONVENTION OF (III).

I. General. The 1970s were years of change for the Baptist State Convention of Michigan (BSCM). Fred D. Hubbs, after serving for more than 18 years as executive secretary, resigned effective Dec. 31, 1970. He had become the first executive secretary of the convention when it organized in 1957 with 52 churches. When he resigned, the convention had 175 churches and 58 missions with a combined membership of 32,000.

Robert B. Wilson succeeded Hubbs as executive secretary (now executive director), Jan. 1, 1971. Prior to his election, Wilson had served as the state director of missions for eight years and before that as an area missionary in the northern section of the state for four years.

The BSCM experienced a second change in 1975 when the staff moved into a new headquarters building in Southfield, a northern Detroit suburb. The office complex, with 8,000 square feet and costing $288,000, was purchased from an insurance company. This was the first time in its history that the convention had been housed in an office-type building. Prior to the move, the staff was housed 12 years in Priscilla Inn, a residence for women, in downtown Detroit.

EUGENE BRAGG

II. Program of Work. *Division Changes.* — The BSCM had an executive board consisting of 27 members until 1972. In that year the board was increased to 36 excluding the convention officers. The executive committee was made up of the convention officers and the chairmen of the standing committees. In 1975 the convention decided that the immediate past president should also be a member of the executive committee.

Until 1972 the convention divided its program of work into four divisions: Administration, Missions, Religious Education, and Special Ministries. In 1972 the Special Ministries Division was eliminated, leaving the other three. The Missions Division became the Cooperative Missions Division, and the Religious Education Division became the Church Development Division. In 1976 the Administration Division became the Services Division. The office of evangelism was placed directly under the executive director and given division status.

Evangelism. —The work of evangelism continues to be a top priority of the BSCM. W. B. Oakley served as secretary of evangelism from Jan. 1, 1963, to Apr., 1974, when he retired to serve at Bambi Lake Assembly. Jim Coldiron succeeded him and began serving, Nov. 1, 1974.

In 1975 the convention established an office of evangelism with responsibility for permeating every area of the convention's life. The title of the leader was changed from secretary to director. The director relates directly to the executive director. He has the responsibility of leading the programs of evangelism development, personal evangelism, and mass evangelism. He works with the division directors, department directors, area directors of missions, and elected state and associational leaders in planning and promoting evangelism in all the work of the convention.

The BSCM celebrated its 20th anniversary in 1977, which was designated as a year of evangelism. Area crusades were held in the major cities of Detroit, Pontiac, Flint, Lansing, Grand Rapids, and Roseville, Apr. 24-May 1. Simultaneous crusades were held in churches and chapels the week of May 1-8, 1977. Pastors, singers, and laypersons from Arkansas, Florida,

Kentucky, and Oklahoma led the local crusades.

In 1979 Michigan was part of the year of evangelism in the North Central States Missions Thrust. Simultaneous crusades were conducted, Apr. 1-8. Forty vocational evangelists led the crusades in the Detroit Association. Pastors and singers came from many states to lead the other local crusades. There was a 12 percent increase in baptisms over 1978.

An evangelism intern program was developed in the office of evangelism. Jack Parrott came to this position, Jan. 1, 1977. He served in developing ministries with young adults, youth, and children. He returned to Southern Baptist Theological Seminary, Feb. 1, 1978. Ron Roy began serving as evangelism intern, Sep. 1, 1978. Both young men were products of the work in Michigan.

The BSCM cooperates with the SBC in developing the use of volunteers. On Apr. 1, 1978, Barney and Jessie Anderson were appointed as Mission Service Corps volunteers in Michigan. Anderson, a retired schoolteacher, had developed a volunteer program for the state of Tennessee with senior adults. He developed a volunteer strategy for the BSCM to utilize the service of volunteers coming to Michigan and those who are in Michigan. The service of volunteers will be strategic to the convention in the decades ahead.

JIM COLDIRON

Church Development Division.—The 1970s were years of consolidation as well as change in the program of work of the BSCM. The convention's Long-range Study Committee appointed in 1970 recommended that all church programs and Baptist Student Union be brought together in the Church Development Division, along with the support services (Church Administration, Church Architecture, Library, Family Ministries, Vocational Guidance, Recreation, Weekday Education, and Bus Outreach).

In Nov., 1975, Bill Chambers, a native of Fort Worth, TX, was elected to serve as director of Bible Teaching (Sunday School) and Brotherhood, beginning Dec. 1. Sunday School work had been led for 20 years by division director Joe Watson. The 1976 annual reports indicated a Sunday School enrollment of 29,211, an all-time high. Metro Reach and ACTION had given a new surge to Sunday School growth. In Aug., 1977, Bill Chambers resigned to return to the pastorate. Bill Moore, director of the Interracial Department of the BSCM, became director of Brotherhood. John Auvenshine, native of Lansing, MI, became the director of the Bible Teaching and Music Department and was made responsible for Weekday Early Education, Feb. 1, 1979. Joe Watson, director of the Religious Education Division, 1958-71, became director of the Church Development Division in 1971.

In 1971 William P. Oakley, a native of Dyer, TN, succeeded Harold Crane as state Church Training director. When Oakley returned to the pastorate in 1973, Jack H. Elliott, originally from Arkansas and Texas, succeeded him. Elliott envisioned the development of a new generation of indigenous Baptist leadership by strengthening the combined opportunities of youth and student work. Church Training enrollments declined in the early 1970s, reaching a low of 5,064 in 1975. This trend was reversed, however, and a significant milestone was marked in 1980 with an emphasis on maturing disciples. During that year, all associations and one-third of the congregations participated in a simultaneous Church Training growth project.

Jack H. Elliott also served as state student director throughout the 1970s. Others who served briefly as full-time campus Baptist Student Union directors were Art Fowler, Wayne State University (WSU); David Hazelwood (WSU); Barry Harper, Michigan State University (MSU); Linda Phillips, Eastern Michigan University (EMU); Richard Flint, WSU; and Brenda Moyer (MSU). The high point of the decade was a BSU enrollment of 348 at 16 campuses in 1972-73, the year of Campus ReaLife, an emphasis on campus evangelism. BSU was intermittently active at 29 Michigan campuses during the decade, averaging 11 campuses each year. It continued without interruption at four major universities: University of Michigan, MSU, EMU, and WSU. The following institutions also reported BSU at some time during the 1970s: Central, Detroit, Michigan Tech, Northern, Oakland, and Western universities; Albion, Delta, John Wesley, Nazareth, Northwest Michigan, Shaw, Soumi, and the Flint area colleges; Henry Ford, Jackson County, Kalamazoo Valley, Lansing, Macomb County, Monroe County, Oakland County, Schoolcraft, and Washtenaw County community colleges; Northwood Institute; and Detroit Institute of Technology.

The decade was one of growth for Woman's Missionary Union in Michigan. In 1979, 3,313 women and girls were enrolled in 300 separate WMU organizations. Total attendance at the three midwinter retreats for Baptist Women and Baptist Young Women approached 1,000. Two weeks of girls' mission camp attracted over 200 campers and counselors during 1979. Upon her retirement as Michigan WMU director in Dec., 1978, Frances Brown (*q.v.*) was succeeded by Joyce Mitchell, a native of Michigan, Jan. 1, 1979. Nine different women have served as state WMU presidents since the first election in 1957. These have included (with the year of their election) Josephine Culley, 1957; Eula Hicks, 1963; Harriette Harp, 1964; Violet Cross, 1966 and 1970; Cecile Brown, 1968; Hilda Hamilton, 1971; Mary Sue Sickafus, 1974; Amy Wilkinson, 1975; and Dorothy Sample, 1978.

JOE WATSON, JACK ELLIOTT,
and JOYCE MITCHELL

Cooperative Missions Division.—The BSCM has adopted a three-goal emphasis around which it performs its work: Sharing Christ, strengthening churches, and starting new congregations. One of the major thrusts of the Cooperative

Missions Division has been to lead in an aggressive church extension program. Billy Whitt, employed as the director of the Cooperative Missions Division, Aug. 1, 1979, succeeded Harold Crane, who had served since 1971. Whitt gave direct attention to starting new congregations and to supervising the other mission personnel.

The convention adopted a goal of 400 churches by 1990, twice the number of churches in 1980. In order to accomplish such a large goal, the convention plans to use more bivocational pastors, seminary teams, seminary van students, pastors receiving church pastoral aid, and other groups to assist Michigan Baptists. The seminary van program has been utilized in starting new congregations and providing for full-time pastors as they complete seminary training. Each weekend, two vans of students from Southern Baptist Theological Seminary go to Michigan to provide leadership for small new congregations. They receive theological training during the week and practical training on the weekends. The van ministry has been made possible by joint participation of the Home Mission Board, Southern Seminary, and the BSCM. Joanne LeGette, a new church extension intern, has been added to the missions staff. She cultivates fields and begins new work in the "thumb" area of the state.

In 1980 the Language Missions Department, under the direction of Eugene Bragg, reported 11 language congregations and 10 deaf ministries. The department has continued its efforts to establish new language congregations. W. T. Moore, director of the convention's Interracial Department, reported 26 black congregations affiliated with the BSCM in 1980. There were more than 40 integrated Southern Baptist congregations in the state.

The operation of Priscilla Inn as a home for working women and women with emotional problems was enhanced when Joyce Mitchell, a missionary of the HMB, came as director in June, 1973. Hundreds of women made their homes at Priscilla Inn, some for as long as 10 years. Ministry to the women included opportunities for spiritual growth, counseling, and socialization. Volunteers from numerous churches made these ministries possible. In Oct., 1978, the state convention, acting on the recommendation of a study committee, sold Priscilla Inn to a private investment company. The door to ministry at the inn is still open since the Baptist Center volunteers currently relate to the residents. The Baptist Center ministry has continued to reach out to many people in the inner city of Detroit under the leadership of Lowell Lawson, director, and Trudy Johnson, associate director. Scores of volunteer workers from the churches have contributed time and talents to this ministry.

BILLY WHITT

Services Division. —The forerunner of the Services Division of the BSCM was the Administration Division. Under the leadership of the convention's executive secretary, the Administration Division was responsible for Bambi Lake, Baptist Foundation, and programs of stewardship, evangelism, and communication of the BSCM. Stewardship, evangelism, and communication were considered departments in the structure. A Special Ministries Committee of the executive board was set up to give assistance to the administration of business services, Bambi Lake, and the Baptist Foundation. While these were not departments, they were the responsibility of the Administration Division director. The director was assigned the task of developing stewardship in the churches; assisting in church budget development; promoting the Cooperative Program in the churches; promoting estate planning and assisting in writing individual wills; developing public media; and relating to the editor, Robert Wilson, in the publication of the *Michigan Baptist Advocate.*

In the 1976 annual meeting of the state convention, the messengers approved a recommendation of the executive board to change the name of the Administration Division to Services Division. This name change also required a change of name for the corresponding committee of the executive board. In addition to the name change, the division was also restructured with four departments—Stewardship, Baptist Foundation, Communications, Bambi Lake, and Business Operations. Robert Wilson then served as director of the latter two departments. Later Bambi Lake was assigned to Roy Adams with responsibility for property development and program correlation. Working closely with Leon Fuller, manager of facilities and services, the director was responsible for efficient and smooth operation of the camp.

In 1978 Roy Adams became the director of the Services Division, relieving the executive director, Robert Wilson, to give himself to other matters such as management of finance and administration of the overall convention. The director has the added responsibility of overseeing the maintenance of the Baptist Building, the Baptist Center, and the mission apartment building.

A new department, a pilot extension Baptist Book Store, was begun in 1980 with Wanda Adkins as manager. The 300-square-foot store will stock an inventory of approximately $30,000.

ROY ADAMS

Mission Apartment Building. —The mission apartment building, owned and operated by the BSCM, is located in Southfield, MI, one mile south of the state convention offices. This four-unit building was dedicated during the annual meeting of the state convention, Nov. 14, 1979.

In the summer of 1975, Owen Cooper, past president of the SBC, offered the apartment concept to Michigan Baptist leaders as a challenge. The idea behind the plan was to have a building in which Mission Service Corps and other volunteers might live while serving the churches. In addition, one apartment was to be reserved for a foreign missionary-in-residence

MICHIGAN STATISTICAL SUMMARY

EUGENE BRAGG

Year	Associations	Churches	Church Membership	Baptisms	SS Enrollment	VBS Enrollment	CT Enrollment	WMU Enrollment	Brotherhood Enrollment	Ch. Music Enrollment	Mission Gifts	Total Gifts	Value Church Property
1969	12	161	34,198	2,075	26,702	17,363	10,225	4,193	1,600	2,755	$ 399,548	$2,967,695	$14,461,546
1970	13	168	34,522	1,888	26,633	13,559	9,171	3,930	1,560	2,836	406,868	3,145,771	15,871,758
1971	13	169	35,563	2,222	26,024	16,002	7,876	3,371	1,720	3,116	549,262	3,441,130	16,430,078
1972	13	169	37,384	2,286	27,312	17,207	7,470	3,710	1,686	3,865	538,214	3,733,774	17,865,886
1973	13	170	38,096	1,795	25,507	15,335	6,631	3,561	1,441	3,920	589,725	3,846,051	18,612,508
1974	13	174	39,567	2,033	26,235	16,639	5,515	3,340	1,483	3,766	614,171	4,098,060	21,164,791
1975	13	176	40,315	1,963	26,567	19,551	5,064	3,327	1,287	3,938	677,136	4,357,388	23,099,676
1976	13	173	41,239	1,921	29,211	15,910	5,337	3,500	1,448	3,734	791,661	4,757,240	24,652,113
1977	14	181	42,654	1,980	29,137	17,387	5,542	3,436	1,221	3,767	934,851	5,205,371	26,614,869
1978	14	182	42,614	1,595	27,875	17,635	5,726	3,531	1,268	4,045	1,027,202	5,770,852	27,886,269
1979	14	185	44,552	1,840	27,533	16,434	5,763	3,717	1,202	3,920	1,285,844	6,309,055	30,455,119
1980	14	188	46,689	2,495	26,877	16,294	6,727	4,131	1,889	4,171	1,386,307	6,714,744	38,534,150

family on furlough. This concept was approved by the BSCM in Nov., 1975.

Immediate plans were set in motion to raise funds to finance the project. Cooper made a substantial financial contribution. Contributions from members and friends of the churches of the BSCM, including Cooper, have amounted to more than $97,000.

Construction was begun in Nov., 1978. Contractors did most of the construction, but many volunteers from Michigan Southern Baptist churches helped in such projects as wall-papering, painting, hanging drapes and curtains, and landscaping. The total project cost $212,200. The building stands as a monument to the commitment of Michigan Southern Baptists to the cause of Christ in and through the Bold Mission Thrust effort. This facility should contribute to the strengthening of existing churches and chapels, to the starting of new congregations across the state, and to the reaching of many for Christ.

ROY ADAMS

MICHIGAN ASSOCIATIONS (III).
I. New Associations. NORTHLAND ASSOCIATION. Organized on Oct. 22, 1977, with six churches. Four of these churches were from Bay Area Association, and two were from the Woodland Association. Northland is composed of 21 counties in the upper section of the lower peninsula. Ten of the counties were formerly in Woodland Association and 11 were in Bay Area Association. In 1980, 8 churches reported 110 baptisms, 766 members, $135,338 total gifts, $22,645 mission gifts, and $518,500 property value.

II. Changes in Associations. BAY AREA ASSOCIATION. The geographical area was cut from 19 counties to 8 when Northland Association was organized in 1977.

WOODLAND ASSOCIATION. The geographical area was reduced from 20 counties to 10 when Northland Association was organized in 1977.

BILLY WHITT

MICHIGAN BAPTIST ADVOCATE. News journal of the Baptist State Convention of Michigan. The periodical was launched on Jan. 27, 1955, as the front page of the *Arkansas Baptist*. Fredrich David Hubbs, the first editor of this news page, was succeeded in Apr., 1955, by James Johnson, pastor of Liberty Baptist Mission in Detroit. Johnson continued as editor until July, 1957. Truett Smith was elected editor in Aug., 1957. Under his leadership the paper became a bimonthly, beginning with the Jan. 15, 1958, issue. Also under his leadership the name was changed to the *Michigan Baptist Advocate* with the first issue of Jan., 1960. When Smith moved to Lansing as pastoral missionary in July, 1961, Hubbs became editor again.

In Feb., 1964, the *Advocate* began as an in-house publication. Subscriptions numbered approximately 3,000. When Robert Wilson succeeded Hubbs as executive secretary of the Baptist State Convention of Michigan in Jan., 1971, he also became editor of the *Advocate*. In Jan., 1977, the state convention began sending the *Advocate* free of charge to every Southern Baptist family in the state. The 1980 circulation was 8,850.

EUGENE BRAGG

MICROFILM, MAJOR BAPTIST COLLECTIONS OF THE HISTORICAL COMMISSION, SBC.

The microfilm program of the Historical Commission, begun in 1952, expanded during the 1970s. The commission continues to gather a large collection of evangelical and Baptist materials from Eastern and Western Europe. Over 1,000 items were in this collection in 1981. An extensive collection of black Baptist items were filmed in 1975, including all of the extant annuals of the three major black Baptist conventions. A special Baptist colonial records project resulted in adding numerous early American Baptist materials to the collection. The filming of state papers and church and associational records and minutes continued. The missionary correspondence and records of the Baptist Missionary Society (Great Britain), 1792-1900, were filmed in 1981. The Historical Commission continues to make available microfilm copies of Baptist material which it has permission to duplicate.

A. RONALD TONKS

MID-AMERICA BAPTIST THEOLOGICAL SEMINARY.

An independent, Southern Baptist-oriented seminary located in Memphis, TN. B. Gray Allison is president. Founded in 1971 in Louisiana as the School of the Prophets, the seminary assumed its present name upon relocating in Little Rock, AR, in 1972. It moved to Memphis in 1975, occupying in 1976 its present facilities at 1255 Poplar Avenue. With a teaching staff of 13 professors and 7 instructors, the seminary offers degree programs in theology (M.Div., Th.D.) and religious education (M.A.), as well as diploma studies (Dip.Th., Dip.R.E.). Student enrollment in 1980 was 241. The seminary is a candidate for accreditation by the Southern Association of Colleges and Schools.

DANIEL H. HOLCOMB

MID-CONTINENT BAPTIST BIBLE COLLEGE

(III; cf. West Kentucky Baptist Bible Institute, Vol. II). O. C. Markham (*q.v.*), president, 1957-76, was succeeded by Wendell Holmes Rone, Sr., the school's graduate dean. The board of trustees consists of two persons each from 14 associations of Southern Baptist churches in four states (Kentucky, Illinois, Missouri, and Tennessee), and all faculty and staff members are required to be active in churches in friendly cooperation with Southern Baptist causes. Operating on the trimester plan, the school enrolled 150 in 1979.

R. CHARLES BLAIR

MID-MISSIONS, BAPTIST

(cf. Mid-Missions, Vols. II, III). At the beginning of the 1980s, Baptist Mid-Missions had approximately 1,100 missionaries serving in 40 countries. Of these, 350 were located in North America. The primary church-planting activities are supplemented by medical work, education—elementary, secondary, Bible and seminary levels—linguistics, translation, and printing. An aviation ministry exists in four countries.

Approved fields are Central African Republic, Republic of Chad, Ghana, Ivory Coast, Liberia, Australia, New Zealand, Mariana Islands and Guam, Bangladesh, Hong Kong, India, Japan, Korea, Taiwan, Jordan, Austria, England, Finland, France, Germany, Ireland, Italy, The Netherlands, Norway, Portugal, Scotland, Spain, Sweden, Eastern Europe, Argentina, Brazil, Peru, Venezuela, Ecuador, Mexico, Honduras, Dominican Republic, Haiti, Jamaica, Puerto Rico, St. Lucia, St. Vincent, five provinces of Canada, 31 states of the United States, and the South Pacific.

The official organ is *The Harvest*, published quarterly. Headquarters are in Cleveland, OH.

ALLAN E. LEWIS

MIDDLETON, ROBERT LEE

(b. Terry, NC, Apr. 4, 1894; d. Nashville, TN, Apr. 23, 1979). Denominational executive and author. Son of Edwin Lee Middleton and Mary Eva (Rigsby) Middleton, he married Sarah Edwards, Oct. 15, 1921. They had one daughter, Sally. In 1921 Middleton operated the Baptist Book Store in Raleigh, NC, while employed as an accountant for the state mission board of North Carolina Baptists. On Aug. 15, 1925, he became head of the accounting department of the Sunday School Board, Nashville. Later, he served as director of the business division, retiring in 1962. He is buried in Woodlawn Cemetery, Nashville, TN.

GOMER R. LESCH

MIDWESTERN BAPTIST THEOLOGICAL SEMINARY

(III). Midwestern's board of trustees has 35 members, 25 from states qualified for representation and 10 local trustees residing within 300 miles of Kansas City, MO. The persons serving as president of the board between 1970 and 1980 were C. Harold Mann of Missouri, 1970-71, S. W. Eubanks of Arkansas, 1971-72, Carlos Bradley of Missouri, 1973-74, Dan Rainbolt of Missouri, 1974-76, R. G. Puckett of Maryland, 1976-78, and James W. Tharp of Missouri, 1978-80. Mann, Bradley, and Tharp were laymen, and the others were ordained ministers.

Administration.—President M. J. Berquist formally retired on July 31, 1972, but, at the trustees' request, remained in office until his successor assumed the presidency on Feb. 1, 1973. Berquist was the seminary's first president, administering its affairs for 16 years.

Midwestern's second president is Milton Ferguson, native of Oklahoma, graduate of

Oklahoma Baptist University (B.A., 1951) and Southwestern Baptist Theological Seminary (B.D., 1954; Th.D., 1959), and teacher of theology and philosophy of religion at Southwestern Seminary, 1956-72.

The seminary's administrative staff was enlarged between 1970 and 1980, with the three major administrative officers being directly responsible to the president; they are academic dean, administrator of internal affairs, and dean of students and registrar. In 1971 Roy L. Honeycutt, Jr., became the school's first academic dean. John C. Howell succeeded him as acting dean in 1975 and became dean in 1976. In 1975 C. W. Scudder, formerly a teacher at Southwestern Seminary, became administrator of internal affairs. In 1978 Scudder's title became vice-president for business development. Working under Scudder's direction in 1980 were Kenneth Kerr in financial services, Wray MacLeod in physical plant services, and Maggie Alexander in food services. Lavell Seats continued as registrar and dean of students. External affairs were under the president's direct supervision; in 1980 these included public relations under the direction of Robert Desbien, alumni affairs and program coordination under the direction of Alta Morrow, and planning under the direction of James Fuller. In 1978 a full-time office for denominational services, including placement of students and alumni, opened for the first time. Paul Lambert, formally an associational executive, directed this program.

Instructional Program.—Since 1970 Midwestern has continued its programs leading to M.Div. and M.R.E. degrees and to diplomas in theology and religious education. In 1971 Midwestern dropped its Th.M. program. In full consultation with accrediting agencies, the seminary developed in 1971, and initiated in 1972, a program leading to a D.Min. degree. Based on a basic seminary degree (M.Div. or M.R.E.), the D.Min. program emphasizes professional competence in ministry. A D.Min. candidate must satisfy the requirements of five seminars (worship and preaching, interpretation and teaching, pastoral care, administration, and mission to society); engage in programs of supervision in an institutional setting and a ministry setting; and develop, conduct, analyze, and report on a ministry project. The M.Div. and M.R.E. programs serve around 90 percent of all students.

Following an intensive review of the curriculum, the seminary reduced the number of semester hours for the M.Div. degree from 96 to 88 hours, beginning with the 1971-72 school year. In the 1970s the seminary expanded its requirements in supervision, or fieldwork, and in 1978 a faculty member (Doran McCarty) became a full-time director of supervised ministry. In 1979 the seminary authorized a program of continuing education.

In 1971 the seminary instituted a new plan for scheduling classes in all work except that leading to the D.Min. degree. Becoming known in school circles within a few years as the "Midwestern Plan," it calls for scheduling a two-hour course in a four-week period (two hours per day) or an eight-week period (one hour per day). In 1977 the faculty decided to continue the four-week plan as the basic instructional unit, but the scheduling of eight-week units increased in the late 1970s. This scheduling came under review during the seminary's decennial self-study in 1980.

Accreditation.—Since 1966 Midwestern has enjoyed unqualified accreditation by the Association of Theological Schools (ATS). In Mar., 1971, the school received full accreditation from the North Central Association of Colleges and Secondary Schools (NCACSS), a voluntary, nongovernmental association for the maintenance of quality education. In 1979 the seminary began its decennial self-study to satisfy ATS and NCACSS requirements for continued accreditation; the reevaluation by these accrediting agencies is scheduled for 1981. Self-study committees consist of trustee, administrative, faculty, student, and alumni personnel.

Faculty.—Since 1970 numerous changes have occurred in Midwestern's faculty. Of the 17 faculty members serving in 1970, 11 have continued since election between 1958 and 1960; two died (B. A. Sizemore, Jr. (*q.v.*), in 1976 and Clifford Ingle (*q.v.*) in 1977); one retired (Dewitt Matthews in 1977); and three resigned to accept positions elsewhere (Philip Briggs in 1971, Roy Honeycutt in 1975, and Everett Reneer in 1975). The following were elected to the full-time faculty after 1970: G. Temp Sparkman in religious education and church administration, 1972- , C. Roy Woodruff in psychology and pastoral care, 1976-78, Ben F. Philbeck in Old Testament, 1977-79, Delos Miles in evangelism, 1978- , F. William Ratliff in theology and philosophy, 1978- , Maynard Campbell as instructor, 1977-79, and later as assistant professor in preaching, 1979- , Thomas Smothers in Old Testament, 1979- , J. Thomas Meigs in pastoral care, 1979- , and Bob I. Johnson in church administration, 1979- ; Sam Balentine is a full-time instructor in Hebrew, 1979- . The seminary has continued its sabbatical program, initiated in 1965.

The seminary's scheduling of courses for four-week periods has enabled it to use the temporary teaching services of many scholars and specialists. Called adjunctive personnel, these include persons serving in denominational positions, pastorates, and other ministries. The enlargement of the seminary's program of supervision has resulted in the enlistment of pastors and other specialists, most of whom reside in or near Kansas City, to assist in supervision.

Enrollment.—Since 1970 the seminary's annual cumulative enrollment has been as follows: 272 in 1970-71, 331 in 1971-72, 370 in 1972-73, 457 in 1973-74, 441 in 1974-75, 450 in 1975-76, 486 in 1976-77, 573 in 1977-78, 623 in 1978-79, and 669 in 1979-80. Some of the increase was

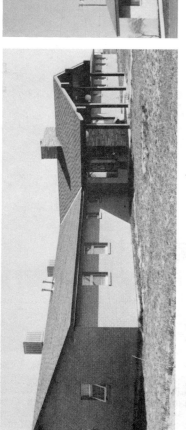

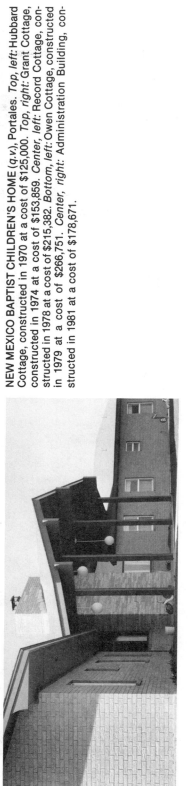

NEW MEXICO BAPTIST CHILDREN'S HOME (q.v.), Portales. *Top, left:* Hubbard Cottage, constructed in 1970 at a cost of $125,000. *Top, right:* Grant Cottage, constructed in 1974 at a cost of $153,859. *Center, left:* Record Cottage, constructed in 1978 at a cost of $215,382. *Bottom, left:* Owen Cottage, constructed in 1979 at a cost of $266,751. *Center, right:* Administration Building, constructed in 1981 at a cost of $178,671.

MIDWESTERN BAPTIST THEOLOGICAL SEMINARY (*q.v.*), Kansas City, MO. *Top:* The Classroom Building, Faculty Offices, and Student Center complex features 16 newly-built faculty offices, renovated classrooms, a curriculum lab, and expanded bookstore and cafeteria facilities. *Center:* The new Child Development Center provides day care for preschoolers of seminary families. *Bottom:* The renovated and redecorated residence hall, which houses 75 single students, is complete with lounge, game room, kitchen, and guest rooms.

due to the addition of the D.Min. program in 1972, but most was due to increases in other degree programs.

Alumni.—As of 1979, Midwestern had conferred 1,175 degrees, including 923 M.Div. (including former B.D.) degrees, 201 M.R.E. degrees, and 56 D.Min. degrees. Most graduates enter some local church ministry (pastoral, religious education, youth work, or others). As of Jan., 1980, 48 Midwestern graduates were serving as appointees of the Foreign Mission Board, SBC, and three were in orientation for foreign mission service. Home Mission Board, SBC, appointees in active service included 25 missionaries and seven missionary associates.

Presidents of Midwestern's national alumni association since 1970 have included Frank Kirkland, Don Wideman, John Dowdy, Jr., Richard Dayringer, Thomas E. Burgdorf, David Bunch, Jerry L. Scruggs, Jimmie Lynn Martin, and Duane E. Trimble. Except for Dowdy, who served two years, each served one year. As the number of Midwestern graduates increased, state and regional meetings of alumni developed. Alumni associations are in 12 state convention areas. Chartered under the national organization, each state association has its own officers.

In the 1970s Midwestern alumni began to appear in greater frequency in denominational offices, both elective and appointive, in the Southern Baptist Convention and affiliated state conventions. Jimmie Lynn Martin was the first alumnus elected to the presidency of a state convention—Kansas-Nebraska Convention of Southern Baptists, 1972-74. In 1977 Paul Swadley became the first Midwestern graduate to serve as president of the Missouri Baptist Convention, and in 1979 Don Wideman became president of this convention. In 1977 R. Rex (Peck) Lindsey became executive director of the Kansas-Nebraska Convention of Southern Baptists. He was the first Midwestern alumnus to serve as the chief administrative officer of a state convention.

Campus and building.—The size of Midwestern's campus remained as it was in 1970 until the sale of eight acres to Kansas City, MO, in 1979. Located in a triangular wedge formed by I-29 and Vivion Road, these acres were not being used in seminary programs. The city plans to erect a picturesque fountain on this site, as a new addition to the "City of Fountains." The city has widened Oak Street along the west side of the campus, thus improving traffic flow. The creation of a new international airport 12 miles northwest of the campus has made Midwestern's facilities more visible in a metropolitan area of 1,400,000 persons.

Building programs since 1970 include the establishment of a modular home park with 35 homes of one and two bedroom units for student families, 1972-73, erection of a faculty office building and renovation of former office space for classroom use, 1977, renovation of the residence hall, 1978, and construction of a center for child development and family life, 1980. Capital needs funds from the SBC financed the office building, renovation of the residence hall, and most of the Child Development Center. Funds from a loan, repaid from rental fees, financed the construction of the apartments.

Sources of Income and Expenditures.—The major source of Midwestern's income is the SBC Cooperative Program which accounted for 93.3 percent of the school's income in 1959, 85.8 percent in 1964, 82.0 percent in 1969, 75.3 percent in 1974, and 77.4 percent in 1979. Income from student fees for the same years amounted to 6.0 percent, 5.6 percent, 4.5 percent, 8.7 percent, and 9.8 percent, respectively. Income from auxiliary enterprises in 1964, 1969, 1974, and 1979 amounted to 5.4 percent, 5.1 percent, 5.5 percent, and 6.1 percent, respectively. Endowments and other sources account for the remainder of Midwestern's income. The school's total income was $566,558 in 1969, $900,866 in 1974, and $1,600,018 in 1979.

The following is illustrative of expenditures in recent years. Of total income in 1969, 22.2 percent was for administration; 57.3 percent for academics; 12.2 percent for operations and plant maintenance; and 7.7 percent for auxiliary enterprises. In 1974 for the same purposes, percentages were 23.2 percent, 45.7 percent, 10.9 percent, and 5.8 percent, respectively; and for 1978, 20 percent, 50.1 percent, 15 percent, and 7 percent, respectively.

Status in Baptist Life.—Since the doctrinal controversy focusing on a member of Midwestern's faculty in the early 1960s, the seminary's status in Baptist life has appeared to improve. As the number of Midwestern's graduates increased, they became active at all levels of Southern Baptist life. This helped to overcome the ill effects of the doctrinal controversy of the early 1960s.

Several Midwestern personnel were conspicuously active in Baptist affairs beyond campus life—as interim pastors, revival preachers, conference leaders, and writers of curriculum materials. President Ferguson spoke at numerous denominational gatherings and was the devotional leader at all sessions of the Missouri Baptist Convention in 1979. J. Morris Ashcraft became noted for his work in theology of stewardship, and he directed a special fund-raising effort for the Child Development Center, 1979-80. William B. Coble has been a featured writer of Sunday School lessons in Missouri Baptists' weekly paper, *Word and Way*, for several years. John C. Howell developed a widely recognized ministry of family life conferences and became one of Southern Baptists' leading writers on the subject of marriage and family life. M. Pierce Matheney, Jr., became a leading figure in Midwest Missions, a special project of Midwestern students in smaller and younger state conventions during recess and summer periods. Doran McCarty served on the Missouri Baptist Historical Commission and also on the executive board of the Missouri Baptist Convention, 1976-79. G. Hugh Wamble testified on behalf of

Missouri Baptists on such legislative matters as parochial aid, liquor control, and gambling. He served as chairman of the Missouri Christian Life Commission, 1971-74, president of the Missouri Baptist Convention, 1973-75, at a time when the convention revised its controlling documents, and member of the Baptist Joint Committee on Public Affairs. Such activities by seminary personnel brought good will to the school and enhanced its ministry.

Prospects.—The seminary entered the 1980s with the largest faculty and student body in its history. The declining number of church vocation volunteers in senior Southern Baptist colleges—from 5,063 in 1974-75 to 3,796 in 1979-80—indicates either that the number of such volunteers is declining or that an increasing number of such volunteers are seeking collegiate training in other institutions. In facing this reality, Midwestern is intensifying recruitment efforts, for any decline now showing up at the college level will reach seminaries in a student generation. The seminary remains committed to the motto publicized in its catalog for over two decades: "In the Heart of America for the Hearts of the World."

G. HUGH WAMBLE

MILLER, IVER ELVIN (b. Mt. Vernon, IL, May 12, 1899; d. Eldorado, IL, Dec. 21, 1977). Pastor and denominational leader. Son of Elvin Oscar and Vallie Palmer Miller, he attended Ewing College, Ewing, IL, 1922-25. He married Mabel Lavern Burden, April 24, 1922. They had three children: Elvin Wesley, Averil Dean, and Vern Edra.

Denominational posts included the board of directors, Illinois Baptist State Association, 1934-48; president, IBSA, 1945-47; associate secretary, IBSA, 1938; and member of the Education Commission, SBC, 1935-48. Along with Harrison Croslin, Sr., and others, he led in the organization of the Illinois Baptist Foundation. He also contributed to the founding of the Southern Illinois College of the Bible at Southern Illinois University in 1938. Pastorates in Illinois included the First Baptist Churches of Jonesboro, Mt. Carmel, Pinckneyville, Eldorado, McLeansboro, and North Benton Baptist. He was a gifted pastor-evangelist. Statistical reports indicate that he baptized about 563 people during his ministry. Miller retired in 1962. He is buried in the East Salem Cemetery, Mt. Vernon, IL.

MYRON D. DILLOW

MINISTER OF MUSIC. Song leader, music director, assistant pastor, choir director, and other titles have been used in Baptist churches to identify the person responsible for music leadership. Following World War I, Southern Baptist churches began employing staff persons to provide full-time leadership in music and educational programs. However, these staff members also served as assistants to pastors, and helped visit unsaved and un-churched persons as well as the sick and bereaved. In only a few instances were these staff associates ordained ministers.

Some of the earliest of these individuals received their music training at Moody Bible Institute. The impact of this school on these churches came through their evangelistic zeal and their preference for hymnals and songbooks from publishers in Chicago and the Midwest. The training of church music leaders in Southern Baptist schools began in 1915 at Southwestern Baptist Theological Seminary, and through the 1920s and 1930s, church music began slowly to gain momentum.

By the 1940s churches increasingly accepted the title, minister of music. Dedicated, creative individuals developed music programs that provided opportunities both for musical expression by persons with musical talents and for music education of children and youth. Other churches saw the potential of this activity, and the demand for trained church musicians increased greatly. In local churches, summer assemblies, youth retreats, and other settings, an increasing number of young people gave evidence that they had felt God's call to a church leadership role in music as a vocation.

As the number of ministers of music increased, ordination for them became a matter of concern. Some churches ordained their ministers of music, some to the "gospel ministry," others to the "gospel ministry in music," or to the "music ministry." Because ministers of music and other professional staff persons in some churches have been ordained, while those in similar positions in other churches have not, some confusion and misunderstanding have existed.

While many churches have a minister of music who devotes time and energies solely to planning and conducting the music program, other churches have combined two or three areas of work—minister of music and education, minister of music and youth, minister of music and recreation, and others. The position of minister of music and youth is one that emerged in the late 1960s.

The rapid growth of church music and the mobility of those involved in it make it difficult to give accurate information about the number of persons so engaged. Recent information reveals that churches reported 9,066 ministers of music, most full time but many part time. There were also others, both full and part time, who were combination ministers of music and education; and ministers of music and youth. This indicates that there are 4,395 full-time church staff persons who are giving part or all of their time to the music ministry, and there are 8,614 salaried part-time church staff persons who are giving leadership to one or more church programs.

The minister of music works in a supportive role to the total program of the church. This staff member is responsible for the church's music ministry as it provides music experiences in the congregational services, as it develops musical skills, attitudes, and understandings of persons of all age groups in the church family, as it ministers to the needs of people through the medium of music, and as it represents the church in the community and the world.

WILLIAM J. REYNOLDS

MINISTERS, COUNSELING OF. Ministers have feelings of inadequacy, insecurity, and confusion, and they experience loneliness and isolation. Consequently, ministers need counseling. Jack Carson, a Texas pastor, as early as 1966, called this need to the attention of the SBC Executive Committee. He said that ministers "would welcome as official and confidential a place to turn to receive . . . Christian concern." E. H. Westmoreland, also of Texas, raised the issue again in 1971 before the SBC. He called for "the establishment of a counseling ministry for pastors and other church-related vocational workers and their families."

Through 1979, 16 state conventions had assigned responsibilities to persons to assist ministers. Most are titled Church-Minister Relations Directors (secretaries). Although much of the service has been through small group work, the most effective service has been done on a one-to-one basis. The Sunday School Board provides counseling for ministers and their spouses through the Career Guidance Section. This counseling includes advice on marital and family difficulties; early, mid-career, and retirement assessment and counseling; forced termination by churches; conflict and stress needs; and career adjustment and changes. The Foreign Mission Board, Home Mission Board, Annuity Board, and Seminary Extension Department provide specialized counseling for ministers interested in missions, vocational change, retirement, and other distinctive personal and vocational needs.

Churches want their ministers to grow and are happy for them to work for personal growth. A few churches in the SBC provide personal development financial assistance. Ministers recognize counseling as a vehicle of personal growth. It is no longer a stigma but a symbol of growth in ministry.

BIBLIOGRAPHY: Louis McBurney, *Every Pastor Needs a Pastor* (1977).

BROOKS FAULKNER

MINISTERS, LICENSING OF. In colonial America the licensing of ministers had both secular and ecclesiastical implications. In those colonies where a state church prevailed, dissenting ministers had to secure a license from the government and could preach only in certain locations and under specific circumstances. Baptists and other nonconformist clergy frequently ignored the licensing requirements and were persecuted, sometimes imprisoned, for preaching without proper credentials. Licensing was a means whereby the state sought to register and control dissenting ministers.

Apart from its political implications, licensing by churches or church bodies is often a way in which many Protestant denominations monitor and validate the authenticity of a minister's call before the granting of ordination. The Saybrook Platform of 1708 indicated the use of licenses among New England Congregationalists. The Platform, which established a common government and confession of faith for the New England churches, also required that county associations oversee the licensing and ordination of candidates for ministry.

In *The Customs of Primitive Churches* (1774), Baptist historian Morgan Edwards (*q.v.* III) indicated that the licensing of preachers was common among Baptists in colonial America. According to Edwards, licenses permitted the new minister to preach in public. Licensing represented the first formal stage on the way to a ministerial vocation.

Early Baptists and other American Protestants generally acknowledged at least five qualities necessary for an authentic call to the ministry: A valid religious experience, good character, genuine sense of call, correct doctrine, and adequate preparation. A license provided the candidate with the necessary credentials while permitting the sponsoring church to verify spiritual maturity. Most congregations considered the licentiate a duly recognized minister, able to perform most pastoral tasks. Some groups did forbid the nonordained to administer baptism or communion.

Congregationalists and Presbyterians normally grant licenses through their respective associations or presbyteries. Methodists license new preachers at the yearly general conference, while Baptists approve licenses through a vote of the local church. In Baptist churches, candidates for ministry are often licensed but not ordained until they receive a formal call to a particular congregation.

BILL J. LEONARD

MINISTERS, PLACEMENT OF. In the past, churches called ministers from among their membership or upon recommendations from recognized Baptist leaders or groups. Normally, at present, a selection committee locates, screens, and recommends prospects, but final decisions remain with the total congregation and the minister. Baptist agencies assist, at most, in introducing churches and ministers.

State conventions have become more actively involved since the mid-1960s, and now almost half the conventions maintain an office of church-minister relations. In others the executive secretary or missions director bears the responsibility. They avoid the term "placement," but maintain and distribute information about churches or ministers, usually without evaluation or recommendation. Questionnaires completed on a voluntary basis by churches or ministers provide the bulk of information shared. Convention personnel cooperate closely with area missionaries, seminaries, and colleges, seeking to extend the supply of prospects while remaining sensitive to local needs and conditions. Some conventions have extended the range of services to include such things as counseling, conferences, and studies.

Initial placement has not reached the critical stage, but relocation for many ministers is virtually impossible. As age increases above 50 or special difficulties arise, some ministers are forced into secular jobs or locked into insecure, unchallenging positions. Personnel distribution remains a problem also, providing an overabundance of ministers in areas and functions where demands are least. Pioneer areas and mission boards recruit with meager responses; educational and music positions remain unstaffed. Placement of women and divorced ministers may present the greatest challenge for the next decade, but placement in all aspects will remain a critical problem for Southern Baptists for the foreseeable future.

BIBLIOGRAPHY: Claude L. Howe, Jr., "The Call, Placement, and Tenure of Ministers," *Baptist History and Heritage* (Jan., 1980).

CLAUDE L. HOWE, JR.

MINISTRIES STUDY CENTER, OVERSEAS. See OVERSEAS MINISTRIES STUDY CENTER.

MINISTRY, BIVOCATIONAL. See BIVOCATIONAL MINISTRY.

MINISTRY, CONTINUING EDUCATION FOR. See CONTINUING EDUCATION FOR MINISTRY.

MINNESOTA-WISCONSIN SOUTHERN BAPTIST FELLOWSHIP. *Beginnings.*—In Aug., 1953, four families in Madison, WI, contacted Illinois area missionary, Harold E. Cameron, requesting assistance in starting a Southern Baptist church. Immanuel Baptist Church (now Midvale) constituted on Sep. 20, with 19 charter members as the first church in the two-state area. Other churches soon followed. Because Illinois was heavily involved in mission work in the greater Chicago area and Indiana, the local churches in Minnesota-Wisconsin in July, 1956, sent a letter to Texas Baptists appealing for sponsorship. Messengers from six Wisconsin churches and one newly organized Minnesota church were seated at the Baptist General Convention of Texas in Corpus Christi, Nov., 1956. Wisconsin-Minnesota Baptist Association was organized, Oct. 15, 1956, with seven churches and 411 members. BGCT joined the Home Mission Board to provide support through financial aid and the appointment of Frank B. Burress as area missionary.

Organization.—Minnesota-Wisconsin Southern Baptist Fellowship organized, Nov. 15, 1969, in La Crosse, WI, with 31 congregations, 4,225 members, and a local budget of $53,440. Membership increased to 5,743 in 44 congregations by 1973, when Burress was elected coordinator and the fellowship office was established in Madison, WI. Thereafter, churches channeled Cooperative Program and other missions offerings

through the Madison office. The office moved to Rochester, MN, in 1975, with Otha Winningham elected coordinator in July. D. E. Strahan, elected Feb., 1977, as Church Services director, assisted in developing religious education programs until his retirement, Dec., 1978.

Structure.—With BGCT approval, the fellowship in 1978 adopted a revised organizational structure to transfer administration of BGCT and Home Mission Board funding to the Rochester office. The fellowship adopted a $639,266 budget in 1979 including financial resources from BGCT, HMB, and other agencies.

The fellowship organized its programs into four departments: Missions, Church Services, Evangelism, and Student Work. Winningham directed the Missions and Evangelism Departments in addition to serving as coordinator-treasurer. Other staff included David Turner, elected May, 1979, as language program leader in the Missions Department; James E. Rennell, elected Jan., 1979, served as Church Services director (Sunday School, Church Training, and related programs) until 1980. Billy J. Chambers was elected in 1981; John Nance, elected May, 1978, served as Student Work director; and Betty Turnbull, elected July, 1976, served as volunteer director, Woman's Missionary Union, until 1979. Ruth Harris served as volunteer director, 1979-81. Betty Lynn Cadle became full-time WMU director in 1981. The HMB and the fellowship participated in the employment of five directors of missions for field service in the six associations.

The fellowship had 92 churches and chapels with 10,300 members, a total operating budget of $777,918, and a weekly state paper, the Minnesota-Wisconsin edition of the *Baptist Standard*, in 1980.

See also TEXAS, BAPTIST GENERAL CONVENTION OF.

OTHA WINNINGHAM

MISSIOLOGY. The study of Christian missions, embracing the pooling of knowledge, understanding skills, and techniques provided by the social and behavioral sciences, by regional studies, and by a wide range of professions.

The American Society of Missiology, founded in 1972 and inaugurated in 1973, is the professional association for mission studies in North America. The society holds an annual meeting for study and discussion of vital issues in missions and publishes a quarterly journal, *Missiology: An International Review*.

First published in 1973, *Missiology* is a scholarly publication that is distinctively multidisciplinary (history, theology, anthropology, communication theory, religious encounter, ecumenics, and methodology), interconfessional (work from Catholic, conciliar, and conservative-evangelical spheres), and practical (not just theoretical reflection, but applied mission science).

More than 2,700 missiologists (600 of whom are members of the American Society of Missiology) and a constituency of 600 key libraries worldwide use *Missiology*. The editor is Arthur F. Glasser and the editorial offices are located in Pasadena, CA.

ARTHUR F. GLASSER

MISSIOLOGY, AMERICAN SOCIETY OF. See AMERICAN SOCIETY OF MISSIOLOGY.

MISSION CHALLENGE COMMITTEE. Upon recommendation of its Executive Committee, the 1974 SBC authorized a special committee of 21 persons, seven appointed by the president and seven by each of the mission boards, to study the plans of the boards, measure Southern Baptists' human and financial resources and potential for mission advance, and develop a missions challenge to Southern Baptists in the final quarter of this century.

Members of the committee were Warren C. Hultgren, chairman; J. D. Grey; Helen Fling; Irene Landes; W. O. Vaught, Jr.; James G. Harris; Owen Cooper; J. R. White; Glen E. Braswell; Travis S. Berry; E. H. Westmoreland; M. Hunter Riggins, Jr.; Emma S. Stratton; Russell H. Dilday, Jr.; Carl E. Bates; Nell Bowen; M. Dale Allen; Gene Garrison; Grayson Glass; and Lewis I. Myers. Resource persons serving with the committee were Porter Routh, Albert McClellan, Baker James Cauthen, Arthur B. Rutledge, Jesse Fletcher, and Fred B. Moseley.

The committee developed three background papers: (1) "Southern Baptist Mission Work in the Next 25 Years," (2) "Southern Baptist Denominational Cooperation in Missions," and (3) "Southern Baptist Commitment and Involvement in Missions." The committee made its final report to the 1976 Convention.

Among the 15 recommendations adopted were: (1) That the Convention set as its primary missions challenge that every person in the world shall have the opportunity to hear the gospel of Christ in the next 25 years; (2) that the Convention reaffirm the place and responsibility of the local church in missions, and call upon its agencies to reinforce this concept; (3) that the mission boards be requested to undertake seriously the creative addition of new patterns of work that will help accomplish the objective of the primary mission challenge; and (4) that the agencies work together to discover and implement plans for a broader based missions education to reach all the members of the churches. These recommendations led to the formation of Bold Mission Thrust in 1977.

See also BOLD MISSION THRUST.

FRED B. MOSELEY

MISSION EDUCATION PROMOTION CONFERENCE (III). See GRADED SERIES CONFERENCE.

MISSION FRIENDS (III). Since 1970 the Woman's Missionary Union, SBC, organization for boys and girls birth through five years or school entrance. *Start* is the publication for leaders in Mission Friends.

The WMU emphasis, "Minding the Future," in 1976-77 sought to enlist more preschoolers in Mission Friends and to increase adult members' and leaders' awareness of their personal responsibility for preschoolers.

Two materials additions occurred. In 1978-79 WMU began a new Mission Friends parent publication, *Share* (later changed to Mission Friends *Share*, a take-home piece for three, four, and five-year-olds). That same year two Mission Friends books were added for use in the Foreign Mission Graded Series and Home Mission Graded Series.

In 1979 Mission Friends organizations totaled 14,264 with a membership of 121,454.

EVELYN BLOUNT

MISSION SERVICE CORPS. The Mission Service Corps (MSC) grew out of the Missions Challenge report to the 1976 SBC which requested that SBC agencies develop opportunities for long-and short-term involvement of laypersons in missions ministries. The 1977 SBC adopted the following recommendation of the SBC Executive Committee:

We recommend that the Southern Baptist Convention, working in cooperation with the state conventions, seek to enlist by 1982 5,000 persons, groups of churches, or churches who would agree to provide and fund 5,000 mission volunteers who would go for one or two years, either in the United States or overseas, in an effort to reach the objectives of the Bold Mission Thrust. It is hoped that the churches will also encourage an increase in Cooperative Program giving by some percentage each year and that the churches will seek as a goal to double their Cooperative Program gifts during this same period of time as projected by the Stewardship Commission.

The Mission Volunteer Committee, chaired by W. Ches Smith, III, of Tifton, GA, recommended that the project be named Mission Service Corps and that the major responsibility be given to the state mission boards, Home Mission Board, and Foreign Mission Board for the enlistment and utilization of the volunteers.

A national office with Ralph West as MSC process coordinator was established at the HMB to serve both boards. David T. Bunch was elected to lead the MSC for the HMB, and Lewis Meyers for the FMB.

The significant factors related to the MSC are:

1. The approval of funding of short-term volunteers by individuals, churches, associations, and others.

2. All personnel classified as MSC are subject to approval of the FMB or the HMB.

3. All assignments are approved by the state conventions, HMB, or FMB.

4. MSC personnel serve under the supervision of long-term missions personnel.

5. The MSC plan is intended to be an integral part of the mission programs of the mission agencies.

6. At the beginning of 1980, it was apparent that the goal of 5,000 volunteers would not be met. In the spring of 1980 the goal of 2,500 volunteers by the HMB and 1,000 volunteers by the FMB was established as a goal through 1982.

7. As of Apr. 1, 1980, 261 persons had been approved and assigned through the HMB and were serving in 40 states, Puerto Rico, American Samoa, and Canada; and 50 had been assigned through the FMB to 26 countries.

See also MISSION CHALLENGE COMMITTEE.

GERALD PALMER

MISSION 70. A national conference on world missions for students and young adults held Dec. 28-31, 1969, in Atlanta, GA, and supported by the Southern Baptist Foreign Mission Board, Home Mission Board, Woman's Missionary Union, Brotherhood Commission, and the Programs of Vocational Guidance and Student Work of the Sunday School Board. Ed Seabough served as executive coordinator.

LLOYD HOUSEHOLDER

MISSIONARY RESEARCH, INTERNATIONAL BULLETIN OF. See INTERNATIONAL BULLETIN OF MISSIONARY RESEARCH.

MISSIONARY USE OF RADIO AND TELEVISION. See RADIO AND TELEVISION, MISSIONARY USE OF.

MISSIONS (II, III). Some mission agencies gave strong emphasis in the 1970s to strategy and long-range planning, particularly for the rest of the century. They sought to make methodology more comprehensive and flexible and attempted new approaches. The great cities came in for more consideration, as did new fields, such as evangelism, church growth, lay leadership training, mass media (the printed page, radio, television, and other audiovisual techniques), theological education by extension, students and other young people, benevolent ministries, and agricultural work.

Missionary staffs tended to increase in some instances, decrease in others. Some missionary agencies were forced to curtail missionary appointments. Others managed to forge ahead. For the latter, career appointments increased, but growth was proportionately greater in short-term categories, which tended to proliferate. Mission efforts were reinforced by nonmissionary personnel living in overseas settings.

Missionary roles changed somewhat, and further changes were predicted. The work of missionaries, in some cases, changed from leading to supporting the emerging national leadership. Some of their best work was done in generating ideas, effort, and enthusiasm for national programs and causes—often in secondary roles or behind the scenes.

Irresponsible charges that American missionaries were agents of the Central Intelligence Agency were made in the public press and otherwise. Those making the charges were not careful to make distinctions; therefore, all missionaries came under suspicion. Mission agencies came to the defense of their missionaries. The Southern Baptist Foreign Mission Board, for example, reaffirmed the board's "long-standing position of non-involvement of its missionary representatives in political affairs," cautioned its missionaries to refrain from "any relationship with intelligence operations of any nation (including the United States) or with political movements in the nations where they serve," and advised President Gerald R. Ford of its action.

Soaring inflation at home and abroad and other problems did their deadly work. It cost more to do the same things. Progress in the work, wherever it occurred, brought added costs. Devaluation of the United States dollar caused special pressures on mission funds. Rising costs caused urgently needed adjustments in such items as missionary support, field budgets, capital needs allocations, and administrative and promotional expenses.

Since many health problems could only be solved by preventing them from occurring, "curative medicine" gave place to a greater extent to "preventive medicine" in medical missions.

The world's hunger problem intensified dramatically. Disasters of calamitous proportions (hurricanes, floods, droughts, earthquakes, wars, violence, and others) seemed to occur with growing frequency. Christians became more acutely aware of the needs of others and their obligation to alleviate their suffering, whether by gifts or volunteer service.

More, but not enough, Christians came to see that missions is the responsibility of each Christian and each church; that churches exist for the purpose of world outreach and kingdom extension; and that the world is big enough to require the efforts of all Christians and Christian groups.

Meanwhile, the world's population and human misery escalated alarmingly. Although devotees to other religions multiplied, as did adherents to no identifiable religion, Christ's mandate, which includes the whole world, remained in force.

BIBLIOGRAPHY: Frank K. Means and R. Keith Parks, *Sequel: The Decade of the Seventies (1981)*; "A Statement of Foreign Mission Board Philosophy" (adopted by FMB in June, 1978).

FRANK K. MEANS

MISSIONS, ASSOCIATION OF PROFESSORS OF. Growing out of a much older regional fellowship of professors of missions in the Atlantic seaboard area, the Association of Professors of Missions was organized in Louisville, KY, in 1952. Its purpose is "to promote among its members fellowship, spiritual life, and professional usefulness."

Until 1974 the association met biennially, usually in conjunction with the meeting of the American Association of Theological Schools. Membership was restricted to professors of missions in institutions affiliated with the AATS and to "other qualified persons" upon invitation of the executive committee. In 1972 membership was officially opened to "all professors of missions" and "other qualified persons." Two years later, the constitution was revised to provide for annual meetings, preferably preceding or following the meeting of the American Society of Missiology.

The organization of the latter in the early 1970s and the publication of its journal, *Missiology,* have effected other changes in the association. It no longer publishes its proceedings, and it focuses more sharply than previously upon the teaching of missions.

Regional fellowships continue to supplement the purpose of the association. A wide spectrum of membership is included, both Protestant and Catholic, mostly from the United States but also including Canada. Southern Baptist professors of missions are heavily involved in the association.

E. LUTHER COPELAND

MISSIONS, BAKER JAMES CAUTHEN CHAIR OF WORLD. See CAUTHEN, BAKER JAMES, CHAIR OF WORLD MISSIONS.

MISSIONS, SCHOOLS OF (II). See WORLD MISSIONS CONFERENCES.

MISSIONS CONFERENCES, STUDENT. See CONFERENCES, STUDENT MISSIONS.

MISSIONS CONFERENCES, WORLD. See WORLD MISSIONS CONFERENCES.

MISSIONS DIGEST. A monthly newsletter begun in Nov., 1979, to provide missions information and assistance in using that information. *Missions Digest* contains current missions reports, excerpts, and condensations from SBC missions periodicals, and references and guidelines for best use of missions information and materials. The newsletter is a cooperative project of five SBC agencies: Brotherhood Commission, Woman's Missionary Union, Sunday School Board, Home Mission Board, and Foreign Mission Board. Its purpose is to help the denomination reach its Bold Mission Thrust objective of making the gospel known to all mankind by the year 2000. Monthly circulation in 1980 to pastors, ministers of education, and associational directors of missions was 41,000.

MIKE DAVIS

MISSIONS EDUCATION COUNCIL. A coordination group of Woman's Missionary Union, Brotherhood Commission, Home Mission Board, Foreign Mission Board, and Sunday School Board for a comprehensive missions education strategy. In 1976 the SBC approved recommendations from the Missions Challenge Committee (appointed in 1974) directing these agencies to strengthen biblical understandings of missions and implement plans for a broader-based missions education. After study, the

agencies formed the council in 1977 with executive and administrative groups and five permanent work groups to implement a coordinated curriculum design, communication with pastors and staff, a national merchandising plan, program designs, and testing approaches. The groups have met since 1977.

See also MISSION CHALLENGE COMMITTEE.

BOBBIE SORRILL

MISSISSIPPI ASSOCIATIONS (II, III).
I. New Associations. NORTHWEST. Organized in 1980 by merger of DeSoto and Tate Associations comprised of churches in DeSoto and Tate Counties. In 1980, 49 churches reported 749 baptisms, 18,288 members, $4,000,888 total gifts, $545,075 mission gifts, and $14,380,000 property value.

II. Changes in Associations. DESOTO. Dissolved in 1980 to merge with Tate and form Northwest Association.

TATE. Dissolved in 1980 to merge with DeSoto and form Northwest Association.

WEBSTER COUNTY. Name changed from Zion on Oct. 21, 1975.

ZION. Name changed to Webster County on Oct. 21, 1975.

LYNN E. MAY, JR.

MISSISSIPPI BAPTIST CONVENTION (II, III).
I. History. In 1969 the convention included 76 associations, 1,886 churches, and a membership of 531,206. In 1979 there were 76 associations, 1,915 churches, and 612,773 members. In the same period, total church income increased from $39,259,198 to $105,764,509, Cooperative Program receipts increased from $3,704,010 to $9,961,221, and the value of church property increased from $171,691,195 to $435,793,524.

W. Douglas Hudgins, executive secretary-treasurer, 1969-73, was the great stabilizer after hurricane Camille in 1969 and the recession of 1970. E. Earl Kelly, pastor of Ridgecrest Baptist Church, Jackson, succeeded Hudgins, Nov. 13, 1973. The following have served as president of the convention since 1969: John McCall, Vicksburg, 1969-70; Glenn Perry, Philadelphia, 1971-72; David Grant, Jackson, 1973-74; James Richardson, Leland, 1975-76; Robert Hamblin, Tupelo, 1977-78; and Bill Causey, Jackson, 1979.

II. Capital Additions. The 1969 convention authorized the appointment of an Assembly Study Committee. Beverly Tinnin, Meridian, committee chairman, recommended that the assembly be reconstructed on the old site at Pass Christian. In 1972 a Capital Funds Campaign was authorized. Following a successful campaign to raise $1,250,000 which had been directed by David Grant, Jackson, the 1974 convention voted to rebuild Gulfshore Baptist Assembly. The Gulfshore Construction Committee, Brooks Wester, Hattiesburg, chairman, completed the assignment, and the assembly was dedicated, May 5, 1978. James L. Sullivan,

Nashville, was the dedication speaker. During construction other properties on Henderson Point were secured, and 1979 property appraisals exceeded $5,000,000.

A new 600-bed facility costing $35,000,000 was dedicated, Jan. 25, 1976, and named Mississippi Baptist Medical Center.

Baptist Children's Village acquired two new satellite campuses: Farrow Manor, Inc., Tate County, was purchased in 1976; and the Dickerson place, Lincoln County, was purchased in 1979.

Five student centers were added during the 1970s. The Neilson home in Oxford was purchased and refurbished as a student center for the University of Mississippi in Oct., 1972. New centers were dedicated at Itawamba Junior College, Mar. 22, 1970; Copiah-Lincoln Junior College, June 27, 1976; Northeast Mississippi Junior College, Sep. 26, 1976; and Delta State University, Apr. 29, 1979. At the end of the decade the Mississippi Baptist Convention Board owned 12 student centers with a value of $2,700,000.

Central Hills Baptist Retreat began operations in 1979, and the first construction phase was completed on 360 acres of land near Kosciusko at a cost of $1,500,000 in 1980.

The property value of the four Mississippi Baptist colleges increased from $18,382,519 in 1969 to $27,491,513 in 1979. Mississippi College acquired a large downtown Jackson building to be used by the School of Law. William Carey College purchased Gulf Coast Military Academy property, Gulfport, in 1976 and began a satellite operation named William Carey College on the Coast.

The value of all fixed assets of the Mississippi Baptist Convention increased from $34,141,059 in 1969 to $86,823,454 in 1979.

III. Organization and Personnel. W. Douglas Hudgins and A. L. Nelson, comptroller-business manager, programmed a model computer operation for all convention board records in the early 1970s.

E. Earl Kelly led the board in a reorganization of the convention board staff in 1974. Chester Vaughn, program director, was assigned the supervision of personnel and programs of those departments responsible for assisting churches in the areas of church program organizations (Church Music, Church Training, Church Administration, and Sunday School), and missions and evangelism organizations (Baptist Student Ministries, Brotherhood, Cooperative Missions, Cooperative Ministries with National Baptists, Evangelism, and Woman's Missionary Union). Kelly gave supervision to all other areas of work while giving direction to the entire staff. Later, three new departments were added: P. C. Perkins, director of Church-Minister Relations, Nov. 1, 1975; Leon Emery, director of Church Administration, Jan. 1, 1977; and Frank Simmons, manager of Gulfshore Baptist Assembly, Jan. 1, 1978. In 1978 the Department of Cooperative Ministries with

National Baptists was deleted, when Dick Brogan, director, became president of the Mississippi Baptist Seminary. Brogan had served as director since the retirement of W. P. Davis, Sep. 1, 1971.

The 1974 convention secured a new charter for the Mississippi Baptist Seminary to create an independent biracial institution. Operational expenses of the seminary were to be shared by the Mississippi Baptist Convention, the Home Mission Board, and the nine black national state conventions. Believing the best interests of both black and white Baptists could best be served by this arrangement, nine trustees were selected from the Mississippi Convention and one from each of the nine black conventions.

Roy Collum succeeded Gordon Sansing as director of evangelism, Mar. 1, 1970. Sansing had become pastor of First Baptist Church, Grenada, Sep. 15, 1969.

Edwina Robinson, executive secretary of Woman's Missionary Union, retired, May 1, 1971, and was succeeded by Marjean Patterson.

Joe Odle (q.v.) retired as editor of *The Baptist Record*, Aug. 31, 1976, and was succeeded by Donald McGregor. Paul Harrell became director of Brotherhood work upon the retirement of Elmer Howell, Jan. 31, 1977. W. R. Roberts, annuity secretary, retired, May 31, 1978. Bill Sellers, Roberts' successor, was assigned to the Church-Minister Relations Department. Jerry Merriman succeeded Ralph Winders as director of student work, May 31, 1979, a position Winders had held for 22 years.

Carey Cox, secretary of the Mississippi Baptist Foundation, retired, Dec. 31, 1976, and was replaced by Harold Kitchings. R. A. McLemore (q.v.) left the presidency of Mississippi College in 1968 to become the director of the State Department of Archives and History, and Lewis Nobles was selected as his successor. Lowrey Compere, president of Clark College, retired, July 18, 1977. He was succeeded by S. L. Harris of Fort Worth, TX, Apr. 1, 1978. Harris resigned, Dec. 31, 1978, and was succeeded by A. C. Johnson.

IV. Decade of Advance. The 1974 convention adopted the slogan, "Decade of Advance," and goals were set to challenge each Mississippi Baptist church to give measured and regular increases to meet the urgent and pressing needs in Mississippi and the world during the years 1975-84. Later this thrust was merged with the SBC's Bold Mission Thrust, and significant results were recorded.

The Foreign Mission Board held one of its semiannual meetings in Jackson in Apr., 1973, and concluded with a a missionary appointment service in the City Auditorium.

In 1974 the convention transferred the titles and responsibility for the care of all real estate owned by the Board of Ministerial Education to the trustees and administrations of the four Baptist colleges. Of the 6,359 students enrolled in the four colleges in 1979, 383 were ministerial students.

MISSISSIPPI STATISTICAL SUMMARY

Year	Associations	Churches	Church Membership	Baptisms	SS Enrollment	VBS Enrollment	CT Enrollment	WMU Enrollment	Brotherhood Enrollment	Ch. Music Enrollment	Mission Gifts	Total Gifts	Value Church Property
1969	76	1,881	531,206	15,529	317,729	165,784	144,438	56,079	18,769	61,451	$ 6,580,305	$ 39,259,198	$171,691,195
1970	76	1,883	536,667	15,237	313,994	133,092	137,935	51,854	18,700	61,691	6,573,434	41,425,173	179,787,184
1971	76	1,887	545,700	18,308	308,852	147,830	126,435	48,675	20,122	61,384	7,364,825	45,498,709	189,667,795
1972	76	1,885	558,742	19,178	311,475	134,041	124,632	47,554	19,786	65,182	7,857,271	50,596,007	199,885,942
1973	76	1,889	570,644	18,351	316,612	142,999	125,414	47,450	21,073	71,042	8,990,370	54,796,961	217,524,324
1974	76	1,881	580,892	16,674	319,987	143,411	128,213	49,429	21,774	74,666	10,554,065	61,945,880	244,247,801
1975	76	1,889	586,560	17,656	325,052	147,300	129,324	51,327	22,848	78,872	11,499,236	68,048,490	269,637,804
1976	76	1,894	595,010	16,252	336,649	144,592	129,428	50,996	22,732	81,308	12,620,516	75,655,511	304,159,096
1977	76	1,903	606,609	13,949	336,428	144,664	127,374	51,453	22,529	81,824	13,925,251	84,178,082	341,145,548
1978	76	1,907	606,106	13,583	332,263	139,290	126,704	50,943	22,085	84,898	15,889,656	92,680,318	387,362,603
1979	76	1,915	612,773	15,801	336,607	143,309	128,515	51,001	23,521	87,804	18,081,163	105,764,509	435,793,524
1980	75	1,925	620,312	17,363	341,213	148,559	129,033	52,336	25,539	92,412	20,228,230	116,750,514	480,679,175

ESTEEN QUINN and MARY ELIZABETH CLAYBURN

Two color mission films were produced in 1975: "The Whale That Came to Mississippi" and "Missions—A New Day in Mississippi."

During the 1970s the state of Mississippi experienced a series of natural disasters. The Brotherhood Department trained and equipped a disaster task force. During the Apr., 1979, flood, 23,185 meals were served flood victims. Special offerings totaling $1,034,000 were expended to assist victims of fires, floods, hurricanes, and tornadoes.

Between 1975 and 1979, $452,306 were spent on new church sites and chapel trailers. The sites were donated by newly organized churches.

State mission ministries were provided for the major ethnic and language groups in the state: American Indians, Chinese, deaf, Latin Americans, seamen, and Vietnamese. "Good News Mississippi," a joint thrust of Mississippi Baptists and National Baptists to evangelize the state, was a significant biracial religious thrust in 1979.

At the conclusion of 1979 all student directors on state campuses were employed by the convention board. The Baptist programs were being promoted by 126 employees of the convention board in all 76 associations.

BIBLIOGRAPHY: Richard A. McLemore, *A History of Mississippi Baptists, 1780-1970* (1971).

EARL KELLY

MISSISSIPPI BAPTIST FOUNDATION

(II, III). On Apr. 1, 1980, the Principal Funds Account registered $6,186,840. Earnings for distribution to Mississippi Baptist and Southern Baptist causes from 1945 through Mar. 31, 1980, totaled $5,326,878. Fifty percent of current earnings go to Christian education, 40 percent to missions, and 10 percent to recipients of charitable remainder trusts. The foundation's operating budget comes from the Cooperative Program. The executive committee of the nine-member board of trustees invests the principal funds, thereby deleting investment costs. The foundation renders all its ministries as a free service. In 1977 Harold T. Kitchings succeeded Carey Cox as the foundation's executive secretary.

HAROLD T. KITCHINGS

MISSISSIPPI BAPTIST MEDICAL CENTER

(cf. Mississippi Baptist Hospital, Vols. II, III). The new $35,000,000 Mississippi Baptist Medical Center was dedicated, Jan. 25, 1976. On Feb. 1, 1976, patients were moved to the medical center. The 600-bed facility, the largest, private general hospital in Mississippi, maintains approximately 1,500 employees.

The six-floor medical center includes a 19-room surgical suite, 16-bed intensive care unit, 12-bed coronary care unit, and 12-bed out-patient surgery unit. The cardiovascular department has two heart catheterization laboratories and a seven-bed cardiovascular surgery recovery room. The obstetrics-gynecology area includes five nurseries and an alternative birth suite for childbirth in a homelike atmosphere. The emergency area includes an operating room, nine special procedure rooms, a small lab, and a 10-bed holding area. Patient treatment areas include laboratories, radiology, respiratory therapy, physical therapy, and blood bank. Ancillary areas include staff development classrooms, data processing, business office, chapel, cafeteria, medical records, building service, materials management, engineering, gift shop, and administrative offices.

In 1976 the Progressive Care Unit closed, and a 28-bed Chemical Dependency Unit for the treatment of alcohol and drug abuse opened. Inclusion of a program for teenage abusers in 1979 and expansions in 1977 and 1979 increased capacity to 74 beds.

New departments created in 1977 were social services, patient education, public relations, and nurse recruiting. In 1978 plans were undertaken to build a radiation therapy center adjacent to the existing medical center for treatment of cancer patients. A fund drive conducted in Dec., 1978, raised over $1,000,000 toward the $2,600,000 project, completed in early 1981.

Land, buildings, equipment, and other assets are valued at $54,525,264. Patient income in 1979 was $36,819,802. Cooperative Program gifts totaled $138,000. Charity work totaled $2,874,468.

JEAN MAY

MISSISSIPPI BAPTIST ORPHANAGE (II). See BAPTIST CHILDREN'S VILLAGE, THE.

MISSISSIPPI BICENTENNIAL BELL. The Mississippi Liberty Bell, one of 53 identical replicas of the Liberty Bell cast in France in 1950 and presented to the people of Mississippi, rang at two SBC meetings—Miami in 1975, and Norfolk in 1976. John Lee Taylor, Mississippi Foreign Mission Board member, heard W. O. Vaught, board president, mention the Order of Business Committee's plans for a liberty bell in the convention's sessions, June 10-12, 1975. Earl Kelly, Mississippi Baptist Convention Board's executive secretary-treasurer, and Taylor asked Governor William Waller for the loan of the Mississippi Liberty Bell. Heber Ladner, secretary of state and capital commission chairman, announced the commission's unanimous vote granting permission for the loan of the bell to the Mississippi Baptist Convention and the SBC.

The Home and Foreign Mission Boards shared the expense of remounting the bell on a steel yoke. Ford Motor Company provided a truck for transportation and insurance. Traveling 50,000 miles through 23 states, the bell appeared in state Baptist conventions in Alabama, Mississippi, Georgia, Oklahoma, and Arkansas; at bicentennial rallies; at Sunday School and music conventions; at historic sites in Philadelphia, PA, Washington, DC, Richmond, VA, and Greenville, SC; at the Arkansas-Texas

A. & M. football game; and at a patriotic rally, July 4, 1976, in Little Rock.

Upon its return home July 6, 1976, with special ceremonies, a plaque of appreciation from the SBC was permanently attached.

C. B. HAMLET, III

MISSISSIPPI COLLEGE (II, III). The college enrollment increased from 2,304 in 1969 to 3,124 in 1979. Enrollment in the graduate school exceeded 1,000 by 1979, and library holdings climbed to 177,000 volumes. In 1979, 728 degrees were awarded. The institutional budget rose from $3,100,000 in 1969 to $7,500,000 in 1979, and the Annual Fund increased dramatically from 664 donors giving $60,000 in 1969 to 2,200 giving $400,000 in 1979. Three major buildings—the Learning Resources Center, Cockroft Hall (home economics and nursing), and the A. E. Wood Coliseum—were added. Administrative reorganization led to the creation of four vice-presidencies: Academic Affairs, 1969, Business Affairs, 1974, Student Affairs, 1974, and Graduate and Special Programs, 1978.

Between 1969 and 1979, five schools were organized: the School of Nursing, 1969, the School of Business, 1975, the Graduate School, 1975, the School of Law, 1975, and the School of Education, 1977.

Two major financial campaigns conducted successfully were the Commitment Campaign for $3,000,000 and Breakthrough for $5,000,000. A $4,500,000 building in downtown Jackson, given to Mississippi College School of Law by the United Gas Pipeline Company in 1978, was completely renovated in 1979.

New degree programs at the education specialist level were introduced in the areas of school administration, guidance and counseling, elementary education, English, mathematics, and social sciences. Offerings at the master's level during the decade expanded with six new areas added.

In 1976 the Lilly Endowment granted Mississippi College over $100,000 for a three-year faculty development program. In 1977 the Southern Regional Education Board awarded the college a two-year faculty evaluation grant. The college established a Division of Continuing Education in 1975, and by 1979 more than 1,500 students were participating in credit and noncredit courses.

The Gulf South Athletic Conference accepted the college as a member in 1972. In 1976, 1977, and 1979, the men's track team won the conference championship; in 1978 the men's basketball team earned the same honors; and in 1979 the football team earned the championship. The college added Frierson Baseball Field and a new practice football field to its athletic facilities.

The campus grew by 220 acres in 1973 with the acquisition of the Clinton Waterways Experiment Station property, designed for recreation and academic use. The following year radio station WHJT-FM went on the air in Decem-

GULFSHORE BAPTIST ASSEMBLY (*q.v.*), Pass Christian, MS. New facilities were dedicated May 5, 1978. The main building, completed in late 1977 and named the Chester L. Quarles Administration Building, accommodates 344 persons. Value of the assembly property in July, 1981, was $4,993,860.

MISSISSIPPI COLLEGE (*q.v.*), Clinton. Provine Chapel houses the college's Department of Religion.

MISSISSIPPI BAPTIST MEDICAL CENTER (*q.v.*), Jackson. New facilities occupied in 1976. Valued at $37,000,000 in mid-1981. With a 600-bed capacity, it is Mississippi's largest privately owned hospital.

ber. In 1976 the college was named the first bicentennial campus in the state when it began the celebration of the nation's bicentennial, its own sesquicentennial, and its 125th anniversary as a Baptist-owned institution of higher education.

Lewis Nobles has served as college president since 1968.

EDWARD L. MCMILLAN

MISSOURI, CHRISTIAN LIFE COMMISSION OF (III). Since its inception, the commission has had two basic concerns in implementing its five primary programs (family, human rights, economics, moral concepts, and citizenship). These concerns have been for legislation (both state and national) and personal ethical awareness. In its earlier years, the legislative concern was dominant. Beginning in the middle of the 1970s, a more nearly equal emphasis existed. Willard Reine has served as legislative consultant for the commission since 1977. The 1979 report to the Missouri Baptist Convention indicated a major concern for world hunger. In the light of major food crises in many lands, Missouri Baptists gave more than $150,000 to this cause in response to the commission's appeal. With obvious disintegration of the family, the commission concerned itself in 1980 with conferences and emphases on the family.

W. C. LINK, JR.

MISSOURI ASSOCIATIONS (II).
I. New Associations. CANE CREEK-STODDARD. Organized in 1971 by the merger of Cane Creek and Stoddard Associations. In 1980, 37 churches reported 245 baptisms, 9,727 members, $1,079,135 total gifts, $174,013 mission gifts, and $5,030,500 property value.
LINN-LIVINGSTON. Organized in 1975 by the merger of Linn County and Livingston Associations. In 1980, 29 churches reported 237 baptisms, 7,802 members, $914,533 total gifts, $190,967 mission gifts, and $4,354,855 property value.
TRI-COUNTY. Organized in 1976 by the merger of Christian County and Stone-Taney County Associations. In 1980, 47 churches reported 320 baptisms, 8,493 members, $1,368,929 total gifts, $267,487 mission gifts, and $4,740,000 property value.
II. Changes in Associations. BURBOISE. Organized in 1851, the association disbanded in 1969. Its churches joined Dixon and Miller Associations.
CAMDEN COUNTY. Organized in 1889, the association disbanded and became a part of Lamine Association in 1979.
CANE CREEK. Organized in 1857, the association merged with Stoddard Association in 1971 to form Cane Creek-Stoddard Association.
CHRISTIAN COUNTY. Organized as Bethel Association in 1853 (with name changes to Southwest Bethel in 1869 and then to Christian County in 1889), it merged with Stone-Taney

County Association in 1976 to form Tri-County Association.
DAVIESS. Organized in 1901, the association disbanded and became a part of the North Grand River Association in 1970.
LINN COUNTY. Organized in 1872, the association merged with Livingston Association in 1975 to form Linn-Livingston Association.
LIVINGSTON. Organized in 1872, the association merged with Linn Association in 1975 to form Linn-Livingston Association.
STODDARD. Organized in 1894 as Stoddard County Association (name changed to Stoddard in 1966-67), the association merged with Cane Creek Association in 1971 to form Cane-Creek-Stoddard Association.
STONE-TANEY. Organized in 1923 as Stone-County Association (name changed to Stone-Taney in 1956-57), the association merged with Christian County Association in 1976 to form Tri-County Association.

JIM GOODSON

MISSOURI BAPTIST CHILDREN'S HOME (II, III). In 1969 a second group home for boys was built at a farm location. In 1972 a day-care center for children aged two through six was opened on campus. It operated until June, 1978, with license for 50 children. In 1979, 436 children were served through residential-group homes, foster-adoptive services, and ministries to unmarried parents.

In Dec., 1974, Edgar Blake retired as administrator. Howard Meyer succeeded him in Jan., 1975, and resigned Sep., 1978. He was succeeded by Allen Harrelson in Nov., 1979. The Psychological Family Services Department operated from Sep., 1975, through 1979 with Thomas Trimble as director. The goal of this department was counseling families with difficulties and preserving family units. In 1976 an open-air recreational center and a gazebo were built on campus.

MRS. HOMER DELOZIER

MISSOURI BAPTIST CHURCH PLANNING, BUILDING, AND FINANCE SERVICES (cf. Missouri Baptist Convention, Vol. III). The department has been combined and enlarged to include building planning consultation services in cooperation with the Church Architecture Department, Sunday School Board. Maximum building fund loans were increased to $75,000. Services available to churches include counsel in all stages of planning, building, or financing.

ELWOOD G. KELLEY

MISSOURI BAPTIST COLLEGE (cf. Hannibal-LaGrange College, Vol. I; Missouri Baptist College, Vol. III). A four-year, coeducational, liberal arts college, occupying an 81-acre campus in Creve Coeur, a suburb of St. Louis, MO.

Merger with Hannibal-LaGrange College in 1967 was dissolved, Apr. 10, 1973, restoring

Hannibal-LaGrange College and establishing a one-campus college known as Missouri Baptist College. In 1971 the college had introduced a third-year level of work and in 1972 a fourth, granting bachelor's degrees to 29 persons, May 13, 1973.

A severe financial crisis resulted in the suspending of operations on Aug. 17, 1974. Under the leadership of J. Edwin Hewlett, then pastor of Southwestern Baptist Church, a campaign for funds was launched among churches of the St. Louis area. In one week, $400,000 in cash and pledges to be paid over a period of three years was received. On Aug. 25, 1974, the trustees voted to reopen the college. Classes began on schedule, Sep. 4, with 331 students, compared to 415 for the previous spring, a budget reduced from $1,223,000 to $889,000, and full-time faculty reduced from 33 to 13. In the collapse, president Frank B. Kellogg, who had succeeded L. A. Foster in 1970, resigned, and Robert S. Sutherland, chairman of behavioral sciences, was appointed acting president and dean. In 1976 he was named president and acting dean.

Achieving candidacy by North Central Association in 1974, full accreditation was granted in Apr., 1978. In 1973 a building was completed to house classrooms, faculty offices, student lounge, cafeteria, and chapel; and in 1979 the college's first residence facilities, to house 50 men and 50 women, were completed. The total enrollment for the fall semester, 1979, was 434, including 110 students in a nursing certificate program of Missouri Baptist Hospital.

GORDON PSALMONDS

MISSOURI BAPTIST CONVENTION (III; cf. Missouri Baptist General Association, Vol. II).

I. Revision of Convention Structure. Revisions in the convention begun in the late 1960s were completed in the 1970s. During the tenure of Earl O. Harding (q.v.), convention executive secretary, 1954-73, much centralizing of organizational structure occurred. Restiveness over this centralized control led the executive committee of the convention in 1973 to authorize the formation of a Structure and Reorganization Committee to study the structure and reorganization of the convention. While the study was in process, the death of Harding, Aug. 12, 1973, came as a shock to the convention. H. L. McClanahan and then T. W. Nelson served as interim secretaries while both reorganization and promotion work of the convention went forward.

Many changes in structure came quickly, but in Columbia in 1973 the Structure and Reorganization Committee was enlarged to 15 members with representatives from religious, educational, and business communities asked to serve. Many specific instructions were given this committee at the Columbia convention. A lengthy report and the implementation of many authorized changes came at the annual meeting in Joplin, Oct., 1974.

The 1974 minutes reflected the major changes brought about as a result of the Columbia convention and showed concern about management policies during the Harding years. Primary was a $1,040,000 debt owed to the Missouri Baptist Building fund by the executive board which had borrowed to refurbish its office building. Most dissatisfaction quieted after business reorganization in the convention; the selection of Rheubin L. South as executive director, Feb. 17, 1975; the adoption of new management and direction policies for the *Word and Way,* the state paper, when Bob Terry became editor, Aug. 25, 1975; and the creation of a Business Service Division with Roger W. Hall chosen as director, June 1, 1975.

Other major concerns of the convention in following years were Bold Mission Thrust, the use of state, tax-supported scholarships by Baptists attending Baptist colleges, the development of a convention-sponsored counseling service apart from child care programs, and a cooperative effort with Baptists of Taiwan to engage in concerted evangelism over a three-year period.

In 1974 the Executive Board was instructed to organize and conduct its work through five standing committees: Administrative Committee, Church Development Committee, Missions and Evangelism Development Committee, Communications Committee, and Inter-Agency Committee.

The Administrative Committee was responsible for fiscal affairs, personnel management, stewardship and Cooperative Program promotion, and general services.

The Church Development Committee's work included Sunday School, Church Training, Church Music, Woman's Missionary Union, Brotherhood, World Missions Conferences, pastoral skill development, general church administration, church library, Christian recreation, architectural advisory services, and Windermere programming.

The Missions and Evangelism Development Committee's responsibility included associational directors of missions, state missions activities, location and organization of new churches, coordination of all student activities, location and operation of student centers, campus ministries and ministers, work with National Baptists, special direct missions assistance to metroplex areas, supplemental pastoral support, and location and supervision of student summer missionaries.

The Communications Committee's area of responsibility was the convention's Christian Life Commission, the *Word and Way,* the departments, agencies, and institutions, communications of state Executive Board concerns to the churches, general public relations, and civic and business leaders in Missouri.

The Inter-Agency Relations Committee's responsibility included the Executive Board's relations with the convention agencies and institutions and newly proposed agencies and institutions.

The staff structure was to be headed by an executive director elected by the Executive Board and an administrative staff consisting of the executive directors of various programs, the directors of the office of general program coordination and of general stewardship and Cooperative Program Promotion, and division directors.

The continuing implementation and expansion of the work structure and reorganization was passed to a standing committee for continuing review.

II. Recurring Problems. Some recurring problems appear to have reached a solution. The question of dual alignment of the churches was decided with single alignment the policy of the convention. The publishing of a detailed budget of the convention was begun, and in the 1979 annual a detailed report was provided. The problem of separation of church and state as related to the institutions of the convention was resolved by the "Public Aid" and Government Involvement Study Committee report in 1979. The uses of government funds were to be in keeping with the nature and purpose of the institution, and no government funds were to be accepted that diverted an institution from its distinctive Baptist nature and purpose or which infringed upon the institution's right to use religion as a criterion in employee selection or use of facilities.

III. Program Development and Personnel Changes. Following 1970 a major reorganization of program emphasis occurred. Realignment of responsibilities was effected under Divisions of Management, Service, Church Development, Evangelism, Associational Administration, Stewardship Promotion, and Bond and Loan Service. John Crutchfield became division director for Church Development, responsible for coordinating the work of Sunday School, Church Training, Baptist Men, Woman's Missionary Union, Church Music, and Student Ministries. Bill Marshall became secretary of Student Work. In 1971 John Crutchfield replaced Luther B. Dyer in the Evangelism Division. Fred D. Hubbs became director of Associational Administration. Billy T. Hargrove become director of Stewardship, succeeding W. H. Allison who had served ably for many years. In 1972 the Church Development Division became Program Services with H. L. McClanahan succeeding Crutchfield, who moved to the Evangelism Division. Bob Woolley succeeded Dale C. Brubaker, who retired from the Church Music Department.

Much change in personnel occurred in 1973-74 following the death of Earl Harding. McClanahan became interim secretary; Jean Lee, director of new Library Services Department; Elwood Kelley, secretary of Brotherhood; Howard Mayer, secretary of Church Administration; and Alberta Gilpin, secretary of Woman's Missionary Union.

Other personnel changes occurring were:

Charles Johnson became Student Ministries director, 1974; Harold T. Copeland, director of a new Church Media Center, and Harvey Wright, Annuity and Insurance Department director, both in 1975; Harold Souther, director of Church Development, Paul Harvey, Brotherhood director, and James Goodson, Mission's Department director, all in 1976; George Worrell, Evangelism director, 1977; and Jim Fitzmaurice, Baptist Press manager, and Frank Denton, Foundation director, 1978.

IV. Expansion and Changes. A Church-Minister Relations Department was inaugurated, Mar., 1979, providing to both churches and ministers a place of contact and counsel. A counseling service begun by the Missouri Baptist Children's Home, Bridgeton, indicated that a definite need existed within the state, but the expenses exceeded the resources of the institution. A convention committee seeking to find a place within program structure called for additional study.

The decade was marked by expansion in all institutions, and many facilities were renovated as well as expanded. The work in Iowa grew under the encouragement of the convention and many of the churches.

Hannibal-LaGrange College, Hannibal, began an extension center in St. Louis which developed into Missouri Baptist College, St. Louis, chartered in 1964, for a time a dual-campus college with campuses at St. Louis and Hannibal. The dual campus arrangement was dissolved, Apr. 10, 1973. Hannibal-LaGrange was rechartered as a junior college, and Missouri Baptist College was established as a one-campus college. Christian emphases and the training of Christian leadership have received new commitment by the Baptist colleges of the state. All added new buildings and equipment during the decade.

The role of the Baptist colleges in the convention was also redefined during the decade. At the center of a healthy relationship between colleges and the convention was the recognition that a college and a church are not identical in their purposes, methods of approach, composition of membership, and internal administration. By means of complementary roles, each contributes to the Christian mission in the world. A covenant relationship was declared as basic to a reasonable response each may expect from the other.

There was little change in the percentages given through the SBC or allocated to the institutions and programs of the state convention during the decade.

The Bold Mission Thrust proposed by the SBC in 1976 was begun in Missouri by the calling of a task force in July, 1977, by the executive director. The six objectives adopted were: (1) give every person in Missouri an opportunity to hear and respond to the gospel; (2) provide a New Testament-based fellowship of believers for all people; (3) encourage mission participation; (4) determine volunteer utilization;

MISSOURI STATISTICAL SUMMARY

Year	Associations	Churches	Church Membership	Baptisms	SS Enrollment	VBS Enrollment	CT Enrollment	WMU Enrollment	Brotherhood Enrollment	Ch. Music Enrollment	Mission Gifts	Total Gifts	Value Church Property
1969	81	1,820	510,013	16,867	338,645	175,969	112,989	64,544	19,019	42,660	$ 6,540,548	$36,735,761	$159,497,969
1970	81	1,825	515,554	15,362	333,425	157,465	111,299	59,873	18,341	43,030	6,730,608	38,323,889	165,711,833
1971	80	1,831	524,021	17,129	324,885	155,988	91,728	59,006	19,880	43,578	7,794,006	41,741,843	176,465,394
1972	79	1,826	534,106	20,277	330,920	158,654	92,107	57,336	19,268	47,067	8,362,447	45,944,724	189,089,916
1973	79	1,840	545,179	19,359	331,234	160,573	86,591	53,915	18,124	49,723	8,897,862	46,931,978	200,361,765
1974	79	1,842	553,979	18,573	331,390	166,370	84,567	53,567	17,525	51,680	9,826,237	52,270,049	215,353,201
1975	82	1,844	565,626	19,433	333,781	168,857	79,890	52,386	17,146	53,246	10,740,677	57,304,921	243,356,385
1976	81	1,848	571,794	18,000	345,160	159,286	80,053	52,133	17,232	54,177	11,651,558	63,863,073	266,019,861
1977	80	1,853	578,442	15,331	340,041	148,216	72,914	50,827	16,702	53,679	12,924,632	69,372,518	292,080,079
1978	80	1,855	584,596	14,635	331,452	154,403	73,422	47,820	15,936	57,324	13,764,852	75,097,320	319,994,870
1979	79	1,872	589,277	15,387	329,277	152,944	72,140	47,701	16,031	57,886	15,706,740	82,501,013	366,846,466
1980	79	1,881	600,514	20,784	336,013	159,770	74,390	49,385	17,570	61,072	17,782,723	91,463,049	413,203,304

DAVID O. MOORE

(5) equip the saints to do the work of God in the world; and (6) build a significant financial base to accomplish Bold Mission Thrust. The response to the thrust has been increasing.

The Department of Student Ministries was reorganized in 1975. The new approach had two outstanding features. One was that student ministries in Missouri would be carried out in "closest cooperation with local Baptists." Therefore, local area Student Work Advisory Committees were established throughout the state. The other feature of reorganization was that the Student Ministries program would be directed to the entire state. The number of BSU's grew from 33 in 1975 to 55 in 1980. Charles H. Johnson is state director.

V. New Baptist Building. The new Baptist Building in Jefferson City, completed and entered for service, June, 1971, was the culmination of a movement begun in 1955 when first drawings were made. In 1969 the convention voted unanimously to purchase the building known as the Missouri Motor Hotel for $531,155, which was paid from the general fund of the convention. After study, the final plan approved included remodeling all eight floors, replacing the heating and air-conditioning system, and adding new furniture for an estimated cost of $2,660,000. The actual cost was $2,615,713, which included $212,566 for furnishings and equipment.

MONTE PETERSON and CHARLES H. JOHNSON

MISSOURI BAPTIST CONVENTION, ANNUITY BOARD WORK OF (III). Harvey J. Wright succeeded J. W. Fisher as annuity secretary in 1977 upon Fisher's retirement. A new retirement plan was added in 1978. In 1979 over 64 percent of Missouri churches were enrolled in Annuity Board plans. A total of 1,518 individuals were participating in all plans.

HARVEY J. WRIGHT

MISSOURI BAPTIST CREDIT UNION (III). The 1970s brought growth and stability. Membership increased from 501 to 1,098 (119 percent), assets increased from $191,443 to $784,483 (310 percent), and the board of directors declared a six percent quarterly dividend for 1979. Bob Wooley served as president of the board in 1980, and Dolores Dake served as manager.

ELWOOD G. KELLEY

MISSOURI BAPTIST FOUNDATION (II, III). Thomas W. Nelson retired as executive director-treasurer, Dec. 31, 1978, and was succeeded by Frank Denton. Assets under management, Jan. 1, 1969, were valued at $4,704,618. On Dec. 31, 1979, this figure was $14,371,560. During the same period, the number of trust funds increased from 113 to 217. These funds were received by living trusts or by wills from donors for the benefit of Missouri Baptist and Southern Baptist agencies and institutions.

THOMAS W. NELSON

MOBILE COLLEGE (*q.v.*), Mobile, AL. *Top:* Entrance Marker, dedicated in the fall of 1980, features a five-foot bronze seal. *Bottom:* J. L. Bedsole Library, dedicated in 1971, houses approximately 60,000 volumes.

BIRMINGHAM BAPTIST AS-
SOCIATION BUILDING, Bir-
mingham, AL. Acquired in
1980.

MARY ESSIE STEPHENS
ACTIVITIES CENTER at
Shocco Springs Baptist Assembly, Talladega, AL. Built
in 1980.

MISSOURI BAPTIST GENERAL AS-SOCIATION (II). See MISSOURI BAPTIST CONVENTION.

MISSOURI BAPTIST HISTORICAL COMMISSION (III; cf. Missouri Baptist Historical Society, Vol. II). In 1980 Pamela Finlay was part-time archivist, and Hubert Inman Hester was curator of the commission's collection. In 1970 the commission published *These Missouri Baptists,* edited by Hester, as volume six of *Missouri Baptist Biography.* In the early 1970s it released three volumes of the *Journal of Missouri Baptist History.* The commission conducted statewide oral history conferences in 1972 and 1978 and a Baptist heritage conference in 1979.

L. DOUGLAS MCGLAUGHLIN

MISSOURI BAPTIST HOSPITAL (II, III). By 1969 the new ultramodern Missouri Baptist Hospital was involved in an expansion program extending over a 10-year period. The $6,500,000 East Wing provided another 144 beds, an enlarged X-ray suite, an eight-bed coronary care unit, an emergency room, and an outpatient department. This expansion also gave the hospital the ability to develop much needed services—pulmonary function laboratory, gastroenterology department, and respiratory therapy department.

The $8,500,000 West Wing, nearing completion in 1980, was the last of the construction program under the master plan developed in 1960. The hospital, now a 500-bed facility well furnished and equipped, includes oncology, coronary care, medical and surgical intensive care, and psychiatric units. Robert J. Guy, executive director since Mar., 1962, died in Feb., 1976, and was succeeded by Norman E. McCann.

NORMAN E. McCANN

MISSOURI HOME FOR AGED BAPTISTS (III). See BAPTIST HOME, THE.

MITCHELL, BENJAMIN FRANKLIN (b. Jewell, GA, Oct. 1, 1901; d. Louisville, KY, July 26, 1972). Pastor and denominational worker. The son of Robert Henry and Sarah Jane Chapman Mitchell, farmers, he married Marguerite Tasker, May 2, 1922. They had five children: Ben F., Jr., Robert, Barbara, Lala, and Margaret. He attended the University of Louisville and The Southern Baptist Theological Seminary (Th.M. Certificate, 1940). He served Shively and Clifton Heights Baptist Churches in Louisville, 1936-53, and was superintendent of missions and evangelism of Long Run Association, 1953-67. He is buried at Jewell, GA.

LEO T. CRISMON

MIXIM, GEORGE A. BERUMEN (b. Zacatecas, Mexico, June 13, 1876; d. Brownsville, TX, Sep. 12, 1958). Pastor. Reared a Roman Catholic, he excelled in studies at Colegio Militar, Mexico City, and worked as a bookkeeper and mining engineer. He married Josefina Rocha, Apr. 20, 1898. They had one daughter, Josefina de Saenz, and one adopted daughter, Herlinda. Ordained July 23, 1899, by the Zacatecas Church, he helped in the theological school at Torreon and served a church at Muzquiz. He emigrated to the United States in May, 1914, serving a short time as pastor in El Paso, TX. He moved to Brownsville in Feb., 1915, where he served as pastor until his death.

ERNEST E. ATKINSON

MOBILE COLLEGE (III). In 1970 the enrollment surpassed 500; in the fall of 1979, 1,074 were enrolled. The original campus consisted of 400 acres, but a land gift from Scott Paper Company increased the campus to 685 acres. The Bedsole Library was dedicated in 1971 with holdings of 33,000 volumes, increasing to 72,000 by 1980. Other facilities added during the 1970s were the Men's Housing Village, Flag Center, Student Activities Building, olympic-size pool, and a home for missionaries on furlough.

The number of full-time faculty members increased from 31 in 1970 to 56 in 1979. An associate degree in nursing was first offered in 1973 and a bachelor's degree in nursing in 1978. Support from the Alabama Baptist State Convention increased proportionately with the growth of the school from $273,000 in 1970 to $723,000 in 1979. The operating budget increased during the same period from $588,000 to $2,462,000.

WILLIAM K. WEAVER, JR.

MOFFATT, FREDERICK THOMAS, SR. (b. Dundee, Scotland, Aug. 8, 1898; d. Frankfort, KY, Oct. 1, 1970). Pastor. Son of William Moffatt, cobbler, and Jean Moffatt, he migrated to America in 1921. He attended Carson-Newman College (B.A., 1926). On June 4, 1926, he married Mary Lenora Martin. They had three sons: Fred T., Jr., John William, and James R. His pastorates included Grace Baptist Church, Byington, Knox County, TN, 1925-26; Horse Cave, KY, 1927-30; First Church, Jellico, TN, 1930-35; First Church, Lake Charles, LA, 1935-37; and First Church, Frankfort, KY, 1937-61. After his retirement, Moffatt served as executive director of the Kentucky State Parole Board. He is buried at Frankfort, KY.

LEO T. CRISMON

MONTANA, SOUTHERN BAPTISTS IN. See NORTHERN PLAINS BAPTIST CONVENTION.

MONTGOMERY BAPTIST HOSPITAL (III). See BAPTIST MEDICAL CENTER, MONTGOMERY, AL.

MOON, FREDERICK DOUGLAS (b. Fallis, OK, May 4, 1896; d. Oklahoma City, OK, Dec. 16, 1975). Black Baptist educator. The son of Polly Twiggs and Henry Clay Moon, former slaves in Arkansas, he attended Langston University (B.S., 1921) and the University of Oklahoma (M.A.). In 1935 he married Leeashia Margurite Harris. They had one daughter. Moon was principal of black schools at Crescent, 1921-31; Wewoka, 1931-40; and Oklahoma City, 1940-61. He held membership in numerous community, civic, and professional organizations. The first black to serve on the Oklahoma City board of education, 1972-74, he was president his last year on the board.

In 1962-67, Moon served as the first executive secretary-treasurer of the Oklahoma Baptist State Convention of National Baptists. He led in starting the National Baptist Falls Creek encampment, 1963-71; started the Baptist Student Union at Langston in 1963; and led in building Camp Burge near Oklahoma City in 1966. He is buried in Tracie Hill Cemetery, Oklahoma City, OK.

J.M. GASKIN

MOORE, JOHN THOMAS (b. Monroe County, MO, Aug. 6, 1864; d. Portland, OR, Sep. 14, 1938). Pastor and denominational executive. Son of John Franklin Moore and Ann Eliza Welch, farmers, he married Mary Alice Howard, July 22, 1888. After her death in 1892, he married Idella Adeline Howard, May 16, 1893. Moore helped organize a Baptist convention in Eastern Oregon which in 1893 sought affiliation with SBC. The request was refused by the SBC in 1894. Moore later affiliated with the Landmark body in Texarkana, which he served as executive, 1927-31. Returning to Portland in 1932, he soon organized Pacific Coast Baptist Bible Institute. Moore was president and pastor at time of his death. He edited the *Pacific Coast Baptist,* 1935-38. He is buried in Lincoln Memorial Cemetery, Portland, OR.

ROY L. JOHNSON

MOORE, KARL HILDRETH (b. Venus, TX, Dec. 11, 1893; d. Ardmore, OK, Apr. 11, 1971). Pastor and military chaplain. Son of Madison McNeely and Sara Hodges Moore, he was educated at Decatur College, Baylor University (B.A., 1918), and Southwestern Baptist Theological Seminary (Th.M., 1921; Th.D., 1924). He married Jennie Ross on Mar. 9, 1916. Their children were Karleen and Jennie. A United States Army chaplain in World War I and a Navy chaplain in World War II, he also served as pastor of churches in Wilson, 1926-29, and Blackwell, 1929-31, OK; Denton, 1931-34, and Brownwood, 1934-43, TX; and Ardmore, OK, 1945-57. He wrote one book, *The Overcoming Christ* (1940). He is buried in Hillcrest Cemetery, Ardmore, OK.

J. M. GASKIN

MOORE, WALTER LANE (b. Quitman, LA, June 22, 1905; d. Macon, GA, Jan. 6, 1978). Pastor and writer. The son of Richard T. Moore, a dairyman, and Clara Lane Moore, he graduated from Louisiana Polytechnic Institute

(1927) and attended Southwestern Baptist Theological Seminary (1925-27). He and Miriam McCall were married on Aug. 1, 1927. They had three children: Carol, Martha, and Walter L., Jr.

Moore served as pastor of the First Baptist churches of Waynesboro, GA, 1934-39; Cedartown, GA, 1939-47; Waycross, GA, 1947-51; Meridan, MS, 1951-59; and Vineville Baptist Church, Macon, GA, 1959-70. He held many positions in the Southern Baptist Convention and the Georgia Baptist Convention, including president of the Georgia Convention, 1968-70; trustee of Southwestern Baptist Theological Seminary, 1947-51; chairman of the Committee on Order of Business for the SBC, 1958; and member of the Executive Committee, SBC, 1958-59.

His writings included *Courage and Confidence from the Bible* (1951); *Outlines for Preaching* (1965); daily devotions for *Christian Herald* magazine, 1948-1951; a weekly devotional column in *The Christian Index,* 1941-1951; "Sermon Suggestions," *Quarterly Review,* 1954-1972; and curriculum materials for the Sunday School Board, SBC, for 30 years. Moore is buried in Rosehill Cemetery, Macon, GA.

HOWARD P. GIDDENS

MORAL ALERT. See CHRISTIAN CITIZENSHIP CORPS.

MORGAN, LEONARD LAFAYETTE (b. Rutherford County, NC, Oct. 6, 1894; d. Raleigh, NC, May 27, 1978). State convention leader. Son of Hampton and Sarah Morgan, farmers, he began his ministry as an associational field worker in Robeson County, NC, in 1927. He served the North Carolina Baptist State Convention as Sunday School secretary, 1936-56, and as its first secretary of the Church Building and Planning Department from 1957 until retirement in 1961. He was affectionately known as "Mr. Sunday School."

Under Morgan's leadership, Sunday Schools in North Carolina grew from 2,437 in 1936 to 3,266 in 1956. He led summer enlargement campaigns, teacher training, church building improvement, and the first state Vacation Bible School clinic. He was a deacon and lay leader at Tabernacle Baptist Church, Raleigh, NC. Educated at Mars Hill and Wake Forest Colleges, he married Foy Johnson on Aug. 15, 1927. Their two children were Martha and Leonard, Jr. He is buried in Montlawn Cemetery, Raleigh, NC.

MYRA MOTLEY PRINCE

MOROCCO, MISSION IN (III). In 1980 two Southern Baptist missionary couples served in Morocco. They served two small American-European congregations and managed a book store (the only one in the country authorized to import Christian books). For several months a missionary taught English in a Moroccan university. Direct evangelism among Moroccans is forbidden, and there are no visible Moroccan churches. However, the number of Moroccan Christians is growing slowly. A new believer usually traces his conversion back to Christian radio broadcasts, Bible correspondence courses, and contact with Christians.

J. D. HUGHEY

MORRIS, SAMUEL FALLS (b. Cushing, OK, May 8, 1917; d. Topeka, KS, Dec. 27, 1973). Missionary to the Indians. The son of Grover and Clara Morris, farmers, he attended Chilocco Indian School, OK, and Oklahoma Baptist University (B.A., 1950). After serving in the United States Air Force, 1942-45, he worked as a councilman on the Sauk and Fox tribes. Appointed by the Home Mission Board, he served various Indian congregations for 25 years. He married Olelah Mae Cornell in 1944. Their children were Samuel, David, Joseph, and John. He is buried at Shawnee, OK.

B. FRANK BELVIN

MOSTELLER, JAMES DONOVAN (b. Adairsville, GA, Sep. 3, 1915; d. New Orleans, LA, Jan. 1, 1977). Pastor, college and seminary professor, and administrator. Son of Linnie Mosteller and Andrew James Mosteller, auto mechanic, he attended Oglethorpe University, Atlanta, GA (B.A., 1940; M.A., 1941), and Northern Baptist Theological Seminary (B.D., 1949; Th.D., 1951). He did additional study at the University of Chicago Divinity School and at Oxford University in England where he was Lilly postdoctoral fellow, 1964-65, and honorary fellow at Regents Park College, 1972-73. On Dec. 22, 1941, he married Iris Edmunds. They had two children, James Donovan, Jr., and Iris.

Mosteller served several rural churches in Georgia, 1940-44. He was pastor of Calvary Baptist Church, Chicago, IL, 1945-49. His career in education began with appointment in 1940 to the faculty of Oglethorpe University, where he taught literature and journalism. He was acting dean and professor of English and Bible at Brewton-Parker Junior College in Georgia, 1942-44. He taught church history at Northern Seminary, 1947-67, and served as dean of the faculty, 1956-65. Mosteller joined the faculty of New Orleans Baptist Theological Seminary in 1967 and served as professor of church history until his death in 1977. He also served as dean of the School of Theology, 1969-72, and as acting president, 1970-71.

Mosteller was a member of the American Society of Church History, the American Baptist Historical Society, the Southern Baptist Historical Society, and Phi Kappa Delta. In addition to numerous articles and book reviews, he wrote the following books: *A History of the Kiokee Baptist Church* (1952), *Life in the Kingdom* (1959), *Our Heritage and Our Hope* (1967), and *Handmaiden of the King* (1972). He is buried in the cemetery of Pine Grove Baptist Church, Thomson, GA.

STAN RUSHING

MOUNT BAKER BAPTIST ASSEMBLY (III). The location of the camp made it impractical for use by churches in some parts of Oregon and Washington. The annual allocation of $14,000 for the assembly also caused complaints. A committee studied the issue and recommended that the property be sold in favor of a site closer to Portland, OR. Opposition arose and the idea was dropped. Complaints continued until the convention deeded 80 acres of the property to Puget Sound Association in Nov., 1978. Mount Baker, Capilano, and Puget Sound Associations now conduct seven weeks of summer camps on the site. A master plan to upgrade the assembly to accommodate 1,000 people has been presented to Whatcom County for approval.

O. RAY HARRIS

MOUSER, WILLIAM HENRY (b. Cameron, Indian Territory, OK, Sep. 20, 1893; d. Shafter, CA, July 20, 1977). Layman and philanthropist. The son of George W. Mouser, a minister, and Ella Bunn Mouser, he married Ann Montgomery West, Nov. 12, 1916. They had one son, Albert.

Mouser and his father and brother were charter members of the Orthodox Missionary Baptist Church of Shafter (later called First Southern Baptist Church), established May 10, 1936. This church was the site for the formation both of the San Joaquin Valley Missionary Baptist Association, Apr. 13, 1939, California's first modern-day Southern Baptist association, and the Southern Baptist General Convention of California, Sep. 13, 1940. He became a deacon when a young man, and for 30 years he directed the music in his own church. While his formal training was limited, he knew the old do-re-mi method and he taught singing schools in many churches.

A successful farmer, Mouser served on the Executive Board of the California Convention. He made provisions in his will for a large portion of his estate to be administered by the California Baptist Foundation to benefit Southern Baptist causes in California. He is buried in Olivewood Cemetery, Riverside, CA.

FLOYD LOONEY

MOZAMBIQUE, MISSION IN. Ernest and Janice (Thompson) Harvey were assigned to Mozambique in 1970 but lived in South Africa until 1973, when they obtained residence permits. In 1975 a Marxist government was installed in newly-independent Mozambique. John and Jean (Howard) Poe arrived in Aug., 1975, but left three weeks later because of political pressures. The Harveys, on furlough when the Poes left, moved to Kenya to renew efforts to obtain reentry permission. By 1977 that permission had not been granted, and the Mozambique mission was dissolved. Most Baptist churches continued to operate. In 1980 radio programs were being broadcast into Mozambique from Trans World Radio in Switzerland.

JOY NEAL

MULKEY, PHILIP (b. near Halifax, NC, May 14, 1732; d. c.1805). Pastor of the first Separate Baptist church in South Carolina. Son of Philip and Sarah Mulkey, he married Ann Ellis of Lunenburg County, VA, c.1749. They had five children: David, Jonathan, Sarah, Philip, and Marty. Reared an Anglican, Mulkey became a Baptist in 1756 under the influence of Shubal Stearns (*q.v.* I), who led his ordination in 1757.

Mulkey and 12 others moved from North Carolina to Little River of Broad, SC, where they organized a church in Aug., 1759. The church moved in 1762 to its present location in Union County and took the name Fairforest. It survives today as Upper Fairforest. Fairforest Church became the center of Separate Baptist expansion in South Carolina. Mulkey's Tory sympathies forced him and his family to flee South Carolina about 1775. They went to Washington County, NC (later TN). Mulkey's life after 1778 is obscure.

LOULIE LATIMER OWENS

MURDOCH, JOHN COCHRAN (b. Antreville, SC, Feb. 5, 1916; d. Savannah, GA, Mar. 30, 1977). Minister and child care executive. The son of L. Earle and Annie Cochran Murdoch, farmers, he attended Erskine College (A.B., 1937) and The Southern Baptist Theological Seminary (Th.M., 1940). He spent his entire ministry in service to the Connie Maxwell Children's Home and the Connie Maxwell Baptist Church, both in South Carolina. Employed by the children's home in 1940 as field representative, later assistant superintendent-treasurer and executive director, he was pastor of Connie Maxwell Church, 1946-75.

Murdoch served also as vice-president and president of the South Carolina Baptist Convention, and president, South Carolina Baptist Historical Society. He was also a leader in South Carolina Christian Action Council and the Christian Action and Public Affairs Committees. His influence in professional child care services is reflected in the various offices which he held: president of South Carolina Welfare Forum; president of Southeastern Child Care Association; president of Child Care Executives of Southern Baptists; and member of the membership panel of the Child Welfare League of America.

Murdoch lectured in workshops in practically every state. He wrote numerous articles on child care. He married Frances Bolton, of Greenwood, SC, May 23, 1970. He is buried in Connie Maxwell Cemetery, Greenwood, SC.

SAM M. SMITH

MUSGRAVE, MARY TROVILLION (b. Brownfield, IL, Aug. 23, 1891; d. Harrisburg, IL, Nov. 17, 1975). Free-lance writer, pastor's wife, and radio announcer. Daughter of Ferris and Carrie Clanahan Trovillion, she married J. A. Musgrave, a Baptist minister, in 1941. They had no children. As a free-lance writer she con-

tributed to the *Paducah Sun-Democrat, The Herald-Enterprise, The American Magazine, Kessinger's Midwest Review, St. Louis Post-Dispatch, St. Louis Globe Democrat, Evansville Courier and Press,* and various farm magazines. She was coauthor of her family history, *The Silver Horse.*

After her husband suffered a paralytic stroke in July, 1945, she assumed his position and worked for 25 years as announcer and coordinator of *The Baptist Hour,* a daily religious broadcast over radio station WEBQ, Harrisburg, IL, dating back to 1925. She retired in Aug., 1970. She is buried in the Sunset Hill Cemetery, Harrisburg, IL.

MYRON D. DILLOW

MUSIC, BAPTIST (II, III). The music ministry of Southern Baptists continued to expand during the 1970s. In 1970 W. Hines Sims retired as secretary of the Church Music Department of the Sunday School Board after 24 years of service. William J. Reynolds succeeded him in 1971 and led the department until his retirement in 1980.

While the total church music ministry enrollment reported from the churches in 1969 was 1,062,494, in 1979 it was 1,465,774, an increase of 403,280. The number of music directors (both full and part-time) approached 11,000 as the decade ended.

In 1975 Convention Press published the new *Baptist Hymnal.* The Hymnal Committee was made up of five subcommittees with 67 men and women serving as members. The subcommittees were Content Organization, Scripture Readings, Theological and Doctrinal Evaluation, New Material, and Promotion and Interpretation. The hymnal was launched with PraiSing 75, a giant convocation held in Nashville, TN, Mar. 10-13, 1975, with over 10,000 people attending. PraiSing included concerts each night featuring such artists as the Fisk Jubilee Singers, Hale and Wilder, and the Speer Family. Sales of 3,558,580 copies attest the success of the hymnal. The Church Music Department gives 25 free hymnals to each new church and mission that requests them. About 24,500 free hymnals have been distributed under this program. The hymnal has been published in 11 different editions. These are Standard Round Note, Shaped Note, Keyboard/Conductor, Instrumental, Organ, Loose-Leaf, Accompanist's, Pulpit, Large Print, Miniature, and Braille.

From 1969 through 1979, the department broadened and deepened its scope of publishing. In 1969 it was publishing five periodicals: *The Church Musician, The Youth Musician, The Junior Musician, Music for Primaries,* and *The Children's Music Leader.* In 1979 the department published 10 periodicals plus companion recordings and demonstration cassettes. They are (for youth, adults, and their leaders) *The Church Musician, Gospel Choir, Choral Praise, Opus One,* and *Opus Two;* and (for children, preschoolers, and their leaders) *The Music Leader, Music Makers, Young Musicians,* and *Music Time. The*

Cassette Musician is a magazine on cassette for all church music leaders.

Many books and kits were also published under the Convention Press imprint. The most innovative of the Church Study Course materials were the programmed instruction kits for individual learning. The 10 kits covered four areas: Developing Sight-Singing Skills, Developing Vocal Skills, Developing Choral Skills, and Developing Musical Understandings. Another type of kit, the resource kit, was also introduced. It contains an assortment of materials, including books, leaflets, filmstrips, mobiles, posters, and recordings for leaders.

The Church Music Department published a wide variety of recordings, tape tracks, anthems, cantatas, and musicals through Broadman Press. About 1,850 Broadman music titles are now in print. In 1978 Broadman Press held a gospel song competition. About 6,000 entries from 1,600 composers were received. "He Is Lord," written by Judy Ward, was the first-place winner.

Metro Music Emphases were begun in Jan., 1973, with the St. Louis Baptist Association. They have also been held in New Orleans, Dallas, Tampa, Greensboro, Oklahoma City, Denver, and other cities throughout the USA. These emphases help the churches in a metropolitan area understand and use the materials and services of the Church Music Department.

Many music seminars were held in the SSB's Church Program Training Center on age-group work, handbells, worship, pastor-music director relationships, and other specialized areas. The annual music conferences at Ridgecrest and Glorieta continued through the 1970s with two weeks at Ridgecrest in 1969, and a combined attendance of 6,005, and one week at Ridgecrest in 1979 with 2,968 attending. A total of 2,676 people attended the music conference at Glorieta in 1969, and 2,684 attended in 1979.

The 1970s witnessed several trends in church music. One was an increase in instrumental music in the churches. Figures show increases in the number of participants in instrumental groups at 89.7 percent. The number participating in handbell groups has increased 1,344.2 percent.

Another trend was toward more combination staff positions in the churches—music-youth, music-recreation, or music-education. New attention is being given to the needs of these staff members and the churches they serve. Along with this emphasis came a sharpened focus on the volunteer and part-time directors. More seminars were held for them, and new publications were planned to help the volunteer and part-time music director. This work parallels a renewed concern for the needs of smaller churches throughout the SBC.

See also HYMNALS, BAPTIST; PRAISING.

LINDA KONIG AND DAN JOHNSON

MUSIC, MINISTER OF. See MINISTER OF MUSIC.

MUSIC IN MISSIONS (III). The 1970s saw a phenomenal development in Southern Baptist music missions. By 1980 the category of music missionary, initiated by Southern Baptists in 1951, had 112 persons in service, ranked third in number of appointments by the Foreign Mission Board. Southern Baptists have noticeably influenced more than 20 other mission agencies which have appointed music missionaries.

Part of the success of the enterprise grew out of an ambitious program of missionary education by Southern Baptist music activity, including Sunday School Board music publications, mission programs during Church Music Leadership Weeks at the Ridgecrest and Glorieta Conference Centers, and emphases in the annual Southern Baptist Church Music Conference.

Music missions was added to the curriculum of the School of Church Music at Southwestern Baptist Theological Seminary, in 1967, and a music missions publication, *Missionary Notes,* was begun. The establishment of a World Missions and Church Growth Center at Southwestern in 1980 opened the way for further expansion and research in music missions. Annual church music workshops at The Southern Baptist Theological Seminary and New Orleans Baptist Theological Seminary have included an emphasis on music missions.

Musical developments in overseas churches reflected affirming support from many sources. Several state music departments encouraged churches to provide handbells and other equipment for music missionaries.

The 20th anniversary of music missions was observed by a special issue of *The Commission,* Apr., 1971. This FMB journal communicated to Southern Baptists the extraordinary developments in music missions. Celebrating the 20th anniversary of the appointment of Southern Baptists' first music missionaries—Donald and Violet Orr to Colombia—a special service was conducted at Travis Avenue Baptist Church, Fort Worth, TX, with Convention-wide representation.

By the end of the 1970s, most older mission fields had their own Baptist hymnals, except for a few in the Orient which had a long tradition of interdenominational hymnals. Three important hymnals were published during the decade— *New Songs of Praise* in Chinese in Hong Kong, 1973; the *Himnario Bautista* in Spanish at the Baptist Spanish Publishing House, El Paso, TX, in 1978; and the new edition of *Cantor Cristao* in Portuguese in Rio de Janeiro in 1978. Each of these hymnals was intended to serve all national constituencies using these languages.

The Chinese hymnal published in Hong Kong had dual notation (staff notation and numeral notation), both widely used in the Orient. The Chinese and Spanish hymnals had multinational committees. Most significantly, all three hymnals included a large number of indigenous hymns, which may have accounted for the tremendous success of these publications. Both the Baptist Spanish Publishing House, El Paso, TX, and the Argentine Baptist publishing house, Amanecer, produced a series of indigenous songbooks. Several national conventions issued music handbooks; the Japan Baptist Convention published five. Several less ambitious collections of hymns were also published in Africa during the 1970s. As the 1980s began, hymnals were being planned in a number of African languages.

The use of indigenous music increased rapidly around the world. Indigenous hymns appeared in published form in Zambia, Malawi, Japan, and Korea. Music missionaries in at least 14 countries reported the widespread use of indigenous musical instruments. The guitar, always popular in mission work, emerged as a prominent church instrument in most countries where Southern Baptists are engaged in missionary enterprises. Music missionaries encouraged the use of indigenous music through contests, choir festivals, publications, and public performances of works by national composers.

The development of organized music programs in many churches occurred in South America and the Orient. In Brazil the seminaries in Recife and Rio de Janeiro were granting church music degrees regularly, and the demand for ministers of music was greater than the seminaries could meet. In Japan the minister of music was emerging as a church-related vocation. In Africa church music conferences and festivals were exceedingly popular. Several countries reported music conferences for bush churches. National conventions were occasionally dominated by joyous performances by choirs from local churches that, at times, became an "all night hymn sing." In Argentina the national convention sponsored three-month area music institutes in major cities. Japan celebrated a "church music year" in 1973 and has had an annual nationwide music clinic since. All areas except Africa were holding regular music camps. Associational and national church music festivals became regular events on all continents.

Continent-wide music missions conferences were held in South America in 1973, in Asia in 1973 and 1978, and in East Africa in 1978. At these conferences significant contributions were made by both nationals and music missionaries working under appointment by the FMB, SBC. Additional conferences are planned for the 1980s. Many signs point to significant advances in music missions in the coming decade.

T. W. HUNT

MUSICALS, CHRISTIAN. Extended multi-sectional musical works in one or more contemporary popular music styles with narrative or thematic religious text and message. Usually, they utilize solos and choruses and often include spoken dialogue or narration. Accompaniment ranges from piano or small folk-pop group to orchestra and may be performed with live instrumental accompaniment or with prerecorded tape track. Media such as choreography, drama, sound and light effects, and congregational participation are often used.

While there are numerous historical instances of folk-pop styles in the church, the direct line of development of the Christian musical goes back to Geoffrey Beaumont's *20th Century Folk Mass* (1960), which was written and performed in England in 1955. Subsequent use of pop-style church music was identified with the Anglican Church in England and the Roman Catholic and certain evangelical groups in America.

For Heaven's Sake, by Kromer and Silver (1961), is a direct antecedent of the Christian musical. Called "a musical revue," it contained a sequence of scenes involving dramatic Christian satire with songs and dialogue in popular language. The "sing out" and folk groups of the 1960s encouraged the further development of Christian folk-pop music.

Good News, compiled, arranged, and partly composed by Bob Oldenburg (1967), was labeled a "Christian folk-musical" and represented a culmination of the trends of the times and also served as a signal of the direction of youth music in the church for years to come.

Of the numerous Christian musicals written after *Good News,* noteworthy ones included *Tell It Like It Is,* by Ralph Carmichael and Kurt Kaiser (1969), the first to gain national media attention; *Life,* by Otis Skillings (1970), one of the first to produce a tape track accompaniment; and *Celebrate Life,* by Buryl Red and Ragan Courtney (1972), which combined live and taped accompaniment and blended in more traditional church styles. Seasonal, worship-celebration, and music drama "musicals" were composed. Christian musicals, usually conceived for youth choirs, were published also for children, adult, and senior adult groups. The use and development of Christian musicals peaked during the mid-1970s, but such musicals remained a significant part of the repertoire of many church music programs.

PHILLIP LANDGRAVE

N

NAME CHANGE STUDY, SOUTHERN BAPTIST CONVENTION. See SOUTHERN BAPTIST CONVENTION NAME CHANGE STUDY.

NANEY, RUPERT FIREBURN LEROY (b. Yellville, AR, Dec. 9, 1890; d. Oklahoma City, OK, Feb. 10, 1978). Pastor and denominational leader. The son of James Harvey and Nancy Keeter Naney, farmers, he graduated from Ouachita Baptist University (A.B., 1915). He served as pastor of Olivet Church, Oklahoma City, 1925-48; Lookout Mountain Church, Chattanooga, TN, 1948-50; and Nichols Hills, Oklahoma City, 1950-66. He was president of the Oklahoma Baptist Convention, 1936-38, and vice-president of the SBC, 1939-40. He is buried in Memorial Park Cemetery, Oklahoma City, OK.

AUGUIE HENRY

NATIONAL ASSOCIATION OF FREE WILL BAPTISTS. See FREE WILL BAPTISTS, NATIONAL ASSOCIATION OF.

NATIONAL BAPTIST CONVENTION, U.S.A., INC. (II). The largest black denomination in the United States with a membership of 6,300,000 in 27,000 churches. This body has its headquarters in Chicago, IL. Joseph Harrison Jackson has served as president since 1953.

Through its National Baptist Foreign Mission Board, located in Philadelphia, PA, this convention sponsors 676 churches and related facilities in seven African nations and three tropical American countries, including the Republic of South Africa, Liberia, Malawi, Ghana, Lesotho, Swaziland, Sierra Leone, Jamaica, the Bahama Islands, and Nicaragua. William J. Harvet, III, serves as corresponding secretary of this foreign mission work.

In 1961 a group of pastors separated from the convention to form the Progressive National Baptist Convention, U.S.A., Inc. Mostly young pastors, they coalesced around the leadership and ideals of Martin Luther King, Jr., and sought a more active participation in the civil rights struggles of the time.

The National Baptist Convention, U.S.A., Inc., carries on its work through a series of seven boards: Foreign Mission Board, Home Mission Board, Evangelistic Board, Benefit Board, Educational Board, Sunday School Publishing Board, and Training Union Board. American Baptist Theological Seminary at Nashville, TN, is a joint project of the SBC and the National Baptist Convention, U.S.A., Inc.

See also PROGRESSIVE NATIONAL BAPTIST CONVENTION, U.S.A., INC.

MAYNARD P. TURNER, JR., and LEON MCBETH

NATIONAL BAPTIST CONVENTION, U.S.A., INC., FOREIGN MISSION BOARD (III). William Harvey is the executive secretary. The board has missions located in the Caribbean Islands and Africa (Ghana, Liberia, Malawi, Swaziland, and South Africa). There are approximately 24 missionaries with Liberia being the largest mission. The board operates from a budget of more than $600,000, received from special offerings given by churches. In addition to agricultural, educational, and medical missions, teams of laymen and ministers go on evangelistic tours and conduct special projects. Offices are in Philadelphia, PA.

EMMANUEL L. MCCALL

NATIONAL BAPTIST CONVENTION OF AMERICA (II). A major black denomination with 12,400 churches and about 3,500,000 members. James C. Sams serves as president. The convention promotes its programs through seven boards: Home Mission, Foreign Mission, Baptist Training Union, National Baptist Publishing, Evangelical, Benevolent, and Educational. The official denominational organ is *The National Baptist Union Review,* published in Nashville, TN. Convention-sponsored foreign mission stations include Haiti, Jamaica, Panama, Virgin Islands, Cameron, and Liberia in West Africa.

MARVIN C. GRIFFIN

NATIONAL BAPTISTS, HOME MISSION BOARD PROGRAM OF WORK WITH (III). See BLACK CHURCH RELATIONS, HOME MISSION BOARD PROGRAM OF.

NATIONAL CONFERENCE ON BOLD CHRISTIAN EDUCATION AND BOLD MISSIONS. See HIGHER EDUCATION, TRENDS AMONG BAPTISTS IN.

NATIONAL STEWARDSHIP SEMINARS. See STEWARDSHIP SEMINARS, NATIONAL.

NATIONWIDE BAPTIST DIGEST. A monthly paper published in Nashville, TN, from Jan., 1947, through Nov., 1952, under the editorship of Livingston Mays and Russell

Bradley Jones. Known at first as *Southwide Baptist Digest,* 1947-50, it was viewed as a supplement to state Baptist papers, not as a substitute for them. Pledging total support to the SBC, the paper reprinted many articles directly from state papers as it provided news and inspiration.

MARK R. CONYERS

NEBRASKA, SOUTHERN BAPTISTS IN. See KANSAS-NEBRASKA CONVENTION OF SOUTHERN BAPTISTS.

NEGRO BAPTISTS IN LOUISIANA. Black Baptist churches in Louisiana are aligned with three national conventions: National Baptist Convention, USA, Inc.; National Baptist Convention of America; and Progressive National Baptist Convention.

The Louisiana Baptist Convention has had a Department of Work with National Baptists since 1954 when W. R. Grigg became director. Robert Ferguson succeeded Grigg in 1957 and served until 1959, when Tom Pfeifer became director. Harvey Hoffman, on Mar. 15, 1978, became the fourth director. The department's ministries may be summarized as follows:

1. Establishes dialogue between National and Southern Baptist churches, associations, and state conventions.

2. Develops cooperative ministries between Southern and National Baptists at every level of organization.

3. Develops materials to promote understanding and appreciation of one another's heritage.

4. Administers scholarships for National Baptist students preparing for church-related vocations.

5. Provides information and training to churches, associations, and conventions through printed materials, audiovisuals, news releases, workshops, and seminars.

6. Provides leadership training through pastors' conferences and assemblies.

Fifteen regional missionaries appointed by the Home Mission Board, SBC, work under the leadership of the director to achieve these goals. In an effort to enhance pastoral training, the Wilburn Hoffman, Sr., lectureship has been established at United Theological Seminary in Monroe. Funds bequeathed by Hoffman's widow are administered through the Louisiana Baptist Convention. They provide annual lectures on preaching by nationally known ministers, black and white.

HARVEY W. HOFFMAN

NEGRO BAPTISTS IN VIRGINIA. In 1980 three principal Negro Baptist conventions existed in Virginia. The Virginia Baptist State Convention (VBSC) with 300 churches supports Virginia Seminary and College in Lynchburg. The Baptist General Convention of Virginia (BGCV) with 576 churches is oriented toward Virginia Union University, Richmond, founded by American Baptists. From the beginning the university cooperated with the Baptist General Association of Virginia (BGAV), the SBC, and the American Baptist Churches. The SBC has provided financial assistance for scholarships and Bible teachers. In 1969 the school of theology was aligned with Union Theological Seminary and the Presbyterian School of Christian Education to form the Richmond Theological Center. This school, which became one of only three Negro seminaries in the United States with full accreditation, had 85 students in 1979. Paul Clark became the first director of Christian education for the BGCV with assistance from BGAV in 1973. The Goodwill Convention, composed of pastors and churches which retain membership with VBSC and BGCV, is the organ of the National Baptist Convention of the U.S.A., Inc., programs in Virginia.

The Tri-Convention Committee, formed in 1967 from the three Negro bodies, sponsored evangelism conferences, 1967-72, and four statewide awareness and fellowship meetings in Richmond in 1968, 1970, 1975, and 1980. The Jackson Ward Ministry, a cooperative effort of BGCV, BGAV, Woman's Missionary Union of Virginia, the Richmond Baptist Association, and Fifth Street Baptist Church, provided social ministries in downtown Richmond, 1970-76. In 1979 the BGCV moved Johnson's Boys' Camp to BGAV's Camp Piankatank for cooperative sponsorship.

In 1968 three Negro churches became dually aligned with BGAV. In 1979, 21 churches were aligned. The first conference on "Stewardship for Black Churches" was held at Eagle Eyrie in 1977 and 1979 by BGCV assistance and produced its own stewardship materials.

PHILLIP E. RODGERSON

NESS, ROWLAND MCDOWELL (b. Baltimore, MD, Sep. 30, 1909; d. Baltimore, MD, Nov. 22, 1976). Layman. The son of Sarah Wahmann and Charles M. Ness, a businessman, he attended the Friends School (Quaker) and Johns Hopkins University (A.B., 1932). He married Louise Linthicum, niece of Joshua Levering (*q.v.* II), Feb. 7, 1935. They had one child, Louise. Ness served most of his adult life in the University Baptist Church, Baltimore, where he was a deacon, Sunday School teacher and director, usher, and member of the Mission Board, Baptist Convention of Maryland, serving as its president, 1958-60.

Ness served as president of the Maryland Baptist Children's Aid Society more than 20 years, was chairman of *The Maryland Baptist* Committee, and was a trustee of the Baptist Home. After service in the United States Army, he was discharged in 1945 with the rank of colonel. He became an insurance broker, serving as vice-president of his firm until his retirement in 1975. Deeply devoted to Baltimore and Maryland, he assisted in many civic projects. He was a member of the Hopkins Club, the Merchants Club, and the Engineering Society of Baltimore. Ness is buried in the cemetery of Saters Baptist

Church, Lutherville, the oldest Baptist church in Maryland.

R. G. PUCKETT

NEVADA ASSOCIATIONS.

I. New Associations. LAHONTAN. Organized Oct. 19, 1979, as one of four associations formed out of Northern Nevada Association. Located in a rural area of the state, Lahontan in 1980 reported 10 churches, 4 missions, 53 baptisms, 1,384 members, $210,106 total receipts, and $29,319 mission gifts.

NORTHEAST. Organized Oct. 19, 1979, out of Northern Nevada Association. In 1980, 9 churches and 11 missions reported 103 baptisms, 837 members, $299,617 total receipts, and $70,947 mission gifts.

NORTHERN NEVADA. Organized July 19, 1955, as Nevada Baptist Association at Lakeshore Baptist Church, Tahoe Valley, CA, by the six Nevada churches and one California church from the Feather River Association: First Baptist Church, Carson City; Calvary Baptist Church, Hawthorne; First Southern Baptist Church, Reno; Temple Baptist Church, Sparks; First Baptist Church, Winnemucca; First Baptist Church, Yerington, all in Nevada, and Lakeshore Baptist Church of Tahoe Valley, CA. This association later included additional churches around Lake Tahoe in California and Nevada as well as a church in Twin Falls, ID. The name was changed in 1977 to the Northern Nevada Baptist Association. L. B. Sigle, former missionary for the Feather River Baptist Association, was Nevada Association's first missionary, 1955-69. His successor, Robert A. Wells, served until 1979 when the association was divided into four associations, one retaining the name *Northern,* as adopted in 1977. When the Nevada Convention was organized in 1978, Northern had 28 churches with 5,137 members. In 1980, 9 churches and 2 missions reported 127 baptisms, 1,724 members, $318,853 total gifts, and $55,792 mission gifts.

SOUTHERN NEVADA. Organized Oct., 1955, in Boulder City as Lake Mead Association by churches in Kingman, AZ, and Needles, CA, as well as Southern Nevada. By 1964 Lake Mead served only Southern Nevada churches and in Oct., 1977, messengers changed the name to Southern Nevada Baptist Association. In 1979, 22 churches and 6 missions reported 636 baptisms, 9,445 members, $1,585,420 total receipts, and $354,863 mission gifts.

SPOONER. Organized Oct. 19, 1979, by churches in the Carson City area formerly affiliated with Northern Association. In 1980, seven churches and one mission reported 178 baptisms, 1,537 members, $292,638 total receipts, and $33,807 mission gifts.

II. Changes in Associations

LAKE MEAD. See Southern Nevada.

NEVADA. See Northern Nevada.

DONALD H. LEDBETTER

NEVADA BAPTIST. Monthly, 16-page newspaper published by the Nevada Baptist Convention since 1979. Vern Miller, longtime newspaper publisher in Nevada, became part-time editor in Mar., 1979. In 1980 paid circulation exceeded 2,000. The Every Church Member Family Plan is promoted. The *Nevada Baptist* is a member of the Nevada Press Association and the Baptist Press.

ERNEST B. MYERS

NEVADA BAPTIST CONVENTION.

I. Southern Baptist Beginnings. At the close of World War II, Southern Baptist families connected with the several military bases in Nevada played a leading role in beginning Southern Baptist churches in the state. In 1947 Southern Baptist families employed at the United States Naval Base at Babbitt (located just outside of Hawthorne) recognized the need for a church. Ben E. Felts, Sr., and Lester Hampton, two Baptist deacons from the South, helped to begin the first church which was organized as an independent Baptist church on Oct. 25, 1947. Through the influence of these two Southern Baptist laymen, the congregation voted to affiliate with Southern Baptists on Aug. 14, 1948. Fred McCalley and Wiley Hinton of the Home Mission Board aided in this endeavor. This church joined the Sacramento Valley Association in California.

By 1955 enough Southern Baptist churches had been organized in Nevada to form two associations in the state. The first, organized in the north, was named Nevada Baptist Association. Shortly thereafter, Lake Mead Association was organized in Southern Nevada. Thus began a unique relationship in evangelizing Nevada. Because of the vast distances in the state, the Lake Mead Association in the south affiliated with the Arizona Southern Baptist Convention, and the Nevada Association affiliated with The Southern Baptist General Convention of California.

On Apr. 27-28, 1964, the pastors of the two associations met in the Temple Baptist Church of Sparks for the purpose of organizing a fellowship that became the forerunner of the Nevada Baptist Convention. A. B. Cash of the Home Mission Board, E. W. Hunke, Jr., of the Arizona Convention, and D. Wade Armstrong of California represented the denomination at this meeting.

The growth of the churches in Nevada eventually prompted leaders to recognize the need for a state convention. Although many contributed to this growth, one main factor stood out—dedicated pastors and missionaries who came and stayed long enough to grow churches. Charles H. Ashcraft started and served as pastor of First Southern Church in Las Vegas for 10 years; Don Loving served as missionary for Lake Mead Association for over a year, and then served the Redrock Church of Las Vegas for more than 15 years; Donald W. Mulkey started and led the Twin Lakes Church in Las Vegas for more than 16 years; Crile Dean served Temple Church of Sparks for more than 11 years; Donald H. Ledbetter has led the Calvary Church of Elko for over 15 years; LaVern A. Inzer served as a pastor and missionary in Northern Nevada for more than 20 years; L. B. Sigle (*q.v.*) served as associational missionary and pastored missions in Northern Nevada for more than 15 years; M. E. McGlamery has served as associational missionary in Southern Nevada for over eight years; and Robert A. Wells has served as associational missionary in Northern Nevada for over 10 years.

On Apr. 29, 1976, the Nevada Baptist Fellowship met in the First Southern Baptist Church of Reno. E. W. Hunke, Jr., of the HMB met with the leaders of the fellowship, along with Robert Hughes of California and Roy Sutton of Arizona. At this meeting a committee was appointed to begin a study concerning the possible organization of a state convention.

At the annual fellowship meeting on Apr. 28, 1977, in the Calvary Baptist Church in Las Vegas, a motion was passed that a new convention be organized in 1978, and begin operation, Jan. 1, 1979. A joint meeting of the newly appointed convention study committee was held with California, Arizona, and HMB representatives, Apr. 29, 1977. This committee was composed of A. Rudy Duett, chairman, Donald Ledbetter, Paul Lewis, Tom Bacon, Mike Proctor, Rex Langston, and Evelyn Newell from the Northern Association; and Robert Holmes, Donald Mulkey, Tom Popelka, Stanley Unruh, Don Loving, and Bruce Castleberry from the Southern Association. The committee decided to seek a letter of intent from all the churches who would favor affiliation with the proposed convention.

During its Oct. 11, 1977, meeting in Tonopah, the state convention committee decided that the constituting date would be Oct. 16-17, 1978. Committees to obtain personnel, draw up a constitution, formulate a budget, and recommend the location of the state headquarters were set into motion. By Oct., 1978, these committees had completed their work. Governor Mike O'Callaghan proclaimed the week of Oct. 15-21, 1978, as Southern Baptist Week in Nevada. On Oct. 16 messengers from all over the state gathered at the Redrock Church in Las Vegas for the purpose of organizing a state convention in Nevada.

II. Formation of the Convention. The convention was opened with A. Rudy Duett, pastor, First Southern Church, Reno, and president of the Nevada Baptist Fellowship, presiding. A motion to constitute was read by Tom Popelka, pastor, West Oakey Church, Las Vegas. The Nevada Area Baptist Convention was constituted with 71 churches and missions which had a total church membership of 13,318. Almost 400 persons were present to organize this 34th state convention affiliated with the Southern Baptist Convention. The new convention later dropped the word *Area* from its name.

Messengers elected the following executive committee (later called executive board) for the new convention: Robert Holmes, Henderson; Stanley Unruh, Las Vegas; Don Loving, Las Vegas; Don Mulkey, Las Vegas; Calfrey Collins, Battle Mountain; Tom Bacon, Hawthorne;

Evelyn Newell, Fernley; J. Paul Lewis, Carson City; Rex Langston, Sparks; Tom Popelka, Las Vegas; and A. Rudy Duett, Reno, as chairman. The convention also elected Duett as its first president. Tom Bacon, pastor of the oldest Southern Baptist church in Nevada, located at Hawthorne, was elected vice-president. Robert Hughes, executive director of the Baptist General Convention of California, represented one parent convention. Roy Sutton, executive director of the Arizona Southern Baptist Convention, represented the other parent convention. Ernest B. Myers was elected as executive director-treasurer of the new convention on a recommendation of the search committee presented by chairman Don Mulkey. Operation of the convention began on Jan. 1, 1979. Temporary offices were located at Temple Baptist Church, Sparks. The convention purchased a residence at 895 North Center Street in Reno, renovated it, and in Dec., 1979, occupied the new offices.

III. Program of Work. *Executive Board.*—The executive board serves as the convention ad interim and as the convention's operating board for its general programs not specifically assigned elsewhere. The board has authority to act for the convention between sessions, except that it cannot impose its will upon the convention by contravening any action of the convention taken at its regular session.

The board is composed of 12 members, one third of whom are laypersons, elected at the annual meetings. Members are eligible for two consecutive three-year terms. One third are elected each year.

Annual reports are made to the convention concerning the total convention program, operating programs entrusted to the board, and such other matters as the board deems necessary and proper. It annually recommends to the convention a budget for distribution of all undesignated resources of the convention. The board employs all convention personnel, except the executive director-treasurer, as is necessary to achieve the purpose of the convention. To carry out the functions of the convention, an executive director-treasurer is employed by the convention to serve as the chief executive officer for the executive board, the chief administrator, and program officer for the executive board staff.

Leadership and Program Development.—Ernest Boyd Myers, as executive director, soon led the executive board and convention to acknowledge and accept basic priorities for the new state body. Myers emphasized that the convention's task was twofold: (1) to strengthen existing churches, and (2) to help churches start new missions and churches.

The convention employed Charles L. McKay as its first director of Missions and Stewardship. His enthusiasm and wisdom helped provide a climate for mission advance and stewardship participation. McKay led in stewardship and Cooperative Program promotion, enabling both large and small churches and missions to identify their commitment to world missions through the Cooperative Program. The first year was a banner year in Cooperative Program giving, exceeding the budget set by the convention.

The purchase of the property on North Center Street was a big step in providing Nevada Southern Baptists with a resource center for their operation as a convention. Purchased with funds given by the Arizona and California Conventions, the property was extensively remodeled for use as the Nevada Baptist Convention Center. Its location in the heart of the city, across the street from the University of Nevada at Reno, and one block off Interstate 80, made it an ideal location.

Nevada Baptists gave over $20,000 to help with expenses in remodeling and renovation. Friends of Nevada made sizable contributions. Many Baptists responded to the call to "Give a Day's Pay" in this campaign.

Mel C. Craft, Jr., was employed on Mar. 15, 1979, and served until 1980 in the Christian Education leadership responsibilities. He was asked to coordinate and develop the calendar for the convention. His specific program assignments included Sunday School, Church Music, Church Administration, Family Life, Recreation, Baptist Student Ministries, and Weekday Education. Adrian W. Hall succeeded Craft beginning as director of Sunday School, Dec. 15, 1980.

Myer's jobs included the assignments of Church Architecture and Brotherhood along with his duties as executive director-treasurer.

The need for an official journal or state paper was soon evident. Vern Miller was elected editor of the *Nevada Baptist* in Mar., 1979. He brought years of newspaper experience to the office. The *Nevada Baptist* is published monthly.

Nevada Baptists set a goal for 25 new church-type missions during 1980-81. Strong churches and associations in Mississippi, Arkansas, Texas, Arizona, Oklahoma, and South Carolina began to share their resources, mating the strong with the weak.

The convention held its first annual meeting at the historic First Baptist Church of Hawthorne on Oct. 30-31, 1979. A. C. Queen, regional evangelism director for the Nevada Baptist Convention and the Utah-Idaho Convention, reported an increase in the number of baptisms in the churches. Other program leaders also reported gains during the convention's first year. Special workers for Sunday School, Church Training, and Church Music were enlisted. Special training was made available, enabling them to be a part of the convention team to train associational and church workers for all age groups. By mid 1980, training had been provided for 700 church leaders.

Nancy Hall, director of Woman's Missionary Union on a part-time basis, leads a creative WMU program which includes Acteens, Girls in Action and Mission Friends. Clinics, training sessions for leadership, and promotion of mission information regarding mission offerings are at the heart of this program of work.

A. Rudy Duett was elected to serve as Church Training, Baptist Student Ministry, Church Recreation, and Media Center director on Nov. 13, 1979. Duett, formerly pastor of First Southern Baptist Church, Reno, and the convention's first president, brought to this position a broad knowledge of Nevada Baptist life. He directs the BSU program on the University of Nevada at Reno campus and supervises the BSU program at the University of Nevada Las Vegas campus. Pam Phinney Gatling, a product of that program, serves as part-time advisor for the Las Vegas BSU.

Donald W. Mulkey was elected Nov. 13, 1979, to succeed McKay as director of Missions and Stewardship. Mulkey, long-time pastor of Twin Lakes Church in Las Vegas, and the convention's second president, began his new work with the convention Jan. 1, 1980.

At the start of 1980 the programs of the convention emerged with purpose, balance, focus, and energy. Continuing to experience growth, the convention reported that year 52 churches and 26 missions with 15,299 members, 1,092 baptisms, 15,299 enrolled in Sunday School, 2,146 in Church Training, church property valued at $12,470,705, total gifts of $2,555,593, and mission gifts of $554,728.

See also ARIZONA SOUTHERN BAPTIST CONVENTION; CALIFORNIA, SOUTHERN BAPTIST GENERAL CONVENTION OF.

DONALD H. LEDBETTER
A. RUDY DUETT,
MEL C. CRAFT, JR.

NEW ENGLAND, BAPTIST GENERAL ASSOCIATION OF. In 1960 Southern Baptists formed their first church in New England, the Screven Memorial Church in Portsmouth, NH. Growth for Southern Baptists in New England has not been rapid. In the beginning much of the work grew out of transplanted Southern Baptists' desire for a church that met their spiritual needs. Many of them were transient; they made their contribution and then moved on, leaving their beginnings to others who came after them to develop the work more fully.

The first two Southern Baptist associations in New England were the Northeastern Baptist District Association formed Apr. 29, 1960, and the New England Baptist Association in 1962 under the leadership and direction of the Baptist Convention of Maryland (BCM) and the Home Mission Board. The latter organization dissolved in 1967 with the creation of the Baptist General Association of New England (BGANE). James H. Currin serves as executive director. Four associations—Massachusetts, Southeastern New England, Upper New England, and Western Connecticut—comprise the BGANE. In 1980 these associations, each with a director of missions, had 74 churches and chapels and 7,694 members of churches.

Today the BGANE occupies a building located on the property which was the birthplace of Luther Rice (q.v. II). The property contains 10 acres in addition to a plot of four acres made available for the Rice Memorial Baptist Church in Northborough, MA.

The stated purpose of the BGANE, as indicated in its constitution, is "to provide a means of cooperation among member churches in the work of spreading the gospel at home and abroad, and the spiritual growth and development of the churches through programs of missions, evangelism, religious education, and stewardship. This body shall strive to effect a close cooperation with the BCM and the SBC, with which bodies the BGANE declares itself to be in friendly cooperation."

Along with the BCM, the boards and agencies of the SBC and the Baptist General Association of Virginia in a "sister relationship" stand committed to assist the work in New England. All have a special interest in New England, a territory of six states and 12,000,000 people.

See also MARYLAND, BAPTIST CONVENTION OF; VIRGINIA BAPTIST GENERAL ASSOCIATION OF.

ROY GRESHAM

NEW ENGLAND BAPTIST, THE. See MARYLAND BAPTIST, THE.

NEW HAMPSHIRE, SOUTHERN BAPTISTS IN. See MARYLAND, BAPTIST CONVENTION OF; NEW ENGLAND, BAPTIST GENERAL ASSOCIATION OF.

NEW JERSEY, SOUTHERN BAPTISTS IN. See NEW YORK, BAPTIST CONVENTION OF; PENNSYLVANIA-SOUTH JERSEY, BAPTIST CONVENTION OF.

NEW MEXICO, BAPTIST CONVENTION OF (II, III).

I. History. Churches and missions grew from 290 with a membership of 91,958 in 1970 to 323 with a membership of 104,407 in 1979. The budget grew from $626,169 in 1970 to $1,306,148 in 1979. As in former years, churches in 1970 did not respond with gifts to the point where budgets were being met. With a full staff complement, including five full-time Baptist Student Union directors, the 1970 state mission offering in the fall had to be diverted to clear up the budget deficit. This had been the practice in the past.

R. Y. Bradford, executive director (formerly called executive secretary-treasurer), launched a program for the consolidation of staff and services, and the matter of a possible reorganization of the entire staff structure was placed in the hands of a special study committee.

In the Nov., 1970, meeting of the convention, held in Alamogordo, the special study committee's report was adopted. It in effect canceled two staff positions and consolidated two others. Those canceled were associate state Sunday School secretary and state BSU director. Those consolidated were Evangelism and Brotherhood. Additionally, full-time BSU directors at Highlands University and New Mexico Western University were eliminated, and the work in those locations was placed in the hands of student assistants. The convention also reorga-

nized the state staff into positions of executive director-treasurer, business manager, and five division directors: Special Ministries (Children's Home), Baptist Foundation and Church Loan Corporation, Communication, Education, and Missions. The new structure provided for one associate in the Education Division, to be in charge of Church Training and Church Music, and two associates in the Mission Division, one to head Evangelism-Brotherhood work and the other the state Woman's Missionary Union director. The convention instructed Bradford, in cooperation with the Policy-Personnel Committee of the State Mission Board, to name the people to staff these positions. Those named shortly thereafter were:

Division of Special Ministries, Bert E. Edmison, former assistant administrator of the Mexican Baptist Children's Home in San Antonio, TX. He succeeded Walker C. Hubbard (q.v.), June 15, 1971. Hubbard had served as superintendent of the children's home for 37 years.

Division of Foundation and Church Loan Corporation, John D. Ratliff. He succeeded William C. Ribble, who retired, Feb. 11, 1971, after 12 years as head of the work. Ratliff had been his associate since 1969.

Division of Communication, C. Eugene Whitlow. He had been editor of the *Baptist New Mexican* and director of public relations since June, 1967.

Division of Education, Edward E. Storm, Jr. He had been elected associate Sunday School director in 1953 and state Sunday School secretary in 1962 upon the retirement of William J. Lites (q.v. III). The new staff assignment made him directly responsible for Sunday School and BSU work along with Church Administration and Church Architecture. Charles F. Polston was named his associate to head up Church Training, Church Music, Family Ministries, Vocational Guidance, and work with the mentally retarded. Polston had been state Training Union and Church Music secretary for 22 years.

Division of Mission Ministries, Felix Wagner. He came to the post from the pastorate of a church in Florida. The division includes three departments responsible for (1) Language Missions, (2) Evangelism and Brotherhood, and (3) WMU. Wagner took the Evangelism-Brotherhood work; a former Home Mission Board missionary to New Mexico, James W. Nelson, was assigned the Language Mission work; and Vanita M. Baldwin, who had been state WMU director prior to the organizational restructure, was retained in that department.

Howard C. Sivells, who had been state Brotherhood secretary for 17 years, retired, Mar. 1, 1971.

Jeff Rutherford, who had been secretary of promotion and stewardship, was retained in that role until his retirement, Dec. 31, 1973.

Further organizational changes during the decade included the retirement of executive director R. Y. Bradford, Dec. 31, 1974, and his replacement by Chester O'Brien, Amarillo, TX, superintendent of missions, who took office, Jan. 1, 1975.

Division of Mission Ministries associate, Vanita M. Baldwin, resigned effective Jan. 2, 1977, to accept the state leadership of WMU in Florida. She was succeeded by Aquilla A. Brown, director of Baptist Women in the South Carolina WMU.

Lemuel E. Lawson joined the Division of Mission Ministries staff as an associate in charge of Brotherhood and Evangelism in July, 1973. He came from a similar position with the state Convention of Baptists in Indiana.

Henry C. Reavis, who had been manager of the Baptist Book Store in Albuquerque for 35 years, and who during New Mexico Baptists' lean years had served in a variety of executive positions, including assistant to the executive secretary, editor of the *Baptist New Mexican,* supervisor of the children's home in Portales, supervisor of the Baptist hospital in Clovis, and acting corresponding secretary of the convention, died, Apr. 10, 1972.

John D. Ratliff resigned as director of the Baptist Foundation and Church Loan Corporation, July 1, 1975, and was replaced by Gary L. Inman, a Las Cruces Savings and Loan Company official.

The State Mission Board, the convention ad interim, changed its name, Nov. 6, 1975, to State Executive Board.

The result of the organizational restructuring in 1970 soon began to surface. Tight monetary controls imposed by the executive director moved the convention from a position of operational deficits to one of spending no more than receipts from the churches, and other sources, would allow. The state mission offering, which had been used for years to make up budget deficits, was divested of this role and began to be used for real missionary causes and activities.

The recovery of the convention's financial stability has enabled it to reemploy full-time student directors at Highlands University and New Mexico Western University. These two positions had been discontinued in the 1970 shuffle.

The convention is virtually without debt of any kind and has acquired extensive holdings in this 10-year period. New and permanent BSU buildings on five university campuses in the state are debt free. The convention's two camps, Inlow Youth Camp in the Manzano Mountains and Sivells Baptist Camp in the Sacramento Mountains, are also virtually debt free. The Baptist Building in Albuquerque has been renovated, and adjoining properties on both sides have been purchased and converted into landscaped parking lots.

II. Mission Emphases. Missionary work among the ethnic population of the state intensified and grew in the 1970s. In addition to blacks and Spanish Americans, there are numerous tribes of American Indians. An intensive pro-

NEW MEXICO STATISTICAL SUMMARY

Year	Associations	Churches	Church Membership	Baptisms	SS Enrollment	VBS Enrollment	CT Enrollment	WMU Enrollment	Brotherhood Enrollment	Ch. Music Enrollment	Mission Gifts	Total Gifts	Value Church Property
1969	16	243	92,196	3,166	51,756	29,552	22,704	8,482	3,717	7,209	$ 967,208	$ 6,088,396	$28,188,090
1970	16	244	91,587	2,909	50,259	24,526	20,006	7,804	3,257	7,196	990,422	6,425,499	29,180,593
1971	16	248	92,894	3,475	49,195	25,568	16,986	7,096	3,291	7,295	1,185,695	6,796,377	30,958,046
1972	16	250	94,089	4,052	49,702	27,055	16,271	6,716	3,229	7,150	1,244,291	7,832,330	31,502,732
1973	15	252	96,498	3,505	49,946	29,248	14,732	6,315	2,988	7,530	1,444,582	7,903,438	33,497,870
1974	15	252	97,522	3,312	48,932	27,693	14,517	6,243	2,534	7,982	1,604,443	8,633,734	36,350,345
1975	15	253	98,553	3,768	48,931	29,273	13,187	5,821	2,718	7,940	1,801,187	9,794,673	39,375,649
1976	15	249	98,768	3,349	51,983	26,782	13,282	5,851	2,541	7,788	2,024,276	10,853,536	43,778,537
1977	15	251	102,412	3,109	50,833	26,303	13,106	5,623	2,513	8,199	2,205,928	12,018,067	50,871,786
1978	15	250	103,205	3,011	48,081	29,285	12,873	5,769	2,515	8,434	2,320,149	13,425,404	56,635,056
1979	15	249	105,413	3,069	48,335	25,354	12,871	5,809	2,641	8,915	2,907,701	15,388,948	64,303,600
1980	15	250	108,188	4,204	52,048	28,211	13,142	5,654	2,905	9,310	3,108,679	17,344,051	73,069,063

HAZEL B. MORROW

gram has resulted in the gaining of considerable witness opportunities to these ethnics.

The HMB during the decade appointed three full-time missionaries to work under the direction of the state convention's director of missions. All salaries and other expenses are shared on the basis of 27 percent being paid by the state convention and 73 percent by the HMB.

One of these missionary appointees heads up Christian Social Ministries in the state. Because of the large ethnic population of New Mexico, one of the great needs is literacy missions, and literacy mission programs have been begun in Las Cruces, Albuquerque, Socorro, Magdalena, Espanola, and other places.

Another missionary appointee was selected to work with the deaf and to promote a ministry to the ever-increasing number of internationals entering the state, especially Laotians and Vietnamese who have immigrated to New Mexico. Oriental missions now include two in Albuquerque and one in Clovis, plus outreach ministries for smaller cities in the state through the use of audiovisuals. The ministry to the deaf includes two summer camps annually, plus an annual family retreat for the deaf at Inlow Camp. The minister helps coordinate Bible study at the State School for the Deaf, Santa Fe.

Also under the direction of the missionary appointees is the work of seminary extension centers, which have increased from 1 to 11 during the decade and students from 11 to 224. Approximately 50 percent of the students are of ethnic origins. A day-care center at Southwest Indian Polytechnic Institute, Albuquerque, was begun in Nov., 1978, to provide facilities for Indians enrolled at the institution. It is named Carrie Vaughan Youth Center in honor of Carrie Vaughan who was for many years president of WMU in Virginia. (Over the years, numerous mission gifts from the Virginia WMU have been received in New Mexico for work among the ethnic populations.)

Another missionary thrust has been made by using modular chapels to begin new missionary activities where the congregations are small. The first of two was bought in May, 1979, and located at San Rafael, and the second at a point between Farmington and Bloomfield.

Another missionary objective has been the continuation of Indian family camps which were started in the state in 1945. During the 1970s, attendance at the annual camp at Inlow Youth Camp increased to 350-450. The camp features Bible studies, mission study, fellowship, and recreation. The majority of the Indian leadership, both pastoral and lay persons, usually come from these camps.

Missions emphasis has included the preparation and distribution of audio materials such as tapes of the New Testament in Spanish which have been placed in the hands of Spanish pastors and leaders in the state; and tapes in the Navajo Indian language which have been distributed to all Navajo leadership.

As the result of an intensive missionary thrust

slanted toward the ethnic population of New Mexico, together with the results from other mission activities, an annual average of 1,521 professions of faith took place during the 1970s.

The mission thrust of the New Mexico Convention has coincided with the SBC Bold Mission Thrust, and all energies and resources available for advancing mission causes have been carefully and studiously employed. The large ethnic population of the state has pressed increasing demands for missionaries upon missionary leadership. This has been met by increased appointments of HMB missionaries, and a significant shift from Anglo missionaries to indigenous leadership. As a result, mission evangelism prospects for the ethnic population of New Mexico are very encouraging.

C. EUGENE WHITLOW

NEW MEXICO ASSOCIATIONS (II, III).
I. New Associations. PECOS VALLEY. Formed in 1972 out of South Pecos Valley and North Pecos Valley Associations. In 1979, 35 churches reported 290 baptisms, 16,974 members, $1,913,954 total gifts, $351,464,000 mission gifts, and a total property value of $9,291,800.

II. Changes in Associations. NORTH PECOS VALLEY. Disbanded in 1972 for churches to form Pecos Valley Association.

SOUTH PECOS VALLEY. Disbanded in 1972 for churches to form Pecos Valley Association.

BETTY J. WILSON

NEW MEXICO BAPTIST CHILDREN'S HOME. The 1970s brought transition to the children's home. Walker Clarence Hubbard (*q.v.*) and Dorothy, his wife, retired as superintendent and matron of the home in 1971 after serving 34 years each. Bert Edmison became superintendent, May 1, 1971, and continues to hold this position. In 1970 the state mission offering was designated to pay off the indebtedness of the home and establish a separate account for its operation.

Passage of a recommendation by the Executive Mission Board, Jan., 1972, to sell a tract of land owned by the home began a trend of upgrading the facilities of the children's home. Four new cottages were built to provide better facilities for the children and house parents. Each cottage provides for 12 children and an apartment for the house parents. These cottages were built at a total cost of approximately $800,000 without incurring any indebtedness. An administration building costing $178,000 is under construction, and a mobile home off campus has been purchased for the use of house parents on their days off.

The population of the children's home also changed during the 1970s. Whereas the home was founded to give "homelike care for homeless children of white parentage," the home now ministers to children regardless of parentage. The population has also changed numerically. The home now ministers to its capacity, 48 children. Care is not provided for high school graduates, as was previously done. The children's home now consists of approximately 300 acres and has a property valuation of $1,750,000.

HERBERT E. BERGSTROM

NEW MEXICO BAPTIST FOUNDATION. The first full-time director, W. C. Ribble, was succeeded by J. D. Ratliff in 1971. Gary L. Inman succeeded Ratliff in 1975. Eighteen directors, elected by the Baptist Convention of New Mexico, serve three-year terms. Selected members of the business community, they govern and manage the work of the foundation. Their time and service are donated without remuneration.

Each investment of foundation funds is carefully studied and approved by the office staff, after which it is presented to the investment committee which makes the final determination. Each investment is screened from a moral point of view, and no investments are made in the liquor or tobacco industries or in any business or industry which reflects upon the Christian purposes served by the foundation.

The foundation's operating budget is funded partially by New Mexico Cooperative Program receipts with the balance being produced by fees charged to trusts and endowments. On Sep. 30, 1979, the assets of the foundation totaled $2,558,445. For the year ended Sep. 30, 1979, the total payouts of the foundation were $266,184.

The board of directors is also responsible for the New Mexico Baptist Church Loan Corporation which was chartered in Oct., 1959, to assist churches in acquiring various forms of financing. As of Sep. 30, 1979, the assets of the corporation totaled $177,652.

See also NEW MEXICO, BAPTIST CONVENTION OF, VOLS. II, III.

GARY L. INMAN

NEW MEXICO BAPTIST HISTORY COMMITTEE (cf. New Mexico Baptist Historical Society, Vol. I). The committee was reactivated, Jan., 1979, by action of the executive board of the Baptist Convention of New Mexico. Betty Danielson serves as chairman with Herbert Bergstrom, Bonnie Ball O'Brien, and John Ransdell as members. Recent accomplishments of this committee include cross-referencing of the archives in the Baptist Building and the addition to the files of a copy of the *New Mexico Baptist Annual* for 1906, long missing from the local collection.

A total of 488 letters from four pioneer missionaries who served between 1849 and 1852 (Hiram Walter Read, Lewis Smith, John Milton Shaw, and Samuel Gorman) were copied from microfilm and added to the state's Baptist history collection. Two books written by O'Brien, *Harry P. Stagg: Christian Statesman* (1976) and *Promises Kept* (1978), presented a narrative history of Baptist work in New Mexico through the leadership of Stagg, executive secretary, 1938-67, and through the lives of 10 Baptist leaders of that era.

BETTY DANIELSON

NEW MEXICO BAPTIST STUDENT WORK. (III; cf. New Mexico Bible Chairs, Vol. II) The Education Ministries Division, including Sunday School, Church Training, Church Music, and student work, was formed in the organizational restructuring of the Baptist Convention of New Mexico in 1971. With no full-time state student director, student work, combined with Sunday School, became the responsibility of the division director, Edward E. Storm, Jr., who had been with the Sunday School Department since 1953. Three full-time campus directors and five student assistants were employed. The Portales director served only on that campus; directors at Albuquerque and Las Cruces visited universities in Las Vegas and Silver City, respectively, two days each week, teaching Bible and directing the work. Construction of the new student center in Albuquerque, which allowed the Baptist Student Union to move from the residence it had used for several years, was approved in Apr., 1972.

In July, 1973, after a comprehensive study of philosophy and objectives of student work in New Mexico, the study committee recommended to the state mission board that credit Bible teaching be discontinued at four schools, but retained at Portales, where direct credit was given by Eastern New Mexico State University. Directors major on noncredit Bible study groups, campus evangelism and outreach, and Christian growth of council members and other BSU students. Part-time directors were employed at Las Vegas and Silver City.

In 1975 full-time directors were employed at Las Vegas and Silver City. Volunteers have directed BSU's on branch campuses at Roswell, Alamogordo, Gallup, Farmington, and Carlsbad, and at Hobbs Junior College, New Mexico Technical Institute at Socorro, the College of Santa Fe, Southwest Indian Polytechnic Institute in Albuquerque, and the University of Albuquerque. There are still 10 schools with no Baptist work.

Associational student work committees serve to correlate the work of the BSU, and churches in each association relate to a college or university.

EDWARD E. STORM, JR.

NEW MEXICO OPPORTUNITY CAMPS. See OPPORTUNITY CAMPS (NEW MEXICO).

NEW ORLEANS BAPTIST THEOLOGICAL SEMINARY (II, III). During the 1970s New Orleans Seminary experienced administrative changes, completed a structural reorganization, engaged in extensive curricular revision, and utilized expanded resources while securing a reaffirmation of accreditation and launching additional programs and ministries.

Administrative changes.—The trustees elected Grady Coulter Cothen, president of Oklahoma

Baptist University, as the seminary's sixth president on Sep. 17, 1970. The first alumnus to serve in that capacity, Cothen possessed a broad background of denominational experience as pastor, state executive director, college president, and popular preacher. Assuming his duties on Nov. 15, the new president indicated a determination to enhance the academic integrity and administrative efficiency of the institution.

President Cothen appointed a curriculum revision committee on Jan. 22, 1971, that involved the total faculty and selected students in an extensive study. "New Orleans Baptist Theological Seminary is engaged in perhaps the most rigorous reevaluation of its purposes, organization, and curricula in its history," he reported to the Southern Baptist Convention in 1972. Administrative recommendations resulted eventually in assigning specific areas of responsibility to an executive vice-president and vice-presidents for academic affairs, business affairs, student affairs, and development. Academic reorganization and curricular adjustments also emerged from the study, beginning what Cothen described as "a new era" in seminary life.

Cothen resigned effective May 1, 1974, to become president of the Sunday School Board. Ray P. Rust, the executive vice-president, served as chief administrative officer until Jan. 1, 1975, when Landrum P. Leavell, II, became the seventh president of the institution. Also an alumnus, Leavell had strong family ties with the seminary where his uncle, Roland Q. Leavell (*q.v.* III), had been president for 12 years, 1946-58. A popular pastor and denominational leader, Leavell served at First Baptist Church, Wichita Falls, TX, for 11 years before coming to New Orleans. His practical and pastoral interests strengthened trends already in operation at the seminary. Under his leadership student enrollment has increased significantly, campus facilities have been improved, accreditation has been reaffirmed, and new programs have been initiated. Basic seminary goals involving "academic excellence and a warm spiritual atmosphere" remain unchanged.

Structural Reorganization.—Until 1972 the seminary functioned academically in three schools (Theology, Religious Education, and Church Music) with a dean for each. The schools had field and departmental units. A new divisional structure became operative with the fall semester of 1972-73 consisting of five divisions: Biblical Studies, Theological and Historical Studies, Pastoral Ministries, Religious Education Ministries, and Church Music Ministries. Departmental units remained intact; but several departments were shifted to more appropriate divisions, and departments function without heads essentially as areas of study. Instead of school deans, divisional chairmen appointed by the president are responsible to the vice-president for academic affairs, who has general oversight of and responsibility for the academic programs of the seminary. The School of Chris-

tian Training, reinstituted in 1976, functions under a director who reports to the president.

Revised committee structures accompanied changes noted above. Standing committees nominated by a committee on committees include appropriate administrative members, faculty representatives from the divisions, and in some cases students. President Leavell chairs the admissions council and the chapel and lecture committee. A committee for student enlistment and alumni affairs reports to the executive vice-president. The vice-president of student affairs receives assistance from the student affairs committee. Other standing committees function under the direction of the vice-president for academic affairs. These include committees for faculty affairs and academic affairs, library, field education, continuing education, and doctoral admissions. Additional ad hoc committees plan and supervise the pastors and student missions conferences, publish *The Theological Educator,* and sponsor other projects. These committees function both in an advisory and policy-making capacity so that together with an administrative council they provide supervision and input for internal operations of seminary life.

Curricular Adjustments.—A major revision of degree programs and curricular offerings resulted from the institutional study previously described. The seminary offered six graduate degree programs at the beginning of the decade: Master of Theology, Master of Religious Education, Master of Church Music, Specialist in Education, Doctor of Theology, and Doctor of Education. Diploma programs in Christian theology, religious education, and church music existed also for students without college degrees. The school structure and degree requirements tended to isolate students studying theology, religious education, or church music. Faculty members became convinced that the isolation carried over into churches with detrimental results after the students graduated.

The Basic Studies Program designed and initiated in 1972 addressed this problem. The program, required for all students, involved a full year of study in courses designed to develop competencies considered necessary for effective ministry. Interdisciplinary in nature and in part team taught, the courses are designed to encourage students to share in a unified ministry. Some courses have been refined or changed, and requirements for music students have been reduced, but the Basic Studies Program remains an integral part of the seminary curriculum.

Incorporation of the Basic Studies courses and concern for practical ministry alongside academic excellence led to adjustments in the various programs of study and in degree terminology. The three-year Master of Theology degree became the Master of Divinity (M.Div.), incorporating Basic Studies, a core curriculum, and electives. Students select a divisional major in keeping with their vocational interests and goals. Terminology for master's programs in

BAPTIST CONVENTION OF NEW YORK (*q.v.*), Exchange House, Lake Placid. Part of Adirondack Resort Ministries.

CHOWAN COLLEGE (*q.v.*), Murfreesboro, NC. Jesse Helms Physical Education Center. Completed in 1980 at cost of $2,750,000; serves as center for physical education classes and intramural and varsity sports programs for over 1,000 students.

NEW ORLEANS BAPTIST THEOLOGICAL SEMINARY (q.v.), LA. *Bottom, left:* J. D. and Lillian Grey Missionary Home became official part of campus, May 4, 1980. Provides housing for J. D. Grey Library and furloughing missionaries. *Top, right:* John T. Christian Library, completed in 1975, houses over 200,000 items. *Top, left:* Roland Q. Leavell Chapel. Completed in 1975 with addition of steeple patterned after FBC of Providence, RI. *Bottom, right:* New Student Center. Secured on May 26, 1981, contains 119,000 square feet. Center occupies top floor.

religious education and church music remained unchanged, but students desiring a three-year program may receive the M.Div. degree with a major in religious education. Also, students specializing in religious education or church music may complete a minor in the other area, preparing for a combination ministry. Specialist degrees beyond the master's level terminated with the reorganization in 1972.

Alterations in the Doctor of Theology degree program have not been substantial except for a reduction in areas of specialization. The same could be said for the Doctor of Education in Religious Education or Psychology and Counseling, but the Ed.D. in Church Music Education became the Doctor of Musical Arts (D.M.A.) in 1980.

A major addition at the doctoral level has been the launching of the Doctor of Ministry degree program (D.Min.). Initiated in 1972 and radically revised three years later, the D.Min. represents a professional degree program designed to promote excellence in the practice of ministry. Components include an interdisciplinary colloquium that introduces and inaugurates the program, two classical seminars, a course focusing on research techniques and project design, a professional seminar, a project conceived as a specific and substantial act of ministry within the vocational task of the student, and an extensive project report.

Twenty-five students enrolled for this degree the first year, and enrollment peaked in 1977 at 199. Seminars have been offered not only on campus but in several other areas: Tampa, Jacksonville, and Orlando, FL; Atlanta, GA; Birmingham, AL; Jackson, MS; Shreveport, LA; and Memphis, TN. Bradford Curry has directed this program since 1974.

A School of Christian Training for students without college degrees functioned from 1955 to 1959. Then, diploma programs continued with these students attending master's level classes. Because of widespread concern in the SBC for providing courses of study for the large number of ministers with limited training, the seminary reactivated the School of Christian Training in 1976, securing Fred B. Moseley as director and creating faculty positions for teachers. The school began offering the Associate of Divinity degree (A.Div.) in 1980. A limited number of courses also are offered in off-campus settings, currently in Tupelo, MS; Marietta, GA; Birmingham, AL; and Miami, FL (Ethnic Branch).

Reaffirmed Accreditation.—Negotiations were initiated on Nov. 30, 1973, for a joint review of the seminary by the Southern Association of Colleges and Schools and the Association of Theological Schools. Seminary programs had been accredited by the latter since 1953 and the former since 1965. A team representing both agencies visited the campus in Apr., 1975. Seminary personnel cooperated fully in the evaluation and in responding to various recommendations. The agencies affirmed full accreditation for all academic programs, including the newly initiated Doctor of Ministry.

The National Association of Schools of Music first accredited basic seminary music programs in 1966 and the doctorate four years later. A periodic review by this agency secured a reaffirmation of accreditation and approval for replacing the Ed.D. degree program with the D.M.A. in 1980. Also, Southern Association representatives visited the campus in 1980 to evaluate the School of Christian Training. Academic programs of the school received approval, as did the proposed A.Div. degree.

Faculty and Students.—Students and faculty comprise essential resources for any educational institution. The quantity and quality of both increased substantially at the seminary during the 1970s. Thirty-seven faculty members signed the Articles of Religious Belief, and 31 remained on the faculty as the decade ended. Supplementary personnel also assisted the resident faculty, providing expertise and support for programs of study on and off campus. Permanent faculty added, including four who signed the Articles at the 1980 convocation, were: Harry J. Rowe, F. Eugene Brasher, Fisher H. Humphreys, Earl M. Owen, Jr., Grady C. Cothen, J. Terry Young, Bobby D. Box, Bobby Ell Adams, Paul W. Stevens, Victor Bradford Curry, Carroll Benton Freeman, Sr., William Benjamin Rogers, Jr., Landrum Pinson Leavell, II, Clinton Colgate Nichols, Jerry J. Breazeale, Harold T. Bryson, Cos H. Davis, Jr., Billy E. Simmons, Billy Kenneth Smith, Carlton L. Winbery, H. Leroy Yarbrough, Fred B. Moseley, Charles E. Graham, Mrs. Ann Daniel Carlino, Talmadge D. Butler, Al Washburn, Bernard M. Spooner, Donald Waylon Bailey, Don H. Stewart, C. Ferris Jordan, Bart C. Neal, Thomas A. Berry, Linda Patricia Shipley, James L. Minton, Monte Thomas Starkes, Luther Maxwell Dorr, Sr., Daniel H. Holcomb, Clay Corvin, Robert L. Hamblin, Macklyn W. Hubbell, and Ted D. Wylie. The trustees in 1979 adopted the statement on the Baptist Faith and Message as a "supplement or corollary" to the Articles of Religious Belief.

The seminary continues to maintain a liberal sabbatical leave policy, and some assistance is provided faculty members who attend meetings of professional societies. Faculty development seminars are conducted regularly, addressing a variety of needs and issues. The seminary journal, *The Theological Educator,* provides a channel for publication and a media for informing readers of developments in a variety of disciplines. The number and diversity of books, articles, and other materials produced annually give evidence that the faculty is contributing to theological scholarship. At the same time, their involvement in churches, denominational activities, and practical service indicates their commitment to vital Christian ministry.

Accumulative student enrollment increased every academic session in the decade, totaling 738 in 1970-71 and exceeding 1,600 in 1979-80.

Graduates from about 200 colleges and universities scattered throughout the nation and in several foreign countries were studying at New Orleans Seminary, and a substantial number of these anticipated mission service after graduation. Since 1921, 13.5 percent of the career appointees of the Foreign Mission Board have been graduates of New Orleans Seminary while a sizable group has served under the Home Mission Board. Vocational goals vary, of course, but the majority of students still prepare for ministry in and through the local church. Relatively few graduate before serving in some capacity on a church staff, with the result that initial placement and transition to full-time ministry is a comparatively simple process following graduation.

Students have participated to some extent in influencing seminary policies and procedures during the decade. On several occasions student representatives discussed proposed curriculum changes with the academic vice-president and division chairmen. Some standing committees include students with voice and vote, and the Student Body Association functions effectively through elected officers. Unrest that characterized the 1960s has been minimal during the 1970s as students have reflected individualized, conservative tendencies evident throughout the nation.

Material and physical resources.—Total revenues of the seminary slightly exceeded $1,000,000 in 1969-70 but approached $4,000,000 in 1979-80. The Cooperative Program remains the major source of income but not to the extent contributed previously. Operating funds provided through the Cooperative Program for the year beginning the decade totaled $885,208 compared to $2,303,923 as the decade ended, but the percentage of total income from the Cooperative Program dropped from 85.6 percent to 58.7 percent. Other sources of income include student fees, gifts, endowment, and auxiliary enterprises. In 1980 the seminary was engaged in a campaign to raise $2,000,000 for endowment and capital needs. Response to the campaign was very positive, giving every indication that the goal would be exceeded.

Library facilities more than doubled with the completion of an adjacent unit in 1975. Library shelving capacity increased to 300,000 volumes with seating for 297 persons. The collection presently totals about 150,000 volumes along with another 90,000 pieces of material (microfilm, museum pieces, and others). The music library was transferred into the new unit in 1976, and an archaeological museum was established the following year. The library also includes a media center and a radio station (WBSN-FM, begun in 1979).

Most other academic and administrative buildings have been renovated or altered. Alterations of the Frost Administration Building provided facilities for administrative units while renovations in the Dodd Building made available additional faculty offices. Changes in the Bunyan Building included construction of a preaching chapel and several seminar rooms as well as the alteration of some classrooms. Most of this construction was completed by 1975, but the Preschool Education Center was renovated in 1976-77, the School of Christian Training building became operational in 1977, and a student lounge was completed the same year.

Recreational facilities for the seminary community have been greatly improved and expanded. A total renovation of the gymnasium and installation of modern equipment made provisions for skating, television, weight lifting, pool, sauna, and other activities. Playground areas have been improved, four lighted tennis courts constructed, and a junior Olympic-size swimming pool completed. Construction of a new student center at a cost of $3,000,000 is projected for 1982 and should free space for classrooms and offices and accommodate an enlarged food service area, student store, medical clinic, post office, and other facilities.

Availability of student housing reached a critical stage as the student body expanded. Purchase of the Gentilly Apartments in 1978 made available 64 additional apartments for married students. Carey Hall, the women's dormitory, has been totally renovated. Construction of the J. D. and Lillian Grey Missionary Residence was completed in 1980, affording housing for furloughing missionary couples. The latter structure also houses Grey's library.

Other improvements in physical resources are evident to members of the seminary community. The most visible additions seen by outsiders, however, are the attractive addition to the library and the spire that adorns the chapel, completed in 1975.

Retrospect and Prospect.—The seminary maintained a healthy relationship with its various constituencies and a strong academic program during the past decade. President Leavell and academic vice-president J. Hardee Kennedy, along with other administrators, provided excellent leadership and encouraged careful planning as seminary life diversified and became more complex.

Alumni officers established an annual workshop on campus in 1972 that has contributed to their planning and supporting a variety of activities at the national and state levels. Churches continue to encourage members called of God to attend New Orleans or another Southern Baptist seminary and look to their graduates when ministers are needed. The Southern Baptist Convention selects responsible trustees, provides funds, and chooses alumni for prominent leadership positions in denominational life. The general public has been responsive to and supportive of seminary activities.

The seminary is busier than in previous eras. Activities proceed virtually year round as interterms, workshops, and special programs multiply. Night classes lengthen hours of the day and new programs extend the geographical bounds of seminary life to Israel, Oxford, and other places. Off-campus centers and clinical programs provide courses of study for students without college degrees or for those seeking doctorates.

Predictions for the next decade should be regarded as highly tentative, but prospects at the present appear bright. A capable administration, stable and competent faculty, and an eager, expanding student body provide the basis for optimism. A need for additional space is already foreseen and will increase as the enrollment rises. Funds to supplement those provided through the Cooperative Program will likely be required to a greater extent if the inflationary spiral continues.

Tension between the demand for professional training and academic competence may increase, and the diversification and expansion in terms of programs and places will no doubt continue. Hopefully, the seminary will respond creatively to its statement of purpose by "fulfilling its responsibility as an academic community, a denominational agency, and a fellowship of faith."

CLAUDE L. HOWE, JR.

NEW TESTAMENT CRITICISM. See BIBLICAL CRITICISM, NEW TESTAMENT.

NEW TESTAMENT LITERATURE (II).
New Testament studies in the mid to late 1970s and early 1980s have moved beyond strict historical-critical concerns to a fresh consideration of the documents of the New Testament as literature. Literary types found in the New Testament, such as narrative and poetry, are being considered as parts of a larger linguistic pattern of meaning. Redaction critics and structuralists have made major contributions to this trend. Structuralism, for example, seeks meaning in the language of a text apart from the concerns of date, authorship, place of writing, and purpose. Three helpful works in this area are Edgar V. McKnight, *Meaning in Texts* (1978); Richard A. Spencer (ed.), *Orientation by Disorientation* (1980); and Robert C. Tannehill, *The Sword of His Mouth* (1975).

BIBLIOGRAPHY: William A. Beardslee, *Literary Criticism of the New Testament* (1978). Norman R. Petersen, *Literary Criticism for New Testament Critics* (1978).

DONALD E. COOK

NEW YORK, BAPTIST CAMPUS MINISTRY IN (cf. New York, Baptist Student Work in, Vol. III). During the 1970s, campus ministry expanded to more than 60 campuses and saw the first state student convention held Oct., 1971, at the Vassar Road Baptist Church. Pastors, faculty, administrative personnel, and students served as volunteer directors on most of these campuses.

Following the resignation of Caby Byrne in Aug., 1970, Alton Harpe began his ministry at the United States Military Academy at West Point in Jan., 1971. Following the abolition of compulsory chapel at the academy in 1974, a Baptist worship service began which has attracted over 100 cadets and staff in addition to the ongoing campus ministry.

In a move to bolster campus ministry, the Baptist Convention of New York employed William Roy Dunning in Feb., 1975, as the state director of campus ministries and church music.

Another full-time campus minister, Quentin Lockwood, Jr., came to the work in New York City, Oct., 1976, to replace M. Ray Gilliland who took a position with the Metropolitan New York Baptist Association.

In Sep., 1977, John Tudor Walsh came to be campus minister at Princeton University and soon developed a strong student group.

Of special note are the US-2 volunteers who served during the decade: Larry Hudson, Potsdam; Marian Osborne, Potsdam; Michael Perry, Potsdam; Judy Chin, international students, New York City; Ron Sisk, New York University, New York City; Aron Teel, Rochester; and W. June Campbell, Rochester.

In Dec., 1980, the Baptist Convention of New York asked William Roy Dunning to become director of the Education Division and Quentin Lockwood, Jr., to become the state director of Campus Ministries.

QUENTIN LOCKWOOD, JR.

NEW YORK, BAPTIST CONVENTION OF (III).
I. History. Steady growth occurred in the Baptist Convention of New York in the decade following its organization in 1969. From 10,494 members in 70 churches and 27 chapels in 1969, the convention grew to 175 churches and 67 chapels with 19,200 members in 1980. From 1970 to 1980 the churches reported 12,884 baptisms.

The convention's territory includes most of Northern New Jersey and the southern tip of Connecticut, because these areas relate to the Greater New York City complex. Many of the members of the churches in these two states work in New York City.

Paul S. James, first executive secretary of the convention, served, 1970-75. A native New Yorker, James led the convention in organizing for growth. Under his leadership, the convention organized two major divisions of work, Education and Missions. John Tubbs served as director of the Education Division, 1970-78. Jon Meek served as director of the Missions Division, 1970-80. In 1975 Paul James retired after serving in New York as pastor, director of missions for Metropolitan New York Association, and executive secretary of the convention for a total of 18 years.

Jack P. Lowndes suceeded James as executive secretary of the convention. A native Georgian, Lowndes began his work, Mar. 1, 1975, coming from the pastorate of Memorial Baptist Church of Arlington, VA. While pastor in Virginia, Lowndes had served two terms as president of the directors of the Home Mission Board, SBC.

II. Program of Work. From the beginning of work in the territory of the convention, a commitment has existed to share the gospel with all peoples. Because many of the people in the convention territory speak a language other than English as their mother language, the convention added a language program leader, Leobard Estrada, in 1971 and assigned him to the Missions Division. There are now over 60 churches and chapels which use a language other than English as the basic language, and 18 different languages are represented. Manual Alonso now serves as language program leader. Most of these churches are in the New York City area. The goal of the language program is to add churches in at least one new language each year.

In 1973 the convention added a Ministry to Internationals in addition to the language program. Elias Golonka was elected to serve in this position with primary emphasis to be given to the personnel at the United Nations. This work enables the convention to have a limited ministry to most of the nations of the world. Golonka, who speaks several languages, continues to serve in this position. Over 150 nations have membership in the United Nations.

Within the convention's territory, there are 287 campuses and over 1,200,000 students attending college or graduate school full time. Ministering to students is an important part of the work of the convention. In 1975 William R. Dunning was elected to serve as the first full-time campus minister for the convention. He also served as the first state music director. These ministries were placed in the Education Division.

The convention continued to give strong emphasis to evangelism. In order to assist the churches in sharing the gospel, the convention added an Evangelism Division in 1976. This action gave the convention three major divisions: Education, Evangelism, and Missions. Elected by the convention to serve as director of the division was Daniel Sanchez. At the time, Sanchez was serving as associate director in the language division of the Home Mission Board, SBC.

From the beginning of the convention in 1969, Woman's Missionary Union has been a part of the convention's work. In 1976 the convention voted to employ a WMU director. Gloria Grogan, a native of Virginia, was elected as the first director. The WMU department is in the Missions Division.

When the convention was organized in 1969, the six associations represented were Adirondack, Central, Frontier, Greater Rochester, Metropolitan New York, and Southern Tier. By 1979 each of these associations had a director of missions. In 1980 Norman Bell served Adirondack; J. T. Davis, Central; Clifford Matthews, Frontier; Norman Beckham, Greater Rochester; Quinn Pugh, Metropolitan New York; and John Simmons, Southern Tier. Each association has continued to add new churches and chapels. In 1980 two new associations were organized out of the Central Association. The Greater Syracuse Association was organized to serve Syracuse and the surrounding counties, and the Hudson Valley Association was organized with churches from the Albany-Schenectady area.

The offices of the convention are located in Syracuse in a downtown office building. The convention has voted to seek to secure its own building in keeping with its growth. A study committee has recommended that the offices remain in the Syracuse area.

Since its beginning in 1969, the convention has maintained a close relationship with the Home Mission Board, SBC. The convention has a cooperative agreement with the HMB on mission work. The convention and board jointly agree on funds for the mission work administered by the convention. This includes appointed missionaries, summer student missionaries, and aid for pastors. There is also assistance for staff personnel to administer these programs.

The convention also works with the Sunday School Board, SBC, in educational ministries. The board assists the convention in staff salaries and in other ways. In 1980 the convention elected William R. Dunning to serve as director of its Education Division.

The convention supports and works with all SBC agencies, boards, and commissions. Where there is no staff person assigned to a particular program, it is administered through the office of the executive secretary-treasurer.

At its 1979 session, the convention voted to sign a contract with the SSB for an extension Baptist Book Store. For some time the convention had felt the need for a book store to help the churches and had adopted resolutions requesting a book store.

The extension Book Store is an experiment for the board and the convention. The convention operates the store and the board has responsibility for providing stock. The convention receives a commission on total sales. The store began operations in the basement of the First Baptist Church of Syracuse in Jan., 1980. The first year sales totaled over $19,000. Mrs. Jack Lowndes serves as the manager of the store.

The convention observed its 10th anniversary in 1979 at Syracuse with a number of past presidents present. A highlight of the meeting was the presentation of a convention hymn by Ken Medima who had composed "We Belong" especially for the occasion.

The convention is supported by gifts from the churches to the convention budget. Each year since its beginning, the convention has increased the percentage of its budget given to SBC causes. The budget adopted for 1970, the first full year of operation as a convention, totaled $422,060. The budget adopted for 1980 totaled $1,470,479.

The Georgia Baptist Convention voted to enter a sister state relationship with the Baptist Convention of New York in 1978. This relationship has brought help from the convention, associations, and churches of Georgia to the convention, associations, and churches in the

NEW YORK STATISTICAL SUMMARY

Year	Associations	Churches	Church Membership	Baptisms	SS Enrollment	VBS Enrollment	CT Enrollment	WMU Enrollment	Brotherhood Enrollment	Ch. Music Enrollment	Mission Gifts	Total Gifts	Value Church Property
1969	—	—	—	—	—	—	—	—	—	—	—	—	—
1970	6	74	10,348	830	9,731	10,273	3,762	1,814	565	1,368	$232,343	$1,712,996	$ 5,503,550
1971	6	78	11,182	952	9,922	11,894	2,890	1,616	625	1,543	378,772	1,980,520	6,379,285
1972	6	85	12,874	1,028	10,661	15,938	2,757	2,075	782	1,990	470,169	2,650,181	8,409,788
1973	6	91	14,263	1,117	11,167	10,962	2,480	2,038	898	2,265	521,754	2,282,650	10,050,470
1974	6	98	15,818	1,341	11,940	12,222	2,478	2,219	846	2,855	549,248	2,500,882	12,040,195
1975	6	100	17,026	1,508	12,725	13,932	2,517	2,406	1,163	2,986	684,289	2,845,306	12,676,402
1976	6	106	18,286	1,185	13,782	13,253	2,349	2,299	1,100	2,870	653,243	2,993,127	13,918,312
1977	6	118	18,537	1,108	13,381	9,994	2,383	2,389	1,090	3,120	686,803	3,382,320	16,678,822
1978	6	128	18,553	1,266	12,963	10,798	2,709	2,237	837	2,886	781,425	3,744,847	16,986,806
1979	6	134	18,154	1,110	13,084	9,793	2,540	2,402	989	2,692	769,463	4,049,664	20,436,542
1980	6	140	18,822	1,357	12,749	11,986	2,576	1,997	900	2,543	942,462	4,439,543	20,779,565

JACK P. LOWNDES

territory of the Baptist Convention of New York.

The *New York Baptist* is the official publication of the convention. Published monthly in Syracuse, the paper seeks to keep the members of the churches informed about convention activities, as well as SBC news and news of general interest. The paper is a member of the Baptist Press Association. Jack Lowndes serves as editor.

JACK P. LOWNDES

NEW YORK ASSOCIATIONS.

I. New Associations. GREATER ROCHESTER. Organized in Oct., 1969, by three churches and two missions in the Rochester area from Frontier Association. In 1980 eight churches reported 51 baptisms, 748 members, $213,000 total gifts, and $22,633 mission gifts.

GREATER SYRACUSE. Organized in Oct., 1980, by churches from Central Association to serve Syracuse and surrounding counties. In 1980 seven churches reported 82 baptisms, 675 members, $167,989 total gifts, and $41,899 mission gifts.

HUDSON. Organized in Oct., 1980, by churches from Central Association in the Albany-Schenectady area. In 1980 four churches reported 37 baptisms, 314 members, $186,252 total gifts, and $34,347 mission gifts.

II. Changes in Associations. CENTRAL. Churches in the Albany-Schenectady area and those in Syracuse and surrounding counties withdrew in 1980 to form two new associations, Greater Syracuse and Hudson. Central continued to serve churches in the Albany-Schenectady area, and those in Syracuse and surrounding counties withdrew in 1980 to form two new associations, Greater Syracuse and Hudson. Central continued to serve churches in the Rome-Utica area.

See also NEW YORK, METROPOLITAN BAPTIST ASSOCIATION, Vol. III; NEW YORK, SOUTHERN BAPTISTS IN UPSTATE, Vol. III.

LYNN E. MAY, JR.

NEW YORK RESORT MINISTRIES. The Baptist Convention of New York helped provide a ministry for the 1980 Winter Olympics at Lake Placid, NY. In keeping with its goals to share the gospel and establish churches where needed, the convention decided that a church should be established in Lake Placid—a resort area with a permanent population of 3,000 with many thousands more visiting in the general area both summer and winter.

In 1977 David and Mary Ann Book, missionaries of the Home Mission Board, SBC, were assigned to Lake Placid. Ken and Marilyn Prickett, area consultants for the Home Mission Board, were living in the area. With the help of these two couples and numerous volunteers, a ministry was developed for the Olympics during which the village housed approximately 1,800 athletes from 35 nations. Another 14,000 members of the official Olympics family also crowded into Lake Placid. The Baptist Convention of New York purchased a house on Main Street which became a place of ministry to approximately 50,000 people who crowded into the village to see the Olympics. Witnessing, counseling, and other ministries were provided. As a result of these efforts, a Baptist church was organized in Lake Placid, the first since 1938, with David Book serving as pastor. The church is in the Adirondack Baptist Association, Baptist Convention of New York.

See also RESORT MISSIONS.

JACK P. LOWNDES

NEWMAN, ALBERT SIDNEY (b. Anacoco, LA, Feb. 10, 1894; d. Shreveport, LA, Jan. 4, 1971). Educator and pastor. The son of Mary Newman and John Newman, a merchant, he attended Louisiana College (B.A., 1926) and Baptist Bible Institute (Th.M., Th.D.). He was superintendent of Acadia Baptist Academy and principal of public high schools, serving also as pastor of West Lake Church, 1936-39, and Temple Church, Ruston, 1939-42. He was secretary of Louisiana Convention Brotherhood, 1945-54. He married Rebecca May, June 18, 1916. Their children were Esthman and Marna. He is buried in Greenwood Cemetery, Ruston, LA.

GRADY E. WELCH, SR.

NICARAGUA, MISSION IN. Prior to 1976, Southern Baptist ministries in Nicaragua were limited to occasional visits of missionaries from the Bahamas and Costa Rica to the 128-year-old Ebenezer Baptist Church on Corn Island. Following Managua's earthquake in Dec., 1972, Southern Baptists responded with massive relief help, volunteer work crews, and the assistance of missionaries from neighboring countries. Southern Baptist missionaries began a Christian literature ministry in Managua in Aug., 1976, upon request of the Nicaragua Baptist Convention. Stanley and Glenna (Morgan) Stamps transferred there from Ecuador. The Baptist Culture Center was serving as a wholesale deposit of the Baptist Spanish Publishing House and as a retail outlet for Bibles, religious books, and Christian literature. A Bible correspondence course and film ministry complemented the center's witness, and the missionaries participated in local church and convention activities. A music ministry was inaugurated in early 1980.

STANLEY D. STAMPS

NIGER REPUBLIC, MISSION IN. Soon after the opening of the mission in 1973 with the transfer of two missionary couples from Nigeria to Maradi, the great Sahel drought struck Niger. A relief program including food and emergency medical help claimed most of the time of the missionaries. Unsuccessful efforts were made to establish a trade school in Maradi. One missionary couple left because of health problems, and the remaining couple

transferred to Niamey, working largely with nomadic Tuaregs who were contacted during the drought. Response is slow in this solidly Muslim nation.

JOHN E. MILLS

NIGERIA, MISSION IN (II, III). Missionaries declined from 218 in 1969 to 130 in 1979, but Baptist growth in Nigeria continued unabated, reporting 1,250 churches with 300,000 members. Increasingly, missionaries were serving in consultant roles. Most primary and high schools and teacher training institutions begun by Baptists were absorbed into a government educational system, but missionaries continued to serve in some with good results. Government increased its role in medical institutions, but missionaries continued to serve effectively in the Ogbomosho and Eku hospitals, the nursing school in Eku, the Kersey Children's Home, and the Baptist Health Service in Ogbomosho. In 1980, the mission was emphasizing pastoral training in a degree program at the Nigerian Baptist Seminary in Ogbomosho, in pastors' schools in Kaduna, Oyo, Eku, and Owerri, and through Theological Education by Extension. Radio, television, adult education, and student work were playing important roles.

JOHN E. MILLS

NONEVANGELICALS, HOME MISSION BOARD PROGRAM OF WORK RELATED TO (III). See INTERFAITH WITNESS, HOME MISSION BOARD PROGRAM OF.

NORMAN COLLEGE. See GEORGIA, BAPTIST CONVENTION OF THE STATE OF.

NORTH AMERICAN BAPTIST ASSOCIATION (II). See BAPTIST MISSIONARY ASSOCIATION OF AMERICA.

NORTH AMERICAN BAPTIST CONFERENCE (cf. North American Baptist General Conference, Vol. II). A fellowship of churches predominantly German in origin, formerly called the North American Baptist General Conference. In 1978 the 21 associations and 355 churches affiliated with this body had 57,241 members. The congregations are located in the United States and Canada, with the greatest strength centered in the states of Michigan, the Dakotas, and California and in the provinces of Alberta and British Columbia. During the preceding nine years the conference had added eight churches and 2,161 members.

The group is conservative in theology and has preserved its ethnic heritage to a considerable degree. The conference offices are in Oakbrook Terrace, IL. Peter E. Fehr is moderator; John Binder, executive secretary.

BIBLIOGRAPHY: R. J. Kerstan, "Historical Factors in the Formation of the Ethnically Oriented North American Baptist General Conference" (Ph.D. dissertation, Northwestern University, 1971). M. L. Leuschner, "North American Baptist General Conference," *Baptist Advance,* ed. D. C. Woolley (1964).

CHESTER RAYMOND YOUNG

NORTH AMERICAN BAPTIST FEL-LOWSHIP (III). The fellowship, organized in 1966, consists of representatives of nine Baptist bodies in North America: American Baptist Churches in the U.S.A., General Association of General Baptists, National Baptist Convention of America, Progressive National Baptist Convention, Inc., North American Baptist Conference, Seventh Day Baptist General Conference, and the Southern Baptist Convention, all in the USA; and Baptist Federation of Canada and National Baptist Convention of Mexico.

Carl W. Tiller, an associate secretary of the BWA, became secretary of the fellowship following the retirement of Frank H. Woyke in 1971. He was succeeded in turn by Charles F. Wills in 1978.

Chairmen in the past decade, and the member bodies they represent, have been: Gideon K. Zimmerman, North American Baptist Conference, 1970-72; Sloan S. Hodges, Progressive National Baptist Convention, 1972-74; Robert C. Campbell, American Baptist Churches in the U.S.A., 1974-76; Ernest K. Bee, Seventh Day Baptist General Conference, 1976-78; R. Fred Bullen, Baptist Federation of Canada, 1978-80; and Carolyn Weatherford, SBC, 1980.

Primary goals and objectives of the fellowship have been to help Baptist leaders of the continent to know each other better and to plan through sharing sessions for cooperative efforts toward common goals. The fellowship has sponsored a quarterly supplement to *The Baptist World.*

Fellowship representatives have engaged in a series of theological conversations with representatives of the Lutheran Council in the USA. These dialogues began in 1978 and are expected to continue twice annually through 1981, with the stated purpose "to encourage greater understanding between the confessional bodies. The goal will be clarification, not consensus."

C. E. BRYANT

NORTH AMERICAN BAPTIST GENERAL MISSIONARY SOCIETY, INC. Founded in 1883 with a Baptist tradition of planting churches and involvement in personal and small group evangelism, this society is engaged in related ministries such as education, medicine, and funds transmittal. The headquarters are located in Villa Park, IL, with Richard Schilke as general secretary. *Baptist Herald* is the monthly periodical. Ninety-seven missionaries are under appointment to four overseas mission fields. The oldest is Japan, where work began in 1951, and the largest is Cameroon. Total income is approximately $900,000 with $800,000 being spent overseas.

See also NORTH AMERICAN BAPTIST GENERAL CONFERENCE, VOL. II; NORTH AMERICAN BAPTIST CONFERENCE, VOL. IV.

M. THOMAS STARKES

NORTH AMERICAN BAPTIST WOMEN'S UNION (III). The union, an organiza-tion within the Baptist World Alliance, grew in the 1970s with the addition of national groups from Trinidad, the Bahamas, and Guyana. Quinquennial assemblies were held in Toronto, Canada, 1972, and Freeport, Grand Bahamas, 1977. The 1972 meeting, with over 2,500 in attendance, reflected the current BWA emphasis on reconciliation. Letha Casazza, of Washington, DC, was elected to a five-year term as president.

The 25th anniversary assembly in 1977 was the first to be held outside the North American continent. Marena Belle Williams, of Kansas City, MO, was elected president; Judith Clanton, vice-president; Florence Korb, secretary; and Helen Fling, treasurer. The union has continued to promote the Day of Prayer the first Monday in November. The offering on this occasion has steadily increased; in 1979 more than $119,000 was collected.

DORIS DEVAULT

NORTH CAROLINA, BAPTIST STATE CONVENTION OF (II, III).
I. History. W. Perry Crouch retired as general secretary-treasurer of the convention, Dec. 31, 1975, after 12 years of service, being succeeded by Cecil A. Ray, who came to this position from the staff of the Baptist General Convention of Texas.

The largest statistical achievements in 1969-79 were in finances. Total gifts increased 136 percent and mission gifts 143 percent, accompanied by an inflation rate of 108 percent for the same period. Church membership increased 9.5 percent, Brotherhood 23.8 percent, and Church Music 39.6 percent. Baptisms declined 21.7 percent, Sunday School 8.9 percent, Vacation Bible School 1.7 percent, Woman's Missionary Union 8.8 percent, and Church Training 37.3 percent.

II. Important Issues and Developments. *Baptismal Issue.*—Five items shared the limelight during this period. First came the baptismal issue in 1971-74. A committee appointed in 1972 reported in 1973 11 churches with a few unimmersed members and/or a membership policy making this possible. However, the convention consistently voted down attempts in 1971, 1973, and 1974 to amend the constitution so as to exclude such churches from convention membership.

Wake Forest University.—The second important item was a changed relationship between the convention and Wake Forest University. The general board appointed a special committee in July, 1977, to study certain problems and report to the annual sessions in 1977, 1978, and 1979. A further controversy erupted after the Wake Forest board of trustees, on Dec. 9, 1977, approved the use of $85,000 of a federal grant for construction of a greenhouse, an action which the 1977 convention had opposed. During 1978, however, "the Executive Committee received a request from Wake Forest University trustees asking for a changed relationship with self perpetuating board of trustees." This was referred to the Council on Christian Higher Education, which appointed a subcommittee which entered into negotiations with representatives of Wake Forest. This produced a delicately balanced compromise arrangement, adopted with one amendment by the 1979 annual session. Some of the most important points in the document are: (1) The relationship changed from "an institution of the convention to an institution related to the convention by means of a . . . covenant;" (2) no Cooperative Program funds for Wake Forest after Jan. 1, 1981, leaving each individual church to decide whether 6.04 percent of its Cooperative Program money will go to Wake Forest; (3) all trustees of Wake Forest still elected by the convention, but with a new option whereby up to one-third may be "members of any evangelical Christian denomination" anywhere.

Selection of Leaders.—The third important item concerned changes in the selection of leaders. After a two-year study, the 1977 convention voted restrictions on the number of committee and board members from each church, including bylaw changes expressing the desire "that . . . at least 25 percent of members [nominated] to the various boards, agencies and institutions [come] from churches under 400 members." In 1978 this was changed to 400 resident members. A committee on trustee selection proposed in 1979 extensive changes in the process. Final action was deferred to 1980, with the agreement that the plan is already being implemented.

Bold Mission Thrust.—A fourth important item was participation in the Bold Mission Thrust adopted by the SBC in 1977, involving the doubling of Cooperative Program gifts by 1982 and doubling "at least two more times by the year 2000," with the purpose of "sharing the gospel of Jesus Christ with every person in the world by the year 2000." The state convention adopted these same goals in 1977, along with doubling baptisms by 1982 and various other decisions to implement these plans. Closely related to this was a major adjustment in special offerings. In 1977 and 1978 the goal for the State Missions Offering was greatly enlarged to liquidate convention indebtedness, especially on Caraway Conference Center, opened in Jan., 1977. In 1979 the offering became North Carolina Missions Offering, the goal was $2,000,000, and it included what had previously been six separate offerings for state missions, hospital, homes for aging, children's homes, Christian education, and Heck-Jones (Woman's Missionary Union).

Baptist History.—The fifth important item was Baptist history. The 1976 annual session celebrated the nation's bicentennial with four dramatic presentations entitled "Crossroads of Baptist History." On Mar. 21, 1980, a special session met in Greenville, celebrating the 150th anniversary of the founding of the convention in that city, Mar. 26, 1830. The 1981 annual session will meet jointly with the Baptist General Convention (black), with separate business sessions, as was done in 1974.

III. Program of Work. *Administration.*— The general board, composed of persons living in every association, has "power to act for the convention . . . between sessions." This board, working through its committees, especially its executive committee, employs staff members and works with them in promoting each facet of work. Cecil A. Ray is the chief administrative officer; since 1977 he has been assisted by Roy J. Smith, the first associate general secretary. The Department of Pastor-Church Relations is part of this administrative unit.

Division of Business Management.—Leon P. Spencer, after 20 years of service as director of this division, retired, Dec. 31, 1973, being succeeded by Richard D. Smith, formerly director of the Church Building Planning Department. In Jan., 1974, the convention dedicated extensive additions and renovations done to its office building. In addition to supervision of the building, mail room, print shop, and telephone service, this division includes management of Camp Caraway and Conference Center in Asheboro and North Carolina Baptist Assembly in Southport. The departments of Retirement Planning and Data Processing are in this division, and much of the work was converted to computer in 1975. Program-based budgeting began with the 1977 budget.

Division of Church Programs.—Nathan C. Brooks, Jr., after 10 years as director of this division, retired, Dec. 31, 1976, being succeeded by Burrel Lucas, who had been director of the Sunday School Department. Departments now include Church Building Planning, Church Music, Church Training, Sunday School, and close cooperation with WMU.

Woman's Missionary Union.—Sara Ann Hobbs, after 10 years as executive director of WMU, became director of Estate Planning for the North Carolina Baptist Foundation in Aug., 1977, being succeeded by Nancy Curtis, who previously served as Baptist Young Women director.

Division of Communications.—William H. Boatwright became director of this new division in 1977 after seven years as director of the Department of Public Relations. The division includes an extensive and well-equipped audiovisual department.

Division of Evangelism.—Julian S. Hopkins *(q.v.)* retired, Dec. 31, 1969, after 13 years as director of this division, being succeeded by William C. Lamb. The division includes departments of Youth and Renewal Evangelism, and Evangelism Development.

Division of Missions.—Howard J. Ford, after 12 years as director of this division, retired, Dec. 31, 1978, being succeeded by Sara Ann Hobbs, formerly with WMU and North Carolina Baptist Foundation. This division maintains area missionaries and includes departments for Associational Development, Brotherhood, Chaplaincy and Language Ministries, Church Extension, Fruitland Baptist Bible Institute and Conference Center, and Special Ministries.

Division of Stewardship.—Ottis J. Hagler *(q.v.)*

NORTH CAROLINA STATISTICAL SUMMARY

Year	Associations	Churches	Church Membership	Baptisms	SS Enrollment	VBS Enrollment	CT Enrollment	WMU Enrollment	Brotherhood Enrollment	Ch. Music Enrollment	Mission Gifts	Total Gifts	Value Church Property
1969	80	3,455	1,016,250	28,015	733,229	358,497	167,375	148,217	43,756	108,758	$12,045,588	$ 76,857,407	$ 367,327,320
1970	80	3,449	1,023,147	27,358	717,993	287,139	157,449	138,856	44,887	110,189	12,572,821	81,504,202	398,643,435
1971	80	3,443	1,034,322	29,551	698,853	298,832	126,147	135,452	50,485	112,279	14,058,264	89,413,398	411,307,839
1972	80	3,461	1,046,302	31,978	693,176	284,350	119,230	136,768	50,824	125,676	15,683,929	98,921,298	441,039,174
1973	80	3,457	1,059,605	29,357	693,874	283,553	112,207	137,142	53,335	131,851	17,732,644	106,660,669	489,435,012
1974	80	3,444	1,071,724	28,927	688,463	299,313	108,650	138,318	54,605	138,241	19,369,639	116,548,480	558,606,800
1975	80	3,447	1,082,175	30,217	694,835	307,121	106,084	141,857	56,695	142,396	20,640,847	123,917,525	610,307,952
1976	80	3,458	1,093,578	26,244	695,682	292,739	102,430	143,304	56,627	144,384	22,569,709	137,891,913	675,424,349
1977	80	3,462	1,099,651	22,543	685,627	277,973	94,878	139,662	54,901	141,768	24,971,253	148,233,311	727,600,309
1978	80	3,463	1,105,972	22,202	669,520	280,344	97,151	137,185	55,042	146,157	27,297,850	160,945,785	811,955,943
1979	80	3,468	1,110,890	21,900	659,458	276,768	96,581	134,973	54,204	148,741	30,108,483	176,556,137	911,550,964
1980	80	3,475	1,118,305	24,997	654,689	284,402	101,715	134,620	57,095	152,467	33,545,564	190,267,208	1,008,645,215

LAMAR J. BROOKS

resigned as director of this division in 1970 because of disability. Work was continued through the Department of Stewardship in the Division of Church Programs and the Department of Stewardship Promotion under Administration. In Sep., 1977, this became a division again, with O. D. Martin, Jr., as the new director.

Division of Youth and Campus Ministries.—After nine years as director of the Department of Campus Ministry, James Y. Greene became the first director of this division in 1977. There are 24 campus ministers and departments for Personnel Development, Commuter Student Ministry, Specialized Student/Church Ministries, Student Ministries, and Youth Ministries.

Council on Christian Higher Education.—Ben C. Fisher resigned as executive secretary, Sep., 1970, to become executive secretary of the Education Commission, SBC, being succeeded by T. Robert Mullinax, Mar. 1, 1971. The institutions are: Campbell University, Chowan College, Gardner-Webb College, Mars Hill College, Meredith College, Wake Forest University, and Wingate College.

Council on Christian Social Services.—The general secretary-treasurer was acting executive secretary of this council until Roy J. Smith became the first associate general secretary in 1977, thus also becoming executive secretary of this council. The institutions are: Baptist Children's Homes of North Carolina, Inc., North Carolina Baptist Hospitals, Inc., and North Carolina Baptist Homes, Inc.

Council on Christian Life and Public Affairs.— The general secretary-treasurer was acting executive director of this council until Mar. 1, 1973, when Charles V. Petty became the first full-time director. In 1979 he was succeeded by W. Douglas Cole, director of the Department of Christian Family Life. Other departments are Christian Citizenship Education and Aging.

Agencies.—Two convention agencies, separate from the above structure, are *Biblical Recorder, Inc.* and North Carolina Baptist Foundation.

Convention Presidents.—The following served as convention presidents, 1970-80: John E. Lawrence, Raleigh; Thomas M. Freeman, Dunn; Allen A. Bailey, Charlotte; Coy C. Privette, Kannapolis; C. Mark Corts, Winston-Salem; and Cecil E. Sherman, Asheville.

LAMAR J. BROOKS

NORTH CAROLINA ASSOCIATIONS (II, III). In 1980, 80 associations were cooperating with the Baptist State Convention of North Carolina. No changes of name occurred and no new associations were formed in the 1970s.

JOHN R. WOODARD

NORTH CAROLINA BAPTIST ASSEMBLY. Consecutive directors have been Richard K. Redwine, Fred Smith, and Tom McKay. Rebuilding of Lantana Lodge into a facility for adults, 1971, erection of the Rachel Hatch Auditorium, 1968, and building of a new dining room, 1978, improved the physical plant greatly.

See also NORTH CAROLINA, BAPTIST STATE CONVENTION OF, VOL. III.

NATHAN C. BROOKS, JR.

NORTH CAROLINA BAPTIST FOUN-DATION (II, III). Edwin S. Coates became executive secretary in 1972, succeeding C. Gordon Maddrey. Assets in trust totaled $5,100,000 in 1979.

EDWIN S. COATES

NORTH CAROLINA BAPTIST HIS-TORICAL COLLECTION. The collecting of North Carolina Baptist historical materials in the Wake Forest University Library began in 1885 with the formation of the North Carolina Baptist Historical Society. In 1959 the collection was designated the official depository for North Carolina Baptist historical materials. James Nicholson was the first director. In 1964 John R. Woodard became the director. In 1970 the collection was officially named The Ethel Taylor Crittenden Collection in Baptist History to honor her work in developing its contents. The collection has an active program.

JOHN R. WOODARD

NORTH CAROLINA BAPTIST HOMES, INC. (III). An institution of the Baptist State Convention of North Carolina providing a Christian life-care ministry for persons 65 and older, primarily those belonging to Baptist churches. In 1980 William A. Poole completed 20 years as executive director. In June, 1980, 300 individuals were being served through four facilities in Winston-Salem—Resthaven Home, Hayes Home, an apartment complex, and a central skilled nursing facility for all six homes—plus homes in Albemarle, Hamilton, Yanceyville, and Asheville.

Since 1970, the addition of 20 nursing-care beds, four duplex apartments, and the Asheville home with a capacity of 49 increased the homes' population 39 percent. The operating budget increased 267 percent over this period. Support comes from Cooperative Program funds (1.28 percent), the North Carolina missions offering, resident income (76 percent in 1980), and personal, memorial, and estate gifts.

W. A. POOLE

NORTH CAROLINA BAPTIST HOS-PITAL (cf. North Carolina Baptist Hospitals, Inc., Vols. II, III). More than 22,000 patients are admitted each year. About 35,000 patients are seen in the emergency room. Clinical visits by ambulatory patients exceed 178,000 annually.

See also BOWMAN GRAY SCHOOL OF MEDICINE.

RUSSELL BRANTLEY

NORTH CAROLINA BAPTIST HOSPI-TAL SCHOOL OF PASTORAL CARE. See SCHOOL OF PASTORAL CARE.

NORTH CENTRAL STATES MISSIONS THRUST. The North Central States Missions Thrust grew out of the Fellowship of Great Lakes States, originally founded when the state directors of missions felt a need for a time of fellowship and sharing. In Jan., 1961, Harold Cameron of Illinois, Arthur Walker of Ohio, Robert Wilson of Michigan, and George Staton of Indiana had their first meeting.

In Jan., 1969, the meeting included the state executive secretaries: James H. Smith of Illinois, Ray Roberts of Ohio, Fred Hubbs of Michigan, and E. Harmon Moore of Indiana. The element of fellowship was primary with times of sharing successes and failures in the pioneer areas. A togetherness emerged.

Out of the fellowship came the "Great Lakes Day" at The Southern Baptist Theological Seminary. The seminary designated a day each spring as "Great Lakes Day," and executive secretaries and directors of missions visited the campus to interview students. One of the executive secretaries annually spoke in chapel on the challenge of ministry in the Great Lakes states.

Early in 1972, Tommy Coy, data consultant for the Planning Section of the Home Mission Board, began an analysis of the 1970 Illinois census. In Dec., 1972, the raw data was shared with James H. Smith, executive secretary of Illinois, and Charles Chaney, director of the newly created Church Extension Division of Illinois Baptists. The data revealed 419 cities in Illinois with a population between 1,000 and 150,000 with no evangelical church, and that 24 percent of the population had as their mother tongue a language other than English. Of the 11,200,000 total population, over 1,500,000 were blacks, concentrated primarily on the south side of Chicago. The data gave information by county and for the major cities by census tract.

The information was shared with the Great Lakes States Fellowship in Jan., 1973. The other states immediately decided to seek similar information. The time had come for a united effort to reach the North Central States with the gospel.

The state directors of missions in 1974 agreed to change the name from "Great Lakes States" to "North Central States." They also invited the directors of missions in the Wisconsin-Minnesota Southern Baptist Fellowship and the Iowa Southern Baptist Fellowship to join the North Central States Fellowship.

The directors of missions met, June 3, 1974, in Indianapolis, IN, to develop strategy based on the new data from the HMB. They agreed to invite representatives from Southern Baptist agencies to attend the next annual meeting. R. V. Haygood, director of missions for Indiana, was to serve as convener and chairman.

The Jan., 1975, meeting in Indianapolis was attended by representatives from the HMB, Sunday School Board, Brotherhood Commission, Radio-Television Commission, and Woman's Missionary Union. The concept of "doubling" became the objective: double the num-

FALLS CREEK BAPTIST CONFERENCE CENTER (*q.v.*), Davis, OK. Lodge II.

OKLAHOMA CITY RETIREMENT CENTER, Oklahoma. Activity Building.

OKLAHOMA BAPTIST UNIVERSITY (*q.v.*), Shawnee. Mabee Learning Center.

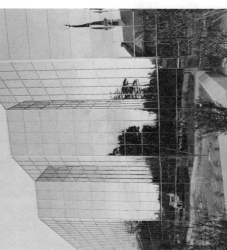

NORTH CAROLINA BAPTIST HOMES, INC. (q.v.). *Left:* Hayes Home Campus, Winston-Salem. Duplex apartment constructed in 1977 for younger retirees. *Right:* Western North Carolina Home, Asheville. Opened in 1979; has a capacity for 49 older adults.

NORTH CAROLINA BAPTIST HOSPITALS, INC. (q.v.), Winston-Salem. Bowman Gray School of Medicine, Focus Building. Houses the Clinical Pastoral Education Division of the Department of Pastoral Care.

NORTHERN PLAINS BAPTIST CONVENTION (q.v.) BUILDING, Rapid City, SD. Purchased for $65,000 in May, 1972. Completely paid for by Oct., 1976.

ber of churches, double membership, double Sunday School enrollment, double finances, and double every organization. The time frame was to be 1974-89, and the objective was to double the 1974 statistics.

A special meeting of the fellowship was held in Miami Beach, FL, June 11, 1975, during the SBC. The directors of missions recommended that a coordinator be hired for the first phase through 1979 and that the SSB and HMB each be asked to contribute $20,000 annually for four years beginning with 1976. The SSB immediately agreed. The HMB was reluctant, fearing the possibility of setting a precedent.

A special meeting in Sep., 1975, in Detroit considered hiring a coordinator and selecting the major emphasis for the first phase. The group unanimously agreed to have the four executive secretaries serve a one-year term each as coordinator. Travel and other expenses were to be reimbursed, but there would be no remuneration for service. The SSB contributed $20,000; the HMB, $10,000; and WMU, $2,500, annually for four years, 1976-79.

E. Harmon Moore served in 1976. The emphasis was to promote the concept of doubling. In 1977 it was to start 400 new church-type missions; Robert Wilson was coordinator. James H. Smith coordinated the emphasis of Sunday School enlargement through new Sunday Schools and the Sunday School Action Plan in 1978. Ray Roberts led an intensive effort for evangelism in 1979.

A special mass meeting was held the first week of each January in the city of the coordinating executive secretary for that year. In 1976 it was in Indianapolis with state staff members, associational directors of missions, moderators, and representatives from the Southern Baptist agencies attending.

In 1977 the group met in Kalamazoo, MI, along with 400 pastors who had agreed to try to lead their churches to start a new mission.

The 1978 meeting was in Springfield, IL. Charles Chaney and Ron Lewis of the Illinois staff led a church growth seminar for invited pastors who had committed their churches to growth through Sunday School expansion.

The 1974 annuals indicated 1,784 Southern Baptist churches in the seven North Central States. The goal was to double that number in 15 years. The 2,000th church was constituted in Milford, MI, Dec. 16, 1979, with Dale Gross as its bivocational pastor who served the mission from its beginning. The occasion was attended by Harold Bennett, executive secretary of the SBC Executive Committee, Grady Cothen, SSB, and Carolyn Weatherford, WMU. On the last day of 1979, there were 2,000 churches and 340 church-type missions.

JAMES H. SMITH

NORTH DAKOTA, SOUTHERN BAPTISTS IN. See NORTHERN PLAINS BAPTIST CONVENTION.

NORTH GREENVILLE COLLEGE (cf. North Greenville Junior College, Vols. II, III). The 1970s brought to North Greenville Junior College a third (Harold Eugene Lindsey, 1970-75) and a fourth (George Silver, 1975-80) president and a shortened name in 1972 as the word *Junior* was deleted from the charter which was revised under the direction of Lindsey.

The Advisory Board and Ryan B. Eklund, vice-president for development, promoted a vigorous capital needs campaign. Campus beautification was a major concern as additional landscaping and building renovation was done. White Hall, 1971, and Neves Dining Hall, 1972, were renovated while the gymnasium was completely remodeled and named the Joe F. Hayes, Jr., Gymnasium, 1976.

The Donnan Building, 1975, was renovated, adding an executive suite and needed classrooms when the library was moved into the spacious Edwin F. Averyt Learning Center, 1974. Other new buildings constructed during these years were the Walter Brashier Apartments, 1973, and the Grange Cothran Maintenance Building, 1974. Additional improvements on the campus included five hard-surface tennis courts and paved parking areas for faculty, staff, students, and visitors.

In 1973 North Greenville College opened a Downtown Extension in the Wade Hampton Mall which was moved to the Insurance Building at 135 South Main Street in Aug., 1977. This move was made possible when Walter Brashier donated the 10-story building to the college. The first three floors of the newly-named NGC Building were converted into classrooms and administrative offices for North Greenville College at Greenville.

During the academic year 1977-78, a 10-year self-study was conducted, and a visiting committee reaffirmed the accreditation of the college by the Southern Association of Schools and Colleges. Graduates continued to transfer to leading colleges and universities, and many continued to prepare for careers in Christian vocations.

During the last half of the decade, faculty salaries were raised, professional development was stressed, and 30 percent of the faculty enrolled in doctoral programs. The curriculum was broadened to include Cooperative-Experiential Education in the fields of church-related vocations as the most popular vocational choices. Of the total enrollment, 477 were from South Carolina, 55 were from other states, and 15 were international students. Baptists still outnumbered other denominations with 306 being members of Baptist churches.

S. C. BRISSIE

NORTHERN PLAINS ASSOCIATIONS (cf. Northern Plains Baptist Associations, Vol. III).

I. New Associations. BIG HORN (WY). Organized Sep. 22, 1979, by five churches and one mission in Northwest Wyoming which withdrew from Yellowstone Association. In 1980 six churches reported 47 baptisms, 882 members, $172,408 total gifts, and $38,483 mission gifts.

BIG SKY (MT). Organized Sep. 28, 1970, by three churches in Southeast Montana which withdrew from Yellowstone Association. In 1980 five churches reported 87 baptisms, 655 members, $201,832 total gifts, and $37,830 mission gifts.

ENERGY BASIN (WY). Organized Oct. 17, 1973, in South Central Wyoming by churches withdrawing from Frontier Association, Green River Association, and three new churches constituting at that time. In 1980 seven churches reported 67 baptisms, 548 members, $178,700 total gifts, and $22,293 mission[1] gifts.

LAKE REGION (SD). Organized Sep. 23, 1978, by six churches and three missions in Northeastern South Dakota which had been affiliated with East River Association. In 1980 seven churches reported 54 baptisms, 450 members, $115,703 total gifts, and $39,661 mission gifts.

OAHE (SD). Organized Sep. 23, 1978, by five churches and three missions in Central South Dakota which had been affiliated with East River Association. In 1980 six churches reported 59 baptisms, 348 members, $156,971 total gifts, and $30,573 mission gifts.

SIOUXLAND (SD). Organized Sep. 23, 1978, by four churches in Southeastern South Dakota which had been affiliated with East River Association. In 1980 seven churches reported 70 baptisms, 522 members, $140,895 total gifts, and $12,845 mission gifts.

WIND RIVER (WY). Organized Sep. 22, 1979, by three churches and three missions in West Central Wyoming which withdrew from Yellowstone Association. In 1980 four churches reported 58 baptisms, 750 members, $176,690 total receipts, and $59,339 mission gifts.

II. Changes in Associations. EAST RIVER (SD). Organized Nov. 2, 1964, by messengers from four churches east of the Missouri River which withdrew from South Dakota Association of Southern Baptists. On Sep. 23, 1978, the association disbanded as the churches withdrew to form Oahe, Siouxland, and Lake Region Associations in South Dakota.

YELLOWSTONE (WY). Organized in 1961 by messengers from six churches which had previously been in Old Faithful Association. On Sep. 22, 1979, the churches withdrew to form the Wind River and Big Horn Associations in Wyoming. Yellowstone Association continued in Central Montana.

DON HARMS

NORTHERN PLAINS BAPTIST. Bimonthly periodical of the Northern Plains Baptist Convention, published at Rapid City, SD. It began publication in Jan., 1976, with John P. Baker as editor. Nicy Murphy succeeded Baker as editor in Feb., 1976. Roy W. Owen became editor in Jan., 1977. By Jan., 1980, the subscription list totaled about 3,400. News of the Northern Plains Baptist Convention was first published in the *Rocky Mountain Baptist,* the Colorado Baptist General Convention paper.

ROY W. OWEN

NORTHERN PLAINS BAPTIST CONVENTION (III).
I. History. The convention had 75 churches when it was constituted in Nov., 1967. That number increased slowly at first. By the end of 1971 there were only 81 churches. Five new churches were added each year in 1973 and 1974. The total then was 93. By 1978 the number of new churches reached double digits when 13 were constituted. By Sep., 1980, however, churches totaled 153, more than double the number when the convention began. The number of associations grew from 13 in 1967 to 18 by the end of 1979.

Church membership also increased. In 1972 baptisms surpassed 1,000 for the first time, and total membership reached 14,293. By 1977 baptisms surpassed 1,500, and the membership had grown to 19,254. During 1979-80 convention churches baptized 2,125 persons, and church members totaled 23,205.

Directors of Missions Changes.—Convention growth brought accompanying personnel changes. Directors of associational missions in 1969 included Leroy Smith (*q.v.*), Montana; J. T. Burdine, North Dakota; Wilson Parker, South Dakota; and O. R. Delmar, Wyoming. In 1969 Leroy Smith resigned. Glenn Field succeeded him in 1971, coming from the pastorate of Arapahoe Road Baptist Church, Littleton, CO. Parker was elected director of missions for the convention in May, 1972. Henry Chiles became the South Dakota director of associational missions the same year. He had been pastor of Central Baptist Church of Bearden, Knoxville, TN, for 23 years. Chiles and his church had been strongly supporting work in Northern Plains for several years.

W. J. Hughes became director of associational missions for the three associations of Big Sky, Hi-Line, and Yellowstone in Eastern Montana in 1975. He came from serving as pastoral missionary in Wyoming. Glenn Field continued to work with the three associations of Glacier, Treasure State, and Triangle in Western Montana.

In Apr., 1976, Charles Crim came from the pastorate of Monroe Avenue Baptist Church, Green River, WY, to serve the three associations of Southern Wyoming: Energy Basin, Frontier, and Green River. O. R. Delmar continued work with the two associations in Northern Wyoming: Old Faithful and Yellowstone, which became Big Horn, Old Faithful, and Wind River in 1979.

Carl Ellison joined the team of directors of associational missions in North Dakota in 1976 upon the resignation of J. T. Burdine. Ellison had been serving as pastor of Mountain Springs Baptist Church, Piedmont, SC.

Convention Staff Changes.—The 1970s brought numerous personnel changes in the office staff in Rapid City, SD. In May, 1972, Wilson

Parker became director of missions, Brotherhood, and stewardship—responsibilities previously handled by executive director John P. Baker. D. G. McCoury joined the staff in Feb., 1971, as director of Church Training, student ministries, and family ministries. This work had formerly been directed by Bob Lawrence who continued to direct Sunday School, music, architecture, and recreation. McCoury had formerly served as pastor of Loma Vista Baptist Church, Kansas City, MO. In 1974 June Highlan moved into the newly-created position of executive assistant. She had been working as Baker's secretary and bookkeeper since Mar., 1968. Both Bob Lawrence and D. G. McCoury resigned at the end of 1974 to accept positions with the Colorado Baptist General Convention.

In June, 1975, Don L. Plott, pastor in Provo, UT, became director of the Teaching/Training Division, which would then consist of three persons. His two associates, Michael McCrocklin and Pete W. Fast, were elected in the fall of 1975. Fast came from Applewood Baptist Church, Wheat Ridge, CO, where he had been minister of music and education. McCrocklin had been working as a student director in Texas. Plott resigned in May, 1976. John W. Thomason replaced him, Aug. 1, 1976. Thomason came from an eight-year pastorate of Trinity Baptist Church, Billings, MT. C. Clyde Billingsley was elected missions director effective Jan. 1, 1977. At the time of his election he was serving in a similar position in the Utah-Idaho Convention.

At the end of 1976, John P. Baker, executive director, and Nicy Murphy, Woman's Missionary Union director, retired. Honoring the two retirees highlighted the convention's annual meeting in Nov., 1976. Roy W. Owen succeeded Baker and began his duties, Oct. 15, 1976. Owen came from the Colorado Convention where he had been serving as associate executive director. Dolores J. Gilliland became WMU director in Jan., 1977. At the time of her election she was teaching high school English in Rapid City.

Staff changes continued. McCrocklin resigned in Sep., 1977, to accept a position with the Iowa Southern Baptist Fellowship. Ben Early came in Apr., 1978, to replace McCrocklin. Early's programs included student ministries, family ministry, church architecture, and church recreation. He came from the pastorate of Trinity Baptist Church, Grand Junction, CO. Fast resigned in May, 1978, to accept a church staff position in Portland, OR. On Sep. 1, 1978, Charles E. Sharp succeeded Fast. Sharp came from serving as a professor at Mobile College, Mobile, AL. The program areas he directed were church music, Church Training, and church media. Don Harms was hired to fill the new position of associate in the missions division. His responsibilities included the programs of evangelism and Brotherhood. He came from the pastorate of Southwest Park Baptist Church, Abilene, TX.

Student Work.—Persons coming to do student work multiplied in the 1970s. Mary Risinger, a US-2 missionary, worked at the University of South Dakota, Vermillion, in 1969 and was transferred to Billings, MT, in 1970. In Aug., 1969, Carrol Smith resigned as director at the University of Wyoming, Laramie. A US-2 couple, the Steve Davidsons, then served that campus. Dave Medders followed them in Aug., 1976. Joe Glaze went as director for the University of North Dakota in 1973. The Billings' work was assumed by another US-2 worker, Steve Wilson. When his term ended, Robert Foster became full-time director.

Student work at South Dakota State University, Brookings, began in 1972. Woodrow Northcutt served as director. He came from a five-year pastorate of the First Baptist Church, Shelby, MT. That Baptist Student Union purchased a student center in 1976. Reggie Bowman became the first full-time director at Montana State University, Bozeman, MT, in 1977. John Christy started student work at the University of South Dakota in 1978. Directors who came in 1979 included Cecil Spencer, South Dakota State University; Bob Agee, Rapid City area; Steve Kavli, Fargo, ND, and Moorhead, MN; and Lenny Spenst, University of Montana, Missoula. In addition to these, pastors and other volunteers do student work on about 15 campuses.

Language Missions.—Missions personnel have continued to expand the work of the convention among special groups. Language missions have flourished. The Balard Whites started work on the Cheyenne River Reservation in South Dakota in 1966. They constituted First Baptist Church, Eagle Butte, Aug. 10, 1969. A new sanctuary was dedicated there, May 6, 1973. The work at LaPlant grew stronger, and a new building was dedicated there, June 27, 1976. Work on the Pine Ridge Reservation in South Dakota began in 1969 when A. L. Davis began a ministry at Sharp's Corner. In May, 1971, he started another mission in the town of Pine Ridge. Harold Heiney moved to Pine Ridge as pastor in Aug., 1971. Red Shirt village requested a ministry, and Davis started work there in 1972. Lakota Baptist Church, Pine Ridge, constituted in June, 1974, and dedicated a new building in 1975.

John Miller, pastor of Baptist Temple, Mandan, ND, helped initiate work on the Standing Rock Reservation in that state. During the summer of 1970, sites were acquired at the towns of Fort Yates and Cannon Ball. Mobile chapels provided meeting places. Ted and Mona Samples served both places from 1975 until 1977, when Bill Tiger arrived as pastor. The Samples moved to Fort Washakie, WY, to begin work on the Wind River Reservation. Calvin Sandlin became pastor of Sioux Baptist Church, Rapid City, SD, following the retirement of A. L. Davis at the end of 1976. In 1977 Wilbert Robertson became pastor of the Indian mission at Sisseton, SD.

In Montana the R. L. Meffords began serving on the Northern Cheyenne Reservation in

1967. They began the Morning Star Baptist Chapel, Lame Deer. They resigned in 1978 to accept the pastorate of Temple Baptist Church, Ellsworth Air Force Base, SD. The First Baptist Church of Shelby began to minister on the Blackfeet Reservation. A Vacation Bible School revealed the potential and led to an ongoing Bible study by pastor Jack Park in 1976. In late 1976 Preston and Pat North began serving and located in Browning, MT.

In Aug., 1978, the Jack Cowards were appointed as catalytic language missionaries to Billings, MT. They worked with Morning Star Baptist Chapel. In addition, they began work with Orientals, Spanish-speaking, and Indian people in Billings, along with work on the Crow Reservation. Developments in 1980 included the dedication of a new building at Poplar, MT, on the Fort Peck Reservation. The Oliver Marsons minister there. James White was called to be pastor of Haines Avenue Baptist Church (formerly Sioux Baptist Chapel). The Sandlins began work on the Rosebud Reservation in South Dakota.

Other Developments.—Ronald D. Hefner began the first Christian social ministry in the convention in Casper, WY, in July, 1974. In addition to his work with the Baptist Center in North Casper, he served as Christian social ministries consultant for the convention. Randy Foster succeeded Hefner in 1978 and settled in Jackson, WY, to begin a church and a resort ministry.

Several career foreign missionaries went from places of service in the convention. John V. "Johnny" and Diana Norwood, Central Baptist Church, Lewistown, MT, and Eddie and Judy Neese, Westside Baptist Church, Great Falls, MT, were appointed to Indonesia. Robert and Judy McEachern, Hillcrest Baptist Church, Riverton, WY, went to Korea. Ronald and Delinda Miller, First Baptist Church, Harlowton, MT, went to Malawi. Michael and Stephanie Reeder, members of Knollwood Baptist Church, Rapid City, SD, were appointed to Columbia. Alice Creecy, a member of Highland Baptist Church, Great Falls, MT, was appointed to Hong Kong. Bernie and Annette Fairchild went to Jordan. Fairchild is a pharmacist. They volunteered while members of Trinity Baptist Church, Missoula, MT.

The convention purchased a new office building in 1972 and completed payment for it in 1976. Located at 924 Quincy, Rapid City, SD, it replaced the old building which was completely inadequate to house the offices of the rapidly growing new convention.

The convention began publishing its own paper, the *Northern Plains Baptist,* in Jan., 1976.

II. Program of Work.—The executive director-treasurer works as the chief administrative officer. In addition, he serves as editor of the *Northern Plains Baptist.*

The division directors provide leadership for the Business Services, Missions, and Teaching/Training Divisions. The Business Services Division director works as office manager, book-

keeper, and executive assistant. The Missions Division director promotes the programs of missions and stewardship. One associate in the division promotes evangelism and Brotherhood. A second associate promotes Woman's Missionary Union. The director of the Teaching/Training Division promotes Sunday School, Vacation Bible School, and church administration. One associate in the division promotes Church Training, music, and church media services. A second associate promotes family ministry, Baptist student ministries, church recreation, and church architecture.

Missions.—Six directors of associational missions lead in encouraging and coordinating the work of 18 associations in the convention. Eight language missionaries work with Indian people in 11 locations. One catalytic missionary lives in Billings, MT, developing work with Spanish-speaking persons and Orientals.

Stewardship.—The Stewardship Department encourages persons and churches to be responsible stewards. This department makes churches aware of the Cooperative Program and encourages giving on a percentage basis.

Evangelism.—The Evangelism Department promotes evangelism in the local churches through a convention evangelism conference, area conferences, and associational clinics. Emphases include revival meetings, lay evangelism schools, TELL witness training, and lifestyle witnessing.

Brotherhood.—The Brotherhood Department conducts an annual convention, area conferences, and associational clinics.

Woman's Missionary Union.—The WMU Department conducts an annual convention. WMU programs provide missions education for girls and women. Numerous persons on the convention level and in the associations do this work.

Sunday School.—Priority areas for this department include enlisting and training associational age-level teams, starting new Sunday Schools, and training workers in the churches. Twin concerns are the enrollment of new persons and the improvement of Bible teaching and learning.

Vacation Bible School.—This department provides an extensive program each year to train VBS workers. Mission VBS and Backyard Bible Clubs receive high priority.

Church Administration.—This department provides help for pastors in personal growth, skill development, church council training, and career guidance. Deacon training and youth ministry are other areas of work. This department also works to encourage vocational guidance in the churches.

Church Training.—This department gives major emphasis to beginning new Church Training programs. Special attention has been given recently to the *Survival Kit for New Christians.* Equipping God's people for service is another important facet of the work.

Church Music.—Special attention to planning worship services claimed the attention of pastors

NORTHERN PLAINS STATISTICAL SUMMARY

Year	Associations	Churches	Church Membership	Baptisms	SS Enrollment	VBS Enrollment	CT Enrollment	WMU Enrollment	Brotherhood Enrollment	Ch. Music Enrollment	Mission Gifts	Total Gifts	Value Church Property
1969	13	76	11,540	864	9,527	8,525	4,671	1,755	577	847	$ 126,422	$1,076,023	$ 4,749,211
1970	13	79	12,373	773	9,759	8,467	4,600	1,532	526	894	142,839	1,167,597	5,045,831
1971	14	81	12,974	925	9,870	9,970	3,415	1,592	610	1,190	206,761	1,354,644	5,658,642
1972	14	83	14,247	1,078	10,231	11,722	3,382	1,555	562	1,317	274,765	1,542,412	5,811,240
1973	14	88	14,891	1,055	10,600	12,763	2,936	1,596	697	1,201	303,709	1,641,264	6,507,251
1974	15	91	15,580	1,093	10,747	10,585	2,919	1,694	746	1,422	465,003	1,884,084	7,472,950
1975	15	96	16,408	1,080	11,328	13,588	2,979	1,942	853	1,474	544,949	2,158,427	8,970,295
1976	15	106	17,907	1,185	12,756	13,255	2,633	2,075	870	1,410	555,008	2,726,388	10,977,490
1977	15	114	19,201	1,582	14,901	14,032	2,696	2,049	813	1,756	644,030	3,396,232	13,734,781
1978	15	129	20,942	1,358	16,067	13,828	3,207	2,117	776	1,960	807,847	3,979,572	17,244,919
1979	17	134	21,778	1,468	15,666	14,673	3,791	2,035	1,015	1,989	1,001,670	4,727,098	20,186,946
1980	18	151	23,373	2,079	16,038	14,956	3,737	2,292	882	2,206	1,015,571	5,279,373	25,026,812

JUNE HIGHLAN

and music directors in two retreats last year. This department conducts choral clinics and workshops for church music leaders.

Student Ministries.—This department helps conduct Baptist student work on 27 campuses. Full-time directors serve four campuses, while the rest of the directors are volunteer or part time. Evangelism is the major thrust on the campuses along with development of Christians.

Family Ministry.—Programs for marriage enrichment and family enrichment have recently been augmented by programs for single persons and senior adults. The program has been multiplied through trained special workers.

Church Architecture.—This program offers consultation to churches engaged in building programs. Church architecture provides additional help in the areas of church building beautification and energy conservation.

Church Recreation.—This program helps churches plan, promote, and conduct social gatherings. Drama and puppetry also receive attention.

Church Media.—This program helps churches with beginning or improving their libraries. It stresses using books, tracts, and periodicals in outreach.

JOHN W. THOMASON

NORTHERN PLAINS BAPTIST FOUNDATION. An organization authorized by the Northern Plains Baptist Convention executive board in May, 1973, and incorporated, Nov. 8, 1973, with offices in Rapid City, SD. Leslie T. Crozier, Charles P. Harkins, and Jerry M. Glass were named as directors. John P. Baker, succeeded in Jan., 1977, by Roy W. Owen, was its registered agent. The first gift of more than $2,400 was from state missions offerings. Assets in Dec., 1979, totaled $31,707.

ROY W. OWEN

NORTHINGTON, MARY EVELYN (b. Clarksville, TN, May 15, 1885; d. Clarksville, TN, Nov. 28, 1974). State Woman's Missionary Union leader. Daughter of Michael Carr Northington, a merchant, and Nannie Neblett, she attended the Female Academy, Clarksville, TN, and graduated from WMU Training School, Louisville, KY. She served as Tennessee WMU fieldworker, 1908-13, and as WMU secretary for Illinois, 1915-20, and Alabama, 1920-23, before joining the staff of Tennessee WMU as executive secretary-treasurer in 1923. She served in this post for 30 years. The Tennessee WMU now gives $500 scholarships in her name to each Tennessee Baptist college. She is buried in Greenwood Cemetery, Clarksville, TN.

MARY JANE NETHERY

NORTHRIP, RAY ULMAN (b. Weatherford, OK, May 15, 1909; d. Ada, OK, Jan. 21, 1969). Physician and lay leader. The son of John Whitley and Ellen Fitzgerald Northrip, he attended Oklahoma Baptist University (B.S., 1932) and the University of Oklahoma School of Medicine (M.D., 1936). He was a partner in the Sugg Clinic at Ada, OK, 1949-69, after service in Ogbomosho, Nigeria, as a medical missionary, 1938-42. On Jan. 19, 1946, he married Mildred Crittenden. They had two children, Jann and Dennis.

Active in Ada's First Baptist Church where he was a deacon, Northrip was state Brotherhood president in 1953. He served as camp physician and medical director at Falls Creek Assembly, 1950-68. He is buried in Memorial Park Cemetery, Ada, OK.

J. M. GASKIN

NORTHWEST ASSOCIATIONS (cf. Oregon-Washington, Baptist General Convention of, Vol. II; Oregon-Washington Associations, Vol. III).

I. New Associations. PUGET SOUND. Organized May 5, 1975, by churches formerly in Evergreen and Mt. Rainier Baptist Associations, WA, following an initial meeting of messengers from the churches in Mar., 1975. Population and economic growth of King and Pierce County, WA, which spilled over into Snohomish and Thurston Counties, WA, made coordinated work of the two associations involved in this area desirable.

After consultation with the Northwest Baptist Convention and Home Mission Board personnel, pastors in Evergreen and Mt. Rainier Associations led the churches to dissolve those associations, form Puget Sound Association, and develop a single metropolitan mission program. In 1980, 50 churches and 15 missions reported 789 baptisms, 13,684 members, $2,818,578 total gifts, $446,483 mission gifts, and $18,411,700 property value.

II. Changes in Associations. EVERGREEN. Organized in 1950 in Northwest Washington, the association disbanded in 1975 in order for its churches to help form Puget Sound Association.

MOUNT RANIER. Organized in 1968 in the Olympia-Tacoma area, the association disbanded in 1975 in order for its churches to help form Puget Sound Association.

OREGON TRAIL. Organized in 1974 by three Oregon churches, Pendleton of Pendleton, Trinity Baptist Church of LaGrande, and New Hope of Baker, in an effort to create more involvement of churches in associational work and to assist the weaker churches. The association dissolved in 1979 when its churches returned to the Columbia Basin Association.

GALEN IRBY and O. RAY HARRIS

NORTHWEST BAPTIST CONVENTION (cf. Oregon-Washington, Baptist General Convention of, Vols. II, III). The Northwest Baptist Convention is the largest state convention among Southern Baptists in land area, with churches in Oregon, Washington, Northern Idaho, Northern California, the four western provinces of Canada, and one church in Mon-

tana. From the state office in Portland to the farthest church, Fellowship Baptist Church, Winnipeg, Manitoba, Canada, are some 2,500 miles.

I. History. In the past decade the membership of the churches in the NWBC grew from 41,279 to 65,000. The number of churches grew from 216 to 269, and church-type missions from 49 to 79. The Sunday School enrollment gained 27.7 percent, from 34,131 to 43,611.

The 1970s in the Northwest were marked by the dynamic leadership of the executive director, Dan C. Stringer. He became the leader in Apr., 1971, following the short administration of William Eugene Grubbs. Grubbs was executive secretary from Dec., 1968, to Dec., 1970, when he resigned to accept a position with the Foreign Mission Board, SBC.

Stringer resigned in the fall of 1979 to go to the Florida Baptist Convention as executive director. On June 6, 1980, Cecil Sims, the director of Canadian Missions for the NWBC, was elected the new NWBC executive director by a called state convention at Mill Park Baptist Church, Portland, OR.

The following served as president of the convention during the 1970s: Carrol E. Bolin, Jack H. Stuart, Cecil Sims, William O. Crews, Allen Schmidt, and Roy Phillip Masters Belcher.

II. Program of Work. *Evangelism.*—Lewis Steed resigned as director of evangelism in 1970 after serving for many years in this position. The job was upgraded to director of Evangelism Division, and Steed was followed by Howard Ramsey in 1972. Ramsey served until he resigned in 1979 to go to the Evangelism Division of the Home Mission Board.

Communications Division.—C. E. Boyle retired as editor of the *Northwest Baptist Witness* (formerly known as the *Pacific Coast Baptist,* and briefly as the *Northwest Baptist*) in 1976 after having served for 22 years. In Nov., 1976, William O. Crews began serving as director of communication for the convention and editor of the paper. He resigned in Aug., 1978, to become pastor of Magnolia Avenue Baptist Church, Riverside, CA. Herb Hollinger, a pastor from Issaquah, WA, and a native of Idaho, began serving in 1979. He expanded the ministry of the paper.

Church Services Division.—In 1972 Bob Flegal came from Arizona to be the director of the Church Services Division and a leader in Sunday School work. Under his leadership, the Sunday School enrollment rose from 34,131 to 43,611, a 27.7 percent increase. Woman's Missionary Union, Brotherhood, Student Work, and Church Training are also under this division.

Student Work.—The 1970s witnessed phenomenal growth in student work in the NWBC. Sam Fort served as Baptist Student Union director for the convention. In 1969 organized BSU groups were on 17 campuses, with 440 students reported to have been involved in the ongoing campus BSU program and approximately 1,400 students involved in at least one BSU-sponsored event on campus. By 1978-79, 2,700 students were involved in the ongoing BSU program with 11,000 students attending at least one BSU function. In 1978-79, there were 10 full-time BSU directors and five volunteers.

The summer missions program during this 10-year period included 91 BSU-sponsored summer missionaries sent out by the Northwest BSU. Giving to summer missionaries increased from $2,000 in 1969 to more than $8,000 in 1979.

The coming of Robert Cannon in 1975 to the University of Saskatchewan BSU was significant. Providing his own support, he led in the development of embryonic BSU's across Canada, 1975-79. Five strong BSU's resulted in this five-year period, all with full-time directors.

Woman's Missionary Union.—Sara Wisdom came from the Arkansas Baptist Convention staff to be WMU director in 1972 and has continued in this position. In 1969 the WMU membership was 4,433; by 1972 it had declined to 3,624, but this downward trend was reversed. In every year since 1972, membership gains have occurred. In 1979 WMU membership was reported as 4,453.

Missions Division.—In 1969 W. C. Carpenter was the director of the Division of Missions. He resigned in 1978 to take another assignment in Lewiston, ID, prior to retirement. Bill Peters became the new director. The most outstanding development was the beginning of a new work starter program.

Language Missions.—In the late 1960s, the NWBC created a new position of general language missionary. Harold Hitt was employed to fill this position. A new era of attention was focused on language missions by the Northwest.

By the end of 1969, a total of 10 places had some type of language ministry. The first ongoing deaf work was started at Calvary Baptist, Renton, WA, by Jim and Irene Stark. The first Chinese church in the Northwest was begun at Vancouver, British Columbia, under Jonathan Cheung.

The next year, the Vancouver Chinese Church was organized, and a new work was begun among the Spanish in Walla Walla, WA. In 1971 two new language works were started among the Spanish in Seattle, WA, and internationals in Eugene and Corvallis, OR.

In 1972 six new language works were begun, the most significant being the international seamen's ministry by the First Baptist Church, Lacey, WA (Port of Olympia), with Fern Powers and Carole Rodgers. This became a nationwide pattern.

In 1973 eight new language works were started, including the one among urban Indians in Portland, OR, by Harold Hitt. The international seamen's ministry continued to grow. Allen Elston, missionary to the Warm Springs Indians, was featured in the May, 1973, issue of *Home Missions* magazine.

In 1974 eight new language ministries were

initiated; Andrew Viera came as catalytic missionary to the Seattle area. The deaf work saw an increased interest while US-2ers Stan and Lynn Stepleton were in the convention.

In 1975 the First Baptist Church of the Deaf in Portland became the first independent deaf church in the SBC. Korean work was started in Tacoma under the leadership of Joseph Cho. A second Chinese church was begun in Edmonton, Alberta. Language units in existence at the end of 1975 totaled 22.

Korean and Japanese work at First Baptist Church, Lakewood, Tacoma, WA, experienced rapid growth in 1976 and 1977. In 1977 James Booth became pastor of the First Baptist Church of the Deaf in Portland, OR. He resigned in 1980 to go to Louisiana.

Deaf work in the Northwest saw another change with the coming of Fred DeBerry as associate pastor to the deaf at Calvary Baptist Church, Renton, WA, in 1978. This church has more than 50 deaf members. In the same year, Metropolitan Baptist, Portland, OR, began a ministry to the Hmong people from Laos. In addition, three new Korean works were started in Oregon.

Sponsorship of Indo-Chinese refugees by Northwest churches made important strides during 1979. Churches in Washington were second only to Texas; and with Oregon added, the Northwest was the leader among Southern Baptists. At the end of 1979, there were 40 places of language work in the convention.

Christian Social Ministries.—Elmer L. Whiten was one of only two state staff members to have continuous services from 1969 to 1980. He is associate director in the Cooperative Missions Division and works in the field of Christian Social Ministries.

Associational Missions.—Also under the Missions Division in 1980 were 14 directors of associational missions. Only Omer E. Hyde, Gilbert Skaar, and O. Ray Harris served through the 1970s as directors of associational missions in the NWBC. In July, 1980, O. Ray Harris retired as the missionary in the Puget Sound Baptist Association, which is in the Seattle-Tacoma area. Harris served more than 20 years in this post. He was succeeded by David Holden from Iowa. Holden arrived, July, 1980.

Northwest Baptist Foundation.—Harry Bonner, a longtime pastor in the Northwest, came to the Northwest Baptist Foundation as director and also as the stewardship director for the convention. During the 1970s, a dramatic increase occurred in the NWBC Cooperative Program gifts, increasing from $292,429 in 1970 to $972,355 in 1979. The portion forwarded to the national SBC Cooperative Program increased even more dramatically from $58,486 in 1970 to $281,983 in 1979.

Institutional Changes.—The convention took steps to divest itself of institutions with the transfer of Mt. Baker Baptist Assembly and the Seattle Student Center to the Puget Sound Baptist Association, and the transfer of Bailey

NORTHWEST STATISTICAL SUMMARY

Year	Associations	Churches	Church Membership	Baptisms	SS Enrollment	VBS Enrollment	CT Enrollment	WMU Enrollment	Brotherhood Enrollment	Ch. Music Enrollment	Mission Gifts	Total Gifts	Value Church Property
1969	22	214	39,237	2,273	33,153	23,315	14,464	4,517	1,229	3,432	$ 436,814	$ 3,337,803	$16,058,430
1970	22	222	41,296	2,396	33,501	21,539	14,719	4,300	1,232	3,873	480,495	3,631,490	17,742,299
1971	22	232	43,551	2,716	33,362	21,514	11,883	3,907	1,471	3,565	662,618	4,196,876	19,192,678
1972	22	234	44,641	2,874	32,408	23,081	10,834	3,597	1,119	3,532	736,197	4,498,421	20,737,776
1973	22	240	46,531	2,761	32,744	23,591	9,885	3,591	1,139	4,301	815,648	4,782,090	24,120,452
1974	23	246	49,043	3,193	35,521	26,459	10,741	3,626	1,398	4,835	1,001,258	5,413,685	27,401,128
1975	22	247	52,146	3,400	37,217	28,173	10,688	3,806	1,492	5,154	1,168,786	6,374,637	31,542,925
1976	22	249	54,972	3,288	40,989	22,198	10,975	3,911	1,579	4,982	1,390,259	7,340,643	36,055,651
1977	22	250	58,631	3,619	42,534	23,071	10,734	3,933	1,466	5,810	1,733,312	8,587,410	44,360,627
1978	22	261	61,667	3,853	42,174	23,094	10,369	4,193	1,547	6,532	1,843,141	10,225,056	51,951,158
1979	21	272	64,694	3,752	43,537	23,400	10,607	4,503	1,721	6,718	2,187,108	12,037,105	65,611,484
1980	21	285	67,138	4,436	46,967	25,309	11,459	4,579	1,786	7,000	2,749,682	13,042,149	74,492,638

SAM A. HARVEY

Memorial Boys Ranch to a non-Baptist group of trustees.

The location of the state Baptist office was changed in 1976 with the sale of the building on N.W. 29th Avenue and the purchase of the present Baptist Building at 1033 N.E. 6th Avenue. Following extensive remodeling, the building houses staff offices, and printing and secretarial areas, and provides a 5,000-square-foot parking garage. A conference and training area seats approximately 150 persons.

In 1980 a seminary satellite of Golden Gate Baptist Theological Seminary, Mill Valley, CA, was opened in Portland, OR. Called the Northwest Center, Ernest Loessner came as the first director. The format is unique, having as its main purpose the recruitment of pastors and church staff for the Northwest. Plans are to open a second location, possibly in Seattle, as soon as possible. Original funding for the Northwest Center came from the 1979 Sylvia Wilson State Mission Offering which raised an unprecedented $100,000.

Baptist Book Store.—Mildred Baker, the only manager the Baptist Book Store in the Northwest has ever had, retired in 1980. Originally located in Portland, OR, the store was moved across the Columbia River to Vancouver, WA, because of tax problems.

Canadian Committee.—In 1979 the Canadian Committee of the NWBC recommended to the convention that it be dissolved because it was no longer needed with the opening of Canada for help from the national SBC agencies. This committee had for years administered a limited mission program in Canada funded by the late William Fleming and the NWBC.

A unique feature of the convention is that it has cooperating churches in two nations, the United States and Canada. In 1977 the SBC voted to permit its boards to work, without restraint, on request from churches or Baptist bodies in Canada. The Canadian churches have been a cooperating part of the NWBC for many years, yet the Canadian churches cannot be seated at the SBC. In 1978 Cecil Sims, longtime pastor in the Northwest, went to give general direction to the Southern Baptist work in Canada. He served until his election as executive director of the NWBC in1980.

See also CANADIAN BAPTISTS; CANADIAN SOUTHERN BAPTISTS; CANADIAN—SBC RELATIONS.

SAM A. HARVEY

NORTHWEST BAPTIST FOUNDATION (III). The foundation provided approximately $300,000 in construction loans to 94 churches from 1968 to 1975. In the early 1970s the foundation began to provide estate planning seminars and private counsel to Northwest Baptists. These emphases have resulted in the establishment of student scholarship funds and trusts benefiting various aspects of Northwest Southern Baptist work. Harry G. Bonner continues as executive director. The Mar. 31, 1980, balance for the foundation was $725,600.

HARRY BONNER

NORTHWEST BAPTIST WITNESS (cf. *Pacific Coast Baptist,* Vol. III). State paper of the Northwest Baptist Convention. In an attempt to identify the paper more closely with the convention, messengers in the 1974 annual meeting approved changing *Pacific Coast Baptist* to *Northwest Baptist.* After further debate, the final name for the paper was approved by the 1975 convention as the *Northwest Baptist Witness.* A major change in the publication came at the end of 1976 when C. E. Boyle retired after 26 years as editor. At that time the *Witness* also became a part of a newly-created Division of Communications, which included the convention's printing department, public relations, and other communication-related work.

With the first issue of 1977 William O. Crews became editor. Crews had most recently served as president of the convention and was pastor of Metropolitan Baptist Church, Portland, OR. He served as director of the Division of Communications as well as editor of the *Witness.* Sep. 6, 1978, marked another change in the paper as Dan C. Stringer, the convention's executive director-treasurer, became interim editor upon the resignation of Crews. Stringer relinquished the editorship, Mar. 1, 1979, upon the arrival of Herb Hollinger as editor. Hollinger had been pastor of Foothills Baptist Church, Issaquah, WA, for more than five years.

The first issue under Hollinger's editorship introduced a new tabloid format. In conjunction with his appointment, the convention's Executive Board also approved a major change in distribution of the paper. Effective Jan. 1, 1980, all families of Northwest Baptist churches began receiving the paper with the costs absorbed by the churches' gifts to the Cooperative Program.

HERB HOLLINGER

NORTHWEST CENTER OF GOLDEN GATE BAPTIST THEOLOGICAL SEMINARY. See GOLDEN GATE BAPTIST THEOLOGICAL SEMINARY, NORTHWEST CENTER OF.

NORWOOD, JOSEPHINE CARROLL (b. Knightsdale, NC, Sep. 26, 1913; d. Richmond, VA, Nov. 8, 1978). State Woman's Missionary Union leader, speaker, and writer. Daughter of James Nathaniel and Hattie Lee (Wilson) Norwood, she graduated from Richmond Professional Institute of the College of William and Mary (B.S., 1949). In 1949-50 she studied at WMU Training School, Southern Baptist Theological Seminary, and the University of Louisville.

In 1950 Norwood was elected associate secretary of WMU of Virginia. She was responsible for the camping program, Business Women's Federation work, and the interracial work for the state until 1954, when she was elected executive secretary-treasurer of the WMU of Maryland. She served there until her retirement in 1978. Under her leadership, Maryland WMU developed Camp Wo-Me-To into a year-round family camp. She developed and guided the entire WMU program in all 11 states in the Northeast pioneer area beginning in 1957.

An avid Baptist historian, she led the Maryland WMU, in cooperation with WMU of the SBC, to place a bronze marker on the marble slab covering the grave of Annie Armstrong (*q.v.* I) in Baltimore. She compiled a collection of historical items, writings, books, and church records of Maryland Baptist history. This collection in the Maryland Baptist Building was named the Josephine Carroll Norwood History Collection in her memory. She served on the Historical Commission, SBC, 1972-80. She is buried in Forest Lawn Cemetery, Richmond, VA.

ELIZABETH LEIGHTON WILLING

NUESTRA TAREA. Monthly missions publication of the Language Department, Woman's Missionary Union, SBC, for Spanish-speaking people in the USA. The magazine's offices are located at the national WMU headquarters, Birmingham, AL.

Supported by the Home Mission Board, the magazine originated in San Antonio, TX. The first issue was published in 1955 with Esther B. Moye as editor. One of the associate editors was Martha Thomas Ellis, who later became editor and then consulting editor. In 1968 the offices moved to HMB headquarters, Atlanta, GA. That same year Doris Díaz joined the magazine as administrative editor. The magazine moved to its present location in 1972. Díaz continued as editor until 1975 when she became director of the newly formed Language WMU Department. Since 1975 there have been three editors: Carmen González, Grace E. Márquez, and Gladys Caballero.

DORIS DÍAZ

O

OAK HILL ACADEMY (II, III). A Virginia Baptist boarding school for grades 8 through 12 located in Grayson County, VA. The academy has 15 buildings on a 240-acre rural campus and serves students with special needs in a Christian community environment. When the school celebrated its centennial in 1978, enrollment was 200 students, some of whom came from foreign countries.

The school is fully accredited by the Virginia Department of Education and the United States goverment for teaching foreign students. Each student has an individual faculty advisor. The board of trustees, composed entirely of Virginia Baptists, was increased from 15 to 24 in 1975. Total assets on May 31, 1979, were $1,830,107. Robert B. Isner has served as president since Aug. 1, 1966.

JOHN S. MOORE

ODLE, JOE TAFT (b. West Frankfort, IL, Aug. 19, 1908; d. Jackson, MS, Mar. 24, 1980). Pastor, editor, author. Son of Harry Odle, Baptist pastor, and Winona (Dillon) Odle, he graduated from Union University, Jackson, TN (B.A., 1930), and studied at Southern Baptist Theological Seminary (1934). Mississippi College awarded him an honorary degree (D.D., 1949). He married Mabel Riley at Lone Oak, KY, July 17, 1930. Their children were Joe Thomas and Sarah. His pastorates included churches in Illinois and Tennessee (during high school and college); Kentucky (Barlow and Bandana, 1930-32; East, Paducah, 1932-43); and Mississippi (First, Crystal Springs, 1943-47; First, Gulfport, 1947-56).

He was associate executive-secretary, Mississippi Baptist Convention Board, 1956-59. He edited the *Baptist Record* from 1959 until his retirement in 1976. His editorial, "Smoke Over Mississippi" (Aug. 6, 1964), won two national press association awards. He was known as a strong defender of basic Baptist doctrines. Books he wrote include *It's a Great Life: Don't Miss It!* (1967); *Is Christ Coming Soon?* (1971); *Why I Am a Baptist* (1972); *The Coming of the King* (1974); and *Church Member's Handbook* (1941). Over 2,000,000 copies of the handbook had been sold by 1979.

Odle was vice-president, 1953, and recording secretary, 1977-79, of the Mississippi Baptist Convention; president of the Southern Baptist Press Association, 1971; and a member of Rotary. He is buried in Lakewood Memorial Cemetery, Jackson, MS.

ANNE WASHBURN MCWILLIAMS

OFFUTT, GARLAND KIMBLE, SR. (b. Jefferson County, KY, May 7, 1908; d. Jeffer-son County, KY, June 23, 1976). Pastor. The son of Elmore Thevalle Offutt, a minister, he was baptized by his father at Pleasant Green Baptist Church, Lexington, KY, in 1918. He studied at Kentucky State College (A.B.) and Simmons University (B.Th.). He was the first black to graduate with the Th.D. degree from Southern Baptist Theological Seminary, 1948. He served with the Home Mission Board and taught at the American Baptist Theological Seminary and at Simmons University. He served as pastor of churches in Bracktown and Ashland, KY. From 1948 to 1976 he was assistant pastor and pastor of West Chestnut Street Baptist Church, Louisville.

Offutt married Catherine Wilson. They had one son, Garland. Following her death, he married Laura Carter, Mar. 9, 1969. He is buried in Greenwood Cemetery, Lexington, KY.

WILLIAM H. ROGERS

OGDEN, HENRY ELLIS (b. Brownwood, TX, Oct. 6, 1887; d. Baxter Springs, KS, Mar. 8, 1966). Pastor. The son of Paul and Martha Virginia Ogden, farmers, he married Mary Ella Lewelling in 1908 in Rotan, TX. This marriage ended in divorce after 12 years. In 1924 he married Alta Pearl Spidell. His pastorates included Chanute, Caney, and Baxter Springs, KS; Blake Church near Avilla, MO; Bykota Church near Carthage, MO; Mound Valley, KS; Mindenmines, MO; and Key West, FL.

While Ogden was pastor of First Church, Baxter Springs, KS, 1935-48, he baptized 693 people, an average of one per week for more than 13 years. He also led this church to organize one of the earliest bus ministries during World War II. He wrote and published many hymns, including "Christ of Calvary," "Leaning on the Everlasting Arms," and "Since Jesus Came Into My Heart,"—the latter two not the familiar hymns by the same titles.

During Ogden's pastorate, the Baxter Springs Church established five missions: Sunnyside, Star, Westside in Baxter Springs, Riverton, all in Kansas, and Hockerville, OK. Riverton and Westside (now Fellowship Baptist Church) are still active.

On Oct. 4, 1958, he married Lillian Potter (Duffel) at Chetopa, KS. He is buried at Galena, KS.

GERALD DYER

OHIO, BAPTIST FOUNDATION OF THE STATE CONVENTION OF BAPTISTS IN. The first gift to the foundation, $1,600 in church bonds, was received in 1969 to establish a memorial fund for a retired pastor's wife who had died. In the first 10 years of operation, the foundation served as trustee for 18 different funds. In 1980 the corpus of funds held totaled $60,600, and earnings for designated causes reached $11,122.

The Baptist causes benefiting from the funds are as follows: foreign missions, Baptist Student Union field work, beginning new churches, state missions, scholarships, seminaries, and the general fund which is designated by the trustees on an annual basis. Property valued at $300,000 was also received and transferred to Baptist Benevolence, Inc., to begin a retirement center. The foundation's operating budget comes from state convention Cooperative Program receipts. Darty F. Stowe continues as executive director.

See also OHIO, STATE CONVENTION OF BAPTISTS IN, VOL. III.

DARTY F. STOWE

OHIO, STATE CONVENTION OF BAPTISTS IN (II, III).

As the 1970s began, churches and missions in Western Pennsylvania and the part of West Virginia contiguous to Ohio were affiliated with the State Convention of Baptists in Ohio. In 1970 state conventions were formed in those states, and Ohio no longer sponsored the churches and missions. In all, about 100 congregations once classified with Ohio went into two new state conventions. This temporary statistical loss to Ohio in a number of churches, missions, and organizational memberships was recouped later in the decade.

As the 1970s closed, Ohio had 452 churches and 111 missions associated with its statewide Southern Baptist ministry. Total membership of churches and missions topped 100,000 for the first time during the decade. The 1970s ended with Ray E. Roberts, the convention's only executive secretary, having announced his forthcoming retirement.

1970.—In 1970 Gilbert E. Wilder, at that time associate Sunday School director for the state convention, became director of the Department of Church Training and Music. He was still serving in that capacity as 1980 began. Grady Evans, then regional director for student ministries on campuses in Southwestern Ohio (the Cincinnati-Hamilton-Dayton area), was called in 1970 to become director of the Student Ministries Department for the state convention, a post he still held as the decade ended.

Orville H. Griffin, area director of missions for Cincinnati, moved in 1970 to Dayton as director of missions for the association serving that city and several surrounding counties. Nelson E. Russell, associate in the state convention Missions Department, succeeded Griffin in 1970 as director of missions for Cincinnati Baptist Association and Southern Hills Baptist Association. Charles E. Magruder, a native Ohioan, formerly missions director in Buffalo, NY, while that area was under Ohio's sponsorship, moved to Columbus, OH, to become director of missions for Capital City Baptist Association. Both

Russell and Magruder continued in these posts through the 1970s.

Members of the First Baptist Church, West Jefferson, near Columbus, observed their sesquicentennial in Nov., 1970. Although the church was 150 years old, it had been affiliated with Southern Baptists only since 1959.

1971.—In Mar., 1971, Arlie Carter resigned as manager of Seneca Lake Baptist Assembly, the convention-sponsored encampment in East Central Ohio. He had been manager more than three years. Carter was succeeded by Clyde Bowen, a Dayton pastor for 11 years.

The executive board of the state convention, meeting in Apr., 1971, realigned associational boundaries and called Frank Miller, a pastor in the greater Cincinnati metro area, as director of missions for Erie and Summit Baptist Associations, with offices in Akron. Miller was still in the position as 1979 ended.

John Tollison, director of missions for the state of Delaware (an association of the Baptist Convention of Maryland), came, Dec. 1, 1971, as director of missions for two associations (Cuyahoga and Northern Ohio) covering the greater Cleveland metro area and some cities just west of Cleveland. Earlier Tollison had been director of missions in the Syracuse, NY, area, when Southern Baptists there were associated with the Ohio Convention. Tollison remained in Cleveland throughout the rest of the decade.

1972.—The first Lay Evangelism School in the convention, held Mar. 13-17, 1972, was hosted by churches in the greater Columbus area. More than 1,000 attended. Southern Baptists in Ohio launched a new venture in May, 1972, by setting up a Baptist Bible Institute educational program at Seneca Lake Baptist Assembly. The following quarter of 1972, the executive board elected James R. Pinkley, Jr., as missions director for Maumee Valley Baptist Association, which encompassed Toledo and adjoining Northwestern Ohio. Pinkley came from a similar post in Kentucky. Pinkley was still serving in this position at the close of the 1970s. A record of more than 450 men attended the Laymen's Witnessing Retreat, an annual event, in Aug., 1972. Robert Hall, for 14 years missons director in Southeast Ohio, was reassigned to an area along Lake Erie in North Central Ohio. The area included a section between Cleveland and Toledo but did not include either of those cities. The executive board worked out this realignment in Nov., 1972.

1973.—Three new area directors of missions were called during 1973. William Murray, a pastor in Warren in Northeast Ohio, was assigned to Muskingum Valley and Scioto Valley Baptist Associations. His call was effective Apr. 1.

Don Davidson, pastor at Defiance, Ohio, was called, effective Sep. 1, 1973, as director of missions for Steel Valley Baptist Association, whose principal city is Youngstown. He succeeded Ross Hughes, who retired.

Clifford B. Coleman, a pastor at McArthur within the region affected, was called, effective Oct. 16, 1973, as director of missions in Scioto Valley Baptist Association, after the association, formerly paired with Muskingum Valley Baptist Association, was assigned its own missions director.

Ohio's first Youth Evangelism Celebration, held in Columbus, drew about 1,000 youth.

Charles Raley resigned as director of the Sunday School Department, July 16, 1973. Michael R. Collins, an associate in the Sunday School Department of the Florida Baptist Convention, was elected to succeed Raley and took office, Dec. 1, 1973.

Clyde Bowen, manager of Seneca Lake Baptist Assembly, resigned effective Sep. 3, 1973, to accept the pastorate of a church in Sidney, OH.

The 400th church affiliated with the convention was constituted in Worthington, a suburb of Columbus, on Sep. 9, 1973.

1974.—The convention's 20th anniversary year (1974) featured an emphasis on evangelism. In the same year, the convention adopted the report of its future program committee, which included a new staff organization chart. At the same time, the convention voted to send the *Ohio Baptist Messenger* into the home of every church family in Ohio at state Cooperative Program expense. Formerly, it went only into homes of families in churches subscribing to the paper for their members. This decision helped double the circulation of the *Ohio Baptist Messenger* before the end of the decade.

The convention established 10-year goals for baptisms, new congregations started, and organizational activities. The convention's endorsement of a $375,000 bond issue for First Baptist Church of Huber Heights (a section of Dayton) was the largest the convention had ever endorsed. For the first time, more than $1,000,000 in Cooperative Program gifts came in from churches during 1974.

1975.—In Jan., 1975, the state convention executive board voted to make Ohio Baptist Bible Institute, started three years earlier to supplement the seminary extension ministry, a part of the new Boyce Bible School, Louisville, KY.

Harold Hamilton resigned as manager of Seneca Lake Baptist Assembly effective Mar. 1, 1975, and former manager Clyde Bowen returned for a second time to the assembly managership effective May 26, 1975.

On May 29, 1975, Flanery and Ethel Brooks of Mason, OH, conditionally deeded their 65-acre farm, valued at more than $250,000, to the state convention. The principal condition was that the property be used to establish a retirement center, under convention sponsorship, for Baptist senior citizens. The state convention at this point had no institutional ministry.

1976.—Three members of the state convention staff announced their retirement during the first half of 1976. They were L. H. Moore, editor, *Ohio Baptist Messenger;* W. Leonard Stigler, director of evangelism and stewardship; and Mrs. A. L. Kirkwood, director of Woman's Missionary Union.

The state convention budget in 1976 exceeded $2,000,000 for the first time. Converts baptized totaled 8,147 for the previous associational year, a record which still stood at the end of the 1970s. Total membership of affiliated churches and missions reached 110,126.

Personnel changes were paramount in 1976. Rondel T. Martin, Youngstown pastor, was called to the convention staff as director of Brotherhood when William H. Slagle, who held the post, was assigned a newly created staff position as properties manager. Martin's appointment was effective Feb. 2, 1976. Helen Allan became the new WMU director, and Theo Sommerkamp the new editor of the *Ohio Baptist Messenger.*

Slagle resigned as director of property management and was succeeded by Virgil Barnett, Cleveland pastor, Sep. 1. Four new directors of missions were elected—Paul Nevels, longtime Ohio pastor, for Southern Hills Baptist Association; Joe Baker, Dayton pastor, for Greater Dayton Baptist Association; Don Gillis, Huron pastor, for Miami Valley and Southwestern Baptist Associations; and William Barner of Indiana for Buckeye Central Baptist Association.

Nevel's appointment enabled Nelson Russell to devote full time to Cincinnati Baptist Association. Barner's coming enabled Gary Harden to devote full time to being missions director for West Central Baptist Association. Previously both Russell and Harden served a two-association area.

Gillis succeeded L. H. Gardner, who moved out of the state, and Baker succeeded Orville H. Griffin, elected to succeed W. Leonard Stigler as convention director of evangelism and stewardship.

Myrtle Anderson, manager of the Baptist Book Store in Ohio, retired. The Sunday School Board of the Southern Baptist Convention named Royce Dodd of Texas to succeed her, effective Oct., 1976. Jon H. Fisher succeeded Dodd in 1977.

First sessions of the new Columbus branch of Boyce Bible School were opened in the fall of 1976, using a Baptist-owned building adjacent to the state convention office building.

1977.—In 1977 membership of Far Hills Baptist Church, Dayton, the largest among Southern Baptists in Ohio, topped 3,000. Virgil Barnett resigned in 1977 as director of property management and returned to the pastorate. The position was left unfilled. Circulation of the *Ohio Baptist Messenger* moved past the 25,000 mark for the first time in 1977.

1978.—In 1978 the Home Mission Board designated Cleveland as one of a select number in its Key Cities program for planning expanded metropolitan ministries. At the 1978 convention Ray E. Roberts announced his forthcoming retirement, effective in June, 1980. He had been the only executive secretary of the state convention.

1979-80.—In 1979 Ohio and six other states in the North Central Mission Thrust engaged in a special year of evangelism. This was Ohio's year to coordinate the annual emphasis of the NCMT.

OHIO STATISTICAL SUMMARY

Year	Associations	Churches	Church Membership	Baptisms	SS Enrollment	VBS Enrollment	CT Enrollment	WMU Enrollment	Brotherhood Enrollment	Ch. Music Enrollment	Mission Gifts	Total Gifts	Value Church Property
1969	22	399	86,815	6,979	80,138	53,239	31,614	12,178	4,608	9,557	$1,010,705	$8,351,580	$35,805,016
1970	21	402	90,735	7,261	79,263	51,012	28,131	11,077	4,307	9,998	1,086,428	8,997,955	38,220,708
1971	17	370	86,413	7,108	72,203	52,399	20,458	9,277	4,013	9,146	1,581,824	8,982,491	37,716,672
1972	17	381	91,540	7,505	72,484	54,234	18,955	9,234	4,246	9,947	1,671,177	9,644,670	42,338,293
1973	17	389	98,246	7,598	75,719	49,619	18,100	9,504	4,208	11,144	1,782,670	10,627,369	46,978,603
1974	17	401	104,024	8,117	78,353	54,118	18,463	9,523	4,350	11,594	2,078,090	11,876,355	53,512,630
1975	18	413	110,104	8,147	81,692	58,572	17,889	10,179	4,615	11,626	2,049,821	12,827,682	60,223,161
1976	18	422	115,002	7,207	88,067	51,842	16,690	9,919	5,217	11,374	2,342,287	14,577,605	71,251,568
1977	18	435	118,113	5,969	89,960	48,910	16,336	9,683	4,612	11,765	2,730,645	16,048,037	78,144,006
1978	18	443	120,568	5,381	87,061	45,424	15,385	9,903	4,483	11,419	2,822,147	17,081,354	84,820,232
1979	18	450	124,036	6,294	85,219	43,551	15,533	9,535	4,553	12,249	3,232,993	19,232,962	96,678,055
1980	18	450	128,119	7,428	87,438	46,959	16,073	10,048	4,973	13,150	3,718,272	20,863,425	110,793,566

THEO SOMMERKAMP

The state convention session in 1979 celebrated the 25th anniversary of the convention. The executive board elected Tal D. Bonham, evangelism director for Oklahoma Baptists, to succeed Roberts as executive secretary, effective Apr. 1, 1980.

Plans for a fund drive for the proposed Baptist retirement center, to have been called Brookhaven, were indefinitely postponed for lack of interest in establishing the institution. Maude Skinner became Ohio's first Mission Service Corps volunteer. She was also the first in the entire SBC assigned to Japan. Harold and Marjorie Lloyd of Montgomery, AL, were the first MSC appointees to come to Ohio. They worked as church planters in Mount Gilead, seat of the last county in Ohio lacking a Southern Baptist church or mission.

See also PENNSYLVANIA-SOUTH JERSEY, BAPTIST CONVENTION OF; WEST VIRGINIA CONVENTION OF SOUTHERN BAPTISTS.

BIBLIOGRAPHY: L. H. Moore, *The History of Southern Baptists in Ohio* (1979).

THEO SOMMERKAMP

OHIO ASSOCIATIONS (II, III).

I. New Associations. NORTHWEST. Organized Oct. 12, 1974, by six churches and four missions formerly affiliated with the Maumee Valley Baptist Association. In 1979 eight churches reported 99 baptisms, 1,136 members, $300,567 total gifts, $30,533 mission gifts, and $1,168,000 property value.

II. Changes in Associations. CINCINNATI. Name changed from Greater Cincinnati in 1972.

CUYAHOGA. Changed name to Greater Cleveland Association in 1973.

FRONTIER. Located in New York State, this association affiliated with the Baptist Convention of New York when the convention was organized in Sep., 1969.

GREATER CINCINNATI. Name changed to Cincinnati in 1972.

GREATER CLEVELAND. Name changed from Cuyahoga in 1973.

GREATER HUNTINGTON. Comprised of churches in West Virginia, this association affiliated with the West Virginia Convention of Southern Baptists when that convention was formed in Oct., 1970.

GREATER PITTSBURG. Comprised of churches in the Pittsburg, PA, area, this association affiliated with the Baptist Convention of Pennsylvania-South Jersey when that convention was organized in Oct., 1970.

GREATER ROCHESTER. Comprised of churches in the Rochester, NY, area, this association affiliated with the Baptist Convention of New York when that convention was formed in Sep., 1969.

PIONEER. Comprised of West Virginia churches, this association affiliated with the West Virginia Convention of Southern Baptists when that convention was organized in Oct., 1970.

UPPER OHIO VALLEY. Comprised of West Virginia churches, this association affiliated with the West Virginia Convention of Southern Baptists when that convention was organized in Oct., 1970.

ARTHUR L. WALKER

OHIO BAPTIST BUILDERS. An organization of volunteer workers formed in June, 1977, by Rondel T. Martin, director, Brotherhood Department, State Convention of Baptists in Ohio, to help needy churches or missions erect their first buildings.

Enlisting a superintendent and team, Ohio Baptist Builders strives to put the building under roof in six days as well as construct inside partitions, baptistry, and platform. The local congregation must prepare the building foundation and provide room and board for the volunteer builders while on the site.

The first church assisted was New Life Baptist Church in Mansfield, OH, within a few weeks after Ohio Baptist Builders was formed. Through the 1979 season the organization had assisted nine churches in Ohio.

Ohio Baptist Builders primarily assists churches which cannot afford the cost of contract labor. Building superintendents for projects are men with professional construction experience, and many other workers are also experienced, although this is not a requirement for a helper. The superintendents and other volunteers are recruited from within memberships of Ohio Southern Baptist churches, with 139 persons on the ready list.

Although basically for men, participation is not limited to men. Women and children sometimes assist in construction.

THEO E. SOMMERKAMP

OHIO BAPTIST MESSENGER, THE (III). L. H. Moore, elected editor of this Ohio Baptist newspaper in 1966, retired in 1976. During those years circulation grew from 6,300 to 24,441. In 1975 financial support of the paper was changed from the traditional church family plan—in which churches paid for subscriptions for their members—to full convention support, by which the paper was sent to each family without cost to the churches.

Theo E. Sommerkamp became editor in 1976. In 1980 the format of the paper was changed from newsmagazine style to a tabloid newspaper. The circulation was 27,000 in Apr., 1980.

L. H. MOORE

OHRN, ARNOLD THEODORE (b. Raymond, WI, Jan. 22, 1889; d. Berkeley, CA, July 31, 1963). Baptist World Alliance leader. His father was J. A. Ohrn, a pastor. After attending the University of Oslo (M.A., M.Th.), he taught at Baptist Theological Seminary, Oslo, 30 years and also served as general secretary of Baptist Union of Norway. While serving as general secretary of the BWA in Washington, 1948-60, he was one of four ministers from the United States to visit Baptist churches in the Union of Soviet Socialist Republics in Aug.,

1955, the first such visit by a religious group following the Russian revolution.

C. E. BRYANT

OKINAWA, MISSION IN (III). On May 15, 1972, the United States government returned Okinawa to Japanese control. Baptist work continued much as before. Southern Baptist English-language church work expanded to include cooperation with the Okinawa Baptist Convention. In 1977 William and Mary Louise (Gulley) Medling completed 33 years of missionary service, 13 in Okinawa. They were the first missionaries to be retired from Okinawa. The Naha Calvary Church (English language) disbanded in 1977 because of the reduction of United States military forces. The Okinawa Baptist Convention has 18 churches and a membership of 1,564, including three English-language churches. Missionaries total seven, including one journeyman.

GEORGE H. HAYS

OKLAHOMA, ASSEMBLIES AND CAMPS IN. Oklahoma Baptists' white, Indian, and black youth are served by 24 organized assemblies and camps. This figure does not include several camps operated by Free Will, Landmark, and Independent Baptists.

Burge.—Located 25 miles northeast of Oklahoma City on 42 acres of land, Camp Burge began in 1959 when Mary Burge gave the land to New Hope Church, Oklahoma City. The camp opened in 1961. The title changed to East Zion Association (Black) in 1961, and to the Oklahoma Baptist State Convention (Black) in 1966. In 1979, facilities included the original land, a dormitory, chapel, assembly building, dining room, and caretaker's home, all valued at $300,000. Camps for all ages run from June to autumn. Total campers in 1979 were 700, with a $10,000 budget provided from the state convention's Cooperative Program.

Caddo.—Red Rock Canyon Youth Camp, operated by the Caddo Association, began in 1964. In 1979 there were 179 campers. Out of a $4,200 budget, a rental of $531 was paid the state park service for use of facilities. The association's board governs the camp. In 1980 there were 420 campers.

Central.—The Central Association holds a junior youth camp annually at Roman Nose State Park. In 1979 a budget of $3,200 cared for 169 campers.

Choctaw-Chickasaw Indian.—Since 1962 a camp for Choctaw-Chickasaw Indian youth has been held at Kiamichi Assembly. The 1979 budget of $1,000 was provided by participating Indian churches.

Davis.—Camp Davis is located three miles south of Haskell, OK, on a 22-acre tract of land. Named for its founder, Charles H. Davis, the camp is owned by the Creek District Baptist Association (Black), of which Davis has been moderator 54 years (since 1926). The camp was founded in 1963. Property consists of the original land and five buildings, including a chapel, and is valued at $30,000. In 1979 a $3,000 budget supported by churches in the association provided for 500 campers.

Deaf.—In 1958, Leslie Gunn, Oklahoma missionary to the deaf, founded the state camp for the deaf at Falls Creek with 25 campers. Ages are 10-20, with sessions held at Falls Creek from the beginning except 1970-75 when the camp was held at Camp Hudgens and 1979 at Lela Assembly. Since 1978, Randy Cash, director of ministries for the Oklahoma Baptist Conference for the Deaf and Blind, has been camp director. The normal attendance most years has been 100. The $500 annual budget comes from Woman's Missionary Union offerings and the state deaf conference.

East Central.—East Central Association began holding an annual camp at Kiamichi Assembly in 1959. The $1,800 budget comes from churches of the association and from registration fees.

Gibson (I, III).—Facilities include a dining hall with storm shelter, recreation area, swimming pool, tabernacle, offices, guest cottage, caretaker's home, ball courts, shop building, amphitheater, and eight church-owned cabins. In 1979 the budget was $29,000, property value was $300,000, and total registration was 200.

Grand Lake (I, III).—Property consists of 65 acres of land, a dining hall, tabernacle, six teaching shelters, playground, swimming pool, and 24 cabins. In 1979 total registration was 891. Financial support in 1980 was provided by registration fees and $15,575 from the association's budget. Property value is about $300,000.

Great Plains.—Indian youth from the Comanche, Kiowa, Caddo, Delaware, and Wichita tribes rent for $400 per year the facilities of Southwest Assembly for an encampment. Since 1967, the Great Plains Indian Fellowship has functioned as successor to the extinct (since 1963) Great Plains Indian Association. David B. Warren, Home Mission Board worker with internationals in Oklahoma, is adviser and in 1979 Amon Harjo was camp director. Attendance was 40. A budget of $850 was provided by supporting churches and Oklahoma WMU.

Green Country (formerly Disney, III).—The name was changed from Disney to Green Country Assembly, Sep. 10, 1977. Property consists of 45 acres of land, dining hall, tabernacle, swimming pool, dormitories, recreation area, teaching pavilions, and church-owned cabins, all valued at $125,000 in 1980. Income in 1979 was $27,940 from registration fees and churches in Rogers and Craig-Mayes Associations. The 1979 registration was 725, and the 1980 budget was $27,472.

Indian Falls Creek.—The Indian Falls Creek Assembly began in 1947 when 333 Indians met on the Falls Creek Assembly grounds. It has met annually since that date. The peak registration was 1,419 in 1964. In 1979 the record number of 40 tribes was represented with 1,280 campers. Total registrations for the years 1947-79 were 29,018.

Kamp Kay.—July 22-26, 1945, Perry Association started Kamp Kay at Camp McFadden seven miles east of Ponca City. Registration was 150. Since 1947 the camp has been sponsored by Kay Association, and it moved to Lela Assembly in 1961. In 1979 a rental of $200 was paid Lela Assembly out of a $1,500 budget for 93 campers.

Lela.—Located seven miles west of Pawnee, Camp Lela was transferred to Cimarron Association by the Home Mission Board, SBC, in 1964. Property in 1979 consisted of 40 acres of land and seven buildings valued at $172,500. Total registration for six weeks of camp and 27 retreats in 1979 was 1,779. The 1980 budget of $10,805 was provided from camper fees and the Cimarron Association's budget.

Muskogee-Seminole-Wichita Indian.—Located on 40 acres of land near Henryetta, OK, the Muskogee-Seminole-Wichita Indian Assembly was founded in 1959. Owned by the Muskogee-Seminole-Wichita Indian Association in Oklahoma, there are 30 buildings to house campers, provide dining services, and serve as classrooms. Property value in 1980 was about $300,000.

Northwestern (II, III).—In 1979 Northwestern Assembly's property consisted of 40 acres of land four miles northeast of Vici, OK, a tabernacle, dining hall, four dormitories, swimming pool, and tennis court—all valued at $300,000. In 1979 there were 170 campers. The 1980 budget was $35,000.

Perry.—In 1952 Perry Association began its own camp when it discontinued joint operation of Kamp Kay with Kay Association. Sessions are held at Lela Assembly for an annual rental of $377. In 1979 a budget of $2,667 provided for 129 campers.

Southwest (II, III).—In 1979 there were 17 buildings on 17 acres of land adjacent to Lake Lugert, which is leased for $350 per year. Property value in 1979 was $400,000. The operating budget was $20,115. Al Wilson became resident manager in 1979.

Southwest Indian.—In 1979 the Southwest Indian encampment was started at the Arapaho powwow grounds near Colony, OK. Max Malone was director for 65 youth from the Cheyenne and Arapaho tribes.

Spanish.—Since 1964 a statewide Spanish camp has been held at the Southwest Assembly grounds. A 1979 budget of $1,500 included $400 rental for facilities. Funds were provided from registration and the Baptist General Convention of Oklahoma.

Ta-Na-Ha.—Camp Ta-Na-Ha was founded by the WMU of Capital Association in 1972 by the purchase of 80 acres of land for $60,000. The camp began for Acteens, Girls in Action, and Royal Ambassadors. Ownership was transferred to the association in 1974. Land and a large metal building, four miles east of Arcadia, were valued at $400,000 in 1979. Expenditures in 1978-79 were $15,447.

See also CAMP HUDGENS; CAMP NUNNY-CHA-HA (OKLAHOMA); CHEROKEE ASSEMBLY; FALLS CREEK ASSEMBLY; KIAMICHI BAPTIST ASSEMBLY; TULAKOGEE ASSEMBLY, OKLAHOMA.

BIBLIOGRAPHY: J. M. Gaskin, *Baptist Milestones in Oklahoma* (1966); *The Falls Creek Story* (1967); *Sights and Sounds of Falls Creek* (1980).

                                        J. M. GASKIN

OKLAHOMA, BAPTIST GENERAL CONVENTION OF (II, III).

When Joe L. Ingram became executive director in 1971, he led the convention to revise the structure of its program of work. Major program developments since 1969 are described below.

Annuity.—Roscoe C. Miller directed annuity promotion and services, 1957-72. The convention's board voted, Oct. 5, 1972, to establish the office of Annuity and Ministerial Services effective Jan. 1, 1973, with Johnson Thomas Roberts as director. In cooperation with the Annuity Board, SBC, the office keeps church leadership informed of the Annuity Board plans, which are designed to provide insurance and retirement needs for staff members and their families. The office maintains a biographical data file on ministers and other church staff; provides brochures on the work of pulpit committees; keeps current files on retired ministers available for supply work; assists churches in securing pulpit supplies upon request; counsels pastors and pulpit committees when requested; and encourages and assists church staff members in the field of continuing education.

J. T. ROBERTS

Brotherhood.—This department reported a low enrollment for the state in 1969 with work in 446 churches. In 1970 the new Grouping-Grading Plan was put in effect when Brotherhood assumed responsibility for first, second, and third grade Royal Ambassadors. In 1971 Mission Education Dialogues (MEDs) were conducted in each state association to interpret mission education for men and boys, 503 churches reported men's work, and the department set up a statewide disaster relief program.

In 1972 reports indicated 677 pastors and staff attended the MEDs, and 125 new units of men/boys' work were begun. That year 739 churches reported Brotherhood work with an enrollment of 18,165. In 1972 a lay couples' retreat began in place of the state Brotherhood convention.

Laddie Adams succeeded Henry Chennault, May 1, 1973. That year the department assumed administrative responsibility for the world missions conferences. Bob Banks left Oklahoma in 1974 for a post with the Brotherhood Commission, SBC, and Adams was elected director. Paul McCullough became associate in charge of Royal Ambassador work, Mar. 1. Lay renewal work was scheduled in 46 churches in 1975. In 1977 the anniversary of RA work in Oklahoma was the theme for the RA congress. That was the last year of the lay couples' retreat.

In 1978 joint area leadership training conferences with Woman's Missionary Union were begun in 15 locations, giving more than 700 men training in missions action and missions education. A statewide men's rally began at Falls Creek with over 600 in attendance.

World missions conferences are held in six to nine associations each year on a five-year rotating cycle. In 1979 Brotherhood and RA work were reported in 559 churches.

LADDIE ADAMS

Child Care.—This department is a multiple-service agency helping children and families in crisis. Most children served are dependent and neglected; some are emotionally disturbed; a few need supervision. Children are served without regard to race, color, creed, or national origin. About 10 percent are Indian, 5 percent black, and 5 percent Mexican-American. The agency is licensed by Oklahoma's Department of Human Services. The convention board serves as the governing body.

Lowell D. Milburn has been department director since 1969. In 1979 Christian guidance was provided for 634 children in four institutions. This number included 92 in foster care, 71 unwed mothers, 29 adoptions, and family counseling and aid. The 1979 budget was $1,732,000. Financial support comes from three main sources: Cooperative Program, endowment, and the annual Mother's Day offering. Other sources are birthday offerings, memorials, sponsorships, and special gifts. In 1978 the convention published a history of this work entitled *The Child Care Ministry of Oklahoma Baptists,* by J. M. Gaskin.

LOWELL D. MILBURN

Cooperative Missions.—J. T. Roberts served as secretary of the Department of Missions until Dec. 31, 1972. The convention changed the name of the department to Cooperative Missions, Jan. 1, 1973, and appointed Robert Eugene Haskins, who had been language missions director since Jan. 16, 1970, as director. Associational services, world missions conferences, in-service guidance, and seminary extension were assigned to other departments. The director assumed leadership for language missions, chaplaincy, Christian Service Corps and other volunteer programs, interfaith witness, church extension, resort missions, and the US-2 program.

Bob W. Lovejoy succeeded John W. Brill, Apr. 1, 1971, as department associate director. He works with National Baptists, church-community ministries, and student summer missions.

In 1978 Oklahoma involvement in Mission Service Corps, a new program of Southern Baptists to enlist 5,000 short-term missions volunteers by 1982, was assigned to this department. In 1979 the Refugee and Immigration Services program was assumed by the department with Bob W. Lovejoy named coordinator.

ROBERT E. HASKINS

Evangelism.—John Allen Pennington was the convention's first secretary of evangelism and established a basic growth pattern by giving consistent emphasis to simultaneous revivals. This was followed by the Personal Evangelism Institute in 1969-70 to provide witness training for lay persons and counseling youth at Falls Creek.

In 1971-72, a major thrust was given personal

witness training through TELL schools, youth witness training, counseling materials written for Falls Creek, and cooperation with churches and associations in developing a renewal strategy. The years 1973-79 saw renewed interest in local church revivals and area crusades with continued emphasis on training through TELL schools, TELL witness, and WOW. The state evangelism conference and the youth evangelism conferences have grown in numbers and influence. These strategies, implemented into the "Growing an Evangelistic Church" concept, have resulted in a balanced approach in evangelism and some of Oklahoma's best years in baptisms. The department has led in crusades and witness training in work in some new states, South Africa, England, and Hong Kong.

Directors of evangelism since 1948 have been John Allen Pennington, 1948-69; Jerold Robert McBride, 1969-71; Charles Billy Hogue, 1971-73; Tal D. Bonham, 1973-79; and Jerry Don Abernathy, 1980-   . Associate directors have included Joe Lynn Ford, 1972-74, and Clyde R. Cain, 1974-   .

CLYDE R. CAIN

Master Plan.—In 1978 Executive Director Joe L. Ingram proposed what he called a "Master Plan" for the 1980s. The plan projected an increase in Cooperative Program giving to $20,000,000, and a $25,000,000 endowment campaign to be completed by 1985. The campaign was designed to secure endowment and increased annual funds for Oklahoma Baptist institutions and agencies on a percentage basis to fill the gap between income and expenses caused by inflation. On June 1, 1979, M. Judson Cook became general director for the Master Plan. Cook had worked in promotion and fund raising for the Child Care Department since 1956.

M. JUDSON COOK

Music.—Under the leadership of Eugene Monroe Bartlett, Jr., church music enrollment in Oklahoma churches increased from 40,084 in 1969 to 55,788 in 1979.

While on furlough from service as music missionary in Kenya, East Africa, Glenn T. Boyd was appointed associate director in June, 1976, joining Bartlett and Mary June Tabor, assistant, who was employed in 1951. Boyd served until June, 1977, when he returned to Kenya. Paul D. Magar became associate in Jan., 1978. He came from the staff of Olivet Church, Oklahoma City.

In the annual session of the state convention in Nov., 1979, Bartlett announced his retirement, which became effective in the spring of 1980 after 26 years of service. The convention's board elected Boyd to succeed Bartlett, effective Sep. 1, 1980.

PAUL D. MAGAR

Planning and Promotion.—Established in the reorganization in 1972, this office is headed by Lyle Garlow, associate executive director of the convention. Areas of work assigned to the office are Cooperative Program promotion, steward-

ship promotion, associational services, church administration, coordinated promotion planning, and calendar coordination. Public relations, an original assignment, was transferred in 1979 to the *Baptist Messenger.* Planning and promotion relate to convention departments involved in church programming: Brotherhood, Church Music, Cooperative Missions, Evangelism, Religious Education, and Woman's Missionary Union—a convention auxiliary with department status. Relating associational services to the Planning and Promotion office has given strength and greater visibility to associational work and the role of directors of missions. Glenn Brown, associate director since 1972, is responsible for stewardship promotion and church administration.

LYLE GARLOW

Religious Education.—The years 1969-80 were marked by new growth in Sunday School enrollment. After a decline, 1964-71, enrollment began an upswing, and by 1978 a new all-time high was reached with 340,811 reported. This growth trend continued through 1979. The decline in Church Training was reversed, with an increase reported in 1979.

Besides Sunday School and Church Training, other areas of work assigned to this department since 1973 include church building consultation, Falls Creek's annual program, library services, Vacation Bible Schools, and recreation. On July 8, 1971, Bill C. Haggard succeeded Lyle Garlow as Religious Education director.

In 1980 department workers included Darlene Koch, childhood education, since 1970; Ann Gardner, youth education, since 1975; and Billy Allen, adult education, since 1977.

BILL C. HAGGARD

Retirement Centers and Chaplaincy.—Retirement centers and nursing homes are operated in Oklahoma City, Hugo, and Owasso under a committee of the convention's board of directors. The committee recommends appointment of chaplains to these centers and to the seven hospitals operated by the Baptist Health Care Corporation of Oklahoma. The Baptist Retirement Center at Oklahoma City, opened in 1965, is operated by Baptist Laymen's Corporation. Don Donalson is administrator. Sam Garner administers the Hugo Golden Age Home, opened in 1958. The Tulsa Baptist Retirement Center at Owasso, a 96-unit apartment complex, opened in 1978 and is run by the Baptist Laymen's Corporation of Tulsa. Monroe Palmer is director.

JOE L. INGRAM

Student Work.—The Student Department operated 28 Baptist student centers in the state in 1980, and provided funds for 49 full-time and three part-time campus ministers and associates who served students as counselors and teachers. Seventeen of these directors were recent products of BSU work in Oklahoma.

Through the BSUs across Oklahoma, students are involved in worship, Bible study, missions, work with internationals, ministry teams,

OKLAHOMA STATISTICAL SUMMARY

Year	Associations	Churches	Church Membership	Baptisms	SS Enrollment	VBS Enrollment	CT Enrollment	WMU Enrollment	Brotherhood Enrollment	Ch. Music Enrollment	Mission Gifts	Total Gifts	Value Church Property
1969	41	1,366	544,983	17,644	317,282	149,026	122,931	44,697	15,412	40,084	$ 5,780,224	$ 33,993,596	$148,089,704
1970	41	1,368	546,872	17,746	311,910	112,259	113,569	40,506	14,832	40,585	5,920,880	35,625,161	154,140,549
1971	41	1,374	560,522	18,652	310,091	122,055	101,152	38,263	16,460	40,302	6,952,887	38,411,987	163,157,811
1972	41	1,386	575,747	21,586	312,505	119,940	99,021	36,830	18,184	42,875	7,339,317	42,919,893	172,672,042
1973	41	1,388	583,937	19,495	314,483	124,194	94,500	35,337	17,995	46,919	8,173,634	43,907,421	184,095,122
1974	41	1,386	597,310	19,812	317,474	126,080	93,192	35,981	17,502	47,827	9,143,582	50,330,982	201,693,698
1975	41	1,391	610,687	20,843	318,400	132,954	93,109	35,604	17,295	48,443	10,077,488	55,689,971	229,526,084
1976	41	1,394	623,832	21,491	331,814	124,732	89,870	34,721	17,513	50,313	11,591,851	64,133,978	258,500,678
1977	41	1,398	632,462	19,334	334,545	122,506	89,065	33,762	16,852	52,235	13,487,965	74,422,888	289,824,240
1978	41	1,409	639,120	18,940	340,811	125,902	90,050	32,647	16,146	52,690	14,578,497	80,463,527	329,619,825
1979	41	1,419	659,152	21,231	339,906	130,260	88,330	33,131	15,729	55,788	17,165,036	92,595,167	382,946,271
1980	41	1,426	674,766	25,431	349,901	136,185	89,324	32,804	17,581	57,195	18,854,139	107,633,688	438,730,300

LYLE GARLOW

and evangelism. Oklahoma BSU students had a 1980 goal of $71,750 designated to help the Student Department send out 55 summer missionaries in 1980 and to send support to 15 BSUs in new convention areas. Teams of students from several campuses assisted new BSUs in California, Kansas, Colorado, Nebraska, and New Mexico. Three teams were scheduled to go on mission trips to Mexico City, Belize, and Taiwan.

New BSU centers were recently constructed at Carl Albert Junior College at Poteau; Phillips University, Enid; and Tulsa Junior College, Tulsa. Plans in 1980 called for new buildings to be constructed at El Reno, Seminole, Oklahoma Baptist University, Oral Roberts University at Tulsa, Oklahoma City University, Connors State College at Warner, and Southeastern State University at Durant. The 1980 value of BSU centers in Oklahoma was over $5,000,000.

Gifts through the convention's Cooperative Program provided $635,000 in 1980 for student work. An additional $500,000 was provided by area associations, churches, and individuals. The projected Cooperative Program receipts for BSU in 1981 were $742,000. The increased amount over 1980 was designated for hiring full-time directors at El Reno Junior College and Connors State. Funds were earmarked for the immediate construction of facilities at Warner, Seminole, and El Reno.

BSUs across Oklahoma ministered to approximately 12,000 students in 1979. Enrollment of Baptist students in Oklahoma colleges and universities was 26,000. These figures reflected an appreciable increase over 1969 when there were 5,000 BSU students out of a Baptist student enrollment of 21,000.

ROBERT E. LEE

BILIOGRAPHY: J. M. Gaskin, *Baptist Milestones in Oklahoma* (1966).

J. M. GASKIN

OKLAHOMA ASSOCIATIONS (II, III).

I. New Associations. ATOKA-COAL. Formed at Atoka, Oct. 16, 1978, from former Atoka Association, retaining same area of Atoka and Coal Counties. In 1980, 25 churches reported 297 baptisms, 6,347 members, $767,396 total gifts, and $72,638 mission gifts.

CAPITAL. Formed Oct. 16, 1970, at Western Hills Church, Oklahoma City, by vote to change name from Oklahoma County in which county the state capital is located. In 1980, 116 churches reported 5,760 baptisms, 129,712 members, $23,147,191 total gifts, and $2,549,904 mission gifts.

GRADY. Organized in 1975 at Amber by vote to change name from Chicasaw. In 1980, 19 churches reported 299 baptisms, 10,080 members, $1,546,726 total gifts, and $240,674 mission gifts.

WASHINGTON-OSAGE. Organized at Dewey, Oct. 19, 1976, out of Delaware-Osage by 33 churches. In 1980, 33 churches reported 511 baptisms, 16,265 members, $3,239,751 total gifts, and $442,584 mission gifts.

II. Changes in Associations. ATOKA. Name changed to Atoka-Coal, Oct. 16, 1978.

CHICKASAW. Name changed, Oct. 14, 1975, to Grady, with same area of Grady County retained.

DELAWARE-OSAGE. Name changed, Oct. 19, 1976, to Washington-Osage to define more clearly the area served.

OKLAHOMA COUNTY. Name changed to Capital at Western Hills Church, Oklahoma City, Oct. 16, 1970.

J. M. GASKIN

OKLAHOMA BAPTIST FOUNDATION
(II, III). See BAPTIST FOUNDATION OF OKLAHOMA, THE.

OKLAHOMA BAPTIST HISTORICAL COMMISSION (II).
In 1976 Jesse Marvin Gaskin was employed as the first director of history, and the Oklahoma Baptist Collection was housed in a new library at Oklahoma Baptist University. In 1979 the collection had approximately 30,000 items. Oklahoma's Cooperative Program allocated $32,000 to the commission in 1980 for operations.

J. M. GASKIN

OKLAHOMA BAPTIST HISTORICAL SOCIETY (III).
The society meets annually during the yearly meeting of the state convention. Membership in 1979 was 203.

J. M. GASKIN

OKLAHOMA BAPTIST UNIVERSITY
(II, III). The administration of Grady Coulter Cothen ended, Sep., 1970, when he resigned to become president of New Orleans Baptist Theological Seminary. In June, 1971, William Graydon Tanner was elected president and served until Sep., 1976. He resigned to become executive director-treasurer of the Home Mission Board, SBC. Tanner was followed by Ernest Eugene Hall, who assumed his duties as the 12th president of OBU on Oct. 15, 1977. The interim presidents of this period were Robert Lee Lynn, 1970-71, and William Everett Neptune, 1976-77.

The main source of support for the operating budget is the Baptist General Convention of Oklahoma, which allocated $1,408,750 for that purpose in 1979-80. The total budget for 1980-81 was $7,419,526. Endowment funds stood at $10,701,160 as of Jan. 1, 1980.

During the 1970s the university received $8,440,000 in gifts and grants, the largest single gift being $500,000 in 1974 by the J. E. and L. E. Mabee Foundation of Tulsa, OK. Several major building programs were completed during the decade, including a University Center, 1970; the Mabee Fine Arts Center, 1971; the Mabee Learning Center, 1976; the West University Apartments Complex, 1977; and a new physical plant center, 1978. In Jan., 1980, work was begun on a $3,000,000 renovation of two older dormitories on the campus. This was the first phase of a projected $10,000,000 expansion program designed to include a new health, physical education, and recreation-activities complex, expected to be started in 1980-81. The plan includes a total of 19 projects.

Enrollment during the 1970s followed a pattern of rise and decline. From an enrollment of 1,642 in Sep., 1969, the number reached a record high of 1,818 in the fall of 1975. After that a decline set in and continued to a low of 1,531 in the fall of 1979. The university graduated 279 seniors in 1978-79.

In Sep., 1970, a new liberal arts curriculum was implemented, emphasizing greater integration of knowledge, and introducing the 4-1-4 calendar in the school year. The curriculum was further revised in 1978-79 with emphasis on a general education core and a return to the three-hour credit base. The faculty in 1980 consisted of 125 members, 97 of whom were full time and 49 holding doctoral degrees.

The 100,000th volume to the OBU library was dedicated in May, 1975. As of Aug., 1979, total holdings were 122,310 bound volumes and a volume equivalent in microfilm of 23,371, making a total of 145,681 volumes. The library is a member of the Ohio College Library Center service and also serves as a depository for government documents and for the Oklahoma Baptist Collection.

William R. Pogue, OBU alumnus, participated in the 84-day Skylab III space mission in 1973-74. David L. Boren, associate professor of political science and an OBU faculty member since 1969, was elected governor of Oklahoma in Nov., 1974. Boren is now a United States senator from Oklahoma.

BIBLIOGRAPHY: J. N. Owens, *Annals of OBU* (1956).

E. W. THORNTON

OKLAHOMA CHILDREN'S HOMES (cf.
Oklahoma Baptist Orphans' Home, Vol. I; Oklahoma Baptist Children's Home, Vol. III). As a licensed institution and child-placing agency, each of the three Oklahoma Baptist children's homes provides children opportunities for group living in cottages on campus, foster home placement, adoptive placement, or assistance in returning to their own family homes, when possible.

On Mar. 11, 1978, the Oklahoma City Home commemorated its 75th year of ministry to children with the dedication of the new I. L. Yearby Counseling Center. From its 40-acre campus in northwest Oklahoma City, over 4,000 boys and girls have received care since 1906. The home has 16 new and modernized brick buildings—including nine cottages, a recreation-education building with a gymnasium, a swimming pool, and the Administration Building with the new Counseling Center—and provides family-style living for 100 children. James V. Browning has served as the administrator of the home since Aug., 1954.

The J. Ray Smiths of Tulsa provided 92 acres

of land for beginning the Baptist Children's Home of Owasso, OK, Apr. 22, 1973. Five cottages, Mabee Administration-Counseling Center, a commissary, and a swimming pool have been completed. Mike Nomura, a former resident of Oklahoma Boys Ranch Town, became superintendent in Nov., 1974. Child care services and unwed mother care in Northeastern Oklahoma are administered through the Owasso Home.

Oklahoma Baptists' fourth child care institution was spearheaded by a gift of land and $200,000 from Governor Raymond Gary in 1977. In three years the Madill Home has grown to a campus of five cottages, an administration building, the superintendent's residence, a swimming pool, and a commissary. Jerry T. Bradley has served as superintendent of the home since May, 1977. The home provides all types of services to children in Southern and Southeastern Oklahoma.

The number of children served in each of the children's homes and their operating budgets in 1979 were as follows: Oklahoma City, 150 children, $513,000; Owasso, 83 children, $236,690; and Madill, 56 children, $186,000.

BIBLIOGRAPHY: J. M. Gaskin, *The Child Care Ministry of Oklahoma Baptists* (1978).

JAMES V. BROWNING

OKLAHOMA HOSPITALS. See HOSPITALS, OKLAHOMA.

OKLAHOMA INDIAN BAPTISTS. See INDIAN BAPTISTS, OKLAHOMA.

OKLAHOMA LAYMEN'S CORPORATIONS. See LAYMEN'S CORPORATIONS, OKLAHOMA.

OKLAHOMA SCHOOL OF RELIGION, THE (cf. Oklahoma School of Religion, Vols. II, III). Located in Tulsa, the Oklahoma School of Religion opened Dec. 1, 1975, with 25 students as a reorganized institution which formerly operated at Langston, OK. In 1979-80, a faculty of 12 taught 160 resident students. Satellite centers at Muskogee, Langston, Pauls Valley, Oklahoma City, Hennepin, and Ardmore increased the faculty to 32 with 400 students. Operated by the Oklahoma Baptist State Convention (Negro), the school offers a basic A.A. degree in religion.

J. M. GASKIN

OLD TESTAMENT CRITICISM. See BIBLICAL CRITICISM, OLD TESTAMENT.

OMAN, STIRTON (b. Nashville, TN, Feb. 26, 1902; d. Cat Cay, Bahamas, Mar. 18, 1977). Layman and denominational leader. Son of John Oman, Jr. and Bessie (Bond) Oman, farmers, he married Frances Allen, Dec. 27, 1921. They had five children: Frances, Ann, Betty, Stirton, Jr., and Jack. He graduated from Montgomery Bell Academy, Nashville, TN (1920), and was awarded an honorary LL.D degree from Pepperdine College (1968). He was both chairman of the board of Oman Construction Company in Nashville and president of the Southern Baptist Foundation, 1955-57, 1959-66, and 1970-75. He is buried in Mt. Olivet Cemetery, Nashville.

CHRISTINE M. BESS

ONEIDA BAPTIST INSTITUTE (cf. Oneida Institute, Vols. II, III). A seven-year academy (beginning with grade six) located at Oneida, KY. Its enrollment, which comes from all parts of the nation and several foreign countries, grew from 185 students in the fall of 1969 to 374 in 1979. The institute is the fastest-growing boarding school in the United States. Each student is required to work 11½ hours weekly in a labor program. During the 1970s seven major buildings were constructed, and four others were renovated. The budget for 1969-70 was $235,000; a decade later, $1,062,000. Assets increased by almost 300 percent during that period. Barkley Moore, a 1958 graduate of Oneida, succeeded David C. Jackson as the president, Aug. 1, 1972. Moore had served in the Peace Corps in Iran during 1964-70.

CHESTER RAYMOND YOUNG

OPPORTUNITY CAMPS (NEW MEXICO). Begun, in 1965 H. C. Sivells, then Brotherhood secretary of the Baptist Convention of New Mexico, and Perry Denton, a layman from Carlsbad, the camps were intended for boys 9-13 years of age who were convicted of a crime but not committed to a correctional institution. The purpose was to change their behavior and direction of life through discussion of law and authority, evangelism, and physical exercise under the guidance of Christian counselors.

Today, the philosophy remains the same. Girls' camps have been added, and children who have not had some arrest record may become campers. The camps are volunteer-directed and depend upon volunteer counselors and state police officers assigned to help in the camps.

The first opportunity camp was held at the Royal Ambassador Camp (now Sivells Baptist Camp) near Cloudcroft in Aug., 1965. Of 28 boys attending, 20 made professions of faith. In 1968 the program was enlarged to two camps for boys which were also held at Sivells Camp. One of these camps subsequently was moved to Inlow Youth Camp near Tajique in 1972. In 1973 laymen of the San Juan Baptist Association began a boys' opportunity camp at their associational campground, Hesperus Baptist Camp. This camp serves in that association and is entirely managed, staffed, and financed by that association. The first opportunity camp for girls was held at Sivells in 1974, and a second girls' camp was added at Inlow in 1978.

The operation of the camps depends upon the

involvement of New Mexico pastors and laypersons who act in every capacity. Most funding comes from designated gifts of churches and individuals, and the remainder from BCNM missions funds. Associational committees provide finances and recruit campers and counselors. Statewide committees recruit staff and plan programs. Associational committees provide follow-up.

JAMES GOODNER

ORAL HISTORY, LOUISIANA BAPTIST. See LOUISIANA BAPTIST ORAL HISTORY.

ORAL HISTORY AMONG SOUTHERN BAPTISTS. During the 1970s Southern Baptists began several efforts to tape record and preserve oral memoirs for both present and future use. Led by Baylor University and the Historical Commission, SBC, research activity of this kind won general acceptance in the SBC.

The Baylor University Program for Oral History was the first organized oral history work in the SBC. Starting in 1970, its Religion and Culture Project included studies of Texas Baptist leaders and agencies. In the fall of 1973, the Historical Commission, SBC, hosted a Baptist Oral History Workshop which signaled the start of oral history projects by Baptist agencies and on the campuses of Southern Baptist colleges, universities, and seminaries. The Historical Commission staff then began holding workshops for Baptists in various states and during summer sessions at Glorieta and Ridgecrest Baptist Conference Centers, in addition to their interviewing activity with former SBC presidents. Several state Baptist historical societies and SBC agencies began oral history work. The Apr., 1975, joint meeting of the commission and the Southern Baptist Historical Society centered around the theme of Baptist oral history, which also became the focal point of the July, 1975, issue of *Baptist History and Heritage.*

Additional steps in developing Baptist oral history occurred during the 1970s. The Bowman Gray School of Medicine at Wake Forest University organized an oral history project on the history of medicine at the North Carolina institution. The Baptist General Convention of Texas funded the Texas Baptist Oral History Consortium (a network of Baptist colleges, academies, and Southwestern Baptist Theological Seminary) to develop a more comprehensive, statewide effort. Some of its oral memoirs became available on microfilm through the Historical Commission. In 1978 the State Missions Commission, BGCT, funded the Mexican Baptist Oral History Project, a bilingual effort to gather primary source material for a forthcoming book. Both the Texas consortium and the Mexican Baptist projects worked out of offices on the Baylor campus under general guidelines of the Historical Committee of the Texas convention. The consortium's most recent emphasis has been on interviewing retired missionaries living in Texas.

Oral history has become a popular, valuable approach to the study of the Baptist heritage. Many Baptist organizations now view oral history as one of the best ways of recording and preserving Baptist history.

See also HISTORICAL COMMISSION, SBC.

THOMAS L. CHARLTON

ORAL HISTORY CONSORTIUM, TEXAS BAPTIST. See TEXAS BAPTIST ORAL HISTORY CONSORTIUM.

ORDINATION OF WOMEN. See WOMEN, ORDINATION OF SOUTHERN BAPTIST.

OREGON-WASHINGTON, BAPTIST GENERAL CONVENTION OF (II, III). See NORTHWEST BAPTIST CONVENTION.

OREGON-WASHINGTON ASSOCIATIONS (III). See NORTHWEST ASSOCIATIONS.

ORGANIZATION MANUAL, SOUTHERN BAPTIST CONVENTION. See SOUTHERN BAPTIST CONVENTION ORGANIZATION MANUAL.

ORIENTATION, CHURCH MEMBER. See CHURCH MEMBER ORIENTATION.

ORTEGON, SAMUEL MIJARES (b. El Paso, TX, Apr. 30, 1903; d. Los Angeles, CA, May 19, 1978). Chaplain, pastor, educator, and denominational worker. Educated at the University of Southern California (B.A., 1930; Th.M., 1932; M.A., 1933; Ph.D., 1949). He served as captain in the United States Army, 1943-46, in the South Pacific and Japan. He taught sociology and was department chairman at Spanish American Baptist Seminary, 1930-38; Eastern Baptist College, 1946-58; Hardin-Simmons University, 1959; Upland College, 1959-60; and California Baptist College, 1961-77.

Ordained in 1927 by the Belvedere Park Baptist Church, Los Angeles, CA, which he pastored, 1925-30, he was pastor of the First Mexican Baptist Church of Los Angeles, 1930-38. He directed Spanish-speaking work for the American Baptist Convention in Southern California, 1938-43. He married Eliva Martinez, and they had two daughters, Priscilla and Yvette. Ortegon is buried in Rose Hills Cemetery, Los Angeles County, CA.

STEPHEN P. CARLETON

OUACHITA BAPTIST UNIVERSITY (III; cf. Ouachita Baptist College, Vol. II). During the 1970s Ouachita turned away from the problems of the late 1960s: Less-than-ideal denominational relations, financial deficits, and enrollment decline. The school experienced progress and new strength in virtually all aspects of institutional life. The administration of president Daniel R. Grant included Ben M. Elrod, vice-president for development; Carl Goodson, vice-president for academic affairs; Ed Coulter, vice-president for administration;

and B. Aldon Dixon, dean of students, during most of the decade.

The Arkansas Baptist State Convention increased its Cooperative Program support for the university from less than $480,000 in 1969 to more than $1,100,000 in 1979. A convention-sponsored advancement campaign, 1971-72, led by W. O. Vaught, Jr., Rheubin South, and Alvin (Bo) Huffman, raised nearly $7,000,000, including specialized area campaigns. Ouachita earmarked one-third of the campaign funds for operating purposes other than the physical plant.

A new long-range campus plan was adopted in 1971, featuring a "megastructure" in the heart of the campus, combining beauty, utility, and economy. By 1979 four of the five proposed buildings in the megastructure had been completed at a cost of $5,000,000 with a remaining indebtedness of less than $100,000. In addition to construction of these new buildings (Evans Student Center, Lile Hall, Mabee Fine Arts Center, and McClellan Hall), several existing structures were renovated and expanded.

Student enrollment increased from 1,320 in 1969 to 1,619 in 1979, with an all-time record number living on the campus. During the 1970s Ouachita consistently ranked in the top three colleges and universities in Arkansas in the number of National Merit Scholars enrolled. More than 300 students (approximately 20 percent of the enrollment) were preparing for church vocations, and in 1978 more of the record number of new foreign missionary appointees from the Southern Baptist Convention came from Ouachita than from any other college or university in the United States. Ouachita's athletic teams competed well in the Arkansas Intercollegiate Conference, winning the All-sports Trophy for three consecutive years at the end of the decade.

Other special achievements during the 1970s included the establishment of a cooperative program with neighboring Henderson State University, making possible more specialized courses of study for students; the establishment of a student exchange program between Ouachita and Seinan Gakuin University in Fukuoka, Japan; and the establishment of the Ouachita Student Foundation.

DANIEL R. GRANT

OUR MISSION FIELDS. First official publication of Woman's Missionary Union, SBC. To provide a complete and well-planned monthly missionary program, this quarterly magazine began in July, 1906, with Fannie E. S. Heck (*q.v.* I) as editor and a circulation of 6,000 copies. Demand for this periodical increased so rapidly that the 7,000 and 9,000 copies printed of the second and third issues were insufficient. Sunbean Band programs and suggestions "for young ladies" appeared in the second issue, and in 1908 programs for boys were added. Claris I. Crane (*q.v.*) was editor, 1912-14. In Oct., 1914, the magazine was superseded by the monthly *Royal Service.*

DORIS DEVAULT

OVERSEAS MINISTRIES STUDY CENTER. A non-denominational residential center in Ventor, NJ, for continuing education of persons engaged in Christian world mission. Established in 1923 as a memorial to William Howard Doane, the famous composer of gospel songs such as "Tell Me the Old, Old Story" and "To God Be the Glory," the center was known originally as "The Houses of Fellowship." The study programs and residential facilities, which include 38 furnished apartments, are open to missionaries of all boards, societies, and denominations. The center is intended for the intellectual and spiritual renewal of missionaries and their families on furlough, and overseas church leaders who have come to North America on special missionary assignment or to study. All persons admitted into residence are expected to spend at least half their time in study and to respect any differing opinions held by others. Each year several hundred persons participate in the short intensive seminars, consultations, and study conferences dealing with a broad range of vital issues in world mission.

Overseas Ministries Study Center is a member of the Society for the Advancement of Continuing Education for Ministry, and has affiliate status in the Association of Theological Schools in the United States and Canada. It publishes the *International Bulletin of Missionary Research,* a scholarly journal of worldwide circulation and influence.

GERALD H. ANDERSON

OWENS, JAMES NEWTON (b. Bare Branch, TN, Aug. 3, 1883; d. Shawnee, OK, July 12, 1972). Baptist layman and teacher. Son of John and Martha (Walker) Owens, he was educated at the University of the South (B.A., M.A.) and received the Doctor of Humanities degree from Oklahoma Baptist University in 1953. He was the beloved ideal of Oklahoma Baptist University students who affectionately knew him as "Uncle Jimmy." He taught at OBU for 36 years, serving as professor of modern languages. His chief publication, *Annals of Oklahoma Baptist University* (1956), remains the main source of OBU's history. From his marriage, July 24, 1912, to Julia Spencer came five children: James N., Jr., Julia S., John J., Martha J., and Robert J. He is buried in Resthaven Memorial Garden, Shawnee, OK.

E. W. THORNTON

P

PACIFIC COAST BAPTIST (III). See NORTHWEST BAPTIST WITNESS.

PACT. International prayer partner plan for Crusade of the Americas, 1968-69. At the request of the SBC, Woman's Missionary Union organized PACT for 1968-69 revivals. PACT linked individuals, churches, church organizations, and families in intercession for the crusade. Leaflets printed in English, Spanish, and Portugese resulted in requests for prayer partners from 49 states and 29 countries.

See also CRUSADE OF THE AMERICAS, VOL. III.

DORIS DEVAULT

PALM BEACH ATLANTIC COLLEGE (III). In Sep., 1969, Palm Beach Atlantic College began its second academic year. In 1972 the trustees elected Warner Earle Fusselle as the second president. He succeeded Jess Moody. The college received its accreditation from the Southern Association of Colleges and Schools in 1972. The E. C. Blomeyer Library continued to grow during Fusselle's administration, and the college continued to purchase property that eventually would house new buildings.

In Jan., 1978, George R. Borders was named president. Borders came from Stetson University where he had served in various administrative capacities for the previous 12 years. In Dec., 1978, the college received a 10-year reaffirmation of its accreditation from the Southern Association. In Sep., 1979, Palm Beach received $25,000 from the special state missions offering of the Florida Baptist Convention.

In 1980 the college functioned with four major divisions: Humanities, Social Sciences, Natural Sciences, and Professional Sciences. Within these four divisions there are 12 majors and several minors. Students come from 29 states and 16 foreign countries. Fifty-five percent of the students are Baptists; the remaining 45 percent represent the other major denominations in America.

Palm Beach grew in several ways during the 1970s. The size of the student body and faculty increased significantly. The physical plant expanded from three borrowed buildings to 38 buildings. The value of the library grew from $200,000 to $2,500,000, and the endowment grew from $100,000 to $1,500,000. The college has graduated 605 students since the first graduating class of 1972.

GEORGE BORDERS

PALMER, JOHN NORRIS (b. Blue Mountain, MS, July 13, 1898; d. Baton Rouge, LA, Oct. 9, 1971). Pastor and denominational leader. Son of David M. and Mamie (Norris) Palmer, he was converted in 1909 and ordained in 1917 by Lowerey Memorial Baptist Church, Blue Mountain, MS. He graduated from Mississippi College (B.A., 1920) and The Southern Baptist Theological Seminary (Th.B., 1922; Th.M., 1928). Honorary doctorates were conferred by Mississippi College (D.D., 1930) and Louisiana College (LL.D., 1949). He married Margaret Emerson, July 7, 1924. They had no children.

Spanning six decades, Palmer served pastorates in Mississippi, Kentucky, Tennessee, and Louisiana, including First Church, Baton Rouge, LA, 1933-71. President of the Louisiana Baptist Convention, 1941-42, he also was a member of its executive board and a trustee of Louisiana College. He served further on the SBC Executive Committee, Sunday School Board, Foreign Mission Board, and Home Mission Board. A world traveler, Palmer visited 50 states and over 100 countries on all continents. Aristocratic in looks, dress, and demeanor, he was a pulpit craftsman. He was at his best as a board member who saw through issues and summarized to consensus. His strongest contributions were to evangelism and missions through the local church and the denomination. He is buried in Hernando Cemetery, Hernando, MS.

G. AVERY LEE

PANAMA, MISSION IN (cf. Panama and Canal Zone, Missions in, Vol. III). Agreeing that Panama should relate to the Foreign Mission Board, Home Mission Board and FMB administrators worked harmoniously between 1972 and 1975 to effect a transfer that would cause minimum disruption to the Baptist work in Panama. Foreign missionaries Ervin and Ruth (Tyson) Hastey worked with HMB superintendent Joe Carl Johnson to accomplish the transfer, Jan. 1, 1975. Promptly, missionaries transferred from five Latin American countries to work with Hastey. While honoring HMB commitments, the FMB changes included accelerated release of the Baptist Clinic on Ailigandi to the Panamanian government, expansion of Cresta Mar Encampment, purchase of a convention building, and opening a book store, Sep., 1979. Twenty-three foreign missionaries and one home missionary were working with 57 churches, 66 missions, 71 pastors, and 6,245 members as the 1980s began.

A. CLARK SCANLON

PARA-CHURCH GROUPS AND SOUTHERN BAPTISTS. Para-church groups seem to flourish in the soil of twentieth-century American Christianity. Para-church groups are organizations that exist alongside of and parallel to the church and overlap the functions, goals, and membership of the church. Several qualities characterize these organizations. They often represent a kind of entrepreneurship in which gifted leaders have rallied a constituency, perhaps by the medium of radio or television. Often they garner support from members of established denominations as well as independent congregations. Usually, they are unrelated to, unconcerned with, and unaccountable to the procedures and structures of denominations.

Many para-church organizations are single-issue groups—centering their attention on such causes as Bible distribution, world hunger, or family concerns; or directing their energies toward particular target groups such as athletes, teenage drug addicts, or black Americans. In some instances, a broadly stated objective such as evangelism may become the rationale for multifaceted programs that change the para-church group into a mini-denomination.

Many of these groups are familiar. Bible Study Fellowship, the Billy Graham Evangelistic Association, Bread for the World, Campus Crusade for Christ, Child Evangelism Fellowship, Evangelicals for Social Action, Faith at Work, Full-Gospel Businessmen's Fellowship, Institute of Basic Youth Conflicts, Inter-Varsity Christian Fellowship, Navigators, World Vision, Yokefellows, and Youth for Christ are representative para-church groups.

Several educational institutions are para-church in character and present a particular challenge to Southern Baptists. Four such schools are Mid-America Baptist Theological Seminary, Luther Rice Theological Seminary, the California Graduate School of Theology, and the Criswell Center for Biblical Studies.

Responses to para-church groups are both negative and positive. Many persons see these groups as harmful. They siphon time, energy, money, and people from Southern Baptist causes. Some feel that such groups can be allies to the denomination by pointing out next steps for Southern Baptists to take. Others see some para-church groups as a positive channel for joining with other evangelical Christians to share the gospel. Yet others view some of these groups as responses to deeply felt needs which the church is not meeting.

Many persons feel that Southern Baptists are vulnerable to para-church groups. While no statistics are available, substantial indications suggest that this assessment is true. Southern Baptists need a balanced approach to para-church groups which will: (1) Analyze and evaluate them; (2) inform the Baptist constituency about them; (3) affirm that which is good and commendable within them and challenge that which is not; and (4) evaluate and develop Southern Baptist programs in light of the needs of people.

BIBLIOGRAPHY: Nathan Larry Baker, "Baptist Polity and Para-Church Organizations," *Baptist History and Heritage* (July, 1979).

NATHAN LARRY BAKER

PARADISE VALLEY BAPTIST RANCH.
See ARIZONA SOUTHERN BAPTIST CONVENTION.

PARAGUAY, MISSION IN (II, III). The year 1970 marked the 50th anniversary of Baptist work in Paraguay and the 25th anniversary of Southern Baptist work there. The mission and the Paraguay Convention experienced relationship problems but also found areas of common concern and mutual cooperation. Betty Missena, pastor's wife, was elected first woman president of the convention. Paraguayan Baptists experienced an interdenominational evangelistic crusade which reported 5,000 decisions, dedicated a new radio and television studio, increased Spanish broadcasts, and added broadcasts in Guarani.

A family planning center and visiting nurse program were set up, a hospital chapel was dedicated, a private outpatient clinic and laboratory wing were opened, the school of nursing was officially recognized, the residency program was reestablished, and the mobile clinic was reactivated. Seminary students from surrounding countries attended classes in clinical pastoral education. A goodwill center was established in a poorer section of Asuncion.

FRANK K. MEANS

PARKER, JOHN BRUTON (b. Corinth, MS, May 28, 1884; d. El Paso, TX, Dec. 10, 1979). Home and foreign missionary. He served as pastor of churches in Texas and New Mexico before and after serving in Brazil, 1917-23. Parker was also associational missionary in New Mexico, 1926-32; and missionary to the Spanish of New Mexico, 1932-45, and Texas, 1946-63.

LOYD CORDER

PASTORAL CARE (II, III).
I. Definition. The following definitions of pastoral care by Southern Baptists express the diversity in contemporary definitions of this ministry. Wayne Oates defines pastoral care as "the Christian pastor's combined fortification and confrontation of persons as persons in times of both emergency crisis and developmental crisis." "Pastoral care and counseling," according to Edward Thornton, "are forms of religious ministry which integrate the findings of behavioral science and theology in the effort to prepare the way for divine-human encounter in the midst of human crises." C. W. Brister writes, "Pastoral care is the mutual concern of Christians for each other and for those in the world for whom Christ died. Protestant pastoral care views the church itself as minister and the pastor as a servant of servants." In sum, pastoral care is an expression of Christian ministry toward persons in crisis.

Pastoral care today integrates the findings of behavioral science and theology and is guided by these behavioral science assumptions: A developmental view of personality, awareness of unconscious processes, and a belief that empathic listening is central to a helping relationship. Pastoral care, however, seeks to prepare persons for divine-human encounter; therefore, its guidance comes primarily from theological and not psychological assumptions. God is understood to be the ultimate comforter, confronter, and helper. Protestant definitions of pastoral care also affirm the priesthood of believers and encourage activation of the laity as agents of pastoral care. Pastoral counseling is a specialized form of pastoral care; it is care provided in a formal relationship which has specified time limits, a private place, and a clear counselor-counselee contract.

II. Beginnings of Modern Pastoral Care Among Southern Baptists, 1894-1945. A scientifically-based understanding of human personality and of therapy emerged around the turn of the century and began to have an impact on the training of ministers in America in the 1920s. This new point of view led to the training of ministers on the basis of direct pastoral experience under close supervision. The supervision was guided by a clinical method which involved disciplined procedures for observation, an awareness of one's own bias, and a method of relating theory to practice.

Theodore F. Adams (q.v.).—The year 1930 was possibly the first important contact of Southern Baptist ministry with a scientifically-informed pastoral care. In that year Theodore F. Adams attended a summer pastor's conference at the University of Chicago where he met Otis Rice, chaplain of St. Luke's Hospital, New York City. "He lectured about the new concept in pastoral counseling," said Adams, "and for the first time in my life I learned it was more important to listen than to talk." Adams was then an American Baptist pastor in Toledo, OH. In 1936 he became pastor of the First Baptist Church, Richmond, VA. He continued his studies in pastoral care and in 1948 led the church to establish a staff position for visitation, evangelism, and counseling, a position filled by early doctoral graduates in pastoral care from Southern Baptist Theological Seminary: Lyn Elder, 1948-51; Myron Madden, 1951-54; and O. J. Hodges, 1955-59.

Graduate Theses in Psychology of Religion and Pastoral Care.—Evidence of the influence of the behavioral sciences on Southern Baptist theological education appeared first in the field of the psychology of religion. The first graduate level thesis in psychology of religion in a SBC seminary appeared at Southern Seminary in 1894, written by Dexter G. Whittinghill and entitled "Old Testament Psychology." Between 1894 and 1940, nine other theses in the psychology of religion were written, eight more at Southern Seminary and one at Southwestern Baptist Theological Seminary. Martin L. Fergeson's 1943 thesis at Southwestern Seminary, "Modern Schools of Psychology and their Influence upon the Functions of the Minister," signaled a shift of focus toward pastoral care. A dramatic increase in theses in pastoral care occurred after World War II. At that time a major curriculum innovation was occurring at Southern Seminary.

Gaines S. Dobbins (q.v.).—The first theological educator among Southern Baptists to express a sustained interest in the psychology of religion and pastoral care was Gaines S. Dobbins. He joined the Southern Seminary faculty in 1920 and found the prevailing teaching method "too content-centered and inadequately oriented toward equipping the student for effectiveness in pastoral ministries." In his search for a better method, he secured a leave to study under George Albert Coe at Columbia University and to take additional courses from John Dewey, E. L. Thorndike, and Harrison S. Elliott. In the late 1930s Dobbins became interested in clinical pastoral education (CPE), a learning innovation which gave theological students direct supervision in the practice of pastoral care, usually in the setting of a general or a mental hospital. In 1937 he and W. O. Carver (q.v. I) invited Seward Hiltner, then director of the Council for Clinical Training (CCT), to visit Southern Seminary. Soon thereafter the seminary sought to launch a CPE program at Louisville General Hospital; however, a CCT accredited supervisor was not available.

In 1943 Dobbins was teaching a class in the psychology of religion and giving particular attention to Anton Boisen's idea of theological education through "the study of living human documents." Dobbins received a call from the superintendent of Louisville General Hospital asking for student volunteers who might serve as attendants and orderlies on the psychiatric unit to replace personnel who had left for military service. Dobbins recruited students from his psychology of religion class. Work in that psychiatric ward became the first clinically-based theological study in Southern Baptist theological education. Dobbins selected Wayne E. Oates to supervise his fellow students; and Spafford Ackerly and E. E. Landis of the Department of Psychiatry, University of Louisville Medical School, provided clinical supervision.

Wayne E. Oates.—Wayne E. Oates took his first quarter of CPE under Ralph Bonacker, a CCT chaplain supervisor at Norton Infirmary, Louisville, KY, in 1944. The following academic year, 1944-45, Bonacker and Oates—Oates under Dobbins's faculty sponsorship—offered the first unit of CPE at Southern Seminary. In the summer of 1945, Dobbins arranged for Oates and Richard K. Young (q.v.) to take CPE from Anton Boisen and William Andrew at Elgin State Hospital, Elgin, IL. That same year Oates was appointed an instructor in pastoral care on the seminary faculty. In 1946 he made application to Frederick Kuether of the CCT for supervisory accreditation in order to have the appropriate credentials to establish an indigenous program of CPE in institutions near Southern Seminary. Kuether rejected his request. Undeterred by this denial of CCT credentials, Oates set about to legitimatize CPE by encompassing it within the seminary's academic program. He based the accreditation of CPE supervisors upon completion of an advanced degree in pastoral care. Only 15 months after being turned down as a CCT supervisor, Oates was directing a seminary program in pastoral care which included the offering of CPE in four different hospitals.

III. Establishment of Pastoral Care as an Accepted Specialty Among Southern Baptists, 1945-60. *Marriage and Family Ministry.* — Scientifically-informed pastoral care made its earliest impact on Southern Baptist ministry in the area of family life. In 1936 Theodore Adams inaugurated an annual Christian family life emphasis at First Baptist Church, Richmond, VA. This ministry was informed by his increasing knowledge of behavioral science research into marriage and the family. In the aftermath of disruptions caused in families in his community during World War II, D. Swan Haworth, then pastor of the First Baptist Church, Vicksburg, MS, devoted considerable attention to family life enrichment. In 1948 he organized what was probably the first family life conference in the SBC.

Among a number of professional persons invited to participate in the conference was Hugh Brim, director of the Social Service Commission of the SBC. The conference became a model for Brim in his promotion of other such conferences, and Wayne Oates used this conference format as the basis of his first course in marriage and family counseling at Southern Seminary in 1952.

Hospital Chaplaincies and CPE. — Hospital chaplaincies and CPE became the leading edge of the spread of a scientifically-informed, clinically-trained pastoral care. CPE is analogous to the clinical education of medical students. It attends to the personal identity of the student as well as to the development of pastoral skills. CPE met a learning need for seminarians which was not being met in more traditional theological education. Early expansion of CPE by Southern Baptist chaplain supervisors unfolded as these first programs were begun by: Wayne Oates at Kentucky Baptist Hospital, Louisville, KY, 1946; Oates and Myron Madden at Kentucky State Hospital, Danville, KY, 1947; Oates and Richard Young at North Carolina Baptist Hospital, Winston-Salem, NC, 1947; Aaron Rutledge at Central State Hospital, Louisville, KY, 1948; Don Corley at Southern Baptist Hospital, New Orleans, LA, 1951; Joe Luck, chaplain at Memorial Baptist Hospital, Houston, TX, who contracted for supervisors from the Institute of Religion to provide CPE beginning in 1954; George Bowdler at Baptist Hospital, Columbia, SC, 1955; John Boyle at Louisville General Hospital, Louisville, KY, 1956; E. Augustus Verdery at Georgia Baptist Hospital, Atlanta, GA, 1956; and Howard Linton at Hermann Hospital, Houston, TX, 1956.

Professorships in Pastoral Care. — Professorships in pastoral care developed rapidly in the decade following World War II. Southern Seminary appointed Wayne Oates in 1948, Samuel Southard in 1957, and D. Swan Haworth in 1960. New Orleans Baptist Theological Seminary appointed John M. Price, Jr. *(q.v.),* in 1949 and Harold Rutledge in 1950. Central Baptist Seminary secured instruction from R. Lofton Hudson, 1950-54. Southwestern Seminary named Franklin M. Segler in 1951 and C. W. Brister in 1957. Southeastern Baptist Theological Seminary named Richard K. Young to a part-time appointment in 1953. In 1954 Golden Gate Baptist Theological Seminary appointed Lyn Elder. After opening its doors in 1958, Midwestern Baptist Theological Seminary employed Everett V. Reneer in 1962.

Pastoral Counseling. — As a separate function of ministry, pastoral counseling has appeared among Southern Baptists in three institutional forms: (1) As an extension of hospital chaplaincies and CPE programs, (2) in a separate counseling center, and (3) as the assignment of a church staff member. The First Baptist Church, Richmond, VA, named a minister of counseling to its staff in 1948, marking the first pastoral counseling position established by Southern Baptists. Other early pastoral counseling positions also arose. David Edens became minister of counseling, Trinity Baptist Church, San Antonio, TX, in 1957. In 1958 R. Lofton Hudson organized the Midwest Christian Counseling Service, Kansas City, MO, the third pastoral counseling center in the nation. Rhea Gray established the Personal Counseling Service of New Albany, IN, in 1959. That same year O. J. Hodges formed the Ozark Christian Counseling Service, Springfield, MO.

IV. New Experiments in Pastoral Care by Southern Baptists, 1960-80. During the 1960s and 1970s, Southern Baptists continued to develop CPE programs and counseling positions. At the same time new experiments occurred.

Professional Associations. — Professional associations became a prominent feature for Southern Baptist specialists in pastoral care. In 1957 Southern Baptist CPE supervisors formed the Southern Baptist Association for CPE (SBACPE) in Nashville, TN. In 1965 the association changed its name to the Association of Clinical Pastoral Educators to reflect its increasing ecumenical membership. In 10 years the original membership of 18 had grown to 80, and the association had become a national accrediting body. In 1967 it dissolved itself to merge with the Association for Clinical Pastoral Education (ACPE), an organization unifying four CPE accrediting groups. Southern Baptists provided leadership in forming the ACPE and in its continuing development. In 1980 Southern Baptist supervisors constituted 14.4 percent of the ACPE membership with 101 members.

In 1964 Southern Baptist pastoral counselors participated in the organization of the American Association of Pastoral Counselors (AAPC). In 1980 they made up 10.6 percent of the association membership with 140 members. Southern Baptist hospital chaplains played a leading role in the formation of the College of Chaplains of the American Protestant Hospital Association (APHA). Charles Phillips, a Southern Baptist minister, served as executive director of the College of Chaplains, 1967-80, and since 1973 has been the chief executive officer of the APHA.

CPE in the Military Chaplaincy. —CPE in the military chaplaincy developed primarily out of initiatives by Southern Baptist chaplains. The following programs came from these initiatives: The first CPE program in the Army at Walter Reed Army Medical Center, Washington, DC, 1969, by T. Dick Denson; CPE at Brooke Army Medical Center, San Antonio, TX, 1970, by Max E. Burgin; CPE at Fort Knox, KY, 1973, by Eugene Allen; CPE at the United States Army Chaplain Center and School, Fort Hamilton, NY, by Max Burgin in 1975. Because only the Army of the three service branches provides CPE, these programs also serve Navy and Air Force chaplains.

Denominational Support for Pastoral Care. — Denominational support for pastoral care began to extend beyond the seminaries and hospitals during the 1960s and 1970s. The Chaplain's Commission of the Home Mission Board appointed L. L. McGee in 1962 as the first secretary of hospital chaplaincy. This office oversees denominational endorsement of hospital chaplains and pastoral counselors and serves as liaison between them and the SBC. In 1969 the District of Columbia Baptist Convention established a pastoral counseling service in cooperation with the Washington Pastoral Counseling Service and under the leadership of S. Lewis Morgan, Jr. In 1971 the Georgia Baptist Convention contracted with the Department of Pastoral Services, Georgia Baptist Hospital, to provide pastoral counseling to church related professional persons.

James L. Cooper was employed by the Baptist General Convention of Texas in 1971 to provide pastoral counseling for Baptist ministers and their families. The Union Baptist Association, Houston, TX, created the Center for Counseling in 1975 with associational and state convention funds and named Howard Hovde its director in 1976. Also in 1976 the Sunday School Board named Jerry W. Brown director of personal and professional growth for ministers, with responsibility for programs of pastoral care for church related professionals undergoing mid-career stress. In 1977, through the leadership of Sandra Harvey, the HMB began funding Resources for Family Growth, Columbia, MD, as a pilot project in family ministry. In 1980 the North Carolina Baptist Convention first contracted with the School of Pastoral Care, North Carolina Baptist Hospital, to provide pastoral counseling to convention ministers and their families.

V. Assessment. In 1980 Richard L. Hester and Andrew D. Lester surveyed Southern Baptist members of the ACPE and AAPC for historical data for this research and to secure the opinion of this group concerning the most no-table persons, programs, and books in the history of pastoral care among Southern Baptists. Of 215 questionnaires mailed, 112, or 53 percent, were returned. When asked to name the three persons they regarded as most influential in the history of pastoral care among Southern Baptists, respondents named the following (percent figure shows the proportion of responses of questionnaires returned): Wayne E. Oates, 96 percent; Myron Madden, 46 percent; Richard K. Young, 46 percent; and E. Augustus Verdery, 21 percent.

Asked to name the three most influential centers for training in pastoral care among Southern Baptists, the respondents cited: North Carolina Baptist Hospital, 80 percent; the CPE cluster associated with Southern Seminary, 60 percent; Southern Baptist Hospital in New Orleans, 46 percent; and Georgia Baptist Medical Center, 43 percent.

Responses to the question of three important model pastoral counseling programs shaped by Southern Baptists yielded these: North Carolina Baptist Hospital, 62 percent; counseling programs related to Southern Seminary, 37 percent; Georgia Baptist Medical Center, 30 percent; and Southern Baptist Hospital, 23 percent.

The bibliography at the end of this article lists in order the books cited by respondents in answer to the question of the most valuable books in pastoral care authored by Southern Baptists.

VI. Conclusions. Southern Baptist specialists in pastoral care have made contributions to this field and to the life of the church far beyond the limits of the denomination. Their leadership has been national and interdenominational.

Southern Baptist leadership in pastoral care has opened a door to significant ecumenical cooperation between Southern Baptists and persons in other denominations. By the early 1960s, the SBACPE had an interdenominational membership. In 1967 it merged itself into a totally ecumenical group, the ACPE. Southern Baptists have invested themselves in the ecumenical constituency of the AAPC and the College of Chaplains of the APHA and have, since World War II, moved progressively into chaplaincy positions in non-Baptist institutions. Pastoral counseling positions outside local congregations have opened yet another door to ecumenical engagement. This transcending of denominational boundaries has provided a new and important channel of communication and cooperation with non-Baptists which had not existed before.

Associated with the advantages of ecumenical involvement has been the liability of a loss of close denominational involvement. The Southern Baptist chaplain of an institution or pastoral counselor in a counseling center is accountable to institutional executives and boards of trustees on the one hand and to professional associations on the other. This leaves open the question of how these persons relate to a congregation or to the denomination. Southern Baptist polity does not provide structures which make clear how pastoral care specialists employed outside a congregation or denominational agency are related to the denomination. In the absence of such structures, the pastoral care specialist too often ends up without a sense of inclusion in the mainstream of denominational life and without accountability to the constituency with which he or she is identified in ministry.

Pastoral care has also been a doorway through which the behavioral sciences have influenced Southern Baptist pastors and churches by providing scientifically-based understandings of human personality and of effective patterns of helping. The model of helping introduced by pastoral care has been largely dependent upon the medical profession. This model has tended to overemphasize the professional role of the minister, to conceive of helping as basically a one-to-one relationship, and therefore to neglect the principle of the priesthood of believers and the importance of the Christian community as a source of healing.

BIBLIOGRAPHY: Wayne E. Oates, *The Christian Pastor* (1953, 1964). Myron Madden, *The Power to Bless* (1969). Edward E. Thornton, *Professional Education for Ministry: A History of Clinical Pastoral Education* (1970). C. W. Brister, *Pastoral Care in the Church* (1964). Richard K. Young and Albert L. Meiburg, *Spiritual Therapy* (1960). Edward E. Thornton, *Theology and Pastoral Counseling* (1964). Richard K. Young, *The Pastor's Hospital Ministry* (1954). Wayne E. Oates, *The Psychology of Religion* (1973); *Protestant Pastoral Counseling* (1962); *When Religion Gets Sick* (1970); (ed.) *An Introduction to Pastoral Counseling* (1959); *Religious Factors in Mental Illness* (1955); *Religious Dimensions of Personality* (1957); *Pastoral Counseling* (1974).

RICHARD L. HESTER, C. W. BRISTER,
WALTER C. JACKSON, III,
ANDREW D. LESTER, and AUGUSTUS VERDERY

PASTORS' CONFERENCE, SOUTHERN BAPTIST. See SOUTHERN BAPTIST PASTORS' CONFERENCE.

PATE, MAVIS ORISCA (b. Ringgold, LA, Dec. 23, 1925; d. Gaza, Jan. 16, 1972). Missionary nurse. The daughter of Brady and Mattie Pate, she attended Northwestern State College of Louisiana (R.N., 1945; B.S., 1952), Centenary College, and Southwestern Baptist Theological Seminary. Appointed a missionary, 1964, she served four months in Thailand while waiting to enter Pakistan. During her second term in Pakistan, she transferred to Gaza Baptist Hospital as operating room supervisor and instructor of nursing. While traveling for the hospital, she was ambushed and shot by Arab guerillas. She is buried behind the Gaza hospital nurses' quarters.

KATHRYN E. CARPENTER

PATRICK, WILEY JONES, JR. (b. Macon County, MO, Jan. 3, 1840; d. Pike County, MO, Aug. 13, 1913). State Baptist executive. Son of Wiley Jones and Margaret (Shortle) Patrick, he married Elizabeth Ann Withers, Mar. 8, 1866. After her death, Dec. 1,

1872, he married Amanda E. Ustick, June 2, 1875. His children by his first wife were Pryor Claye and Bower Reynolds; by his second wife they were Margaret, Laura, and Ruth. He attended William Jewell College (1863-64).

Patrick was elected corresponding secretary of the Missouri Baptist General Association, 1865-66; he served on the association's Board of Missions, 1879-1913; was appointed a delegate from Missouri to the Baptist World Alliance, 1911; and was a member of the board of managers of the Missouri Baptist Historical Society, 1886-1913. He wrote and edited a number of biographical and historical books. He served as chaplain of the Missouri Senate, 1873-75. He is buried at Bowling Green, MO.

MRS. DAVID ANDREW DEXHEIMER

PAYNE, ERNEST ALEXANDER (b. London, England, Feb. 19, 1902; d. London, England, Jan. 14, 1980). British Baptist historian and denominational leader. The son of Alexander William Payne, a businessman, he was educated at Kings College, London (B.A.), Regent's Park College, London (B.D.), St. Catherine's and Mansfield College, Oxford (B.Litt.), and University of Marburg, Germany. St. Andrews University awarded him the D.D. degree in 1944. He married Winifred Mary Davies in 1930. They had one child, Ann.

Unable to accept foreign missionary service, he became pastor at Bugbrooke, Northampton, in 1928. He joined the headquarters staff of the Baptist Missionary Society in 1932 as secretary of the Youth Department. In 1936 he became editorial secretary of the BMS. He joined the tutorial staff of Regent's Park College, Oxford, in 1940 in the area of historical theology. He received appointment as university lecturer at Oxford in 1946 in that field as well as in comparative religion and modern missions.

Payne served as general secretary of the Baptist Union of Great Britain and Ireland, 1951-67. While general secretary he continued to work to overcome the damage done to churches during World War II and helped rebuild Baptist church life in Great Britain at all levels. He was instrumental in helping to improve ministerial training, develop new areas of evangelism, and strengthen ecumenical ties. He served as vice-president of the Baptist World Alliance, 1965-70. Active in the World Council of Churches, he served as president, 1968-75. In 1968 he was made a Companion of Honour by the Queen. He was president of the Baptist Union of Great Britain and Ireland, 1977-78, and president of the Baptist Historical Society.

A prolific author of books, pamphlets, and articles, Payne's major books included: *The Saktas* (1933); *The Church Awakes* (1942); *The Free Church Tradition in the Life of England* (1944); *The Fellowship of Believers* (1944); *Henry Wheeler Robinson* (1946); *The Anabaptists of the 16th Century* (1949); *The Baptists of Berkshire* (1952); *James Henry Rushbrooke* (1954); *The Baptist Union: A Short History* (1959); *Veteran Warrior* (a memoir of B. Grey Griffith) (1962); *Free Churchmen Unre-*

pentant and Repentant (1965); *The World Council of Churches* (1970); and *Out of Great Tribulation: Baptists in the Soviet Union* (1974).

BIBLIOGRAPHY: L. G. Champion, *Outlook for Christianity* (1967).

BILL J. LEONARD

PEACE, WAR AND (cf. Peace and Southern Baptists, Vols. II, III; War and Peace, Vol. II). In the 1970s the SBC passed numerous resolutions related to peace. During the early years of the decade, the Vietnam War was the primary focus. These resolutions expressed a commitment to pray for peace and encouraged the President, national leaders, and the United Nations in their efforts to stop the war. In 1972 one peace resolution addressed the issues of conscientious objection and conscientious participation, and another asked for prayerful consideration of the amnesty issue in the context of justice for all. Following the war, the 1974 Convention called for redirecting resources from waging war to healing wounds at home and abroad.

In 1978 one resolution expressed support for arms control, slowing the arms race, and diverting funds from building nuclear weapons to meeting human needs. In the same spirit another 1978 SBC resolution expressed support for SALT II and urged Senate ratification.

See also ARMS CONTROL, DISARMAMENT, AND WORLD PEACE and BAPTIST PEACEMAKER, THE.

WILLIAM H. ELDER, III

PEACE AND SOUTHERN BAPTISTS (II, III). See ARMS CONTROL, DISARMAMENT, AND WORLD PEACE.

PEACHTREE-ON-PEACHTREE INN (III). See GEORGIA BAPTIST HOMES, INC.

PEARCY, GEORGE C. (b. Bedford, VA, June 23, 1813; d. Aug. 24, 1871). Foreign missionary. He attended the Virginia Baptist Seminary (now University of Richmond) and Columbian College, Washington, DC. He married Frances Miller, May 30, 1846. Appointed to Canton, China, Nov. 3, 1845, he joined the Shanghai Mission, Nov., 1848, but resigned Jan. 8, 1855, and returned home due to broken health. He is buried in Cedar Forest Cemetery, Pittsylvania, VA.

FRANK K. MEANS

PEARSON, ROBERT DERFEY (b. Scott County, MS, June 14, 1888; d. Macon, MS, Nov. 25, 1979). Pastor. Son of John Pearson, farmer-preacher, and Martha (Buckner) Pearson, teacher-homemaker, he married Willie Mae Watt, Apr. 9, 1909. They had six children: Robert, Glen, Wilbur, Dorothy, William, and John. Following her death in 1964, he married Elizabeth Tumberlinson. Pastor of First Baptist Church, Macon, MS, for 28 years, 1927-55, he served 21 years on the Mississippi Baptist Convention Board with nine of those years on the executive committee and on the Education Commission.

A firm believer in Church Training, Pearson sponsored Baptist Young People's Union and encouraged Mississippi Baptist youth. He attended the University of Mississippi, earning the certificate in pharmacy; Clarke College and Southwestern Baptist Theological Seminary; and studied extensively in Greek and Hebrew. His early pastorates were at Dixon, Stratton, Lena, Longview, and Sturgis—all in Mississippi—and Bright Hope Church, Fort Worth, TX. Moderator of Noxubee County Association in Mississippi, he served as chaplain of Noxubee General Hospital after retirement. He is buried in Odd Fellows Cemetery, Macon, MS.

MRS. EARL (MARJORIE) KELLY

PECK, JAMES CLAUDE (b. Lafayette, LA, 1916; d. Dallas, GA, Aug. 13, 1961). Chaplain. The son of Wilson J. Peck, Sr., a building inspector, he attended the University of Southwestern, Lafayette, LA; Southwestern Baptist Theological Seminary (B.D.); and New Orleans Baptist Theological Seminary (M.R.E.). A pioneer in the field of industrial chaplaincy, he served as an industrial and hospital chaplain in North Carolina before joining the staff of the Home Mission Board in 1959 as secretary of the Institutional and Industrial Chaplaincy. Peck married Betty Kate Lee in 1945. Following her death, he married Helen Dykes in 1954. Their children were Katherine and James Claude, Jr. He is buried in Greenlawn Memorial Park, Lafayette, LA.

CARL HART

PENDERGRAPH, GARLAND ROOSEVELT (b. Durham, NC, Jan. 14, 1908; d. Ridgecrest, NC, June 16, 1972). Pastor, denominational worker, and chaplain. The son of Rose Gooch and Edwin Pendergraph, a dairyman, he attended Wake Forest College (A.B.) and The Southern Baptist Theological Seminary (Th.M., 1937). He married Jackie B. Davis, July 4, 1933. They had three sons: Garland, Jack, and Newton. Following pastorates in New Haven, Benson, and Perryville, KY, he served as an army chaplain in Europe during World War II. He served on the Executive Board of the Kentucky Baptist Convention for 26 years. He is buried in Rest Haven Cemetery, Louisville, KY.

LEO T. CRISMON

PENN-JERSEY BAPTIST. Monthly news journal of the Baptist Convention of Pennsylvania-South Jersey. Beginning in 1971, shortly after the new convention was organized, the publication was issued as a part of *The Maryland Baptist,* official publication of the Baptist Convention of Maryland. In July, 1979, responsibility for printing each monthly edition of the paper shifted to the Harrisburg office of the Pennsylvania-South Jersey Convention. With the Aug., 1979, issue, all eight pages were devoted to state and Southern Baptist Convention news along with more elaborate promotion of the state convention's programs of work. Ellis Bush, executive secretary-treasurer of the convention, serves as editor. Circulation in 1980 approached 8,000.

See also MARYLAND BAPTIST, THE.

ELLIS M. BUSH

PENNSYLVANIA-SOUTH JERSEY ASSOCIATIONS.

CONEMAUGH VALLEY. Formed on Oct. 23, 1977, by messengers from five churches and one mission in the eastern section of the Greater Pittsburgh Baptist Association. This association was organized to serve the seven counties between Indiana and Fulton, in south central Pennsylvania. On Mar. 1, 1980, John W. Stair became the first director of missions for the new association. In 1980 five churches and one mission reported 79 baptisms, 696 members, $207,461 total gifts, $28,322 mission gifts, and $935,000 property value.

DELAWARE VALLEY. Organized Oct. 27, 1962, by messengers from four churches and three missions. The area included seven counties in eastern Pennsylvania and nine counties in southern New Jersey. The association was affiliated with the Baptist Convention of Maryland until 1970 when it joined the newly formed Baptist Convention of Pennsylvania-South Jersey. In 1980, 37 churches and 13 missions reported 390 baptisms, 5,023 members, $1,098,046 total gifts, $194,347 mission gifts, and $4,626,500 property value.

GREATER PITTSBURGH. Organized Sep. 13, 1963, by the messengers from four churches and five missions. The area to be served was approximately 29 counties in western Pennsylvania. The association was affiliated with the State Convention of Baptists in Ohio until it joined the newly formed Baptist Convention of Pennsylvania-South Jersey in 1970. In 1980, 17 churches and 10 missions reported 224 baptisms, 3,234 members, $897,435 total receipts, $142,140 mission gifts, and $3,878,521 property value.

KEYSTONE. Organized Oct. 13, 1962, with messengers present from the four Southern Baptist churches in south central Pennsylvania. The area to be served by this association included approximately 31 counties in central Pennsylvania. The association affiliated with the Baptist Convention of Maryland until 1970 when it joined the newly formed Baptist Convention of Pennsylvania-South Jersey. In 1980, 26 churches and 16 missions reported 621 baptisms, 6,018 members, $1,587,744 total gifts, $285,005 mission gifts, and $5,556,500 property value.

NORTHEAST. Organized on Oct. 25, 1975, when representatives from the Dallas Baptist Church and three missions met in Williamsport, PA. This association was to promote fellowship among the few Southern Baptists in this church and these missions and to promote church extension in the 15-county area of northeastern Pennsylvania. On Nov. 1, 1975, Jack R. Smith became its first director of missions. In 1980 four churches and seven missions reported 105 baptisms, 657 members, $195,540 total gifts, $107,346 mission gifts, and $308,000 property value.

NORTHWEST. Organized Oct. 20, 1974, by three churches and six missions which had previously affiliated with the Greater Pittsburgh Association. The new association was formed to serve the 13 counties in northwestern Pennsylvania. On Aug. 1, 1975, J. Lowell Wright came from Indiana to serve as the first director of missions. In 1980 six churches and eight missions reported 72 baptisms, 1,162 members, $235,540 total gifts, $112,366 mission gifts, and $560,000 property value.

GEORGE WOODROW BULLARD

PENNSYLVANIA-SOUTH JERSEY, BAPTIST CONVENTION OF (III).

I. Southern Baptist Beginnings. Prior to 1958 four known Southern Baptist churches existed in the Pennsylvania-South Jersey area. All were affiliated with either the Baptist Convention of Maryland or the State Convention of Baptists in Ohio. Three of these churches were organized by Maryland Baptists and are now a part of the work of the Baptist Convention of Pennsylvania-South Jersey: The Wrightsdale Church, Peach Bottom, PA, organized in 1933; Oak View Church, Hanover, PA, organized in 1950; and Seven Valleys Church, Seven Valleys, PA, organized in 1952. All three of these congregations cooperated with Maryland Baptists and Southern Baptists through the Susquehanna Baptist Association. The fourth church, the Bolivar Drive Church, Bradford, PA, organized in 1954 through the efforts of Ohio Baptists, was first affiliated with the Erie Association of Ohio Baptists.

A group of Baptist churches was organized in Southeastern Pennsylvania by people who had moved into the area from West Virginia, Southwestern Virginia, Western North Carolina, and Eastern Tennessee. Until 1958 some of these churches related to the Ashe Baptist Association in North Carolina. Since forming the State Line Baptist Association in 1958 (name changed to Eastern Pennsylvania Baptist Association, 1961), they have had little or no contact with Southern Baptists.

In 1957 and 1958, three new areas of Baptist work opened in Pennsylvania which attracted Baptist leadership in Ohio, Maryland, and the Home Mission Board, SBC. The first effort in this new movement began in Pittsburgh in 1957 when the General Shoe Corporation transferred Jack Edens from Nashville, TN, to that Pennsylvania city. In May, 1958, representatives from the HMB and the State Convention of Baptists in Ohio met with Edens at the Greater Pittsburgh Airport to discuss the possibilities of beginning a Southern Baptist church in Pittsburgh. In July, 28 people responded to a newspaper announcement and met for the first time in Soldiers and Sailors Memorial Hall, Pittsburgh, to discuss starting a Southern Baptist mission in that city. The group continued to meet for Bible study and worship. The work experienced steady growth, and the Pittsburgh

Baptist Church was constituted in Oct., 1959. The new church affiliated with the Upper Ohio Association and the State Convention of Baptists in Ohio. Joseph M. Waltz (q.v.), called as the first pastor, began his services in Oct., 1959, under appointment of the HMB.

In Levittown, PA, in late 1957, three Southern Baptist families—the Charles Edmonds, the Paul Martins, and the Robert Wilsons—feeling that Southern Baptist missionary zeal was a quality much needed in this newly developed city, began meeting for Bible study and prayer. The group sought the aid of the HMB, and A. B. Cash, secretary of pioneer missions, visited the area and promised all possible assistance. In Oct., 1958, interested families started a Sunday School which met in the Levittown Public Recreation Association building. A Southern Baptist Army chaplain from McGuire Air Force Base, Wrightstown, NJ, joined the group and acted as minister until Sep., 1959, when the HMB sent Padgett Cope of Alabama to serve as the first pastoral missionary for the greater Philadelphia area. In Mar., 1960, the Delaware Valley Baptist Church was constituted in Levittown. In June, 1960, the church started a mission in Levittown, NJ, now called Willingboro, and in June, 1961, the name of Delaware Valley Baptist Church went to the mission in Levittown, NJ, and the church in Pennsylvania became known as Haines Road Baptist Chapel.

The influx of more and more people from the South and Southwest into the central part of Pennsylvania made necessary a Southern Baptist church in that area. In May, 1958, Frank Brown, a serviceman from Florida, erected a sign at the corner of his block in Middletown, just a few miles from the state capital, Harrisburg, which pointed to his home and read: "Southern Baptist Mission—one block." In the summer of 1959, this group constituted as Valley Baptist Church with 43 members. K. Wiley Jarrell, area missionary for the Susquehanna Association of Maryland, served as the first pastor, on a part-time basis. In Apr., 1960, Ralph Neighbour, Jr., became the first full-time pastor. He later became director of missions for the central and eastern part of Pennsylvania and the southern half of New Jersey.

Southern Baptist associations first arose in Pennsylvania in 1962. Soon after the Valley Baptist Church, Middletown, was constituted, a church was started in Elizabethtown, to be known as Emmanuel Baptist Church. The Country and Town Baptist Church, Camp Hill, and Carlisle Baptist Church were both constituted in 1961. These four churches, with a membership of fewer than 300, organized Keystone Baptist Association in Oct., 1962. Dolan E. Henry (q.v.) came from the pastorate of North Park Baptist Church in Pittsburgh in 1965 to serve as the first full-time director of missions, following Ralph Neighbour who had divided his time between the Keystone and Delaware Valley associations. In the fall of 1970, the association reported 18 churches, 3 missions, and 2,475 church members.

Soon after the Delaware Valley Church moved to Willingboro, NJ, missions were started at Wrightstown, Absecon, and Lakehurst, NJ. During the same period, work was started in Paoli and Chester, PA. By late Oct., 1962, three of these missions had been constituted into churches. Following the annual meeting of the Northeastern Baptist Association in Wrightstown, NJ, the four churches and three missions organized the Delaware Valley Baptist Association with a total church membership of 465. In Sep., 1965, G. W. Bullard came from Gregory Memorial Baptist Church, Baltimore, MD, to serve as the first full-time director of missions. In Oct., 1970, the association reported 15 churches, 11 missions, and 3,200 church members.

Soon after the constitution of Pittsburgh Baptist Church, other churches were started in Monroeville, North Park, Charleroi, Garwood, and in downtown Pittsburgh. In Sep., 1963, the Greater Pittsburgh Baptist Association was formed with 4 churches, 5 missions, and almost 500 church members. Joseph M. Waltz, who had served as the first pastor of the Pittsburgh church and missionary for the area, became the director of missions in Jan., 1964. By Oct., 1970, the association reported 19 churches, 10 missions, and 2,569 church members.

II. Formation of the Convention. The first fellowship meeting initiated to help move in the direction of a convention for Southern Baptists in the northeastern states was held in Manhattan Baptist Church, New York City, Aug., 1960. No definite plans resulted, and the second meeting was held in Syracuse, NY, in May, 1963. A. B. Cash, secretary, department of pioneer missions, HMB, coordinated the plans and served as moderator of the meeting, which was cosponsored by the Baptist Convention of Maryland and the State Convention of Baptists in Ohio. One hundred twenty representatives came from churches in the nine Baptist associations located within the northeastern region. During this meeting a special committee was appointed to study the pros and cons of organizing a regional convention which would include Southern Baptist churches in Pennsylvania, New Jersey, New York, and the New England states. Joseph M. Waltz, Pittsburgh, served as chairman of the committee. This committee met twice during the year at Country and Town Baptist Church, Camp Hill, PA.

One of the first items of business brought before the next annual meeting of the Northeastern Regional Fellowship, meeting in Haines Road Baptist Church, Levittown, PA, Apr. 30-May 1, 1964, was a report of the study committee, recommending that efforts to organize a regional convention be discontinued. This motion caused a great deal of concern as years of planning were suddenly threatened with extinction. The discussion ended with a decision to hold area group meetings following the evening session. During the next morning session, the Pennsylvania-South Jersey group brought a report which suggested that representatives of the churches of Pennsylvania and Southern New Jersey recommend to these churches that a goal be set to organize a state convention in this area as soon as feasible and proper.

The first meeting of the new Pennsylvania-South Jersey Baptist Fellowship took place, Oct. 2-3, 1964, in North Park Baptist Church, Allison Park, Pittsburgh, PA. Sixty church representatives met and with the guidance of A. B. Cash, of the HMB, and the executive secretaries of the sponsoring state conventions, Maryland and Ohio, laid plans for a new state convention. The group discussed 1967 as a possible target year for organization, but no definite decision was made. A steering committee was elected headed by George N. Bagwell, a layman from Absecon, NJ, with Dolan Henry, pastor, North Park Church, as vice-chairman. The committee consisted of the officers of the fellowship, the moderators of the three associations, the directors of missions, and one additional member from each of the associational areas. The committee was to meet in the spring and fall with a general fellowship meeting in the fall of each year.

During the meeting of the fellowship in Oct., 1965, in Country and Town Baptist Church, Camp Hill, PA, reports revealed a total of 41 churches and chapels with approximately 4,000 members. The fellowship agreed that the fall of 1968 be the projected date for forming a state convention to begin functioning on Jan. 1, 1969.

When the committee met in Feb., 1966, evidence was clear that 70 churches and 10,000 members, as suggested by the HMB, would not be a realistic projection for the fall of 1968, and the committee believed that the fellowship should look at the projected date again in the fall meeting.

One hundred seventy-nine representatives from 33 churches attended the Sep. 30-Oct. 1, 1966, fellowship meeting and heard a report that the growth rate had been 18 percent during the year, adding 923 members and 11 new churches and chapels. The fellowship decided to set a new target date of Oct., 1969, for the organization of the new convention.

During its fourth annual meeting at the Monroeville, PA, Baptist Church in Sep., 1967, the fellowship decided to continue the present structure until the fall of 1969, at which time a functioning general state fellowship, with an executive board and a central office, be constituted as a preparatory step to the organization of a state convention in the fall of 1970. This delay of an additional year seemed wise even though there had been a growth rate of 27 percent. The fellowship appointed committees to consider personnel and staff needed, constitution and bylaws, budget, and location and site.

By the time of the meeting in Middletown PA, in Oct., 1968, more concrete plans had been made toward the organization of a convention. A proposed constitution and bylaws were presented for study and action in the fall of 1969; the churches were requested to send their 1968, 1969, and 1970 state mission offerings to

the fellowship rather than to the sponsoring states; the associations were asked to contribute 10 percent of receipts from churches to the fellowship; and the first full-time employee was to be an executive secretary.

The final meeting of the fellowship occurred in Delaware Valley Baptist Church, Willingboro, NJ, in Oct., 1969. Reports indicated that there were 7,406 church members in 43 churches and 32 chapels in the three associations. The fellowship decided to continue on the present schedule to constitute as a state convention in Oct., 1970, and to begin full operation on Jan. 1, 1971. The proposed constitution and bylaws were adopted, and the group proceeded to elect officers and members of an executive board. Standing committees were elected to make preparation for the organizational meeting. The fellowship agreed to elect an executive secretary-treasurer as soon after Jan. 1, 1970, as possible and appointed a special search committee to bring a recommendation to the executive board.

During 1970 the executive board established an office at 3805 Paxton Street, Harrisburg, PA; elected Joseph M. Waltz, director of missions, Greater Pittsburgh Baptist Association, to serve as the first executive secretary, effective Aug. 1, 1970; and appointed a committee to prepare a job description for a director of religious education and to recommend a person to fill the position.

On Oct. 2-3, 1970, 165 messengers and 85 visitors, representing 60 churches and 15 chapels with approximately 8,500 members, witnessed the official organization of the Baptist Convention of Pennsylvania-South Jersey as the 32nd state convention of Southern Baptists. The fellowship constitution and bylaws, adopted a year earlier, became the convention document with minor changes.

Officers were elected as follows: C. Ed Price, Pittsburgh, president; Frank E. Bowman, Camp Hill, first vice-president; Vernon S. Lee, Paoli, second vice-president; Angelo DeiRossi, Harrisburg, recording secretary; Paul A. Maxey, Pittsburgh, assistant recording secretary; and Frank W. Scott, Pittsburgh, historian. The new convention elected an executive board consisting of three members from the churches of each associational area, with two additional members when church membership exceeded 3,000, and up to five members at large with no more than two elected from any associational area. The budget adopted for 1971 anticipated a total income of $120,500 with $96,000 of this amount coming from the churches through the Cooperative Program. The new convention agreed that 20 percent of all undesignated funds would go to the SBC Executive Committee for world missions beyond the state convention area. Four standing committees were appointed: Program, Nominating, Credentials and Registration, and Auditing.

The new executive secretary-treasurer, Joseph M. Waltz, was presented to the convention. He challenged the messengers to continue in their dedication and to accept a goal of 300 churches and 50,000 members by 1980. He suggested an immediate goal of 30 new missions, 2,200 new members, and 1,400 baptisms in 1971. Out-of-state speakers present were Olin T. Binkley, president, Southeastern Baptist Theological Seminary; Roy T. Gresham, executive secretary, Baptist Convention of Maryland; Ray E. Roberts, executive secretary, State Convention of Baptists in Ohio; Arthur B. Rutledge (*q.v.*), executive secretary, HMB; and James L. Sullivan, executive secretary, Sunday School Board.

The women of the churches gathered for a luncheon meeting on Oct. 2, 1970, and organized a state Woman's Missionary Union. Louise Winningham, Harrisburg, was elected president, and Barbara Estep, Elizabethtown, secretary. The associational WMU directors were designated vice-presidents: Dorothy Breedlove, Greater Pittsburgh; Ruth Ward, Keystone; and Mozelle Bullard, Delaware Valley.

III. History of the Convention. The first decade of the convention was characterized by strong and visionary leadership, organizational development, and continued expansion.

Administrative Changes.—Joseph M. Waltz, executive secretary-treasurer, and a combination secretary-bookkeeper were the only employees of the convention when it began functioning in Jan., 1971. He died on Dec. 13, 1971. In Jan., 1972, the executive board elected convention president C. Ed Price to serve as acting executive secretary-treasurer, and asked that a committee be appointed to recommend a person for the office. At a special called meeting in June, 1972, the executive board elected G. W. Bullard, director of missions, Delaware Valley Baptist Association, to serve as executive secretary-treasurer, effective Aug. 1, 1972. In Apr., 1977, Bullard announced his retirement effective May 31, 1978. A search committee was appointed and in Feb., 1978, the executive board elected Ellis M. Bush, executive minister, First Baptist Church, Shreveport, LA, to serve as executive secretary-treasurer elect, Apr. 1-May 31, and then to assume the full responsibility for the position.

Organizational Development.—The convention planned from the beginning that it would promote its work through divisions and that the executive board would adjust its committee arrangements so that a committee could counsel with each division director, or help plan the programs of work not led by a paid director. The first staff division of responsibility came with the election of Larry L. Lewis as director of religious education, effective Feb. 1, 1971. Lewis promoted all the programs of work related to the Sunday School Board, SBC, and the executive secretary-treasurer did the administration, edited the state paper, and promoted the programs related to the HMB. As WMU president, Louise Winningham promoted WMU work on a volunteer basis until Jan., 1973, when she became a part-time director.

In 1973 the executive board approved a cooperative agreement with the HMB which made all missionaries joint employees of the state convention and channeled HMB support through the convention. This step enlarged the organization to three divisions: Communications and Promotion; Missions, with a Department of WMU; and Religious Education.

In anticipation of an expanded staff and new needs for adequate office space and staff services, the convention offices were moved to the Pennsylvania United Church Center, 900 South Arlington Avenue, Harrisburg, PA, on Sep. 1, 1973.

In Jan., 1974, A. C. Queen became the first director of the newly created Communications and Promotion Division.

Walter E. Browning of the Texas Sunday School Division staff became director of the Religious Education Division in Sep., 1974, and plans were soon made for the expansion of the division. A new plan of funding assistance from the SSB made it possible for the convention to add a Department of Training and Music to the Religious Education Division. In Apr., 1975, Harold R. Price came from the First Baptist Church, Rockville, MD, to serve as the first director of this new department.

In Jan., 1976, the responsibility for the program of Christian Social Ministries of the HMB was added to the responsibility of the WMU Department, and financial provisions were made for a full-time director. In Oct., 1976, Bobbie Black, director of associational missions for Powell River Association of Virginia, came as the first full-time director of the Department of WMU/CSM.

Following the resignation of A. C. Queen in 1977, assignments that he had carried were reevaluated, the Communications and Promotion Division was discontinued, and a new Evangelism and Stewardship Division was established. In this new approach, the executive secretary again assumed responsibility for editing the *Penn-Jersey Baptist* in order for the new division director to devote all of his time to the work of evangelism and stewardship. In Nov., 1977, Dan A. Ray, director of missions for Beaver Dam Association in South Carolina came to serve as the first director of the Evangelism and Stewardship Division.

Beginning in Jan., 1978, the organizational structure of the convention provided for a state missions director other than the executive secretary-treasurer. Wilson A. Parker, director of associational missions for the Southern Tier Association of New York, became the convention's first full-time missions director in Mar., 1978. After only a few months, Parker moved to become the executive director of the Iowa Southern Baptist Fellowship.

Peggy Masters of Arkansas, who had joined the Missions Division as director of the Department of WMU/CSM in May, 1978, shared the administrative responsibilities of the division with the executive secretary until May, 1979, when Harold E. Crane, Jr., came from Michigan to serve as director of the division.

Expansion.—When the convention was organized in Oct., 1970, there were 75 churches and chapels in three associations with approximately 8,500 members. In 1980 there were 150 churches and chapels in six associations with approximately 17,000 church members. The budget for 1971 was $120,500 with $96,000 of the total coming from the churches for the Cooperative Program. In 1980 the cooperative gifts from the churches were expected to total $304,000, and the total convention budget was $1,180,805. The percentage of Cooperative Program receipts going to missions through the SBC increased steadily from the beginning 20 percent to 26 percent in the 1980 budget.

IV. Program of Work. The convention elects an executive board and empowers it to administer the programs of work, according to the policies of the convention, employ the necessary personnel, and recommend to the convention an annual budget. Currently, the programs are assigned to the administrative office and three divisions, with the executive secretary-treasurer as the chief administrator. The executive board has a committee which relates to each division and the administrative office.

The executive secretary-treasurer, in addition to his administrative duties, edits the *Penn-Jersey Baptist*, relates to the Annuity Board concerning retirement and insurance programs, promotes endowment giving, and supervises the work of the business office.

The Missions Division works with the directors of associational missions and all other jointly appointed missionaries in the work of associational development, church extension, language missions, and summer mission activities, and supervises the work of the Department of WMU/CSM. The division relates to the HMB in other special activities in the state convention area. The director relates to the Brotherhood Commission and promotes the work of the Baptist Men and Royal Ambassadors, both in the churches and the associations.

The Department of WMU/CSM works with the associational WMU organizations to promote an effective program of missions education and prayer and mission giving involving the women, young women, and girls in the local churches. The department promotes the Lottie Moon Christmas Offering for Foreign Missions and the Annie Armstrong Easter Offering for Home Missions. The department oversees the preparation of material and the promotion of the State Missions Offering. The department encourages associations and churches to discover and meet the needs for ministry in the church communities. The director works closely with the appointed Christian social ministers.

The Division of Religious Education is responsible for the total programs of teaching, training, and development which are jointly promoted by the state convention and the SSB. The director is the staff member directly responsible for the promotion of Sunday School,

PENNSYLVANIA-SOUTH JERSEY STATISTICAL SUMMARY

Year	Associations	Churches	Church Membership	Baptisms	SS Enrollment	VBS Enrollment	CT Enrollment	WMU Enrollment	Brotherhood Enrollment	Ch. Music Enrollment	Mission Gifts	Total Gifts	Value Church Property
1969	—	—	—	—	—	—	—	—	—	—	—	—	—
1970	—	—	—	—	—	—	—	—	—	—	—	—	—
1971	3	51	9,191	905	8,603	7,791	2,247	1,534	627	1,223	$ 341,030	$1,348,000	$ 4,028,837
1972	3	57	9,819	915	9,018	7,140	2,392	1,613	705	1,314	444,432	1,549,562	4,436,500
1973	3	62	10,780	1,145	9,356	11,729	2,405	1,690	598	1,735	417,052	1,685,423	5,927,000
1974	3	67	11,864	1,067	9,995	10,492	2,226	1,812	768	1,586	438,766	1,783,639	7,008,600
1975	4	75	13,017	1,166	10,724	12,068	2,361	1,934	793	1,793	575,144	2,279,001	7,959,975
1976	5	78	14,117	1,193	11,606	10,746	2,442	1,881	762	2,084	646,722	2,374,471	9,514,575
1977	5	83	15,805	1,107	12,308	9,456	2,835	2,199	762	2,235	826,667	2,724,106	10,789,800
1978	6	90	16,068	1,127	12,471	13,749	2,653	2,224	856	2,292	836,298	2,941,016	12,436,039
1979	6	88	16,743	1,215	12,646	11,560	2,656	2,225	993	2,375	809,736	3,348,190	14,012,485
1980	7	95	17,568	1,425	13,906	10,354	3,521	2,207	891	2,938	1,073,742	3,886,277	16,551,021

JUNE RUDICK

Vacation Bible School, Church Administration, and Church Buildings Consultation. The director supervises other staff personnel in the division.

The Department of Training and Music, a part of the Religious Education Division, seeks to encourage Church Training, Church Music, Church Recreation, and Church Media centers in the churches, and Student Ministries on the college campuses. These programs are encouraged through state and associational events as well as local church events.

The Division of Evangelism and Stewardship works closely with the Evangelism Section of the HMB and the SBC Stewardship Commission in promoting these programs of work. Stewardship promotion involves assisting the churches directly and through state and associational training clinics to develop successful financial programs. The promotion of increased giving to world missions through the Cooperative Program is a major emphasis.

Evangelism, a program of seeking to reach the lost and lead them to faith in Jesus Christ, is encouraged by providing state evangelism conferences, associational clinics, mass evangelistic efforts, church revivals, and training in personal soul-winning.

Financial support of the convention program comes from the churches through the Cooperative Program and through an annual State Mission Offering given in connection with a season of prayer observance. The HMB, on the basis of a cooperative agreement with the state convention, contributes the major portion of the total mission budget. The SSB contributes to the support of the Religious Education Division staff members and provides some program assistance. Other program assistance funds come from the WMU and the Brotherhood Commission. Churches, individuals, and some associations from outside the convention area have provided funds for specific programs and have helped sponsor many new missions.

GEORGE WOODROW BULLARD

PEPPER, JAMES MORGAN (b. St. Thomas, NV, Apr. 17, 1884; d. Miami, FL, Feb. 18, 1974). State executive-secretary. His guardian was M. Whalem of St. Joseph, MO. He attended William Jewell College, Liberty, MO (1904-06), and Southern Baptist Theological Seminary (Th.M., 1909). He married Jessie Wright. Their children were James and Virginia. He served as pastor of Three Rivers and Farmington, MO, Baptist churches; Lansdowne Baptist Church, East St. Louis, IL, where he organized four churches and three missions; Maplewood, MO, Baptist Church, and Felda Baptist Church in Collier County, FL, from 1936 to retirement.

Pepper became the second general secretary of the Illinois Baptist State Association, June 1, 1926, when it was virtually bankrupt. Starting all night prayer meetings at the annual meetings of the state association, he reduced the debt from $122,804—plus $24,432 in overdrafts and

$13,789 held out of denominational funds—to $57,988 by Oct. 30, 1929. Exhausted, he resigned, Nov. 30, 1929. He is buried in Flagler Memorial Park, Miami, FL.

B. J. MURRIE

PEREIRA ALVES, ANTONIO (b. Brazil, c. 1886; d. Cuba, 1958). Home missionary. A writer of many books and articles in Spanish, Portuguese, and English, he was converted in Argentina. He arrived in Cuba, 1911; married Elena Sanchez, 1913; served as a pastor in Palmira, Arrieta, Guayos and Cumanayagua, Cuba; and taught literacy near Cumanayagua.

LOYD CORDER

PERRY, EZEL WILLIE (b. Noxubee, MS, May 14, 1882; d. Oklahoma City, OK, Aug. 31, 1969). Black Baptist pastor. Son of Jack and Mary Perry, he married Sarah Jennings. They had seven children. Moving west in 1908, he edited *The Baptist Rival* at Ardmore, OK. After a short pastorate at Woodville, he moved to El Reno, followed by four years at Lawton, then to the pastorate of Tabernacle Church, Oklahoma City, for 42 years, 1915-57. He was president of the Oklahoma Baptist State Convention 43 years, 1919-62. In 1937 he led in founding the Oklahoma School of Religion and was chairman of its trustees until it closed in 1963.

A vice-president of the National Baptist Convention, U.S.A., Inc., 1941-53, in 1949 he was one of the first blacks to give a major address at an SBC meeting.

J. M. GASKIN

PERU, MISSION IN (II, III). Peru's new constitution implied separation of church and state with equality for all religious bodies. Laymen were active in evangelistic campaigns in the coastal cities. The Baptist convention named its first two national home missionaries in 1979, and the churches responded with adequate support. Radio programs on 16 different stations reached a wide audience, and the bookstore ministry grew significantly. Efforts were made to reach the Chinese community in Lima, and new missions were established in the mountain and jungle areas. Seminary enrollment increased, but many churches continued with lay pastors. The convention adopted the theme, "Consolidate and Advance." At the end of 1979, there were 51 churches and 109 missions.

J. BRYAN BRASINGTON

PHILIPPINES, MISSION IN (II, III). Rapid church growth characterized Southern Baptist witness in the Philippines during the 1970s. The number of churches tripled to 522, and church membership reached 33,879. In early 1980, 160 missionaries (career and support) served in the Philippines. The mission emphasized organization of Sunday Schools, widespread literature distribution, home Bible studies, radio and TV programs coupled with correspondence courses, and evangelistic crusades. Three conventions (Chinese, Luzon, and Mindanao) composed of 21 associations emerged by 1980. Philippine Baptist Extension Seminary Training, established in 1972, grew rapidly. Southern Baptist College, M'lang, has prospered, and a second Bible school was established at Dagupan. Agricultural, humanitarian projects, and evangelism on Mindanao have brought response from remote tribes.

WILLIAM T. ROBERSON

PIANI, JOSEPH FRANK. See PLAINFIELD, JOSEPH FRANK.

PIONEER PLANS. See BROTHERHOOD COMMISSION, SBC.

PIPES, JAMES CARTER (b. Wilkes County, NC, Feb. 8, 1887; d. Asheville, NC, Feb. 19, 1971). Pastor and state missionary. Son of William and Ladocia Pipes, farmers, he was converted under the preaching of Isaac Miller, a country preacher. He received a diploma from Mars Hill College (1919). Pipes married Bessie Gregory in 1908. They had two children, James and Beulah. After her death, he married Nora Fagan in 1917. They had three children: Lena, June, and William. Following her death, he married Ruth Sprinkle in 1938. They had one daughter, Lynda Jayne.

Pipes became field secretary for the North Carolina Baptist State Convention in 1937, serving in this position for the next 20 years. After retiring from the North Carolina Convention in 1957, he served for 10 years as chaplain in the hospitals of Asheville, NC. He is buried in the Gabriel's Creek Baptist Church cemetery, Mars Hill, NC.

ERSKINE PLEMMONS

PLACE OF MEETING, SOUTHERN BAPTIST CONVENTION (II, III). See SOUTHERN BAPTIST ANNUAL CONVENTION ARRANGEMENTS.

PLACEMENT OF MINISTERS. See MINISTERS, PLACEMENT OF.

PLAINFIELD, JOSEPH FRANK (b. Martinego, Province Bergamo, Lombardy, Italy, Oct. 15, 1880; d. Traveler's Rest, SC, Dec. 27, 1976). Home missionary to Italians. Born Guiseppi Francesco Piani, he was educated in Italy to the Catholic priesthood and sent to Brazil as a missionary priest, where he became a Baptist in 1904 through the influence of Solomon Ginsberg (q.v.) and W. H. Canada (q.v. III). Plainfield taught in Baptist schools in Brazil until 1906, when he came to the United States. He graduated from William Jewell College (B.A.) and Southern Baptist Theological seminary (Th.D., 1911).

Ordained to the Baptist ministry in 1909, he later returned to Brazil, but came to the USA permanently in 1915, serving with the American Baptist Home Mission Society until 1924 and St. Louis (MO) City Missions until 1926, when he was appointed by the Home Mission Board, SBC, to serve in Tampa, FL. He married Alice Lucas, Jan. 12, 1912. They retired in 1946 and lived in Cleveland, SC, until her death in 1969, when he moved to Traveler's Rest.

BIBLIOGRAPHY: Joseph Frank Plainfield, "Autobiography," unpublished manuscript (Atlanta, Home Mission Board Library). *Home Missions,* Oct. 7, 1976. Plainfield, Joseph Frank file, archives (Home Mission Board Library).

KATE ELLEN GRUVER

PLANNING, CONVENTION EMPHASES PRIORITY. See CONVENTION EMPHASES PRIORITY PLANNING.

POLHILL, LUCIUS McLENDON (b. Hawkinsville, GA, Dec. 19, 1899; d. Richmond, VA, May 9, 1971). Teacher, pastor, and denominational executive. The son of John Carter, II, and Rosa (DeVaughan) Polhill, he graduated, following service in World War I, from Mercer College (B.A., 1920) and Southern Baptist Theological Seminary (Th.M., 1923; Ph.D., 1934). He married Elizabeth Bowne, Aug. 16, 1928. They had two sons, Lucius M., Jr., and John. He was professor of Bible at Bessie Tift College, 1923-31. His pastorates were: Salem Church, Shelby, KY, 1931-34; Vinton Church, Vinton, VA, 1934-36; First Church, Americus, GA, 1936-43; and Deer Park Church, Louisville, KY, 1943-55. He served on the boards of the Georgia and Kentucky Baptist Conventions. He was executive secretary of the Virginia Baptist Board of Missions and Education, 1955-68.

Polhill received honorary degrees from Mercer University (D.D., 1939) and the University of Richmond (D.H.L., 1967). He served as president of SBC state executive secretaries. A member of a number of Convention boards, at the time of his death he was chairman of the administrative committee of the Foreign Mission Board, SBC. He is buried at Tifton, GA.

IRA D. HUDGINS

POLLARD, ROBERT THOMAS (b. Gainesville, AL, Oct. 4, 1860; d. Selma, AL, Jan. 17, 1938). First black Home Mission Board appointee. Son of Robert and Mary Frances Webb Pollard, he graduated from Alabama Normal and Theological School, Selma, AL, in 1884, and Selma University (A.B., 1896). First appointed by I. T. Tichenor (q.v. III) of the HMB as Sunday School missionary, he later served the HMB as a general missionary for Negro Baptists in Alabama. He served as pastor of leading churches in Alabama, was president of Florida Baptist Institute, Live Oak, FL, and twice served as president of Selma University, 1902-11, 1916-29. He was one of 19 blacks attending the first Baptist World Alliance. After retiring from the Selma presidency, he again became a teacher missionary under the HMB.

He married Eliza Washington, Apr. 7, 1887.

They had one son. After Eliza's death in 1927, he married Pinkie Green Calloway, Sep. 4, 1928.

EMMANUEL McCALL

PONDEROSA SOUTHERN BAPTIST ASSEMBLY (III). Located near Monument, CO, the state assembly of Colorado Baptists ended its 19th year of service in 1979. Joe Cherry was business manager-program coordinator. Cherry returned to Ponderosa in 1978 after serving three years as food services director for Glorieta Conference Center. Al Owen served as director of Ponderosa, 1976-78. The facility now has about 700 acres. A master development plan projects a recreation building, motel, rustic camp, additional conference and administrative space, and a retirement center.

JAMES LEE YOUNG

POOL, JAMES CHRISTOPHER (b. Dove, TX, Jan. 26, 1905; d. San Angelo, TX, Jan. 21, 1978). Missionary, seminary administrator. Son of Ulrich Pool, schoolteacher, and Etta (Starges) Pool, homemaker, he was educated at Baylor University (B.A., 1929); Southern Baptist Theological Seminary (Th. M., 1932; Ph.D. 1936); and Peabody College. He married Elizabeth Routh, Dec. 26, 1935. They had three children: Frances, Carolyn, and James Christopher, Jr. Appointed by the SBC Foreign Mission Board, Apr. 19, 1934, he served in Nigeria, 1934-71, and Liberia, 1971-72. While he was principal of the Nigerian Baptist Theological Seminary, Ogbomosho, 1938-71, the building was built, 1955, and the Nigerian seminary became an extension of Southern Seminary in Louisville, KY. He retired, Aug. 1, 1972. He is buried at Lockhart, TX.

FRANK K. MEANS

POOR IN NEW TESTAMENT PERSPECTIVE, THE. In the New Testament the term "poor" (*ptochos*) appears over 30 times depicting persons destitute of material goods and compelled to beg for survival. Occasionally, it describes day laborers (2 Cor. 9:9; Luke 21:2). The poor are often referred to by noting a specific consequence of their indigence, such as hunger or nakedness.

The poor were special objects of concern in the sayings and deeds of Jesus. He assured them of a reversal of circumstances with the arrival of God's rule (Matt. 5:3-12; Luke 6:20-23), challenged his disciples to benevolence (Matt. 6:2; Luke 6:30; 12:33), and made compassionate action a criterion for judgment (Matt. 25:31-46; Luke 16:19-31).

First-century believers, likewise, accepted responsibility for the deprived. The community of goods in Jerusalem (Acts 2:44-45; 4:34-37), the Antiochene relief offering (Acts 11:29-30), and the Pauline collection for the saints (Gal. 2:10; Rom. 15:25-27; 1 Cor. 16:1-4; 2 Cor. 8—9) attested to both creativity of method and imperative of compassion.

See also POVERTY, VOL. III.

BIBLIOGRAPHY: Robert M. Shurden, "The Christian Response to Poverty in the New Testament Era," Ph.D. dissertation, Southern Baptist Theological Seminary, 1970.

ROBERT M. SHURDEN

POPE, CHARLES WESLEY (b. Cedartown, GA, Feb. 16, 1890; d. Knoxville, TN, Oct. 13, 1973). Pastor and state convention executive. Son of John Q. and Elizabeth Newman Pope, farmers, he was educated at Lanier High School, Macon, GA, Mercer University (A.B., M.A.), and Southern Baptist Theological Seminary. He married Mattie Mae Willoughby, Nov. 5, 1911. Their children were Maurice, Hughlan, Stanley, Virginia, and Mary Elizabeth. Ordained by Poplar Springs Baptist Church, Haralson County, GA, 1915, he served as an evangelist, 1915-20, and an instructor in evangelism, Mercer University, 1924-25. His pastorates were Dublin, GA, 1920-24; Concord, Chattanooga, TN, 1926; and First Baptist Church, Jefferson City, TN, 1927-42. He was a member of Tennessee Baptist executive board, a trustee of Carson-Newman College and Harrison-Chilhowee Academy, and a member of the Committee on Committees, SBC.

Pope was author of *The Church and the Kingdom, The Priority of State Missions,* and *Is Life Worth Living?* He was elected executive secretary-treasurer of the Tennessee Baptist Convention in 1942. After his retirement in 1956, he lived in Tallapoosa, GA, until his death in 1973. He is buried at Steadman, GA.

W. FRED KENDALL, SR.

PORNOGRAPHY (III). Southern Baptists have vigorously opposed pornography for a number of years. In recent times, as the quality of pornography has become slicker and sicker, Southern Baptist opposition has become more vigorous than ever. The basis for this opposition is the strong belief that pornography is an attack on God's good gift of sexuality. Southern Baptist opposition to pornography is not antisexual; rather, it is based on support for sexuality when expressed as God intends.

In 1974 the SBC joined the 1953, 1959, and 1968 Conventions in passing a resolution opposing pornography. The 1974 resolution urged Southern Baptists to continue the fight against pornographic materials until these items were removed from society.

In a resolution dealing with the subject of Christian morality, the 1977 SBC expressed its "continuing opposition to such immoral practices as pornography, obscenity, child abuse, and the exploitation of children in pornography."

The 1978 SBC opposed pornography as a "tool of Satan and a growing detriment to the moral climate of our nation and world." The messengers commended citizens' groups and law enforcement agencies that oppose pornography, and they encouraged churches to become involved in the fight against pornography. The 1979 SBC reaffirmed this resolution because "pornography is a moral cancer that continues to threaten the social health of our society."

The SBC has assigned the Christian Life Commission the primary responsibility for opposing pornography. A number of other agencies have joined in this opposition. The CLC continues to provide resource material to help Southern Baptists organize to fight pornography. Through pamphlets, books, and conferences, the commission provides positive teaching about sexuality as an alternative to the degrading and ultimately unfulfilling treatment of sex found in pornographic materials. Staff members of the commission have also testified in support of stronger anti-pornography laws before various legislative bodies.

See also SEXUALITY, HUMAN.

HARRY N. HOLLIS, JR.

PORTER, FREDERICK SEELY (b. Fredericton, New Brunswick, Canada, Feb. 8, 1880; d. Swainsboro, GA, Mar. 5, 1974). Son of Theodore Porter, a pastor, and Elizabeth Estabrooks Porter, he attended Acadia University, Wolfville, Nova Scotia (B.A., M.A., 1906) and Rochester Theological Seminary, Rochester, NY (B.D., 1908). He was ordained while in the seminary. In May, 1908, he married Edith Spurden of Fredericton. They had two daughters, Evelyn and Carol. After graduation from seminary, Porter served as pastor of the Baptist church in Liverpool, Nova Scotia, and Germain Street Baptist Church, St. John, New Brunswick. During World War I, he served as chaplain in the Canadian Army, reaching the rank of major. After three years in service, he became secretary of the British and Foreign Bible Society. From 1924 to 1930, he was pastor of Trinity Baptist Church, Oklahoma City, OK.

In 1930 Porter became pastor of First Baptist, Columbus, GA, serving there until his retirement in 1949. He was president of the Georgia Baptist Convention, a trustee of Mercer University and Shorter College, a member of the Home Mission Board, SBC, and chairman of the *Christian Index* board of directors. He is buried at Columbus, GA.

W. HOWARD ETHINGTON

PORTUGAL, MISSION IN (III). Portuguese Baptists were experiencing steady, but slow, growth at the end of the decade. In 1979 they reported 230 baptisms and a total membership of 3,000. Southern Baptists have helped them construct church buildings, buy two floors of an apartment house for their seminary use, purchase and develop a conference center, and operate a book store. Fourteen Southern Baptist missionaries serving in Portugal were engaged in radio and music work, seminary training, an English-language pastorate in the Azores, and evangelism and church development. Missionaries from Brazil were also working with Portuguese Baptists.

J. D. HUGHEY

POTTER, PAUL EDWIN (b. Webster County, MO, Dec. 19, 1932; d. Santiago, Dominican Republic, July 7, 1971). Missionary. Son of Roy and Lila Potter, farmers, he married Nancy Ann Roper, July 3, 1957. They had two children, Susan and David. A graduate of Southwest Missouri State University (B.A.) and The Southern Baptist Theological Seminary (Th.B.), he was appointed a missionary by the Foreign Mission Board in 1965. He and his wife started a new work in Santiago, Dominican Republic, in Oct., 1966. During the next four years two churches were organized and three missions were established. Following a year's furlough, they returned to Santiago and were murdered in their home, July 7, 1971. He is buried in the Marshfield, MO, City Cemetery.

L. L. RODGERS

POWELL, FRANK MARION (b. New Bloomfield, MO, Mar. 29, 1886; d. Thomasville, NC, Mar. 19, 1973). Pastor and educator. Son of Malinda A. and James Powell, he graduated from William Jewell College (A.B., 1912), The Southern Baptist Theological Seminary (Th.M., 1916; Th.D., 1917), and attended the University of Cincinnati, Chicago University, and Oxford University. He married Kathleen Stone in 1913. They had three children: Frank, Jr., Robert, and Virginia. Powell served as professor of homiletics, 1918-19, and professor of church history, 1919-41, at Southern Seminary; and professor of church history and homiletics at Golden Gate Baptist Theological Seminary, 1949-52. He held numerous pastorates, including Beechmont, Parkland, and Highland, all in Louisville, KY. He is buried at Thomasville, NC.

BILL J. LEONARD

POWELL, ROBERT LEE (b. MS, Jan. 22, 1888; d. Tacoma, WA, July 30, 1970). Pastor. He married Altha Tabbott in 1919. They had four children: Robert, Rosaltha, Jarell, and Maribeth. He attended Mississippi College (B.A.). While pastor of Temple Baptist Church, Tacoma, WA, he served as one of the founders of the Interstate Baptist Mission in 1943. In 1948 the mission was dissolved in favor of the organization of the Baptist General Convention of Oregon (now known as the Northwest Baptist Convention.) The Temple Church did not choose to cooperate with the newly-formed convention. He is buried at Tacoma, WA.

C. E. BOYLE

PRAISING. A four-day church music event held in Nashville, TN, Mar. 10-13, 1975, and sponsored by the Church Music Department of the Sunday School Board. More than 10,000 registrants from 47 states, Brazil, Canada, and Japan participated.

The major feature of PraiSing was the introduction of the *Baptist Hymnal* (1975), which was premiered on Mar. 13, 1975, in Nashville's

2421 Preaching, Changing Emphases in

Municipal Auditorium. Each registrant was given a copy of a special edition of the hymnal. A 600-voice men's chorus made up of The Centurymen and the ministers of music groups from 13 states performed, and the 10,000 registrants sang a dozen hymns that evening.

An unusual feature of PraiSing was singing through the new hymnal. Fifty singing groups shared in a continuous singing of 30 hours and 27 minutes. Every stanza of every hymn in the new hymnal was sung, and all Scripture selections were read aloud.

A major choral work was commissioned from Cecil Effinger, noted American composer. Textual material for the work, *This We Believe,* was selected from the statement on the Baptist Faith and Message (1963). The performance, under the direction of Amerigo Marino, featured the choirs of 12 Southern Baptist schools and the Nashville Symphony Orchestra. Also commissioned were orchestral settings of five favorite Baptist hymn tunes. Francis McBeth, Llewelyn Gomer, Adolphus Hailstork, David Van Vactor, and Robert Ward composed these settings.

In addition to the 19 local church choirs and 13 state singing groups, choirs from the following Southern Baptist educational institutions sang at PraiSing: Baptist Bible Institute, Belmont College, Blue Mountain College, California Baptist College, Carson-Newman College, Dallas Baptist College, Louisiana College, Mars Hill College, Missouri Baptist College, Shorter College, Southwestern Baptist Theological Seminary, and William Carey College.

Concert artists featured during the four-day event were Betty Jean Chatham, Cynthia Clawson, Jerry Clower, David Ford, the Fisk Jubilee Singers, Robert Hale, Myrtle Hall, Jake Hess, Donald P. Hustad, Max Lyall, Russell Newport, Jeannie C. Riley, George Beverly Shea, the Speer Family, Beverly Terrell, Jet Turner, Randall Veazey, and Dean Wilder.

WILLIAM J. REYNOLDS

PRAYER, BAPTIST WOMEN'S WORLD DAY OF. See BAPTIST WOMEN'S WORLD DAY OF PRAYER.

PRAYER MEETING. A prayer meeting is a relatively informal worship service regularly scheduled by a church during the middle of the week, usually on Wednesday evening, which is at least partially devoted to prayer, and in which the laity usually participate more than in the Sunday worship services.

Although Christians have always gathered periodically for prayer, the precise origin of the prayer meeting as a regular worship service of the church is difficult to ascertain. Two precursors that may have influenced Baptists as early as the eighteenth century were the Methodist midweek prayer services, following John Wesley's informal gatherings for prayer, and the earlier Pietist midweek meetings for prayer and Bible study. The earliest precursors were the sixteenth and seventeenth century Puritan "prophesyings" and other meetings for exhor-

tation and prayer involving lay participation and leadership. As Baptists arose out of Puritanism, they continued such lay participation even after the Puritans had stopped it. Some Baptists even cited their determination to continue it as one reason for separating from the Puritans. Baptists at this time, however, tended to incorporate this lay participation into the Sunday worship rather than having separate weekday services.

Baptists had often set aside special days, depending on the occasion, for thanksgiving and prayer or for humiliation, fasting, and prayer. By the latter part of the eighteenth century, they had begun holding regular monthly prayer meetings to pray for revival of religion. The First Baptist Church of Boston may have been the first to make this a regular weekly service when they took action on Oct. 28, 1793, to have a prayer meeting every Monday evening, and not long afterward changed it to Wednesday.

The practice of a midweek prayer meeting spread in the nineteenth century and came to be associated primarily with prayer for revival and missions. Many revivals grew out of these prayer meetings, and missions gained considerable impetus from them. Gradually, however, as pastors tended to dominate, the prayer meeting lost its basic lay orientation, becoming either an abbreviated Sunday service or a Bible study.

In recent years many churches have incorporated a prayer meeting into a midweek family night program including a meal, mission and music activities, and other church meetings to develop a program with full family involvement. Some churches have also sought to make prayer meeting again a more informal gathering with considerable lay participation for the basic purpose of prayer.

See also PRAYER, VOL. II.

G. THOMAS HALBROOKS

PREACHING, CHANGING EMPHASES IN SOUTHERN BAPTIST (cf. Preaching, Southern Baptist, Vols. II, III). Preaching is an act of the church in which the substance of faith is freshly declared and interpreted anew. It is an event—a moment, a meeting, a sudden seeing —in which preacher, listener, message, and social environment come together. Effective proclamation of the good news requires that the gospel be understood both conceptually and contextually. To ground the church's witness upon the premise that mere proclamation alone will suffice is inadequate. Preaching demands a proper regard for the total human matrix and requires an understanding of the mood and mind of the age. Forming and dominating the cultural life of any epoch is a deep preconceptual attitude toward and understanding of human existence. The past decade has brought far-reaching mutations in human consciousness and corresponding changes in the way the gospel is communicated.

The preacher of today addresses a modern spirit that is radically "this worldly." He encounters a raw secularity. An undertone of nihilism subtracts all elements of affirmation. Historical dislocation marks the world, resulting in a break in the vital and nourishing symbols of cultural tradition. The media provide a flooding of imagery and the transmission of meaning that is immediate and instantaneous. Television has become the universal curriculum of the young and old, the common symbolic environment of all people. A kind of "psychic numbing" marks the present with gaps between knowledge and feeling. Population, social, and vocational mobility have disrupted the coherence and supportiveness of social life, with a resulting aloofness and apathy in human relationships. A premium upon privacy translates into nonavailability to others and an abdication of public responsibility.

The total social environment has constricted selfhood and diminished capacity for experience. People are "acting out" an attempted redefinition of human existence in the light of a new set of values centering about freedom and self-realization. All of these developments have profoundly influenced the shape and style of preaching.

Radio and Television.—Southern Baptists increasingly employ radio and television, or feel their influence, in proclaiming the gospel, not only in regular worship services broadcast from the church sanctuary but also in special programs on Sundays and weekdays. Clergy give many daily devotional broadcasts. The Foreign Mission Board appoints media specialists and makes abundant use of radio and television in the denomination's evangelistic programs overseas. Seminary classes make frequent use of closed circuit television for the preaching and evaluation of student sermons.

Massive and continuous exposure to the media today has created a new set of problems revolving around an overreception of information and entertainment to such a degree that vicarious experience dominates direct experience. The ready acceptance of projected images stifles cultural individuality. A swift simultaneity exists in the media—the terse profile, the one-minute commercial, the five-minute news summary—that contrasts sharply with the conventional liturgies of the church that move programmatically according to an order or shape.

By means of television the hearers of the gospel are as much surfeited with pictures as with words; thus the preacher who communicates must become skillful in turning human ears into eyes. Moreover, he will have to become more conversational and personal in approach. Since television has added substantially to the sheer dynamism of culture and has increased restlessness of mind and spirit through employing a much larger ratio of human senses, the verbally dominated worship service is likely to suffer by comparison.

Millions today view the "electronic church" through nationwide programs by celebrated personalities such as Billy Graham. Week by week the services of worship in local churches are televised to viewers in the environs of the church. This massive presentation of the gospel makes a significant impact upon millions of persons who, for various reasons, are not aligned with local churches or are unable to attend churches of their choice.

For all its vast potential, much popular television preaching has its perils. Programs often do little more than expound the slogans and passwords of personalist pietism and encourage a "privatistic" concept of Christian discipleship. One must apply to television preaching the same criteria that one would use to measure all proclamations of the gospel. The preacher perverts the Word in merely plugging peace of mind, huckstering possibility thinking, fostering cultural piety, embracing civil religion uncritically, or endorsing a religion of mere civility. Electronic popular religion often overlooks the conflict between the gospel and unrepentant self-righteousness, offers candy-coated panaceas to complex problems, is unabashedly materialistic, neglects repentance, and proclaims a gospel of adjustment.

Biblical Exposition.—One of the great potentialities in Southern Baptist preaching lies in its heavy stress upon biblical exposition. Effective preaching occurs with primary reference to the Scriptures, which constitute the church's common memory and hope. Controversies over the nature of biblical revelation and authority have obscured or distorted the place of the Bible in preaching and the proper method of biblical exposition. The preacher can use the Bible rather than interpret it. Biblical revelation is rooted not in the frozen rigidity of propositional dogmatics but in a tradition of life and experience. The Bible is the account of the age-long, gracious action of God in seeking to win persons out of bondage to self-centeredness into the spontaneous affirmation of love. The true authority of the preacher's word lies in the divine action that precedes all that is said and done. The gospel is God's act of redemption before it is man's proclamation of it.

For all the emphasis upon biblical preaching, one cannot assume that all Southern Baptist preaching is a faithful rendering of the Word of God. Much preaching degenerates into moralizing, which assumes that the fundamental task of the sermon is to tell people what they should be and do—thus stressing things to be done, virtues to be developed, or beliefs to be held—with an obscuring of the proper relation of law and gospel. Preaching is truly biblical only when the Bible governs the content of the sermon and when the function of the sermon is analogous to that of the text. The Word that was once proclamation is to be brought into fresh proclamation as the preacher seeks to discern and set forth the continuing echo and recurrent message of the text.

Biblical preaching is a matter of "translation" so that the intention of the biblical writer can be expressed anew. Interpretation is the attempt to relate meanings to persons. The relevance of biblical history lies in no small measure in its challenge to conventional assumptions and in its points of difference from, and confrontation with, contemporary life.

Social Issues.—Southern Baptist preaching has increasingly concerned itself with social issues and concerns. The Christian Life Commission has rendered yeoman service in awakening and educating the conscience of Southern Baptists in social awareness and concern. This agency has provided in-depth analyses of current social problems and resources for addressing these issues. With increasing urbanization, congregations must reckon with conditions of decay and blight in inner cities, with racial tensions and rising crime rates. Increasingly suspect is the tidy, individualistic concept of salvation that has lost sight of persons in their social interconnectedness and historical continuity with the whole of life. One cannot easily ignore the objectifications of sin in economic, cultural, and political institutions and structures. The social order consists of inherited attitudes that have come down from generation to generation through customs, laws, and institutions.

The gospel is a call not only to personal liberation from sin but to a transformation of those powers in the economic spheres that are dehumanizing and oppressive. Enslaving ideologies such as racism, sexism, and consumerism afflict suburban captives today. Although people are comfortably cocooned in their modern gadgetry, the present-day malaise is a standing rebuttal to naive hopes or claims that advanced technology is a sufficient condition for excellence in human life. The Christian gospel challenges the faith of people in the "technological fix" and their assumptions that what counts is the measurable, the tangible, and the material. The present environmental degradation is a reminder that no part of nature is isolated from the whole ecological fabric.

People are accountable to God for the care of the earth: "The earth is the Lord's." People are to be over nature as stewards, custodians, and caretakers but under God. Human pride and greed must be effectively prevented from continuing the mad press toward growth in all sectors—population, investment, pollution, and depletion—that will lead ultimately to a rending of the world's social fabric. The Christian commitment of Southern Baptists is a call to cultivate intimations of humanity, qualitative dimensions in experience, and the hope that life can be reorganized in accord with precepts of a deeper spiritual kingdom.

Holistic Vision.—Southern Baptist preaching has become increasingly holistic in its vision and has moved in its objective from merely securing decisions for salvation or church membership to instructing and strengthening persons who have already embraced the Christian gospel and its claims upon life. Traditionally, Southern Baptists have been inclined to compress their theological understanding to a preoccupation with the theme of redemption—at some cost to creation, resurrection, incarnation, nurture, and churchmanship. Much preaching, understand-

ing, and witnessing within the denomination concentrate upon the meaning of atonement. While obvious strengths attend this vision, it suffers from a lack of richness and depth in the formulation of what Christianity means and what the Christian community undertakes.

The evangelical theme in preaching has frequently tended to reduce salvation to something as ethereal as the "soul" and to restrict this to the isolated individual. Sin is interpreted in terms of individual acts rather than as a state of alienation; whereas original sin pertains not to what individuals have done but to what they are, not to their symptomatic behavior but to the sources of that behavior. Moreover, justification by faith is centered not in what individuals must do but in what God has done in setting them free from the bondage of self. The gospel of grace affirms that God has crossed over to persons in their lostness, estrangement, and alienation and has broken the barriers of sin, guilt, and hopelessness, resulting in a dynamic realignment of the forces within the human personality. As a result, Christian obedience becomes not a matter of legalistic striving or straining to meet ideals but of experiencing the freedom in grace to affirm with one's being the truth: You are; therefore you do. Or as Karl Barth phrased it, "Become what you are."

Preaching, then, concerns itself with the wholeness of the person in relation to self, others, and God, expressed in terms of meaning, value, and obligation. Preaching that is alive to this reality will concern itself with the building up, edifying, and confirming of the body of believers and with helping to integrate them into their new life in Christ. Hence more and more sermons are designed to strengthen and instruct those who are already members of the Body of Christ. The strengthening and confirmation of the faithful should have high priority in the preaching of the church; thus the value of sermons on faith and human crises, marriage and family life, and prayer and the devotional life for the enrichment of the people of God.

Missions, Evangelism, and Witness.—Southern Baptist preaching has traditionally laid heavy stress upon missions, evangelism, and the obligation to share a witness in the world outreach of the church. This emphasis has often served to unite the denomination in the face of threatening fractures in other areas. The current Bold Mission Thrust of Southern Baptists represents a serious and sustained commitment to world evangelization. The church's task of evangelism contains a two-fold thrust. Southern Baptists are seeking to relate those outside the church to the God whom the Christian community proclaims and to the meanings and values it represents, and they are also attempting to bring persons at the periphery of the church's life into the center of the Christian community.

Worship and Community.—A significant development among Southern Baptists today is the growing recognition that preaching is to be viewed within the corporateness of worship and that the sermon itself is to be the means of a more cohesive Christian community. The "primacy of preaching" need not suggest an exclusiveness to the preaching function that fragments the service and reduces other acts of public worship to the status of "preliminaries." Preaching is involved in all the moods and movements of worship—adoration, confession, thanksgiving, supplication, intercession, affirmation, and dedication. The preacher is not a "free lance"; he is a spokesman for the Christian community, and he stands responsible to its tradition. He bespeaks the attention of people by virtue of the charge and the gospel given to him and to the church. Paul recognized that he had been "entrusted" with the gospel. In like manner Southern Baptists are not the originators of the gospel but are to be its faithful transmitters. The sermon should be conceived as the living, dynamic confession of the church's faith.

An adequate concept of worship must make an important place for the Christian symbols and ordinances of the church in their interpretative functions in dramatizing the meaning of the gospel. The same gospel preached in the sermon is proclaimed in the Lord's Supper and baptism. The "sensible signs" within the ordinances are "the gospel made visible." The ordinances do not merely stimulate memory; they are expressions of God's self-giving in a gracious, personal relationship. There is something in their meaning that "breaks through language and escapes"—so much so that Christians can say with John Calvin that they prefer to experience them than understand them.

In Christian worship both the spoken word in preaching and the "acted sign" in the ordinances reinforce each other. Together they constitute the Lord's testament of love, his pledge of loyalty, and his covenant of constancy. They remind Christians that that which was begun in the crucible of Golgotha must go forward until "all things are made new."

JOHN W. CARLTON

PREACHING, H. I. HESTER LECTURESHIP ON. Endowed at Golden Gate Baptist Theological Seminary in 1968 by the H. I. Hesters of Liberty, MO, to highlight the importance of preaching in preparation for the ministry. Hester, longtime professor at William Jewell College, 1926-1963, served also as vice-president of Midwestern Baptist Theological Seminary, 1963-1974. The first lectures were delivered by Theodore F. Adams (*q.v.*), Mar., 1969.

HAROLD K. GRAVES

PREMILLENNIALISM AMONG BAPTIST GROUPS (cf. Premillennial Baptist Groups, Vol. II). Premillennialism is an eschatological interpretation of Revelation 20:1-6 which states that Christ will return to earth before he establishes a rule of 1,000 years and is often paralleled by a rigid view of the Bible, rejection of liberal tendencies, and an other-worldly empha-

sis. The two types of premillennialism are historical and dispensational.

Historical premillennialists believe that before the second coming of Christ a great apostasy will occur, accompanied by persecution of the church. Then the church, including resurrected Christians, will be raptured. Christ then will return to destroy the Antichrist, and the sheep and goat judgment (Matt. 25) will occur. The millennial kingdom will begin, Satan will be bound, and the unrighteous nations will be governed. Near the end of the millennium, Satan will be released and will wage war against the saints, only to be destroyed. Then the white throne judgment will take place (Rev. 20:11-15). The new heaven and the new earth will be established and the eternal kingdom of God will begin.

American dispensationalists, influenced by the teachings of C. I. Scofield (1843-1921), hold that Christ will rapture the church before the tribulation. After the tribulation, he will return with his church. The millennial kingdom will be predominately Jewish with headquaters in Palestine and Temple worship in Jerusalem.

Northern-oriented.—Several premillennial groups appeared by separation from the Northern (American) Baptists and fragmentations among the separating groups. The General Association of Regular Churches (*c.* 240,000 members) holds to dispensational premillennialism. The Conservative Baptist Association of America (over 200,000 members) confirms in its doctrinal statement belief in Christ's premillennial return to the world. Two minor premillennial groups are the New Testament Association of Independent Baptist Churches (*c.* 25,000 members) and the Fundamental Baptist Fellowship (*c.* 10,000 members).

Southern-oriented.—SBC agencies and educational institutions of affiliated state conventions do not require a specific millennial interpretation. However, many SBC pastors and churches and some private institutions operated by Southern Baptists, such as the Criswell Center for Biblical Studies, are premillennial.

The Baptist Missionary Association of America (*c.* 200,000 members) adopted a premillennial statement in 1957 as its predominant interpretation but did not make it binding upon affiliated churches nor a test of fellowship between church members. Other premillennial groups are the American Baptist Association (*c.* 200,000 members), the Baptist Bible Fellowship (*c.* 750,000 members), the Orthodox Baptists, and the Southwide Baptist Fellowship (*c.* 130,000 members).

General Baptists. Premillennialism is held by the General Six Principle Baptists (less than 200 members), and by the National Association of Free Will Baptists (*c.* 230,000 members).

See also MILLENNIUM, Vol. II.

BIBLIOGRAPHY: G. R. Beasley-Murray, and others, *Revelation: Three Viewpoints* (1977). W. A. Criswell, *Criswell Study Bible* (1979). C. I. Scofield, *Scofield Reference Bible* (1919, 1966). A. W. Wardin, Jr., *Baptist Atlas* (1980).

SLAYDEN YARBROUGH

PRESCHOOL WORK. See AGE GROUP WORK IN THE CHURCHES.

PRESS ASSOCIATION, SOUTHERN BAPTIST. See SOUTHERN BAPTIST PRESS ASSOCIATION.

PRESTRIDGE, JOHN NEWTON (b. Selma, AL, Feb. 5, 1853; d. Louisville, KY, Oct. 29, 1913). Pastor, educator, and editor. Son of John Elijah and Sarah (McGraw) Prestridge, he was educated at Howard College, AL, (1869-71), and at The Southern Baptist Theological Seminary (1879-83). Ordained in Alabama, he served churches in Kentucky and Texas. After serving the Williamsburg Institute (Cumberland College), 1894-98, he founded and edited *The Baptist Argus,* 1898-1908; aided in organizing the Baptist World Publishing Company, Louisville; and began publishing *The Baptist World,* May 1, 1908. A founder of the Baptist World Alliance, in 1905, he was chosen secretary for America, serving until his death. Prestridge married Frances Clardy, May 17, 1887. He is buried at Hopkinsville, KY.

LEO T. CRISMON

PRICE, JOHN MILBURN, JR. (b. Fort Worth, TX, Feb. 2, 1921; d. Black Mountain, NC, Aug. 29, 1972). Educator. Son of John M. and Mabel Falk Price, his father was director of the School of Religious Education at Southwestern Baptist Theological Seminary. He was a graduate of Baylor University (B.A., 1942), Southwestern Seminary (B.D., 1945; M.R.E., 1946), and New Orleans Baptist Theological Seminary (Th. M., 1947; Th.D. 1948). He married Rebecca Walker, Oct. 15, 1944. They had four children: Rebecca Jane, John M., III, Paul Falk, and David Walker.

Price served as pastor of churches in Texas and Louisiana while attending seminary. He then became a faculty member at New Orleans and taught from 1946 until 1948 when he was named head of the Department of Religious Education. He was named director of the School of Religious Education in 1952 and appointed dean of the School of Religious Education in 1959. From 1946 until 1972, he was professor of psychology and counseling. He led in the development of religious education and psychology and counseling in the curriculum of New Oreleans Seminary.

Price wrote numerous articles for denominational publications and contributed two chapters to the book, *An Introduction to Pastoral Counseling* (1959), edited by Wayne Oates. He experienced failing health and retired from the New Orleans faculty in 1972. Two weeks after moving to Black Mountain, NC, he died and was buried there.

STANLEY JACK WATSON

PRICE, JOHN MILBURN, SR. (b. near Fair Dealing, KY, Nov. 21, 1884; d. Fort Worth, TX, Jan. 12, 1976). Educator, pastor,

and administrator. The son of John and Elizabeth McLeod Price, farmers, he was converted in a revival meeting at Pleasant Hope, KY, Aug. 11, 1899. He began his education at the Maple Springs, KY, schoolhouse and taught school at Cleveland, KY. After graduating from Southern Normal School, Bowling Green, KY (B.S., 1905), he was a high school principal, Marlow, Indian Territory, OK. He later attended Baylor University (B.A., 1911), Brown University (M.A., 1912), and The Southern Baptist Theological Seminary (Th.M., 1915; Th.D., 1919; Ph.D., 1930). In addition to his earned degrees, Baylor University conferred the L.L.D. degree upon him in 1945; California Baptist College conferred the Litt.D. in 1965.

In 1910 Price became part-time pastor at Eagle Springs Church and Bosqueville Church near Waco, TX. In 1912 he was elected Sunday School evangelist for Blood River Association in Kentucky, his home association. In 1915 Southwestern Baptist Theological Seminary called on him to establish and direct a School of Pedagogy. Price accepted and began his ministry in the fall of 1915. He served at this seminary until his retirement, Aug. 1, 1956.

Price married Mabel Falk, July 11, 1916, in Marlow, OK. They had four children: Mabel, John Milburn, Jr., Joe, and James.

In 1921 Price led Southwestern Seminary to establish the first School of Religious Education among Southern Baptists. He was instrumental in beginning the annual meeting of the Texas Baptist Sunday School Convention in 1926, and led in the organization of the Southwestern Baptist Religious Education Association in 1921, and the Southern Baptist Religious Education Association in 1956. In 1946 he called the organizational meeting of the American Association of Schools of Religious Education, serving as its first president.

During his ministry at Southwestern Seminary, Price served for more than 21 years as pastor of Mansfield and Webb Baptist Churches near Fort Worth. He also wrote 13 books. He is buried in Laurel Land Cemetery, Fort Worth, TX.

JOE DAVIS HEACOCK

PRIMITIVE BAPTISTS (II). Teaching that they are apostolic in origin, Primitive Baptists trace their lineage through the Welsh Baptists and the Waldenses. Their Fulton Confession of Faith (1900) was patterned from the Old London Confession (1644) and the Waldensian Confession (1120). Hyper-Calvinists, they teach that all the elect will be regenerated without the gospel, but that there are blessings in obeying the gospel.

Until the 1950s their ministers emphasized the basic doctrines of salvation by grace. Most of the churches met only one Sunday per month, and their pastors usually worked at secular employment. There were few radio broadcasts and few special meetings other than the annual associations. In the late 1950s their leading ministers began to emphasize personal duty and evangelism in addition to the basic doctrines.

In the late 1970s most rural churches were meeting at least two Sundays per month, and most urban churches were meeting every Sunday. Most of the younger ministers serve their churches full time. Several evangelists preach special meetings each year in many of the churches. The present trend seems to be toward more evangelistic meetings, full-time pastors, more radio broadcasts, and meeting every Sunday. Most of their meetinghouses have been rebuilt or improved in recent years. In 1979 they had 21 periodicals, over 100 weekly radio broadcasts, and a membership estimated from 120,000 to 180,000.

See also ALABAMA ASSOCIATIONS.

W. A. PYLES

PRIVATE SCHOOLS MOVEMENT, BAPTIST. See BAPTIST PRIVATE SCHOOLS MOVEMENT.

PROBE. See BROTHERHOOD COMMISSION, SBC.

PROGRAMMING FOR THE CHURCHES (III). *Decade of Change.* — On Oct. 1, 1970, Southern Baptist churches encountered the greatest number of program changes ever experienced in their history. All church programs and materials previously provided by SBC agencies to assist churches were revised and replaced.

The new church programming which produced these changes appeared in the book *A Dynamic Church: Spirit and Structure for the Seventies* (1969), prepared by SBC church program leaders. The guiding philosophy was:

Churches are central in God's plan for world redemption. The place of each church is never more prominent than in a disordered and changing society. God's purpose for churches has not changed. Conditions under which churches must work are changing. Churches must be sensitive to these conditions and adjust their methods and approaches accordingly.

Church Base Design. — When the SBC approved 1969-73 as phase one of the '70 Onward Emphasis, the Inter-Agency Council voted to revise and continue the use of the statements of the church functions and tasks as coordinating agreements for church programming. For the first time SBC agencies had a common base for church programming. A statement of church functions and tasks was updated and endorsed by the Church Programs and Services Subcommittee on the Inter-Agency Council in Sep., 1979. The church functions are worship, proclaim, witness, nurture, educate, and minister. The church tasks are expressed in the structure of the Church Base Design.

Pastoral Ministries. — Most significant steps were made in the 1970s to provide greater assistance to pastors, deacons, and church staff members. "Pastoral Ministries" is a newer term in Southern Baptist life which expresses concepts in the Bible which give each church a sense of wholeness in focusing on the work of proclamation, care, and leadership.

Family Ministry. — Denominational research in the 1970s revealed that family life had become the top critical issue for the 1980s. The Sunday School Board, Home Mission Board, and Christian Life Commission have given major attention to assisting church leadership in areas of family crises, marriage enrichment, and family issues. The SSB organized a new Family Ministries Department in 1975.

Trained Leadership. — Denominational research also revealed that the second greatest concern of Southern Baptist churches was the lack of trained leadership. The Church Training program of the SSB joined with other SBC base programs in programming to meet this need. Programming for this concern accelerated in 1975 when the SSB established Equipping the Saints as one of its long-range priorities.

Missions and Missions Education. — Missions and mission education came into full focus when the 1976 SBC meeting adopted the Mission Challenge report and the Special Report on Missions by the Foreign Mission Board, and reaffirmed the place and responsibility of the local church in missions. The two SBC mission boards, Woman's Missionary Union, Brotherhood, and the SSB were requested to work in developing broader-based missions education to reach all the members of the churches. As a result of this action, the heads of the five SBC agencies organized a Missions Education Council of which they assumed cooperative leadership. The following priorities were established:

1. That a cooperative strategy be developed for communicating with pastors and church staff members concerning missions education.

2. That a comprehensive Convention-wide plan be developed and implemented which would encourage every small church to provide missions education for all its members.

3. That a national plan be developed to inform Southern Baptists of the availability of missions education materials and effectively distribute these materials.

4. That a coordinated missions education curriculum design be developed which would reach all the people in Southern Baptist churches.

5. That a plan for developing and testing missions education approaches be developed.

In Nov., 1979, the Missions Education Council published and distributed the first free *Missions Digest*, a pastor's monthly resource for missions education.

The denominational emphasis on missions in 1977-79 captured the attention of Southern Baptists in their 1977 meeting in Kansas City, Mo. In that Convention Fred Gregg of Washington, DC, spoke of the keen personal interest of President Jimmy Carter in the 1977-79 emphasis on missions. A historic feature of Gregg's presentation included a message from President Carter by videotape. The Convention was so moved that it adopted a goal to enlist 5,000 missions volunteers by 1982. A keen interest of denominational leaders in this goal resulted in extending the mission emphasis into the 1980s. This emphasis became known as Bold Mission Thrust.

In 1978 the SBC ignored its action of the previous year to have an emphasis with a promotion content for 1979-80 on Equipping for Church Advance. In 1978 the interest in missions was so great that the long-range plans for 1979-80 adopted in the 1975 SBC were also abandoned. The 1978 Convention adopted a detailed plan suggesting a local church Bold Mission Thrust planning process which would help Southern Baptists enter mission emphasis to last far into the future.

Evangelism and Church Growth.—By the end of the 1970s, much of the research and planning among Southern Baptist leaders for church growth had been completed. The books *I Want my Church to Grow* (1977) by C. B. Hogue, and *Design for Church Growth* (1977) by Charles L. Chaney and Ron S. Lewis and the paper "Church Growth Concepts" by Oscar I. Romo led the way.

This work introduced Southern Baptists to some of the approaches to church growth developed by Donald A. McGavran. By Dec., 1979, the SSB and the HMB had prepared a joint statement on church growth in the document titled "Growing Southern Baptist Churches." The statement defined church growth, outlined its principles and characteristics, and provided actions a pastor may take in growing a church. The actions toward growth were:

1. Commit yourself as pastor to the church's growth.

2. Cultivate, equip, and challenge the church's leadership teams to accept growth as a priority concern.

3. Know the needs and opportunities for growth.

4. Establish specific growth goals.

5. Develop and personally direct the strategy for growth.

6. Evaluate and continually reshape the church's growth plan.

7. Celebrate the work of the Holy Spirit in the midst of His people.

Starting New Churches.—The starting of new churches accelerated in the late 1970s. One of the most successful approaches was starting new mission fellowships in the form of Bible-study groups.

The Sunday School Department of the SSB in cooperation with the Department of Church Extension of the HMB developed a cooperative strategy of starting new Sunday Schools as a way to plant new churches and new church-type missions. The strategy produced 1,740 new Sunday Schools by the end of 1978.

By 1978 nine well-tested steps had been developed for starting churches. These steps appear in the book *Planting New Churches* (1978) by Jack Redford.

Church Music.—In Mar., 1975, one of the largest national Southern Baptist church music conclaves was conducted. Titled PraiSing '75, a meeting held in Nashville, TN, with approximately 10,000 attending, the conclave included the introduction of the new *Baptist Hymnal*. By the end of the 1970s, Southern Baptist churches had acquired over 3,000,000 copies of the hymnal.

Bible Study.—New efforts were made to establish in-depth Bible study for the masses. In 1975 the SSB established this concern as a top priority and in Oct., 1978, introduced a new Bible study series for adults and youth.

The SSB and Radio and Television Commission launched a new nationwide Bible correspondence strategy in Oct., 1978. By Oct., 1980, over 200,000 persons participated in the correspondence activities, and *At Home with the Bible*, a companion program to interest and enlist the masses in Bible correspondence, received a nationwide airing on radio and television.

Language and Ethnic Churches.—All of the SBC agencies increased their church programming to assist the growing number of non-English speaking, non-white, and ethnic Southern Baptist churches. In 1979 the HMB reported having established 250 congregations and initiated work with five additional ethnic groups in the previous year. During the same period the SSB established an Ethnic Liaison Unit which majors on working with black and non-English speaking Southern Baptist churches. The SSB also organized a language unit to implement a five-year educational publishing and promotion plan to assist non-English speaking churches. This plan included the establishing of a joint working relationship with the Baptist Spanish Publishing House, El Paso, TX.

Stewardship.—The SBC Stewardship Commission reported in 1979 that it had continued growth in its programming to assist churches. This growth, indicated by Cooperative Program annual increases, ranged in the 8-14 percentages from 1976 through 1978. Careful attention went to a new organization for the church stewardship committee to give planned year-round attention to this continuing emphasis in the churches. Churches were helped by the SBC Stewardship Commission with Together We Build, a fund-raising project.

MORTON F. ROSE

PROGRAMMING FOR THE CHURCHES, 1959-69 (III). See CHANNELING DENOMINATIONAL INFORMATION.

PROGRESSIVE NATIONAL BAPTIST CONVENTION, U.S.A., INC. A convention of black Baptists organized, Nov. 14-15, 1961, at Zion Baptist Church, Cincinnati, OH, by 33 representatives from 14 states. Its objectives are "to encourage, support and promote Christian evangelism; Christian missions; Christian education, including the necessary publication and distribution of literature; Christian stewardship; benevolence; human freedom; and other such Christian work as the convention may determine." There are three classes of membership: representative, life, and honorary.

The PNBC established the following boards: Board of Christian Education and Publication, Foreign Mission Bureau, Home Mission Board, and the Pension Plan Board.

The Convention established the following departments: Women Department, Laymen Department, Ushers and Nurses Department, Youth Department, Moderators Department, and Congress of Christian Education.

Commissions of the Convention are the Cooperative Christianity Commission and the Civil Rights Commission.

In 1980 the PNBC had approximately 1,000,000 members in about 1,700 churches in the United States. Many of the churches are affiliated with another Baptist convention. The official journal of the PNBC is the bimonthly *Baptist Progress.*

PNBC distinctives in comparison to other major black Baptist denominations in America include a two-year tenure for major officers, a unified budget, and a full-time executive secretary.

The PNBC headquarters are located in Washington, DC. C. J. Malloy is executive secretary.

See also NATIONAL BAPTIST CONVENTION, U.S.A., INC.; PROGRESSIVE NATIONAL BAPTIST CONVENTION, U.S.A., INC., BAPTIST FOREIGN MISSION BUREAU.

SID SMITH

PROGRESSIVE NATIONAL BAPTIST CONVENTION, U.S.A., INC., BAPTIST FOREIGN MISSION BUREAU. One of four boards of the Progressive National Baptist Convention, U.S.A., Inc., the Foreign Mission Bureau is directed by George F. Bell, Sr. Churches affiliated with the convention support educational and medical missions in the Caribbean Islands and Liberia.

EMMANUEL L. MCCALL

PROPST, FRED (b. Fredericktown, MO, May 12, 1892; d. Atlanta, GA, Feb. 9, 1971). Missionary. Ordained in 1924, Propst attended Marvin College in Missouri and Northern Baptist Seminary, Chicago, IL. He served 40 years in Illinois in associational, state, and city missions. His first wife died in 1955. They had two sons and five daughters. He married Louise Whitmire, Aug. 19, 1957. He served as pastor, Capitol Avenue Baptist Church, Atlanta, GA, before retirement.

JEWELL BEALL

PROTESTANT CHURCH-OWNED PUBLISHERS' ASSOCIATION. A trade association of religious publishing houses owned and operated by their parent Protestant church bodies. It was chartered in Pennsylvania on June 22, 1951, with 24 member houses. The Sunday School Board was influential in its founding. Harold E. Ingraham *(q.v.)* of the SSB was one of the six original incorporators. Since the association's beginning, the SSB has provided the organization with three presidents: Keith C. Von Hagen, 1957-58, Leonard E.

Wedel, 1966-67, and J. Marvin Crowe, 1974-75.

The organization exists to serve the common interest of its member houses. Its most visible cooperative achievement is the development and distribution of the Cooperative Protestant Religious Education Curriculum, a fully graded two-track curriculum produced in cooperation with the Religious Education Advisory Group of the Armed Forces Chaplains Board. This curriculum is currently used at over 300 military installations around the world.

Cumulative sales volume of member houses has increased 80 percent since 1965. The current membership is 30 houses whose cumulative sales are over $235,000,000.

ROBERT M. BOYD

PSYCHOLOGY OF RELIGION. See PASTORAL CARE.

PUBLIC AFFAIRS, ADVOCACY ROLE OF THE CHURCHES IN. The involvement of American churches in public affairs is inevitably rooted in their exercise of religious liberty. The advocacy role of the churches in public affairs is not only a legal right so far as the United States Constitution is concerned, but a divine obligation. For churches this advocacy role has generally been expressed in upholding the free exercise of religion. This is basic to a free church and a free society, the cause of justice for all persons, the interdependence of religious liberty with all human rights, and the relevance of Christian concerns in national and international affairs.

Admittedly, the advocacy role of churches in public affairs has been ambiguous. Often churches have chosen to moralize about society, while remaining aloof from public affairs. A separating of the gospel from politics has existed simultaneously with a disdain for politics and politicians. Increasingly, however, the advocacy role of churches in public affairs came to be regarded as an inescapable responsibility of the churches and to be identified with the prophetic role of religion in a free society.

For Baptists the church is bound to participate in the arena of public affairs because this involvement is integral to the mission and ministry of the church; it is essential to the faith and teachings of the church and its divine mandate to be "the Body of Christ in the world." All human rights, which constitute the ultimate concern of the churches in public affairs, whether individual or corporate, economic or racial, political or religious, are viewed as sacred because of the theological conception that human beings are created in the image of God.

Since 1930, and particularly since World War II, virtually all the major religious denominations in the United States have established offices on public affairs in the nation's capital. The forerunner of the United States Catholic Conference established headquarters in Washington in 1917. Offices of other denominations followed. The Baptist Joint Committee on Public Affairs, an office for the national bodies of Baptists in the United States and Canada, was inaugurated in 1939.

These denominational offices on public affairs in Washington were established to deal with a variety of denominational concerns: the free exercise of religion, immigration, war and peace, religious persecutions and denial of religious liberty abroad, foreign policy and Christian missions overseas, conscientious objection, disarmament, civil rights, economic justice, right-to-work laws, world hunger, human rights and foreign policy, the United Nations, capital punishment, abortion rights, military chaplaincy, taxation and the churches, tax funds and church institutions, and integrity in government, among others. Since the founding of these offices, the political activities of organized religion have gradually become more inclusive, diffused, and sophisticated. Religious denominations have increasingly sought to influence public policy on matters affecting economic and social justice, human rights, war, and peace. Offices on public affairs have become widely recognized agencies of America's religious denominations.

During these years the advocacy role of churches in public affairs has not been confined to the defense and protection of the institutional interests of the churches. Increasingly, they have focused on matters affecting the general welfare of persons at home and abroad. The advocacy role of the churches has been evident on virtually all matters affecting domestic and foreign policy, war and peace, and the entire legislative and political process. In seeking to minister to the whole person in the world, they acknowledge that no aspect of life can be regarded as outside of God's concern, dominion, and power.

In the United States, the First and Fourteenth Amendments forbid the Congress and the states from defining for the churches the nature and scope of their religious mission. Because the churches define their religious mission as including an obligation to speak out on public affairs, they hold that their advocacy role in public affairs is a part of their constitutionally protected religious liberty. The state may not deny or limit that right. Neither may it require that a church give up its right to "the free exercise of religion" under the First Amendment to be eligible to gain a statutory privilege (e.g., tax exemption).

Nevertheless, the advocacy role of churches in public affairs raises many questions among public officials for which legislative remedy is yet to be found. For example, are religious denominations which are directly and substantially involved in public affairs to be regarded as lobbies? With rare exception, namely the Friends Committee on National Legislation, denominational public affairs offices in Washington, DC, have not registered as lobbies. They have not done so for a variety of reasons.

One is that these offices carry on various public affairs programs which are educational in

nature. These include programs in information and denominational services, which are not aimed primarily at influencing public policy. Their purpose is to inform and serve constituencies in the area of public affairs. Furthermore, these offices are not by nature self-serving or motivated by self-interest like some powerful lobbies of noncharitable organizations. For these reasons, among others, legislative remedy must be found to protect the advocacy role of the church in public affairs.

See also PUBLIC AFFAIRS, BAPTIST JOINT COMMITTEE ON.

JAMES E. WOOD, JR.

PUBLIC AFFAIRS, BAPTIST JOINT COMMITTEE ON (cf. Public Affairs Committee, Baptist Joint, Vols. II, III). Now composed of representatives from nine member bodies in North America: American Baptist Churches in the U.S.A., Baptist Federation of Canada, Baptist General Conference, National Baptist Convention of America, National Baptist Convention of the U.S.A., Inc., North American Baptist Conference, Progressive National Baptist Convention, Inc., Seventh-Day Baptist General Conference, and Southern Baptist Convention, the Baptist Joint Committee on Public Affairs (BJCPA) maintains four ongoing service programs: (1) Government relations, (2) denominational services, (3) research services, and (4) information services. It publishes a monthly periodical, *Report from the Capital*; sponsors a biennial Religious Liberty Conference; promotes Religious Liberty Day on Baptist denominational calendars; publishes staff reports and pamphlets on current public affairs issues; and maintains a comprehensive news service.

C. Emanuel Carlson (*q.v.*) retired as executive director in 1971. James E. Wood, Jr., chairman of church-state studies at Baylor University and a former Southern Baptist missionary to Japan, succeeded Carlson in 1972. Wood served as executive director until his resignation in 1980. The BJCPA elected as Wood's successor James M. Dunn, director of the Texas Christian Life Commission, effective Jan. 1, 1981.

Among the many issues faced by the BJCPA during the 1970s, the largest cluster dealt with the increasing tendency of the federal government to intervene into church affairs. In response to such incursions, the BJCPA adopted formal positions insisting that the churches alone may determine the extent of their mission, instructing its staff not to register as lobbyists, calling on Congress to exclude churches from coverage under lobby disclosure legislation, affirming the right of church groups freely to assemble, opposing the calling of a constitutional convention, opposing the National Labor Relations Board's decision that parochial school systems may be forced to allow lay teacher unionization, opposing the Department of Labor's effort to force church schools to pay unemployment taxes, opposing the Internal Revenue Service's ruling on integrated auxiliaries of churches and racial composition of religious schools, and seeking legislation to forbid the Central Intelligence Agency from using missionaries in intelligence gathering.

While generally opposing government intervention into church affairs, the BJCPA continued its historic opposition to unconstitutional government aid to religion. On public aid to nonpublic schools, the BJCPA vigorously opposed tuition tax credits, tuition voucher plans, and state funding of "auxiliary" services. The agency also opposed payment by the city of Philadelphia for construction of a platform on which Pope John Paul II celebrated Mass, opposed use of public funds for the teaching of transcendental meditation, and opposed government funding of solar energy projects by churches and church schools.

In the area of the role of religion in public life, the BJCPA opposed all efforts to circumvent the Supreme Court's decisions forbidding state sponsorship of religious exercises in public schools, participated in a successful court challenge to required chapel attendance in the military academies, and joined another court case challenging state prohibitions on members of the clergy from seeking public office.

In other domestic issues, the BJCPA asked for comprehensive welfare reform, issued a statement on integrity in government in light of the Watergate revelations, affirmed the right to privacy, issued statements on equality of all persons under law, sought full employment for all able and willing to work, called on Congress and the states to fight child abuse and the sexual exploitation of children, and opposed the removal of the public interest standard in proposed revisions of the Communications Act of 1934.

Internationally, the BJCPA protested the escalation of the Vietnam War into Laos, issued several pronouncements supporting basic human rights, urged the Soviet Union to honor its announced commitment to religious liberty and to release imprisoned Baptist pastor Georgi Vins, protested Israel's anticonversion law, sought reversal of a decision by the government of Turkey to expel the only official Baptist representative in the country, urged Congress to pass the Refugee Act of 1979, urged the governments of the United States and Canada to step up efforts to combat world hunger, and urged the United States Senate to pass the SALT II treaty with the Soviet Union and four pending human rights covenants and treaties.

See also PUBLIC AFFAIRS, ADVOCACY ROLE OF THE CHURCHES IN.

BIBLIOGRAPHY: Stan L. Hastey, "A History of the Baptist Joint Committee on Public Affairs, 1946-1971" (dissertation, Southern Baptist Theological Seminary, 1974).

STAN L. HASTEY

PUBLIC FUNDS AND CHURCH INSTITUTIONS. The American colonists recognized the validity of the biblical principle of religious liberty. They incorporated it into the United States Constitution by the First and Fourteenth Amendments in a form which is usually referred to as separation of church and state.

The concept of the separation of church and state relegates to the state the secular functions of government and denies to it any religious role. Baptists have usually maintained that this institutional separation should be absolute. However, the need for financial assistance to carry out certain aspects of the religious mission of the churches has led some Baptists and other concerned citizens to request or demand public funds to maintain or expand institutional services.

Congress, as well as state and local governments, has responded to the logic of the arguments and the political pressures of supporters of public funds for church institutions. Limited success has occurred in finding constitutional ways to provide public funds for church-related elementary and secondary schools. Some church-related institutions of higher education which resisted, on First Amendment grounds, an executive order denying them the power to discriminate on the basis of religion in hiring have taken funds for staff development, research, and campus construction. Church-related hospitals have taken public funds under the Hill-Burton Act of 1946. Day-care centers have used public funds for school lunch programs. Public funds have been channeled into church institutions in numerous other ways.

When public funds are spent, there must be public accounting for those funds. Books of account must be open for inspection. The regulations which go along with public funds (they are usually referred to as conditional grants in aid) have to be enforced. This intrusion of government into church institutions threatens the freedom of those institutions.

At an imprecise point, the use of public funds by church institutions triggers administrative, statutory, and judicial restrictions. A church-related elementary school could lose its right to teach religion, have public prayers, or display religious symbols. A Baptist hospital could have its religious identity obscured. A Baptist college could be required to hire faculty without reference to religious beliefs.

A church and its institutions are free when they are unencumbered by government regulation. If public funds are used by church institutions, those institutions will ultimately lose their freedom.

See also CHURCH-STATE DECISIONS, THE COURTS AND.

JOHN W. BAKER

PUBLIC RELATIONS (III). Baptist state papers (circulation 1,800,000) continued to be the major public relations effort of state conventions. The Baptist Public Relations Association was a thriving organization in 1979 with 315 members. Accredited members of the Public Relations Society of America included six professionals working for Southern Baptist organizations at the beginning of the decade and five times that number at the close. In 1980 Southern Baptist members of the interfaith, international Religious Public Relations Council numbered 42. Baptist public relations personnel initiated the first interfaith Religious Communications Congress, which drew 476 to Chicago, IL, in 1970. They likewise provided major leadership in the second such meeting, Religious Communications Congress/80, which met in Nashville, TN, in 1980. Registration included 1,313 Catholics, Jews, Protestants, and Orthodox from 43 states and 19 countries.

See also BAPTIST PUBLIC RELATIONS ASSOCIATION.

WILMER C. FIELDS

PUBLIC RELATIONS, CHURCH (cf. Publicity, Church, Vol. II). Church public relations "in its truest sense is the practice of telling and living the truth with a group of people in order to ultimately secure a favorable response." Churches use print media such as newsletters, brochures, bulletins, and direct mail; electronic media such as radio and television; displays and exhibits such as billboards and other signs; and personal contacts such as ushers and office receptionists. Many churches have church public relations committees to eval-

uate, plan, and direct their public relations efforts.

MARGUERITE S. BABB

PYE, LILA WESTBROOK (b. Beebe, AR, May 17, 1891; d. Little Rock, AR, June 3, 1972). State Woman's Missionary Union worker. Daughter of Florence Langley and Alex Westbrook, a dentist, she attended Ouachita Baptist College and Galloway College. On Nov. 3, 1917, she married Walter David Pye, who predeceased her, Dec. 31, 1968. Their only child, a son, died in infancy. Pye's official connection with Arkansas WMU began Jan 10, 1916, when she became office secretary. She served as treasurer, 1916-17, and was elected a member of the executive board in 1921. She was acting president, 1923-24. Other elected positions included president, 1924-29; corresponding secretary and treasurer, 1929-37; and treasurer and program editor, 1937-45.

She was the first state president to serve as vice-president of WMU, SBC, 1926-29. During her tenure as state president and corresponding secretary, she served on many planning committees of WMU, SBC. She was the author of several published writings. She is buried in Oakland Cemetery, Little Rock, AR.

NANCY COOPER

R

RACE RELATIONS (II, III). By 1980 at least 3,000 Southern Baptist churches had integrated memberships. In addition, the SBC had about 600 predominantly black churches. Race relations involvement in Southern Baptist life has been mostly between blacks and whites, but other patterns have developed due to expanded ministries among Hispanics and Orientals. The Sunday School Board established an Ethnic Liaison Unit in 1978 to enable the SSB to serve predominantly ethnic churches. The Home Mission Board's Department of Cooperative Ministries with National Baptists promotes cooperative efforts between Southern Baptist churches and the predominately black National Baptist churches.

From 1968 to 1980, the SBC passed several resolutions pertaining to racial issues. Some dealt in a general way with racism and called for all citizens to work for racial justice and for better understanding between the races (1969, 1970, 1971, 1978), while others dealt with specific denominational matters such as minority representation on SBC boards and commissions

(1973, 1974). Resolutions condemning antiSemitism were passed in 1971 and 1972.

See also CIVIL RIGHTS.

JOHN A. WOOD

RADIO AND TELEVISION, MISSIONARY USE OF. Southern Baptists have radio and television ministries in some 50 countries served by missionaries overseas, as well as among language groups in the homeland. They have constructed studios to help in producing quality broadcast materials. Because of the comparative simplicity in production and lower costs involved, Baptists have built more radio than television facilities overseas. Television programs produced in the United States and in other countries have been dubbed into several languages for use in various parts of the world, thus effecting a greater stewardship of available monetary resources.

Shortly after the Radio and Television Commission, SBC, began the JOT children's cartoon series in the United States, the agency granted permission for JOT to be translated and dubbed into Spanish, Portuguese, Chinese, and other languages. When JOT was first broadcast in Taiwan, missionaries there received some 2,500 requests for the surprise offer the first week, and some 7,000 the first month. Contacts were made and hearts were opened to a further gospel witness because of this children's television series. When JOT was dubbed into Spanish, it became PUNITO and has been used throughout the Spanish-speaking world. Follow-up materials were produced by the Baptist Spanish Publishing House in El Paso, TX, for distribution throughout Latin America.

In 1980 a series of television programs in Spanish called "Circulo Tres" (Circle Three) were produced by the Foreign Mission Board in the Radio-TV Commission facilities for use in Latin America. They will be used also on Spanish language television stations in the United States. Plans call for a similar program in Portuguese to be produced for use in connection with special evangelistic campaigns in Brazil and to celebrate 100 years of Baptist work there.

Missionaries and nationals in several African and Asian countries are also finding opportunities for radio and television broadcasts. Lack of funding and trained personnel hinder full utilization of the media.

See also RADIO AND TELEVISION COMMISSION, SBC.

JERRY PILLOW

RADIO AND TELEVISION COMMISSION, SBC

(II, III). This Southern Baptist Convention agency is the world's largest producer of religious programs for broadcast on free air time. Paul M. Stevens retired as president in 1979 after serving as the agency's chief executive for 27 years. The commission chose Jimmy R. Allen, pastor, First Baptist Church, San Antonio, TX, and a former SBC president, as the new president. He took office Jan. 15, 1980. The agency dedicated the Paul M. Stevens Television Studio and Training Center, another 32,000-square foot facility devoted entirely to television, in 1977.

With an operating budget of $3,859,256 in 1980, the commission produces and distributes seven major radio programs and four television productions heard in 10 languages more than 5,000 times a week on some 3,000 radio and television stations across the country. The commission's flagship program, The Baptist Hour, the only one of the commission programs to carry the denominational name, was being broadcast on more than 400 stations in 1980. After 18 years as The Baptist Hour speaker, Herschel H. Hobbs retired in 1976. He was succeeded by Frank Pollard, pastor, First Baptist Church, San Antonio, TX.

While the agency's guiding principle is to proclaim Christ through radio and television, the commission has sought to produce programs which remain true to the biblical injunction to share the gospel and, at the same time, are superior in both entertainment and technology.

Recognizing that many lost listeners would quickly turn away from a preaching program, the commission elected to package its message in nonpreaching formats. This Is the Answer, a series of dramas and documentaries for television, launched in 1956, won numerous industry awards and established the commission's reputation for excellence. This program was replaced by The Human Dimension in 1972.

Programs in Spanish now include La Hora Bautista, Momentos de Meditacion, and Control* Central, a version of MasterControl*. Devotional programs in Polish, Portuguese, Chinese, Filipino, Hungarian, and Navajo have been started as the Home Mission Board has determined needs among minority groups.

The commission's radio program MasterControl* continued to feature cohosts who conducted interviews on a variety of interesting subjects, played good music, and delivered a Christian message almost before their listeners were aware they were hearing a sermon or moral lesson. This show was on more than 800 stations in 1980.

PowerLine features top-of-the-charts music preferred by young people and uses the songs and lyrics as springboards for Christian truths. The half-hour program also contains two short devotional thoughts from the host and encourages listeners with spiritual problems to write for counseling. Carried by 1,205 radio stations across the country, the program is the most popular and spiritually productive program the commission has ever produced.

Country Crossroads features country music, enjoyed by a large segment of the nation. Hosts are Christian comedian Jerry Clower of Yazoo City, MS, a member of Nashville's Grand Ole Opry; and Bill Mack of Fort Worth's WBAP Radio, a country music disc jockey, and a guest host who serves for a six-week period. The guest host replaced country music singer Leroy Van Dyke, who was a cohost on the show for 10 years until resigning in 1979. Country Crossroads currently is on 1,020 stations.

Other half-hour radio productions include Sounds of the Centurymen, featuring The Centurymen singing group and designed for adult listeners in any format radio station; Black Beat, created specifically for the black community and dealing with the spiritual life of the black American; and Streams in the Desert, presenting music for relaxation and reflection. Inspirational thoughts, Christian poetry, and essays are interspersed between the instrumentals and vocals. Additionally, the commission produces several five-minute news programs requested and underwritten by state Baptist conventions. Also produced are spot announcements for both radio and television.

Television productions include JOT, the 4½-minute animated cartoon introduced in 1968. Today, a new generation of young viewers enjoy the show. JOT's name has been changed to Puntito in Spanish for distribution in Latin-American countries and for television stations that broadcast to Spanish-speaking people. In addition to Spanish, JOT is heard in several

RADIO AND TELEVISION COMMIS-SION, SBC (*q.v.*). *Top, right:* Radio show producer working on one of the commission's 12 weekly radio shows. *Center, top:* Television production studio. *Center, bottom:* Video record-ing, editing, and duplication equip-ment. *Above:* Production of "At Home with the Bible," cosponsored with Sunday School Board. *Bottom, right:* Counseling Department em-ployee answering one of about 11,500 counseling requests received an-nually.

COUNTRY AND TOWN BAP-
TIST CHURCH, Camp Hill,
PA. Site of the organization
meeting of the Baptist Con-
vention of Pennsylvania-
South Jersey, Oct. 2-3, 1970.

WHITESTOWN ROAD BAP-
TIST CHURCH, Butler, PA.
Typical of the simple economical architectural style of
new churches in Pennsyl-
vania-South Jersey.

other languages besides English as missionaries use the program as a successful outreach tool. New segments of the show are currently being produced jointly by the commission and the Foreign Mission Board.

The Human Dimension, a half-hour television drama and documentary which deals with some of today's pressing problems—drugs, leisure, aging, divorce—was launched in 1972. Several segments of the series have won numerous industry awards. These programs, first aired in 1977, have been expanded to a half-hour format from the original 15-minute length. *The Athletes* offers contemporary biographies of sports stars. It was created as entertainment and inspiration for the entire family. *Listen* is a series of documentaries exploring things man has learned about mankind and the universe.

In addition, the commission produces and distributes *At Home with the Bible* (both radio and television) for the Sunday School Board, and produces *Circulo Tres* for the FMB. Commission personnel also work with the three major networks—ABC, CBS, and NBC—to air religious programs.

In an effort to gauge the size of its listening audience and to measure the results of its message, commission programs encourage listeners to write the agency. One incentive is free spiritual counseling. The Counseling Department, begun in 1970, has a four-member staff of trained counselors. In the fiscal year 1978-79, out of 208,116 letters received from listeners, a total of 10,468 were from people seeking spiritual assistance. The number of letters from listeners during 1979-80 was the second highest total since the Counseling Department was organized. Of those who responded, 850 were decisions for Christ.

The commission not only encourages listeners to write; it has a program to encourage the broadcast industry to support its work. One of these is the annual Abe Lincoln Awards program, begun in 1970 and held each February in Fort Worth. The Abe Lincoln Awards were created to thank the nation's broadcasters who air the commission's programs on free time and to encourage those broadcasters to continue to serve their local communities through exemplary community service projects.

BEAM International, a monthly newsletter for the industry, is another of the commission's efforts to encourage the best in broadcasting and, at the same time, promote the use of its own programs. Other commission publications include *Trio,* a newsletter mailed quarterly to pastors of churches either broadcasting or planning to broadcast, and *Share,* a quarterly newsletter which describes commission activities for people who support its efforts over and above their regular church giving.

Another facet of the commission's ministry has been to support the local church. Two departments, the Broadcast Services Department and the Broadcast Engineering Department, work directly with churches to help them meet their broadcast needs.

Broadcast Services is an outgrowth of *Time-Rite, Inc.,* a concept to service the radio and television needs of local churches, associations, state conventions, and other SBC agencies.

Broadcast Engineering works with local churches to design top quality sound reinforcement and lighting systems that enable the listener in the sanctuary and the viewer to participate in a more attractive and easier-to-hear worship service.

BONITA SPARROW

RADIO-TELEVISION BIBLE CORRESPONDENCE COURSE. In Oct., 1978, the Sunday School Board, in cooperation with the Radio and Television Commission, launched a radio-television Bible correspondence course.

The radio-television program *At Home with the Bible* is a 30-minute religious broadcast. The format features music by a singing group, A Joyful Sound, the husband-wife musical team of Bill and Jeanine Walker, interviews with special guests, counseling dialogue with John Drakeford of Southwestern Baptist Theological Seminary, and a 10-12 minute Bible-teaching segment led by Frank Pollard, pastor of First Baptist Church, San Antonio, TX.

During the broadcasts, the audience receives an invitation to write for a free copy of the *Home Bible Study Guide,* a monthly publication that contains Bible study material in a programmed instruction format. Each *Guide* contains a review test which respondents are encouraged to complete and send to the Home Bible Study office for analysis. The office returns the results to the respondents.

The financial support for the course comes from the SSB and contributions from respondents. Eventually, the course is expected to become self-supporting through contributions from respondents. No Cooperative Program funds support Home Bible Study.

Production of the broadcast programs takes place in the studios of the Radio and Television Commission. The SSB pays all expenses for the production. In 1980 *At Home with the Bible* received the Award of Merit for Excellence in Television Programming from the National Religious Broadcasters Association.

See also HOME BIBLE STUDY.

ROBERT G. FULBRIGHT

RANKIN, CHARLES HAYS (b. Worthan, TX, Jan. 2, 1926; d. Topeka, KS, July 8, 1972). The son of Frank E. and Candace Rankin, he attended Louisiana College (B.A., 1951) and New Orleans Baptist Theological Seminary (B.D., 1954; Th.M., 1955). He married Gladys Pearl Minor, June 5, 1948. They had five children: Carolyn, James, Cynthia, Rebecca, and Raymond.

Appointed Home Mission Board language missionaries (Spanish), they served at La Junta, CO, 1956-62; Hatch, NM, 1962-63; and Topeka, KS, 1963-67; and in Christian social ministries, Aug. 1, 1967, until his death. He is buried in the city cemetery of Topeka, KS.

FRANK CLAIBORNE

RAY, GEORGE ERNEST, SR. (b. Nolan, TX, Apr. 15, 1907; d. Mancos, CO, July 26, 1971). The son of George W. and Lula (Rice) Ray, he married Tera May Bitters, May 3, 1930. They had two sons, George E., Jr., and Gilbert B. He attended Hardin-Simmons, Baylor, and Southern Methodist Universities, and Southwestern Baptist Theological Seminary. He served as pastor of churches in Illinois, Texas, and Colorado; associational missionary for Dallas (TX) Baptist Association, 1944-48; area missionary for the Western Slope area of the Colorado Baptist General Convention; president of the Colorado Convention in 1968; and chairman of the executive board, Colorado Convention. Ray also held other state and associational positions. He is buried in Grove Hill Cemetery, Dallas, TX.

WAYNE WILLIAMS

RAY, LEWIS CLINTON (b. Mammoth Cave, KY, Sep. 7, 1895; d. Louisville, KY, Aug. 19, 1978). Pastor. Son of James Andres and Mary Ellen Pardue Ray, farmers, he was educated at Bethel College Academy, Georgetown College (A.B.), and Southern Baptist Theological Seminary (Th.M., 1927), all in Kentucky. He married Hettye Green Lindsey, July 6, 1918. Their children were James and Carolyn. Following his wife's death, he married Elva Hawkins, Aug. 10, 1959. After her death, he married Erma Webber Staples, Nov. 27, 1969. Ray served as pastor at Glasgow Junction; Blanket Creek; Locust Grove; Mt. Olivet; Franklin Street, Louisville, 1924-36; Latonia, Covington, 1937-40; and Baptist Tabernacle, Louisville, 1961-72. He was business manager of the *Western Recorder*, 1941-44. He is buried in Cave Hill Cemetery, Louisville, KY.

LEO T. CRISMON

REAVIS, HENRY CLAY (b. Puxico, MO, Sep. 7, 1894; d. Albuquerque, NM, Apr. 10, 1972). Book store manager. Son of James and Ida Mae (Dodds) Reavis, farmers, he attended La Salle Business University, Chicago, IL. He married Mina Edwards, Nov. 26, 1914. They had two children, Ruth and Jessi. On Feb. 1, 1927, Reavis became an employee of the Baptist Convention of New Mexico. He managed the Baptist Book Store in Albuquerque for 35 years, 1927-62. He also led in the opening of Baptist Book Stores in Arizona, California, Oregon, and at Glorieta Baptist Assembly (now Conference Center).

JOHN W. RANSDELL

RECREATION, CHURCH (II, III). Since its beginning in 1954, the work of the Church Recreation Department of the Sunday School Board has contributed to a steady and stable growth of recreation programming in Southern Baptist churches. Church recreation programs today include activities such as parties, banquets, fellowships, sports, games, retreats, arts, crafts, hobbies, camping, drama, puppetry, backpacking, and physical fitness classes.

Following are a few statistics that provide further insight into this growth. More than 14,000 churches annually report a church recreation ministry. A conservative estimate of current capital investment in recreation facilities by Southern Baptist churches is $1,350,000,000 (exclusive of camps and assemblies owned by churches, associations, state conventions, and other SBC bodies). Every state convention has assigned a staff member responsibility for consultation in church recreation ministry. All Southern Baptist seminaries provide course work in church recreation, while several Baptist colleges and universities offer degree programs in church recreation. Both the Foreign and Home Mission Boards include church recreation program orientation for their career and short-term missionaries. More than 50 books and other resources are now available to support the recreation ministry in churches.

Increasing numbers of churches today are recognizing their responsibilities to the whole person—physical, social, mental, and spiritual—and are including in their programs a ministry of recreation to help meet these needs. These churches are using recreation as a channel of support and service to undergird, supplement, and strengthen all of their programs and activities. They are also using recreation as a catalyst to reach those persons for whom recreation is the most effective means of encounter with Christ. Church recreation has become a vehicle for ministry through meeting the needs of the handicapped, the aged, the underprivileged, and through effective use by missionaries to extend the boundary lines of Christian compassion, service, and witness around the world.

Southern Baptists use recreation today as an aid to worship and as a tool for teaching as drama techniques are being applied to communicate the gospel, or as other aspects of recreation become a workshop in daily living or a classroom implementing teaching-learning activity. Further, churches are using recreation as an environment for fellowship, and as an avenue to abundant living through providing joy, fun, relaxation, fellowship, release, restoration, and opportunity for fellowship with the Creator.

BIBLIOGRAPHY: Ray Conner, *A Guide to Church Recreation* (1977).

RAY CONNER

REDFORD, SAMUEL COURTS (b. Calhoun, MO, Sep. 4, 1898; d. Springfield, MO, Apr. 11, 1977). College president and home missions executive. Youngest child of farmer Eugene Redford of Kentucky and Alice Berry of Missouri, a descendant of President Zachary Taylor, he grew up in rural schools and churches near Granite, Lone Wolf, and Edmund, OK. He attended Oklahoma Baptist

EAGLE EYRIE BAPTIST ASSEMBLY (*q.v.*), Lynchburg, VA. Conference Center and Administration Building completed in 1980.

VIRGINIA BAPTIST HOME (*q.v.*), Richmond. Lakewood Manor. A home for the aged completed in 1978.

UNION UNIVERSITY (*q.v.*), Jackson, TN. *Top:* Relocated on a 150-acre campus north of Jackson, Sep., 1975. All academic departments housed under a 160,000-square-foot roof with 700 students residing in adjoining apartments. *Bottom:* George M. Savage Memorial Chapel features a 1,200-seat auditorium for college programs.

University (B.A., 1920; D.D., 1955), the University of Missouri (M.A., 1921), and Southwestern Baptist Theological Seminary (M.R.E., 1927).

Redford married Helen Ruth Ford of Henrietta, TX, May 24, 1921. They had 10 children: Virginia, Elizabeth, John, Rosemary, David, Courts, Jr., Sylvia, Bill, Jeanette, and Carolyn. Redford served as assistant pastor, First Baptist Church, Shawnee, OK, 1921-23; professor of Bible and religious education, Oklahoma Baptist University, Shawnee, 1923-25; professor of religious education, Southwestern Seminary, 1925-27; stewardship and brotherhood secretary of Missouri Baptist Convention, 1927-30; president, Southwest Baptist College, Bolivar, MO, 1930-43; assistant executive secretary-treasurer, Home Mission Board, SBC, 1943-54; and executive secretary-treasurer, HMB, 1954-64.

Other service included: chairman, SBC Inter-Agency Council; member, SBC Jubilee Advance Committee and the Joint Committee on Canadian Work; and SBC representative to Baptist Joint Committee for Jubilee Advance. He was listed in *Who's Who in American Colleges and Universities*, 1936-43, and *Who's Who in America*, 1935-59. He wrote three books: *Spiritual Frontiers* (1948), *Crusade in Home Missions* (1952), and *Home Missions, USA* (1956).

Redford worked tirelessly to keep Southwest Baptist College open during the Depression. While leading the HMB in Atlanta, he directed the "Four Year Crusade, 1955-58" which reported 1,598 new churches; expanded SBC work to all 50 states; increased operational budgets from $1,970,000 to $5,860,000; constituted new state conventions in Colorado, Indiana, Michigan, Ohio, and Utah-Idaho; developed new relationship with state conventions to employ missionaries jointly; established HMB relationship with Canadian Baptists and Puerto Rico; increased home missionaries from 936 to 2,353; enlarged chaplaincy ministries to civilians; and improved the loan funds corpus from $2,800,000 to $16,600,000. Redford is buried at Bolivar, MO.

EDMUND WILLIAM HUNKE, JR.

REED, WESTON COSBY (b. Jackson County, NC, Apr. 24, 1893; d. Kinston, NC, Aug. 30, 1970). Child-care executive. Son of J. P. and Marcella Reed, farmers, he married Mellie Parker in 1916. They had three children: Mary Nell, Marcella, and Olin. He attended Wake Forest College (B. A., 1925) and Peabody College. In 1943, following a short pastorate at First Baptist Church, Maiden, NC, Reed began serving the Baptist Children's Homes of North Carolina, first at Kennedy Home, Kinston, NC, and later as general superintendent of the system. Following his retirement in 1958 until his death, he continued his interest in the children's homes, serving as a consultant and updating their history in a book entitled *Love in Action* (1973). He is buried at Sylva, NC.

MARSE GRANT

REESE, JOSEPH (b. Kent County, PA, 1732; d. Mar. 5, 1795). Pioneer preacher and revolutionary patriot. He came to the Congaree area in South Carolina in 1745. Converted to Baptist views under the preaching of Philip Mulkey, he was ordained by Oliver Hart and Evan Pugh. Longtime pastor of the Congaree Baptist Church, he won Richard Furman (*q.v.* I) to the Baptist faith. He was active for the colonial cause during the American Revolution.

J. GLENWOOD CLAYTON

REFUGEE RESETTLEMENT. The Home Mission Board established the Office of Immigration and Refugee Service as a part of the Language Missions Department in 1970. This office seeks "to provide leadership and assistance to immigrants who are seeking to reside and/or enter the United States." The office led churches and associations to sponsor over 500 families from Cuba, Europe, Africa, Asia, and Latin America during the 1970s to help them find new homes and new hope in Christ. These efforts are in cooperation with other volunteer organizations. Post-resettlement includes assistance to sponsors and refugees to help the newcomers understand and contribute to the life of the nation.

OSCAR ROMO

REGULAR BAPTIST CHURCHES, GENERAL ASSOCIATION OF (II). A fellowship whose churches are found in all the states except Alabama, Hawaii, Mississippi, and South Carolina, and which is dedicated to separation "from worldliness and ecclesiastical apostasy." Its constituency is concentrated in the Middle West—in Iowa, Michigan, Illinois, Indiana, and Ohio. In 1979 these associated churches numbered 1,554; their membership 243,141. During the 1970s the association increased by 193 churches and 50,646 members.

This denomination represents a protest against liberal doctrine and centralized, denominational polity. Although fundamentalist in theology, its Council of Eighteen rejected a move in the mid-1970s to make strict Calvinism a test for receiving new congregations.

This group channels its missionary efforts through six independent agencies, such as Baptist Mid-Missions and the Association of Baptists for World Evangelism. Its educational work is done through nine independent schools. The fellowship publishes its own Sunday School literature. In 1979 Paul N. Tassell succeeded Joseph M. Stowell as the national representative.

CHESTER RAYMOND YOUNG

REGULAR BAPTISTS, OLD. A denomination which descends from United Baptists, who were formed in 1786-1801 by the union of Regular and Separate Baptists. Almost all its associations and churches carry the term "Old Regular." This name distinguishes the group from those Baptists whom they consider doctrinally unsound.

The oldest association of this denomination is New Salem, organized in 1825 as a United Baptist body. It changed its name to Regular in 1854 and to Old Regular in 1870. Most of the Old Regular Baptist churches are located in Kentucky, North Carolina, Virginia, and West Virginia. A 1980 survey identified 24 associations, 366 churches, and 19,770 members.

Old Regular Baptists regard conversion as an adult experience. A person is usually saved after a lengthy period of "deep conviction of heart and mind because of his sins." During this process the sinner suffers and agonizes until God produces spiritual rebirth. The "travailing" may continue a week, a month, a year, or longer.

Old Regular Baptists are Calvinists who do not hold to particular election. In their doctrinal statements many associations disavow any biblical interpretation which makes "God partial, directly or indirectly."

See also REGULAR BAPTISTS, Vol. II; REGULAR BAPTISTS, CURRENT, Vol. II; UNITED BAPTISTS, Vols. II, IV.

CHESTER RAYMOND YOUNG

REID, ALFRED SANDLIN (b. Orlando, FL, Oct. 26, 1924; d. Greenville, SC, Mar. 7, 1976). Educator. Son of Ulysses Eugene, a Baptist minister, and Rhoda Wilkinson Reid, he attended the University of Miami (B.Ed., 1948) and the University of Florida (M.A., 1950; Ph.D., 1952). He married Nathalie Rozran, July 10, 1948. They had two children, Miriam and Martha. He taught English and literature at Furman University, 1955-76, serving as department chairman, 1972-73. He wrote seven books, including two books of poetry. Shortly before his death, he completed a history of Furman University, *Furman University: Toward a New Identity* (1976). He is buried in Woodlawn Memorial Park, Greenville, SC.

J. GLENWOOD CLAYTON

REID, AVERY HAMILTON (b. Estill Fork, AL, Oct. 17, 1892; d. Montgomery, AL, Apr. 4, 1975). State convention executive. The son of Joseph Barrett Reid and Susan Caroline Hinshaw, farmers, he attended Howard College (A.B., 1917) and The Southern Baptist Theological Seminary (Th.M., 1922). He married Ruby Vardaman, Oct. 12, 1926. They had two children, Hamilton Vardaman Reid and Rachel Dell Reid Avery.

Ordained to the ministry, Sep. 6, 1912, Reid was pastor of First Baptist Church, Sylacauga, AL, 1922-28, and South Avondale, Birmingham, AL, 1928-39. In 1940 he became vice-president of Howard College. In 1944 he led a campaign to pay off the state convention's indebtedness; this was achieved in 1945. While serving as president of the state convention, 1943-45, he was elected executive secretary, effective Jan. 1, 1945, thus serving 10 months in

a dual capacity as president and executive secretary.

Under Reid's leadership the program of the convention and the associational and city mission program were expanded. Departments of Music, Evangelism, Stewardship, Ministers Retirement, and Negro Work were begun. Student centers were established at the senior colleges at Tuscaloosa, Troy, Auburn, and Florence; constitutional amendments provided for women representatives on the Executive Board and Administration Committee. Cooperative Program gifts increased from $349,272 in 1944 to $3,574,970 in 1963, the year of his retirement.

As a writer, he contributed a regular column to *The Alabama Baptist*. He was author of *Baptists in Alabama: Their Organization and Witness* (1967). Reid is buried in Greenwood Cemetery, Montgomery, AL.

GEORGE E. BAGLEY

RELIGION, STATE SPONSORSHIP OF. See STATE SPONSORSHIP OF RELIGION.

RELIGIOUS EDUCATION (II, III).
   I. New Directions, 1969-80. The 1970s witnessed significant change in the field of religious education. During the 1950s and 1960s, attention given to theological foundations was of general dimension. Theological emphasis in the 1970s became much more specific. The theology of hope, coupled with future-oriented psychology, sociology, and education, encouraged religious educators to seek ways to mold the future through nurture rather than to allow the future to mold it. Process theology called forth concepts of process pedagogy and andragogy. In some denominations liberation theology gave its concern of liberation for both oppressed and oppressors to religious educators who saw the learning community as the environment in which truth could provide new ways of achieving reconciliation and freedom.

The new values-clarification approach in public education provided stimulus for a new approach to religious valuing for some denominational agencies. Moral and ethical education gained parallel attention. Many efforts were made, and plans set forth, to gain acceptance for teaching about religion in the public schools, and if possible, to provide learning opportunities in moral and ethical decision making as well.

Although religious educators had earlier given much attention to developmental psychology, in this decade they sought a clearer focus of the stages of faith development. Studies of religious and moral awakenings in children, of moral and faith development of youth, of theological awareness, and of change factors in moral character provided a clearer understanding for Christian leadership to attempt its work and ministry, and gave strong support to proactive focus in learning and to self-directed learning.

Religious educators in the 1970s took into

serious account the sociological effect of cultural pluralism, social change, and social conflict. Socialization, as an educational process, and the concept of experimental involvement, through social action and ministry, received serious consideration.

Awareness of population change caused serious additional consideration to be given to ministry with senior citizens through education for aging, retirement, and death and dying. Leadership roles, skills aptitudes, and competencies received close attention, as did leadership enlistment and development and leadership motivation and commitment. New curriculum materials of a variety of qualities and dimensions, produced by the denominations and by independent publishers, appeared in abundance.

ROBERT POERSHKE

II. Curriculum Trends. A diversity of terms, such as decentralization, simplification, cooperation, and ethnic awareness, could characterize the religious educational curricula of the 1970s. The various developers and producers of religious educational materials tried various directions to meet the expressed needs of a pluralistic society.

John Westerhoff and Donald Miller explored the idea of shifting church school education from a public school model to a model of religious socialization. Under the aegis of an interdenominational partnership known as Joint Educational Development (JED), 12 of the 14 participating denominations developed a curriculum called CE:SA or Christian Education: Shared Approaches. Its aim was to provide a comprehensive and integrated educational curriculum plan to strengthen the nurture and witness of the church. Its four broad areas included Knowing the Word, Interpreting the Word, Living the Word, and Doing the Word.

Southern Baptists introduced in Oct., 1978, a new curriculum series for youth and adults entitled Bible Book Series. This venture was an effort to provide Bible study for the masses, using a book-by-book format. In addition, the Sunday School Board entered television and home Bible study with the production of a 30-minute weekly television program and workbook Bible study materials available by mail order. This move was part of a larger trend to explore the curriculum possibilities of electronic media.

Southern Baptists, American Baptists, and United Methodists are among the denominations producing ethnic materials. The primary thrust has been to produce Hispanic materials, although some Asian materials are also being developed.

In 1980 a curriculum rooted in black liberation theology and jointly produced by the Black Educational Resources Development Project (BERD) and the Office of Black Mission Development in the United Presbyterian Program Agency was being field-tested and was scheduled for release in Sep., 1981.

Finally, the Episcopal Church is exploring the concept of individual churches developing their own personalized curriculum offerings.

G. Campbell Wycoff articulated a consensus that seemed to develop among curriculum designers in the 1970s. "It is the function of curriculum to provide a plan for developing, maintaining, and enhancing those understandings, attitudes, and skills that serve the church's purposes in worship, witness, and work."

RICHARD W. HARMON

III. Teaching Methodologies. In recent years much of the teaching-learning process has concerned itself with structure, process, content, and with outcomes in terms of what happens to individual learners. The entire field of instructional methodology has been guided by efforts to measure Christian personality growth in the following areas: (1) Growth in knowledge of the Christian faith, (2) growth in understanding of the Christian faith and its meaning for life, and (3) growth in attitude toward the Christian faith and its application for life. Increased use of the following methods in Christian education give evidence of this developing trend.

Programmed Instruction. —Programmed instructional materials involve small steps, usually building one upon the other, active responding on the part of the pupil, immediate knowledge of results, self-pacing, and program testing. Many denominations now produce programmed materials. Most of the materials relate to some phase of leader training.

Because of high costs in developing and testing materials, they deal with subjects of continuing value. Most materials used in Theological Education by Extension in missions use one or more of the formats of programmed instruction. The scarcity of trained writers and the validation costs involved will probably prevent the widespread use of programmed instruction in developing Sunday School and Church Training materials for group or class members. However, much material already exists for the training of church leaders such as teachers, committee members, and church officers. Current trends seem to suggest the use of many of the principles used in programmed instruction but to reflect flexibility in the use of the principles.

Instructional Systems and Packages. — Technically, programmed instruction and computer-assisted instruction fall in the category of instructional system. The term refers here to validated instructional packages of a considerably less complex nature. Based on specific objectives and limited for the most part to teaching knowledge and understanding it, these packets do much to improve the quality of teaching. Churches whose leaders lack training could make helpful use of such packages.

The packages have a format different from the quarterly normally used in the churches' educational organizations. Usually they make use of mulitmedia approaches. Some use printed words and pictures. Others use audiotapes along with student response books. Others use videotapes, audiotapes, filmstrips, and other media correlated into one package. Churches will need packages which either individuals or groups can use. Such flexibility comes to fruition in leadership guides which accompany the materials.

The SSB developed the new Equipping Centers for Church Training and the Home Bible Study Correspondence Course around a modified systems approach. Equipping Centers are organizational units of the Church Training program which consist of a variety of learning approaches grouped around a central Bible-related subject. The Home Bible Study Correspondence Course provides valid, self-paced Bible study by correspondence. The studies, coordinated with a weekly television program, involve the whole family in Bible study on great themes and books of the Bible. Because of the increased economy and flexibility of multi-media, instructional systems and packages offer promise to churches, especially in the area of leadership training.

Computer-assisted and Computer-managed Instruction.—In 1978 the Methodist Church experimented with the use of computer-assisted instruction through use of PLATO computer terminals in association with Control Data Corporation. They tested units of study in doctrine and in human sexuality. Denominational agencies of the future could provide banks of computerized courses which churches could receive through computer terminals in a media center. In fact, the future could bring such instructional materials into homes as computer systems become more and more feasible in regard to costs. Churches will face the problem of properly relating these electronic approaches and the need for growth in a fellowship of learners. A computer can do certain things, but it cannot provide a caring fellowship in which the most significant learning takes place.

Experiential Learning.—This approach to education stresses the practical use of what a person has learned. More Bible study seems to focus on reflection about what the Bible says about life and its meaning. Experiential Bible study focuses on the Scriptures by asking the pupil, "What does this verse say to you about your life situation this day? Tomorrow?"

Discipleship training focuses on one-to-one Bible study and guidance in the Christian life. It stresses how to appropriate meaning for life from Bible study. The continuing learning activities in the Southern Baptist Curriculum Design focus on exploring the content of God's revelation as recorded in the Bible; discovering increasing meaning, value, and relevance in the biblical revelation; appropriating personally the meaning and value of the biblical revelation; and applying in all relationships the meaning, value, and relevance of the biblical revelation.

See also LIBERATION THEOLOGY; RELIGIOUS EDUCATION ASSOCIATIONS, SOUTHERN BAPTIST.

LEROY FORD and WILLIAM A. SMITH

RELIGIOUS EDUCATION ASSOCIATIONS, SOUTHERN BAPTIST (cf. Religious Education, Professional Associations, Vol. II). Annual meetings of Southern Baptist religious educators have taken place since the early 1920s for fellowship, counsel, and the study and improvement of the work of religious education. The beginnings of such meetings were in the form of regional gatherings, called associations.

The earliest regional association, the Southwestern Baptist Religious Education Association, organized in 1921, reported 347 members in 1979. The second oldest regional association, the Eastern Baptist Religious Education Association, begun in the 1940s as the Southeastern Baptist Religious Education Association, reported 141 members in 1979. The youngest regional group, the Western Baptist Religious Education Association, formed in 1951, reported 61 members in 1979. Another regional group, the Midwestern Baptist Religious Education and Music Association, formed in 1969, disbanded in the early 1970s.

Many other religious education associations exist in associational and state convention groupings and meet monthly or annually for fellowship and programs.

The Southern Baptist Religious Education Association, formed in 1956, cosponsored with the Sunday School Board a National Conference on Christian Education Ministry, RENEW '75, held in Houston, TX, Feb., 1975. The highest attendance for an annual meeting was 582 when the association met in Atlanta, GA, in 1977.

See also MIDWESTERN BAPTIST RELIGIOUS EDUCATION AND MUSIC ASSOCIATION, VOL. III.

WILLIAM G. CALDWELL

RELIGIOUS HERALD, THE (II, III). Weekly news journal of Virginia Baptists. On Jan. 1, 1980, the circulation was 46,333. The budget plan, used in 391 churches, accounted for 35,017 subscriptions. In 1980 postal rates had increased 1,250 percent since 1970 and continued to drive up costs. Since Sep. 1, 1970, Thomas E. Miller has served as associate to the editor, Julian H. Pentecost.

JOHN D. EDENS

RELIGIOUS LIBERTY (II, III). After nearly 200 years of interpretation, the simply written limitations of the religion clauses of the First Amendment, in the opinion of many, are not clearly understood or observed by government. Churches have had to remain alert to potential violations. The Baptist Joint Committee on Public Affairs attempts to alert Baptists whenever religious liberty and the separation of church and state are threatened by government action. Examples of threats to religious liberty in the 1970s follow.

Advocacy of ideas and not the quest for special favor led Baptists over the past decade to oppose legislation permitting the use of public monies to finance religious education. They successfully opposed a congressional "voucher" plan which would have provided each schoolchild with a voucher representing an equal share of education tax funds. These were to be used to purchase an education in either a private or public school. The proposal was followed by an attempt to give a "tax credit" to parents who paid tuition to private or parochial schools. Baptist opposition to both of these plans sprang from the belief that they would unconstitutionally "establish" a religion, that they would jeopardize the public school system, and that they contributed negatively to social cohesion.

Some legislation and attendant regulations have tended to presume that government understands better than a church what constitutes its religious mission and to threaten lifting of tax exempt status as a weapon for enforcement. Early in the decade, the question arose over what constituted an "integrated auxiliary" of a church and which mission projects, such as retirement housing, were, in fact, integral to its religious witness. In 1976, and again in 1979, the issue of church mission surfaced in terms of the church's claim to the right to speak out on issues of public policy. Proposed regulation of churches in the exercise of their right to influence legislation was viewed by Baptists as a restriction on their understanding of mission.

In 1976 the Baptist Joint Committee on Public Affairs also argued on that basis against a bill placing a percentage ceiling on the amount of its budget that a church might spend to influence legislation. An additional threat to the freedom of a church to define mission for itself came through the proposed revenue procedure to withdraw tax exempt status of church-operated schools which did not comply with mandates on racial quotas. While the committee's sympathies lie in favor of full integration, its concern in this case was the integrity of religious liberty.

The limit on government against its entanglement in the internal affairs of a church also was at issue in the 1970s. California was successfully opposed in its attempt to regulate how a church spends its money. Attempts by several states to regulate how churches raise money and by the federal government to establish for churches which solicit or receive funds through the mails uniform accounting methods and disclosure of their books of account were defeated.

VICTOR TUPITZA

R. E. MILAM BAPTIST STUDENT CENTER. Adjoining the University of Washington campus, the center, former building of Delta Upsilon Fraternity, was purchased in 1965 by the Baptist General Convention of Oregon-Washington. In 1973 the center was renamed and later dedicated as the R. E. Milam Baptist Student Center in honor of Robert Edward Milam, pioneer Baptist leader and first executive secretary-treasurer of the convention of Southern Baptists in the Northwest. In 1978 the convention deeded the center to Puget Sound Baptist Association for continued use as

a Baptist student center. The two bodies cooperate in student ministries.

ROBERT STAPP

RENFROE, JOHN JEFFERSON DEYAMPERT (b. Montgomery County, AL, Aug. 30, 1830; d. Birmingham, AL, June 2, 1888). Pastor and chaplain. The son of a "stock minder," he received limited formal education, studying only briefly at Professor John's Scientific Institute in Tuskeegee, AL. He served as pastor of churches in Calhoun and Cherokee Counties, AL, 1852-57, before beginning a long pastorate at First Church, Talladega, AL, 1858-60, 1864-86, where he was instrumental in the creation of the state Sunday School Board and the state Mission Board. His last pastorate was at Southside Church, Birmingham, 1887-88.

Renfroe served in numerous capacities, including Confederate chaplain in Virginia, 1862-64; corresponding editor of the *Christian Index* and *Southwestern Baptist*, 1866-73; associate editor and editor of *The Alabama Baptist*, 1873-76 and 1886-87, respectively; secretary and president of the state Sunday School Board, 1871-72 and 1873-75, respectively; president of the state Mission Board, 1876-80; and clerk and vice-president of the state convention, 1873 and 1875-76, 1880, 1882, 1885-87, respectively.

Renfroe married Elsie Lee Renfroe. They had eight children: Graves, Theodosia, Curry, Annie, Crockette, John, Elsie Lee, and Ruby. He is buried in Oak Hill Cemetery, Talladega, AL.

WALTER BELT WHITE

REPRESENTATION, SOUTHERN BAPTIST CONVENTION BASIS OF (I, III). The basis of member representation to the SBC has remained unchanged since 1969, but registration requirements were revised. As early as 1930 the bylaws of the Convention stated that Convention secretaries were to enroll "the members of the Convention who shall present themselves with proper evidence of their right to be enrolled." An amendment in 1946 provided for the enrollment of "messengers who present proper credentials from the churches." Bylaw 8(1) was amended in 1980 by specifying "churches cooperating with the Southern Baptist Convention," and requiring that "each messenger shall register in person by presenting a completed and signed Southern Baptist Convention messenger registration card."

LEE PORTER

RESEARCH, HOME MISSION BOARD DIVISION OF (cf. Survey and Special Studies, Department of, Vol. III). The primary source of Home Mission Board research in 1970 was the Survey and Special Studies Department. Staff efforts were divided between interdenominational religious surveys in metropolitan areas and special studies for associations and HMB staff. Most studies were descriptive reports combining insights from church statistics, census documents, and public planners.

In 1971 staff members were divided into the Survey and Special Studies Department, Program Implementation Section, and the Planning Services Department, Planning Section. In late 1972 Planning Services was dissolved, and the staff became consultants in planning and research. In 1975 the Office of Evangelism, Surveys, and Special Studies was established when the Evangelism Section was formed. The three research offices were centralized in 1979 as the Research Division, Planning Section. Staff assignments were made to service all four HMB sections.

Two philosophical shifts occurred during the decade: massive religious surveys became extinct and church growth theories began to be researched. Research staff serving during the decade included: Leonard G. Irwin, 1959-70; William A. Powell, 1962-72; Orrin D. Morris, 1963-72; 1979- ; Donald F. Mabry, 1965-75; Tommy R. Coy, 1968-77; Paul W. Stuart, 1972-76; Leonard O. Hinton, Jr., 1973- ; Phillip B. Jones, 1976- ; C. Kirk Hadaway, 1978- ; and Clay L. Price, 1979- .

See also STUDY AND RESEARCH IN THE SBC.

ORRIN D. MORRIS

RESORT MINISTRIES, NEW YORK. See NEW YORK RESORT MINISTRIES.

RESORT MISSIONS. A Christian ministry and witness in a resort setting. A resort may be a national park, a campground, a state park, a ski slope, a lake, a state fair, or any place where people spend their leisure time. The Special Mission Ministries Department of the Home Mission Board promotes this work.

R. DONALD HAMMONDS

RETIREMENT CENTERS, BAPTIST. Baptist retirement centers began in 1880 with the Baptist Home of the District of Columbia. In the 1950s many Baptist state conventions established homes for the aged. In 1978, 24 facilities operated in the District of Columbia, Florida, Georgia, Kentucky, Louisiana, Maryland, North Carolina, Oklahoma, South Carolina, Tennessee, Texas, and Virginia.

According to need, one can receive services ranging from housekeeping to complete convalescent nursing. Private quarters are available.

Responding to the needs found in retirement centers, Southern Baptists formed the Southern Baptist Association of Executives of Homes for the Aging in 1963. The SBC Christian Life Commission provided support until 1972 when the work was shifted to the Home Mission Board. The professional organization was dormant, 1972-75. A newly expanded organization, Southern Baptist Association of Ministries with the Aging (SBAMA), emerged in 1976 and 1977. The dominant group in the SBAMA remains the executives of the homes for the aging. SBAMA membership is for church and denominational, long-term care/housing, and educational institutions.

JERRY M. STUBBLEFIELD

REVIEW AND EXPOSITOR (II, III). Recent managing editors have included Guy H. Ranson, 1957-58; J. J. Owens, 1959-65; Frank Stagg, 1965-70, 1974-75; David L. Mueller, 1976; and E. Glenn Hinson, 1970-73, 1976- . Since 1959, *Review and Expositor* has used a thematic approach, devoting one annual issue to the January Bible study theme of the SBC. In recent years the journal has gained international attention. The circulation in 1980 was approximately 6,000.

E. GLENN HINSON

REYNOLDS, HANNAH ELIZABETH (b. Anniston, AL, Feb. 14, 1893; d. Greenville, SC, Feb. 10, 1977). Woman's Missionary Union executive. The daughter of Oliver Mallory and Eliza Smith Reynolds, she attended WMU Training School, Louisville, KY. For seven years she was young people's secretary for Alabama WMU. She became young people's secretary in 1929 for Louisiana. The same year she was elected WMU corresponding secretary for Louisiana Southern Baptists. Her first office was a room in the administration building of Baptist Bible Institute, New Orleans.

In 1943 Reynolds moved to Shreveport where WMU and other Louisiana Convention offices were housed until their relocation to Alexandria in 1948. Under her leadership, WMU purchased camp property and began a state offering for scholarships. Following her retirement in 1954, the offering was named the Hannah Reynolds Offering for Christian Education. She is buried in Highland Cemetery, Anniston, AL.

KATHRYN E. CARPENTER

RHODE ISLAND, SOUTHERN BAPTISTS IN. See MARYLAND, BAPTIST CONVENTION OF AND NEW ENGLAND, BAPTIST GENERAL ASSOCIATION OF.

RHODESIA, MISSION IN (III). See ZIMBABWE, MISSION IN.

RICHARDSON, VERNON BRITT (b. Portsmouth, VA, May 19, 1914; d. Richmond, VA, Dec. 6, 1970). Pastor, denominational and civic leader. The son of Norman B. and Lillian Bell (Britt) Richardson, he graduated from the University of Richmond (B.A., 1935) and Crozer Theological Seminary (B.D., 1938). Ordained in Portsmouth in 1938, his pastorates were Westhampton Church, Richmond, VA, 1940-43; University Church, Baltimore, MD, 1946-64; and River Road Church, Richmond, 1965-70.

Richardson married Frances M. Martin, July 17, 1944. They had two children, Frances and Vernon Britt, Jr. During World War II he served as a Navy chaplain. He was a member of the Foreign Mission Board, SBC; Radio and

Television Commission, SBC; Education Commission, SBC; board of trustees, University of Richmond, serving as vice-rector; president, State Mission Board, Baptist Convention of Maryland, 1960; and a member of the President's committee for the employment of the handicapped, 1961-67.

The University of Richmond awarded him the honorary D.D. degree (1949). He is buried at Midlothian, VA.

IRA D. HUGHES

RIDGECREST BAPTIST CONFERENCE CENTER (cf. Ridgecrest Baptist Assembly, Vols. II, III). The Sunday School Board has continued to develop the Ridgecrest facility and to assure increased use on an economically sound basis. Beginning in 1970, the total operating cost of the assembly, including auditorium, conference, and exhibit space, was placed on a cost recovery basis from charges to guests. Ridgecrest Assembly became a part of the newly created Assemblies Division, Oct. 1, 1971, to strengthen administrative support. In July, 1972, the name changed to Ridgecrest Baptist Conference Center to implement further the concept of a year-round center operated for training, worship, denominational fellowship, evangelism, retreats, and spiritual growth.

Major facilities added since 1969 include a new recreation area, 1974, a second 32-unit Royal Gorge Apartment complex, 1974, Maple Lodge, 1974, Spruce Lodge, 1975, Walnut Lodge, 1975, and Lambdin Auditorium, 1979. Facilities given major renovation since 1969 include Spilman Auditorium, 1972, conference space in Crystal Springs and over the dining hall, 1978, Auditorium Annex and conference rooms, 1979, and Woodland Lodge, 1979.

Approximately 50,000 guests participated in 216,000 days of conferences during 1978-79. Summer conferences accounted for 167,300 guest days and fall-winter-spring conferences for 49,000. Kenneth McAnear continues as manager.

ROBERT M. TURNER

RIGGS, MILFORD (b. Kenton County, KY, Sep. 5, 1866; d. St. Louis, MO, Aug. 7, 1947). Administrator of home for aged. Son of James and Elizabeth Longmoor Riggs, farmers, he married Mary Dudley Rees, Oct. 15, 1891. Their children were Milford Dudley, Russell, Robert Longmoor and Milford, Jr. He attended Georgetown College (A.B. and A.M., 1890) and The Southern Baptist Theological Seminary (1888-89). He served as pastor in Council Bluffs, IA, and St. Louis, Boonville, Harrisonville, Joplin, Lexington, and Ironton, MO.

Riggs did field work for Missouri Baptist Orphan's Home, Pattonville, 1905-09. He helped organize young people's work, which later became the Baptist Young People's Union of Missouri. While pastor at Ironton, he and his wife established the Missouri Baptist Home for Aged Baptists in 1913, adopted later as a benev-olent institution of the Missouri Baptist General Association. He was superintendent of this institution until his retirement in 1932. He is buried in Memorial Park Cemetery, St. Louis.

WILLIAM R. RIGGS

RILEY, EMMA CAMILLE (b. Water Valley, MS, Feb. 26, 1879; d. Little Rock, AR., Sep. 8, 1968). Educator and philanthropist. Daughter of William H. and Caroline Sumner Riley, farmers, she graduated from Central College (A.B., 1902). After teaching school for several years, she entered the political field and served in the office of the Secretary of State under six Arkansas governors. She became the first woman Deputy Secretary of State in May, 1924. Riley served on Ouachita Baptist University's board of trustees for 15 years. A generous benefactor of this school, she was a member of the First Baptist Church, El Dorado, Little Rock City Women's Club, Bookfellows, Arkansas Art Center, Delta Kappa Gamma Teachers Sorority, and the Business and Professional Women's Club. She is buried at El Dorado, AR.

T. S. MEDLIN

RIO GRANDE RIVER MINISTRY. State mission effort of the Baptist General Convention of Texas initiated in 1968 as a three-year project with funds from the 1967 state mission offering. The project gained impetus when Hurricane Beulah devastated the Rio Grande Valley in 1967. Elmin K. Howell has directed the work since May, 1968. During the first full year, over 5,000 Texas Baptists and 150 churches participated.

The purpose of the ministry is to provide coordination of services, supplies, resources, personnel, and training of local leaders through the six Baptist associations along the Texas side of the border. Principles and guidelines of international cooperation were set up in 1969 by the Foreign Mission Board and approved by the BGCT. The ultimate goal of the ministry is the indigenization of services—agricultural, medical, and doctrinal—through leadership training in the local church. Equipment and legal services are provided by Los Hermanos de la Frontera, a volunteer lay liaison corporation.

More than 136 missions have been established along the border since the ministry began; over 20 churches have come out of those missions. In 1968 there were 24 Mexican pastors preaching in 35 congregations; in 1980 there were approximately 112 pastors preaching in over 200 congregations. The river ministry has made an impact on 225 churches within the nine Baptist associations on both sides of the border.

ELMIN K. HOWELL

RIVERSIDE BAPTIST CENTER. A multiple-ministries center (a 1976 expansion of Riverside Spanish Mission) in Grand Junction, CO, sponsored through Grand Valley Association, with bivocational pastor Eddie Scroggins as director. In 1978 June Scroggins, wife of Eddie Scroggins, was employed as a home missionary and director of weekday ministries for the center. She and the Riverside Weekday Ministries Program are under the auspices of the Colorado Baptist General Convention. The Southern Baptist Home Mission Board owns the building.

The family ministries part of the center includes work with juveniles, families in crisis, and the mentally handicapped. An outreach effort brings people to the center and its chapel program through child and community help projects. Literacy, mission education, and refugee services are other activities.

JAMES LEE YOUNG

ROBERTS, DAVID BENJAMIN (b. Caldwell County, NC, July 22, 1904; d. Asheville, NC, Feb. 23, 1976). Associational missionary. The son of Joseph and Emma Roberts, farmers, he attended Wake Forest College (B.A.) and Southern Baptist Theological Seminary (Th.G.). He taught school in Rutherford County, NC, for 12 years and served as interim pastor of several churches. He was pastor of Tuckasegee Baptist Church in Mt. Holly, NC, for two years and Bull Creek Baptist Church in Madison County, NC, for nine years.

Roberts served the French Broad Association, 1946-70, first as associational field worker and then as associational missionary. He led the churches into greater cooperation with the denomination, such as 100 percent participation in Vacation Bible School and the Cooperative Program. He married Wilford Alexander, Sep. 29, 1940. They had one son, Clyde. Roberts is buried in the cemetery of Bull Creek Baptist Church, Mars Hill, NC.

H. PAGE LEE

ROBINSON, JAMES ROY (b. Gaffney, SC, Dec. 29, 1908; d. Greenville, SC, June 9, 1976). Student leader, pastor, and assistant to college president. Son of Georgia Hawkins Robinson and James Robinson, a textile worker, he attended Gardner-Webb Junior College, Furman University (B.S., 1933; D.D., 1957), and The Southern Baptist Theological Seminary (Th.M., 1943). He married Nelle Sapoch, Dec. 28, 1932. They had two daughters, Helen and Mary.

Robinson served as Baptist Student Union secretary for Florida, 1935-39; pastor of Vinton Baptist, Vinton, VA, 1943-46; First Baptist, Greer, SC, 1946-56; Citadel Square Baptist, Charleston, SC, 1956-62; and First Baptist, Hickory, NC, 1962-71. He was assistant to the president of Gardner-Webb College, 1972-74. He served as vice-president of the South Carolina Baptist Convention, 1953, and as trustee of North Greenville College, Baptist College at Charleston, Southeastern Baptist Theological Seminary, and the Annuity Board, SBC. He is buried in Wood Memorial Park, Greer, SC.

STEWART B. SIMS, SR.

ROCKY MOUNTAIN BAPTIST (III). Ovid Luer Bayless, editor since 1962, retired on Mar. 1, 1977. Larry R. Jerden, elected to succeed him, assumed the office that day and resigned effective after the May 13, 1977, issue of the paper. James Lee Young, feature editor for Baptist Press, became editor on July 1, 1977. A loss in circulation resulted when the Northern Plains Baptist Convention began publishing its own paper in 1976. Circulation at the end of 1979 was 9,400.

JAMES LEE YOUNG

RODRIGUEZ, GARCIA ALFREDO SIMON (b. Cuba, 1884; d. Sancti Spiritus, Cuba, 1935). Cuban Baptist pastor and writer. Ordained as a minister, Mar. 31, 1907, Rodriguez served churches in Santo Domingo, Santa Clara, Cruces, Pinar del Rio, Sagua la Grande, and Sancti Spiritus. He served on a committee to study the formation of a Cuban Baptist Convention and participated in the writing of its constitution in Feb., 1905. He made his most significant contribution to Cuban Baptist life through his voluminous writings and translations of curricula for Bible study and manuals for the training of Sunday School teachers.

J. DAVID FITE

ROLLINS, RUTH WYRICK (b. Waynesville, MO, July 19, 1895; d. Waynesville, MO, Mar. 28, 1978). Woman's Missionary Union leader. The daughter of Mary Patterson and Martin Wyrick, cattle ranchers, she married Thomas Rollins, May 31, 1920. They had no children. They moved to Oklahoma, serving in Baptist churches in Bartlesville, Ponca City, and Okmulgee. In 1941 they moved to Gary, IN. They were affiliated with various Baptist groups until 1950, when they joined First Southern Baptist Church, Hammond. She served on the board of directors of the Illinois Baptist State Association.

In preparation for the organization of the state convention, Illinois and Kentucky missions directors appointed her promotional chairman for Indiana in 1957. She presided at a preconvention meeting of WMU for Indiana Southern Baptist churches and planned for the organizational meeting. She was elected president in Apr., 1959. After 18 months she resigned, moving to Arizona for her husband's health. After his death in 1961, she returned to Waynesville, MO. She is buried there in Memorial Park Cemetery.

MRS. E. W. SPRINGS

RONDEAU, WILLIAM (b. London, England, Apr. 6, 1779; d. Livingston County, KY, Mar. 11, 1859). Pioneer preacher. Converted in England, Rondeau was ordained about 1812. He married Ann Arkinstall, also of England. They sailed in 1819 to America, where they traveled west to Golconda, IL. Here they settled on Rondeau Island in 1830 with their 10 children: Ebenezer, Charles, Sarah, James, John,

William, Theophilus, Mehitabel, Mary, and Immanuel. Rondeau traveled around southern Illinois and western Kentucky, preaching in backwoods areas and evangelizing and establishing churches. He is buried in the Old Golconda, IL, cemetery.

RONALD L. NELSON

ROTHWELL, ANDREW (b. Delaware County, PA, Nov. 11, 1801; d. Washington, DC, May 21, 1883). Prominent Baptist layman and church founder in Washington, DC. Orphaned at an early age, he was reared by Henry Paschall of Kingsessing, PA, where he learned farming, but he had only three months schooling per year. William Stoughton (*q.v.* II) baptized him in Philadelphia at age nine. At 17 Rothwell was apprenticed to William Frey, a Philadelphia printer. In 1822 he moved to Washington where he became a compositor in the office of Gales and Seaton, printers and publishers of *The National Intelligencer.* He married Susan Borrows in 1824. Later he married Ann Dewees. His children included Eleanor Dewees, Eliza Cornelia, George Washington, Emily Judson, and Fannie R. He joined Second Baptist Church in June, 1824, was elected deacon, and served as church clerk for many years. Although Sunday School work was connected with Second Church as early as 1815, Rothwell, its first recorded superintendent, was instrumental in leading the church to take over the full responsibility "for the school which is held in this house."

In 1828, associated with Thomas W. Ustick, he began publication of a newspaper, *The Washington City Chronicle and Literary Depository,* which was short-lived. He became collector of taxes for the city, and also published in 1828 a compendium of all laws passed by Congress to that date relating to the District of Columbia. He also worked in the Navy Department.

Rothwell became a close friend of Luther Rice (*q.v.* II) and caught his spirit of outreach and vision. Churches established in Washington under Rothwell's leadership were: Third (1842), Thirteenth Street (1853), Fifth (1855), Calvary (1863), and North (1874). He was a member of the board of trustees of Columbian College, 1835-83, serving as secretary and/or treasurer for several terms. In 1877 he helped organize the Columbia Association, now the District of Columbia Baptist Convention. He also actively promoted several benevolent institutions in Washington. In 1867 he published *A History of the Baptist Institutions of Washington City.* Rothwell contributed significantly to the growth of Baptists in the city of Washington for over 40 years. He is buried in Prospect Hill Cemetery in Washington, DC.

FRANCES BECK

ROYAL AMBASSADOR CONGRESSES, NATIONAL. National meetings for Royal Ambassadors are held about every five years. Six congresses have been held: Atlanta, GA, 1953; Fort Worth, TX, 1958; Washington, DC, 1963; Oklahoma City, OK, 1968; St. Louis, MO,

1973; and Nashville, TN, 1979. General purposes of the congresses are to promote feelings of national unity within the Royal Ambassador program and to provide inspirational and missions-related events for Royal Ambassadors. Congress programs include presentations by Christian performers, athletes missionaries, and other inspirational speakers; exhibits; crafts; and special events related to the locale in which the congresses are held.

MIKE DAVIS

ROYAL SERVICE (II, III). See WOMAN'S MISSIONARY UNION, AUXILIARY TO SBC.

RURAL-URBAN MISSIONS, HOME MISSION BOARD PROGRAM OF (III). The Rural-Urban Missions Department became a program in the Division of Associational Services in 1971 and a department of the Associational Missions Division in 1976. Leaders of the program have been Roy Owen, 1971; Larry Bryson, 1971-74; James Nelson, 1974-79; and Quentin Lockwood, 1979-   .

The program works with rural-urban associations (those with population centers of less than 50,000) and with open country, village, small town, and small city churches. It assists associations and newer state conventions in the recruiting, training, appointing, and funding of directors of associational missions, and in providing materials, conferences, and research and pilot projects to aid the small church and the rural-urban association.

Other responsibilities are: Providing materials for and training the Associational Missions Committee; In-Service Guidance Program in 6 seminaries, 3 Bible schools, and 39 colleges, providing field guidance for students who serve rural-urban churches; bivocational pastor relations with J. T. Burdine, Jr., as national consultant; and external relationships to regional and national organizations that are concerned with rural and small town life and nonmetropolitan churches.

The department provides correlation for all HMB programs relating to the rural-urban area through the Rural-Urban Council.

See also RURAL MISSIONS, VOL. II.

QUENTIN LOCKWOOD

RUSHING, FINIS REED (b. Marion, KY, Oct. 8, 1905; d. Russellville, KY, Oct. 6, 1976). State convention missionary. The son of Finis Franklin and Mary Ellen Van Hooser Rushing, farmers, he was converted in 1921, called to full-time service in 1923, and ordained in Caldwell County, Mar. 30, 1925. He was a graduate of Western Kentucky University (A.B., 1933) and attended The Southern Baptist Theological Seminary, 1933-34 and 1934-35. He married Elizabeth Ermine P'Pool in June, 1928. Their children were Mary Ellen and Kyle Wayne. Rushing served as a missionary of the Kentucky Baptist Convention for 30 years, 1946-76.

A. B. COLVIN

RUST, EVERETT WARREN (b. Covington, KY, Sep. 29, 1915; d. Mesa, AZ, Apr. 5, 1979). Pastor and denominational worker. The son of Mae Rust and Everett Rust, a building contractor, he attended Carson-Newman College (A.B., 1944) and The Southern Baptist Theological Seminary (M.Div., 1948). He served as a pastor for 31 years, 1940-71, in Tennessee, Kentucky, and Missouri, serving on the executive boards of each state, and as a trustee of Southern Seminary, 1952-61, Carson-Newman College, 1957-62, and Golden Gate Baptist Theological Seminary, 1965-71. He also served on the study committee for the Baptist Faith and Message, 1962-63.

In 1971 Rust joined the staff of the Home Mission Board as director of the Metropolitan Missions Department. Under his administration, Southern Baptists awoke to the demanding socioeconomic and spiritual needs of American cities. He served as department director until May, 1977, when failing health forced him to move to Arizona. He continued to serve the department as assistant director until his death.

Rust married Anna Lee Morris, Oct. 3, 1936. They had one daughter, Sandra Lee. He is buried in Forest Lawn Cemetery, Erlanger, KY.

DON HAMMER

RUTLEDGE, ARTHUR BRISTOW (b. San Antonio, TX, Apr. 30, 1911; d. Gainesville, GA, Nov. 23, 1977). Missions executive. The son of painter-paperhanger Abram Burl Rutledge and Sarah Priscella Graham, he was converted, baptized, called to the ministry, and ordained in San Antonio's Central Baptist Church. Having attended Briscoe and Crockett grade schools, Washington Irving Junior High School, and Breckenridge High School, all in San Antonio, he was a graduate of Baylor University (B.A., 1936), Southern Baptist Theological Seminary (Th.M., 1939), and Southwestern Baptist Theological Seminary (Th.D., 1944).

While preaching at a Latin-American Baptist mission, Rutledge met volunteer worker Vesta Mae Sharber and married her in Somerset, TX, June 8, 1936. They had three children: Arthur, David, and Frances.

Rutledge led nine Baptist churches during his 27-year pastoral ministry: Old Rock Church, Somerset, TX, 1930-32; Belfalls Church, Nolanville, TX, 1933-36; Somerset Church, Somerset, TX, 1935-36; Long Run Church, Vevay, IN, 1937-40; First Church, Royse City, TX, 1940-42; Central Church, San Antonio, TX, 1942-45; and First Church, Marshall, TX, 1945-57. He served as stewardship and direct missions secretary for the Baptist General Convention of Texas, 1957-59; as missions division director, Home Mission Board, SBC, 1959-64; and as the 14th executive director, HMB, SBC, 1965-76.

Other denominational service included: Moderator, Soda Lake Baptist Association, TX, 1947-49; trustee, East Texas Baptist College, Marshall, TX, 1946-57; trustee, Bishop Col-

lege, Marshall, TX, 1947-57; member, executive board, BGCT, 1946-49, 1954-57, chairman, 1955-57; chairman, Christian Life Commission, BGCT, 1950-55; member, Radio and Television Commission, SBC, 1948-51; member, Foreign Mission Board, SBC, 1954-57; member, North American Baptist Fellowship, 1966-76; and member, Baptist Joint Committee on Public Affairs, 1965-76, chairman, 1974-76.

Rutledge received distinguished alumnus awards from both Southwestern and Southern Seminaries, and the Distinguished Service Award of the SBC Christian Life Commission, 1973. He was listed in *Who's Who in America,* 1968-77; *Who's Who in the South and Southwest,* 1971-77; *The Blue Book,* 1970-77; and *Dictionary of International Biography,* 1972-77. He wrote three books: *Homes That Last* (1952), *Mission to America* (1969), and *Tomorrow Starts Today* (1975).

In his 12 years as HMB executive director, the staff of 50 doubled and its budget of $6,500,000 tripled. Rutledge formulated the HMB's 14 mission guidelines; formalized cooperative agreements with state conventions; moved from direct to cooperative missions; enlisted blacks, ethnics, and women as HMB staff members; expanded HMB programs to include Associational Administrative Services, Christian Social Ministries, Interfaith Witness, Evangelism Development, Mass Evangelism, and Personal Evangelism; elevated evangelism in a more flexible HMB structure; established a Planning Section to develop a "single-uniform national mission program"; implemented goal-oriented planning under themes, "Direction '77," "Crossing Barriers," and "Bold Mission Thrust"; purchased HMB building at 1350 Spring Street, N.W., Atlanta, GA; initiated volunteer enlistment programs; reached out to refugees; instituted HMB disaster relief fund; improved relations with other denominations; and provided HMB library and heritage rooms for historical treasures.

Rutledge died on Thanksgiving Eve, Nov. 23, 1977. His wife, Vesta, died six weeks earlier on Oct. 3, 1977. Both are buried in Forest Lawn Memorial Park, Newnan, GA.

See also HOME MISSION BOARD, SBC.

EDMUND WILLIAM HUNKE, JR.

RWANDA, MISSION IN. In 1977 Earl and Jane (Winchester) Martin arrived in Kigali as Southern Baptists' first missionaries to Rwanda. They were assigned to assist in establishing a Baptist work in the capital city and strengthening nearby rural churches. A building which formerly housed a furniture factory was purchased and renovated to provide space for a church and weekday activities. With the coming of additional missionaries, plans call for expansion into other parts of the country and into services such as veterinary medicine, agriculture, media, and youth ministries. Eight missionaries were serving in 1979.

JOY NEAL

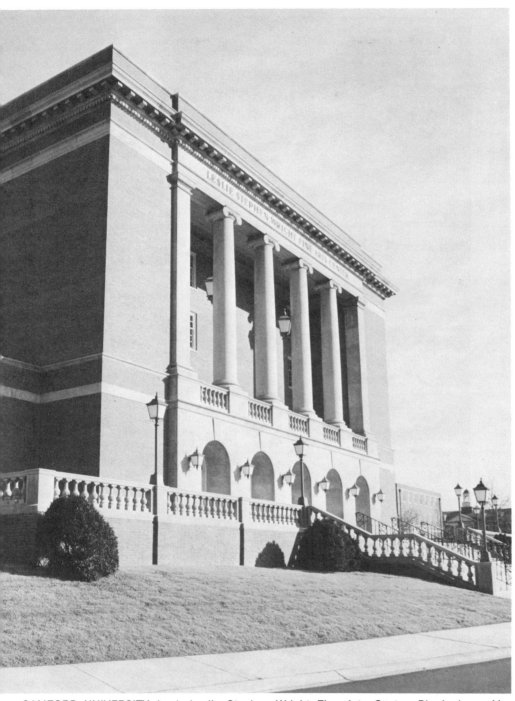

SAMFORD UNIVERSITY (*q.v.*), Leslie Stephen Wright Fine Arts Center, Birmingham, AL. Dedicated in 1976. Features a 3,000-seat auditorium, a 300-seat theater, and academic facilities for the Art Department and the Department of Speech and Dramatic Arts.

MOUNTAIN BROOK BAPTIST CHURCH, Birmingham, AL. The Dotson M. Nelson Christian Life Center, completed in 1975, is at the extreme right. The visiting missionary residence can be seen beyond the parking lot at the top of the picture.

S

SACRED HARP (III). Three developments occurred during the 1970s related to the tradition of the 1844 oblong shape-note tunebook, *The Sacred Harp.* The Sacred Harp Publishing Company, Bremen, GA, issued a new edition of the *Original Sacred Harp* (Denson Revision) in 1971. By far the most widely used during the 1970s was the Denson Revision, issued in 1936, and based on the 1911 edition of Joe S. James. Other editions of the Denson Revision were published in 1960 and 1966. The second most widely used version of the Sacred Harp is the "Cooper" book, and the least used is the "J. L. White" book. In 1978 the most definitive work on the Sacred Harp was published by the University of Georgia Press, *The Sacred Harp: A Tradition and Its Music,* by Buell Cobb.

In 1980 there were about 500 annual singings (many two-day singings) and 200 regularly scheduled night singings or fifth-Sunday singings. A four-day National Sacred Harp Singing Convention was held in Birmingham, AL, June 26-29, 1980. More than 1,200 singers gathered in the Leslie Wright Fine Arts Auditorium, Samford University, for the largest gathering in the history of this tradition. Hugh McGraw and Claude H. Rhea were responsible for planning and coordinating this event.

See also SHAPE-NOTE HYMNODY.

WILLIAM J. REYNOLDS

SADLER, GEORGE WASHINGTON (b. Laneview, VA, Oct. 10, 1887; d. Richmond, VA, July 18, 1975). Missionary and mission administrator. Son of William Burke Sadler and Fannie Faucett Sadler, farmers, he attended Richmond College (B.A., 1910; M.A., 1911), The Southern Baptist Theological Seminary (Th.M., 1914), and Teacher's College, Columbia University (M.A., 1928). Appointed to Nigeria by the Foreign Mission Board in 1914, he did educational work until interrupted by World War I. As an army chaplain in France, he was decorated for bravery in 1918.

Sadler married Annie Laurie Maynard, Aug. 5, 1919. He taught Bible at Westhampton College, Richmond, VA, while awaiting travel to Nigeria. A daughter, Henrietta, was born in 1920, and a son, George William, in 1921, after their arrival in Nigeria. From 1921 to 1931, he served as principal of the Baptist college and seminary in Ogbomosho. Family health problems forced his resignation in 1932, when he became pastor of Second Baptist Church, Liberty, MO.

In 1939 the FMB named Sadler secretary for Africa, Europe, and the Near East. For 18 years he supervised missions in this area, opening new work in seven countries and increasing missionary personnel threefold.

During 1949-50, the Sadlers lived in Ruschlikon, Switzerland, while he served as acting president of the new International Baptist Theological Seminary. After retiring as area secretary in 1958, he was special representative to Europe until 1960, when he returned to Virginia to serve several churches as interim pastor.

Sadler authored *A Century in Nigeria* (1950). He is buried in Hollywood Cemetery, Richmond, VA.

CORNELL GOERNER

SALLEE, ANNIE JENKINS (b. Waco, TX, Feb. 28, 1877; d. Waco, TX, Mar. 1, 1967). Pioneer missionary to China. The daughter of Jessie Speight Jenkins and Warwich Jenkins, a judge, she attended Baylor University (B.S., 1897; M.A., 1899). After teaching one year in Moody, TX, and two years at Decatur Baptist College, she attended Baptist Missionary Training School, Chicago, IL, graduating in 1905. She was appointed by the Foreign Mission Board to China that same year. She married William Eugene Sallee, Sep. 18, 1906, in China. They had no children. They moved to Kaifeng, Honan Province, 1908, where they helped found the Interior China Mission.

Annie Sallee founded one of the first girls' boarding schools in China, the Annie Jenkins Sallee Memorial School for Girls. She also founded an industrial school for women in Kaifeng. Imprisoned by the Japanese for nine months during World War II, she returned to the United States, Aug., 1943. She taught Sunday School in Waco and Dallas until her death. She is buried in Oakwood Cemetery, Waco, TX.

L. KATHERINE COOK

SAMFORD UNIVERSITY (III; cf. Howard College, Vol. I). The largest private institution of higher learning in Alabama, Samford made dramatic strides during the 1970s. The enrollment increased from 2,676 in 1969 to 3,886 in 1979, and the annual operating budget increased from $4,400,000 to $13,400,000.

Improvements made in the academic program included institution of a January-term program, revival and strengthening of the honors program, creation of two learning resources centers, institution of an Air Force ROTC, annexation of the Ida V. Moffett School of Nursing, and inauguration of an adult studies program which awarded the Associate and Bachelor of General Studies degrees in several areas, including Paralegal Studies. A sixth-year degree in teacher education (Educational Specialist) was instituted. Majors in Early Childhood Education were approved for both undergraduate and graduate programs. Career-oriented concentrations were established in interior design, religious education, computer science, international business, environmental science, communications, church recreation, public affairs, and public administration. A Bachelor of Science in Anesthesia was offered in cooperation with the Baptist Medical Centers.

Throughout the decade construction work hastened completion of the master plan adopted in the 1940s. Completed were the Dwight M. Beeson Building (business, history), the second unit of the Ralph W. Beeson Student Center, the Leslie Stephen Wright Fine Arts Center (3,000-seat auditorium, 300-seat theatre), the second unit of Memory Leak Robinson Hall (law), and the Orlean Bullard Beeson Building (education, home economics). The palatial Bush home was deeded to the university for a president's residence. In 1979 Leslie S. Wright began his 22nd year as president.

LEE N. ALLEN

SAN MARCOS BAPTIST ACADEMY (III; cf. San Marcos Academy, Vol. II). Since its founding in 1907, the academy has offered education in a Christian environment to boys and girls from all over the world. The nonprofit coeducational institution for students in grades 3-12 is owned by the Baptist General Convention of Texas.

The academy is the largest boarding school in Texas with 350 students from 20 countries, 15 states, and 80 cities in Texas. The school also enrolls 30 day students. The academic program is organized with emphasis towards college admissions. A junior ROTC program is required for boys in the Upper School (grades 9-12), with a modified military program for the other boys. Recently, the academy sold the present campus to Southwest Texas State University. A new campus, under construction in 1980, was scheduled for occupancy, Dec., 1981. Jack Byrom, the president, has served since 1965.

JIMMIE SCOTT

SÁNCHEZ, JOSÉ M. (b. Cienfuergos, Cuba, May 13, 1913; d. West Palm Beach, FL, Feb. 18, 1976). Cuban Baptist pastor and educator. Son of Jose Sanchez and Maria Sofia Gonzales, he married Norma Nogues. A graduate of the Baptist Theological Seminary of Western Cuba, the University of Havana, and Southwestern Baptist Theological Seminary (M.R.E., 1953), he was responsible for the expansion of Sunday School work among Cuban Baptists during the 1950s. He was professor of education at the Baptist Theological Seminary of Western Cuba.

J. DAVID FITE

SANDERS, FRANCES MARIAN (b. Colleton County, SC, Aug. 8, 1923; d. New Or-

leans, LA, July 4, 1973). Missionary to Mexico. Daughter of Mary Clayton and Guy S. Sanders, a building contractor, she was a graduate of the University of South Carolina (B.A., 1943) and of New Orleans Baptist Theological Seminary (M.R.E., 1947). She served as a public school teacher, Cope, SC, as a summer mission worker in South Louisiana, and as a state and home missionary among the French in South Louisiana and the Spanish in Northwest Louisiana.

Appointed by the Foreign Mission Board in 1954, she began her missionary service the following year in the Mexican Baptist Theological Seminary at Torreon. The library of the seminary, relocated in Mexico City, was named Marian Sanders Memorial Library. During furloughs she was a frequent speaker at encampments and before mission groups. She is buried in Colston Baptist Church cemetery near Bamberg, SC.

PERRY R. SANDERS

SASSER, ROBERT EDWARD (b. Laurel County, KY, July 5, 1911; d. Columbus, GA, Oct. 8, 1979). Pastor and associational leader. The son of Rose and Taylor Sasser, farmers, he married Maude Estep, Dec. 27, 1931. They had six children: Kizzie, Elizabeth, Rosemary, John, Hugh, and Bobby. He served as pastor of Blooming Grove Baptist Church, Brookville, IN, organized Western Avenue Church, Connersville, and in 1940 led five churches in Indiana and Ohio to organize Whitewater Association. He was a leader in organizing the Indiana Association of Missionary Baptists in 1951. He is buried in Slate Hill Cemetery, London, KY.

CLARENCE BROCK

SATELLITES, COMMUNICATIONS. See COMMUNICATIONS SATELLITES.

SCHMIDT, HERBERT (b. Vanderburg County, IN, July 22, 1899; d. Evansville, IN, Feb. 4, 1976). Pioneer missionary and pastor. Son of George and Mary Schmidt, farmers, he attended Evansville public schools and The Southern Baptist Theological Seminary. In Sep., 1922, he married Hazel Croft. They had two daughters, Betty and Delores. Ordained by Walnut Street Baptist Church, Evansville, he served as pastor of this congregation, 1923-32, and of Audubon Church, Henderson, KY, 1932-45.

Schmidt led in beginning the following churches that affiliated with the Indiana Convention: Vann Avenue, Keck Avenue, Bethany, Northeast Park, North Park, Harwood, Trinity, and New Bethel, all in Evansville; First Church of Elberfeld, and Mt. Vernon and Cypress churches.

His denominational service included city missionary, West Kentuckiana Association, 1946-57; and city missionary, East St. Louis, IL, 1957-64. After retirement he served as interim pastor of churches in the Evansville area. He is buried in Park Lawn Cemetery, Evansville, IN.

MRS. E. W. SPRINGS

SCHOOL OF PASTORAL CARE. The School of Pastoral Care of North Carolina Baptist Hospital, established in 1947, has locations in Winston-Salem, Fayetteville, Raleigh, Morganton, and Charlotte. It extends the ministry of the church through hospital chaplaincy, pastoral counseling, and marriage and family enrichment. The school enhances the ministry of the church by offering various levels of clinical pastoral education to clergy and lay leaders. The school is fully accredited through the Association of Clinical Pastoral Education and the American Association of Pastoral Counselors.

                                                        CALVIN KNIGHT

SCHROEDER, GEORGE WILLIAM (b. Pinckneyville, IL, Oct. 28, 1913; d. Memphis, TN, May 29, 1971). State and national Brotherhood executive. Son of Adele and George H. Schroeder, a locomotive engineer, he was a graduate of Southern Illinois University (B.A., 1945; M.A., 1946). He married Lorraine Wilson, June 11, 1932. They had three children: Harriet, George, and Lawson.

Schroeder served as president of the Illinois Baptist State Association Brotherhood in 1939 and was elected Brotherhood secretary of the Illinois Baptist State Association in 1940 and associate secretary of the Brotherhood Commission, SBC, in 1946. He assumed the duties of executive secretary of the national agency, Jan. 1, 1952. During his 19 years as the national Brotherhood leader, Schroeder set three goals which he accomplished. They were to provide a suitable home for Brotherhood work, to develop a challenging program for Southern Baptist men and boys, and to lead men to put that program into practice. During his first seven years as executive secretary, he edited the quarterly *Brotherhood Journal.* He also wrote two books, *Brotherhood Guidebook* (1949) and *You Can Speak for God* (1958).

Schroeder was chairman of the Men's Department of the Baptist World Alliance in 1967. He is buried in Mueller Hill Cemetery, Pinckneyville, IL.

                                                        ROY JENNINGS

SCOTLAND, MISSION IN. Scottish Baptists date from the 1600s, but their growth has been slow. In 1979 there were 150 churches with 14,000 members. They were making progress in stewardship and were showing interest in evangelism and church development. In 1977 a Southern Baptist missionary couple, James E. and Barbara (Paige) Spaulding, went to Scotland on invitation of leaders of the Baptist Union to work among American and Scottish oil workers. The International Baptist Church in Aberdeen soon came into being. A second missionary couple started a Scottish Baptist church in a section of Aberdeen where there had never been Baptist work. Journeymen and volunteers have also accepted assignments in Scotland.

                                                        J. D. HUGHEY

SCOTT, DANIEL JEFFERSON (b. Madison County, IL, Feb. 22, 1878; d. Altus, OK,

Dec. 9, 1959). Pastor and educator. The son of George and Harriett Savage Scott, he married Maude Ethel Paden in 1908. Their children were Ross, Catherine, and Maude. He served as pastor of churches in St. Marys, IL; Birchtree, Edinburgh, and Memphis, MO; and Burleson and Joshua, TX.

A graduate of LaGrange College (B.D., 1913) and Southwestern Baptist Theological Seminary (1915), he returned to LaGrange as president. The college faced a financial crisis, and he led the effort to raise the necessary funds, build a new dormitory, and create an endowment fund. During the Depression in 1931, Scott and his wife undertook the task of bringing the Home for Aged Baptists, Ironton, MO, from a state of bankruptcy to solvency, leaving over $400,000 in endowment upon his retirement as superintendent in 1953. He is buried in Rest Lawn Cemetery, Jackson County, OK.

                                                        MRS. CLYDE RUSSELL

SCOTT, KEMP (b. Washington County, VA, June 20, 1790; d. Carroll County, MO, Apr. 13, 1864). State Baptist leader. His mother was Dorcas Scott and his father's first name is unknown. In 1810 he moved to Barren County, KY. Here he married Anna Alle on May 24, 1810, and to them 12 children were born. Baptized into the Baptist church at Glover's Creek, May 19, 1811, he was ordained by Cumberland River Church, Monroe County, KY, Dec. 3, 1820.

Scott moved to Missouri in 1824, settling in Cooper County. A strong advocate of missions and Sunday Schools, he was one of the signers of the constitution of the newly organized Baptist Central Society of Missouri in 1834 (which became the General Association of United Baptists of Missouri in 1839). He was hired as the first general agent, 1837-38. He is buried in the cemetery of Bethlehem Baptist Church, Carrollton, MO.

                                                        L. DOUGLAS MCGAUGHLIN

SCOUTING, ASSOCIATION OF BAPTISTS FOR. A scouting program organized in 1954 by Joe Carrington, Austin, TX, to encourage scouting in Baptist churches and to offer religious programs: God and Family, God and Church, God and Life. Originally focused on SBC churches, the association now includes other Baptist churches throughout the United States. Al Lineberry, Greensboro, NC, is president; H. M. "Smoky" Eggers, scouter and Baptist layman, is executive director; Owen Cooper, Yazoo City, MS, is president-emeritus. Offices are in Fort Worth, TX.

                                                        OWEN COOPER

SEEDS. Founded in late 1977 as a ministry of Oakhurst Baptist Church, Decatur, GA, with coeditors Gary Gunderson and Andy Loving, *Seeds* is "a magazine for Southern Baptists concerned about hunger." Publishing bimonthly and issuing the newsletter *Sprouts* in alternate months, *Seeds* explores world hunger and the Christian response to it. *Seeds* also supports a hunger education ministry in local churches and coordinates communication on hunger issues among a network of correspondents.

See also HUNGER, WORLD.

RONALD D. SISK

SEMINARY ALLOCATION AND DISTRIBUTION FORMULA. The "seminary formula" is a process utilized by the Executive Committee, SBC, as an aid in determining the appropriate allocation and distribution of Cooperative Program funds to and among the six Southern Baptist seminaries. The development of such a formula was initiated by the Executive Committee in the 1950s. It has undergone several major studies and revisions; the current formula (1981) resulted from a three-year review during 1972-75.

The formula utilizes enrollment data from each Southern Baptist seminary and the average educational and general expenditure per student in accredited seminaries in the United States and Canada. The enrollment data from each seminary, based on the total credit hours earned over a three-year period, is combined and averaged to provide a numerical or quantitative data base. The average educational cost per student in accredited seminaries is used to provide a dollar figure, a "benchmark," for allocation purposes. The formula provides each of the six seminaries a full unit of funding (the "benchmark" dollar figure) for the first 300 full-time equivalent students. The amount then decreases to a minimum of one fifth of a funding unit for students greatly in excess of the average enrollment of the six seminaries.

The seminaries present their funding request, based on the application of the formula, to the Executive Committee, SBC. The committee considers the request along with those of all SBC agencies. Historically, the seminaries' requests, based on the formula, have been funded at less than 100 percent. The formula, therefore, serves as a guideline, not a mandate, to the committee as it recommends a total allocation budget to the messengers of the annual SBC.

MILTON FERGUSON

SEMINARY EXTENSION DEPARTMENT (III). Seminary Extension experienced significant growth during the 1970s. The number of students climbed from 4,379 in 1969-70 to 10,505 in 1978-79, when they represented all 50 states and 23 foreign countries. The number of extension centers increased from 192 in 1967-70 to 392 in 1979-80.

An expanding curriculum during the 1970s increased Seminary Extension's flexibility as an educational system. In addition to the college-level courses already being offered, a Basic Curriculum Series was introduced in 1971. These courses are in areas normally included in a theological curriculum, but they are written in a vocabulary suitable for persons with limited formal education or for whom English is a sec-ond language. In 1971 Seminary Extension published the first of 11 basic courses in Spanish. Four basic curriculum courses were adapted and translated into Vietnamese in 1979.

Provision of learning resources for seminary graduates received increased attention during the 1970s. Identified first as the Continuing Education Curriculum, it was retitled the Personal-Career Development Curriculum in 1975, and the CESA Series (Continuing Education for Seminary Alumni) in 1979. The major emphasis in this system is upon helping seminary-trained ministers to develop personal learning programs and to find resources and programs which can help them achieve goals in their personal learning programs.

A Convention-wide emphasis on Bold Mission Thrust in the late 1970s gave rise in 1980 to the Bold Mission Support System. This system provides special ministry educational support for SBC programs or agencies leading out in Bold Mission Thrust. The first course, developed in cooperation with the Home Mission Board's Church Extension Department, was entitled "How to Plant a Church."

From early in its history, Seminary Extension has offered diploma programs to encourage students to complete successfully prescribed courses of study. Two such programs are offered in the Basic Curriculum System. The College-level Curriculum System includes study programs leading to the Diploma in Pastoral Ministries, Diploma in Educational Ministries, Diploma in Biblical Studies, and an advanced diploma. Home study students may enroll for an entire sequence at one time, with automatic shipment of a new course as each one is completed. Extension centers are encouraged to plan course offerings which make it possible for a student to earn a diploma in a maximum of four years.

Although Seminary Extension is not a degree-granting program, it does encourage its qualified, nondegree students, if feasible, to continue their education for ministry by enrolling for study at a Baptist college or seminary. Many fully-accredited colleges and universities accept toward their degree program credits which students earn through taking Seminary Extension courses. With five of the six Southern Baptist seminaries, a student can earn up to half of all diploma (nondegree) requirements by taking courses with Seminary Extension.

The academic quality of Seminary Extension's courses has received endorsements from three nationally-recognized educational bodies. In 1972 the Accrediting Commission of the National Home Study Council accredited the Seminary Extension Home Study Institute. The Commission reviewed and renewed the accreditation in 1977. After a comprehensive evaluation in 1973, Seminary Extension received institutional membership in the National University Extension Association (now the National University Continuing Education Association).

Southern Baptist seminary faculty members plan and write almost all Seminary Extension courses. College-level courses also use one or more standard college or seminary textbooks. Teachers of college-level courses must have a minimum of a master's degree. An extension center must meet prescribed educational standards to be certified by Seminary Extension.

Raymond M. Rigdon became director of the department in 1969. A major staff reorganization in 1970 moved the department from a pattern of general associates who worked in four major regions of the United States to associates in charge of Seminary Extension's two delivery systems (extension centers and home study). In 1972 J. C. Bradley and J. Ralph Hardee were the first to fill these new positions. In 1975 Howard P. Colson assumed the newly-created position of assistant to the director for educational services. In 1976 Bob I. Johnson succeeded Bradley as associate director for extension centers, and Robert L. Lamb succeeded Hardee as home study associate. A new position of associate director for communications was filled in 1977 by E. Lee Holloway, III. In 1979 James L. Ryan succeeded Johnson in extension center work, and James E. Reed succeeded Lamb in the home study area. The Home Mission Board provides, on a part-time basis, Seminary Extension consultants who work with language-group pastors and black pastors.

In addition to full-time staff members, Seminary Extension extends its ministry through state Seminary Extension representatives and home study instructors. Since 1975, 20 state conventions have designated staff persons to represent Seminary Extension work within their respective states. Seminary Extension Department staff members work with these representatives in planning and in promoting all aspects of Seminary Extension work in their respective states. The Seminary Extension Home Study Institute uses the services of approximately 18 instructors, most of whom are staff members of SBC agencies located in Nashville. Almost all of these instructors have earned doctoral degrees in the areas in which they provide instruction.

Through the versatility of its two delivery systems—extension centers and the Home Study Institute—the Seminary Extension Department makes ministry education opportunities accessible to ministers in every section of the SBC and in many other sections of the world.

See also CONTINUING EDUCATION FOR MINISTRY.

E. LEE HOLLAWAY, III

SENECA LAKE BAPTIST ASSEMBLY
(III). Conference Center owned and operated by the State Convention of Baptists in Ohio. Present facilities include an 11-room lodge, chapel, two dorms, seven cabins, a manager's home, a recreational building, a large swimming pool, and a modern water and sewage system. The facilities accommodate 300-400 persons and are usable year round. The assembly has several natural gas wells which it uses for heating. All property (totaling 203 acres) and buildings are owned by the state convention. Other groups or

individuals do not build or own buildings, although they may rent the facilities when not in use. The property is valued at approximately $900,000. Operational funds are derived from registration fees and from the state convention. The operating budget for 1980 was $125,886.

Managers during the 1970s were Arlie Carter, 1967-71; Clyde Bowen, 1971-73; Harold W. Hamilton, 1973-74; and Clyde Bowen, 1975- . All of the managers, except Harold W. Hamilton, were pastors.

The program is similar to that of other states. The 1980 schedule included 11 weeks of assemblies for Royal Ambassadors, Girls in Action, Acteens, youth, musicians, and families. The Boyce Bible School extension uses the facilities for a week in the spring each year. Other events are scheduled on weekends during the summer and winter. In 1979, 3,889 persons registered for a full or partial week.

JAMES E. TAULMAN

SENEGAL, MISSION IN (III). In 1979, 13
missionaries worked largely through three centers in Dakar-Pikine, and in the newly opened station in Bignona. Besides Bible study and worship services, activities included reading rooms, youth clubs, English classes, sewing classes, health classes, a program of recreation, student work directed at the University of Dakar, and a weekly radio broadcast.

JOHN E. MILLS

SEPARATE BAPTISTS IN CHRIST, GENERAL ASSOCIATION OF (cf. Separate
Baptists, Current, Vol. II; Separate Baptists in Christ, Current, Vol. III). The General Association, organized in 1912, consisted in 1979 of seven district associations with 98 churches and about 9,000 members, most of whom are found in Kentucky. During the 1970s the General Association increased by 13 churches and about 1,400 members, adding to its ranks in 1975 the Christian Unity Association, whose churches are located in Western North Carolina and Virginia. This association had corresponded with Separate Baptists for some 30 years. The reception of this formerly independent group, however, accounted for only a minor part of the growth of the General Association during the 1970s.

Separate Baptists favor district associations over the General Association as the prime depository of ecclesiastical authority. This tendency shows up prominently in the associations' control over the ordination of ministers and the maintenance of their orthodoxy. By this system congregational autonomy gives way to doctrinal uniformity.

See also SEPARATE BAPTISTS, Vol. II.

BIBLIOGRAPHY: J. O. Renault, "The Changing Patterns of Separate Baptist Religious Life, 1803-1977," Baptist History and Heritage (Oct., 1979).

CHESTER RAYMOND YOUNG

SEPARATISTS, ENGLISH. See BAPTIST
BACKGROUNDS.

SEVENTH DAY BAPTIST GENERAL CONFERENCE

SEVENTH DAY BAPTIST GENERAL CONFERENCE (cf. Seventh Day Baptists, Vols. II, III). Seventh Day Baptists observed their 300th anniversary in America with a pilgrimage to Newport, RI, their first location, at the conclusion of the 1971 General Conference. Also in conjunction with that meeting was the first gathering of the delegates to the Seventh Day Baptist World Federation, consisting of 12 national conferences of Seventh Day Baptists. The early 1970s also saw publication of two important books: Herbert E. Saunders' *The Sabbath: Symbol of Creation and Re-Creation* (1970), the first major treatment of Sabbath observance by a Seventh Day Baptist in several decades, and Albert N. Rogers' *Seventh Day Baptists in Europe and America, Vol. III* (1972), an update of the standard Seventh Day Baptist history.

Voicing concern about the political activities of the National and World Councils of Churches, the conference voted in 1973 and 1976, respectively, to withdraw from the councils. At the same time, however, Seventh Day Baptists reaffirmed their general support of ecumenism and voted to participate more actively in the various Baptist interdenominational organizations.

Never a large movement, Seventh Day Baptists had declined from their greatest number of about 10,000 in 1900 to about 5,000 in 1975. However, in 1976 they voted to participate in "Commitment to Growth," a program of education and exercise in church growth designed by consultants from Fuller Evangelistic Association. Since the program's inception Seventh Day Baptists have organized 12 new churches, ordained 15 new pastors, and voted to double their size in the coming "Decade of Discipleship."

See also SEVENTH DAY BAPTIST MISSIONARY SOCIETY.

THOMAS L. MERCHANT

SEVENTH DAY BAPTIST MISSIONARY SOCIETY

SEVENTH DAY BAPTIST MISSIONARY SOCIETY. Formed in 1842, the society traces its roots to the first meeting of the Seventh Day Baptist General Conference in 1802. In earlier years the home field was primary, but interest in foreign missions began in 1844, with missionaries appointed to China in 1847. The 1980 budget was $190,000, and six missionaries were serving in Malawi and the Philippines. Aid goes to churches and national workers in Burma, Guyana, India, Jamaica, Malawi, Mexico, and the Philippines. Consultation is provided to national leaders in Australia, Canada, Kenya, Korea, Nigeria, and South Africa. Leon R. Lawton is executive vice-president, with offices in Westerley, RI.

See also SEVENTH DAY BAPTISTS, VOLS. II, III; SEVENTH DAY BAPTIST GENERAL CONFERENCE, VOL. IV.

J. TERRY YOUNG

SEWELL, WARREN P.

SEWELL, WARREN P. (b. Randolph County, AL, Oct. 29, 1888; d. Atlanta, GA, July 17, 1973). Businessman and philanthropist. The son of Willis C. and Willie Sewell, farmers, he attended Graham, Alabama, schools and Bowdon, GA, College. He organized Sewell Manufacturing Company, which he sold to his brother, Roy B. Sewell, Sr. He then organized Warren Sewell Manufacturing Company in Bowdon, GA. The brothers became competitors, but they remained close to one another.

Sewell was a member of Druid Hills Baptist Church, Atlanta. His pastor, Louie Newton, described him as a deacon who was eager to have a part in his church and denomination. He became a large contributor to Georgia Baptist Hospital and Georgia Baptist colleges.

He married Ava Lee Fowler, June 19, 1912. They had three children: Ava, Charlotte, and Warren. Following her death, he married Ina Morgan, Nov. 2, 1961.

W. L. CLINTON

SEX EDUCATION

SEX EDUCATION (III). See SEXUALITY, HUMAN.

SEXUALITY, HUMAN

SEXUALITY, HUMAN (cf. Sex Education, Vol. III). The subject of human sexuality received wide attention by Southern Baptist churches and agencies during the 1970s. Three major theological themes run through most Southern Baptist treatments of sexuality: (1) God the Creator has created sexuality for human enrichment, communication, and procreation, and he calls humans to celebration and stewardship of sexuality; (2) God acting as Judge condemns the misuse of sexuality as sin, and he calls humans to repent of sexual sins and to work to oppose the misuse of sexuality in society; and (3) God acting as Redeemer provides the means by which humans can express sexuality responsibly, and he calls human beings to express love and to work through the church to provide responsible teaching about sexuality.

In SBC resolutions passed in the 1970s, attention to sexuality focused most often on its misuse. There were resolutions against pornography and against homosexuality. The 1977 SBC asked "churches to speak out against this permissiveness of the new morality and, under the leadership of pastors and parents, supplement and reinforce the sex education taught in the home in order to strengthen the biblical teachings of chastity before marriage and fidelity to marriage vows."

Through a number of printed materials and conferences, the Christian Life Commission, the Sunday School Board, and other Southern Baptist agencies have provided Christian resources on human sexuality.

See also PORNOGRAPHY.

HARRY N. HOLLIS, JR.

SEYCHELLES, MISSION IN

SEYCHELLES, MISSION IN. A chain of islands in the Indian Ocean form the Republic of Seychelles. In June, 1977, William and Susan (Bowman) Steeger moved to Mahe, the largest island, to begin Baptist work. They were joined in Feb., 1978, by Raymond and Lauralee

(Horner) Lindholm, who then left in April when the government would not approve their application to start a community development program. Steeger taught in a government secondary school and developed private Bible study groups. In Sep., 1978, the Steegers, unable to accept a government requirement to promote socialist theory in all classes, left the island, halting Baptist work.

JOY NEAL

SHAPE-NOTE HYMNODY (cf. Shape Note Music, Vol. II).

A tradition of rural American sacred music using unorthodox notation, shape-note hymnody refers to two major bodies of music: (1) an earlier corpus of eighteenth-century psalm tunes, fuguing tunes, and anthems of the Northeast, combined with folk hymns of the frontier South and Midwest, published in four-shape notation, a system initiated in Little and Smith's *Easy Instructor* (Philadelphia, 1801):

```
fa    sol   la    fa    sol   la    mi    fa
1     2     3     4     5     6     7     1
```

and (2) a later body of music which appeared after the Civil War, published in seven-shape notation. Many notations were published, but the one which prevailed was that of Aiken's *Christian Minstrel* (Philadelphia, 1846):

```
do    re    mi    fa    sol   la    si (ti)  do
1     2     3     4     5     6     7        1
```

Shape notes were invented to simplify the task of learning to read vocal music. The shapes of the noteheads represented the solmization syllables, thus eliminating the necessity of learning the staff lines and spaces and the key signatures. Singing school teachers published numerous oblong tunebooks in four-shape notation in the pre-Civil War period. Three tunebooks of this period are William Walker's (*q.v.* II) *Southern Harmony* (Spartanburg, SC; printed, New Haven, CT, and Philadelphia, PA, 1835-54); Benjamin Franklin White (*q.v.* II) and Elisha J. King's *Sacred Harp* (Hamilton, GA; printed, Philadelphia, PA, 1844-59; later editions in southern locations to 1971); and John Gordon McCurry's (*q.v.* II) *Social Harp* (Hart County, GA; printed, Philadelphia, PA, 1855). The compilers of these three books were well-known singing school teachers in the area where they lived, and they were Baptists. *Southern Harmony* survives in an annual singing at Benton, KY. *Sacred Harp*, by far the most popular shape-note tunebook, is used at numerous singings in the South, especially in Alabama, Georgia, and Mississippi.

The scholarly labors of George Pullen Jackson and others have made the older shape-note hymnody of the pre-Civil War period widely known and appreciated as an important tradition of indigenous American music. An increasing number of these folk hymn tunes are found in current denominational hymnals, such as *Baptist Hymnal* (1975 ed.)—e.g., FOUNDATION, WONDROUS LOVE, ARISE, and BEACH SPRING.

Such melodies, related to Anglo-American folksong, were absorbed from oral tradition by singing school teachers who notated and harmonized them, setting them to hymn texts. Other shape-note hymns, designated revival spirituals by Jackson, are folk hymns which have been simplified through repetitions; these are products of frontier revivalism. Revival spirituals in *Baptist Hymnal* (1975 ed.) are WARRENTON, PROMISED, and SHOUT ON.

After the Civil War, influences from the more urban North brought about the use of seven-shape notation and with it more European-influenced music. One representative tunebook of this period and type is William Walker's *Christian Harmony* (1866, 1972), published in his own seven-shape notation. *Christian Harmony* is still used in several southern states, especially Alabama.

By the 1970s, seven-shape songbooks of gospel hymns were being published in the Shenandoah Valley and farther South. A leading publisher of shape-note gospel music from the 1880s was Anthony J. Showalter of Dalton, GA, composer of the music to "Leaning on the Everlasting Arms." Leading twentieth-century shape-note gospel music publishers are the James D. Vaughan Music Publisher, Lawrenceburg, TN, 1912-64, and the Stamps-Baxter Music Company of the Zondervan Corporation, Dallas, TX, 1926-present.

The continuing popularity of shape notes in the South is evident in the publication of hymnals in shape notes, such as the *Broadman Hymnal* (1940) and the *Baptist Hymnal* (1975).

See also SACRED HARP.

HARRY ESKEW

SHARE. See WOMAN'S MISSIONARY UNION, AUXILIARY TO SBC.

SHELL, ROBERT LEE (b. Glen Allen, MO, Mar. 2, 1895; d. Ironton, MO, Sep. 11, 1977). Pastor. The son of T. A. and Rachel Shell, he attended Will Mayfield College, Marble Hill, MO. He married Nettie Long, Oct. 28, 1915. They had one son, Earl Lee. He served as pastor of First Church, Esther; First Church, Bismarck; First Church, Desloge; and First Church, Malden—all in Missouri. He was the first director of missions for Franklin Baptist Association, organizing numerous missions and strengthening work in that area.

Shell served also as director of missions, Pulaski Association, Missouri, and as first director of public relations for the Home for Aged Baptists, Ironton, MO. In his retirement years, he served as interim pastor of numerous Missouri churches. He is buried in Old Trace Creek Cemetery, Bullinger County, MO.

JACQUELYN HUFFMAN

SHELTON, KEITH DELANO (b. Tulsa, OK, Dec. 7, 1933; d. Phoenix, AZ, June 28, 1978). Pastor and foreign missionary. The son of Flora Shelton and Elbert Shelton, a merchant, he attended Oklahoma Baptist University (B.S., 1955), Southwestern Baptist Theological Seminary (B.D., 1962; M.Div., 1972), and Golden Gate Baptist Theological Seminary (D.Min., 1978). He married Anna Lee Inez Painton of Aztec, NM, Aug. 27, 1954. They had four children: Steven, Richard, Karen, and Lisa.

Shelton was appointed by the Foreign Mission Board in 1965 as a missionary to Trujillo, Peru, where he was director of the Baptist seminary. Returning to the states on medical leave in 1974, he became director of metropolitan missions for Central Association of Southern Baptists, Phoenix, AZ, in 1977. He is buried in Resthaven Cemetery, Glendale, AZ.

JOE CAUSEY

SHERRILL, OWEN MILAS (b. Kennett, MO, Dec. 22, 1909; d. Kennett, MO, Sep. 16, 1979). Pastor. The son of Poy and Mary Pool Sherrill, he attended William Jewell College (A.B.), The Southern Baptist Theological Seminary (B.D., 1942), and the University of Missouri. He married Vinda Bennett, May 30, 1937. They had one daughter, Joan. He served as pastor of First Church, Kennett; Savannah Avenue, St. Joseph; First Church, Charleston; First Church, Portageville; and First Church, Flat River—all in Missouri. He served as a pastoral missionary in Massachusetts under the Home Mission Board, 1960-64.

Sherrill served also as director of missions, Black River Association, Missouri; trustee of Southern Seminary; trustee and second vice-president, Missouri Baptist Children's Home; executive board and committee member of the Missouri Baptist Convention; and first moderator of the New England Baptist Association formed in 1962. He is buried in Memorial Cemetery, Dunklin County, MO.

JACQUELYN HUFFMAN

SHOCCO SPRINGS ASSEMBLY (III). See ALABAMA ASSEMBLIES (SHOCCO).

SHORT, WILLIAM THOMAS (b. Irving, KS, Jan. 28, 1884; d. Shawnee, OK, Feb. 19, 1947). Layman and college professor. Son of Thomas Benton and Martha (Paul) Short, he graduated from Oklahoma Baptist State College, Blackwell (A.B., 1911) and joined its faculty the same year. Short earned an M.A. degree from Oklahoma University in 1940. He served on the faculties of three other Oklahoma schools: Cary College, Oklahoma City, 1911; Southwest Baptist College, Mangum, 1912-14; and Oklahoma Baptist University, 1915-47, serving the latter as acting dean and registrar, 1943-44. Short also taught at Decatur Baptist College, Decatur, TX, 1914-15.

On Aug. 10, 1910, Short married Clara Sheriff. They had three daughters: Eunice, Willene,

and Jaxie. He is buried in Fairview Cemetery, Shawnee, OK.

E. W. THORNTON

SHORTER COLLEGE (II, III). Under the leadership of president Randall H. Minor, the college has grown in enrollment, property value, and endowment. The average yearly enrollment from 1969 to 1979 was 838, with an all-time high of 989 in 1977-78. Two new structures have been completed: the Livingston Library in 1976 and the Minor Fine Arts Building in 1980. Property value increased to $7,654,775 in 1979. Endowment then totaled $3,790,037, part of which was provided by the Georgia Baptist Convention. Total expenditures for 1978-79 were $2,542,080. After more than forty years of distinguished service to the college, three members of the faculty and staff retired: Martha Griffin, Emmie Louise Lovell, and Louise Thompson.

Four degree programs were added: Bachelor of Science, Bachelor of Science in Elementary Education, Bachelor of Church Music, and Bachelor of Music Education. One degree, Bachelor of Science in Medical Technology, was terminated. In connection with an expanding program in business administration and economics, a night school was initiated. From 1969 to 1979, degrees were awarded to 1,366 persons.

ROBERT GARDNER

SIGLE, LEONARD BONNIE (b. Hobart, OK, Feb. 24, 1905; d. Pasco, WA, July 15, 1975). Pastor and church planter. Raised in Clinton, OK, where he was converted at First Baptist Church at age 14, he surrendered to the ministry two years later under the preaching of his pastor, Harry Morgan. He served his first church while still in high school. Sigle was educated at Oklahoma Baptist University (1927), Howard Payne College, and Southwestern Baptist Theological Seminary (1930). During college and seminary days, he was pastor of several churches in Texas and Oklahoma.

During his last year at the seminary, the First Baptist Church, Klamath Falls, OR, called him upon the recommendation of Sigle's roommate and a native son of Klamath Falls, R. E. Milam. Sigle was pastor of the Klamath Falls church for five years. After 18 months, he married Edrie E. Wilson of Mitchell, OR. They had three sons. He also started the *Pacific Coast Baptist,* now known as the *Northwest Baptist Witness.* He was also active in the two independent Baptist associations in the area. After leaving this church, he spent four years as a missionary, supported by direct offerings of churches. He preached and started churches in California, Oregon, and Washington.

In 1939 Sigle began a pastorate at First Baptist Church, Longview, WA, leading the church to start several new churches. In 1941 he became missionary of the newly formed Interstate Baptist Mission and started churches in Washington. In 1945 he moved to California to start churches in Turlock and Modesto, finally deciding to cooperate with the new Southern Baptist work in California. In 1948 he became a Southern Baptist area missionary and started 11 churches.

Later Sigle transferred to Nevada, where he started a number of churches. When he retired as a missionary, he moved to Sumner, Washington, where he started another church. Failing eyesight forced his retirement from the active pastorate.

Sigle spent more than 40 years as a pastor, church planter, and missionary. He started more than 40 churches, most of which became Southern Baptist.

SAM A. HARVEY

SILER, ADAM TROY (b. Tacketts Creek, KY, Feb. 13, 1870; d. Williamsburg, KY, Nov. 16, 1953). Attorney, banker, and Baptist layman. The son of Mary Blakely Siler and Terrell Siler, farmers, he attended National Norman University, Lebanon, OH (B.S., 1892). He taught several years in Whitley County, KY, schools and served as county superintendent, 1893-1901. Siler read law in the office of James N. Sharp, Williamsburg, and was admitted to the bar in 1898. He combined practicing law with banking, coal mining, and grocery wholesaling. An active lawyer and a trustee of Cumberland College for 50 years, he served as moderator of the General Association of Baptists in Kentucky, 1944 and 1945.

He married Minnie Chandler in 1897. They had three children: Lilliam, Eugene, and Irma. In 1926 he married Minnie Murphy. He is buried in Highlands Cemetery, Williamsburg, KY.

CHESTER RAYMOND YOUNG

SILVA, JOSE B. (b. Matanzas, Cuba, Feb. 13, 1885; d. Atlanta, GA, Apr. 30, 1968). Home missionary. Baptized in Texas, 1907, Silva served as pastor of First Mexican Baptist Church, Austin, TX, 1908-16. He married Emilia Cantos of Cuba, 1909. He served Clark Memorial Baptist Church (Cuban), Ybor City, FL, 1911-c. 1914 and 1933-50; also three churches in Cuba, c. 1914-33.

LOYD CORDER

SINGAPORE, MISSION IN. See MALAYSIA-SINGAPORE, MISSION IN.

SINGERS, EVANGELISTIC. See EVANGELISTIC SINGERS.

SINGLETON, GORDON GRADY (b. Blufton, GA, June 15, 1890; d. Waco, TX, June 1, 1977). College president and professor. The son of P. H. and Anna Hammack Singleton, farmers, he attended the University of Georgia (B.S.) and Columbia University (Ph.D., 1925). In 1920 he married Hallie Jenkins. They had no children. After working for the Georgia Department of Education, he taught in the graduate schools of the University of Georgia, Emory University, Peabody College, and Mercer Uni-

versity. He was president of Mary Hardin-Baylor College, 1937-52. He then taught for 10 years in the school of education, Baylor University, retiring in 1963.

Singleton served as president of the Independence Association in Texas, 1957-70, the Texas Council of Church-Related Colleges, and the Southern Association of Colleges for Women. In 1974 he received the Elder Statesman Award from the Baptist General Convention of Texas. He is buried in Oakwood Cemetery, Waco, TX.

TRAVIS L. SUMMERLIN

SIVELLS BAPTIST CAMP. Purchased by the Baptist Convention of New Mexico in 1963, Sivells Baptist Camp contains 160 acres in Cox Canyon, 13 miles from Cloudcroft in South Central New Mexico on Highway 24. Originally named "Royal Ambassador Camp," the name was changed in 1972 in honor of the convention's Brotherhood secretary, Howard C. Sivells, who served the state for 17 years. Located high in the Sacramento Mountains at an altitude of approximately 8,000 feet, the camp is situated on the canyon floor, with mountains and tall pines on either side. The camp is open all year for retreats, training, church and family groups, and summer and winter activities.

Facilities include the old ranch buildings; barn, garage, and corrals. The original ranch house burned in 1973 and was replaced with a modern, spacious mobile unit which serves as the resident manager's home. Other buildings include the dining hall, large dormitory, office, shop, and a crafts building which houses the store, library, first aid station, nurse's quarters, leather craft, wood craft, photography and dark room, restrooms, and showers. The faculty building has eight motel-type rooms with adjoining baths. Archery and riflery are included in the camping program, each with a special facility. The latest building, completed in 1979, is a self-contained unit which includes a chapel seating 150, a large multipurpose room with a fireplace, conference room, and small kitchen. It also includes two small dormitories, which accommodate 16 people each, and bath facilities. Total value of land, buildings, and equipment is $450,000.

THEODORE K. ROBERTS

SIZEMORE, BURLAN ARTHUR, JR. (b. Centerville, MO, May 6, 1933; d. Kansas City, MO, Mar. 21, 1976). Educator and minister. Son of Burlan A. Sizemore, a forest ranger, and Florence Bold Sizemore, a secretary, he attended Southwest Baptist College (A.A., 1952), William Jewell College (B.A., 1954), and Southern Baptist Theological Seminary (B.D., 1957; Th.D., 1963). On June 5, 1954, he married Dorothy Jean Johnson of Jefferson City, MO. They had four children: Sherry, Cynthia, Burlan A., III, and Rebecca. He was student pastor of Baptist churches in Missouri, Kentucky, and Indiana, 1952-60; and taught Bible and philosophy at Georgetown College, 1960-68; and Old Testament and Hebrew at Midwestern Baptist Theological Seminary, 1968-76.

Following Sizemore's death in an auto accident, Midwestern Seminary established the Burlan A. Sizemore, Jr., Lectureship in Biblical Studies, financed by popular subscription, as a memorial. He is buried in White Chapel Memorial Gardens, Kansas City, MO.

G. HUGH WAMBLE

SKINNER, RUEL TIPTON (b. Callaway County, KY, Sep. 16, 1892; d. Tampa, FL, Dec. 20, 1978). Pastor, editor, and denominational leader. Son of James Edward and Emily (Miller) Skinner, he received his college and ministerial training at Columbia College (later merged with Stetson University) and Union University.

Skinner served as pastor in McMinnville, Watertown, and Milan, TN; Central Park, Birmingham, AL; and First Baptist, Bowling Green, KY, before becoming editor of the *Western Recorder*, July 1, 1946. He retired as editor July 1, 1957, and spent his remaining years in Florida. He was first married to Glenna Owen who died in 1953. Their children were Sarah, Elsie, James W., William O., and Thomas Eugene. In 1956 he married Irene Hale. He is buried at Bowling Green, KY.

C. R. DALEY

SKYCROFT. See MARYLAND CONFERENCE, RETREAT, CAMPING CENTER—SKYCROFT.

SLAUGHTER, JOHN LAWRENCE (b. Fannin, MS, Aug. 28, 1897; d. Boulder, CO, May 29, 1979). Pastor and denominational leader. The son of Jeffie and John Slaughter, farmers, he attended Mississippi State College (B.S.) and The Southern Baptist Theological Seminary (Th.M., Th.D.). He married Margaret Elizabeth Hooker of Richmond, VA, Sep. 12, 1923. Their children were John, Jr., and Jane. He was pastor of Leigh Street Church, Richmond, VA; First Baptist, Birmingham, AL; and First Baptist, Spartanburg, SC. He also served as administrative assistant at Anderson College, 1968-72, and second vice-president, SBC, 1960. He is buried in Fort Logan National Cemetery.

DON KIRKLAND

SLAUGHTER, MARGARET ELIZABETH HOOKER (b. Richmond, VA, Sep. 2, 1899; d. Boulder, CO, Nov. 15, 1976). Teacher and Woman's Missionary Union leader. The daughter of Minnie Jane Cottrell and Edmund Hooker, building contractor, she attended Westhampton College, University of Richmond (B.A., 1922) and WMU Training School. She married John Lawrence Slaughter, Sep. 12, 1923. Their children were John and Jane. She served on the resident board of WMU, SBC, 1949-52; chairman, bylaws committee, WMU,

SBC, 1950-54; member, executive committee, WMU, SBC, 1949-52; vice-president of South Carolina WMU, 1952-58. She is buried in Fort Logan National Cemetery, Denver, CO.

LILLIE MAE ROBERTS DUNCAN

SMITH, BUDD ELMON (b. Johnston County, NC, Feb. 9, 1910; d. Johnston County, NC, Aug. 5, 1976). College president. The son of James L. and Hettie Smith, farmers, he married Ethel Lillie Knott, Dec. 27, 1943. They had two sons, James and William. Smith was a Phi Beta Kappa graduate of the University of North Carolina (B.A., 1931; Ph.D., 1942; M.A., 1943). He served a term as superintendent of public schools in Oxford, NC, and on the faculty of Wake Forest University in the science division.

Smith served as president of Wingate College, Wingate, NC, 1953-76. His civic and professional service included involvement in the Southern Association of Colleges and Schools, the Education Commission, SBC, and Union County's Industrial Commission. He was committed to the junior college system and to helping the average person develop to his full potential. He is buried at Benson, NC.

J. DEWEY HOBBS

SMITH, FRANCIS LEROY (b. Waco, TX, Mar. 23, 1914; d. Phoenix, AZ, May 16, 1976). Pastor and denominational worker. The son of Florence and J. J. Smith, farmers, he graduated from Baylor University (B.S., 1940) and attended Southwestern Baptist Theological Seminary. He married Claudine Thornton, June 18, 1933, in Lockney, TX. They had two children, Ronald and Patricia.

Smith served as pastor for 15 years in Texas, Arkansas, and Louisiana. He was secretary of evangelism for the Arizona Southern Baptist Convention, 1948-56, and president of Grand Canyon College, 1950-52. In 1959 he moved to Denver, CO, to serve as secretary of evangelism for the Colorado Baptist Convention. Smith was first director of metropolitan missions for Denver Baptist Association, 1957-64. As director of missions for Montana, 1966-70, he helped organize the Northern Plains Baptist Convention. He spent one year in Las Vegas, NV, as director of metropolitan missions, 1971. He became director of metropolitan missions for Central Baptist Association, Phoenix, AZ, in 1972. During his ministry he founded or assisted in the founding of more than 100 churches. He is buried in Resthaven Cemetery, Glendale, AZ.

JOE CAUSEY and CHARLES E. SHARP

SMITH, KATHERINE SAMFORD (b. Troy, AL, May 22, 1900; d. Monroeville, AL, Nov. 23, 1978). Woman's Missionary Union leader and philanthropist. The daughter of Kate Park Samford and William H. Samford, a judge, she was a graduate of Woman's (now Huntington) College (A.B.), Montgomery, AL. She married Albert J. Smith, Oct. 15, 1924.

They had two children, Albert J., Jr., and Katherine.

She served as a member, Alabama WMU Executive Board, 1935-75; Alabama WMU president, 1957-63; Executive Board and Administration Committee, Alabama Baptist State Convention, 1957-63; and Foreign Mission Board, SBC, 1957-63. She also rewrote the state WMU bylaws, reorganizing employed staff and updating Executive Board procedures.

Smith provided substantial financial assistance for women enrolled in Baptist colleges. She established travel scholarships for state WMU staff members. She is buried in Monroeville Cemetery, Monroe County, AL.

MARY ESSIE STEPHENS

SMITH, LESTER ELISHA, SR. (b. Gilmer County, GA, Sep. 10, 1896; d. Atlanta, GA, Dec. 19, 1974). Pastor and denominational leader. Son of William B. and Roxianne Debord Smith, farmers, he attended Locust Grove Institute and Mercer University (B.A., 1923). He married Leone Smith, Aug. 29, 1923. They had two children: Renva and Lester E., Jr.

After student pastorates in Georgia, Smith became pastor of First, Lawrenceville, for three years. He served as pastor of Park Avenue (formerly Woodward Avenue) in Atlanta, 1927-66, and as pastor emeritus until his death in 1974. He served as assistant recording secretary of the Georgia Baptist Convention, 1944-60, and recording secretary, 1960-70; trustee of Tift College; and two terms as a member of the Home Mission Board, SBC. Mercer University awarded him the D.D. degree in 1950. During his ministry, Park Avenue shared in establishing White Oak Hills, Parkwood Hills, Boulevard Heights, and Woodlawn churches in Atlanta, and First Southern Baptist Church of Omaha, NB.

He is buried in Chestnut Grove Baptist Church cemetery, Grayson, GA.

A. TROY ACREE

SMITH, LUCIEN CHRISTIAN (b. Chataignier, LA, Jan. 18, 1883; d. Pineville, LA, Sep. 30, 1973). "Apostle to the French." Son of David Christian and Marie (Soileau) Smith, he married Anna Quinalty, Sep. 6, 1905. They had three daughters: Yelia, Elva, and Lula. A comfortable rice farmer, Smith was converted from Catholicism in 1910 and organized the first French Baptist church in Louisiana in his home community that year. He graduated from Louisiana College (B.A., 1923) and Baptist Bible Institute, New Orleans, LA (1925). Smith served as field missionary for the Louisiana Baptist Convention, 1913-36, and under the Home Mission Board, 1936-52. He helped begin over 20 churches in South Louisiana.

CARL E. CONRAD

SMITH, OSCAR BLAKE (b. Jasper, AR, Jan. 19, 1902; d. Ithaca, NY, June 23, 1973). Pastor. Son of Otis Smith and Mamie Niobe Boomer, he married Dora Alberta Riley on Dec. 15, 1925. They had five sons: John, Riley, Warren, Paul, and Benjamin. After graduating from Ouachita College (B.A., 1925) and Yale University (B.D., 1929), he served as pastor in Crossett, AR, 1925; Bridgeport, CT, 1926-27; Rockville, CT, 1927-29; Mexico, MO, 1929-31; Fayetteville, AR, 1936-40; Conway, AR, 1940-43; and University Church, Austin, TX, 1943-69. He served as president of Hardin College for Women, Mexico, MO, 1930-32. He is buried in the Austin, TX, Memorial Cemetery.

WILLIAM L. PITTS

SMITH, PRYOR BOYD (b. Benton, TN, July 1, 1895; d. Riverside, CA, Mar. 5, 1971). Pastor and educator. Son of farmer and preacher Green Berry Smith and Ida Smith, he married Ocie Viola Moler, Sep. 27, 1916. They had five children: Boyd, Joy, Joan, Deo, and Jonita. He was a graduate of Oklahoma Baptist University (B.A., 1929). Howard Payne College conferred the Doctor of Divinity degree on him in 1955. Ordained in 1921 by the Custer City Baptist Church, Custer City, OK, he served as pastor of churches in Oklahoma, Kansas, and California, including Journeycake Memorial Baptist, Dewey, OK; First Baptist, Ikemah, OK; Central Baptist, Lawton, OK; First Southern Baptist, Glendale, CA; First Baptist, Manhatten Beach, CA; and Central Baptist, Inglewood, CA. In Oklahoma he served as moderator of two associations, Okfuskee, 1938, and Comanche, 1947.

He served as president of California Baptist College from its founding in El Monte, CA, in 1950 until 1957. The college moved to Riverside, CA, in 1955. He also served on the board of trustees of Golden Gate Baptist Theological Seminary, 1951-54.

STEPHEN P. CARLETON

SMITH, ROBERT LEE (b. Childress, TX, Sep. 25, 1911; d. Conroe, TX, Nov. 13, 1979). Home missions pioneer and pastor. The son of Florence and J. J. Smith, farmers, he attended Baylor University (B.S., 1941). He married Lois Opal Thornton, Lockney, TX, Sep. 2, 1933. Their children were Douglass and Reba. He was appointed area missionary by the Home Mission Board for Wyoming and South Dakota, 1955-67. He is buried at Conroe, TX.

JAMES W. PHILLIPS

SMITHERMAN, NELLIE NORTON (b. Jordan, KY, Sep. 1, 1887; d. Shreveport, LA, Aug. 13, 1974). Philanthropist. Daughter of William Hamilton, a schoolteacher, and Corrine Miles Norton, she attended New Orleans Baptist Theological Seminary. She married James Emory Smitherman, Sr. (q.v. III), Jan. 8, 1948. Active in music circles, First Baptist Church, Shreveport, and Caddo Baptist Mission Center, she gave a portion of the money for the Richard W. Norton Library built at Louisiana College in 1955 in memory of her grandfather, a Baptist minister. She provided for several other educational and religious causes in her will. She is buried in Forest Park Cemetery, Shreveport, LA.

JOHN G. ALLEY

SOCIAL ISSUES, LOUISIANA BAP-TISTS AND. See LOUISIANA BAPTISTS AND SOCIAL ISSUES.

SOUTH AFRICA, MISSION IN. In 1820 European settlers started the first Baptist church in South Africa, and in 1877 the Baptist Union of South Africa was organized. Harrison and June (Summers) Pike, arriving in 1977, were the first Southern Baptist missionaries assigned to South Africa, although Marion Fray, field representative for all of Southern Africa, and his wife Jane (Dawley) had moved there in 1974, and missionaries assigned to Angola and Mozambique had lived in Johannesburg for short periods beginning in 1971. By 1980 missionary activity had been established in Johannesburg, Cape Town, and Port Elizabeth. The 17 missionaries taught in theological colleges, worked in church development, and managed a regional guest house and purchasing service for missions in adjacent countries.

JOY NEAL

SOUTH CAROLINA ASSOCIATIONS (II, III).

I. New Associations. WOODRUFF. Organized in 1979 with 13 churches from the Spartan, Greer, and Laurens Associations, and is located in the northwestern part of the state. In 1980, 13 churches reported 83 baptisms, 3,133 members, $469,157 total gifts, $58,196 mission gifts, and $2,222,111 property value.

II. Changes in Associations. COLUMBIA METRO. A name change in 1976 from the Fairfield to the Columbia Metro Association. In 1979, 62 churches reported 34,984 members, 854 baptisms, $7,083,816 total gifts, $834,789 mission gifts, and $39,482,694 property value.

BARNWELL-BAMBERG. A name change in 1978 from the Barnwell to the Barnwell-Bamberg Association. In 1979, 38 churches reported 167 baptisms, 9,934 members, $1,650,941 total gifts, $241,857 mission gifts, and $8,235,631 property value.

LUTHER RICE AREA. Three associations, Ridge, Reedy River, and Edgefield formed the Luther Rice Area Missions Program in 1976. Together they support one director of missions. Named for a pioneer in missions, in 1979, 57 churches reported 171 baptisms, 13,224 members, $2,297,170 total gifts, $263,719 mission gifts, and $11,228,315 property value.

NEWMAN LARRY BRYSON

SOUTH CAROLINA BAPTIST CONVENTION (III; cf. South Carolina, State Convention of the Baptist Denomination in, Vol. II). The convention celebrated its 150th anniversary in 1971 as the oldest state convention in

the SBC. The observance included a historical pageant and release of a new convention history, *Saints of Clay: The Shaping of South Carolina Baptists,* by Loulie Latimer Owens. Cooperative Program receipts increased from $5,300,000 in 1970 to slightly more than $11,000,000 in 1979.

General Board Staff.—The convention's general board staff continues to work principally from the Baptist Building at 907 Richland Street, Columbia. Highlights of changes within this staff include: A. Harold Cole's becoming executive secretary, succeeding Horace G. Hammett, 1970; two complete restructurings to attain increased efficiency, 1974 and 1978; addition of a consultant on church-minister-denomination relationships to facilitate church-staff placement and counsel churches encountering internal strife, 1972; addition of a director of stewardship development and Cooperative Program promotion, 1972; addition of area campus ministers to the staff under direction of the Campus Ministry Department director, formerly sponsored by local churches and associations, 1974; adoption of long-range planning and program budgeting, 1974; expansion of the Missions Department to include language, deaf, and interracial ministry, 1975, with one current staff member to help rural churches discover mission opportunities and another to work with volunteer mission workers and in resort areas; expansion of the Public Relations Office with the addition of a newswriter, 1975, and an audiovisuals worker to oversee distribution of tracts, films, and other items for the entire staff, 1978; addition of a support services coordinator to oversee accounting, reprographics, word processing, mail and telephone services, and properties management, 1978; and combining of Sunday School and Church Training Departments into a Teaching-Training-Ministries Department under one director, 1977. In 1978 the staff became the first state convention staff in the SBC to use a word processing print communications system.

Missions.—In 1977 the Missions Department staff helped start the first Spanish-speaking church affiliated with the state convention. Ports ministries were begun at Georgetown, Charleston, and Port Royal with a US-2 worker assigned by the Home Mission Board to work with about 150 lay volunteers. Christian social ministry workers had been placed in nine South Carolina cities in cooperation with the Home Mission Board by the end of 1979.

Conference Center.—White Oak Conference Center, a 1,006-acre retreat and meeting center near Winnsboro, first approved by the convention in 1971, opened for operation in 1979. Providing for almost 5,000 visitors the first year, facilities include a dining hall-meeting room complex; administration building housing a book store and snack bar; two motel units; a group house; a multipurpose picnic shelter; a pool; and a lake. Long-term development will continue in planned phases. In 1979 the convention deeded 164 acres of adjoining land to

SOUTH CAROLINA STATISTICAL SUMMARY

Year	Associations	Churches	Church Membership	Baptisms	SS Enrollment	VBS Enrollment	CT Enrollment	WMU Enrollment	Brotherhood Enrollment	Ch. Music Enrollment	Mission Gifts	Total Gifts	Value Church Property
1969	44	1,593	579,375	15,588	415,954	199,508	142,542	101,625	34,824	67,038	$ 8,151,443	$ 50,372,046	$235,421,545
1970	44	1,599	587,304	16,327	411,425	168,338	134,535	98,300	35,144	66,786	8,668,948	54,090,183	250,232,904
1971	43	1,597	592,839	17,801	401,604	159,100	116,653	95,454	39,480	68,746	9,451,975	58,159,119	259,501,761
1972	43	1,605	603,515	19,477	407,267	169,590	117,178	95,621	40,217	72,927	10,531,961	64,845,866	277,765,218
1973	43	1,605	613,331	16,814	402,201	167,549	113,820	93,910	40,545	77,272	11,580,638	67,712,828	303,644,943
1974	43	1,620	620,006	17,385	402,823	169,574	112,613	94,759	40,573	79,653	12,983,294	75,252,243	342,345,506
1975	43	1,632	630,799	19,799	406,389	182,271	114,004	97,058	41,567	84,157	13,779,351	81,343,743	379,379,064
1976	43	1,647	640,704	16,391	411,235	169,878	112,814	98,273	41,930	85,515	15,205,834	91,331,064	411,530,621
1977	43	1,651	645,589	14,603	408,059	165,444	109,004	97,112	41,991	87,730	16,514,174	98,291,465	447,551,117
1978	43	1,656	648,783	13,429	401,835	165,616	108,165	95,104	40,999	87,831	18,102,890	107,404,187	488,097,257
1979	43	1,671	655,181	14,639	399,684	165,853	104,319	92,967	41,194	89,582	19,835,208	117,884,237	549,384,496
1980	43	1,682	659,571	15,698	399,671	167,680	104,562	92,389	41,457	90,998	22,083,377	127,878,880	608,223,806

THOMAS J. BRANNON

Woman's Missionary Union, state auxiliary, to use in establishing a new camp which ultimately will replace the existing Camp Rawls, an aging facility in Aiken County.

Buildings.—The Baptist Building was renovated in 1977. A new building on the block was constructed by the convention for a Baptist Book Store, formerly housed in the Baptist Building. All land on the Baptist Building block, except for a church building affiliated with another denomination, was bought and landscaped. A new student center was built adjacent to Clemson University in Clemson, 1978.

Institutions and Agencies.—In the area of institutions and agencies, the convention did an indepth study in 1976 and 1977 which resulted in the adoption of 21 recommendations regarding their future. The recommendations set general directions for the institutions' growth, such as instructing the two convention-sponsored junior colleges not to consider changing to senior college status; that audits for the convention's four colleges be done by the same firm and copies of the audits be sent to the convention's executive secretary-treasurer; that Connie Maxwell Children's Home trustees exercise extreme caution in replacing existing cottages, so that they may not find themselves with a larger campus than needed, and others.

The study also suggested creating a new office called South Carolina Baptist Ministries for the Aging, Inc., to oversee the convention's ministry to senior adults. This umbrella office oversees the existing Bethea Home for the aging in Darlington and will develop new work. In 1979 the office obtained property and buildings in Laurens to use in developing a new home for senior adults.

Government funding for the convention's four colleges received widespread attention in the early 1970s. This culminated in establishing a permanent watchdog committee in 1977 designed to oversee government funding and prevent excessive church-government entanglements in college funding. The four colleges are Furman University, Baptist College at Charleston, North Greenville College, and Anderson College.

Special Emphases.—A study on the role of women in convention churches and in public life was presented to the 1979 annual convention session as information. In 1979 the convention adopted a new annual fund-raising program to combat world hunger. Under the program plastic banks fashioned as rice bowls were distributed to Baptist families and used to collect money for hunger needs. Funds collected will be used on a percentage basis: 85 percent to the Foreign Mission Board for overseas needs, 10 percent to the Home Mission Board for needs in the USA, and 5 percent to the state convention's Missions Department for state needs.

A. HAROLD COLE

SOUTH CAROLINA BAPTIST HISTORICAL SOCIETY, JOURNAL OF. The journal began in 1975 as an annual publication of the society. Its purposes are to stimulate interest in South Carolina Baptist history by providing an outlet for publication of articles, reprinting significant primary documents to make them more accessible to scholars, and publicizing the accessions to the Baptist historical collection in the Furman University Library. J. Glenwood Clayton, curator of the Baptist historical collection, serves as editor. The annual issues appear in November.

J. GLENWOOD CLAYTON

SOUTH CAROLINA BAPTIST HOSPITALS (cf. South Carolina Baptist Hospital, Vols. II, III). In 1978 the South Carolina Baptist Hospitals changed the organization to a corporate structure with corporate titles, and William Arthur Boyce, who had served as administrator since 1957, was named president. James Victor Dorsett became executive vice-president in charge of the Columbia Division, and Parker Sherman Hendricks became executive vice-president in charge of the Easley Division.

In the Columbia Division, phase III of an expansion program, which was completed in 1974, provided facilities for purchasing, engineering, EKG, EEG, physical therapy, and medical records. A professional building to provide office space for physicians in private practice and a parking building were completed in 1977 and named in honor of William A. Boyce. Other improvements included the renovation and modernization of many of the older facilities, the initiation of the Hospice Program (Home Health Licensure) in 1979, and the relocation and construction of a new surgical suite, intensive care area, and respiratory therapy department.

Renovation and expansion occurred in the Easley Division as well. The Easley Baptist Hospital opened a critical care unit in Feb., 1974. The most recent expansion occupied in Oct., 1977, included a new emergency department, medical records department, and physicians' library.

WILLIAM A. BOYCE

SOUTH CAROLINA BAPTIST MINISTRIES FOR THE AGING (cf. Bethea Baptist Home, Vols. I, III). Archie Brickle, superintendent and treasurer of Bethea Baptist Home since 1964, retired, Jan. 15, 1974. During his administration, the home developed physically and financially. J. Thomas Garrett joined the staff in June, 1968, as assistant superintendent and treasurer. He became superintendent and treasurer, Jan. 15, 1974.

In Nov., 1977, the South Carolina Convention asked the trustees of the Bethea Home to form a new organization to provide a wider ministry. The trustees changed the charter and the constitution of Bethea Home to South Carolina Baptist Ministries for the Aging, Inc. On Sep. 21, 1978, J. Thomas Garrett was elected executive director of the new organization. Bethea Baptist Home is now a division of the larger organization.

Following a long search for a site for a new home in the Piedmont area of the state, a merger was formed between the South Carolina aging ministry and the Christian Retirement Center, Inc., Laurens, SC. The center conveyed to the Baptist organization 11 acres of property near downtown Laurens and $300,000 in cash. The Baptist group in turn purchased an additional 48 acres of surrounding property.

This acquired facility will eventually accomodate 400 persons. In 1980 the first phase was scheduled to open in mid-1983. Projected total costs were $7,000,000.

Joseph Wheeler McDade was elected administrator of Bethea Baptist Home, Nov., 1978, and James W. Overbay was elected administrator for the Baptist Home at Laurens, Mar., 1980.

THOMAS GARRETT

SOUTH DAKOTA, SOUTHERN BAPTISTS IN. See NORTHERN PLAINS BAPTIST CONVENTION.

SOUTH TEXAS CHILDREN'S HOME (I, III). This multiservice child care agency, comprised of three campuses and a staff of 41 administered by executive director A. J. Green, Jr., ministered to 495 children and families in 1980. The Boothe Campus in Bee County is licensed to provide residential care for 130 children and youth. The Marshall Campus provides group foster care. The Roberts Memorial Children's Shelter in Corpus Christi is an emergency care facility. Services include family foster care, adoptions, and ministries to stressed families. As an agency of the Baptist General Convention of Texas, this institution receives support for its programs and facilities from the convention, individuals, businesses, and endowment.

A. J. GREEN, JR.

SOUTH VIETNAM, MISSION IN. In 1971 Hue was added to the list of cities where missionaries were based. Baptist social ministries were organized in 1971, pulling together and expanding the variety of ministries being carried on in each area. In 1973 the Vietnam Baptist Theological Seminary projected a program of Theological Education by Extension with learning centers in eight cities. The escalation of the Vietnam War resulted in the takeover of South Vietnam by Communist forces in Apr., 1975. At that time there were 38 churches reporting approximately 3,000 Christians. The 32 missionaries, 4 journeymen, and 2 volunteers evacuated the country. By late 1979, 24 of these were reassigned to other countries or the home office. Eight accepted other positions in the United States.

LEWIS MYERS

SOUTH WEST AFRICA, MISSION IN (III). The Windhoek Church supported a mission in Walvis Bay until 1975 when that congre-

SOUTHEASTERN BAPTIST THEOLOGICAL SEMINARY (*q.v.*), Wake Forest, NC. *Top, left:* Broyhill Hall. Formerly Lea Laboratory of Wake Forest College. Renovated and renamed in 1980-81. *Top, right:* Library. Renovated and expanded in 1976-77. *Bottom, left:* Student Townhouses. Completed in 1980. *Bottom, right:* Women's Dormitory. Completed in 1970.

WHITE OAK CONFERENCE
CENTER (*q.v.*), guest house
near Winnsboro, SC. Opened
in 1979; includes 48 rooms.

BAPTIST COURIER (q.v.)
BUILDING, Greenville, SC.
Completed in 1979, this
3,000-square-foot building
houses the offices of the
state newspaper of the South
Carolina Baptist Convention.

gation organized as a church and called its own pastor. The Windhoek Church dedicated a building in 1978 and soon called a South African pastor. In 1976 John and Clara (Huckaby) Schoolar moved to Tsumeb to assist pastor E. Kandume in work with the Ovambo people, including the church Kandume had started in Oshakati in 1973 and preaching points in the surrounding area. In 1979 a volunteer couple arrived to give pastoral leadership to an international community in Swakopmund.

JOY NEAL

SOUTHEAST TEXAS, BAPTIST HOSPITAL OF (Beaumont) (II, III).

In 1974 the Baptist Hospital School of Nursing affiliated with the Lamar University School of Nursing. In 1977 the hospital added an acute care wing and a business office wing which cost more than $8,000,000, bringing the total capacity to 387 beds and 50 bassinets. The addition houses a surgical suite, emergency department, cardiac intensive care unit, heart catheterization labs, and beds for surgical and medical patients. In 1979 the hospital reached the 30-year mark of Christian service. Services became more specialized with the addition of the care unit and an alcohol rehabilitation center. A section of the hospital's staff was trained in the area of burn treatment.

MARSHA K. JEPSON

SOUTHEASTERN BAPTIST THEOLOGICAL SEMINARY (II, III).

During the decade 1970-79, Southeastern Seminary experienced a doubling of its student enrollment, an enlargement of its faculty, the inauguration of a new president, the adoption of two new degrees, the institution of evening classes, the reconstruction of its library building, and the achievement of regional accreditation.

In 1970 William L. Lumpkin delivered the Carver-Barnes lectures in March, W. Randall Lolley preached the commencement sermon in May to 139 graduates and their guests, and the alumni met in Colorado Springs, CO, in June with 406 attending.

The 20th academic session began, Sep. 15, 1970, with an enrollment of 520. Jerry L. Niswonger assumed duties as director of development, and O. L. Cross became business manager. In cooperation with the Baptist State Convention of North Carolina, a seminar on contemporary evangelism was held in October. Charles L. Taylor and Edward Hughes Pruden taught as visiting professors; guest lecturers included Edwin H. Tuller, Robert S. Denny, Ray C. Petry, James L. Sullivan, and Russell F. Aldwinckle. In Mar., 1971, the trustees, under the presidency of Claud B. Bowen, approved a program of study leading to the D.Min. degree. In May 103 seniors graduated, and in June alumni and friends of Wake Forest University gathered on the old campus for a "family reunion."

In Sep., 1971, the seminary opened with 552 students enrolled. David Mein was a visiting professor; James M. Gustafson, J. Archie Hargraves, Stuart C. Henry, C. Penrose St. Amant, and Henry McKennie Goodpasture were guest lecturers. During the year alumni contributions amounted to $15,568. The trustees accepted a $75,000 bequest from the estate of Talcott W. Brewer of Raleigh, NC. The Sunday School Board cosponsored a church library clinic in April. One hundred and ten graduated on May 25. Richard K. Young (q.v.), associate professor of pastoral care, and John T. Wayland, professor of Christian education, retired on July 31.

The fall enrollment in 1972 was 581. Raymond E. Brown, a Roman Catholic scholar, delivered the fall lectures, and a Jewish-Christian colloquium was conducted in October. Guest lecturers included Clifton J. Allen, Johannes Christian Hoekendijk, John R. Claypool, John Coleman Bennett, and Norman W. Porteous. The trustees voted to enlarge and renovate the library building. Theodore F. Adams (q.v.) delivered the Founder's Day address. Elected to the faculty were: Thorwald Lorenzen, assistant professor of New Testament; J. Colin Harris, assistant professor of Christian education; and Robert L. Richardson, assistant professor of field education. Harwood Cochrane of Richmond, VA, gave $221,287 for the endowment of the Harwood Cochrane Fund. Among the 188 graduates in May were 28 who received the seminary's first D.Min. degrees. In July Frank M. Swett retired as superintendent of buildings and grounds, and Annie S. Earp retired as residence counselor.

The seminary's 23rd year, 1973-74, began with an enrollment of 634. David W. Lee was elected superintendent of buildings and grounds, and Ruth Preslar Lawrence became residence counselor. Guest lecturers included: Carlyle Marney, Wayne E. Oates, Letha Casazza, Baker James Cauthen, D. E. King, C. F. D. Moule, Manuel L. Scott, and James Ralph Scales. W. Alan Tuttle was elected assistant librarian. George W. Braswell, Jr., and Richard A. Spencer joined the faculty as associate professor of church history and assistant professor of New Testament interpretation, respectively. Olin T. Binkley retired as president of the seminary; in May W. Randall Lolley, pastor of the First Baptist Church, Winston-Salem, NC, was elected president, effective Aug. 1, 1974. That spring 143 seniors graduated. John E. Steely was appointed academic coordinator to fill the office of dean, left vacant by the resignation of Raymond Bryan Brown (q.v.), who continued his teaching duties.

The fall enrollment in 1974 was 857. Classes for laypersons were changed from meeting on Monday during the day to Thursday evenings; 194 were enrolled. Rachael F. Nash retired after serving 19 years as assistant to the registrar. Guest lecturers were: G. Henton Davies, Charles E. Boddie, Jaroy Weber, Donald G. Miller, James T. Cleland, N. Gordon Cosby,

Roger Lincoln Shinn, and Moshe Kochavi. Twenty thousand dollars were received from the estates of J. B. (*q.v.* III) and Emily K. Lansdell (*q.v.*) Weatherspoon. Richard L. Hester was elected professor of pastoral care and psychology of religion. The J. Clyde Turner (*q.v.*) endowment fund was established with a gift of $15,000. Carl Hudson of Bunkie, LA, was elected chairman of the board of trustees. Alumni contributed $11,137 in their annual drive. In May the seminary family was saddened by the deaths of Elaine Sheffield Nations, wife of Archie L. Nations, and Rena Cheek Bland, wife of Thomas A. Bland. Commencement exercises were held for 181 graduates. John I Durham and John W. Carlton conducted classes for the seminary that summer at Oxford University, and B. Elmo Scoggin directed a study tour of the holy land. Albert L. Meiburg was elected dean of the faculty, and Rodney V. Byard was chosen as assistant to the president for institutional development.

Southeastern's silver anniversary, 1975-76, began with an enrollment of 976 including 190 in the evening classes. A trustee-faculty-administration retreat was held in October at Boone, NC, and the executive committee of the Baptist World Alliance met on the Southeastern campus in November.

W. Randall Lolley delayed his inauguration as the seminary's third president until Mar. 11, 1976, to coincide with the 25th anniversary of the seminary's founding. The lectures on preaching and the practice of ministry were renamed the Theodore F. Adams (*q.v.*) Lectures and were given in February by Clarence Cranford. The eighth annual alumni giving program totaled $26,888. Glenn T. Miller joined the faculty as assistant professor of church history. Justo L. and Catherine Gonzales, Howard N. Lee, Lewis S. Ford, John Killinger, Robert McAfee Brown, and James David Fite were guest lecturers. The graduating class of 1976 consisted of 191 men and women. The Charles S. Coleman Holy Land Study Fund was established with a gift of $25,000. Peggy Walker Branch was elected the first woman to serve on the seminary's board of trustees. Almost 400 persons attended the annual alumni luncheon in Norfolk, VA, in June. The North Carolina Baptist Ministers' Wives held their 14th annual retreat on campus in August.

In Sep., 1976, Alan Preston Neely signed the seminary's Abstract of Principles as professor of missions, Donald G. Myers began his duties as assistant director of field education, and W. Perry Crouch was named development counselor. Fall enrollment was 997, including 108 women. Guest lecturers were: Arthur B. Rutledge (*q.v.*), Brooks Hays, Carolyn Weatherford, Gardner Taylor, Erik Routley, Baker James Cauthen, and T. F. Torrence. In October the trustees accepted funds for the establishment of the J. Nixon Daniel (*q.v.*) Memorial Scholarship and approved a faculty recommendation that the name of the two-year program of study be changed from Certificate in Theology to Associate of Divinity degree. The trustees also approved a program to endow a professorship of evangelism and the creation of a development council. Alumni gave $21,349 in their ninth annual program. Forty-five students participated in a program of studies in urban ministry, conducted in Washington, DC, with James O. Duncan as resident coordinator; facilities were provided at the Capitol Hill-Metropolitan Baptist Church.

In Mar., 1977, the enlarged and renovated Denny Hall, which houses the seminary's library, was dedicated. The trustees adopted a plan of action, proposed from a two-year long range planning process, for the development of the campus; Tom Brandon of Sherman, TX, was elected chairman of the trustees. Over 100 participated in the 13th annual pastors' seminar in February. In May 242 seniors graduated, and in June 250 attended the alumni luncheon in Kansas City, MO. Enrollment in summer school reached 372 and 322 for the two sessions.

The first volume of *Southeastern Studies*, entitled "Toward A.D. 2,000: Emerging Directions in Christian Ministry," was released in the fall of 1977. Enrollment reached 1,150 students. T. Furman Hewitt joined the faculty as associate professor of Christian ethics, and Robert D. Dale became associate professor of pastoral leadership and church ministries. Bruce P. Powers was elected associate professor of Christian education. Lydia S. Renn retired after serving 18 years as secretary in the field education office. Leander E. Keck, R. Keith Parks, Gene E. Bartlett, Olin T. Binkley, and Pope A. Duncan gave special lectures. Raymond Bryan Brown (*q.v.*), distinguished professor of New Testament interpretation, died on Dec. 16. In Jan., 1978, 40 Roman Catholic priests participated in an institute on preaching held on Southeastern's campus. Spring enrollment was 1,073, and the alumni gifts totaled $18,734. G. Thomas Halbrooks was elected assistant professor of church history, and James W. Good was chosen professor of church music. The trustees approved a Master of Divinity with Church Music degree program and accepted the gift of an Americana Schulmerich Carillon from A. J. Fletcher of Raleigh, NC, given in memory of his parents, James Floyd (*q.v.*) and Louisa Barker Fletcher, and in honor of A. C. Reid, who taught philosophy at Wake Forest University for 46 years and who served as visiting professor at Southeastern. The trustees also authorized the construction of 100 townhouses for students and elected John M. Rich as the seminary attorney to succeed John G. Mills, Jr., who had served for more than 21 years.

The following endowment funds were established: Charles Howard, David Finley, Ruth M. Wilson, I. N. Patterson, and Pamplico Baptist Church. W. Robert Spinks was appointed director of financial development, and John W. Tresch was appointed associate professor of evangelism. The graduating class of 1978 consisted of 260, and Sue Fitzgerald of Mars Hill College was presented the seminary's first citation for excellence in Christian ministry. In July J. Leo Green, distinguished professor of Old Testament interpretation, and Garland A. Hendricks, professor of church-community development and director of field education, retired; and Theodore F. Adams concluded 10 years as visiting professor of preaching. Pauline P. Hobgood retired after 10 years as dormitory counselor. Charles T. Dorman was appointed director of student-field ministry, and Claude Y. Stewart, Jr., was chosen assistant professor of theology. Suzanne Martin Davis became associate director of student-field ministries.

The 28th academic year began, Sep. 5, 1978, with an enrollment of 1,120 students. Special lecturers included: Robert G. Bratcher, William M. Pinson, Jr., Harold A. Carter, Jimmy R. Allen, and Fred B. Craddock. In October the trustees approved a $3,500,000 capital-endowment campaign for recycling the seminary's 145 year-old campus, and the construction of housing for married couples. Ben F. Philbeck was elected professor of Old Testament interpretation. A visiting professorship in missions was established with a gift from A. J. Fletcher of Raleigh, NC. The Raymond Brown Memorial Scholarship program was established with funds given earlier by Harwood Cochrane of Richmond, VA; the Edward A. McDowell, Jr. (q.v.), Greek Prize was established with gifts from the McDowell friends and family. In addition to being accredited by the Association of Theological Schools of the United States and Canada, 1958, Southeastern Seminary received full accreditation by the Southern Association of Schools and Colleges in Dec., 1978. Alumni gifts totaled $52,787.

William Terry Martin became technical services librarian, and the first Student Wives Emphasis week in honor of Esther Jilson Adams was held in Feb., 1979. E. T. Vinson of Greenville, NC, was elected the first alumnus chairman of the board of trustees, and Robert H. Culpepper was elected professor of theology. In April Ellis W. Hollon (q.v.), professor of philosophy of religion, died from injuries sustained in a motorbike accident. In May, Ben C. Fisher gave the commencement charge to 250 graduates, and the urban studies workshop was held in New York City. Twenty Southeastern students participated in a program of church extension in cooperation with the Home Mission Board for 12 weeks during the summer. Summer school enrollment was 335 for the first session and 326 for the second session. In July James E. Tull retired as professor of theology, and Ruth P. Lawrence retired as residence counselor. William P. Clemmons and Malcolm O. Tolbert joined the faculty as associate professor of Christian education and professor of New Testament, respectively.

In the fall of 1979, 1,215 students enrolled at Southeastern. The Kresge Foundation of Troy, MI, granted $100,000 for the renovation of Lea Laboratory to be renamed Broyhill Hall. Guest lecturers included Robert T. Young, Finlay M. Graham, James B. Ashbrook, James Leo Gar-

rett, and Helen Emery Falls. Thomas H. Graves joined the faculty as assistant professor of philosophy of religion. In cooperation with the Sunday School Board, a vocational guidance workshop was held in October. Hubert and Lola Ledford of Raleigh, NC, gave $250,000. The trustees voted to name the renovated and relocated student center for these two friends of the seminary. Wayne F. Murphy became director of planned giving. A conference on biblical authority was planned for Jan., 1980, with Herschel H. Hobbs, Donald E. Cook, and W. Randall Lolley delivering the major addresses.

At the close of 1979 Southeastern had a faculty of 34, with 27 additional instructors and visiting professors. Its library included 120,000 volumes of books and periodicals, plus microcards and microfilms of 80,000 more volumes. The seminary is grateful for its partnership with Southern Baptists in having granted 4,155 degrees to 3,828 men and women.

JAMES H. BLACKMORE

SOUTHEASTERN KENTUCKY BAPTIST HOSPITAL. A general hospital housed in municipally owned facilities at Corbin, KY, and nominally related to the Mount Zion Baptist Association. Baptist trustees have controlled the institution since it opened, Aug. 25, 1952. The 15 trustees nominate their successors. Such nominations are then routinely confirmed by the association. Merrill Hubert Rayburn has administered the hospital since Oct., 1974.

CHESTER RAYMOND YOUNG

SOUTHER, MILDRED ESTELLE CURTIS (b. Ponca City, OK, Jan. 17, 1913; d. Salt Lake City, UT, July 28, 1975). Seminary professor, musician, and professional worker with children. The daughter of the E. O. Curtises of Butte Falls, OR, Souther attended Oklahoma Baptist University (A.B., 1932), Southwestern Baptist Theological Seminary (M.R.E., M.S.M., 1938), and New Orleans Baptist Theological Seminary (D.R.E., 1965). On June 16, 1934, she married William H. Souther. They had two children, Joy and William.

From 1954 to 1958 Souther served as director of primary and beginner work at First Baptist Church, Dallas, TX. In 1959 she was director of children's work of the Training Union Department, Baptist General Convention of Texas. She taught from 1960 to 1975 in children's work at New Orleans Seminary and also directed the Demonstration School. She is buried in Restland Cemetery, Dallas, TX.

HAROLD LEE RUTLEDGE

SOUTHERN ASSOCIATION OF BAPTIST COLLEGES AND SCHOOLS, THE (II). See SOUTHERN BAPTIST COLLEGES AND SCHOOLS, THE ASSOCIATION OF.

SOUTHERN BAPTIST ADVOCATE. A monthly newsmagazine begun in Aug., 1980, and published at Dallas, TX. Founded and edited by Russell Kaemmerling, the publication promotes conservative views in its discussion of current issues among Southern Baptists. Its contents include articles, news items, editorials, open letters, and book reviews. The publication has no official ties with the SBC.

ROBERT L. THOMMARSON

SOUTHERN BAPTIST ASSOCIATION OF CHRISTIAN SCHOOLS. Day school representatives organized the Southern Baptist Association of Christian Schools in Feb., 1980, electing as president Charles W. Freeman, headmaster, Second Baptist School, Houston, TX. Having no official SBC affiliation, the association of church schools, school administrators, and pastors seeks to provide fellowship, exchange information, communicate purposes, and enhance the Christian school image.

See also BAPTIST PRIVATE SCHOOLS MOVEMENT.

G. THOMAS HALBROOKS

SOUTHERN BAPTIST ASSOCIATION OF MINISTRIES WITH THE AGING. See AGING.

SOUTHERN BAPTIST ASSOCIATION OF STATE EXECUTIVE SECRETARIES. While state executive secretaries held informal annual meetings prior to 1945, these gatherings lacked a clear plan of organization and did not have well-defined programs. No minutes were recorded in early meetings. The purpose was a fellowship in which those having similar responsibilities could have an unhindered discussion of matters concerning the work of the denomination.

As denominational work became more complex following World War II, the association organized more formally. Initially the president was elected for two years, later for one year. In earlier years the emphasis of the association was on the exchange of ideas. As the denomination grew, and as state conventions expanded in programs, the association began to do more than exchange ideas. The emphases and programs thought to be positive for the denomination received approbation and promotion.

More recently, the association's agenda has included resolutions or statements on matters of concern in the denomination, particularly matters relating to the Cooperative Program. By 1980 the typical agenda was: prayer for the total work of the churches, administrative procedures, problems relating to Baptist related institutions, effective promotional methods, and concern for those bearing heavy denominational responsibilities.

RICHARD M. STEPHENSON

SOUTHERN BAPTIST CHURCH MUSIC CONFERENCE. An annual meeting of church musicians, the Southern Baptist Church Music Conference (SBCMC) was officially organized in 1957. W. Hines Sims, secretary of the Church Music Department, Sunday School Board, and Paul McCommon, secretary of the Department of Church Music, Georgia Baptist Convention, were the two principal founders of the SBCMC.

At the 1956 pre-SBC meeting of the Southern Baptist state music secretaries in Kansas City, MO, Sims appointed McCommon as chairman of a committee to study the formation of a conference of Southern Baptist church musicians. In Dec., 1956, the committee formulated plans for the first meeting to be held prior to the SBC meeting in Chicago, IL, the following year, and then publicized their plans.

The SBCMC convened for its organizational meeting, May 27, 1957, at the Conrad Hilton Hotel in Chicago, adopted a constitution, and elected the following officers: McCommon as president; Dwight Phillips, W. Plunkett Martin, and V. F. Forderhase as vice-presidents of the local church, educational, and denominational divisions; and Nettie Lou Crowder as secretary-treasurer.

Throughout its history the SBCMC has attempted to provide an organizational format where interaction between local church musicians, music educators, and denominational musicians of the Southern Baptist fellowship can take place. This has been accomplished through panel discussions, addresses, concerts, recitals, demonstrations, and interest sessions which constitute the program content of the annual sessions. Presidents of the SBCMC have been McCommon, Dwight Phillips, T. W. Dean, Gene Bartlett, James D. Woodward, Donald Winters, Bob Burroughs, Carl Perry, Donald C. Brown, Paul Bobbitt, James C. McKinney, and Thad Roberts, Jr.

Some developments in the history of the SBCMC which are of particular importance include the granting of honorary memberships (to individuals who have made outstanding contributions to the cause of Southern Baptist church music), begun during the presidency of Dwight Phillips; the establishment of the *Journal of the Southern Baptist Church Music Conference* during the presidency of T. W. Dean; and the anthem series commissioned during the presidency of James D. Woodward.

CLEAMON R. DOWNS

SOUTHERN BAPTIST COLLEGE (II, III). In 1973 H. E. Williams, who founded the college and served for 32 years as its president, announced his retirement, and the board of trustees named D. Jack Nicholas as the second president of the institution.

During the 1970s, four major new buildings were added to the campus: Maddox Fine Arts Center, 1975; Mabee Student Center, 1977; a married student apartment complex, 1977; and a president's home, 1979. Also, three additional tennis courts were constructed, and several of the World War II military buildings were torn down. In 1980 the 185-acre campus consisted of 44 permanent buildings.

The curriculum expanded during the 1970s with the addition of six new degree programs at the associate degree level: Applied Science, Business Management, Music, Recreation, Church Recreation, and Secretarial Science. However, the college basically remains a liberal arts, coed junior college with a special program for older students training for the rural and bivocational ministry. The holdings of the Felix Goodson Library increased from 29,800 in 1970 to 52,000 in 1980.

The enrollment of the college during the 1970s reflected the national trends of the period. After reaching a low on-campus fall enrollment of 287 in 1973, slow, steady growth produced an on-campus fall enrollment of 383 in 1979.

Southern Baptist College was one of the beneficiaries of the campaign sponsored by the Arkansas Baptist State Convention with the aim of raising $4,000,000 through the Baptist churches of Arkansas for the benefit of Ouachita Baptist University and Southern Baptist College. Southern received $720,982 as a direct result of this campaign. The convention increased its support of the college from $76,000 in 1970 to $293,000 in 1979.

In 1979 the college, with the approval of the state convention, launched the Bold Advancement Campaign, a 10-year resource development plan. The goal is to raise $5,600,000 during the 10-year period, 1979-89. Of the $5,600,000, a total of $2,000,000 is designated for capital improvements, $1,000,000 for general operations, and $2,600,000 for endowment.

In 1979 the college also embarked upon an effort to develop a five-year, long-range master plan of programs and physical facilities. The college is accredited by the North Central Association of Colleges and Secondary Schools.

D. JACK NICHOLAS

SOUTHERN BAPTIST COLLEGES AND SCHOOLS, THE ASSOCIATION OF.

(III; cf. Southern Association of Baptist Colleges and Schools, The, Vol. II). The association emphasized the Christian purpose of member institutions throughout the 1970s. This resulted in the National Colloquium on Christian Education in 1976, publication of *Study of Southern Baptist Colleges and Universities*, 1976-77, and the National Conference on Bold Christian Education and Bold Missions in 1979.

During 1979-80, the association participated with representatives of 22 other denominations in the National Congress of Church-Related Colleges and Universities. This involved two national meetings examining issues facing the institutions and publication of *Church and College: A Vital Partnership* (1980).

An updated history of the Education Commission, SBC, and the association written by H. I. Hester and entitled *Partners in Purpose and Progress* was published in 1977. Hester also endowed the Hester Lecture Series in 1972. The endowed series contributes to the association by bringing outstanding speakers to the annual meeting.

In addition to officers elected annually, the executive director-treasurer of the Education Commission serves the association as executive secretary. Ben C. Fisher retired as executive secretary in 1978 and was succeeded by Arthur L. Walker, Jr.

ARTHUR L. WALKER, JR.

SOUTHERN BAPTIST CONFERENCE OF DIRECTORS OF MISSIONS. See DIRECTORS OF MISSIONS, SOUTHERN BAPTIST CONFERENCE OF.

SOUTHERN BAPTIST CONVENTION, THE (II, III). Southern Baptist church membership increased from 11,489,613 in 1969 to 13,379,073 in 1979. This was a significant gain of 1,889,460 members, or 16.44 percent. Total gifts also increased from $809,608,812 to $2,085,955,800, a gain of $1,276,346,988, or 157 percent. Per capita giving increased from $70.46 to $155.89, a gain of $85.43, or 121 percent. Some of the stewardship gains for the decade may be attributed to inflation.

Baptisms reached the highest point in history in 1972 when 445,725 were baptized into the churches. They also reached the lowest point in 30 years when 336,050 were baptized in 1978. This compared to 334,892 in 1949. The average baptisms for the 11 years 1969-79 was 388,063. This compared with an average of 379,352 for 1959-69, and an average of 384,340 for 1949-59. The ratio of baptisms per 100 enrolled in Sunday School was 5.0 in 1979 and 4.96 in 1978. Generally, the churches held traditional revival meetings, though they were somewhat shortened. At the end of the decade, there were very few two-week meetings, and most revivals were from Sunday through Wednesday or Friday. Larger churches seem to hold fewer revivals than smaller ones.

General church involvement among Southern Baptists was somewhat diminished. Church Training enrollment declined from 2,343,595 to 1,752,026 for the period. This was a loss of 591,569, or 25 percent. This was evenly spread over the 10-year period and averaged 59,156 per year. Woman's Missionary Union enrollment declined from 1,291,221 to 1,086,785, a loss of 204,436, or 15.83 percent. Brotherhood enrollment showed a gain from 430,339 in 1969 to 469,315 in 1979, an increase of 38,976, or 9.05 percent. Vacation Bible School enrollment was down from 3,648,255 to 3,197,517, a loss of 450,708, or 12.35 percent. Most of the VBS loss, however, was between 1969 and 1970. Between 1970 and 1979, the average annual loss was only 14,919, or 0.46 percent.

Church music involvement showed significant gain. In 1969 enrollment was 1,062,494 and in 1979, 1,465,774, a gain of 403,280, or 37.95 percent. This was an average annual gain of 40,328 persons.

Sunday School involvement did not decline as much as some other church organizations. In 1969 enrollment was 7,418,067 and in 1979, 7,317,960, a loss of 100,107, or 1.349 percent. In 1976 the enrollment was 7,458,375, as compared with the all-time high enrollment of 7,761,165 in 1967. At the end of the decade there were signs of renewed interest in Sunday School. Leaders were giving more attention to the promotion of enrollment.

Church curriculum and organizations were radically changed. For many years a single curriculum prevailed for most church organizations, but in 1970 multiple curricula were introduced. Sunday School offered both the Convention Uniform Series and the Life and Work Series. Life and Work became available at two different levels, regular and advanced. Late in the decade a third series was offered, the Bible Book Series. The availability of this new material greatly increased interest in Sunday School Bible study. The new offerings were accompanied with changes in age groupings. The old groupings were replaced with Preschool (1-5), Children (6-11), Youth (12-17), Young Adults (18-29), Median Adults (30-59), and Senior Adults (60-up). Woman's Missionary Union, Church Training, and Brotherhood underwent similar changes in curriculum materials and age grading.

Church construction greatly increased with family-life centers as the new element in church buildings. In 1969 church property was valued at $3,900,472,691 and in 1979, $9,609,575,477, a gain of $5,608,575,477, or 14.4 percent. This reflected both gains in new buildings and inflation. In 1975 the churches reported 6,083 recreation and activities buildings. These included both large gymnasiums and smaller craft buildings. At least 7 percent of the churches, about 2,500, were projected to have had a person serving in an educational capacity at the end of the decade. The increase in recreation and facilities and staff was in keeping with a national trend for organizations to provide more facilities for youth. It also reflected the increased awareness of athletics as a factor in good health. Churches generally were assuming more interest in the welfare of the total person.

Busing became a way of life for many churches. In the early part of the decade, churches bought and used buses as a means of enlisting people in Sunday School. Most of the busing programs were targeted toward children. By 1977 about 6,801 churches owned buses. As fuel shortages developed and gasoline became more expensive, there was some decline in the rate of new bus programs. However, an increase occurred in the purchase of vans and buses as aids to programs for youth and senior citizens. By 1979 most larger churches owned buses or vans for use in church activity programs.

The "super church" became the ideal for many pastors and congregations. In many cities during the decade, large churches developed with involved programs designed to care for the total person. Usually, these churches dominated the religious life of their communities. Their programs included active evangelism, weekday Bible study, elementary education, family services, recreational centers, radio and television programs, mammoth music programs, and extensive youth activities. Most of them made extensive use of television and were

HISTORICAL TABLE OF THE SOUTHERN BAPTIST CONVENTION, 1971-81

Date	Place of Meeting	Registration	Presidents	Secretaries	Preachers
1971	St. Louis, Missouri	13,716	Carl E. Bates, North Carolina	Clifton J. Allen, Tenn.; W. Fred Kendall, Tenn.	John R. Claypool, Kentucky
1972	Philadelphia, Pennsylvania	13,153	Carl E. Bates, North Carolina	Clifton J. Allen, Tenn.; W. Fred Kendall, Tenn.	E. Hermond Westmoreland, Texas
1973	Portland, Oregon	8,871	Owen Cooper, Mississippi	Clifton J. Allen, N. C.; W. Fred Kendall, Tenn.	Dotson M. Nelson, Jr., Alabama
1974	Dallas, Texas	18,190	Owen Cooper, Mississippi	Clifton J. Allen, N. C.; W. Fred Kendall, Tenn.	R. J. Robinson, Georgia
1975	Miami Beach, Florida	16,421	Jaroy Weber, Texas	Clifton J. Allen, N. C.; W. Fred Kendall, Tenn.	Jimmy Allen, Texas
1976	Norfolk, Virginia	18,637	Jaroy Weber, Texas	Clifton J. Allen, N. C.; W. Fred Kendall, Tenn.	Warren Hultgren, Oklahoma
1977	Kansas City, Missouri	16,271	James L. Sullivan, Tennessee	Clifton J. Allen, N. C.; W. Fred Kendall, Tenn.	William Self, Georgia
1978	Atlanta, Georgia	22,872	Jimmy R. Allen, Texas	Martin B. Bradley, Tenn.; Lee Porter, Tenn.	Jesse Fletcher, Texas
1979	Houston, Texas	15,947	Jimmy R. Allen, Texas	Martin B. Bradley, Tenn.; Lee Porter, Tenn.	William Hinson, Louisiana
1980	St. Louis, Missouri	13,844	Adrian P. Rogers, Tennessee	Martin B. Bradley, Tenn.; Lee Porter, Tenn.	H. Edwin Young, Texas
1981	Los Angeles, California	13,529	Bailey E. Smith, Oklahoma	Martin B. Bradley, Tenn.; Lee Porter, Tenn.	James L. Monroe, Florida

SOUTHERN BAPTIST CONVENTION (*q.v.*), 1978, Atlanta, GA. A total of 22,872 registered messengers made this the largest SBC meeting in history.

PRESIDENTS
of the
SOUTHERN BAPTIST CONVENTION
1971-1982

CARL E. BATES
1971-72

OWEN COOPER
1973-74

JAROY WEBER
1975-76

JAMES L. SULLIVAN
1977

JIMMY R. ALLEN
1978-79

ADRIAN P. ROGERS
1980

BAILEY E. SMITH
1981-82

almost wholly dependent on the automobile for transportation. All the talents and resources of the congregation were organized to support the church and its programs.

Many of these churches have been extraordinarily successful. For many smaller churches, they became the models to be followed. At the end of the decade, there was no sign of letup in this general trend. Sometimes the super churches were criticized by other local pastors because of the tendency of members of smaller churches to transfer membership to the larger, more active ones. These transfers seemed especially true of younger church members with growing families.

The charismatic movement of the 1970s touched many Southern Baptist churches. Interest in the movement began in the 1960s and reached its climax in Southern Baptist life about 1975 when charismatics in the churches was selected by Baptist state editors as the number one news story of the year. In 1976 five churches in Alabama, Texas, Louisiana, Kentucky, and Florida sponsored a national charismatic conference of Baptists involved in charismatics. In 1974 Jaroy Weber, SBC president, declared that Southern Baptists had elasticity to deal with the problem. He said the movement had arisen because of misunderstanding of the doctrines of the Holy Spirit and gifts. Some churches were expelled from local associations for charismatic involvement. Many churches had to deal with the problem in their own congregations.

Church renewal brought new life to many congregations. Early in the decade a new form of revival was introduced into the churches, sometimes called the Lay Renewal Movement and sometimes simply church renewal. Though the movement started in private lay groups, it soon became an important part of the Home Mission Board and Brotherhood Commission work. The program utilized large numbers of lay persons in local churches on a volunteer basis. Usually, the sessions lasted Friday through Sunday and were led by lay persons from other churches who paid their own travel expense. The programs were devotionally centered and made little or no provision for the enlistment of lost people, except that after the renewal experience some churches were led to undertake broader and more direct evangelistic actions.

In 1977, 1,657 churches reported a lay renewal week from the previous year. The principal sponsor has been the Brotherhood Commission. Most pastors report that their churches have been greatly revived as a result of the renewal experiences.

Revival in Bible study deepened the spiritual consciousness of many of the churches. Soon after the Sunday School Board introduced the new Bible study curriculum in 1970, a widespread interest in the study of the Bible arose. Classes for Bible study spread beyond normal church hours. Some of those were held in homes, in backyards, and in places of business.

Some church members joined para-denominational groups, and in some instances this promoted divisiveness in the churches, especially when the classes were held on church premises. The problems appeared to be subtle doctrinal differences promoted by the sponsors and veiled criticism of nonparticipants as being less spiritual and less Christian.

A popular denominational Bible study program was instituted in Oct., 1979, by the SSB. Known as Home Bible Study, it was television based and by 1980 had enrolled 200,000 members in correspondence study. It was designed as a self-study program with a fully developed curriculum. Some leaders feel that Southern Baptists were much more Bible conscious in the early 1980s than they were at the end of the 1970s. Part of the revival of interest in Bible study was accompanied by a noticeable conservative trend in attitudes toward the Bible.

Men became increasingly active in the denomination, especially in church renewal and in mission work. In 1969 the SBC Executive Committee sponsored a Lay Utilization Study. A conference of laymen in Nashville, TN, on Dec. 3-5, 1970, called for increased awareness and use of men in church and denominational service. This was the beginning of a rising wave of interest in the use of men in organized Baptist life. At the end of the decade, concluding in the spring of 1980, the Brotherhood Commission conducted 10 regional meetings seeking better ways to use Baptist laymen, especially in missions. The SBC Executive Committee conducted a meeting of business executives seeking ways to use men of unusual ability in Bold Mission Thrust. Signs seem to point to the increased involvement of laymen in Southern Baptist programs of the 1980s.

Doctrinal debate seemed to dominate the decade. Seven out of 10 top Southern Baptist news stories of the decade involved internal strife. Four of the seven, and 15 other top stories, involved doctrinal problems such as biblical orthodoxy, creedalism, the charismatic movement, the role of women in ministry, debate over open communion, and acceptance of non-Baptist baptisms in some churches. The decade opened in 1970 with Baptists meeting at Denver, CO, and debating over Volume 1 of the *Broadman Bible Commentary*. That same year the Christian Life Commission was called to question over its involvement in a debate with Playboy magazine representatives on the magazine's philosophy and situation ethics. The decade ended with debate over the doctrinal integrity of some seminary professors and the question of inerrancy.

Social issues continued to receive wide attention, perhaps best seen in the range of resolutions adopted by the SBC, 1967-80. A partial listing of these is as follows:

Abortion: 1967, 1971, 1974, 1976, 1977, 1978, 1979, 1980.

Alcohol: 1968, 1969, 1970, 1971, 1972, 1973, 1974, 1975, 1976, 1979.

Anti-Semitism: 1972.

NUMBER OF SOUTHERN BAPTIST CHURCHES REPORTING MAJOR ITEMS—1980

SBC and State Conventions	Total No. Reporting Churches	Baptisms	Additions by Letter	Ongoing Sunday School	VBS	Church Training	Ongoing WMU	Ongoing Brotherhood	Ongoing Church Music	Tithes, Offerings and Special Gifts	Mission Expenditures	Church Property	Pastors	Church Debt	Cooperative Program
SBC	35,420	30,069	30,651	34,950	27,933	21,648	23,999	16,858	27,302	34,491	34,170	33,548	32,005	16,134	31,658
Open Country and Village	17,768	13,767	14,191	17,461	.....	9,061	9,607	5,879	11,678	17,205	16,975	16,732	15,883	4,878	15,230
Town	4,023	3,656	3,690	4,004	.....	2,642	3,212	2,236	3,491	3,976	3,970	3,917	3,659	1,993	3,843
City (2,500-9,999 pop.)	3,471	3,246	3,288	3,453	.....	2,507	2,873	2,232	3,064	3,429	3,402	3,340	3,166	2,259	3,272
City (10,000-49,999)	5,001	4,680	4,718	4,962	.....	3,696	4,115	3,305	4,489	4,917	4,875	4,779	4,561	3,563	4,682
City (50,000 or more)	5,157	4,720	4,764	5,070	.....	3,742	4,192	3,206	4,580	4,964	4,948	4,780	4,736	3,441	4,631
Alabama	2,985	2,445	2,536	2,931	2,341	2,239	1,858	1,478	2,139	2,902	2,860	2,823	2,693	1,168	2,557
Open Country and Village	1,897	1,439	1,521	1,851	.....	1,261	941	672	1,165	1,830	1,806	1,780	1,696	499	1,554
Town	279	246	247	278	.....	238	235	187	241	278	274	270	253	139	261
City (2,500-9,999 pop.)	246	235	234	245	.....	221	202	188	222	243	238	237	231	159	220
City (10,000-49,999 pop.)	297	279	280	293	.....	270	239	215	263	291	286	287	266	192	277
City (50,000 or more)	266	246	254	264	.....	249	241	216	248	260	256	249	247	179	245
Alaska	39	34	35	37	32	26	28	20	33	36	37	36	37	20	35
Open Country and Village	8	6	6	8	.....	4	3	3	5	8	8	7	8	5	7
Town	4	4	4	4	.....	1	3	4	3	3	3	3	4	1	3
City (2,500-9,999 pop.)	7	4	6	6	.....	5	5	2	6	6	6	6	7	3	5
City (10,000-49,999 pop.)	6	5	5	5	.....	4	4	1	6	5	6	6	4	1	6
City (50,000 or more)	14	14	14	14	.....	12	13	10	13	14	14	14	14	10	14
Arizona	230	213	210	229	182	157	161	118	182	224	223	217	203	140	220
Open Country and Village	32	24	23	32	.....	14	14	7	13	32	29	29	31	13	29
Town	35	33	33	35	.....	18	23	14	27	34	35	33	30	12	34
City (2,500-9,999 pop.)	39	38	39	39	.....	32	30	24	34	39	39	39	35	20	39
City (10,000-49,999 pop.)	35	33	32	35	.....	29	29	26	31	35	35	34	29	26	35
City (50,000 or more)	89	85	83	88	.....	64	65	47	77	84	85	82	78	69	83
Arkansas	1,240	1,071	1,096	1,231	965	936	664	398	845	1,226	1,212	1,189	1,118	548	1,176
Open Country and Village	703	551	568	694	.....	466	232	100	364	691	677	656	630	191	649
Town	176	171	171	176	.....	147	124	66	144	176	176	176	157	92	170
City (2,500-9,999 pop.)	119	114	118	119	.....	105	108	83	110	118	118	117	112	81	118
City (10,000-49,999 pop.)	143	139	142	143	.....	130	119	90	133	142	142	141	128	102	141
City (50,000 or more)	99	96	97	99	.....	88	81	59	94	99	99	99	91	82	98
California	938	827	814	920	576	577	615	389	793	888	879	836	846	604	803
Open Country and Village	41	32	33	41	.....	16	15	10	26	39	38	38	35	18	33
Town	90	75	76	90	.....	40	44	23	74	87	88	83	79	42	86

City (2,500-9,999 pop.)	136	122	126	135	…	83	88	44	114	130	130	129	126	80	127
City (10,000-49,999 pop.)	298	265	260	294	…	193	209	128	260	290	283	268	274	211	265
City (50,000 or more)	373	333	319	360	…	245	259	184	319	342	340	318	332	253	292
Colorado	164	153	152	164	121	117	118	87	134	161	157	155	149	117	156
Open Country and Village	15	11	14	15	…	7	7	3	9	15	15	15	12	8	14
Town	38	35	33	38	…	22	23	15	28	36	37	37	34	21	37
City (2,500-9,999 pop.)	27	25	24	27	…	20	17	14	23	26	24	24	25	17	24
City (10,000-49,999 pop.)	34	33	33	34	…	27	27	20	29	34	33	33	32	31	33
City (50,000 or more)	50	49	48	50	…	41	44	35	45	50	48	46	46	40	48
District of Columbia	50	36	38	41	31	17	36	14	33	40	41	40	46	30	19
Open Country and Village	…	…	…	…	…	…	…	…	…	…	…	…	…	…	…
Town	…	…	…	…	…	…	…	…	…	…	…	…	…	…	…
City (2,500-9,999 pop.)	…	…	…	…	…	…	…	…	…	…	…	…	…	…	…
City (10,000-49,999 pop.)	…	…	…	…	…	…	…	…	…	…	…	…	…	…	…
City (50,000 or more)	50	36	38	41	31	17	36	14	33	40	41	40	46	30	19
Florida	1,536	1,400	1,436	1,317	1,179	1,154	1,149	906	1,370	1,517	1,509	1,460	1,377	832	1,455
Open Country and Village	494	424	442	485	…	346	300	219	398	490	485	475	434	160	460
Town	180	170	171	179	…	128	143	106	166	178	175	172	161	90	170
City (2,500-9,999 pop.)	179	171	174	177	…	143	154	131	169	179	178	174	162	119	176
City (10,000-49,999 pop.)	294	276	282	291	…	220	243	202	282	290	292	283	265	216	287
City (50,000 or more)	389	359	367	385	…	317	309	248	355	380	379	356	355	247	362
Georgia	2,944	2,443	2,549	2,889	2,359	1,820	2,099	1,654	2,257	2,880	2,809	2,841	2,679	1,223	2,355
Open Country and Village	1,740	1,320	1,414	1,693	…	929	1,044	740	1,153	1,691	1,630	1,674	1,563	485	1,299
Town	278	252	255	277	…	186	238	195	249	275	274	271	254	125	255
City (2,500-9,999 pop.)	278	259	263	277	…	208	242	221	256	277	272	270	263	182	238
City (10,000-49,999 pop.)	422	399	404	418	…	315	374	332	384	416	412	412	390	294	365
City (50,000 or more)	226	213	213	224	…	182	201	166	215	221	221	214	209	137	198
Hawaii	39	37	36	38	25	23	25	15	33	37	38	36	33	27	38
Open Country and Village	1	1	1	1	…	…	1	1	1	1	1	1	1	1	1
Town	6	6	5	6	…	3	3	2	4	5	6	5	4	3	6
City (2,500-9,999 pop.)	8	7	7	8	…	3	5	4	7	8	8	8	6	6	8
City (10,000-49,999 pop.)	14	13	13	13	…	9	8	5	11	13	13	12	12	8	13
City (50,000 or more)	10	10	10	10	…	8	8	3	10	10	10	10	10	9	10
Illinois	896	704	711	884	634	346	525	308	655	867	867	840	786	426	798
Open Country and Village	352	229	229	348	…	78	144	65	201	342	341	332	294	62	313
Town	146	121	125	145	…	59	93	51	117	142	141	141	131	80	134
City (2,500-9,999 pop.)	156	139	144	155	…	78	127	84	134	156	155	151	142	111	148
City (10,000-49,999 pop.)	155	141	142	154	…	88	105	75	138	151	152	146	136	117	145
City (50,000 or more)	87	74	71	82	…	43	56	33	65	76	78	70	83	56	58

NUMBER OF SOUTHERN BAPTIST CHURCHES REPORTING MAJOR ITEMS—1980

SBC and State Conventions	Total No. Reporting Churches	Baptisms	Additions by Letter	Ongoing Sunday School	VBS	Church Training	Ongoing WMU	Ongoing Brotherhood	Ongoing Church Music	Tithes, Offerings and Special Gifts	Mission Expenditures	Church Property	Pastors	Church Debt	Cooperative Program
Indiana	270	238	248	266	209	152	179	126	215	265	259	253	241	205	249
Open Country and Village	38	31	32	37	....	16	22	15	28	36	34	33	34	25	31
Town	49	42	40	47	....	22	26	20	32	47	45	46	38	33	43
City (2,500-9,999 pop.)	43	38	40	43	....	21	28	17	36	43	43	42	41	39	42
City (10,000-49,999 pop.)	74	68	70	74	....	58	59	42	63	73	71	69	71	56	71
City (50,000 or more)	66	59	66	65	....	35	44	32	56	66	66	63	57	52	62
Kansas-Nebraska	219	192	201	214	165	148	161	111	192	214	213	212	190	142	209
Open Country and Village	24	18	19	24	....	15	14	8	21	24	24	24	19	3	24
Town	43	34	36	41	....	23	27	17	40	42	41	42	37	24	41
City (2,500-9,999 pop.)	42	35	38	41	....	28	33	18	33	41	41	40	32	31	40
City (10,000-49,999 pop.)	55	50	53	53	....	37	44	32	47	53	52	53	50	39	51
City (50,000 or more)	55	55	55	55	....	45	43	36	51	54	55	53	52	45	53
Kentucky	2,141	1,808	1,787	2,107	1,751	910	1,262	779	1,610	2,061	2,042	1,999	1,944	763	1,862
Open Country and Village	1,453	1,161	1,147	1,425	....	500	684	368	982	1,383	1,368	1,337	1,316	377	1,217
Town	206	188	187	205	....	104	176	122	180	203	204	200	195	95	196
City (2,500-9,999 pop.)	155	152	146	155	....	90	132	95	145	153	153	151	140	90	149
City (10,000-49,999 pop.)	168	159	158	167	....	108	135	97	157	168	164	163	148	113	153
City (50,000 or more)	159	148	149	155	....	108	135	97	146	154	153	148	145	88	147
Louisiana	1,313	1,136	1,178	1,303	1,018	971	827	516	988	1,298	1,271	1,262	1,164	579	1,205
Open Country and Village	769	622	656	759	....	514	380	196	499	759	735	730	683	228	683
Town	150	139	141	150	....	125	116	68	131	150	149	149	125	69	146
City (2,500-9,999 pop.)	111	107	109	111	....	90	90	69	99	109	108	109	98	73	103
City (10,000-49,999 pop.)	140	134	135	140	....	119	119	95	129	139	139	139	127	106	136
City (50,000 or more)	143	134	137	143	....	123	122	88	130	141	140	135	131	103	137
Maryland	283	261	258	280	221	154	236	151	256	275	275	257	264	194	267
Open Country and Village	50	44	44	50	....	25	36	18	44	48	48	47	47	34	43
Town	33	30	32	33	....	18	30	18	30	33	33	32	31	26	33
City (2,500-9,999 pop.)	35	33	30	35	....	18	32	22	33	35	35	34	32	26	35
City (10,000-49,999 pop.)	93	90	90	93	....	49	80	56	86	92	91	83	86	76	90
City (50,000 or more)	72	64	62	69	....	44	58	37	63	67	68	61	68	32	66
Michigan	187	157	158	184	121	111	132	85	132	166	166	162	169	116	157
Open Country and Village	15	10	11	14	....	5	8	4	7	14	13	12	11	8	10
Town	12	10	7	11	....	4	6	5	8	11	11	11	11	10	11

City (2,500-9,999 pop.)	22	22	21	22	……	14	17	8	14	21	21	21	19	14	20
City (10,000-49,999 pop.)	78	65	69	78	……	49	57	39	58	74	71	71	73	50	69
City (50,000 or more)	60	50	50	59	……	39	44	29	45	46	50	47	55	34	47
Mississippi	1,922	1,595	1,655	1,879	1,472	1,489	1,205	915	1,612	1,889	1,875	1,855	1,716	804	1,770
Open Country and Village	1,341	1,046	1,094	1,299	……	960	700	483	1,057	1,314	1,299	1,286	1,194	404	1,211
Town	180	167	174	179	……	156	159	126	171	177	180	176	156	93	176
City (2,500-9,999 pop.)	134	127	127	134	……	121	111	100	126	134	132	131	122	106	128
City (10,000-49,999 pop.)	221	210	216	221	……	208	191	169	212	219	218	216	203	164	211
City (50,000 or more)	46	45	44	46	……	44	44	37	46	45	46	46	41	37	44
Missouri	1,877	1,543	1,534	1,858	1,502	1,027	1,262	753	1,475	1,851	1,849	1,790	1,701	709	1,763
Open Country and Village	1,077	782	768	1,060	……	442	561	240	726	1,058	1,056	1,023	951	188	989
Town	262	246	251	262	……	178	236	160	245	262	262	256	245	141	258
City (2,500-9,999 pop.)	160	153	152	158	……	129	141	107	148	157	157	150	146	100	152
City (10,000-49,999 pop.)	137	132	132	137	……	103	117	93	126	135	135	131	132	112	133
City (50,000 or more)	241	230	231	241	……	175	207	153	230	239	239	230	227	168	231
Nevada	50	46	46	49	35	30	28	22	35	49	49	45	43	42	48
Open Country and Village	8	4	6	7	……	2	1	……	3	7	8	8	4	7	7
Town	4	4	4	4	……	1	1	……	3	4	4	4	3	4	4
City (2,500-9,999 pop.)	10	10	10	10	……	8	8	8	10	10	10	9	10	10	10
City (10,000-49,999 pop.)	10	10	10	10	……	6	5	3	5	10	10	9	9	8	10
City (50,000 or more)	18	18	16	18	……	13	13	11	14	18	17	15	17	13	17
New Mexico	250	224	226	245	198	175	162	120	189	244	245	234	219	112	236
Open Country and Village	74	56	61	71	……	32	25	17	41	72	72	66	60	13	67
Town	29	27	25	29	……	21	18	12	23	29	29	29	26	12	28
City (2,500-9,999 pop.)	37	36	34	36	……	25	29	21	29	35	36	33	29	17	35
City (10,000-49,999 pop.)	83	79	80	83	……	76	68	51	71	82	83	81	78	54	81
City (50,000 or more)	27	26	26	26	……	21	22	19	25	26	25	25	26	16	25
New York	131	107	101	120	69	62	85	52	90	116	118	103	116	80	108
Open Country and Village	10	7	7	9	……	3	2	……	6	8	9	9	8	5	8
Town	8	8	7	8	……	2	6	2	6	8	8	8	8	6	8
City (2,500-9,999 pop.)	14	14	12	14	……	7	8	6	8	14	14	12	13	11	14
City (10,000-49,999 pop.)	57	48	47	54	……	30	46	27	40	54	53	46	51	39	50
City (50,000 or more)	42	30	28	35	……	20	23	17	30	32	34	28	36	19	28
North Carolina	3,418	2,812	2,877	3,393	2,972	1,509	2,573	1,829	2,893	3,320	3,296	3,237	3,100	1,360	2,902
Open Country and Village	2,160	1,689	1,700	2,140	……	796	1,438	913	1,697	2,079	2,058	2,019	1,946	648	1,733
Town	313	271	286	312	……	158	283	210	298	308	310	305	295	135	293
City (2,500-9,999 pop.)	252	225	236	252	……	149	222	182	237	251	249	244	230	147	236
City (10,000-49,999 pop.)	353	321	333	351	……	202	319	272	338	346	345	338	321	210	324
City (50,000 or more)	340	306	322	338	……	204	311	252	323	336	334	331	308	220	316

NUMBER OF SOUTHERN BAPTIST CHURCHES REPORTING MAJOR ITEMS—1980

SBC and State Conventions	Total No. Reporting Churches	Baptisms	Additions by Letter	Ongoing Sunday School	VBS	Church Training	Ongoing WMU	Ongoing Brotherhood	Ongoing Church Music	Tithes, Offerings and Special Gifts	Mission Expenditures	Church Property	Pastors	Church Debt	Cooperative Program
Northern Plains	151	135	131	148	109	74	94	57	96	146	148	141	144	102	143
Open Country and Village	9	5	6	7		1	3		3	8	9		9	2	8
Town	36	30	26	36		11	14	9	16	34	35	32	34	21	33
City (2,500-9,999 pop.)	42	37	38	41		21	27	16	28	40	41	39	40	30	40
City (10,000-49,999 pop.)	49	48	46	49		29	38	23	36	49	48	47	46	37	47
City (50,000 or more)	15	15	15	15		12	12	9	13	15	15	14	15	12	15
Northwest	283	254	258	280	199	175	189	111	216	281	276	260	255	190	270
Open Country and Village	22	19	20	22		10	11	3	14	22	22	20	19	12	20
Town	38	30	28	37		20	17	9	25	37	35	35	35	17	33
City (2,500-9,999 pop.)	56	54	54	56		38	40	24	47	55	55	51	48	37	54
City (10,000-49,999 pop.)	95	88	91	94		65	73	42	76	95	94	88	86	74	94
City (50,000 or more)	72	63	65	71		42	48	33	54	72	70	66	67	50	69
Ohio	446	407	407	443	334	231	324	233	346	436	435	418	397	347	414
Open Country and Village	51	47	46	50		23	34	22	38	50	49	48	46	39	46
Town	53	49	43	53		29	39	28	43	53	53	51	47	38	52
City (2,500-9,999 pop.)	69	61	60	69		39	54	36	52	68	69	63	60	54	67
City (10,000-49,999 pop.)	127	117	120	126		64	88	71	98	125	126	122	111	107	122
City (50,000 or more)	146	133	138	145		76	109	76	115	140	138	134	133	109	127
Oklahoma	1,391	1,226	1,235	1,389	1,084	1,030	884	587	918	1,342	1,337	1,292	1,258	597	1,323
Open Country and Village	627	496	508	626		365	272	131	265	590	591	561	552	137	583
Town	250	244	242	250		220	192	131	212	249	248	245	226	116	247
City (2,500-9,999 pop.)	160	150	150	159		136	131	91	128	157	154	152	148	99	154
City (10,000-49,999 pop.)	174	169	169	174		157	146	120	156	172	170	165	162	121	169
City (50,000 or more)	180	167	166	180		152	143	114	157	174	174	169	170	124	170
Penn.-So. Jersey	94	81	80	91	59	63	73	48	86	91	90	87	83	70	87
Open Country and Village	9	9	7	9		6	5	5	9	9	9	9	9	5	9
Town	7	7	7	7		1	7	6	7	7	7	7	5	6	7
City (2,500-9,999 pop.)	17	14	16	17		12	12	4	15	16	16	16	15	14	16
City (10,000-49,999 pop.)	35	31	31	34		28	30	24	34	34	34	34	30	28	33
City (50,000 or more)	26	20	19	24		16	19	9	21	25	24	21	24	17	22
South Carolina	1,678	1,455	1,487	1,671	1,493	1,243	1,478	1,218	1,531	1,668	1,652	1,640	1,531	865	1,552
Open Country and Village	950	784	789	945		638	799	624	824	944	934	932	863	377	863
Town	175	155	162	175		136	164	120	166	175	174	173	160	96	167

City (2,500-9,999 pop.)	168	159	166	167		137	156	139	161	167	166	163	158	108	160
City (10,000-49,999 pop.)	244	229	231	244		217	226	214	242	242	239	233	223	176	231
City (50,000 or more)	141	128	139	140		115	133	121	138	140	139	139	127	108	131
Tennessee	2,716	2,358	2,343	2,679	2,188	1,723	1,619	1,094	1,794	2,587	2,551	2,553	2,454	1,041	2,275
Open Country and Village	1,625	1,333	1,313	1,600		861	751	428	839	1,518	1,497	1,502	1,444	405	1,285
Town	247	229	226	247		190	194	131	203	246	246	246	232	106	236
City (2,500-9,999 pop.)	198	193	195	198		161	159	125	175	196	194	190	180	125	185
City (10,000-49,999 pop.)	287	276	278	285		239	237	196	260	283	275	281	269	194	259
City (50,000 or more)	359	327	331	349		272	278	214	317	344	339	334	329	211	310
Texas	3,944	3,330	3,505	3,884	2,907	2,295	2,622	1,926	2,778	3,842	3,834	3,740	3,611	1,967	3,711
Open Country and Village	1,376	964	1,120	1,345		504	544	312	606	1,335	1,336	1,277	1,251	298	1,300
Town	521	481	493	516		317	421	291	445	514	516	510	489	257	506
City (2,500-9,999 pop.)	447	414	421	443		300	375	295	371	441	437	433	405	283	429
City (10,000-49,999 pop.)	617	579	572	610		447	495	413	519	603	601	591	556	452	584
City (50,000 or more)	983	892	899	970		727	787	615	837	949	944	929	910	677	892
Utah-Idaho	73	62	63	72	45	41	49	33	51	71	69	67	63	44	66
Open Country and Village	3	2	2	2		3	1		1	2	1	2	1	1	1
Town	12	10	9	12		3	6	4	4	12	11	10	9	5	11
City (2,500-9,999 pop.)	18	15	17	18		10	12	7	12	18	18	18	14	12	17
City (10,000-49,999 pop.)	22	19	19	22		15	16	13	19	22	22	21	22	17	20
City (50,000 or more)	18	16	16	18		12	14	8	15	17	17	16	17	9	17
Virginia	1,425	1,200	1,184	1,418	1,265	573	1,202	665	1,251	1,407	1,396	1,381	1,287	602	1,338
Open Country and Village	778	586	572	776		213	605	270	622	771	758	755	696	209	719
Town	142	126	127	142		54	128	78	134	141	141	141	128	63	139
City (2,500-9,999 pop.)	63	63	62	63		39	58	34	63	63	63	63	56	40	61
City (10,000-49,999 pop.)	162	156	156	161		92	153	108	160	159	159	156	151	116	156
City (50,000 or more)	280	269	267	276		175	258	175	272	273	275	266	256	174	263
West Virginia	74	65	64	73	67	42	60	31	65	71	71	72	66	53	70
Open Country and Village	16	15	12	16		8	10	1	11	15	15	16	16	11	14
Town	17	14	15	16		6	14	5	15	16	16	13	13	13	16
City (2,500-9,999 pop.)	21	19	19	21		16	20	13	19	21	21	21	19	15	21
City (10,000-49,999 pop.)	16	13	14	16		11	12	8	16	15	15	15	15	11	15
City (50,000 or more)	4	4	4	4		1	4	4	4	4	4	4	3	3	4
Puerto Rico[1]	23	14	12	23	5	8	15	9	9	23	21	15	22	15	21
Open Country and Village															
Town	4	2	2	4		1	3	1	1	4	3	2	4	2	3
City (2,500-9,999 pop.)	2			2						2	1		2		1
City (10,000-49,999 pop.)	6	6	5	6		2	4	3	3	6	6	5	5	5	6
City (50,000 or more)	6	6	5	11		5	8	5	4	11	11	8	11	8	11

[1] Not a state convention but to be shown as part of SBC statistics.
Statistics from *The Quarterly Review*, July, 1981.

COOPERATIVE PROGRAM RECEIPTS DISTRIBUTED TO SBC AGENCIES, 1970-80

	1970	1971	1972*	1972-73	1973-74	1974-75	1975-76	1976-77	1977-78	1978-79	1979-80
Foreign Mission Board	$14,113,351	$14,863,351	$11,147,513	$16,702,020	$18,940,308	$20,057,126	$22,800,937	$24,538,347	$27,053,910	$29,849,359	$33,657,712
Home Mission Board	5,431,037	5,464,242	4,252,196	6,081,433	6,806,955	7,521,422	8,550,293	9,602,815	11,025,801	12,549,644	13,680,054
Annuity Board	200,000	176,165	132,124	179,098	190,488	222,628	278,339	255,100	264,030	300,000	325,000
Golden Gate Seminary	578,632	675,119	430,813	624,127	785,567	866,182	1,054,856	1,197,159	1,236,017	2,868,509	2,603,733
Midwestern Seminary	558,866	712,891	505,065	644,254	929,254	974,205	880,156	1,384,664	1,185,259	1,562,921	1,334,683
New Orleans Seminary	945,348	1,141,715	915,309	1,296,928	1,376,824	1,548,182	1,749,220	1,870,671	1,964,821	2,111,017	2,353,004
Southeastern Seminary	752,461	879,993	978,136	1,256,418	1,178,573	1,335,930	1,409,204	1,757,431	1,882,398	2,088,364	2,927,487
Southern Seminary	1,231,055	1,434,236	1,390,986	1,804,668	1,770,957	2,145,256	2,522,437	2,810,063	2,902,715	3,006,890	3,978,540
Southwestern Seminary	1,467,588	1,694,015	1,426,840	2,027,760	2,321,547	2,513,138	2,970,279	3,390,740	4,147,585	3,781,229	4,193,056
Special Seminary Endowment	—	—	—			—				74,000	126,000
Southern Baptist Foundation	81,600	81,600	61,200	83,537	92,592	105,697	120,170	127,500	153,814	170,000	181,900
American Seminary	95,000	95,000	71,250	97,235	103,503	111,519	126,788	127,500	141,008	150,000	160,500
Brotherhood Commission	288,310	301,086	251,931	332,175	433,790	401,143	456,065	484,700	544,247	576,654	673,250
Christian Life Commission	173,400	200,000	150,000	214,917	243,777	272,977	310,352	329,600	364,821	420,000	449,400
Education Commission	127,500	135,000	101,250	145,028	164,382	183,925	209,107	244,900	258,418	290,000	310,300
Historical Commission	104,040	115,000	86,250	123,831	140,453	156,046	177,410	188,800	207,015	220,000	235,400
Radio-TV Commission	1,342,826	1,507,036	1,264,257	1,663,961	1,889,894	1,935,293	2,223,738	2,698,369	3,031,653	3,014,893	3,301,516
Stewardship Commission	84,660	125,000	93,750	140,704	177,673	196,160	223,764	230,000	278,061	275,000	294,250
Public Affairs Committee	113,628	120,000	90,000	146,387	146,387	167,280	190,753	204,100	225,612	255,000	272,850
SBC Operating Budget	200,000	225,000	168,750	255,811	337,635	400,143	471,853	498,000	551,199	602,000	704,000
Other	36,000	24,078	38,704	30,046	6,250	—	—	—	—	—	—
	$27,925,302	$29,970,527	$23,556,324	$33,832,931	$38,036,809	$41,114,252	$46,725,721	$51,940,459	$57,418,384	$64,165,480	$71,762,635

*9-month budget year when fiscal year changed from calendar year to year beginning in October and ending in September.

TIMOTHY A. HEDQUIST

SOUTHERN BAPTIST SUMMARY—1969-80

	Churches	Membership	Baptisms	SS Enrollment	VBS Enrollment	CT Enrollment	WMU Enrollment	Brotherhood Enrollment	Ch. Music Enrollment	Mission Gifts	Total All Gifts	Church Property
1969	[2]34,335	11,489,613	368,225	7,418,067	3,648,255	2,343,595	[1]1,291,221	430,339	1,062,494	133,224,335	809,608,812	3,900,472,691
1970	[2]34,360	11,629,880	368,863	7,290,447	3,212,436	2,228,217	[1]1,199,813	422,527	1,076,487	138,500,883	857,098,689	4,127,738,253
1971	[2]34,441	11,826,463	409,659	[3]7,141,453	3,241,917	2,106,855	[3]1,137,586	[3]451,538	1,088,980	[3]160,546,250	935,044,620	4,307,682,773
1972	[2]34,534	12,067,284	445,725	[3]7,177,651	3,240,514	2,044,445	[3]1,125,641	[3]454,272	1,088,980	[3]174,772,885	1,023,146,829	4,601,622,835
1973	[2]34,665	12,297,346	413,990	7,182,550	3,239,973	1,949,640	[1]1,102,432	461,080	1,173,004	193,549,922	1,136,238,734	5,022,607,547
1974	[2]34,734	12,515,842	410,482	7,190,829	3,354,681	1,904,986	[1]1,115,149	460,713	1,252,628	219,389,030	1,258,557,004	5,614,906,403
1975	[2]34,902	12,735,663	421,809	7,281,532	3,491,376	1,886,177	[1]1,133,587	476,002	1,304,068	237,617,406	1,387,339,703	6,221,128,761
1976	[2]35,073	12,922,605	384,496	7,458,375	3,275,013	1,850,406	[1]1,139,034	478,981	1,354,944	262,373,823	1,545,977,274	6,897,558,829
1977	[2]35,255	13,083,199	345,690	7,430,931	3,193,877	1,778,179	[1]1,118,085	473,309	1,372,598	289,372,474	1,691,206,562	7,605,102,513
1978	[2]35,404	13,196,979	336,050	7,338,046	3,179,015	1,775,701	[1]1,094,966	466,698	1,382,104	316,919,377	1,869,701,706	8,455,626,539
1979	[2]35,605	13,379,073	368,738	7,317,960	3,197,517	1,752,026	[1]1,086,785	469,315	1,424,693	356,207,790	2,085,955,800	9,609,575,477
1980	[2]35,831	13,606,808	429,742	7,433,405	3,338,824	1,795,619	[1]1,100,243	495,666	1,465,774	401,499,506	2,315,149,038	10,768,305,191

[1]Figures include statistics from the church as well as college and or hospital BYWs.
[2]Nonreporting churches are included. "Nonreporting" refers to those still affiliated with the Convention, but who have not submitted a report for three or more years.
[3]The data is not comparable to previous years. See page 36 in July, 1972, issue of *The Quarterly Review*.
Statistics from *The Quarterly Review*, July 1981.

Child Abuse: 1978, 1979.

Developmentally Disabled and Mentally Ill: 1978.

Family Life and Sex Education: 1969, 1975, 1978.

World Hunger: 1975, 1977, 1978, 1979, 1980.

From 1965 to 1979, Southern Baptists passed more than 150 resolutions on about 50 subjects. Most of these dealt with social problems. Southern Baptists did much more than pass resolutions. The CLC and the Home and Foreign Mission Boards were heavily involved in Christian social work. Several state conventions sponsored disaster relief programs that utilized relief vans staffed by Baptist laymen. The denomination engaged in a world hunger emphasis and offering. The decade also saw a great deal of denominational activity to alleviate the problems of the aging. Several significant conferences and seminars were held in the 1970s. These included the Conference on the Aging, Nashville, TN, 1974; the Convocation on World Hunger, Ridgecrest, 1978; and the Consultation on Women in Church-related Vocations, Nashville, 1978.

In addition, the CLC conducted annual seminars on social issues, well attended and widely heralded as among the best in the nation. Southern Baptists appear to have solved the problem of conflict between social service and evangelism. Most see the two as complementary and not contradictory.

Seminaries reached an all-time high in enrollments. This came in 1978-79 when 10,954 persons were enrolled in the six schools. These included 1,876 women. These students were taught that year by 303 full-time faculty members. At the beginning of the decade, the enrollment stood at 5,848 including 628 women, and there were 234 faculty members.

State conventions grew stronger in influence and resources. In 1969 there were 30 cooperating state conventions, and in 1980, 34. The new ones were New York, 1969, Pennsylvania-South Jersey, 1970, West Virginia, 1970, and Nevada, 1978. The resources of the state conventions reached an all-time high. The 34 state conventions own 435 pieces of property, most of it public service institutions such as colleges, hospitals, homes for children, and others. The total value was $1,332,755,539, and endowment for these public service institutions stood at $560,283,052.

Bold Mission Thrust was the principal denominational emphasis at the close of the decade, and was the outgrowth of an Executive Committee Study Committee of Fifteen appointed in 1970. From this committee emerged the Missions Challenge Committee appointed by the SBC in 1974. The broad outline of Bold Mission Thrust was approved by the SBC at Norfolk, VA, in 1976. Detailed operations plans were approved in 1977, 1978, 1979, and 1980. Probably as much has been said and written about Bold Mission Thrust as any other program ever adopted by Southern Baptists. At the beginning of the 1980s, the plan was struggling against the threat of rapidly rising inflation and indifference in the churches, but there were signs that the plan was moving forward. One very great barrier was the threat of secular inundation of the religious spirit.

The Cooperative Program made gains in the face of inflation, recession, and less emphasis by some churches. In 1969 total gifts to the undesignated Cooperative Program were $78,220,474. In 1979 they were $184,169,263, a gain of $105,948,789, or 135 percent for the decade. This was an average annual increase of $10,594,878. However, much of the gain came in the late 1970s as inflation increased. The proportion of the Cooperative Program going to state and SBC causes remained relatively unchanged over the 10-year period. In 1969, 35.1 percent went to SBC causes and in 1979, 34.8 percent. Gifts by local churches through the Cooperative Program dropped from 9.28 percent of their total gifts in 1969 to 8.28 percent in 1979.

Designated contributions to SBC causes increased during the decade. In 1969 Southern Baptists designated $22,297,719 for their agencies, most of it through the Lottie Moon and Annie Armstrong offerings. In 1979 they designated $54,910,904, a gain of $32,613,185, or 146 percent. Note that this is 10 percentage points more than the percentage gain of the SBC Cooperative Program. It perhaps reflects a natural penalty associated with the complexity of a structure such as the Cooperative Program, and perhaps also the relative ease with which leaders can personalize special offerings.

Three study committees indicated some concern with the Convention's structural arrangements. The first was the Executive Committee Study Committee of Fifteen appointed in 1970, the second, the Convention's Mission Challenge Committee appointed in 1974, and the third, the Convention's Committee of Seven appointed to study the Executive Committee in 1974. Much of what came from these three efforts was the updating of Convention directions set in 1955-59 when the SBC in 1958 and 1959 adopted the recommendations of the Committee to Study the Total Southern Baptist Programs. On the whole the studies of the three committees of the 1970s showed that Southern Baptists were properly self-critical but well pleased with their present agency and program structures.

Leadership in the SBC and the state conventions did an almost complete rollover in the years 1970-80. Only two SBC agency heads at the beginning of the 1970s still held office 10 years later. They were Foy Valentine of the Christian Life Commission and Duke K. McCall of Southern Baptist Theological Seminary. Not since the 1950s have there been so many leadership changes in so short a period.

See also BOLD MISSION THRUST; CANADIAN–SBC RELATIONS; CONVENTION EMPHASIS PRIORITY PLANNING; COOPERATIVE PROGRAM; COOPERATIVE PROGRAM ALLOCATION BUDGET PLANNING; EXECUTIVE COMMITTEE, SBC; INTER-AGENCY COUNCIL; PROGRAMMING FOR THE CHURCHES; SEMINARY ALLOCATION AND DISTRIBUTION FORMULA; SOUTHERN BAPTIST CONVENTION ANNUAL ARRANGEMENTS; SBC, BASIS OF REPRESENTATION; SBC CAPITAL NEEDS; SBC CONSTITUTION, BYLAWS, and BUSINESS and FINANCIAL PLAN CHANGES; SBC LEADERSHIP CHANGES; SBC LOGO; SBC NAME CHANGE; SBC ORGANIZATIONAL MANUAL; SBC VOTING PROCEDURES; SOUTHERN BAPTISTS, GROWTH OF; TRUSTEESHIP.

BIBLIOGRAPHY: Robert A. Baker, *The Southern Baptist Convention and Its People, 1607-1972* (1974). Albert McClellan, *Meet Southern Baptists* (1978).

ALBERT MCCLELLAN

SOUTHERN BAPTIST CONVENTION ANNUAL ARRANGEMENTS (cf. Place of Meeting, Southern Baptist Convention, Vols. II, III). Bylaw 20 (5) (d) of the SBC Constitution and Bylaws charges the Executive Committee to "recommend to the Convention a time and place and to have oversight of the arrangements for the meetings of the Convention." Normally, the messengers to the annual Convention vote on sites five years in advance of meetings. However, due to the difficulty of securing space in some cities, at times cities have been considered six or seven years prior to meetings.

Over the years the Convention has established requirements for a host city. The current guidelines, adopted by the Convention in 1976, are: (1) A guarantee of 6,500 hotel and motel rooms, with the majority within walking distance or a 10-minute bus ride; and (2) a main auditorium which will seat at least 16,000 people and provide proportionate exhibit space.

The process to select a host city takes nine months. In the September meeting of the Executive Committee, the Convention Arrangements Workgroup of the Administrative and Convention Arrangements Subcommittee reviews all invitations received from the various cities asking to host the annual meeting. Each city's invitation must be accompanied by an invitation from a local Baptist association or group of associations or from the state convention in which the city is located. The cities that satisfy the requirements are then asked to submit to the workgroup specific proposals by the February meeting of the Executive Committee. At the February meeting the workgroup selects from the submitted proposals and makes a recommendation to the Administrative and Convention Arrangments Subcommittee, which in turn makes a recommendation to the full Executive Committee. SBC messengers vote in June on the recommendation of the Executive Committee for the host city.

TIM HEDQUIST

SOUTHERN BAPTIST CONVENTION BASIS OF REPRESENTATION. See REPRESENTATION, SOUTHERN BAPTIST CONVENTION BASIS OF.

SOUTHERN BAPTIST CONVENTION CAPITAL NEEDS. In Feb., 1945, the SBC Executive Committee noted the capital needs campaigns being conducted by several SBC agencies and approved a systematic survey of capital needs of all agencies. The following September a special committee reported $20,750,000 long-range capital needs for seven agencies (Foreign Mission Board, Home Mission Board, Relief and Annuity Board, Southern Baptist Theological Seminary, Southwestern Baptist Theological Seminary, Baptist Bible Institute, and American Baptist Theological Seminary). The committee also reported $3,062,000 needed in 1946 by the seven agencies.

In December of the same year, the Executive Committee approved a motion that all 1946 SBC Cooperative Program receipts above $3,000,000 be divided among the seven agencies for capital needs purposes. This was the beginning of the SBC Capital Needs program that has turned about $80,000,000 of Cooperative Program funds to SBC agencies for capital needs purposes, 1946-80. Among other things, this money has provided funds for rebuilding three older seminaries and constructing three newer ones.

Since 1946 the Convention has approved seven capital needs programs: 1946-51, $11,151,783; 1952-53, $21,000,000; 1959-63, $23,500,000; 1965-68, $8,955,000; 1969-73, $5,000,000; 1974-78, $4,977,500; and 1979-84, $16,705,985. Altogether 14 agencies have participated in the program. Since 1965 all capital needs for the FMB and HMB have been included in their operation budgets except for the 1969-73 program in which the HMB's church loan fund was included for $1,000,000.

See also COOPERATIVE PROGRAM ALLOCATION BUDGET PLANNING.

ALBERT MCCLELLAN

SOUTHERN BAPTIST CONVENTION CONSTITUTION, BYLAWS, AND BUSINESS AND FINANCIAL PLAN CHANGES. The 1845 SBC constitution provided for two mission boards and called for the election of their trustees by the Convention. Convention membership was based on contributions by individuals and "collateral societies" or "bodies." The rules of order had more to do with procedure for the annual meeting than for the operation of the agencies. The reorganization of the SBC Executive Committee in 1927 brought plans for better business operation, but it was not until the 1939 SBC meeting that the Business and Financial Plan was approved.

The plan provides for budget development, audits, capital investments, gift annuities, special solicitations, trust funds, reserves, financial reports to the Convention, new enterprises, and other matters. It states that the Executive Committee "shall recommend to the Convention an operating budget." Prior to 1959 the Executive Committee recommended a comprehensive budget to the Convention which included the budgets of all the agencies. The SBC changed this in 1959 when it was recognized that the Executive Committee was not in a position to approve agency budgets.

The SBC revised its constitution in 1946 to provide for the rotation of trustees and directors of the agencies for three-year terms. Certain exceptions for technical reasons were provided. Those elected were limited to two consecutive terms, but could be elected again after remaining off for one year. In 1968 the SBC amended the constitution to provide four-year terms, amended the bylaws to make more precise the makeup and the method of appointment of the Credentials Committee, and also amended the bylaws to provide that no person could serve as a trustee who is responsible for the administration of funds received from that agency or who receives full or partial salary from that agency.

A 1971 bylaw amendment provided that the Resolutions Committee should be appointed 60 days before the Convention and that copies of proposed resolutions should be mailed to the chairman 30 days before the Convention. In 1972 a bylaw change provided that motions dealing with the work of agencies be referred to the agencies for report, unless the Convention by a two-thirds vote decides on immediate consideration. This eased the problem of debating issues without full information. Agencies are required to report on the study procedures along with any proposed changes to the next annual session.

A 1975 bylaw change provided that a person who rotates off as a director of one agency cannot be named as a director of another agency until one year has elapsed. In that same year the constitution and bylaws were also amended to reduce the number of local members on a board from 18 to 12, and to increase the number of representatives from states with more than 250,000 members.

In 1977 the SBC amended the constitution and bylaws to remove sexist language and to make it clear that women were eligible to serve in any SBC office.

In 1978 the SBC incorporated Convention Procedure into the laws, and the bylaws were rearranged to provide for a more logical sequence. The voting procedure was revised to provide that "if an officer does not receive a majority of votes cast on the first ballot, subsequent ballots should carry the names of those who are included in the top 50 percent of the total votes cast on the previous ballot."

A 1979 constitutional amendment provided that the same provisions would apply to the boards as apply to the other agencies regarding the charter provisions for membership on their boards. This made it possible, if approved by the Convention, for some of the boards to reduce their size.

See also SOUTHERN BAPTIST CONVENTION, THE.

PORTER ROUTH

SOUTHERN BAPTIST CONVENTION LEADERSHIP CHANGES. A heavy turnover of SBC agency chief executives occurred in the 1970s. The top leadership positions changed in 18 of the 20 organizations during the decade. Five of them changed twice—positions at New Orleans Baptist Theological Seminary and the Brotherhood, Stewardship, Education, and American Baptist Theological Seminary Commissions. Only two of the agency chief executives on duty at the beginning of 1970 were still in office at the beginning of 1980. They were Duke K. McCall, who became president of The Southern Baptist Theological Seminary in 1951, and Foy D. Valentine, who became executive secretary-treasurer of the Christian Life Commission in 1960.

Retirees during the decade included some chief executives of 20 or more years tenure— Baker James Cauthen of the Foreign Mission Board, 1954-79; Porter Routh of the Executive Committee, 1951-79; Paul M. Stevens of the Radio and Television Commission, 1953-79; James L. Sullivan of the Sunday School Board, 1953-75; Alma Hunt of the Woman's Missionary Union (SBC Auxiliary), 1948-74; Harold K. Graves of Golden Gate Baptist Theological Seminary, 1952-77; and Robert Naylor of Southwestern Baptist Theological Seminary, 1958-78.

Heavy turnover was also evident in top state convention leadership posts. The president or administrative executive changed at least once in the 1970s in 27 of 46 senior colleges. Editors of 26 of the 34 state Baptist newspapers changed (including four founded in the 1970s). Seventy persons were editors of state Baptist newspapers in the 1970s. Executives of 21 of the 34 state Baptist conventions changed (including three founded in the 1970s). Three other state Baptist executive secretaries had announced retirements for 1980.

ROBERT J. O'BRIEN and VERN C. MYERS

SOUTHERN BAPTIST CONVENTION LOGO. At its June, 1978, meeting in Atlanta, GA, the Southern Baptist Convention approved the first official logo or insignia for the denomination. The design is a combination of a cross, the world, and an open Bible. Inspiration for it came from a metal sculpture on the front of the SBC Building, Nashville, TN. The design was chosen from hundreds of suggestions and 64 proposals from 14 Baptist artists. Registered with the United States Patent Office as "a collective mark" for the exclusive use of Southern Baptists, its use is voluntary.

WILMER C. FIELDS

SOUTHERN BAPTIST CONVENTION NAME CHANGE STUDY. During the annual SBC meeting in 1974, W. A. Criswell of Texas moved that a committee of seven be appointed to study the possibility of changing the name of the SBC. Porter Routh of Tennessee offered a substitute motion that the study be approved

and that the study be made by a seven-member committee already approved to study and evaluate the Executive Committee. The substitute passed.

A survey conducted by the committee showed that a majority of Southern Baptists opposed a name change. While some newer areas of the Convention favored a name change, older and larger states opposed change as much as nine to one. Fifty-two different names were suggested. The committee completed its study and reported to the 1975 SBC meeting that "in light of its findings it is the committee's considered judgment that the name of the Southern Baptist Convention should not be changed at this time."

Reasons given for retaining the present name included: (1) Opposition to a name change by the vast majority of Southern Baptists; (2) association of the present name with certain doctrinal positions, traditions, and emphases; (3) the danger of other groups claiming the present name should it be dropped; (4) the difficulty of communicating a name change; (5) the difficulties related to inserting a new name into the charters of all official documents and the related legal ramifications; and (6) the absence of a consensus on a suitable new name.

HAROLD C. BENNETT

SOUTHERN BAPTIST CONVENTION ORGANIZATION MANUAL. The Convention bylaws require the SBC Executive Committee to maintain an Organization Manual subject to the following conditions: (1) define the responsibilities of each agency for conducting programs and performing other functions, and (2) cite Convention authority for these assignments. The Organization Manual was begun in 1959 and completed in 1967 when all the program statements were approved as a whole by the Convention. Revised annually and printed in limited numbers, copies are available from the SBC Executive Committee.

ALBERT MCCLELLAN

SOUTHERN BAPTIST CONVENTION VOTING PROCEDURES. The 1892 Convention adopted a change in the bylaws specifying that the officers of the Convention "shall be elected by ballot." This requirement, deleted in 1955, was reinstated in 1958. The Convention amended its procedure in 1962 to provide for printed ballots. Charges of voting irregularities at the 1964 Convention led to a revision of the registration process. The Convention has used data processing cards as ballots since 1965.

A Credentials Committee, recommended in 1965, was approved in 1968. The Convention added an item on tellers to its procedures in 1965, but in 1978 consolidated this item and the one on voting with the bylaw entitled "election of officers." In 1980 the Convention adopted a separate bylaw on voting which specified various acceptable methods of voting and forbade voting by proxy. By Convention request, the Executive Committee studied "the need for a bylaw or a change in Convention procedures to make vote tabulations public" and in 1977 secured approval of a bylaw requiring announcement of tabulations. The recording secretary now reports to the Convention the tabulation of all votes taken by ballot.

In 1952 the Convention amended Article V of the constitution to read: "The first vice-president shall be voted upon and elected after the election of the president has taken place; and the second vice-president shall be voted upon and elected after the election of the first vice-president has taken place."

Prior to 1978 when three or more individuals were nominated, a second ballot was usually taken with the names of the two persons receiving the highest vote on the first ballot. That year the Convention changed the bylaw to read: "If an officer does not receive a majority of votes cast on the first ballot, subsequent ballots should carry the names of those who are included in the top 50 percent of the total votes cast on the previous ballot."

Charges of registration and voter irregularities in 1979 prompted an investigation by the registration secretary of the Convention. He found no massive illegal registration but uncovered numerous registration problems. A few messengers had registered twice; some churches had more messengers than the constitution allowed; and some registered, although they were not elected by their churches.

In 1980 changes were made in the registration process to assure that the constitutional provisions concerning registration were followed by all messengers. The Convention amended its bylaws to require "each messenger to register in person by presenting a completed and signed Southern Baptist Convention Messenger Registration Card."

LEE PORTER

SOUTHERN BAPTIST EDUCATOR, THE (II, III).

This bimonthly newsmagazine of the Education Commission, SBC, carries analytical articles on religious, economic, legal, social, or educational trends affecting Christian education, as well as news and feature articles concerning the 72 Southern Baptist-related seminaries, colleges, and schools. The 1980 circulation was about 8,300. The Association of Southern Baptist Colleges and Schools provides a subscription for all faculty and trustees of the schools.

H. REX HAMMOCK

SOUTHERN BAPTIST FOUNDATION. (I, III).

The assets held by the foundation for agencies, institutions, and individuals increased from $11,020,708 at the end of 1969 to $23,361,150 on Sep. 30, 1979. Income produced by these assets for Baptist causes increased from $529,729 to $1,733,862 during the same period. Increasing assets and rising interest rates throughout the economy contributed to this income growth.

The trend of many trust institutions in the 1960s to admit as many accounts as possible into a pooled fund was reversed in the late 1970s. The historically high interest rates precipitated this change. Therefore, the foundation encouraged the various SBC agencies to transfer endowment, reserve, and capital needs funds from the pooled fund to individually managed accounts. This enabled the foundation to invest for each agency so as to reflect more accurately its particular investment objective.

The report of the Committee of Fifteen in 1974 to the Executive Committee, SBC, resulting from consultation with SBC agencies contained several recommendations concerning the foundation. After considerable discussion and meetings with the Committee of Fifteen, the Association of Baptist Foundation Executives, and other interested persons, the Executive Committee, SBC, adopted an amended recommendation in Feb., 1975, as follows:

(1) That the Executive Committee inform the Southern Baptist Convention Foundation (a) that in its opinion the Foundation is fully empowered by its program statement to inform the membership of the Southern Baptist Convention of its services, and (b) that the Foundation should do all it can to implement its program statement, also keeping in mind the needs of the state foundations; (2) That the Executive Committee ask the Convention to request the Foundation to work with the Executive Committee to the end that a percentage of its investment income be used toward funding the expenses of operating the Foundation; (3) That it be recognized that leadership for developing a strategy for raising money from private sources for both SBC and state conventions is the program responsibility of the Stewardship Commission, and needs no special implementation at this time.

The automation of the trust accounting system in 1979 ensured the continuation of providing the broad range of services enumerated in the program of work. The decline from 13.85 percent in 1969 to 9.80 percent in 1979 of the ratio of budget allocation to income produced by foundation assets demonstrated the improving efficiency of providing those services. The operating budget, provided in its entirety by the Cooperative Program, grew from $80,000 in 1969 to $170,000 in 1979.

Kendall Berry retired as the foundation's executive on Dec. 31, 1976, after nine years of service. Funds under management more than doubled during this period and income tripled. The foundation elected Hollis E. Johnson, III, an investment manager from Nashville, TN, as the fifth full-time chief executive to begin service, Jan. 1, 1977.

HOLLIS E. JOHNSON, III

SOUTHERN BAPTIST HISTORICAL SOCIETY (II).

Encouraging the recording and preserving of Baptist history, the society reported 682 members in 1980. It works and meets annually with the Historical Commission, SBC. Membership, which is open to individuals, churches, and institutions, provides use of the Dargan-Carver Library and subscriptions to

Baptist History and Heritage and *The Quarterly Review.*

See also HISTORICAL COMMISSION, SBC.

JAMES E. TAULMAN

SOUTHERN BAPTIST JOURNAL. Published monthly by the Baptist Faith and Message Fellowship since Dec., 1973, this publication seeks to expose and counter "liberalism" within the SBC. It typically carries editorials, articles, book reviews, and reader responses. William A. Powell, the paper's founder and current editor, commenced the journal in Buchanan, GA. Although it identifies itself as a Southern Baptist publication, it has no official connection with the SBC.

ROBERT L. THOMMARSON

SOUTHERN BAPTIST PASTORS' CONFERENCE (III). The conference, continuing to meet just prior to the Southern Baptist Convention, provides a time of inspirational preaching, a consideration of problems related to the pastoral ministry, and an emphasis on evangelism and missions. While some pastors have complained in recent years about the negative rather than inspirational nature of many messages, and have expressed concern about the present value of the conference, present officers are taking steps to get the conference program back on its original course. The conference grows in numbers. Difficulty faces the arrangements committee to find a place sufficient for the attendance. The budget runs into thousands of dollars. The conference may well be called the "preacher's revival."

BIBLIOGRAPHY: Gerald Martin, *"Sir, We Would See Jesus": The Story of the Southern Baptist Pastors' Conference* (1968).

HERSCHEL H. HOBBS

SOUTHERN BAPTIST PERIODICAL INDEX (III). The 1970s were years of growth and change for this annual publication of the Historical Commission, SBC. The number of periodicals included in the index has expanded to 47. Since 1974, the index has been a product of the commission's Baptist Information Retrieval System.

CHARLES W. DEWEESE

SOUTHERN BAPTIST PRESS ASSOCIATION (II). An organization composed of 35 Baptist publications affiliated with Baptist state conventions and Baptist Press. In 1979 the organization's constitution was changed so the membership was composed of the publications rather than the editors of these publications and their assistants. The change also eliminated the category of associate membership, which had been composed of the editors of publications of various SBC agencies.

The association meets three times each year: a three-day workshop in February held at various places in the nation on invitation of one of the member publications, and brief meetings during the annual SBC meeting and during the

September meeting of the SBC Executive Committee. The office of vice-president was changed to president-elect in 1971. The association is basically for fellowship, although the members often pass resolutions related to the ministry and interest of the Baptist state papers. The program committee for the annual workshops is composed of the officers and the host editor.

ALVIN C. SHACKLEFORD

SOUTHERN BAPTIST RESEARCH FELLOWSHIP. See STUDY AND RESEARCH IN THE SBC.

SOUTHERN BAPTIST THEOLOGICAL SEMINARY, ENDOWED CHAIRS OF. Through endowed chairs Southern Seminary receives support for designated professorships apart from Cooperative Program funds. Although types of endowments vary, a fully funded chair provides salary, office facilities, and secretarial services for the professor. Chairs are named by or for donors, outstanding professors, or religious leaders.

The seminary holds permanent endowment for the following chairs: Joseph Emerson Brown (Christian Theology), 1880; William Owen Carver (Missions and World Religions), 1900; David T. Porter (Church History), 1903; Basil Manly, Jr. (Religious Education), 1906; James Buchanan Harrison (New Testament), 1933; John R. Sampey (Old Testament), 1938; Woman's Missionary Union (Social Work Education), 1963; William Walker Brookes (Church and Community), 1963; Billy Graham (Evangelism), 1965; Gaines S. Dobbins (Church Administration), 1976; Victor and Louise Lester (Preaching), 1977; Lawrence and Charlotte Hoover (Pastoral Care), 1978; and Ellen Edens McCall (Prayer and Personal Devotion), 1979.

Chairs endowed by others (corpus not held by the seminary) include V. V. Cooke (Organ), 1975; and Carolyn King Ragan (Church Music), 1979. Chairs for visiting professors include: Robert Roble (Christian Preaching), 1938; Warren Sewell (Pastoral Studies), 1971; John and Margaret Slaughter (Theology), 1979; and C. J. and Lillian Godsey (New Testament), 1980.

BILL J. LEONARD

SOUTHERN BAPTIST THEOLOGICAL SEMINARY, THE (II, III). In the 1970s continuity with established traditions and change to meet new circumstances marked the life of Southern Seminary. The salient characteristic of the seminary in this decade was growth. This growth, both quantitative and qualitative, included a new student influx, physical construction and renovation, financial campaigns, academic revision and experimentation, administrative restructuring, new forms of student ministry, and sensitivity to growing issues in theological education, such as spiritual formation and the role of women in Christian ministry.

SOUTHWESTERN BAPTIST THEOLOGICAL SEMINARY (*q.v.*), Fort Worth, TX. Goldia and Robert Naylor Children's Center. Constructed in 1972-73 at a cost of $750,000.

SOUTHERN BAPTIST THEOLOGICAL SEMINARY (*q.v.*), Louisville, KY. *Top:* Cooke Hall, built in 1970, provides faculty offices, teaching studios, and rehearsal rooms for the seminary's School of Church Music. *Bottom:* Heeren Recital Hall, a 225-seat auditorium located on the second floor of Cooke Hall. Features a 45-rank Schlicker organ.

Much of the growth at Southern Seminary in the 1970s was a response to meet the needs of a burgeoning student body. The enrollment for the academic year 1969-70 was 1,575. Ten years later that figure had zoomed to 2,880. The largest increase occurred during the middle of the decade. In 1973-74 Southern's total enrollment was 1,637. Three years later, in 1976-77, the statistics had increased by more than 1,000 to 2,796. The latter figure secured Southern Seminary's status as the largest independent college or graduate school in Kentucky.

All of the elements contributing to this increase are not known, but the resurgence of religious interest among American college students in the late 1960s and early 1970s constituted a major factor. By the latter years of the decade, an expected leveling off in enrollment had occurred. In spite of the slowdown, Southern was the third largest accredited seminary in North America in 1980.

Physical Facilities.—The record growth of the student body during the decade heightened demands for physical facilities. On Oct. 20, 1970, the cornerstone for the new Church Music Building, Cooke Hall, was officially placed. Named for V. V. Cooke, Sr., a longtime benefactor of the seminary, the new building contained 16,000 square feet of floor space, joined by an arcade to Alumni Memorial Chapel.

A new comprehensive Child Care Center opened at the seminary, Aug. 30, 1971. The center was located in Rankin Hall, which had been thoroughly renovated and equipped for child care needs. While obviously designed to meet the needs of children in the community, the Child Care Center also served as a demonstration school for future ministers who would be concerned with the spiritual and physical nurture of children.

Erected in 1926, Norton Hall underwent major renovations during the decade. These renovations provided for administrative offices, the modernization of classroom facilities, and the improvement of faculty offices. The Carver Building was also renovated, providing accommodations for the Boyce Bible School and the Office of Business Affairs, which was moved from Norton Hall. The renovation of the Carver Building was part of a new campus master plan adopted by the board of trustees in Apr., 1978. This plan called for physical improvements in seminary property over the next 11 years totaling more than $8,000,000.

Living conditions for seminary students also demanded enhancement and enlargement. This was accomplished by the renovation of apartments in Seminary Village and by the construction of the new Springdale Apartment Complex opened in 1978.

A pivotal date for the seminary, as well as the entire Louisville community, was Apr. 3, 1974. A devastating tornado ripped through Louisville, causing extensive damage to buildings and trees on the seminary campus. Campus offices and housing were without heat and light for 10 days, and no classes were held, Apr. 4-22. While injuries to seminary families were minimal, praise for seminary students who assisted nearby neighbors in the Crescent Hill community was widely acknowledged. Damage to seminary property was estimated at $1,000,000.

Academic Life.—Development in the academic programs at Southern Seminary during the 1970s reflected various factors: the general trends in theological education, Southern Seminary's constant attempt to coordinate theoretical and practical knowledge, the diversification of ministerial callings, a desire to make theological education accessible to the noncollege graduate, the attempt to extend theological education beyond the local campus, and a general upgrading of academic excellence in the context of spiritual commitment.

The growing need for specialized programs of study led to three new degree programs. In Apr., 1971, the seminary trustees approved the Doctor of Ministry (D.Min.) degree and authorized the faculty to develop the program for implementation by the fall of 1972. While implemented in 1972 and evolving throughout the decade, the D.Min. has remained an advanced professional degree with emphasis on competency in ministry.

For a number of years the Doctor of Theology (Th.D.) was the highest degree awarded by the School of Theology. In 1971 the Welch Report ranked Southern Seminary's Th.D. among the 16 leading established programs in graduate theological education in the United States and Canada. Beginning in 1974-75, the Ph.D. replaced the Th.D. as the graduate degree in theology with a focus on research and teaching. While not an entirely new degree program, the Ph.D. contained features not present in the older Th.D. program. Among these was a requirement that Ph.D. students had to do a part of their graduate seminars in a university setting.

In 1978 the trustees approved a third new degree, the Master of Divinity in Religious Education (M.Div./R.E.). Designed for church staff members other than pastors, this three-year program required more intensive biblical, historical, and theological studies than the traditional Master of Religious Education (M.R.E.) degree. The M.Div./R.E. has proven to be a very popular degree program.

In the fall of 1979 the M.Div. degree program underwent revision in order to keep pace with the trend of vocational specialization in ministry. Six new "tracks" were built into the M.Div. degree. These six tracks were (1) pastor, (2) campus ministry, (3) church and denominational staff ministry, (4) chaplain-pastoral counselor ministry, (5) missions ministry, and (6) Christian social ministry. Also a seminary-wide course entitled "Formation for Christian Ministry" was required for students in all three schools—Theology, Religious Education, and Church Music—of the seminary. The "Track" system within the M.Div. degree accented

Southern's interest in the various forms of ministry while the "Formation" course stressed the spiritual development required of all types of ministers.

A major new development occurred at Southern Seminary in 1973 when the board of trustees authorized the initiation of Boyce Bible School. Offering a diploma program and designed for students who have not completed college or seminary degree programs, Boyce Bible School provides a comprehensive education for women and men preparing for effective ministry in Southern Baptist churches. Since its beginning the school has had three directors: Allen W. Graves, James Ryan, and David Q. Byrd. The school is named for James P. Boyce (q.v. I), first president of Southern Seminary and one committed to seeing that the seminary would provide educational opportunity for noncollege graduates.

Southern Seminary also acted in the 1970s to extend its ministry beyond the local campus in Louisville. In Apr., 1977, the trustees voted to revise and reactivate a long-standing relationship with the Nigerian Baptist Theological Seminary in Ogbomosho, Nigeria. The new relationship called for Southern Seminary to grant degrees to students who complete specific academic programs offered by the Nigerian Seminary. Acting to extend itself within the states as well as overseas, Southern Seminary began, in 1979, to offer off-campus credit courses at Carson-Newman College in Jefferson City, TN. Under the leadership of Provost Roy L. Honeycutt, Jr., Southern Seminary also coordinated a new program in off-campus theological education for all six Southern Baptist seminaries. Expected to be fully operational by Aug., 1981, this new program is designed to meet the need for theological training in pioneer areas of the SBC and is motivated by the spirit of Bold Mission Thrust.

Two other areas marked the enrichment and intensification of the academic dimension of Southern Seminary in the 1970s. One related to the Boyce Centennial Library which in 1974 became a charter member of SOLINET. SOLINET (Southeastern Library Network) is a computerized library cataloging project which makes available the catalog listing of every item in the libraries of the 100 member schools. Southern Seminary became one of six theological schools with access to the facilities of SOLINET. In 1975 Andrew B. Rawls became audiovisual librarian at Southern Seminary. The first person to hold the position on a full-time basis, he has supervised the seminary's rapidly growing instructional resources in electronic and film media and materials. The J. Graham Brown Foundation of Louisville provided a $100,000 grant to enlarge and improve the instructional media facilities of the Boyce Library in 1979.

Finally, endowed chairs of instruction, which multiplied in the 1970s, have enriched the total seminary life. These new endowed chairs and their dates of beginning are as follows: the War-ren P. Sewell Visiting Professorship in Pastoral Studies, 1971; the J. Clyde Turner Visiting Professorship in Christian Preaching, 1974; the V. V. Cooke Chair of Organ, 1975; the Gaines S. Dobbins Chair of Church Administration, 1976; the Victor and Louise Lester Chair of Christian Preaching, 1978; the Ellen Edens McCall Chair of Prayer and Personal Devotion, 1978; the Carolyn King Ragan Chair of Church Music, 1979; the Lawrence and Charlotte Hoover Chair of Pastoral Care, 1979; the John L. and Margaret H. Slaughter Visiting Professorship in Christian Theology, 1979; the C. F. Barry Chair of Christian Communication, 1980; and the C. J. and Lillian B. Godsey Visiting Professorship in New Testament Interpretation, 1980.

Financial Development.—A crucial area for Southern Seminary, as with all theological education in America, in the 1970s was that of escalating costs. The SBC Executive Committee announced in Feb., 1971, that the 1972 allocations to the denomination's boards and agencies for operating expenses would be frozen at the 1971 level. This placed the seminary's financial situation at a critical point and impacted faculty-staff salaries, as well as general services to students and alumni.

While the decade began with a gloomy financial picture, various efforts were made throughout the decade to improve the situation. Students began a Student Development Council while the seminary organized the Century Club and the John A. Broadus Society. The Century Club is a published list of friends and alumni who contribute $100 or more per year. The John A. Broadus Society is a similar list of persons giving over $1,000 per year.

A swelling enrollment in the student body led the seminary to launch a Resources for Excellence Campaign with a $10,000,000 goal. Begun in 1977, this effort was directed at individuals, foundations, and corporations. By 1980 the goal had been surpassed.

Administration.—By Sep., 1980, Duke K. McCall began his 30th year as president of Southern Seminary. Under his leadership, and in response to a recommendation from an accrediting committee, a new administrative structure had been implemented in Aug., 1972. The new plan called for three vice-presidents to supervise the noninstructional operations of the seminary and a provost to coordinate the academic life of the three schools of Theology, Religious Education, and Music. Badget Dillard was named vice-president for business affairs; Wesley M. Pattillo, vice-president for development; and Allen W. Graves, vice-president for student affairs.

William E. Hull became the seminary's first provost, serving simultaneously in that capacity and as dean of the School of Theology. In 1975 Hull resigned to assume the pastorate of the First Baptist Church of Shreveport, LA. Roy L. Honeycutt, Jr., formerly dean at Midwestern Baptist Theological Seminary, became dean of the School of Theology in 1975 and provost of the seminary in 1976. While the provost has served as the chief academic officer of the seminary, each of the three schools has been headed by its own dean. William E. Hull, 1969-75, Roy L. Honeycutt, Jr., 1975-80, and Walter B. Shurden, 1980- , have served successively as dean of the School of Theology. Ernest J. Loessner, 1970-73, Ralph C. Atkinson, 1973-76, Allen W. Graves, 1976-80, and Jack H. McEwen, 1980- , have served as dean of the School of Religious Education. Forrest H. Heeren served as dean of the School of Church Music, 1953-81. Milburn Price, formerly chairman of the Department of Music at Furman University, succeeded Heeren in 1981.

Tensions at the seminary between faculty and administration appeared in the early 1970s. Various factors, intensified by the resignation of Wayne E. Oates from the faculty, led President McCall to suggest a study by the Faculty Affairs Committee of the elements contributing to faculty morale. In a report to the seminary faculty, Nov. 26, 1973, this committee highlighted the problem of "low faculty morale." Attributing morale problems to administrative philosophy and style and a faculty feeling of noninvolvement in decision-making processes, the committee's report was approved by the seminary faculty.

Responding to the report, the president requested the faculty to name an Ad Hoc Advisory Committee to the President to make a thorough study of the morale situation. Over a period of several months the Ad Hoc Committee made specific proposals relating to increased participation of the faculty in seminary governance, including the use of a search committee process for employing new faculty. After sensitive and extensive negotiations, the problems were brought to a satisfactory conclusion by the close of academic year 1973-74. The latter half of the decade has been marked by high faculty morale, openness of communication between faculty and administration, and a genuine affirmation of the administrative leadership.

In the closing years of the decade, the SBC was embroiled in the so-called inerrancy debate. A controversy regarding the interpretation and nature of Holy Scripture, the debate had significant political overtones for the Convention. Because of President Duke K. McCall's leadership in opposing the tactics of the inerrancy advocates, Southern Seminary was very much at the center of the conflict. In an effort to open communication between the seminary and its critics, McCall and Southern Seminary hosted a Heart of America Bible Conference on the Louisville campus in 1979. Little, if any, progress was made at the conference in settling the controversial issue. The debate continued into 1981 with McCall remaining a prominent personality in the Convention-wide struggle.

Growing Areas of Interest.—Among the many developing areas of interest at the seminary in the 1970s, two, in particular, stand out. They are (1) student ministries and (2) women in theological education.

In 1973-74 a program was inaugurated at Southern Seminary to send seminary students to serve as foreign missionaries during the summers. Continuing throughout the decade, three goals have dominated the summer missions program: (1) to aid in specific ways with mission points overseas, (2) to increase the missions consciousness at the seminary, and (3) to provide specific opportunities for seminary students to discern God's will for their lives regarding a missionary career.

Students have also been engaged in mission outreach in the United States through a summer church extension ministry. Revival teams have been organized and dispatched under the leadership of evangelism professor Lewis Drummond. In cooperation with the state convention in Michigan, a weekend van ministry had developed. Several students travel together in a van each weekend to serve in pioneer work among Michigan Southern Baptists.

The emerging new role of women in theological education and in Christian ministry was reflected at Southern Seminary in the 1970s. Whereas women have traditionally been enrolled in the School of Religious Education, an increasing number have entered the M.Div. degree program in the School of Theology. By 1980 five women were serving on the faculty of the School of Religious Education. Two women, Elaine Dickson and Elizabeth Lambert, served as dean of student affairs at the seminary.

Fay Woody Leach became the first woman to receive a doctorate from the seminary in Dec., 1970. She received the Ed.D. from the School of Religious Education. By Dec., 1980, three women had received the Ph.D., and a growing number of women were entering that degree program. Marie Mathis, a longtime president of Woman's Missionary Union, SBC, 1956-63, 1969-75, and a former member of its staff, 1963-69, received the seminary's E. Y. Mullins Denominational Service Award in 1971. The first woman to receive that award, she was also the first woman ever to deliver the commencement address at Southern Seminary.

Faculty.—Faculty members in order of election since 1970 were:
McSwain, Larry Lee (1940-), 1970- ; Simmons, Paul Dewayne (1936-), 1970- ; Clinard, Gordon (1922-73), 1970-72; Allerton, Thomas D. (1935-) 1972-75; Vaughn, W. Judson (1943-), 1972-73; Beasley-Murray, George R. (1916-), 1973- ; Drummond, Lewis A. (1926-), 1973- ; Tupper, E. Frank (1941-), 1973- ; Atkinson, Ralph C., Jr. (1934-), 1973-76; Culpepper, R. Alan (1946-), 1974- ; Rowatt, G. Wade, Jr. (1943-), 1974- ; Guinn, G. Earl (1912-), 1975- ; Honeycutt, Roy L., Jr. (1926-), 1975- ; Smith, G. Douglas (1939-), 1975- ; Hawn, Charles M. (1948-), 1975-77; Thornton, Edward E. (1925-), 1975- ; Leonard, Bill J. (1946-), 1975- ;

Hartsell, Robert L. (1930-   ), 1975-78; Perkey, Bart N. (1945-   ), 1975-78; Munro, Joyce Huth (1946-   ), 1975-78; Bennett, F. Russell (1929-   ), 1975-   ; Easley, E. Lucie (1950-   ), 1976-   ; Blevins, James Lowell (1936-   ), 1976-   ; Cunningham, Richard B. (1932-   ), 1976-   ; Shurden, Walter B. (1937-   ), 1976-   ; Stassen, Glen Harold (1936-   ), 1976-   ; Hardee, J. Ralph (1935-   ), 1976-   ; Davis, Olivia Temple (1943-   ), 1976-77; Boud, Ronald E. (1941-   ), 1976-   ; Lester, Andrew D. (1939-   ), 1977-   ; Garland, David E. (1947-   ), 1977-   ; Rogers, Robin Kent (1947-   ), 1977-   ; Turner, Ronald A. (1946-   ), 1977-   ; Tuck, William Powell (1934-   ), 1978-   ; Harton, R. Michael (1946-   ), 1978-   ; Chapman, Kathryn (1940-   ), 1978-   ; Aleshire, Daniel O. (1947-   ), 1978-   ; Jones, Boyd M. (1953-   ), 1978-   ; Bailey, Raymond H. (1938-   ), 1979-   ; Gerbrandt, Carl (1940-   ), 1979-   ; Omanson, Roger L. (1946-   ), 1979-   ; George, Timothy F. (1950-   ), 1979-   ; White, Ernest O. (1929-   ), 1980-   ; Borchert, Gerald L. (1932-   ), 1980-   ; McEwen, Jack (1927-   ), 1980-   ; Borchert, Doris (1936-   ), 1980-   ; Garland, Diana (1950-   ), 1980-   ; Bates, Carl E. (1914-   ), 1981-   ; Price, J. Milburn (1938-   ), 1981-   .

See also BOYCE BIBLE SCHOOL.

WALTER B. SHURDEN

SOUTHERN BAPTISTS, GROWTH OF, (cf. Growth of Southern Baptists, Vols. I, III). Southern Baptists grew from a membership of 351,951 in 1845 to 13,606,808 in 1980. The number of churches increased from 4,126 in 1845 to 35,831 in 1980. From 1969 to 1980 Southern Baptists increased by 2,117,195 members and 1,496 churches and continued to be the largest Protestant group in the United States.

Sunday School enrollment increased from 7,418,067 in 1969 to 7,433,405 in 1980. Church Training enrollment stood at 1,795,619 in 1980, compared to 2,343,595 in 1969. Woman's Missionary Union enrollment stood at 1,100,043 in 1980 compared to 1,291,221 in 1969, and Brotherhood enrollment increased from 430,339 to 495,666 in the same period. Vacation Bible School enrollment was 3,648,225 in 1969 compared to 3,338,824 in 1980. In 1969, 18,074 churches reported a music ministry; by 1980 the number had increased to 27,302 churches with an enrollment of 1,527,397. In 1979, 17,964 churches reported having a church library compared to 14,140 churches in 1969.

Another indication of the growth of Southern Baptists was the increase in total gifts and mission gifts through the churches. Total gifts in 1969 were $809,608,812 of which $133,224,335 was reported as mission gifts. In 1980 total gifts were $2,315,149,038 including $401,499,506 in mission gifts. Total per capita gifts increased from $70.46 in 1969 to $170.15 in 1980.

Cooperative Program receipts in 1980 were $207,284,435, an increase from $78,220,474 in 1969. Of these receipts, $71,762,635 was distributed to Convention-wide causes compared to $27,433,440 in 1969.

The home and foreign mission programs experienced tremendous growth in the 1970s. Foreign missionary personnel increased from 2,490 in 1969 to 3,059 in 1980. The Lottie Moon Offering increased from $15,297,558 in 1969 to $40,597,113 in 1979. The number of home missionaries increased from 2,235 in 1969 to 2,970 in 1980.

The Sunday School Board is responsible for 16 programs of work, including the operation of 65 book stores and two Convention-wide conference centers at Ridgecrest and Glorieta. Approximately 71,000,000 copies of periodicals were published in 1980 compared to 81,000,000 in 1969.

Southern Baptist seminaries reported a total enrollment of 11,634 in 1980-81 plus 10,554 enrolled through seminary extension centers, and property valued at $80,027,441. In 1969 enrollment was 12,041 and property was valued at $48,147,260.

Forty-six Southern Baptist senior colleges and universities reported a total enrollment of 139,753 in 1980 compared with 83,699 enrolled in 43 schools in 1969. Property value increased from $403,351,213 in 1969 to $776,722,176 in 1980.

Twenty Baptist junior colleges, academies, and Bible schools reported a total enrollment of 13,735 in 1980 with property valued at $84,290,377; in 1969, 14,403 were enrolled in 23 schools with property valued at $59,335,936.

Twenty-three Southern Baptist hospitals reported a total bed capacity of 11,966 in 1980. In 1969, 43 hospitals had a total bed capacity of 14,920.

Thirty-two Southern Baptist retirement facilities reported a capacity of 4,728 with residents totaling 4,170 in 1980. Forty-six Baptist children's homes (main and branch) reported 2,817 residents, plus 2,158 children living off campus. In 1969 Southern Baptists had 16 homes for aged and 27 children's homes.

Southern Baptists had 34 state conventions in 1980, an increase from 30 in 1969, with churches in all 50 states and in Canada.

JEAN HUDGENS

SOUTHERN CALIFORNIA CENTER OF GOLDEN GATE BAPTIST THEOLOGICAL SEMINARY. See GOLDEN GATE BAPTIST THEOLOGICAL SEMINARY, SOUTHERN CALIFORNIA CENTER OF.

SOUTHWEST BAPTIST COLLEGE (II, III). The years 1969-79 constituted a period of growth for the college in program development, administrative reorganization, student enrollment, and building construction.

Inaugurated in 1968, James L. Sells served as president until the fall of 1979, when he was named chancellor and Harlan Spurgeon became president. Under Sells' leadership the college received full accreditation in Apr., 1970, by the North Central Accreditation Association. In 1972 the college began to reorganize the academic area into schools with the formation of the Courts Redford School of Theology and Church Vocations. Other schools followed: Music and Fine Arts; Business, Education, and Social Sciences; and Arts and Sciences. Programs in church recreation, church music, and evangelism also developed in the mid-1970s.

In 1977 the Marietta Meller's Dining Commons, which seats 600, was completed on the Shoffner Campus. The Parents' Association Dining Room in the same structure provides facilities for smaller dining functions. The Mabee Chapel, which seats 1,300, was completed and dedicated, Nov. 18, 1979. The building includes a large classroom which can be divided into two rooms seating about 60 persons each, a preaching laboratory with facilities for videotaping, stage shop and dressing areas, and the Redford School of Theology complex. The stage can handle complete dramatic, worship, and musical events. A bell tower was added in front of the chapel in the winter of 1979. Both the dining commons and the chapel were part of the second century emphasis initiated in 1973.

As 1979 ended, Southwest was completing plans for two additional structures to be built in the early 1980s—a classroom and administration complex to house the Education for Business and Community Leadership program and a World Missions and Evangelism Conference Center.

In 1978-79 the college had an enrollment of 1,559. In the May, 1979, commencement, 257 persons graduated. In 1980 Southwest had 72 full-time faculty members and 20 part-time teachers. Approximately 30 percent had earned doctorates. The Estep Library contained a total of 73,300 volumes. The college consists of 123 acres on two campuses and a total of 33 buildings, with a net worth of $14,959,504. The total budget for 1978-79 was $5,262,935.

H. K. NEELY

SOUTHWESTERN BAPTIST THE-OLOGICAL SEMINARY (II, III). The most impressive development in the life of Southwestern Seminary during the past decade has been the growth of the student body. The cumulative enrollment for the school year 1970-1971 was 2,171, which was only 75 students more than the previous year. However, during the 1970s the enrollment virtually doubled. The total cumulative enrollment for 1979-80 was 4,336. All three schools experienced substantial growth. Enrollment in the School of Theology rose from 1,384 to 2,035; the School of Religious Education from 577 to 1,501; and the School of Church Music from 210 to 399. Off-campus study centers established by the seminary during this period, with 299 students in 1979-80, account for only a small fraction of the increase. Much of the history of Southwestern during these years revolves around the attempt to keep

pace with the multiplicity of needs presented by such rapid growth in the student load.

Curriculum.—While the three-school structure of the seminary has remained unchanged, the curricula have undergone extensive revision. After a three-year curriculum study in the School of Theology, the M.Div. degree program was changed in 1972 to allow more flexibility for the individual student. Eighteen semester hours of electives were scheduled for the third year, out of a total of 88 needed for graduation. Students were first admitted to a new doctoral degree program in the fall of 1972. The new degree, designated Doctor of Ministry, was intended to supplement the basic theological degree by a program of study designed to develop skills for ministry informed by the classical theological disciplines.

Since its introduction, the curriculum for the D.Min. has undergone some revision while retaining its basic distinctives. The program requires 24 hours of seminars, on and off the campus, and the successful completion of a professional project.

With the adoption of the D.Min. degree, the Th.M. was discontinued and the faculty began a careful review of the Th.D. degree. As a result of this study, a newly designed Ph.D. replaced the traditional Th.D. The new degree was tailored specifically for those whose vocational goals called for knowledge and experience in research and teaching in the theological disciplines. Complementary study on the graduate level in a university setting was also incorporated into this degree program.

The three schools of Southwestern are not as separate as they might appear. Students enrolled in one of the schools are required to take prescribed courses in each of the other schools. Certain degrees are combined degrees, the programs of which have been structured by the faculties of the school involved. The seminary catalog currently lists two such degrees: M.Div. with church music concentration and M.R.E. with a church music minor. The D.Min. degree is also open to M.R.E. students who meet the requirements of the degree. Each of the three schools provides a special curriculum for a limited number of diploma students.

The off-campus study centers are entirely new to Southwestern. Southwestern's first center was opened in the fall of 1975 on the campus of Houston Baptist University. A second center followed in 1976 at Oklahoma Baptist University. A third began classes in San Antonio facilities provided by the Mexican Baptist Bible Institute in 1977. These centers are staffed by Southwestern faculty members on a limited schedule of Monday classes only.

Faculty.—By necessity, the faculties of the three schools were forced to augment their forces rapidly in order to meet the demands of the new degree programs, the off-campus study centers, and the greatly enlarged student body. Hence, to the elected faculty the seminary has added guest professors, adjunct teachers, and teaching fellows. By 1980 the School of Theology faculty numbered 48 members, 2 guest professors, 9 adjunct teachers, and 12 teaching fellows. The School of Religious Education counted 21 faculty members, 13 adjunct teachers, and 1 teaching fellow. The School of Church Music listed 20 faculty, 2 guest professors, and 8 teaching fellows. The total teaching staff, including all categories listed above, numbered 136.

In making additions to the faculty, the seminary has attempted to keep faith with Southern Baptists. It seeks to balance the academic and devotional aspects of the seminary's life. Each new faculty member is asked to declare himself in substantial agreement with the doctrinal position of the SBC by signing the seminary's Articles of Faith, which are those adopted by the SBC at Kansas City, MO, in 1963. Each faculty member is also expected to be involved actively in the life of his church and denomination. The measure of this involvement is impossible to overestimate. Members of Southwestern's faculty are constantly in demand in a wide spectrum of denominational activity, such as Sunday School Board consultants, Bible teachers, evangelists, interim pastors, and interim ministers of education and music.

Apparently no segment of denominational life has escaped the impact of Southwestern due to the expertise of the members of its faculty. Faculty members bring to their tasks a backlog of thorough preparation and experience enriched by continuing study. While most faculty members hold at least one degree from Southwestern, many also have earned degrees from some of the major universities and seminaries in the United States and Europe.

A generous sabbatical leave program has made possible postdoctoral studies for tenured faculty in numerous institutions in a variety of cultural settings and countries. The result has been a faculty of increased productivity and recognition. Evidence of this fact is seen in the literary output during the past decade. During these years, faculty members have contributed to numerous Sunday School and Church Training curriculum materials, engaged in two Bible translation projects, translated and edited German monographs, and written textbooks for their own classes in at least a half dozen disciplines. Forty-four faculty publications have been reviewed in the *Southwestern Journal of Theology* during this period. In addition, numerous articles and book reviews by faculty members have appeared in this journal as well as other scholarly publications.

A number of recent activities have honored certain members of the faculty. The first was the publication in 1976 of a *Festschrift, The Lord's Free People,* in honor of Robert A. Baker, professor of church history and member of the faculty since 1942. *The Lord's Free People* has two distinctions: It is the first *Festschrift* ever published by the faculty of the School of Theology, and the essays were all contributed by Baker's former students with the exception of the one written by Baker himself. T. B. Maston, retired professor of Christian ethics, was honored by a *Festschrift* in 1979 which was largely the result of the efforts of his former students.

A new lecture series on preaching and pastoral ministry was inaugurated in 1976 by the trustees in honor of Jesse and Fannie Northcutt. In 1979 Northcutt was named the first E. Hermond Westmoreland professor of preaching.

Fleming Library.—Integral to the academic life of Southwestern is Fleming Library with its holdings of 465,255 items. The library is in reality a complex of libraries and archives. Fleming Library serves as the depository for the Texas Baptist Historical Collection. The Music Library, housed in Cowden Hall, the Audio-Visual Learning Center and the Southern Baptist Curriculum Materials Center, located in Price Hall, are all a part of the library.

The facilities of the library have not been able to meet the increased demands of a burgeoning student body. Plans are now underway to construct an entirely new facility which will provide for the multiplicity of needs which are at present inadequately met. A new library building will also make available additional space for much needed classrooms and offices for faculty and administration.

Administration.—After 20 years at the helm of Southwestern, Robert E. Naylor retired in 1978. President Naylor came to Southwestern as a student in 1928. He graduated in 1932 with his Th.M. degree and his bride of less than two years, the former Goldia Geneva Dalton. From 1941 to 1958 he served on the seminary's board of trustees. At the time of his election to the presidency of Southwestern, Naylor was chairman of the trustees. He was also pastor of Travis Avenue Baptist Church. Thus, he brought to his new position an intimate acquaintance with the seminary and its internal affairs. He provided the seminary with forceful and theologically conservative leadership.

In 1973 the administrative structure of the seminary was changed. The reorganization called for four vice-presidents: public affairs, academic affairs, business affairs, and student affairs. Five major buildings and the J. Howard Williams Student Village apartment complex were constructed under Naylor's leadership. Two of these buildings, the Goldia and Robert Naylor Children's Building, 1973, and the Recreation-Aerobics Center, 1979, were built during the last 10-year period.

Two years before his retirement, Naylor led the trustees to launch a campaign to increase the seminary's endowment by $5,000,000 and provide an additional $3,000,000 for capital needs by 1980. The campaign raised more than $9,000,000 in pledges and gifts.

Russell Hooper Dilday, Jr., became the sixth president of Southwestern on Aug. 1, 1978. Dilday came to the presidency of Southwestern from Second Ponce de Leon Baptist Church in Atlanta, GA, where he had served as pastor since 1969. Both the new president and his wife, the former Betty Doyen, are natives of Texas. Dilday holds two degrees from Southwestern,

SOUTHWESTERN BAPTIST THEOLOGICAL SEMINARY (q.v.), Fort Worth, TX. *Top:* J. Howard Williams Memorial Student Village. One of several housing areas for married and single students. *Bottom:* Recreation-Aerobics Center. Opened in Jan., 1979, the $1,600,000 facility provides recreational and physical fitness programs for students, faculty and staff, and their families.

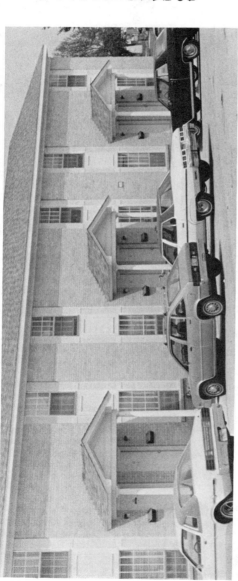

SOUTHWESTERN BAPTIST THEOLOGICAL SEMINARY (*q.v.*), Fort Worth, TX. New Library Center. When completed in July, 1982, this $6,600,000 facility will house the world's largest theological library with more than 700,000 volumes.

including the Ph.D. He also served as alumni president of the Georgia Southwestern Alumni Association and Southwestern's National Alumni Association. President-elect Dilday spent seven months on the campus getting acquainted with his new responsibilities and the most pressing needs of the seminary prior to assuming the reins of the seminary.

Upon taking office, Dilday moved without hesitation to strengthen both the administration and the faculty. A new office, that of executive vice-president, was created in order to increase the efficiency and coordination of various aspects of the administrative life of the seminary. Lloyd Elder was brought from the Baptist General Convention of Texas to serve as the seminary's first executive vice-president. The title of vice-president for academic affairs was changed to academic affairs and provost. Upon Jesse Northcutt's retirement from that post, John P. Newport was invited back to the faculty to assume that position. John Earl Seelig's title was changed from vice-president for public affairs to vice-president for administrative affairs. Wayne Evans remained vice-president for business affairs. With the election of Lawrence Klempnauer as vice-president for student affairs, the roster of vice-presidents was completed in 1980.

As the 1980s dawned under Dilday's leadership, Southwestern's faculty was in the process of accelerated expansion. Dilday brought to the seminary a pastoral understanding of the needs of people as well as that of the academic process. Hence, his administration gave every evidence of dedication both to the highest academic standards and an unswerving support of what Baptists are about in the world today. His sensitivity and identity with the purpose and goals of the SBC will help Southwestern maintain the role in denominational life which it has assumed since its earliest days. Evidence of the far-reaching vision of the new president was found in *The President's Report: One Plus Five* (1979).

Trustees and Advisory Council.—Such an enterprise as Southwestern represents could not begin to fulfill its destiny without strong support groups. Thirty-six trustees elected by the SBC are responsible to the denomination for the overall operation of the seminary. These same trustees also provide a strong source of support for faculty and administration. Since 1959 an Advisory Council, made up of prominent Christian laymen and businessmen, has brought increased acceptance and additional financial undergirding to the seminary in Texas and particularly in the Fort Worth-Dallas metroplex.

Finances.—The cost of seminary education at Southwestern is a major expenditure for the denomination. For example, the new Recreation-Aerobics Center cost $2,219,073. Of this amount, $447,800 came from Cooperative Program funds. The remainder came from a variety of sources, including four local foundations. Without the Cooperative Program the seminary could not operate. The receipts from this source have steadily increased during the past 10 years.

For the 1969-70 school year, the seminary received $1,302,575. The educational and general expenditure for that year reported to the SBC was $2,246,847. The corresponding figures for 1979-80 were: Cooperative Program receipts, $4,115,661; educational and general expenditures, $7,206,826. During the same period the endowment increased from $6,551,731 to $16,638,958 as of Sep. 1, 1979.

Alumni.—Obviously, Southwestern is big business. It resembles a corporate structure in its administrative functions and personnel. However, its success or failure is not measured in terms of capital gains or losses but first, in terms of learning and personal development in preparation for ministry; second, the number of graduates; and third, the quality of service those graduates who minister in the name of Christ render around the world.

No adequate criteria exist by which to measure the effectiveness of the learning process. The diploma or degree earned indicates that the minimal requirements for graduation have been met. Graduates of all three schools in 1969-70 numbered 413. In 1979-80 the number of graduates had risen to 817. The total number graduating during this period was 6,613. This brings the total number of Southwestern graduates from its beginning through July, 1980, to 18,911. When former students are added to the alumni roster, the figure for all students becomes 37,435. Of this number 27,274 were engaged in some form of vocational Christian ministry in 1979. Approximately 50 percent (1,541) of the career missionaries appointed by the Foreign Mission Board received their education at Southwestern.

While Southwestern has always been known for graduates willing to serve in the most demanding and inconspicuous posts either as missionaries or as bivocational ministers, today Southwestern graduates are also prominent in SBC leadership. Four of the six Southern Baptist seminaries are headed by Southwestern graduates. Southwestern continues to make a significant contribution to the life of the Convention and its agencies through its graduates.

W. R. ESTEP

SOUTHWESTERN JOURNAL OF THEOLOGY, THE (II, III). Managing editors have been William L. Hendricks, 1967-71; Leon McBeth, 1971-74; F. B. Huey, Jr., 1975-78; Bert Dominy, 1978-80; and James Brooks, 1981-   . Robert E. Naylor served as editor-in-chief, 1958-79. He was succeeded by Russell H. Dilday.

The format of the journal is thematic. In an effort to meet the needs of students and pastors, as well as teachers, the fall issues have focused on the book of the Bible selected for the January Bible Study emphasis in Southern Baptist churches. Recent editions have been the Letters of John (1970), Job (1971), Galatians (1972), Colossians (1973), Acts (1974), Hosea (1975),

Romans (1976), Exodus (1977), Mark (1978), Ephesians (1979), and Philippians (1980).

The spring issues have been devoted to a wide range of topics such as Stewardship (1971), Prayer (1972), The Ministry Today (1973), Interpreting the Bible (1974), Creative Trends in Ministry (1975), Religion in American Culture (1976), Baptiists Deal with Controversial Issues (1977), Salvation (1978), Christology (1979), Current Issues in New Testament Scholarship (1980), and Current Issues in Old Testament Scholarship (1981).

During the last 10 years, the journal has increased in circulation from 2,200 to 3,000.

BERT DOMINY

SOUTHWIDE BAPTIST DIGEST. See NATIONWIDE BAPTIST DIGEST.

SOWELL, ERMINE BAGBY (b. Sao Paulo, Brazil, July 25, 1881; d. Porto Alegre, Brazil, Aug. 18, 1939). Foreign missionary. The daughter of Anne (*q.v.* I) and W. B. Bagby (*q.v.* I), missionaries to Brazil, she attended Baylor College (B.A., 1903), and was married to Sidney McFarland Sowell (*q.v.* II), missionary to Argentina, Mar. 26, 1906. They had four children: Benjamin, Anne, Maurice, and John. She is buried in the Baptist Cemetery, Porto Alegre, Brazil.

FRANK K. MEANS

SPAIN, MISSION IN (II, III). The end of 1979 found Baptists numbering 7,674 and having contributed more than $1,000,000. Thirty-two missionaries were cooperating with the Spanish Baptist Union, which encouraged self-support on the part of the churches. Several missionary couples were engaged in pioneer evangelism work in cities where previously no Baptist witness existed. In 1978 a five-year plan of evangelism was begun. New work opened in Badajoz and Vigo, and Jose Borras became the first Spaniard elected president of the Spanish Baptist Theological Seminary in Alcobendas near Madrid. Broadcasting work, a music ministry, and work in the Canary Islands were other ministries of Baptists in Spain as the new decade began.

ELISE NANCE BRIDGES

SPANISH BAPTIST PUBLISHING HOUSE (II). See BAPTIST SPANISH PUBLISHING HOUSE.

SPECIAL MISSION MINISTRIES, HOME MISSION BOARD DEPARTMENT OF (III). With the reorganization of the Home Mission Board on Jan. 1, 1971, R. Donald Hammonds succeeded E. Warren Woolf as department director. With that reorganization also came the responsibility of resort missions. Growing interest in volunteer involvement has led the department to provide varied opportunities for the volunteer. The purpose of the department can best be summed up as providing correlation for the discovery of need, recruiting and assigning volunteers in missions in support of other HMB programs and providing leadership resources and personnel for resort missions, special events with mission opportunity, and student work in newer convention areas.

R. DONALD HAMMONDS

SPRING MEADOWS CHILDREN'S HOME (II, III). In 1969 J. D. Herndon, superintendent of the home since 1959, became director of development for the Kentucky Baptist Board of Child Care. In 1970 new administrative offices were built on the Spring Meadows campus to house the central administrative portion of the Kentucky Baptist Board of Child Care. Superintendents of the home have included George Gray, 1970-71; Robert Elliott, 1972-74; Wayne Crosby, 1974-76; and Jesse Hatfield, 1977- .

The program has evolved over the years in response to the needs of youth and children of Kentucky. Initially caring for dependent, orphaned children, today's program focuses on teenagers from broken or troubled homes. In 1976 the Board of Child Care adopted a 10-year long-range plan to ensure a program that continues to provide a relevant ministry.

WILLIAM E. AMOS

SPRING STREET USA. A nationally syndicated "religious variety" television series of 34 shows launched by the Home Mission Board in 1973. The program, deriving its name from the HMB's Atlanta Spring Street address, was produced cooperatively by the HMB, responsible for show content, and the Radio and Television Commission, responsible for production and distribution. The show format included music by the 12-member group, "Spring Street Singers," guest interviews, and a message by Kenneth Chafin, program host and former HMB evangelism secretary. Buryl Red composed and directed much of the music. Funding shortages forced production to stop in 1975.

C. B. HOGUE

SPRINGER, RUDOLPH ARDEN (b. Midlothian, TX, Aug. 2, 1905; d. Natchez, MS, Apr. 1, 1973). Denominational leader. Son of George Andrew and Elizabeth (Busby) Springer, farmers, he married Margaret Ward, Aug. 3, 1925. Their children were Jeanine and Diane. He began denominational work in 1923 as young people's worker and financial secretary at Cliff Temple Baptist Church, Dallas, TX. From 1928 to 1938, he served as educational director for three Texas Baptist churches. He became treasurer of the Baptist General Convention of Texas, July 1, 1938, and served in this capacity until his retirement, Dec. 31, 1970. During part of this time, 1938-45, he also served as Brotherhood secretary for Texas.

Springer received honorary degrees from East Texas Baptist College (L.L.D., 1949) and the

University of Corpus Christi (L.L.D., 1959). He is buried at Dallas, TX.

JAY L. SKAGGS

SRI LANKA, MISSION IN. This island located off the southern tip of India was known as Ceylon when Baptist work was introduced by the Baptist Missionary Society of London in 1812. Its name was changed to the Republic of Sri Lanka in 1972, although political independence was received from England in 1948. In 1977 a Southern Baptist missionary couple serving in Thailand was invited to serve fraternally in a consultant role in church development to the Baptists of Sri Lanka. Another couple came later. By the end of 1980, there were 22 Baptist churches with a total of 2,000 Baptists in the country.

JOY SOUTHER CULLEN

ST. KITTS, MISSION IN. These two islands, St. Kitts and Nevis, are part of the Leeward Islands and lie between the Caribbean Sea and the open Atlantic. William Connor started the Baptist work in St. Kitts in the early 1960s. Today the work includes three Baptist churches and three missions. Southern Baptists have related to the work on St. Kitts through financial gifts and building teams. The Baptist work on Nevis also began in the 1960s.

LESTER C. BOYD

ST. MARTIN, MISSION IN. This Caribbean island is divided between Dutch and French-speaking populations. Baptist churches function on both sides of the island. Southern Baptist missionaries maintained residence there for approximately nine months in 1978-79, but permanent missionary presence was not established.

W. W. GRAVES

ST. VINCENT, MISSION IN. Work on St. Vincent began in Jan., 1977, with the arrival of Donald G. and Maudie (Greenwalt) Overstreet. They initiated Bible studies, and in a few months the first church began meeting regularly on Sundays. Various ministries developed, including a full music program, a prison ministry, and a Sunday School program. The church has grown steadily. Missionaries Larry and Wanda (Seay) Lee assumed responsibility for the work when the Overstreets returned to the USA for medical leave. Orvell and Susan (Ward) Bryant arrived in May, 1978, beginning work in a rural village in the north of the island. The church there has grown steadily, and a new building was under construction in 1980. One of the ministries in this area was a community health program.

ORVELL BRYANT, JR.

STAKELY, SARAH JESSIE DAVIS (b. Richmond County, GA, Jan. 23, 1861; d. Montgomery, AL, June 6, 1929). Woman's Missionary Union and civic leader. The daughter of Sarah Ann and William H. Davis, a pastor, she attended Southern Female College, LaGrange, GA (A.B., 1881). On Feb. 15, 1882, she married Charles A. Stakely (q.v. II). She bore two sons, Davis Fonville and Charles, Jr., and three daughters, Anne Kilpatrick, Frances Sloan, and Flora McIver.

Active in WMU work, Stakely was fourth president of the Convention-wide organization, 1899-1903. Later she served as president of Alabama WMU, 1908-20. A charter member of the Daughters of the American Revolution, she was chaplain general in 1896 and was a lifelong member. In Montgomery she was a member of the No Name Literary Club. She is buried at Montgomery, AL.

LEE N. ALLEN

STANDARDS OF EXCELLENCE (II). See ACHIEVEMENT GUIDES.

STARK, EARL LEE (b. Prescott, KS, Nov. 8, 1899; d. Oklahoma City, OK, Aug. 23, 1973). Pastor and denominational worker. The son of John William and Minnie Coleman Stark, he attended Moody Bible Institute (1922-24) and Oklahoma Baptist University (B.A., 1928). On Nov. 1, 1929, he married Ion Veretta Bell. He served Oklahoma pastorates at Lawton, 1933-37, Woodward, 1937-46, and Holdenville, 1946-53. He was the first field secretary for the Oklahoma Baptist Children's Home, 1954-55, and field secretary for the Oklahoma Baptist Foundation, 1956-68. He is buried in Memorial Park Cemetery, Oklahoma City, OK.

J. M. GASKIN

START (III). See WOMAN'S MISSIONARY UNION, AUXILIARY TO SBC.

STATE EVANGELISM CONFERENCES. See EVANGELISM CONFERENCES, STATE.

STATE EXECUTIVE SECRETARIES, SOUTHERN BAPTIST ASSOCIATION OF. See SOUTHERN BAPTIST ASSOCIATION OF STATE EXECUTIVE SECRETARIES.

STATE SPONSORSHIP OF RELIGION. Few church-state problems have persisted over the past decade more than state sponsorship of religion, particularly religious exercises in public schools. One explanation for the ongoing debate over the proper role of religion in public life focuses on the natural tension between the establishment clause and the free exercise clause of the First Amendment. The nation's founders, concerned about keeping government out of religion in any official sense, sensed the necessity of guaranteeing that no person should be discriminated against for holding any religious view or no religious view at all.

Another explanation centers on the debate over whether the USA is a "Christian" nation. Throughout American history the view has been widely held that the USA is the "new Israel," with an accompanying conviction of the messianic role of America.

Baptists have challenged these popular views as theologically and historically bankrupt. Some of the most influential of the nation's founders recalled unfavorable Old World experiences where church and state were united or closely allied. So they determined that in the new nation there would be no official connection between the two.

Theologically, Baptists and others have argued that no modern state can validly be viewed as ancient Israel's successor. Beyond that, Baptists have resisted any effort to declare the USA a "Christian" nation because of their emphasis on biblical principles such as the freedom of each individual before God, the voluntary nature of true faith, the prophetic role of religion in the life of the nation, and the priesthood of the believer.

Over the past two decades, most of this continuing struggle has focused on religious exercises in public schools. The controversy dates to 1962 and 1963 with two United States Supreme Court decisions, *Engel* v. *Vitale*, 1962, and *Abington School District* v. *Schempp*, 1963. The Court declared that the state may not write and require the saying of prayers nor require the reading of the Bible for devotional purposes.

Both *Engel* and *Schempp*, nevertheless, cite specific examples of what is permissible and consistent with the First Amendment religion clauses. Among the permitted practices are use of the Bible as a reference in teaching secular subjects, use of the Bible for its literary and historic qualities, study of comparative religion and history of religions, recitation of historical documents containing references to God, and singing of anthems that include the composers' professions of faith in God. The Court in summary encouraged "the propriety . . . of the teaching *about* religion, as distinguished from the teaching *of* religion, in the public schools."

Efforts have originated in Congress, nevertheless, to overturn the effect of the Supreme Court rulings. One method chosen by Court opponents has been the proposal of a constitutional amendment to permit "voluntary" prayer in schools and other public buildings. In 1971 such an amendment passed the United States Senate but failed in the House of Representatives when it fell 28 votes short of the necessary two-thirds majority. Although similar constitutional amendments have been introduced in each Congress since then, proponents have failed thus far. Another device opponents of the Court's prayer and Bible reading decisions have attempted to use is to remove the issue from the jurisdiction of federal courts.

In a number of other legal tests during the 1970s, federal courts, including the Supreme Court, declined to go further in declaring unconstitutional other expressions of piety in the public sphere. Atheist Madalyn Murray O'Hair, for example, failed in her legal challenges to forbid astronauts from reading the Bible and praying publicly from space; to eliminate the phrase, "so help me God," from judicial oaths; and to remove the motto, "In God We Trust," from United States coins and currency.

A federal district court in Richmond, VA, ruled in 1974 that invocations and benedictions at public school graduation exercises do not violate the prohibition against an establishment of religion. This conclusion was similar to that reached two years earlier by a federal district court in Pennsylvania on grounds that attendance at such ceremonies is voluntary.

At least two cases during the decade established the right of states or local school boards to provide for a period of voluntary silent meditation as part of a daily routine in public schools.

In cases involving religious symbols in public places, court rulings held in 1976 that it is permissible to display a cross on city property and, in 1979, that schools may display nativity scenes during the Christmas season as examples of a common religious and cultural heritage.

STAN L. HASTEY

STETSON UNIVERSITY (II, III). In 1970 John E. Johns became president after serving for several months as acting president. He served until 1976, when he resigned to become president of Furman University. George R. Borders, vice-president for student affairs, served as chief administrative officer until July, 1977, when Pope A. Duncan became president. Johns left the university with no financial deficits and a small surplus. Despite inflation, under Duncan's leadership the university ended the decade with new buildings, salary increases, and plans for a fundraising campaign. Gifts to Stetson through the Florida Baptist Convention increased from $397,054 in 1969 to $661,231 in 1979. Total student enrollment reached a record high in 1979 of 3,009.

The physical plant expanded with the completion in 1974 of the Edmunds Activity Center, at a cost of $1,650,000, with a seating capacity of 4,300 for athletic events, concerts, and convocations. The renovation of Flagler Hall has been completed. At a cost of almost $600,000, the university improved Stover Theater, is completely renovating DeLand Hall, and has acquired a new building to house the Gillespie Museum of Minerals. A new classroom building was erected at the College of Law at St. Petersburg, and the space and acquisitions at the law library have been sharply increased.

Total enrollment at Stetson remained steady during the 1970s, although requirements for admission have been raised slightly. Tuition costs have increased, but with more than $2,000,000 annually in financial aid to the students, the load has not been crushing.

The Florida Baptist Convention and Stetson University cooperate closely on many fronts. Stetson's Extension Division of Christian Education offers a variety of courses on the Bible, church history, and theology to a large number of churches throughout the state. The teachers involved in this program are invited to the campus each year for a conference and workshop, and a Baptist Leadership Conference is held at Stetson each year. Stetson regularly assists churches through student evangelistic teams and vocational guidance programs for pastors and high school guidance counselors. The Religion Department is deeply and constantly involved in a variety of church and convention activities.

Stetson's School of Music began the decade with the new facilities of Presser Hall, dedicated in 1970. Many of the young men and women who become professional music directors in the churches of Florida and elsewhere are trained by the School of Music. Graduates from the school also join the faculties of high schools and community colleges in Florida. Each year, in cooperation with the Florida Baptist Convention, the School of Music holds a Church Music workshop. Enrollment in the school has almost doubled since the low point in the 1960s, and two new faculty members have been added.

Stetson's physical education and athletic programs have grown considerably, especially for young women, since the Edmunds Center was opened in 1974. Stetson's basketball, baseball, and women's tennis teams have competed successfully with some of the best teams in the country.

The School of Business Administration grew in enrollments and in public esteem during the 1970s. The university's weakest point remains its lack of a large income-producing endowment. The present administration is making plans to remedy this problem.

GILBERT L. LYCAN

STEWARDSHIP COMMISSION, SBC (III). Growth characterized the commission in the 1970s. The staff tripled, and the operational budget increased from $250,000 in 1970 to $1,554,000 in 1980.

The commission achieved greater acceptance and stability, partly through some of the tests made of the agency. In 1972 and 1973 the SBC reconsidered whether the commission was a viable SBC agency. At both annual SBC meetings, an overwhelming majority voted against a recommendation to dissolve the commission.

Merrill D. Moore, who had been executive director-treasurer of the commission since its formation, retired in 1971. His successor, James V. Lackey, resigned as director after two years in that office. In early 1974, A. R. Fagan became the third executive director-treasurer of this young agency.

Several significant developments in the commission's relationships occurred during the 1970s. One of the most important was the cultivation of relationships with persons responsible for stewardship promotion in the various state conventions. These state convention stewardship promotion persons bear their own expenses in meeting with the commission staff four times a year for detailed work on the production of materials. These materials therefore reflect the thinking of a broad perspective of Southern Baptist life.

Another development has been that of a strong supportive role to the work of the foundations in the Convention. In this relationship the commission staff has become a resource to these foundations for the production of promotional materials which they use across the Convention.

Annually, the commission provides a seminar for the staff of the foundations and for development officers of Southern Baptist institutions. The seminar brings together program personnel with expertise in estate planning, tax regulations, promotional techniques, and management of investments. These seminars are planned primarily to upgrade the skills of persons in these areas of ministry.

In the 1970s the commission's work in each of its three program areas grew statistically at a rapid pace. In 1970 funds raised for capital projects were $2,119,000. In 1979 the amount was $30,251,151, with a total for the decade of $127,215,099. In stewardship development, total church gifts in 1970 were $850,000,000, while in 1979 they reached $2,222,000,000, a growth of 161.41 percent. Cooperative Program giving experienced a growth of 130.35 percent from $80,000,000 in 1970 to $184,281,000 in 1979.

See also STEWARDSHIP PROMOTION: THE GREAT CHALLENGE PROGRAM; STEWARDSHIP SEMINARS, NATIONAL; TOGETHER WE BUILD.

A. R. FAGAN

STEWARDSHIP PROMOTION: THE GREAT CHALLENGE PROGRAM. A local church budget project which lets church members help decide the direction of their church's ministries. Its use, beginning in 1975, fulfilled the need for an effective budget promotion program for small and mid-size churches.

The program was developed and tested in 1974 primarily by E. Stanley Williamson (q.v.), director of stewardship development for the Stewardship Commission, SBC. Pilot programs conducted that year in the Northwest Baptist Convention and the Arizona Southern Baptist Convention proved successful. In 1975 the Great Challenge Program was part of a special stewardship program in the Baptist State Convention of Michigan. Since then eight other state conventions have used it during major year-long stewardship emphases. By 1979, 13 additional state conventions had incorporated it into their ongoing stewardship promotion.

The three-Sunday program features biblical preaching by the pastor, stewardship testimonies by selected laypersons, distribution of stewardship tracts, and the preparation and adoption of the church's budget. The main activity is an informal fellowship dinner program directed by a trained leader from outside the church.

During the dinner program, church members select priorities for the upcoming budget year.

They also suggest a giving goal for the new year and indicate the percentage of their church's income they would like to see given to missions through the Cooperative Program. The program concludes with members making giving commitments on unsigned cards. All this information is processed and announced during the program. These results are forwarded to the budget committee as it completes its work on the proposed budget.

ERNEST D. STANDERFER

STEWARDSHIP SEMINARS, NATIONAL. Three national stewardship seminars held in the 1970s provided in-depth Bible study that has shaped much of Southern Baptists' recent stewardship teaching and programs. The purpose for the first, held Apr. 27-30, 1971, at Glorieta Baptist Conference Center, was to examine biblical truths concerning the Christian's role in the material world and to discover appropriate responses.

The second seminar was held April 28-May 2, 1975, at Lake Yale Baptist Assembly in Florida. This, too, was a Bible study seminar designed to discover the appropriate Christian understanding of and response to the challenge of the support of missions by studying the biblical teachings on the subject and representative responses in the life of the churches.

Writers for the 1971 and 1975 seminars were selected by the seminar committee, chaired by Michael Speer of the Stewardship Commission, SBC. Approximately two years' preparation and writing time was given to each seminar.

Two writers prepared studies for both of these seminars, J. Morris Ashcraft (Midwestern Baptist Theological Seminary) and Richard B. Cunningham (Golden Gate and Southern Baptist Theological Seminaries). Other writers for 1971 were: Ray Summers (Baylor University), Jack Taylor (pastor, San Antonio, TX), J. Leo Green (Southeastern Baptist Theological Seminary), James Leo Garrett, Jr. (Southern Seminary), Lory Hildreth (pastor, Texarkana, TX), J. Henry Parker (pastor, Orlando, FL), Brooks H. Wester (pastor, Hattiesburg, MS), H. Franklin Paschall (pastor, Nashville, TN), Cecil A. Ray (Stewardship Division, Baptist General Convention of Texas), and Jerry Horner (Southwest Baptist College).

Other writers for 1975 were: Clyde T. Francisco (Southern Seminary), Lee Gallman (Samford University), L. Jack Gray (Southwestern Baptist Theological Seminary), Albert L. Cardwell (pastor, Macon, GA), C. Penrose St. Amant (Baptist Theological Seminary, Ruschlikon, Switzerland), Franklin D. Pollard (pastor, Dallas, TX), Grady C. Cothen (Sunday School Board), John Bunn (Campbell College), Daniel H. Holcomb (Oklahoma Baptist University), Harold S. Songer (Southern Seminary), and James E. Tull (Southeastern Seminary).

Studies from the first seminar were published in a book entitled *Resource Unlimited* (1972), edited by William L. Hendricks. *Mission Unlim-*

ited (1976), edited by J. Morris Ashcraft, combined the papers from the second seminar. Approximately 57,000 copies of the two volumes were distributed to pastors by the Stewardship Commission and participating state conventions.

The third seminar was held April 26-30, 1976, at Ridgecrest Baptist Conference Center. Its purpose was to examine the truths discovered in the two previous seminars and how to apply these truths to methods that individual Christians, churches, and the denomination could use. The program was organized around five theme assemblies: Prayer, led by Joe Burnett (Charlotte, NC); People, William Clemmons (Louisville, KY); Finances, Charles Tidwell (Fort Worth, TX); Education, Lawson Hatfield (Little Rock, AR); and Church Programs, Keener Pharr (Jacksonville, FL).

These three seminars grew out of the conviction of stewardship leaders that the Bible is the base of authority for a theology of stewardship and mission support. These studies led to new convictions and emphases on stewardship and missions.

See also STEWARDSHIP COMMISSION, SBC.

CECIL A. RAY

STEWARDSHIP TRENDS IN THE 1970s. See GIVING TRENDS IN THE 1970s.

STEWART, JOHN WILLIAM (b. Randolph County, AL, Feb. 20, 1854; d. Birmingham, AL, Oct. 13, 1928). Pastor and denominational leader. The son of Milton Alexander and Jane (Holmes) Stewart, he obtained his early education in Randolph County schools, was graduated from Howard College (B.A., 1884), and studied at The Southern Baptist Theological Seminary, 1884-86. Ordained in 1881, he served part-time Alabama pastorates, 1886-88. In 1888 he became pastor of Evergreen Baptist Church, Evergreen, AL. On Oct. 1, 1891, he married Mary Leigh Crook. They had four children: John W., Jr., Crook, Grace, and Mary.

A founder of Louise Short Baptist Widows and Orphans Home (Alabama Baptist Children's Home), Stewart resigned his pastorate to become first superintendent of the institution, Mar. 8, 1893. He served in this capacity until Jan. 1, 1910, when he moved to Birmingham. In 1917 he was called back as superintendent and remained until 1923. He is buried at Birmingham, AL.

BIBLIOGRAPHY: A. K. Walker and J. O. Colley, *The Story of the Alabama Baptist Children's Home* (1945).

T. W. COLLIER

STILLEY, STEPHEN (b. Somerset County, MD, 1765; d. Saline County, IL, July, 1841). Pioneer preacher. Son of tobacco farmers, John and Grace Sountain Stilley, he married Elizabeth Whitford, Feb. 9, 1791, in Craven County, NC. They had four children: Alfred, Stephen, Jr., Ann, and Rebecca. Moving to Livingston County, KY, he became a charter member of Old Salem Baptist Church in 1805. He crossed into Illinois territory and on July 19, 1806, helped constitute the Big Creek Baptist Church, now known as the First Baptist Church of Elizabethtown, the oldest active Baptist church in Illinois. He is buried on his old home place in Saline County, IL.

RONALD L. NELSON

STONEHAM, JOSEPH DILLARD (b. Fort Worth, TX, May 19, 1903; d. Fletcher, NC, Sep. 29, 1973). Denominational leader. The son of Joseph Dillard and Lurline Bozeman Stoneham, he was converted at age 10. He graduated from Bryan Street High School, Dallas, TX, and the University of Texas (B.B.A.). Stoneham married Frances Frank, June 4, 1937. He was a deacon of First Baptist Church, Dallas, where he lived for 63 years. After serving 12 years as director of Relief and Annuitants Services, Annuity Board, SBC, he retired in 1970. He is buried at Dallas, TX.

LARRY CRISMAN

STROUD, JOSEPH OLIVER (b. Laurens, SC, Aug. 10, 1922; d. Raleigh, NC, Mar. 11, 1977). State convention leader. Son of Jesse and Ella Stroud, farmers, he was educated at North Greenville Junior College (1939-41), Furman University (B.A., 1943), and Southwestern Baptist Theological Seminary (1944-46). Stroud then served four North Carolina Baptist churches as minister of music and education: Florence, Forest City, 1946-48; First Church, Belmont, 1948-51; College Avenue, Lenoir, 1951-54; and First Church, Statesville, 1954-56. On Apr. 1, 1956, he became the first director of the Church Music Department, Baptist State Convention of North Carolina, a position he held until his death.

Stroud married Rachel Garrett on Dec. 19, 1943. They had two children, Claire Ella and Joseph Oliver. He is buried in the Warrior Creek Baptist Church cemetery, Laurens, SC.

CHARLES GATWOOD

STUDENT ACTIVITIES, GOLDEN GATE BAPTIST THEOLOGICAL SEMINARY (II). Student activities are many and varied. Although many are spontaneous or are an outgrowth of academic programs, most activities are planned by the Student Association.

Each spring the Student Association elects its officers. Representatives from all segments of the student body (married students, single students, and students who live off campus), compose the association. Student leaders publish a newspaper called *The Current*, carry out Student Council activities, plan and lead a World Mission Conference, and plan other activities to enhance student life. Such activities include picnics, film series, socials, prayer meetings, town hall meetings, and family enrichment conferences.

The Missions Fellowship, an organization which promotes missions awareness among students, holds monthly meetings featuring missionaries, films, and promoting causes such as world hunger relief.

Seminary Women's Fellowship is an organization of student wives and single women who promote activities for the women of the seminary and their families. Craft fairs, personal growth awareness, and seminary adjustment are activities and concerns addressed by this group. This organization operates a used clothing store on campus with the proceeds going to student scholarships.

Other active groups include a Fine Arts Committee, Hymn Society, and SHARE (Seminary Hunger and Relief Effort). An emphasis on religious drama resulted in the presentation in 1980 of *Everyman*, a medieval morality play.

A prayer line ministry is another student-planned activity. Each semester students sign up to become part of an intercessory prayer ministry. Prayer requests are taken from all over the world.

Students engage in music concerts each semester as part of their academic training. The Concert Choir, Men's Chorus, Oratorio Chorus, and ensembles present other music concerts which are both entertaining and enlightening for the entire community.

Several recreation areas on campus provide students an opportunity to engage in freetime activities. An intramural sports program is promoted by the students.

All standing faculty committees have student members.

F. DANIEL BOLING, JR.

STUDENT ACTIVITIES, NEW ORLEANS BAPTIST THEOLOGICAL SEMINARY (II, III). Student activities at New Orleans Seminary took more definite shape in 1973 when the trustees elected a dean of student affairs. Various aspects of student life previously handled by several members of the faculty and administrative staff were assigned to one office. In 1976 this title was upgraded to vice-president for student affairs. Financial aid for students in the form of grants, loans, and off-campus secular work became the responsibility of this office. State clubs, which earlier met on missionary day, began meeting on a monthly basis. The clubs elected their own officers and worked with representatives from the various state Baptist conventions to promote dissemination of information regarding church work positions in the respective states, and in other ways provided for times of fellowship and inspiration.

Opportunities for involvement in worship and lecture series were provided through chapel services three times a week; the Layne Lectures, Tharp Lectures, and Gurney Lectures; and two missionary days each school year. Spiritual emphasis week, held at the beginning of the third term, was sponsored by the Student Body Association. A mission fellowship met once a month to hear mission speakers, share fellowship, and in other ways encourage missions.

Campus recreational facilities have been improved substantially. The gymnasium floor was replaced with one suitable for skating. A vigorous program of volleyball, basketball, and other gym sports was available. An addition to the gym provided facilities for Ping-Pong, pool, table games, TV lounge, weight lifting, sauna, and whirlpool. Further, four lighted tennis courts and a baseball diamond were on campus. A swimming pool was completed recently, ceramic classes were made available, and students with musical talent could participate in choir programs.

During the 1970s the Student Body Association was an active organization. Each spring the students elected a president, vice-president, and secretary-treasurer, as well as representatives from their particular dormitories and streets of residence. At the election time the students also chose classmates to serve on faculty committees and those who would lead chapel services for two weeks at the end of the semester.

During the period 1970-80, students continued to combine their formal theological training with current involvement in ministry. Many commuted to churches far distant from the seminary. Others served in churches surrounding the seminary and in Home Mission Board ministries in the city. This provided both practical experience and financial help to meet seminary living expenses.

PAUL W. STEVENS

STUDENT ACTIVITIES, THE SOUTHERN BAPTIST THEOLOGICAL SEMINARY (II).

Student activities at Southern Seminary serve to complement and supplement the students' academic experiences. The diversity both in the backgrounds and interests of students was reflected in the diversity of student activities during the decade 1970-79.

Worship was an integral part of student life. In chapel services held three times each week, members of the seminary community gathered for worship led by the faculty, staff, students, pastors, and denominational leaders. Emphasis weeks heightened interest and awareness in special areas. The Francisco Preaching Awards provided opportunities for students to compete in the area of sermon preparation with the winners preaching their sermons in chapel services during student preaching week. During missions emphasis week home and foreign missionaries visited the campus to share experiences and stimulate interest in missions.

Special lectureships brought to the campus each year persons of national and international reputation who presented new ideas and perspectives. Weekly concerts and recitals presented by the students and faculty of the School of Church Music and by special guests helped to broaden student awareness of the musical world.

The student missions committee planned, organized, and administered student missions activities. Several hundred college students with special interests in missions traveled to the campus for a weekend of missions study and activity at each annual missions conference. Beginning in 1974 the committee provided the impetus and financial support for 10 to 15 students to work directly each summer with missionaries on home and foreign fields. Missions activities were primarily self-supporting through student fund-raising efforts, many of which became social events for the seminary community.

The student government association was led by officers elected by members of the student body. The association organized and stimulated many campus activities in accordance with its purposes of building community, heightening social awareness, enhancing communication within the seminary community, and encouraging individual and community spiritual growth. Intramural athletic competition, campus social events, spiritual life retreats, social action efforts, and special interest clubs were particularly popular means for meeting association goals.

Evening school, an important element of campus life for married students, was designed to provide theological, biblical, and practical training for student spouses. An associate-in-ministry certificate was awarded to those spouses who completed a prescribed course of study.

ELISABETH E. LAMBERT

STUDENT ACTIVITIES, SOUTHWESTERN BAPTIST THEOLOGICAL SEMINARY (II, III).

Coming from more than 490 colleges and universities, from 50 states and 6 continents, student enrollment grew from 2,096 in 1969-70 to 4,154 in 1978-79, with a total of 5,773 graduates during this period. The enrollment ratio of men to women continued near 84-16, whereas the married-single ratio changed from 75-25 in 1969 to 67-33 in 1979.

The seminary enlarged the student affairs division to facilitate the total development of student ministers, focusing upon two areas: spiritual development and vocational placement. To provide supportive leadership, three new offices were added: vice-president, chaplain, and Recreation-Aerobics Center director.

In 1978 the $2,000,000 Recreation-Aerobics Center was completed and has an average of 3,700 per week participating in its programs. The indoor-outdoor facility provides for swimming, basketball, volleyball, racquetball, table games, instructional activities, football, soccer, softball, tennis, and jogging tracks.

The student council gives leadership to the activities of the student body and to its 21 student clubs and groups. Initiated in this decade were an annual blood drive, an intercessory prayer ministry, a student-to-student orientation program, and the National Baptist Student Fellowship. Campus opportunities also include chapel services, revivals, mission weeks, lectureships, recitals, banquets, retreats, orientations, films, picnics, publications, and special activities.

The Pioneer Penetration and summer missions programs annually provide service opportunities for more than 200 students in all sections of the United States. Among the 5,500 Southern Baptist churches located within a 200-mile radius of Fort Worth, TX, students fill more than 1,300 staff positions and countless other field work and volunteer assignments. The seminary assists in such placement and in campus and secular employment.

LLOYD ELDER

STUDENT MINISTRY, INTERNATIONAL. See INTERNATIONAL STUDENT MINISTRY.

STUDENT MISSIONS CONFERENCES. See CONFERENCES, STUDENT MISSIONS.

STUDY AND RESEARCH IN THE SBC (III).

I. Background. The past decade has brought an apparent stabilization of the framework within which study and research activity occurs in the SBC.

In the 1960s much planning and execution of research by denominational groups and agencies paralleled the formal program and subprogram structure. The concept of study and research was derived from, or was a part of, the subprogram purview of many agencies. Organizational components and staff assignments existed to implement or support program research needs. Coordination and communication of research concerns were pursued through the Inter-Agency Council's Coordinating Committee, specifically through a standing Study and Research Work Group.

During the 1970s there was a gradual pulling back from the concept of administering and coordinating study and research in close identification with the program and subprogram structure. Early in the decade a reorganization of the Coordinating Committee resulted in the elimination of the work group dealing with research. Both the Home Mission and Sunday School Boards have evolved in their research directions but in recent years have opted for a functional approach to organizing for research. The research effort is centralized in each agency, with the component having primary responsibilities related to corporate directional planning as well as to the operational research needs of programs.

Research activity has emerged in several state conventions, perhaps stimulated by information needs in an era of extreme change and uncertainty. Also, the popularization and enlarged application of computers in a number of conventions have enhanced the interest and possibilities for certain types of research activity.

The Foreign Mission Board has taken steps to develop a limited, but ongoing, research capacity to provide information crucial to its planning and operations.

A void created by the discontinuance of the Coordinating Committee's Study and Research Work Group in the early 1970s likely led to the formation of the Southern Baptist Research Fellowship in 1977.

II. Selected Responsibilities in Research.

RESEARCH SERVICES DEPARTMENT, SUNDAY SCHOOL BOARD. The department is one of the SSB's oldest continuing components. Since its inception in 1920, denominational statistics, research, and selected mailing list responsibilities have claimed the resources and energy of department personnel. A separate system for compiling Vacation Bible School statistics was assigned to the department in 1965. The latest addition to the work areas was the processing of Church Study Course Award requests in 1971.

A major reorganization within the SSB in 1971 led to a lessening of resources allocated to the research segment of the department's work. Nevertheless, a section of five professional researchers was retained and is currently intact, with the replacement of only one person experienced during the period. Stability and heightened experience of this team have made it a valuable asset for the SSB and denomination. The department staff now consists of 22 persons.

During most of the 1970s the department was a part of the Church Services and Materials Division, primarily serving the needs of components in that division. In 1977 the department became part of the Office of Planning and began to focus more on (1) meeting general needs and (2) executing operational research for all board components. Assistance, upon request, to other SBC agencies has continued.

Futures research is a developing area of interest and involvement for the department; personnel have monitored the burgeoning activity and methodological development related to future studies.

A careful process is used for attaching priorities to research project requests received. These priorities are important input into the annual allocation of funds available for research. Traditionally, diverse methodologies are used in conducting research—psychological, sociological, marketing, attitudinal-opinion, and statistical. Projects typically fall into such categories as (1) input to long-range planning (2) product evaluation, (3) publication readership measurement, (4) assessment of new product ideas, (5) program evaluation, (6) customer feedback, and (7) opinion and attitude studies.

Projects in recent years have involved such subjects as characteristics and basic attitudes of Southern Baptists, pastors' family relationships, SSB image among Southern Baptists, test of Equipping Center concept, feasibility of a pastoral care journal, needs of small Sunday Schools, senior adult ministry in the churches, needs for mission education, discipleship leader training evaluation, and profile of black Southern Baptists.

Department personnel maintain relationship and affiliation with groups of other religious research professionals and with general research associations. The SSB, through its research department, jointly sponsored the Church

Membership Study 1980 with four other groups. This effort will culminate in a publication detailing denominational membership, number of churches, and population in each county of the United States. Also, the department has been active in the formation and leadership of the Southern Baptist Research Fellowship.

MARTIN B. BRADLEY

BAPTIST JOINT COMMITTEE ON PUBLIC AFFAIRS. The program of Research Services of the Baptist Joint Committee on Public Affairs was created in 1965 when it became evident that the vast amount of information on church-state relations and public affairs concerns of the denomination required specialists to pull together and analyze that information.

The research undertaken is usually of the library-legal-analytical type and is related primarily to current governmental activities. Therefore, the research products are generally not statistical, but they have a solid data base and are not valuational.

From its beginning in 1939, the agency has maintained vertical files on church-state matters. These are probably the largest research resources of their kind in the country. A highly specialized library is also maintained. The Library of Congress and the Supreme Court Library—only a city block from the agency's office—provide exhaustive research materials.

Research Services serves the Program of Governmental Relations in a number of ways. It is responsible for the preparation of testimony given before congressional committees and administrative agencies. It also drafts and files legal briefs with the Supreme Court and lower courts in those church-state cases in which Baptist interests or principles are involved.

Research Services is also charged with the responsibility of providing information and documentation on issues for the agency's programs of Denominational Services and Information Services.

In addition, Research Services produces in-depth studies of church-state issues of particular importance to Baptists. Typical of these are "Government and the Mission of the Churches: The Problem of 'Integrated Auxiliaries' " and "Nontheistic Religions and the First Amendment."

The research facilities of the Baptist Joint Committee are made available to scholars, Southern Baptist agencies, state conventions, and churches through direct research or through the agency's response to research inquiries.

JOHN W. BAKER

CHRISTIAN LIFE COMMISSION, SBC. From its beginning, the Christian Life Commission has maintained a strong emphasis on researching social issues. In recent years research has been done through surveys, public hearings, consultations with specialists on specific social issues, study leaves, memberships in professional so-

cieties dealing with social concerns (which give access to their data banks), and keeping extensive up-to-date files on ethical concerns.

The commission's professional staff have specific research responsibilities pertinent to their particular job assignments. A staff position, director of research and editorial services, was added in 1977 to give emphasis to general research.

The agency has published results of research as resource papers; three major pamphlet series, resource packets dealing with issues such as hunger, television, and citizenship; scores of articles in SBC periodicals; and a newsletter entitled *Light*.

A mail answering service to all Southern Baptists and others in search of information on social problems is provided.

WILLIAM M. TILLMAN, JR.

DIVISION OF RESEARCH, HOME MISSION BOARD. The primary source of research at the HMB in 1970 was the Department of Survey and Special Studies. Leonard G. Irwin, director of the department since 1962, was promoted to director, Planning and Coordination Section in 1971. His four associates were separated into two units: (1) William A. Powell became director, Survey and Special Studies Department in the Program Implementation Section with Donald F. Mabry as his associate; and (2) Orrin D. Morris became director, Planning Services Department in the Planning and Coordination Section with Tommy R. Coy as his associate.

Powell and Mabry specialized in telephone area religious surveys, descriptive studies for associational planning, and research for leaders in their section. Morris and Coy specialized in research for long-range planning at the HMB and assistance to the regional coordinators in missions and evangelism planning with state conventions.

When Powell transferred to the Evangelism Division in 1972, Mabry became director and Paul W. Stuart was employed as his associate. Later that year, Morris became a regional coordinator and the Planning Services Department was dissolved. Coy became planning consultant, and Leonard O. Hinton, Jr., was elected research consultant in 1973. Both units continued the same functions; however, much effort was given to developing applications of computer tapes from the Census Bureau to denominational planning. Data on denominations were used to form two indexes (Evangelism Index and Church Index) whereby the need for evangelical witness and new churches in every county in the nation would be studied.

New directions evolved in 1975. Mabry joined the Florida staff. The HMB's Survey and Special Studies Department was retitled Office of Missions Surveys and Special Studies. The Evangelism Section was formed and the Office of Evangelism Survey and Analysis established. Hinton transferred to direct that office. Phillip B. Jones was elected research consultant (Jones had been data processing assistant in the Planning Section, 1973-75). By this time, the inter-denominational religious surveys had become extinct and the research staff was located in three section offices. Planning Section personnel provided research for the Services Section staff.

In 1976 Stuart accepted a pastorate in Arkansas. The missions office was thereafter manned by Clay L. Price, who had been research assistant since 1974 (a nonstaff position).

In 1977 Coy resigned to join the staff of the Christian Broadcasting Network in Virginia. In 1978 C. Kirk Hadaway was elected research and data management consultant in the Planning Section.

On Jan. 1, 1979, the research staff was centralized in the Planning Section as the Research Division. Morris became director with four other staff members: Jones, planning researcher; Hinton, evangelism services researcher; Price, missions researcher (elected to staff); and Hadaway, researcher, data development. The primary thrust of the research remained the same except for (1) efforts to test church growth assumptions, (2) extensive cross-referencing of the large volume of reports produced during previous years, and (3) assignment of services for all four sections.

ORRIN D. MORRIS

EDUCATION COMMISSION, SBC. The assigned function to provide studies on denominational relations, finances, curriculum, management, public relations, and recruitment of students results in annual reports on Baptist school enrollments, church vocation volunteers, finances, and distribution of state convention education funds. Requested research is conducted on individual school problems, regional accreditation, regulatory and legal concerns, and dissertation subjects. Faculty benefits were studied in the early 1970s.

The commission published the *Study of Southern Baptist Colleges and Universities, 1976-77,* following the National Colloquim on Christian Education, 1976. Conducted by Earl J. McGrath, stated purposes of colleges were studied and programs assessed in terms of purposes. Study of assets, revenue sources, and expenditures, a part of the McGrath Study, was continued annually with John Minter Associates through 1979.

A 1979 survey of campus religious activities, mission activities, and mission courses was made for the National Conference on Bold Christian Education and Bold Missions.

ARTHUR L. WALKER, JR.

HISTORICAL COMMISSION, SBC. Research is a vital program of the Historical Commission. The commission regularly responds to requests for information from individuals, churches, associations, state conventions, SBC agencies, and other bodies. For example, at the request of the SBC Executive Committee during the decade, the commission prepared two major research papers, "Fund Raising Campaigns for State Baptist Institutions of Higher Education,

1965-74'' and ''Resume of Events of the Boards of the Southern Baptist Convention, 1962-1971.''

The commission's Baptist Information Retrieval System aids researchers by providing printouts of bibliographical references on selected topics and/or persons. Special assistance goes to students, writers, and other researchers using the Dargan-Carver Library, which contains the best single collection of Southern Baptist historical materials that exists. Because of its involvement in historical research, the commission is represented on the Southern Baptist Research Fellowship.

The commission does not do genealogical research. Other kinds of queries for data receive careful attention.

CHARLES W. DEWEESE

III. Research by State Conventions. The need for research has been a developing interest on the part of state convention leaders. This has surfaced because of the importance given to research by governmental, industrial, and educational institutions on a regional and national level during the past decade. The influence of the Research Services Department of the SSB and Division of Research of the HMB has definitely had a positive effect on the need for research by state leaders in helping decision makers in solving problems and in long-range planning.

The following are examples of the kind of survey and research being done:
1. Outside Groups: These include studies done by educational institutions, market specialists, and others.
2. Inventory of giving records of churches and associations.
3. Use of associational church letter data. Several state conventions are storing church letter data on computer or electronic memory typewriters.
4. Inventories of new mission-church sites needed and where they are located.
5. A large number of state conventions are helping associations prepare surveys to be used in associational strategy planning.

In order to respond to the need of additional research, many state conventions are employing well-qualified people. With the employment of staff, new computing technology and the increased need for long-range planning, the 1980s will bring an acceleration of research being done by state conventions.

J. V. THOMAS

IV. Statistics and Records. The Research Services Department (formerly called Department of Survey, Statistics, and Information and later the Research and Statistics Department) of the SSB, under the leadership of Martin B. Bradley, continued in the 1970s to attach a great deal of importance to the accurate and thorough collection, analysis, and dissemination of denominational statistics. As a result, Southern Baptists remain today as one of the leading denominations in this field. In yearly meetings involving statisticians from various denominations, Southern Baptists were frequently called on to share the "inner workings" of their statistical process.

The UCL (Uniform Church Letter) remained the principal tool for gathering statistics about Southern Baptists and their churches. During the decade the UCL was held to the general length of 150 items on Part A and a standard format for both parts A and B. One section of Part A, consisting of approximately 21 items, was designated as a rotation section to allow for new items to be added and other items taken off. This was in keeping with the general position of a fixed UCL length which was felt early in the decade to be necessary in order that increasing demand for space not balloon the UCL to an impractical length and complexity.

Labels similar to those used on federal income tax forms were introduced to cut costs and speed up processing. Also, a short-form UCL was inaugurated early in the decade both to save costs through a standard size of 8½ x 11 and to concentrate all instructions for filling out the UCL in a relatively new instruction booklet.

In 1978 the use of microfiche replaced microfilm for the use and preservation of selected statistics for each church. Microfilming was used from 1946 through 1977. The microfiche provides for faster data retrieval and a reduction in production costs.

Training of associational clerks continued to be emphasized to ensure more accurate statistics. These training efforts were expanded to cover more state convention meetings of associational leadership.

Because the Census Bureau does not gather information on religious affiliation, Southern Baptists participated in both a 1971 and a 1980 Church Membership Study. These reports show, for participating denominations, the number of churches, church membership, and population in each county of the United States.

The role statistics and records played in the 1970s in the planning process of Southern Baptist agencies appears to have been significant.

JAMES A. LOWRY

V. Futures Research. The 1960s and 1970s witnessed an accelerated world interest and involvement in studying the future. Underlying most, if not all, futures studies are the positions that (1) studies are for the purpose of understanding possible alternative futures, not predicting them, and (2) actions taken now contribute to or help shape one's future.

In Mar., 1977, the SSB, under the leadership of President Grady C. Cothen, convened a futuristic conference for selected agency and state convention leaders. This event heightened the concern for denominational responsibilities in confronting and shaping issues of the future.

Preparation in the late 1970s of the IMPACT '80s document, under the working leadership of Albert A. McClellan, Orrin D. Morris, and

Morton F. Rose, helped focus Southern Baptists' thinking on possible future issues for churches and their environments. This document was a product and example of selected futures research methods.

The Research Services Department, a component in the SSB's Office of Planning, now projects formal futures research activity integral to the board's long-range planning. Futures research has also become a continuing interest of the HMB's Research Division.

MARTIN B. BRADLEY

VI. Southern Baptist Research Fellowship. Concerned individuals met in Dallas, TX, June 27, 1977, to discuss the possibility of organizing a research fellowship related to Southern Baptists. The second meeting, Dec. 1-2, 1977, in Dallas provided the setting for discussing a proposed purpose and constitution of the research fellowship. The Southern Baptist Research Fellowship was officially organized by the adoption of the constitution and the election of officers on June 10, 1978, in Atlanta, GA.

The purpose of the fellowship is to provide an informal forum for Southern Baptists with professional interest in religious research. The membership includes Southern Baptists whose work relates to the execution or the use of research and statistics. The fellowship's quarterly, *The Newsletter*, contains the latest information available related to research projects and reports conducted by the many different organizations within Southern Baptist life.

The fellowship meets annually, usually before the SBC. Each year an outstanding contributor to research within the denomination is recognized.

The first officers of the fellowship included Leonard G. Irwin, president; J. V. Thomas, program vice-president; James Lowry, membership vice-president; Orrin D. Morris, editor, *Research News Bulletin*; Roy Jennings, secretary-treasurer; and Martin B. Bradley, award chairperson.

LEONARD G. IRWIN

STUDY COURSES (II). See CHURCH STUDY COURSE.

STUMPH, CALOWA WILLIAM (b. Purdy, TN, Oct. 16, 1878; d. Albuquerque, NM, Nov. 4, 1972). Pastor and missionary. Son of Loritta Stumph and John Wesley Stumph, watchmaker and justice of the peace, he was converted in Aug., 1897. He was called to preach, then entered Southwestern Baptist University (now Union University, B.S., 1906). He married Delia Etta Beville, Nov. 14, 1906. They had one child, Roy.

Following pastorates in Tennessee, Louisiana, Mississippi, Missouri, and Texas, the Stumphs moved to Clovis, NM, Mar., 1921, when he became pastor of the First Baptist Church. In Dec., 1922, he was elected corresponding secretary of the Baptist Convention of

New Mexico and served until 1931. During this tenure additional duties included: treasurer of the convention; editor, *Baptist New Mexican;* superintendent, Baptist Orphans' Home and Clovis Baptist Hospital; manager, Baptist Book Store; and president, Montezuma College. Stumph was listed in *Who's Who in America* in 1928. A member of the original framing committee of 39 proposing the Cooperative Program in 1925, Stumph attended the SBC in Miami, FL, in 1960 when the program's 35th year was celebrated. He was the only one of the eight remaining members able to attend.

After serving pastorates in New Mexico and Arizona, he returned to New Mexico in 1933 as a missionary to the Indians under the direction of the Home Mission Board, and served churches at Alamo, Albuquerque, and Isleta. In 1938 he was appointed superintendent of the board's Spanish and Indian work in New Mexico and Arizona. He retired in 1951 but continued to edit the *All-Indian Baptist* until 1955. He then contributed monographs to *Encyclopedia of Southern Baptists* (1958).

Following the death of his first wife, he married Jessie Douglas of Tulsa, OK, in 1957. For 24 years before his death, he was a member of Fruit Avenue Baptist Church, Albuquerque. He is buried in Sunset Memorial Park, Albuquerque, NM.

JOHN W. RANSDELL

SUDAN, MISSION IN. Sudan, Africa's largest country, remained closed to Southern Baptists until 1980. Samuel and Virginia (Currey) Cannata arrived in Pibor Post, near the Ethiopian border, in March. Ronald D. and Judy (Bailey) Bodenhamer joined them three months later. Both couples had previously served in Ethiopia. The two couples' assignment was to participate in a development-evangelism project with the Murle tribespeople in cooperation with other mission groups. Cannata, a physician, and Judy Bodenhamer, a medical technologist, were to design a primary health care program, while Ronald Bodenhamer was to provide agricultural services. The couples' first task was to learn the Murle language, which had only recently been reduced to writing.

JOY NEAL

SUNDAY SCHOOL (II, III). The 1970s were a period of adjustment and experimentation with new approaches for Southern Baptist Sunday Schools. Early in the decade numerous changes were introduced in Sunday School work, including a new grouping-grading plan, new curriculum materials, and a delineation of Sunday School tasks in the churches. The resulting adjustment period plus continued social and cultural changes in the nation caused Sunday School enrollment to remain relatively stable during the decade. Enrollment was

7,290,447 in 1970 and 7,317,960 in 1979.

A number of the new approaches introduced during the 1970s were efforts to reach previously unreached persons for Bible study. In 1970 many churches began to use buses and intense visitation to reach people. These efforts usually succeeded mainly in reaching large numbers of children. During 1970-71 the Sunday School Department of the Sunday School Board began to assist churches in operating bus outreach programs and in assimilating the children into Sunday School and worship services. The increase in Sunday School enrollment in 1971-72 was generally credited to the bus outreach emphasis.

During 1971-72 the promotion of associational Bible conferences was incorporated into the ongoing work of the Sunday School Department of the SSB. State conventions and associations joined in the promotion, providing an opportunity for both small and large churches to participate in Bible study in a large group setting supplemental to ongoing Sunday School.

In 1972 October was designated outreach month in the denominational calendar, providing opportunity for Sunday Schools to give major attention to enlargement and outreach during this month each year. In 1973, after several years of inter-program planning, the week between the last Sunday of September and the first Sunday in October was reassigned to Sunday School to be promoted as Sunday School Preparation Week. This enabled the Sunday School program to begin planning for a major effort in preparation and outreach each fall and to continue this emphasis through October.

Materials and promotional plans for Backyard Bible Clubs were introduced in 1973. The materials consist of Bible stories, contemporary stories, pictures, songs, and easy-to-follow teaching steps for the leader. Many churches began using the Backyard Bible Club as a first contact with children who were later enrolled in mission Vacation Bible Schools, church Vacation Bible Schools, or Sunday School.

In 1975-76 a new approach to prospect discovery and enlistment was utilized on a widespread basis. This approach, known as AC-TION, called for enrolling persons in Sunday School anytime, anywhere the persons agreed to be enrolled. Persons who agreed to be enrolled were placed on the roll of the appropriate Sunday School class or department before the next Sunday. During the first full year of promotion by the Sunday School Department of the SSB, more than 2,000 churches used the ACTION plan to enroll persons for Bible study. Sunday School enrollment increases during the 1975-76 year were the largest since 1969.

In Feb., 1977, a major denominational effort was launched to encourage the starting of new Sunday Schools. A goal was set to start 3,000 new Sunday Schools between Feb., 1977, and Sep. 30, 1979. This effort involved the cooperation of the Sunday School Department of the SSB, state convention Sunday School departments, associational leaders, and local church leaders. As a result, 3,013 new Sunday Schools were reported. This was more than three times the number reported during the preceding three years.

A new curriculum line for adults and youth which was introduced in Oct., 1978, provided a book-by-book study of the entire Bible in nine years. Work was begun in 1977 to give greater emphasis to the evangelistic role of Sunday School workers in a church. Materials for Preparation Week in 1978 were designed to help Sunday School workers recognize and take advantage of evangelistic opportunities.

In 1977 A. V. Washburn retired as secretary of the Sunday School Department of the SSB, a position he had held since 1958. In Feb., 1978, Harry Piland was named director of the department.

A promotion to recognize annually the fastest growing Sunday Schools in the SBC was begun in 1978. The first recognitions were made in 1980.

New task statements for Sunday School adopted in 1979 were: (1) reach persons for Bible study, (2) teach the Bible, (3) witness to persons about Christ and lead persons into church membership, (4) minister to Sunday School members and nonmembers, (5) lead members to worship, and (6) interpret and undergird the work of the church and the denomination.

Southern Baptist Sunday School work entered the 1980s with a renewed emphasis on outreach and evangelism. Denominational, state, and associational promotion plans designed to achieve a total Sunday School enrollment of 8,500,000 by the end of 1985 were developed.

DONALD F. TROTTER

SUNDAY SCHOOL BOARD, SBC (II, III). The 1970s were years of transition in leadership for the Sunday School Board. James L. Sullivan, president, and J. M. Crowe, executive vice-president, retired, Feb. 1, 1975, after 22 years of service. SSB trustees elected Grady C. Cothen as president, Feb., 1974, and W. O. Thomason as executive vice-president, July, 1974. In Feb., 1977, James W. Clark succeeded Thomason, who resigned in Nov., 1976.

In 1980 the SSB was carrying out its work through 16 programs assigned by the SBC. The organization was streamlined for effectiveness, with programs reduced from the 25 which were operative from 1965 to 1972.

I. History Since 1969. Sullivan devoted the closing years of his administration to refining the organization so that the new administration would be able to effect a smooth transition and to reviewing the personal goals he had set for his tenure to assure the achievement of those that were possible.

In programming, the administration approached the 1970s with a simplified plan of organization for all church programs, a more flexible grouping-grading plan to meet the needs of churches of varying sizes, and a new curriculum for all church program organizations.

Sullivan had established 13 objectives for his administration. They were: (1) Achieve numerical growth in church education organizations, (2) correlate programs and activities of church organizations, (3) relate all program organizations to the local church as an integral part of the church's life, (4) produce the best in religious education materials, (5) provide diversity in education and publication to meet diverse needs of churches, (6) staff the SSB with capable people with commitment to SSB and SBC objectives, (7) establish in-house training for SSB employees, (8) provide necessary buildings and equipment, (9) provide adequate salaries, (10) provide a favorable internal climate with help for solving employees' problems, (11) consolidate operations to avoid duplication, (12) increase public relations efforts, and (13) operate economically with increased productivity.

All these goals were achieved to Sullivan's satisfaction, except for his feeling that numerical growth in church program organizations had not been as rapid or as significant as he had hoped.

Soon after Cothen took office as president, he articulated four areas which he intended to give priority treatment during his administration: (1) In-depth Bible study for the masses, (2) equipping the saints, (3) support and enrichment for family life, and (4) aid and encouragement for pastors and church staff members. During the first five years of the Cothen administration, these priorities were implemented through special financial, staffing, and programming efforts.

In-depth Bible Study for the Masses.—The SSB promoted the ACTION Plan for increasing Sunday School enrollment, introduced a new Bible Book Study curriculum for adults and young people, initiated a radio-television Bible correspondence course, undertook Sunday School growth campaigns in each association, and exceeded by Sep., 1979, a three-year goal to establish 3,000 new Sunday Schools.

Equipping the Saints for the Work of the Ministry.—Equipping Centers introduced into the Church Training program met with successful response. The New Day for Training emphasis resulted in the formation of 528 new Church Training programs in the SBC.

Support and Enrichment of Family Life.—The Program of Family Ministry Development became the 16th program of work for the SSB in June, 1976. A new Family Ministry Department had been incorporated into the board's organization in June, 1975. Emphasis went to Christian Home Week as an observance throughout the SBC, to family life conferences and retreats, and to new monthly periodicals, *Mature Living,* started in Oct., 1977, and *Christian Single,* begun in Oct., 1979.

Aid and Encouragement for Pastors and Church Staff Members.—The SSB held consultations for career assessment and development. In 1977-78, 10,146 pastors participated in conferences related to this priority.

SUNDAY SCHOOL BOARD (*q.v.*), Nashville, TN. *Top:* Baptist Book Store, Mobile, AL. The nationwide chain of Baptist Book Stores has grown to 65 outlets, adding nine stores and four mail order centers since 1969. *Center, right:* Frost Building, Nashville, TN. Refurbished and reoccupied by the SSB in 1980, the SSB first occupied the building in 1914 and later leased it to SBC agencies and Nashville businesses. *Center, left:* Glorieta Baptist Conference Center, NM, and *Bottom:* Ridgecrest Baptist Conference Center, NC, had more than 58,000 guests in year-round conferences during 1980.

SUNDAY SCHOOL BOARD (*q.v.*) OFFICES, Nashville, TN. Located on 18 acres of property in downtown Nashville. Not shown is the Board's Operations Building which provides a warehouse, offices, and is a distribution center for over 164,000,000 pieces of literature published each year.

Other Developments.—Centrifuge, a week-long 14-hour per day camping program, was introduced at Glorieta and Ridgecrest in the summer of 1979. In the 19 weeks of both conference centers in 1980, 9,373 youth and sponsors attended.

On May 1, 1979, the SSB acquired the Holman Bible Publishing Company at a cost of $2,200,000. For the first time in history, the board was equipped to carry out one of the basic elements of its mission—the production and distribution of Bibles.

For only the third time in history, the Glorieta and Ridgecrest Baptist Conference Centers operated with a net contribution ($61,846) rather than a budgeted loss in the 1979-80 fiscal year.

The board continued to cooperate in denominational efforts. It gave support in planning and conducting Mission '70, a world missions conference held in Atlanta, GA, Dec. 28-31, 1969. Major financial, planning, periodical, and programming support was given to Bold Mission Thrust. The board was involved similarly in the denomination's Convocation on World Hunger held at Ridgecrest Baptist Conference Center, Nov. 20-21, 1978.

In 1978-79, the SSB and Brotherhood Commission, at the request of the Executive Committee, SBC, carried out a joint study on the feasibility of consolidating the work of the commission with that of the SSB. The Executive Committee accepted the report from the study committee that a merger would not be in the best interests of the commission and the churches.

The SSB initiated a Business Systems Planning study in 1978, with a nine-person internal team studying the board's information resources and needs. A comprehensive report issued, July 14, 1978, identified and defined 11 key resources of the board, 14 major business processes, and 127 subprocesses. The report recommended thhe establishment of an integrated SSB Information Systems Network, with a prioritized list of systems to be developed in support of the network. Establishment of a data base and data communication environment and an integrated information network was also recommended. Implementation of the report began as soon as it was completed.

Subsequently, the SSB employed the A. T. Kearney Company to conduct a feasibility study which was used to determine priorities in implementing new information systems.

In Feb., 1977, SSB trustees approved establishment and funding at each of the six seminaries a chair of religious education or denominational relations. The professor occupying the chair would: (1) Furnish liaison to the faculty and student body for the SSB, (2) keep religious education and music faculties current on SSB programs, resources, and materials, (3) work with the seminary library in the interest of maintaining a curriculum library, (4) hold an annual literature interpretation clinic, and (5) hold an annual workshop with graduating se-

niors to interpret materials, programs, and resources. The concept was established for a minimum period of five years with the intention of making the arrangement permanent.

In March and April of 1979, trustees approved employment of Edutel Communications and Development, Inc., to conduct a technological review of print media distribution and telecommunications services with recommendations for future uses. The study was completed in early 1980, concluding that the media used by the board are particularly suited to the mission of the SSB; that the board must examine new developments in communications to see how to adapt to them in the years to come; that no immediate action is imperative; and that time and effort need to be given to potential uses of new technologies.

Finance and Sources of Income.—From its beginning, the SSB has been self-sustaining with respect to finances and has made appropriations to other SBC causes from the earnings it has derived from its programs of publishing and distribution. In 1969-70, the board's sales and other income amounted to $38,383,000. The 1980-81 budget called for a total income of $107,599,000.

Never has the SSB been a recipient of Cooperative Program funds. The Program of Cooperative Education and Promotion Work with State Boards has in effect served to free Cooperative Program funds for other purposes. This program provided the following sums to state conventions for promotion in the areas where the SSB and the states have mutual interest: 1969-70, $947,597; 1970-71, $949,638; 1971-72, $958,458; 1972-73, $958,878; 1973-74, $982,218; 1974-75, $1,384,666; 1975-76, $1,611,470; 1976-77, $1,612,257; 1977-78, $1,637,250; 1978-79, $1,715,614; and 1979-80, $1,733,060.

Funds provided to the SBC operating budget under the Program of SBC Support amounted to $606,639 in 1979-80. Of this amount, $200,000 was to be used to increase endowments of two seminaries. This compares with an allocation of $384,209 in 1969-70.

A new formula for the allocation of these funds was adopted in 1974, calling for 33⅓ percent of the first $1,000,000 contributed by the SSB to the Program of Cooperative Education and Promotion Work with State Conventions, plus 10 percent of such funds in excess of $1,000,000 to be contributed to the SBC Operating Budget.

Tax Problems.—Tax problems in Nashville, TN, continued to be a matter for litigation. The case which began in 1969 with an assessment against all Davidson County properties of the SSB was not concluded until 1974. The Supreme Court of Tennessee ruled in June of that year that religious publishing houses must pay taxes on all property not used strictly for their denominational work. The decision did not spell out clearly the areas of property which were exempt. After the SSB asked the court to reconsider portions of its decision, a clarifying opinion was issued in Aug., 1974, stating that an activity must be "directly related to the religious program or work of the institution in order for property to be exempt."

A final determination of additional tax was worked out according to a formula suggested by the court, and in which the SSB and Metropolitan Nashville tax assessors arrived at an agreeable figure. Portions of SSB property such as a part of the administrative area for the Baptist Book Store operation; executive offices; and other areas identifiable as relating to work beyond the denominational thrust of the SSB's central ministry are thus subject to property taxes. The SSB paid about $120,000 to the Metropolitan Nashville government in property taxes in 1980.

In 1969 the SSB filed a complaint in the state of New Mexico contesting a tax assessment of $10,000,000 against the Glorieta Baptist Conference Center property. In Nov., 1969, a tax bill of $133,940 was received for Glorieta. The SSB agreed to a liability for $302 for the property occupied by the washateria, and contested the remainder of the bill.

In Sep., 1970, the tax lawsuit was settled by compromise, the SSB agreeing to taxation of the property occupied by the guest washateria, service station, and gift shop. The final agreement, signed Feb. 3, 1971, stated, "Glorieta Baptist Assembly is legally considered a religious, nonprofit institution and therefore untaxable under New Mexico law."

The BECOMING Episode.—In 1971 President Sullivan made a decision as editor-in-chief of all SSB publications to revise an issue of *Becoming* and *Becoming for Leaders.* A photograph in *Becoming,* picturing a black male and two white female students was, according to Sullivan, subject to misinterpretation which could seriously hinder the study objectives of the periodical. Similarly, a portion of the study material might have been misinterpreted. Revisions in both areas were made before the periodicals were shipped to the churches. In a report to the trustee executive committee, Sullivan pointed to a "potential misinterpretation of a combination of elements: photographic content, photographic technical quality, and textual material in each of the periodicals. . . . Taken together they created what we considered an intolerable situation."

Reaction ensued to the effect that the SSB was taking a position inconsistent with biblical principles concerning race relations. The SSB received an unusually heavy amount of critical mail during the time the episode was in focus in the secular and denominational press.

The Broadman Bible Commentary Controversy.—The first volume of this 12-volume commentary was the subject of discussion, debate, and Convention action at the 1970 and 1971 SBC sessions. Considerable time, energy, and funds were expended in responding to the expressed desires of SBC messengers.

The Baptist Faith and Message.—In July, 1969, the trustees implemented the action of the SBC with respect to The Baptist Faith and Message.

The action stated: "The Sunday School Board instructs its employees to see that programs or tasks assigned to them are carried out in a manner consistent with and not contrary to the statement of faith adopted by the Convention in Kansas City in 1963." Subsequently, all employees dealing with doctrinally-related materials signed a copy of commitment to abide by The Baptist Faith and Message. New employees in this category signed the statement as a condition of employment.

In Jan., 1970, the trustees unanimously granted the president authority to add to the staff of the editorial secretary sufficient personnel "to give all manuscripts one more analytical evaluation prior to publication." Later that year, H. Leo Eddleman, past president of New Orleans Baptist Theological Seminary, was named "doctrinal reader" for the board. Following his retirement in 1972, the responsibility was renamed, becoming "manuscript analyst," and transferred to the Church Services and Materials Division.

II. Program of Work. The SBC revised and approved program statements for the work of the SSB in 1971 to provide clearer and more succinct statements, reducing the number of programs from 25 to 15. Subsequent organizational changes aligned the board's internal management structure to correspond more closely with the program statements. A 16th program, Family Ministry Development, was added in 1976, reflecting the high level of interest in the SBC in finding solutions to problems of family life.

Program of Book Store Operation.—In addition to the traditional concept of providing book store buildings, sales floors, and mail order centers for distribution of products to customers, innovative distribution channels were explored. Lifeway Direct Sales was one such channel. Another was the establishment of contract stores in associational and state convention offices. As leases expired or buildings became outdated, some Baptist Book Stores were moved or new branches were established in suburban areas where adequate parking was available and highway access easier.

The Program of Book Store Operation in 1979-80 provided 43 percent ($40,974,791) of the board's total receipts, with a net contribution of $2,465,289, 52 percent of the funds provided to the board for capital needs and other designated purposes.

Program of Broadman Publishing.—The SSB took the unprecedented step of purchasing a Bible publishing company in 1979. The board set up this operation as a separate division for management purposes and elected E. Odell Crowe as director of the Holman Division in Oct., 1980. The division is included in the Program of Broadman Publishing for SBC reporting purposes. In acquiring the Holman Bible Publishing Company, the SSB added about 410 book and Bible titles and about 11,400 new customer accounts. The acquisition necessitated the establishment of a new computer-based accounts receivables system with on-line capability.

In the 1979-80 fiscal year, the Program of Broadman Publishing accounted for 12 percent of the board's total sales, with a net contribution of $1,086,974, 23 percent of the total funds available from operations for the board.

Program of Church Services and Material Development.—In 1979 four divisions—Bible Teaching, Christian Development, Church and Staff Support, and Conference Center—were reorganized into a new relationship under Morton F. Rose, who was elected vice-president for Church Programs and Services.

The CPS office includes the work and supervision of the coordinator of the inter-agency function of Coordinated Promotion Planning (CPP), with Lynn M. Davis as coordinator since 1974. The CPP process continues to work with state conventions and SBC programs, giving attention to Bold Mission Thrust, 1979-82, and planning for BMT, 1982-85. The SSB is committed to giving priority support to involvement in BMT in cooperation with other SBC agencies. A task group involving CPS personnel is at work evaluating what has been done and what should be done concerning assisting small churches.

The SSB has developed liaison work with ethnic groups in the Southern Baptist constituency through an Ethnic Liaison Unit, established in Feb., 1978. Through this unit, significant progress has been made in improving communications with black Southern Baptists. In cooperation with the SSB's Research Services Department, the Uniform Church Letter for the first time provided information on black membership in Southern Baptist churches. Liaison work with Spanish and Asian Baptists in the United States is beginning. Work with other groups is planned.

The SSB began to clarify and strengthen working relationships between the Seminary Extension Department and CPS components. Contact persons were enlisted from CPS components to assist the SED in developing three new courses: "Youth Education in a Church," "Adult Education in a Church," and "The Educational Ministry of a Church."

The Church Program Training Center continues to conduct advanced conferences and seminars for pastors, church staff members, and denominational leaders.

The SSB provided five Foreign Mission Board publishing houses with galley proofs of selected SSB periodicals for use in developing materials in languages of the overseas areas.

The concept of channeling noncurriculum material for other agencies continues to develop. A channeling process coordinator, Robert A. Orr, handled provision of periodical space for a large number of the requests received.

Program of Sunday School Development.—This program continues to support the traditional enrollment, new class organization, and teaching-learning improvement emphases which have produced growth in Southern Baptist Sunday Schools throughout the years. At the same time, new approaches have been developed to try to reverse the declining enrollment trends of 1977, 1978, and 1979 following gradual increases from 1971 through 1976.

The SSB introduced the Bible Book Series in 1978 as a third curriculum option. This series is basically a content approach to Bible study. All 66 books of the Bible are scheduled for study in three three-year cycles. Some study from both Old and New Testaments is included each year.

Home Bible Study was a new development which reached large numbers of people through correspondence Bible lessons. This effort received first promotion through the new radio and television program, "At Home with the Bible." The SSB funded these outreach efforts by a program reserve fund set up in the SSB budget by the trustees upon the recommendation of President Cothen. Contributions were solicited from persons who responded to the programs and the courses, but the projects were not self-sustaining by 1980.

The Sunday School Department continued to give emphasis to BMT and the Cooperative Program through its curriculum materials and through ongoing field service events, as well as through Associational Bold Mission Bible Conferences.

Vacation Bible School promotion, Weekday Bible Study, and other special Bible teaching projects continue to receive attention through the Program of Sunday School Development.

Program of Church Training Development.—SBC action in 1972 changed the name of the program from the Program of Training Union Promotion. Terminology changes in the SSB organization and publications and in organizations in state conventions, associations, and churches were subsequently made to achieve consistency. Training Unions in churches became Training Groups.

The *Survival Kit for New Christians* was published in 1980, providing a beginning for follow-up and discipleship training for new Christians. Other new member training materials were being redesigned to focus on discipleship and responsible church membership.

This program provides major support for BMT through a long-range Equipping Center curriculum framework, emphasis on church growth in 1981-82 age-group periodicals, and emphasis on the family and ministry in 1982-83 age-group periodicals. Baptist Doctrine Studies in 1981 emphasized the doctrine of the church.

Program of Church Music Development.—Consistent increase in involvement of persons in Church Music programs distinguished this program from other church educational ministries.

New administrative guidance products were released in Jan., 1980—*Building an Effective Music Ministry, Building an Effective Older Children's Choir, Building an Effective Younger Children's Choir,* and *Building an Effective Preschool Choir.* A related text for part-time and volunteer music directors, *And a Music Director, Too,* was released in May, 1980.

Program of Church Administration Development.—This program now includes the Program of Vocational Guidance. Major emphasis goes to the SSB priority, "Aid and encouragement for pastors and church staff members." Primary attention also goes to equipping deacons for ministry in their churches.

In 1979 the first National Conference for Church Secretaries was held in Nashville, with about 700 secretaries attending.

Work with the church council continued with pilot testing of a church council training approach. Weekday education in the churches continued to receive emphasis, with a new Christian School Series curriculum being used in 100 schools in 1980. The Southern Baptist Association of Christian Schools was organized in 1980 in connection with a Christian school management seminar.

Reginald Milton McDonough was elected secretary of the Church Administration Department in 1977 to succeed Howard Bryce Foshee, who became director of the new Christian Development Division.

Program of National Student Ministries.—In addition to its ongoing efforts in student ministry, this program was completing development of student Bible study materials and the plan for their introduction in 1981. Ten-year goals called for 1,500 student ministries with 1,150 directors by 1987.

Program of Church Architecture Service.—Consultation with churches continues to be at the heart of this service. In 1978-79, 3,669 individual churches and denominational organizations were assisted through consultation. The main material piece for the program, *Church Properties/Building Guidebook,* was revised to include material on energy conservation in church buildings. Rowland E. Crowder replaced W. A. Harrell *(q.v.)* as secretary of the Church Architecture Department upon Harrell's death in 1971.

Program of Church Library Development.—This program includes the educational and promotional aspects of the program of audiovisual education service. Production and distribution functions of that program are now with the Program of Broadman Publishing.

Terminology has been changed in this program as the concept of the library's responsibility has broadened from books and other printed matter to all types of educational media. Many churches operate audio and videocassette ministries as part of their church media library service. Some churches use the media library for ordering and distributing educational curriculum materials.

A new product in 1979, produced by the Church Media Library Department, was *Choice Creations Tracts,* 50 new titles designed for persons to use in outreach and ministry. Written by a representative group of Southern Baptists, these tracts relate to such areas as salvation, Christian life, doctrine, ministry, and family. The former Program of Bible and Tract Distribution is now handled principally by this program.

The Church Media Library Department maintains the media centers at Ridgecrest and Glorieta Baptist Conference Centers.

Program of Church Recreation Development.—In 1971 the SSB elected Ray Conner to succeed Bob M. Boyd as secretary of the Church Recreation Department. One of the remarkably successful efforts of this program was the initiation of Centrifuge at Ridgecrest and Glorieta Conference Centers in the summer of 1979. Centrifuge is a week long, 14-hour per day youth camping program that includes Bible study, worship, music, drama, mission education, outdoor education, overnight backpacking, sports, games, crafts, campfires, musicals, films, puppetry, and more. Many youths made professions of faith in Christ during these weeks; others made Christian vocation decisions and acknowledged life rededication and commitment. On the first day for 1980 reservation acceptance, both conference centers were completely filled for Centrifuge, with more than 8,000 youth on the waiting list. Studies were under way to add satellite meetings on one or two college campuses.

Program of Family Ministry Development.—The SSB added this program in 1976, a work which had been accomplished previously under the Programs of Sunday School and Church Training Promotion. The 1976 action gave the Family Ministry function higher visibility and status, in keeping with a renewed effort to provide solutions for the continuing problems in family relationships throughout the United States.

Program of Conference Center Operation.—In 1979 the SSB grouped this program with the Bible Training, Christian Development, and Church and Staff Support Divisions for administrative purposes. Robert M. Turner was elected director of the Conference Center Division in Jan., 1978, succeeding Bob M. Boyd.

Program of Cooperative Education and Promotion Work with State Boards.—(See discussion of this program in **History** section of this article.)

Program of Southern Baptist Convention Support.—Payments made by the SSB to this program, providing the SSB share of the operation expenses of the SBC, grew from $384,209 in 1970 to $606,639 at the end of the 1979-80 fiscal year.

Program of Sunday School Board General Management.—In Feb., 1973, the trustees approved changes in title for the top SSB executives. The executive secretary-treasurer became president; associate executive secretary-treasurer became executive vice-president; the president of trustees became chairman; and the chairman of the local executive committee became vice-chairman of trustees.

As of Sep. 30, 1980, there were 1,506 regular employees, compared to 1,483 in 1970. In this period when the budget of the SSB increased about 2.5 times, from $38,383,000 to $96,201,000, the number of employees increased only slightly less than 2 percent.

Agency Organization and Personnel.—Three of the SSB's four division directors retired in 1971 and 1972: W. L. Howse (*q.v.*), Education Division, Keith C. Von Hagen, Book Store Division, and Herman L. King, Publishing Division. To evaluate the organization in the light of these retirements, the SSB appointed a marketing organization study group, Nov., 1968, to formulate a recommendation concerning an organizational structure to implement the marketing concept at the SSB. The group was composed of W. O. Thomason, Wayne H. Chastain, Herman L. King, Ras B. Robinson, Jay O. Turner, Keith C. Von Hagen, with J. M. Crowe as chairman.

The marketing component was defined as "a philosophy of business which states that the customers' wants/needs satisfaction is the economic, social, and moral justification for the Board's existence. This concept means that it is the wants/needs of the marketplace and not the desire of the Board to sell its products that is the predominantly important thing. Consequently, all Board activities in planning, production, and finance, as well as in marketing, must be devoted to, first, determining what the customers' wants/needs are and then to satisfying these wants/needs while still making sufficient earnings to provide adequate working capital, fixed assets, and reserve to carry on the work of the Board."

The marketing organization study group recommended that the SSB move in the direction of a product line organization as rapidly as the size and growth of the SSB would permit because of the following advantages of a product line organization: (1) Accountability for earnings can be placed in the responsibility of specific managers because these managers are in position to control the internal factors affecting earnings; (2) minimizes interdivision and interdepartment conflicts; (3) unifies and concentrates marketing efforts; (4) offers possibilities for better customer service; (5) makes possible financial information relating to earnings accountability; (6) easier to delegate authority without creating conflicts; (7) provides more direct line of communication; (8) places responsibility for coordination at lower levels; (9) better morale because of clearer assignments; and (10) enables the Executive Office to spend more time in corporate management.

Based on the recommendations of the marketing organization study group, the desire to simplify the organizational structure of the SSB by eliminating overlapping and conflicting responsibilities, and the desire to fix total accountability in division directors for the success of their program, their supporting materials and services, and the board's operation, the administration recommended and the trustees approved in actions taken in Aug., 1970, Jan., 1971, and July, 1971, a new organizational structure. This new organization was headed by the Executive Office, with the Office of Personnel and Office of Public Relations as staff offices, and the Assemblies Division, Broadman Division, Church Services and Materials Division, and Management Services Division as line operating divisions. The Church Services and Materials Division included a Church Program Organization Group, a Church Program Services Group, and a Central Support Group.

In the Church Program Services Group were the Church Administration, Church Architecture, Church Library, and Church Recreation Departments. In the Central Support Group were the Art, Materials Services, Promotional Materials, and Research Services Departments. National Student Ministries was also included in this division.

The office of editorial secretary was transferred to a staff relationship to the director of the Church Services and Materials Division in Feb., 1972. Howard P. Colson served in the position from Clifton J. Allen's retirement in 1969 until his own retirement in 1975.

In Feb., 1973, the Office of Personnel and the Manpower Development Department of the Management Services Division were merged into the Personnel Department and placed in the Management Services Division. Kenton C. Hofmeister was elected Personnel Department manager in Mar., 1974. In June, 1974, the trustees approved a reorganization of the Book Store Division into six regional departments which coincided with the new regional mail centers being developed by the United States Postal Service.

President Cothen recommended in July, 1975, a reorganization of the Church Services and Materials Division for four reasons: (1) Response from the field indicated a lack of visibility for program leaders; (2) high cost for executive management and special staff in the division; (3) difficulty of strategic planning; and (4) the division director, Allen B. Comish, had stated he would welcome an opportunity to consider reorganization.

New reporting relationships for departments were established. A new Family Ministries Department was formed, and Joseph Hinkle was elected secretary.

Two new offices, Finance and Planning, were established. E. DeVaughn Woods was elected vice-president for Finance, and Morton F. Rose was elected director of Planning. The work of the editorial secretary became a responsibility of the director of Planning at this time.

President Cothen assigned Elaine Dickson the task of studying the Church Services and Materials Division organizations to define problems and suggest solutions. In Feb., 1977, outcomes of the study were expressed in terms of the following needs: (1) An organization which is adaptable and flexible enough to act effectively in response to emerging needs and/or opportunities; (2) an organization which enables divisions to act out of their independence with other divisions within the board and particularly with other denominational units—SBC, state, and association; (3) an organization capable of providing correlated materials and services which contribute to wholeness of experience for churches and for individuals, and an organization which can handle that correlation at division level or below; (4) an organization in which accountability and freedom to act is assigned as far out in the organization as is feasible; and (5) an organization which is able to accommodate the demands for internal leadership and for external leadership.

SSB trustees approved the new divisional organization, Feb. 1, 1977. Robert G. Fulbright was elected director of the Bible Teaching Division, and Howard B. Foshee director of the Christian Development Division. In June of that year, J. Ralph McIntyre was elected director of the Church and Staff Support Division.

The Office of Public Relations was renamed Office of Communications in Feb., 1977, and Lloyd T. Householder was elected director. Gomer R. Lesch, who had directed the office since its establishment, was named special assistant to the Executive Office.

A further refinement in the organization took place in Aug., 1979, when the positions of vice-president for Church Programs and Services and vice-president for Marketing and Distribution were established. Morton F. Rose was elected vice-president for Church Programs and Services, with four divisions reporting to him— Bible Teaching, Christian Development, Church and Staff Support, and Conference Center. The Broadman, Book Store, and Holman Divisions were included under the vice-president for Marketing and Distribution. Jimmy D. Edwards was elected to this position in Feb., 1981.

In Feb., 1980, Richard Kay was elected director of the Office of Planning.

A study of the Personnel Department was undertaken in Sep., 1979. In Feb., 1980, President Cothen reported completion of the study to the trustees, who implemented his recommendation to relate the Personnel Department to the Executive Office, with Gomer R. Lesch as liaison.

III. Organizational Leadership, June 1, 1981. ADMINISTRATIVE STAFF. Grady C. Cothen, president; James W. Clark, executive vice-president; Gomer R. Lesch, special assistant; Morton F. Rose, vice-president for Church Programs and Services; (vacant), director, Bible Teaching Division; Howard B. Foshee, director, Christian Development Division; J. Ralph McIntyre, director, Church and Staff Support Division; Robert M. Turner, director, Conference Center Division; Lloyd T. Householder, director, Office of Communications; E. DeVaughn Woods, vice-president for Finance; Richard Kay, director, Office of Planning; Jimmy D. Edwards, vice-president for Publishing and Distribution; E. Dessel Aderholt, director, Broadman Division; Bill Graham, director, Book Store Division; E. Odell Crowe, director, Holman Division; (vacant), director, Management Services Division.

EXECUTIVE MANAGEMENT GROUP. All of the above administrative staff members and the following:

Personnel Department.—Steve Lawrence, manager.

Bible Teaching Division.—Jerry Ross, manager, Art Department; Harry Piland, director, Sunday School Department; Billie Pate, manager, Management Support Group, Sunday School Department; Donald Trotter, manager, Sunday School Administration Group; Max Caldwell, manager, Youth-Adult Group, Sunday School Department; Muriel Blackwell, manager, Preschool-Children Group, Sunday School Department.

Christian Development Division.—Roy Edgemon, director, Church Training Department; Art Criscoe, manager, Management Support Section, Church Training Department; Joe Hinkle, secretary, Family Ministry Department; Charles Roselle, secretary, and Ed Rollins, manager, National Student Ministries.

Church and Staff Support Division.—(vacant), secretary, Church Administration Department; Rowland Crowder, secretary, Church Architecture Department; Mancil Ezell, secretary, Church Media Library Department; Wesley Lee Forbis, secretary, Church Music Department; Ray Conner, secretary, Church Recreation Department.

Conference Center Division.—Larry Haslam, manager, Glorieta Baptist Conference Center; Ken McAnear, manager, Ridgecrest Baptist Conference Center.

Office of Finance.—Don Early, manager, Investment Office.

Office of Planning.—Martin Bradley, manager, Research Services Department.

Broadman Division.—Crawford Howell, manager, Broadman Sales Department; Andy Dodson, manager, Broadman Marketing Services Department; Johnnie Godwin, manager, Broadman Products Department.

Book Store Division.—(vacant), manager, Operations Department; Elaine Dickson, manager, Direct Sales Department; (vacant), manager, East Central Region; Al Crawford, manager, Southern Region; Jay Turner, manager, Southeastern Region; Paul Webb, manager, Southwestern Region; Robert Mendenhall, manager, Western Region.

Management Services Division.—Peggy Self, manager, Accounting and Control Department; Jim Shull, manager, Administrative Services Department; John Jackson, manager, Procurement Department; Hilton Austin, manager, Property Management; Van Simpson, manager, Systems Department; David Turner, manager, Material Services Department.

Credit Union.—The Baptist Board Employees Credit Union was established in 1954. Board employees and retirees and their families, as well as employees of other SBC agencies in Tennessee and their families, are eligible for membership. Total assets as of Oct. 1, 1980, were $8,377,231; total members were 2,683. Four employees work with manager Jim Holder.

Personnel.—The following professional and managerial workers retired before 1970 but were not mentioned in Volume III of this *Encyclopedia* (figures indicate year of retirement and total number of years service at the board): 1966, E. A. Herron (manager, Glorieta, 16); 1967, Eurabee Odom (assistant editor, 11), and Willard K. Weeks (manager, Ridgecrest, 16); and 1968, Blanche Mays (book store manager, 23).

Retired in 1970 were Hardie Bass, Jr. (chief architect, 24); Herman Burns (managing art director, 41); Lorell Burns (book store manager, 23); Harvey Gibson (field services staff consultant, 19); Julian Johnson (foreman, 28); Maribelle Jones (book store manager, 35); W. Hines Sims (secretary, Church Music Department, 24).

In 1971, Ava Arrington (stock room supervisor, 6); Emmett Golden (purchasing agent, 36); Ollie Lowenstein (proofreader, 31); and Keith C. Von Hagen (director, Book Store Division, 42).

In 1972, Annie Ward Byrd (senior editorial coordinator, 31); Kate Carter (book store manager, 21); Wallace Greene, Jr. (music promotion specialist, 26); Imogene Greer (book store manager, 26); Herman L. King (director, Publishing Division, 33); Richard Sellars (book store manager, 15); and Althea Smith (proofreader, 41).

In 1973, Helen Conger (librarian, 28); May Detherage (book store manager, 27); Eva Giles (advertising production coordinator, 25); Clifford A. Holcomb (associational music consultant, 20); Roland C. Hudlow (general officers consultant, 12); Harriet McLean (copy editor, 17); Charles R. Miller, Jr. (art supervisor, 27); Samuel Shanko (instrumental consultant, 12); and Leonard E. Wedel (director, Office of Personnel, 28).

In 1974, Eunice E. Ausbrooks (office supervisor, 19); Lloyd E. Barnes (building consultant, 18); Mabel King Beeker (assistant editor, 26); Katherine Burkhardt (proofreader, 17); Jo Alice Haigh (editor, 20); Young H. Lang (Broadman salesman, 10); Virginia Martin (book store manager, 30); Leon Mayo (foreman, 47); Clara Odom (buyer, 19); Joan Rittenhouse (book store manager, 22); Ada Rutledge (preschool consultant, 18); Edith Steele (bibliography researcher, 28); and Loren R. Williams (music sales specialist, 22).

In 1975, Zelah Amos (proofreader, 18); Howard P. Colson (editorial secretary, 25); J. M. Crowe (executive vice-president, 21); Marian Keegan (archivist, 14); Martha Miner (book store manager, 22); James L. Sullivan (president, 21); and Pauline Summers (supervisor-office assistant, 41).

In 1976, Myrtle A. Anderson (book store manager, 23); Alta Faircloth (assistant music editor, 24); Jo Gwin (book store manager, 35); Rubena Horn (occupational nurse, 20); Dewey Kilby (artist, 6); and Idus V. Owensby (Church Administration consultant, 15).

In 1977, Saxe Adams (preschool music consultant, 15); Allen B. Comish (director, Church Services and Materials Division, 10); Louise Ellerker (adult curriculum editor, 36); Philip B. Harris (secretary, Church Training Department, 24); Robert Jackson (photography supervisor, 20); Nora Padgett (preschool consultant, 22); Lillian L. Patterson (supervisor-office assistant, 21); Mildred J. Schreiner (art design supervisor, 38); H. S. Simpson (manager, Materials Services Department, 40); Howard T. Tomlin (supervisor, Accounts Payable, 22); and A. V. Washburn (secretary, Sunday School Department, 44).

In 1978, Dolores J. Baker (design editor, 23); Robert Chaudoin (supplies promotion specialist, 11); John Demerich (employee benefits consultant, 33); Marie Hedgecoth (editor, 25); Alma May Scarborough (editor, 22); and Wayne E. Todd (secretary, Church Media Library Department, 19).

In 1979, Lola A. Allen (book store manager, 28); Everett B. Barnard (personnel counselor, 18); Arnold Durbin (manager, Mail Order Center, 25); William J. Fallis (chief editor, general religious books, 35); Joseph Green (development facilitator, 25); William F. Kautzman (master artist-designer, 20); and Mary Lou Roof (book store manager, 34).

In 1980 Mildred I. Baker (book store manager, 34); D. P. Brooks (editor, 20); Forrest Marker (assistant editor, 13); William J. Reynolds (secretary, Church Music Department, 25); Charles Treadway (senior consultant, Pastoral Ministries, 28); Paul Turner (supervisor, special projects, 25); Bruce Whitfield (inventory specialist, 27); and Helen Young (preschool consultant, 31).

IV. Periodicals Launched, 1970-80. GENERAL PUBLICATIONS. Quarterlies: *Living with Children* (1978-). *Living with Preschoolers* (1973-). *Living with Teenagers* (1978-). Monthlies: *Christian Single* (1979-). *Mature Living* (1977-).

LEADERSHIP MATERIALS. Quarterlies: *Children's Worship Resource Kit* (1978-). *Collage* (1977-79). *Motivators for Sunday School Workers* (1978-). *Sunday School Growth Journal* (1980-). *Workers' Meeting Resource Kit* (1977-).

PERSONAL READING. Quarterlies: *encounter!* (1972-). *Open Windows, Large Print* (1976-).

SUNDAY SCHOOL QUARTERLIES. *Adult Life and Work Cassette* (1979-). *Adult Life and Work Resource Kit* (1977-). *Beginning* (1980-). *Bible Book Study Commentary* (1979-). *Bible Book Study for Adult Teachers* (1978-). *Bible Book Study for Adults* (1978-). *Bible Book Study for Adults, Large Print* (1980-). *Bible Book Study for Adult Teachers Resource Kit* (1979-). *Bible Book Study for Youth* (1978-). *Bible Book Study for Youth Teachers* (1978-). *Bible Book Study for Youth Teachers Resource Kit* (1978-). *Bible Book Study Guide* (1980-). *Bible Discoverers Recording* (1979-). *Bible Learners Recording* (1979-). *Bible Searchers Recording* (1979-). *Bible Study for Bible Discoverers Teachers* (1980-). *Bible Study for Bible Learners Teachers* (1980-). *Bible Study for Bible Searchers Teachers* (1980-). *Broadman Comments* (1976-). *Cassette for Bible Discoverers* (1976-). *Cassette for Bible Learners* (1976-).

Cassette for Bible Searchers (1976-). *Context* (1970-74); succeeded by *Collegiate Bible Study*. *El Interprete* (1978-). *El Interprete Maestro* (1979-). *Extended Session for Babies and Toddlers* (1980-). *Extended Session for 2's and 3's* (1980-). *Extended Session for 4's and 5's* (1980-). *Guide B for Preschool Teachers Resource Kit* (1978-). *Guide C for Preschool Teachers* (1973-). *Guide C for Preschool Teachers Resource Kit* (1978-). *Invitation to Bible Study* (1970-73). *Layman's Bible Book Commentary* (1979-). *People* (1970-73). *Points for Emphasis* (1976-). *Resource Kit for Bible Discoverers* (1972-). *Resource Kit for Bible Learners* (1972-). *Resource Kit for Bible Searchers* (1972-). *Studying Adult Life and Work Lessons* (1970-). *Sunday School Lesson Illustrator* (1974-79); succeeded by *Biblical Illustrator*. *Sunday School Resource Kit for Teaching Deaf Children* (1976-). *Sunday School Resource Kit for Teaching the Mentally Retarded* (1979-). *Your Invitation* (1970-73). *Youth in Action: Department Director's Resource Kit* (1978-). *Youth in Action Resource Kit* (1973-). *Youth in Discovery: Department Director's Resource Kit* (1978-). *Youth in Discovery Resource Kit* (1973-). *Youth in Search* (1970-73). *Youth in Search Teacher* (1970-73).

CHURCH TRAINING QUARTERLIES. *Adult Church Training Guide* (1972-73). *Alive* (1970-72); succeeded by *Come Alive*. *Alive for Leaders* (1970-72); succeeded by *Come Alive for Leaders*. *Baptist Adults* (1971-). *Baptist Adults Resource Kit* (1977-). *Baptist Young Adults Resource Kit* (1978-). *Baptist Youth* (1973-). *Baptist Youth Kit for Leaders* (1973-). *Becoming* (1970-73). *Becoming for Leaders* (1970-73). *Becoming Kit for Leaders* (1972-73). *Care Kit for Leaders* (1972-). *Come Alive Kit for Leaders* (1972-). *Exploring B Kit for Leaders* (1970-). *Exploring C Kit for Leaders* (1970-). *Now* (1970-73). *Now for Leaders* (1970-73). *Skill* (1970-73). *Source* (1973-80). *Source Resource Kit* (1977-80). *Young Adults in Training* (1973-). *Young Adults in Training Resource Kit* (1977-).

CHURCH MUSIC QUARTERLIES. *The Cassette Musician* (1978-). *Choral Overtones* (1970-74); succeeded by *Choral Praise*. *Choral Overtones Recording* (1970-74); succeeded by *Choral Praise Recording*. *Choral Tones* (1970-74); succeeded by *Gospel Choir*. *Choral Tones Recording* (1970-74); succeeded by *Gospel Choir Recording*. *Demo Cassette* (1978-). *Glory Songs* (1980-). *Glory Songs Recording* (1980-). *Music Makers Recording* (1972-). *Music Makers Resource Kit* (1979-). *Music Time* (1979-). *Opus One* (1970-). *Opus One Recording* (1970-). *Opus Two* (1970-). *Opus Two Recording* (1970-). *Preschool Music Recording* (1972-). *Preschool Music Resource Kit* (1980-). *Young Musicians Recording* (1970-).

V. Periodicals Launched or Current, Oct., 1980. GENERAL PUBLICATIONS. Quarterlies: *Church Recreation*. *Living with Children*. *Living with Preschoolers*. *Living with Teenagers*. *Media: Library Services Journal*. *Proclaim*. *The Quarterly Review*. *Search*. Monthlies: *The Deacon*. *Christian Single*. *Church Administration*. *Home Life*. *Mature Living*. *The Student*.

GENERAL PUBLICATIONS (SPANISH). Produced by Baptist Spanish Publishing House and distributed by SSB: *Ancla (The Anchor)*. *El Hogar Cristiano (The Christian Home)*. *El Promotor De Educacion Cristiano (The Promoter of Christian Education)*. *Respuesta (The Answer)*.

LEADERSHIP MATERIALS. Quarterlies: *Children's Worship Resource Kit*. *The Cassette Musician*. *Children's Leadership*. *Motivators for Sunday School Workers*. *Preschool Leadership*. *Worker's Meeting Resource Kit*. *Youth in Discovery: Department Director's Resource Kit*. *Youth in Action: Department Director's Resource Kit*. *Youth Leadership*. *The Youth Teacher: Department Director's Resource Kit*. Monthlies: *Adult Leadership*. *The Church Musician*. *Church Training*. *Sunday School Growth Journal*. *Sunday School Leadership*.

PERSONAL READING. Weeklies: *Adventure*. *More*. Quarterlies: *Bible Reader's Guide*. *encounter! Open Windows*. *Open Windows, Large Print*. Monthly: *event*.

SUNDAY SCHOOL QUARTERLIES. *Adult Bible Teacher*. *Adult Bible Study*. *Adult Life and Work Cassette*. *Adult Life and Work Resource Kit*. *The Adult Teacher*. *Advanced Bible Study*. *Beginning*. *Bible Book Study Commentary*. *Bible Book Study for Adult Teachers*. *Bible Book Study for Adult Teachers Resource Kit*. *Bible Book Study for Adults*. *Bible Book Study for Adults, Large Print*. *Bible Book Study for Youth*. *Bible Book Study for Youth Teachers*. *Bible Book Study for Youth Teachers Resource Kit*. *Bible Discoverers*. *Bible Discoverers Recording*. *Bible Discoverers Teacher*. *Bible Learners*. *Bible Learners Recording*. *Bible Learners Teacher*. *Bible Lesson Digest*. *Bible Searchers*. *Bible Searchers Recording*. *Bible Searchers Teacher*. *Bible Study for Bible Discoverers Teacher*. *Bible Study for Bible Learners Teacher*. *Bible Study for Bible Searchers Teacher*. *Bible Study Leaflet*. *Bible Study Pocket Commentary*. *Biblical Illustrator*. *Broadman Comments*. *Cassette for Bible Discoverers*. *Cassette for Bible Searchers*. *Extended Session for Babies and Toddlers*. *Extended Session for 2's and 3's*. *Extended Session for 4's and 5's*. *Growing*. *Guide A for Preschool Teachers*. *Guide B for Preschool Teachers*. *Guide B for Preschool Teachers Resource Kit*. *Guide C for Preschool Teachers*. *Guide C for Preschool Teachers Resource Kit*. *Layman's Bible Book Commentary*. *Living*. *Look and Listen*. *On the Wing*. *Points for Emphasis*. *Resource Kit for Bible Learners*. *Resource Kit for Bible Discoverers*. *Resource Kit for Bible Searchers*. *Senior Adult Bible Study*. *Simplified Bible Study*. *Studying Adult Life and Work Lessons*. *Sunday School Adults*. *Sunday School Lessons Simplified*. *Sunday School Resource Kit for Teaching Deaf Children*. *Sunday School Resource Kit for Teaching the Mentally Retarded*. *Sunday School Youth A*. *Sunday School Youth B*. *Sunday School Young Adults*. *Sunday School Senior Adults*. *Teaching Pictures for Bible Discoverers*. *Teaching Pictures for Bible Learners*. *Teaching Pictures for Bible Searchers*. *Test Your Knowledge Life and Work*. *Young Adult Bible Study*. *Youth in Action*. *Youth in Action Resource Kit*. *Youth in Action Teacher*. *Youth in Discovery*. *Youth in Discovery Resource Kit*. *Youth in Discovery Teacher*. *Youth Teacher Resource Kit*. *The Youth Teacher*.

SUNDAY SCHOOL QUARTERLIES (SPANISH). Produced and distributed by SSB: *Adultos en la Escuela Dominical (Sunday School Adults)*. *El Maes-*

tro de Adultos (The Adult Teacher). Produced by the Baptist Spanish Publishing House and distributed by SSB: *A Delante! (Forward!*—ages 18-29). *Conquistadores (Conquerors*—ages 9-11). *Conquistadores para Maestros de Primarios (Conquerors—Teachers of Primaries). El Expositor Biblico para Alumnos Maestro (Bible Expositor for Adults Pupil Book). El Expositor Biblico para Maestros (Bible Expositors Teachers Book). El Maestro de Adultos (Adult Teacher). Lecciones Biblicas (Biblical Readings). Lecciones Ilustradas para Maestro de Parvulos (Illustrated Lessons—Teachers of Children). Nuestros Ninos (Our Children*—ages 6-8). *Nuestros Ninos para Maestro de Principiantes (Our Children—Teacher).*

CHURCH TRAINING QUARTERLIES. *Baptist Adults. Baptist Adults Resource Kit. Baptist Young Adults. Baptist Young Adults Resource Kit. Baptist Youth. Baptist Youth Kit for Leaders. Care. Care for Leaders. Care Kit for Leaders. Come Alive. Come Alive for Leaders. Come Alive Kit for Leaders. Exploring A. Exploring A for Leaders. Exploring A Kit for Leaders. Exploring C. Exploring C for Leaders. Exploring C Kit for Leaders.*

CHURCH TRAINING QUARTERLIES (SPANISH). Produced and distributed by SSB: *La Fe Bautista (The Baptist Faith).* Produced by Baptist Spanish Publishing House and distributed by SSB: *Accion! (Action!) Ahora! (Now!). Cuaderno de Actividades* (workbook—ages 4-8). *Revista pare Parvulos y Principiantes* (ages 4-8). *Revista para Uniones de Primarios* (ages 9-11).

CHURCH MUSIC QUARTERLIES. *Choral Praise. Choral Praise Recording. Demo Cassette. Glory Songs. Glory Songs Recording. Gospel Choir. Gospel Choir Recording. Music Makers. Music Makers Recording. Music Makers Resource Kit. Music Time. Opus One. Opus One Recording. Opus Two. Opus Two Recording. Preschool Music Recording. Preschool Music Resource Kit. Young Musicians. Young Musicians Recording.*

See also ARCHITECTURE, CHURCH; AUDIOVISUALS/ELECTRONIC MEDIA; BOOK STORES, BAPTIST; BROADMAN BIBLE COMMENTARY; BROADMAN PRESS; CHURCH ADMINISTRATION; CHURCH TRAINING; EQUIPPING CENTERS; CONVENTION PRESS; CURRICULUM, SOUTHERN BAPTIST CHURCH; DARGAN-CARVER LIBRARY; EXCEPTIONAL PERSONS, MATERIALS FOR USE WITH; FAMILY MINISTRY; GLORIETA BAPTIST CONFERENCE CENTER; HOLMAN BIBLE PUBLISHING COMPANY; HOME BIBLE STUDY; INTERNATIONAL STUDENT MINISTRY; LANGUAGE PUBLISHING; LIBRARY, CHURCH; MUSIC, BAPTIST; RADIO-TELEVISION BIBLE CORRESPONDENCE COURSE; RECREATION, CHURCH; RIDGECREST BAPTIST CONFERENCE CENTER; SUNDAY SCHOOL; URBAN CHURCH STUDIES, CENTER FOR; VACATION BIBLE SCHOOL; VOCATIONAL GUIDANCE, PROGRAM OF.

								GOMER R. LESCH

SUNDAY SCHOOL LESSONS, UNIFORM (II). See UNIFORM SERIES, COMMITTEE ON.

SUNDAY SCHOOL'S 200th ANNIVERSARY. The development of the Sunday School is to a great extent the history of Christian education in America. Robert Raikes, traditionally considered to be the father of the modern Sunday School movement, opened a school in Gloucester, England, in 1780. Raikes, an Anglican layman, began his Sunday School for poor, illiterate, working children who worked six days a week and ran wild in the streets on Sunday.

Bicentennial celebrations of the Sunday School movement in 1980 were worldwide. In England the celebration began formally in London with a ceremony at the statue of Robert Raikes. A book was written by Frank Booth entitled, *Robert Raikes of Gloucester* (1980).

Among Southern Baptists in America, recognition of the 200th Anniversary of Sunday School focused in the areas of promotion, publications, and enlargement through Bold Mission Thrust. Bold Mission Thrust in relationship to Sunday School enlargement emphasized starting new Sunday Schools and establishing new classes or departments in existing Sunday Schools.

For Southern Baptists the Sunday School remains the largest major education and outreach program organization of the churches with an enrollment of 7,300,000 in 1980. The bicentennial year found Sunday School growth stable.

								ALVA G. PARKS

SURINAM, MISSION IN. Surinam, formerly called Dutch Guiana, achieved independence from the Dutch on Nov. 25, 1975. Slightly larger than Illinois and located on the northeast coast of South America, the country has a multiracial society of about 400,000, including Hindustani, Creole, Javanese, Bush-Negroes, Chinese, Amerindians, and others. Dutch is the official language, although many are spoken. Religions include Hinduism, Islam, Roman Catholicism, and Moravian Brethren. Southern Baptists began work in Paramaribo, the capital, in 1971. Since then two churches, one mission, and several preaching points have been established. Work among English and Chinese-speaking peoples has begun. In early 1980, nine career missionaries were assigned to Surinam.

								FREDERICK E. DAY

SURLES, HENRY FLOYD (b. near Dillon, SC, May 19, 1882; d. Darlington, SC, May 20, 1973). Pastor and denominational leader. Son of William Pinkney, a farmer, and Phoebe Jane Coates Surles, he attended Furman University (B.A., 1908) and The Southern Baptist Theological Seminary (Th.M., 1911). For 42 years he was pastor of seven churches in Kentucky, Missouri, Kansas, and South Carolina. From 1939 to 1963, he served either as assistant secretary or secretary of the South Carolina Baptist Convention. Surles married Sue Olmstead, May 31, 1911. Their children were Lucille and Henry Floyd, Jr. He is buried in Springwood Cemetery, Greenville, SC.

								OLLIN J. OWENS

SWEDISH BAPTISTS IN NORTH AMERICA. See BAPTIST GENERAL CONFERENCE; CANADIAN BAPTISTS.

SWITZERLAND, BAPTIST CENTER (cf. Baptist Center, Switzerland, Vol. III). In the 1970s, the Baptist Theological Seminary, the main unit of this center at Ruschlikon, survived serious financial problems caused mainly by a decline in the value of the dollar. The faculty continued to be both American and European. In 1980 a distinguished European, C. Ronald Goulding, became interim president.

The executive board is responsible to both the European Baptist Federation and the Foreign Mission Board, SBC. The president of the German-speaking Baptist Union of Switzerland is a Ruschlikon seminary professor.

The European Baptist Press Service, a radio recording studio, international conferences, the office of the FMB's field representative, and a growing role in evangelism add to the significance of the Ruschlikon Baptist Center. In 1980, 16 Southern Baptist missionaries were living and working in Switzerland.

J. D. HUGHEY

T

TAIWAN (FORMOSA), MISSION IN (III; cf. Formosa, Mission in, Vol. I). Tragedy struck the mission in 1973 when Gladys Hopewell was brutally murdered by a cook. Chiang Kai Shek, leader of the country, died in 1975. The Christian testimony in his will stirred revival fires led by Chow Lien Hwa, Baptist seminary teacher and pastor. A new Chinese Baptist hymnbook served to unify and strengthen the churches. The Chinese Baptist Convention sent a missionary couple to Korea, a program of Theological Education by Extension was launched, and a ministry among the Hakka Chinese began. The radio-television studio in Taipei produced its first motion picture, installed video cassette equipment, and began a daily radio program. At the end of the decade the missionary count was 107, including five journeymen.

GEORGE H. HAYS

TALBIRD, HENRY (b. Nov. 7, 1811, Hilton Head Island, SC; d. Oct. 14, 1890, Switzerland, FL). Minister, soldier, and educator. Son of Sarah E. Talbird and Henry Talbird, a manufacturer, he was a descendant of pioneer settlers of South Carolina. He attended Madison (now Colgate) University, New York (A.M., 1841). Following pastorates in Tuscaloosa, AL, 1842, and Montgomery, AL, 1843-52, he became professor of theology at Howard College, succeeding T. F. Curtis (q.v. III), and was soon elected second president, succeeding S. S. Sherman (q.v. III). His marriage, Jan. 15, 1845, to Mary C. Griffin, wealthy widow, linked him and the college to the planter aristocracy.

During the Civil War Talbird served as captain of the Seventh Alabama Infantry Regiment and colonel of the 41st Alabama Regiment.

Failing health forced him to return to pulpits in rural Alabama. Subsequent pastorates were in Henderson, KY, 1868-71; Lexington, MO, 1872-84; and Starke, FL, 1884-87. He is buried at Switzerland, FL.

LEE N. ALLEN

TALIAFERRO, HARDIN EDWARDS (b. Surry County, NC, 1811; d. Loudon, TN, Nov. 2, 1875). Preacher, editor, and writer. The son of Sallie and Charles Taliaferro, farmers, he attended an academy in Madisonville, TN. In 1834 he married Elizabeth Henderson. They had two daughters, Nancy and Adelaide. For 20 years he served as pastor of churches in Coosa River Association, Alabama. His literary penchant led him to join his brother-in-law, Samuel Henderson (q.v. III), in 1856 as "junior editor" of *South Western Baptist*.

A summer's visit in 1857 to his native region kindled memories of his happy boyhood, and he began writing the comic/folk sketches contained in *Fisher's River (North Carolina) Scenes and Characters, by Skitt,* "Who Was Raised Thar" (1859), a masterpiece of southwestern humor. While Taliaferro edited the *South Western Baptist,* 1859-62, its weekly pages reflected his light-heartedness and uncompromising orthodoxy. About 1872 he returned to Tennessee and was active in the Loudon church until his death.

RICHARD WALSER

TANZANIA, MISSION IN (cf. East Africa, Mission in, Vol. III). Separate mission organizations were formed in Tanzania and Kenya in 1978. The seminary at Arusha continued serving all of East Africa. Tanzanian missionaries also operated several Bible schools and a seminary extension program. Agricultural projects in Arusha, Kasulu, and Kyela responded to Tanzania's physical needs. Dar es Salaam's community center emphasized adult education. From the opening of Mbeya Baptist Hospital in 1960 until the Baptist mission transferred it to the government in 1979, almost 20,000 inpatients and more than 300,000 outpatients received treatment. Medical clinics continued in the Mbeya and Kigoma regions. An evangelistic project among the Sukuma people in northwestern Tanzania resulted in 56 new churches and 2,575 baptisms in an eight-week period in 1979. In a plan called "Shoulder to Shoulder," Tanzania's 23,000 Baptists entered the 1980s with a goal of 100,000 Baptists in Tanzania by the year 2000. Seventy-nine missionaries were serving in 1979.

JOY NEAL

TARDY, WILLIAM T. (b. Drew County, AR, June 8, 1872; d. Marshall, TX, Feb. 24, 1919). Pastor. The son of A. B. Tardy, a country doctor and farmer, and Mary S. Vaughn Tardy, he attended Ouachita Baptist College. He married Daisy Mobberly, Feb. 12, 1895. They had six children: W. T., Jr., James, Joseph, Francis, Harold, and Margaret. Although he served as pastor in churches in Arkansas and Louisiana, most of his pastorates were in Texas: Longview, Palestine, Greenville, Paris, Nacogdoches, and Marshall. He was one of the founders of the College of Marshall, later East Texas Baptist College. He is buried in Greenwood Cemetery, Longview, TX.

C. GWIN MORRIS

TELEVISION. The issue of the moral dimensions of television broadcasting became a major concern of Southern Baptists in the 1970s.

Messengers to the 1977 SBC adopted recommendations presented by the Christian Life Commission on television and morality. These recommendations grew out of hearings held in Richmond, VA; Jackson, MS; San Francisco, CA; and the Dallas-Fort Worth, TX, area. The recommendations called Southern Baptists to confront television's moral challenge, to utilize special study materials prepared by the CLC, to encourage churches to ask members to use careful moral judgment about the kind of television programs watched, to communicate with those in the industry responsible for television programming, and to urge Southern Baptists to join with others to support the good and eradicate the evil in television programming.

In the fall of 1977, the CLC launched a Help for Television Viewers campaign. Resource packets of material were sent to every Southern Baptist pastor. Many churches ordered additional packets. The packet itself became news and was discussed on national television, in major newspapers throughout the country, and in national magazines. Millions of pieces of the material have been distributed to people concerned about television morality throughout the nation.

In 1979 the SBC passed a resolution commending people in the television industry working to provide morally responsible programming, supporting legislation to uphold the public interest in television regulations, and opposing legislation removing restraints from an industry "that has proven its unwillingness to restrain itself."

In its Help for Television Viewers program, the CLC has worked closely with the Southern Baptist Radio and Television Commission.

HARRY N. HOLLIS, JR.

TELEVISION, CABLE. Cable television (community antenna television, CATV) was developed in the late 1940s in communities unable to receive TV signals because of certain terrain or distance features relative to available TV stations. The signals thus captured were then distributed via cable to subscribers for a fee. By the time of the effective date for the current Federal Communications *Cable Television Report and Order*, Mar. 31, 1972, many additional services were coming on line, pay cable being the most important economically.

While the Federal Communications Commission does not follow a licensing procedure regarding cable TV systems, it does require a "certificate of compliance," and provides minimum standards for franchises issued by local governments. These standards relate to the process of selecting a franchisee, franchise duration, fees, establishment of a construction timetable, rates charged to subscribers, and procedures for handling subscriber complaints.

At the present time, there are over 4,200 operating cable systems in the United States, serving some 10,200 communities. Another 1,300 systems are approved but not built. Operating systems currently reach about 15,100,000 subscribers, accounting for over 44,000,000 people or 20 percent of the nation's TV households. Pay cable is on approximately 2,000 systems and reaches 5,000,000 subscribers in 49 states.

In 1976 there were 357 Southern Baptist churches utilizing cable systems, providing primarily the Sunday morning and evening worship services. Recent estimates suggest as many as 1,500 SBC churches now using cable.

The Radio and Television Commission, SBC, continues to assist the churches in their use of cable systems through the provision of programming, consultation, production, and channel management and planning. The ministry options are endless, including local children's programs, Bible study courses, promotional training, educational training, music programs, Christian news service, SBC programming such as the Sunday School Board's *At Home with the Bible* series, and community specials, as a part of the church's outreach.

See also RADIO AND TELEVISION COMMISSION, SBC.

CHARLES RODEN

TELEVISION, MISSIONARY USE OF. See RADIO AND TELEVISION, MISSIONARY USE OF.

TELEVISION IN RELIGION AND SOUTHERN BAPTISTS.

During the 1970s the term "electronic church" described a growing phenomenon in American religious life, namely, the efforts of numerous Christian groups and individuals to communicate the gospel via mass media. Christian broadcasting began in the 1920s as church services and other evangelical programs were produced for radio. By 1979 there were over 1,000 religious radio stations, 25 Christian television outlets, and thousands of religious radio and television programs produced by denominations, local churches, and individual Christians. Many of these groups affiliate with the National Religious Broadcasters, founded in 1944, which coordinates activities and lobbying efforts for over 850 members who produce about 70 percent of all religious broadcasting in America. The Radio and Television Commission, SBC, is a member, although not an active participant, in the NRB.

The Christian Broadcasting Network, founded in 1960 by Marion "Pat" Robertson, is the largest distributor of religious television programming. The network's most successful program, the *700 Club,* represents a new style of religious broadcasting with host, guests, audience participation, and telephone counseling.

Other TV evangelists with multimillion dollar budgets increasingly purchased television time rather than rely on public service programming given by local stations. The Radio and Television Commission once relied heavily on such free time, producing limited series or specials rather than weekly programs. The declining availability of free time has led the commission to reevaluate its current procedures.

The impact of electronic religion on contemporary Christianity continues to be evaluated and debated.

BILL J. LEONARD

TENNESSEE ASSOCIATIONS (II, III).

I. New Associations. SHILOH. Organized Jan. 3, 1975, by representatives from 26 churches of Hardin County and McNairy Associations, meeting with First Baptist Church, Crump. The new association adopted a constitution and bylaws and policies related to the work of the director of associational missions. The first annual meeting was held Oct. 16-17, 1975. Separate actions by Hardin County and McNairy Associations on Oct. 19, 1974, provided for the merger of the two associations. In 1979, 37 churches reported 274 baptisms, 8,675 members, $1,191,806 total gifts, $133,859 mission gifts, and $4,872,680 property value.

SULLIVAN. Organized Oct. 7, 1974, at First Baptist Church, Kingsport, by representatives of 16 churches located in the Kingsport area of Sullivan County and previously affiliated with Holston Association. Chartered by the state of Tennessee as Sullivan Baptist Association, Incorporated, the association has a written constitution and bylaws and subscribes to The Baptist Faith and Message statement of the SBC of 1963. In 1979, 17 churches reported 228 baptisms, 10,198 members, $2,179,732 total gifts, $484,980 mission gifts, and $10,957,493 property value.

II. Changes in Associations. CLINCH. This association of only two churches held its sixth and final meeting on Oct. 23, 1971, at Kyles Ford, and ceased to exist when the two churches were received into the fellowship of Holston Valley Association, Sep. 23, 1972.

HARDIN COUNTY. Seventh and final session held Oct. 17, 1974. Merged with McNairy to form Shiloh, Jan. 3, 1974.

MCMINN. Name changed to McMinn-Meigs Association of Baptists, Incorporated, in annual meeting, Oct. 20, 1977, to better identify the geographical area of the association (McMinn and Meigs Counties).

MCNAIRY. Organized in 1924, the association merged with Hardin County Association in 1975 to form Shiloh Association.

LESLIE R. BAUMGARTNER

TENNESSEE BAPTIST CHILDREN'S HOMES, INC.

(II, III). About 500 dependent and neglected children receive care annually on four campuses and through their related services. The campuses are located at Franklin, Memphis, and Chattanooga. The 500 acres of land plus buildings and equipment were valued at $4,962,287 in 1979. The budget for 1978-79 was $1,429,197, and the per capita cost of care was $5,598. The ministry is supported through the Cooperative Program and an annual Mother's Day offering in the churches, supplemented by personal gifts, bequests, and memorials. The children attend public schools and churches off the campuses.

This ministry of benevolence and missions is a multiservice program, including group care, foster homes, adoptions, family counseling, and work with unwed mothers. Services are available to children of all races and creeds.

E. B. BOWEN

TENNESSEE BAPTIST CONVENTION (II, III).

I. History. During the past decade, the Tennessee Baptist Convention grew numerically, financially, and in programs and services. From 1969 to 1979, the number of churches increased from 2,699 to 2,760 and membership from 880,802 to 995,625. Total gifts more than doubled in this period from $7,483,374 to $19,073,848.

Leadership.—After serving as executive secretary-treasurer since Nov. 1, 1956, W. Fred Kendall retired, Dec. 31, 1972. He was succeeded, Jan. 1, 1973, by Ralph E. Norton, who served until his retirement, Dec. 31, 1978. Tom J. Madden became executive secretary-treasurer, Jan. 1, 1979.

Directors of the various administrative and state missions areas of the Executive Board during the 1970s were: Business Office, Glenn A. Jenkins, 1968-72, James M. McDonald,

1972-   ; Cooperative Program and Stewardship Promotion, W. C. Summar, 1969-75, O. M. Dangeau, 1976-   ; *Baptist and Reflector* editors, James A. Lester, 1968-74, Alvin C. Shackleford, 1976-   ; Program Services, Wallace E. Anderson, 1960-   ; Protection Plans, Paul R. Phelps, 1966-71, Vern B. Powers, 1971-   ; Tennessee Baptist Foundation, Jonas L. Stewart, 1968-   ; Brotherhood, Roy J. Gilleland, Jr., 1956-76, Archie D. King, 1977-   ; Church Music, Frank G. Charton, 1955-   ; Church Training, Charles L. Norton, 1943-75, Johnnie Hall, Jr., 1976-   ; Evangelism, F. M. Dowell, Jr., 1956-76, Malcolm McDow, 1977-   ; Missions, Leslie R. Baumgartner, 1960-   ; Student, Glenn Yarbrough, 1969-   ; and Sunday School, Wendell W. Price, 1965-   . Several departments have expanded their programs and personnel. The number of employees increased from 67 at the close of 1969 to 101 in 1979, excluding directors of missions and student directors who are jointly employed by associations.

Significant Events.—On Mar. 23, 1971, a special service was held to transfer ownership of the restored Sinking Creek Baptist Church, the oldest extant church in Tennessee of any faith (built before 1779), from a historical society in Elizabethton to the convention.

A History of the Tennessee Baptist Convention, by W. Fred Kendall, was authorized and published by the convention to commemorate its centennial in 1974.

The centennial convention session convened in Murfreesboro, Nov. 12-14, 1974, to celebrate the organization of the convention in that city in Apr., 1874. Major features included a film which depicted the overall work of the convention and a pageant which portrayed the 100 years of convention history.

The convention was called into a special session, Apr. 5, 1979, the first called convention since Aug. 12, 1874, to deal with a financial situation that developed in the initial planning of Belmont Plaza, a housing facility built by the Tennessee Baptist Service Corporation for retired persons.

Aug. 4, 1979, marked the 10th anniversary of the official opening of the executive board building in Brentwood. During the 1970s, convention work grew to the point that building space became a problem. A long-range study of present utilization and future expansion of the building has begun.

II. Program of Work. *Growth of Student Work.*—Developments in the Department of Student Work included the expansion of Baptist Student Union into the state's community colleges. Active BSU programs exist on the campuses of nine of the state's 10 community colleges.

The staff has increased in size. A director serves on each of the community college campuses, five of them in full-time appointments. The first full-time staff associate was employed at the University of Tennessee in Knoxville. Five graduate assistant scholarships have been budgeted, with workers appointed to various campuses.

The work with black students has become an official and integral part of the BSU program. The long-existing work with the historically black schools in Nashville was assigned to the department. Workers to develop black fellowship groups within BSU were provided at Knoxville and Memphis.

Student missions has continued as a vital part of Baptist Student Union. Tennesseans have sent about 40 young people each year for mission appointments of at least 10 weeks duration and about 250 each year in short-term mission projects. Students have made significant contributions toward alleviating world hunger, particularly in Bangladesh and Brazil.

Student center buildings were designed and constructed at Columbia, Murfreesboro, Cleveland, and Chattanooga. Temporary units were provided at Jackson State, Motlow State, and Roane State Community Colleges, and in Nashville.

Convention Ministries Division.—This office was established by action of the Executive Board in 1975. The director is responsible to the executive secretary-treasurer and provides leadership in coordination and correlation to the following departments: Brotherhood, Church Training, Evangelism, Missions, Student, Sunday School, and Music. Woman's Missionary Union, an auxiliary, relates in a cooperative effort. Tom Madden served as the first director, 1976-78. After assuming the duties of executive secretary-treasurer, he was succeeded by Carroll C. Owen, in Apr., 1979.

Church-Ministers Information Department.—The convention approved the establishment of this department and its program statement in 1975. The primary responsibility of the department is to supply information upon request to churches about pastors and other church staff personnel and to be available for counseling to both church and staff personnel regarding matters of ministry. J. William Harbin assumed the position as director of the department in 1976.

Church Media Services, Church Recreation, and Historical Society.—Jean Adkinson, consultant, served under the direction of the director of the Convention Ministries Division, 1977-81.

Public Affairs and Christian Life.—Jerry M. Self, 1978, became the consultant in the areas of family life, citizenship, human relations, separation of church and state, alcohol and drug abuse, and moral-social issues. This position is presently assigned to the office of *Baptist and Reflector.*

Missions Department.—Ministry of the Missions Department was enlarged and strengthened in 1977 by the employment of Ruben J. Cãnas to head the program of Language Missions and Interfaith Witness and the transfer of Jarvis Hearn to the Brentwood office from Seymour, TN, to enhance the ministry to the deaf.

Committee Organization of the Tennessee Baptist Convention.—The eight standing committees of the convention, along with the Executive Board, carry out the work of the convention between sessions. These committees are: Arrangements, Audits, Boards, Committees, Constitution and Bylaws, Credentials, Journal, and Resolutions. Each committee is composed of 15 members.

The Executive Board, composed of 99 members, meets five times a year in regularly scheduled meetings and at other times when it is called. There are 25 members from each of the three sections of the state and 24 who are, as nearly as possible, distributed in proportion to the Baptist population in the three sections as reported to the preceding convention. The convention president and president of WMU serve as ex officio members. Each member is recommended by a Nominating Committee to serve on one of the following standing committees of the board: Christian Services, Denominational Cooperation, Education, Public Affairs and Christian Life, State Missions, and Tennessee Baptist Program. The seventh standing committee, the Administrative Committee, is composed of chairmen of the other six standing committees, the president and vice-president of the Executive Board, president of the convention, and nine at-large members who are recommended by the Nominating Committee.

Budget Process.—One of the major responsibilities of the Executive Board is to recommend a Cooperative Program budget to the convention. A percentage division of funds is approved for SBC and state causes prior to budget preparation. There are no preferred items deleted before the percentage division is approved. Requests for state programs are submitted to the office of the executive secretary-treasurer and are reviewed by committees assigned to the four budget areas (Administrative, State Missions, Education, and Christian Services) on the basis of priority needs, not percentage. The Tennessee Baptist Program Committee reviews recommendations from the other committees in light of income of the past year, the projected income for the coming year, and the overall convention program before making recommendations to the Executive Board. The Executive Board makes the final recommendation to the convention. The proposed budget is printed in the state paper at least two weeks before the annual session of the convention.

Special Committees.—In 1970 a special committee was appointed to study the constitution and bylaws of the convention and was made a standing committee of the convention in 1973.

The Centennial Steering Committee was appointed in 1970 to make plans for the centennial celebration during the 1974 session of the convention in Murfreesboro.

In 1971 a committee was appointed to study the establishment of a ministry to senior citizens. The following year the committee recommended that a ministry to the aging be created and, as a result of further study, the Tennessee Baptist Service Corporation was chartered in 1974.

TENNESSEE STATISTICAL SUMMARY

Year	Associations	Churches	Church Membership	Baptisms	SS Enrollment	VBS Enrollment	CT Enrollment	WMU Enrollment	Brotherhood Enrollment	Ch. Music Enrollment	Mission Gifts	Total Gifts	Value Church Property
1969	69	2,699	880,802	25,780	535,154	228,589	197,565	80,969	26,090	74,194	$ 9,093,179	$ 58,797,580	$277,640,229
1970	69	2,698	892,001	28,077	531,902	217,880	191,609	76,229	25,738	75,681	9,479,468	61,947,368	289,013,418
1971	69	2,711	902,780	29,708	522,057	221,325	166,470	72,278	27,354	76,139	11,044,298	68,714,306	300,885,363
1972	68	2,722	917,579	32,185	524,962	221,953	163,218	72,039	27,910	81,945	12,091,786	75,166,553	325,280,031
1973	68	2,741	931,516	28,967	521,885	223,271	155,780	70,924	28,013	87,424	13,474,818	79,687,505	361,938,317
1974	68	2,746	942,711	29,994	521,607	233,297	154,895	72,159	28,742	91,984	14,913,630	87,820,389	400,554,314
1975	68	2,750	957,771	31,365	528,239	246,005	155,164	74,958	30,488	97,024	16,299,391	97,174,969	439,892,865
1976	68	2,758	970,619	27,902	537,124	236,963	156,684	75,208	30,147	99,861	17,809,865	108,601,494	484,261,087
1977	68	2,760	977,641	23,482	532,538	226,113	151,413	74,134	29,953	100,516	19,529,898	118,600,488	531,099,270
1978	68	2,756	984,707	23,166	527,373	225,121	148,739	73,717	29,685	104,400	21,120,662	131,673,784	584,944,422
1979	68	2,759	995,564	26,305	521,750	234,041	146,036	72,881	29,856	106,607	23,773,792	144,669,382	668,079,680
1980	68	2,765	1,013,890	30,443	529,583	245,298	148,118	74,281	30,897	111,259	26,414,505	159,139,343	742,489,583

JEAN ADKINSON

In 1972 the convention authorized the appointment of a special committee to study the system of representation on boards and committees as compared with that of other states and the SBC. Public hearings were conducted in each of the three sections of the state. As a result of the study, changes were made in the constitution of the convention and in various charters: the Executive Board was increased from 75 to 99, convention committees were increased from 9 to 15, and no person could serve on more than one committee or board except Baptist Memorial Hospital in Memphis and the Tennessee Baptist Foundation, according to their charter requirements.

The Tennessee Baptist Program Committee was given a special assignment in 1972 to prepare program statements which defined functions, objectives, and relationships of the various program areas of the convention's work. These statements were adopted by the convention in annual session as bylaws to be amended only by convention action. As other programs have emerged, new program statements have been adopted. Revisions of program statements are made according to the procedure for amending bylaws.

A Church Staff Salary Study Committee, consisting of 15 laymen (five from each section of the state), was nominated by the Committee on Committees in 1973. Results of the study were printed and distributed in booklet form to all convention churches in 1974. A follow-up study was made in 1977, and, again, findings were made available to all churches.

A Reorganization Study Committee of the Executive Board was appointed in 1974. A complete study was made of the organization and relationships of departments and agencies whose offices were housed within the Executive Board building. The division concept was adopted, and the first to be established was the Convention Ministries Division with Tom Madden as director. The Central Administrative Division was left under the guidance of the executive secretary-treasurer for the present time.

A Committee on World Hunger was approved by the convention in 1978 and appointed by the convention. This committee has led Tennessee Baptists to be more aware of world hunger, and it recommends definite ways that needs can be met.

Due to a financial crisis involving Belmont Plaza, a retirement high rise and a project of the Tennessee Baptist Service Corporation, the Belmont Plaza Study Committee was appointed to explore solutions, investigate options, and bring recommendations to the called convention in Apr., 1979. Final disposition of the facility was approved by the Executive Board, Mar. 13, 1980.

TOM MADDEN

TENNESSEE BAPTIST FOUNDATION
(II, III). Jonas L. Stewart continues as executive secretary-treasurer. Assets on Jan. 1, 1980,

were about $9,000,000. Income distributed in 1979 was $563,384. Administrative expenses are paid from Cooperative Program income. All earned income from trusts and other funds goes to the cause designated by the donor. The budget for 1979-80 called for expenditures of $149,311.

JONAS STEWART

TENNESSEE BAPTIST HISTORICAL SOCIETY (II, III). During the 1970s the society worked to establish an official relationship with the Tennessee Baptist Convention. A permanent history committee, recommended in the society's report to the convention, was approved in Memphis, 1973. Convention bylaws were adopted at this same meeting which disqualified nearly all active members of the Tennessee Baptist Historical Society from serving on a committee. The history committee was withdrawn at the 1976 convention in Murfreesboro. Further efforts to establish some relation to the convention brought suggestions of an auxiliary relationship. The society was not favorable to it. Considerable discussion with the convention Executive Board and committees of the board led to the presentation of a program statement which was approved upon recommendation from the board.

Jean Adkinson was employed by the state convention in May, 1977, to direct the historical work in the state. Her other duties included church media and recreation. A union catalog of Baptist materials was completed. Two chapters of the society meet regularly—East Tennessee at Carson-Newman College and Middle Tennessee at Brentwood.

JOHN D. BOLTON

TENNESSEE BAPTIST SERVICE CORPORATION. This organization became an institution of the Tennessee Baptist Convention upon the recommendation of a study committee composed of Marvin Robertson, Charles Earl, Virgil Peters, Robert Orr, Gaye L. McGlothlen, Tom Madden, Willene Peek, and Clarence Stewart. Tom Madden served as chairman. Upon recommendation of this committee, the executive board of the convention called for the establishment of the TBSC during the annual meeting of Tennessee Baptists, Nov. 12, 1974, in Murfreesboro, TN: Gene Kerr presented a general report; Gaye L. McGlothlen presented the bylaws; Ralph McIntyre presented the charter; Virgil Peters presented recommendations; and Tom Madden presented philosophy.

The convention accepted the report, established the TBSC, and elected 15 directors: Tom Madden, Tullahoma; Gaye L. McGlothlen, Nashville; Virgil Peters, Franklin; Ralph McIntyre, Chattanooga; Clarence Stewart, Pulaski; Robert Orr, Dyersburg; Marvin Robertson, Bolivar; David E. Stewart, Brownsville; Ann Weiland, Brentwood; Hamilton Traylor,

Maryville; Bill Delaney, Columbia; Harley Fite, Jefferson City; W. A. Catlett, Dandridge; Ed Meier, Memphis; and Leonard Wedel, Franklin. Tom Madden served as chairman.

TBSC was chartered as a not-for-profit corporation in Tennessee, Dec. 2, 1974. The incorporators were Ralph Norton, Gene Kerr, and Robert C. Taylor. The purposes of the corporation as stated in the charter are:

the establishment and support of any religious, charitable and educational activities that will promote the advancement or well-being of mankind, either directly, or indirectly through its cooperation with public or private agencies having like purposes or objects, including but not limited to: to provide elderly persnot limited to: to provide elderly persons with housing facilities and services specially designed to meet the physical, social, psychological and spiritual needs of the aged, and to contribute to their health, security, happiness, spiritual well-being, and usefulness in longer living. To operate and maintain buildings and residences to provide for the personal and nursing care of people of advanced age, who by reason of illness or physical infirmity are unable to care for themselves. To provide information on facilities for churches and associations.

The program statement of TBSC states that its purpose is "to foster care for retirees and elderly people in a Christian environment which will be conducive to creative living. The services and facilities of this program shall be designed to provide the residents with security and comfort, freedom from doubt and fear, and a sense of purpose and fulfillment so as to contribute to the spiritual and social well-being of the individual."

Gene Kerr, assistant to the executive secretary of the TBC, was elected executive director-treasurer of the TBSC at its first meeting in Brentwood, Dec. 2, 1974. W. E. Darby became Gene Kerr's assistant, July 1, 1976, serving in that capacity until he succeeded Kerr as executive director-treasurer, Dec. 31, 1977, upon Kerr's retirement.

The TBSC has operated Baptist Health Care Center, a 101-bed intermediate care nursing home in Lenoir City, TN, since Feb., 1979. It also sponsors a retirement village, Deer Lake, in Nashville, TN.

Belmont Plaza, a 123-unit congregate care high-rise apartment building, was conceived and planned by the special committee which recommended the establishment of the TBSC. The plans were completed and executed by the first board of directors elected by the TBC. The contract for the facility was let to Joe M. Rodgers and Associates, Inc., on Mar. 8, 1977. Due to faulty legal work and improper financial planning, the facility was unable to open when completed, Jan. 12, 1979. It was transferred to a group of private investors, May 15, 1980.

WADE DARBY

TEXAS, BAPTIST GENERAL CONVENTION OF (II, III).

I. History. In 1969 the convention included 120 associations and 3,897 churches with a membership of 1,868,235. In 1979 there were 118 associations and 3,982 churches with 2,172,284 members. Total Cooperative Program income increased from $19,714,096 in 1969 to $44,892,182 in 1979, with the total value of church property going from $609,303,423 to $1,502,993,742 during the same period.

Leadership.—On Jan. 1, 1974, James H. Landes succeeded Thomas A. Patterson as executive secretary of the BGCT. Landes had served pastorates in Texas and Alabama and had also been president of Hardin-Simmons University. The title of the chief executive officer was changed to executive director by action of the 1975 convention.

Rudolph A. Springer (q.v.) retired as treasurer of the BGCT in Dec., 1970, a position he had held for 32 years. He was succeeded by Jay L. Skaggs, convention controller.

The following served as presidents of the convention during this period: Jimmy R. Allen, San Antonio, 1970-71; Landrum P. Leavell, Wichita Falls, 1972-73; Ralph M. Smith, Austin, 1974-75; James G. Harris (q.v.), Fort Worth, 1976; and Milton E. Cunningham, Houston, 1977-79. James Gordon Harris died, July 31, 1977, in the midst of his term as president. Serving as BGCT executive board chairmen were B. J. Martin, Pasadena, 1969; James Gordon Harris (q.v.), Fort Worth, 1970-71; Travis Berry, Plano, 1972-73; Lloyd Elder, Fort Worth, 1974; C. Grayson Glass, Galveston, 1975-76; Ed Brooks Bowles, Beaumont, 1977-78; and D. L. Lowrie, Texarkana, 1979.

Study Committees.—The decade 1969-79 saw numerous study committees appointed to deal with specific issues arising within the convention. A President's Committee, 1969, brought recommendations on a new procedure for the selection of the BGCT executive secretary. This new method adopted called for a 15-member search committee to bring a recommendation to the executive board regarding a new executive secretary. This new method was used first in 1973 in the selection of James H. Landes. A Committee to Define Church Membership, 1969, and a Special Committee to Define a Regular Missionary Baptist Church, 1976, both brought reports seeking to clarify what the BGCT constitution means by the term, "regular missionary Baptist churches." The charismatic issue was the occasion for the appointment of the 1976 committee. A 1969 Committee to Study the Cooperative Program suggested various ways to discover and develop the total resources of Texas Baptists through a new plan known as Channels of Compassion. An Urban Strategy Committee, 1971, recommended the creation of an Urban Strategy Council to coordinate an ongoing convention program to meet pressing urban needs in the state. In 1971 a Pastoral Care Committee recommended the "establishing of a church-staff information service" and that a "coordinator of counseling service for ministers and families be employed." James L. Cooper became coordinator of the Ministers Counseling Service in 1972. The

Church/Staff Information Service was implemented in 1977 with William E. Norman as director.

A report of an Institution Study Committee in 1974-75 resulted in a name change for the Christian Education Commission and Human Welfare Commission, making both of them coordinating boards. A procedure for release of institutions was also adopted by the convention. An Annuity Study Committee, 1974, recommended the establishment of a permanent annuity committee to seek further improvement in the retirement program of Texas pastors. A Baptist Student Union Study Committee, 1976, advocated a closer working relationship between the state division of student work and the local association in carrying out the BSU program in the state. A Special Church-State Study Committee was appointed in 1978 to study and update convention guidelines concerning relations of Baptist institutions and government agencies. No major changes were recommended. A Convention Study Committee was named in 1979 to consider: (1) The role of the executive director, (2) staff structure and budget, (3) future space needs of the executive board staff, and (4) energy-related problems.

An updated Texas Baptist history, *The Blossoming Desert: A Concise History of Texas Baptists,* by Robert A. Baker was published in 1970.

II. Review of Work. Article II of the BGCT constitution states, "The object of this body shall be to awaken and stimulate among the churches the greatest possible activity in evangelism, missions, Christian education and benevolent work and enterprises." During the period 1969-79, this stated purpose of the BGCT was basically carried out through actions of the various boards, commissions, and committees under the guidance of the 180-member executive board.

State Missions Commission.—In 1969 the BGCT State Missions Commission helped to promote the Crusade of the Americas. The commission also began to provide financial assistance to associations to help place associational directors of education on their staffs. In 1970 over 15,000 youth attended and participated in the state Youth Music Festival. The Pastor/Builder program was enlarged to three persons who serve as both pastor and building supervisor for new or needy church situations.

A program of assistance, education, and encouragement to Mexican border communities in their agricultural development, begun in 1971, included farming methods, animal husbandry, and water supplies. That year the commission also began a furloughing missionary program in which foreign missionaries on furlough worked as staff associates in stewardship promotion. A mobile disaster relief unit was provided and staffing developed. Special associational allocations through the state missions offering were initiated to help advance local missions in the associations. A Mission Starter program was begun to help increase new church starts. Urban strategy planning was developed, and a

program of personal evangelism was begun. An outreach consultant was added, and Sunday School became a division of work.

In 1973 the commission began the Youth Super Summer emphasis in which youth and youth leaders received intensive witness training and practice. Over 25,000 attended the Youth Evangelism Conference. More than 12,000 people attended the state Sunday School convention.

The commission led the state in 1974 to celebrate the 50th anniversary of the Cooperative Program in a series of informational and inspirational rallies. It also accelerated New Mission/New Church expansion with larger financial help and increased field support in surveys and studies.

In 1975 the commission conducted an Archway to the 80's leadership convocation for associational leaders, preparing the way for goal-setting and program formulation for the years ahead. A graded series of new-convert training materials (Spanish and English versions) were specially designed to be used among Spanish-speaking converts. A program of medical services for the Rio Grande River Ministry was adopted with a part-time state coordinator. The Mexican Rural Work Committee (Big Bend) and the El Paso Border Ministries Committee were authorized and funded to manage River Ministry coordination and program in those areas.

In 1976 the commission used a Spanish-language hymnal initiated and produced with the combined efforts of the Foreign Mission Board, Sunday School Board, and the Home Mission Board. By 1977 church expansion support with $1,000,000 for a single year reached a new level of progress in assisting new church starts. The commission recognized the 20th year of cooperative work and support with the SSB for starting 96 new Sunday Schools in 1976-77 and 152 in 1977-78. Church Training was recognized as Texas Baptists earned the largest increase in 1977-78 in Baptist Doctrine Church Study Course Awards.

In 1978 the commission assisted the beginning of associational staff to serve five associations in Minnesota-Wisconsin. Also adopted was the report of the joint Unification Study Committee of the Mexican Baptist Convention and the BGCT. New emphasis was given to providing additional funding to assist the Baptist Church Loan Corporation to meet new church and mission loan requests. The commission also led in the response to the invitation of the FMB to work with Baptists in Brazil in their centennial emphasis to double their work between 1977 and 1982; the Mission Service Corps promotion led to the first group of Mission Service Corps volunteers in America being sent from Texas to Brazil in 1979. The Bold Mission Thrust emphasis in church goal setting, new work acceleration, and missions giving growth were promoted in the associations and churches. March was set aside as Sunday School growth month, and the first year saw a gain of over

7,000 against a loss the previous year of 11,000. The bilingual staff was enlarged once again to bring the total bilingual staff, both professional and secretarial, to 11 people, or 12 percent of the State Missions Commission staff.

Charles P. McLaughlin has served as director of the State Missions Commission since 1964. In 1974 C. Wade Freeman retired from the Division of Evangelism following 27 years of service. He was succeeded by L. L. Morriss. Lory Hildreth became director of the Stewardship Division in 1976 to replace Cecil A. Ray who resigned to become executive director of the Baptist State Convention of North Carolina. In 1979 Bernard M. Spooner was named director of the Sunday School Division, succeeding John T. Sisemore, who retired.

Christian Education Coordinating Board.—Two significant institutional changes occurred during the 1970s. In 1970 the BGCT voted to divest itself of the Baylor School of Dentistry, Dallas. In 1971 the BGCT voted to free the University of Corpus Christi from convention ties, thus making it possible for the school to become a state university. After 10 years as director of the Christian Education Coordinating Board, Woodson Armes retired at the end of 1977. Donald Anthony became director in Jan., 1978, and served until his death on Nov. 24, 1978. Since that time James Basden has served as interim director. Two shifts in leadership characterized the 1970s in the Division of Student Work, one of the facets of the Christian education program of Texas Baptists. On Dec. 31, 1978, W. F. Howard retired from the directorship of the division, a position which he had occupied for 31 years. Chester L. "Chet" Reames was appointed division director, effective Jan. 1, 1976, serving until Aug. 3, 1978, when he died in an automobile accident. Jack Greever succeeded him on June 14, 1979.

In a time of declining college enrollment throughout the country, enrollment in the eight Texas Baptist colleges and universities increased during the 1970s.

Human Welfare Coordinating Board.—The 1970s saw several changes in the work of the Human Welfare Coordinating Board, the most visible being the official name change in 1975 from commission to Coordinating Board, along with some changes in responsibilities and reporting. By mutual consent, the BGCT released one hospital, Memorial Baptist Hospital in Houston, from convention sponsorship. The chaplaincy program there was retained as a convention entity. Building and expansion programs took place at all hospitals: Hillcrest Baptist Hospital, Waco; Baylor University Medical Center, Dallas; Baptist Hospital of Southeast Texas, Beaumont; High Plains Hospital, Amarillo; Hendrick Medical Center, Abilene; Baptist Memorial Hospital System, San Antonio; and Baptist Memorial Geriatric Center, San Angelo. Chaplaincy programs were initiated at Bexar County Hospital, San Antonio; Texas Medical Center, Houston; and a Spanish-speaking chaplain was added to the staff at Valley Baptist

Medical Center, Harlingen. Several of the hospitals began to utilize the concept of the hospital authority and the issuance of tax exempt revenue bonds to help with capital indebtedness.

All of the children's homes—Buckner's in Dallas, Texas Baptist Children's Home in Round Rock, Mexican Baptist Children's Home in San Antonio, and South Texas Children's Home in Beeville—opened group emergency shelters for children in crisis situations. A notable film, *Where There Is Love,* was made, depicting effective child care on the campus of a Texas Baptist children's home.

Anniversaries celebrated were Hendrick Medical Center, 50th; Valley Baptist Medical Center, 50th; Baylor University Medical Center, 75th; and Buckner Baptist Benevolences, 100th.

The BGCT recognized the retirement of T. H. Morrison, Jr., president of Valley Baptist Medical Center, in 1979 after 47 years in the field of health care in Texas. James Basden has served as director of the Human Welfare Coordinating Board since its beginning in 1960.

III. Special Events. Special BGCT activities having widespread interest during the past decade include the following.

Crusade of the Americas.—Revivals and encounter crusades in 1969 were highly productive in Texas Baptist churches. A highlight of the crusade was the distribution in Texas of 1,459,000 copies of *Good News for Modern Man.* This was the largest number of Bibles distributed in a given time and place in the history of the American Bible Society.

Good News Texas/Living Proof.—This major convention-wide evangelistic emphasis in 1977 had the stated purpose "to share the gospel with Texas in an intensive way and attempt to strengthen the churches and lead new converts and other church members into Christian discipleship growth." One of the unusual features of Good News Texas was a $1,500,000 mass media campaign which included Living Proof testimonies by well-known people on television and radio, advertising in newspapers and magazines, billboard messages, and direct mail pieces. Local church revivals climaxed the evangelistic thrust in the spring of 1977. An evaluation of Good News Texas indicates it may have been somewhat less than it was designed and hoped to be, but that "it was Texas Baptists doing what they have always done, but doing it on a larger scale and using newer methods."

Bold Mission Thrust.—This SBC movement, begun in 1977, is designed to help "Southern Baptists understand, accept and become involved in the mission to enable every person in the world to have opportunity to hear and respond to the gospel of Christ by the year 2000." Texas Baptist churches joined in this SBC emphasis by setting goals for increasing Sunday School enrollment, baptisms, new churches and missions, and financial support for local, state, and world missions. The BGCT established a Mission Service Corps office to assist in enlist-

TEXAS STATISTICAL SUMMARY

Year	Associations	Churches	Church Membership	Baptisms	SS Enrollment	VBS Enrollment	CT Enrollment	WMU Enrollment	Brotherhood Enrollment	Ch. Music Enrollment	Mission Gifts	Total Gifts	Value Church Property
1969	120	3,897	1,868,235	56,407	1,132,219	519,651	412,281	160,880	60,754	161,617	$24,082,419	$141,039,327	$ 609,303,423
1970	120	3,867	1,901,465	58,133	1,109,663	496,138	381,148	125,360	60,348	166,408	25,063,072	147,300,569	635,742,562
1971	118	3,854	1,930,840	65,054	1,093,997	480,326	307,284	136,170	59,754	167,381	29,804,405	159,289,073	658,445,515
1972	118	3,844	1,965,723	67,446	1,096,204	476,338	289,024	133,316	60,074	173,698	31,074,678	172,437,029	694,494,114
1973	118	3,855	2,001,022	60,868	1,091,000	460,743	265,487	129,413	60,802	183,206	34,832,963	194,038,436	750,493,607
1974	118	3,852	2,037,791	58,908	1,089,009	471,101	255,371	128,175	58,880	182,114	40,639,025	219,300,076	837,146,202
1975	118	3,914	2,073,841	58,828	1,096,310	512,704	248,266	129,973	58,203	188,539	43,527,134	243,169,125	917,409,202
1976	116	3,935	2,100,830	54,372	1,134,908	485,459	236,079	131,313	58,273	192,116	47,710,887	273,530,584	1,033,959,115
1977	116	3,942	2,124,800	52,599	1,136,015	465,848	221,332	130,675	59,537	191,531	52,744,679	300,476,390	1,153,234,263
1978	117	3,961	2,149,404	51,988	1,124,975	458,653	221,659	129,027	59,540	196,965	58,308,842	338,083,210	1,288,878,162
1979	118	3,982	2,172,284	58,693	1,132,068	454,740	217,872	125,764	57,962	197,481	66,986,346	381,840,597	1,502,993,742
1980	119	4,012	2,228,728	67,138	1,159,418	493,689	227,066	128,732	63,060	206,815	77,658,603	413,164,690	1,709,760,487

WILLIAM E. NORMAN

ing short-term mission volunteers for the Bold Mission Thrust effort. Further involvement in Bold Mission Thrust by Texas Baptists included the acceptance of an invitation to participate in the Brazilian evangelism campaign during the period 1978-81. A Mission to Brazil office was established to coordinate the Texas response to requests from the Brazil convention for assistance in carrying out their crusade.

Family Life Task Force.—Established in 1977 to project plans for a convention-wide family life emphasis in 1978-79, this group's specific objectives were: (1) To reaffirm marriage and family from a biblical perspective, (2) to raise the awareness level of family concerns in the local church, and (3) to encourage churches to respond in redemptive ministry to contemporary families. A family life resource guide was prepared to assist the local church in its ministry to families. Six regional family life conferences were held in the state during 1979-80.

JAMES H. LANDES and W. E. NORMAN

TEXAS, THE BAPTIST FOUNDATION OF (cf. Texas Baptist Foundation, Vols. II, III). In 1979 the foundation distributed income totaling $12,330,000 to Baptist institutions and agencies. During the same period, income totaling $2,518,000 was paid to individuals who had transferred money or property to the foundation under agreements that will provide them or others with an income for life after which the funds will serve designated Baptist causes. The book value of the foundation's assets on Dec. 31, 1979, exceeded $203,000,000. Lynn Craft has been president since 1976.

CLIFF ELKINS

TEXAS ASSOCIATIONS (II).
I. **New Associations.** ABILENE. Organized Oct., 1957, with 32 churches located in Taylor County and previously affiliated with Sweetwater Association. It has a written constitution and articles of faith and employs a director of missions. In 1979, 37 churches and one mission reported 624 baptisms, 27,108 members, $5,105,756 total receipts, $700,556 mission gifts, and $21,579,000 property value.

BI-STONE. Organized Oct. 10, 1961, with 29 churches located in Freestone and Limestone Counties and previously affiliated with Freestone-Leon and Limestone Associations. It has a written constitution but no articles of faith and employs a director of missions. In 1979, 22 churches and one mission reported 134 baptisms, 7,504 members, $1,151,004 total receipts, $200,355 mission gifts, and $4,502,000 property value.

CAPROCK. Organized Dec. 9, 1960, with 31 churches located in Briscoe, Floyd, Motley, Crosby, Dickens, and Garza Counties and previously affiliated with Dickens and Floyd Associations. It has a written constitution but no articles of faith and employs a director of missions. In 1979, 19 churches and three missions reported 114 baptisms, 7,374 members, $967,585 total receipts, $243,848 mission gifts, and $3,850,000 property value.

EMMANUEL. Organized Feb. 6, 1962, with 15 churches located in Tyler, Jasper, Newton, and Hardin Counties and previously affiliated with New Bethel, Orange, Southeast Texas, and Trinity River Associations. It has a written constitution but no articles of faith and employs a director of missions. In 1979, 27 churches and one mission reported 530 baptisms, 12,508 members, $1,948,966 total receipts, $302,387 mission gifts, and $6,619,000 property value.

FRIO RIVER. Organized Oct. 10, 1962, with 36 churches located principally in Zavala, Frio, Atascosa, Dimmit, LaSalle, McMullen, Webb, and Duval Counties and previously affiliated with Atascosa and Winter Garden Associations. It has a written constitution but no articles of faith and employs a director of missions. In 1979, 39 churches and 14 missions reported 310 baptisms, 10,510 members, $1,428,912 total receipts, $302,936 mission gifts, and $6,081,000 property value.

GOLDEN TRIANGLE. Organized in Nov., 1966, with 63 churches located principally in Orange, Jefferson, Jasper, and Newton Counties and previously affiliated with Southeast Texas and Orange Associations. It has a written constitution and articles of faith and employs a director of missions. In 1979, 85 churches and three missions reported 1,488 baptisms, 67,128 members, $10,947,057 total receipts, $1,724,859 mission gifts, and $51,090,000 property value.

GREGG. Organized Oct. 14, 1955, with 32 churches located in Gregg County and previously affiliated with Soda Lake Association. It has a written constitution and articles of faith and employs a director of missions. In 1979, 35 churches and one mission reported 875 baptisms, 26,503 members, $5,787,846 total receipts, $910,336 mission gifts, and $26,584,000 property value.

HARMONY-PITTSBURG. Organized in 1968 with 65 churches located principally in Titus, Morris, Camp, Wood, Upshur, and Rains Counties and previously affiliated with Harmony and Pittsburg Associations. It has a written constitution and articles of faith and employs a director of missions. In 1979, 60 churches reported 421 baptisms, 19,964 members, $3,107,489 total receipts, $603,690 mission gifts, and $11,399,000 property value.

LEON. Organized Oct. 16, 1961, with seven churches located in Leon County and previously affiliated with Freestone-Leon Association. It has a written constitution but no articles of faith and employs a director of missions. In 1979, six churches reported 57 baptisms, 1,733 members, $220,409 total receipts, $40,134 mission gifts, and $680,000 property value.

LLANOS ALTOS. Organized Oct. 19, 1960, with 36 churches located in Parmer, Castro, Bailey, and Lamb Counties and previously affiliated with Tierra Blanca, West Plains, and Staked Plains Associations. It has a written constitution but no articles of faith and employs a

director of missions. In 1979, 33 churches and two missions reported 211 baptisms, 12,475 members, $1,769,014 total receipts, $384,531 mission gifts, and $7,225,000 property value.

MIDLAND. Organized Oct. 9, 1960, with 18 churches located in Midland County and previously affiliated with Permian Basin Association. It has a written constitution and articles of faith and employs a director of missions. In 1979, 16 churches and five missions reported 261 baptisms, 15,745 members, $3,268,031 total receipts, $940,031 mission gifts, and $9,300,000 property value.

ODESSA. Organized Oct. 3, 1960, with 29 churches located principally in Ector County and previously affiliated with Permian Basin Association. It has a written constitution but no articles of faith and employs a director of missions. In 1979, 22 churches and two missions reported 466 baptisms, 21,969 members, $3,947,436 total receipts, $528,566 mission gifts, and $12,797,000 property value.

PANFORK. Organized Sep. 16, 1975, with 22 churches located in Gray, Wheeler, Donley, Collingsworth, and Hall Counties and previously affiliated with North Fork and Panhandle Associations. It has a written constitution but no articles of faith and employs a director of missions. In 1979, 22 churches and three missions reported 193 baptisms, 9,073 members, $1,217,313 total receipts, $253,033 mission gifts, and $4,113,000 property value.

RIO GRANDE VALLEY. Organized Oct. 1, 1975, with 54 churches located in Starr, Hidalgo, Willacy, and Cameron Counties and previously affiliated with Lower Rio Grande and Magic Valley Associations. It has a written constitution and employs a director of missions. In 1979, 60 churches and 42 missions reported 876 baptisms, 26,203 members, $4,617,559 total receipts, $1,225,511 mission gifts, and $17,721,000 property value.

SABINE VALLEY. Organized Oct. 22, 1927, with 24 churches located in San Augustine, Sabine, Jasper, and Newton Counties and previously affilliated with Central Missionary and Sabine-Neches Associations. It has a written constitution but no articles of faith and employs a director of missions. In 1979, 28 churches and two missions reported 277 baptisms, 9,514 members, $1,436,882 total receipts, $246,491 mission gifts, and $5,307,000 property value.

SOUTH PLAINS. Organized Oct. 19, 1960, with 30 churches located in Cochran, Hockley, and Terry Counties and previously affiliated with Brownfield and Hockley-Cochran Associations. It has a written constitution but no articles of faith and employs a director of missions. In 1979, 24 churches and seven missions reported 280 baptisms, 11,924 members, $1,827,234 total receipts, $410,403 mission gifts, and $9,825,000 property value.

WEST CENTRAL. Organized Oct. 19, 1971, with 35 churches located in Fisher, Jones, Kent, and Stonewall Counties and previously affiliated with Stonewall-Kent, Fisher, and Jones Associations. It has a written constitution but no articles of faith and employs a director of missions. In 1979, 30 churches and three missions reported 192 baptisms, 9,879 members, $1,139,723 total receipts, $220,749 mission gifts, and $4,620,000 property value.

WICHITA-ARCHER-CLAY. Organized Oct. 22, 1964, with 50 churches located in Wichita, Archer, and Clay Counties and previously affiliated with Wichita-Archer and Clay Associations. It has a written constitution and articles of faith and employs a director of missions. In 1979, 51 churches and two missions reported 723 baptisms, 37,194 members, $5,588,154 total receipts, $1,031,779 mission gifts, and $23,206,000 property value.

II. Changes in Associations. ATASCOSA. Merged with Winter Garden in Oct., 1962, to form Frio River Association.

BAYLOR-KNOX. Merged with Throckmorton-Young at end of 1964 associational year to form Southern Association.

BOWIE. Organized as Red River-Texarkana Association in 1929, it adopted its present name in 1967.

BROWNFIELD. Disbanded in 1960 during reorganization of former District 9 and became part of Lubbock and South Plains Associations.

CENTRAL MISSIONARY. Organized as Central Baptist Association in 1849. At one time it included churches in Shelby, Nacogdoches, Sabine, San Augustine, and Angelina Counties. In Oct., 1904, the association adopted a new constitution under name of Central Missionary Baptist Association. It merged with Sabine-Neches in Oct., 1927, to form Sabine Valley Association.

CLAY. Merged with Wichita-Archer at end of 1964 associational year to form Wichita-Archer-Clay Association.

DICKENS. Disbanded in 1960 during reorganization of former District 9 and became part of Caprock Association.

FISHER. Merged with Jones and Stonewall-Kent in Oct., 1971, to form West Central Association.

FLOYD. Disbanded in 1960 during reorganization of former District 9 and became part of Caprock and Staked Plains Associations.

FREESTONE-LEON. Became part of Bi-Stone and Leon Associations in 1961.

G.A.Y. Changed name to Permian Association in 1975.

HARMONY. Merged with Pittsburg in 1968 to form Harmony-Pittsburg Association.

HOCKLEY-COCHRAN. Disbanded in 1960 during reorganization of former District 9 and became part of South Plains Association.

JONES. Merged in Oct., 1971, with Fisher and Stonewall-Kent to form West Central Association.

LAMAR. Changed name to Red River Valley on Oct. 9, 1967.

LIMESTONE. Became part of Bi-Stone Association in 1961.

LOWER RIO GRANDE. Divided in 1957—30 churches of lower valley continued to use name

Lower Rio Grande, 22 other churches chose name of Magic Valley. In 1975 Lower Rio Grande reunited with Magic Valley to form Rio Grande Valley Association.

MAGIC VALLEY. Organized in Oct., 1957, with 22 churches and 14 missions from Lower Rio Grande Association. Reunited with that association in 1975 to form Rio Grande Valley Association.

NORTH FORK. Merged with Panhandle on Sep. 16, 1975, to form Panfork Association.

ORANGE. Merged with Southeast Texas in Nov., 1966, to form Golden Triangle Association.

PANHANDLE. Merged with North Fork on Sep. 16, 1975, to form Panfork Association.

PERMIAN. Organized as G.A.Y. Association in 1943 and adopted present name in 1975.

PERMIAN BASIN. Disbanded at close of 1960 associational year to form Midland and Odessa Associations.

PITTSBURG. Merged with Harmony in 1968 to form Harmony-Pittsburg Association.

RED RIVER-TEXARKANA. Changed name to Bowie Association at 1967 associational meeting.

RED RIVER VALLEY. Organized as Lamar Association in 1887 and adopted present name on Oct. 9, 1967.

SABINE-NECHES. Organized in 1924 with seven churches in Jasper, Newton, and Orange Counties, it merged with Central Missionary in Oct., 1927, to form Sabine Valley Association.

SALT FORK. Organized as Southern Association in 1964 and adopted present name in 1978.

SOUTHEAST TEXAS. Merged with Orange in Nov., 1966, to form Golden Triangle Association.

SOUTHERN. Organized in 1964 by the merger of Baylor-Knox and Throckmorton-Young Associations, it changed its name to Salt Fork in 1978.

STONEWALL-KENT. Merged with Fisher and Jones in Oct., 1971, to form West Central Association.

THROCKMORTON-YOUNG. Merged with Baylor-Knox at end of 1964 associational year to form Southern Association.

TIERRA BLANCA. Disbanded in 1960 during reorganization of former District 9 and became part of Llanos Altos and Staked Plains Associations.

WICHITA-ARCHER. Merged with Clay at end of 1964 associational year to form Wichita-Archer-Clay Association.

WILBARGER-FOARD. Joined Red Fork Association at end of 1964 associational year.

WINTER GARDEN. Merged with Atascosa in Oct., 1962, to form Frio River Association.

ELLEN KUNIYUKI BROWN

TEXAS BAPTIST CHILDREN'S HOME (II, III). This agency of the Baptist General Convention of Texas has provided daily care and Christian nurture to dependent and neglected children since 1950. Multiple services include campus care, emergency care, foster care, adoption, group home care, and family services. Dedicated to serving families in crisis, the home provides services to over 500 children each year. Financial support is provided through the Cooperative Program and by gifts from churches and interested individuals.

CHARLES I. WRIGHT

TEXAS BAPTIST CHURCH LOAN CORPORATION. A self-supporting agency of the Baptist General Convention of Texas approved in 1951 by the executive board. The corporation serves new and small churches in Texas, Minnesota, and Wisconsin with long-term financing. The corporation does not receive Cooperative Program money for operations. Money used for loans is borrowed from various lending institutions. During the 1970s, 192 loans were funded, totaling over $15,000,000. Total assets of the corporation increased during this same period by 57 percent to over $16,000,000.

BRUCE W. BOWLES

TEXAS BAPTIST DISASTER RELIEF PROGRAM. See DISASTER RELIEF PROGRAM, TEXAS BAPTIST.

TEXAS BAPTIST ENCAMPMENTS (cf. Texas Baptist Camps, Vol. III). A total of 25 encampments were operating in Texas in 1979, an increase of three from 1970. During the summer of 1979, 185,718 people attended these encampments, with 5,380 making professions of faith in Christ and 774 giving their lives to church-related vocations. Operated independently by a local association, each of these encampments has a full-time resident manager. In 1964 these camps requested that a closer relationship be developed with the Baptist General Convention of Texas. The state convention assigned this relationship to the Special Services Division.

In 1972 the name of Camp Leuders changed to Big Country Baptist Assembly, and Red River Encampment changed to Chaparral. In 1973 Chaparral became Chaparral Assembly, and El Paso Association Encampment became Aspendale Ranch. In 1975 Menard Encampment opened at Miles, TX. Lake Tomahawk Encampment began operation at Baytown, TX, in 1976. Timberline Encampment opened at Bullard, TX, in 1978.

R. HOOPER DILDAY

TEXAS BAPTIST HISTORICAL SOCIETY. The first Texas Baptist Historical Society, constituted Nov. 10, 1938, with W. W. Barnes (q.v. III) as president, ceased functioning early in World War II. L. R. Elliott (q.v. III) led in a second organization on Oct. 21, 1953, at San Antonio, but after a few years it became inactive. On Nov. 1, 1977, the society was reactivated at Fort Worth with Robert L. Baker as president, followed by Thomas L. Charlton and

Royce Measures, with Keith C. Wills as secretary-treasurer.

D. D. TIDWELL

TEXAS BAPTIST MEMORIALS GERIATRIC CENTER (III). With an addition to the hospital in 1978 and a new skilled nursing facility in 1981, the center has expanded its ministry to include 315 beds in the hospital and nursing home units, space for 175 persons in the Moody Memorial Retirement Center (Hotel Cactus), and 151 living units in the 55 cottages and 48 duplexes of Baptist Memorials Village located on the Main Campus in San Angelo. The center ministers to over 600 retired and elderly persons from 24 states through its facilities and a staff of 300 employees who work under the direction of hospital and nursery home administrator W. D. McDonald, retirement administrator James Orr, and executive director Taylor Henley.

TAYLOR HENLEY

TEXAS BAPTIST MEN (III). Robert E. Dixon has served as executive director since 1970. He succeeded W. L. "Wimpy" Smith. Presidents of Texas Baptist Men since its organization in 1968 have been Roy Akers, Luman Holman, C. J. Humphrey, Joe Lenamon, and Olen Miles. The organization achieves its objectives through vice-presidents for Royal Ambassadors, Baptist Young Men, retirees, lay-led revivals, lay renewal, agricultural missions, prison ministries, disaster relief, and lay involvement through the Foreign and Home Mission Boards.

R. E. DIXON

TEXAS BAPTIST ORAL HISTORY CONSORTIUM. Begun in 1975 by the Historical Committee of the Baptist General Convention of Texas, the consortium involves 12 Baptist colleges and institutions in gathering information through oral history research. Depositories, including the Texas Collection at Baylor University and the Fleming Library at Southwestern Baptist Theological Seminary, hold the tapes and transcripts of over 35 oral memoirs. Over 75 series of interviews were in process in 1980. Research includes the histories of Texas Baptist institutions, agencies, churches, associations, and revival movements; projects on the fundamentalist era; the National Baptist Convention of Texas; retired missionaries in Texas; the women's movement; and a specially-funded Mexican Baptist oral history project. Thomas L. Charlton, of Baylor University, serves as consortium director.

L. KATHERINE COOK

TEXAS CHRISTIAN LIFE COMMISSION. See CHRISTIAN LIFE COMMISSION (TEXAS).

THAILAND, MISSION IN (cf. Thailand, Southern Baptist Mission in, Vols. II, III). The Thailand Baptist Mission has continued to major on making disciples and establishing churches. By the end of 1980, the work of the 60 career and 13 short-term missionaries had resulted in over 1,600 members in 24 churches and 45 smaller Christian groups organized into the Thailand Baptist Churches Association. The seminary and other leadership training programs support the churches' growth. Outreach institutions such as the hospital, mass communications, and the student center witness through ministry to thousands of people. Between 1975 and 1980, ministries to Cambodian and Vietnamese refugees distributed over $1,000,000 in aid, resulted in over 2,500 baptisms, and led to official recognition of Baptists by the government. A Bangkok Urban Strategy has been developed to plant more churches in the capital city.

RONALD C. HILL

THEOLOGICAL EDUCATION, TRENDS AMONG BAPTISTS IN (cf. Theological Education, Vol. II). A review of theological education in the 1960s and 1970s reveals significant new trends, directions, and patterns. They are related to changes in nomenclature, the introduction of new degrees, off-campus educational efforts, growing enrollments, diversity of teaching methods, emphasis on continuing education, and other facets of theological education.

Degrees.—Pursuant to action taken by the Association of Theological Schools (ATS), SBC seminaries in 1967 adopted the Master of Divinity (M.Div.) degree to replace the Bachelor of Divinity (B.D.), the basic theological degree. The rationale for the change noted that the professional-graduate work taken in the seminaries was post-baccalaureate and should be appropriately recognized. Provision was made for B.D. graduates to obtain the M.Div. by exchange.

In 1974 Southern Baptist Theological Seminary and Southwestern Baptist Theological Seminary introduced the Doctor of Philosophy (Ph.D.) nomenclature to replace the traditional Doctor of Theology (Th.D.). Several factors prompted the change, but basically the Ph.D. was perceived by many as a stronger credential for prospective teachers in colleges and seminaries and was better understood by educators. The revised doctoral curriculum which accompanied the change required that some study would be done in a university setting. Provision was made for earlier Th.D. graduates to obtain the Ph.D. by exchange.

Similarly, in the 1960s schools of Religious Education moved to replace the Doctor of Religious Education (D.R.E.) with the Doctor of Education (Ed.D.). In the schools of Church Music the older Doctor of Church Music (D.C.M.) was phased out in favor of the Doctor of Musical Arts (D.M.A.).

In 1972 the Doctor of Ministry (D.Min.) degree was introduced as an advanced professional degree in the practice of ministry. Different from the traditional degrees which emphasized the classical theological studies, the D.Min. was approved by ATS in 1970. Offered

in the six SBC seminaries, the program is composed of seminars, ministry under supervision, and a field project (thesis) related to an aspect of ministry.

By 1980 two seminaries offered an associate degree for students lacking a baccalaureate degree but who completed two years of divinity studies. It represented an incentive for those who could not qualify for the master's degree because they lacked the prerequisite degree, and it gave recognition to the advanced level of seminary studies.

Off-Campus Theological Education.—Of major importance in the 1970s was the development of off-campus programs of theological education. Designated centers, satellites, and modules, they were fashioned according to need and resources to offer degree and diploma studies at sites distant from the main campus. The first off-campus center, begun in 1973 in Garden Grove (greater Los Angeles), CA, by Golden Gate Baptist Theological Seminary, was named the Southern California Center. Subsequently, Golden Gate and the other SBC seminaries individually sponsored off-campus studies in Atlanta, GA; Houston, TX; Miami, FL; Phoenix, AZ; Portland, OR; San Antonio, TX; Shawnee, OK; Tampa, FL; and elsewhere. In 1980 the six seminaries agreed to sponsor jointly a limited program of studies in Baltimore, MD; Detroit, MI; Chicago, IL; and Jackson, TN.

Such programs had the advantage of taking theological education to pastors and others where they lived and ministered, but they also raised concerns over adequate faculty staffing, funding, library resources, and providing a setting for learning comparable to that found on campus. Simultaneously, accrediting bodies adopted strict guidelines regulating such extension programs and seeking to ensure their academic excellence.

Enrollments.—The number of students enrolled in SBC seminaries continued to climb to record levels during the 1960s and 1970s. The 1960 enrollment totaled 5,954. In the fall, 1980, a total of 9,700 enrolled with a projection of about 11,000 for the full session. This number represented approximately 20 percent of the total enrollment of 194 seminaries in the United States and Canada which belong to ATS.

During this period the number of women increased in all programs, especially the M.Div. In 1980 females accounted for 17 percent of the total enrollment in the six seminaries. This trend caused questions to be raised over the place of women in ministry and the limited opportunities for employment by Southern Baptist churches.

Burgeoning enrollments brought pressures on seminary faculties and facilities, especially classrooms and student housing.

Other Trends.—Seminary faculties expressed a serious interest in developing programs of continuing theological education. The usual approach was to utilize special lectures, conferences, workshops, short-term courses, and the like, and to give Continuing Education Units

(CEU's) for the time invested. The CEU's are not convertible to academic units or semester hours. In some instances a director was appointed to coordinate this program.

The seminaries also maintained a keen interest in the accreditation of their degree programs as they held membership not only in the major professional accrediting body (ATS) but also obtained membership in the various regional accrediting agencies. Those institutions with major music programs were accredited by the National Association of Schools of Music (NASM). Membership in such accrediting bodies encouraged high academic standards and gave graduates full recognition of their degrees by other institutions of higher learning.

The growing use of visiting teachers in short terms and summer school permitted the exchange of professors and the sharing of ideas. The plan also enabled seminaries to utilize specialists from churches and the denomination to provide expertise, enrich the curriculum, and add course options not otherwise available to students.

As new types of ministries emerged, new emphases developed, and the need of new studies became apparent, seminaries sought to alter and update curricula and programs. Every aspect and organization of church and denominational life were likely to have their counterpart in a seminary course. Through such flexibility and adjustment, theological education was infused with new vitality, and training for ministry was kept relevant.

Faculties continued to wrestle with the issue of providing for students a balance between the traditional disciplines and the practical (ministry) studies, recognizing thereby the necessity of both in educating ministers for church-related tasks. A certain softening of the lines between these two areas of curriculum and programs issued in a new openness to one another. As a result, along with classroom study and academic excellence, seminaries stressed the need of opportunities for specific ministry under supervision. These have taken the form of experimental courses, "practical activities," "ministry practice," and internships, with just the right formula still to be found.

In addition, new emphasis went to missions and evangelism. Missions majors were created, and new dimensions of the missions task were studied. In the field of evangelism seminaries added new courses and evangelism professors.

Another concern focused on the need for "spiritual formation" in students preparing for ministry. The object was to find ways to motivate students to deepen their spiritual life and to provide them with resources to achieve this.

Techniques of teaching seemed to multiply in the period. A survey of teaching methods included the use of interdisciplinary panels, case studies, group activities, games simulation, psychodrama, dialogical exchanges, and contracted assignments. Of course, the lecture as a method was not abandoned, but there was an effort to develop student-centered and more creative methods of instruction.

A new cooperative relationship between the seminaries and other agencies of the SBC emerged as manifested through joint faculty conclaves from the six seminaries sponsored by the Sunday School Board, greater use of board and agency staff personnel as adjunct faculty, and the creation of a liaison faculty position in each seminary sponsored by the SSB. Communication improved, consultation increased, and mutual tasks and interests were shared.

The seminaries also sought ways to acknowledge their partnership with Baptist colleges, universities, and national student ministries in the larger task of theological education. The Bible schools, too, shared the task by providing for those students unable to attend college and seminary.

During the period increasing scrutiny was directed toward seminary faculties regarding their doctrinal views. Interest centered primarily on the issue of the inerrancy of the Scriptures. In 1980 the SBC adopted a resolution exhorting "the trustees of seminaries . . . to faithfully discharge their responsibility to carefully preserve the doctrinal integrity of our institutions. . . ." Pursuant to this action, seminary faculties, administrations, and trustees reaffirmed their commitment to the Baptist Faith and Message statement adopted by the SBC in 1963.

In the 1970s a growing awareness of the presence of blacks and ethnic minorities developed. Seminaries tried to recruit students from these groups and to provide courses and organize conferences to become familiar with the heritage and needs of minority groups.

The Seminary Extension Department has filled the role of auxiliary to the seminaries in offering educational opportunities to pastors without seminary training, to seminary graduates who want to continue or update their studies, and to lay church leaders interested in such study on a college level. Through this means thousands of students have added to their Bible knowledge and improved their effectiveness in ministry.

In recent years an increase has occurred in schools not controlled by the SBC but designed to educate pastors and others for SBC churches. Those with the greatest influence are Luther Rice Seminary, Mid-America Baptist Seminary, and Criswell Center for Biblical Studies.

BIBLIOGRAPHY: W. Morgan Patterson, "Changing Preparation for Changing Ministry," *Baptist History and Heritage* (Jan., 1980).

W. MORGAN PATTERSON

THEOLOGICAL EDUCATOR, THE. A journal of theology and ministry published twice a year by the faculty of New Orleans Baptist Theological Seminary. During the 50th anniversary of the founding of the seminary, 1967-68, the faculty published an *Anniversary Bulletin*. It included an article entitled "Toward the Future" by J. Hardee Kennedy, dean of the School of Theology. One of Kennedy's proposals was that the faculty begin to publish a theological journal. The *Anniversary Bulletin* became the first volume of the new journal, which took the name of *The Theological Educator* with the appearance of the second volume in 1969. Single issues were published annually, 1969-72, and two issues have been published each year since 1973. The annual fall issue relates to the forthcoming January Bible Study book, and the spring issue deals with selected topics. An editorial committee produced the journal, 1969-75. Since 1975, Fisher Humphreys has served as editor.

FISHER HUMPHREYS

THEOLOGY, LIBERATION. See LIBERATION THEOLOGY.

THEOLOGY (CONSERVATIVE), RESURGENCE OF. See CONSERVATIVE THEOLOGY, RESURGENCE OF.

THIBODEAUX, LAWRENCE (b. Branch, LA, Mar. 3, 1911; d. Laurel, MS, Aug. 28, 1968). Pastor. Born to French Catholic parents, Louvinia Thibodeaux and Maurice Thibodeaux, later a pioneer Baptist preacher to the French-speaking people of Southwest Louisiana, he was a graduate of Louisiana State University (M.S.) and also attended New Orleans Baptist Theological Seminary. He helped organize what is now the Louisiana Baptist French Radio Ministry, and was one of 12 radio preachers, 1954-55. Married to Virginia LeBlanc, they had two sons, Lawrence and David. He organized and served numerous churches in South Louisiana, including Thibodaux First and Christ Church, Houma, LA.

W. L. SEWELL

THORNTON, EVERETT WHITFIELD (b. Sidney, IA, June 9, 1893; d. Shawnee, OK, Oct. 2, 1980). Educator and historian. The son of M. M. and Eura Hiatt Thornton, he graduated from Sidney High School (1911), Des Moines College (B.A., 1916), the University of Chicago (M.A., 1927), and Iowa State University (Ph.D., 1933). He married Verdelle Case, June 12, 1920, at Des Moines. The couple had two sons, Lowell and Edward.

Thornton's teaching career included Centerville, IA, high school, 1916-18; superintendent of Farragut, IA, public schools, 1919-21; missionary teacher in Central Philippine College, 1921-26; dean and history instructor at Fort Dodge Junior College, Fort Dodge, IA, 1927-32; political science instructor at Sioux Falls College, Sioux Falls, SD, 1934-42; and professor of history, Oklahoma Baptist University, 1942-66. Thornton was OBU archivist, 1966-78; author of 24 published articles on history; a veteran of World War I; and member of the Southern Baptist Historical Commission, 1971-73. He is buried in Fairview Cemetery, Shawnee, OK.

J. M. GASKIN

TIBBS, ALBERT ELIAS (b. Columbus, GA, Oct. 22, 1901; d. Greenville, SC, Oct. 11, 1972). The son of Harry A., an engineer, and Mattie Holt Tibbs, he attended Furman University (B.A., 1922), Princeton Theological Seminary (Th.B., 1925), and New Orleans Baptist Theological Seminary (Th.D., 1936). On July 6, 1930, he married Annie Nell Wyatt. They had three children, Albert E., Jr., Harry, and Mary.

Tibbs taught at New Orleans Seminary, 1930-48, and moved to Furman University in 1948 to become dean and teach philosophy. He relinquished the deanship in 1961 to return to full-time teaching, retiring in 1970. He was elected president of the South Carolina Baptist Convention in 1949. He is buried in Springwood Cemetery, Greenville, SC.

J. GLENWOOD CLAYTON

TIFT COLLEGE (II, III). A 1972 capital funds program provided for the renovation of Hardin Library in 1973, Roberts Chapel in 1977, and Ponder Hall in 1979. It also provided for a new administration-classroom building on the site of Tift Hall.

Other developments during the 1970s included a new Schantz pipe organ, the gift of Gerald Saunders and D. Abbott Turner, dedicated in Roberts Chapel in 1978; a coeducational Evening Division begun in 1977; and a Bachelor of Science in Nursing degree program begun in 1979. Community service programs included the Monroe County Mental Health Clinic, which opened in 1971, and community service courses offered by the Evening Division, which began in 1979. In Apr., 1980, the front circle of the campus was dedicated as an historic site and listed officially in the National Register of Historic Places.

The 1979 graduating class totaled 84 plus 29 in the first Evening Division commencement. The total 1979 fall quarter enrollment of 741 included 489 on campus, 102 in the Evening Division, and 131 at Georgia Baptist Hospital School of Nursing in Atlanta.

Total assets in 1979 exceeded $18,000,000 including an endowment of $3,266,984. The income for 1979 was $2,234,330. Robert W. Jackson continues as president.

B. CARROLL CARTER

TIMERITE, INC. (III). The agency continues to serve Southern Baptists in accordance with the program statement of the Radio and Television Commission, providing broadcast media consultation, production, and marketing to churches, associations, state conventions, and their duly authorized institutions. In order to service the changing needs of the SBC, several strategic decisions were made between 1972 and 1976.

The regional office concept began undergoing modification in view of the commission's desire to establish TimeRite firmly in the minds of Southern Baptists as a unity within itself, and to provide services as economically as possible. By Oct., 1972, the western office in Fresno, CA, had been moved to Dallas, TX, where all operations continued under the direction of the regional representative. The eastern office in Wilmington, NC, continued to function until the summer of 1979.

The operations of TimeRite, Inc., were directed as of Oct. 1, 1976, to media buying and marketing research, with all other services relative to point IV of the commission's program statement being handled by the Special Projects Department, which from Jan., 1979, has been known under the name Broadcast Services. In addition, Oct. 1, 1977, marked the completion of TimeRite's move into the commission's building in Fort Worth, TX. The Dallas office was subsequently closed in Dec., 1978.

See also RADIO AND TELEVISION COMMISSION, SBC.

CHARLES RODEN

TINKLE, AMANDA ARVILLA (b. Benton, AR, Sep. 12, 1908; d. Little Rock, AR, Jan. 12, 1979). Missionary. The daughter of Andrew and Dora Bell Tinkle, farmers, she graduated from the Nursing School of Arkansas Baptist Hospital (1931). Commissioned as a missionary, Dec. 3, 1938, she served in Shaki, Okuto, Iwo, and Ogbomosho, Nigeria, dispensing medicine, treating lepers, training nurses, financing many Nigerians' education, and evangelizing in the bush country. She retired, Oct. 6, 1973. She is buried in the cemetery of Kentucky Baptist Church, Saline County, AR.

VIRGINIA PREDDY BELLUE

TOGETHER WE BUILD. Capital fund-raising service. The 1970s brought a new approach to building programs in Southern Baptist churches. The 1969 SBC authorized the Stewardship Commission to employ a staff to assist churches in *Together We Build* programs. The work of the 1960s had been researching and developing this service. The 1970s brought implementation and refinement. *Together We Build* became an effective professional capital fund-raising service which provided maximum spiritual and financial assistance to Southern Baptist churches. It has enabled churches to build the facilities they need while significantly reducing long-term indebtedness and large interest payments.

The major thrust of fund-raising efforts in 1970 was in the Kansas-Nebraska Convention of Southern Baptists which confronted a convention-backed bond mortgage that was unsecured. Through a united effort, over $600,000 was raised and the financial crisis was eliminated. Churches have saved hundreds of thousands of dollars in interest and principal payments as a result of this service provided by the Stewardship Commission.

The commission expanded the staff of its office of Endowment and Capital Giving in 1971 by employing Fred M. Chapman of Nashville, TN,

and Kenneth R. Mullins of Tulsa, OK, to join Ben G. Gill, who had been a consultant since 1969. Twenty-five churches were assisted in raising $4,842,000. In 1972 consultants assisted a state Baptist institution in fund raising for the first time. They achieved the first million-dollar program in 1973 by assisting the First Baptist Church of Augusta, GA, in raising $1,330,000.

As the demand for services provided by the *Together We Build* program continued to grow, the commission employed additional consultants: two in 1972; one in 1973, 1975, and 1976; three in 1977 and 1978; and one in 1979, with the latter specializing in institutional fund raising. The program in 1975 established a working relationship with the Church Loans Division of Church Extension Department of the Home Mission Board, and the Church Architecture Department of the Sunday School Board. In 1976 the first regional office for *Together We Build* was established in Washington, DC. That year consultants assisted 75 churches in raising $12,589,301. Responding to increasing requests for assistance year by year, they helped 103 churches raise $30,251,151 through the *Together We Build* program in 1979.

Directors of the *Together We Build* program have been William H. Pitt, Sr., 1969-70; Ben G. Gill, 1970-73; Robert Capra, 1973-74; and Fred M. Chapman, 1974- .

See also STEWARDSHIP COMMISSION, SBC.

FRED M. CHAPMAN

TOGO, MISSION IN (III). By 1979 churches and preaching stations in Togo numbered 45 with 1,284 members. The missionary staff numbered 21 located in four stations. New programs of work included literacy, student work, and agricultural evangelism. The Baptist Pastor's School in Lome served all of French-speaking West Africa and was directing a program of Theological Education by Extension for the entire area. A Bible correspondence course, a Baptist center and reading room, and an audiovisual program were proving effective for the mission.

JOHN E. MILLS

TORTOLA, MISSION IN. Tortola is one of the British Virgin Islands lying between the Caribbean Sea and the open Atlantic. English is spoken. Baptist work on Tortola bagan in the early 1960s by independent Baptist missionaries from the USA who started six churches. Southern Baptist work began with filling a request from Mt. Carmel Baptist Church for an interim pastor. Missionaries Lester and Fonda (Bice) Boyd arrived in Tortola on Dec. 31, 1976. The work of developing the leadership of Mt. Carmel Baptist Church was completed at the end of 1980, when the leadership was turned over to a lay leader.

LESTER E. BOYD

TOWNSEND, HEPHZIBAH JENKINS (b. Charleston, SC, 1780; d. Edisto Island, SC,

Mar. 4, 1847). Founder of first home and foreign mission society for women in the South. Daughter of Daniel Jenkins, an Army captain, and Hephzibah Frampton Jenkins, she married Daniel Townsend about 1794. They had six children: John, Susan, Mary, Amarinthia, Daniel, and Theodoria. Inspired by her pastor, Richard Furman (q.v. I), Townsend organized by 1811 the Wadmalaw and Edisto Female Mite Society which contributed to foreign missions and the Charleston Association's missionary fund. Later she gathered the Auxiliary Education Society for the support of ministerial students. She organized a Baptist church on Edisto Island and erected the building at her own expense. It became an all-black congregation which still survives. She is buried in the church cemetery.

LOULIE LATIMER OWENS

TRANSKEI, MISSION IN. Southern Baptist involvement in Transkei began in response to a request from the Baptist church in Umtata, the capital. Planning for a multiracial outreach, church leaders contacted Marion Fray, Foreign Mission Board field representative for Southern Africa, asking that Southern Baptists consider sending a pastor. Eugene and Lavonne (Thompson) Meacham moved from Malawi in Oct., 1979, to accept this responsibility. The same month, Dudley and Rebecca (Reagan) Phifer, who had also served in Malawi, moved to Umtata to work with the Baptist Union of Transkei in church development. In December, Dennis McCall, an extended-term volunteer, arrived for a year's service in agricultural ministries.

JOY NEAL

TRINIDAD AND TOBAGO, MISSION IN (III). Differences in mission philosophy led to a decision to cease cooperation with the Trinidad Baptist Union in 1976. Mission efforts were concentrated in the northern section of the island. In 1980 two couples were assigned to Trinidad, with three churches and two missions reporting 184 members. Emphasis on leadership training, evangelism, and church development continued to be the main thrusts. Three young people were students in Barbados Baptist College. A national fellowship body was being organized.

JEAN HOLLEY JACOBS

TRIPP, EDGAR FRANKLIN (b. Scott County, AR, Mar. 12, 1894; d. Montgomery, AL, July 8, 1975). Pastor and denominational leader. Son of Synthia Coffey and William J. Tripp, he was educated at Ouachita Baptist College and Oklahoma Baptist University. Ordained in 1911 by First Baptist Church, Wynnewood, OK, Tripp married Elvira Whitaker, June 23, 1912. Their children were Ramona, Ann Elizabeth, Kuma, Nancy, and Frank, Jr. He served as a pastor in Hickory, Sulphur Springs, Kingston, Yale, and Idabelle,

all in Oklahoma; Monroe and Minden, LA; St. Joseph, MO, 1929-38; and Montgomery, AL, 1938-47. He originated and promoted the Hundred Thousand Club.

After serving as a captain in the Medical Administrative Corps of the United States Army, 1942-43, he resumed the Montgomery pastorate until elected executive secretary of the Hospital Commission of the SBC, 1947-59. Upon retirement he established the Montgomery Baptist Hospital. President of Louisiana and Alabama Baptist Conventions, he also served 16 years on the SBC Executive Committee, and was first vice-president of the SBC, 1935. He is buried at Montgomery, AL.

LEE N. ALLEN

TRUETT-McCONNELL COLLEGE (cf. Truett-McConnell Junior College, Vols. II, III). In 1972 Ronald Edsel Weitman became president, succeeding Warner Earle Fusselle. The college's accreditation was reaffirmed in 1970 by the Southern Association of Colleges and Schools, and in 1980 the college was in a process of self-study for another 10-year reaffirmation of its accreditation.

Net value of the physical facilities of the 1979 audit was $2,728,128. A recreational complex consisting of swimming pool, weight room, bath house, athletic field, and six tennis courts was completed in 1975.

In 1973 the college began classes in locations off campus as a service to the people in the mountain communities. By 1980 classes were being held in six off-campus locations, in addition to classes in a local correctional facility for men. In 1980 TMC's enrollment was 650, and the college offered associate degrees in liberal arts, music, general studies, business, and applied sciences.

EDNA HOLCOMB

TRUMAN, HARRY S (b. Lamar, MO, May 8, 1884; d. Independence, MO, Dec. 26, 1972). Thirty-third president of the United States. Son of John Anderson and Martha Ellen (Young) Truman, a farming couple, he spent his youth near Grandview and in Independence, MO, and attended the Baptist church adjoining his grandfather Solomon Young's farm and First Presbyterian Church, Independence. Truman's Southern forebears helped found the "family" church (First Baptist) at Grandview, MO, which Truman joined in 1902, maintaining membership there throughout his life. He preferred the tenets and simple, nonliturgical practices of Baptists.

Truman attended the University of Kansas City Law School, 1921-23. He married Elizabeth (Bess) Wallace, 1919. They had one child, Mary Margaret. He worshiped at the First Baptist Church, Washington, DC, as well as private military chapels. He appointed a committee on religion and welfare in the armed forces. A controversial action proposed a permanent ambassador to the Vatican. He is buried in the court-yard of Truman Library, Independence, MO.

WILLIAM CUTHBERTSON

TRUSTEESHIP. On May 10, 1845, the first SBC constitution approved an article on trustees or "board of managers" that called for Convention election of agency trustees. This principle is still one of the main factors in SBC polity.

The 1979 constitution states that the trustees are authorized to elect required officers and staff executives and to adopt bylaws. Article VI and Bylaw 16 provide requirements for the election of trustees. Other guidelines include the following: "All officers shall be subject to the control and direction of their directors in matters pertaining to the work and obligations of the board, institution, or commission." Further, all funds must be deposited in a depository or depositories approved by the directors, and "The treasurer shall not pay out money except as the directors may order and direct."

Trustees must be members of cooperating Baptist churches. "All incorporated agencies of the Convention shall be required to comply with the letter and spirit of the Constitution insofar as it is not in conflict with the statute law of the state in which an agency is incorporated." Trustees must be elected by the Convention, and no agency can change the trustee requirements of its charter without the prior consent of the SBC.

PORTER W. ROUTH

TUCKER, CLIFFORD ELIOT (b. Memphis, TN, Oct. 28, 1926; d. New Orleans, LA, Oct. 1, 1971). Seminary music professor. The son of Ollie Duggin and Ernest Shreeves Tucker, a lithographer, he married Susan Dorris, Nov. 29, 1957. They had no children. He was a graduate of Southwestern University (B.M., 1949) and Juilliard School (M.S., 1952). He served as organist-pianist at Bellevue Baptist Church, Memphis, TN, 1941-51, and as organist-choirmaster, Calvary Baptist Church, New York City, 1952-58. In addition, he served as staff accompanist for a Memphis radio station and a local theater group.

Tucker joined the music staff at New Orleans Baptist Theological Seminary in 1958, serving until 1968. While at New Orleans, he also served as organist-choirmaster in various churches and accompanied for oratorio performances. His musical recordings include *A Singing Faith, The Creation, How Beautiful Upon the Mountains, Dawn of Redeeming Grace, Hymn of Praise,* and *Hear My Prayer.* He is buried in Memorial Park, Memphis, TN.

HARRY L. ESKEW

TUCKER, JEREMIAH H. (b. Limestone County, AL, Nov. 14, 1829; d. Keachie, LA, May 31, 1881). Minister and educator. After attending Union University in Tennessee, he taught in Mississippi and Texas and moved to Louisiana in 1855 to teach at Mt. Lebanon University. Pastorates included First Church of Shreveport and Keachie Church. He served as moderator of Grand Cane Association, president of the Louisiana Convention, and president of Keachie Female College. His father was George Tucker, a minister. He married Anna M. Jenkins in 1858. After her death, he married Mary Jenkins in 1866.

GLEN LEE GREENE

TULAKOGEE ASSEMBLY, OKLA-HOMA (cf. Tulakogee Baptist Assembly, Vols. II, III). Dual ownership since 1947 by Muskogee and Tulsa Associations ended for Tulakogee Apr. 7, 1976, when Tulsa paid Muskogee $50,000 and assumed a $70,000 debt on the assembly. A committee of the Tulsa Association governs the assembly. Land is leased from the United States Corps of Engineers for $1.00 per year. The dorms, cabins, dining room, and conference complex are valued at $500,000. The 1980 budget was $60,000.

J. M. GASKIN

TURKEY, MISSION IN (III). For 12 years the Galatian Baptist Mission in Ankara was the only point of Baptist witness in Turkey. In 1979 the government refused to renew the resident visas of the missionary couple serving there. The fellowship consisted primarily of American military service personnel, although other nationalities were represented. The work has been temporarily suspended, but mission administrators hope the government will again allow another fellowship to exist.

ELISE NANCE BRIDGES

TURNER, JOHN CLYDE (b. Statesville, NC, Mar. 31, 1878; d. Raleigh, NC, Feb. 1, 1974). Pastor and state convention leader. Son of John and Nancy Turner, farmers, he married Bertha Hicks in 1908. They had no children. He attended Wake Forest College (A.B., 1908) and The Southern Baptist Theological Seminary (Th.M., 1905). Turner was pastor of churches in Fisherville and Newport, KY, 1902-07; Tattnall Square Church, Macon, GA, 1907-10; and First Church, Greensboro, NC, 1910-48. In addition to serving as president of the Baptist State Convention of North Carolina, 1929-32, he served as a trustee of Southern Seminary for 31 years and as a trustee of Wake Forest College for 25 years.

Turner wrote seven books: *A Truth in a Smile* (1941), *The Gospel of the Grace of God* (1943), *Soul-winning Doctrines* (1943), *Our Baptist Heritage* (1945), *The New Testament Doctrine of the Church* (1951), *These Things We Believe* (1956), and *A Century of Service* (1959).

While serving as pastor in Greensboro, he led the First Baptist Church to give at least one dollar to outside mission causes for every dollar used for the church's ministry in that city. Shortly after his death, church members made a memorial gift of $50,000 to Southern Seminary to establish a visiting professorship in evangelical ministry and preaching. He is buried in Oakwood Cemetery, Raleigh, NC.

SARAH PARKER

TYNER, BUNYAN YATES (b. Robeson County, NC, Dec. 1, 1882; d. Raleigh, NC, June 22, 1973). Educator. The son of Louis and Martha Tyner, farmers, he attended Buies Creek Academy (diploma, 1904), Wake Forest College (A.B., 1908), Columbia University Teachers' College (M.A., 1912), and Peabody College (1930). He married the former Mary Lee Bivens, July 28, 1909.

Tyner's longest teaching tenure was at Meredith College where he chaired the education department, 1932-54. He was second principal of Wingate Academy (now College), 1908-11, and first director of the Meredith-Wake Forest-Mars Hill summer school, Mars Hill, NC, 1935-41. Tyner and others of his family created the Tyner Chair of Bible at Campbell College (now University) in 1964. He was a lifetime deacon of First Church, Raleigh. He is buried in Montlawn Memorial Park, Raleigh, NC.

CAROLYN C. ROBINSON

U

UGANDA, MISSION IN (III). In 1972 Southern Baptists had 27 missionaries in Uganda; by 1978 there were only four. In 1973 the predominantly Muslim government intensified pressures on Christian groups. In 1977 all except four religious bodies were banned. Baptist churches could not meet, but missionaries were allowed to stay. Webster and Betty (Wilt) Carroll and James and Linda (Clarkson) Rice remained, operating social ministries and a Bible correspondence school. Church primary schools were allowed to continue. In 1979 after a change of government, new national leaders encouraged churches to lead in Uganda's spiritual reconstruction. Baptist leaders met for planning. About a third of 300 congregations had survived the ban. A massive relief program that summer met critical physical needs and paved the way for immediate and long-range evangelistic efforts. Bible schools were reopened. New missionaries came. By early 1980, 14 missionaries were working with Uganda Baptists to rebuild and strengthen their witness.

JOY NEAL

UNIFORM SERIES, COMMITTEE ON (III; cf. Sunday School Lessons, Uniform, Vol. II). This interdenominational group provides a plan for Bible study to help persons know the content of the Bible, understand its message, and be aware of God as revealed in Jesus Christ. In 1980 the chairman was a Southern Baptist, Wilbur C. Lamm. Committee membership totaled 67 persons from 24 denominations, 14 of whom were from the editorial staff of the Sunday School Board. During the years the SSB has been a part of the committee, all lesson materials published by the board have been written and edited by Southern Baptists.

Questions have been raised through the years concerning the relationship of the committee to the National Council of Churches. Some denominations with committee memberships are also Council members. Others, like Southern Baptists, are not. The Council's office in New York City provides clerical assistance to the committee, but there is no connection between the committee and other Council operations, policies, or activities.

WILBUR C. LAMM

UNION UNIVERSITY (II, III). In the fall of 1975, Union moved its campus eight miles from the central downtown location it had occupied since 1825 to a 150-acre site in north Jackson. The modern campus features a 150,000-square foot educational complex with all academic facilities under a single roof. Instead of dormitories, rows of apartments feature a private bedroom for each student. The university launched two subsequent expansion campaigns, one in 1978 and the other in 1979, to relieve overcrowded conditions and increase resident enrollment from 554 to 700. In 1979 Union also constructed its first married student apartments for 20 couples.

For the fall of 1979, the university had an enrollment of 1,158 and a record full-time equivalent of 1,078, a plant valued at $11,736,503, and an endowment of $1,690,561. The operating budget for the 1980-81 school year reached $5,061,677. In 1980 the school graduated its first class of baccalaureate level nursing students. Robert E. Craig has served as president since 1967.

ROBERT E. CRAIG

UNITED BAPTISTS (II). The majority of United churches are located in Kentucky, West

Virginia, Tennessee, and Missouri. This denomination probably has as many as 40 district associations. Statistics for 1980 showed 517 churches with 53,665 members.

Even though United Baptists are moderate Calvinists, they display some theological variety. Many of their associations hold that Christ tasted death for every man, while others are not as specific. One group is premillennial, but another strongly disavows that position. The West Union Association, which has 6,508 communicants, replaced a brief doctrinal statement in 1968 with the entire New Hampshire Confession of Faith.

BIBLIOGRAPHY: W. M. Patterson, "Small Baptist Groups in Kentucky," in L. T. Crismon, ed., *Baptists in Kentucky, 1776-1976* (1975). A. W. Wardin, Jr., *Baptist Atlas* (1980).

CHESTER RAYMOND YOUNG

UNITED NATIONS—NON-GOVERNMENTAL OBSERVER. From its very inception the United Nations was seen as including within its community not only governments but the citizenry of the nations formally represented. For the United Nations to carry out its work on the issues of world peace, human rights, international justice, and social progress, the support and understanding of the citizens of the world are essential prerequisites. To facilitate the process of communicating with citizens and to tap the expertise of various groups, the Non-Governmental Observer program was developed. The SBC participates in the program through the Christian Life Commission.

WILLIAM H. ELDER, III

UNIVERSITY OF CORPUS CHRISTI (II, III). See CORPUS CHRISTI, UNIVERSITY OF.

UNIVERSITY OF RICHMOND (II, III). In 1969 the university received the largest personal gift in the history of American higher education: $50,000,000 from trustee E. Claiborne Robins and his family. Of this amount, $40,000,000 was designated for use as endowment.

E. Bruce Heilman was inaugurated as fifth president of the university in the fall of 1971. He moved quickly to launch a campaign to raise another $50,000,000 for capital improvements and upgrading of programs. By 1980, eight years into a 10-year fund drive involving more than 5,000 volunteers across the country, the university had raised a total of $54,000,000. This made possible an unprecedented era of building on the campus. Fourteen campus structures were renovated, and five new buildings were constructed from 1970 to 1980. Among the capital improvements were an $8,000,000 science center, a $10,000,000 sports center, a $4,600,000 university commons, two women's dormitories at a total cost of $6,000,000, a $4,200,000 renovation of the Boatwright Memorial Library including a major addition to the building, and a $2,500,000 reno-

vation of three old science buildings into an academic and administrative complex.

By 1973 a new master plan for physical development of the 350-acre campus was approved. Faculty salaries were advanced. Academic offerings were increased and strengthened in a steady movement toward excellent education, especially in the undergraduate programs. Eighty-five percent of faculty members held Ph.D. degrees in 1980.

As the university approached its sesquicentennial year in 1980, enrollment stood at approximately 6,200. Approximately 1,000 students were women undergraduates. In 1979 the School of Business Administration was renamed the E. Claiborne Robins School of Business Administration. Total assets on June 30, 1979, were $178,420,272.

WILLIAM L. LUMPKIN

UPPER VOLTA, MISSION IN. Bryant and Ina (Martin) Durham arrived in Ouagadougou in 1971 to begin Baptist work. Extensive use of a Bible correspondence course as a means of entry was especially successful with high school students. Agricultural work and relief ministries in the Koudougou area, including feeding and well digging, produced converts and churches. Scripture knowledge, agriculture, and small crafts were taught in a rural training center. A convention organized in 1977. A third station was opened in 1979 at Tenkoudougou. Volunteers contributed in relief work and building projects. New projects included student work and literacy. Churches and preaching stations numbered 45 with 1,485 members. Missionaries totaled 14.

JOHN E. MILLS

URBAN CHURCH STUDIES, CENTER FOR. A joint venture of several SBC agencies, designed to help Baptist churches at home and abroad more effectively reach persons for Christ and congregationalize the urban areas of the world.

Grady C. Cothen, president of the Sunday School Board, and William G. Tanner, president of the Home Mission Board, convened an exploratory meeting on May 21, 1979, with representatives of Woman's Missionary Union, the Foreign Mission Board, the Brotherhood Commission, and the seminaries to discuss the possibility of developing a research-training center to strengthen the growth of inner-city churches in transition. This meeting was an outgrowth of earlier conversations and meetings in which Cothen and Tanner discussed their mutual concerns about attacking the problems of the inner city. Further meetings resulted in an agreement in 1980 to establish a Center for Urban Church Studies.

The center has four objectives: (1) to conduct research in the area of urban concerns; (2) to review present models of urban ministry and to design and test other models; (3) to suggest materials and products and serve as an information resource center for Baptist agencies, state conventions, associations, churches at home, and national Baptist groups abroad; and (4) to provide training which deals with the "how to" in effectively reaching persons for Christ and congregationalizing the urban areas of the world.

The center is operated by a board of directors designated by the participating SBC agencies. Directors at the outset were Morton Rose, SSB; James Nelson, HMB; Winston Crawley, FMB; June Whitlow, WMU; Norman Godfrey, BC; and G. Willis Bennett, chairman, representing the six seminaries.

Larry L. Rose, executive director of the Waco, TX, Baptist Association, was appointed to direct the center on Jan. 1, 1981. Rose and a small staff are housed at the SSB in Nashville.

GRADY C. COTHEN

URBAN—RURAL MISSIONS. See RURAL-URBAN MISSIONS, HOME MISSION BOARD PROGRAM OF.

URUGUAY, MISSION IN (II, III). The mission adopted a zonal plan in the 1970s, dividing the country into eight areas assigned to specific missionaries who maintained contact with and gave encouragement to the churches and their leaders. Relations with national leaders improved. Mass media ministries received a boost. Two journalism workshops were held. The Mass Communications Center, Montevideo, opened in 1978. Two Christian films, shown on leading television stations, drew a record viewer response. Hundreds requested correspondence courses offered on radio broadcasts. Extensive newspaper ads informed the public about Baptists, their beliefs, and programs of work. In 1978 Baptists joined hands with other denominations in sponsoring an interdenominational evangelistic crusade. Over 5,000 decisions were registered, and the churches were strengthened. Thirty missionaries were serving in 1979.

FRANK K. MEANS

UTAH-IDAHO ASSOCIATIONS (III).
I. New Associations. WHISPERING PINES. Organized Apr. 25, 1972, by messengers representing Emmanuel Church, Cottonwood, ID; Mountain Shadows Mission, Grangeville, ID; and Pine Ridge Church, Kamiah, ID. Twenty-one persons attended the organizational meeting. Member churches previously had been associated with the Boise Valley Association until geographical factors and travel distances seemed to make it practical to form this new association. In 1979 six churches and two missions reported 46 baptisms, 287 members, $120,002 total gifts, $44,909 mission gifts, and $406,500 property value.

II. Changes in Associations. MID STATE. Organized in 1968 by two churches in Central Utah, First Southern, Dragerton, and First Baptist, Price, and merged with the Gideon Baptist Association in 1970. In 1975 the Price church joined the Utah Baptist Association, and in 1979

the Dragerton (city renamed East Carbon in 1974) Church joined the Utah Baptist Association.

OVAL WALKER

UTAH-IDAHO SOUTHERN BAPTIST CONVENTION (III).
I. Convention Operations. In 1979 the nine associations were served by four area directors of missions. Richard Ashworth served Gideon, Rainbow, and Utah Associations. Mayo Brown served Salt Lake Association. Earl Jackson served Golden Spike and Eastern Idaho. Roy Ferguson served Boise Valley, Magic Valley, and Whispering Pines.

Seventy-nine churches, reporting a total membership of 13,408, baptized 736 and gave $192,562 through the Cooperative Program, $23,891 for state missions, $17,984 for home missions, and $36,109 for foreign missions.

The state convention gives 20 percent of Cooperative Program receipts for SBC causes. The Home Mission Board assists in funding joint programs with the convention under a 94 percent-8 percent agreement. The Sunday School Board helps in the funding of some religious education programs. The convention budget income reported in 1979 was $694,762 from all sources, $96,936 in restricted funds, and $791,698 total income. Budget expenses were $650,025; restricted funds expenditures, $111,436; reserves expended, $18,949; and total expenditures, $780,410. The convention has no indebtedness.

II. Convention Property and Funds. The convention offices are located in the debt-free building at 986 South Fourth East in Salt Lake City, UT, purchased in 1972. In 1972 the convention received from the HMB land and a building at 2119 South 1700 East, Salt Lake City, subject to a gift lien contract. This property was used as collateral in the purchase of the present office building. In 1976 the convention was released from the gift lien. In 1975 the convention purchased from the HMB 4.2 acres of undeveloped land at 1950 West 4700 South in Salt Lake City. In 1977 the convention paid the HMB in full for the land after selling 1.6 acres. A Baptist Building Fund was established in 1978 in preparation for the relocation of convention offices in larger facilities.

A Utah-Idaho SBC Loan Fund was established in 1972 on receipt by the convention of $25,475 inheritance from James P. and Maud S. Bridges. The fund has increased to $43,083 with the interest being used for new work loans. Ten loans have been made from the fund; five paid in full.

A Trust and Memorial Fund was established in 1965 by convention Executive Board action and currently has assets of $25,817. Individuals and institutions may invest in the fund and receive semiannual interest payments. Loans up to $3,000 from the fund may be authorized by an elected committee. Larger loans may be approved by the Executive Board.

III. Program of Work. The Executive Board with 19 members elected by the convention messengers to serve three-year rotating terms has general supervision of convention work. The board acts for the convention in the interim between sessions. The executive secretary-treasurer, elected by the board, serves an indefinite tenure. He also serves as editor of the state paper, *Utah-Idaho Southern Baptist Witness;* as director of evangelism; and as administrator of the Trust and Memorial Fund. The executive secretary-treasurer since 1969 has been Darwin E. Welsh. The assistant executive and assistant editor is Anita Lemke, elected in 1970.

In 1977 the HMB appointed A. C. Queen missionary to assist the Utah-Idaho Convention and Nevada Baptists, preparing to organize a new convention, in evangelism development. A Good News Utah-Idaho Crusade in 1979 directed by Queen contributed to 736 baptisms. The crusade included lay evangelism schools, Scripture distribution, and simultaneous revivals. Queen also initiated an annual youth evangelism conference.

The convention director of missions, stewardship, and Brotherhood is M. Bruce Gardner, elected May 4, 1978. C. Clyde Billingsley served in this position, Mar., 1975, to Dec., 1976. John P. Baker served as interim director from Jan., 1978, to July, 1978.

The Baptist Concern Center, Salt Lake City, is directed by Carl and Judy Holden. The Christian Social Ministries work at Sun Valley-Ketchum, ID, directed by Joe and Pam Owen, was initiated in Feb., 1978, as a direct result of a feasibility study completed by Chuck Clayton, western field representative for the Special Mission Ministries Department of the HMB, and was promoted through the 1975 state missions offering.

In Nov., 1978, Willis and Rebecca Blair were appointed by the convention to serve as new work starters in Meridian, ID. The Blairs are the first missionaries to be employed and paid entirely by the Utah-Idaho Convention. The salary comes from a new work reserve which was established through state mission offerings received since 1975.

The Spanish work in Utah is under the direction of Salvador and Elodia Cano. Spanish work in Idaho is directed by Huron and Edie Polnac. There are three Spanish missions in Utah and two in Idaho.

The Fort Hall Indian Mission, Blackfoot, ID, for the Shoshone-Bannock Indians, is directed by Mike and Virginia McKay. The Intermountain Baptist Indian Chapel, which ministers to students of the Intermountain Indian School, Brigham City, UT, is directed by Bruce and Bea Conrad. Work with the Ute-Ouray tribes is conducted at Roosevelt, UT. This work, under the leadership of John Blake, was organized, Nov. 7, 1976, as the convention's first language church.

Yam Yee and HipToc Lee serve the Chinese Baptist Mission, Salt Lake City. Elizabeth Watkins, veteran missionary to Japan for 41 years,

UTAH-IDAHO STATISTICAL SUMMARY

Year	Associations	Churches	Church Membership	Baptisms	SS Enrollment	VBS Enrollment	CT Enrollment	WMU Enrollment	Brotherhood Enrollment	Ch. Music Enrollment	Mission Gifts	Total Gifts	Value Church Property
1969	9	63	8,595	459	6,624	3,881	3,140	1,129	270	640	$ 79,999	$ 665,252	$ 3,267,700
1970	8	64	9,118	493	6,212	4,402	2,649	1,133	353	799	84,426	727,403	3,142,100
1971	8	64	9,511	547	6,355	4,930	2,103	1,100	454	922	137,986	746,618	3,035,300
1972	8	62	9,916	570	6,416	5,223	2,111	1,085	406	781	148,489	835,437	3,404,100
1973	9	67	10,473	604	6,356	5,596	2,040	1,143	314	1,122	160,034	968,172	4,070,100
1974	9	64	11,058	698	6,526	5,631	1,906	1,257	299	852	220,481	1,074,086	4,537,900
1975	9	64	11,768	726	6,616	5,514	1,799	1,085	392	912	276,229	1,359,370	5,495,635
1976	9	64	12,287	607	7,165	5,382	1,963	1,108	490	889	309,366	1,435,483	6,476,900
1977	9	68	12,650	617	7,172	4,543	1,726	1,123	501	1,180	292,673	1,561,792	7,685,900
1978	9	69	12,585	676	7,387	5,103	1,852	1,127	513	1,256	332,966	1,857,430	10,162,250
1979	9	72	13,437	741	7,522	4,491	1,768	1,099	442	1,347	485,215	2,284,329	11,205,700
1980	9	73	14,616	901	8,085	5,033	2,182	1,278	599	1,354	496,693	2,300,150	13,561,500

ANITA LEMKE

directs the Japanese work in Salt Lake City. A ministry to the Koreans was initiated in May, 1976, under the direction of John and Prisca Lee. In June, 1976, a Korean mission was started with three families and has grown to 54 adult members.

Director of Sunday School, Student Ministries, Church Administration, and Church Architecture is Guy D. Ward, elected in 1969. Student work is organized on 13 campuses in the two-state convention. David Barnes served as Baptist Student Ministries director from Jan., 1972, to June 15, 1974. Both the BSU and the Charles H. Ashcraft Chair of Bible, initiated in 1979, meet in the University Baptist Church building in Boise, ID. The Chair of Bible, which offers seminary credit through the SBC Seminary Extension Department, operates under the direction of the Boise Valley Association. Instructors are Dan Robinson and Huron Polnac.

William H. Souther became the director of Church Training and Church Music, June 1, 1975. Under Souther's direction a bicentennial choir was organized in 1975 and performed for a rally held at the Salt Palace in Salt Lake City on July 4, 1976, and other occasions. The choir was later renamed the Intermountain Baptist Choir. Many members travel over 200 miles for rehearsals. The choir sang for the Glorieta Baptist Conference Center during Church Music Week in 1979. Since 1976, the *Messiah* has become an annual music feature in Salt Lake City at Christmas. Other productions have been at Sun Valley and Burley, ID.

The Woman's Missionary Union operates as a department of the convention and has been under the direction of Gernice Ward since 1969. Fifty-three churches and missions have WMU work. Extensive leadership is offered once a year on the state level, and annual leadership training is encouraged in each association. Training is provided by a WMU promotional committee which consists of volunteers who are elected WMU officers and associational WMU directors. Special focus is given to Acteens through an annual house party. Acteens have been taken to the two National Acteen Convocations sponsored by WMU, SBC.

In 1979 the Golden Gate Baptist Theological Seminary Center, housed through the Chair of Religion at the University Baptist Church, Salt Lake City, was established with C. E. Autrey as director and professor. Students enrolled in the Salt Lake City satellite enjoy the same privileges and relationships of accreditation and opportunities that are presently a part of the program at the Mill Valley campus in California.

SBC Seminary Extension Department courses are also offered at the Salt Lake City Chair of Religion. Seminary Extension Department courses have been offered also at Pocatello, ID, and two locations in Salt Lake City. The P. O. Bocker Memorial Library with over 3,000 volumes is available to all center students.

IV. Special Activities. A Greater Salt Lake Crusade for Christ was held, July 26-Aug. 2, 1970, at the Salt Palace in Salt Lake City. The crusade was sponsored by the convention, the HMB, and 35 churches and missions of the Salt Lake and Golden Spike Associations. C. E. Autrey was the evangelist. Attendance for the crusade was 6,396; there were 300 decisions, including 45 professions of faith.

In 1971 the convention launched a youth mission pilot program. Four volunteers, Benton Welsh, from Salt Lake City, UT, and Diana Rhodes, Sam Ashcraft, and Sharon Phillips from North Little Rock, AR, were enlisted for one year's mission service with their parents and churches paying their expenses. The youth were commissioned on Sep. 11, 1971, in Salt Lake City. Benton and Sam served in the Northwest Baptist Convention under the general supervision of W. C. Carpenter; Diana and Sharon served in Utah under the supervision of Darwin E. Welsh. The pilot project was monitored by the HMB and later developed into the Sojourner Program.

A long-range planning program was adopted by the convention in 1974 with the statement of mission as follows:

> The Mission of the Utah-Idaho Southern Baptist Convention is to help churches carry out the Great Commission of God: (1) By helping to strengthen churches at the point of need in fulfilling world mission through cooperative effort. (2) By helping churches visualize and meet the need to establish new mission points with existing resources. (3) By helping to lead churches to experience a real togetherness (fellowship) so that goals may be set and reached in a continuous effort.

A. C. QUEEN

UTAH-IDAHO SOUTHERN BAPTIST WITNESS. Official newspaper of the Utah-Idaho Southern Baptist Convention. The first issue was published, Feb. 10, 1965, under editor Charles H. Ashcraft. Darwin E. Welsh became the editor on Sep. 15, 1969. Anita Lemke was elected associate editor, Nov. 9, 1970. In 1974 the four-page publication was changed from 23 to 22 issues per year, published semi-monthly with one issue in November and December. The 1979 budget was $8,105 with a circulation of 3,066. In Jan., 1980, the *Witness* was changed to an eight-page monthly publication.

ANITA LEMKE

V

VACATION BIBLE SCHOOL (II, III). During the 1970s the Sunday School Board expanded Vacation Bible School to include Church VBS, Mission VBS, and Backyard Bible Clubs. The total number of all VBS projects in 1979 was 35,681 with a total enrollment of 3,197,517. These projects reported a $1,412,316 total mission offering and 55,680 professions of faith. VBS continues to be one of the leading evangelistic activities conducted by Southern Baptist churches.

The annual church VBS curriculum provides for 10 sessions of Bible study for all ages including adults. Optional five-session pupils' books were offered for the first time in 1979.

Two five-session mission VBS curricula are available for alternate use in locations outside the church community with preschoolers, children, and youth not in Sunday School. Churches reported 2,870 mission schools in 1979. Many associations now provide training in mission VBS, as well as church VBS work.

Three sets of Backyard Bible Club materials are available for use with children for one and one half hours a day for five days. In 1979, 5,287 Backyard Bible Clubs were reported. One purpose of these clubs is to enroll the children and their families in Sunday School.

The Projects Promotion Section, Sunday School Department, SSB, is responsible for the general promotion of VBS work. Since 1969, Harold C. Marsh, section supervisor, has correlated each year from six to eight regional VBS institutes that train approximately 400 state VBS special workers. These workers, under the direction of the state Sunday School departments, conduct conferences in state VBS clinics for aproximately 9,000 associational VBS leaders who train approximately 110,000 church VBS leaders each year.

Arthur Burcham has served as general VBS consultant since 1968. In 1978 H. Wayne Etheridge succeeded William R. Cox as editor of general VBS materials. Age-group VBS editorial and field service responsibilities rest with the respective age-group sections in the Sunday School Department.

ARTHUR BURCHAM

VALLEY BAPTIST ACADEMY (III). Since 1970 a continuous expansion of the school's physical plant and ministry has occurred. Located in Harlingen, TX, the campus has been enlarged to 90 acres. A library-learning center, five faculty housing units, and a gymnasium have been added. Students are from the United States, Mexico, Central America, South America, and islands of the Caribbean. A high percentage go from the school to institutions of higher learning.

H. E. GARY

VALLEY BAPTIST MEDICAL CENTER (cf. Valley Baptist Hospital, Harlingen, TX, Vols. II, III). Valley Baptist Hospital became Valley Baptist Medical Center in 1975. Also in 1975, the Diagnostic and Therapeutic Center was opened to physicians on the medical center's staff. A $12,000,000 expansion program began in Sep., 1977, including a new and enlarged surgical suite, another critical care unit, new emergency and outpatient units, an enlarged and relocated radiology department, expansion of the food service department, expansion of the power plant, and 76 new patient beds.

In 1978 the Valley Baptist Medical Development Corporation, including the Watson W. Wise Memorial Renal Dialysis Center, was organized. The medical center has 278 beds, with assets in excess of $32,000,000. Benjamin M. McKibbens became president and chief executive officer in 1977.

RANDY BAKER

VAN DYKE, EDWARD TOWNSEND (b. Albany, OH, Feb. 12, 1918; d. Athens, OH, Feb. 20, 1979). Businesn and prominent Ohio Baptist layman. Son of Arthur O. and Ethel (Townsend) Van Dyke, farmers, he was a graduate of Mountain State Business College, Parkersburg, WV, and of the Management Institute, Washington, DC. He married Edith McConnell of Edith, OH, Apr. 25, 1939. They had one daughter, Sue Osborne.

Van Dyke rendered significant service among Ohio Baptists. A charter member of the First Baptist Church, Athens, when it was constituted, Dec. 30, 1952, he served as a deacon of this church and was also chairman of the building committee. He was in demand throughout the state as a lay speaker. In addition to serving on the executive board of the State Convention of Baptists in Ohio, and on the board of the state Baptist Foundation, he was also a trustee of the SBC Brotherhood Commission. He gave hours of his time to help construct the facilities of the Seneca Lake Baptist Assembly and served later as its food manager. He is buried in Alexander Cemetery, Albany, OH.

CHARLES E. MAGRUDER

VAN NESS, NOBLE (b. Atlanta, GA, Mar. 31, 1897; d. Vinalhaven, ME, Sep. 13, 1976). Denominational publishing executive. Son of

Frances Tabb and Isaac Jacobus Van Ness (*q.v.* II), he married Bethann Faris, Mar. 28, 1928, in Ardmore, PA. They had three children: Caroline, John, and Lucy. A graduate of Vanderbilt University (B.S.), he served as instructor and coach at Mars Hill College before joining the Sunday School Board, Nashville, in 1922. Following his retirement in 1965, he and his wife moved to the island of Vinalhaven, ME.

GOMER R. LESCH

VAN ROYEN, RUSSELL GLENN (b. Howard, KS, Feb. 21, 1898; d. San Antonio, TX, Aug. 19, 1978). Home missionary. Son of Robert James and Nora Bell (McNabney) Van Royen, he married Edith Ile Hylton, Feb. 20, 1918. An alumnus of Central Baptist Seminary (1922), he served churches in Kansas and Texas, 1917-41; was rural evangelist for Texas Baptist General Convention, 1941-44; and served with the Home Mission Board, SBC, as first secretary of visual education, 1944-49; field worker, 1950; superintendent of work in Panama and the Canal Zone, 1951-59; field worker for language missions, 1960-64; and leader in refugee resettlement, 1962-64. Following his retirement from the HMB, Van Royen served in the Texas Baptist Convention River Front Ministry at Presidio, 1966-76. He is buried in Sunset Memorial Park, San Antonio, TX.

LOYD CORDER

VENEZUELA, MISSION IN (II, III). As the 1970s came to a close, Baptist work was continuing to grow throughout the country. A close relationship existed between nationals and missionaries. The Venezuelan Baptist Convention had a strong missionary vision with emphasis on reaching all Venezuela for Christ. Substantial increases in baptisms and church membership were occurring each year. The radio ministry was touching thousands annually, and groups were learning by radio to organize into missions and churches. Listener response came from countries throughout Latin America. The home mission offering was increasing each year and in 1980 supported eight full-time home missionary couples. At the beginning of 1980, there were 70 churches and 65 missions.

J. BRYAN BRASINGTON

VERMONT, SOUTHERN BAPTISTS IN. See MARYLAND BAPTIST CONVENTION OF; NEW ENGLAND, BAPTIST GENERAL ASSOCIATION OF.

VIOLENCE (III). Violence affects every individual in the United States and around the world. Violence may be defined as the exercise of force which causes damage or abuse to people, principles, property, or something of value.

In recent years many people have come to understand violence in this wider sense. This understanding has led to the realization that besides physical violence there are also a number of nonphysical forms of violence that concerned Christians must seek to eliminate.

In 1975 the SBC adopted a resolution on violence which called on "the American people to recognize the dreadful consequences of violence in our nation." The resolution commended the Federal Communications Commission for holding hearings on broadcast violence, opposed psychological and verbal violence, called on advertisers not to sponsor violent programs, and urged Southern Baptist churches to communicate the fact that Jesus Christ is the only hope to replace violence with lasting peace.

The Christian Life Commission, SBC, gives continuing attention to problems related to violence through its publications and conferences.

HARRY N. HOLLIS, JR.

VIRGINIA, BAPTIST GENERAL ASSOCIATION OF (II, III).
I. History. On Nov. 1, 1971, the General Association established an office of Church-Minister Relations, which was placed under the program operation of the Virginia Baptist General Board in 1974. On Nov. 12, 1975, the General Association voted to change its financial operation from the calendar year to the fiscal year—Dec. 1 to Nov. 30. In Nov., 1976, the General Association established a churchwide state mission offering to be taken in September of each year, promoted jointly by the Virginia Baptist General Board and Woman's Missionary Union of Virginia. This offering reached over $350,000 annually by the end of 1979. H. Doyle Chauncey became treasurer of the General Association on Jan. 1, 1979, succeeding James T. Todd. The treasurer's office computerized its operations on June 5, 1979, and by the end of 1979 had formulated plans to computerize the record and mailing systems of the Virginia Baptist General Board. Richard M. Stephenson continues as executive director of the General Board.

In 1979 there were 43 district associations with 1,458 churches and missions, with a membership of 571,137, cooperating with the General Association. Contributions in 1979 through the Cooperative Program were nearly double those of 1969, as were total missions gifts. In 1979 Cooperative Program receipts were $8,222,341, and total missions gifts were $11,684,645. Total gifts received by churches of Virginia in 1979 were $82,879,037, which was more than double the amount received in 1969.

II. Program of Work. Elected by the Baptist General Association of Virginia, the General Board serves as manager for all matters committed to its trust and has the authority to make and implement plans that it deems judicious, provided such plans are in accord with its own charter and the constitution and bylaws of the General Association. The board holds title to all properties of the General Association and may also act in interim for the General Association. The board develops its own program consistent with the overall purpose of the General Association as stated in its constitution: "The object of the General Association shall be to furnish the

Baptist churches of Virginia a medium of cooperation for the propagation of the Gospel of Jesus Christ, and for the advancement of the Redeemer's Kingdom by all methods in accord with the Word of God.'' The board is composed of members nominated by a General Association committee on boards and committees and elected by the General Association. In addition, 12 persons serve as members of the board by virtue of office. There are two categories of board members elected by the General Association: (1) Eight members at large from eight different associations, and (2) associational members elected in accord with the bylaws of the board:

> One member from the area of each cooperating district association; providing, however, that no association formed after September 1, 1969, shall have members elected to the General Board from its area unless and until it has at least 5,000 members who give at least $20,000 through the Cooperative Program annually. When the Cooperative Program gifts from the churches of an association reach $150,000 annually, an additional member shall be elected and when the Cooperative Program gifts from the churches of an association reach $500,000 annually, one more member shall be elected (maximum of three associational members).

The staff of the General Board implements the various programs approved by the board. A new staff structure adopted in 1979 contained four divisions: Church Programs, General Promotion, Ministries, and Business Management. Church Programs includes Baptist Men, Church Training, Bible Teaching, Church Music, and Church Administration (a new area). New programs and emphases have been developed over the last decade in the ongoing work of the General Board. Eagle Eyrie, the all-year assembly facilities for Virginia Baptists, is operated as a part of the Division of Church Programs. A new small conference and administrative building has been erected at Eagle Eyrie which greatly increases the service of the conference center to small groups.

In 1979 Church Administration was upgraded to a full department of work. The primary focus of Church Administration is in the area of pastoral ministries. This includes providing resources for pastors, staff persons, ministers' wives, church secretaries, deacons, church councils, and general church leadership. This program also relates to ministers of youth and coordinates four annual projects: Junior High Weekend, Senior High Weekend at Eagle Eyrie, Youth Week, and Summer Worker Orientation.

During the 1970s, Virginia Baptists developed an overall evangelism strategy with emphasis upon a continuous program of witnessing and development in Christian discipleship. In 1973 the first full-time director of evangelism was employed. Evangelism, a part of the Division of General Promotion, is a vital and integral part of the total General Board program. "Growing Evangelistic Churches in Virginia" is a priority of the evangelism office.

VIRGINIA STATISTICAL SUMMARY

Year	Associations	Churches	Church Membership	Baptisms	SS Enrollment	VBS Enrollment	CT Enrollment	WMU Enrollment	Brotherhood Enrollment	Ch. Music Enrollment	Mission Gifts	Total Gifts	Value Church Property
1969	44	1,433	529,135	14,134	395,684	178,621	71,953	95,623	20,310	49,598	$ 7,039,361	$40,669,616	$212,328,145
1970	44	1,434	533,465	13,656	386,345	150,617	64,883	91,194	18,896	51,045	7,102,348	42,317,557	226,787,270
1971	43	1,415	533,650	14,873	363,615	147,890	45,948	87,065	19,688	50,920	7,713,510	46,129,255	232,988,421
1972	43	1,411	540,705	16,081	358,711	144,649	41,852	84,568	18,974	54,070	8,419,135	49,718,892	252,454,993
1973	43	1,416	549,732	15,828	354,490	143,814	39,677	82,755	19,157	57,904	9,144,524	52,581,664	272,984,727
1974	43	1,412	554,559	14,649	345,646	153,871	37,850	82,047	18,422	60,526	10,075,157	56,712,706	312,349,444
1975	43	1,407	562,578	15,532	345,230	147,904	36,743	80,826	18,952	61,858	10,971,533	62,354,752	340,359,758
1976	43	1,417	568,244	13,277	342,474	138,347	34,910	79,547	19,029	61,905	11,817,370	68,240,530	375,416,246
1977	43	1,429	573,333	12,359	339,567	138,862	32,277	76,141	18,208	62,016	12,445,685	73,471,055	411,180,221
1978	43	1,429	574,940	10,977	332,157	134,724	35,269	73,090	17,630	62,518	13,403,094	78,686,657	448,694,048
1979	43	1,431	579,273	11,342	327,298	135,706	35,177	70,501	17,171	63,957	14,683,203	86,389,281	496,615,801
1980	43	1,435	584,866	13,126	324,060	138,971	39,534	69,313	17,981	66,329	16,052,394	92,708,282	551,662,320

HAZEL MALLORY

At the 1971 meeting of the General Association, a recommendation to establish what is now called the Pastor-Church Relations Office was overwhelmingly adopted, showing the intense concern of ministers and lay persons in this vital area. A notable achievement in ministry support was the formation of a ministers' unemployment fund in 1972. The fund was begun with an allocation of $12,500 from the General Board with a matching amount from the Curtis English family. The fund provides emergency aid for ministers in situations of forced termination of pastorates. In 1973 the General Association entered a contractual agreement with the Institute of Pastoral Care to provide a cost-sharing pastoral counseling and referral service for ministers and their immediate families.

Twenty regional stewardship seminars were held across the state in 1979 under the leadership of the Division of General Promotion, and over 900 pastors participated in these meetings during the month of May. These meetings are held annually.

In the Ministries Division the missions area concentrated its work in the 1970s in the fast developing urban corridor, that narrow strip of land on both sides of I-95 from Alexandria to Petersburg and on both sides of I-64 from Richmond to Virginia Beach. This area, which comprises only 15 percent of the land area of the state, contained 58 percent of the population by 1970. In 1971 the General Association adopted a goal to establish 58 new churches in this area. At the end of 1979, 36 new churches and missions had been established. Continuing emphasis was indicated for this work by the employment of the first director of metropolitan missions in 1979. At the beginning of the decade, only 15 of the 43 associations had directors of associational missions; in 1979, 28 had directors, and 5 associations had employed a second professional person to lead in Christian social ministries.

Virginia Baptists have established through the Department of Christian Life Concerns an extensive legislative network to inform Virginia Baptists on legislative concerns and their impact on the quality of life in Virginia.

In 1979 the programs for Church Training were separated from the Department of Teaching and Training (now the Department of Bible Teaching), and a new area of work with greater emphasis on training in the churches was formed into a Department of Church Training.

Near the end of the decade several programs were started or expanded significantly. Work with senior citizens greatly increased. A Senior Citizen's Week at Eagle Eyrie has become a significant expansion of the assembly program. Work with retarded persons has had increasing interest and involvement. In 1980 a committee was working out plans for the beginning of care centers for retarded adults. As the decade ended, the newest program expansion was the inauguration of a videotape program with major staff assignment in this area of work.

BIBLIOGRAPHY: Reuben E. Alley, *A History of Baptists in Virginia* (1974).

JOHN C. IVINS
and RICHARD M. STEPHENSON

VIRGINIA, NEGRO BAPTISTS IN. See NEGRO BAPTISTS IN VIRGINIA.

VIRGINIA ASSOCIATIONS (II, III). At the beginning of 1980, Virginia had 43 associations, one less than in 1969. In 1970 Mountain State Association in West Virginia joined the new West Virginia Baptist Convention.

JOHN D. EDENS

VIRGINIA BAPTIST CHILDREN'S HOME (II, III). In the decade of the 1970s, licensed capacity was reduced from 180 to 100 children in group care. There were 10 cottages with a maximum of 10 children per cottage in 1980. Two additional eight-bed cottages have been designated for emergency care services since 1978. The average age of children upon admission to the group care program was 14.6, and the average stay was two years.

In 1978 the board of trustees adopted a three-year plan to blanket the state with five regional child and family care centers. These served distressed families with professional Christian services, using the campus-style group care facilities at Salem as a backup with special care services primarily for teenagers. Emphasis was on preventive programs and intensive crisis intervention services to prevent long-term separation of children from their families. On Sep. 30, 1979, total assets were $4,714,874. The operating budget for 1979-80 was $1,060,000. Capital outlay for the decade was negligible; however, one cottage was razed and a new one completed in 1979 at a cost of $300,000.

R. FRANKLIN HOUGH, JR.

VIRGINIA BAPTIST EXTENSION BOARD, INC. (cf. Virginia Extension Board, Inc., Vols. II, III). For 40 years the board has made loans to assist churches in financing building programs. During the 1970s the board also bought land sites for new churches. Seventy-six churches held loans in 1980. Assets in 1979 were $2,669,688.

RICHARD M. STEPHENSON

VIRGINIA BAPTIST FOUNDATION (II, III). The executive director's office has been in Richmond since its removal from Petersburg in Mar., 1971, when Ernest L. Honts became executive director, succeeding James R. Bryant. Robert L. Mobley has been executive director since June, 1976. Foundation assets continued to increase and totaled $5,212,546 on Dec. 31, 1979. Annual income in 1979 reached $320,247, of which $219,941 was distributed. Beneficiaries included the Foreign Mission Board, SBC, Virginia Baptist Children's Home, and Virginia Baptist Homes. The bulk of the foundation's assets are received from proceeds of wills and trusts of Virginia Baptists.

STERLING H. MOORE

VIRGINIA BAPTIST HISTORICAL SOCIETY (II, III). The society celebrated its centennial in 1976. In Aug., 1979, it selected its first full-time executive director, Frederick J. Anderson. Executive secretaries of the society in the 1970s were Woodford B. Hackley (q.v.), 1954-74, and Ernest C. Bolt, Jr., 1975-79. The society's quarters at the University of Richmond were renovated and doubled in size in 1976 to accommodate the increasing collection of archival materials. In 1980 the society acquired microfilming equipment for further preservation of records.

On June 15, 1980, the society promoted its preservation work and the appreciation of Baptist history by sponsoring the first statewide Virginia Baptist Heritage Day. Under the editorship of Woodford B. Hackley, 1962-71, and John S. Moore, 1972-   , the society's annual journal, *The Virginia Baptist Register,* has published over 100 articles of original research principally on early Baptist history in Virginia. Since 1972 the society has published a newsletter, *The Chronicle.*

FREDERICK J. ANDERSON

VIRGINIA BAPTIST HOMES (III; cf. Virginia Baptist Home, Vol. II). After the retirement of the general superintendent, F. B. LeSueur, in Dec., 1969, Charles E. Neal, former administrator of the Newport News home, became executive director. In Mar., 1970, R. Furman Kenney became administrator of the Newport News home. The position of associate executive director was added to the general office staff in 1972. Raleigh O. Baker became administrator of the Culpeper home after the death of L. T. Saunders in 1978. The homes acquired an additional tract of 253 acres from the estate of trustee E. Turpin Wills. This was added to the Kinloch Farm operation at Culpeper in 1975, making a total of 600 acres.

In 1974 the Newport News home was enlarged to house an additional 94 residents. A new 52-bed health care unit was also dedicated at the Newport News home on May 6, 1979. In 1978 a third home, Lakewood Manor in Richmond, was completed with Albert E. Simms as administrator. The Hurt Gerontology Center was established in 1974, and W. L. Howse, III, became director of the education, training, and resource center. On Sep. 29, 1978, the homes observed the 30th anniversary of the first home at a celebration in Culpeper.

In 1979 the total fixed assets of the three homes were $17,500,000 with a combined resident capacity of 850. Sources of income included funds received from residents, Cooperative Program receipts, and special gifts and income through wills and legacies.

CHARLES E. NEAL

VIRGINIA BAPTIST HOSPITAL (II, III). Virginia Baptist Hospital's School of Nurs-

ing announced in 1979 that plans were underway to cooperate with Lynchburg College to offer the baccalaureate degree in nursing, with the college using the hospital facilities. The School of Nursing would cease to exist in 1982, having graduated more than 1,000 students. The hospital's School of Pastoral Care became nationally accredited during the 1970s, offering three programs in pastoral training. An agreement with Lynchburg General Hospital in 1972 placed responsibility for obstetrical services for all of central Virginia on the Virginia Baptist Hospital.

In Oct., 1972, a newborn intensive care nursery began operation. The hospital was given the first newborn transport vehicle in the state. The obstetrical philosophy of the hospital is family-centered care with participation of fathers and sibling visitation. During the 1970s construction and renovation provided for self-care, coronary care, intensive care, psychiatry, obstetrical facilities, a dietary and cafeteria complex, and an enlarged pharmacy. Charles S. Elliott, administrator for over 25 years, retired on May 3, 1980, and was succeeded by George W. Dawson. Total assets for the year ending Sep. 30, 1979, were $18,957,998.

MARTHA P. MOORE

VIRGINIA BAPTIST REGISTER, THE (III). Annual publication of the Virginia Baptist Historical Society, it continues to publish material relating to Virginia Baptist history. Most of the articles deal with early Baptist work in the state. An anniversary edition, published in 1976, included a history of the Virginia Baptist Historical Society which celebrated its centennial that year. A separate index is published every five years. Articles have featured John Williams' (q.v. II) journal; Morgan Edwards' (q.v. III) Virginia notebook; and Jeremiah Walker (q.v.), John Williams, John Leland (q.v.), John Asplund (q.v. III), Samuel Harris (q.v. I), and Robert Baylor Semple (q.v. II). Woodford B. Hackley (q.v.) retired as editor at the end of 1971 and was succeeded by John S. Moore of Lexington, VA.

JOHN S. MOORE

VIRGINIA INTERMONT COLLEGE (II, III). In the 1970s, the school moved from a two-year college for women to a four-year coeducational institution offering the bachelor's degree in over 20 fields of study. It was accredited as a four-year college by the Southern Association of Colleges and Schools in 1972. More than 600 students from 35 states and 10 foreign countries registered for the regular day program in 1980. The B.A. degree program in social work received accreditation from the Council of Social Work Education in 1979. Library holdings in 1978 included 59,044 volumes.

The operating budget in 1979 was about $3,000,000. Total assets on June 30, 1979, were $7,233,070. Floyd V. Turner, who began as president in July, 1956, resigned on June 30, 1979, and was succeeded by Kenneth D. Glass.

JOHN S. MOORE

VOCATIONAL GUIDANCE, PROGRAM OF (III). The Program of Vocational Guidance assists churches in educating persons in the Christian meaning of vocation, in providing occupational information, and in offering guidance and counseling with emphasis on church-related vocations. The Career Guidance Section of the Church Administration Department was assigned the program in 1975. Initially, vocational guidance focused on the entrants to church-related vocations. The focus has broadened significantly. Now helps are offered to persons who are in vocational transition or in mid-career crises, as well as to those who are changing church-related vocations, assessing their careers, or facing retirement.

The program develops suggested principles, methods, and procedures for vocational guidance patterns for churches. Life Commitment Month in April is an example of these efforts. Training modules in vocational guidance have been developed to assist leaders in churches and denominational positions.

BROOKS FAULKNER

VOLLMER, ALBERT MARTYN (b. Louisville, KY, June 2, 1894; d. Louisville, KY, July 14, 1974). The son of Mary Meyer, a merchant, and Stephen Vollmer, Jr., a carpenter, he attended Georgetown College (A.B., 1927) and The Southern Baptist Theological Seminary (Th.G., 1927). He married Geneva Rizpah Hillenbrand, Oct. 23, 1918. Their children were Nellie, Albert Martyn, II, and Robert. Pastor of First Baptist Church, Dyersburg, TN, 1935-46, he served as first executive secretary of the Kentucky Baptist Foundation, 1946-64. Assets increased from $6,500 to $2,100,000 during his tenure. He is buried in Resthaven Cemetery, Louisville, KY.

LEO T. CRISMON

VOTING PROCEDURES, SOUTHERN BAPTIST CONVENTION. See SOUTHERN BAPTIST CONVENTION VOTING PROCEDURES.

W

WADE, THOMAS JEFFERSON (b. Atoka County, OK, Dec. 30, 1893; d. Hugh, OK, Dec. 8, 1957). Choctaw Indian and missionary to Indians in Oklahoma. The son of Agnes Wade and Able Wade, a Presbyterian minister, he became a Baptist in 1936. Under appointment by the Home Mission Board, 1941-56, he served among the Ponca, Otoe, and Shawnee Indians. He married Myrtle Hopkins, and they had seven children. He preferred to lead in revitalizing failing churches and establishing churches on new fields. He is buried in Mt. Olive Cemetery, Hugo, OK.

B. FRANK BELVIN

WAITE, FLORIDA (b. Pensacola, FL, Sep. 6, 1892; d. Pensacola, FL, Nov. 2, 1977). Denominational leader. Daughter of Frederick Waite, carpenter, and Elizabeth Waite, she taught high school and served later as educational director in her home church, First Baptist, Pensacola, FL. She came to the Sunday School Board, Nashville, as office secretary and associate editor in 1933. On Nov. 1, 1943, she became the first secretary of the newly organized Church Library Service in the Division of Education and Promotion, a position she held

until retiring in 1957. She is buried in St. John's Cemetery, Pensacola, FL.

See also LIBRARY, CHURCH, VOL. II.

MANCIL EZELL

WAKE FOREST UNIVERSITY (III; cf. Wake Forest College, Vol. II). Growth and development continued throughout the 1970s. Significant developments occurred in the governance of the university, especially in its relationship to the Baptist State Convention of North Carolina. According to a document approved by the convention in 1979, the new relationship had the following features: (1) Wake Forest would no longer be an institution of the convention but would be related to the convention by a "covenant"; (2) The institution would no longer receive Cooperative Program funds from the convention after Jan. 1, 1981, unless individual churches designated part of their Cooperative Program money to it; and (3) All trustees of Wake Forest would still be elected by the convention, but one third could be "members of any evangelical church" anywhere.

The Charles H. Babcock Graduate School of Management became the university's third professional school, joining the School of Law and the Bowman Gray School of Medicine. The

Graduate School offered the master's degree in 19 departments and the Ph.D. in eight. The total 1979-80 enrollment of Wake Forest reached 4,734. The operating budget was $66,364,000, the endowment $56,983,000, and the property value $84,992,000. The library contained 746,000 volumes. Grants from the Z. Smith Reynolds Foundation increased to $1,020,000 per year; scholarship aid increased fourfold to $2,500,870. Four new buildings, including the fine arts center named for current president James R. Scales, were erected during the 1970s.

See also NORTH CAROLINA, BAPTIST STATE CONVENTION OF.

HENRY S. STROUPE

WALKER, JEREMIAH (b. Fauquier County, VA, June 28, 1746; d. Elbert County, GA, Sep. 20, 1792). Separate Baptist preacher, author, organizer of churches, and crusader for religious liberty in Virginia. Son of James and Elizabeth Walker, he was baptized on Apr. 16, 1766, at Grassy Creek Church, Granville County, NC, and soon began to preach. Ordained on Dec. 11, 1769, he became pastor of the Nottoway Church, Amelia County, VA. Walker drafted petitions and appeared before the Virginia House of Burgesses in behalf of religious toleration. Imprisoned at Chesterfield County, VA, for preaching without a license, he gained great popularity among dissenters. He and his associates led in the organization of 20 to 30 churches.

Due to a moral lapse, he left Virginia in 1783 and settled in Elbert County, GA. In Georgia his earlier Arminian views became more pronounced. He withdrew from the Georgia Baptist Association and organized the General Baptist Association, founded on Arminian principles, in 1791. In the same year he published *The Fourfold Foundation of Calvinism Examined and Shaken*. Walker married Jane Graves by whom he had seven children. He is buried in Elbert County, GA.

JOHN S. MOORE

WALTERS, FRANCIS RUSSELL (b. La Follette, TN, May 22, 1879; d. Manchester, KY, Feb. 11, 1970). Pastor. Son of Joseph Marion and Elizabeth Tiller Walters, he was converted and baptized in 1895. Ordained in 1905, he was pastor of the Manchester, KY, Baptist Church for 54 years and of 18 other churches, serving as many as seven at one time. Also a missionary of the Kentucky Baptist Convention, 1909-49, Walters was unfailing in his response to calls for help from churches or communities. He averaged preaching once a day for more than 25 years. Walters married Lettie Newport, Dec. 24, 1906. Their children were Gifford J., Francis R., Jr., Jan, and Dorcas. He is buried at La Follette, TN.

A. B. COLVIN

WALTZ, JOSEPH MARVIN (b. Madison, IN, Sep. 1, 1925; d. Hershey, PA, Dec. 13, 1971). State convention executive. The son of Joseph Berresford and Mayme Waltz, he was a graduate of Georgetown College (A.B., 1946) and Southern Baptist Theological Seminary (B.D., 1949). He served as pastor of churches in Kentucky before moving to Ohio in 1954. He served as president of the State Convention of Baptists in Ohio, 1958-61.

Waltz moved to Pittsburgh, PA, in 1959 to lead Pittsburgh Baptist Church and to direct Southern Baptist work in Western Pennsylvania. In 1964 he became director of missions for the Greater Pittsburgh Baptist Association. He served as first executive secretary-treasurer of the Baptist Convention of Pennsylvania-South Jersey from Jan., 1971, until his death. He married Jane Marie Geiger, Aug. 23, 1946. They had four children: Marvin, Carol, David, and Lynn. He is buried in Hershey Cemetery, Hershey, PA.

DAVID C. WALTZ

WAR. See PEACE, WAR AND.

WARING, WILLIAM TORRINGTON, II (b. Dutch Flats, CA, Aug. 16, 1891; d. Scottsdale, AZ, Mar. 17, 1961). Pastor and pioneer in Chicago and Great Lakes area. Son of W. T. Waring, an importer, he married Sally Pryor Beard, June, 1927. He was pastor of First Baptist Church, Pinckneyville, IL, 1935-40, and First Church, Anna, IL, 1940-44. After a brief stint as superintendent of evangelism for Illinois Baptists and a city missionary, Peoria, IL, Waring became director of education and enlistment for Great Lakes Baptist Association. He was the first SBC agent to unify and strengthen Southern Baptist churches in Chicago and the northern Great Lakes states. He is buried at Phoenix, AZ.

CHARLES L. CHANEY

WARREN, CASPER CARL (b. Sampson County, NC, May 28, 1896; d. Charlotte, NC, May 20, 1973). Pastor and SBC president. The son of Richard Moore Warren, a retail grocer, and Rosella Strickland Warren, he was a graduate of Wake Forest College (L.L.B., 1917; B.A., 1920) and Southern Baptist Theological Seminary (Th.M., 1925; Th.D., 1928). He married Mary Lashbrook Strickland, Aug. 25, 1925. They had three children: Casper Carl, Jr., A. Eugene, and Mary Virginia Warren Poe. After her death, he married Sibyl Brame Townsend, Jan. 19, 1962.

Warren's pastorates included Lexington Avenue Church, Danville, KY, 1928-38; Immanuel Church, Little Rock, AR, 1938-43; and First Church, Charlotte, NC, 1943-58. As SBC president, 1956-57, Warren challenged the Convention to establish 30,000 preaching points by 1964, the jubilee year of Baptists in America. He became director of the resulting "30,000 Movement," resigning his Charlotte pastorate. Warren also served as a trustee of various institutions in Arkansas and North Carolina, president of North Carolina Baptists, trustee and alumni association president of Southern Seminary, and the first president of the board of trustees of Southeastern Baptist Theological Seminary. He wrote *Glimpses of Glory* (1961). In retirement he served as interim pastor in the Charlotte area. He is buried in Evergreen Cemetery, Charlotte, NC.

MARY WARREN POE and SIBYL B. WARREN

WASHINGTON, SOUTHERN BAPTISTS IN. See NORTHWEST BAPTIST CONVENTION.

WATTS, JAMES WASHINGTON (b. Laurens, SC, Feb. 26, 1896; d. Darlington, SC, Oct. 16, 1975). Scholar and author. The son of Clara (Dial) and John Drayton Williams Watts, farmers, he married Mattie Leila Reid, June 30, 1920. Their children were John, Bryson, and Betty.

Watts graduated from Furman University (B.A., 1915) and Southern Baptist Theological Seminary (Th.M., 1922; Ph.D., 1933). Beginning in 1917 he did YMCA Army work which led to an appointment as Army chaplain and a commission as first lieutenant. Watts and his wife served in Palestine under appointment by the Foreign Mission Board, 1923-28. Unable to return to Palestine after a furlough because of health problems and the reduced resources of the board, he served during 1929-30 as assistant pastor of First Baptist Church, Greenville, SC. Later he pursued doctoral studies at Southern Seminary.

In 1931 Watts became professor of Old Testament and Hebrew at the Baptist Bible Institute (now New Orleans Baptist Theological Seminary). With this decision he launched a career of scholarly teaching and writing, interim administrative responsibilities, and leadership in theological education, continuing with the institution for 36 years. He was a member of a small group of heroic teachers and staff who maintained the operation of the school during the Great Depression. Twice he served as acting president, first in 1942-43, following the administration of W. W. Hamilton (*q.v.* III), and again in 1946 before Roland Q. Leavell (*q.v.* III) assumed office. His special contribution was in curriculum development and qualitative academic standards. His recommendation to President Hamilton led to the organization of the Inter-Seminary Council for Southern Baptist seminaries.

Watts' published works include: *Living of the Gospel* (1938), *A Survey of Old Testament Teaching* (1947), *A Survey of Syntax in the Hebrew Old Testament* (1951), *A Distinctive Translation of Genesis* (1963), *In the House of the Lord: Psalm 23* (1965), *Exodus—A Distinctive Translation with Interpretative Outline* (1977), *Isaiah—A Distinctive Translation with Interpretative Outline* (1977), and *Glimpses of God* (1977). The last three volumes (edited by John D. W. Watts) were published after his death. He is buried in Chestnut Ridge Cemetery near Laurens, SC.

J. HARDEE KENNEDY

WAYLAND, JAMES HENRY (b. Randolph County, MO, Apr. 22, 1863; d. Plainview, TX, Feb. 6, 1948). Physician and philanthropist. Son of Joseph H. and Catherine (Gates) Wayland, farmers, he completed his medical training at Kentucky School of Medicine (1886). He married Sarah Frances Tucker. They had nine children. A physician in Plainview, TX, for 35 years, he led efforts to found a Baptist school. He made an initial donation of $10,000 and about 25 acres of land west of Plainview. Construction of Wayland Literary and Technical Institution began in Apr., 1909. The school opened for the first grade through junior college, Sep. 27, 1910, with 62 students. The name changed to Wayland Baptist College in 1911. He is buried in Plainview Cemetery.

ESTELLE OWENS

WAYLAND BAPTIST COLLEGE (III; cf. Wayland College, Vol. II). Under president Roy C. McClung, Wayland grew in the 1970s. School properties, valued at $8,841,769 included 29 permanent buildings on the main campus and 13 other permanent housing units, with two other buildings under construction in 1980. Enrollment increased every year during the decade, reaching an all-time high of 1,376 students in 1979. The college, on its 80-acre campus in Plainview, TX, offered four degrees in 32 major fields and 23 minor fields of study, and maintained programs at four off-campus extension centers. The trustees adopted the college's first $5,000,000 budget for the 1980-81 year. Endowments totaled $5,358,297 in 1980.

EDDIE OWENS

WAYMAN, HARRY CLIFFORD (b. Independence, KY, Apr. 10, 1881; d. Sarasota, FL, Apr. 7, 1959). Seminary professor and college president. Son of Stanton and Jennie French Wayman, farmers, he married Margaret Belle Biggerstaff in Aug., 1906. Their children were Harry and Margaret. A graduate of Georgetown College (A.B.) and Southern Baptist Theological Seminary (Th.M., 1914; Th.D., 1927), he taught at Southern Seminary, 1915-23. He served as president of William Jewell College, 1923-28, resigning amid the fundamentalist-modernist controversy. He served also as pastor of the First Baptist churches of Newport, KY, and Sarasota, FL. He is buried in Manasota Memorial Park, Bradenton, FL.

TIMOTHY GEORGE

WEATHERSPOON, EMILY KILPATRICK LANSDELL (b. Hephzibah, GA, Nov. 17, 1913; d. Augusta, GA, June 10, 1973). Missionary and educator. Daughter of Rinaldo Addison and Ruth Kilpatrick Lansdell, she graduated from Coker College (A.B., 1933). Graduate study at the University of Georgia, Duke University (M.A., 1938), and Columbia University preceded her appointment to China in 1943 by the Foreign Mission Board. She studied Chinese language and literature at the University of California and at Yale University (M.A., 1946) before sailing to China, where she taught English at the University of Shanghai.

She left China, Feb. 15, 1949. Following service as a college representative of the Foreign Mission Board, she became, in July, 1951, president of Woman's Missionary Union Training School, which, in 1953, became Carver School of Missions and Social Work. Leaving Carver School in 1957, she taught missions for three years at Southeastern Baptist Theological Seminary. There she married Jesse Burton Weatherspoon (q.v. III) on Apr. 14, 1962. Following his death in 1964, she joined the faculty of Georgia Southwestern College in 1967. There she taught until shortly before her death. She is buried in the Hephzibah, GA, cemetery.

H. EUGENE MCLEOD

WEBSTER, PERLEY (b. Haverhill, MA, Oct. 23, 1902; d. Portland, OR, June 29, 1979). Layman and church builder. The son of Louise Webster and Charles Webster, a drayman, he became a member of First Baptist Church, Melbourne, FL. He married Glenn Joiner, Oct. 28, 1924. They had one daughter, Miriam. Webster sold his dry cleaning business and moved his family to Oregon in 1943 during World War II. He helped construct buildings for pioneer churches in Klamath Falls and Portland, OR, and Longview, WA. He is buried in Skyline Memorial Gardens, Portland, OR.

ROBERT N. STAPP

WEEK OF PRAYER FOR FOREIGN MISSIONS AND LOTTIE MOON CHRIST-MAS OFFERING. A week observed annually in Southern Baptist churches in December to emphasize foreign missions. Urged by Lottie Moon (q.v. II) in 1888, the newly-formed Woman's Missionary Union asked women to collect missions offerings during Christmas and bring them to a society meeting in January. The goal was $2,000. The $3,315 offering sent three missionaries to China.

Since 1888, the Week of Prayer has been observed. The offering was named the Lottie Moon Christmas Offering in 1918. In 1926 the week was moved from January to December. After 1928, it was preceded by study of a foreign missions book. A permanent date was set in 1953.

The Foreign Mission Board determined and recommended to WMU the offering object each year. In the early years, the offering was mainly for missions work in China. During the 1920s and 1930s, it paid off debts, returned missionaries to the field, and paid salaries.

Until 1957, the week was a WMU observance. With an era of prayer during the Third Jubilee Advance, 1958-64, WMU led local churches to observe the week. Goals became church goals. In 1968 WMU became responsible for leading churches in special missions projects. The 1979 offering was

$40,597,113. The following listing of gifts shows a total of $446,320,058 from 1888 to 1979.

See also WOMAN'S MISSIONARY UNION, AUXILIARY TO SOUTHERN BAPTIST CONVENTION.

BOBBIE SORRILL

LOTTIE MOON CHRISTMAS OFFERING AND ANNIE ARMSTRONG EASTER OFFERING, 1888-1980

Dates	Lottie Moon Christmas Offering	Annie Armstrong Easter Offering
1888	$ 3,315	
1889	2,659	
1890	4,320	
1891	4,984	
1892	5,068	
1893	3,596	
1894	3,454	
1895	4,501	
1896	3,708	
1897	4,356	
1898	4,493	
1899	5,309	
1900	6,355	
1901	6,088	
1902	7,534	
1903	10,957	
1904	11,787	
1905	14,016	
1906	17,522	
1907	21,272	$ 10,488
1908	26,300	13,572
1909	27,921	17,199
1910	25,283	18,590
1911	28,943	19,898
1912	31,875	19,180
1913	38,035	16,941
1914	27,661	15,742
1915	36,147	14,016
1916	40,986	19,819
1917	44,110	20,225
1918	53,687	25,042
1919	68,768	30,687
1920	40,092	39,949
1921	28,615	21,102
1922	29,583	18,129
1923	42,206	23,010
1924	48,677	23,705
1925	306,376	27,631
1926	246,152	83,739
1927	172,457	89,061
1928	235,274	92,560
1929	190,130	78,639
1930	200,799	92,645
1931	170,724	99,576
1932	143,331	77,355
1933	172,512	68,197
1934	213,925	100,255
1935	240,455	106,564
1936	292,401	118,359
1937	290,219	135,364
1938	315,000	147,791
1939	330,424	159,189
1940	363,746	167,904
1941	449,162	206,168
1942	562,609	239,729
1943	761,269	312,761
1944	949,844	401,079
1945	1,201,962	468,801
1946	1,381,048	529,047
1947	1,503,010	558,677
1948	1,669,683	654,432
1949	1,745,682	690,229

1950	2,110,019	704,436
1951	2,668,051	874,788
1952	3,280,372	991,484
1953	3,602,554	1,119,864
1954	3,957,821	1,212,434
1955	4,628,691	1,256,254
1956	5,240,745	1,574,890
1957	6,121,585	1,741,859
1958	6,762,448	1,676,353
1959	7,706,847	2,126,085
1960	8,238,471	2,226,165
1961	9,315,754	2,553,723
1962	10,323,591	2,891,184
1963	10,949,857	3,049,283
1964	11,870,649	3,193,953
1965	13,194,357	3,573,146
1966	13,760,146	4,033,079
1967	14,664,679	4,088,470
1968	15,159,206	4,682,554
1969	15,297,558	5,045,782
1970	16,220,104	4,966,984
1971	17,833,810	5,345,551
1972	19,664,972	6,059,603
1973	22,232,757	6,884,357
1974	23,234,093	8,130,141
1975	26,169,421	8,491,653
1976	28,763,809	9,631,011
1977	31,938,553	10,745,967
1978	35,919,605	12,282,228
1979	40,597,113	14,171,637
1980	44,700,339	16,479,032
Total	$491,020,397	$157,877,034

DORIS DEVAULT

WEEK OF PRAYER FOR HOME MISSIONS AND ANNIE ARMSTRONG EASTER OFFERING. A week observed annually in Southern Baptist churches the first week of March to emphasize home missions. The first Week of Self-Denial for Home Missions in 1895 grew out of the need expressed by Woman's Missionary Union's executive committee for a second period of intercession to increase missions gifts and interest. Responding to Home Mission Board secretary Isaac Taylor Tichenor's (q.v. II) appeal about the $25,000 board debt and possible withdrawal of missionaries, WMU decided to use the results of the week for this emergency. More than the $5,000 requested was received.

In 1903 WMU changed the name to Week of Prayer and Special Effort for Home Missions. After 1928, it was preceded by study of a home missions book. In 1922 the offering was renamed Thank Offering, and in 1934 it became known as the Annie Armstrong Offering for Home Missions, named for WMU's first corresponding secretary (q.v. I). In 1953 a permanent date was set.

Until 1957 the week was a WMU observance. With an era of prayer during the Third Jubilee Advance, 1958-64, WMU led churches to observe the week, and offering goals became church goals. In 1969 the offering was linked with Easter, and Easter was added to the name. Reported offerings increased from $10,488 in 1907 to $16,479,032 in 1980.

See also WOMAN'S MISSIONARY UNION, AUXILIARY TO SOUTHERN BAPTIST CONVENTION.

BOBBIE SORRILL

WEEKDAY EDUCATION IN THE CHURCHES (cf. Weekday Religious Education, Vol. II; Weekday Bible Study, Vol. III). Weekday education is a term that describes programs operating Monday through Friday in Southern Baptist churches which minister to children from birth through grade 12. The programs include infant care, day care, kindergarten, Mother's Day Out, Tuesday-Thursday school, and Christian school (grades 1-12). The purposes of weekday education are education, outreach, care, and mission. It is intended to be a ministry of the church as well as a service to the community.

The program is unique in that fees are generally paid for services rendered. This causes major differences in the way weekday education is related to the church as contrasted with other church programs. The administration of a major budget, control of faculty, and use of space for large enrollments lead to a complex and comprehensive church ministry.

The Sunday School Board has recognized this field since 1954 when James C. Barry of the Sunday School Department began providing materials and training to churches involved in some form of weekday education. In 1973 the Church Administration Department assumed responsibility for the work under the direction of William H. Halbert, Jr. In 1980 more than 3,000 churches were involved in weekday education. To provide for growth in day care and Christian schools, a full line of curriculum resources was produced for administration, teaching, subject, and pupil areas.

Studies by the SSB have revealed the following about the status of weekday education in Southern Baptist churches. Weekday education ministries include a variety of programs composed of varying sizes of enrollments and staffs, serving different age groupings on diverse operating schedules. In most cases in the past, the kindergarten program was the first program operated by the church. Now day care seems to be the principal program used to launch the ministry. Most of the programs operate five days a week. However, some of the nursery schools and Tuesday-Thursday schools operate on a two-or-three-day-per-week schedule.

Regarding the growth of weekday education, one study revealed that 10 years is the longest period any school surveyed has existed. About two-thirds of the kindergarten programs have been in operation five years or more.

In most churches the programs are considered a ministry and they operate in shared facilities with church program organizations. The majority of weekday education programs are self-supporting, relying on fees and tuition. The average educational background for a teacher in a church-related program is a college degree.

WILLIAM H. HALBERT, JR.

WEEKS, WILLIE PORTMAN (b. Calhoun County, MS, Feb. 14, 1885; d. Sacramento, CA, Sep. 16, 1970). Early Southern Baptist pastor in the West. He attended Southwestern Baptist Theological Seminary (1922-24). Ordained in 1909 in New Mexico, he was pastor at Durant, Calvin, Dustin, and Prague, OK; Rodeo, CA; and Sweet Home and Klamath Falls, OR. On Aug. 26, 1907, he married Lilly Bell Pool. She died in 1911. On Dec. 31, 1917, he married Eunice Maude Lane. They had seven children.

Weeks was host pastor for the first annual meeting of the Baptist General Convention of Oregon (now the Northwest Baptist Convention), held at First Baptist Church, Sweet Home, OR, Nov., 1948.

SAM A. HARVEY

WELCH, OLIVER (b. Madison County, VA, Apr. 27, 1791; d. Talladega County, AL, Apr. 23, 1874). Pastor and pioneer denominational leader. The son of Elizabeth Terrell Welch and Nathaniel Welch, a farmer and builder, he served several rural churches in Virginia before moving to Talladega County, AL, in 1834. Pastor of the Talladega Church (now Alpine) for more than 35 years, he was a leader in the Coosa River Association.

On Sep. 18, 1810, Welch married Elizabeth Mallory. They had nine children: Mary, Nathaniel, William, James, Mallory, Hannah, Varanda, Uriel, and Oscar. A granddaughter, Maud Reynolds McLure (q.v. II), was the first principal of Woman's Missionary Union Training School. In 1838 Welch married Theresa B. Jennings, who died shortly thereafter. In 1849 he married a widow, Sarah T. Finley, who died in 1861. Welch is buried in the family graveyard, Kingston Plantation, near Alpine, AL.

WALTER BELT WHITE

WEST KENTUCKY BAPTIST BIBLE INSTITUTE (II). See MID-CONTINENT BAPTIST BIBLE COLLEGE.

WEST VIRGINIA ASSOCIATIONS (III). **New Associations.** ALLEGHENY. Constituted in Sep., 1970, with eight congregations and 592 members. In 1980, 12 congregations reported 73 baptisms, 1,380 members, $214,924 total gifts, and $41,989 total mission gifts.

EASTERN PANHANDLE. Constituted in a meeting at Berkeley Springs in 1977 by seven churches which had been connected with the Upper Ohio Valley Baptist Association of West Virginia. In 1980, 10 congregations reported 117 baptisms, 560 members, $177,928 total gifts, and $70,982 total mission gifts.

IMMANUEL. Formed Oct. 20, 1977, by churches from Upper Ohio Valley, Pioneer, and Greater Huntington Associations. In 1980, 10 congregations reported 77 baptisms, 1,131 members, $286,781 total gifts, and $39,291 total mission gifts.

MONONGAHELA. Organized in the First Southern Baptist Church of Fairmont in 1977 by churches which had been affiliated with the Upper Ohio Valley Baptist Association of West Virginia. In 1980 eight congregations reported

81 baptisms, 975 members, $255,247 total gifts, and $32,775 total mission gifts.

TUG VALLEY. Formed on June 3, 1975, at East Williamson Baptist Church by six churches which had been affiliated with Pike Association in Kentucky and Mountain State Association in West Virginia. In 1980 seven congregations reported 58 baptisms, 1,432 members, $200,885 total gifts, and $36,123 total mission gifts.

FLOYD TIDSWORTH, JR.

WEST VIRGINIA BAPTIST FOUNDATION. Established at the annual meeting of the West Virginia Convention of Southern Baptists in Nov., 1977, and incorporated in 1978, the foundation is the trust agency of the state convention. It encourages Christian estate planning through the writing of wills, creation of living trusts, endowment gifts, and annuities. Its services include presentations of programs in the churches, and to groups, along with personal assistance in estate planning, drawing of wills and agreements, and coordination with attorneys as to bequests and trusts for specific Baptist causes.

The corporate structure of the foundation provides for nine directors, a president, vice-president, secretary, and treasurer, along with the necessary committees. Elmo Cox was elected president and operations officer at the organizational meeting and has continued to serve in this capacity. The incorporating directors were: Dayne Aldridge, John Caldwell, Elmo Cox, John Lewelling, John Robinson, Sr., Richard R. Rockwell, Frank F. Waddell, Jr., James W. Walls, and William White.

The budget for the foundation comes from the state convention. All income received from investments is paid to the beneficiary or Baptist cause on a quarterly, semiannual, or annual basis.

ELMO COX

WEST VIRGINIA CONVENTION OF SOUTHERN BAPTISTS (III). **I. History.** *Formation of the Convention.*—The West Virginia Convention of Southern Baptists was formed at the fourth annual session of the Baptist General Association of West Virginia, Oct. 29-30, 1970, at Witcher Baptist Church, Belle, WV. With the association's president, Tom Lang, pastor of First Baptist Church, Fairlea, WV, the 57 messengers constituted as a convention on Oct. 29. It became the 33rd state convention cooperating with the SBC. Initially, the convention asked John I. Snedden and Francis Tallant to "continue in their present capacities, sharing leadership responsibilities in cooperation with the Executive Board."

George Bulson, then pastor of Ceres Baptist Church, was elected as the convention's first president. Other action of that historic session was the approval of a philosophy of work which established evangelism as the number one priority, with starting new work as number two, and enlisting and training workers as number three. Individual attention to the needs of churches was also emphasized. The first approved budget of the state convention was $176,524 of which $70,950 was to be received from Cooperative Program gifts of the churches and approximately $105,000 from SBC boards and agencies and special offerings. At the time of constitution there were 62 congregations, including 51 churches and 11 missions, with a membership of 13,187.

Development.—Steady growth during the 1970s increased total congregations to 95, including 71 churches, 24 missions, and a constituency of 18,229. The 1980 budget totaled $661,880 with $305,003 anticipated from West Virginia church Cooperative Program gifts and $356,877 from other sources.

Personnel.—The convention functioned without an executive secretary-treasurer during its first year of operation. In 1971 the convention elected to this position John I. Snedden, who served until retirement, Dec. 31, 1979.

Francis R. Tallant served as director of religious education through Feb., 1973, when he resigned to become executive director of the Warren Association in Kentucky.

Tom Lang, pastor of Fairlawn Baptist Church, Parkersburg, and past president of the convention, succeeded Tallant in March. To meet the need for additional personnel and with additional funding available from the Sunday School Board, the convention employed Jackson C. Walls, minister of education and youth of First Baptist Church, Fairborn, OH, as the first associate in the Religious Education Division.

In 1973 Floyd Tidsworth, Jr., area missionary in the state, became director of missions work, succeeding Snedden, who had assumed the position of executive secretary earlier. Ola Cox (*q.v.*) became the first state Woman's Missionary Union director in 1972, serving on a part-time basis. Delores Lynn Palmer became the first full-time WMU and campus ministries director, Feb. 1, 1975. Two full-time campus ministers added to the staff were Z. Clinton Fugate at Marshall University, Huntington, and Jess Wood at West Virginia University, Morgantown.

Upon the resignation of Tom Lang in 1976, Jackson Walls was named director of religious education and John Auvenshine of Michigan became associate. Auvenshine resigned in Jan., 1979, to return to a similar position in Michigan, and in June, 1979, C. Thomas Young became associate in religious education.

John I. Snedden retired, Dec. 31, 1979. Thomas Erle Halsell, director of evangelism, State Convention of Baptists in Indiana, became executive secretary-treasurer elect, Oct. 1, 1979, and assumed full convention leadership, Jan. 1, 1980. He leads the present staff of five program leaders, two campus ministers, five area missionaries, and five office secretaries.

Property Purchase.—In 1976 the convention purchased a house and 48-acre parcel of ground known as the Ramsey farm for $100,000. The property, now known as the Elkview property, is located at the interchange of Interstate 79 and Frame Road, 10 miles northeast of Charleston, WV, and is the future site of the West Virginia state offices. A portion of this property is being sold to a developer with plans to build a shopping center, motel, and restaurant. The convention expects to receive enough cash from the sale of this portion of the property to help finance the building of a facility in the early 1980s to house the state offices.

II. Program of Work. Programs expanded as enlarged resources and personnel became available and as the needs grew through the starting of new churches and the development of all churches. The 1980 program of work was as follows:

Administration.—The administrative body of the convention is the Executive Board composed of 20 members from various areas throughout the state. They are elected for a three-year term and are ineligible for reelection for one year after they have completed a term. Paid workers of the convention are ineligible for board membership. The convention grants the board authority to function in its cooperative work and handle its affairs between the annual meetings. The board appoints all missionaries and other employees and has the responsibility of fixing all salaries of convention employees and determining their job responsibilities.

The officers of the convention are the president, two vice-presidents, and recording secretary-historian. These are elected annually and serve as officers of the Executive Board. In the first meeting of the board following the annual meeting of the state convention, the president has the responsibility of appointing committees, including Administrative, Finance, and a committee for each of the various department or phases of the work of the convention. The Cooperative Program budget is recommended by the board to the convention for adoption.

The convention's executive secretary-treasurer is chief administrative and promotional agent of the convention and board. As treasurer, he is in charge of all properties and funds of the convention under the supervision of the board, keeps a record of receipts and disbursements, and makes a written report annually to the board and convention.

On Jan. 1, 1980, Thomas E. Halsell became the second executive secretary-treasurer, succeeding John I. Snedden. In West Virginia the executive secretary-treasurer also serves as director of evangelism.

The West Virginia Southern Baptist.—This is the monthly newspaper of the convention in West Virginia and operates under the supervision of the State Paper Committee of the Executive Board. The purpose of *The West Virginia Southern Baptist* is to publish religious news, Baptist doctrine, and to promote the work of the convention. Since 1975 Jackson C. Walls has been editor. Circulation climbed to 6,000 in 1980.

Annuity.—Until 1978 annuity and insurance for state staff employees were administered through the Ohio Convention. The West Virginia state office now administers, promotes, and educates in matters related to annuity for both state staff and church staff personnel. This is included in the responsibilities of the state executive secretary-treasurer.

Missions Division.—The convention's Missions Division includes all programs related to the Home Mission Board except evangelism. This division also encompasses Woman's Missionary Union, stewardship promotion, and Brotherhood. In addition to the overall administrative responsibilities for all the work of the division, the division director is personally responsible for the work in church extension, language work, direct missions, and all work related to the missions section of the HMB. He also directs the Brotherhood work and stewardship promotion. The top priority in West Virginia is starting new work, with a goal of doubling West Virginia congregations by the end of 1985.

Stewardship promotion consists of providing conferences, tracts, audiovisuals, and other resources to encourage and educate churches and associations in New Testament stewardship lifestyle. The Great Challenge program of stewardship has been used effectively in the churches of the state.

The objective of the Brotherhood work is to assist the associations and churches in developing a program of missionary education and mission activity for men and boys.

The WMU and Christian Social Ministries departments are included in the Missions Division, and in 1979 Maxine Bumgarner became director. The WMU department is charged with the responsibility of mission education and involvement of women and girls and the promotion of the three major special offerings, Lottie Moon for foreign missions, Annie Armstrong for home missions, and Ola Cox for state missions.

Christian Social Ministries work is conducted on a limited basis in West Virginia. Mark McAllister, under the direction of the state director, is serving in the Braxton County area while serving a small congregation. He returned to the state after serving in Worcester, MA, in a similar position.

Religious Education Division.—This division includes all program areas related to the Sunday School Board, SBC, and is directed by Jackson C. Walls. In addition to the overall direction of the division, he is personally responsible for Sunday School, Church Architecture, Church Media Services, and Family Ministry. The primary emphasis in Sunday School work is starting new Sunday Schools by encouraging churches to start satellite Bible studies and the use of Sunday School contract workers to start work in areas where there is no Southern Baptist work; also training of workers in the associations and churches.

Church Architecture involves conferences and on-site visits to consult with pastors and building committees on all aspects of church building, from buying property to beautification of present facilities.

WEST VIRGINIA STATISTICAL SUMMARY

Year	Associations	Churches	Church Membership	Baptisms	SS Enrollment	VBS Enrollment	CT Enrollment	WMU Enrollment	Brotherhood Enrollment	Ch. Music Enrollment	Mission Gifts	Total Gifts	Value Church Property
1971	6	53	13,863	925	9,002	6,764	1,638	1,484	603	1,436	$149,151	$1,135,348	$ 4,369,650
1972	6	54	14,626	894	9,113	8,132	1,512	1,809	600	1,483	176,089	1,228,468	4,270,450
1973	6	53	14,965	916	9,306	8,038	1,373	1,936	517	1,654	235,383	1,341,020	5,051,750
1974	6	58	15,940	912	9,558	7,482	1,809	1,784	556	1,841	256,597	1,551,740	6,123,250
1975	6	62	16,600	1,011	10,226	8,775	1,661	1,861	590	1,896	275,842	1,850,023	6,712,830
1976	6	64	16,779	751	10,088	8,463	1,686	1,862	540	1,808	357,358	2,307,659	8,188,900
1977	9	66	17,708	705	11,066	6,163	1,528	2,038	620	1,978	461,379	2,391,701	10,299,500
1978	9	69	17,856	643	10,580	8,206	1,515	1,816	444	2,005	478,624	2,412,406	11,432,500
1979	9	74	18,334	627	10,465	8,813	1,240	1,710	592	2,278	459,988	2,829,930	13,361,350
1980	9	76	19,183	898	11,483	9,319	1,619	1,958	627	2,218	601,470	3,224,521	13,852,000

KAY BOYD

Church Media Services encourages churches to create new libraries and provides resources to upgrade existing libraries.

Family Ministry provides resources to encourage higher quality family life and to deal with family problems. Churches are encouraged to plan and conduct family life conferences. An annual state singles retreat was started in 1979.

The areas of Church Training, Church Music, Church Administration, and Church Recreation are directed by C. Thomas Young, associate director of religious education. Young came to the convention in June, 1979.

Church Training is committed to assisting the churches and associations in training leadership, instructing new Christians and church members, and training church members in doctrine, polity, and Baptist history.

Church Music provides resources, conferences, and personal consultation for the purpose of training music leadership and improving the overall music ministries of West Virginia churches and associations.

A primary objective of Church Administration is to encourage churches to develop a functioning church council, to develop effective deacons, and improve skills of pastors and other church staff members.

Church Recreation assists churches in identifying the role of banquets, fellowships, drama, and recreation as a valid asset to the life of the church fellowship.

Campus Ministries became a part of the Religious Education Division by vote of the Executive Board in 1979. Until then it had been housed in the Missions Division. Z. Clinton Fugate, director of the Campus Ministries Department, also serves as campus minister at Marshall University and supervises the full-time campus minister serving at West Virginia University. Jess Wood was in that position until his resignation in July, 1980. Campus Ministries is committed to the evangelization and Christian development of college students on all state college campuses, using both paid and volunteer campus ministers.

Evangelism. — The evangelism work of West Virginia is directed by Thomas E. Halsell, who is also the executive secretary-treasurer. Halsell came to this position, Jan. 1, 1980. This department gives encouragement to the evangelistic programs of the churches by promoting revivals and providing the annual state evangelistic conference and associational evangelism clinics.

                                    JACKSON C. WALLS

WESTERN RECORDER (II, III). Chauncey R. Daley has served as editor of this Kentucky Baptist paper since July 1, 1957. Bobby S. Terry was associate editor from Sep. 26, 1968, until Sep. 14, 1975, when he became editor of *Word and Way,* the Missouri Baptist paper. James H. Cox has been associate editor since Sep. 15, 1975. George A. Price was business and circulation manager from July, 1966, until his resignation in Aug., 1972. Price was succeeded by Paul Whitler, Jr., on Aug. 25, 1972.

In 1977 *Western Recorder* discontinued doing its own printing, a practice followed since 1919. It also changed from a magazine to a tabloid format. Sources of anticipated income for 1979-80 were: Subscriptions, $173,000; Cooperative Program allotment, $134,000; advertising, $17,000; and other income, $4,000. The weekly circulation in 1980 was approximately 60,000.

                                    C. R. DALEY

WESTMORELAND, E. HERMOND, CHAIR OF EVANGELISM. A chair established in 1978 at Golden Gate Seminary honoring Westmoreland (*q.v.*), who had served as a trustee of Golden Gate for 14 years and as chairman of the trustee building committee responsible for developing the Strawberry Point campus. The major emphases of the chair are to train church leaders in evangelism, develop student evangelism teams, and provide resources for evangelism conferences. G. William Schweer was named the first occupant of the chair.

                                    STANTON H. NASH

WESTMORELAND, EDWIN HERMOND (b. Booneville, AR, Sep. 9, 1905; d. Sugar Land, TX, Aug. 28, 1976). Pastor and denominational leader. Son of Ed Westmoreland, a county clerk, and Jane Leftwich, he married Madie Merle Tull, Aug. 30, 1927. They had two children, Jackson Tull and Jareth Elaine. He graduated from Ouachita College (B.A., 1927) and The Southern Baptist Theological Seminary (Th.M., 1930). He held three pastorates: Monticello, AR; Leland, MS; and South Main, Houston, TX, 1938-71. He served as president of the Baptist General Convention of Texas, 1958-59, and as vice-president of the SBC, 1953-54. He is buried in Forrest Park West, Houston, TX.

                                    WILLIAM L. PITTS

WHARTON, MORTON BRYAN (b. Culpeper County, VA, Apr. 5, 1839; d. Atlanta, GA, July 20, 1908). Pastor, editor, and diplomat. Son of Malcolm Hart and Susan Roberts Colvin Wharton, farmers, he attended Richmond College (A.B., 1861) to prepare for the ministry. On Aug. 2, 1864, he married Mary Belle Irwin of Georgia. They had one daughter. After serving as an evangelist with the Virginia Colportage Society in the Confederate army, he was pastor at Bristol, TN; Eufaula, AL (twice); Walnut Street Church, Louisville, KY; Greene Street Church, Augusta, GA; First Church, Montgomery, AL; Freemason Street Church, Norfolk, VA; and co-pastor at Brantly Baptist Church, Baltimore, MD, with Henry M. Wharton (*q.v.* II).

He acquired partial interest in J. W. Burke and Company, publisher of *Kind Words.* A year later, 1881, he was appointed consul in Sonneberg, Germany. He returned to Georgia, 1883-84, as part owner and editor of the *Christian Index.* Author of books of sermons, travel accounts, and poems, he was credited with coining the word *pastorium*. Wharton is buried at Eufaula, AL.

LEE N. ALLEN

WHITE, BLANCHE SYDNOR (b. Dinwiddie County, VA, Feb. 19, 1891; d. Richmond, VA, May 12, 1974). State Woman's Missionary Union executive. The daughter of William Richard and Annie (Hone) White, she served as office secretary, Foreign Mission Board, SBC, 1908-22; first field worker, WMU, SBC, 1922-24; and executive secretary, Virginia WMU, 1925-49.

Baptized in 1904 at Sharon Baptist Church, Petersburg Association (VA), White united with First Baptist Church, Richmond, VA, in 1908. Her formal schooling was mainly in private schools under tutors. She completed the prescribed course at Smithdeal Business College, Richmond. White led in the development of the state WMU of Virginia. During years of indebtedness of the Southern Baptist and Virginia Baptist mission agencies, she raised significant funds for payment of debts and for support of existing and new mission work. As early as 1934, a black woman was housed in the Virginia WMU office, serving as field worker for joint mission efforts of black and white Baptist women.

Other state work begun by White included establishment of goodwill centers, use of volunteers for summer evangelistic efforts (first in 1937), and placement of the first Baptist student secretary on a college campus in Virginia. In her retirement years she and Olive Brunson Martin (*q.v.*) led in the reorganization and expansion of the Women's Department, Baptist World Alliance.

White indexed *The Religious Herald* from 1828 to 1874. Her extensive research resulted in her compiling histories for churches, district associations, state and associational Woman's Missionary Union units, and BWA. She wrote at least 50 books, plus scores of articles for Baptist publications. White was a popular speaker. In 1951 the University of Richmond conferred on her the Litt.D. degree. She is buried in Blandford Cemetery, Petersburg, VA.

CARRIE S. VAUGHAN

WHITE OAK CONFERENCE CENTER. A "grassroots" interest during the late 1960s among South Carolina's Baptist church leaders and the request of the South Carolina Baptist Religious Education Association (SCBREA) caused the 1971 South Carolina Baptist Convention (SCBC) to "look with favor on the idea of seeking to provide a state assembly," and to begin setting aside capital funds for development. The first donation to the future conference center came from E. R. Eller in 1972. A fund-raising drive among convention churches during 1976 produced an additional $202,630.

In 1973 the SCBC appointed "a Committee of 10 to consider the feasibility . . . of a Convention Center (Assembly), and to study for a minimum of two years to develop master plans for a

Conference Center, including location, funding and development." Committee members elected were: Henry Finch, Jr., chairman; Vivian Andrews; William O. Duckworth; L. Lamar King; Lewis Martin, Jr.; P. L. McCall, Sr.; L. H. Miller, Jr.; Lonnie H. Shull, Jr.; Stewart B. Simms, Sr.; and Patsy Waters. They visited 40 of 70 suggested sites, often accompanied by Charles Stott (professional camp planner from Raleigh, NC), who was employed to help in site selection and later in development of the master plan. Upon recommendation of the committee, the 1974 SCBC voted to buy 731 acres of land at White Oak in Fairfield County at a cost of $367,695; and in 1975, an additional 275 acres were purchased for $137,500.

In 1975 James L. Beacham, director of McCall Royal Ambassador Camp for 11 years, was elected director of the conference center. The SCBC approved the firm of Neal Architects, Inc., and adopted a master plan.

In 1977 a 25-acre lake was completed as part of the first of seven phases of construction and development, and a dedication service was held for the first completed building, the McCall Multipurpose Shelter (named for Belle W. and Peter Leroy McCall, Sr.), which was used by about 800 persons during that year. Also in 1977, the SCBC voted to begin construction on the third and fourth phases as early as possible in 1978, and to convey to the state Woman's Missionary Union at no cost a 165-acre tract of land across the road from the conference center for use in establishing a camp.

Construction began in 1978 and continued through the summer of 1979 on more roads; electrical, water, and sewage systems; administration building; dining hall; 48 motel rooms; a group house; recreational areas; swimming pool; and other facilities.

The first conference was held by the SCBREA, Apr. 27-29, 1979; and Jimmy Allen, then president of the SBC, was the principal speaker at the dedication service held on May 12 and attended by 800-900 people.

The first year's overnight attendance was 7,251. General board departments sponsored 47 conferences with an attendance of 4,331; attendance from 79 local church groups was 2,171; and there were 12 other groups with an attendance of 749. Three thousand others attended day conferences and/or used the picnic shelter.

JAMES L. BEACHAM

WHITE, RANSOM KELLY (b. Connellys Springs, NC, May 12, 1893; d. Franklin, VA, Feb. 22, 1979). Pastor and educator. The son of Mariah Harris and Rufus T. Harris, minister and farmer, he attended Buie's Creek Academy, Wake Forest College (B.A., 1917; M.A., 1919), and The Southern Baptist Theological Seminary (Th.M., 1920; Th.D., 1922). On Sep. 12, 1918, he married Vesta Charles Benthall. They had no children.

White served as pastor of Siloam Church, Marion, AL, 1922-26; First Church, Bessemer,

AL, 1926-28; Belmont Heights Church, Nashville, TN, 1928-46; and First Church, West Palm Beach, FL, 1946-52. In 1952 he became the first president of Belmont College, serving until 1959.

White held many denominational positions, including trustee of Howard College, Tennessee College, and Cumberland University; president, Tennessee State Mission Board; president, Tennessee Baptist Convention, 1943-44; and member, Foreign Mission Board. He is buried in a family cemetery near Conway, NC.

HERBERT GABHART

WHITE, WILLIAM RICHARDSON (b. Brownsboro, TX, Dec. 2, 1892; d. Waco, TX, Mar. 24, 1977). Pastor and educator. Son of Gibson and Kittie Dorman White, he was a graduate of Howard Payne University (B.A., 1917) and Southwestern Baptist Theological Seminary (Th.M., 1922; Th.D., 1927). He married Edna V. Woods, Jan. 17, 1916. She died Dec. 16, 1948. He married Catherine W. Tarwater, June 20, 1950. She died, Sep. 14, 1970. He married Ioda Mohr, Aug. 28, 1971.

Ordained to the ministry in 1911, his pastorates included Broadway Baptist, Fort Worth, TX, 1931-35; First Baptist, Oklahoma City, OK, 1935-40; and First Baptist, Austin, TX, 1945-48. He was also professor of missions, Southwestern Seminary, 1923-27; executive secretary, Baptist General Convention of Texas, 1929-31; president, Hardin-Simmons University, 1940-43; editorial secretary, Sunday School Board, SBC, 1943-45; and president, 1948-61, and chancellor, 1961-63, of Baylor University. He was author of *The Royal Road to Life* (1938), *Broadman Comments* (1945-48), *Baptist Distinctives* (1946), and *That the World May Know* (1947).

For 10 years after retirement, White wrote comments on the Sunday School lesson for the *Baptist Standard* and the *Baptist and Reflector*. He is buried in Oakwood Cemetery, Waco, TX.

W. J. WIMPEE

WILLIAM CAREY COLLEGE (II, III). J. Ralph Noonkester elected in 1956, continues as president. The college offers five baccalaureate degrees, two master's degrees, and the specialist in education degree. In 1969 the college added the B.S. in nursing, merging with Mather School of Nursing, Southern Baptist Hospital, New Orleans, LA. The fifth baccalaureate degree, the B.F.A., was introduced in 1975. In 1970 the college began a program of graduate studies, introducing the M.Mus. degree. Four years later the board of trustees authorized a program leading to the M.Ed. degree, and, in 1978, the Spec.Ed. degree became a part of the academic program. In 1979 the Department of Psychology and the Graduate Division were finalizing plans to introduce a third master's degree, the M.A. in counseling psychology, in the fall of 1980.

In 1969 the college was divided into the School of Arts and Sciences, the School of Music, and the School of Nursing. In 1976 the Department of Business was enlarged and renamed the School of Business Administration; the Graduate Division was formed with all graduate work brought under the auspices of the dean of graduate studies; and the Division of Continuing Education was established.

In June, 1976, William Carey purchased the Gulf Coast Military Academy property, Gulfport, MS, and dedicated its new acquisition, renamed William Carey College on the Coast, in Aug., 1976. Carey on the Coast is a regional campus serving commuting students at both the undergraduate and graduate levels. It occupies 20 acres of beachfront property and includes four major educational buildings, three frame houses, a swimming pool, and additional storage buildings.

During the 1970s, two academic buildings and an addition to the science building were completed on the Hattiesburg campus. Three other buildings were renovated, and a modular unit was added. In 1970 both Fairchild Education-Psychology Building and the addition to Green Science Hall were finished. In 1973 Tatum Court Administration Building was renovated; Mary Ross Infirmary was revamped into offices for the Department of Business; and the Thomas Business Building was constructed. In 1976 renovation of Lawrence Hall was begun. Once a men's dormitory, this building now houses the campus post office, book store, nurse's office, and administrative offices and curriculum laboratory for Special Services, a remedial academic program.

In Aug., 1977, a modular unit was added adjoining Fairchild Hall for use by the Carey Child Development Center. Construction of a $9,000,000 educational complex, which will house the Carey School of Nursing, was begun in 1979 at Southern Baptist Hospital, New Orleans. Enrollment at William Carey College tripled during the decade. In the fall of 1969, 893 students were enrolled; total enrollment in the fall of 1979 was 2,631. The 1969-70 budget was $1,500,000; the 1979-80 budget was $5,275,500.

JO LAURIN DAVIS

WILLIAM JEWELL COLLEGE (II, III). Thomas S. Field assumed the presidency in Aug., 1970, and served until June, 1980. J. Gordon Kingsley, Jr., academic dean of the college, became president, July 1, 1980.

The 1970s were years of unusual growth and development. New curriculum design and education for individual achievement provided greater opportunity for a student's personal intellectual growth and a fresh educational renewal for the college. The adoption of this proposal aroused considerable interest in academic circles.

A nursing education program inaugurated in 1970 had 95 degree-seeking students in 1980. The college graduated 178 nurses during the decade. The department was accredited by the National League of Nursing in 1977.

In 1972 the William Jewell College Parents' Association was established.

In 1973 the college established the first full-time development department, which has recorded more than $5,000,000 in cash and pledges in the current fund drive.

The college observed its 125th anniversary with a festival of achievement in the spring, 1974. Governor Christopher Bond proclaimed the week of May 19-23 as William Jewell Week in Missouri.

Construction of a music building was finished in the summer of 1975 at a cost of $1,400,000 and was dedicated as the Pillsbury Music Center on Nov. 15, 1975. The music program received accreditation by the National Association of the Schools of Music in 1978.

In Sep., 1977, the college launched a capital fund drive known as the William Jewell Tomorrow Campaign. Designed to raise $10,000,000 over a five-year period to meet long-range building and operating needs of the college, more than one-half was received by May, 1980. The first phase of this program was the erection of a $4,000,000 physical activities facility, completed in the fall of 1980.

Jewell Hall, the first building on the campus, was placed on the National Register of Historic Places in 1978.

Foreign study programs existed with Regents Park College of Oxford University, Wolfson College of Cambridge University, Harlaxton College in England, and at Seinan Gakuin University in Japan.

A fine arts series brought annually to the campus and the Kansas City metropolitan area premier performing artists of the world.

By 1979 general endowment increased to $12,000,000, the operating budget to $7,057,000, receipts from the Missouri Baptist Convention to $650,000, enrollment for the fall semester to 1,704, full-time faculty to 86, and degrees awarded to 308.

H. I. HESTER

WILLIAMS, JOHN DAVIS (b. Granville County, NC, c. 1800; d. Wetumpka, AL, Oct. 7, 1870). Pastor, editor, and educator. Son of Thomas, Jr., and Elizabeth Williams, he made a commitment to the Baptist ministry at an early age. After 1818 he moved to Harrison County, VA, serving as an itinerant evangelist and later as pastor of Reedy Creek Baptist Church, 1822-27, and other churches. In 1824 he married Mary Johnson Grigg. They had four children: Thomas, Robert, Martha, and Indianna.

Following other Virginia pastorates, including Petersburg, 1931-35, Williams moved to Wetumpka, AL, as pastor of Coosa River (now First) Baptist Church, 1936-39. He established and edited a religious newspaper *Family Visiter* [sic], 1838-39. During 1857-58 he published *Southern Dial,* a magazine advocating a biblical defense of slavery. He wrote frequently for various denominational papers, organized the first school in Wetumpka, and promoted railroad development in Central Alabama. He is buried at Wetumpka, AL.

LEE N. ALLEN

WILLIAMS, WILLIAM HARRISION. (b. Charlottesville, VA, Oct. 31, 1879; d. Charlotte, NC, Aug. 24, 1974). Pastor. Son of William Harrision and Matilda (Silcox) Williams, his father served as pastor of a Baptist church in Charlottesville. He married Anne Laura McChord, Sep. 10, 1910. They had two children, McChord and William Harrison, III. He graduated from William Jewell College, Liberty, MO (A.B. 1901) and The Southern Baptist Theological Seminary (Th.M., 1904).

Williams served pastorates in Kentucky and Missouri. In 1928 he came from the First Baptist Church, St. Joseph, MO, to Pritchard Memorial Baptist Church, Charlotte, NC. He served as second vice-president of the SBC, 1940-1946, and was a member of the Foreign Mission Board, the Home Mission Board, and the SBC Executive Committee. A past president of the North Carolina State Convention, 1941, he served as a trustee of many of the institutions and schools of the convention. He is buried in Evergreen Cemetery, Charlotte, NC.

JAMES S. POTTER

WILLIAMSON, EDGAR STANLEY, II (b. Anaconda, MT, Nov. 9, 1920; d. Nashville, TN, Apr. 30, 1977). Denominational worker. The son of Edgar Stanley (q.v. III) and Rowena (Armstrong) Williamson, he attended Ouachita Baptist University (B.A., 1942) and Southwestern Baptist Theological Seminary (M.R.E., 1949; D.R.E., 1950). He married Virginia Kilby, Nov. 17, 1945. Their children were Diana, Stan, and Jo Anne. Minister of education, 1945-52, in Arkansas, Texas, Tennessee, and Oklahoma, he also worked at the Sunday School Board as superintendent of Intermediate Sunday School work, secretary of cooperative field promotion, and secretary of Broadman Films. He served as director of stewardship development, Stewardship Commission, SBC, 1971-77. He is buried in National Cemetery, Nashville, TN.

BARBARA CONNER

WILLINGHAM, EDWARD BACON (b. Richmond, VA, Oct. 30, 1899; d. New York, NY, Nov. 16, 1972). Pastor and missionary statesman. The son of Robert J. (q.v. II) and Corneille (Bacon) Willingham, he graduated from the University of Richmond (B.A., 1921) and The Southern Baptist Theological Seminary (Th.M., 1924). He did graduate study at Washington University, St. Louis, MO, and Union Theological Seminary, New York, NY. He married Harriet Sharon, Aug. 25, 1929. They had two children, Harriet and Edward B., Jr.

Willingham taught Bible at the University of Richmond, 1924-26, and was field secretary, Virginia Baptist Board of Missions and Education, 1926-28. His pastorates were: Rivermont Avenue Church, Lynchburg, VA, 1928-32; Delmar Church, St. Louis, MO, 1932-40; Fifth Avenue Church, Huntington, WV, 1940-45; and National Baptist Memorial Church, Washington, DC, 1945-55. He was general secretary, American Baptist and Woman's American Baptist Foreign Mission Societies, 1955-65.

Willingham served on the Foreign Mission and the Relief and Annuity Boards, SBC; board of trustees, Southern Seminary; and the Baptist Joint Committee on Public Affairs. He was president, West Virginia Baptist Convention, and from 1955 to 1960 was western treasurer, Baptist World Alliance. He is buried in Hollywood Cemetery, Richmond, VA.

R. STUART GRIZZARD

WILSON, CLARENCE GEORGE (b. Santee, NB, Sep. 21, 1903; d. Albuquerque, NM, Sep. 28, 1958). Sioux Indian concert singer. The son of Jacob and Agnes Wilson, he attended the University of South Dakota and the University of Kansas and studied music at several conservatories. He married Maggie Howard, 1925; then Geneva Groom, 1935. His children were Winona, George, Margery, Lonah, and Richard. Converted in 1928 during a concert trip to the Southwest, he served under the Home Mission Board in New Mexico for five years. After working as an evangelist for nine years, he returned to the HMB and the Indians in Albuquerque and Santa Fe areas. He is buried at Albuquerque, NM.

B. FRANK BELVIN

WILSON, NORVEL W. (b. Pendleton County, VA, Oct. 20, 1834; d. New Orleans, LA, Sep. 6, 1878). Denominational leader and pastor. Of Methodist parents, he joined the Moravians but became a Baptist in 1857. He was ordained in Pittsylvania County, VA, Aug. 11, 1858. He served three country churches until Jan., 1861, when he became pastor at Chapel Hill, NC. He married in June, 1861. Wilson became pastor at Farmdale, VA, in 1867 and three years later succeeded J. B. Jeter (q.v. I) at Grace Church, Richmond. By the time of his resignation nearly five years later, a church resolution indicated that he had preached 386 sermons and delivered 139 lectures in the church, had baptized 162 with 100 others having professed conversion, and had encouraged the church to contribute about $40,000 to church and benevolent causes.

Wilson became pastor of Coliseum Place Church, New Orleans, in 1875. When yellow fever raged in the city in 1875, he ministered to his congregation until he was finally felled by the disease himself.

J. D. GREY

WILSON, SYLVIA ABEENE (b. Roseburg, OR, June 3, 1900; d. Portland, OR, May 30, 1977). State WMU leader. Daughter of William Henry Abeene, a railroad worker, and

Mrs. Abeene, she was a graduate of Multnomah School of the Bible, Portland, OR. She married Burt G. Thompson, Aug., 1918. They had two daughters, Doris Lorraine and Lois Eileen. Later she married William H. Wilson, Oct. 21, 1932. After Wilson's death in 1944, she began to study and promote Southern Baptist world missions. She served as president of Woman's Missionary Union of the Northwest Baptist Convention from July, 1948, to Oct., 1964.

The convention in its annual session, Nov. 9, 1977, renamed the Northwest Missions Offering the Sylvia Wilson Missions Offering. She is buried in Lincoln Memorial Park, Portland, OR.

ROLAND HOOD

WINDERMERE BAPTIST ASSEMBLY (III). The state Baptist assembly in Missouri serves an average of 18,000 persons per year. In 1976 a new policy and program statement was developed, emphasizing a commitment to spiritual, moral, mental, and physical development. New programs instituted were Youth Development, Over 60s Conferences, Older Children Music Camp, Summer Missionaries Conference, Weekday Early Education Workshops, Single Adult Conference, Marriage Enrichment Workshops, and Special Worker's Training Conferences. Improved physical properties include a refurbished dining hall, auditorium, and children's building. Income in 1979 was $531,000.

ARTHUR KOEHLER

WINDWARD ISLANDS, MISSION IN. See BARBADOS, MISSION IN; DOMINICA, MISSION IN; GRENADA, MISSION IN; ST. VINCENT, MISSION IN.

WING, JOHN WILLIAM (b. Edgefield County, SC, Nov. 9, 1884; d. Atlanta, GA, Aug. 12, 1963). Denominational worker. Son of Marion L. and Mary G. Wing, farmers, he attended Draughons Business College, Atlanta. As business manager at the Home Mission Board, 1921-54, he saw the work grow from 4 to 16 operation phases and yearly receipts increase from $200,000 to $3,000,000. He married Marilu Beckham, July 22, 1908. Their children were Jerome, James, and Julia. He is buried in Westview Cemetery, Atlanta, GA.

LEONOAR C. ADAMS

WINGATE COLLEGE (cf. Wingate Junior College, Vols. II, III). A four-year, coeducational Baptist college fully accredited in liberal arts and sciences. About 1,500 students study on the 300-acre campus with 31 buildings. Thomas E. Corts became president in 1974 upon the retirement of Budd E. Smith (q.v.). In 1977 the school admitted its first junior class and then awarded its first four-year degrees in 1979. Degrees are offered in 12 fields. A special program allows sophomores at midterm to study abroad briefly as a follow-up to cluster-group courses. About 85 percent of Wingate's students come from North Carolina and seven percent from South Carolina. Endowment doubled in the 1970s to $5,300,000.

THOMAS E. CORTS

WISCONSIN, SOUTHERN BAPTISTS IN. See MINNESOTA-WINCONSIN SOUTHERN BAPTIST FELLOWSHIP.

WOMAN'S MISSIONARY UNION, AUXILIARY TO SBC (cf. Woman's Missionary Union, Vols. II, III). The year 1970 saw members of WMU in churches fitted comfortably into a new grouping-grading plan which carried different organizational structure and terminology.

Early in the decade the WMU executive board reworded WMU tasks to sharpen the expression of a church's total missions responsibility. Officially approved by the Coordinating Committee of the Inter-Agency Council, the WMU tasks, which describe what should be included in a church missions program for women, girls, and preschool children, were stated as follows: Teach missions, engage in mission action, support world missions through praying and giving, and provide and interpret information regarding the work of the church and denomination.

In answer to requests from the field, the executive board restudied the tasks and revised them in Jan., 1973. While it does not show up in the statement of the first task, spiritual development, a fourth division of scope for teaching missions, was added. The concept of task two was enlarged, and the task statement became, "to engage in mission action and direct evangelism." The third task was changed to a simple statement, "Support missions," but reflected no change in concept.

WMU closely adhered to these tasks, representing the basis of all WMU work, in shaping activities, products, and curriculum for all age levels, and implemented them through all WMU magazines: *Royal Service, Dimension, Contempo, Accent* and *Accent Leader Edition, Aware, Discovery, Start,* Mission Friends *Share,* and *Nuestra Tarea.*

WMU's adjustment to the new grouping-grading system necessitated a redesign of its individual achievement plans. The new plans, Mission Adventures and Studiact, replaced Girls' Auxiliary Forward Steps and Young Women's Auxiliary Citation.

Because of declining enrollment in WMU organizations in the early 1970s, enlistment and enlargement became key emphases. Giant Step, a plan to increase membership, number of organizations, and subscriptions to WMU magazines in churches, was conducted for a two-year period, 1972-74. Also during the 1970-79 period each age-level organization had an emphasis on enlargement—*a tempo* for Baptist Young Women in 1975-76; "Minding the Future" for Acteens, Girls in Action, and Mission Friends in 1976-77; and "Baptist Women Year in the Church" for Baptist Women in 1978-79.

At the close of this 10-year period, the WMU executive board approved a national enlargement plan which called for additional personnel and funding. The plan, jointly sponsored by WMU, SBC, and state WMUs, was devised to contact every church not reporting WMU on the church letter to the association about the possibility of organizing WMU work. Outstanding women in each state were selected and trained to be StarTeam members to contact each church not reporting WMU work. Specialized enlargement materials were developed by the WMU staff in consultation with state WMU staffs. Evelyn Blount, who served as assistant to the Education Division director, was selected to give leadership to this gigantic enlargement undertaking. These enlistment-enlargement emphases showed positive results in WMU organization and membership statistics during the decade.

WMU enrollment stood at 1,086,785 with 80,195 age-level organizations in 1979. Breakdowns were as follows: Baptist Women, 494,273 enrolled in 26,183 organizations; Baptist Young Women, 70,231 enrolled in 6,410 organizations; Campus BYW, 924 enrolled in 53 organizations; Acteens, 115,944 enrolled in 13,115 organizations; Girls in Action, 202,857 enrolled in 20,170 organizations; Mission Friends, 121,454 enrolled in 14,264 organizations; and 81,102 general WMU officers.

On Jan. 1, 1972, Doris Díaz, former Home Mission Board editor of Spanish WMU materials, moved to Birmingham. She became WMU language missions consultant with specific responsibilities for editing Spanish materials, and for field services among Spanish-speaking and other language groups. In 1974 when the staff was restructured, Díaz became Language Department director in the Education Division and an editor, editorial assistant, and secretary were employed. This work, in addition to the work of the promotion associate in new areas, was funded by the HMB and directed by WMU.

In 1972 in an effort to strengthen mission action, WMU and the HMB jointly sponsored 15 national mission action workshops in various areas of the nation.

At the close of the 1971-72 church year, the Sunday School Board discontinued the World in Books catalog, provided by its Sales and Advertising Department. It was replaced by a WMU Materials Catalog, listing all WMU materials available from Baptist Book Stores.

The executive board changed its bylaws in Jan., 1973, to allow for more involvement of laywomen in laying broad plans for the development of the total WMU program as it is recommended to churches. This change made it possible for the president to appoint annually a work group, called the Dated Plan Work Group, composed of laywomen to meet in Birmingham, AL, to help in developing activities, products, and curriculum for all age levels for a given year.

This same year the Promotion Division underwent reorganization. The name was changed to Education Division, and five departments were created—General Administration, Adult, Youth, Children and Preschool, and Art. Each department had a supervisor with appropriate age-level personnel serving in the department.

In Feb., 1973, Margaret Bruce, long-time employee of WMU, retired. A native of Tennessee, she had been elected as young people's secretary in May, 1948. Later she directed Woman's Missionary Society work; then assumed the title of Baptist Women director when organizations were renamed. Upon her retirement she had served WMU, SBC, 25 years.

In Jan., 1974, the WMU executive board approved a new basic program design for Associational WMU.

Alma Hunt concluded her service as WMU executive secretary, Oct. 5, 1974. She had begun her work in 1948; thus serving 26 years in this capacity. During those years WMU made significant strides in its work. The operational base was enlarged, both financially and physically. The professional staff grew, WMU membership in churches increased, cooperation with other agencies was encouraged and strengthened, intense interprogram study, design, and implementation were carried on, WMU program statement and related activities were approved, new emphasis on mission action was developed, changes were made in the structure of WMU in the church in order to reflect the changing times, and a new approach for development of annual curriculum and activities for a church was begun. Being a writer and speaker, Alma Hunt also made outstanding personal contributions to the work of WMU.

On Oct. 7, 1974, Carolyn Weatherford, executive director for Florida WMU, became WMU, SBC's, fifth executive secretary. (The executive board changed the title to executive director, Jan. 14, 1976.) At that time Marie Mathis, WMU president, and Weatherford announced a major reorganization in office management. Two assistants to the executive secretary were named. Catherine Allen was given responsibilities in public and employee relations, and June Whitlow was made responsible for planning and research. La Venia Neal was named treasurer. The Education Division, designated to handle program design, promotion, and development of publications, was restructured with Bobbie Sorrill as director. A Customer Services Division was created to handle production of publications, inventory, sales, and shipping. Mary Hines became director. These five persons plus Weatherford comprised the top management group, the Executive Council. In Apr., 1979, Neal retired as treasurer, and Audrey Cowley succeeded her in June, 1979.

In her first annual meeting address as executive secretary, June, 1975, Weatherford examined the heart of this union that is both "women" and "missionary" and found it destined for long life.

In June, 1975, Marie Mathis, who had served two terms and a total of 13 years as president, retired. During her years of leadership, she had played a vital role in inter-agency programming and had linked WMU closely to the affairs of the Women's Department of the Baptist World Alliance.

Christine Gregory, Danville, VA, was elected to succeed Mathis as president. During her tenure of office, Gregory led the executive board in upgrading salaries and fringe benefits of WMU employees. A major accomplishment in this time was the establishment and funding of the WMU Employee Orientation, Training, and Enrichment Plan. Several employees have been awarded the opportunity for extended enrichment.

Early in her administration Weatherford led the agency to set priorities and write objectives for each. Priorities chosen for 1977-78 were Enlistment-Enlargement Plan, Missions Education Strategy, Marketing Plan, Finances, and Base of Operation. The next planning cycle's priorities included Enlargement Plan, Life-Changing Commitments Plan, Church Professional Leadership Development Plan, and Base of Operation Plan. The headquarters staff, executive board, state WMU leaders, and church WMU leaders contributed to the development of these priorities. The priorities served as criteria for the establishment of new programs, production of new materials, and allocation of new monies for the remainder of the decade.

Also contributing input to these objectives was a long-range planning committee appointed by Gregory to give specific direction to WMU's centennial in 1988. Those serving on the Direction '88 Committee were: Sara Frances Anders, Pineville, LA; Maxine Barber, Johnson, KS; Clyde Bizzell, Dallas, TX; W. C. Fields, Nashville, TN; Christine Gregory, Danville, VA; Linda Hood Hix, Oklahoma City, OK; Jewell Jennings, Lebanon, TN; Mauriece Johnston, San Antonio, TX; Jack Lowndes, Syracuse, NY; William O'Brien, Richmond, VA; Marjean Patterson, Jackson, MS; Brenda Staver, El Toro, CA; and Evelyn Thompson, Richmond, VA.

In 1975-76 the WMU executive board recommended that an organizational plan for Campus Baptist Young Women be developed and materials produced to implement the design. In consultation with National Student Ministries Department of the SSB, WMU developed a flexible organization structure suited to the needs of students. The organization structure was piloted on selected college campuses and was put into full operation in the 1978-79 school year.

Also in 1975-76 WMU designed plans for its participation in North Central Missions Thrust, a plan of seven North Central states to double their churches and membership. A prayer project plan and a share-the-leader plan were developed and promoted, and funds were contributed to this thrust.

In Aug., 1976, Ethalee Hamric, editor of *Di-*

mension, retired. Hamric had previously served as editor of *Royal Service.*

On Oct. 1, 1976, WMU entered an agreement with the Book Store Division of the SSB to discontinue retail sales of WMU materials from the WMU Building in Birmingham. This was a three-year experiment for the Baptist Book Store to sell all WMU materials. The agreement was studied at the end of the three-year period, and it was made permanent.

A $500,000 addition to the WMU office building was constructed in 1977 with a service of dedication taking place, Jan. 11, 1978.

In 1977 the WMU Conference at Glorieta combined with Brotherhood into a Bold Mission Leadership Conference. This conference continued to be joint through the remainder of the decade, whereas the Ridgecrest WMU Conference remained a conference planned and promoted by WMU.

In Sep., 1977, Helen Fling assumed the position of promotion associate in new areas following the retirement of Bernice Elliott in August of that year.

In 1976-77 the WMU executive board approved a volunteer program utilizing volunteers from churches in the Birmingham area in the WMU Building for various kinds of routine responsibilities, and Bernice Elliott was secured to coordinate the plan.

In Jan., 1978, Margaret Perkins was introduced as a consultant in Cooperative Ministries with National Baptists. The HMB made this agreement with WMU possible by funding this work and allowing the consultant's work to be directed by WMU. (The title of WMU consultant for cooperative ministries with National Baptists was changed to WMU consultant, black church relations in June, 1980.)

WMU voted in Jan., 1977, to participate with other boards and agencies in sponsoring a World Hunger Day in Southern Baptist churches.

WMU participated with several other boards and agencies in sponsoring a Consultation on Women in Church-related Vocations in Nashville, TN, Sep. 20-22, 1978. An official response relative to the findings of this consultation was approved by the WMU executive board in Jan., 1979.

During the 1970s WMU personnel worked with personnel of other agencies to complete correlated plans for assisting the churches in implementing the denomination's emphases. Appropriate materials to support the emphases of 1970-79 were produced and information was channeled through existing WMU materials.

As a result of the recommendations of the Missions Challenge Committee in 1976, WMU personnel worked with personnel of the two missions boards, Brotherhood Commission, and the SSB in planning a strategy for discovering and implementing plans for a broader-based missions education to reach all members of Southern Baptist churches. The Missions Education Council, formed at the SBC level in 1977, was composed of the following groups:

Executive, administrative, program design, research and development, promotion, marketing, and curriculum. A staff assistant, Katharine Bryan, was employed to perform staff work for designing, launching, and sustaining cooperative work in missions education done by the five agencies.

The executives of the five agencies identified five areas of cooperation: (1) That a cooperative strategy be developed for communicating with pastors and church staff members, (2) that a comprehensive Convention-wide plan be developed and implemented which would encourage every church to provide missions education for all its members, (3) that a national marketing plan be developed to inform Southern Baptists of the availability of missions education materials and effectively distribute the materials, (4) that a coordinated missions education curriculum design be developed which would reach all the people in Southern Baptist churches, and (5) that a plan for developing and testing missions education approaches be developed.

During this decade WMU participated in interprogram design work by working with other church program organizations through the Coordinating Committee of the Inter-Agency Council.

WMU work expanded in the 1970s with the organization of state WMUs in West Virginia, 1970; Pennsylvania-South Jersey, 1970; and Nevada, 1978.

BIBLIOGRAPHY: Alma Hunt and Catherine Allen, *History of Woman's Missionary Union* (rev., 1974).

JUNE WHITLOW

WOMAN'S MISSIONARY UNION, Auxiliary to the Alabama Baptist State Convention (II, III). The Alabama WMU sponsors the Lottie Moon Christmas Offering ($942,866 in 1969; $2,156,236 in 1979), the Annie Armstrong Easter Offering ($315,621 in 1969; $1,034,924 in 1979), the Kathleen Mallory Offering for work in Alabama, a scholarship fund for young women preparing for vocational Christian service and enrolled in Baptist colleges and seminaries, and ministers' wives enrolled in Howard College extension centers. The WMU also provides gift magazine subscriptions for Alabama home and foreign missionaries; Christmas gifts to children of missionaries enrolled in Alabama schools, and to needy retired ministers and their wives or widows; and support to miscellaneous causes as needs arise.

Work with black Baptists has been a priority of Alabama WMU. Financial and planning assistance was provided regularly for black mission activities including a youth camping project until 1971, when a biracial committee projected National Baptists' assuming responsibility for the camping program. Through an Executive Board committee, Inter Baptist Fellowship, cooperative work continues.

Ministries include training volunteers for teaching nonreaders; ministering to economically disadvantaged, victims of alcohol and drug abuse, juvenile delinquents, prisoners, and others with special needs; and financial and personnel assistance to the South Alabama mission field, seaman's ministry in Mobile, and a migrant ministry.

A chapel, dining hall, living quarters for the camp director, business office, and library were completed in July, 1980, at the girls' camp at Shocco Springs.

State presidents of the WMU have been Isabel Triplitt, Salem, 1968-73; Hermione Jackson, Birmingham, 1973-78; and Camilla Lowry, Auburn, 1978- .

MARY ESSIE STEPHENS

WOMAN'S MISSIONARY UNION, Auxiliary to the Arkansas Baptist State Convention (II). WMU in Arkansas entered the 1970s with its purpose—to promote Christian missions through organizations of Woman's Missionary Union—firmly intact.

The tasks of this organization remained the same. The name, Woman's Missionary Union, was retained for the overall organization. But age-level names, age divisions, titles, and materials experienced changes.

Arkansas WMU is supported through the ABSC budget and governed between annual meetings by an executive board, which determines year-by-year emphases. These emphases include leader-member training in such basics as enlistment, enlargement, mission study, mission action, and mission support on national, state, district, association, and church levels.

Activities sponsored by the organization include resident camping experiences scheduled for Girls in Action and Acteens at Ferncliff, Siloam Springs, and, beginning in 1964, at Camp Paron; house parties, retreats, and chartered bus trips to Glorieta and Ridgecrest Conference Centers; national WMU annual meetings; and the North American Baptist Women's Union meeting, in Toronto in 1972, planned for women and young women groups.

Establishment of the Nancy Cooper Scholarship Fund, announced at the 1974 annual meeting in recognition of Cooper's 26 years as executive secretary and treasurer, resulted in gift scholarships for volunteers for missions or church-related vocations or for internationals studying at Ouachita Baptist University or Southern Baptist College. Thirty scholarships, plus three others made possible by individual gifts, were granted during 1969-79.

The Lillian May Scholarship Fund, begun in 1917, furnished nine loan scholarships, 1969-79, to young women doing graduate study in Southern Baptist seminaries, and 29 gift scholarships to native Arkansans under regular appointment by either of the SBC's mission boards studying for credit in seminary or college.

Continuing an annual project, WMU subscribed for a magazine of their choice for missionaries from Arkansas. Offerings given during annual meetings and budgeted amounts made this possible. In 1979, 66 foreign missionaries, eight home missionaries, and 10 retired missionaries were recipients.

In promoting Bold Mission Thrust, WMU set as a priority the beginning of mission education in 150 churches without WMU organizations. Each association was challenged to begin WMU organizations in five of these churches. Bold state goals for the three special mission offerings resulted in increased giving. When Bold Mission Thrust penetrated the WMU staff, a year's leave of absence and $6,000 were granted Willene Pierce, Adult Division director, to serve as Mission Service Corps volunteer with Indians in Oklahoma.

Nancy Cooper served as executive secretary and treasurer, 1949-75. She was succeeded by Julia Ketner, 1975- . WMU presidents who have served since 1957 are Elma Cobb, 1957-64 (75th anniversary president); Mrs. Roy E. Snider, 1964-69; Mrs. J. A. Hogan, 1969-74; Mrs. George Tharel, 1974-76; Mrs. James Sawyer, 1976-79; and Mrs. Boyd Margason, 1969- .

Beginning with the 1980s, WMU is responding to the theme, "Life Changing Commitments," and is continuing to assist churches and associations in establishing, conducting, enlarging, and improving WMU work in the organizations of Woman's Missionary Union.

RUBY HERRICK SNIDER

WOMAN'S MISSIONARY UNION, Auxiliary to the Baptist Convention of Maryland (III; cf. Woman's Missionary Union, Auxiliary to the Maryland Baptist Union Association, Vol. II). The 1971-72 centennial year of Maryland WMU set the pace for mission advances and achievements. Steadily increasing gifts to world missions through special offerings promoted by the WMU, 1970-79, totaled: Annie Armstrong Easter Offering, $914,723; Lottie Moon Christmas Offering, $1,934,616; and Kathryn Barnes Offering for State Missions, $516,276. New Baptist conventions which developed out of Maryland Baptist work received strength from existing WMU organizations in 42 churches in New York and in 47 churches in Pennsylvania-South Jersey.

Students received 87 scholarship loans from endowed funds and state missions offerings. During this decade two former scholarship loan recipients were appointed for service with Southern Baptist mission boards. The BWC (Business Women's Circles), Captain and Mrs. John T. Willing, and Hattie Wilson Norwood Memorial Scholarship funds, dedicated Apr. 7, 1970, were first granted in 1971; Centennial Memorial Scholarship was first granted in 1977.

Other centennial highlights included updating the written history of the state WMU, celebrating Camp Wo-Me-To's 25th anniversary, and placing a historical marker on the Baltimore Greenmount Cemetery grave of Annie Walker Armstrong (*q.v.* I).

Josephine Carroll Norwood (*q.v.* I), who served as executive director, 1956-78, was succeeded by Betty Lynn Cadle in Feb., 1979.

BETTY LYNN CADLE

WOMAN'S MISSIONARY UNION, Auxiliary to the Baptist Convention of New Mexico (II, III). The 1970s brought several personnel changes to New Mexico WMU. In Mar., 1977, Lera Turner of Tennessee became director of Acteens, Girls in Action, and Mission Friends. In June, 1977, Vanita Baldwin resigned after 16 years as director of the state's WMU to become director of Florida's WMU. She was succeeded in Jan., 1978, by Aquilla Brown, Baptist Women's director of South Carolina. Glee Capehart succeeded Ofa Hopkins as office secretary in Jan., 1979.

State WMU presidents have been Helen Lee Lambirth, Elida, 1966-71, 1978- ; Vora Hartley, Clovis, 1971-74; and Lynette Thompson, Fort Sumner, 1974-78.

Acteens and Girls in Action engage in a week of camp at Inlow Youth Camp and at Sivells Baptist Camp. Home and foreign missionaries provide current mission information. A Mother-Daughter Missions Weekend is provided for girls in grades one through three along with their mothers.

WMU provides an annual Queen's Court and Encounter for Acteens and sponsors a couple's retreat, involving Baptist Young Women and young Baptist men.

In 1979, 36 Acteens went to Kansas City, MO, to participate in the National Acteen's Conference. This was the first group of New Mexico Acteens to attend a national function.

Two WMU leadership camps provide specialized training for WMU and age-level officers in addition to adult members. Mission Friends activities and a missions day camp for girls and boys in grades one through three are also held.

An Associational WMU Age-level Symposium, started in 1979, prepares associational officers to train in their respective age levels.

Saturated Training was initiated in 1978. The WMU staff goes into an association church by church to design a program of WMU which meets the needs of the individual church.

Through the WMU State Activity Fund, $2,500 in scholarships go annually to young women and men in college and seminary.

At the end of 1979, 468 WMU organizations in the state had 5,090 members.

AQUILLA A. BROWN

WOMAN'S MISSIONARY UNION, Auxiliary to the Baptist General Association of Virginia (II, III). During the 1970s, WMU of Virginia launched its centennial celebration with 100 days of prayer from Dec. 8, 1973, to Mar. 19, 1974, the opening day of the annual meeting. Three centennial memorials in missions were adopted: (1) foreign—a building to house the training center of Hong Kong Baptist Theological Seminary in memory of Blanche Sydnor White (q.v.); (2) home—a building at Zuni Indian Reservation in New Mexico in honor of Carrie Sinton Vaughan; and (3) state—enlargement of staff at Clinchco and Trammel Baptist Centers, and enlargement of facilities at Manassas Baptist Center.

The third history of Virginia WMU, *Light Three Candles* by Juliette Mather, was published in 1973. Three veteran state missionaries retired: Elizabeth Thomas, Allie Candler, and Emma Lou McCraw. Two outstanding leaders died in the 1970s: Olive Brunson Martin (q.v.), president of Virginia WMU, 1925-29, 1935-46, and first president, Women's Department, Baptist World Alliance, 1948-60; and Blanche Sydnor White, executive secretary, Virginia WMU, 1925-50. Four presidents served during this 10-year period: Emma Stratton, 1964-71, Christine Gregory, 1971-75, Mary Jane Thurman, 1975-78, and Jane Clarke, 1979- .

In 1971 WMU agreed to present an annual request for operating expenses to the budget committee of the Baptist General Association of Virginia. Previously the organization was supported by recall of funds not to exceed 5 percent of the gifts of the membership through the Cooperative Program.

Kathryn Bullard became the sixth executive secretary in Mar., 1975 (title later changed to executive director-treasurer), succeeding Carrie S. Vaughan, who served, 1958-75. Changes and additions occurred in the professional leadership. Sue Hutton, GA and Mission Friends director, resigned in 1977 after eight years of service. Ann Kilner became Acteens director, June 1, 1976. Maxine Bumgarner was Baptist Women and Baptist Young Women director, 1977-79. Linda Morgan served as GA and Mission Friends director, 1978-79. Rees Watkins became editorial and research secretary in 1975 after 26 years as a youth director.

In 1976 the state missions study committee recommended that the Virginia state missions offering be cosponsored by WMU and the Virginia Baptist General Board. In Mar., 1978, the long-range camping committee recommended that WMU procure property centrally located in the state and build a new camp for year-round use. The state missions committee recommended that the Baptist work at Clinchco be continued under the sponsorship of a local church and the Wise Association, looking toward being constituted into a church.

A committee to study Baptist Women work asked in 1979 that plans be given for bold enlistment of all women in Baptist Women work and that the Federation of Baptist Business Women's Circles on the state level be disbanded.

REES WATKINS

WOMAN'S MISSIONARY UNION, Auxiliary to the Baptist General Convention of Oklahoma (II). During the years 1970-77, Oklahoma's WMU held its annual session in the spring. Beginning Nov. 13-14, 1978, the annual session was moved back to the week of the state convention's meeting in the autumn. In 1979, 1,085 churches reported WMU work with 33,131 members. Titles for state WMU workers were changed in 1970 to correspond with the names of organizations: Baptist Young Women director, Acteen director, and Mission Friends-Girls in Action director. The Baptist Women director was added, May 1, 1973. The state secretary's title was changed to director, Apr. 22, 1975.

Special ongoing projects each year include Camp Nunny-Cha-ha, training sessions in cooperation with the Brotherhood Department of the convention in 15 regional state meetings, and promotion of three missions offerings. In 1979 these offerings totaled $1,518,294 for the Lottie Moon Offering for Foreign Missions; $466,098 for the Annie Armstrong Offering for Home Missions, and $269,582 for the Edna McMillan (q.v. III) Offering for State Missions. The 1980 operating budget of $157,797 was provided from the state convention's Cooperative Program. Abbie Louise Green has been director since 1963.

HELEN GASKIN

WOMAN'S MISSIONARY UNION, Auxiliary to the Baptist General Convention of Texas (II, III). State directors of Mission Friends and Girls in Action in the 1970s were Claudia Jones Swain, 1970-77; Nell Carter Branum, 1978-79; and Marsha Spradlin, 1979- . Acteens directors were Sheryl Churchill, 1970-76, and Barbara Curnutt, 1977- . Baptist Young Women directors were Katharine Bryan, 1970-77, and Dorothy Miller, 1978- . Baptist Women directors were Katharine Bryan, 1975-77, and Dorothy Miller, 1978- . Eula Mae Henderson continued as executive secretary-treasurer with a title change in 1977 to executive director-treasurer.

In 1976 the State WMU Centennial Committee, Jean Kemp, of Belton, chairman, set forth the 1980 centennial goals for the state organization as well as local and associational goals for the years 1976-80. The state activities included the 25th anniversary of the WMU House Party at Baylor University in 1978 with 2,309 attending; six regional mini-house parties in the spring of 1979; and the release of a WMU history, *A Pilgrimage of Faith* by Inez Boyle Hunt, who had served as state WMU president, 1968-72.

Mauriece Johnston, San Antonio, served as state president, 1972-76, and Huis Coy, Houston, became president in 1976. Following her husband's death, she married Elvis Egge of Corsicana in 1978. She continues her service as state president.

The Mary Hill Davis Offering for State Missions exceeded $1,000,000 in 1973; the 1979 offering amounted to $1,964,481. In 1979 the Annie Armstrong Easter Offering went beyond $2,000,000 for the second year, and the Lottie Moon Christmas Offering reached $6,691,436.

Scholarships for black and Hispanic students continued to Baptist schools in Texas with funds from the Mary Hill Davis Offering along with the support of the River Ministry begun in 1967.

The state officers, the associational WMU directors plus six members-at-large, compose the WMU Executive Board. The state organization for Spanish-speaking women, a part of Texas WMU, had the following presidents: Hortense Palomo, 1967-71; Teresa Luna, 1971-75; Mary Godsey, 1975-79; and Marcella Casarez, 1979- .

EULA MAE HENDERSON

WOMAN'S MISSIONARY UNION, Auxiliary to the Georgia Baptist Convention (II, III). The 1970 organizational structure of WMU was reflected in the staff positions: directors for Baptist Women-Baptist Young Women, Acteens, Girls in Action-Mission Friends, and executive director-treasurer.

Presidents since 1969 have been Nell Bowen, 1970-75; Genet Barron, 1975-80; and Rachel Howard, 1980- . Dorothy Pryor has served as executive director-treasurer since 1963. Language WMU work has grown. WMU has sponsored internationals at the annual international student conference. Janice Singleton seminary scholarships, awarded annually, have gone to two women or missionary children in alternate years. Attendance at the annual area interracial observances of the Baptist Women's Day of Prayer exceeds 1,000. Staff members are given mission tours. Attendance is increasing at annual meetings and at leadership training and age-level events.

WMU provides summer camps at WMU-owned Camp Pinnacle, Clayton, and sponsors tours to national Acteens conferences and to North American Baptist Women's Union meetings. Leadership training teams have gone to the sister states of New York and Indiana and to other conventions.

Anticipating its centennial in 1984, the Georgia WMU has authorized a history and launched enlistment plans to increase the present membership of 107,072 in 7,655 organizations and 2,083 churches.

DOROTHY PRYOR

WOMAN'S MISSIONARY UNION, Auxiliary to the Kentucky Baptist Convention (cf. Woman's Missionary Union, Auxiliary to the General Association of Baptists in Kentucky, Vol. II). In 1958 the staff included a Sunbeams-Girls Auxiliary director and a Young Woman's Auxiliary-Woman's Missionary Society director. Two years later the staff was expanded to include a director for each age-level organization. A camp for girls at Cedarmore, begun with two cabins in 1958, was completed in 1976 with facilities for 225. Named Cedar Crest, the camp includes 11 cabins, a dining hall, 3 unit shelters, an administration building, and a swimming pool.

The first WMU report to be presented by a woman in the history of the Kentucky Baptist Convention occurred in 1962. Julia Woodward, Kentucky WMU president, gave the report. Odessa Ferguson, executive secretary of the Kentucky WMU since 1947, retired in 1970. She was succeeded by Kathryn Jasper, a Somerset, KY, native, whose title became executive director. The annual state missions offering became the Eliza Broadus Offering for State Missions in 1976. It was named for a leader who had greatly influenced both Kentucky and SBC WMU work.

Kentucky WMU traces its origin to the first statewide effort exerted for the cause of missions among women affiliated with the General Association of Baptists in Kentucky (now Kentucky Baptist Convention). The 100th anniversary of Kentucky WMU was celebrated in 1978. A hundred days of prayer began the celebration. A highlight of the year was the showing of a film *Bridgebuilders,* produced by Kentucky WMU to show who Kentucky Baptists are and what they believe and do.

Significant in the centennial year was the printing of a WMU history, *Proclaiming Christ, 1878-1978,* by Dixie Bale Mylum. The climax of the 1978 annual meeting was the presentation of a pageant, "Let the Woman Keep Silent/Go Tell," by Helen Graves. This also recounted the history of Kentucky WMU.

Continued interest in mission education has resulted in increased giving. Over $2,000,000 was given through the state and home and foreign mission offerings in 1978-79. Records for 1978-79 show an enrollment of 50,120 in WMU in Kentucky, an increase of 1,100 over the year before. The number of WMUs rose to 1,292.

KATHRYN JASPER

WOMAN'S MISSIONARY UNION, Auxiliary to the Louisiana Baptist Convention (II, III). In 1970 age-level organizations became Baptist Women, Baptist Young Women, Acteens, Girls in Action, and Mission Friends. The first annual state BYW Conference was held in 1971, as was the first state meeting for Acteens. That year saw the first annual state WMU Prayer Retreat at Camp Tall Timbers. The first session of the 1976 prayer retreat was the dedication of the new Kathryn E. Carpenter Chapel at Tall Timbers.

Since 1970 staff members have been an executive secretary-treasurer (now executive director-treasurer) and two age-level directors. Kathryn E. Carpenter has served in the executive position since 1955. Age-level directors, 1969-79, included Sylvia Thigpen, Barbara Hayes, Kaye Johnson, Margaret Parsons, Aline Fuselier, Ann Thomason, and Frances Grafton. During this period WMU presidents were Frances Daigle Conrad, Lucille Keith McNair, and Joyce Litton Foreman.

Scholarships provided by the Hannah Reynolds (*q.v.* IV). Offering total annually: Louisiana College, 75; SBC seminaries, 25; and mission field seminaries, 25. This offering in 1979 for the first time exceeded $50,000. Four years earlier the Lottie Moon Christmas Offering exceeded $1,000,000 and in 1979 was $1,626,993. The Georgia Barnette State Mission Offering in 1979 totaled $318,385—the largest ever. Allocations from this offering went to mission church construction, land purchases, deaf ministry,

French and Spanish radio programs, resort and ethnic ministries, and the WMU Camp.

KATHRYN E. CARPENTER

WOMAN'S MISSIONARY UNION, Auxiliary to the Missouri Baptist Convention (cf. Woman's Missionary Union, Auxiliary to the Missouri Baptist General Association, Vol. II). The regrouping-grading, started in 1969, became operative in 1970 and brought changes in WMU staff positions, elected WMU officers, and the executive committee. The staff shifted to directors of Baptist Women, Baptist Young Women, Acteens, Girls in Action, and Mission Friends to relate to church organizations. The elected state officers were president, vice-president, secretary, and an executive committee of 12 area members and 10 members at large. Missouri WMU celebrated its 50th anniversary in 1973 in the First Baptist Church, Poplar Bluff. Six charter members were present. The host church presented a pageant, "Missouri WMU Fifty Years Ago."

In 1973 Mary Bidstrup, executive secretary, retired after 25 years, and Alberta Gilpin succeeded her. Additional staff are Debbie Bailey and Donna Maples. Missouri WMU provided student loans to 38 mission volunteers for seminary training, available because of local WMU gifts to the Madge N. Truex Fund.

NELL CONSTANZ

WOMAN'S MISSIONARY UNION, Auxiliary to the South Carolina Baptist Convention (II). Several bylaw amendments in 1957 created four departments of work: Woman's Missionary Society, Young Woman's Auxiliary, Girls Auxiliary, and Sunbeam Band. Hannah Brummitt Hills joined the staff, Jan. 1, 1970, as WMU administrative assistant and WMS director. On Oct. 1, 1970, South Carolina WMU moved with WMU, SBC, into the new pattern of organizations.

Regional organizations were discontinued in 1959, though geographical representation is maintained for the state nominating committee and board of trustees of Camp Rawls and through 10 vice-presidents on the executive board. Forty-four associational WMU's hold semiannual and age-level meetings.

Leadership training has been a major focus since 1956. Basic leadership courses introduced by WMU, SBC, 1959-60, were supplemented by advanced training developed by the state WMU, 1961-67. Annual institutes at Camp Rawls train associational and church WMU leaders.

The 25th anniversary of Camp Rawls was observed, June 4, 1966. A long-range study of future needs of the camp culminated in an offer from the South Carolina Baptist Convention in Nov., 1977, to deed to WMU 164.6 acres of the White Oak Conference Center property for a new WMU camp. WMU accepted this offer on Mar. 20, 1978, and in Mar., 1980, the name La Vida was chosen. An architect was employed, and funding was provided through the Mrs. J. D.

Chapman Offering for State Interests and designated gifts from WMU members.

The centennial of the state WMU, 1974-75, had as its theme, "Commemoration . . . Commission . . . Commitment." WMU received the general award of the South Carolina Baptist Historical Society for its overall program of celebration. An outgrowth of the observance was the publication in Mar., 1980, of the official WMU history, *The Eternal Now,* by Kathryn A. Greene.

In 1977 South Carolina WMU was recognized by WMU, SBC, as leading all other states in percentage of churches with WMU work—88.6 percent. Membership in 1979 totaled 92,985 in 6,302 organizations. Gifts to WMU-promoted offerings that year were: Lottie Moon Christmas Offering for Foreign Missions, $2,672,638; Annie Armstrong Easter Offering for Home Missions, $1,001,948; and Mrs. J. D. Chapman Offering for State Interests, $496,997.

Presidents since 1957 have been: Nelle Blakely Ashmore, 1957-63; Frances Greer Eller, 1963-68; Nora Brown Byrd, 1968-71; Kathryn Abee Greene, 1971-76; and Mildred Cone Bomar, 1976. Two persons have served as executive secretaries: Ruth Provence, 1955-73, and Hannah Brummitt Hills, 1973-   .

RUTH PROVENCE

WOMAN'S MISSIONARY UNION, Auxiliary to the Tennessee Baptist Convention (II). In Jan., 1959, 85,535 women and young people in 1,534 Tennessee churches were enrolled in WMU organizations: Woman's Missionary Society, 45,350; Young Woman's Auxiliary, 6,180; and Girls Auxiliary, 18,105. There were 1,518 Sunbeam Bands. In addition to leadership clinics at the state and associational levels, a state GA Queen's Court, and YWA House Parties, WMU conducted eight weeks of camp for young people at Camps Linden and Carson. From 1961 to 1967, a state WMU Retreat was held at Gatlinburg.

Mary Jane Nethery joined the Tennessee staff in Aug., 1967, as executive secretary-treasurer after the resignation of Mary Mills in February. At that time there were four professional staff positions in addition to the executive secretary-treasurer: WMS director, YWA director, GA director, and Sunbeam Band director. In 1969 WMU moved to the new Executive Board building at 205 Franklin Road in Brentwood where they now occupy a suite of offices on the second floor. Tennessee WMU currently has six professional positions and three full-time office staff positions.

In 1961 multiple societies in WMS were introduced to take the place of the Business Women's Circle Federation. In Oct., 1968, WMS assumed the structural changes designed for use in the new Grouping and Grading Plan to begin Oct., 1970; circles became groups. From 1959 to 1969, the overall enrollment showed a decrease of 5.3 percent. The enrollment peak of 96,531 came in 1964. WMU sustained its largest losses during the four transitional years,

1967-71, with an 18,707 or 20.5 percent member loss, most from WMS and Baptist Women. Four metropolitan areas accounted for approximately 50 percent of the total losses. New organizations were Mission Friends (preschool), Girls in Action (ages 6-11), Acteens (ages 12-17), Baptist Young Women (ages 18-29), and Baptist Women (adults). Brotherhood assumed responsibility for Royal Ambassadors, thus accounting for another 4,000-5,000 of the total member loss. Statistics for the first nine years after the changes showed a stabilizing of Baptist Women, a 50 percent growth in BYW, a 4 percent growth in Mission Friends, and an 18 percent loss in Acteens.

Since 1959, Tennessee WMU has awarded 154 Mary Northington (*q.v.*) scholarships totaling $67,000, 44 Belmont-endowed scholarships totaling $9,000, and 82 graduate loan scholarships totaling $32,200. In 1974 graduate loans became graduate scholarships and all past loan debts were waived. Since 1966, WMU has awarded 10 medical scholarships at a total of $5,700. In 1974-75 WMU began selection of scholarship recipients at Harrison-Chilhowee Baptist Academy, although previous allocations for workshops and scholarships had been made. Sixty-five scholarships totaling $20,500 have been awarded since that time. The latest scholarship offered through Tennessee WMU is the Studiact scholarship, awarded to graduating seniors who have achieved the high level of Studiact work.

Many opportunities for training are offered each year at the WMU House Party, BYW House Parties, Career Baptist Women Meeting, and specialized training conferences. Acteens Summit Meetings, GA-la's, and GA and Acteens Camps provide special missions education for young people involved in the WMU organizations.

MARY JANE NETHERY

WOMEN, ORDINATION OF SOUTHERN BAPTIST. The first woman ordained to the gospel ministry by a Southern Baptist church apparently was Addie E. Davis. A 1963 B.D. graduate of Southeastern Baptist Theological Seminary, she was ordained by Watts Street Baptist Church of Durham, NC, on Aug. 9, 1964.

The real movement toward the ordination of women in the Southern Baptist Convention did not begin until the early 1970s. Between 1964 and 1972 records indicate that only one other woman was ordained by a Southern Baptist church. This action was later rescinded. While no definitive count of the number ordained exists, Helen Lee Turner, of Virginia Intermont College, compiled a list of 58 persons in 1979.

The ordination of women has caused controversy in the SBC since the real crux of the women-in-ministry issue lies at the point of ordination. In Southern Baptist history ordination has been viewed as a local church matter. Opposition to the ordination of women has formed at the associational level as a result of this view of ordination. At least one association, the South District Association in Kentucky, has withdrawn fellowship from a church for ordaining a woman. Ordained women ministers are not currently seen as the norm among Southern Baptists.

BIBLIOGRAPHY: Leon McBeth, *Women in Baptist Life* (1979).

C. ANNE DAVIS

WOMEN DEACONS. The 1970s saw renewed emphasis upon women deacons in Southern Baptist churches. Many churches ordained women to the diaconate, and a number of churches elected women to chair the deacon group.

Ordaining women as deacons is not a new practice in Baptist life. Some of the earliest Baptist confessions of faith specified that women as well as men may serve as deacons. Typical was the English Baptist confession of 1611, which provided for "Deacons Men, and Women." In 1774 Morgan Edwards (*q.v.* III) published a book entitled *Customs of Primitive Churches* which showed that many Baptist churches in America had women deacons or deaconesses. Most of these were among the Separate Baptists in the South.

The acceptance of women as deacons or deaconesses continued among early Southern Baptists. In 1846 R. B. C. Howell (*q.v.* I) published *The Deaconship* in which he gave scriptural and practical reasons why Southern Baptist churches should have deaconesses. The work of deaconesses, according to Howell, consisted mostly in benevolence, missions, and ministry to women.

The practice of electing deaconesses diminished after 1900 but never ceased entirely among Southern Baptists. Several factors probably contributed to the decline of the deaconess role: A change in the work of deacons from ministry roles to management; adverse reactions to the suffragette movement of the times; emergence of the modern church committee structure which allowed women on benevolence and baptism committees to render essentially the same functions they had previously rendered as deaconesses; and the formation of Woman's Missionary Union in 1888, which gave women another organized structure through which to exercise leadership.

The question of ordaining women deacons has been controversial in the 1970s. Attention was drawn to the question by the periodical *The Deacon*, which devoted its Apr., 1973, issue to the question, "Should Churches Elect Women as Deacons?" While no exact statistics are available, it appears that the ordination of women deacons is increasing, involving hundreds of churches in several states.

Some question arises as to the relationship of "deaconess" and "woman deacon." Some churches use the terms to designate the same office, with the only difference being gender. Others use "deacon" to describe the ordained

office of men, and "deaconess'" to describe a subordinate, nonordained office for women. For the most part those Baptists in the South in the 1700s and 1800s who accepted or advocated any diaconal role for women meant them to be deaconesses in the subordinate sense of that word. However, those women ordained in the past decade have usually been on a basis of full equality with male deacons, and are called deacons rather than deaconesses.

Not all Southern Baptists approve of women deacons. Those who do approve cite historical precedent and Scripture passages, such as Romans 16:1, 1 Timothy 3:11, and 1 Timothy 5:9-10. Those who oppose also cite Scripture, often the same passages with different interpretations. The SBC has never taken any official stand on this question, since Baptist polity leaves ordination to the local church.

See also DEACON, MINISTRY OF THE.

BIBLIOGRAPHY: C. W. Deweese, *The Emerging Role of Deacons* (1979). Leon McBeth, *Women in Baptist Life* (1979).

LEON MCBETH

WOMEN IN CHURCH-RELATED VOCATIONS, CONSULTATION ON. A consultation, held Sep. 20-22, 1978, in Nashville, TN, to address the changing roles and rising demands of women in missions, ministry, and other Baptist professions. The consultation emerged from discussions of the Missions Coordination Subcommittee of the Inter-Agency Council in 1977-78. All SBC agencies were invited to participate in sponsoring this first Convention-wide forum on women. The following joined as sponsors: Baptist Joint Committee on Public Affairs, Brotherhood Commission, Christian Life Commission, Foreign Mission Board, Historical Commission, Home Mission Board, Radio and Television Commission, Southeastern Baptist Theological Seminary, Southern Baptist Theological Seminary, Sunday School Board, and Woman's Missionary Union.

The meeting was geared to provide SBC agencies a body of findings for use in employment, policy making, educational programs, and vocational guidance. More than 300 persons paid registration fees. Among them were SBC and state convention executives, pastors, college and seminary faculty, and students. More than two-thirds were women, approximately 15 of whom were ordained or seeking ordination for ministerial professions.

Two consultation-sponsored research projects were unveiled. A survey of 700 women employed by SBC entities revealed some discontent but generally satisfied views. More than 50 consultation women protested the survey's conclusions. Another study identified sexism in some SSB publications. Addresses, research, and discussion summaries were published in a volume of findings distributed to registrants and widely sold in later months.

The steering committee was chaired by Catherine B. Allen, WMU; with Winston Crawley, FMB; Orrin Morris, HMB; Morton Rose, SSB; Ronald Tonks, Historical Commission; Clarence Duncan, Radio and Television Commission; Alan Neely, SEBTS; Harry Hollis, CLC; Connie Davis, Brotherhood Commission; and Stan Hastey, BJCPA. Bobbie Sorrill, WMU, chaired the program and research committee; Martha Jo Glazner, SSB, chaired the arrangements committee; La Venia Neal, WMU, chaired the finance committee; Elaine Furlow, HMB, chaired the findings committee; and Johnni Johnson Scofield, FMB, chaired the publicity and publications committee.

BIBLIOGRAPHY: *Findings, Consultation on Women in Church-Related Vocations* (1978).

CATHERINE B. ALLEN

WOMEN IN MINISTRY, BAPTIST.

Women have performed various types of ministry in Baptist life, both officially and unofficially from the beginning of Baptist history.

In England, where Baptists originated as a separate denomination, some Baptist women were active in ministry in the seventeenth century. For example, among the General Baptists some women preached, even though there was opposition. John Smyth, founder of the earliest known Baptist church, said bluntly that "women are not permitted to speak in the church in time of prophecy." In his *Gangraena,* directed against Baptists, the Presbyterian scholar Thomas Edwards mentioned as one scandal against Baptists that they allowed "she preachers." He cited Baptist women who preached, baptized, and engaged in public teaching of Scripture. Among English Baptists the practice of women who preached was never widespread and tended to diminish after 1750. The practice has been revived in this century. The shortage of Baptist pastors after World War II led some Baptist women to assume full pastoral functions.

In Colonial America Baptist women had a limited speaking role. In 1774 Morgan Edwards (*q.v.* III) published his *Customs of Primitive Churches,* a description of Baptist churches in the new land. He indicated that women served as deaconesses and sometimes as eldresses but did not "preach" in any formal manner. Another Baptist historian, David Benedict (*q.v.* III), recorded that after 1800 the speaking roles of both Baptist women and laymen dimished in favor of a more professional clergy.

Women were known to preach, exhort, and pray among the Separate Baptists of the South between 1750 and 1800. Martha Marshall, wife of Daniel Marshall (*q.v.* II) and sister of Shubal Stearns (*q.v.* II), the two most important founders of Separate Baptists, was a popular preacher and exhorter whose public addresses usually melted listeners to tears. When Separate Baptists and Regular Baptists discussed uniting in the late eighteenth century, one barrier was the ministerial roles of women.

Freewill Baptists were the first Baptists in this country to grant full ordained status to women. The American Baptist Churches (formerly, Northern Baptist Convention) began to ordain women in the nineteenth century, including Edith Hill Booker in 1894, Margaret M. Joshua in 1921, and Gwendolyn Rich Thomas in 1940. Since then they have allowed ministerial status to women, though the number remains small. The more conservative Baptist groups and National Baptists generally do not recognize women as ministers. Some Baptist groups in Europe recognize women ministers, but the practice is generally not encouraged. Women ministers, while not unknown, are rare among Baptists in Latin America.

Women have been ordained as ministers in Southern Baptist churches since 1964 when Addie Davis was ordained in North Carolina, but women were active in many phases of ministry long before that. They served as teachers, counselors, chaplains, ministers of music, ministers of education, and in other ministry roles, including pastoral roles. Some women who serve in these roles are ordained, but most are not. In 1980 about 2,000 women were enrolled in SBC seminaries, many of them in theological degree programs.

A new development among Southern Baptists is the husband-wife ministry team in which both are ordained. In some cases the husband does the preaching, while the wife ministers in music or education, but in others they share all ministerial work, including preaching and pastoral counseling, and are called co-pastors. In 1980 there were perhaps a dozen such husband-wife teams known to be active in Southern Baptist churches, and a few others under appointment as missionaries.

Southern Baptist attitudes about women in ministry seem to be changing. As late as the 1920s, many Southern Baptists felt women should have no speaking role before mixed groups. A 1977 survey by Clay L. Price of the Home Mission Board, SBC, revealed that over 75 percent of Southern Baptists who responded felt women should be ordained for such roles as youth work, religious education, and social ministries. About 18 percent felt women should be ordained and called as pastors. Two-thirds of the respondents felt acceptance of women in ministry would increase in the future.

BIBLIOGRAPHY: Leon McBeth, *Women in Baptist Life* (1979). *Baptist History and Heritage,* Special issue, "The Role of Women in Baptist History" (Jan., 1977).

LEON MCBETH

WOMEN IN NEW TESTAMENT PERSPECTIVE.

Jesus called men and women to discipleship and servanthood; and except for the twelve, he prescribed no offices or forms for ministry. He rejected cultic restrictions that excluded women from worship and from even touching the Scriptures. Internalizing good and evil, he undercut the idea that menstruation renders one defiled or defiling. He publicly affirmed a woman who touched him, although she suffered an issue of blood. He ignored the rabbinical teaching that men should talk little with women. He talked openly with a woman at Jacob's well, to the astonishment of his disciples. He affirmed Mary's right to the "word," without disaffirming Martha's role as hostess. He accepted the service of women during his earthly ministry and as risen Christ commissioned Mary Magdalene to proclaim to the apostles the good news that he was not dead but alive.

The early church struggled between the ideal of full freedom and responsibility of women in Christ (Gal. 3:28) and traditional patterns restricting women. Women served as prophetesses (Acts 2:1-18; 21:9), instructors of men (Acts. 18:26), deacons (Rom. 16:1), and co-workers with Paul (Phil. 4:2). As the church moved from its early fluidity toward developing structures, restrictions upon women increased, with codes regulating dress, speech, and authority.

BIBLIOGRAPHY: Evelyn and Frank Stagg, *Woman in the World of Jesus* (1978).

EVELYN and FRANK STAGG

WOMEN'S DEPARTMENT OF THE BAPTIST WORLD ALLIANCE. See BAPTIST WORLD ALLIANCE, WOMEN'S DEPARTMENT OF THE.

WOMEN'S MOVEMENTS AND SOUTHERN BAPTISTS. Scholars usually date movements toward rights for women from 1792, when Mary Wollstonecraft published *A Vindication of the Rights of Women.* Shortly after, Baptist women launched the first organized women's movement in the United States. Mary Webb led 14 Baptists and six Congregationalists to form the Boston Female Society for Missionary Purposes in 1800. Soon an exclusively Baptist group, the Boston women fostered development of 120 other women's missionary organizations. Thus, at the outset of women's movements, Baptist women found missions to be the harbor for activism.

A Baptist became a role model for the adventurous American woman. She was Ann Hasseltine Judson (*q.v.* I). Her exploits beginning in 1812 as the first American female Baptist missionary lifted expectations of generations of Protestant women. Ann Judson gave women a mirror for exploring their own situations and finding acceptable ways around their subjugation. The feminism they saw developing in the USA could be safely projected in service abroad, where mistreatment of women was by infidels, not by Christians.

Luther Rice (*q.v.* II), colleague of Adoniram (*q.v.* I) and Ann Judson, planted women's mission societies throughout the Atlantic states. By the second Baptist Triennial Convention in 1817, 110 of the 187 cooperating mission societies were women's organizations.

Secular feminism arose outside Southern Baptist environs among Quakers, Northerners, and abolitionists. When the SBC was formed in 1845 to cut ties with those opposing slavery, it also cut lines of communication with feminism. The formal launching of the feminist movement—the Women's Rights Convention of 1848—nevertheless was followed in 1849 by the appointment of the first woman SBC missionary. The Foreign Mission Board sent Harriet A. Baker (*q.v.* I) to China as an experiment. After her troubled resignation in 1853, FMB policy until 1872 prohibited appointment of single women; women married to missionaries did not have a status as missionaries.

Southern Baptists helped open educational doors for women. Occasional churches and several state conventions established female schools. For example, Virginia Baptists sponsored Hollins College, Richmond Female Institute, and Albemarle Female Institute. These schools aired women's rights issues to assure the students that their education was for use only in the home.

Many churches did not permit women to vote on or to discuss church business, and missionary societies were not encouraged because public speaking by women was akin to abolitionist models. The Civil War brought change. Leading Baptists spoke for rights of women in employment. Church-related careers for women were proposed, but developed only in missions, slowly.

Northern feminists were ignored when Congress granted the vote to black males, so women organized in 1869 to fight militantly for suffrage. Concerned about the balance of political power, Southern Baptists did not throw their support to woman suffrage.

As suffrage associations were formed, nearly every denomination except the SBC formed a woman's missionary organization. Northern Baptist women organized the Woman's American Baptist Foreign Mission Society in 1871 and the Woman's Baptist Home Mission Society in 1873 and 1877. They began tapping southern support and appointed southern women as missionaries. Ann Graves (*q.v.*) routed the new movement belatedly into Southern Baptist circles. She fostered Woman's Mission to Woman in Baltimore, mother society for the rise of women's influence in SBC life. This group petitioned the FMB to reverse its policy and appoint Lula Whilden of South Carolina and Edmonia Moon (*q.v.* II) of Virginia in 1872. Wherever these women had contacts, vigorous financial backing sprang up.

The SBC, seeing needed financing, began in 1872 to take encouraging note of women's work, leading to grudging acceptance of the 1888 formation of Woman's Missionary Union, Auxiliary to SBC. WMU was formalized during violent Southern Baptist debates of the 1870s and 1880s on "the woman question." The suffrage movement and the woman's temperance movement antagonized southern men and made a specter of female leadership. At the root was fear of women's ordination and of changing home patterns. Women mission leaders avoided the debate. Annie Armstrong (*q.v.* I) personally refused to speak in an audience that included men, basing her belief on scriptural grounds.

The rise of WMU paralleled the rise of women's clubs in the United States. Fannie E. S. Heck (*q.v.* I), president of WMU, SBC, between 1892 and 1915, was a founder of the woman's club of Raleigh, NC, and was prominent in other civic groups. She translated secular models into rapid expansion of WMU. Yet she dodged questions about suffrage, only acknowledging that women's roles were changing.

The first feminine voice in SBC sessions was heard in 1905. Minnie Elliott of Phoenix, AZ, spontaneously seized the floor. A newsman recorded the incident; the SBC secretary did not. In 1916 Kathleen Mallory (*q.v.* II) and Maude Reynolds McLure (*q.v.* II) addressed the SBC.

Ratification of the Woman Suffrage Amendment was in sight before the SBC gave women a denominational vote in 1918, although women had been delegates to the Convention as early as 1877. State conventions were ahead (Kentucky in 1869 and all but four states by 1900). WMU leaders were ambivalent about admission to the SBC, fearing that WMU's power for mission support might shrink, but they fought successfully in 1921-22 for women to be placed on Convention boards.

Assuming that the vote would win women full rights, feminists mounted no serious movements for 40 years. But their hopes were unfulfilled in both church and society. The 1963 publication of *The Feminine Mystique* by Betty Friedan opened what came to be called the women's liberation movement or women's movements. In 1964 the Civil Rights Act banned discrimination against women. The National Organization for Women was organized in 1966, pressuring for "consciousness raising" and political action. The passage of the Equal Rights Amendment by Congress in 1972 and the Supreme Court's 1973 proabortion decision stimulated Southern Baptist debate of pre-1888 intensity. Coinciding with the publication of *The Feminine Mystique,* the SBC elected its first woman officer, Marie Mathis of Texas, as second vice-president, and passed an unprecedented resolution honoring her service as president of WMU, SBC. However, the liberation movement may have reduced women's visibility in the SBC. Convention programs in 1956, 1957, and 1958 showed extensive activity by women as speakers and in business. From then until 1977 no woman was placed in a speech-making or public-praying role. Only WMU leaders and a few women on SBC committees spoke in routine Convention business sessions.

Meanwhile the denomination turned out significant publications on women's issues. Among influential ones were *The Baptist Program,* Oct., 1970; *The Quarterly Review,* Spring, 1970; *Home Missions,* May, 1972; *The Deacon,* Apr., 1973; *The Commission,* Nov., 1974; *Review and Expositor,* Winter, 1975; *Baptist History and Heritage,* Jan., 1977; and numerous WMU magazines. Since 1975, more than 50 articles on women's roles have appeared each year in SBC periodicals and Broadman Press has published at least two dozen books on the topic. The Seminary Extension curriculum in 1977 added a course, "Women in the Church."

In 1972, as the Equal Rights Amendment was passed, Marie Mathis was nominated for president of the SBC—the only woman nominated to date. She was defeated. Convention sessions of 1973, 1974, and 1975 included controversies on women, including ordination, biblical interpretation, abortion, the ERA, and changing roles. Jessie Tillison Sappington, Houston, TX, was outspoken on several of these issues. After the 1973 Convention approved her resolution that women were created for the glory of man, to occupy different functions, the SBC Christian Life Commission in 1974 asked the SBC to condemn discrimination against women. Various CLC proposals were either tabled or defeated, but the CLC followed with a conference on "Christian Freedom for Women and Other Human Beings."

Pro-women supporters nominated Helen Long Fling of New York, former president of WMU, SBC, as second vice-president of the SBC in 1973 and as first vice-president in 1974. She was defeated in the run-off election each time. In 1975 Myra Gray Bates of North Carolina became the first woman to nominate a winning candidate for Convention office, and was elected herself as second vice-president in 1976. Anita Bryant Green of Florida was defeated in a bid for first vice-president in 1978. No other woman attempted Convention office until Christine Burton Gregory of Virginia, retiring president of WMU, SBC, was elected first vice-president in 1981. In Florida, Nevada, and District of Columbia Baptist Conventions, women have served as president.

The number of women on boards of the SBC rose from 2.5 percent in 1961 to 8.1 percent in 1980-81. The first woman to chair a Convention committee was Virginia Robinson Chandler of Nebraska, who headed the Denominational Calendar Committee in 1975 and 1976. Marian Gibbs Grant of North Carolina was the first woman on the Order of Business Committee. Elected in 1976, she became chairman for the 1978 Convention. Her influence was felt immediately when a woman was invited to lead in prayer in 1977. Nine women spoke and prayed in 1980, when two women were on the Order of Business Committee. In 1980 Margaret Fraser Bryan of Tennessee became the first woman to chair a SBC board, the Southern Baptist Commission on the American Baptist Theological Seminary.

The most progressive action concerning women was the Consultation on Women in Church-Related Vocations of 1978. Partly in reaction, Joyce Gentry Rogers, whose husband Adrian was SBC president, organized the Mid-Continent Christian Women's Concerns Conference in Memphis, TN, in May, 1980. More than 4,000 women attended the conservative program.

The percentage of women registered as messengers to SBC Conventions was as low as 33.5

percent in 1968 and as high as 42.1 percent in 1978.

The number of single women serving as foreign missionaries declined during the recent women's movements. In traditional days of 1948, 27 percent of the SBC foreign missionaries were single women. By 1958, they comprised only 18 percent of the force; by 1980 they had declined to 8.63 percent. Linked with research of Sarah Frances Anders showing a decline in employment of women in church and denominational jobs, the figures paint a negative picture.

Changes for women meant changes for WMU. From a peak enrollment of 1,509,484 in 1964-65, WMU declined to 1,100,043 members in 1979-80. Major changes in organizational approaches stabilized membership at the 1,100,000 level after 10 years of decline.

See also WOMEN, CONVENTION PRIVILEGES OF, Vol. II; WOMEN, ORDINATION OF SOUTHERN BAPTIST; WOMEN DEACONS; WOMEN IN CHURCH-RELATED VOCATIONS, CONSULTATION ON; WOMEN IN MINISTRY, BAPTIST.

BIBLIOGRAPHY: Leon McBeth, *Women in Baptist Life* (1979). Thematic issue on "The Role of Women in Baptist History," *Baptist History and Heritage* (Jan., 1977). Thematic issue on "Women and the Church," *Review and Expositor* (Winter, 1975).

CATHERINE B. ALLEN

WOODWARD, GEORGE HOMER (b. Earlington, KY, May 21, 1890; d. Riverside, CA, Dec. 16, 1969). Pioneer California pastor. The son of Aaron Eldridge Petit Woodward and Laura Frances Crabtree, farmers, he married Oma Fillbeck, Nov. 25, 1909, in Blytheville, AR. They had five children: Laurabelle, Ometa, Gerald, Clinton, and Elizabeth.

Woodward established merchandising outlets for a nationally-known department store and was later manager of one of these stores. He helped to pioneer Southern Baptist work in Arizona. In 1941 he went to Riverside, CA, to manage a store. Soon he established First Southern Baptist Church, now known as Palm Baptist Church, where he remained as pastor for nine years. From there he went to Indio, CA, to serve as pastor of the newly-organized Wallace Memorial Baptist Church. He returned to Riverside about 1954, where he organized Temple (now Calvary) Baptist Church and served as its pastor until his retirement.

Woodward served as a member of the Executive Board of the Southern Baptist General Convention of California. He wrote the report on Christian education for the state convention in 1942, which led to the founding of California Baptist College eight years later. He is buried in Olivewood Cemetery, Riverside, CA.

FLOYD LOONEY

WORD AND WAY (II, III). Official journal of the Missouri Baptist Convention. W. Ross Edwards retired as editor on July 31, 1975. Elene Stone, an employee since 1948, was named interim editor. During the interim, the convention's executive board voted to change the publication's structure and moved it from a department of work to a program of the executive board, solely responsible to the board's Communications Committee.

Bobby Sweede Terry, associate editor of the *Western Recorder,* was named editor of *Word and Way* effective Aug. 25, 1975. The newspaper's staff has expanded and now includes a managing editor, two newswriters, administrative secretary, accountant, and a five-member mailing crew. The number of pages printed has increased 25 percent since 1975 and now averages 500 tabloid pages annually. The paper is jointly financed through Cooperative Program allocations and funds generated by subscriptions and advertising.

BOBBY S. TERRY

WORLD BAPTIST FELLOWSHIP (cf. Fundamental Baptist Fellowship, The, Vol. I). The World Baptist Fellowship consists of 1,250 independent, fundamental congregations. The WBF reflects the continuing influence of J. Frank Norris (*q.v.* II), described as one of the most controversial figures in American religious history. Some 2,500 churches directly or indirectly owe their origin or inspiration to Norris. In addition to those churches within the WBF, an even larger ratio of churches are affiliates of the Baptist Bible Fellowship, Springfield, MO, due to a WBF division in 1950, and an unknown number of churches have chosen to remain independent of any national organization. The official publication of the WBF is *The Fundamentalist.*

The WBF maintains the Arlington Baptist College, Arlington, TX, with an average annual enrollment above 500 students. The college has a 52-acre campus, and is certified by the state of Texas to offer the Bachelor of Arts and the Bachelor of Science degrees. Graduates of the college have built some of the largest churches in America. The official publication of the college is the *Media.*

The WBF expresses its missionary interest through its mission agency with headquarters on the college campus. Currently, 80 missionary families are at work in 24 foreign countries. The agency serves as a clearinghouse in a liaison relationship between the missionary and the supporting churches. The official publication of the agency is the *Reaper's Report.*

See also BAPTIST BIBLE FELLOWSHIP, Vol. I.

BIBLIOGRAPHY: R. W. Barber and W. Martin, *The Man and The Movement* (1977). B. V. Bartlett, *The Beginnings: A Pictorial History of the Baptist Bible Fellowship* (1975). G. W. Dollar, *A History of Fundamentalism in America* (1973). R. E. Falls, *A Fascinating Biography of J. Frank Norris* (1975). C. A. Russell, *Voices of American Fundamentalism* (1976). E. L. Towns, *The Christian Hall of Fame* (1971). WBF Mission Agency, *Directory of Supporting Churches* (1979).

WAYNE MARTIN

WORLD BAPTIST FELLOWSHIP MISSION AGENCY. Organized in 1928, the agency is supported by independent fundamentalist Baptist churches, and is primarily engaged in planting indigenous churches. The agency also is involved in broadcasting, correspondence courses, education, and evangelism. In 1980, 166 missionaries were serving in Australia, Brazil, Colombia, Costa Rica, Ecuador, France, Germany, Guatemala, Honduras, Indonesia, Japan, New Zealand, Philippines, Spain, and the United Kingdom. Total income in 1979 was $2,029,368. Robert O. Schmidt is director. Offices are located in Arlington, TX.

J. TERRY YOUNG

WORLD EVANGELISM, ASSOCIATION OF BAPTISTS FOR (II, III). The association had 502 career missionaries in 1980, including 68 single women. In addition, there are short-term missionaries. Missionaries serve in 17 countries, Brazil being the largest with 107 missionaries. Three new countries were entered in 1979—Argentine, Gambia, and Portugal— with plans made to enter Norway. New work was also begun in the United States. Major types of ministry include aviation, theological education, medicine, Bible translation work, and church planting. Work is also done with the deaf, blind, students, satellite cities, river villages, industrial personnel, refugees, and prisoners. Wendell W. Kempton is president. Total income in 1979 was $5,043,629. Offices are located in Cherry Hill, NJ.

HELEN E. FALLS

WORLD HUNGER. See HUNGER, WORLD.

WORLD MISSION JOURNAL. See BROTHERHOOD COMMISSION, SBC.

WORLD MISSIONS CONFERENCES (III). Since 1974, the Brotherhood Commission, SBC, has been responsible for correlating the promotion of these conferences which bring missionary personnel in contact with local churches. The commission established a World Missions Conference Department and elected James W. Hatley as director in June, 1976. Promoted as a five-to-seven-session associational program, the conferences involve churches in the simultaneous study of age-graded mission materials, followed by a missionary speaker. In 1979 the conferences were held in 3,389 churches, attracting 1,082,060 persons. The plan is to offer all Southern Baptist churches an opportunity to participate in a World Missions Conference at least every five years.

JAMES W. HATLEY

WORRELL, ADOLPHUS SPALDING (b. Newton County, GA, Mar. 3, 1831; d. Louisville, KY, July 31, 1908). Evangelist, educator, and editor. The son of William Green and Martha Melton Worrell, he attended Mercer University (A.B., 1855; A.M., 1858). He married Mary L. Sheed, Sweetwater, TN, in 1864. They had two daughters and one son. He taught at Mississippi College and Union University before becoming president of Mt. Lebanon University in LA, 1865-66. He was also president of Lexington Baptist Female College in Kentucky,

1868-71; California Baptist College, 1873-75; Mt. Pleasant College in Missouri, 1878-80; and Buckner College in Arkansas, 1882-83.

Worrell edited or published *Soldier's Friend*, Atlanta, GA, 1860s; *Louisiana Baptist*, 1865-66; *The Baptist Sentinel* in Kentucky, 1868-71; *Western Recorder* in Kentucky, 1871-72; *The Evangel*, San Francisco, CA, 1870s; and *Gospel Witness* in Kentucky, 1893-1908. He translated the New Testament (1904). Believing in divine healing through faith only, he refused medication and the care of physicians.

LEE N. ALLEN

WORTHINGTON, ALFRED (b. Union Parish, LA, Jan. 25, 1884; d. Oklahoma City, OK, Aug. 28, 1966). Missionary to the Indians. The son of William Spiller and Mary Ellen Worthington, farmers, he attended Ouachita College (A.B.) and Southwestern Baptist Theological Seminary (B.D.). Under appointment by the Home Mission Board, he served Osages and Pawnees, 1930-45. After moving to Newkirk, OK, he was Baptist religious work director, Chilocco Indian School. He is buried at Newkirk, OK.

B. FRANK BELVIN

WRIGHT, ABRAHAM (b. Pana, IL, Feb. 10, 1896; d. Litchfield, IL, Sep. 5, 1975). Educator, pastor, and missionary. Son of William H. and P. A. Wright, he graduated from Shurtleff College (Ph.B., 1921) and the University of Illinois (M.A., 1931). He married Mae Keel, May 31, 1916. They had five children: Harold O., Ralph E., Richard E., Ruth, and Lucille. Wright was superintendent, public schools, Brookport, IL, 1924-31, while serving rural churches in Massac County.

After serving as pastor of First Baptist Church, Nashville, IL, four years, Wright lived in Gillespie, IL, 1935-43, leading rural churches and serving half time as missionary for Macoupin Association, organizing five new churches. After moving to Benld, he was appointed a language missionary by the Home Mission Board, Nov. 10, 1945. He is buried at Nokomis, IL.

MRS. W. E. LEE

WRIGHT, FRANCIS EVERETT (b. DeQueen, AR, Apr. 19, 1915; d. Jackson, TN, May 15, 1976). Educator. Son of Gerden Gate, an accountant, and Ellen Beesley Wright, a teacher, he attended Baylor University (B.A., 1942) and Peabody College (M.A., 1948; Ed.D., 1954). On June 5, 1941, he married Mildred Cooper of Waco, TX. They had one daughter, Kay. He served as pastor of Baptist churches in Grapeland, TX, 1941-42, and West, TX, 1946-47, and as an Air Force chaplain, 1943-46. As an educator, he served as personnel counselor at Northwestern State College in Louisiana, 1948-50; dean of men at Baylor University, 1950-52; academic dean, 1954-63, and president, 1963-67, of Union University; and president, Jackson State Community College, Jackson, TN, 1967-76. He is buried in Ridgecrest Cemetery, Jackson, TN.

G. HUGH WAMBLE

WYOMING, SOUTHERN BAPTISTS IN. See NORTHERN PLAINS BAPTIST CONVENTION.

Y

YATES, KYLE MONROE (b. Apex, NC, Feb. 7, 1895; d. Waco, TX, Feb. 15, 1975). Seminary and university professor, pastor, and denominational leader. Son of William Manly and Della Jones Yates, he was a graduate of Wake Forest College (A.B., 1916; A.M., 1917); Southern Baptist Theological Seminary (Th.M., 1920; Th.D., 1922); and the University of Edinburgh (Ph.D., 1932). He received numerous honorary degrees. Ordained in 1916, he served as pastor of several churches in North Carolina and Kentucky, 1917-28; Walnut Street Church in Louisville, KY, 1942-46; and Second Church in Houston, TX, 1946-56.

Yates was professor of Old Testament at Southern Seminary, 1922-42; distinguished professor at Baylor University, 1956-71; second vice-president of the SBC, 1955; one of the major translators of the Revised Standard Version, and a prolific author. Among his best remembered books were: *The Essentials of Biblical Hebrew* (1938), *Preaching from the Prophets* (1942), *Preaching from the Psalms* (1948), *Studies in Psalms* (1953), *Preaching from Great Bible Chapters* (1957), and *Preaching from John's Gospel* (1964). He married Margaret Webb Sharp, Aug. 24, 1922. Their children were Kyle, Jr., and Ellen. He is buried in Oakwood Cemetery, Waco, Texas.

KYLE M. YATES, JR.

YATES, WILLIAM FRANKLIN (b. Ray County, MO, Aug. 21, 1877; d. Richmond, MO, Aug. 11, 1979). Banker, farmer, and philanthropist. Son of James T. and Janie (Richardson) Yates, farmers, he attended William Jewell College (B.A.). He married Willie Barron. They had one son, James. Following her death in 1951, he married Helen Allene Weary, Mar. 31, 1967. He served as president of Exchange Bank, Richmond, 1901-79, and as Sunday School superintendent, First Baptist Church, Richmond, for 51 years. He was a trustee of William Jewell College, 1942-79, and manager of the investment portfolio for the college. He is buried in the Richmond, MO, cemetery.

DAVID O. MOORE

YEMEN, MISSION IN (cf. Yemen Arab Republic, Mission in, Vol. III). The Baptist Hospital in Jibla continued to be recognized as one of the best in the country. As the 1980s began, its clinics were always crowded, and its 80 beds were usually occupied. In 1977 fire damage required a $225,000 appropriation from the Foreign Mission Board. Restrictions on Christian witnessing continued, but a service in Arabic, the only one in the country, was permitted on Sunday evenings. Bibles and Scripture portions were being distributed discreetly. In 1980, no Baptist church existed in Yemen, but 20 missionaries were assigned to the country.

J. D. HUGHEY

YORK, THEODORE HUGHES, SR. (b. Marietta, GA, Feb. 27, 1903; d. Canton, OK, June 23, 1962). Home missionary. After serving as a volunteer lay worker with Italians in Tampa, FL, York married Mary Carolyn Patch, 1931. He was a missionary with Armenia Avenue Baptist Church (Italian), Tampa, 1943-55; and with the Indians of Utah, 1955-56, and Oklahoma, 1956, until his death.

LOYD CORDER

YOUNG, RICHARD KNOX (b. Roxboro, NC, Sep. 18, 1913; d. Roxboro, NC, Dec. 31, 1974). Hospital chaplain and educator. He married Mary Frances Vickers, Nov. 13, 1935. They had three children: Vicky, Richard K., Jr., and David. Young attended Wake Forest College (B.A., 1943) and The Southern Baptist Theological Seminary (B.D., 1946; Th.D., 1952). He also studied clinical pastoral education at Elgin State Hospital, Elgin, IL, under Anton T. Boisen and W. R. Andrews.

Young became chaplain at North Carolina Baptist Hospital, Sep. 1, 1946. The next year he helped establish the first clinical pastoral education program in North Carolina. Through the School of Pastoral Care, he trained more than 1,000 pastors and missionaries. He became the first professor of pastoral care at Southeastern Baptist Theological Seminary in 1953, a post he held concurrently with his hospital chaplaincy until his retirement in 1971.

He served as president of the Southern Baptist Hospital Chaplains' Association and of the College of Chaplains of the American Protestant Hospital Association, 1956. He was the author of *The Pastor's Hospital Ministry* (1954) and coauthor with Albert L. Meiburg of *Spiri-*

tual Therapy (1960). He is buried in Providence Baptist Cemetery, Roxboro, NC.

ALBERT L. MEIBURG

YOUTH WORK, BAPTIST (III). See AGE-GROUP WORK IN THE CHURCHES.

Z

ZAMBIA, MISSION IN (III). Missionaries in Zambia expanded into new locations and types of ministry in the 1970s. In Lusaka the radio studio began television programming, student ministries were conducted on several campuses, a program of church music development was initiated, and a hostel for missionary children was opened. Kalwa farm near Serenje, historically associated with the Moffat and Livingstone families, was given to the Baptist mission. Agricultural ministries began there and at Petauke. Theological education took place through the seminary near Lusaka, through training centers at Petauke and Serenje, and through Theological Education by Extension, based in Kabwe. By 1979 Bible Way Correspondence School had enrolled almost 8,000 students. For short periods missionaries lived at Zambezi, in the west, and Livingstone, in the south. At the end of 1979, 43 missionaries, living in five of the nine provinces, worked with approximately 5,400 members of 80 churches.

JOY NEAL

ZICKRICK, JEROME SEARIGHT (b. Texas City, TX, Oct. 2, 1913; d. Shawnee, OK, Mar. 13, 1979). College administrator. Son of Fred and Edith Price Zickrick, he married Mary Faye Allee, Oct. 18, 1935. They had one son, Leon. He attended Oklahoma Baptist University (A.B., 1944) and the University of Oklahoma (M.A., 1948). He served as a teacher and administrator at Oklahoma Baptist University, 1944-79. He is buried in Resthaven Park, Shawnee, OK.

HELEN THAMES RALEY

ZIMBABWE, MISSION IN (cf. Rhodesia, Mission in, Vol. III). After years of internal warfare, Zimbabwe was born, Apr. 18, 1980. Advance in the 1970s included establishing a Bible correspondence school, Theological Education by Extension, and a midwifery school. The national convention assumed responsibility for operating Sanyati schools and appointed its first home missionary. The war affected mission work by limiting travel in rural areas, closing all clinics except one, and forcing Sanyati Secondary School and the seminary in Gwelo to relocate temporarily. On June 15, 1978, Archie G. Dunaway was fatally stabbed at Sanyati. Following Dunaway's death missionaries moved from Sanyati. African personnel continued to operate the hospital and school, and missionaries Maurice Randall and John Monroe made periodic visits. After the war the mission and convention planned a mission thrust into refugee settlements in Salisbury. The seminary announced plans to establish a degree program. The mission made personnel requests for both replacement and expansion.

JOY NEAL